MySQL

The definitive guide to using, programming, and administering MySQL 4 databases

Second Edition

Paul DuBois

DEVELOPER'S
LIBRARY

Sams Publishing, 800 East 96th Street, Indianapolis, Indiana 46240

MySQL

Second Edition

Copyright © 2003 by Sams Publishing

International Standard Book Number: 0-7357-1212-3

Library of Congress Catalog Card Number: 2001095496

Printed in the United States of America

First printing: January 2003

Third printing with corrections August 2003

06 05 04 03   7 6 5 4

Interpretation of the printing code: The rightmost double-digit number is the year of the book's printing; the rightmost single-digit number is the number of the book's printing. For example, the printing code 03-1 shows that the first printing of the book occurred in 2003.

Trademarks

Warning and Disclaimer

Associate Publisher
Stephanie Wall

Acquisitions Editor
Katie Purdum

Managing Editor
Charlotte Clapp

Development Editor
Chris Zahn

Senior Project Editor
Lori Lyons

Copy Editor
Pat Kinyon

Senior Indexer
Cheryl Lenser

Proofreader
Linda Seifert

Composition
Stacey Richwine-DeRome

Design
Gary Adair

Contents At a Glance

TABLE OF CONTENTS

IV   Appendixes

About the Author

Paul DuBois is a writer, database administrator, and leader in the Open Source community. In addition to *MySQL*, he is also the author of *MySQL and Perl for the Web*, *MySQL Cookbook*, *Using csh and tcsh*, and *Software Portability with imake*.

About the Technical Reviewers

These reviewers contributed their considerable hands-on expertise to the entire development process for *MySQL,* Second Edition. As the book was being written, these dedicated professionals reviewed all the material for technical content, organization, and flow. Their feedback was critical to ensuring that the book fits our readers' need for the highest-quality technical information.

Shane Kirk obtained his B.S. in Computer Science from the University of Kentucky. He currently lives in Cincinnati, Ohio, working as a database administrator and software developer for Opinion One (www.opinionone.com), a software company whose focus is developing market research software and solutions.

Dr. Hang T. Lau is an adjunct professor in the Computer Science Department at Concordia University in Montreal, Canada. He has worked in industry as a system scientist for more than 20 years in areas including telecommunication network planning, speech recognition applications in telecommunication, and transport access radio network systems.

Acknowledgments

Acknowledgments are presented here by edition.

First Edition

This book benefited greatly from the comments, corrections, and criticisms provided by the technical reviewers: David Axmark, Vijay Chaugule, Chad Cunningham, Bill Gerrard, Jijo George John, Fred Read, Egon Schmid, and Jani Tolonen. Special thanks goes to Michael "Monty" Widenius, the principal MySQL developer, who not only reviewed the manuscript, but also fielded hundreds of questions that I sent his way during the course of writing the book. Naturally, any errors that remain are my own. I'd also like to thank Tomas Karlsson, Colin McKinnon, Sasha Pachev, Eric Savage, Derick H. Siddoway, and Bob Worthy, who reviewed the initial proposal and helped shape the book into its present form.

The staff at New Riders are responsible first for conceiving this book and then for turning my scribblings into the finished work you hold in your hands. Laurie Petrycki acted as Executive Editor. Katie Purdum, Acquisitions Editor, helped me get under way and took the heat when I missed deadlines. Leah Williams did double duty not only as Development Editor but as Copy Editor; she put in many, many late hours, especially in the final stages of the project. Cheryl Lenser and Tim Wright produced the index. John Rahm served as Project Editor. My thanks to each of them.

Most of all, I want to express my appreciation to my wife, Karen, for putting up with another book, and for her understanding and patience as I disappeared, sometimes for days on end, into "the writing zone." Her support made the task easier on many occasions, and I am pleased to acknowledge her contribution; she helped me write every page.

Second Edition

For the second edition, the technical reviewers once again played a crucial role in finding errors and making corrections and clarifications. Hang Lau and Shane Kirk served as reviewers. I'd also like to thank Monty Widenius, Alexander Barkov, Jani Tolonen, and the other MySQL developers for patiently enduring my many questions and supplying answers that made their way into these pages.

The New Riders staff that brought this edition to life were Stephanie Wall, Associate Publisher; Chris Zahn, Development Editor; Lori Lyons, Senior Project Editor; Pat Kinyon, Copy Editor; Cheryl Lenser, Indexer; and Stacey Richwine-DeRome, Compositor.

And, as always, my wife Karen provided the behind-the-scenes support that readers do not see, but without which this book would be much poorer.

Tell Us What You Think

As the reader of this book, *you* are our most important critic and commentator. We value your opinion and want to know what we're doing right, what we could do better, what areas you'd like to see us publish in, and any other words of wisdom you're willing to pass our way.

You can email or write me directly to let me know what you did or didn't like about this book—as well as what we can do to make our books stronger.

Please note that I cannot help you with technical problems related to the topic of this book, and that due to the high volume of mail I receive, I might not be able to reply to every message.

When you write, please be sure to include this book's title and author as well as your name and phone or email address. I will carefully review your comments and share them with the author and editors who worked on the book.

Email: opensource@samspublishing.com

Mail: Mark Taber
            Associate Publisher
            Sams Publishing
            800 East 96th Street
            Indianapolis, IN 46240 USA

Introduction

A relational database management system (RDBMS) is an essential tool in many environments, from the more traditional uses in business, research, and education contexts, to newer applications, such as powering search engines on the Internet. However, despite the importance of a good database for managing and accessing information resources, many organizations have found them to be out of reach of their financial resources. Historically, database systems have been an expensive proposition, with vendors charging healthy fees both for software and for support. In addition, because database engines often had substantial hardware requirements to run with any reasonable performance, the cost was even greater.

In recent years, the situation has changed on both the hardware and software sides of the picture. Personal computers have become inexpensive but powerful, and a whole movement has sprung up to write high-performance operating systems for them that are available for the cost of an inexpensive CD, or even free over the Internet. These include several BSD UNIX derivatives (FreeBSD, NetBSD, OpenBSD) as well as various forms of Linux (RedHat, Caldera, LinuxPPC, to name a few).

Production of free operating systems to drive personal computers to their full capabilities has proceeded in concert with—and to a large extent has been made possible by—the development of freely available tools such as gcc, the GNU C compiler. These efforts to make software available to anyone who wants it have resulted in what is now called the Open Source movement, and which has produced many important pieces of software. For example, Apache is the most widely used Web server on the Internet. Other Open Source successes are the Perl general-purpose scripting language and PHP, a language that is popular due largely to the ease with which it allows dynamic Web pages to be written. These all stand in contrast to proprietary solutions that lock you into high-priced products from vendors that don't even provide source code.

Database software has become more accessible, too. Database systems such as PostgreSQL are available for free. More recently, commercial vendors such as Informix and Oracle have begun to offer their software at no cost for operating systems such as Linux. (However, these latter products generally come in binary-only form with no support, which lessens their usefulness.)

Another entry into the no-to-low cost database arena is MySQL, a SQL (Structured Query Language) client/server relational database management system originating from Scandinavia. MySQL includes a SQL server, client programs for accessing the server, administrative tools, and a programming interface for writing your own programs.

MySQL's roots began in 1979, with the UNIREG database tool created by Michael "Monty" Widenius for the Swedish company TcX. In 1994, TcX began looking around for a SQL server for use in developing Web applications. They tested some commercial servers, but found all too slow for TcX's large tables. They also took a look at mSQL, but it lacked certain features TcX required. Consequently, Monty began developing a new server. The programming interface was designed explicitly to be similar to the one used by mSQL because several free tools were available for mSQL; by using a similar interface, those same tools could be used for MySQL with a minimum of porting effort.

In 1995, David Axmark of Detron HB began to push for TcX to release MySQL on the Internet. David also worked on the documentation and on getting MySQL to build with the GNU `configure` utility. MySQL 3.11.1 was unleashed on the world in 1996 in the form of binary distributions for Linux and Solaris. Today, MySQL works on many more platforms and is available in both binary and source form. The company MySQL AB has been formed to provide distributions of MySQL and to offer support and training services.

And MySQL continues to develop. The addition of features such as transactions, row-level locking, foreign key support, and replication has caused people who once would have considered only "big engine" databases for their applications to give MySQL a second look.

MySQL is an Open Source project that can be used for free under most circumstances, for which reason it enjoys widespread popularity in the Open Source community. But MySQL's popularity isn't limited to Open Source enthusiasts. Yes, it runs on personal computers (indeed, much MySQL development takes place on inexpensive Linux systems). But MySQL is portable and runs on commercial operating systems (such as Solaris, Mac OS X, and Windows) and on hardware all the way up to enterprise servers. Furthermore, its performance rivals any database system you care to put up against it, and it can handle large databases with millions of records.

MySQL lies squarely within the picture that now unfolds before us: freely available operating systems running on powerful but inexpensive hardware, putting substantial processing power and capabilities in the hands of more people than ever before, on a wider variety of systems than ever before. This lowering of the economic barriers to computing puts powerful database solutions within reach of more people and organizations than at any time in the past. Organizations that once could only dream of putting the power of a high-performance RDBMS to work for them now can do so for very little cost. This is true for individuals as well. For example, I use MySQL with Perl, Apache, and PHP on my Apple iBook running Mac OS X. This allows me to carry my work with me anywhere. Total cost: the cost of the iBook.

Why Choose MySQL?

If you're looking for a free or inexpensive database management system, several are available from which to choose: MySQL, PostgreSQL, one of the free-but-unsupported engines from commercial vendors, and so forth. When you compare MySQL with other database systems, think about what's most important to you: Performance, support, features (SQL conformance, extensions, and so forth), licensing conditions and restrictions, and price all are factors to take into account. Given these considerations, MySQL has many attractive features to offer:

- **Speed.** MySQL is fast. The developers contend that MySQL is about the fastest database you can get. You can investigate this claim by visiting http://www.mysql.com/benchmark.html, a performance-comparison page on the MySQL Web site.

- **Ease of use.** MySQL is a high-performance but relatively simple database system and is much less complex to set up and administer than larger systems.

- **Query language support.** MySQL understands SQL, the language of choice for all modern database systems.

- **Capability.** Many clients can connect to the server at the same time. Clients can use multiple databases simultaneously. You can access MySQL interactively using several interfaces that let you enter queries and view the results: command-line clients, Web browsers, or X Window System clients. In addition, a variety of programming interfaces are available for languages such as C, Perl, Java, PHP, and Python. You can also access MySQL using applications that support ODBC (Open Database Connectivity), a database communications protocol developed by Microsoft. Thus, you have the choice of using prepackaged client software or writing your own for custom applications.

- **Connectivity and security.** MySQL is fully networked, and databases can be accessed from anywhere on the Internet, so you can share your data with anyone, anywhere. But MySQL has access control so that people who shouldn't see your data can't. To provide additional security, MySQL now supports encrypted connections using the Secure Sockets Layer (SSL) protocol.

- **Portability.** MySQL runs on many varieties of UNIX, as well as on other non-UNIX systems, such as Windows and OS/2. MySQL runs on hardware from home PCs to high-end servers.

- **Small size.** MySQL has a modest distribution size, especially compared to the huge disk space footprint of certain commercial database systems.

- **Availability and cost.** MySQL is an Open Source project, freely available under the terms of the GNU General Public License (GPL). This means that MySQL is free for most in-house uses. (If you want to sell MySQL or services that require it, that is a different situation and you should contact MySQL AB.)

- **Open distribution.** MySQL is easy to obtain; just use your Web browser. If you don't understand how something works or are curious about an algorithm, you can get the source code and poke around in it. If you don't like how something works, you can change it. If you think you've found a bug, report it; the developers listen.

What about support? Good question—a database isn't much use if you can't get help for it. Naturally, I'd like to think this book is all the assistance you'll ever need. But, realistically, you'll have questions that I never thought of or didn't have room to cover. You'll find that other resources are available and that MySQL has good support. MySQL is freely available, but you're not on your own when you install it:

- The *MySQL Reference Manual* is included in MySQL distributions and also is available online. The *Reference Manual* regularly receives good marks in the MySQL user community. This is important, because the value of a good product is diminished if no one can figure out how to use it.

- Training classes and technical support contracts are available from MySQL AB, for those who prefer or require formal arrangements.

- There is an active mailing list to which anyone may subscribe. The list has many helpful participants, including several MySQL developers. As a support resource, many people find this list sufficient for their purposes.

The MySQL community, developers and non-developers alike, is very responsive. Answers to questions on the mailing list often arrive within minutes. When bugs are reported, the developers generally release a fix quickly, and fixes become available immediately over the Internet. Contrast this with the often-frustrating experience of navigating the Byzantine support channels of the big vendors. (You've been there? Me, too. I know which alternative I prefer when I have a question about a product. Being put on hold at a vendor's convenience has no appeal compared to being able to post a question to a mailing list and check for replies at my convenience.)

MySQL is an ideal candidate for evaluation if you are in the database-selection process. You can try MySQL with no risk or financial commitment. Yet, if you get stuck, you can use the mailing list to get help. An evaluation costs some of your time, but that's true no matter what database system you're considering— and it's a safe bet that your installation and setup time for MySQL will be less than for many other systems.

Already Running Another RDBMS?

If you're currently running another database system, should you convert to MySQL? Not necessarily. If you're happy with your current system, why bother to switch? But if you feel constrained by what you're using, you definitely should consider MySQL. Perhaps performance of your current system is a concern, or it's proprietary and you don't like being locked into it. Perhaps you'd like to run on hardware that's not supported by your current system, or your software is provided in binary-only format and you'd really prefer to have the source available. Or maybe it just costs too much! All of these are reasons to look into MySQL. Use this book to familiarize yourself with MySQL's capabilities, ask some questions on the MySQL mailing list, and you'll probably find the answers you need to make a decision.

If you are considering switching from another SQL database to MySQL, check out the comparison page on the MySQL Web site at http://www.mysql.com/information/crash-me.php. Then check the chapters in this book that deal with MySQL's data types and dialect of SQL. You may decide that the version of SQL supported by your current RDBMS is too different and that porting your applications would involve significant effort.

Part of your evaluation should be to try porting a few examples, of course, because it may turn out not to be as difficult as you think—even if your database is an older one that doesn't understand SQL. One such experience I've had required converting a record management system from an RDBMS that wasn't SQL-based. There wasn't any language similarity at all to take advantage of, and some of the data types had no SQL equivalent. This project involved conversion of the network access methods and dozens of screen-based entry programs and canned queries. It took perhaps a month and a half of full-time effort. That's not bad.

Tools Provided with MySQL

The MySQL distribution includes the following tools:

- **A SQL server.** This is the engine that powers MySQL and provides access to your databases.
- **Client programs for accessing the server.** An interactive program allows you to enter queries directly and view the results, and several administrative and utility programs help you run your site. One utility allows you to control the server. Others let you import or export data, check access permissions, and more.
- **A client library for writing your own programs.** You can write clients in C because the library is in C, but the library also provides the basis for third-party bindings for other languages.

In addition to the software provided with MySQL itself, MySQL is used by many talented and capable people who like writing software to enhance their productivity and who are willing to make that software available. The result is that you have access to a variety of third-party tools that make MySQL easier to use or that extend its reach into areas such as Web site development.

What You Can Expect from This Book

By reading this book, you'll learn how to use MySQL effectively so that you can get your work done more productively. You'll be able to figure out how to get your information into a database, and you'll learn how to formulate queries that give you the answers to the questions you want to ask of that data.

You don't need to be a programmer to understand or use SQL. This book will show you how it works. But there's more to understanding how to use a database properly than just knowing SQL syntax. This book emphasizes MySQL's unique capabilities and shows how to use them.

You'll also see how MySQL integrates with other tools. The book shows how to use MySQL with PHP or Perl to generate dynamic Web pages created from the result of database queries. You'll learn how to write your own programs that access MySQL databases. All of these enhance MySQL's capabilities to handle the requirements of your particular applications.

If you'll be responsible for administrating a MySQL installation, this book will tell you what your duties are and how to carry them out. You'll learn how to set up user accounts, perform database backups, and make sure your site is secure.

Road Map to This Book

This book is organized into four parts.

Part I: General MySQL Use

- **Chapter 1, "Getting Started with MySQL and SQL."** Discusses how MySQL can be useful to you, and provides a tutorial that introduces the interactive MySQL client program, covers the basics of SQL, and demonstrates MySQL's general capabilities.

- **Chapter 2, "Working with Data in MySQL."** Discusses the column types that MySQL provides for describing your data, properties and limitations of each type, when and how to use them, how to choose between similar types, expression evaluation, and type conversion.

- **Chapter 3, "MySQL SQL Syntax and Use."** Every major RDBMS now available understands SQL, but every database engine implements a slightly different SQL dialect. This chapter discusses SQL with particular emphasis on those features that make MySQL distinctive.

- **Chapter 4, "Query Optimization."** How to make your queries run more efficiently.

Part II: Using MySQL Programming Interfaces

- **Chapter 5, "Introduction to MySQL Programming."** Discusses some of the application programming interfaces available for MySQL and provides a general comparison of the APIs that the book covers in detail.

- **Chapter 6, "The MySQL C API."** How to write C programs using the API provided by the client library included in the MySQL distribution.

- **Chapter 7, "The Perl DBI API."** How to write Perl scripts using the DBI module. Covers standalone scripts and CGI scripts for Web site programming.

- **Chapter 8, "The PHP API."** How to use the PHP scripting language to write dynamic Web pages that access MySQL databases.

Part III: MySQL Administration

- **Chapter 9, "Introduction to MySQL Administration."** What the database administrator's duties are and what you should know to run a site successfully.

- **Chapter 10, "The MySQL Data Directory."** An in-depth look at the organization and contents of the data directory, the area under which MySQL stores databases and status files.

- **Chapter 11, "General MySQL Administration."** How to make sure your server starts up and shuts down properly when your system does. Also includes instructions for setting up MySQL user accounts, and discusses log file maintenance, configuring the InnoDB tablespace, server tuning, running multiple servers, and setting up replication servers.

- **Chapter 12, "Security."** What you need to know to make your MySQL installation safe from intrusion, both from other users on the server host and from clients connecting over the network. Describes how to set up your MySQL server to support secure connections over SSL.

- **Chapter 13, "Database Backups, Maintenance, and Repair."** Discusses how to reduce the likelihood of disaster through preventive maintenance, how to back up your databases, and how to perform crash recovery if disaster strikes in spite of your preventive measures.

Part IV: Appendixes

- **Appendix A, "Obtaining and Installing Software."** Where to get and how to install the major tools described in the book.

- **Appendix B, "Column Type Reference."** Descriptions of MySQL's column types.

- **Appendix C, "Operator and Function Reference."** Descriptions of the operators and functions that are used to write expressions in SQL statements.

- **Appendix D, "SQL Syntax Reference."** Descriptions of each SQL statement that MySQL understands.

- **Appendix E, "MySQL Program Reference."** Descriptions of the programs provided in the MySQL distribution.

- **Appendix F, "C API Reference."** Descriptions of data types and functions in the MySQL C client library.

- **Appendix G, "Perl DBI API Reference."** Descriptions of methods and attributes provided by the Perl DBI module.

- **Appendix H, "PHP API Reference."** Descriptions of the functions that PHP provides for MySQL support.

- **Appendix I, "Internet Service Providers."** What to consider when choosing an ISP that provides MySQL access. What to consider when operating as an ISP providing MySQL services to customers.

How to Read This Book

Whichever part of the book you happen to be reading at any given time, it's best to try out the examples as you go along. If MySQL isn't installed on your system, you should install it or ask someone to do so for you. Then get the files needed to set up the sampdb sample database to which we'll be referring throughout the book. Appendix A, "Obtaining and Installing Software," says where you can obtain all the components and has instructions for installing them.

If you're a complete newcomer to MySQL or to SQL, begin with Chapter 1, "Getting Started with MySQL and SQL." This provides you with a tutorial introduction that grounds you in basic MySQL and SQL concepts and brings you up to speed for the rest of the book. Then proceed to Chapter 2, "Working with Data in MySQL," and Chapter 3, "MySQL SQL Syntax and Use," to find out how to describe and manipulate your own data so that you can exploit MySQL's capabilities for your own applications.

If you already know some SQL, you should still read Chapter 2 and Chapter 3. SQL implementations vary, and you'll want to find out what makes MySQL's implementation distinctive in comparison to others with which you may be familiar.

If you have experience with MySQL but need more background on the details of performing particular tasks, use the book as a reference, looking up topics on a need-to-know basis. You'll find several of the appendixes especially useful for reference purposes.

If you're interested in writing your own programs to access MySQL databases, read the API chapters, beginning with Chapter 5, "Introduction to MySQL Programming." If you want to produce a Web-based front end to your databases for easier access to them, or, conversely, to provide a database back end for your Web site to enhance your site with dynamic content, check out Chapter 7, "The Perl DBI API," and Chapter 8, "The PHP API."

If you're evaluating MySQL to find out how it compares to your current RDBMS, several parts of the book will be useful. Read the data type and SQL syntax chapters in Part I to compare MySQL to the SQL that you're used to, the programming chapters in Part II if you have custom applications, and the administrative chapters in Part III to assess the level of administrative support a MySQL installation requires. This information is also useful if you're not currently using a database but are performing a comparative analysis of MySQL along with other database systems for the purpose of choosing one of them.

If you want access to MySQL and are seeking an Internet Service Provider (ISP) who offers it, see Appendix I, "Internet Service Providers," for some tips on how to choose one. This appendix also provides advice to service providers who want to provide MySQL to attract new customers or serve existing ones better.

Versions of Software Covered in This Book

As of this writing, the current general release of MySQL is the 4.0 version series, and active development is taking place in the 4.1 series. This book covers them both, as well as earlier 3.22 and 3.23 features.

For the other major packages discussed here, any recent versions should be sufficient for the examples in this book. Current versions are:

Package	Version
Perl DBI	1.32
Perl MySQL DBI driver	2.1020
PHP	4.2.3
Apache	1.3.27/2.0.43
CGI.pm	2.87

All the software discussed in this book is available on the Internet. Appendix A, "Obtaining and Installing Software," provides instructions for getting MySQL, Perl DBI support, PHP, Apache, and CGI.pm onto your system. This appendix also contains instructions for obtaining the sample database that is used in examples throughout this book, as well as the example programs that are developed in the programming chapters.

Conventions Used in This Book

Typographical conventions used in this book are as follows:

`Monospaced` font indicates hostnames, filenames, directory names, commands, options, and Web sites. Where commands are shown as you enter them, **`bold monospaced`** font indicates the part you enter. *`Italicized`* font in commands indicates where you should substitute a value of your own choosing.

In commands, the prompt indicates how the command is run. The `%` prompt is used for most commands; in general, these may be run either from your UNIX shell or from the DOS prompt. More specialized prompts are `#`, which indicates a command run as the UNIX `root` user, and `C:\>` to indicate a command intended specifically for Windows. SQL statements that are issued from the `mysql` program are shown with the `mysql>` prompt.

In SQL statements, SQL keywords and function names are written in upper-case. Database, table, and column names are written in lowercase. In syntax descriptions, square brackets (`[]`) indicate optional information.

The term "Windows NT-based systems" stands collectively for the family of Windows variants that are based on Windows NT, which currently includes Windows NT, 2000, and XP. It does not include Windows 95, 98, or Me.

Additional Resources

This book aims to tell you virtually everything you'll need to know about MySQL. But if you have a question the book doesn't answer, where should you turn?

Useful resources include the Web sites for the software you need help with:

Package	Primary Web Site
MySQL	`http://www.mysql.com/documentation/`
Perl DBI	`http://dbi.perl.org/`
PHP	`http://www.php.net/`
Apache	`http://www.apache.org/`
CGI.pm	`http://stein.cshl.org/WWW/software/CGI/`

These sites contain pointers to various forms of information, such as reference manuals, frequently asked-question (FAQ) lists, and mailing lists:

- **Reference manuals.** The primary documentation included with MySQL itself is the Reference Manual. It's available in several formats, including an online version. PHP's manual comes in several forms, too. The DBI module and its MySQL-specific driver are documented separately. The DBI document provides general concepts. The MySQL driver document discusses capabilities specific to MySQL.

- **FAQs.** There are FAQs for DBI, PHP, and Apache.

- **Mailing lists.** Several mailing lists centering around the software discussed in this book are available. It's a good idea to subscribe to the ones that deal with the tools you want to use. It's also a good idea to use the archives for those lists that have them. When you're new to a tool, you will have many of the same questions that have been asked (and answered) a million times, and there is no reason to ask again when you can find the answer with a quick search of the archives.

Instructions for subscribing to the mailing lists vary, but you can find information at the URLs shown here:

Package	Mailing List Instructions
MySQL	http://www.mysql.com/documentation/
Perl DBI	http://dbi.perl.org/
PHP	http://www.php.net/support.php
Apache	http://www.apache.org/foundation/mailinglists.html

- **Ancillary Web sites.** Besides the official Web sites, some of the tools discussed here have ancillary sites that provide more information, such as sample source code or topical articles. Check for a "Links" area on the official site you're visiting.

Using the Online MySQL Reference Manual

Be sure to check the online MySQL Reference Manual occasionally for information on the latest improvements to MySQL. The manual is updated continually as changes are made.

I

General MySQL Use

1

Getting Started with MySQL and SQL

THIS CHAPTER PROVIDES AN INTRODUCTION to the MySQL relational database management system (RDBMS) and to the Structured Query Language (SQL) that MySQL understands. It lays out basic terms and concepts you should understand, describes the sample database we'll use for examples throughout the book, and serves as a tutorial that shows you how to use MySQL to create a database and interact with it.

Begin here if you are new to databases and perhaps uncertain whether or not you need one or can use one. You should also read the chapter if you don't know anything about MySQL or SQL and need an introductory guide to get started. Readers who have experience with MySQL or with database systems might want to skim through the material. However, everybody should read the "A Sample Database" section to become familiar with the purpose and contents of the sampdb database that is used repeatedly throughout the book.

How MySQL Can Help You

This section describes situations in which the MySQL database system is useful. This will give you an idea of the kinds of things MySQL can do and the ways in which it can help you. If you don't need to be convinced about the usefulness of a database system—perhaps because you've already got a problem in mind and just want to find out how to put MySQL to work helping you solve it—you can proceed to the "A Sample Database" section later in this chapter.

A database system is essentially just a way to manage lists of information. The information can come from a variety of sources. For example, it can represent research data, business records, customer requests, sports statistics, sales reports, personal hobby information, personnel records, bug reports, or student grades. However, although database systems can deal with a wide range of information, you don't use such a system for its own sake. If a job is easy to do already, there's no reason to drag a database into it just to use one. A grocery list is a good example; you write down the items to get, cross them off as you do your shopping, and then throw the list away. It's highly unlikely that you'd use a database for this. Even if you have a palmtop computer, you'd probably keep track of a grocery list by using its notepad function rather than its database capabilities.

The power of a database system comes into play when the information you want to organize and manage becomes voluminous or complex and your records become more burdensome than you care to deal with by hand. Clearly this is the case for large corporations processing millions of transactions a day; a database is a necessity under such circumstances. But even small-scale operations involving a single person maintaining information of personal interest may require a database. It's not difficult to think of scenarios in which the use of a database can be beneficial because you needn't have huge amounts of information before that information becomes difficult to manage. Consider the following situations:

- Your carpentry business has several employees. You need to maintain employee and payroll records so that you know whom you've paid and when, and you must summarize those records so that you can report earnings statements to the government for tax purposes. You also need to keep track of the jobs your company has been hired to do and which employees you've scheduled to work on each job.

- You run a network of automobile parts warehouses and need to be able to tell which ones have any given part in their inventories so that you can fill customer orders.

- As a toy seller, you're particularly subject to fad-dependent demand for items that you carry. You want to know what the current sales trajectory is for certain items so that you can estimate whether to increase inventory (for an item that's becoming more popular) or decrease it (so you're not stuck with a lot of stock for something that's no longer selling well).

- That pile of research data you've been collecting over the course of many years needs to be analyzed for publication, lest the dictum "publish or perish" become the epitaph for your career. You want to boil down large amounts of raw data to generate summary information and to pull out selected subsets of observations for more detailed statistical analysis.

- You're a popular speaker who travels the country to many types of assemblies, such as graduations, business meetings, civic organizations, and political conventions. You give so many addresses that it's difficult to remember what you've spoken on at each place you've been, so you'd like to maintain records of your past talks and use them to help you plan future engagements. If you return to a place where you've spoken before, you don't want to give a talk similar to one you've already delivered there, and a record of each speech would help you avoid repeats. You'd also like to note how well your talks are received. (Your address "Why I Love Cats" at the Metropolitan Kennel Club was something of a dud, and you don't want to make that mistake again the next time you're there.)

- You're a teacher who needs to keep track of grades and attendance. Each time you give a quiz or a test, you record every student's grade. It's easy enough to write down scores in a gradebook, but using the scores later is a tedious chore. You'd rather avoid sorting the scores for each test to determine the grading curve, and you'd really rather not add up each student's scores when you determine final grades at the end of the grading period. Counting each student's absences is no fun, either.

- The organization for which you are the secretary maintains a directory of members. (The organization could be anything—a professional society, a club, a repertory company, a symphony orchestra, or an athletic booster club.) You generate the directory in printed form each year for members, based on a word processor document that you edit as membership information changes. You're tired of maintaining the directory that way because it limits what you can do with it. It's difficult to sort the entries in different ways, and you can't easily select just certain parts of each entry (such as a list consisting only of names and phone numbers). Nor can you easily find a subset of members, such as those who need to renew their memberships soon—if you could, it would eliminate the job of looking through the entries each month to find those members who need to be sent renewal notices. Also, you'd really like to avoid doing all the directory editing yourself, but the society doesn't have much of a budget and hiring someone is out of the question. You've heard about the "paperless office" that's supposed to result from electronic record keeping, but you haven't seen any benefit from it. The membership records are electronic, but, ironically, aren't in a form that can be used easily for anything *except* generating paper by printing the directory!

These scenarios range from situations involving relatively small amounts to large amounts of information. They share the common characteristic of involving tasks that can be performed manually but that could be performed more efficiently by a database system.

What specific benefits should you expect to see from using a database system such as MySQL? It depends on your particular needs and requirements—and as illustrated by the preceding examples, those can vary quite a bit. Let's look at a type of situation that occurs frequently and so is fairly representative of database use. Database management systems are often employed to handle tasks such as those for which people use filing cabinets. Indeed, a database is like a big filing cabinet in some ways, but one with a built-in filing system. There are some important advantages of electronically maintained records over records maintained by hand. For example, if you work in an office setting in which client records are maintained, the following are some of the ways MySQL can help you in its filing system capacity:

- **Reduced record filing time.** You don't have to look through drawers in cabinets to figure out where to add a new record. You just hand it to the filing system and let it put the record in the right place for you.

- **Reduced record retrieval time.** When you're looking for records, you don't search through each one yourself to find the ones containing the information you want. Suppose you work in a dentist's office. If you want to send out reminders to all patients who haven't been in for their checkup in a while, you ask the filing system to find the appropriate records for you. Of course, you do this differently than if you were talking to another person to whom you'd say, "Please determine which patients haven't visited within the last 6 months." With a database, you utter a strange incantation:

  ```
  SELECT last_name, first_name, last_visit FROM patient
  WHERE last_visit < DATE_SUB(CURDATE(),INTERVAL 6 MONTH);
  ```

  That can be pretty intimidating if you've never seen anything like it before, but the prospect of getting results in a second or two rather than spending an hour shuffling through your records should be attractive. (In any case, you needn't worry. That odd-looking bit of gobbledygook won't look strange for long. In fact, you'll understand exactly what it means by the time you've finished this chapter.)

- **Flexible retrieval order.** You needn't retrieve records according to the fixed order in which you store them (by patient's last name, for example). You can tell the filing system to pull out records sorted in any order you like—by last name, insurance company name, date of last visit, and so on.

- **Flexible output format.** After you've found the records in which you're interested, there's no need to copy the information manually. You can let the filing system generate a list for you. Sometimes you might just print the information. Other times you might want to use it in another program. (For example, after you generate the list of patients who are overdue on their dental visits, you might feed this information into a word processor that prints out notices that you can send to those patients.) Or you might be interested only in summary information, such as a count of the selected records. You don't have to count them yourself; the filing system can generate the summary for you.

- **Simultaneous multiple-user access to records.** With paper records, if two people want to look up a record at the same time, the second person must wait for the first one to put the record back. MySQL gives you multiple-user capability so that both can access the record simultaneously.

- **Remote access to and electronic transmission of records.** Paper records require you to be where the records are located or for someone to make copies and send them to you. Electronic records open up the potential for remote access to the records or electronic transmission of them. If your dental group has associates in branch offices, those associates can access your records from their own locations. You don't need to send copies by courier. If someone who needs records doesn't have the same kind of database software you do but does have electronic mail, you can select the desired records and send their contents electronically.

If you've used database management systems before, you already know about the benefits just described, and you may be thinking about how to go beyond the usual "replace the filing cabinet" applications. The manner in which many organizations use a database in conjunction with a Web site is a good example. Suppose your company has an inventory database that is used by the service desk staff when customers call to find out whether you have an item in stock and how much it costs. That's a relatively traditional use for a database. However, if your company puts up a Web site for customers to visit, you can provide an additional service—a search page that allows customers to determine item pricing and availability. This gives customers the information they want, and the way you provide it is by searching the inventory information stored in your database for the items in question—automatically. The customer gets the information immediately, without being put on hold listening to annoying canned music or being limited by the hours your service desk is open. And for every customer who uses your Web site, that's one less phone call that needs to be handled by a person on the service desk payroll. (Perhaps the Web site can pay for itself this way?)

But you can put the database to even better use than that. Web-based inventory search requests can provide information not only to your customers but to your company as well. The queries tell you what customers are looking for, and the query results tell you whether or not you're able to satisfy their requests. To the extent that you don't have what they want, you're probably losing business. Consequently, it makes sense to record information about inventory searches—what customers were looking for and whether you had it in stock. Then you can use this information to adjust your inventory and provide better service to your customers.

Another Web-based application for databases is to serve up banner advertisements in Web pages. I don't like them any better than you do, but the fact remains that they are a popular application for MySQL, which can be used to store advertisements and retrieve them for display by a Web server. In addition, MySQL can perform the kind of record keeping often associated with this activity by tracking which ads have been served, how many times they've been displayed, which sites accessed them, and so on.

So how does MySQL work? The best way to find out is to try it for yourself, and for that we'll need a database to work with.

A Sample Database

This section describes the sample database we'll use throughout the rest of this book. It gives you a source of examples you can try out as you learn to put MySQL to work. We'll draw examples primarily from two of the situations described earlier:

- **The organizational secretary scenario.** We need something more definite than "an organization," so I'll make one up with these characteristics: It's composed of people drawn together through a common affinity for United States history (called, for lack of a better name, the U.S. Historical League). The members maintain their affiliation by renewing their memberships periodically on a dues-paying basis. Dues go toward the expenses incurred by the League, such as publication of a newsletter, *Chronicles of U.S. Past*. The League also operates a small Web site, but it hasn't been developed very much. Thus far, the site has been limited to basic information, such as what the League is about, who the officers are, and how people can join.

- **The grade-keeping scenario.** During the grading period, you administer quizzes and tests, record scores, and assign grades. Afterward, you determine final grades, which you turn in to the school office along with an attendance summary.

Now let's examine these situations more closely in terms of two requirements:

- You have to decide what you want to get out of the database—that is, what goals you want to accomplish.

- You have to figure out what you're going to put into the database—that is, what data you will keep track of.

Perhaps it seems backward to think about what comes out of the database before considering what goes into it. After all, you must enter your data before you can retrieve it. But the way you use a database is driven by your goals, and those are more closely associated with what you want to get from your database than with what you put into it. You certainly aren't going to waste time and effort putting information into a database unless you're going to use it for something later.

The U.S. Historical League

The initial situation for this scenario is that you as League secretary maintain the membership list using a word processing document. That works reasonably well for generating a printed directory but limits what else you can do with the information. You have the following objectives in mind:

- You want to be able to produce output from the directory in different formats, using only information appropriate to the application. One goal is to be able to generate the printed directory each year—a requirement the League has had in the past that you plan to continue to carry out. You can think of other uses for the information in the directory, too— for example, to provide the current member list for the printed program that's handed out to attendees of the League's annual banquet. These applications involve different sets of information. The printed directory uses the entire contents of each member's entry. For the banquet program, you need to pull out only member names (something that hasn't been easy using a word processor).

- You want to search the directory for members whose entries satisfy various criteria. For example, you want to know which members need to renew their memberships soon. Another application that involves searching arises from the list of keywords you maintain for each member. These keywords describe areas of U.S. history in which each member is particularly interested (for example, the Civil War, the Depression, civil rights, or the life of Thomas Jefferson). Members sometimes ask you for a list of other members with interests similar to their own, and you'd like to be able to satisfy these requests.

- You want to put the directory online at the League's Web site. This would benefit both the members and yourself. If you could convert the directory to Web pages by some reasonably automated process, an online version of the directory could be kept up to date in a more timely fashion than the printed version. And if the online directory could be made searchable, members could look for information easily themselves. For example, a member who wants to know which other members are interested in the Civil War could find that out without waiting for you to perform the search, and you wouldn't need to find the time to do it yourself.

I'm well aware that databases are not the most exciting things in the world, so I'm not about to make any wild claims that using one stimulates creative thinking. Nevertheless, when you stop thinking of information as something you must wrestle with (as you do with your word processing document) and begin thinking of it as something you can manipulate relatively easily (as you hope to do with MySQL), it has a certain liberating effect on your ability to come up with new ways to use or present that information:

- If the information in the database can be moved to the Web site in the form of an online directory, you might be able to make information flow the other way. For example, if members could edit their own entries online to update the database, you wouldn't have to do all the editing yourself, and it would help make the information in the directory more accurate.

- If you stored email addresses in the database, you could use them to send email to members who haven't updated their entries in a while. The messages could show members the current contents of their entries, ask them to review it, and indicate how to make any needed modifications using the facilities provided on the Web site.

- A database might help you make the Web site more useful in ways not even related to the membership list. The League publishes a newsletter, *Chronicles of U.S. Past,* that has a children's section in each issue containing a history-based quiz. Some of the recent issues have focused on biographical facts about U.S. presidents. The Web site could have a children's section, too, where the quizzes are put online. Perhaps this section could even be made interactive by putting the information from which quizzes are drawn in the database and having the Web server query the database for questions to present to visitors.

Well! At this point the number of uses for the database that you're coming up with may make you realize that you could be getting a little carried away. After pausing to come back down to earth, you start asking some practical questions:

- **Isn't this a little ambitious?** Won't it be a lot of work to set this up? Anything's easier when you're just thinking about it and not doing it, of course, and I won't pretend that all of this will be trivial to implement. Nevertheless, you'll have done everything we've just outlined by the end of this book. Just keep one thing in mind: It's not necessary to do everything all at once. We'll break the job into pieces and tackle it a piece at a time.

- **Can MySQL do all these things?** No it can't, at least not by itself. For example, MySQL has no direct Web-programming facilities. But even though MySQL alone cannot do everything we've discussed, you can combine MySQL with other tools that work with it to complement and extend its capabilities.

  We'll use the Perl scripting language and the DBI (database interface) Perl module to write scripts that access MySQL databases. Perl has excellent text-processing capabilities that allow for manipulation of query results in a highly flexible manner to produce output in a variety of formats. For example, we can use Perl to generate the directory in Rich Text Format (RTF), a format that can be read by all kinds of word processors.

  We'll also use PHP, another scripting language. PHP is particularly adapted to writing Web applications, and it interfaces easily with databases. This allows you to run MySQL queries right from Web pages and to generate new pages that include the results of database queries. PHP works well with Apache (the most popular Web server in the world), making it easy to do things such as presenting a search form and displaying the results of the search.

  MySQL integrates well with these tools and gives you the flexibility to choose how to combine them to achieve the ends you have in mind. You're not locked into some all-in-one suite's components that have highly touted "integration" capabilities but that actually work well only with each other.

- **And, finally, the big question—how much will all this cost?** The League has a limited budget, after all. This may surprise you, but it probably won't cost anything. If you're familiar with the usual ken of database systems, you know that they're generally pretty pricey. By contrast, MySQL is usually free. (See the *MySQL Reference Manual* for specific details.) The other tools we'll use (Perl, DBI, PHP, Apache) are free, so, all things considered, you can put together a useful system quite inexpensively.

The choice of operating system for developing the database is up to you. Virtually all the software we'll discuss runs under both UNIX (which I use as an umbrella term that includes BSD UNIX, Linux, Mac OS X, and so on) and Windows. The few exceptions tend to be shell or batch scripts that are specific to either UNIX or Windows.

Now let's consider the other situation for which we'll be using the sample database.

The Grade-Keeping Project

The initial scenario here is that as a teacher, you have grade keeping responsibilities. You want to convert the grading process from a manual operation using a gradebook to an electronic representation using MySQL. In this case, the information you want to get from a database is implicit in the way you use your gradebook now:

- For each quiz or test, you record the scores. For tests, you put the scores in order so that you can look at them and determine the cutoffs for each letter grade (A, B, C, D, and F).

- At the end of the grading period, you calculate each student's total score, sort the totals, and then determine grades based on them. The totals might involve weighted calculations because you probably want to count tests more heavily than quizzes.

- You provide attendance information to the school office at the end of the grading period.

The objectives are to avoid manually sorting and summarizing scores and attendance records. In other words, you want MySQL to sort the scores and perform the calculations necessary to compute each student's total score and number of absences when the grading period ends. To achieve these goals, you'll need the list of students in the class, the scores for each quiz and test, and the dates on which students are absent.

How the Sample Database Applies to You

If you're not particularly interested in the Historical League or in grade keeping, you may be wondering what any of this has to do with you. The answer is that these example scenarios aren't an end in themselves. They simply provide a vehicle by which to illustrate what you can do with MySQL and tools that are related to it.

With a little imagination, you'll see how example database queries apply to the particular problems you want to solve. Suppose you're working in that dentist's office I mentioned earlier. You won't see many dentistry-related queries in this book, but you will see that many of the queries you find here apply to patient record maintenance, office bookkeeping, and so on. For example, determining which Historical League members need to renew their memberships soon is similar to determining which patients haven't visited the dentist for a while. Both are date-based queries, so once you learn to write the membership-renewal query, you can apply that skill to writing the delinquent-patient query in which you have a more immediate interest.

Basic Database Terminology

You may have noticed that you're already several pages into a database book and still haven't seen a whole bunch of jargon and technical terminology. In fact, I still haven't said anything at all about what "a database" actually looks like, even though we have a rough specification of how our sample database will be used. However, we're about to design that database and then we'll begin implementing it, so we can't avoid terminology any longer. That's what this section is about. It describes some terms that come up throughout the book so that you'll be familiar with them. Fortunately, many relational database concepts are really quite simple. In fact, much of the appeal of relational databases stems from the simplicity of their foundational concepts.

Structural Terminology

Within the database world, MySQL is classified as a relational database management system (RDBMS). That phrase breaks down as follows:

- The database (the "DB" in RDBMS) is the repository for the information you want to store, structured in a simple, regular fashion:
  - The collection of data in a database is organized into tables.
  - Each table is organized into rows and columns.
  - Each row in a table is a record.
  - Records can contain several pieces of information; each column in a table corresponds to one of those pieces.
- The management system (the "MS") is the software that lets you use your data by allowing you to insert, retrieve, modify, or delete records.
- The word "relational" (the "R") indicates a particular kind of DBMS, one that is very good at relating (that is, matching up) information stored in one table to information stored in another by looking for elements common to each of them. The power of a relational DBMS lies in its

ability to pull data from those tables conveniently and to join information from related tables to produce answers to questions that can't be
answered from individual tables alone.

Here's an example that shows how a relational database organizes data into
tables and relates the information from one table to another. Suppose you
run a Web site that includes a banner advertisement service. You contract
with companies that want their ads displayed when people visit the pages on
your site. Each time a visitor hits one of your pages, you serve an ad embedded in the page that is sent to the visitor's browser and assess the company a
small fee. To represent this information, you maintain three tables (see Figure
1.1). One table, `company`, has columns for company name, number, address,
and telephone number. Another table, `ad`, lists ad numbers, the number for
the company that "owns" the ad, and the amount you charge per hit. The
third table, `hit`, logs each ad hit by ad number and the date on which the ad
was served.

Some questions can be answered from this information using a single table. To
determine the number of companies you have contracts with, you need count
only the rows in the `company` table. Similarly, to determine the number of hits
during a given time period, only the `hit` table need be examined. Other questions are more complex and it's necessary to consult multiple tables to determine
the answers. For example, to determine how many times each of the ads for
Pickles, Inc. was served on July 14, you'd use all three tables as follows:

1. Look up the company name (Pickles, Inc.) in the `company` table to find
   the company number (14).

2. Use the company number to find matching records in the `ad` table so
   you can determine the associated ad numbers. There are two such ads,
   48 and 101.

3. For each of the matched records in the `ad` table, use the ad number in
   the record to find matching records in the `hit` table that fall within the
   desired date range, and then count the number of matches. There are
   three matches for ad 48 and two matches for ad 101.

Sounds complicated! But that's just the kind of thing at which relational database systems excel. The complexity is actually somewhat illusory because each
of the steps just described really amounts to little more than a simple matching
operation—you relate one table to another by matching values from one
table's rows to values in another table's rows. This same simple operation can
be exploited in various ways to answer all kinds of questions: How many different ads does each company have? Which company's ads are most popular?

How much revenue does each ad generate? What is the total fee for each company for the current billing period?

Now you know enough relational database theory to understand the rest of this book, and we don't have to go into Third Normal Form, Entity–Relationship Diagrams, and all that kind of stuff. (If you want to read about such things, I suggest you begin with the works of C.J. Date or E.F. Codd.)

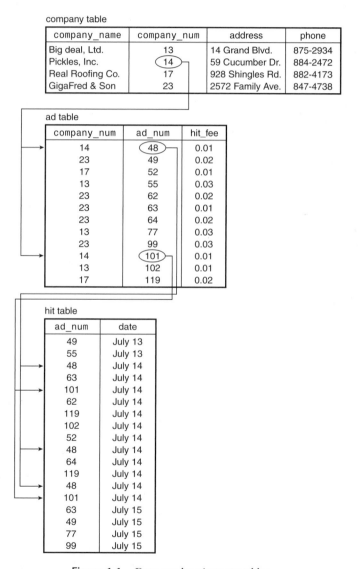

Figure 1.1   Banner advertisement tables.

Query Language Terminology

To communicate with MySQL, you use a language called SQL (Structured Query Language). SQL is today's standard database language, and all major database systems understand it. SQL supports many different kinds of statements, all designed to make it possible to interact with your database in interesting and useful ways.

As with any language, SQL may seem strange while you're first learning it. For example, to create a table, you need to tell MySQL what the table's structure should be. You and I might think of the table in terms of a diagram or picture, but MySQL doesn't, so you create the table by telling MySQL something like this:

```
CREATE TABLE company
(
    company_name  CHAR(30),
    company_num   INT,
    address       CHAR(30),
    phone         CHAR(12)
);
```

Statements like this can be somewhat imposing when you're new to SQL, but you need not be a programmer to learn how to use SQL effectively. As you gain familiarity with the language, you'll look at CREATE TABLE in a different light—as an ally that helps you describe your information, not as just a weird bit of gibberish.

MySQL Architectural Terminology

When you use MySQL, you're actually using two programs, because MySQL operates using a client/server architecture:

- The server program, mysqld, is located on the machine where your databases are stored. It listens for client requests coming in over the network and accesses database contents according to those requests to provide clients with the information they request.
- Clients are programs that connect to the database server and issue queries to tell it what information they want.

The MySQL distribution includes the database server and several client programs. You use the clients according to the purposes you want to achieve. The one most commonly used is mysql, an interactive client that lets you issue queries and see the results. Two administrative clients are mysqldump, which dumps table contents into a file, and mysqladmin, which allows you to check on the status of the server and performs administrative tasks, such as telling the server to shut down. The distribution includes other clients as well. If you have application requirements for which none of the standard clients is suited, MySQL also provides a client-programming library so that you can write your own programs. The library is usable directly from C programs. If you prefer a language other than C, interfaces are available for several other languages— Perl, PHP, Python, Java, C++, and Ruby, to name a few.

MySQL's client/server architecture has certain benefits:

- The server provides concurrency control so that two users cannot modify the same record at the same time. All client requests go through the server, so the server sorts out who gets to do what and when. If multiple clients want to access the same table at the same time, they don't all have to find and negotiate with each other. They just send their requests to the server and let it take care of determining the order in which the requests will be performed.

- You don't have to be logged in on the machine where your database is located. MySQL understands how to work over the Internet, so you can run a client program from wherever you happen to be, and the client can connect to the server over the network. Distance isn't a factor; you can access the server from anywhere in the world. If the server is located on a computer in Australia, you can take your laptop computer on a trip to Iceland and still access your database. Does that mean anyone can get at your data just by connecting to the Internet? No. MySQL includes a flexible security system, so you can allow access only to people who should have it. And you can make sure those people are able to do only what they should. Perhaps Sally in the billing office should be able to read and update (modify) records, but Phil at the service desk should be able only to look at them. You can set each person's privileges accordingly. If you do want to run a self-contained system, just set the access privileges so that clients can connect only from the host on which the server is running.

Beginning with MySQL 4, you have another option for running the server. In addition to the usual `mysqld` server that is used in a client/server setting, MySQL includes the server as a library, `libmysqld`, that you can link into programs to produce standalone MySQL-based applications. This is called the embedded server library because it's embedded into individual applications. Use of the embedded server contrasts with the client/server approach in that no network is required. This makes it easier to create and package applications that can be distributed on their own with fewer assumptions about their external operational environment. On the other hand, it should be used only in situations where the embedded application is the only one that will need access to the databases managed by the server.

The Difference Between MySQL and mysql

To avoid confusion, I should point out that MySQL refers to the entire MySQL RDBMS and `mysql` is the name of a particular client program. They sound the same if you pronounce them, but they're distinguished here by capitalization and typeface differences.

Speaking of pronunciation, MySQL is pronounced "my-ess-queue-ell." We know this because the MySQL Reference Manual says so. On the other hand, SQL is pronounced "sequel" or "ess-queue-ell," depending on who you ask. I'm not going to take sides. Pronounce it how you like, but be prepared for the eventuality that you'll run into someone who will correct you and inform you of the "proper" pronunciation! (I myself pronounce it as "sequel," which is why I use constructs like "a SQL query" rather than "an SQL query.")

A MySQL Tutorial

You have all the background you need now; it's time to put MySQL to work!

This section will help you familiarize yourself with MySQL by providing a tutorial for you to try. As you work through the tutorial, you will create a sample database and some tables and then interact with the database by adding, retrieving, deleting, and modifying information in the tables. During the process of working with the sample database, you will learn the following things:

- **The basics of the SQL language that MySQL understands**. (If you already know SQL from having used some other RDBMS, it would be a good idea to skim through this tutorial to see whether MySQL's version of SQL differs from the version with which you are familiar.)

- **How to communicate with a MySQL server using a few of the standard MySQL client programs**. As noted in the previous section, MySQL operates using a client/server architecture in which the server runs on the machine containing the databases and clients connect to the server over a network. This tutorial is based largely on the `mysql` client program, which reads SQL queries from you, sends them to the server to be executed, and displays the results so you can see what happened. `mysql` runs on all platforms supported by MySQL and provides the most direct means of interacting with the server, so it's the logical client to begin with. Some of the examples also use `mysqlimport` and `mysqlshow`.

This book uses `sampdb` as the sample database name, but you may need to use a different name as you work through the material. For example, someone else on your system already may be using the name `sampdb` for their own database, or your MySQL administrator may assign you a different database name. In either case, substitute the actual name of your database for `sampdb` whenever you see the latter in examples.

Table names can be used exactly as shown in the examples, even if multiple users on your system have their own sample databases. In MySQL, it doesn't matter if other people use the same table names, as long as each of you uses your own database. MySQL will keep the tables straight and prevent you from interfering with each other.

Obtaining the Sample Database Distribution

This tutorial refers at certain points to files from the "sample database distribution" (also known as the `sampdb` distribution, after the name of the `sampdb` database). These files contain queries and data that will help you set up the sample database. See Appendix A, "Obtaining and Installing Software," for instructions on getting the distribution. When you unpack it, it will create a directory named `sampdb` containing the files you'll need. I recommend that you change location into that directory whenever you're working through examples pertaining to the sample database.

Preliminary Requirements

To try the examples in this tutorial, a few preliminary requirements must be satisfied:

- You need to have the MySQL software installed.
- You need a MySQL account so that you can connect to the server.
- You need a database to work with.

The required software includes the MySQL clients and a MySQL server. The client programs must be located on the machine where you'll be working. The server can be located on your machine, although that is not required. As long as you have permission to connect to it, the server can be located anywhere. If you need to get MySQL, see Appendix A for instructions. If your network access comes through an Internet service provider (ISP), find out whether the provider offers MySQL as a service. If not and your ISP won't install it, check Appendix I, "Internet Service Providers," for some guidelines on choosing a more suitable provider.

In addition to the MySQL software, you'll need a MySQL account so that the server will allow you to connect and create your sample database and its tables. (If you already have a MySQL account, you can use that, but you may want to set up a separate account for use with the material in this book.)

At this point, we run into something of a chicken-and-egg problem. To set up a MySQL account to use for connecting to the server, it's necessary to connect to the server. Typically, this is done by connecting as the MySQL root user on the host where the server is running and issuing a GRANT statement to create a new MySQL account. If you've installed MySQL on your own machine and the server is running, you can connect to it and set up a new sample database administrator account with a username of sampadm and a password of secret as follows (change the name and password to those you want to use, both here and throughout the book):

```
% mysql -p -u root
Enter password: ******
mysql> GRANT ALL ON sampdb.* TO 'sampadm'@'localhost' IDENTIFIED BY 'secret';
```

The mysql command includes a -p option to cause mysql to prompt for the root user's MySQL password. Enter the password where you see ****** in the example. (I assume that you have already set up a password for the MySQL root user and that you know what it is. If you haven't yet assigned a password, just press Enter at the Enter password: prompt. However, having no root password is insecure and you should assign one as soon as possible.)

The GRANT statement just shown is appropriate if you'll be connecting to MySQL from the same machine where the server is running. It allows you to connect to the server using the name sampadm and the password secret and gives you complete access to the sampdb database. However, GRANT doesn't create the database; we'll get to that a bit later.

If you don't plan to connect from the same host as the one where the server is running, change localhost to the name of the machine where you'll be working. For example, if you will connect to the server from the host asp.snake.net, the GRANT statement should look like this:

```
mysql> GRANT ALL ON sampdb.* TO 'sampadm'@'asp.snake.net' IDENTIFIED BY 'secret';
```

If you don't have control over the server, ask your MySQL administrator to set up an account for you. Then substitute the MySQL username, password, and database name that the administrator assigns you for sampadm, secret, and sampdb throughout the examples in this book.

More information on the GRANT statement, setting up MySQL user accounts, and changing passwords can be found in Chapter 11, "General MySQL Administration."

Establishing and Terminating Connections to the Server

To connect to your server, invoke the `mysql` program from your shell (that is, from your UNIX prompt or from a DOS console under Windows). The command is as follows:

```
% mysql options
```

I use `%` throughout this book to indicate the shell prompt. That's one of the standard UNIX prompts; another is `$`. Under Windows, the prompt that you'll see will be something like `C:\>`.

The `options` part of the `mysql` command line might be empty, but more probably you'll have to issue a command that looks something like the following:

```
% mysql -h host_name -p -u user_name
```

You may not need to supply all those options when you invoke `mysql`, but it's likely that you'll have to specify at least a name and password. Here's what the options mean:

- `-h host_name` (alternate form: `--host=host_name`)

  The server host you want to connect to. If the MySQL server is running on the same machine where you are running `mysql`, this option normally can be omitted.

- `-u user_name` (alternate form: `--user=user_name`)

  Your MySQL username. If you're using UNIX and your MySQL username is the same as your login name, you can omit this option; `mysql` will use your login name as your MySQL name.

  Under Windows, the default user name is ODBC, which is unlikely to be a useful default for you. Either specify a `-u` option on the command line or add a default to your environment by setting the USER variable. For example, you can use the following `set` command to specify a user name of sampadm:

  ```
  C:\> set USER=sampadm
  ```

  If you place this command in your AUTOEXEC.BAT file, it will take effect whenever you start up Windows and you won't have to issue it at the prompt.

- `-p` (alternate form: `--password`)

  This option tells `mysql` to prompt you for your MySQL password. For example:

  ```
  % mysql -h host_name -p -u user_name
  Enter password:
  ```

When you see the `Enter password:` prompt, type in your password. (It won't be echoed to the screen, in case someone's looking over your shoulder.) Note that your MySQL password is not necessarily the same as your UNIX or Windows password. If you omit the `-p` option, `mysql` assumes you don't need one and doesn't prompt for it.

An alternate form of this option is to specify the password value directly on the command line by typing the option as `-pyour_pass` (alternate form: `--password=your_pass`). However, for security reasons, it's best not to do that. For one thing, the password becomes visible to others that way.

If you do decide to specify the password on the command line, note particularly that there is *no space* between the `-p` option and the following password value. This behavior of `-p` is a common point of confusion because it differs from the `-h` and `-u` options, which are associated with the word that follows them whether or not there is a space between the option and the word.

Suppose that my MySQL username and password are `sampadm` and `secret`. If the MySQL server is running on the same host, I can leave out the `-h` option and the `mysql` command to connect to the server looks like this:

```
% mysql -p -u sampadm
Enter password: ******
```

After I enter the command, `mysql` prints `Enter password:` to prompt for my password, and I type it in (the `******` indicates where I type `secret`).

If all goes well, `mysql` prints a greeting and a `mysql>` prompt indicating that it is waiting for me to issue queries. The full startup sequence is as follows:

```
% mysql -p -u sampadm
Enter password: ******
Welcome to the MySQL monitor.  Commands end with ; or \g.
Your MySQL connection id is 7575 to server version: 4.0.4-log

Type 'help;' or '\h' for help. Type '\c' to clear the buffer.
mysql>
```

To connect to a server running on some other machine, it's necessary to specify the hostname using an `-h` option. If that host is `cobra.snake.net`, the command looks like this:

```
% mysql -h cobra.snake.net -p -u sampadm
```

In most of the examples that follow that show a `mysql` command line, I'm going to leave out the `-h`, `-u`, and `-p` options for brevity and assume that you'll supply whatever options are necessary.

After you establish a connection to the server, you can terminate your session any time by typing QUIT:

```
mysql> QUIT
Bye
```

You can also quit by typing \q or (on UNIX) by pressing Ctrl-D.

When you're just starting to learn MySQL, you'll probably consider its security system to be an annoyance because it makes it harder to do what you want. (You must obtain permission to create and access a database, and you must specify your name and password whenever you connect to the server.) However, after you move beyond the sample database used in this book to entering and using your own records, your perspective will change radically. Then you'll appreciate the way that MySQL keeps other people from snooping through (or worse, destroying) your information.

There are ways to set up your account so you don't have to type in connection parameters each time you run mysql. These are discussed in the "Tips for Interacting with mysql" section later in this chapter. The most common method for simplifying the connection process is to store your connection parameters in an option file. You may want to skip ahead to that section right now to see how to set up such a file.

Issuing Queries

After you're connected to the server, you're ready to issue queries. This section describes some general things you should know about interacting with mysql.

To enter a query in mysql, just type it in. At the end of the query, type a semicolon character (';') and press Enter. The semicolon tells mysql that the query is complete. After you've entered a query, mysql sends it to the server to be executed. The server processes the query and sends the results back to mysql, which displays the result for you.

The following example shows a simple query that asks for the current date and time:

```
mysql> SELECT NOW();
+---------------------+
| NOW()               |
+---------------------+
| 2002-09-01 13:54:24 |
+---------------------+
1 row in set (0.00 sec)
```

mysql displays the query result and a line that shows the number of rows the result consists of and the time elapsed during query processing. In subsequent examples, I usually will not show the row-count line.

Because `mysql` waits for the semicolon as a statement terminator, you need not enter a query all on a single line. You can spread it over several lines if you want:

```
mysql> SELECT NOW(),
    -> USER(),
    -> VERSION()
    -> ;
+---------------------+-------------------+---------------+
| NOW()               | USER()            | VERSION()     |
+---------------------+-------------------+---------------+
| 2002-09-01 13:54:37 | sampadm@localhost | 4.0.4-beta-log |
+---------------------+-------------------+---------------+
```

Note how the prompt changes from `mysql>` to `->` after you enter the first line of the query. That tells you that `mysql` thinks you're still entering the query, which is important feedback—if you forget the semicolon at the end of a query, the changed prompt helps you realize that `mysql` is still waiting for something. Otherwise, you'll be waiting, wondering why it's taking MySQL so long to execute your query, and `mysql` will be waiting patiently for you to finish entering your query! (`mysql` has a couple of other prompts as well; they're all discussed in Appendix E, "MySQL Program Reference.")

For the most part, it doesn't matter whether you enter queries using uppercase, lowercase, or mixed case. The following queries are all equivalent:

```
SELECT USER();
select user();
SeLeCt UsEr();
```

The examples in this book use uppercase for SQL keywords and function names, and lowercase for database, table, and column names.

When you invoke a function in a query, there must be no space between the function name and the following parenthesis:

```
mysql> SELECT NOW ();
ERROR 1064: You have an error in your SQL syntax near '()' at line 1
mysql> SELECT NOW();
+---------------------+
| NOW()               |
+---------------------+
| 2002-09-01 13:56:36 |
+---------------------+
```

These two queries look similar, but the first one fails because the parenthesis doesn't immediately follow the function name.

Another way to terminate a query is to use \g rather than a semicolon:

```
mysql> SELECT NOW()\g
+---------------------+
| NOW()               |
+---------------------+
| 2002-09-01 13:56:47 |
+---------------------+
```

Or you can use \G, which displays the results in vertical format:

```
mysql> SELECT NOW(), USER(), VERSION()\G
*************************** 1. row ***************************
      NOW(): 2002-09-01 13:56:58
     USER(): sampadm@localhost
  VERSION(): 4.0.4-beta-log
```

For a query that generates short output lines, \G is not so useful, but if the lines are so long that they wrap around on your screen, \G can make the output easier to read.

If you've begun typing in a multiple-line query and decide you don't want to execute it, type \c to clear (cancel) it:

```
mysql> SELECT NOW(),
    -> VERSION(),
    -> \c
mysql>
```

Notice how the prompt changes back to mysql> to indicate that mysql is ready for a new query.

You can store queries in a file and tell mysql to read queries from the file rather than from the keyboard. Use your shell's input redirection facilities for this. For example, if I have queries stored in a file named myfile.sql, I can execute its contents as follows:

```
% mysql < myfile.sql
```

You can call the file whatever you want. I use the .sql suffix as a convention to indicate that a file contains SQL statements.

Executing mysql this way is something that will come up in the "Adding New Records" section later in this chapter when we enter data into the sampdb database. It's a lot more convenient to load a table by having mysql read INSERT statements from a file than to type in each statement manually.

The remainder of this tutorial shows many queries that you can try out for yourself. These are indicated by the mysql> prompt before the query, and such examples are usually accompanied by the output of the query. You should be able to type in these queries as shown, and the resulting output should be the same. Queries that are shown without a prompt are intended simply to illustrate a point, and you need not execute them. (You can try them out if you like; if you use `mysql` to do so, remember to include a terminator such as a semicolon at the end.)

> **When Do You Need a Semicolon?**
>
> Most queries shown in this book end with a semicolon, which is a convenient way of indicating where each query ends (particularly for multiple-statement examples). It also parallels the way you'd enter the queries should you try them from the `mysql` program. But semicolons are not part of the SQL syntax for the statements, so when you issue a query in another context, such as from within a Perl or PHP script, you should omit the semicolon. If you do not, an error will most likely occur.

Creating the Database

We'll begin by creating the `sampdb` sample database and the tables within it, populating its tables, and performing some simple queries on the data contained in those tables. Using a database involves several steps:

1. Creating (initializing) the database
2. Creating the tables within the database
3. Interacting with the tables by inserting, retrieving, modifying, or deleting data

Retrieving existing data is easily the most common operation performed on a database. The next most common operations are inserting new data and updating or deleting existing data. Less frequent are table creation operations, and least frequent of all is database creation. However, we're beginning from scratch, so we must begin with database creation, the least common thing, and work our way through table creation and insertion of our initial data before we get to where we can do the really common thing—retrieving data.

To create a new database, connect to the server using `mysql` and then issue a CREATE DATABASE statement that specifies the database name:

```
mysql> CREATE DATABASE sampdb;
```

You'll need to create the `sampdb` database before you can create any of the tables that will go in it or do anything with the contents of those tables.

Does creating the database select it as the default (or current) database? No, it doesn't, as you can see by executing the following query:

```
mysql> SELECT DATABASE();
+------------+
| DATABASE() |
+------------+
|            |
+------------+
```

To make `sampdb` the default database, issue a `USE` statement:

```
mysql> USE sampdb;
mysql> SELECT DATABASE();
+------------+
| DATABASE() |
+------------+
| sampdb     |
+------------+
```

The other way to select a database is to name it on the command line when you invoke `mysql`:

```
% mysql sampdb
```

That is, in fact, the usual way to name the database you want to use. If you need any connection parameters, specify them before the database name. For example, the following two commands allow the `sampadm` user to connect to the `sampdb` database on the local host and on `cobra.snake.net`:

```
% mysql -p -u sampadm sampdb
% mysql -h cobra.snake.net -p -u sampadm sampdb
```

Unless specified otherwise, all the examples that follow assume that when you invoke `mysql`, you name the `sampdb` database on the command line to make it the current database. If you invoke `mysql` but forget to name the database on the command line, just issue a `USE sampdb` statement at the `mysql>` prompt.

Creating Tables

In this section, we'll build the tables needed for the `sampdb` sample database. First, we'll consider the tables needed for the Historical League and then those for the grade-keeping project. This is the part where some database books start talking about Analysis and Design, Entity-Relationship Diagrams, Normalization Procedures, and other such stuff. There's a place for all that, but I prefer just to say we need to think a bit about what our database will look like—what tables it should contain, what the contents of each table should be, and some of the issues involved in deciding how to represent our data.

The choices made here about data representation are not absolute. In other situations, you might well elect to represent similar data in a different way, depending on the requirements of your applications and the uses to which you intend to put your data.

Tables for the Historical League

Table layout for the Historical League is pretty simple:

- **A `president` table**. This contains a descriptive record for each U.S. president. We'll need this for the online quiz on the League Web site (the interactive analog to the printed quiz that appears in the children's section of the League's newsletter).

- **A `member` table**. This is used to maintain current information about each member of the League. It'll be used for creating printed and online versions of the member directory, sending automated membership renewal reminders, and so on.

The president Table

The `president` table is simpler, so let's discuss it first. This table will contain some basic biographical information about each United States president:

- **Name**. Names can be represented in a table several ways. For example, we could have a single column containing the entire name or separate columns for the first and last name. It's certainly simpler to use a single column, but that limits you in some ways:
    - If you enter the names with the first name first, you can't sort on last name.
    - If you enter the names with the last name first, you can't display them with the first name first.
    - It's harder to search for names. For example, to search for a particular last name, you must use a pattern and look for names that match the pattern. This is less efficient and slower than looking for an exact last name.

  To avoid these limitations, our `president` table will use separate columns for the first and last names.

  The first name column will also hold the middle name or initial. This shouldn't break any sorting we might do because it's not likely we'll want to sort on middle name (or even first name). Name display should work properly, too, because the middle name immediately follows the first name regardless of whether a name is printed in "Bush, George W." or in "George W. Bush" format.

  There is another slight complication. One president (Jimmy Carter) has a "Jr." at the end of his name. Where does that go? Depending on the format in which names are printed, this president's name is displayed as "James E. Carter, Jr." or "Carter, James E., Jr." The "Jr." doesn't associate with either first or last name, so we'll create another column to hold a name suffix. This illustrates how even a single value can cause problems when you're trying to determine how to represent your data. It also shows why it's a good idea to know as much as possible about the type of data values you'll be working with before you put them in a database. If you have incomplete knowledge of what your data look like, you may have to change your table structure after you've already begun to use it. That's not necessarily a disaster, but in general it's something you want to avoid.

- **Birthplace (city and state).** Like the name, this too can be represented using a single column or multiple columns. It's simpler to use a single column, but as with the name, separate columns allow you to do some things you can't do easily otherwise. For example, it's easier to find records for presidents born in a particular state if city and state are listed separately.

- **Birth date and death date.** The only special problem here is that we can't require the death date to be filled in because some presidents are still living. MySQL provides a special value NULL that means "no value," so we can use that in the death date column to signify "still alive."

The member Table

The member table for the Historical League membership list is similar to the president table in the sense that each record contains basic descriptive information for a single person. But each member record contains more columns:

- **Name.** We'll use the same three-column representation as for the president table: last name, first name, and suffix.

- **ID number.** This is a unique value assigned to each member when a membership first begins. The League hasn't ever used ID numbers before, but now that the records are being made more systematic, it's a good time to start. (I am anticipating that you'll find MySQL beneficial and that you'll think of other ways to apply it to the League's records. When that happens, it'll be easier to associate records in the member table with other member-related tables you may create if you use numbers rather than names.)

- **Expiration date.** Members must renew their memberships periodically to avoid having them lapse. For some applications, you might use the date of the most recent renewal, but this is not suitable for the League's purposes. Memberships can be renewed for a variable number of years (typically one, two, three, or five years), and a date for the most recent renewal wouldn't tell you when the next renewal must take place. In addition, the League allows lifetime memberships. We could represent these with a date far in the future, but NULL seems more appropriate because "no value" logically corresponds to "never expires."

- **Email address**. Publishing these addresses will make it easier for those members that have them to communicate with each other more easily. For your purposes as League secretary, these addresses will allow you to send out membership renewal notices electronically rather than by postal mail. This should be easier than going to the post office and less expensive as well. You'll also be able to use email to send members the current contents of their directory entries and ask them to update the information as necessary.

- **Postal address**. This is needed for contacting members that don't have email (or who don't respond to it). We'll use columns for street address, city, state, and Zip code.

  I'm assuming that all League members live in the United States. For organizations with a membership that is international in scope, that assumption is an oversimplification, of course. If you want to deal with addresses from multiple countries, you'll run into some sticky issues having to do with the different address formats used for different countries. For example, Zip code is not an international standard, and some countries have provinces rather than states.

- **Phone number**. Like the address fields, this is useful for contacting members.

- **Special interest keywords**. Every member is assumed to have a general interest in U.S. history, but members probably also have some special areas of interest. This column records those interests. Members can use it to find other members with similar interests.

Creating the Historical League Tables

Now we're ready to create the Historical League tables. For this we use the CREATE TABLE statement, which has the following general form:

```
CREATE TABLE tbl_name ( column_specs );
```

`tbl_name` indicates the name you want to give the table. `column_specs` provides the specifications for the columns in the table, as well as any indexes (if there are any). Indexes make lookups faster; we'll discuss them further in Chapter 4, "Query Optimization." For the president table, the CREATE TABLE statement looks like this:

```
CREATE TABLE president
(
    last_name    VARCHAR(15) NOT NULL,
    first_name   VARCHAR(15) NOT NULL,
    suffix       VARCHAR(5) NULL,
```

```
    city        VARCHAR(20) NOT NULL,
    state       VARCHAR(2) NOT NULL,
    birth       DATE NOT NULL,
    death       DATE NULL
);
```

If you want to type in that statement yourself, invoke mysql, making sampdb the current database:

```
% mysql sampdb
```

Then enter the CREATE TABLE statement as just shown, including the trailing semicolon so that mysql can tell where the end of the statement is.

To create the president table using a prewritten description, use the create_president.sql file from the sampdb distribution. This file is located in the sampdb directory that is created when you unpack the distribution. Change location into that directory and then run the following command:

```
% mysql sampdb < create_president.sql
```

Whichever way you invoke mysql, specify any connection parameters you may need (hostname, username, or password) on the command line preceding the database name.

Each column specification in the CREATE TABLE statement consists of the column name, the data type (the kind of values the column will hold), and possibly some column attributes.

The two column types used in the president table are VARCHAR and DATE. VARCHAR(n) means the column contains variable-length character (string) values, with a maximum length of n characters each. You choose the value of n according to how long you expect your values to be. state is declared as VAR-CHAR(2); that's all we need if states are entered using their two-character abbreviations. The other string-valued columns need to be wider to accommodate longer values.

The other column type we've used is DATE. This type indicates, not surprisingly, that the column holds date values. However, what may be surprising to you is the format in which dates are represented. MySQL expects dates to be specified in 'CCYY-MM-DD' format, where CC, YY, MM, and DD represent the century, year within the century, month, and date. This is the ANSI SQL standard for date representation (also known as ISO 8601 format). For example, a date of July 18, 2002 is specified in MySQL as '2002-07-18', not as '07-18-2002' or '18-07-2002'.

The only attributes we're using for the columns in the president table are NULL (values can be missing) and NOT NULL (values must be filled in). Most columns are NOT NULL because we'll always have a value for them. The two columns that can have NULL values are suffix (most names don't have one) and death (some presidents are still alive, so there is no date of death).

For the member table, the CREATE TABLE statement looks like this:

```
CREATE TABLE member
(
    member_id    INT UNSIGNED NOT NULL AUTO_INCREMENT,
    PRIMARY KEY (member_id),
    last_name    VARCHAR(20) NOT NULL,
    first_name   VARCHAR(20) NOT NULL,
    suffix       VARCHAR(5) NULL,
    expiration   DATE NULL DEFAULT '0000-00-00',
    email        VARCHAR(100) NULL,
    street       VARCHAR(50) NULL,
    city         VARCHAR(50) NULL,
    state        VARCHAR(2) NULL,
    zip          VARCHAR(10) NULL,
    phone        VARCHAR(20) NULL,
    interests    VARCHAR(255) NULL
);
```

Type that statement into mysql or execute the following command to use the prewritten file from the sampdb distribution:

```
% mysql sampdb < create_member.sql
```

In terms of column types, most columns of the member table except two are not very interesting because they are created as variable-length strings. The exceptions are member_id and expiration, which exist to hold sequence numbers and dates, respectively.

The primary consideration for the member_id membership number column is that each of its values should be unique to avoid confusion between members. An AUTO_INCREMENT column is useful here because then we can let MySQL generate unique numbers for us automatically when we add new members. Even though it just contains numbers, the declaration for member_id has several parts:

- INT signifies that the column holds integers (numeric values with no fractional part).
- UNSIGNED disallows negative numbers.
- NOT NULL requires that the column value must be filled in. (This means that no member can be without an ID number.)
- AUTO_INCREMENT is a special attribute in MySQL. It indicates that the column holds sequence numbers. The AUTO_INCREMENT mechanism works like this; If the value for the member_id column is missing

(or NULL) when you create a new member table record, MySQL automatically generates the next sequence number and assigns it to the column. This makes it easy to assign IDs to new members, because MySQL will do it for us.

The PRIMARY KEY clause indicates that the member_id column is indexed to allow fast lookups and that each value in the column must be unique. The latter property is desirable for member ID values, because it prevents us from using the same ID twice by mistake. (Besides, MySQL requires every AUTO_INCREMENT column to have some kind of unique index, so the table definition is illegal without one.)

If you don't understand that stuff about AUTO_INCREMENT and PRIMARY KEY, just think of them as giving us a magic way of generating an ID number for each member. It doesn't particularly matter what the values are, as long as they're unique. (When you're ready to learn more about how to declare and use AUTO_INCREMENT columns, Chapter 2, "Working with Data in MySQL," covers them in detail.)

The expiration column is a DATE. It has a default value of '0000-00-00', which is a non-NULL value that means no legal date has been entered. The reason for this is that expiration can be NULL to indicate that a member has a lifetime membership. If we don't specify otherwise, a column that can contain NULL also has NULL as its default value. That's not desirable in this case; if you created a new member record but forgot to specify the expiration date, MySQL would fill in the expiration column with NULL automatically—thus making the member a lifetime member! By specifying that the column has a default value of '0000-00-00' instead, we avoid this problem. That also gives us a value we can search for periodically to find records for which the expiration date was never properly entered.

Now that you've told MySQL to create a couple of tables, check to make sure that it did so as you expect. In mysql, issue the following query to see the structure of the president table:

```
mysql> DESCRIBE president;
+------------+-------------+------+-----+------------+-------+
| Field      | Type        | Null | Key | Default    | Extra |
+------------+-------------+------+-----+------------+-------+
| last_name  | varchar(15) |      |     |            |       |
| first_name | varchar(15) |      |     |            |       |
| suffix     | varchar(5)  | YES  |     | NULL       |       |
| city       | varchar(20) |      |     |            |       |
| state      | char(2)     |      |     |            |       |
| birth      | date        |      |     | 0000-00-00 |       |
| death      | date        | YES  |     | NULL       |       |
+------------+-------------+------+-----+------------+-------+
```

In some versions of MySQL, the results from DESCRIBE include additional information showing access privilege information. I've not shown that here because it makes the lines too long to display without wrapping around.

The output looks pretty much as we'd expect, except that the information for the state column says its type is CHAR(2). That's odd; wasn't it declared as VAR-CHAR(2)? Yes, it was, but MySQL has silently changed the type from VARCHAR to CHAR. The reason for this has to do with efficiency of storage space for short character columns, which I won't go into here. If you want the details, check the discussion of the ALTER TABLE statement in Chapter 3, "MySQL SQL Syntax and Use." For our purposes here, there is no difference between the two types. The important thing is that the column stores two-character values.

If you issue a DESCRIBE member query, mysql will show you similar information for the member table.

DESCRIBE is useful when you forget the name of a column in a table or need to know its type or how wide it is and so on. It's also useful for finding out the order in which MySQL stores columns in table rows. That order is important when you use INSERT or LOAD DATA statements that expect column values to be listed in the default column order.

The information produced by DESCRIBE can be obtained in different ways. It may be abbreviated as DESC or written as an EXPLAIN or SHOW statement. The following statements are all synonymous:

```
DESCRIBE president;
DESC president;
EXPLAIN president;
SHOW COLUMNS FROM president;
SHOW FIELDS FROM president;
```

These statements also allow you to restrict the output to particular columns. For example, you can add a LIKE clause at the end of a SHOW statement to display information only for column names that match a given pattern:

```
mysql> SHOW COLUMNS FROM president LIKE '%name';
+------------+-------------+------+-----+---------+-------+
| Field      | Type        | Null | Key | Default | Extra |
+------------+-------------+------+-----+---------+-------+
| last_name  | varchar(15) |      |     |         |       |
| first_name | varchar(15) |      |     |         |       |
+------------+-------------+------+-----+---------+-------+
```

The '%' character used here is a special wildcard character that is described later in the "Pattern Matching" section. Similar restrictions can be used with DESCRIBE and EXPLAIN as well; for the exact syntax, see Appendix D, "SQL Syntax Reference."

The SHOW statement has other forms that are useful for obtaining different types of information from MySQL. SHOW TABLES lists the tables in the current database, so with the two tables we've created so far in the sampdb database, the output looks like this:

```
mysql> SHOW TABLES;
+------------------+
| Tables_in_sampdb |
+------------------+
| member           |
| president        |
+------------------+
```

SHOW DATABASES lists the databases that are managed by the server to which you're connected:

```
mysql> SHOW DATABASES;
+-----------+
| Database  |
+-----------+
| menagerie |
| mysql     |
| sampdb    |
| test      |
+-----------+
```

The list of databases varies from server to server, but you should see at least sampdb and mysql. You created sampdb yourself, and the database named mysql holds the grant tables that control MySQL access privileges.

The mysqlshow utility provides a command-line interface to the same kinds of information that the SHOW statement displays. With no arguments, mysql-show displays a list of databases:

```
% mysqlshow
+-------------+
|  Databases  |
+-------------+
| menagerie   |
| mysql       |
| sampdb      |
| test        |
+-------------+
```

With a database name, it shows the tables in the given database:

```
% mysqlshow sampdb
Database: sampdb
+-----------+
|  Tables   |
+-----------+
| member    |
| president |
+-----------+
```

With a database and table name, `mysqlshow` displays information about the columns in the table, much like the SHOW COLUMNS statement.

Tables for the Grade-Keeping Project

To see what tables are required for the grade-keeping project, let's consider how you might write down scores when you use a paper-based gradebook. Figure 1.2 shows a page from your gradebook. The main body of this page is a matrix for recording scores. There is also other information necessary for making sense of the scores. Student names and ID numbers are listed down the side of the matrix. (For simplicity, only four students are shown.) Along the top of the matrix, you put down the dates when you give quizzes and tests. The figure shows that you've given quizzes on September 3, 6, 16, and 23, and tests on September 9 and October 1.

students		scores						
		Q	Q	T	Q	Q	T	
ID	name	9/3	9/6	9/9	9/16	9/23	10/1	...
1	Billy	14	10	73	14	15	67	...
2	Missy	17	10	68	17	14	73	...
3	Johnny	15	10	78	12	17	82	...
4	Jenny	14	13	85	13	19	79	...
...	...	...	...	...	...	...	...	...

Figure 1.2   Example gradebook.

To keep track of this kind of information using a database, we need a `score` table. What should records in this table contain? That's easy. For each row, we need student name, the date of the quiz or test, and the score. Figure 1.3 shows how some of the scores from the gradebook look when represented in a table like this. (Dates are written the way MySQL represents them, in `'CCYY-MM-DD'` format.)

`score` table

name	date	score
Billy	2002-09-23	15
Missy	2002-09-23	14
Johnny	2002-09-23	17
Jenny	2002-09-23	19
Billy	2002-10-01	67
Missy	2002-10-01	73
Johnny	2002-10-01	82
Jenny	2002-10-01	79

Figure 1.3   Initial `score` table layout.

However, there is a problem with setting up the table in this way because it leaves out some information. For example, looking at the records in Figure 1.3, we can't tell whether scores are for a quiz or a test. It could be important to know score types when determining final grades if quizzes and tests are weighted differently. We might try to infer the type from the range of scores on a given date (quizzes usually are worth fewer points than a test), but that's ugly because it relies on inference and not something explicit in the data.

It's possible to distinguish scores by recording the type in each record, for example, by adding a column to the `score` table that contains 'T' or 'Q' for each row to indicate "test" or "quiz," as in Figure 1.4. This has the advantage of making the type of score explicit in the data. The disadvantage is that this information is somewhat redundant. Observe that for all records with a given date, the score type column always has the same value. The scores for September 23 all have a type of 'Q', and the scores for October 1 all have a type of 'T'. This is unappealing. If we record a set of scores for a quiz or test this way, not only will we be putting in the same date for each new record in the set, we'll be putting in the same score type over and over again. Ugh. Who wants to enter all that redundant information?

score table

name	date	score	type
Billy	2002-09-23	15	Q
Missy	2002-09-23	14	Q
Johnny	2002-09-23	17	Q
Jenny	2002-09-23	19	Q
Billy	2002-10-01	67	T
Missy	2002-10-01	73	T
Johnny	2002-10-01	82	T
Jenny	2002-10-01	79	T

Figure 1.4   `score` table layout, revised to include score type.

Let's try an alternative representation. Instead of recording score types in the `score` table, we'll figure them out from the dates. We can keep a list of dates and use it to keep track of what kind of "grade event" (quiz or test) occurred on each date. Then we can determine whether any given score was from a quiz or a test by combining it with the information in our event list; just match the date in the `score` table record with the date in the `event` table to get the event type. Figure 1.5 shows this table layout and demonstrates how the association works for a `score` table record with a date of September 23. By matching the record with the corresponding record in the `event` table, we see that the score is from a quiz.

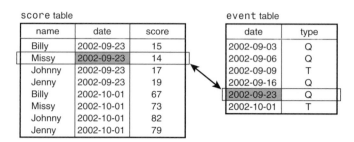

Figure 1.5 score and event tables, linked on date.

This is much better than trying to infer the score type based on some guess; instead, we're deriving the type directly from data recorded explicitly in our database. It's also preferable to recording score types in the score table because we must record each type only one time, rather than once per score record.

However, now we're combining information from multiple tables. If you're like me, when you first hear about this kind of thing, you think, "Yeah, that's a cute idea, but isn't it a lot of work to do all that looking up all the time; doesn't it just make things more complicated?"

In a way, that's correct; it is more work. Keeping two lists of records is more complicated than keeping one list. But take another look at your gradebook (see Figure 1.2). Aren't you already keeping two sets of records? Consider the following facts:

- You keep track of scores using the cells in the score matrix, where each cell is indexed by student name and date (down the side and along the top of the matrix). This represents one set of records; it's analogous to the contents of the score table.

- How do you know what kind of event each date represents? You've written a little 'T' or 'Q' above the date, so you're also keeping track of the association between date and score type along the top of the matrix. This represents a second set of records; it's analogous to the event table contents.

In other words, even though you may not think about it as such, you're really not doing anything different with the gradebook than what I'm proposing to do by keeping information in two tables. The only real difference is that the two kinds of information aren't so explicitly separated in the paper-based gradebook.

The page in the gradebook illustrates something about the way we think of information and about the difficulty of figuring out how to put information in a database. We tend to integrate different kinds of information and interpret them as a whole. Databases don't work like that, which is one reason why they sometimes seem artificial and unnatural. Our natural tendency to unify information makes it quite difficult sometimes even to realize when we have multiple types of data instead of just one. Because of this, you may find it a challenge to "think as a database thinks" about how your data should be represented.

One requirement imposed on the `event` table by the layout shown in Figure 1.5 is that the dates be unique because each date is used to link together records from the `score` and `event` tables. In other words, you cannot give two quizzes on the same day, or a quiz and a test. If you do, you'll have two sets of records in the `score` table and two records in the `event` table, all with the same date, and you won't be able to tell how to match `score` records with `event` records.

That problem will never come up if there is never more than one grade event per day. But is it really valid to assume that will never happen? It might seem so; after all, you don't consider yourself sadistic enough to give a quiz and a test on the same day. But I hope you'll pardon me if I'm skeptical. I've often heard people claim about their data, "That odd case will never occur." Then it turns out the odd case does occur on occasion, and usually you have to redesign your tables to fix problems that the odd case causes.

It's better to think about the possible problems in advance and anticipate how to handle them. So, let's suppose you might need to record two sets of scores for the same day sometimes. How can we handle that? As it turns out, this problem isn't so difficult to solve. With a minor change to the way we lay out our data, multiple events on a given date won't cause trouble:

1. Add a column to the `event` table and use it to assign a unique number to each record in the table. In effect, this gives each event its own ID number, so we'll call this the `event_id` column. (If this seems like an odd thing to do, consider that your gradebook in Figure 1.2 already has this property; the event ID is just like the column number in your gradebook score matrix. The number might not be written down explicitly there and labeled "event ID," but that's what it is.)

2. When you put scores in the `score` table, record the event ID rather than the date.

The result of these changes is shown in Figure 1.6. Now you link together the `score` and `event` tables using the event ID rather than the date, and you use the `event` table to determine not just the type of each score but also the date on which it occurred. Also, it's no longer the date that must be unique in the `event` table, it's the event ID. This means you can have a dozen tests and quizzes on the same day, and you'll be able to keep them straight in your records. (No doubt your students will be thrilled to hear this.)

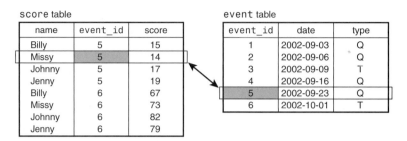

Figure 1.6   `score` and `event` tables, linked on event ID.

Unfortunately, from a human standpoint, the table layout in Figure 1.6 seems less satisfactory than the previous ones. The `score` table is more abstract because it contains fewer columns that have a readily apparent meaning. The table layout shown earlier in Figure 1.4 was easy to look at it and understand because the `score` table had columns for both dates and score types. The current `score` table shown in Figure 1.6 has columns for neither. This seems highly removed from anything we can think about easily. Who wants to look at a `score` table that has "event IDs" in it? That just doesn't mean much to us.

At this point, you reached a crossroads. You're intrigued by the possibility of being able to perform grade-keeping electronically and not having to do all kinds of tedious manual calculations when assigning grades. But after considering how you actually would represent score information in a database, you're put off by how abstract and disconnected the representation seems to make that information.

This leads naturally to a question: "Would it be better not to use a database at all? Maybe MySQL isn't for me." As you might guess, I will answer that question in the negative, because otherwise this book will come to a quick end. But when you're thinking about how to do a job, it's not a bad idea to consider various alternatives and to ask whether you're better off using a database system such as MySQL or something else, such as a spreadsheet program:

- The gradebook has rows and columns, and so does a spreadsheet. This makes the gradebook and a spreadsheet conceptually and visually very similar.

- A spreadsheet program can perform calculations, so you could total up each student's scores using a calculation field. It might be a little tricky to weight quizzes and tests differently, but you could do it.

On the other hand, if you want to look at just part of your data (quizzes only or tests only, for example), perform comparisons such as boys versus girls, or display summary information in a flexible way, it's a different story. A spreadsheet doesn't work so well, whereas relational database systems perform those operations easily.

Another point to consider is that the abstract and disconnected nature of your data as represented in a relational database is not really that big of a deal, anyway. It's necessary to think about that representation when setting up the database so that you don't lay out your data in a way that doesn't make sense for what you want to do with it. However, after you determine the representation, you're going to rely on the database engine to pull together and present your data in a way that is meaningful to you. You're not going to look at it as a bunch of disconnected pieces.

For example, when you retrieve scores from the `score` table, you don't want to see event IDs; you want to see dates. That's not a problem. The database will look up dates from the `event` table based on the event ID and show them to you. You may also want to see whether the scores are for tests or quizzes. That's not a problem, either. The database will look up score types the same way—using the event ID. Remember, that's what a relational database system like MySQL is good at—relating one thing to another to pull out information from multiple sources to present you with what you really want to see. In the case of our grade-keeping data, MySQL does the thinking about pulling information together using event IDs so that you don't have to.

Now, just to provide a little advance preview of how you'd tell MySQL to do this relating of one thing to another, suppose you want to see the scores for September 23, 2002. The query to pull out scores for an event given on a particular date looks like the following:

```
SELECT score.name, event.date, score.score, event.type
FROM score, event
WHERE event.date = '2002-09-23'
AND score.event_id = event.event_id;
```

Pretty scary, huh? This query retrieves the student name, the date, score, and the type of score by joining (relating) score table records to event table records. The result looks like this:

```
+--------+------------+-------+------+
| name   | date       | score | type |
+--------+------------+-------+------+
| Billy  | 2002-09-23 |    15 | Q    |
| Missy  | 2002-09-23 |    14 | Q    |
| Johnny | 2002-09-23 |    17 | Q    |
| Jenny  | 2002-09-23 |    19 | Q    |
+--------+------------+-------+------+
```

Notice anything familiar about the format of that information? You should; it's the same as the table layout shown in Figure 1.4. And you don't need to know the event ID to get this result. You specify the date you're interested in and let MySQL figure out which score records go with that date. So if you've been wondering whether all the abstraction and disconnectedness loses us anything when it comes to getting information out of the database in a form that's meaningful to us, it doesn't.

Of course, after looking at that query, you might be wondering something else, too. Namely, it looks kind of long and complicated; isn't writing something like that a lot of work to go to just to find the scores for a given date? Yes, it is. However, there are ways to avoid typing several lines of SQL each time you want to issue a query. Generally, you figure out once how to perform a query such as that one and then you store it so that you can repeat it easily as necessary. We'll see how to do this in the "Tips for Interacting with mysql" section later in this chapter.

I've actually jumped the gun a little bit in showing you that query. It is, believe it or not, a little simpler than the one we're really going to use to pull out scores. The reason for this is that we need to make one more change to our table layout. Instead of recording student name in the score table, we'll use a unique student ID. (That is, we'll use the value from the "ID" column of your gradebook rather than from the "Name" column.) Then we create another table called `student` that contains name and `student_id` columns (Figure 1.7).

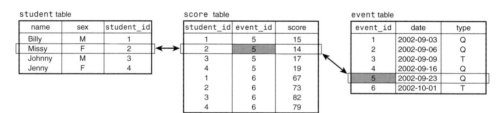

Figure 1.7   `student`, `score`, and `event` tables, linked on student ID and event ID.

Why make this modification? For one thing, there might be two students with the same name. Using a unique student ID number helps you tell their scores apart. (This is exactly analogous to the way you can tell scores apart for a test and quiz given on the same day by using a unique event ID rather than the date.) After making this change to the table layout, the query we'll actually use to pull out scores for a given date becomes a little more complex:

```
SELECT student.name, event.date, score.score, event.type
FROM event, score, student
```

```
WHERE event.date = '2002-09-23'
AND event.event_id = score.event_id
AND score.student_id = student.student_id;
```

If you're concerned because you don't find the meaning of that query immediately obvious, don't be. Most people wouldn't. We'll see the query again after we get further along into this tutorial, but the difference between now and later is that later you'll understand it. And, no, I'm not kidding.

You'll note from Figure 1.7 that I added something to the student table that wasn't in your gradebook; it contains a column for sex. This will allow for simple things like counting the number of boys and girls in the class or more complex things like comparing scores for boys and girls.

We're almost done designing the tables for the grade-keeping project. We need just one more table to record absences for attendance purposes. Its contents are relatively straightforward: a student ID number and a date (see Figure 1.8). Each row in the table indicates that the given student was absent on the given date. At the end of the grading period, we'll call on MySQL's counting abilities to summarize the table's contents to tell us how many times each student was absent.

absence table

student_id	date
2	2002-09-02
4	2002-09-15
2	2002-09-20

Figure 1.8   absence table.

Now that we know what our grade-keeping tables should look like, we're ready to create them. The CREATE TABLE statement for the student table is as follows:

```
CREATE TABLE student
(
    name        VARCHAR(20) NOT NULL,
    sex         ENUM('F','M') NOT NULL,
    student_id  INT UNSIGNED NOT NULL AUTO_INCREMENT,
    PRIMARY KEY (student_id)
);
```

Type that statement into mysql or execute the following command:

```
% mysql sampdb < create_student.sql
```

The CREATE TABLE statement creates a table named student with three columns, name, sex, and student_id.

name is a variable-length string column that can hold up to 20 characters. This name representation is simpler than the one used for the Historical

League tables; it uses a single column rather than separate first name and last name columns. That's because I know in advance that no grade-keeping query examples will need to do anything that would work better with separate columns. (Yes, that's cheating. I admit it.)

sex represents whether a student is a boy or a girl. It's an ENUM (enumeration) column, which means it can take on only one of the values listed in the column specification: 'F' for female or 'M' for male. ENUM is useful when you have a restricted set of values that a column can hold. We could have used CHAR(1) instead, but ENUM makes it more explicit what the column values can be. If you forget what the possible values are, issue a DESCRIBE *tbl_name* statement. For an ENUM column, MySQL will display the list of legal enumeration values.

By the way, values in an ENUM column need not be just a single character. The type column could have been declared as something like ENUM('female', 'male') instead.

student_id is an integer column that will contain unique student ID numbers. Normally, you'd probably get ID numbers for your students from a central source, such as the school office. We'll just make them up, using an AUTO_INCREMENT column that is declared in much the same way as the member_id column that is part of the member table created earlier.

Note that if you really were going to get student ID numbers from the office rather than generating them automatically, you could declare the student_id column without the AUTO_INCREMENT attribute. But leave in the PRIMARY KEY clause to disallow duplicate IDs.

The event table looks like this:

```
CREATE TABLE event
(
    date        DATE NOT NULL,
    type        ENUM('T','Q') NOT NULL,
    event_id    INT UNSIGNED NOT NULL AUTO_INCREMENT,
    PRIMARY KEY (event_id)
);
```

To create the table, type that statement into mysql or execute the following command:

```
% mysql sampdb < create_event.sql
```

All the columns are declared as NOT NULL because none of them can be missing.

The date column holds a standard MySQL DATE value, in '*CCYY-MM-DD*' (year-first) format.

type represents score type. Like sex in the student table, type is an enumeration column. The allowable values are `'T'` and `'Q'`, representing "test" and "quiz."

event_id is an AUTO_INCREMENT column declared as a PRIMARY KEY, similar to student_id in the student table. Using AUTO_INCREMENT allows us to generate unique event ID values easily. As with the student_id column in the student table, the particular values are less important than that they be unique.

The score table looks like this:

```
CREATE TABLE score
(
    student_id  INT UNSIGNED NOT NULL,
    event_id    INT UNSIGNED NOT NULL,
    PRIMARY KEY (event_id, student_id),
    score       INT NOT NULL
);
```

Type that statement into mysql or execute the following command:

```
% mysql sampdb < create_score.sql
```

The student_id and event_id columns are INT (integer) columns indicating the student and event to which each score applies. By using them to link to the student and event tables, we'll be able to tell the student name and event date. We've also made the combination of the two columns a PRIMARY KEY. This ensures that we won't have duplicate scores for a student for a given quiz or test. Also, it'll be easier to change a score later. For example, when a score is entered incorrectly, we can clobber the old record when we put in the new records by using MySQL's REPLACE statement. It's not necessary to do a DELETE coupled with an INSERT; MySQL does it for us.

Note that it's the combination of event_id and student_id that is unique. In the score table, neither value is unique by itself. There will be multiple score records for each event_id value (one per student) and multiple records for each student_id value (one for each quiz and test).

score is an integer column. That is, I'm assuming score values are always integers. If you wanted to allow scores such as 58.5 that have a fractional part, you'd use one of the floating-point column types, such as FLOAT or DECIMAL, instead.

The absence table for attendance looks like this:

```
CREATE TABLE absence
(
    student_id  INT UNSIGNED NOT NULL,
    date        DATE NOT NULL,
    PRIMARY KEY (student_id, date)
);
```

Type that statement into `mysql` or execute the following command:

```
% mysql sampdb < create_absence.sql
```

The `student_id` and `date` columns are both declared as `NOT NULL` to disallow missing values. We make the combination of the two columns a primary key so that we don't accidentally create duplicate records. After all, it wouldn't be fair to count a student absent twice on the same day!

Adding New Records

At this point, our database and its tables have been created. Now we need to put some records into the tables. However, it's useful to know how to check what's in a table after you put something into it, so although retrieval is not covered in any detail until the next section, you should know at least that the following statement will show you the contents of any table *tbl_name*:

```
SELECT * FROM tbl_name;
```

For example:

```
mysql> SELECT * FROM student;
Empty set (0.00 sec)
```

Right now, `mysql` indicates that the table is empty, but you'll see a different result after trying the examples in this section.

There are several ways to add data to a database. You can insert records into a table manually by issuing `INSERT` statements. You can also add records by reading them from a file, either in the form of pre-written `INSERT` statements that you feed to `mysql` or as raw data values that you load using the `LOAD DATA` statement or the `mysqlimport` utility.

This section demonstrates each method of inserting records into your tables. What you should do is play with all of them to familiarize yourself with them and to see how they work. After you're done trying out the methods, go to the end of the section and run the commands you find there to drop the tables, recreate them, and load them with a known set of data. By doing so, you'll make sure the tables contain the same records that I worked with while writing the sections that follow, and you'll get the same results shown in those sections. (You may want to skip directly to the end of this section if you already know how to insert records and just want to populate the tables.)

Let's start adding records by using `INSERT`, a SQL statement for which you specify the table into which you want to insert a row of data and the values to put in the row. The `INSERT` statement has several forms:

- You can specify values for all the columns:
  ```
  INSERT INTO tbl_name VALUES(value1,value2,...);
  ```

For example:

```
mysql> INSERT INTO student VALUES('Kyle','M',NULL);
mysql> INSERT INTO event VALUES('2002-9-3','Q',NULL);
```

With this syntax, the VALUES list must contain a value for each column in the table, in the order that the columns are stored in the table. (Normally, this is the order in which the columns were specified in the table's CREATE TABLE statement.) If you're not sure what the column order is, issue a DESCRIBE *tbl_name* statement to find out.

You can quote string and date values in MySQL using either single or double quotes. The NULL values are for the AUTO_INCREMENT columns in the student and event tables. Inserting a "missing value" into an AUTO_INCREMENT column causes MySQL to generate the next sequence number for the column.

MySQL versions from 3.22.5 up allow you to insert several rows into a table with a single INSERT statement by specifying multiple value lists:

```
INSERT INTO tbl_name VALUES(...),(...),... ;
```

For example:

```
mysql> INSERT INTO student VALUES('Abby','F',NULL),('Kyle','M',NULL);
```

This involves less typing than multiple INSERT statements and is also more efficient for the server to execute.

- You can name the columns to which you want to assign values and then list the values. This is useful when you want to create a record for which only a few columns need to be set up initially.

```
INSERT INTO tbl_name (col_name1,col_name2,...) VALUES(value1,value2,...);
```

For example:

```
mysql> INSERT INTO member (last_name,first_name) VALUES('Stein','Waldo');
```

As of MySQL 3.22.5, this form of INSERT allows multiple value lists too:

```
mysql> INSERT INTO student (name,sex) VALUES('Abby','F'),('Kyle','M');
```

Any column not named in the column list is assigned a default value. For example, the preceding statements contain no values for the member_id or student_id columns, so MySQL will assign the default value of NULL. (member_id and student_id both are AUTO_INCREMENT columns, so the net effect in each case is to generate and assign the next sequence number, just as if you had assigned NULL explicitly.)

- As of MySQL 3.22.10, you can name columns and values in
  `col_name=value` form.

  ```
  INSERT INTO tbl_name SET col_name1=value1, col_name2=value2, ... ;
  ```

For example:

```
mysql> INSERT INTO member SET last_name='Stein',first_name='Waldo';
```

Any column not named in the SET clause is assigned a default value. You
cannot insert multiple rows using this form of INSERT.

Another method for loading records into a table is to read them directly from
a file. For example, if you have a file named `insert_president.sql` that contains INSERT statements for adding new records to the `president` table, you
can execute those statements like this:

```
% mysql sampdb < insert_president.sql
```

(The `insert_president.sql` file can be found in the `sampdb` distribution.)
If you're already running `mysql`, you can use a SOURCE command to read the
file:

```
mysql> SOURCE insert_president.sql;
```

SOURCE requires MySQL 3.23.9 or newer.

If you have the records stored in a file as raw data values rather than as INSERT
statements, you can load them with the LOAD DATA statement or with the
`mysqlimport` utility.

The LOAD DATA statement acts as a bulk loader that reads data from a file. Use
it from within `mysql`:

```
mysql> LOAD DATA LOCAL INFILE 'member.txt' INTO TABLE member;
```

Assuming that the `member.txt` data file is located in your current directory on
the client host, this statement reads it and sends its contents to the server to be
loaded into the `member` table. (`member.txt` can be found in the `sampdb` distribution.)

By default, the LOAD DATA statement assumes that column values are separated
by tabs and that lines end with newlines (also known as linefeeds). It also
assumes that the values are present in the order that columns are stored in the
table. It's possible to read files in other formats or to specify a different column
order. See the entry for LOAD DATA in Appendix D for details.

LOAD DATA LOCAL won't work if your MySQL is older than version 3.22.15
because that's when the capability of reading files from the client was added to
LOAD DATA. (Without the LOCAL keyword, the file must be located on the
server host and you need a server access privilege that most MySQL users
don't have.) In addition, as of MySQL 3.23.49, the LOCAL capability may be

present but disabled by default. If the LOAD DATA statement results in an error, try again after invoking mysql with the --local-infile option—for example:

```
% mysql --local-infile sampdb
mysql> LOAD DATA LOCAL INFILE 'member.txt' INTO TABLE member;
```

If that doesn't work, either, the server also needs to be told to allow LOCAL. See Chapter 11 for information on how to do this.

The mysqlimport utility acts as a command line interface to LOAD DATA. You invoke mysqlimport from the shell, and it generates a LOAD DATA statement for you:

```
% mysqlimport --local sampdb member.txt
```

This won't work if your MySQL is older than version 3.22.15 because the --local option requires LOAD DATA LOCAL. As with the mysql program, if you need to specify connection parameters, indicate them on the command line preceding the database name.

For the command just shown, mysqlimport generates a LOAD DATA statement to load member.txt into the member table. That's because mysqlimport determines the table name from the name of the data file using everything up to the first period of the filename as the table name. For example, member.txt and president.txt would be loaded into the member and president tables. This means you should choose your filenames carefully or mysqlimport won't use the correct table name. For example, you may want to load member1.txt and member2.txt into the member table, but mysqlimport would think it should load them into tables named member1 and member2. You could, however, use names like member.1.txt and member.2.txt, or member.txt1 and member.txt2.

After you have tried the record-adding methods just described, you should re-create and load the sampdb database tables so that their contents are the same as what the next sections assume. From your shell, execute the following commands:

```
% mysql sampdb < create_president.sql
% mysql sampdb < insert_president.sql
% mysql sampdb < create_member.sql
% mysql sampdb < insert_member.sql
% mysql sampdb < create_student.sql
% mysql sampdb < insert_student.sql
% mysql sampdb < create_score.sql
% mysql sampdb < insert_score.sql
% mysql sampdb < create_event.sql
% mysql sampdb < insert_event.sql
% mysql sampdb < create_absence.sql
% mysql sampdb < insert_absence.sql
```

If you don't want to type those commands individually (which is not unlikely), try the following under UNIX:

```
% sh init_all_tables.sh sampdb
```

Or try the following under Windows:

```
C:\> init_all_tables.bat sampdb
```

If you need to specify connection parameters, list them on the command line before the database name.

Retrieving Information

Our tables are created and loaded with data now, so let's see what we can do with that data. The SELECT statement allows you to retrieve and display information from your tables, in as general or specific a manner as you like. You can display the entire contents of a table

```
SELECT * FROM president;
```

or you can select as little as a single column of a single row:

```
SELECT birth FROM president WHERE last_name = 'Eisenhower';
```

The SELECT statement has several clauses (or parts), which you combine as necessary to retrieve the information in which you're interested. Each of these clauses can be simple or complex, so SELECT statements as a whole can be simple or complex. However, you may rest assured that you won't find any page-long queries that take an hour to figure out in this book. (When I see arm-length queries in something I'm reading, I generally skip right over them, and I'm guessing you do the same.)

The general form of SELECT is as follows:

```
SELECT what to select
FROM table or tables
WHERE conditions that data must satisfy;
```

To write a SELECT statement, specify what you want to retrieve and then some optional clauses. The clauses just shown (FROM and WHERE) are the most common ones, although others can be specified as well, such as GROUP BY, ORDER BY, and LIMIT. Remember that SQL is a free-format language, so when you write your own SELECT queries, you need not put line breaks in the same places I do.

The FROM clause is usually present, but it need not be if you don't need to name any tables. For example, the following query simply displays the values of some expressions. These can be calculated without reference to any table, so no FROM clause is necessary:

```
mysql> SELECT 2+2, 'Hello, world', VERSION();
+-----+--------------+----------------+
| 2+2 | Hello, world | VERSION()      |
+-----+--------------+----------------+
|   4 | Hello, world | 4.0.4-beta-log |
+-----+--------------+----------------+
```

When you do use a FROM clause to specify a table from which to retrieve data, you'll also indicate which columns you want to see. The most "generic" form of SELECT uses * as a column specifier, which is shorthand for "all columns." The following query retrieves all colums from the student table and displays them:

```
mysql> SELECT * FROM student;
+-----------+-----+------------+
| name      | sex | student_id |
+-----------+-----+------------+
| Megan     | F   |          1 |
| Joseph    | M   |          2 |
| Kyle      | M   |          3 |
| Katie     | F   |          4 |
 ...
```

The columns are displayed in the order that MySQL stores them in the table. This is the same order in which the columns are listed when you issue a DESCRIBE student statement. (The ... at the end of the example indicates that the query returns more rows than are shown.)

You can explicitly name the column or columns you want to see. To select just student names, do the following:

```
mysql> SELECT name FROM student;
+-----------+
| name      |
+-----------+
| Megan     |
| Joseph    |
| Kyle      |
| Katie     |
 ...
```

If you name more than one column, separate them with commas. The following statement is equivalent to SELECT * FROM student, but names each column explicitly:

```
mysql> SELECT name, sex, student_id FROM student;
+-----------+-----+------------+
| name      | sex | student_id |
+-----------+-----+------------+
| Megan     | F   |          1 |
| Joseph    | M   |          2 |
| Kyle      | M   |          3 |
| Katie     | F   |          4 |
 ...
```

You can name columns in any order:

```
SELECT name, student_id FROM student;
SELECT student_id, name FROM student;
```

You can even name a column more than once if you like, although generally that's kind of pointless.

MySQL allows you to select columns from more than one table at a time. We'll get to this in the "Retrieving Information from Multiple Tables" later in this chapter.

Column names are not case sensitive in MySQL, so the following queries are equivalent:

```
SELECT name, student_id FROM student;
SELECT NAME, STUDENT_ID FROM student;
SELECT nAmE, sTuDeNt_Id FROM student;
```

On the other hand, database and table names *may* be case sensitive; it depends on the file system used on the server host. Windows filenames are not case sensitive, so a server running on Windows does not treat database and table names as case sensitive. A server running on UNIX treats database and table names as case sensitive because UNIX filenames are case sensitive. (An exception to this occurs under Mac OS X; filenames on HFS+ file systems are not case sensitive, whereas filenames on UFS file systems are.) If you want to have MySQL treat database and table names as not case sensitive, see the "Operating System Constraints on Database and Table Naming" section in Chapter 10, "The MySQL Data Directory."

Specifying Retrieval Criteria

To restrict the set of records retrieved by the SELECT statement, use a WHERE clause that specifies criteria for selecting rows. You can select rows by looking for column values that satisfy various criteria. You can look for various types of values. For example, you can search for numbers:

```
mysql> SELECT * FROM score WHERE score > 95;
+------------+----------+-------+
| student_id | event_id | score |
+------------+----------+-------+
|          5 |        3 |    97 |
|         18 |        3 |    96 |
|          1 |        6 |   100 |
|          5 |        6 |    97 |
|         11 |        6 |    98 |
|         16 |        6 |    98 |
+------------+----------+-------+
```

Or you can look for string values. (Note that string comparisons normally are not case sensitive.)

```
mysql> SELECT last_name, first_name FROM president
    -> WHERE last_name='ROOSEVELT';
+-----------+------------+
| last_name | first_name |
+-----------+------------+
| Roosevelt | Theodore   |
| Roosevelt | Franklin D.|
+-----------+------------+
mysql> SELECT last_name, first_name FROM president
    -> WHERE last_name='roosevelt';
+-----------+------------+
| last_name | first_name |
+-----------+------------+
| Roosevelt | Theodore   |
| Roosevelt | Franklin D.|
+-----------+------------+
```

Or you can look for dates:

```
mysql> SELECT last_name, first_name, birth FROM president
    -> WHERE birth < '1750-1-1';
+------------+------------+------------+
| last_name  | first_name | birth      |
+------------+------------+------------+
| Washington | George     | 1732-02-22 |
| Adams      | John       | 1735-10-30 |
| Jefferson  | Thomas     | 1743-04-13 |
+------------+------------+------------+
```

It's also possible to search for a combination of values:

```
mysql> SELECT last_name, first_name, birth, state FROM president
    -> WHERE birth < '1750-1-1' AND (state='VA' OR state='MA');
+------------+------------+------------+-------+
| last_name  | first_name | birth      | state |
+------------+------------+------------+-------+
| Washington | George     | 1732-02-22 | VA    |
| Adams      | John       | 1735-10-30 | MA    |
| Jefferson  | Thomas     | 1743-04-13 | VA    |
+------------+------------+------------+-------+
```

Expressions in WHERE clauses can use arithmetic operators (Table 1.1), comparison operators (Table 1.2), and logical operators (Table 1.3). You can also use parentheses to group parts of an expression. Operations can be performed using constants, table columns, and function calls. We will have occasion to use several of MySQL's functions in queries throughout this tutorial, but there are far too many to show here. See Appendix C, "Operator and Function Reference," for a complete list.

Table 1.1   **Arithmetic Operators**

Operator	Meaning
+	Addition
–	Subtraction
*	Multiplication
/	Division
%	Modulo (remainder after division)

Table 1.2   **Comparison Operators**

Operator	Meaning
<	Less than
<=	Less than or equal to
=	Equal to
<=>	Equal to (works even for NULL)
!= or <>	Not equal to
>=	Greater than or equal to
>	Greater than

Table 1.3   **Logical Operators**

Operator	Meaning
AND	Logical AND
OR	Logical OR
XOR	Logical ExclusiveOR
NOT	Logical negation

When you're formulating a query that requires logical operators, take care not to confuse the meaning of the logical AND operator with the way we use "and" in everyday speech. Suppose you want to find "presidents born in Virginia and presidents born in Massachusetts." That question is phrased using "and," which seems to imply that you'd write the query as follows:

```
mysql> SELECT last_name, first_name, state FROM president
    -> WHERE state='VA' AND state='MA';
Empty set (0.36 sec)
```

It's clear from the empty result that the query doesn't work. Why not? Because what it really means is "Select presidents who were born both in Virginia and in Massachusetts," which makes no sense. In English, you might express the query using "and," but in SQL, you connect the two conditions with OR:

```
mysql> SELECT last_name, first_name, state FROM president
    -> WHERE state='VA' OR state='MA';
+------------+--------------+-------+
| last_name  | first_name   | state |
+------------+--------------+-------+
| Washington | George       | VA    |
| Adams      | John         | MA    |
| Jefferson  | Thomas       | VA    |
| Madison    | James        | VA    |
| Monroe     | James        | VA    |
| Adams      | John Quincy  | MA    |
| Harrison   | William H.   | VA    |
| Tyler      | John         | VA    |
| Taylor     | Zachary      | VA    |
| Wilson     | Woodrow      | VA    |
| Kennedy    | John F       | MA    |
| Bush       | George H.W.  | MA    |
+------------+--------------+-------+
```

This disjunction between natural language and SQL is something to be aware of, not just when formulating your own queries, but also when writing queries for other people. It's best to listen carefully as they describe what they want to retrieve, but you don't necessarily want to transcribe their descriptions into SQL using the same logical operators. For the example just described, the proper English equivalent for the query is "Select presidents who were born either in Virginia or in Massachusetts."

The NULL Value

The NULL value is special. It means "no value," so you can't assess it against known values the way you can assess two known values against each other. If you attempt to use NULL with the usual arithmetic comparison operators, the result is undefined:

```
mysql> SELECT NULL < 0, NULL = 0, NULL != 0, NULL > 0;
+----------+----------+-----------+----------+
| NULL < 0 | NULL = 0 | NULL != 0 | NULL > 0 |
+----------+----------+-----------+----------+
|     NULL |     NULL |      NULL |     NULL |
+----------+----------+-----------+----------+
```

In fact, you can't even compare NULL against itself because the result of comparing two unknown values cannot be determined:

```
mysql> SELECT NULL = NULL, NULL != NULL;
+-------------+--------------+
| NULL = NULL | NULL != NULL |
+-------------+--------------+
|        NULL |         NULL |
+-------------+--------------+
```

To perform searches for NULL values, you must use a special syntax. Instead of using = or != to test for equality or inequality, use IS NULL or IS NOT NULL. For example, you can find presidents who are still living using the following query because we have represented their death dates as NULL in the president table:

```
mysql> SELECT last_name, first_name FROM president WHERE death IS NULL;
+-----------+------------+
| last_name | first_name |
+-----------+------------+
| Ford      | Gerald R   |
| Carter    | James E.   |
| Reagan    | Ronald W.  |
| Bush      | George H.W.|
| Clinton   | William J. |
| Bush      | George W.  |
+-----------+------------+
```

To find names that have a suffix part, use IS NOT NULL:

```
mysql> SELECT last_name, first_name, suffix
    -> FROM president WHERE suffix IS NOT NULL;
+-----------+------------+--------+
| last_name | first_name | suffix |
+-----------+------------+--------+
| Carter    | James E.   | Jr.    |
+-----------+------------+--------+
```

MySQL 3.23 and up has a special MySQL-specific <=> comparison operator that is true even for NULL-to-NULL comparisons. The preceding two queries can be rewritten to use this operator as follows:

```
mysql> SELECT last_name, first_name FROM president WHERE death <=> NULL;
+-----------+------------+
| last_name | first_name |
+-----------+------------+
| Ford      | Gerald R   |
| Carter    | James E.   |
| Reagan    | Ronald W.  |
| Bush      | George H.W.|
| Clinton   | William J. |
| Bush      | George W.  |
+-----------+------------+
mysql> SELECT last_name, first_name, suffix
    -> FROM president WHERE NOT (suffix <=> NULL);
+-----------+------------+--------+
| last_name | first_name | suffix |
+-----------+------------+--------+
| Carter    | James E.   | Jr.    |
+-----------+------------+--------+
```

Sorting Query Results

Every MySQL user notices sooner or later that if you create a table, load some records into it, and then issue a SELECT * FROM *tbl_name* statement, the records tend to be retrieved in the same order in which they were inserted. That makes a certain intuitive sense and, as a result, it's natural to make the assumption that retrieval of records in insertion order is a principle that you can rely on. But you can't, because the assumption is incorrect. For example, if you delete and insert rows after loading the table initially, those actions likely will change the order in which the server returns the table's rows. (Deleting records puts "holes" of unused space in the table, which MySQL tries to fill later when you insert new records.)

The principle that you *can* rely on is this: There is no guarantee about the order in which the server will return rows, unless you specify one yourself. To do so, add an ORDER BY clause to the statement that defines the sort order you want. The following query returns president names, sorted lexically (alphabetically) by last name:

```
mysql> SELECT last_name, first_name FROM president
    -> ORDER BY last_name;
+------------+--------------+
| last_name  | first_name   |
+------------+--------------+
| Adams      | John         |
| Adams      | John Quincy  |
| Arthur     | Chester A.   |
| Buchanan   | James        |
...
```

You can specify whether to sort a column in ascending or descending order by using the ASC or DESC keywords after column names in the ORDER BY clause. For example, to sort president names in reverse (descending) name order, use DESC as follows:

```
mysql> SELECT last_name, first_name FROM president
    -> ORDER BY last_name DESC;
+------------+--------------+
| last_name  | first_name   |
+------------+--------------+
| Wilson     | Woodrow      |
| Washington | George       |
| Van Buren  | Martin       |
| Tyler      | John         |
...
```

Ascending order is the default if you specify neither ASC nor DESC for a column name in an ORDER BY clause.

Query output can be sorted on multiple columns, and each column can be sorted in ascending or descending order independently of any other. The following query retrieves rows from the `president` table, sorts them by reverse state of birth, and by last name within each state:

```
mysql> SELECT last_name, first_name, state FROM president
    -> ORDER BY state DESC, last_name ASC;
+------------+---------------+-------+
| last_name  | first_name    | state |
+------------+---------------+-------+
| Arthur     | Chester A.    | VT    |
| Coolidge   | Calvin        | VT    |
| Harrison   | William H.    | VA    |
| Jefferson  | Thomas        | VA    |
| Madison    | James         | VA    |
| Monroe     | James         | VA    |
| Taylor     | Zachary       | VA    |
| Tyler      | John          | VA    |
| Washington | George        | VA    |
| Wilson     | Woodrow       | VA    |
| Eisenhower | Dwight D.     | TX    |
| Johnson    | Lyndon B.     | TX    |
...
```

If you sort a column that may contain NULL values, where will they appear in the sort order? It depends. As of MySQL 4.0.2, they'll always sort at the beginning, even if you specify DESC. Prior to that, they sort at the beginning for ascending sorts and at the end for descending sorts.

If you want to ensure that NULL values will appear at a given end of the sort order, add an extra sort column that distinguishes NULL from non-NULL values. For example, to sort presidents by death date but put living presidents (those with NULL death dates) at the beginning of the sort order, use the following query:

```
mysql> SELECT last_name, first_name, death FROM president
    -> ORDER BY IF(death IS NULL,0,1), death;
+------------+---------------+------------+
| last_name  | first_name    | death      |
+------------+---------------+------------+
| Ford       | Gerald R      | NULL       |
| Carter     | James E.      | NULL       |
| Reagan     | Ronald W.     | NULL       |
| Bush       | George H.W.   | NULL       |
| Clinton    | William J.    | NULL       |
| Bush       | George W.     | NULL       |
| Washington | George        | 1799-12-14 |
| Adams      | John          | 1826-07-04 |
...
| Truman     | Harry S.      | 1972-12-26 |
| Johnson    | Lyndon B.     | 1973-01-22 |
| Nixon      | Richard M     | 1994-04-22 |
+------------+---------------+------------+
```

To put living presidents at the end instead, use the following query:

```
mysql> SELECT last_name, first_name, death FROM president
    -> ORDER BY IF(death IS NULL,1,0), death;
+------------+--------------+------------+
| last_name  | first_name   | death      |
+------------+--------------+------------+
| Washington | George       | 1799-12-14 |
| Adams      | John         | 1826-07-04 |
...
| Truman     | Harry S.     | 1972-12-26 |
| Johnson    | Lyndon B.    | 1973-01-22 |
| Nixon      | Richard M    | 1994-04-22 |
| Ford       | Gerald R     | NULL       |
| Carter     | James E.     | NULL       |
| Reagan     | Ronald W.    | NULL       |
| Bush       | George H.W.  | NULL       |
| Clinton    | William J.   | NULL       |
| Bush       | George W.    | NULL       |
+------------+--------------+------------+
```

The `IF()` function evaluates an expression and returns the value of its second or third argument, depending on whether the expression is true or false. For the first query, `IF()` evaluates to `0` for `NULL` values and `1` for non-`NULL` values, which places all `NULL` values ahead of all non-`NULL` values. For the second query, it does the opposite, placing all `NULL` values after all non-`NULL` values. This strategy can be used as of MySQL 3.23.2, which is the first version that allows expressions in `ORDER BY` clauses.

Limiting Query Results

When a query returns many rows, but you want to see only a few of them, the `LIMIT` clause is useful, especially in conjunction with `ORDER BY`. MySQL allows you to limit the output of a query to the first n rows of the result that would otherwise be returned. The following query selects the five presidents who were born first:

```
mysql> SELECT last_name, first_name, birth FROM president
    -> ORDER BY birth LIMIT 5;
+------------+------------+------------+
| last_name  | first_name | birth      |
+------------+------------+------------+
| Washington | George     | 1732-02-22 |
| Adams      | John       | 1735-10-30 |
| Jefferson  | Thomas     | 1743-04-13 |
| Madison    | James      | 1751-03-16 |
| Monroe     | James      | 1758-04-28 |
+------------+------------+------------+
```

If you sort in reverse order, using ORDER BY birth DESC, you'd get the five
most recently born presidents instead:

```
mysql> SELECT last_name, first_name, birth FROM president
    -> ORDER BY birth DESC LIMIT 5;
+-----------+------------+------------+
| last_name | first_name | birth      |
+-----------+------------+------------+
| Clinton   | William J. | 1946-08-19 |
| Bush      | George W.  | 1946-07-06 |
| Carter    | James E.   | 1924-10-01 |
| Bush      | George H.W.| 1924-06-12 |
| Kennedy   | John F     | 1917-05-29 |
+-----------+------------+------------+
```

LIMIT also allows you to pull a section of records out of the middle of a result
set. To do this, you must specify two values. The first value is the number of
records to skip at the beginning of the result set, and the second is the number
of records to return. The following query is similar to the previous one but
returns 5 records after skipping the first 10:

```
mysql> SELECT last_name, first_name, birth FROM president
    -> ORDER BY birth LIMIT 10, 5;
+-----------+------------+------------+
| last_name | first_name | birth      |
+-----------+------------+------------+
| Tyler     | John       | 1790-03-29 |
| Buchanan  | James      | 1791-04-23 |
| Polk      | James K.   | 1795-11-02 |
| Fillmore  | Millard    | 1800-01-07 |
| Pierce    | Franklin   | 1804-11-23 |
+-----------+------------+------------+
```

To pull a randomly selected record from the president table, use ORDER BY
RAND() in conjunction with LIMIT:

```
mysql> SELECT last_name, first_name FROM president
    -> ORDER BY RAND() LIMIT 1;
+-----------+------------+
| last_name | first_name |
+-----------+------------+
| McKinley  | William    |
+-----------+------------+
```

Ordering by the result of a formula like this works for MySQL 3.23.2 and
later. Prior to that, you must use a workaround that involves generating an
additional column containing random numbers. See the "Overriding
Optimization" section in Chapter 4 for details.

Calculating and Naming Output Column Values

Most of the preceding queries have produced output by retrieving values from tables. MySQL also allows you to calculate an output column value as the result of an expression. Expressions can be simple or complex. The following query evaluates a simple expression (a constant) and a more complex expression involving several arithmetic operations and a couple of function calls:

```
mysql> SELECT 17, FORMAT(SQRT(3*3+4*4),0);
+----+-------------------------+
| 17 | FORMAT(SQRT(3*3+4*4),0) |
+----+-------------------------+
| 17 | 5                       |
+----+-------------------------+
```

Expressions can also refer to table columns:

```
mysql> SELECT CONCAT(first_name,' ',last_name),CONCAT(city,', ',state)
    -> FROM president;
+----------------------------------+-------------------------+
| CONCAT(first_name,' ',last_name) | CONCAT(city,', ',state) |
+----------------------------------+-------------------------+
| George Washington                | Wakefield, VA           |
| John Adams                       | Braintree, MA           |
| Thomas Jefferson                 | Albemarle County, VA    |
| James Madison                    | Port Conway, VA         |
...
```

This query formats president names as a single string by concatenating first and last names separated by a space and formats birthplaces as the birth cities and states separated by a comma.

When you use an expression to calculate a column value, the expression becomes the column's name and is used for its heading. That can lead to a very wide column if the expression is long (as the preceding query illustrates). To deal with this, you can assign the column a different name using the AS *name* construct. Such names are called column aliases. The output from the previous query can be made more meaningful as follows:

```
mysql> SELECT CONCAT(first_name,' ',last_name) AS Name,
    -> CONCAT(city,', ',state) AS Birthplace
    -> FROM president;
+-----------------------+-------------------------+
| Name                  | Birthplace              |
+-----------------------+-------------------------+
| George Washington     | Wakefield, VA           |
| John Adams            | Braintree, MA           |
| Thomas Jefferson      | Albemarle County, VA    |
| James Madison         | Port Conway, VA         |
...
```

If the column alias contains spaces, you'll need to put it in quotes:

```
mysql> SELECT CONCAT(first_name,' ',last_name) AS 'President Name',
    -> CONCAT(city,', ',state) AS 'Place of Birth'
    -> FROM president;
+-----------------------+-------------------------+
| President Name        | Place of Birth          |
+-----------------------+-------------------------+
| George Washington     | Wakefield, VA           |
| John Adams            | Braintree, MA           |
| Thomas Jefferson      | Albemarle County, VA    |
| James Madison         | Port Conway, VA         |
...
```

Working with Dates

The principal thing to keep in mind when it comes to dates in MySQL is that it always represents them with the year first. July 27, 2002 is represented as `'2002-07-27'`. It is not represented as `'07-27-2002'` or as `'27-07-2002'`, as you might be more used to writing.

MySQL provides several ways to perform operations on dates. Some of the things you can do are as follows:

- Sort by date. (We've seen this several times already.)
- Look for particular dates or a range of dates.
- Extract parts of a date value, such as the year, month, or day.
- Calculate the difference between dates.
- Compute a date by adding or subtracting an interval from another date.

Some examples of these operations follow.

To look for particular dates, either by exact value or compared to another value, compare a DATE column to the value you're interested in:

```
mysql> SELECT * FROM event WHERE date = '2002-10-01';
+------------+------+----------+
| date       | type | event_id |
+------------+------+----------+
| 2002-10-01 | T    |        6 |
+------------+------+----------+
mysql> SELECT last_name, first_name, death
    -> FROM president
    -> WHERE death >= '1970-01-01' AND death < '1980-01-01';
+-----------+------------+------------+
| last_name | first_name | death      |
+-----------+------------+------------+
| Truman    | Harry S.   | 1972-12-26 |
| Johnson   | Lyndon B.  | 1973-01-22 |
+-----------+------------+------------+
```

To test or retrieve parts of dates, you can use functions such as YEAR(), MONTH(), or DAYOFMONTH(). For example, I can find presidents who were born in the same month that I was (March) by looking for dates with a month value of 3:

```
mysql> SELECT last_name, first_name, birth
    -> FROM president WHERE MONTH(birth) = 3;
+-----------+------------+------------+
| last_name | first_name | birth      |
+-----------+------------+------------+
| Madison   | James      | 1751-03-16 |
| Jackson   | Andrew     | 1767-03-15 |
| Tyler     | John       | 1790-03-29 |
| Cleveland | Grover     | 1837-03-18 |
+-----------+------------+------------+
```

The query can also be written in terms of the month name:

```
mysql> SELECT last_name, first_name, birth
    -> FROM president WHERE MONTHNAME(birth) = 'March';
+-----------+------------+------------+
| last_name | first_name | birth      |
+-----------+------------+------------+
| Madison   | James      | 1751-03-16 |
| Jackson   | Andrew     | 1767-03-15 |
| Tyler     | John       | 1790-03-29 |
| Cleveland | Grover     | 1837-03-18 |
+-----------+------------+------------+
```

To be more specific—down to the day—I can combine tests for MONTH() and DAYOFMONTH() to find presidents born on my birthday:

```
mysql> SELECT last_name, first_name, birth
    -> FROM president WHERE MONTH(birth) = 3 AND DAYOFMONTH(birth) = 29;
+-----------+------------+------------+
| last_name | first_name | birth      |
+-----------+------------+------------+
| Tyler     | John       | 1790-03-29 |
+-----------+------------+------------+
```

This is the kind of query you'd use to generate one of those "these famous people have birthdays today" lists such as you see in the Entertainment section of your newspaper. However, for the current date, you don't have to plug in a specific day the way the previous query did. To check for presidents born today, no matter what day of the year today is, compare their birthdays to the month and day parts of CURDATE(), which always returns the current date:

```
SELECT last_name, first_name, birth
FROM president WHERE MONTH(birth) = MONTH(CURDATE())
AND DAYOFMONTH(birth) = DAYOFMONTH(CURDATE());
```

You can subtract one date from another, which allows you to find the interval between dates. For example, to determine which presidents lived the longest, subtract the birth date from the death date. To do this, convert birth and death to days using the `TO_DAYS()` function and take the difference:

```
mysql> SELECT last_name, first_name, birth, death,
    -> TO_DAYS(death) - TO_DAYS(birth) AS age
    -> FROM president WHERE death IS NOT NULL
    -> ORDER BY age DESC LIMIT 5;
+-----------+------------+------------+------------+-------+
| last_name | first_name | birth      | death      | age   |
+-----------+------------+------------+------------+-------+
| Adams     | John       | 1735-10-30 | 1826-07-04 | 33119 |
| Hoover    | Herbert C. | 1874-08-10 | 1964-10-20 | 32943 |
| Truman    | Harry S.   | 1884-05-08 | 1972-12-26 | 32373 |
| Madison   | James      | 1751-03-16 | 1836-06-28 | 31150 |
| Jefferson | Thomas     | 1743-04-13 | 1826-07-04 | 30397 |
+-----------+------------+------------+------------+-------+
```

To convert age in days to approximate age in years, divide by 365 (the `FLOOR()` function used here chops off any fractional part from the age to produce an integer):

```
mysql> SELECT last_name, first_name, birth, death,
    -> FLOOR((TO_DAYS(death) - TO_DAYS(birth))/365) AS age
    -> FROM president WHERE death IS NOT NULL
    -> ORDER BY age DESC LIMIT 5;
+-----------+------------+------------+------------+------+
| last_name | first_name | birth      | death      | age  |
+-----------+------------+------------+------------+------+
| Adams     | John       | 1735-10-30 | 1826-07-04 |   90 |
| Hoover    | Herbert C. | 1874-08-10 | 1964-10-20 |   90 |
| Truman    | Harry S.   | 1884-05-08 | 1972-12-26 |   88 |
| Madison   | James      | 1751-03-16 | 1836-06-28 |   85 |
| Jefferson | Thomas     | 1743-04-13 | 1826-07-04 |   83 |
+-----------+------------+------------+------------+------+
```

In this particular case, the age values happen to correspond to true age at death. But the calculation used in the query may not always do so, because years are not always exactly 365 days long. To calculate ages as we normally think of them, take the difference between the year parts of the dates and then subtract one if the calendar day of the death date occurs earlier than that of the birth date:

```
mysql> SELECT last_name, first_name, birth, death,
    -> (YEAR(death) - YEAR(birth)) - IF(RIGHT(death,5) < RIGHT(birth,5),1,0)
    -> AS age
    -> FROM president WHERE death IS NOT NULL
    -> ORDER BY age DESC LIMIT 5;
```

```
+-----------+------------+------------+------------+------+
| last_name | first_name | birth      | death      | age  |
+-----------+------------+------------+------------+------+
| Adams     | John       | 1735-10-30 | 1826-07-04 |   90 |
| Hoover    | Herbert C. | 1874-08-10 | 1964-10-20 |   90 |
| Truman    | Harry S.   | 1884-05-08 | 1972-12-26 |   88 |
| Madison   | James      | 1751-03-16 | 1836-06-28 |   85 |
| Jefferson | Thomas     | 1743-04-13 | 1826-07-04 |   83 |
+-----------+------------+------------+------------+------+
```

The IF() expression used here performs the calendar day test based on a simple substring comparison of the last five characters of the dates. This works for two reasons. First, MySQL treats dates as strings if you pass them to a string function—in this case, RIGHT(), which returns the rightmost n characters of a string. Second, MySQL produces dates with a fixed number of digits in each of their subparts. The comparison would not work if leading zeroes were not present for month and day values less than 10.

Taking a difference between dates is also useful for determining how far dates are from some reference date. That's how you can tell which Historical League members need to renew their memberships soon. Compute the difference between their expiration dates and the current date, and if it's less than some threshold value, a renewal will soon be needed. The following query finds memberships that are due for renewal within 60 days:

```
SELECT last_name, first_name, expiration FROM member
WHERE (TO_DAYS(expiration) - TO_DAYS(CURDATE())) < 60;
```

To calculate one date from another, you can use DATE_ADD() or DATE_SUB(). These functions take a date and an interval and produce a new date, for example:

```
mysql> SELECT DATE_ADD('1970-1-1', INTERVAL 10 YEAR);
+----------------------------------------+
| DATE_ADD('1970-1-1', INTERVAL 10 YEAR) |
+----------------------------------------+
| 1980-01-01                             |
+----------------------------------------+
mysql> SELECT DATE_SUB('1970-1-1', INTERVAL 10 YEAR);
+----------------------------------------+
| DATE_SUB('1970-1-1', INTERVAL 10 YEAR) |
+----------------------------------------+
| 1960-01-01                             |
+----------------------------------------+
```

A query shown earlier in this section selected presidents who died during the 1970s, using literal dates for the endpoints of the selection range. That query can be rewritten to use a literal starting date and an ending date calculated from the starting date and an interval:

```
mysql> SELECT last_name, first_name, death
    -> FROM president
    -> WHERE death >= '1970-1-1'
    -> AND death < DATE_ADD('1970-1-1', INTERVAL 10 YEAR);
+-----------+------------+------------+
| last_name | first_name | death      |
+-----------+------------+------------+
| Truman    | Harry S.   | 1972-12-26 |
| Johnson   | Lyndon B.  | 1973-01-22 |
+-----------+------------+------------+
```

The membership-renewal query can be written in terms of DATE_ADD():

```
SELECT last_name, first_name, expiration FROM member
WHERE expiration < DATE_ADD(CURDATE(), INTERVAL 60 DAY);
```

Earlier in this chapter, a query was presented for determining which of a dentist's patients haven't been in for their checkups in a while:

```
SELECT last_name, first_name, last_visit FROM patient
WHERE last_visit < DATE_SUB(CURDATE(),INTERVAL 6 MONTH);
```

That query may not have meant much to you then. Is it more meaningful now?

Pattern Matching

MySQL supports pattern matching operations, which allows you to select records without supplying an exact comparison value. To perform a pattern match, you use special operators (LIKE and NOT LIKE), and you specify a string containing wild card characters. The character '_' matches any single character, and '%' matches any sequence of characters (including an empty sequence). Pattern matches using LIKE or NOT LIKE are not case sensitive.

The following pattern matches last names that begin with a 'W' or 'w' character:

```
mysql> SELECT last_name, first_name FROM president
    -> WHERE last_name LIKE 'W%';
+------------+------------+
| last_name  | first_name |
+------------+------------+
| Washington | George     |
| Wilson     | Woodrow    |
+------------+------------+
```

On the other hand, the following pattern match is erroneous:

```
mysql> SELECT last_name, first_name FROM president
    -> WHERE last_name = 'W%';
Empty set (0.00 sec)
```

The query demonstrates a common error, which is to use a pattern with an arithmetic comparison operator. The only way for such a comparison to succeed is for the column to contain exactly the string `'W%'` or `'w%'`.

This pattern matches last names that contain 'W' or 'w' anywhere in the name, not just at the beginning:

```
mysql> SELECT last_name, first_name FROM president
    -> WHERE last_name LIKE '%W%';
+------------+------------+
| last_name  | first_name |
+------------+------------+
| Washington | George     |
| Wilson     | Woodrow    |
| Eisenhower | Dwight D.  |
+------------+------------+
```

This pattern matches last names that contain exactly four characters:

```
mysql> SELECT last_name, first_name FROM president
    -> WHERE last_name LIKE '____';
+-----------+------------+
| last_name | first_name |
+-----------+------------+
| Polk      | James K.   |
| Taft      | William H. |
| Ford      | Gerald R   |
| Bush      | George H.W.|
| Bush      | George W.  |
+-----------+------------+
```

MySQL also provides another form of pattern matching based on regular expressions, which are described in the section that discusses the REGEXP operator in Appendix C.

Setting and Using SQL Variables

MySQL versions 3.23.6 and up allow you to set variables using query results, which provides a convenient way to save values for use in later queries. Suppose you want to find out which presidents were born before Andrew Jackson. To determine that, you can retrieve his birth date into a variable and then select other presidents with a birth date earlier than the value of the variable:[1]

---

1. This problem could be solved in a single query using a join, but we're not to the point of writing joins yet. Besides, sometimes it's just easier to use a variable.

```
mysql> SELECT @birth := birth FROM president
    -> WHERE last_name = 'Jackson' AND first_name = 'Andrew';
+-----------------+
| @birth := birth |
+-----------------+
| 1767-03-15      |
+-----------------+
mysql> SELECT last_name, first_name, birth FROM president
    -> WHERE birth < @birth ORDER BY birth;
+------------+------------+------------+
| last_name  | first_name | birth      |
+------------+------------+------------+
| Washington | George     | 1732-02-22 |
| Adams      | John       | 1735-10-30 |
| Jefferson  | Thomas     | 1743-04-13 |
| Madison    | James      | 1751-03-16 |
| Monroe     | James      | 1758-04-28 |
+------------+------------+------------+
```

Variables are named using `@name` syntax and assigned a value in a `SELECT` statement using an expression of the form `@name := value`. The first query therefore looks up the birth date for Andrew Jackson and assigns it to the `@birth` variable. (The result of the `SELECT` still is displayed; assigning a query result to a variable doesn't cause the query output to be suppressed.) The second query refers to the variable and uses its value to find other president records with a lesser birth value.

Variables also can be assigned using a `SET` statement, although in this case either = or := are allowable as the assignment operator:

```
mysql> SET @one_week_ago = DATE_SUB(CURDATE(),INTERVAL 7 DAY);
mysql> SELECT CURDATE(), @one_week_ago;
+------------+---------------+
| CURDATE()  | @one_week_ago |
+------------+---------------+
| 2002-09-03 | 2002-08-27    |
+------------+---------------+
```

Generating Summaries

One of the most useful things MySQL can do for you is to boil down lots of raw data and summarize it. MySQL becomes a powerful ally when you learn to use it to generate summaries because that is an especially tedious, time-consuming, error-prone activity when done manually.

One simple form of summarizing is to determine which unique values are present in a set of values. Use the `DISTINCT` keyword to remove duplicate rows from a result. For example, the different states in which presidents have been born can be found as follows:

```
mysql> SELECT DISTINCT state FROM president ORDER BY state;
+-------+
| state |
+-------+
| AR    |
| CA    |
| CT    |
| GA    |
| IA    |
| IL    |
| KY    |
| MA    |
| MO    |
| NC    |
| NE    |
| NH    |
| NJ    |
| NY    |
| OH    |
| PA    |
| SC    |
| TX    |
| VA    |
| VT    |
+-------+
```

Another form of summarizing involves counting, using the COUNT() function.
If you use COUNT(*), it tells you the number of rows selected by your query. If
a query has no WHERE clause, COUNT(*) tells you the number of rows in your
table. The following query shows how many members are listed in the
Historical League membership table:

```
mysql> SELECT COUNT(*) FROM member;
+----------+
| COUNT(*) |
+----------+
|      102 |
+----------+
```

If a query does have a WHERE clause, COUNT(*) tells you how many rows the
clause matches. The following query shows how many quizzes you have given
to your class so far:

```
mysql> SELECT COUNT(*) FROM event WHERE type = 'Q';
+----------+
| COUNT(*) |
+----------+
|        4 |
+----------+
```

COUNT(*) counts every row selected. By contrast, COUNT(*col_name*) counts only non-NULL values. The following query demonstrates these differences:

```
mysql> SELECT COUNT(*),COUNT(email),COUNT(expiration) FROM member;
+----------+--------------+-------------------+
| COUNT(*) | COUNT(email) | COUNT(expiration) |
+----------+--------------+-------------------+
|      102 |           80 |                96 |
+----------+--------------+-------------------+
```

This shows that while the member table has 102 records, only 80 of them have a value in the email column. It also shows that six members have a lifetime membership. (A NULL value in the expiration column indicates a lifetime membership, and because 96 out of 102 records are not NULL, that leaves six.)

As of MySQL 3.23.2, you can combine COUNT() with DISTINCT to count the number of distinct values in a result. For example, to count the number of different states in which presidents have been born, do the following:

```
mysql> SELECT COUNT(DISTINCT state) FROM president;
+-----------------------+
| COUNT(DISTINCT state) |
+-----------------------+
|                    20 |
+-----------------------+
```

You can produce an overall count of values in a column or break down the counts by categories. For example, you may know the overall number of students in your class as a result of running the following query:

```
mysql> SELECT COUNT(*) FROM student;
+----------+
| COUNT(*) |
+----------+
|       31 |
+----------+
```

But how many students are boys and how many are girls? One way to find out is by asking for a count for each sex separately:

```
mysql> SELECT COUNT(*) FROM student WHERE sex='f';
+----------+
| COUNT(*) |
+----------+
|       15 |
+----------+
mysql> SELECT COUNT(*) FROM student WHERE sex='m';
+----------+
| COUNT(*) |
+----------+
|       16 |
+----------+
```

However, although that approach works, it's tedious and not really very well suited for columns that might have several different values. Consider how you'd determine the number of presidents born in each state this way. You'd have to find out which states are represented so as not to miss any (SELECT DISTINCT state FROM president) and then run a SELECT COUNT(*) query for each state. That is clearly something you don't want to do.

Fortunately, MySQL can count, using a single query, how many times each distinct value occurs in a column. For our student list, we can count boys and girls as follows:

```
mysql> SELECT sex, COUNT(*) FROM student GROUP BY sex;
+------+----------+
| sex  | COUNT(*) |
+------+----------+
| F    |       15 |
| M    |       16 |
+------+----------+
```

The same form of query tells us how many presidents were born in each state:

```
mysql> SELECT state, COUNT(*) FROM president GROUP BY state;
+-------+----------+
| state | COUNT(*) |
+-------+----------+
| AR    |        1 |
| CA    |        1 |
| CT    |        1 |
| GA    |        1 |
| IA    |        1 |
| IL    |        1 |
| KY    |        1 |
| MA    |        4 |
| MO    |        1 |
| NC    |        2 |
| NE    |        1 |
| NH    |        1 |
| NJ    |        1 |
| NY    |        4 |
| OH    |        7 |
| PA    |        1 |
| SC    |        1 |
| TX    |        2 |
| VA    |        8 |
| VT    |        2 |
+-------+----------+
```

When you count values this way, the GROUP BY clause is necessary; it tells MySQL how to cluster values before counting them. You'll just get an error if you omit it.

The use of COUNT(*) with GROUP BY to count values has a number of advantages over counting occurrences of each distinct column value individually:

- You don't have to know in advance what values are present in the column you're summarizing.
- You need only a single query, not several.
- You get all the results with a single query, so you can sort the output.

The first two advantages are important for expressing queries more easily. The third advantage is important because it affords you flexibility in displaying your results. By default, MySQL uses the columns named in the GROUP BY to sort the results, but you can specify an ORDER BY clause to sort in a different order. For example, if you want number of presidents grouped by state of birth but sorted with the most well-represented states first, you can use an ORDER BY clause as follows:

```
mysql> SELECT state, COUNT(*) AS count FROM president
    -> GROUP BY state ORDER BY count DESC;
+-------+-------+
| state | count |
+-------+-------+
| VA    |     8 |
| OH    |     7 |
| MA    |     4 |
| NY    |     4 |
| NC    |     2 |
| VT    |     2 |
| TX    |     2 |
| SC    |     1 |
| NH    |     1 |
| PA    |     1 |
| KY    |     1 |
| NJ    |     1 |
| IA    |     1 |
| MO    |     1 |
| CA    |     1 |
| NE    |     1 |
| GA    |     1 |
| IL    |     1 |
| AR    |     1 |
| CT    |     1 |
+-------+-------+
```

When the column you want to sort by is determined by a summary function, you can give the column an alias and refer to the alias in the ORDER BY clause. The preceding query demonstrates this, where the COUNT(*) column is aliased as count. Another way to refer to such a column is by its position in the output. The previous query could have been written as follows instead:

```
SELECT state, COUNT(*) FROM president
GROUP BY state ORDER BY 2 DESC;
```

I don't find that referring to columns by position leads to very understandable queries. Also, if you add, remove, or reorder output columns, you must remember to check the ORDER BY clause and fix the column number if it has changed. Aliases don't have this problem.

If you want to group results using GROUP BY with a calculated column, you can refer to it using an alias or column position, just as with ORDER BY. The following query determines how many presidents were born in each month of the year:

```
mysql> SELECT MONTH(birth) AS Month, MONTHNAME(birth) AS Name,
    -> COUNT(*) AS count
    -> FROM president GROUP BY Name ORDER BY Month;
+-------+-----------+-------+
| Month | Name      | count |
+-------+-----------+-------+
|     1 | January   |     4 |
|     2 | February  |     4 |
|     3 | March     |     4 |
|     4 | April     |     4 |
|     5 | May       |     2 |
|     6 | June      |     1 |
|     7 | July      |     4 |
|     8 | August    |     4 |
|     9 | September |     1 |
|    10 | October   |     6 |
|    11 | November  |     5 |
|    12 | December  |     3 |
+-------+-----------+-------+
```

Using column positions, the query would be written as follows:

```
SELECT MONTH (birth), MONTHNAME(birth), COUNT(*)
FROM president GROUP BY 2 ORDER BY 1;
```

COUNT() can be combined with ORDER BY and LIMIT to find, for example, the four most well-represented states in the president table:

```
mysql> SELECT state, COUNT(*) AS count FROM president
    -> GROUP BY state ORDER BY count DESC LIMIT 4;
+-------+-------+
| state | count |
+-------+-------+
| VA    |     8 |
| OH    |     7 |
| MA    |     4 |
| NY    |     4 |
+-------+-------+
```

If you don't want to limit query output with a LIMIT clause but rather by looking for particular values of COUNT(), use a HAVING clause. HAVING is similar to WHERE in that it specifies conditions that must be satisfied by output rows. It differs from WHERE in that it can refer to the results of summary functions like COUNT(). The following query will tell you which states are represented by two or more presidents:

```
mysql> SELECT state, COUNT(*) AS count FROM president
    -> GROUP BY state HAVING count > 1 ORDER BY count DESC;
+-------+-------+
| state | count |
+-------+-------+
| VA    |     8 |
| OH    |     7 |
| MA    |     4 |
| NY    |     4 |
| NC    |     2 |
| VT    |     2 |
| TX    |     2 |
+-------+-------+
```

More generally, this is the type of query to run when you want to find duplicated values in a column (or to find non-duplicated values, use HAVING count = 1.)

There are summary functions other than COUNT(). The MIN(), MAX(), SUM(), and AVG() functions are useful for determining the minimum, maximum, total, and average values in a column. You can even use them all at the same time. The following query shows various numeric characteristics for each quiz and test you've given. It also shows how many scores go into computing each of the values. (Some students may have been absent and are not counted.)

```
mysql> SELECT
    -> event_id,
    -> MIN(score) AS minimum,
    -> MAX(score) AS maximum,
    -> MAX(score)-MIN(score)+1 AS range,
    -> SUM(score) AS total,
    -> AVG(score) AS average,
    -> COUNT(score) AS count
    -> FROM score
    -> GROUP BY event_id;
+----------+---------+---------+-------+-------+---------+-------+
| event_id | minimum | maximum | range | total | average | count |
+----------+---------+---------+-------+-------+---------+-------+
|        1 |       9 |      20 |    12 |   439 | 15.1379 |    29 |
|        2 |       8 |      19 |    12 |   425 | 14.1667 |    30 |
|        3 |      60 |      97 |    38 |  2425 | 78.2258 |    31 |
|        4 |       7 |      20 |    14 |   379 | 14.0370 |    27 |
|        5 |       8 |      20 |    13 |   383 | 14.1852 |    27 |
|        6 |      62 |     100 |    39 |  2325 | 80.1724 |    29 |
+----------+---------+---------+-------+-------+---------+-------+
```

This information might be more meaningful if you knew whether the `event_id` values represented quizzes or tests, of course. However, to produce that information, we need to consult the `event` table as well; we'll revisit this query in the next section, "Retrieving Information from Multiple Tables."

Summary functions are fun to play with because they're so powerful, but it's easy to get carried away with them. Consider the following query:

```
mysql> SELECT
    -> state AS State,
    -> AVG((TO_DAYS(death)-TO_DAYS(birth))/365) AS Age
    -> FROM president WHERE death IS NOT NULL
    -> GROUP BY state ORDER BY Age;
+-------+-----------+
| State | Age       |
+-------+-----------+
| KY    | 56.208219 |
| VT    | 58.852055 |
| NC    | 60.141096 |
| OH    | 62.866145 |
| NH    | 64.917808 |
| NY    | 69.342466 |
| NJ    | 71.315068 |
| TX    | 71.476712 |
| MA    | 72.642009 |
| VA    | 72.822945 |
| PA    | 77.158904 |
| SC    | 78.284932 |
| CA    | 81.336986 |
| MO    | 88.693151 |
| IA    | 90.254795 |
+-------+-----------+
```

The query selects presidents who have died, groups them by state of birth, figures out their age at time of death, computes the average age (per state), and then sorts the results by average age. In other words, the query determines, for non-living presidents, the average age of death by state of birth.

And what does that demonstrate? It shows only that you can write the query. It certainly doesn't show that the query is worth writing. Not all things you can do with a database are equally meaningful; nevertheless, people sometimes go query-happy when they find out what they can do with their database. This may account for the rise of increasingly esoteric (and pointless) statistics on televised sporting events over the last few years. The sports statisticians can use their databases to figure out everything you'd ever want to know about a team and also everything you'd *never* want to know. Do you really care which third-string quarterback holds the record for most interceptions on third down when his team is leading by more than 14 points with the ball inside the 15-yard line in the last two minutes of the second quarter?

Retrieving Information from Multiple Tables

The queries we've written so far have pulled data from a single table. But MySQL is capable of working much harder for you. I've mentioned before that the power of a relational DBMS lies in its ability to relate one thing to another because that allows you to combine information from multiple tables to answer questions that can't be answered from individual tables alone. This section describes how to write queries that do that.

When you select information from multiple tables, you're performing an operation called a *join*. That's because you're producing a result by joining the information from one table to the information in another. This is done by matching up common values in the tables.

Let's work through an example. Earlier, in "Tables for the Grade-Keeping Project" section, a query to retrieve quiz or test scores for a given date was presented without explanation. Now it's time for the explanation. The query actually involves a three-way join, so we'll build up to it in two steps. In the first step, we construct a query to select scores for a given date as follows:

```
mysql> SELECT student_id, date, score, type
    -> FROM event, score
    -> WHERE date = '2002-09-23'
    -> AND event.event_id = score.event_id;
+------------+------------+-------+------+
| student_id | date       | score | type |
+------------+------------+-------+------+
|          1 | 2002-09-23 |    15 | Q    |
|          2 | 2002-09-23 |    12 | Q    |
|          3 | 2002-09-23 |    11 | Q    |
|          5 | 2002-09-23 |    13 | Q    |
|          6 | 2002-09-23 |    18 | Q    |
...
```

The query works by finding the event record with the given date and then using the event ID in that record to locate scores that have the same event ID. For each matching event record and score record combination, the student ID, score, date, and event type are displayed.

The query differs from others we have written in two important respects:

- The FROM clause names more than one table because we're retrieving data from more than one table:
  ```
  FROM event, score
  ```

- The WHERE clause specifies that the event and score tables are joined by matching up the event_id values in each table:
  ```
  WHERE ... event.event_id = score.event_id
  ```

Notice how we refer to the event_id columns using *tbl_name.col_name* syntax so that MySQL knows to which tables we're referring. (event_id occurs in both tables, so it's ambiguous if used without a table name to qualify it.) The other columns in the query (date, score, type) can be used without a table qualifier because they appear in only one of the tables and thus are unambiguous.

I generally prefer to qualify every column in a join to make it clearer (more explicit) which table each column is part of, and that's how I'll write joins from now on. In fully qualified form, the query looks like the following:

```
SELECT score.student_id, event.date, score.score, event.type
FROM event, score
WHERE event.date = '2002-09-23'
AND event.event_id = score.event_id;
```

The first-stage query uses the event table to map a date to an event ID and then uses the ID to find the matching scores in the score table. Output from the query contains student_id values, but names would be more meaningful. By using the student table, we can map student IDs onto names, which is the second step. Name display is accomplished using the fact that the score and student tables both have student_id columns, allowing the records in them to be linked. The resulting query is as follows:

```
mysql> SELECT student.name, event.date, score.score, event.type
    -> FROM event, score, student
    -> WHERE event.date = '2002-09-23'
    -> AND event.event_id = score.event_id
    -> AND score.student_id = student.student_id;
+-----------+------------+-------+------+
| name      | date       | score | type |
+-----------+------------+-------+------+
| Megan     | 2002-09-23 |    15 | Q    |
| Joseph    | 2002-09-23 |    12 | Q    |
| Kyle      | 2002-09-23 |    11 | Q    |
| Abby      | 2002-09-23 |    13 | Q    |
| Nathan    | 2002-09-23 |    18 | Q    |
...
```

This query differs from the previous one as follows:

- The student table is added to the FROM clause because it is used in addition to the event and score tables.

- The student_id column was unambiguous before, so it was possible to refer to it in either unqualified (student_id) or qualified (score.student_id) form. Now it is ambiguous because it is present in both the score and student tables, so it *must* be qualified as score.student_id or student.student_id to make it clear which table to use.

- The WHERE clause has an additional term specifying that score table records are matched against student table records based on student ID:

  ```
  WHERE ... score.student_id = student.student_id
  ```

- The query displays the student name rather than the student ID. (You could display both if you wanted to, of course.)

With this query, you can plug in any date and get back the scores for that date, complete with student names and the score type. You don't have to know anything about student IDs or event IDs. MySQL takes care of figuring out the relevant ID values and using them to match up table rows automatically.

Another task the grade-keeping project involves is summarizing student absences. Absences are recorded by student ID and date in the absence table. To get student names (not just IDs), we need to join the absence table to the student table, based on the student_id value. The following query lists student ID number and name along with a count of absences:

```
mysql> SELECT student.student_id, student.name,
    -> COUNT(absence.date) as absences
    -> FROM student, absence
    -> WHERE student.student_id = absence.student_id
    -> GROUP BY student.student_id;
+------------+-------+----------+
| student_id | name  | absences |
+------------+-------+----------+
|          3 | Kyle  |        1 |
|          5 | Abby  |        1 |
|         10 | Peter |        2 |
|         17 | Will  |        1 |
|         20 | Avery |        1 |
+------------+-------+----------+
```

Note: Although I'm supplying a qualifier in the GROUP BY clause, it isn't strictly necessary for this query. GROUP BY refers to output columns, and there is only one such column named student_id, so MySQL knows which one you mean.

The output produced by the query is fine if we want to know only which students had absences. But if we turn in this list to the school office, they may say, "What about the other students? We want a value for every student." That's a slightly different question. It means we want to know the number of absences, even for students that had none. Because the question is different, the query is different as well.

To answer the question, we can use LEFT JOIN rather than a regular join. LEFT JOIN tells MySQL to produce a row of output for each row selected from the table named first in the join (that is, the table named to the left of the LEFT

JOIN keywords). By naming the `student` table first, we'll get output for every student, even those who are not represented in the `absence` table. To write this query, use LEFT JOIN between the tables named in the FROM clause (rather than separating them by a comma) and add an ON clause that says how to match up records in the two tables. The query is as follows:

```
mysql> SELECT student.student_id, student.name,
    -> COUNT(absence.date) as absences
    -> FROM student LEFT JOIN absence
    -> ON student.student_id = absence.student_id
    -> GROUP BY student.student_id;
+------------+----------+----------+
| student_id | name     | absences |
+------------+----------+----------+
|          1 | Megan    |        0 |
|          2 | Joseph   |        0 |
|          3 | Kyle     |        1 |
|          4 | Katie    |        0 |
|          5 | Abby     |        1 |
|          6 | Nathan   |        0 |
|          7 | Liesl    |        0 |
...
```

Earlier, in the "Generating Summaries" section, we ran a query that produced a numeric characterization of the data in the score table. Output from that query listed event ID but did not include event dates or types, because we didn't know then how to join the `score` table to the `event` table to map the IDs onto dates and types. Now we do. The following query is similar to one run earlier, but shows the dates and types rather than simply the numeric event IDs:

```
mysql> SELECT
    -> event.date,event.type,
    -> MIN(score.score) AS minimum,
    -> MAX(score.score) AS maximum,
    -> MAX(score.score)-MIN(score.score)+1 AS range,
    -> SUM(score.score) AS total,
    -> AVG(score.score) AS average,
    -> COUNT(score.score) AS count
    -> FROM score, event
    -> WHERE score.event_id = event.event_id
    -> GROUP BY event.date;
+------------+------+---------+---------+-------+-------+---------+-------+
| date       | type | minimum | maximum | range | total | average | count |
+------------+------+---------+---------+-------+-------+---------+-------+
| 2002-09-03 | Q    |       9 |      20 |    12 |   439 | 15.1379 |    29 |
| 2002-09-06 | Q    |       8 |      19 |    12 |   425 | 14.1667 |    30 |
| 2002-09-09 | T    |      60 |      97 |    38 |  2425 | 78.2258 |    31 |
| 2002-09-16 | Q    |       7 |      20 |    14 |   379 | 14.0370 |    27 |
| 2002-09-23 | Q    |       8 |      20 |    13 |   383 | 14.1852 |    27 |
| 2002-10-01 | T    |      62 |     100 |    39 |  2325 | 80.1724 |    29 |
+------------+------+---------+---------+-------+-------+---------+-------+
```

You can use functions, such as COUNT() and AVG(), to produce a summary over multiple columns, even if the columns come from different tables. The following query determines the number of scores and the average score for each combination of event date and student sex:

```
mysql> SELECT event.date, student.sex,
    -> COUNT(score.score) AS count, AVG(score.score) AS average
    -> FROM event, score, student
    -> WHERE event.event_id = score.event_id
    -> AND score.student_id = student.student_id
    -> GROUP BY event.date, student.sex;
+------------+-----+-------+---------+
| date       | sex | count | average |
+------------+-----+-------+---------+
| 2002-09-03 | F   |    14 | 14.6429 |
| 2002-09-03 | M   |    15 | 15.6000 |
| 2002-09-06 | F   |    14 | 14.7143 |
| 2002-09-06 | M   |    16 | 13.6875 |
| 2002-09-09 | F   |    15 | 77.4000 |
| 2002-09-09 | M   |    16 | 79.0000 |
| 2002-09-16 | F   |    13 | 15.3077 |
| 2002-09-16 | M   |    14 | 12.8571 |
| 2002-09-23 | F   |    12 | 14.0833 |
| 2002-09-23 | M   |    15 | 14.2667 |
| 2002-10-01 | F   |    14 | 77.7857 |
| 2002-10-01 | M   |    15 | 82.4000 |
+------------+-----+-------+---------+
```

We can use a similar query to perform one of the grade-keeping project tasks—computing the total score per student at the end of the semester. The query looks like this:

```
SELECT student.student_id, student.name,
SUM(score.score) AS total, COUNT(score.score) AS n
FROM event, score, student
WHERE event.event_id = score.event_id
AND score.student_id = student.student_id
GROUP BY score.student_id
ORDER BY total;
```

There is no requirement that a join be performed between different tables. It might seem odd at first, but you can join a table to itself. For example, you can determine whether any presidents were born in the same city by checking each president's birthplace against every other president's birthplace:

```
mysql> SELECT p1.last_name, p1.first_name, p1.city, p1.state
    -> FROM president AS p1, president AS p2
    -> WHERE p1.city = p2.city AND p1.state = p2.state
    -> AND (p1.last_name != p2.last_name OR p1.first_name != p2.first_name)
    -> ORDER BY state, city, last_name;
```

```
+-----------+-------------+-----------+-------+
| last_name | first_name  | city      | state |
+-----------+-------------+-----------+-------+
| Adams     | John Quincy | Braintree | MA    |
| Adams     | John        | Braintree | MA    |
+-----------+-------------+-----------+-------+
```

There are two tricky things about this query:

- It's necessary to refer to two instances of the same table, so we create table aliases (p1 and p2) and use them to disambiguate references to the table's columns.

- Every president's record matches itself, but we don't want to see that in the output. The second line of the WHERE clause disallows matches of a record to itself by making sure the records being compared are for different presidents.

A similar query finds presidents who were born on the same day. However, birth dates cannot be compared directly because that would miss presidents who were born in different years. Instead, use MONTH() and DAYOFMONTH() to compare month and day of the birth date:

```
mysql> SELECT p1.last_name, p1.first_name, p1.birth
    -> FROM president AS p1, president AS p2
    -> WHERE MONTH(p1.birth) = MONTH(p2.birth)
    -> AND DAYOFMONTH(p1.birth) = DAYOFMONTH(p2.birth)
    -> AND (p1.last_name != p2.last_name OR p1.first_name != p2.first_name)
    -> ORDER BY p1.last_name;
+-----------+------------+------------+
| last_name | first_name | birth      |
+-----------+------------+------------+
| Harding   | Warren G.  | 1865-11-02 |
| Polk      | James K.   | 1795-11-02 |
+-----------+------------+------------+
```

Using DAYOFYEAR() rather than the combination of MONTH() and DAYOFMONTH() would result in a simpler query, but it would produce incorrect results when comparing dates from leap years to dates from non-leap years.

The joins performed thus far have combined information from tables that have some meaningful logical relationship, but meaningfulness is in the eye of the beholder—that is, you. MySQL doesn't know (or care) whether or not the joined tables have anything to do with each other. For example, you can join the event table to the president table to find out whether you gave any quizzes or tests on a president's birthday:

```
mysql> SELECT president.last_name, president.first_name,
    -> president.birth, event.type
    -> FROM president, event
```

```
    -> WHERE MONTH(president.birth) = MONTH(event.date)
    -> AND DAYOFMONTH(president.birth) = DAYOFMONTH(event.date);
+-----------+------------+------------+------+
| last_name | first_name | birth      | type |
+-----------+------------+------------+------+
| Carter    | James E.   | 1924-10-01 | T    |
+-----------+------------+------------+------+
```

It turns out you did. But so what? This illustrates that MySQL will happily crank out results, whether they make any sense or not. Just because you're using a computer, it doesn't automatically mean that results from a query are useful or worthwhile. Fortunately or unfortunately, we still must think about what we're doing.

Deleting or Updating Existing Records

Sometimes you want to get rid of records or change their contents. The DELETE and UPDATE statements let you do this. This section discusses how to use them.

The DELETE statement has the following form:

```
DELETE FROM tbl_name
WHERE which records to delete;
```

The WHERE clause that specifies which records should be deleted is optional. But if you leave it out, all records in the table are deleted, which means the simplest DELETE statement is also the most dangerous:

```
DELETE FROM tbl_name;
```

That query wipes out the table's contents entirely, so be careful with it! To delete specific records, use the WHERE clause to select the records in which you're interested. This is similar to using a WHERE clause in a SELECT statement to avoid selecting the entire table. For example, to specifically delete from the president table only those presidents born in Ohio, use the following query:

```
mysql> DELETE FROM president WHERE state='OH';
Query OK, 7 rows affected (0.00 sec)
```

If you're not really sure which records a DELETE statement will remove, it's often a good idea to test the WHERE clause first by using it with a SELECT statement to find out which records it matches. This can help you ensure that you'll actually delete the records you intend (and only those records). Suppose you want to delete the record for Teddy Roosevelt. Would the following query do the job?

```
DELETE FROM president WHERE last_name='Roosevelt';
```

Yes, in the sense that it would delete the record you have in mind. No, in the sense that it also would delete the record for Franklin Roosevelt. It's safer to check the WHERE clause with a SELECT statement first, like this:

```
mysql> SELECT last_name, first_name FROM president
    -> WHERE last_name='Roosevelt';
+-----------+-------------+
| last_name | first_name  |
+-----------+-------------+
| Roosevelt | Theodore    |
| Roosevelt | Franklin D. |
+-----------+-------------+
```

From that you can see the need to be more specific:

```
mysql> SELECT last_name, first_name FROM president
    -> WHERE last_name='Roosevelt' AND first_name='Theodore';
+-----------+------------+
| last_name | first_name |
+-----------+------------+
| Roosevelt | Theodore   |
+-----------+------------+
```

Now you know the proper WHERE clause to select the desired record, so the DELETE query can be constructed correctly:

```
mysql> DELETE FROM president
    -> WHERE last_name='Roosevelt' AND first_name='Theodore';
```

This seems like a lot of work to delete a record, doesn't it? Better safe than sorry! (This is the type of situation in which you'll want to minimize typing through the use of copy and paste or input line-editing techniques. See the "Tips for Interacting with mysql" section later in this chapter for more information.)

To modify existing records, use UPDATE, which has the following form:

```
UPDATE tbl_name
SET which columns to change
WHERE which records to update;
```

The WHERE clause is just as for DELETE. It's optional, so if you don't specify one, every record in the table will be updated. For example, the following query changes the name of each of your students to George:

```
mysql> UPDATE student SET name='George';
```

Obviously, you must be careful with queries like that, so normally you'll add a WHERE clause to be more specific about which records to update. Suppose you recently added a new member to the Historical League but filled in only a few columns of his entry:

```
mysql> INSERT INTO member (last_name,first_name)
    -> VALUES('York','Jerome');
```

Then you realize you forgot to set his membership expiration date. You can fix that with an UPDATE statement that includes an appropriate WHERE clause to identify which record to change:

```
mysql> UPDATE member
    -> SET expiration='2001-7-20'
    -> WHERE last_name='York' AND first_name='Jerome';
```

You can update multiple columns with a single statement. The following UPDATE modifies Jerome's email and postal addresses:

```
mysql> UPDATE member
    -> SET email='jeromey@aol.com',street='123 Elm St',city='Anytown',
    -> state='NY',zip='01003'
    -> WHERE last_name='York' AND first_name='Jerome';
```

You can also "unset" a column by setting its value to NULL (assuming the column allows NULL values). If at some point in the future Jerome later decides to pay the big membership renewal fee that allows him to become a lifetime member, you can mark his record that way by setting his expiration date to NULL ("never expires"):

```
mysql> UPDATE member
    -> SET expiration=NULL
    -> WHERE last_name='York' AND first_name='Jerome';
```

With UPDATE, just as for DELETE, it's not a bad idea to test a WHERE clause using a SELECT statement to make sure you're choosing the right records to update. If your selection criteria are too narrow or too broad, you'll update too few or too many records.

If you've tried the queries in this section, you'll have deleted and modified records in the sampdb tables. Before proceeding to the next section, you should undo those changes. Do that by reloading the tables using the instructions at the end of the "Adding New Records" section earlier in this chapter.

Tips for Interacting with mysql

This section discusses how to interact with the mysql client program more efficiently and with less typing. It also describes how to connect to the server more easily, how to enter queries without typing each one by hand, and how to change the prompt if you don't like the default prompt.

Simplifying the Connection Process

It's likely that you need to specify connection parameters, such as hostname, username, or password when you invoke mysql. That's a lot of typing just to run a program and it gets tiresome very quickly. There are several ways to minimize the amount of typing necessary to establish a connection to the MySQL server:

- Store connection parameters in an option file.
- Repeat commands by taking advantage of your shell's command history capabilities.
- Define a `mysql` command line shortcut using a shell alias or script.

Using an Option File

As of version 3.22.10, MySQL allows you to store connection parameters in an option file. Then you don't have to type the parameters each time you run `mysql`; they are used just as if you had entered them on the command line. A big advantage of this technique is that the parameters will also be used by other MySQL clients, such as `mysqlimport`. In other words, an option file makes it easier to use not just `mysql` but many other programs as well.

Under UNIX, you set up an option file by creating a file named `~/.my.cnf` (that is, a file named `.my.cnf` in your home directory). Under Windows, create an option file named `my.cnf` in the root directory of the C drive or named `my.ini` in your Windows system directory (that is, `C:\my.cnf` or `%SYSTEM%\my.ini`). An option file is a plain text file, so you can create it using any text editor. The file's contents look something like the following:

```
[client]
host=server_host
user=your_name
password=your_pass
```

The `[client]` line signals the beginning of the client option group; any lines following it are read by MySQL client programs to obtain option values through the end of the file or until a different option group begins. Replace *server_host*, *your_name*, and *your_pass* with the hostname, username, and password that you specify when you connect to the server. For example, `.my.cnf` might look like this:

```
[client]
host=cobra.snake.net
user=sampadm
password=secret
```

The `[client]` line is required to define where the option group begins, but lines that define parameter values are optional. You can specify just the ones you need. For example, if you're using UNIX and your MySQL username is the same as your UNIX login name, there is no need to include a `user` line. If you connect to localhost, no `host` line is necessary.

After creating the option file, an additional precaution you should take under UNIX is to set the file's access mode to a restrictive value to make sure no one else can read or modify it. Either of the following commands make the file accessible only to you:

```
% chmod 600 .my.cnf
% chmod u=rw,go-rwx .my.cnf
```

More information on option files may be found in Appendix E.

Using Your Shell's Command History

Shells such as `tcsh` and `bash` remember your commands in a history list and allow you to repeat commands from that list. If you use such a shell, your history list can help you avoid typing entire commands. For example, if you've recently invoked `mysql`, you can execute it again, as follows:

```
% !my
```

The `!` character tells your shell to search through your command history to find the most recent command that begins with "my" and reissue it as though you'd typed it again yourself. Some shells also allow you to move up and down through your history list using the Up arrow and Down arrow keys (or perhaps Ctrl-P and Ctrl-N). You can select the command you want this way and then press Enter to execute it. `tcsh` and `bash` have this facility, and other shells may as well. Check the documentation for your shell to find out more about using your history list.

Using Shell Aliases and Scripts

If your shell provides an alias facility, you can set up a short command name that maps to a long command. For example, in `csh` or `tcsh`, you can use the `alias` command to set up an alias named `sampdb` like this:

```
alias sampdb 'mysql -h cobra.snake.net -p -u sampadm sampdb'
```

The syntax for `bash` is slightly different:

```
alias sampdb='mysql -h cobra.snake.net -p -u sampadm sampdb'
```

Defining the alias makes the following two commands equivalent:

```
% sampdb
% mysql -h cobra.snake.net -p -u sampadm sampdb
```

Clearly, the first is easier to type than the second. To make the alias take effect each time you log in, put the alias command in one of your shell's startup files (for example, `.tcshrc` for `tcsh`, or `.bash_profile` for `bash`).

Under Windows, a similar technique is to create a shortcut that points to the `mysql` program and then edit the shortcut properties to include the appropriate connection parameters.

Another way to invoke commands with less typing is to create a script that executes `mysql` for you with the proper options. In UNIX, a shell script that is equivalent to the `sampdb` alias just shown looks like this:

```
#! /bin/sh
exec mysql -h cobra.snake.net -p -u sampadm sampdb
```

If you name the script `sampdb` and make it executable (with `chmod +x sampdb`), you can type `sampdb` at the command prompt to run `mysql` and connect to my database.

Under Windows, a batch file can be used to do the same thing. Name the file `sampdb.bat` and put the following line in it:

```
mysql -h cobra.snake.net -p -u sampadm sampdb
```

This batch file can be run either by typing `sampdb` at the prompt in a DOS console or by double-clicking its Windows icon.

If you access multiple databases or connect to multiple hosts, you can define several aliases, shortcuts, or scripts, each of which invokes `mysql` with different options.

Issuing Queries with Less Typing

`mysql` is an extremely useful program for interacting with your database, but its interface is most suitable for short, single-line queries. It's true that `mysql` itself doesn't care whether or not a query spreads across multiple lines, but long queries aren't much fun to type. Nor is it very entertaining to enter a query, even a short one, only to discover that you must retype it because it has a syntax error. There are several techniques you can use to avoid needless typing and retyping:

- Use `mysql`'s input line-editing facility.
- Use copy and paste.
- Run `mysql` in batch mode.

Using the mysql Input Line Editor

`mysql` has the GNU Readline library built in to allow input line editing. You can manipulate the line you're currently entering or you can recall previous input lines and re-enter them, either as is or after further modification. This is convenient when you're entering a line and spot a typo; you can back up within the line to correct the problem before pressing Enter. If you enter a query that has a mistake in it, you can recall the query, edit it to fix the problem, and then resubmit it. (This is easiest if you type the entire query on one line.)

Some of the editing sequences you will find useful are shown in Table 1.4, but there are many input editing commands available besides those shown in the table. You can read about them in the command editing chapter of the bash manual, available online from the GNU Project Web site at http://www.gnu.org/manual/.

Table 1.4 **mysql Input Editing Commands**

Key Sequence	Meaning
Up arrow or Ctrl-P	Recall previous line
Down arrow or Ctrl-N	Recall next line
Left arrow or Ctrl-B	Move cursor left (backward)
Right arrow or Ctrl-F	Move cursor right (forward)
Escape B	Move backward one word
Escape F	Move forward one word
Ctrl-A	Move cursor to beginning of line
Ctrl-E	Move cursor to end of line
Ctrl-D	Delete character under cursor
Delete	Delete character to left of cursor
Escape D	Delete word
Escape Backspace	Delete word to left of cursor
Ctrl-K	Erase everything from cursor to end of line
Ctrl-_	Undo last change; may be repeated

The following example describes a simple use for input editing. Suppose you've entered this query while using mysql:

```
mysql> SHOW COLUMNS FROM persident;
```

If you notice that you've misspelled president as persident before pressing Enter, press Left arrow or Ctrl-B a few times to move the cursor left until it's on the s. Then press Delete twice to erase the er, type re to fix the error, and press Enter to issue the query. If you press Enter before you notice the misspelling, that's not a problem. After mysql displays its error message, press up arrow or Ctrl-P to recall the line and then edit it as just described.

Under Windows, the Readline editing capabilities are not available in mysql. (If you're using a Windows NT-based system, mysql will support the arrow keys for moving up and down through input lines or left and right within lines, but not the other editing commands.) To take advantage of the full set of input editing commands, you can use the `mysqlc` program, which is like `mysql` but is built with the Cygnus libraries that include Readline support. For details on making sure `mysqlc` is installed correctly, see the entry for `mysql` in Appendix E.

Using Copy and Paste to Issue Queries

If you work in a windowing environment, the text of queries that you find useful can be saved in a file and recalled by copy and paste operations. Simply perform the following steps:

1. Invoke `mysql` in a terminal window or a DOS console window.
2. Open the file containing your queries in a document window (for example, I use `vi` on UNIX, `gvim` on Windows, and BBEdit on Mac OS).
3. To execute a query stored in your file, select it in the document and copy it. Then switch to your terminal window or DOS console and paste the query into `mysql`.

The procedure sounds cumbersome when written out like that, but when you're actually carrying it out, it provides a way to enter queries quickly and with no typing.

This technique also allows you to edit your queries in the document window, and it allows you to construct new queries by copying and pasting pieces of existing queries. For example, if you often select rows from a particular table but like to view the output sorted in different ways, you can keep a list of different ORDER BY clauses in your document window and then copy and paste the one you want to use for any particular query.

You can use copy and paste in the other direction, too (from your terminal window to your query file). When you enter lines in `mysql`, they are saved in a file named `.mysql_history` in your home directory. If you manually enter a query that you want to save for further reference, quit `mysql`, open `.mysql_history` in an editor, and then copy and paste the query from `.mysql_history` into your query file.

Running mysql in Batch Mode

It's not necessary to run `mysql` interactively. `mysql` can read input from a file in non-interactive (batch) mode. This is useful for queries that you run periodically because you certainly don't want to retype such a query every time you run it. It's easier to put it into a file once and then have `mysql` execute the contents of the file as needed.

Suppose you have a query that finds Historical League members who have an interest in a particular area of U.S. history by looking in the interests column of the member table. For example, to find members with an interest in the Great Depression, the query could be written as follows:

```
SELECT last_name, first_name, email, interests FROM member
WHERE interests LIKE '%depression%'
ORDER BY last_name, first_name;
```

Put the query in a file interests.sql and then run it by feeding it to mysql as follows:

```
% mysql sampdb < interests.sql
```

By default, mysql produces output in tab-delimited format when run in batch mode. If you want the same kind of tabular ("boxed") output you get when you run mysql interactively, use the -t option:

```
% mysql -t sampdb < interests.sql
```

If you want to save the output, redirect it to a file:

```
% mysql -t sampdb < interests.sql > output_file
```

To use the query to find members with an interest in Thomas Jefferson, you could edit the query file to change depression to Jefferson and then run mysql again. That works okay as long as you don't use the query very often. If you do, a better method is needed. One way to make the query more flexible is to put it in a shell script that takes an argument from the script command line and uses it to change the text of the query. That parameterizes the query so that you can specify the interests value when you run the script. To see how this works, write a little shell script, interests.sh:

```
#! /bin/sh
# interests.sh - find USHL members with particular interests
if [ $# -ne 1 ]; then echo 'Please specify one keyword'; exit; fi
mysql -t sampdb <<QUERY_INPUT
SELECT last_name, first_name, email, interests FROM member
WHERE interests LIKE '%$1%'
ORDER BY last_name, first_name;
QUERY_INPUT
```

The third line makes sure there is one argument on the command line; it prints a short message and exits otherwise. Everything between <<QUERY_INPUT and the final QUERY_INPUT line becomes the input to mysql. Within the text of the query, the shell replaces the reference to $1 with the argument from the command line. (In shell scripts, $1, $2, and so on refer to the command arguments.) This causes the query to reflect whatever keyword you specify on the command line when you run the script.

Before you can run the script, you must make it executable:

```
% chmod +x interests.sh
```

Now you don't need to edit the script each time you run it. Just tell it what you're looking for on the command line:

```
% interests.sh depression
% interests.sh Jefferson
```

The `interests.sh` script can be found in the `misc` directory of the `sampdb` distribution. An equivalent Windows batch file, `interests.bat`, is provided there as well.

Changing the mysql Prompt

As of MySQL 4.0.2, you can change the primary `mysql` prompt if you don't like it. For example, to include the name of the current database in the prompt, use the `PROMPT` command as follows and then select different databases to see how the prompt follows the current selection:

```
% mysql
mysql> PROMPT \d>\_
PROMPT set to '\d>\_'
(none)> USE sampdb;
Database changed
sampdb> USE test;
Database changed
test>
```

The `PROMPT` keyword is followed by the prompt string that you want to use. Within the string, sequences that begin with backslashes indicate special prompt options. The `\d` and `\_` sequences signify the current database name and a space; for a complete list of available options, see the entry for `mysql` in Appendix E.

Where to Now?

You know quite a bit about using MySQL now. You can set up a database and create tables. You can put records into those tables, retrieve them in various ways, change them, or delete them. But the tutorial in this chapter only scratches the surface, and there's still a lot to know about MySQL. You can see this by considering the current state of our `sampdb` database. We've created it and its tables and populated them with some initial data. During the process we've seen how to write some of the queries we need for answering questions about the information in the database. But much remains to be done. For example, we have no convenient interactive way to enter new score records for the grade-keeping project or new member entries for the Historical League directory. We have no convenient way to edit existing records. And we still can't generate the printed or online forms of the League directory. These tasks and others will be revisited in the upcoming chapters, particularly in Chapter 7, "The Perl DBI API," and Chapter 8, "The PHP API."

Where you go next in this book depends on what you're interested in. If you want to see how to finish the job we've started with our Historical League and grade-keeping projects, Part II, "Using MySQL Programming Interfaces," covers how to write MySQL-based programs. If you're going to serve as the MySQL administrator for your site, Part III of this book, "MySQL Administration," deals with administrative tasks. However, I recommend acquiring additional general background in using MySQL first, by reading the remaining chapters in Part I, "General MySQL Use." These chapters discuss how MySQL handles data, provide further information on the syntax and use of query statements and show how to make your queries run faster. A good grounding in these topics will stand you in good stead no matter the context in which you use MySQL—whether you're running `mysql`, writing your own programs, or acting as a database administrator.

2

Working with Data in MySQL

VIRTUALLY EVERYTHING YOU DO IN MySQL involves data in some way or another because the purpose of a database management system is, by definition, to manage data. Even a simple SELECT 1 statement involves expression evaluation to produce an integer data value.

Every data value in MySQL has a type. For example, 37.4 is a number, and 'abc' is a string. Sometimes data types are explicit, as when you issue a CREATE TABLE statement that specifies the type for each column you declare as part of the table:

```
CREATE TABLE mytbl
(
    int_col  INT,       /* integer-valued column */
    str_col  CHAR(20),  /* string-valued column */
    date_col DATE       /* date-valued column */
);
```

Other times, data types are implicit, such as when you refer to literal values in an expression, pass values to a function, or use the value returned from a function:

```
INSERT INTO mytbl (int_col,str_col,date_col)
VALUES(14,CONCAT('a','b'),20020115);
```

The INSERT statement shown here performs the following operations, all of which involve data types:

- It assigns the integer value 14 to the integer column int_col.
- It passes the string values 'a' and 'b' to the CONCAT() function. CONCAT() returns the string value 'ab', which is assigned to the string column str_col.
- It assigns the integer value 20020115 to the date column date_col. The assignment involves a type mismatch, so MySQL performs an automatic type conversion that converts the integer 20020115 to the date '2002-01-15'.

To use MySQL effectively, it's essential to understand how MySQL handles data. This chapter describes the types of data values that MySQL can handle and discusses the issues involved in working with those types:

- The general kinds of values MySQL can represent, including the NULL value.
- The specific data types MySQL provides for table columns and the properties that characterize each column type. Some of MySQL's column types are fairly generic, such as the BLOB string type. Others, such as AUTO_INCREMENT integer types and the TIMESTAMP date type, behave in special ways that you should understand to avoid being surprised.
- MySQL support for working with different character sets.
- Choosing column types appropriately for your tables. It's important to know how to pick the best type for your purposes when you build a table, and when to choose one type over another when several related types might be applicable to the kind of values you want to store.
- MySQL's rules for expression evaluation. MySQL provides a wide range of operators and functions that you can use in expressions to retrieve, display, and manipulate data. The rules for expression evaluation include the rules governing type conversion that come into play when a value of one type is used in a context requiring a value of another type. It's important to understand when type conversion happens and how it works; some conversions don't make sense and result in meaningless values. Assigning the string '13' to an integer column results in the value 13, but assigning the string 'abc' to that column results in the value 0 because 'abc' doesn't look like a number. Worse, if you perform a comparison without knowing the conversion rules, you can do considerable damage, such as updating or deleting every row in a table when you intend to affect only a few rows.

Two appendixes provide additional information to supplement the discussion here about MySQL's column types, operators, and functions. These are Appendix B, "Column Type Reference," and Appendix C, "Operator and Function Reference."

The examples used throughout this chapter use CREATE TABLE extensively. The statement should be reasonably familiar to you because we used it in the tutorial section of Chapter 1, "Getting Started with MySQL and SQL." See also the entry for CREATE TABLE in Appendix D, "SQL Syntax Reference." Several examples also use ALTER TABLE to modify the structure of tables. This statement too is discussed in the appendix as well as in Chapter 3, "MySQL SQL Syntax and Use."

MySQL supports several table types, which differ in their properties. In some cases, the way you use a particular column type will be determined or influenced by the table type. This chapter refers to table types on occasion, but a more detailed description of the available types and their characteristics can be found in Chapter 3.

MySQL Data Types

MySQL knows about several data types—that is, general categories in which values can be represented. These include numbers, string values, temporal values such as dates and times, and the NULL value.

Numeric Values

Numbers are values such as 48 or 193.62. MySQL understands numbers specified as integers (with no fractional part) or floating-point values (with a fractional part). Integers can be specified in decimal or hexadecimal format.

An integer consists of a sequence of digits with no decimal point. In numeric contexts, an integer can be specified as a hexadecimal constant and is treated as a 64-bit integer. The syntax for specifying hexadecimal values is given in the next section, "String (Character) Values," because they are treated as strings by default.

A floating-point number consists of a sequence of digits, a decimal point, and another sequence of digits. One sequence of digits or the other can be empty, but not both.

MySQL understands scientific notation. This is indicated by immediately following an integer or floating-point number with 'e' or 'E', a sign character ('+' or '-'), and an integer exponent. 1.34E+12 and 43.27e-1 are numbers in legal scientific notation. The number 1.34E12 is also legal even though it is missing a sign character before the exponent, but only as of MySQL 3.23.26. Prior to that version, a sign character is required.

Hexadecimal numbers cannot be used in scientific notation: The 'e' that begins the exponent part is also a legal hex digit and thus would be ambiguous.

Any number can be preceded by a minus sign ('-') to indicate a negative value.

String (Character) Values

Strings are values, such as `'Madison, Wisconsin'`, or `'patient shows improvement'`. You can use either single or double quotes to surround a string value. The ANSI SQL standard specifies single quotes, so statements written using them are more portable to other database engines.

Several escape sequences are recognized within strings and can be used to indicate special characters, as shown in Table 2.1. Each sequence begins with a backslash character ('\') to signify a temporary escape from the usual rules for character interpretation. Note that a NUL byte is not the same as the NULL value; NUL is a zero-valued byte, whereas NULL is the absence of a value.

Table 2.1 **String Escape Sequences**

Sequence	Meaning
\0	NUL (ASCII 0)
\'	Single quote
\"	Double quote
\b	Backspace
\n	Newline (linefeed)
\r	Carriage return
\t	Tab
\\	Backslash
\Z	Ctrl-Z (Windows EOF character)

To include either kind of quote character within a string, you can do one of three things:

- Double the quote character if the string is quoted using the same character:

```
'I can''t'
"He said, ""I told you so."""
```

- Quote the string with the other quote character; in this case, you do not double the quote characters within the string:

```
"I can't"
'He said, "I told you so."'
```

- Escape the quote character with a backslash; this works regardless of the quote characters used to quote the string:

```
'I can\'t'
"I can\'t"
"He said, \"I told you so.\""
'He said, \"I told you so.\"'
```

Hexadecimal constants can be used to specify string values. There are two different syntaxes for such constants. The first consists of '0x' followed by one or more hexadecimal digits ('0' through '9' and 'a' through 'f'). For example, 0x0a is 10 decimal, and 0xffff is 65535 decimal. Non-decimal hex digits can be specified in uppercase or lowercase, but the leading '0x' cannot be given as '0X'. That is, 0x0a and 0x0A are legal, but 0X0a and 0X0A are not. In string context, pairs of hexadecimal digits are interpreted as ASCII codes, converted to characters, and the result is used as a string. In numeric context, a hexadecimal constant is treated as a number. The following statement illustrates both uses:

```
mysql> SELECT 0x616263, 0x616263+0;
+----------+------------+
| 0x616263 | 0x616263+0 |
+----------+------------+
| abc      |    6382179 |
+----------+------------+
```

As of MySQL 4.0, string values can also be specified using the ANSI SQL notation X'*val*', where *val* consists of pairs of hexadecimal digits. As with 0x notation, such values are interpreted as strings but can be used as numbers in a numeric context:

```
mysql> SELECT X'616263', X'616263'+0;
+-----------+-------------+
| X'616263' | X'616263'+0 |
+-----------+-------------+
| abc       |     6382179 |
+-----------+-------------+
```

Unlike 0x notation, the leading 'x' is not case sensitive:

```
mysql> SELECT X'61', x'61';
+-------+-------+
| X'61' | x'61' |
+-------+-------+
| a     | a     |
+-------+-------+
```

From MySQL 4.1 and later, string values can be specified to lie within a particular character set. Before that, string values are interpreted using the server's default character set. The "Character Set Support" section later in this chapter discusses issues related to character sets in more detail.

Date and Time (Temporal) Values

Dates and times are values such as `'2002-06-17'` or `'12:30:43'`. MySQL also understands combined date/time values, such as `'2002-06-17 12:30:43'`. Take special note of the fact that MySQL represents dates in year-month-day order. This often surprises newcomers to MySQL, although this format is the ANSI SQL standard (also known as ISO 8601 format). You can display date values any way you want by using the `DATE_FORMAT()` function, but the default display format lists the year first, and input values must be specified with the year first.

The NULL Value

`NULL` is something of a "typeless" value. Generally, it's used to mean "no value," "unknown value," "missing value," "out of range," "not applicable," "none of the above," and so on. You can insert `NULL` values into tables, retrieve them from tables, and test whether a value is `NULL`. However, you cannot perform arithmetic on `NULL` values; if you try, the result is `NULL`.

MySQL Column Types

Each table in a database is made up of one or more columns. When you create a table using a `CREATE TABLE` statement, you specify a type for each column. A column type is more specific than a data type, which is just a general category, such as "number" or "string." A column type precisely characterizes the kind of values a given table column can contain, such as `SMALLINT` or `VARCHAR(32)`.

MySQL's column types are the means by which you describe what kinds of values a table's columns contain, which in turn determines how MySQL treats those values. For example, if you have numeric values, you can store them using a numeric or a string column type, but MySQL will treat the values somewhat differently depending on how you store them. Each column type has several characteristics:

- What kind of values you can store in it

- How much space values take up, and whether the values are fixed-length (all values of the type taking the same amount of space) or variable-length (the amount of space depending on the particular value being stored)
- How values of the type are compared and sorted
- Whether the type allows NULL values
- Whether the type can be indexed

The following discussion surveys MySQL's column types briefly in a broad overview and then describes in more detail the properties that characterize each type.

Overview of Column Types

MySQL provides column types for values from all the general data type categories except the NULL value. NULL spans all types in the sense that the property of whether a column can contain NULL values is treated as a type attribute.

MySQL has numeric column types for both integer and floating-point values, as shown in Table 2.2. Integer columns can be signed or unsigned. A special attribute allows sequential integer column values to be generated automatically, which is useful in applications that require a series of unique identification numbers.

Table 2.2 **Numeric Column Types**

Type Name	Meaning
TINYINT	A very small integer
SMALLINT	A small integer
MEDIUMINT	A medium-sized integer
INT	A standard integer
BIGINT	A large integer
FLOAT	A single-precision floating-point number
DOUBLE	A double-precision floating-point number
DECIMAL	A floating-point number, represented as a string

MySQL string column types are shown in Table 2.3. Strings can hold anything, even arbitrary binary data such as images or sounds. Strings can be compared according to whether or not they are case sensitive. In addition, you can perform pattern matching on strings. (Actually, in MySQL you can perform pattern matching on any column type, but it's most often done with string types.)

Table 2.3 **String Column Types**

Type Name	Meaning
CHAR	A fixed-length character string
VARCHAR	A variable-length character string
TINYBLOB	A very small BLOB (binary large object)
BLOB	A small BLOB
MEDIUMBLOB	A medium-sized BLOB
LONGBLOB	A large BLOB
TINYTEXT	A very small text string
TEXT	A small text string
MEDIUMTEXT	A medium-sized text string
LONGTEXT	A large text string
ENUM	An enumeration; column values may be assigned one enumeration member
SET	A set; column values may be assigned multiple set members

MySQL date and time types are shown in Table 2.4, where CC, YY, MM, DD hh, mm, and ss represent century, year, month, day, hour, minute, and second. For temporal values, MySQL provides types for dates and times (either combined or separate) and timestamps (a special type that allows you to track when changes were last made to a record). There is also a type for efficiently representing year values when you don't need an entire date.

Table 2.4 **Date and Time Column Types**

Type Name	Meaning
DATE	A date value, in '$CCYY\text{-}MM\text{-}DD$' format
TIME	A time value, in '$hh\text{:}mm\text{:}ss$' format
DATETIME	A date and time value, in '$CCYY\text{-}MM\text{-}DD$ $hh\text{:}mm\text{:}ss$' format
TIMESTAMP	A timestamp value, in $CCYYMMDDhhmmss$ format
YEAR	A year value, in $CCYY$ format

Creating Tables

To create a table, issue a CREATE TABLE statement and specify a list of the columns that make up the table. Each column has a name and a type, and various attributes can be associated with each type. The following example creates a table named mytbl containing three columns named f, c, and i:

```
CREATE TABLE mytbl
(
    f FLOAT(10,4),
    c CHAR(15) NOT NULL DEFAULT 'none',
    i TINYINT UNSIGNED NULL
);
```

The syntax for declaring a column is as follows:

```
col_name col_type [col_attributes] [general_attributes]
```

The name of the column, `col_name`, is always first in the definition. The precise rules for naming columns are given in the "MySQL Naming Rules" section of Chapter 3. Briefly summarized, column names can be up to 64 characters long and can consist of alphanumeric characters from the server's default character set, as well as the underscore and dollar sign characters ('_' and '$'). Function names (words such as `POS` and `MIN`) are not reserved and can be used as column names; but keywords, such as `SELECT`, `DELETE`, and `CREATE`, normally are reserved and cannot be used, but as of MySQL 3.23.6, you can include other characters within a name or use reserved words by enclosing the name within backtick ('`') characters. A column name can begin with any character that is legal in a name, including a digit. However, unless quoted within backticks, a name cannot consist entirely of digits because then it would appear to be a number.

The column type `col_type` indicates the specific kind of values the column can hold. The type specifier can also indicate the maximum length of the values you store in the column. For some types, you specify the length explicitly as a number. For others, the length is implied by the type name. For example, `CHAR(10)` specifies an explicit length of 10 characters, whereas `TINYBLOB` values have an implicit maximum length of 255 characters. Some of the type specifiers allow you to indicate a maximum display width (how many characters to use for displaying values). Floating-point types allow the number of decimal places to be specified, so you can control how precise values are.

Following the column type, you can specify optional type-specific attributes as well as more general attributes. These attributes function as type modifiers. They cause MySQL to change the way it treats column values in some way:

- The type-specific attributes that are allowable depend on the column type you choose. For example, `UNSIGNED` is allowable only for numeric types, and `BINARY` is allowable only for `CHAR` and `VARCHAR`.

- The general attributes can be given for any column type, with a few exceptions. You can specify `NULL` or `NOT NULL` to indicate whether a column can hold `NULL` values. For all but `BLOB` and `TEXT` types, you can specify `DEFAULT def_value` to indicate that a column should be assigned the value `def_value` when a new row is created that does not explicitly specify the column's value. The value of `def_value` must be a constant; it cannot be an expression or refer to other columns.

If multiple column attributes are given, there are some constraints on the order in which they may appear. In general, you should be safe if you specify column type-specific attributes such as UNSIGNED or ZEROFILL before general attributes such as NULL or NOT NULL.

The rest of this section discusses the syntax for declaring each of MySQL's column types and the properties that characterize them, such as their range and storage requirements. The type specifications are shown as you use them in CREATE TABLE statements. Optional information is indicated by square brackets ([]). For example, the syntax MEDIUMINT[(M)] indicates that the maximum display width, specified as (M), is optional. On the other hand, for VARCHAR(M), the lack of brackets indicates that (M) is required.

Numeric Column Types

MySQL's numeric column types fall into two general classifications:

- Integer types are used for numbers that have no fractional part, such as 1, 43, -3, 0, or -798432. You can use integer columns for data represented by whole numbers, such as weight to the nearest pound, height to the nearest inch, number of stars in a galaxy, number of people in a household, or number of bacteria in a petri dish.

- Floating-point types are used for numbers that may have a fractional part, such as 3.14159, -.00273, -4.78, or 39.3E+4. You can use floating-point column types for values that may have a fractional part or that are extremely large or small. Some types of data you might represent as floating-point values are average crop yield, distances, money values, unemployment rates, or stock prices.

Integer types are the simplest. Floating-point types are more complex, particularly because their behavior has changed at certain points in MySQL's development.

Floating-point values can be assigned to integer columns but will be rounded to the nearest integer. Conversely, integer values can be assigned to floating-point columns. They are treated as floating-point values with a fractional part of zero.

Table 2.5 shows the name and range of each numeric type, and Table 2.6 shows the amount of storage required for values of each type.

Table 2.5   **Numeric Column Type Ranges**

Type Specification	Range
TINYINT[(M)]	Signed values: −128 to 127 (-2^7 to $2^7 - 1$)
	Unsigned values: 0 to 255 (0 to $2^8 - 1$)
SMALLINT[(M)]	Signed values: −32768 to 32767 (-2^{15} to $2^{15} - 1$)
	Unsigned values: 0 to 65535 (0 to $2^{16} - 1$)

Type Specification	Range
MEDIUMINT[(M)]	Signed values: −8388608 to 8388607 (-2^{23} to $2^{23} - 1$)
	Unsigned values: 0 to 16777215 (0 to $2^{24} - 1$)
INT[(M)]	Signed values: −2147683648 to 2147483647 (-2^{31} to $2^{31} - 1$)
	Unsigned values: 0 to 4294967295 (0 to $2^{32} - 1$)
BIGINT[(M)]	Signed values: −9223372036854775808 to 9223372036854775807 (-2^{63} to $2^{63} - 1$)
	Unsigned values: 0 to 18446744073709551615 (0 to $2^{64} - 1$)
FLOAT[(M,D)]	Minimum non-zero values: ±1.175494351E−38
	Maximum non-zero values: ±3.402823466E+38
DOUBLE[(M,D)]	Minimum non-zero values: ±2.2250738585072014E−308
	Maximum non-zero values: ±1.7976931348623157E+308
DECIMAL([M[,D]])	Varies; range depends on M and D

Table 2.6 **Numeric Column Type Storage Requirements**

Type Specification	Storage Required
TINYINT[(M)]	1 byte
SMALLINT[(M)]	2 bytes
MEDIUMINT[(M)]	3 bytes
INT[(M)]	4 bytes
BIGINT[(M)]	8 bytes
FLOAT[(M,D)]	4 bytes
DOUBLE[(M,D)]	8 bytes
DECIMAL([M[,D]])	M bytes (MySQL < 3.23), M+2 bytes (MySQL ≥ 3.23)

Integer Column Types

MySQL provides five integer types: TINYINT, SMALLINT, MEDIUMINT, INT, and BIGINT. INTEGER is a synonym for INT. These types vary in the range of values they can represent and in the amount of storage space they require. (Types with a larger range require more storage.) Integer columns can be declared as UNSIGNED to disallow negative values; this shifts the range for the column upward to begin at 0.

When you declare an integer column, you can specify an optional display size M. If given, M should be an integer from 1 to 255. It represents the number of characters used to display values for the column. For example, MEDIUMINT(4) specifies a MEDIUMINT column with a display width of 4. If you declare an integer column without an explicit width, a default width is assigned. The defaults are the lengths of the "longest" values for each type.

Note that displayed values are not chopped to fit within *M* characters. If the printable representation of a particular value requires more than *M* characters, MySQL displays the full value.

The display size *M* for an integer column is related only to the number of characters used to display column values. It has *nothing* to do with the number of bytes of storage space required. For example, BIGINT values require 8 bytes of storage regardless of the display width. It is not possible to magically cut the required storage space for a BIGINT column in half by declaring it as BIG-INT(4). Nor does *M* have anything to do with the range of values allowed. If you declare a column as INT(3), that will not restrict it to a maximum value of 999.

The following statement creates a table to illustrate the default values of *M* and *D* for integer column types:

```
CREATE TABLE mytbl
(
    itiny       TINYINT,
    itiny_u     TINYINT UNSIGNED,
    ismall      SMALLINT,
    ismall_u    SMALLINT UNSIGNED,
    imedium     MEDIUMINT,
    imedium_u   MEDIUMINT UNSIGNED,
    ireg        INT,
    ireg_u      INT UNSIGNED,
    ibig        BIGINT,
    ibig_u      BIGINT UNSIGNED
);
```

If you issue a DESCRIBE mytbl statement after creating the table, the number following each type name shows the value that MySQL uses by default in the absence of an explicit display width specifier: [1]

```
+-----------+-----------------------+
| Field     | Type                  |
+-----------+-----------------------+
| itiny     | tinyint(4)            |
| itiny_u   | tinyint(3) unsigned   |
| ismall    | smallint(6)           |
| ismall_u  | smallint(5) unsigned  |
| imedium   | mediumint(9)          |
| imedium_u | mediumint(8) unsigned |
| ireg      | int(11)               |
| ireg_u    | int(10) unsigned      |
| ibig      | bigint(20)            |
| ibig_u    | bigint(20) unsigned   |
+-----------+-----------------------+
```

1. Due to a minor glitch, the display width for BIGINT will be 21 (not 20) if you run this query using a version of MySQL older than 3.23.

Floating-Point Column Types

MySQL provides three floating-point types: FLOAT, DOUBLE, and DECIMAL. Synonymous types are DOUBLE PRECISION and REAL for DOUBLE, and NUMERIC for DECIMAL. Ranges for these types differ from ranges for integer types in the sense that there is not only a maximum value a floating-point type can represent, but also a minimum non-zero value. The minimum values provide a measure of how precise the type is, which is often important for recording scientific data. (There are, of course, corresponding negative maximum and minimum values.)

Floating-point types can be declared as UNSIGNED, although not until MySQL 4.0.2 for FLOAT and DOUBLE. Unlike the integer types, declaring a floating-point type UNSIGNED doesn't shift the type's range upward, it merely eliminates the negative end.

For each floating-point type, you can specify a maximum display size M and the number of decimal places D. The value of M should be from 1 to 255. The value of D can be from 0 to 30, but should be no more than $M-2$. (If you're more familiar with ODBC terms, M and D correspond to the ODBC concepts of "precision" and "scale.")

For FLOAT and DOUBLE, M and D are optional. If they are omitted, these types are treated as follows:

- Prior to MySQL 3.23.6, FLOAT and DOUBLE are treated as FLOAT(10,2) and DOUBLE(16,4) with stored values rounded to 2 and 4 decimals, respectively.
- For MySQL 3.23.6 and later, FLOAT and DOUBLE are stored to the full precision allowed by your hardware.

For DECIMAL, M and D may or may not be optional, depending on your version of MySQL:

- Prior to MySQL 3.23.6, M and D are required for DECIMAL columns.
- For MySQL 3.23.6 and later, if D is omitted, it defaults to 0. If M is omitted as well, it defaults to 10. In other words, the following equivalences hold:

```
DECIMAL = DECIMAL(10) = DECIMAL(10,0)
DECIMAL(n) = DECIMAL(n,0)
```

FLOAT(p) syntax is also allowed for ODBC compatibility. However, the precise behavior of columns specified using this syntax is somewhat complicated:

- Prior to MySQL 3.23, the allowable values of p are 4 and 8, indicating the number of bytes of storage per value. FLOAT(4) and FLOAT(8) are treated as FLOAT(10,2) and DOUBLE(16,4) with stored values rounded to 2 and 4 decimals, respectively.

- For MySQL 3.23.0 to 3.23.5, the allowable values of p are still 4 and 8 and indicate the number of bytes of storage, but FLOAT(4) and FLOAT(8) are treated as single-precision and double-precision columns with values stored to full hardware precision.

- For MySQL 3.23.6 and later, p can range from 0 to 53 and indicates the minimum number of bits of precision required for stored values. For p values from 0 to 24, the column is treated as single-precision. For values from 25 to 53, the column is treated as double-precision.

More confusing still is that MySQL allows FLOAT4 and FLOAT8 as synonyms, but what they are synonyms for depends on your version of MySQL:

- Prior to MySQL 3.23.6, FLOAT4 and FLOAT8 are equivalent to FLOAT(10,2) and DOUBLE(16,4).

- For MySQL 3.23.6 and later, FLOAT4 and FLOAT8 are equivalent to FLOAT and DOUBLE.

If you carefully compare these equivalences to those for FLOAT(4) and FLOAT(8), you'll see that FLOAT4 and FLOAT8 are *not quite* the same as FLOAT(4) and FLOAT(8), although you might have expected them to be.

Checking How MySQL Treats a Type Specification

If you're not sure how your version of MySQL will treat a given floating-point column specification, try the following. Create a table that contains a column defined the way you're wondering about and then use DESCRIBE to see how MySQL reports the type. For example, in MySQL 3.23.0, if you create a column using FLOAT4, you'd see the following:

```
mysql> CREATE TABLE t (f FLOAT4);
mysql> DESCRIBE t;
+-------+------------+------+-----+---------+-------+
| Field | Type       | Null | Key | Default | Extra |
+-------+------------+------+-----+---------+-------+
| f     | float(10,2)| YES  |     | NULL    |       |
+-------+------------+------+-----+---------+-------+
```

In MySQL 3.23.6, you'd see the following instead:

```
mysql> CREATE TABLE t (f FLOAT4);
mysql> DESCRIBE t;
+-------+-------+------+-----+---------+-------+
| Field | Type  | Null | Key | Default | Extra |
+-------+-------+------+-----+---------+-------+
| f     | float | YES  |     | NULL    |       |
+-------+-------+------+-----+---------+-------+
```

The lack of a (M, D) indicator in the latter case indicates that values are stored to the full precision allowed by the hardware.

This technique actually works to see how MySQL treats any column definition, but I have found it most useful for floating-point types.

Choosing Numeric Column Types

When you choose a numeric type, consider the range of values you need to represent and choose the smallest type that will cover the range. Choosing a larger type wastes space, leading to tables that are unnecessarily large and that cannot be processed as efficiently as if you had chosen a smaller type. For integer values, TINYINT is the best if the range of values in your data is small, such as a person's age or number of siblings. MEDIUMINT can represent millions of values and can be used for many more types of values, at some additional cost in storage space. BIGINT has the largest range of all but requires twice as much storage as the next smallest integer type (INT) and should be used only when really necessary. For floating-point values, DOUBLE takes twice as much space as FLOAT. Unless you need exceptionally high precision or an extremely large range of values, you can probably represent your data at half the storage cost by using FLOAT.

Every numeric column's range of values is determined by its type. If you attempt to insert a value that lies outside the column's range, truncation occurs; MySQL clips the value to the appropriate endpoint of the range and uses the result. No truncation occurs when values are retrieved.

Value truncation occurs according to the range of the column type, not the display width. For example, a SMALLINT(3) column has a display width of 3 and a range from –32768 to 32767. The value 12345 is wider than the display width but within the range of the column, so it is inserted without clipping and retrieved as 12345. The value 99999 is outside the range, so it is clipped to 32767 when inserted. Subsequent retrievals retrieve the value 32767.

In general, values assigned to a floating-point column are rounded to the number of decimals indicated by the column specification. If you store 1.23456 in a FLOAT(8,1) column, the result is 1.2. If you store the same value in a FLOAT(8,4) column, the result is 1.2346. This means you should declare floating-point columns with a sufficient number of decimals to give you values as precise as you require. If you need accuracy to thousandths, don't declare a type with only two decimal places.

The DECIMAL type is a floating-point type, but it differs from FLOAT and DOUBLE in that DECIMAL values actually are stored as strings and have a fixed number of decimals. The significance of this fact is that DECIMAL values are not subject to roundoff error the way that FLOAT and DOUBLE columns are—a property that makes DECIMAL especially applicable to currency calculations. The corresponding tradeoff is that DECIMAL values are not as efficient as floating-point values stored in native format that the processor can operate on directly.

The maximum possible range for DECIMAL is the same as for DOUBLE, but the effective range is determined by the values of M and D. If you vary M and hold D fixed, the range becomes larger as M becomes larger. This is illustrated by Table 2.7. If you hold M fixed and vary D, the range becomes smaller as D becomes larger, although the precision increases. This is shown by Table 2.8.

Table 2.7 **How *M* Affects the Range of DECIMAL*(M,D)***

Type Specification	Range (for MySQL < 3.23)	Range (for MySQL ≥ 3.23)
DECIMAL(4,1)	−9.9 to 99.9	−999.9 to 9999.9
DECIMAL(5,1)	−99.9 to 999.9	−9999.9 to 99999.9
DECIMAL(6,1)	−999.9 to 9999.9	−99999.9 to 999999.9

Table 2.8 **How *D* Affects the Range of DECIMAL*(M,D)***

Type Specification	Range (for MySQL < 3.23)	Range (for MySQL ≥ 3.23)
DECIMAL(4,0)	−999 to 9999	−9999 to 99999
DECIMAL(4,1)	−9.9 to 99.9	−999.9 to 9999.9
DECIMAL(4,2)	−.99 to 9.99	−99.99 to 999.99

The range for a given DECIMAL type depends on your version of MySQL. As of MySQL 3.23, DECIMAL values are handled according to the ANSI specification, which states that a type of DECIMAL(M, D) must be able to represent any value with M digits and D decimal places. For example, DECIMAL(4,2) must be able to represent values from −99.99 to 99.99. Because the sign character and decimal point must still be stored, this requires an extra two bytes, so DECIMAL(M, D) values for MySQL 3.23 and later use M+2 bytes. For DECIMAL(4,2), six bytes are needed for the "widest" value (−99.99). At the positive end of the range, the sign byte is not needed to hold a sign character, so MySQL uses it to extend the range beyond that required by the ANSI specification. In other words, for DECIMAL(4,2), the maximum value that can be stored in the six bytes available is 999.99.

There are two special conditions that reduce the DECIMAL storage requirement of M+2 bytes to a lesser value:

- If D is 0, DECIMAL values have no fractional part and no byte need be allocated to store the decimal point. This reduces the required storage by one byte.
- If a DECIMAL column is UNSIGNED, no sign character need be stored, also reducing the required storage by one byte.

For versions of MySQL prior to 3.23, DECIMAL values are represented in a slightly different fashion. A DECIMAL(M,D) column is stored using M bytes per value, and the sign character and decimal point (if needed) are included in the M bytes. Thus, for a type DECIMAL(4,2), the range is −.99 to 9.99 because those cover all the possible 4-character values. If D is 0, no decimal point need be stored, and the byte usually used for that purpose can be used to store another digit. The effect is to extend the range of the column by an extra order of magnitude. (This explains why the pre-3.23 range in Table 2.8 shifts by a factor of 10 for DECIMAL(4,2) compared to DECIMAL(4,1), but by a factor of 100 for DECIMAL(4,1) compared to DECIMAL(4,0). I bet you didn't even notice that!)

Numeric Column Type Attributes

The ZEROFILL attribute can be specified for all numeric types. It causes displayed values for the column to be padded with leading zeros to the display width. You can use ZEROFILL when you want to make sure column values always display using a given number of digits. Actually, it's more accurate to say "a given minimum number of digits" because values wider than the display width are displayed in full without being chopped. You can see this by issuing the following statements:

```
mysql> DROP TABLE IF EXISTS mytbl;
mysql> CREATE TABLE mytbl (my_zerofill INT(5) ZEROFILL);
mysql> INSERT INTO mytbl VALUES(1),(100),(10000),(1000000);
mysql> SELECT my_zerofill FROM mytbl;
+-------------+
| my_zerofill |
+-------------+
|       00001 |
|       00100 |
|       10000 |
|     1000000 |
+-------------+
```

Note that the final value, which is wider than the column's display width, is displayed in full.

The UNSIGNED attribute disallows negative values. It is most often used with integer types. Making an integer column UNSIGNED doesn't change the "size" of the underlying data type's range; it just shifts the range upward. Consider this table specification:

```
CREATE TABLE mytbl
(
    itiny    TINYINT,
    itiny_u  TINYINT UNSIGNED
);
```

itiny and itiny_u are both TINYINT columns with a range of 256 values but differ in the particular allowable values. The range of itiny is −128 to 127, whereas the range of itiny_u is shifted up, resulting in a range of 0 to 255.

UNSIGNED is useful for integer columns into which you plan to store information that doesn't take on negative values, such as population counts or attendance figures. If you use a signed column for such values, you use only half of the column type's range. By making the column UNSIGNED, you effectively double your range. If you use the column for sequence numbers, it will take twice as long to run out of values if you make it UNSIGNED.

You can also specify UNSIGNED for floating-point columns, although the effect is slightly different than for integer columns. The range does not shift upward; instead, the upper end remains unchanged and the lower end becomes zero. A precaution to observe is that you should not use UNSIGNED with FLOAT or DOUBLE columns prior to MySQL 4.0.2. In earlier versions, MySQL allows these types to be declared as UNSIGNED, but doing so may result in unpredictable column behavior. (This prohibition does not apply to DECIMAL.)

One other attribute, AUTO_INCREMENT, can be specified for integer column types only. Use the AUTO_INCREMENT attribute when you want to generate unique identifiers or values in a series. When you insert NULL into an AUTO_INCREMENT column, MySQL generates the next sequence value and stores it in the column. Normally, unless you take steps to cause otherwise, AUTO_INCREMENT values begin at 1 and increase by 1 for each new row. The sequence can be affected if you delete rows from the table. This depends on the table type, which determines whether or not sequence values are reused.

You can have at most one AUTO_INCREMENT column in a table. The column should be NOT NULL, and it should be declared as a PRIMARY KEY or as a UNIQUE key. Also, because sequence values are always positive, you normally declare the column UNSIGNED as well. For example, you can declare an AUTO_INCREMENT column in any of the following ways:

```
CREATE TABLE ai (i INT UNSIGNED AUTO_INCREMENT NOT NULL PRIMARY KEY);
CREATE TABLE ai (i INT UNSIGNED AUTO_INCREMENT NOT NULL, PRIMARY KEY (i));
CREATE TABLE ai (i INT UNSIGNED AUTO_INCREMENT NOT NULL, UNIQUE (i));
```

It is always allowable to declare an AUTO_INCREMENT column explicitly NOT NULL, as shown. However, for versions 3.23 and later, MySQL treats AUTO_INCREMENT columns as NOT NULL automatically.

The behavior of AUTO_INCREMENT columns is discussed further in the "Working with Sequences" section later in this chapter.

Following the attributes just described, which are specific to numeric columns, you can also specify the general attributes NULL or NOT NULL. If you do not specify NULL or NOT NULL for a numeric column, the default is NULL. You can also specify a default value using the DEFAULT attribute. If you do not specify a default value, one is chosen automatically. For all numeric column types, the default is NULL for columns that may contain NULL, and 0 otherwise.

The following table contains three INT columns, having default values of -1, 1, and NULL:

```
CREATE TABLE t
(
    i1 INT DEFAULT -1,
    i2 INT DEFAULT 1,
    i3 INT DEFAULT NULL
);
```

String Column Types

MySQL provides several string types to hold character data. Strings are often used for values like the following:

```
'N. Bertram, et al.'
'Pencils (no. 2 lead)'
'123 Elm St.'
'Monograph Series IX'
```

But strings are actually "generic" types in a sense because you can use them to represent any value. For example, you can use string types to hold binary data, such as images or sounds, or output from gzip, should you want to store compressed data.

Table 2.9 shows the types provided by MySQL for declaring string-valued columns and the maximum size and storage requirements of each type. For variable-length column types, the amount of storage taken by a value varies from row to row and depends on the length of the values actually stored in the column. This length is represented by L in the table.

The extra bytes required in addition to L are the number of bytes needed to store the length of the value. MySQL handles variable-length values by storing both the content of the value and its length. These extra bytes are treated as an unsigned integer. Notice the correspondence between a variable-length type's maximum length, the number of extra bytes required for that type, and the range of the unsigned integer type that uses the same number of bytes. For example, `MEDIUMBLOB` values can be up to $2^{24}-1$ bytes long and require 3 bytes to record the result. The 3-byte integer type `MEDIUMINT` has a maximum unsigned value of $2^{24}-1$. That's not a coincidence.

Table 2.9 **String Column Types**

Type Specification	Maximum Size	Storage Required
`CHAR[(M)]`	M bytes	M bytes
`VARCHAR(M)`	M bytes	$L+1$ bytes
`TINYBLOB, TINYTEXT`	$2^8 - 1$ bytes	$L+1$ bytes
`BLOB, TEXT`	$2^{16} - 1$ bytes	$L+2$ bytes
`MEDIUMBLOB, MEDIUMTEXT`	$2^{24} - 1$ bytes	$L+3$ bytes
`LONGBLOB, LONGTEXT`	$2^{32} - 1$ bytes	$L+4$ bytes
`ENUM('value1','value2',...)`	65535 members	1 or 2 bytes
`SET('value1','value2',...)`	64 members	1, 2, 3, 4, or 8 bytes

For `ENUM` and `SET`, the column definition includes a list of legal values. Attempting to store a value other than those causes the value to be converted to `''` (the empty string). For the other string types, values that are too long are chopped to fit. But string types range from very small to very large, with the largest type able to hold nearly 4GB of data, so you should be able to find something long enough to avoid truncation of your information.[2]

`ENUM` and `SET` values are stored internally as numbers, as detailed later in the "ENUM and SET Column Types" section. Values for the other string types are stored as a sequence of bytes and treated either as bytes or characters, depending on whether the type holds binary or non-binary strings:

- A binary string is treated as a generic sequence of bytes, without respect to any character set. `BLOB` columns hold binary values, as do `CHAR` and `VARCHAR` columns if they are declared with the `BINARY` attribute.

- A non-binary string is treated as a sequence of characters and interpreted with respect to the properties of a particular character set. `TEXT` columns hold non-binary strings, as do `CHAR` and `VARCHAR` columns if they are declared without the `BINARY` attribute. For a single-byte character set, each character takes one byte. For multi-byte character sets, characters can take more than one byte. In MySQL 4.1 and later, columns can be assigned character sets individually. Prior to MySQL 4.1, the server's default character set is used to interpret character strings.

---

2. The effective maximum column size is actually imposed by the maximum packet size of the client/server communication protocol. This value is 16MB prior to MySQL 4, and 1GB for MySQL 4 and later.

Use of a character set causes non-binary strings to be compared and sorted using the character set's collating sequence. By contrast, a binary string has no character set and thus no collating sequence. This results in some differences in the way binary and non-binary strings are interpreted:

- Binary strings are processed byte-by-byte in comparisons based only on the underlying numeric value of each byte. One implication of this property is that binary values are case sensitive, because the lowercase and uppercase versions of a given letter have different numeric codes.

- Non-binary strings are processed character-by-character in comparisons using the character set collating sequence. For most character sets, uppercase and lowercase versions of a given letter have the same collating value, which means that non-binary string comparisons are not case sensitive. Similar characters with different accents also may have the same collating value. For example, 'E' and 'É' compare as the same character in the `latin1` character set.

There are a few character sets that do treat uppercase and lowercase as having different collating values and that distinguish between accent marks: `cp1521csas`, `cp1527ltlvcsas`, `latin1csas`, `maccecsas`, and `macromancsas`. Note that these character set names each end with `csas`, which means "case sensitive, accent sensitive." They're something of a special case, so although elsewhere in this book I discuss non-binary strings as not case sensitive, keep in mind that these character sets exist as exceptions to the rule.

The distinction between characters and bytes can be seen easily by considering the length of a string containing multi-byte characters. For example, in MySQL 4.1 and later, you can use the `CONVERT()` function to generate a string in any available character set. The following statement creates `@s` as a string using `ucs2`, a character set that uses two bytes to encode each character:

```
mysql> SET @s = CONVERT('ABC' USING ucs2);
```

What is the "length" of the string `@s`? It depends. If you measure with `CHAR_LENGTH()`, which is multi-byte aware, you get the length in characters. If you measure with `LENGTH()`, which is not multi-byte aware, you get the length in bytes:

```
mysql> SELECT CHAR_LENGTH(@s), LENGTH(@s);
+-----------------+------------+
| CHAR_LENGTH(@s) | LENGTH(@s) |
+-----------------+------------+
|               3 |          6 |
+-----------------+------------+
```

A binary string has no character set and is treated simply as a sequence of individual bytes. Consequently, the length of the string is the same whether measured in characters or bytes:

```
mysql> SET @s = BINARY CONVERT('ABC' USING ucs2);
mysql> SELECT CHAR_LENGTH(BINARY @s), LENGTH(BINARY @s);
+------------------------+-------------------+
| CHAR_LENGTH(BINARY @s) | LENGTH(BINARY @s) |
+------------------------+-------------------+
|                      6 |                 6 |
+------------------------+-------------------+
```

The difference between lengths in characters and in bytes is significant for interpreting the meaning of string column types. For example, a column declaration of VARCHAR(20) doesn't really mean "20 characters maximum," it means "as many characters as will fit in 20 bytes." For single-byte character sets, the two are the same because the number of characters is the same as the number of bytes. But, for a multi-byte character set, the number of characters can be many less than 20.

The CHAR and VARCHAR Column Types

CHAR and VARCHAR are the most commonly used string types. The difference between them is that CHAR is a fixed-length type and VARCHAR is a variable-length type. Values in a CHAR(M) column each take M bytes; shorter values are right-padded with spaces when they are stored. (Trailing spaces are stripped off on retrieval, however.) Values in a VARCHAR(M) column are stored using only as many bytes as necessary, plus one byte to record the length. Trailing spaces are stripped from VARCHAR values when they are stored; this differs from the ANSI SQL standard for VARCHAR values. (A VARCHAR type for which trailing spaces are not stripped may be introduced in a future version of MySQL.)

CHAR and VARCHAR columns can be declared with a maximum length M from 1 to 255. M is optional for CHAR and defaults to 1 if missing. Beginning with MySQL 3.23, CHAR(0) is also legal. CHAR(0) is useful as a placeholder when you want to declare a column but don't want to allocate space for it if you're not sure yet how wide to make it. You can use ALTER TABLE to widen the column later. A CHAR(0) column can also be used to represent on/off values if you allow it to be NULL. Values in such a column can have two values—NULL or the empty string. A CHAR(0) column takes very little storage space in the table—only a single bit. As of MySQL 4.0.2, VARCHAR(0) is allowable as well, but it's treated as CHAR(0).

Keep two general principles in mind when choosing between CHAR and VAR-CHAR column types:

- If your values are all the same length, VARCHAR actually will use more space due to the extra byte required to record the length of values. On the other hand, if your values vary in length, VARCHAR columns have the advantage of taking less space. A CHAR(n) column always takes n bytes, even if it is empty or NULL.

- If your values don't vary much in length, CHAR is a better choice than VARCHAR if you're using MyISAM or ISAM tables. For such table types, tables with fixed-length rows can be processed more efficiently than tables with variable-length rows.

With a few limited exceptions, you cannot mix CHAR and VARCHAR within the same table. MySQL will even change columns from one type to another, depending on the circumstances. (This is something that other databases do not do.) The principles that apply are as follows:

- Table rows are fixed-length only if all the columns in the table are fixed-length types.

- If even a single column has a variable length, table rows become variable-length as well.

- If table rows are variable-length, any fixed-length columns in the column may as well be converted to variable-length equivalents when that will save space.

What this means is that if you have VARCHAR, BLOB, or TEXT columns in a table, you cannot also have CHAR columns; MySQL silently converts them to VARCHAR. Suppose you create a table as follows:

```
CREATE TABLE mytbl
(
    c1  CHAR(10),
    c2  VARCHAR(10)
);
```

If you issue a DESCRIBE query, the output is as follows:

```
mysql> DESCRIBE mytbl;
+-------+-------------+------+-----+---------+-------+
| Field | Type        | Null | Key | Default | Extra |
+-------+-------------+------+-----+---------+-------+
| c1    | varchar(10) | YES  |     | NULL    |       |
| c2    | varchar(10) | YES  |     | NULL    |       |
+-------+-------------+------+-----+---------+-------+
```

Notice that the presence of the VARCHAR column causes MySQL to convert c1 to VARCHAR as well. If you try using ALTER TABLE to convert c1 to CHAR, it won't work. The only way to convert a VARCHAR column to CHAR is to convert all VARCHAR columns in the table at the same time:

```
mysql> ALTER TABLE mytbl MODIFY c1 CHAR(10), MODIFY c2 CHAR(10);
mysql> DESCRIBE mytbl;
+-------+----------+------+-----+---------+-------+
| Field | Type     | Null | Key | Default | Extra |
+-------+----------+------+-----+---------+-------+
| c1    | char(10) | YES  |     | NULL    |       |
| c2    | char(10) | YES  |     | NULL    |       |
+-------+----------+------+-----+---------+-------+
```

The BLOB and TEXT column types are variable-length like VARCHAR, but they have no fixed-length equivalent, so you cannot use CHAR columns in the same table as BLOB or TEXT columns. Any CHAR column will be converted to VARCHAR.

The exception to non-mixing of fixed- and variable-length columns is that CHAR columns shorter than four characters are not converted to VARCHAR. For example, MySQL will not change the CHAR column in the following table to VARCHAR:

```
CREATE TABLE mytbl
(
    c1 CHAR(2),
    c2 VARCHAR(10)
);
```

You can see this from the output of DESCRIBE:

```
mysql> DESCRIBE mytbl;
+-------+-------------+------+-----+---------+-------+
| Field | Type        | Null | Key | Default | Extra |
+-------+-------------+------+-----+---------+-------+
| c1    | char(2)     | YES  |     | NULL    |       |
| c2    | varchar(10) | YES  |     | NULL    |       |
+-------+-------------+------+-----+---------+-------+
```

The reason columns shorter than four characters are not converted is that, on average, any savings you might gain by not storing trailing spaces are offset by the extra byte needed in a VARCHAR column to record the length of each value. In fact, if all your columns are short, MySQL will convert any that you declare as VARCHAR to CHAR. MySQL does this because the conversion will decrease storage requirements on average and, for MyISAM and ISAM tables, will improve performance by making table rows fixed-length. Suppose you create a table with the following specification:

```
CREATE TABLE mytbl
(
    c0 VARCHAR(0),
    c1 VARCHAR(1),
    c2 VARCHAR(2),
    c3 VARCHAR(3)
);
```

DESCRIBE reveals that MySQL silently changes all the VARCHAR columns to CHAR:

```
mysql> DESCRIBE mytbl;
+-------+---------+------+-----+---------+-------+
| Field | Type    | Null | Key | Default | Extra |
+-------+---------+------+-----+---------+-------+
| c0    | char(0) | YES  |     | NULL    |       |
| c1    | char(1) | YES  |     | NULL    |       |
| c2    | char(2) | YES  |     | NULL    |       |
| c3    | char(3) | YES  |     | NULL    |       |
+-------+---------+------+-----+---------+-------+
```

The BLOB and TEXT Column Types

A "BLOB" is a binary large object—basically, a container that can hold anything you want to toss into it, and that you can make about as big as you want. In MySQL, the BLOB type is really a family of types (TINYBLOB, BLOB, MEDIUMBLOB, LONGBLOB), which are identical except for the maximum amount of information they can hold (see Table 2.9). BLOB columns are useful for storing data that may grow very large or that can vary widely in size from row to row. Some examples are word-processing documents, images and sounds, compound data, and news articles. MySQL also has a family of TEXT types (TINYTEXT, TEXT, MEDIUMTEXT, LONGTEXT). These are similar to the corresponding BLOB types, except that they are associated with a character set and operations on TEXT columns take character set into account. (For MySQL 4.1 and later, this is the character set assigned to the TEXT column itself. Prior to 4.1, it is the server's default character set.) This results in the general differences between binary and non-binary strings that were described earlier. For example, in comparison and sorting operations, BLOB values are case sensitive and TEXT values are not.

BLOB or TEXT columns sometimes can be indexed, depending on the table type you're using:

- MyISAM tables support BLOB and TEXT indexing (for MySQL 3.23.2 and later), as do BDB tables. However, you must specify a prefix size to be used for the index. This avoids creating index entries that might be huge and thereby defeat any benefits to be gained by that index. The exception is that no prefix is specified for FULLTEXT indexes on TEXT columns, because FULLTEXT searches are based on the entire content of the indexed columns.

- ISAM, HEAP, and InnoDB tables do not support BLOB and TEXT indexes.

BLOB or TEXT columns may require special care:

- Due to the typical large variation in the size of BLOB and TEXT values, tables containing them are subject to high rates of fragmentation if many deletes and updates are done. You'll want to run OPTIMIZE TABLE periodically to reduce fragmentation and maintain good performance. See Chapter 4, "Query Optimization," for more information.

- If you're using very large values, you may need to tune the server to increase the value of the max_allowed_packet parameter. See Chapter 11, "General MySQL Administration," for more information. You will also need to increase the packet size for any client that wishes to use very large values. Appendix E, "MySQL Program Reference," describes how to do this for the mysql client program.

The ENUM and SET Column Types

ENUM and SET are special string column types for which values must be chosen from a fixed (predefined) list of allowable strings. The primary difference between them is that ENUM column values must consist of exactly one member of the list of values, whereas SET column values can contain any or all members of the list. In other words, ENUM is used for values that are mutually exclusive, whereas SET allows multiple choices from the list.

The ENUM column type defines an enumeration. ENUM columns can be assigned values consisting of exactly one member chosen from a list of values specified at table-creation time. You can define an enumeration to have up to 65,535 members. Enumerations are commonly used to represent category values. For example, values in a column declared as ENUM('N','Y') can be either 'N' or 'Y'. Or you can use ENUM for such things as answers to multiple-choice questions in a survey or questionnaire, or available sizes or colors for a product:

```
employees ENUM('less than 100','100-500','501-1500','more than 1500')
color ENUM('red','green','blue','black')
size ENUM('S','M','L','XL','XXL')
```

If you are processing selections from Web pages, you can use an ENUM to represent the option that a visitor to your site chooses from a set of mutually exclusive radio buttons on a page. For example, if you run an online pizza ordering service, an ENUM can be used to represent the type of crust a customer orders:

```
crust ENUM('thin','regular','pan style','deep dish')
```

If enumeration categories represent counts, it's important to choose your categories properly when you create the enumeration. For example, when recording white blood cell counts from a laboratory test, you may group the counts into categories as follows:

```
wbc ENUM('0-100','101-300','>300')
```

When a test result comes in as an exact count, you can record the value in the wbc column terms of the category into which the count falls. But you cannot recover the original count if you decide you want to convert the column from a category-based ENUM to an integer column based on exact count. (If you really need the exact count, use an integer column instead.)

The SET type is similar to ENUM in the sense that when you create a SET column, you specify a list of legal set members. But unlike ENUM, each column value can consist of any number of members from the set. The set can have up to 64 members. You can use a SET when you have a fixed set of values that are not mutually exclusive, as they are in an ENUM column. For example, you might use a SET to represent options available for an automobile:

```
SET('luggage rack','cruise control','air conditioning','sun roof')
```

Then, particular SET values would represent those options actually ordered by customers:

```
'cruise control,sun roof'
'luggage rack,air conditioning'
'luggage rack,cruise control,air conditioning'
'air conditioning'
''
```

The final value shown (the empty string) means that the customer ordered no options. This is a legal SET value.

SET column values are represented as a single string. If a value consists of multiple set members, the members are separated in the string by commas. Obviously, this means you shouldn't use a string containing a comma as a SET member.

Other uses for SET columns might be for representing information, such as patient diagnoses or results from selections on Web pages. For a diagnosis, there may be a standard list of symptoms to ask a patient about, and the patient might exhibit any or all of them. For your online pizza service, the Web page for ordering could have a set of check boxes for ingredients that a customer wants on a pizza, several of which might be chosen.

The way you declare the legal value list for an ENUM or SET column is significant in several ways:

- The list determines the possible legal values for the column, as has already been discussed.

- You can insert ENUM or SET values in any lettercase, but the lettercase of the strings specified in the column declaration determines the lettercase of column values when they are retrieved later. For example, if you have an ENUM('Y','N') column and you store 'y' and 'n' in it, the values are displayed as 'Y' and 'N' when you retrieve them. This does not affect comparison or sorting behavior because ENUM and SET columns are not case sensitive.

- The order of values in an ENUM declaration is the order used for sorting. The order of values in a SET declaration also determines sort order, although the relationship is more complicated because column values can contain multiple set members.

- The order of values in a SET declaration determines the order in which set members appear when SET column values consisting of multiple members are displayed.

ENUM and SET are classified as string types because enumeration and set members are specified as strings when you create columns of these types. However, the members are stored internally as numbers and you can operate on them as such. This means that ENUM and SET types are more efficient than other string types because they often can be handled using numeric operations rather than string operations. It also means that ENUM and SET values can be used in either string or numeric contexts.

ENUM members in the column declaration are numbered sequentially beginning with 1. (0 is reserved by MySQL for the error member, which is represented in string form by the empty string.) The number of enumeration values determines the storage size of an ENUM column. One byte can represent 256 values, two bytes can represent 65,536 values. (Compare this to the ranges of the one-byte and two-byte integer types TINYINT UNSIGNED and SMALLINT UNSIGNED.) Thus, the maximum number of enumeration members is 65,536 (counting the error member) and the storage size depends on whether or not there are more than

256 members. You can specify a maximum of 65,535 (not 65,536) members in the ENUM declaration because MySQL reserves a spot for the error member as an implicit member of every enumeration. When you assign an illegal value to an ENUM column, MySQL assigns the error member instead.

The following is an example you can try using the mysql client. It demonstrates that you can retrieve ENUM values in either string or numeric form (which shows the numeric ordering of enumeration members and also that the NULL value has no number in the ordering):

```
mysql> CREATE TABLE e_table (e ENUM('jane','fred','will','marcia'));
mysql> INSERT INTO e_table
    -> VALUES('jane'),('fred'),('will'),('marcia'),(''),(NULL);
mysql> SELECT e, e+0, e+1, e*3 FROM e_table;
+--------+------+------+------+
| e      | e+0  | e+1  | e*3  |
+--------+------+------+------+
| jane   |    1 |    2 |    3 |
| fred   |    2 |    3 |    6 |
| will   |    3 |    4 |    9 |
| marcia |    4 |    5 |   12 |
|        |    0 |    1 |    0 |
| NULL   | NULL | NULL | NULL |
+--------+------+------+------+
```

You can compare ENUM members either by name or number:

```
mysql> SELECT e FROM e_table WHERE e='will';
+------+
| e    |
+------+
| will |
+------+
mysql> SELECT e FROM e_table WHERE e=3;
+------+
| e    |
+------+
| will |
+------+
```

It is possible to declare the empty string as a legal enumeration member. It will be assigned a non-zero numeric value, just as any other member listed in the declaration would be. However, using an empty string may cause some confusion because that string is also used for the error member that has a numeric value of 0. In the following example, assigning the illegal enumeration value 'x' to the ENUM column causes the error member to be assigned. This is distinguishable from the empty string member only when retrieved in numeric form:

```
mysql> CREATE TABLE t (e ENUM('a','','b'));
mysql> INSERT INTO t VALUES('a'),(''),('b'),('x');
mysql> SELECT e, e+0 FROM t;
```

```
+------+------+
| e    | e+0  |
+------+------+
| a    |    1 |
|      |    2 |
| b    |    3 |
|      |    0 |
+------+------+
```

The numeric representation of SET columns is a little different than for ENUM columns. Set members are not numbered sequentially. Instead, each member corresponds to an individual bit in the SET value. The first set member corresponds to bit 0, the second member corresponds to bit 1, and so on. A numeric SET value of 0 corresponds to the empty string. SET members are maintained as bit values. Eight set values per byte can be stored this way, so the storage size for a SET column is determined by the number of set members, up to a maximum of 64 members. SET values take 1, 2, 3, 4, or 8 bytes for set sizes of 1 to 8, 9 to 16, 17 to 24, 25 to 32, and 33 to 64 members.

The representation of a SET as a set of bits is what allows a SET value to consist of multiple set members. Any combination of bits can be turned on in the value, so the value can consist of any combination of the strings in the SET declaration that correspond to those bits.

The following is an example that shows the relationship between the string and numeric forms of a SET column; the numeric value is displayed in both decimal and binary form:

```
mysql> CREATE TABLE s_table (s SET('jane','fred','will','marcia'));
mysql> INSERT INTO s_table
    -> VALUES('jane'),('fred'),('will'),('marcia'),(''),(NULL);
mysql> SELECT s, s+0, BIN(s+0) FROM s_table;
+--------+------+----------+
| s      | s+0  | BIN(s+0) |
+--------+------+----------+
| jane   |    1 | 1        |
| fred   |    2 | 10       |
| will   |    4 | 100      |
| marcia |    8 | 1000     |
|        |    0 | 0        |
| NULL   | NULL | NULL     |
+--------+------+----------+
```

If you assign a value containing substrings that are not listed as set members to a SET column, those strings drop out and the column is assigned a value consisting of the remaining substrings. When you assign values to SET columns, the substrings don't need to be listed in the same order that you used when you declared the column. However, when you retrieve the value later, members will be listed in declaration order. Suppose you declare a SET column to represent furniture items using the following declaration:

```
SET('table','lamp','chair')
```

If you assign a value of 'chair,couch,table' to this column, two things happen. First, 'couch' drops out because it's not a member of the set. Second, when you retrieve the value later, it appears as 'table,chair'. This occurs because MySQL determines which bits correspond to each substring of the value to be assigned and turns them on in the stored value. 'couch' corresponds to no bit and is ignored. On retrieval, MySQL constructs the string value from the numeric value by scanning the bits in order, which automatically reorders the substrings to the order used when the column was declared. This behavior also means that if you specify a set member more than once in a value, it will appear only once when you retrieve the value. If you assign 'lamp,lamp,lamp' to a SET column, it will be simply 'lamp' when retrieved.

The fact that MySQL reorders members in a SET value means that if you search for values using a string, you must list members in the proper order. If you insert 'chair,table' and then search for 'chair,table' you won't find the record; you must look for it as 'table,chair'.

Sorting and indexing of ENUM and SET columns is done according to the internal (numeric) values of column values. The following example might appear to be incorrect otherwise because the values are not sorted in alphanumeric order:

```
mysql> SELECT e FROM e_table ORDER BY e;
+--------+
| e      |
+--------+
| NULL   |
|        |
| jane   |
| fred   |
| will   |
| marcia |
+--------+
```

The placement of the NULL value depends how your version of MySQL sorts NULL values. (See the "Sorting Query Results" section in Chapter 1.)

If you have a fixed set of values and you want them to sort in a particular order, you can exploit the ENUM sorting properties. Represent the values as an ENUM column in a table and list the enumeration values in the column declaration in the order that you want them to be sorted. Suppose you have a table representing personnel for a sports organization, such as a football team, and that you want to sort output by personnel position so that it comes out in a particular order, such as the coaches, assistant coaches, quarterbacks, running backs, receivers, linemen, and so on. Define the column as an ENUM and list the enumeration elements in the order that you want to see them. Sort operations on that column will automatically come out in the order you specify.

For cases where you want an ENUM to sort in regular lexical order, you can convert the column to a non-ENUM string by using CONCAT() and sorting the result:

```
mysql> SELECT CONCAT(e) AS e_str FROM e_table ORDER BY e_str;
+--------+
| e_str  |
+--------+
| NULL   |
|        |
| fred   |
| jane   |
| marcia |
| will   |
+--------+
```

CONCAT() doesn't change the displayed values but has the side effect in this query of performing an ENUM-to-string conversion that alters their sorting properties.

String Column Type Attributes

The BINARY attribute can be specified for the CHAR and VARCHAR types to cause column values to be treated as binary strings (that is, as a string of bytes rather than as a string of characters). A common use for this is to cause column values to be case sensitive.

In MySQL 4.1 and later, you can specify a CHARACTER SET *charset* attribute for CHAR, VARCHAR, and TEXT columns. *charset* should be a valid character set name. The character set may differ among columns. For example, the following table contains latin1, utf8 (Unicode), and sjis (Japanese) columns:

```
CREATE TABLE mytbl
(
    c1  CHAR(10) CHARACTER SET latin1,
    c2  VARCHAR(40) CHARACTER SET utf8,
    t   MEDIUMTEXT CHARACTER SET sjis
);
```

In versions of MySQL for which individual columns may be assigned character sets, DESCRIBE output will show that information:

```
mysql> DESCRIBE mytbl;
+-------+-----------------------------------+------+-----+---------+-------+
| Field | Type                              | Null | Key | Default | Extra |
+-------+-----------------------------------+------+-----+---------+-------+
| c1    | varchar(10) character set latin1  | YES  |     | NULL    |       |
| c2    | varchar(40) character set utf8    | YES  |     | NULL    |       |
| t     | mediumtext character set sjis     | YES  |     | NULL    |       |
+-------+-----------------------------------+------+-----+---------+-------+
```

Binary strings do not have character sets, so the CHARACTER SET attribute is not applicable to CHAR BINARY, VARCHAR BINARY, or any of the BLOB types. Character sets cannot be assigned to ENUM or SET columns, either, because values in such columns are represented numerically.[3]

In MySQL 4.1 and later, every non–binary character column has a character set; one will be assigned, even if you do not specify one explicitly in the column definition. Character sets can be designated at the column, table, database, or server level, so when you create a character column, MySQL determines which character set to assign to it by trying the following rules in order:

1. If the column definition includes a character set, use that set.
2. Otherwise, if the table definition includes a table-level character set other than DEFAULT, use that set.
3. Otherwise, if the database has been assigned a character set other than DEFAULT, use that set.
4. Otherwise, use the server's default character set.

In other words, MySQL searches up through the levels at which character sets can be specified until it finds an explicit character set and then uses that for the column's set. The server always has a default character set, so the search process is guaranteed to terminate at the server level even if no character set is specified explicitly at any of the lower levels.

---

3. The string values that correspond to ENUM and SET values currently are interpreted with respect to the server's default character set. There is work in progress in MySQL 4.1 to allow such columns to be associated with a named character set or to be declared as BINARY— a feature that may in fact be available by the time this book reaches you.

Suppose the server's character set is greek and that the current database has a character set of DEFAULT. The following CREATE TABLE statement specifies no character set at either the column or table level:

```
CREATE TABLE t (c CHAR(10));
```

The database has no explicit set either, so MySQL searches all the way up to the server level to find a character set (greek) to use for the column c. You can verify that with DESCRIBE:

```
mysql> DESCRIBE t;
+-------+-------------------------------+------+-----+---------+-------+
| Field | Type                          | Null | Key | Default | Extra |
+-------+-------------------------------+------+-----+---------+-------+
| c     | char(10) character set greek  | YES  |     | NULL    |       |
+-------+-------------------------------+------+-----+---------+-------+
```

The next statement specifies a table-level character set, so MySQL searches only up to that level to determine that the character set for column c should be cp850:

```
CREATE TABLE t (c CHAR(10)) CHARACTER SET cp850;
```

Again, you can verify that with DESCRIBE:

```
mysql> DESCRIBE t;
+-------+-------------------------------+------+-----+---------+-------+
| Field | Type                          | Null | Key | Default | Extra |
+-------+-------------------------------+------+-----+---------+-------+
| c     | char(10) character set cp850  | YES  |     | NULL    |       |
+-------+-------------------------------+------+-----+---------+-------+
```

Character sets are described further in the "Character Set Support" section later in this chapter.

The general attributes NULL or NOT NULL can be specified for any of the string types. If you don't specify either of them, NULL is the default. However, declaring a string column as NOT NULL does not prevent entry of an empty string. An empty value is different than a missing value, so don't make the mistake of thinking that you can force a string column to contain non–empty values by declaring it NOT NULL. If you require string values to be non-empty, that is a constraint you must enforce from within your own applications.

You can also specify a default value using the DEFAULT attribute for all string column types except the BLOB and TEXT types. If you don't specify a default value, one is chosen automatically. The default is NULL for columns that may contain NULL. For columns that may not contain NULL, the default is the empty string except for ENUM, where the default is the first enumeration member. (For SET, the default when the column cannot contain NULL is actually the empty set, but that is equivalent to the empty string.)

Date and Time Column Types

MySQL provides several column types for temporal values—DATE, DATETIME, TIME, TIMESTAMP, and YEAR. Table 2.10 shows the types provided by MySQL for declaring columns that hold date and time values and the range of legal values for each type. The storage requirements for each type are shown in Table 2.11.

Table 2.10 **Date and Time Column Types**

Type Specification	Range
DATE	'1000-01-01' to '9999-12-31'
TIME	'-838:59:59' to '838:59:59'
DATETIME	'1000-01-01 00:00:00' to '9999-12-31 23:59:59'
TIMESTAMP[(*M*)]	19700101000000 to sometime in the year 2037
YEAR[(*M*)]	1901 to 2155 for YEAR(4), and 1970 to 2069 for YEAR(2)

Table 2.11 **Date and Time Column Type Storage Requirements**

Type Specification	Storage Required
DATE	3 bytes (4 bytes prior to MySQL 3.22)
TIME	3 bytes
DATETIME	8 bytes
TIMESTAMP	4 bytes
YEAR	1 byte

Each date and time type has a "zero" value that is stored when you insert a value that is illegal for the type, as shown in Table 2.12. This value is also the default value for date and time columns that are declared NOT NULL.

Table 2.12 **Date and Time Type "Zero" Values**

Type Specification	Zero Value
DATE	'0000-00-00'
TIME	'00:00:00'
DATETIME	'0000-00-00 00:00:00'
TIMESTAMP	00000000000000
YEAR	0000

MySQL always represents dates with the year first, in accordance with the ANSI SQL and ISO 8601 specifications. For example, December 3, 2004 is represented as '2004-12-03'. MySQL does allow some leeway in the way it allows input dates to be specified. For example, it will convert two-digit year values to four digits, and you need not supply a leading zero digit for month and day values that are less than 10. However, you must specify the year first and the day last. Formats that you may be more used to, such as `'12/3/99'` or `'3/12/99'`, will be interpreted incorrectly. The date interpretation rules MySQL uses are discussed further in the "Working with Date and Time Columns" section later in this chapter.

Time values are returned in the time zone local to the server; MySQL doesn't make any time zone adjustments for the values that it returns to the client.

The DATE, TIME, and DATETIME Column Types

The `DATE`, `TIME`, and `DATETIME` types hold date, time, and combined date and time values. The formats are `'CCYY-MM-DD'`, `'hh:mm:ss'`, and `'CCYY-MM-DD hh:mm:ss'`, where `CC`, `YY`, `MM`, `DD` `hh`, `mm`, and `ss` represent century, year, month, day, hour, minute, and second. For the `DATETIME` type, the date and time parts are both required; if you assign a `DATE` value to a `DATETIME` column, MySQL automatically adds a time part of `'00:00:00'`. (Conversely, if you assign a `DATETIME` value to a `DATE` column, MySQL discards the time part.)

MySQL treats the time in `DATETIME` and `TIME` values slightly differently. For `DATETIME`, the time part represents a time of day. A `TIME` value, on the other hand, represents elapsed time—that's why the range for `TIME` columns is so great and why negative values are allowed.

One thing to watch out for when inserting `TIME` values into a table is that if you use a "short" (not fully qualified) value, it may not be interpreted as you expect. For example, you'll probably find that if you insert `'30'` and `'12:30'` into a `TIME` column, one value will be interpreted from right to left and the other from left to right, resulting in stored values of `'00:00:30'` and `'12:30:00'`. If you consider `'12:30'` to represent a value of "12 minutes, 30 seconds," you should specify it in fully qualified form as `'00:12:30'`.

The TIMESTAMP Column Type

`TIMESTAMP` columns represent values in `CCYYMMDDhhmmss` format, with a range from `19700101000000` to sometime in the year 2037. The range is tied to UNIX time, where the first day of 1970 is "day zero," also known as "the epoch." The beginning of 1970 determines the lower end of the `TIMESTAMP` range. The upper end of the range corresponds to the four-byte limit on UNIX time, which can represent values into the year 2037.[4]

---

4. The upper limit on `TIMESTAMP` values will increase as operating systems are modified to extend the upper range of UNIX time values. This is something that must be addressed at the system library level. MySQL will take advantage of these changes as they are made.

The TIMESTAMP type is so called because it has some special properties for recording when a row is created or modified:

- If you insert a NULL into any TIMESTAMP column, the column value is set automatically to the current date and time.
- The current date and time are also used if you create or update a row without assigning an explicit value to the column, but only for the first TIMESTAMP column in a row.
- For any TIMESTAMP column, you can update its value to the current timestamp by setting it to NULL, or you can defeat timestamping by inserting an explicit date and time value into the column rather than NULL.

A TIMESTAMP column declaration can include a specification for a maximum display width M. Table 2.13 shows the display formats for the allowed values of M. If M is omitted from a TIMESTAMP declaration or has a value of 0 or greater than 14, the column is treated as TIMESTAMP(14). Odd values of M are treated as the next higher even number.

Table 2.13 **TIMESTAMP Display Formats**

Type Specification	Display Format
TIMESTAMP(14)	CCYYMMDDhhmmss
TIMESTAMP(12)	YYMMDDhhmmss
TIMESTAMP(10)	YYMMDDhhmm
TIMESTAMP(8)	CCYYMMDD
TIMESTAMP(6)	YYMMDD
TIMESTAMP(4)	YYMM
TIMESTAMP(2)	YY

The display width for TIMESTAMP columns has nothing to do with storage size or the values stored internally. TIMESTAMP values are always stored in 4 bytes and used in calculations to full 14-digit precision, regardless of the display width. To see this, suppose you declare a table as follows and then insert some rows into it and retrieve them:

```
mysql> CREATE TABLE mytbl (ts TIMESTAMP(8), i INT);
mysql> INSERT INTO mytbl VALUES(20020801120000,3);
mysql> INSERT INTO mytbl VALUES(20020801120001,2);
mysql> INSERT INTO mytbl VALUES(20020801120002,1);
mysql> INSERT INTO mytbl VALUES(20020801120003,0);
mysql> SELECT * FROM mytbl ORDER BY ts, i;
```

```
+----------+------+
| ts       | i    |
+----------+------+
| 20020801 |    3 |
| 20020801 |    2 |
| 20020801 |    1 |
| 20020801 |    0 |
+----------+------+
```

On the face of it, the rows produced by the SELECT statement appear to be sorted in the wrong order—the values in the first column are all the same, so it seems the sort should order the rows according to the values in the second column. This apparently anomalous result is due to the fact that MySQL is using the full 14-digit values inserted into the TIMESTAMP column for sorting. These values are all distinct, so they entirely determine the sort order of the result.

MySQL has no column type that can be set to the current date and time when a record is created and that remains immutable thereafter. If you want to achieve that, you can do it two ways:

- Use a TIMESTAMP column. When you create a new record, set the column to NULL to initialize it to the current date and time:

  ```
  INSERT INTO tbl_name (ts_col, ...) VALUES(NULL, ...);
  ```

  Whenever you update the record thereafter, explicitly set the column to the value it already has. Assigning an explicit value defeats the timestamping mechanism because it prevents the column's value from being automatically updated:

  ```
  UPDATE tbl_name SET ts_col=ts_col WHERE ... ;
  ```

- Use a DATETIME column. When you create a record, initialize the column to NOW():

  ```
  INSERT INTO tbl_name (dt_col, ...) VALUES(NOW(), ...);
  ```

  Whenever you update the record thereafter, leave the column alone:

  ```
  UPDATE tbl_name SET ... anything BUT dt_col here ... WHERE ... ;
  ```

If you want to use TIMESTAMP columns to maintain both a time-created value and a last-modified value, you can do so by using one TIMESTAMP for the time-modified value and a second TIMESTAMP for the time-created value. Make sure the time-modified column is the first TIMESTAMP, so that it's set when the record is created or changed. Make the time-created column the second TIMESTAMP, and initialize it to NOW() when you create new records. That way, its value will reflect the record creation time and will not change after that.

The YEAR Column Type

YEAR is a one-byte column type used for efficient representation of year values. A YEAR column declaration can include a specification for a display width M, which should be either 4 or 2. If M is omitted from a YEAR declaration, the default is 4. YEAR(4) has a range of 1901 to 2155. YEAR(2) has a range of 1970 to 2069, but only the last two digits are displayed. You can use the YEAR type when you want to store date information but only need the year part of the date, such as year of birth, year of election to office, and so forth. When you do not need a full date value, YEAR is much more space-efficient than other date types.

TINYINT has the same storage size as YEAR (one byte), but not the same range. To cover the same range of years as YEAR by using an integer type, you would need a SMALLINT, which takes twice as much space. If the range of years you need to represent coincides with the range of the YEAR type, YEAR is more space-efficient than SMALLINT. Another advantage of YEAR over an integer column is that MySQL will convert two-digit values into four-digit values for you using MySQL's usual year-guessing rules. For example, 97 and 14 become 1997 and 2014. However, be aware that inserting the numeric value 00 into a four-digit YEAR column will result in the value 0000 being stored, not 2000. If you want a value of 00 to convert to 2000, you must specify it in string form as '00'.

Date and Time Column Type Attributes

There are no attributes that are specific to the date and time column types. The general attributes NULL or NOT NULL can be specified for any of the date and time types. If you don't specify either of them, NULL is the default. You can also specify a default value using the DEFAULT attribute. If you don't specify a default value, one is chosen automatically. The default is NULL for columns that may contain NULL. Otherwise, the default is the "zero" value for the type. TIMESTAMP columns are special; the default for the first such column in a table is the current date and time and the "zero" value for any others.

Note that because default values must be constants. you cannot use a function such as NOW() to supply a value of "the current date and time" as the default for a DATETIME column. To achieve that result, set the column value explicitly to NOW() whenever you create a new record or else use a TIMESTAMP column (assuming that the special properties of TIMESTAMP are suitable for your purposes).

Working with Date and Time Columns

MySQL tries to interpret date and time values in a variety of formats, including both string and numeric forms. Table 2.14 shows the allowable formats for each of the date and time types.

Table 2.14 **Date and Time Type Input Formats**

Type	Allowable Formats
DATETIME, TIMESTAMP	`'CCYY-MM-DD hh:mm:ss'`
	`'YY-MM-DD hh:mm:ss'`
	`'CCYYMMDDhhmmss'`
	`'YYMMDDhhmmss'`
	`CCYYMMDDhhmmss`
	`YYMMDDhhmmss`
DATE	`'CCYY-MM-DD'`
	`'YY-MM-DD'`
	`'CCYYMMDD'`
	`'YYMMDD'`
	`CCYYMMDD`
	`YYMMDD`
TIME	`'hh:mm:ss'`
	`'hhmmss'`
	`hhmmss`
YEAR	`'CCYY'`
	`'YY'`
	`CCYY`
	`YY`

Formats that have no century part (CC) are interpreted using the rules described in next section, "Interpretation of Ambiguous Year Values." For string formats that include delimiter characters, you don't have to use '-' for dates and ':' for times. Any punctuation character can be used as the delimiter. Interpretation of values depends on context, not on the delimiter. For example, although times are typically specified using a delimiter of ':', MySQL won't interpret a value containing ':' as a time in a context where a date is expected. In addition, for the string formats that include delimiters, you need not specify two digits for month, day, hour, minute, or second values that are less than 10. The following are all equivalent:

```
'2012-02-03 05:04:09'
'2012-2-03 05:04:09'
'2012-2-3 05:04:09'
'2012-2-3 5:04:09'
'2012-2-3 5:4:09'
'2012-2-3 5:4:9'
```

Note that values with leading zeroes may be interpreted differently depending on whether they are specified as strings or numbers. The string `'001231'` will be seen as a six-digit value and interpreted as `'2000-12-31'` for a DATE and as `'2000-12-31 00:00:00'` for a DATETIME. On the other hand, the number `001231` will be seen as `1231` after the parser gets done with it and then the interpretation becomes problematic. This is a case where it's best to supply a string value `'001231'` or else use a fully qualified value if you are using numbers (that is, `20001231` for DATE and `200012310000` for DATETIME).

In general, you can freely assign values between the DATE, DATETIME, and TIMESTAMP types, although there are certain restrictions to keep in mind:

- If you assign a DATETIME or TIMESTAMP value to a DATE, the time part is discarded.
- If you assign a DATE value to a DATETIME or TIMESTAMP, the time part of the resulting value is set to zero (`'00:00:00'`).
- The types have different ranges. In particular, TIMESTAMP has a more limited range (1970 to 2037), so, for example, you cannot assign a pre-1970 DATETIME value to a TIMESTAMP and expect reasonable results. Nor can you assign values that are far in the future to a TIMESTAMP.

MySQL provides many functions for working with date and time values. See Appendix C for more information.

Interpretation of Ambiguous Year Values

For all date and time types that include a year part (DATE, DATETIME TIMESTAMP, YEAR), MySQL handles values that contain two-digit years by converting them to four-digit years. This conversion is performed according to the following rules:

- Year values from 00 to 69 become 2000 to 2069.
- Year values from 70 to 99 become 1970 to 1999.

You can see the effect of these rules most easily by assigning different two-digit values to a YEAR column and then retrieving the results. This will also demonstrate something you should take note of:

```
mysql> CREATE TABLE y_table (y YEAR);
mysql> INSERT INTO y_table VALUES(68),(69),(99), (00);
mysql> SELECT * FROM y_table;
```

```
+------+
| y    |
+------+
| 2068 |
| 2069 |
| 1999 |
| 0000 |
+------+
```

Notice that `00` was converted to `0000`, not to `2000`. That's because as a number, `00` is the same as `0` and is a perfectly legal value for the `YEAR` type. If you insert a numeric zero, that's what you get. To get `2000` using a value that does not contain the century, insert the string `'0'` or `'00'`. You can make sure MySQL sees a string and not a number by inserting `YEAR` values using `CONCAT()`. This function returns a string result uniformly regardless of whether its argument is a string or a number.

In any case, keep in mind that the rules for converting two-digit to four-digit year values provide only a reasonable guess. There is no way for MySQL to be certain about the meaning of a two-digit year when the century is unspecified. If MySQL's conversion rules don't produce the values that you want, the solution is to provide unambiguous data with four-digit years.

Is MySQL Year-2000 Safe?

MySQL itself is year-2000 safe because it stores dates internally with four-digit years, but it's your responsibility to provide data that result in the proper values being stored in the first place. The real problem with two-digit year interpretation comes not from MySQL but from the human desire to take a shortcut and enter ambiguous data. If you're willing to take the risk, go ahead. It's your risk to take, and MySQL's guessing rules are adequate for many situations. Just be aware that there are times when you really do need to enter four digits. For example, to enter birth and death dates into the `president` table that lists U.S. presidents back into the 1700s, four-digit year values are in order. Values in these columns span several centuries, so letting MySQL guess the century from a two-digit year is definitely the wrong thing to do.

Working with Sequences

Many applications need to use unique numbers for identification purposes. The requirement for unique values occurs in a number of contexts: membership numbers, sample or lot numbering, customer IDs, bug report or trouble ticket tags, and so on.

MySQL's mechanism for providing unique numbers is through `AUTO_INCREMENT` columns that allow you to generate sequential numbers automatically. However, `AUTO_INCREMENT` columns are handled somewhat differently for the various table types that MySQL supports, so it's important to understand not only the general concepts underlying the AUTO_INCREMENT mechanism, but also the differences between table types. This section describes how AUTO_INCREMENT columns work so that you can use them effectively without running into the traps that sometimes surprise people. It also describes how you can generate a sequence without using an AUTO_INCREMENT column.

For versions of MySQL up to 3.23, the only table type available is ISAM. After that, additional table types were introduced—the MyISAM and HEAP types first, and the BDB and InnoDB types later. The discussion here indicates how each table type behaves with respect to AUTO_INCREMENT columns. (For more general information about the characteristics of MySQL's table handlers, see Chapter 3.)

AUTO_INCREMENT for ISAM Tables

AUTO_INCREMENT columns in ISAM tables behave as follows:

- Inserting NULL into an AUTO_INCREMENT column causes MySQL to automatically generate the next sequence number and insert that value into the column. AUTO_INCREMENT sequences begin at 1, so the first record inserted into the table gets a sequence column value of 1 and subsequent records get values of 2, 3, and so forth. Each automatically generated value will be one more than the current maximum value stored in the column.

- Inserting 0 into an AUTO_INCREMENT column has the same effect as inserting NULL. However, this is not guaranteed to be true indefinitely, so it's better to insert NULL.

- Inserting a row without specifying an explicit value for the AUTO_INCREMENT column is the same as inserting NULL into the column.

- If you insert a record and specify a non-NULL, non-zero value for the AUTO_INCREMENT column, one of two things will happen. If a record already exists with that value, an error occurs because values in AUTO_INCREMENT columns must be unique. If a record does not exist with that value, the record is inserted and the sequence continues with the next value after that for subsequent rows. In other words, you can "bump up" the counter by inserting a record with a sequence value greater than the current counter value.

Bumping up the counter can result in gaps in the sequence, but you can also exploit this behavior to generate a sequence that begins at a value higher than 1. Suppose you create an ISAM table with an AUTO_INCRE-MENT column, but you want the sequence to begin at 1000 rather than at 1. To achieve this, insert a "fake" record with a value of 999 in the AUTO_INCREMENT column. Records inserted subsequently will be assigned sequence numbers beginning with 1000, after which you can delete the fake record.

(Why might you want to begin a sequence with a value higher than 1? One reason is to make sequence numbers all have the same number of digits. If you're generating customer ID numbers, and you expect never to have more than a million customers, you could begin the series at 1,000,000. You'll be able to add well over a million customer records before the digit count for customer ID values changes. Other reasons for not beginning a sequence at 1 might have nothing to do with technical considerations. For example, if you were assigning membership numbers, you might want to begin a sequence at a number higher than 1 to fore-stall political squabbling over who gets to be member number 1—by making sure there isn't any such number. Hey, it happens. Sad, but true.)

- If you delete the record containing the largest value in an AUTO_INCRE-MENT column, that value is reused the next time you generate a new value. This is a consequence of the principle that for ISAM tables, each new automatically generated value is one larger than the current maxi-mum value stored in the column. Another consequence is that if you delete all the records in the table, all values are reused, so the sequence starts over beginning at 1.

- If you use UPDATE to set an AUTO_INCREMENT column to a value that already exists in another row, a "duplicate key" error occurs. If you update the column to a value larger than any existing column value, the sequence continues with the next number after that for subsequent records.

- If you use REPLACE to update a record based on the value of the AUTO_INCREMENT column, the AUTO_INCREMENT value does not change. If you use REPLACE to update a record based on the value of some other PRI-MARY KEY or UNIQUE index, the AUTO_INCREMENT column will be updated with a new sequence number if you set it to NULL.

- The value of the most recent automatically generated sequence number is available by calling the LAST_INSERT_ID() function. This allows you to reference the AUTO_INCREMENT value in other statements without knowing what the value is. `LAST_INSERT_ID()` is tied to `AUTO_INCRE-MENT` values generated during the current server session; it is not affected by `AUTO_INCREMENT` activity associated with other clients. If no `AUTO_INCREMENT` value has been generated during the current session, `LAST_INSERT_ID()` returns 0.

The `AUTO_INCREMENT` mechanism for ISAM forms the basis for understanding sequence behavior for the other table types. Those types implement behavior that for the most part is similar to that just described, so keep the preceding discussion in mind as you read on.

AUTO_INCREMENT for MyISAM Tables

MyISAM tables offer the most flexibility for sequence handling. The MyISAM storage format introduces some features that address some of the shortcomings of ISAM tables:

- With ISAM tables, values deleted from the top of the sequence are reused. If you delete the record with the highest sequence number, the new record added gets the same sequence value as the deleted record. This results in sequences that are not strictly monotonic, which is a problem should you need to guarantee that no record be given a number that has been used before. With MyISAM, the values in an automatically generated series are strictly increasing and are not reused. If the maximum value is 143 and you delete the record containing that value, MySQL still generates the next value as 144.

- ISAM sequences always begin at 1 unless you use the fake-record technique mentioned earlier to start the sequence at a higher value. With MyISAM tables, you can specify the initial value explicitly by using an `AUTO_INCREMENT` = *n* option in the `CREATE TABLE` statement. The following example creates a MyISAM table with an `AUTO_INCREMENT` column named `seq` that begins at 1,000,000:

  ```
  CREATE TABLE mytbl
  (
      seq INT UNSIGNED AUTO_INCREMENT NOT NULL,
      PRIMARY KEY (seq)
  ) TYPE = MYISAM AUTO_INCREMENT = 1000000;
  ```

A table can have only one `AUTO_INCREMENT` column, so there is never any ambiguity about the column to which the terminating `AUTO_INCRE-MENT` = *n* option applies, even if the table has multiple columns (as most tables do).

- You can change the current sequence counter for an existing MyISAM table with ALTER TABLE. If the sequence currently stands at 1000, the following statement will cause the next number generated to be 2000:

  ```
  ALTER TABLE mytbl AUTO_INCREMENT = 2000;
  ```

  If you want to reuse values that have been deleted from the top of the sequence, you can do that, too. The following statement will set the counter down as far as possible, causing the next number to be one larger than the current maximum sequence value:

  ```
  ALTER TABLE mytbl AUTO_INCREMENT = 1;
  ```

In addition to overcoming the weaknesses of ISAM sequence handling, the MySQL table handler as of MySQL 3.23.5 supports the use of composite (multiple-column) indexes for creating multiple independent sequences within the same table. To use this feature, create a multiple-column PRIMARY KEY or UNIQUE index that includes an AUTO_INCREMENT column as its last column. For each distinct key in the leftmost column or columns of the index, the AUTO_INCREMENT column will generate a separate sequence of values. For example, you might use a table named bugs for tracking bug reports of several software projects, where the table is declared as follows:

```
CREATE TABLE bugs
(
    proj_name    VARCHAR(20) NOT NULL,
    bug_id       INT UNSIGNED AUTO_INCREMENT NOT NULL,
    description VARCHAR(100),
    PRIMARY KEY (proj_name, bug_id)
) TYPE = MYISAM;
```

Here, the proj_name column identifies the project name and the description column contains the bug description. The bug_id column is an AUTO_INCREMENT column; by creating an index that ties it to the proj_name column, you can generate an independent series of sequence numbers for each project. Suppose you enter the following records into the table to register three bugs for SuperBrowser and two for SpamSquisher:

```
mysql> INSERT INTO bugs (proj_name,description)
    -> VALUES('SuperBrowser','crashes when displaying complex tables');
mysql> INSERT INTO bugs (proj_name,description)
    -> VALUES('SuperBrowser','image scaling does not work');
mysql> INSERT INTO bugs (proj_name,description)
    -> VALUES('SpamSquisher','fails to block known blacklisted domains');
mysql> INSERT INTO bugs (proj_name,description)
    -> VALUES('SpamSquisher','fails to respect whitelist addresses');
mysql> INSERT INTO bugs (proj_name,description)
    -> VALUES('SuperBrowser','background patterns not displayed');
```

The resulting table contents look like the this:

```
mysql> SELECT * FROM bugs ORDER BY proj_name, bug_id;
+--------------+--------+-------------------------------------------+
| proj_name    | bug_id | description                               |
+--------------+--------+-------------------------------------------+
| SpamSquisher |      1 | fails to block known blacklisted domains  |
| SpamSquisher |      2 | fails to respect whitelist addresses      |
| SuperBrowser |      1 | crashes when displaying complex tables    |
| SuperBrowser |      2 | image scaling does not work               |
| SuperBrowser |      3 | background patterns not displayed         |
+--------------+--------+-------------------------------------------+
```

Note that it does not matter that the order of record entry switches between projects. The table numbers bug_id values for each project separately.

If you use a composite index to create multiple sequences, values deleted from the top of a sequence *are* reused. This contrasts with the usual MyISAM behavior of not reusing values.

AUTO_INCREMENT for HEAP Tables

HEAP tables do not support the AUTO_INCREMENT mechanism prior to MySQL 4.1. As of 4.1, AUTO_INCREMENT columns are allowed and behave as follows:

- The initial sequence value can be set with an AUTO_INCREMENT = n option in the CREATE TABLE statement and can be modified after table creation time using that option with ALTER TABLE.
- Values that are deleted from the top of the sequence are not reused.
- Composite indexes cannot be used to generate multiple independent sequences within a table.

AUTO_INCREMENT for BDB Tables

The BDB table handler manages AUTO_INCREMENT columns as follows:

- The initial sequence value cannot be set with an AUTO_INCREMENT = n option in the CREATE TABLE statement. Nor can it be modified using that option with ALTER TABLE.
- Values that are deleted from the top of the sequence are reused.
- Composite indexes can be used to generate multiple independent sequences within a table.

AUTO_INCREMENT for InnoDB Tables

The InnoDB table handler manages AUTO_INCREMENT columns as follows:

- The initial sequence value cannot be set with an AUTO_INCREMENT = n option in the CREATE TABLE statement. Nor can it be modified using that option with ALTER TABLE.
- Values that are deleted from the top of the sequence are not reused.
- Composite indexes cannot be used to generate multiple independent sequences within a table.

Issues to Consider with AUTO_INCREMENT

You should keep the following points in mind to avoid being surprised when you use AUTO_INCREMENT columns:

- AUTO_INCREMENT is not a column type; it's a column type attribute. Furthermore, AUTO_INCREMENT is an attribute intended for use only with integer types. Versions of MySQL earlier than 3.23 are lax in enforcing this constraint and will let you declare a column type such as CHAR with the AUTO_INCREMENT attribute. However, only the integer types work *correctly* as AUTO_INCREMENT columns.

- The primary purpose of the AUTO_INCREMENT mechanism is to allow you to generate a sequence of positive integers, so you should declare AUTO_INCREMENT columns to be UNSIGNED. This also has the advantage of giving you twice as many sequence numbers before you hit the upper end of the column type's range.

  It is possible under some circumstances to generate sequences of negative values using an AUTO_INCREMENT column. But this is an unsupported use of AUTO_INCREMENT and the results are not guaranteed. My own experiments indicate somewhat inconsistent behavior between versions with regard to negative sequences, so even if you achieve the results you want with one version of MySQL, that may change if you upgrade to a newer version. (In other words, attempting to use AUTO_INCREMENT for anything but a sequence of positive integers can result in unpredictable behavior. You have been warned!)

- Don't be fooled into thinking that adding AUTO_INCREMENT to a column declaration is a magic way of getting an unlimited sequence of numbers. It's not; AUTO_INCREMENT sequences are always bound by the range of the underlying column type. For example, if you use a `TINYINT` column, the maximum sequence number is 127. When you reach that limit, your application will begin to fail with "duplicate key" errors. If you use `TINYINT UNSIGNED` instead, you'll reach the limit at 255.

- Clearing a table's contents entirely may reset a sequence to begin again at 1, even for table types that normally to not reuse `AUTO_INCREMENT` values. This can occur for either of the following statements:

```
DELETE FROM tbl_name;
TRUNCATE TABLE tbl_name;
```

The sequence reset occurs due to the way MySQL optimizes a complete table erasure operation: It tosses the data rows and indexes and recreates the table from scratch rather than deleting individual rows. This causes all sequence number information to be lost. If you want to delete all records but preserve the sequence information, you can suppress this optimization by using `DELETE` with a `WHERE` clause that is always true:

```
DELETE FROM tbl_name WHERE 1;
```

This forces MySQL to evaluate the condition for each row and thus delete every row individually.

Forcing Non-Reuse of Sequence Values

What can you do to maintain a strictly increasing series of values for table types that reuse values that are deleted from the top of a sequence? One solution is to maintain a separate table that you use only for generating `AUTO_INCREMENT` values and from which you never delete records. That way, the values in the table are never reused. When you need to generate a new record in your main table, first insert a `NULL` into the sequence number table. Then insert the record into your main table using the value of `LAST_INSERT_ID()` for the column that you want to contain a sequence number:

```
INSERT INTO ai_tbl SET ai_col = NULL;
INSERT INTO main_tbl SET id=LAST_INSERT_ID() ... ;
```

Adding a Sequence Number Column to a Table

Suppose you create a table and put some information into it:

```
mysql> CREATE TABLE t (c CHAR(10));
mysql> INSERT INTO t VALUES('a'),('b'),('c');
mysql> SELECT * FROM t;
```

```
+------+
| c    |
+------+
| a    |
| b    |
| c    |
+------+
```

Then you decide that you want to include a sequence number column in the table. To do this, issue an ALTER TABLE statement to add an AUTO_INCREMENT column, using the same kind of type definition that you'd use with CREATE TABLE:

```
mysql> ALTER TABLE t ADD i INT AUTO_INCREMENT NOT NULL PRIMARY KEY;
mysql> SELECT * FROM t;
+------+---+
| c    | i |
+------+---+
| a    | 1 |
| b    | 2 |
| c    | 3 |
+------+---+
```

Note how MySQL has assigned sequence values to the AUTO_INCREMENT column automatically. You need not do so yourself.

Resequencing an Existing Column

If a table already has an AUTO_INCREMENT column but you want to renumber it to eliminate gaps in the sequence that may have resulted from row deletions, the easiest way to do it is to drop the column and then add it again. When MySQL adds the column, it will assign new sequence numbers automatically, as shown in the previous example.

Suppose a table t looks like the following, where i is the AUTO_INCREMENT column:

```
mysql> CREATE TABLE t (c CHAR(10), i INT NOT NULL AUTO_INCREMENT PRIMARY KEY);
mysql> INSERT INTO t (c)
    -> VALUES('a'),('b'),('c'),('d'),('e'),('f'),('g'),('h'),('i'),('j'),('k');
mysql> DELETE FROM t WHERE c IN('a','d','f','g','j');
mysql> SELECT * FROM t;
+------+----+
| c    | i  |
+------+----+
| b    | 2  |
| c    | 3  |
| e    | 5  |
| h    | 8  |
| i    | 9  |
| k    | 11 |
+------+----+
```

The following ALTER TABLE statement drops the column and then adds it again:

```
mysql> ALTER TABLE t
    -> DROP i,
    -> ADD i INT UNSIGNED AUTO_INCREMENT NOT NULL,
    -> AUTO_INCREMENT = 1;
mysql> SELECT * FROM t;
+------+---+
| c    | i |
+------+---+
| b    | 1 |
| c    | 2 |
| e    | 3 |
| h    | 4 |
| i    | 5 |
| k    | 6 |
+------+---+
```

The AUTO_INCREMENT = 1 clause resets the sequence to begin again at 1. For a MyISAM table (or a HEAP table as of MySQL 4.1), you can use a value other than 1 to begin the sequence at a different value. For other table types, just omit the AUTO_INCREMENT clause, because they do not allow the initial value to be specified this way. The sequence will begin at 1.

Note that although it's easy to resequence a column, there is usually very little reason to do so. MySQL doesn't care whether a sequence has holes in it, nor do you gain any performance efficiencies by resequencing.

Generating Sequences Without AUTO_INCREMENT

Another method for generating sequence numbers doesn't use an AUTO_INCRE-MENT column at all. Instead, it uses an alternate form of the LAST_INSERT_ID() function that takes an argument. (This form was introduced in MySQL 3.22.9.) If you insert or update a column using LAST_INSERT_ID(expr), the next call to LAST_INSERT_ID() with no argument returns the value of expr. In other words, expr is treated as though it had been generated as an AUTO_INCREMENT value. This allows you to generate a sequence number and then retrieve it later in your session, confident that the value will not have been affected by the activity of other clients.

One way to use this strategy is to create a single-row table containing a value that is updated each time you want the next value in the sequence. For example, you can create and initialize the table as follows:

```
CREATE TABLE seq_table (seq INT UNSIGNED NOT NULL);
INSERT INTO seq_table VALUES(0);
```

These statements set up `seq_table` with a single row containing a `seq` value of 0. To use the table, generate the next sequence number and retrieve it as follows:

```
UPDATE seq_table SET seq = LAST_INSERT_ID(seq+1);
SELECT LAST_INSERT_ID();
```

The `UPDATE` statement retrieves the current value of the `seq` column and increments it by 1 to produce the next value in the sequence. Generating the new value using `LAST_INSERT_ID(seq+1)` causes it to be treated like an `AUTO_INCREMENT` value, which allows it to be retrieved by calling `LAST_INSERT_ID()` without an argument. `LAST_INSERT_ID()` is client-specific, so you get the correct value even if other clients have generated other sequence numbers in the interval between the `UPDATE` and the `SELECT`.

Other uses for this method are to generate sequence values that increment by a value other than 1 or that are negative. For example, the following statement can be executed repeatedly to generate a sequence of numbers that increase by 100 each time:

```
UPDATE seq_table SET seq = LAST_INSERT_ID(seq+100);
```

Repeating the following statement will generate a sequence of decreasing numbers:

```
UPDATE seq_table SET seq = LAST_INSERT_ID(seq-1);
```

You can also use this technique to generate a sequence that begins at an arbitrary value by setting the `seq` column to an appropriate initial value.

The preceding discussion describes how to set up a counter using a table with a single row. That's okay for a single counter, but if you want several of them, creating one table per counter leads to needless multiplication of tables. For example, suppose you have a Web site and you want to put some "this page has been accessed *n* times" counters in several pages. You probably don't want to set up a separate counter table for every page that has a counter.

One way to avoid creating multiple counter tables is to create a single table with two columns. One column holds a counter value; the other holds a name that uniquely identifies each counter. You can still use the `LAST_INSERT_ID()` function, but you determine which row it applies to by using the counter name. The table looks like this:

```
CREATE TABLE counter
(
    name  VARCHAR(255) BINARY NOT NULL,
    PRIMARY KEY (name),
    value INT UNSIGNED
);
```

The name column is a string so that you can name a counter whatever you want, and it's declared as a PRIMARY KEY to prevent duplicate names. This assumes that applications using the table agree on the names they'll be using. For Web counters, uniqueness of counter names is ensured simply by using the pathname of each page within the document tree as its counter name. The BINARY attribute causes pathname values to be treated as case sensitive. (Omit it if your system has pathnames that are not case sensitive.)

To use the counter table, insert a row corresponding to each page for which you need a counter. For example, to set up a new counter for the site's home page, do the following:

```
INSERT INTO counter (name,value) VALUES('index.html',0);
```

That initializes a counter named 'index.html' with a value of zero. To generate the next sequence value for the page, use its pathname to look up the correct counter value and increment it with LAST_INSERT_ID(expr) and then retrieve the value with LAST_INSERT_ID():

```
UPDATE counter SET value = LAST_INSERT_ID(value+1) WHERE name = 'index.html';
SELECT LAST_INSERT_ID();
```

An alternative approach is to increment the counter without using LAST_INSERT_ID():

```
UPDATE counter SET value = value+1 WHERE name = 'index.html';
SELECT value FROM counter WHERE name = 'index.html';
```

However, that doesn't work correctly if another client increments the counter after you issue the UPDATE and before you issue the SELECT. You could solve that problem by using a transaction or by putting LOCK TABLES and UNLOCK TABLES around the two statements to block other clients while you're using the counter. But the LAST_INSERT_ID() method accomplishes the same thing more easily. Because its value is client-specific, you always get the value you inserted, not the one from some other client, and you don't have to complicate the code with transactions or locks to keep other clients out.

Character Set Support

Character-based data values are interpreted with respect to a given character set, which determines the allowable characters that can be used. Character sets also have a collating (sorting) order, which affects many types of operations on character values:

- Comparisons: <, <=, =, <>, >=, and >.
- Sorting: ORDER BY, MIN(), MAX().
- Grouping: GROUP BY, DISTINCT.

The character set also affects other aspects of server operation, such as which characters can be used in database, table, and column names, because names normally are constructed from the alphanumeric characters in the server's default character set. (See the "MySQL Naming Rules" section in Chapter 3.)

The level of character set support available to you depends on your version of MySQL. Prior to MySQL 4.1, the server operates using a single character set at a time. As of MySQL 4.1, the server can support multiple character sets simultaneously, and character sets can be specified at the server, database, table, column, or string constant level. For example, if you want a table's columns to use `latin1` by default, but also to include a Hebrew column and a Greek column, you can do that. You can also find out what character sets are available or convert data from one character set to another.

This section describes how to use the character sets that are supported by your server. To configure your server to support the character sets you want, see Chapter 11. That chapter also includes notes on what to do when upgrading to MySQL 4.1 so that you can use the new features with older tables.

Character Set Support Before MySQL 4.1

Prior to MySQL 4.1, data values in MySQL have no explicit character set. Instead, string constants and column values are interpreted with respect to the server's character set. By default, this is the character set selected when the server was built (usually `latin1`), but the built-in value can be overridden at runtime with the `--default-character-set` option. This is very simple but quite limiting. For example, you cannot have a table that stores values using different character sets for different columns.

The single-character-set model also can lead to index-related problems if you change the server's character set after having already created tables and loaded character data into them. These problems occur due to the fact that index values are stored in sorted order, with the order for character columns being determined by the collating sequence of the character set that happens to be in force at the time the index entries are created. Some character sets have different collating sequences than others, so if you load a table while the server is using one character set and then reconfigure the server to use a different set, it's possible that the index entries will no longer be in the correct order with respect to the collating sequence of the new character set. Worse, if you add new rows to the table, the index that was initially created using the sort order of the original character set will be updated using the order of the new set. Consequently, index-based queries may not work correctly.

The solution to this problem is to rebuild the indexes for each existing table that has character-based indexes to use the collating order of the new character set. A table can be converted in various ways:

- Dump the table with `mysqldump`, drop it, and reload it from the dump file. This operation causes the indexes to be rebuilt as the file is reloaded. It works for any table type.

- Drop the indexes and add them again (for example, with `ALTER TABLE`, or with `DROP INDEX` and `CREATE INDEX`). This works for any table type but requires that you know the exact index definitions so that you can re-create them properly.

- For MyISAM tables, you can rebuild indexes by running `myisamchk` with the `--recover` and `--quick` options, together with a `--set-character-set` option that specifies the character set to use. Equivalent alternatives are to use the `mysqlcheck` program with the `--repair` and `--quick` options or a `REPAIR TABLE` statement with the `QUICK` option. `mysqlcheck` and `REPAIR TABLE` are more convenient because the server does the work and it knows which character set to use. `myisamchk` must be run with the tables offline, and you have to specify the character set explicitly.

Despite the many methods available for reordering indexes if you change the server's character set, the fact that you need to do it at all is a bother. MySQL 4.1 eliminates the need.

Character Set Support in MySQL 4.1 and Later

Character set support has been revised considerably in MySQL 4.1 to provide the following features:

- Support for using multiple character sets simultaneously
- The ability to specify character sets at the server, database, table, column, and string constant level, not just at the server level:
  - An `ALTER DATABASE` statement for database character set assignment
  - `CREATE TABLE` and `ALTER TABLE` clauses for table- and column-level character set assignment
- Functions and operators for converting individual values from one character set to another or for determining the character set of a value
- A `COLLATE` operator for treating values in one character set as having the collating order of another character set

- A SHOW CHARACTER SET statement to list all the character sets the server knows about
- Automatic index reordering when character set changes occur
- Unicode support, provided by the utf8 and ucs2 character sets
- Many other new character sets

You cannot mix character sets within a string or use different character sets for different rows of a given column. However, by using a Unicode character set (which represents the encodings for many languages within a single character set), you may be able to implement multi-lingual support of the type you desire.

Specifying Character Sets

Character sets can be assigned at several levels, from the default used by the server down to the set used for individual strings:

- The server's default character set is built in at compile time, and you can override it at server startup time by using a --default-character-set option.
- To specify a default character set for a database, use the following statement:

  ```
  ALTER DATABASE db_name DEFAULT CHARACTER SET charset;
  ```

  charset is the name of a supported character set, or DEFAULT. A value of DEFAULT indicates that the database has no explicit character set; in this case, the server makes database-level character set decisions by referring to the server's default character set.
- To specify a default character set for a table, use a CHARACTER SET table option at table creation time:

  ```
  CREATE TABLE tbl_name (...) CHARACTER SET = charset;
  ```

  charset is the name of a supported character set, or DEFAULT. A value of DEFAULT tells the server to make table-level character set decisions by referring to the database character set.
- Columns in a table can be assigned a character set explicitly with a CHARACTER SET attribute. For example:

  ```
  c CHAR(10) CHARACTER SET charset
  ```

  In this case, the charset value must be the name of a supported character set; it cannot be DEFAULT. However, you can omit the CHARACTER SET attribute entirely, in which case the table-level character set is used. Column types for which a character set can be given are CHAR and VARCHAR (if declared without the BINARY attribute) and the TEXT types.

- String constants can be converted to a given character set using the following notation, where *charset* is the name of a supported character set:

  ```
  _charset str
  ```

  The following examples produce strings in the latin7 and utf8 character sets:

  ```
  _latin7 'abc'
  _utf8 'def'
  ```

  This notation works only for literal quoted strings, not for hexadecimal constants, string expressions, or column values. However, any string can be converted to a designated character set using the CONVERT() function:

  ```
  SELECT CONVERT(str USING charset);
  ```

It's also possible to sort values from given character set using the collating sequence for a different set by using the COLLATE operator. For example, if c is a latin1 column but you want to order it using latin1_de sorting rules, do this:

```
SELECT c FROM t ORDER BY c COLLATE latin1_de;
```

Determining What Character Sets Are In Use

Character set support in MySQL 4.1 and up includes statements for obtaining information at several levels:

- At the server level, you can find out which character sets are available using the following query:

  ```
  SHOW CHARACTER SET;
  ```

  To determine what the server's default character set is, issue the following query:

  ```
  SHOW VARIABLES LIKE 'character_set';
  ```

- The database-level character set for a given database can be obtained as follows:

  ```
  SHOW CREATE DATABASE db_name;
  ```

  If the statement output doesn't indicate a character set, the database's character set has been never been set or has been set explicitly to DEFAULT.

- A table's character set can be discovered two ways:

```
SHOW CREATE TABLE tbl_name;
SHOW TABLE STATUS LIKE 'tbl_name';
```

- Individual character set assignments for a table's columns are displayed by each of the following statements:

```
DESCRIBE tbl_name;
SHOW COLUMNS FROM tbl_name;
SHOW CREATE TABLE tbl_name;
```

- To determine what character set is associated with a string, string expression, or column value, use the CHARSET() function:

```
SELECT CHARSET(str);
```

Unicode Support

One of the reasons there are so many character sets is that different encodings have been developed for different languages. This presents several problems. For example, a given character that is common to several languages might be represented by different numeric values in different encodings. Also, different languages require different numbers of bytes to represent characters. The Latin-1 character set is small enough that every character fits in a single byte, but some languages, such as those used in Japan and China, contain so many characters that they require multiple bytes per character.

The goal of Unicode is to provide a unified character-encoding system within which all languages can be represented in a consistent manner. In MySQL, Unicode support is provided through two character sets:

- UTF-8 is a variable-length format in which characters are represented using from one to four characters. (UTF is an abbreviation for UCS Transformation Format, where UCS is itself an abbreviation for Universal Character Set.) The utf8 character set in MySQL does not include any four-byte characters, although support for them may be added in the future.
- The other Unicode character set in MySQL is UCS2. The ucs2 set represents each character using two bytes, most significant byte first. This character set does not represent characters that require more than two bytes.

Converting Older Tables to MySQL 4.1 Format

If you upgrade a server to MySQL 4.1 or newer, older tables can still be used but will not be able to take full advantage of the improved character set support instituted in 4.1. To rectify this, you should convert them to 4.1 format. Instructions for doing so can be found in Chapter 11.

Choosing Column Types

The "MySQL Column Types" section earlier in this chapter describes the various MySQL column types from which you can choose and the general properties of those types, such as the kind of values they can contain, how much storage space they take, and so on. But how do you actually decide which types to use when you create a table? This section discusses issues to consider that will help you choose.

The most "generic" column types are the string types. You can store anything in them because numbers and dates can be represented in string form. So why not just declare all your columns as strings and be done with it? Let's consider a simple example. Suppose you have values that look like numbers. You can represent these as strings, but should you? What happens if you do?

For one thing, you'll probably use more space because numbers can be stored more efficiently using numeric columns than string columns. You'll also notice some differences in query results due to the different ways that numbers and strings are handled. For example, the sort order for numbers is not the same as for strings. The number 2 is less than the number 11, but the string `'2'` is lexically greater than the string `'11'`. You can work around this by using the column in a numeric context as follows:

```
SELECT col_name + 0 as num ... ORDER BY num;
```

Adding zero to the column forces a numeric sort, but is that a reasonable thing to do? It's a useful technique sometimes, but you don't want to have to use it every time you want a numeric sort. Causing MySQL to treat the column as a number rather than a string has a couple of significant implications. It forces a string-to-number conversion for each column value, which is inefficient. Also, using the column in a calculation prevents MySQL from using any index on the column, which slows down the query further. Neither of these performance degradations occur if you store the values as numbers in the first place. The simple choice of using one representation rather than another has implications for storage requirements, query handling, and processing performance.

The preceding example illustrates that several issues come into play when you choose column types. The following list gives a quick rundown of factors to think about when picking a type for a column.

- **What kind of values will the column hold?** Numbers? Strings? Dates? This is an obvious question, but you must ask it. You can represent any type of value as a string, but as we've just seen, it's likely that you'll get better performance if you use other more appropriate types for numeric values. (This is also true for date and time values.) However, assessing the type of values you're working with isn't necessarily trivial, particularly for other people's data. It's especially important to ask what kind of values the column will hold if you're setting up a table for someone else, and you must be sure to ask enough questions to get sufficient information for making a good decision.

- **Do your values lie within some particular range?** If they are integers, will they always be non-negative? If so, you can use UNSIGNED. If they are strings, will they always be chosen from among a fixed set of values? If so, you may find ENUM or SET a useful type.

  There is a tradeoff between the range of a type and the amount of storage it uses. How "big" a type do you need? For numbers, you can choose small types with a limited range of values, or large types that are essentially unlimited. For strings, you can make them short or long, so you wouldn't choose CHAR(255) if all the values you want to store contain fewer than 10 characters.

- **What are the performance and efficiency issues?** Some types can be processed more efficiently than others. Numeric operations generally can be performed more quickly than string operations. Short strings can be compared more quickly than long strings and also involve less disk overhead. For ISAM and MyISAM tables, performance is better for fixed-length types than for variable-length types.

- **How do you want your values to be compared?** For strings, comparisons can be case sensitive or not case sensitive. You choices here also affect sorting and grouping operations, which are based on comparisons.

- **Do you plan to index a column?** If you do, it affects your choice of table type and column type because indexing properties are not the same for all table handlers. For example, with ISAM tables, you cannot index BLOB and TEXT columns, and indexed columns must be defined as NOT NULL (which affects your ability to use NULL values).

Now let's consider each of these issues in more detail. But before we do, allow me to point something out. You want to make the best column type choices you can when you create a table, but if you make a choice that turns out to be non-optimal, it's not the end of the world. You can use ALTER TABLE to change the type to a better one. This can be as simple as changing a SMALLINT to MEDIUMINT after finding out your data contain values larger than you originally thought. Or it can be more complex, such as changing a CHAR to an ENUM with a specific set of allowed values. In MySQL 3.23 and later, you can use PROCEDURE ANALYSE() to obtain information about your table's columns, such as the minimum and maximum values as well as a suggested optimal type to cover the range of values in a column:

```
SELECT * FROM tbl_name PROCEDURE ANALYSE();
```

The output from this query can help you determine that a smaller type can be used, which can improve the performance of queries that involve the table and reduce the amount of space required for table storage.

What Kind of Values Will the Column Hold?

The first thing you think of when you're trying to decide on a column type is the kind of values the column will be used for, because this has the most evident implications for the type you choose. In general, you do the obvious thing—you store numbers in numeric columns, strings in string columns, and dates and times in date and time columns. If your numbers have a fractional part, you use a floating-point column type rather than an integer type, and so on. But sometimes there are exceptions. The principle here is that you need to understand the nature of your data to be able to choose the type in an informed manner. If you're going to store your own data, you probably have a good idea of how to characterize it. On the other hand, if others ask you to set up a table for them, it's sometimes a different story. It may not be so easy to know just what you're working with. Be sure to ask enough questions to find out what kind of values the table really should contain.

Suppose you're told that a table needs a column to record "amount of precipitation." Is that a number? Or is it "mostly" numeric—that is, typically but not always coded as a number? For example, when you watch the news on television, the weather report generally includes a measure of precipitation. Sometimes this is a number (as in "0.25 inches of rain"), but sometimes it's a "trace" of precipitation, meaning "not much at all." That's fine for the weather report, but what does it mean for storage in a database? You either need to quantify "trace" as a number so that you can use a numeric column type to record precipitation amounts, or you need to use a string so that you can record the word "trace." Or you could come up with some more complicated arrangement, using a number column and a string column where you fill in one column and leave the other one NULL. It should be obvious that you want to avoid that option, if possible; it makes the table harder to understand and it makes query-writing much more difficult.

I would probably try to store all rows in numeric form, and then convert them as necessary for display purposes. For example, if any non-zero amount of precipitation less than .01 inches is considered a trace amount, you could display values from the column as follows:

```
SELECT IF(precip>0 AND precip<.01,'trace',precip) FROM ... ;
```

Some values are obviously numeric, but you must determine whether to use a floating-point or integer type. You should ask what your units are and what accuracy you require. Is whole-unit accuracy sufficient, or do you need to represent fractional units? This may help you distinguish between integer and floating-point column types. For example, if you're representing weights, you can use an integer column if you record values to the nearest pound. You'd use a floating-point column if you want to record fractional units. In some cases, you might even use multiple fields—for example, if you want to record weight in terms of pounds and ounces.

Height is a numeric type of information for which there are several representational possibilities:

- **As a string such as `'6-2'` for a value like "6 feet, 2 inches"**. This has the advantage of having a form that's easy to look at and understand (certainly more so than "74 inches"), but it's difficult to use this kind of value for mathematical operations such as summation or averaging.

- **As one numeric field for feet and another for inches**. This would be a little easier to work with for numerical operations, but two fields are more difficult to use than one.

- **As one numeric field representing inches**. This is easiest for a database to work with, and least meaningful for humans. But remember that you don't have to present values in the same format that you use to work with them. You can reformat values for meaningful display using MySQL's many functions. That means this might be the best way to represent height.

Another type of numeric information is money. For monetary calculations, you're working with values that have dollars and cents parts. These look like floating-point values, but FLOAT and DOUBLE are subject to rounding error and may not be suitable except for records in which you need only approximate accuracy. Because people tend to be touchy about their money, it's more likely you need a type that affords perfect accuracy. You have a couple of choices:

- You can represent money as a DECIMAL(M,2) type, choosing M as the maximum width appropriate for the range of values you need. This gives you floating point values with two decimal places of accuracy.

The advantage of DECIMAL is that values are represented as strings and are not subject to roundoff error. The disadvantage is that string operations are less efficient than operations on values represented internally as numbers.

- You can represent all monetary values internally as cents using an integer type. The advantage is that calculations are done internally using integers, which is very fast. The disadvantage is that you will need to convert values on input or output by multiplying or dividing by 100.

If you need to store date information, do the values include a time? That is, will they *ever* need to include a time? MySQL doesn't provide a date type that has an optional time part; DATE never has a time and DATETIME must have a time. If the time really is optional, use a DATE column to record the date and a separate TIME column to record the time. Then allow the TIME column to be NULL and interpret that as "no time:"

```
CREATE TABLE mytbl
(
    date DATE NOT NULL,     # date is required
    time TIME NULL          # time is optional (may be NULL)
);
```

One type of situation in which it's especially important to determine whether you need a time value occurs when you're joining two tables with a master-detail relationship that are "linked" based on date information.

Suppose you're conducting research involving subjects who come in to your office to be tested. Following a standard initial set of tests, you may run several additional tests, with the choice of tests varying according to the results of the initial tests. You might represent this information using a master-detail relationship in which the subject identification information and the standard initial tests are stored in a master record and any additional tests are stored as rows in a secondary detail table. Then you link together the two tables based on subject ID and the date on which the tests are given.

The question you must answer in this situation is whether you can use just the date or whether you need both date and time. This depends on whether or not a subject may go through the testing procedure more than once during the same day. If so, record the time (say, the time that the procedure begins) using either a DATETIME column or separate DATE and TIME columns that both must be filled in. Without the time value, you will not be able to associate a subject's detail records with the proper master records if the subject is tested twice in a day.

I've heard people claim "I don't need a time; I will never test a subject twice on the same day." Sometimes they're correct, but I have also seen some of these same people turn up later wondering how to prevent detail records from being mixed up with the wrong master record after entering data for subjects who were tested multiple times in a day. Sorry, then it's too late!

Sometimes you can deal with this problem by retrofitting a TIME column into the tables. Unfortunately, it's difficult to fix existing records unless you have some independent data source, such as the original paper records. Otherwise, you have no way to disambiguate detail records to associate them to the proper master record. Even if you have an independent source of information, this is very messy and likely to cause problems for applications you've already written to use the tables. It's best to explain the issues to the table owners and make sure you've got a good characterization of the data values before creating their tables.

Sometimes you may have incomplete data, and this will influence your choice of column types. You may be collecting birth and death dates for genealogical research, and sometimes all you can find out is the year or year and month someone was born or died—not the exact date. If you use a DATE column, you can't enter a date unless you have the full date. If you want to be able to record whatever information you have, even if it's incomplete, you may have to keep separate year, month, and day fields. Then you can enter the parts of the date that you have and leave the rest NULL. Another possibility is available in MySQL 3.23 and later, which allows the day or month and day parts of DATE values to be 0. Such "fuzzy" dates can be used to represent incomplete date values.

Do Your Values Lie Within Some Particular Range?

If you've decided on the general category from which to pick a type for a column, thinking about the range of values you want to represent will help you narrow down your choices to a particular type within that category. Suppose you want to store integer values. The range of your values determines the types you can use. If you need values in the range from 0 to 1000, you can use anything from a SMALLINT up to a BIGINT. If your values range up to 2 million, you can't use SMALLINT, and your choices range from MEDIUMINT to BIGINT. Then you need to pick one type from among the possibilities.

Of course, you could simply use the largest type for the kind of value you want to store (BIGINT for the examples in the previous paragraph). Generally, however, you should use the smallest type that is large enough for your purposes. By doing so, you'll minimize the amount of storage used by your tables, and they will give you better performance because smaller columns usually can be processed more quickly than larger ones. (Reading smaller values requires less disk activity, and more key values fit into the index cache, allowing indexed searches to be performed faster.)

If you don't know the range of values you'll need to be able to represent, you either must guess or use BIGINT to accommodate the worst possible case. (If you guess and the type you choose does turn out to be too small, all is not lost; you can use ALTER TABLE later to make the column bigger.)

In Chapter 1, we created a score table for the grade-keeping project that had a score column for recording quiz and test scores. The table was created using INT to keep the discussion simpler, but you can see now that if scores are in the range from 0 to 100, a better choice would be TINYINT UNSIGNED because that would use less storage.

The range of values in your data also affects the attributes you can use with your column type. If values are never negative, you can use UNSIGNED; otherwise, you can't.

String types don't have a "range" in the same way numeric columns do, but they have a length, and the maximum length you need affects the column types you can use. If your strings are shorter than 256 characters, you can use CHAR, VARCHAR, TINYTEXT, or TINYBLOB. If you want longer strings, you can use a TEXT or BLOB type, but CHAR and VARCHAR are no longer options.

For string columns that you will use to represent a fixed set of values, you might consider using an ENUM or SET column type. These can be good choices because they are represented internally as numbers. Operations on them are performed numerically, which makes them more efficient than other string types. They can also be more compact than other string types, which saves space.

When characterizing the range of values you have to deal with, the best terms are "always" and "never" (as in "always less than 1000" or "never negative") because they allow you to constrain your column type choices more tightly. But be wary of using these terms when they're not really justified. Be especially wary if you're consulting with other people about their data and they start throwing around those two terms. When people say "always" or "never," be sure they really mean it. Sometimes people say their data always have a particular characteristic when they really mean "almost always."

For example, suppose you're designing a table for a group of investigators who tell you, "Our test scores are always 0 to 100." Based on that statement, you choose TINYINT and you make it UNSIGNED because the values are always non-negative. Then you find out that the people who code the data for entry into the database sometimes use −1 to mean "student was absent due to illness." Oops. They didn't tell you that. It may be acceptable to use NULL to represent such values, but if not, you'll have to record a −1 and then you can't use an UNSIGNED column. (This is an instance where ALTER TABLE comes to your rescue!)

Sometimes decisions about these types of cases can be made more easily by asking a simple question: Are there ever exceptions? If an exceptional case ever occurs, even just once, you must allow for it. You will find that people who talk to you about designing a database invariably think that if exceptions don't occur very often, they don't matter. When you're creating a table, you can't think that way. The question you need to ask isn't "How often do exceptions occur?" It's "Do exceptions *ever* occur?" If they do, you must take them into account.

What Are the Performance and Efficiency Issues?

Your choice of column type can influence query performance in several ways. If you keep the general guidelines discussed in the following sections in mind, you'll be able to choose types that will help MySQL process your tables more efficiently.

Numeric Versus String Operations

Numeric operations are generally faster than string operations. Consider comparison operations. Numbers can be compared in a single operation. String comparisons may involve several byte-by-byte or character-by-character comparisons, more so as the strings become longer.

If a string column has a limited number of values, use an ENUM or SET type to get the advantages of numeric operations. These types are represented internally as numbers and can be processed more efficiently.

Consider alternative representations for strings. Sometimes you can improve performance by representing string values as numbers. For example, to represent IP numbers in dotted-quad notation, such as 192.168.0.4, you might use a string. But as an alternative, you could convert the IP numbers to integer form by storing each part of the dotted-quad form in one byte of a four-byte INT UNSIGNED type. Storing integers would both save space and speed lookups. On the other hand, representing IP numbers as INT values might make it difficult to perform pattern matches, such as you might do if you wanted to look for numbers in a given subnet. So you cannot consider only space issues; you must decide which representation is more appropriate based on what you want to do with the values. (Whichever way you choose, the INET_ATON() and INET_NTOA() functions can help convert between the two representations.)

Smaller Types Versus Bigger Types

Smaller types can be processed more quickly than larger types. A general principle is that they take less space and involve less overhead for disk activity. For strings in particular, processing time is in direct relationship to string length.

For columns that use fixed-size types, choose the smallest type that will hold the required range of values. For example, don't use BIGINT if MEDIUMINT will do. Don't use DOUBLE if you only need FLOAT precision. For variable-size types, you may still be able to save space. A BLOB uses 2 bytes to record the length of the value, a LONGBLOB uses 4 bytes. If you're storing values that are never as long as 64KB, using BLOB saves you 2 bytes per value. (Similar considerations apply for TEXT types, of course.)

Fixed-Length Versus Variable-Length Types

Fixed-length and variable-length types have different performance implications, although the particular effects of each depends on the table type.

For MyISAM and ISAM tables, fixed-length types generally can be processed more quickly than variable-length types:

- With variable-length columns, you get more fragmentation of a table on which you perform many deletes or updates due to the differing sizes of the records. You'll need to run OPTIMIZE TABLE periodically to maintain performance. This is not an issue with fixed-length rows.

- Tables with fixed-length rows are easier to reconstruct if you have a table crash. The beginning of each record can be determined because they all are at positions that are multiples of the fixed record size, something that is not true with variable-length rows. This is not a performance issue with respect to query processing, but it can certainly speed up the table repair process.

If you have variable-length columns in a MyISAM or ISAM table, converting them to fixed-length columns will improve performance because fixed-length records are easier to process. Before you attempt to do this, though, consider the following:

- Fixed-length columns are faster but take more space. CHAR(*n*) columns always take *n* bytes per value (even empty ones) because values are padded with trailing spaces when stored in the table. VARCHAR(*n*) columns take less space because only as much space is allocated as is necessary to store each value, plus one byte per value to record the length. Thus, if you are choosing between CHAR and VARCHAR columns, the tradeoff is one of time versus space. If speed is your primary concern, use CHAR columns to get the performance benefits of fixed-length columns. If space is at a premium, use VARCHAR columns. As a rule of thumb, you can assume that fixed-length rows will improve performance even though more space is used. But for an especially critical application, you may want to implement a table both ways and run some tests to determine which alternative actually is better for your particular application.

- You cannot convert just one variable-length column; you must convert them all. Additionally, you must convert them all at the same time using a single ALTER TABLE statement or the attempt will have no effect.

- Sometimes you cannot use a fixed-length type, even if you want to. There is no fixed-length type for strings longer than 255 bytes, for example.

For InnoDB tables, fixed-length and variable-length rows are both stored the same way (as a row header containing pointers to individual column values, plus storage for the values). This means that fixed-length rows aren't any simpler to process. Consequently, the primary performance factor is the amount of storage used for rows. The implication is that variable-length rows will usually be faster for InnoDB tables because they require less space and thus less disk I/O to process.

Indexable Types

Indexes speed up queries, so choose types you can index, at least for columns that you plan to use for comparisons in searches. See the "Do You Plan to Index a Column?" section later in this chapter for more information.

NULL Versus NOT NULL Types

If you declare a column NOT NULL, it can be handled more quickly because MySQL doesn't have to check the column's values during query processing to see whether they are NULL. It also saves one bit per row in the table. Avoiding NULL in columns may make your queries simpler (because you don't have to think about NULL as a special case), and simpler queries generally are processed more quickly.

How Do You Want Your Values to be Compared?

You can often control case sensitivity of string values for comparison and sorting purposes by the type of column you use to store them. The determining factor is whether the column contains binary strings (case sensitive) or non-binary strings (not case sensitive). Table 2.15 shows each binary string type and the corresponding non-binary type. Some types (CHAR, VARCHAR) are binary or not binary according to the presence or absence of the keyword BINARY in the column declaration. The "binary-ness" of other types (BLOB, TEXT) is implicit in the type name.

Table 2.15 **Binary and Non-Binary String Types**

Binary Type	Non-Binary Type
CHAR(*M*) BINARY	CHAR(*M*)
VARCHAR(*M*) BINARY	VARCHAR(*M*)
TINYBLOB	TINYTEXT
BLOB	TEXT
MEDIUMBLOB	MEDIUMTEXT
LONGBLOB	LONGTEXT

If you want to use a column for both case-sensitive and not case-sensitive comparisons, use a non-binary type. Then, whenever you want a case-sensitive comparison, use the BINARY keyword to force a string to be treated as a binary string value. For example, if mycol is a CHAR column, you can compare it different ways. The following comparison is not case sensitive:

```
mycol = 'ABC'
```

But the following comparisons are both case sensitive (note that it doesn't matter which string the BINARY operator is applied to):

```
BINARY mycol = 'ABC'
mycol = BINARY 'ABC'
```

If you have string values that you want to sort in some non-lexical order, consider using an ENUM column. Sorting of ENUM values occurs according to the order in which you list the enumeration values in the column declaration, so you can make the values sort in any order you want.

Do You Plan to Index a Column?

Indexes allow MySQL to process queries more efficiently. Choosing indexes is a topic covered in more detail in Chapter 4, but a general principle is that columns you commonly use in WHERE clauses to select rows are good candidates for indexing.

If you want to index a column or include it in a multiple-column index, there may be constraints on the types you can choose. For example, some table types (InnoDB and ISAM) do not allow indexes on BLOB or TEXT columns, and prior to MySQL 3.23.2, all indexed columns must be declared as NOT NULL. If you find yourself bumping up against these restrictions, you may be able to work around them:

- If you want to use a BLOB or TEXT column but your table type does not allow them to be indexed, check whether your values ever exceed 255 bytes. If not, use a similar VARCHAR column type instead and index that. You can use VARCHAR(255) BINARY for BLOB values and VARCHAR(255) for TEXT values.

- To work around a NOT NULL restriction, if you can designate some value as special, you might be able to treat it as though it means the same thing as NULL. For a DATE column, you might designate '0000-00-00' to mean "no date." In a string column that normally holds only non-empty values, you might designate that the empty string means "missing value." In a numeric column, you might use −1 if the column normally would hold only non-negative values. (Of course, you could not declare the column as UNSIGNED in this case.)

Inter-Relatedness of Column Type Choice Issues

You can't always consider the issues involved in choosing column types as though they are independent of one another. For example, range is related to storage size for numeric types; as you increase the range, you require more storage, which affects performance. Or consider the implications of choosing to use AUTO_INCREMENT to create a column for holding unique sequence numbers. That single choice has several consequences involving the column type, indexing, and the use of NULL:

- AUTO_INCREMENT is a column attribute that should be used only with integer types. That immediately limits your choices to TINYINT through BIGINT.

- AUTO_INCREMENT columns are intended only for generating sequences of positive values, so you should declare them as UNSIGNED.

- AUTO_INCREMENT columns must be indexed. Furthermore, to prevent sequence numbers from being reused, the index must be unique. This means you must declare the column as a PRIMARY KEY or as a UNIQUE index.

- AUTO_INCREMENT columns must be NOT NULL.

All of this means you do not just declare an AUTO_INCREMENT column like this:

```
mycol arbitrary_type AUTO_INCREMENT
```

You declare it like this:

```
mycol integer_type UNSIGNED AUTO_INCREMENT NOT NULL,
PRIMARY KEY (mycol)
```

Or like like this:

```
mycol integer_type UNSIGNED AUTO_INCREMENT NOT NULL,
UNIQUE (mycol)
```

Expression Evaluation and Type Conversion

MySQL allows you to write expressions that include constants, function calls, and references to table columns. These values can be combined using different kinds of operators, such as arithmetic or comparison operators, and terms of an expression can be grouped with parentheses. Expressions occur most commonly in the output column list and WHERE clause of SELECT statements. For example, the following is a query that is similar to one used for age calculations in Chapter 1:

```
SELECT
    CONCAT(last_name, ', ', first_name),
    (YEAR(death) - YEAR(birth)) - IF(RIGHT(death,5) < RIGHT(birth,5),1,0)
FROM president
WHERE
    birth > '1900-1-1' AND DEATH IS NOT NULL;
```

Each column selected represents an expression, as does the content of the WHERE clause. Expressions also occur in the WHERE clause of DELETE and UPDATE statements, the VALUES() clause of INSERT statements, and so on.

When MySQL encounters an expression, it evaluates it to produce a result. For example, (4*3)/(4-2) evaluates to the value 6. Expression evaluation may involve type conversion, such as when MySQL converts the number 960821 into a date '1996-08-21' if the number is used in a context requiring a DATE value.

This section discusses how you can write expressions in MySQL and the rules that govern the various kinds of type conversions that MySQL performs during the process of expression evaluation. Each of MySQL's operators is listed here, but MySQL has so many functions that only a few are discussed. For more information, see Appendix C.

Writing Expressions

An expression can be as simple as a single constant:

```
0       Numeric constant
'abc'   String constant
```

Expressions can use function calls. Some functions take arguments (values inside the parentheses) and some do not. Multiple arguments should be separated by commas. When you invoke a function, there can be spaces around arguments, but there must be no space between the function name and the opening parenthesis:[5]

```
NOW()                    Function with no arguments
STRCMP('abc','def')      Function with two arguments
STRCMP( 'abc', 'def' )   Spaces around arguments are legal
STRCMP ('abc','def')     Space after function name is illegal
```

If there is a space after the function name, the MySQL parser may interpret the function name as a column name. (Function names are not reserved words, and you can use them for column names if you want.) The usual result is a syntax error.

You can use table column values in expressions. In the simplest case, when the table to which a column belongs is clear from context, a column reference can be given simply as the column name. Only one table is named in each of the following SELECT statements, so the column references are unambiguous, even though the same column names are used in each statement:

```
SELECT last_name, first_name FROM president;
SELECT last_name, first_name FROM member;
```

If it's not clear which table should be used, column names can be preceded by the table name. If it's not clear which database should be used, the table name can be preceded by the database name. You can also use these more-specific forms in unambiguous contexts if you simply want to be more explicit:

```
SELECT
    president.last_name, president.first_name,
    member.last_name, member.first_name
```

---

5. Actually, you can tell MySQL to allow spaces after function names by starting the server with the --ansi or --sql-mode=IGNORE_SPACE option. However, this causes function names to be treated as reserved words.

```
FROM president, member
WHERE president.last_name = member.last_name;
SELECT sampdb.student.name FROM sampdb.student;
```

Finally, you can combine all these kinds of values (constants, function calls, and column references) to form more complex expressions.

Operator Types

MySQL includes several kinds of operators that can be used to combine terms of expressions. Arithmetic operators, listed in Table 2.16, include the usual addition, subtraction, multiplication, and division operators, as well as the modulo operator. Arithmetic is performed using BIGINT (64-bit) integer values for +, -, and * when both operands are integers, as well as for / and % when the operation is performed in a context where the result is expected to be an integer. Otherwise, DOUBLE is used. Be aware that if an integer operation involves large values such that the result exceeds 64-bit range, you will get unpredictable results. (Actually, you should try to avoid exceeding 63-bit values; one bit is needed to represent the sign.)

Table 2.16 **Arithmetic Operators**

Operator	Syntax	Meaning
+	a + b	Addition; sum of operands
-	a - b	Subtraction; difference of operands
-	-a	Unary minus; negation of operand
*	a * b	Multiplication; product of operands
/	a / b	Division; quotient of operands
%	a % b	Modulo; remainder after division of operands

Logical operators, shown in Table 2.17, evaluate expressions to determine whether they are true (non-zero) or false (zero). It is also possible for a logical expression to evaluate to NULL if its value cannot be ascertained (for example, 1 AND NULL is of indeterminate value). MySQL allows the C-style &&, ||, and ! operators as alternative forms of AND, OR, and NOT. Note in particular the || operator; ANSI SQL specifies || as the string concatenation operator, but in MySQL it signifies a logical OR operation.[6]

If you use the following expression, expecting it to perform string concatenation, you may be surprised to discover that it returns the number 0:

```
'abc' || 'def'                                      → 0
```

---

6. If you want the ANSI behavior for ||, start the server with the --ansi or --sql-mode=PIPES_AS_CONCAT option.

`'abc'` and `'def'` are converted to integers for the operation, and both turn into 0. In MySQL, use `CONCAT('abc','def')` to perform string concatenation:

`CONCAT('abc','def')`   → `'abcdef'`

Table 2.17   **Logical Operators**

Operator	Syntax	Meaning
AND, &&	a AND b, a && b	Logical intersection; true if both operands are true
OR, ||	a OR b, a || b	Logical union; true if either operand is true
XOR	a XOR b	Logical exclusive-OR; true if exactly one operand is true
NOT, !	NOT a, !a	Logical negation; true if operand is false

Bit operators, shown in Table 2.18, perform bitwise intersection, union and exclusive-OR where each bit of the result is evaluated as the logical AND, OR, or exclusive-OR of the corresponding bits of the operands. (The XOR and ^ exclusive-OR operators are not available until MySQL 4.0.2.) You can also perform bit shifts left or right. Bit operations are performed using BIGINT (64-bit) integer values.

Table 2.18   **Bit Operators**

Operator	Syntax	Meaning
&	a & b	Bitwise AND (intersection); each bit of result is set if corresponding bits of both operands are set
|	a | b	Bitwise OR (union); each bit of result is set if corresponding bit of either operand is set
^	a ^ b	Bitwise exclusive-OR; each bit of result is set only if exactly one corresponding bit of the operands is set
<<	a << b	Left shift of a by b bit positions
>>	a >> b	Right shift of a by b bit positions

Comparison operators, shown in Table 2.19, include operators for testing relative magnitude or lexical ordering of numbers and strings as well as operators for performing pattern matching and for testing NULL values. The `<=>` operator is MySQL-specific and was introduced in MySQL 3.23.

Table 2.19 **Comparison Operators**

Operator	Syntax	Meaning
=	a = b	True if operands are equal
<=>	a <=> b	True if operands are equal (even if NULL)
!=, <>	a != b, a <> b	True if operands are not equal
<	a < b	True if a is less than b
<=	a <= b	True if a is less than or equal to b
>=	a >= b	True if a is greater than or equal to b
>	a > b	True if a is greater than b
IN	a IN (b1, b2, ...)	True if a is equal to any of b1, b2, ...
BETWEEN	a BETWEEN b AND c	True if a is between the values of b and c, inclusive
NOT BETWEEN	a NOT BETWEEN b AND c	True if a is not between the values of b and c, inclusive
LIKE	a LIKE b	SQL pattern match; true if a matches b
NOT LIKE	a NOT LIKE b	SQL pattern match; true if a does not match b
REGEXP	a REGEXP b	Regular expression match; true if a matches b
NOT REGEXP	a NOT REGEXP b	Regular expression match; true if a does not match b
IS NULL	a IS NULL	True if operand is NULL
IS NOT NULL	a IS NOT NULL	True if operand is not NULL

The BINARY operator is available as of MySQL 3.23 and can be used to cast (convert) a string to a binary string. Generally, this is done to render a string case sensitive in comparison or sorting operations. The first of the following comparisons is not case sensitive, but the second and third ones are:

```
'abc' = 'Abc'                          → 1
BINARY 'abc' = 'Abc'                   → 0
'abc' = BINARY 'Abc'                   → 0
```

There is no corresponding NOT BINARY cast. If you expect to use a column both in case-sensitive and in not case-sensitive contexts, use a column type that is not case sensitive and use BINARY for those comparisons that you want to be case sensitive. Alternatively, for a column that is case sensitive, you can use it in a comparison that is not case sensitive by converting both operands to the same lettercase with UPPER() or LOWER():

```
UPPER(col_name) < UPPER('Smith')
LOWER(col_name) < LOWER('Smith')
```

For string comparisons that are not case sensitive, it is possible that multiple characters will be considered equivalent, depending on your character set. For example, 'E' and 'É' might be treated the same for comparison and ordering operations. Binary (case sensitive) comparisons are done using the numeric codes of successive bytes in the values.

Pattern matching allows you to look for values without having to specify an exact literal value. MySQL provides SQL pattern matching using the LIKE operator and the wildcard characters '%' (match any sequence of characters) and '_' (match any single character). MySQL also provides pattern matching based on the REGEXP operator and regular expressions that are similar to those used in UNIX programs such as grep, sed, and vi. You must use one of these pattern-matching operators to perform a pattern match; you cannot use the = operator. To reverse the sense of a pattern match, use NOT LIKE or NOT REGEXP.

The two types of pattern matching differ in important respects besides the use of different operators and pattern characters:

- LIKE is not case sensitive unless at least one operand is a binary string. This is also true for REGEXP, except that prior to MySQL 3.23.4, REGEXP is always case sensitive.
- SQL patterns match only if the entire string is matched. Regular expressions match if the pattern is found anywhere in the string.

Patterns used with the LIKE operator can include the '%' and '_' wildcard characters. For example, the pattern 'Frank%' matches any string that begins with 'Frank':

```
'Franklin' LIKE 'Frank%'                          → 1
'Frankfurter' LIKE 'Frank%'                       → 1
```

The wildcard character '%' matches any sequence of characters, including the empty sequence, so 'Frank%' matches 'Frank':

```
'Frank' LIKE 'Frank%'                             → 1
```

This also means the pattern '%' matches any string, including the empty string. However, '%' will not match NULL. In fact, any pattern match with a NULL operand fails:

```
'Frank' LIKE NULL                                 → NULL
NULL LIKE '%'                                      → NULL
```

MySQL's `LIKE` operator is not case sensitive unless one of its operands is a binary string. Thus, `'Frank%'` matches both of the strings `'Frankly'` and `'frankly'` by default, but matches only one of them in a binary comparison:

```
'Frankly' LIKE 'Frank%'                        → 1
'frankly' LIKE 'Frank%'                        → 1
BINARY 'Frankly' LIKE 'Frank%'                 → 1
BINARY 'frankly' LIKE 'Frank%'                 → 0
```

This differs from the ANSI SQL LIKE operator, which is case sensitive.

The wildcard character can be specified anywhere in the pattern. `'%bert'` matches `'Englebert'`, `'Bert'`, and `'Albert'`. `'%bert%'` matches all of those strings and also strings like `'Berthold'`, `'Bertram'`, and `'Alberta'`. `'b%t'` matches `'Bert'`, `'bent'`, and `'burnt'`.

The other wildcard character allowed with `LIKE` is '_', which matches any single character. The pattern `'___'` matches any string of exactly three characters. `'c_t'` matches `'cat'`, `'cot'`, `'cut'`, and even `'c_t'` (because '_' matches itself).

To match literal instances of the '%' or '_' characters, turn off their special meaning by preceding them with a backslash ('\%' or '_'):

```
'abc' LIKE 'a%c'                               → 1
'abc' LIKE 'a\%c'                              → 0
'a%c' LIKE 'a\%c'                              → 1
'abc' LIKE 'a_c'                               → 1
'abc' LIKE 'a\_c'                              → 0
'a_c' LIKE 'a\_c'                              → 1
```

MySQL's other form of pattern matching uses regular expressions. The operator is `REGEXP` rather than `LIKE`. The most common regular expression pattern characters are as follows:

- The '.' character is a wildcard that matches any single character:

  ```
  'abc' REGEXP 'a.c'                           → 1
  ```

- The [...] construction matches any character listed between the square brackets.

  ```
  'e' REGEXP '[aeiou]'                          → 1
  'f' REGEXP '[aeiou]'                          → 0
  ```

You can specify a range of characters by listing the endpoints of the range separated by a dash ('-') or negate the sense of the class (to match any character not listed) by specifying '^' as the first character of the class:

```
'abc' REGEXP '[a-z]'                           → 1
'abc' REGEXP '[^a-z]'                          → 0
```

'*' means "match any number of the previous thing," so that, for example, the pattern `'x*'` matches any number of 'x' characters:

```
'abcdef' REGEXP 'a.*f'                          → 1
'abc' REGEXP '[0-9]*abc'                         → 1
'abc' REGEXP '[0-9][0-9]*'                       → 0
```

"Any number" includes zero instances, which is why the second expression succeeds.

`'^pat'` and `'pat$'` anchor a pattern match so that the pattern *pat* matches only when it occurs at the beginning or end of a string, and `'^pat$'` matches only if *pat* matches the entire string:

```
'abc' REGEXP 'b'                                → 1
'abc' REGEXP '^b'                               → 0
'abc' REGEXP 'b$'                               → 0
'abc' REGEXP '^abc$'                            → 1
'abcd' REGEXP '^abc$'                           → 0
```

A REGEXP pattern can be taken from a table column, although this will be slower than a constant pattern if the column contains several different values. The pattern must be examined and converted to internal form each time the column value changes.

MySQL's regular expression matching has other special pattern elements as well. See Appendix C for more information.

Operator Precedence

When MySQL evaluates an expression, it looks at the operators to determine the order in which it should group the terms of the expression. Some operators have higher precedence; that is, they are "stronger" than others in the sense that they are evaluated earlier than others. For example, multiplication and division have higher precedence than addition and subtraction. The following two expressions are equivalent because * and / are evaluated before + and -:

```
1 + 2 * 3 - 4 / 5                               → 6.2
1 + 6 - .8                                      → 6.2
```

Operator precedence is shown in the following list, from highest precedence to lowest. Operators listed on the same line have the same precedence. Operators at a higher precedence level are evaluated before operators at a lower precedence level. Operators at the same precedence level are evaluated left to right.

```
BINARY   COLLATE
NOT  !
^
XOR
- (unary minus)   ~ (unary bit negation)
*  /  %
```

```
+    -
<<   >>
&
|
<   <=  =  <=>  !=  <>  >=  >  IN  IS  LIKE  REGEXP  RLIKE
BETWEEN  CASE  WHEN  THEN  ELSE
AND  &&
OR  ||
:=
```

You can use parentheses to override the precedence of operators and change the order in which expression terms are evaluated:

```
1 + 2 * 3 - 4 / 5                              → 6.2
(1 + 2) * (3 - 4) / 5                          → -0.6
```

NULL Values in Expressions

Take care when you use NULL values in expressions, because the result may not always be what you expect. The following guidelines will help you avoid surprises.

If you supply NULL as an operand to any arithmetic or bit operator, the result is NULL:

```
1 + NULL                                       → NULL
1 | NULL                                       → NULL
```

With logical operators, the result is NULL unless the result can be determined with certainty.[7]

```
1 AND NULL                                     → NULL
1 OR NULL                                      → 1
0 AND NULL                                     → 0
0 OR NULL                                      → NULL
```

NULL as an operand to any comparison or pattern-matching operator produces a NULL result, except for the <=>, IS NULL, and IS NOT NULL operators, which are intended specifically for dealing with NULL values:

```
1 = NULL                                       → NULL
NULL = NULL                                    → NULL
1 <=> NULL                                     → 0
NULL LIKE '%'                                  → NULL
NULL REGEXP '.*'                               → NULL
NULL <=> NULL                                  → 1
1 IS NULL                                      → 0
NULL IS NULL                                   → 1
```

---

7. Prior to MySQL 3.23.9, NULL is treated as a false value with logical operators; this behavior may be considered a bug.

Functions generally return NULL if given NULL arguments, except for those functions designed to deal with NULL arguments. For example, IFNULL() is able to handle NULL arguments and returns true or false appropriately. On the other hand, STRCMP() expects non-NULL arguments; if it discovers you've passed it a NULL argument, it returns NULL rather than true or false.

In sorting operations, NULL values group together. However, whether they sort before or after non-NULL values is version dependent, as discussed in the "Sorting Query Results" section in Chapter 1.

Type Conversion

Whenever a value of one type is used in a context that requires a value of another type, MySQL performs extensive type conversion automatically according to the kind of operation you're performing. Type conversion can occur for any of the following reasons:

- Conversion of operands to a type appropriate for evaluation of an operator
- Conversion of a function argument to a type expected by the function
- Conversion of a value for assignment into a table column that has a different type

You can also perform explicit type conversion using a cast operator or function.

The following expression involves implicit type conversion. It consists of the addition operator + and two operands, 1 and '2':

```
1 + '2'
```

The operands are of different types (number and string), so MySQL converts one of them to make them the same type. But which one should it change? In this case, + is a numeric operator; MySQL wants the operands to be numbers and converts the string '2' to the number 2. Then it evaluates the expression to produce the result 3. Here's another example. The CONCAT() function concatenates strings to produce a longer string as a result. To do this, it interprets its arguments as strings, no matter what type they are. If you pass it a bunch of numbers, CONCAT() will convert them to strings and then return their concatenation:

```
CONCAT(1,2,3)                                    → '123'
```

If the call to CONCAT() is part of a larger expression, further type conversion may take place. Consider the following expression and its result:

```
REPEAT('X',CONCAT(1,2,3)/10)                    → 'XXXXXXXXXXXX'
```

CONCAT(1,2,3) produces the string '123'. The expression '123'/10 is converted to 123/10 because division is an arithmetic operator. The result of this expression would be 12.3 in floating-point context, but REPEAT() expects an integer repeat count, so an integer division is performed to produce 12. Then REPEAT('X',12) produces a string result of 12 'x' characters.

A general principle to keep in mind is that MySQL attempts to convert values to the type required by an expression rather than generating an error. Depending on the context, it will convert values of each of the three general categories (numbers, strings, or dates and times) to values in any of the other categories. However, values can't always be converted from one type to another. If a value to be converted to a given type doesn't look like a legal value for that type, the conversion fails. Conversion to numbers of things like 'abc' that don't look like numbers results in a value of 0. Conversion to date or time types of things that don't look like a date or time result in the "zero" value for the type. For example, converting the string 'abc' to a date results in the "zero" date '0000-00-00'. On the other hand, any value can be treated as a string, so it's generally not a problem to convert a value to a string.

MySQL also performs more minor type conversions. If you use a floating-point value in an integer context, the value is converted (with rounding). Conversion in the other direction works as well; an integer can be used without problem as a floating-point number.

Hexadecimal constants are treated as strings unless the context clearly indicates a number. In string contexts, each pair of hexadecimal digits is converted to a character and the result is used as a string. The following examples illustrate how this works:

```
0x61                      → 'a'
0x61 + 0                  → 97
X'61'                     → 'a'
X'61' + 0                 → 97
CONCAT(0x61)              → 'a'
CONCAT(0x61 + 0)          → '97'
CONCAT(X'61')             → 'a'
CONCAT(X'61' + 0)         → '97'
```

In comparisons, treatment of hexadecimal constants depends on your version of MySQL. From MySQL 3.23.22 and later, hex constants in comparisons are treated as numbers:

```
0x0a = '\n'                                          → 0
0xaaab < 0xab                                        → 0
0xaaab > 0xab                                        → 1
0x0a = 10                                            → 1
```

Prior to MySQL 3.23.22, hex constants are treated as binary strings unless compared to a number. Thus, several of the preceding comparisons have a different result when executed under older servers:

```
0x0a = '\n'                                          → 1
0xaaab < 0xab                                        → 1
0xaaab > 0xab                                        → 0
0x0a = 10                                            → 1
```

Some operators force conversion of the operands to the type expected by the operator, no matter what the type of the operands is. Arithmetic operators are an example of this; they expect numbers and the operands are converted accordingly:

```
3 + 4                                                → 7
'3' + 4                                              → 7
'3' + '4'                                            → 7
```

In string-to-number conversion, it's not enough for a string simply to contain a number somewhere. MySQL doesn't look through the entire string hoping to find a number, it looks only at the beginning; if the string has no leading numeric part, the conversion result is 0.

```
'1973-2-4' + 0                                       → 1973
'12:14:01' + 0                                       → 12
'23-skidoo' + 0                                      → 23
'-23-skidoo' + 0                                     → -23
'carbon-14' + 0                                      → 0
```

Be aware that MySQL's string-to-number conversion rule changed as of version 3.23. Currently, numeric-looking strings are converted to floating-point values. Prior to 3.23, they are converted to integer values, with rounding:

```
'-428.9' + 0                                → -428.9 (MySQL ≥ 3.23)
'-428.9' + 0                                → -429   (MySQL < 3.23)
```

The logical and bit operators are even stricter than the arithmetic operators. They want the operators to be not only numeric, but to be integers, and type conversion is performed accordingly. This means that a floating-point number, such as 0.3, is not considered true, even though it's non-zero; that's because the result is 0 when it's converted to an integer. In the following expressions, the operands are not considered true until they have a value of at least 1.

```
0.3 OR .04                                      → 0
1.3 OR .04                                      → 1
0.3 AND .04                                     → 0
1.3 AND .04                                     → 0
1.3 AND 1.04                                    → 1
```

This type of conversion also occurs with the `IF()` function, which expects the first argument to be an integer. This means that values that round to zero will be considered false:

```
IF(1.3,'non-zero','zero')                       → 'non-zero'
IF(0.3,'non-zero','zero')                       → 'zero'
IF(-0.3,'non-zero','zero')                      → 'zero'
IF(-1.3,'non-zero','zero')                      → 'non-zero'
```

To test floating-point values properly, it's best to use an explicit comparison:

```
IF(0.3>0,'non-zero','zero')                     → 'non-zero'
```

Pattern matching operators expect to operate on strings. This means that you can use MySQL's pattern matching operators on numbers because it will convert them to strings in the attempt to find a match.

```
12345 LIKE '1%'                                 → 1
12345 REGEXP '1.*5'                             → 1
```

The magnitude comparison operators (`<`, `<=`, `=`, and so on) are context sensitive; that is, they are evaluated according to the types of their operands. The following expression compares the operands numerically because they are both numbers:

```
2 < 11                                          → 1
```

This expression involves string operands and thus results in a lexical comparison:

```
'2' < '11'                                      → 0
```

In the following comparisons, the types are mixed, so MySQL compares them as numbers. As a result, both expressions are true:

```
'2' < 11                                        → 1
2 < '11'                                        → 1
```

When evaluating comparisons, MySQL converts operands as necessary according to the following rules:

- Other than for the `<=>` operator, comparisons involving NULL values evaluate as NULL. (`<=>` is like `=`, except that NULL `<=>` NULL is true.)

- If both operands are strings, they are compared lexically as strings. Binary strings are compared on a byte-by-byte basis using the numeric value of each byte. Comparisons for non-binary strings are performed character-by-character using the collating sequence of the character set in which the strings are expressed. If the strings have different character sets (as is possible as of MySQL 4.1), the comparison may not yield meaningful results. A comparison between a binary and a non-binary string is treated as a comparison of binary strings.

- If both operands are integers, they are compared numerically as integers.

- As of MySQL 3.23.22, hexadecimal constants are compared as numbers. Before that, hex constants that are not compared to a number are compared as binary strings.

- If either operand is a TIMESTAMP or DATETIME value and the other is a constant, the operands are compared as TIMESTAMP values. This is done to make comparisons work better for ODBC applications.

- Otherwise, the operands are compared numerically as floating-point values. Note that this includes the case of comparing a string and a number. The string is converted to a number, which results in a value of 0 if the string doesn't look like a number. For example, '14.3' converts to 14.3, but 'L4.3' converts to 0.

Date and Time Interpretation Rules

MySQL freely converts strings and numbers to date and time values as demanded by context in an expression, and vice versa. Date and time values are converted to numbers in numeric context; numbers are converted to dates or times in date or time contexts. This conversion to a date or time value happens when you assign a value to a date or time column or when a function requires a date or time value. In comparisons, the general rule is that date and time values are compared as strings.

If the table mytbl contains a DATE column date_col, the following statements are equivalent:

```
INSERT INTO mytbl SET date_col = '2004-04-13';
INSERT INTO mytbl SET date_col = '20040413';
INSERT INTO mytbl SET date_col = 20040413;
```

In the following examples, the argument to the TO_DAYS() function is interpreted as the same value for all three expressions:

```
TO_DAYS('2004-04-10')                          → 732046
TO_DAYS('20040410')                            → 732046
TO_DAYS(20040410)                              → 732046
```

Testing and Forcing Type Conversion

To see how type conversion will be handled in an expression, use the `mysql` program to issue a `SELECT` query that evaluates the expression:

```
mysql> SELECT 0x41, 0x41 + 0;
+------+----------+
| 0x41 | 0x41 + 0 |
+------+----------+
| A    |       65 |
+------+----------+
```

As you might imagine, I did quite a bit of that sort of thing while writing this chapter!

Testing expression evaluation is especially important for statements such as `DELETE` or `UPDATE` that modify records because you want to be sure you're affecting only the intended rows. One way to check an expression is to run a preliminary `SELECT` statement with the same `WHERE` clause that you're going to use with the `DELETE` or `UPDATE` statement to verify that the clause selects the proper rows. Suppose the table `mytbl` has a `CHAR` column `char_col` containing the following values:

```
'abc'
'def'
'00'
'ghi'
'jkl'
'00'
'mno'
```

Given these values, what is the effect of the following statement?

```
DELETE FROM mytbl WHERE char_col = 00;
```

The intended effect is probably to delete the two rows containing the value `'00'`. The actual effect is to delete all the rows—an unpleasant surprise! This happens as a consequence of MySQL's comparison rules. `char_col` is a string column, but `00` in the statement is not quoted, so it is treated as a number. By MySQL's comparison rules, a comparison involving a string and a number is evaluated as a comparison of two numbers. As the `DELETE` statement is performed, each value of `char_col` is converted to a number and compared to `0`. Unfortunately, although `'00'` converts to `0`, so do all the strings that don't look like numbers. As a result, the `WHERE` clause is true for every row, and the `DELETE` statement empties the table. Obviously, this is a case where it would have been prudent to test the `WHERE` clause with a `SELECT` statement prior to executing the `DELETE`, because that would have shown you that too many rows are selected by the expression:

```
mysql> SELECT char_col FROM mytbl WHERE char_col = 00;
+----------+
| char_col |
+----------+
| 'abc'    |
| 'def'    |
| '00'     |
| 'ghi'    |
| 'jkl'    |
| '00'     |
| 'mno'    |
+----------+
```

When you're uncertain about the way a value will be used, you may want to exploit MySQL's expression evaluation mechanism to force conversion of a value to a particular type or to call a function that performs the desired conversion:

- Add `+0` or `+0.0` to a term to force conversion to a numeric value:

  ```
  0x65                                          → 'e'
  0x65 + 0                                      → 101
  0x65 + 0.0                                    → 101.0
  ```

- Use `FLOOR()` to convert a floating-point number to an integer, or add `+0.0` to convert an integer to a floating-point number:

  ```
  FLOOR(13.3)                                   → 13
  13 + 0.0                                      → 13.0
  ```

  If you want rounding instead, use `ROUND()` rather than `FLOOR()`.

- Use `CONCAT()` to turn a value into a string:

  ```
  14                                            → 14
  CONCAT(14)                                    → '14'
  ```

  Or (as of MySQL 4.0.2), use `HEX()` to convert a number to a hexadecimal string:

  ```
  HEX(255)                                      → 'FF'
  HEX(65535)                                    → 'FFFF'
  ```

  You can also use `HEX()` with a string value to convert it to a string of hex digit pairs representing successive bytes in the string:

  ```
  HEX('abc');                                   → '616263'
  ```

- Use `ASCII()` to convert a character to its ASCII value:

  ```
  'A'                                           → 'A'
  ASCII('A')                                    → 65
  ```

  To go in the other direction from ASCII code to character, use `CHAR()`:

  ```
  CHAR(65)                                      → 'A'
  ```

- Use `DATE_ADD()` to force a string or number to be treated as a date:

```
20030101                                → 20030101
DATE_ADD(20030101, INTERVAL 0 DAY)      → '2003-01-01'
'20030101'                              → '20030101'
DATE_ADD('20030101', INTERVAL 0 DAY)    → '2003-01-01'
```

- Generally, you can convert a temporal value to numeric form by adding zero:

```
CURDATE()                               → '2002-09-18'
CURDATE()+0                             → 20020918
CURTIME()                               → '12:05:41'
CURTIME()+0                             → 120541
```

- In MySQL 4.1 and later, you can convert a string from one character set to another by using `CONVERT()` or by prepending a character set identifier to the string:

```
'abc'                                   → 'abc'
CONVERT('abc' USING ucs2)               → '\0a\0b\0c'
CHARSET('abc')                          → 'latin1'
CHARSET(CONVERT('abc' USING ucs2))      → 'ucs2'
CHARSET(_ucs2 'abc')                    → 'ucs2'
```

Conversion of Out-of-Range or Illegal Values

The basic principle is this: Garbage in, garbage out. If you don't verify your data first before storing it, you may not like what you get. Having said that, the following are some general principles that describe MySQL's handling of out-of-range or otherwise improper values:

- For numeric or `TIME` columns, values that are outside the legal range are clipped to the nearest endpoint of the range and the resulting value is stored.

- For date and time columns other than `TIME`, values that are outside the range for the type may be converted to the "zero" value, `NULL`, or some other value. (In other words, the results are unpredictable.)

- For string columns other than `ENUM` or `SET`, strings that are too long are truncated to fit the maximum length of the column. Assignments to an `ENUM` or `SET` column depend on the values that are listed as legal in the column definition. If you assign to an `ENUM` column a value that is not listed as an enumeration member, the error member is assigned instead (that is, the empty string that corresponds to the zero-valued member). If you assign to a `SET` column a value containing substrings that are not listed as set members, those strings drop out and the column is assigned a value consisting of the remaining members.

- For date or time columns, illegal values are converted to the appropriate "zero" value for the type (see Table 2.12).

These conversions are reported as warnings for ALTER TABLE, LOAD DATA, UPDATE, INSERT INTO ... SELECT, and multiple-row INSERT statements. In the mysql client, this information is displayed in the status line that is reported for a query. In a programming language, you may be able to get this information by some other means. If you're using the MySQL C or PHP APIs, you can invoke the mysql_info() function. With the Perl DBI API, you can use the mysql_info attribute of your database connection. The information provided is a count of the number of warnings.

3

MySQL SQL
Syntax and Use

FLUENCY WITH SQL IS NECESSARY FOR EFFECTIVE communication with the
MySQL server, because that is the language that it understands. For example,
when you use a program such as the mysql client, it functions primarily as a
means for you to send SQL statements to the server to be executed. You must
also know SQL if you write programs that use the MySQL interface provided
by your programming language because the interface functions as the means that
allows you to communicate with the server by sending SQL statements to it.

Chapter 1, "Getting Started with MySQL and SQL," presented a tutorial
introduction to many of MySQL's capabilities. This chapter builds on that
material to go into more detail on several areas of SQL implemented by
MySQL. It discusses how to refer to elements of databases, including the rules
for naming and the case sensitivity constraints that apply. It also describes many
of the more important SQL statements that are used for the following types of
operations:

- Creating and destroying databases, tables, and indexes
- Obtaining information about your databases and tables
- Retrieving data using joins, subselects, and unions
- Using multiple-table deletes and updates

- Performing transactions that allow multiple statements to be treated as a unit
- Setting up foreign key relationships
- Using the FULLTEXT search engine

MySQL's SQL statements can be grouped into several broad categories; Table 3.1 lists some representative statements for each. In some cases, a utility program is available that provides a command-line interface to a statement. For example, mysqlshow allows SHOW operations to be performed from the command line. This chapter points out such equivalences where appropriate.

Some of the statements in the table are not covered here because they are more appropriately discussed in other chapters. For example, the administrative statements GRANT and REVOKE for setting up user privileges are dealt with in Chapter 11, "General MySQL Administration." Chapter 12, "Security," provides further details on what privileges are available and what they allow. The syntax for all SQL statements implemented by MySQL is listed in Appendix D, "SQL Syntax Reference." In addition, you should consult the MySQL Reference Manual for additional information, especially for changes made in recent versions of MySQL.

Table 3.1 **Types of SQL Statements Supported by MySQL**

SELECTING, CREATING, DROPPING, AND ALTERING DATABASES
```
USE
CREATE DATABASE
DROP DATABASE
ALTER DATABASE
```

CREATING, ALTERING, AND DROPPING TABLES AND INDEXES
```
CREATE TABLE
DROP TABLE
CREATE INDEX
DROP INDEX
ALTER TABLE
```

GETTING INFORMATION ABOUT DATABASES AND TABLES
```
DESCRIBE
SHOW
```

RETRIEVING INFORMATION FROM TABLES
  SELECT
  UNION

PERFORMING TRANSACTIONS
  BEGIN
  COMMIT
  ROLLBACK
  SET AUTOCOMMIT

MODIFYING INFORMATION IN TABLES
  DELETE
  INSERT
  LOAD DATA
  REPLACE
  UPDATE

ADMINISTRATIVE STATEMENTS
  FLUSH
  GRANT
  REVOKE

The final section of the chapter describes what MySQL does not include—that is, what features it lacks. These are capabilities found in some other databases but not in MySQL. Such features include triggers, stored procedures, and views. Do these omissions mean that MySQL isn't a "real" database system? Some people think so, but in response I'll simply observe that the lack of these capabilities in MySQL hasn't stopped large numbers of people from using it. That's probably because for many or most applications, those features don't matter.

I should also point out that the set of features missing from MySQL continues to shrink over time. For the first edition of this book, the list of missing features included transactions, subselects, foreign keys, and referential integrity. A significant amount of progress has been made in improving MySQL since then, and those capabilities all have been added now. Triggers, stored procedures, and views are scheduled for implementation in the future.

MySQL Naming Rules

Almost every SQL statement refers in some way to a database or its constituent elements. This section describes the syntax rules for referring to databases, tables, columns, indexes, and aliases. Names are subject to case sensitivity considerations, which are described as well.

Referring to Elements of Databases

When you use names to refer to elements of databases, you are constrained by the characters you can use and the length that names can be. The form of names also depends on the context in which you use them. Another factor that affects naming rules is that the server can be started in different naming modes.

- **Legal characters in names.** Unquoted names can consist of any alphanumeric characters in the server's default character set, plus the characters '_' and '$'. Names can start with any character that is legal in a name, including a digit. However, a name cannot consist entirely of digits because that would make it indistinguishable from a number. MySQL's support for names that begin with a number is somewhat unusual among database systems. If you use such a name, be particularly careful of names containing an 'E' or 'e' because those characters can lead to ambiguous expressions. For example, the expression 23e + 14 (with spaces surrounding the '+' sign) means column 23e plus the number 14, but what about 23e+14? Does it mean the same thing, or is it a number in scientific notation?

  Aliases can be fairly arbitrary, but you should quote an alias within single or double quotes if it is a SQL keyword, is entirely numeric, or contains spaces or other special characters.

  As of MySQL 3.23.6, names can be quoted within backtick characters ('`'), which allows use of any character except backtick, ASCII 0, and ASCII 255. This is useful when a name contains special characters or is a reserved word. Quoting a name also allows it to be entirely numeric, something that is not true of unquoted names.

  There are also two additional constraints for database and table names, even if you quote them. First, you cannot use the '.' character because it is the separator in *db_name.tbl_name* and *db_name.tbl_name.col_name* notation. Second, you cannot use the UNIX or Windows pathname separator characters ('/' or '\'). The separator characters are disallowed in database and table names because databases are represented on disk by directories, and tables are represented on disk by at least one file. Consequently, these types of names must not contain characters that are illegal in directory names and filenames. The UNIX pathname separator is disallowed on Windows (and vice versa) to make it easier to transfer databases and tables between servers running on different platforms. For example, suppose you were allowed to use a slash in a table name on Windows. That would make it impossible to move the table to UNIX, because filenames on that platform cannot contain slashes.

- **Name length.** Names for databases, tables, columns, and indexes can be up to 64 characters long. Alias names can be up to 256 characters long.

- **Name qualifiers.** Depending on context, a name may need to be qualified to make it clear what the name refers to. To refer to a database, just specify its name:

```
USE db_name;
SHOW TABLES FROM db_name;
```

To refer to a table, you have two choices. First, a fully qualified table name consists of a database name and a table name:

```
SHOW TABLES FROM db_name.tbl_name;
SELECT * FROM db_name.tbl_name;
```

Second, a table name by itself refers to a table in the default (current) database. If sampdb is the default database, the following statements are equivalent:

```
SELECT * FROM member;
SELECT * FROM sampdb.member;
```

If no database has been selected, naming a table without a database qualifier is illegal because the server cannot tell which database the table belongs to.

To refer to a column, there are three choices: fully qualified, partially qualified, and unqualified. A fully qualified name (written as db_name.tbl_name.col_name) is completely specified. A partially qualified name (written as tbl_name.col_name) refers to a column in the named table. An unqualified name (written simply as col_name) refers to whatever table is indicated by the surrounding context. The following two queries refer to the same pair of column names, but the context supplied by the FROM clause of each statement indicates from which table to select the columns:

```
SELECT last_name, first_name FROM president;
SELECT last_name, first_name FROM members;
```

It's usually unnecessary to supply fully qualified names, although it's always legal to do so if you want. If you select a database with a USE statement, that database becomes the default database and is implicit in every unqualified table reference. If you're using a SELECT statement that refers to only one table, that table is implicit for every column reference in the statement. It's necessary to qualify names only when a table or database cannot be determined from context. For example, if a query refers to tables from multiple databases, any table not in the default database must be referenced using the *db_name.tbl_name* form to let MySQL know which database to look in to find the table. Similarly, if a query uses multiple tables and refers to a column name that is present in more than one table, it's necessary to qualify the name with a table name to make it clear which column you mean.

- **Server startup mode.** If the server has been started with the `--ansi` or `--sql-mode=ANSI_QUOTES` option, names can be quoted with double quotes rather than backticks (although backticks can still be used).

Case Sensitivity in SQL Statements

Case sensitivity rules in SQL statements vary for different parts of the statement and also depend on what you referring to and the operating system of the machine on which the server is running:

- **SQL keywords and function names.** Keywords and function names are not case sensitive. They can be given in any lettercase. The following statements are equivalent:

  ```
  SELECT NOW();
  select now();
  sElEcT nOw();
  ```

- **Database and table names.** Databases and tables in MySQL are implemented using directories and files in the underlying file system on the server host. As a result, case sensitivity of database and table names depends on the way the operating system on that host treats filenames. Windows filenames are not case sensitive, so a server running on Windows does not treat database and table names as case sensitive. Servers running on UNIX usually treat database and table names as case sensitive because UNIX filenames are case sensitive. (An exception is that names in HFS+ file systems under Mac OS X are not case sensitive.)

  You should consider lettercase issues if you create a database on a server with case-sensitive filenames and you might someday move the database to a server where filenames are not case sensitive. For example, if you create two tables named abc and ABC on a UNIX server where those names are treated differently, you would have problems moving the tables to a Windows machine; there, abc and ABC would not be distinguishable because names are not case sensitive. One way to avoid having case sensitivity properties become an issue is to pick a given lettercase (for example, lowercase) and always create databases and tables using names in that lettercase. Then case of names won't be a problem if you move a database to a different server. Another approach to issues of name lettercase is to start the server with the `lower_case_table_names` variable set. This variable is discussed further in Chapter 10, "The MySQL Data Directory."

- **Column and index names.** Column and index names are not case sensitive in MySQL. The following queries are equivalent:

```
SELECT name FROM student;
SELECT NAME FROM student;
SELECT nAmE FROM student;
```

- **Alias names.** Aliases are not case sensitive, except for table aliases. You can specify an alias in any lettercase (upper, lower, or mixed), but you must refer to a table alias using the same lettercase consistently throughout the query.

Regardless of whether or not a database or table name is case sensitive on your system, you must refer to it using the same lettercase throughout a given query. That is not true for SQL keywords, function names, or column and index names, all of which can be referred to in varying lettercase style throughout a query. Naturally, the query will be more readable if you use a consistent lettercase rather than "ransom note" style (`SelECt NamE FrOm ...`).

Selecting, Creating, Dropping, and Altering Databases

MySQL provides several database-level statements: USE for selecting a default database, CREATE DATABASE for creating databases, DROP DATABASE for removing them, and ALTER DATABASE for modifying global database characteristics.

Selecting Databases

The USE statement selects a database to make it the default (current) database for a given connection to the server:

```
USE db_name;
```

You must have some access privilege for the database or you cannot select it. If you do have access to a database, you can use its tables even without selecting the database explicitly by qualifying table names with the database name. For example, to retrieve the contents of the `president` table in the `sampdb` database without selecting the database first, write the query like this:

```
SELECT * FROM sampdb.president;
```

However, it's much more convenient to refer to tables without having to specify a database qualifier.

Selecting a default database doesn't mean it must be the default for the duration of the connection. You can issue any number of `USE` statements to switch back and forth among databases as often as you want, as long as you have access privileges to use them. Nor does selecting a database limit you to using tables only from that database. While one database is the default, you can refer to tables in other databases by qualifying their names with the appropriate database name.

When a connection to the server terminates, any notion by the server of what the default database was disappears. That is, if you connect to the server again, it doesn't remember what database you had selected previously. In fact, that's not even an idea that makes any sense, given that MySQL is multi-threaded and can handle multiple connections from a given user, which can begin and end asynchronously. In this environment, it's not clear what the meaning of "the previously selected database" might be.

Creating Databases

Creating a database is easy; just name it in a `CREATE DATABASE` statement:

```
CREATE DATABASE db_name;
```

The constraints on database creation are that the name must be legal, the database must not already exist, and you must have sufficient privileges to create it.

Dropping Databases

Dropping a database is just as easy as creating one, assuming you have sufficient privileges:

```
DROP DATABASE db_name;
```

However, the `DROP DATABASE` statement is not something you should use with wild abandon. It removes the database and all tables within it. After you drop a database, it's gone forever. In other words, don't try out this statement just to see how it works. If your administrator has been performing database backups regularly, you may be able to get the database back. But I can guarantee that no administrator will be sympathetic if you say, "Uh, I was just playing around with DROP DATABASE to see what would happen, and, uh...can you restore my database for me?"

Note that a database is represented by a directory under the data directory, and the directory is intended for storage of table data. If you drop a database but its name continues to show up when you issue a SHOW DATABASES statement, the reason is most likely that the database directory contains non-table files. DROP DATABASE will not delete such files and, as a result, will not delete the directory either. This means that the database directory will continue to exist, albeit empty of any tables. To really drop the database if this occurs, manually remove any remaining files in the database directory and the directory itself.

Altering Databases

The ALTER DATABASE statement, available as of MySQL 4.1, makes changes to a database's global characteristics or attributes. Currently, the only such characteristic is the default character set:

```
ALTER DATABASE db_name DEFAULT CHARACTER SET charset;
```

charset should be the name of a character set supported by the server, such as greek or sjis. (To find out which sets your server supports, issue a SHOW CHARACTER SET statement.) charset can also be DEFAULT to indicate that the database uses the server-level character set by default. See Chapter 2, "Working with Data in MySQL," for further discussion of character sets and character set levels.

Database attributes are stored in the db.opt file in the database directory.

Creating, Dropping, Indexing, and Altering Tables

MySQL allows you to create tables, drop (remove) them, and change their structure using the CREATE TABLE, DROP TABLE, and ALTER TABLE statements. The CREATE INDEX and DROP INDEX statements allow you to add or remove indexes on existing tables. But before diving into the details for these statements, it's helpful to understand something about the different types of tables that MySQL supports.

Table Types

MySQL supports multiple table handlers, each of which implements a table type that has a specific set of properties or characteristics. The table types actually available to you will depend on your version of MySQL, how it was configured at build time, and the options with which it was started. The current table type handlers and the versions in which they are first available are listed in the following table:

Table Type	MySQL Version First Available
ISAM	All versions
MyISAM	3.23.0
MERGE	3.23.25
HEAP	3.23.0
BDB	3.23.17/3.23.34a
InnoDB	3.23.29/3.23.34a

Two version numbers are listed for BDB and InnoDB. The first number indicates when the table type appeared in binary distributions, the second when it became available in source distributions. MRG_MyISAM and BerkeleyDB are synonyms for MERGE and BDB. (From 3.23.29 through 3.23.36, the InnoDB table type was known as Innobase; thereafter, InnoDB is the preferred name, though Innobase is recognized as a synonym.)

Because MySQL can be configured in different ways, it's quite possible that a server for a given version of MySQL will not support all table types available in that version. See the "Getting Information about Databases and Tables" section later in this chapter to find out how to tell which types a given server actually supports. See the "Selecting Table Handlers" section in Chapter 11 for details on configuring the server.

The general characteristics of MySQL's table types are described in the following sections.

ISAM Tables

The ISAM handler manages tables that use the indexed sequential access method. The ISAM storage format is the original MySQL table type and is the only one available prior to Version 3.23. The ISAM handler has since been superceded by the MyISAM handler; MyISAM tables are the preferred general replacement because they have fewer limitations. The ISAM type is still available but is considered pretty much obsolete. Support for it will fade over time. (ISAM table support has been omitted from the embedded server now, for example, and probably will disappear entirely in MySQL 5.)

MyISAM Tables

The MyISAM storage format is the default table type in MySQL as of version 3.23, unless the server has been configured otherwise.

- Tables can be larger than for the ISAM storage method if your operating system itself allows large file sizes.

- Table contents are stored in machine-independent format. This means you can copy tables directly from one machine to another, even if they have different architectures.

- Relative to ISAM tables, MyISAM relaxes several indexing constraints. For details, see the "Indexing Tables" section later in this section.

- MyISAM format provides better key compression than does ISAM format. Both formats use compression when storing runs of successive similar string index values, but MyISAM also can compress runs of similar numeric index values because numeric values are stored with the high byte first. (Index values tend to vary faster in the low-order bytes, so high-order bytes are more subject to compression.) To enable numeric compression, use the PACK_KEYS=1 option when creating a table.

- MyISAM has more capable AUTO_INCREMENT handling than is available for other table types. The details of this are discussed in the "Working with Sequences" section of Chapter 2.

- For improved table integrity checking, each MyISAM table has a flag that is set when the table is checked by the server or by myisamchk. MyISAM tables also have a flag indicating whether a table was closed properly. If the server shuts down abnormally or the machine crashes, the flag can be used to detect tables that need to be checked. This can be done automatically at server startup time by specifying the --myisam-recover option.

- The MyISAM handler supports full text searching through the use of FULLTEXT indexes.

MERGE Tables

MERGE tables are a means for grouping multiple MyISAM tables into a single logical unit. By querying a MERGE table, you are in effect querying all the constituent tables. One advantage of this is that you can in effect exceed the maximum table size allowed by the file system for individual MyISAM tables.

The tables that make up a MERGE table must all have the same structure. This means the columns in each table must be defined with the same names and types in the same order, and the indexes must be defined in the same way and in the same order. It is allowable to mix compressed and uncompressed tables. (Compressed tables are produced with myisampack; see Appendix E, "MySQL Program Reference.")

A MERGE table cannot refer to tables in a different database.

HEAP Tables

The HEAP storage format uses tables that are stored in memory and that have fixed-length rows, two characteristics that make them very fast. HEAP tables are temporary in the sense that they disappear when the server terminates. However, in contrast to temporary tables created with CREATE TEMPORARY TABLE, HEAP tables are visible to other clients. Several constraints apply to HEAP tables that allow them to be handled more simply and thus more quickly:

- Indexes are used only for comparisons performed with the = and <=> operators. This is due to the use of hashed indexes, which are very fast for equality comparisons but not for range searches with comparison operators such as < or >. Indexes also are not used in ORDER BY clauses for this reason.
- You cannot have NULL values in indexed columns prior to MySQL 4.0.2.
- AUTO_INCREMENT columns cannot be used prior to MySQL 4.1.
- BLOB and TEXT columns cannot be used. Because rows are stored using fixed-length format, you cannot use variable length column types such as BLOB and TEXT. VARCHAR is allowed but is treated internally as the corresponding CHAR type.

BDB Tables

BDB tables are managed by the Berkeley DB handler developed by Sleepycat. The BDB handler offers these features:

- Transaction-safe tables with commit and rollback
- Automatic recovery after a crash
- Page-level locking for good concurrency performance under query mix conditions that include both retrievals and updates

InnoDB Tables

InnoDB tables are the most recent table type added to MySQL. They are managed by the InnoDB handler developed by Innobase Oy. The InnoDB handler offers the following features:

- Transaction-safe tables with commit and rollback.
- Automatic recovery after a crash.
- Foreign key support, including cascaded delete.
- Row-level locking for good concurrency performance under query mix conditions that include both retrievals and updates.
- InnoDB tables are managed within a separate tablespace rather than by using table-specific files like the other table types. The tablespace can consist of multiple files and can include raw partitions. The InnoDB handler, in effect, treats the tablespace as a virtual file system within which it manages the contents of all InnoDB tables.
- Tables can exceed the size allowed by the file system for individual files through use of multiple files or raw partitions in the tablespace.

Table Representation on Disk

Every table, no matter its format, is represented on disk by a file that contains the table's format (that is, its definition). This file has a basename that is the same as the table name and a `.frm` extension. For most table types, a table's contents are stored on disk using other files that are unique to the table. The exceptions are for HEAP and InnoDB tables, for which the `.frm` file is the only one that is uniquely associated with a given table. (HEAP table contents are stored in memory. InnoDB table contents are managed within the InnoDB tablespace in common with other InnoDB tables, not within files specific to a particular table.) The various table types use files with the following extensions:

Table Type	Files on Disk
ISAM	`.frm` (definition), `.ISD` (data), `.ISM` (indexes)
MyISAM	`.frm` (definition), `.MYD` (data), `.MYI` (indexes)
MERGE	`.frm` (definition), `.MRG` (list of constituent MyISAM table names)
HEAP	`.frm` (definition)
BDB	`.frm` (definition), `.db` (data and indexes)
InnoDB	`.frm` (definition)

For any given table, the files specific to it are located in the directory that represents the database to which the table belongs.

Table Type Portability Characteristics

Any table is portable to another server in the sense that you can dump it into a text file with `mysqldump`, move the file to the machine where the other server runs, and load the file to recreate the table. Portability as described in this section means that you can directly copy the files that represent the table on disk to another machine, install them into a database directory, and expect the MySQL server there to be able to use the table. Of course, HEAP tables do not satisfy this definition because their contents are stored in memory, not on disk. Of the other table types, some are portable and some are not:

- ISAM tables are stored in a machine-dependent format, so they are portable only between machines that have identical hardware characteristics.
- BDB tables are not portable because the location of the table is encoded into the table's `.db` file. This makes a BDB table location-specific within the file system of the machine on which the table was created. (That's the conservative view of BDB portability. I have experimented with BDB files in various ways, such as by moving them between database directories, renaming the files to use a different basename, and so on. I have not observed ill effects. But presumably it's better to play it safe and move BDB tables by dumping them with `mysqldump` and re-creating them on the destination machine by reloading the dump file.)
- MyISAM and InnoDB tables are stored in machine-independent format and are portable, assuming that your processor uses two's-complement integer arithmetic and IEEE floating-point format. Unless you have some kind of oddball machine, neither of these conditions should present any real issues. In practice, you're probably most likely to see portability-compromising variation in hardware if you're using an embedded server built for a special-purpose device, as these sometimes will use processors that have non-standard operating characteristics.
- MERGE tables are portable as long as their constituent MyISAM files are portable.

In essence, the portability requirements for MyISAM and InnoDB tables are that they either contain no floating-point columns or that both machines use the same floating-point storage format. "Floating-point" means FLOAT and DOUBLE here. DECIMAL columns are stored as strings, which are portable.

Note that for InnoDB, portability must be assessed at the tablespace level, not at the table level. The InnoDB handler stores the contents of all InnoDB tables within the tablespace rather than within table-specific files. Consequently, it's the InnoDB tablespace files that are or are not portable, not individual InnoDB tables. This means that the floating-point portability constraint applies if *any* InnoDB table uses floating-point columns.

Regardless of a table type's general portability characteristics, you should not attempt to copy table or tablespace files to another machine unless the server has been shut down cleanly. You cannot assume the integrity of your tables if you perform a copy after an unclean shutdown; they may be in need of repair or there may be transaction information still stored in a table handler's log files that needs to be applied or rolled back to bring tables up to date.

Similarly, if the server is running and actively updating tables, the table contents on disk will be in flux and the associated files will not yield usable table copies. In the case of a running server, you may be able to tell it to leave the tables alone while you copy them. For details, see Chapter 13, "Database Backups, Maintenance, and Repair."

Creating Tables

To create a table, use a CREATE TABLE statement. The full syntax for this statement is complex because there are so many optional clauses, but in practice, it's usually fairly simple to use. For example, all of the CREATE TABLE statements that we used in Chapter 1 are reasonably uncomplicated. If you start with the more basic forms and work up, you shouldn't have much trouble.

The CREATE TABLE specifies, at a minimum, the table name and a list of the columns in it—for example:

```
CREATE TABLE mytbl
(
    name   CHAR(20),
    age    INT NOT NULL,
    weight INT,
    sex    ENUM('F','M')
);
```

In addition to the columns that make up a table, you can specify how the table should be indexed when you create it. Another option is to leave the table unindexed when you create it and add the indexes later. (For MyISAM and ISAM tables, that's a good strategy if you plan to populate the table with a lot of data before you begin using it for queries. Updating indexes as you insert each row is much slower for those table types than loading the data into an unindexed table and creating the indexes afterward.)

We have already covered the basic syntax for the CREATE TABLE statement in Chapter 1 and discussed how to write column definitions in Chapter 2. I assume you've read those chapters and won't repeat that material here. Instead, the remainder of this section deals with some important extensions to the CREATE TABLE statement that were introduced beginning with MySQL 3.23 and that give you a lot of flexibility in how you construct tables:

- Table options that modify storage characteristics
- Creation of a table only if it doesn't already exist
- Temporary tables that are dropped automatically when the client session ends
- The capability of creating a table from the result of a SELECT query
- Using MERGE tables

Table Options

As of MySQL 3.23, you can add table options after the closing parenthesis in the CREATE TABLE statement to modify the table's storage characteristics. For example, prior to MySQL 3.23, any table created will be of type ISAM, because that is the only type available. From 3.23 on, you can add a TYPE = *tbl_type* option to specify the type explicitly. For example, to create a HEAP or InnoDB table, write the statement like this (the table type name is not case sensitive):

```
CREATE TABLE mytbl ( ... ) TYPE = HEAP;
CREATE TABLE mytbl ( ... ) TYPE = INNODB;
```

With no TYPE specifier, the server creates the table using its default type. This will be MyISAM unless you reconfigure the server to use a different default, either when you build the server or by giving a --default-table-type option at server startup time. If you specify a table type name that is syntactically legal but for which the handler is unavailable, MySQL creates the table using the default type. If you give an illegal table type, an error results.

Other table options can be given as well. Many of them apply only to particular table types. For example, a MIN_ROWS = *n* option can be used with HEAP tables to allow the HEAP handler to optimize memory usage:

```
CREATE TABLE mytbl ( ... ) TYPE = HEAP MIN_ROWS = 10000;
```

If the handler considers the value of MIN_ROWS to be large, it may allocate memory in larger hunks to avoid the overhead of making many allocation calls.

A complete list of table options is given in the entry for CREATE TABLE in Appendix D.

For an existing table, table options can be used with an ALTER TABLE statement to modify the table's current characteristics. For example, to change
mytbl from its current table type to InnoDB, do this:

```
ALTER TABLE mytbl TYPE = INNODB;
```

The types allowed when you convert a table's type may depend on the feature
compatibility of the old and new types. Suppose you have a MyISAM table
that includes a BLOB column. You will not be able to convert the table to
HEAP format because HEAP tables do not support BLOB columns.

Provisional Table Creation

To create a table only if it doesn't already exist, use CREATE TABLE IF NOT
EXISTS. This feature is available as of MySQL 3.23.0. You can use it for an
application that makes no assumptions about whether a table that it needs has
been set up in advance. The application can go ahead and attempt to create
the table as a matter of course. The IF NOT EXISTS modifier is particularly
useful for scripts that you run as batch jobs with mysql. In this context, a regular CREATE TABLE statement doesn't work very well. The first time the job
runs, it creates the table, but the second time an error occurs because the table
already exists. If you use IF NOT EXISTS, there is no problem. The first time
the job runs, it creates the table, as before. For the second and subsequent
times, table creation attempts are silently ignored without error. This allows the
job to continue processing as if the attempt had succeeded.

Temporary Tables

You can use CREATE TEMPORARY TABLE to create temporary tables that disappear automatically when your session ends. This is handy because you don't
have to bother issuing a DROP TABLE statement explicitly to get rid of the
table, and the table doesn't hang around if your session terminates abnormally.
For example, if you have a canned query in a batch file that you run with
mysql and decide not to wait for it to finish, you can kill the script in the
middle with impunity and the server will remove any temporary tables that
the script creates.

A temporary table is visible only to the client that creates the table. The name
can be the same as that of an existing permanent table. This is not an error,
nor does the existing permanent table get clobbered. Instead, the permanent
table becomes hidden (inaccessible) while the temporary table exists. Suppose
you create a temporary table in the sampdb database named member. The original member table becomes hidden, and references to member refer to the temporary table. If you issue a DROP TABLE member statement, the temporary

table is removed and the original member table "reappears." If you simply disconnect from the server without dropping the temporary table, the server automatically drops it for you. The next time you connect, the original member table is visible again. (The original table also reappears if you rename a temporary table that hides it to have a different name. If the temporary table's new name happens to be that of another permanent table, that table becomes hidden while the temporary table has its name.)

The name-hiding mechanism works only to one level. That is, you cannot create two temporary tables with the same name.

A TEMPORARY table can be created with a particular storage format by using a TYPE option. (Prior to MySQL 3.23.54, a MERGE table cannot be TEMPORARY.)

Prior to MySQL 3.23.2, TEMPORARY is unavailable, so there are no true temporary tables except in the sense that you consider them temporary in your own mind. You must remember to drop such a table yourself. If you forget, the table hangs around until you notice and remove it. Table persistence also occurs if an application creates a table but exits early due to an error before it can drop the table.

Creating Tables from SELECT Query Results

One of the key concepts of relational databases is that everything is represented as a table of rows and columns, and the result of every SELECT is also a table of rows and columns. In many cases, the "table" that results from a SELECT is just an image of rows and columns that scroll off the top of your display as you continue working. But sometimes it is desirable to save a query result in another table so that you can refer to it later.

As of MySQL 3.23.0, you can do that easily. Use a CREATE TABLE ... SELECT statement to cause a new table to spring into existence on-the-fly to hold the result of an arbitrary SELECT query. You can do this in a single step without having to know or specify the data types of the columns you're retrieving. This makes it exceptionally easy to create a table fully populated with the data you're interested in, ready to be used in further queries. For example, the following statement creates a new table named student_f that consists of information for all female students in the student table:

```
CREATE TABLE student_f SELECT * FROM student WHERE sex = 'f';
```

To copy an entire table, omit the WHERE clause:

```
CREATE TABLE new_tbl_name SELECT * FROM tbl_name;
```

Or, to create an empty copy, use a WHERE clause that always evaluates to false:

```
CREATE TABLE new_tbl_name SELECT * FROM tbl_name WHERE 0;
```

Creating an empty copy of a table is useful if you want to load a data file into the original table using LOAD DATA, but you're not sure if you have the options for specifying the data format quite right. You don't want to end up with malformed records in the original table if you don't get the options right the first time! Using an empty copy of the original table allows you to experiment with the LOAD DATA options for specifying column and line delimiters until you're satisfied your input records are being interpreted properly. After you're satisfied, you can load the file into the original table. Do that either by rerunning the LOAD DATA statement with the original table name or by copying the data into it from the copy:

```
INSERT INTO orig_tbl SELECT * FROM copy_tbl;
```

You can combine CREATE TEMPORARY TABLE with SELECT to retrieve a table's contents into a temporary copy of itself:

```
CREATE TEMPORARY TABLE mytbl SELECT * FROM mytbl;
```

That allows you to modify the contents of mytbl without affecting the original, which can be useful when you want to try out some queries that modify the contents of the table, but you don't want to change the original table. To use pre-written scripts that use the original table name, you don't need to edit them to refer to a different table; just add the CREATE TEMPORARY TABLE statement to the beginning of the script. The script will create a temporary copy and operate on the copy, and the server will delete the copy when the script finishes. (One caution to observe here is that some clients, such as mysql, attempt to reconnect to the server automatically if the connection drops. Should this happen when you're working with the temporary table, it will be dropped and the queries executed subsequent to reconnecting will use the original table. Keep this in mind if you have an unreliable network.)

To create a table as an empty copy of itself, use a WHERE clause that is never true in conjunction with CREATE TEMPORARY TABLE ... SELECT:

```
CREATE TEMPORARY TABLE mytbl SELECT * FROM mytbl WHERE 0;
```

Creating a table on-the-fly from the results of a SELECT statement is a powerful capability, but there are several issues to consider when doing this.

With CREATE TABLE ... SELECT, you should use aliases as necessary to provide reasonable column names. When you create a table by selecting data into it, the column names are taken from the columns that you are selecting. If a column is calculated as the result of an expression, the "name" of the column is the text of the expression. Prior to MySQL 3.23.6, the following statement will fail outright, because expressions aren't legal as column names:

```
mysql> CREATE TABLE mytbl SELECT PI();
ERROR 1166: Incorrect column name 'PI()'
```

From 3.23.6 on, column naming rules are relaxed, so the statement will succeed but create a table with an unusual column name:

```
mysql> CREATE TABLE mytbl SELECT PI();
mysql> SELECT * FROM mytbl;
+----------+
| PI()     |
+----------+
| 3.141593 |
+----------+
```

That's unfortunate, because the column name can be referred to directly only by enclosing it within backticks:

```
mysql> SELECT `PI()` FROM mytbl;
+----------+
| PI()     |
+----------+
| 3.141593 |
+----------+
```

To provide a column name that is easier to work with when selecting an expression, use an alias:

```
mysql> CREATE TABLE mytbl SELECT PI() AS mycol;
mysql> SELECT mycol FROM mytbl;
+----------+
| mycol    |
+----------+
| 3.141593 |
+----------+
```

A related snag occurs if you select columns from different tables that have the same name. Suppose tables t1 and t2 both have a column c and you want to create a table from all combinations of rows in both tables. The following statement will fail because it attempts to create a table with two columns named c:

```
mysql> CREATE TABLE t3 SELECT * FROM t1, t2;
ERROR 1060: Duplicate column name 'c'
```

You can provide aliases to specify unique column names in the new table:

```
mysql> CREATE TABLE t3 SELECT t1.c AS c1, t2.c AS c2 FROM t1, t2;
```

Another thing to watch out for is that characteristics of the original table that are not reflected in the selected data will not be incorporated into the structure of the new table. For example, creating a table by selecting data into it does not automatically copy any indexes from the original table, because result sets are not themselves indexed. Similarly, column attributes such as AUTO_INCREMENT or the default value may not be carried into the new table. (Newer versions do better than older ones.) In some cases, you can force specific attributes to be used in the new table by invoking the CAST() function, which is available as of MySQL 4.0.2. The following CREATE TABLE ... SELECT statement forces the columns produced by the SELECT to be treated as INT UNSIGNED, DATE, and CHAR BINARY, which you can verify with DESCRIBE:

```
mysql> CREATE TABLE mytbl SELECT
    -> CAST(1 AS UNSIGNED) AS i,
    -> CAST(CURDATE() AS DATE) AS d,
    -> CAST('Hello, world' AS BINARY) AS c;
mysql> DESCRIBE mytbl;
+-------+------------------+------+-----+------------+-------+
| Field | Type             | Null | Key | Default    | Extra |
+-------+------------------+------+-----+------------+-------+
| i     | int(1) unsigned  |      |     | 0          |       |
| d     | date             |      |     | 0000-00-00 |       |
| c     | char(12) binary  |      |     |            |       |
+-------+------------------+------+-----+------------+-------+
```

You can apply CAST() to column values retrieved from other tables as well. The allowable cast types are BINARY (binary string), DATE, DATETIME, TIME, SIGNED, SIGNED INTEGER, UNSIGNED, and UNSIGNED INTEGER.

As of MySQL 4.1, it's possible to provide even more information about the types that you want the columns in the new table to have by giving explicit definitions for them. Columns in the table are matched with the selected columns by name, so provide aliases for the selected columns if necessary to cause them to match up properly:

```
mysql> CREATE TABLE mytbl (i INT UNSIGNED, d DATE, c CHAR(20) BINARY)
    -> SELECT
    -> 1 AS i,
    -> CURDATE() AS d,
    -> 'Hello, world' AS c;
mysql> DESCRIBE mytbl;
+-------+------------------+------+-----+---------+-------+
| Field | Type             | Null | Key | Default | Extra |
+-------+------------------+------+-----+---------+-------+
| i     | int(10) unsigned | YES  |     | NULL    |       |
| d     | date             | YES  |     | NULL    |       |
| c     | char(20) binary  | YES  |     | NULL    |       |
+-------+------------------+------+-----+---------+-------+
```

Note that this allows you to create character columns that have a different width than that of the longest value in the result set. Also note that the `Null` and `Default` attributes of the columns are different for this example than for the previous one. You could provide explicit declarations for those attributes as well if necessary.

Prior to MySQL 3.23, `CREATE TABLE ... SELECT` is unavailable. If you want to save the results of a `SELECT` in a table for use in further queries, you must make special arrangements in advance:

1. Run a `DESCRIBE` or `SHOW COLUMNS` query to determine the types of the columns in the tables from which you want to capture information.

2. Issue an explicit `CREATE TABLE` statement to create the table into which you want to save the `SELECT` results. The statement should specify the names and types of the columns that the `SELECT` will retrieve.

3. After creating the table, issue an `INSERT INTO ... SELECT` query to retrieve the results and insert them into the table.

Clearly, compared to `CREATE TABLE ... SELECT`, this involves a lot of ugly messing around.

Using MERGE Tables

The MERGE table type, available in MySQL 3.23.25 and up, provides a way to perform queries on a set of tables simultaneously by treating them all as a single logical unit. As described earlier in the "Table Types" section, MERGE can be applied to a collection of MyISAM tables that all have identical structure. Suppose you have a set of individual log tables that contain log entries on a year-by-year basis and that each are defined like this, where *CCYY* represents the century and year:

```
CREATE TABLE log_CCYY
(
    dt     DATETIME NOT NULL,
    info   VARCHAR(100) NOT NULL,
    INDEX (dt)
) TYPE = MYISAM;
```

If the current set of log tables includes `log_1999`, `log_2000`, `log_2001`, `log_2002`, and `log_2003`, you can set up a MERGE table that maps onto them like this:

```
CREATE TABLE log_all
(
    dt     DATETIME NOT NULL,
    info   VARCHAR(100) NOT NULL,
    INDEX (dt)
) TYPE = MERGE UNION = (log_1999, log_2000, log_2001, log_2002, log_2003);
```

The TYPE option must be MERGE, and the UNION option lists the tables to be included in the MERGE table. After the table has been set up, you query it just like any other table, but the queries will refer to all the constituent tables at once. The following query determines the total number of rows in all the log tables:

```
SELECT COUNT(*) FROM log_all;
```

This query determines how many log entries there are per year:

```
SELECT YEAR(dt) AS y, COUNT(*) AS entries FROM log_all GROUP BY y;
```

Besides the convenience of being able to refer to multiple tables without issuing multiple queries, MERGE tables offer some other nice features:

- A MERGE table can be used to create a logical entity that exceeds the allowable size of individual MyISAM tables.

- You can include compressed tables in the collection. For example, after a given year comes to an end, you wouldn't be adding any more entries to the corresponding log file, so you could compress it with myisampack to save space. The MERGE table will continue to function as before.

- Operations on MERGE tables are similar to UNION operations. UNION is unavailable prior to MySQL 4, but MERGE tables can be used in some cases as a workaround.

MERGE tables also support DELETE and UPDATE operations. INSERT is trickier, because MySQL needs to know which table to insert new records into. As of MySQL 4.0.0, MERGE table definitions can include an INSERT_METHOD option with a value of NO, FIRST, or LAST to indicate that INSERT is forbidden or that records should be inserted into the first or last table named in the UNION option. For example, the following definition would cause an INSERT into log_all to be treated as an INSERT into log_2003, the last table named in the UNION option:

```
CREATE TABLE log_all
(
    dt      DATETIME NOT NULL,
    info    VARCHAR(100) NOT NULL,
    INDEX (dt)
) TYPE = MERGE UNION = (log_1999, log_2000, log_2001, log_2002, log_2003)
INSERT_METHOD = LAST;
```

Dropping Tables

Dropping a table is much easier than creating it because you don't have to specify anything about its contents. You just have to name it:

```
DROP TABLE tbl_name;
```

MySQL extends the DROP TABLE statement in some useful ways. First, you can drop several tables by specifying them all on the same statement:

```
DROP TABLE tbl_name1, tbl_name2, ... ;
```

Second, if you're not sure whether or not a table exists, but you want to drop it if it does, you can add IF EXISTS to the statement. This causes MySQL not to complain or issue an error if the table or tables named in the statement don't exist:

```
DROP TABLE IF EXISTS tbl_name;
```

IF EXISTS is particularly useful in scripts that you use with the mysql client. By default, mysql exits when an error occurs, and it is an error to try to remove a table that doesn't exist. For example, you might have a setup script that creates tables that you use as the basis for further processing in other scripts. In this situation, you want to make sure the setup script has a clean slate when it begins. If you use a regular DROP TABLE at the beginning of the script, it would fail the first time because the tables have never been created. If you use IF EXISTS, there is no problem. If the tables are there, they are dropped; if not, the script continues anyway.

Indexing Tables

Indexes are the primary means of speeding up access to the contents of your tables, particularly for queries that involve joins on multiple tables. This is an important enough topic that Chapter 4, "Query Optimization," discusses why you use indexes, how they work, and how best to take advantage of them to optimize your queries. This section covers the characteristics of indexes for the various table types and the syntax you use for creating and dropping them.

Table Type Indexing Characteristics

MySQL provides quite a bit of flexibility in the way you can construct indexes:

- You can index single columns or construct composite indexes from combinations of columns.
- An index can be allowed to contain duplicate values or required to contain only unique values.
- You can have more than one index on a table if you want to be able to look up a values quickly from different columns of a table.

- For string column types other than ENUM or SET, you may elect to index a prefix of a column, that is, only the leftmost *n* bytes. (In fact, for BLOB and TEXT columns, you cannot set up an index unless you do specify a prefix length.) Prefixes can be up to 255 bytes. If the column is mostly unique within the first *n* bytes, you usually won't sacrifice performance, and may well improve it. Indexing a column prefix rather than the entire column can make an index much smaller and faster to access.

Not all table types offer all indexing features. The following table summarizes the indexing properties of the various table types. (The table does not include the MERGE type because MERGE tables are created from MyISAM tables and have similar indexing characteristics.)

Index Characteristic	ISAM	MyISAM	HEAP	BDB	InnoDB
NULL values allowed	No	Yes	As of 4.0.2	Yes	Yes
Columns per index	16	16	16	16	16
Indexes per table	16	32	32	31	32
Maximum index row size (bytes)	256	500	500	500/1024	500/1024
Index column prefixes allowed	Yes	Yes	Yes	Yes	No
BLOB/TEXT indexes allowed	No	Yes (255 bytes max)	No	Yes (255 bytes max)	No

Two numbers are shown for the BDB and InnoDB index row sizes. For these table types, the size is 500 bytes up through 4.0.3 and 1024 bytes thereafter.

The table illustrates some of the reasons why MyISAM storage format generally is to be preferred to the ISAM format that it succeeds. MyISAM relaxes several of the indexing constraints that apply to ISAM tables. For example, with MyISAM tables, you can index columns that contain NULL values, you can index BLOB and TEXT columns, and you can have a larger number of indexes per table.

One implication of the differences in indexing characteristics for the various table types is that, depending on your version of MySQL, you may simply not be able to index certain columns. For example, you can use only ISAM tables if your MySQL is older than 3.23, which means you can't index a column if you want it to be able to contain NULL values. Conversely, if you require an index to have certain properties, you may not be able to use certain types of tables. If you need to index a `BLOB` column, for example, you must use a MyISAM or BDB table.

If you have an existing table of one type but would like to convert it to another type that has more suitable indexing characteristics, use `ALTER TABLE` to change the type. Suppose you have MySQL 3.23 or later but have older tables that were originally created as ISAM tables. You can easily convert them to MyISAM storage format using `ALTER TABLE`, which allows you to take advantage of MyISAM's superior indexing features:

```
ALTER TABLE tbl_name TYPE = MYISAM;
```

Creating Indexes

MySQL can create several types of index:

- **A regular (non-unique) index.** This gives you indexing benefits but allows duplicates.

- **A unique index.** This disallows duplicate values. For a single-column index, this ensures that the column contains no duplicate values. For a multiple-column (composite) index, it ensures that no combination of values in the columns is duplicated among the rows of the table.

- **A `FULLTEXT` index, used when you want to perform full text searches.** This index type is supported only for MyISAM tables. (For more information, see the "Using FULLTEXT Searches" section later in this chapter.)

You can create indexes for a new table when you use `CREATE TABLE`, or add indexes to existing tables with `CREATE INDEX` or `ALTER TABLE`. `CREATE INDEX` was introduced in MySQL 3.22, but you can use `ALTER TABLE` if your version of MySQL is older than that. (MySQL maps `CREATE INDEX` statements onto `ALTER TABLE` operations internally.)

`ALTER TABLE` is the more versatile than `CREATE INDEX`. You can use it to create a regular index, a `UNIQUE` index, a `PRIMARY KEY`, or a `FULLTEXT` index :

```
ALTER TABLE tbl_name ADD INDEX index_name (index_columns);
ALTER TABLE tbl_name ADD UNIQUE index_name (index_columns);
ALTER TABLE tbl_name ADD PRIMARY KEY (index_columns);
ALTER TABLE tbl_name ADD FULLTEXT (index_columns);
```

`tbl_name` is the name of the table to add the index to, and `index_columns` indicates which column or columns should be indexed. If the index consists of more than one column, separate the names by commas. The index name `index_name` is optional, so you can leave it out and MySQL will pick a name based on the name of the first indexed column. ALTER TABLE allows you to specify multiple table alterations in a single statement, so you can create several indexes at the same time. (This is faster than adding them one at a time with individual statements.)

To require that an index contain only unique values, create the index as a PRIMARY KEY or a UNIQUE index. The two types of index are very similar. In fact, a PRIMARY KEY is just a UNIQUE index that has the name PRIMARY. Two differences between the types of index are:

- A table can contain only one PRIMARY KEY because you can't have two indexes with the name PRIMARY. You can place multiple UNIQUE indexes on a table, although it's somewhat unusual to do so.

- A PRIMARY KEY cannot contain NULL values, whereas a UNIQUE index can. If a UNIQUE can contain NULL values, it usually can contain multiple NULL values. The reason for this is that it is not possible to know whether one NULL represents the same value as another, so they cannot be considered equal. (BDB tables are an exception—a BDB table allows only one NULL value within a UNIQUE index.)

CREATE INDEX can add a regular, UNIQUE, or FULLTEXT index to a table, but not a PRIMARY KEY:

```
CREATE INDEX index_name ON tbl_name (index_columns);
CREATE UNIQUE INDEX index_name ON tbl_name (index_columns);
CREATE FULLTEXT INDEX index_name ON tbl_name (index_columns);
```

tbl_name, *index_name*, and *index_columns* have the same meaning as for ALTER TABLE. Unlike ALTER TABLE, the index name is not optional with CREATE INDEX, and you cannot create multiple indexes with a single statement.

To create indexes for a new table when you issue a CREATE TABLE statement, the syntax is similar to that used for ALTER TABLE, but you specify the index-creation clauses as part of the column specification list:

```
CREATE TABLE tbl_name
(
    ... column declarations ...
    INDEX index_name (index_columns),
    UNIQUE index_name (index_columns),
    PRIMARY KEY (index_columns),
    FULLTEXT index_name (index_columns),
    ...
);
```

As with `ALTER TABLE`, the index name is optional in `CREATE TABLE` statements for each `INDEX`, `UNIQUE`, and `FULLTEXT` clause; MySQL will pick an index name if you leave it out.

As a special case, you can create a single-column `PRIMARY KEY` by adding `PRIMARY KEY` to the end of a column declaration. As of MySQL 3.23, you can do the same for a `UNIQUE` index. For example, this statement:

```
CREATE TABLE mytbl
(
    i INT NOT NULL PRIMARY KEY,
    j CHAR(10) NOT NULL UNIQUE
);
```

is equivalent to the following one:

```
CREATE TABLE mytbl
(
    i INT NOT NULL,
    j CHAR(10) NOT NULL,
    PRIMARY KEY (i),
    UNIQUE (j)
);
```

Each of the preceding table-creation examples have specified `NOT NULL` for the indexed columns. For ISAM tables (and for HEAP tables prior to MySQL 4.0.2), that's a requirement because you cannot index columns that may contain `NULL` values. For other table types, indexed columns can be `NULL` as long as the index is not a `PRIMARY KEY`.

To index a prefix of a string column (the leftmost n bytes of column values), the syntax for naming the column in the index definition is `col_name(n)` rather than simply `col_name`. For example, the following statement creates a table with two `CHAR` columns but uses only the first 10 bytes from each in the index created from those columns.

```
CREATE TABLE mytbl
(
    name    CHAR(30) NOT NULL,
    address CHAR(60) NOT NULL,
    INDEX (name(10),address(10))
);
```

Index prefixes are supported for ISAM, MyISAM, HEAP, and BDB tables, but not for InnoDB tables.

Prefix lengths, just like column lengths, refer to bytes rather than characters. The two are the same for single-byte character sets, but not for multi-byte character sets. MySQL will store into an index value as many complete characters as will fit. For example, if an index prefix is 5 bytes long and a column value consists of 2-byte characters, the index value will contain 2 characters, not 2.5 characters.

In some circumstances, you may find it not only desirable but necessary to index a column prefix rather than the entire column:

- Prefixes are necessary for BLOB or TEXT columns in any table type that allows those column types to be indexed. The prefix may be up to 255 bytes long.

- The length of index rows is equal to the sum of the length of the index parts of the columns that make up the index. If this length exceeds the allowable length of index rows, you can make the index "narrower" by indexing a column prefix. Suppose a MyISAM table contains two CHAR(255) columns named c1 and c2, and you want to create an index based on both of them. The length of an index row in this case would be 255+255, which exceeds the MyISAM limit of 500 bytes per index row. However, you can create the index by indexing a shorter part of one or both columns.

Indexing a prefix of a column constrains that changes that you can make to the column later. You cannot shorten the column to a length less than the prefix length without dropping the index and re-creating it using a shorter length for the indexed part of a column. If you index the first 30 bytes of a 40-byte CHAR column but then discover that you never store more than 20 bytes in the column, you might decide to save space in the table by changing the column to be only 20 bytes wide. In this case, you must drop the index first before making the column narrower. Then you can add the index again, indexing 20 or fewer bytes.

Columns in FULLTEXT indexes do not have prefixes. If you specify a prefix length for a FULLTEXT index, it will be ignored.

Dropping Indexes

To drop an index, use either a DROP INDEX or an ALTER TABLE statement. Like the CREATE INDEX statement, DROP INDEX was introduced in MySQL 3.22, is handled internally as an ALTER TABLE statement and cannot be used to affect a PRIMARY KEY. The syntax for index-dropping statements looks like this:

```
DROP INDEX index_name ON tbl_name;
ALTER TABLE tbl_name DROP INDEX index_name;
ALTER TABLE tbl_name DROP PRIMARY KEY;
```

The first two statements are equivalent. The third is used only for dropping a PRIMARY INDEX; it is unambiguous because a table can have only one such key. If no index was created explicitly as a PRIMARY KEY but the table has one or more UNIQUE indexes, MySQL drops the first of them.

Indexes can be affected if you drop columns from a table. If you drop a column that is a part of an index, the column is removed from the index as well. If all columns that make up an index are dropped, the entire index is dropped.

Altering Table Structure

ALTER TABLE is a versatile statement in MySQL, and you can use it to do many things. We've already seen some of its capabilities (for changing table types and for creating and dropping indexes in this chapter, and for renumbering sequences in Chapter 2). You can also use ALTER TABLE to rename tables, add or drop columns, change column types, and more. In this section, we'll cover some of the other features it offers. The full syntax for ALTER TABLE is described in Appendix D.

ALTER TABLE is useful when you find that the structure of a table no longer reflects what you want to do with it. You may want to use the table to record additional information, or perhaps it contains information that has become superfluous. Maybe existing columns are too small, or perhaps you've declared them larger than it turns out you need and you'd like to make them smaller to save space and improve query performance. Or maybe you just typed in the table's name incorrectly when you issued the CREATE TABLE statement. The following are some examples:

- You're running a research project. You assign case numbers to research records using an AUTO_INCREMENT column. You didn't expect your funding to last long enough to generate more than about 50,000 records, so you made the column type SMALLINT UNSIGNED, which holds a maximum of 65,535 unique values. However, the funding for the project was renewed, and it looks like you may generate another 50,000 records. You need to make the type bigger to accommodate more case numbers.

- Size changes can go the other way, too. Maybe you created a CHAR(255) column but now recognize that no value in the table is more than 100 characters long. You can shorten the column to save space.

- You want to convert a table to another type to take advantage of features offered by that type. For example, an ISAM table won't allow NULL values in indexed columns. If you really need to index a column that contains NULL, you can convert it to be a MyISAM table.

The syntax for `ALTER TABLE` is as follows:

```
ALTER TABLE tbl_name action, ... ;
```

Each action specifies a modification you want to make to the table. Some database engines allow only a single action in an `ALTER TABLE` statement, but MySQL allows multiple actions; just separate the actions by commas. This extension to `ALTER TABLE` is useful because some types of table modifications cannot be performed with single-action statements. For example, it's impossible to change all the `VARCHAR` columns to `CHAR` columns by changing them one at a time. You must change them all at once.

The following examples show some of the capabilities of `ALTER TABLE`:

- **Renaming a table.** Use a `RENAME` clause that specifies the new table name:

  ```
  ALTER TABLE tbl_name RENAME TO new_tbl_name;
  ```

  Another way to rename tables is with `RENAME TABLE`, available as of MySQL 3.23.23. The syntax looks like this:

  ```
  RENAME TABLE old_name TO new_name;
  ```

  One thing that `RENAME TABLE` can do that `ALTER TABLE` cannot is rename multiple tables in the same statement. For example, you can swap the names of two tables like this:

  ```
  RENAME TABLE t1 TO tmp, t2 TO t1, tmp TO t1;
  ```

  If you qualify a table name with a database name, you can move a table from one database to another by renaming it. Either of the following statements move the table t from the `sampdb` database to the `test` database:

  ```
  ALTER TABLE sampdb.t RENAME TO test.t;
  RENAME TABLE sampdb.t TO test.t;
  ```

  You cannot rename a table to use a name that already exists, however.

- **Changing a column type.** To change a column type, you can use either a `CHANGE` or `MODIFY` clause. Suppose the column in a table `mytbl` is `SMALLINT UNSIGNED` and you want to change it to `MEDIUMINT UNSIGNED`. Do so using either of the following commands:

  ```
  ALTER TABLE mytbl MODIFY i MEDIUMINT UNSIGNED;
  ALTER TABLE mytbl CHANGE i i MEDIUMINT UNSIGNED;
  ```

  Why is the column named twice in the command that uses `CHANGE`? Because one thing that `CHANGE` can do that `MODIFY` cannot is to rename the column in addition to changing the type. If you had wanted to rename i to j at the same time you changed the type, you'd do so like this:

  ```
  ALTER TABLE mytbl CHANGE i j MEDIUMINT UNSIGNED;
  ```

The important thing with CHANGE is that you name the column you want to change and then specify a complete column declaration, which includes the column name. You must include the name in the declaration, even if it's the same as the old name.

As of MySQL 4.1, you can assign character sets to individual columns, so it's possible to use the CHARACTER SET attribute in a column's definition to change its character set:

```
ALTER TABLE t MODIFY c CHAR(20) CHARACTER SET ucs2;
```

An important reason for changing column types is to improve query efficiency for joins that compare columns from two tables. A comparison is quicker when the columns are both the same type. Suppose you're running a query like the following:

```
SELECT ... FROM t1, t2 WHERE t1.name = t2.name;
```

If t1.name is CHAR(10) and t2.name is CHAR(15), the query won't run as quickly as if they were both CHAR(15). You can make them the same by changing t1.name using either of the following commands:

```
ALTER TABLE t1 MODIFY name CHAR(15);
ALTER TABLE t1 CHANGE name name CHAR(15);
```

Prior to MySQL 3.23, it's essential that joined columns be of the same type, or indexes will not be used for the comparison and the join will run more slowly. But even from 3.23 and later, when indexes can be used in joins between dissimilar column types, a query will still be faster if the types are identical.

- **Converting a table from variable-length rows to fixed-length rows.** Suppose you have a table chartbl that was created like this:

  ```
  CREATE TABLE chartbl (name VARCHAR(40), address VARCHAR(80));
  ```

  The table contains VARCHAR columns and you want to convert them to CHAR columns to see what kind of performance improvements you get. (If the table uses ISAM or MyISAM storage format, fixed-length rows generally can be processed more quickly than variable-length rows.) The problem here is that you need to change the columns all at once in the same ALTER TABLE statement. You can't do them one at a time or the attempt will be ineffective. (Try changing just one of them and then run DESCRIBE chartbl; you'll find that the columns are still defined as VARCHAR!) The reason for this is that if you change a single column at a time, MySQL notices that the table still contains variable-length columns and reconverts the changed column back to VARCHAR to save space. To deal with this, change all the VARCHAR columns at the same time:

```
ALTER TABLE chartbl MODIFY name CHAR(40), MODIFY address CHAR(80);
```

Now DESCRIBE will show that the table contains CHAR columns. It's exactly this type of operation that makes it important that ALTER TABLE support multiple actions in the same statement.

There is a caveat to be aware of when you want to convert a table as just shown: BLOB and TEXT types are variable-length types with no fixed-length equivalent. The presence of any BLOB or TEXT columns in a table will defeat any attempt to convert it to fixed-length row format because even one variable-length column in a table causes it to have variable-length rows.

- **Converting a table from fixed-length rows to variable-length rows.** Suppose you discover that chartbl is indeed faster with fixed-length rows. On the other hand, it takes more storage than you'd like, so you decide to convert it back to its original form to save space. Converting a table in this direction is much easier. You only need to change one CHAR column to VARCHAR and MySQL will convert the other CHAR columns automatically. To convert the chartbl table, either of the following statements will do:

```
ALTER TABLE chartbl MODIFY name VARCHAR(40);
ALTER TABLE chartbl MODIFY address VARCHAR(80);
```

- **Converting a table type.** To convert a table from one storage format to another, use a TYPE clause to change the table's type:

```
ALTER TABLE tbl_name TYPE = tbl_type;
```

tbl_type is a type specifier such as ISAM, MYISAM, HEAP, BDB, or INNODB (lettercase does not matter).

Changing table types can be useful when you upgrade your MySQL installation to a newer version that provides additional table-handling features. For example, if you upgrade from a pre-3.23 version of MySQL to 3.23 or later, your older tables will be in ISAM format. To change them to MyISAM format, use the following statement for each one:

```
ALTER TABLE tbl_name TYPE = MYISAM;
```

Doing this allows you to take advantages of the capabilities that MyISAM offers than ISAM does not. These are discussed earlier in the "Table Types" and "Indexing Tables" sections earlier in this chapter. For example, MyISAM tables are machine independent, so you can move them to other machines by copying table files directly, even if the machines have different hardware architectures. In addition, with MyISAM tables, you can index BLOB and TEXT columns, and indexed columns can contain NULL values.

Another reason to change a table type is to make it transaction-safe. Suppose you have a MyISAM table and discover that an application that uses it needs to perform transactional operations, including rollback in case failures occur. MyISAM tables do not support transactions, but you can make the table transaction-safe by converting it to a BDB or InnoDB table:

```
ALTER TABLE tbl_name TYPE = BDB;
ALTER TABLE tbl_name TYPE = INNODB;
```

ALTER TABLE is useful in many ways, but there are circumstances under which you should not use it. The following are two examples:

- HEAP tables are held in memory and disappear when the server exits. It is not a good idea to convert a table to type HEAP if you require the table to last beyond server shutdown.
- If you use a MERGE table to group a collection of MyISAM tables together, you should avoid using ALTER TABLE to modify any of the MyISAM tables unless you make the same change to all of them, and to the MERGE table as well. The proper functioning of a MERGE table depends on its having the same structure as all of its constituent MyISAM tables.

Getting Information about Databases and Tables

MySQL provides a SHOW statement that has several variant forms that display information about databases and the tables in them. SHOW is helpful for keeping track of the contents of your databases and for reminding yourself about the structure of your tables. You can also use SHOW prior to issuing ALTER TABLE; it's often easier to figure out how to specify a change to a column after you determine the column's current definition.

The SHOW statement can be used to obtain information about several aspects of your databases and tables:

- List the databases managed by the server:
  ```
  SHOW DATABASES;
  ```

- List the tables in the current database or in a given database:
  ```
  SHOW TABLES;
  SHOW TABLES FROM db_name;
  ```

  Note that SHOW TABLES doesn't show TEMPORARY tables.

- Display information about columns or indexes in a table:

  ```
  SHOW COLUMNS FROM tbl_name;
  SHOW INDEX FROM tbl_name;
  ```

  The DESCRIBE `tbl_name` and EXPLAIN `tbl_name` statements are synonymous with SHOW COLUMNS FROM `tbl_name`.

- Display descriptive information about tables in the current database or in a given database:

  ```
  SHOW TABLE STATUS;
  SHOW TABLE STATUS FROM db_name;
  ```

  This statement was introduced in MySQL 3.23.0.

- Display the CREATE TABLE statement that corresponds to the current structure of a table:

  ```
  SHOW CREATE TABLE tbl_name;
  ```

  This statement was introduced in MySQL 3.23.20.

Several forms of SHOW take a LIKE `'pat'` clause allowing a pattern to be given that limits the scope of the output. `'pat'` is interpreted as a SQL pattern that can include the '%' and '_' wildcard characters. For example, the following statement displays the names of tables in the current database that begin with `'geo'`:

```
SHOW TABLES LIKE 'geo%';
```

To match a literal instance of a wildcard character in a LIKE pattern, precede it with a backslash. Generally, this is done to match a literal '_', which occurs frequently in database, table, and column names.

The mysqlshow command provides some of the same information as the SHOW statement, which allows you to get database and table information from the shell:

- List databases managed by the server:

  ```
  % mysqlshow
  ```

- List tables in the named database:

  ```
  % mysqlshow db_name
  ```

- Display information about columns in the named table:

  ```
  % mysqlshow db_name tbl_name
  ```

- Display information about indexes in the named table:

  ```
  % mysqlshow --keys db_name tbl_name
  ```

- Display descriptive information about tables in the named database:

  ```
  % mysqlshow --status db_name
  ```

The `mysqldump` utility allows you to see the structure of your tables in the form of a CREATE TABLE statement (much like SHOW CREATE TABLE). When using `mysqldump` to review table structure, be sure to invoke it with the `--no-data` option so that you don't get swamped with your table's data!

```
% mysqldump --no-data db_name tbl_name
```

If you omit the table name, `mysqldump` displays the structure for all tables in the database.

For both `mysqlshow` and `mysqldump`, you can specify the usual connection parameter options (such as `--host` or `--user`.)

Determining Which Table Types Your Server Supports

ISAM is the only type available before MySQL 3.23. From 3.23 on, MyISAM, MERGE, and HEAP are always available, and availability of the other types can be assessed by means of an appropriate SHOW VARIABLES statement:

```
SHOW VARIABLES LIKE 'have_isam';
SHOW VARIABLES LIKE 'have_bdb';
SHOW VARIABLES LIKE 'have_inno%';
```

If the output from the query shows that the variable has a value of YES, the corresponding table handler is enabled. If the value is something else or there is no output, the handler is unavailable. The use of the pattern `have_inno%` to determine InnoDB availability matches both `have_innodb` and `have_innobase`. (The latter form was used in MySQL 3.23.30 to 3.23.36 before being renamed to `have_innodb`.)

You can use table type information to determine whether your server supports transactions. BDB and InnoDB are the two transaction-safe table types, so check whether their handlers are enabled as described in the preceding discussion.

As of MySQL 4.1, the list of table types is available directly through the SHOW TABLE TYPES statement:

```
mysql> SHOW TABLE TYPES;
+---------+---------+-------------------------------------------------------------+
| Type    | Support | Comment                                                     |
+---------+---------+-------------------------------------------------------------+
| MyISAM  | DEFAULT | Default type from 3.23 with great performance               |
| HEAP    | YES     | Hash based, stored in memory, useful for temporary tables   |
| MERGE   | YES     | Collection of identical MyISAM tables                       |
| ISAM    | YES     | Obsolete table type; Is replaced by MyISAM                  |
| InnoDB  | YES     | Supports transactions, row-level locking and foreign keys   |
| BDB     | YES     | Supports transactions and page-level locking                |
+---------+---------+-------------------------------------------------------------+
```

The `Support` value is `YES` or `NO` to indicate that the handler is or is not available, `DISABLED` if the handler is present but turned off, or `DEFAULT` for the table type that the server uses by default. The handler designated as `DEFAULT` should be considered available.

Checking a Table's Existence or Type

It's sometimes useful to be able to tell from within an application whether or not a given table exists. You can use `SHOW TABLES` to find out:

```
SHOW TABLES LIKE 'tbl_name';
SHOW TABLES FROM db_name LIKE 'tbl_name';
```

If the `SHOW` statement lists information for the table, it exists. It's also possible to determine table existence with either of the following statements:

```
SELECT COUNT(*) FROM tbl_name;
SELECT * FROM tbl_name WHERE 0;
```

Each statement succeeds if the table exists and fails if it doesn't. The first statement is most appropriate for MyISAM and ISAM tables, for which `COUNT(*)` with no `WHERE` clause is highly optimized. (It's not so good for InnoDB or BDB tables, which require a full scan to count the rows.) The second statement is more general because is runs quickly for any table type. Use of these queries is most suitable for use within application programming languages, such as Perl or PHP, because you can test the success or failure of the query and take action accordingly. They're not especially useful in a batch script that you run from `mysql` because you can't do anything if an error occurs except terminate (or ignore the error, but then there's obviously no point in running the query at all).

To determine the type of a table, you can use `SHOW TABLE STATUS` as of MySQL 3.23.0 or `SHOW CREATE TABLE` as of MySQL 3.23.20. The output from both statements includes a table type indicator. For versions older than 3.23.0, neither statement is available; but then the only available table type is ISAM, so there is no ambiguity about what storage format your tables use.

Retrieving Records from Multiple Tables

It does no good to put records in a database unless you retrieve them eventually and do something with them. That's the purpose of the `SELECT` statement—to help you get at your data. `SELECT` probably is used more often than any other in the SQL language, but it can also be the trickiest; the constraints you use to choose rows can be arbitrarily complex and can involve comparisons between columns in many tables.

The basic syntax of the SELECT statement looks like this:

```
SELECT selection_list        # What columns to select
FROM table_list              # Where to select rows from
WHERE primary_constraint     # What conditions rows must satisfy
GROUP BY grouping_columns    # How to group results
ORDER BY sorting_columns     # How to sort results
HAVING secondary_constraint  # Secondary conditions rows must satisfy
LIMIT count;                 # Limit on results
```

Everything in this syntax is optional except the word SELECT and the *selection_list* part that specifies what you want to retrieve. Some databases require the FROM clause as well. MySQL does not, which allows you to evaluate expressions without referring to any tables:

```
SELECT SQRT(POW(3,2)+POW(4,2));
```

In Chapter 1, we devoted quite a bit of attention to single-table SELECT statements, concentrating primarily on the output column list and the WHERE, GROUP BY, ORDER BY, HAVING, and LIMIT clauses. This section covers an aspect of SELECT that is often confusing—writing joins; that is, SELECT statements that retrieve records from multiple tables. We'll discuss the types of join MySQL supports, what they mean, and how to specify them. This should help you employ MySQL more effectively because, in many cases, the real problem of figuring out how to write a query is determining the proper way to join tables together.

One problem with using SELECT is that when you first encounter a new type of problem, it's not always easy to see how to write a SELECT query to solve it. However, after you figure it out, you can use that experience when you run across similar problems in the future. SELECT is probably the statement for which past experience plays the largest role in being able to use it effectively, simply because of the sheer variety of problems to which it applies.

As you gain experience, you'll be able to adapt joins more easily to new problems, and you'll find yourself thinking things like, "Oh, yes, that's one of those LEFT JOIN things," or, "Aha, that's a three-way join restricted by the common pairs of key columns." (I'm a little reluctant to point that out, actually. You may find it encouraging to hear that experience helps you. On the other hand, you may find it alarming to consider that you could wind up thinking in terms like that!)

Many of the examples that demonstrate how to use the forms of join operations that MySQL supports use the following two tables, t1 and t2. They're small, which makes them simple enough that the effect of each type of join can be seen readily:

```
Table t1:      Table t2:
+----+----+    +----+----+
| i1 | c1 |    | i2 | c2 |
+----+----+    +----+----+
|  1 | a  |    |  2 | c  |
|  2 | b  |    |  3 | b  |
|  3 | c  |    |  4 | a  |
+----+----+    +----+----+
```

The Trivial Join

The simplest join is the trivial join, in which only one table is named. In this case, rows are selected from the named table:

```
mysql> SELECT * FROM t1;
+----+----+
| i1 | c1 |
+----+----+
|  1 | a  |
|  2 | b  |
|  3 | c  |
+----+----+
```

Some people don't consider this form of SELECT a join at all and use the term only for SELECT statements that retrieve records from two or more tables. I suppose it's a matter of perspective.

The Full Join

If a SELECT statement names multiple tables in the FROM clause with the names separated by commas, MySQL performs a full join. For example, if you join t1 and t2 as follows, each row in t1 is combined with each row in t2:

```
mysql> SELECT t1.*, t2.* FROM t1, t2;
+----+----+----+----+
| i1 | c1 | i2 | c2 |
+----+----+----+----+
|  1 | a  |  2 | c  |
|  2 | b  |  2 | c  |
|  3 | c  |  2 | c  |
|  1 | a  |  3 | b  |
|  2 | b  |  3 | b  |
|  3 | c  |  3 | b  |
|  1 | a  |  4 | a  |
|  2 | b  |  4 | a  |
|  3 | c  |  4 | a  |
+----+----+----+----+
```

A full join is also called a *cross join* because each row of each table is crossed with each row in every other table to produce all possible combinations. This is also known as the *cartesian product*. Joining tables this way has the potential to produce a very large number of rows because the possible row count is the product of the number of rows in each table. A full join between three tables that contain 100, 200, and 300 rows, respectively, could return 100×200×300 = 6 million rows. That's a lot of rows, even though the individual tables are small. In cases like this, a WHERE clause will normally be used to reduce the result set to a more manageable size.

If you add a WHERE clause causing tables to be matched on the values of certain columns, the join becomes what is known as an *equi-join* because you're selecting only rows with equal values in the specified columns:

```
mysql> SELECT t1.*, t2.* FROM t1, t2 WHERE t1.i1 = t2.i2;
+----+----+----+----+
| i1 | c1 | i2 | c2 |
+----+----+----+----+
|  2 | b  |  2 | c  |
|  3 | c  |  3 | b  |
+----+----+----+----+
```

The JOIN and CROSS JOIN join types are equivalent to the ',' (comma) join operator. For example, the following statements are all the same:

```
SELECT t1.*, t2.* FROM t1, t2 WHERE t1.i1 = t2.i2;
SELECT t1.*, t2.* FROM t1 JOIN t2 WHERE t1.i1 = t2.i2;
SELECT t1.*, t2.* FROM t1 CROSS JOIN t2 WHERE t1.i1 = t2.i2;
```

Normally, the MySQL optimizer considers itself free to determine the order in which to scan tables to retrieve rows most quickly. On occasion, the optimizer will make a non-optimal choice. If you find this happening, you can override the optimizer's choice using the STRAIGHT_JOIN keyword. A join performed with STRAIGHT_JOIN is like a cross join but forces the tables to be joined in the order named in the FROM clause.

STRAIGHT_JOIN can be specified at two points in a SELECT statement. You can specify it between the SELECT keyword and the selection list to have a global effect on all cross joins in the statement, or you can specify it in the FROM clause. The following two statements are equivalent:

```
SELECT STRAIGHT_JOIN ... FROM t1, t2, t3 ... ;
SELECT ... FROM t1 STRAIGHT_JOIN t2 STRAIGHT_JOIN t3 ... ;
```

Qualifying Column References

References to table columns throughout a SELECT statement must resolve unambiguously to a single table named in the FROM clause. If only one table is named, there is no ambiguity because all columns must be columns of that table. If multiple tables are named, any column name that appears in only one table is similarly unambiguous. However, if a column name appears in multiple tables, references to the column must be qualified by the table name using `tbl_name.col_name` syntax to specify which table you mean. Suppose a table mytbl1 contains columns a and b, and a table mytbl2 contains columns b and c. In this case, references to columns a or c are unambiguous, but references to b must be qualified as either `mytbl1.b` or `mytbl2.b`:

```
SELECT a, mytbl1.b, mytbl2.b, c FROM mytbl1, mytbl2 ... ;
```

Sometimes a table name qualifier is not sufficient to resolve a column reference. For example, if you're joining a table to itself, you're using it multiple times within the query and it doesn't help to qualify a column name with the table name. In this case, table aliases are useful for communicating your intent. You can assign an alias to any instance of the table and refer to columns from that instance as `alias_name.col_name`. The following query joins a table to itself, but assigns an alias to one instance of the table to allow column references to be specified unambiguously:

```
SELECT mytbl.col1, m.col2 FROM mytbl, mytbl AS m WHERE mytbl.col1 > m.col1;
```

Left and Right Joins

An equi-join shows only rows where a match can be found in both tables. Left and right joins show matches, too, but also show rows in one table that have no match in the other table. The examples in this section use LEFT JOIN, which identifies rows in the left table that are not matched by the right table. RIGHT JOIN is the same except that the roles of the tables are reversed. (RIGHT JOIN is available only as of MySQL 3.23.25.)

A LEFT JOIN works like this: You specify the columns to be used for matching rows in the two tables. When a row from the left table matches a row from the right table, the contents of the rows are selected as an output row. When a row in the left table has no match, it is still selected for output, but joined with a "fake" row from the right table in which all the columns have been set to NULL. In other words, a LEFT JOIN forces the result set to contain a row for every row in the left table whether or not there is a match for it in the right table. The rows with no match can be identified by the fact that all columns from the right table are NULL.

Consider once again our two tables, t1 and t2:

```
Table t1:        Table t2:
+----+----+      +----+----+
| i1 | c1 |      | i2 | c2 |
+----+----+      +----+----+
|  1 | a  |      |  2 | c  |
|  2 | b  |      |  3 | b  |
|  3 | c  |      |  4 | a  |
+----+----+      +----+----+
```

If we use a cross join to match these tables on t1.i1 and t2.i2, we'll get output only for the values 2 and 3, which appear in both tables:

```
mysql> SELECT t1.*, t2.* FROM t1, t2 WHERE t1.i1 = t2.i2;
+----+----+----+----+
| i1 | c1 | i2 | c2 |
+----+----+----+----+
|  2 | b  |  2 | c  |
|  3 | c  |  3 | b  |
+----+----+----+----+
```

A left join produces output for every row in t1, whether or not t2 matches it. To write a left join, name the tables with LEFT JOIN in between (rather than a comma) and specify the matching condition using an ON clause (rather than a WHERE clause):

```
mysql> SELECT t1.*, t2.* FROM t1 LEFT JOIN t2 ON t1.i1 = t2.i2;
+----+----+------+------+
| i1 | c1 | i2   | c2   |
+----+----+------+------+
|  1 | a  | NULL | NULL |
|  2 | b  |    2 | c    |
|  3 | c  |    3 | b    |
+----+----+------+------+
```

Now there is an output row even for the value 1, which has no match in t2.

LEFT JOIN is especially useful when you want to find *only* those left table rows that are unmatched by the right table. Do this by adding a WHERE clause that looks for rows in the right table that have NULL values—in other words, the rows in one table that are missing from the other:

```
mysql> SELECT t1.*, t2.* FROM t1 LEFT JOIN t2 ON t1.i1 = t2.i2
    -> WHERE t2.i2 IS NULL;
+----+----+------+------+
| i1 | c1 | i2   | c2   |
+----+----+------+------+
|  1 | a  | NULL | NULL |
+----+----+------+------+
```

Normally, what you're really after are the unmatched values in the left table. The NULL columns from the right table are of no interest for display purposes, so you wouldn't bother naming them in the output column list:

```
mysql> SELECT t1.* FROM t1 LEFT JOIN t2 ON t1.i1 = t2.i2
    -> WHERE t2.i2 IS NULL;
+----+----+
| i1 | c1 |
+----+----+
|  1 | a  |
+----+----+
```

LEFT JOIN actually allows the matching conditions to be specified two ways. ON is one of these; it can be used whether or not the columns you're joining on have the same name:

```
SELECT t1.*, t2.* FROM t1 LEFT JOIN t2 ON t1.i1 = t2.i2;
```

The other syntax involves a USING() clause; this is similar in concept to ON, but the name of the joined column or columns must be the same in each table. For example, the following query joins mytbl1.b to mytbl2.b:

```
SELECT mytbl1.*, mytbl2.* FROM mytbl1 LEFT JOIN mytbl2 USING (b);
```

LEFT JOIN has a few synonyms and variants. LEFT OUTER JOIN is a synonym for LEFT JOIN. There is also an ODBC-style notation for LEFT JOIN that MySQL accepts (the OJ means "outer join"):

```
{ OJ tbl_name1 LEFT OUTER JOIN tbl_name2 ON join_expr }
```

NATURAL LEFT JOIN is similar to LEFT JOIN; it performs a LEFT JOIN, matching all columns that have the same name in the left and right tables.

One thing to watch out for with LEFT JOIN is that if the columns that you're joining on are not declared as NOT NULL, you may get problematic rows in the result. For example, if the right table contains columns with NULL values, you won't be able to distinguish those NULL values from NULL values that identify unmatched rows.

As already mentioned, LEFT JOIN is useful for answering "Which values are missing?" questions. When you want to know which values in one table are not present in another table, you use a LEFT JOIN on the two tables and look for rows in which NULL is selected from the second table. Let's consider a more complex example of this type of problem than the one shown earlier using t1 and t2.

For the grade-keeping project first mentioned in Chapter 1, we have a student table listing students, an event table listing the grade events that have occurred, and a score table listing scores for each student for each grade event. However, if a student was ill on the day of some quiz or test, the score table wouldn't have any score for the student for that event, so a makeup quiz or test should be given. How do we find these missing records so that we can make sure those students take the makeup?

The problem is to determine which students have no score for a given grade event and to do this for each grade event. Another way to say this is that we want to find out which combinations of student and event are not represented in the score table. This "which values are not present" wording is a tip-off that we want a LEFT JOIN. The join isn't as simple as in the previous example, though, because we aren't just looking for values that are not present in a single column; we're looking for a two-column combination. The combinations we want are all the student/event combinations, which are produced by crossing the student table with the event table:

```
FROM student, event
```

Then we take the result of that join and perform a LEFT JOIN with the score table to find the matches:

```
FROM student, event
    LEFT JOIN score ON student.student_id = score.student.id
                  AND event.event_id = score.event_id
```

Note that the ON clause allows the rows in the score table to be joined according to matches in different tables. That's the key for solving this problem. The LEFT JOIN forces a row to be generated for each row produced by the cross join of the student and event tables, even when there is no corresponding score table record. The result set rows for these missing score records can be identified by the fact that the columns from the score table will all be NULL. We can select these records in the WHERE clause. Any column from the score table will do, but because we're looking for missing scores, it's probably conceptually clearest to test the score column:

```
WHERE score.score IS NULL
```

We can put the results in order using an ORDER BY clause. The two most logical orderings are by event per student or by student per event. I'll choose the first:

```
ORDER BY student.student_id, event.event_id
```

Now all we need to do is name the columns we want to see in the output, and we're done. Here is the final query:

```
SELECT
    student.name, student.student_id,
    event.date, event.event_id, event.type
```

```
FROM
    student, event
    LEFT JOIN score ON student.student_id = score.student_id
                    AND event.event_id = score.event_id
WHERE
    score.score IS NULL
ORDER BY
    student.student_id, event.event_id;
```

Running the query produces these results:

```
+-----------+------------+------------+----------+------+
| name      | student_id | date       | event_id | type |
+-----------+------------+------------+----------+------+
| Megan     |          1 | 2002-09-16 |        4 | Q    |
| Joseph    |          2 | 2002-09-03 |        1 | Q    |
| Katie     |          4 | 2002-09-23 |        5 | Q    |
| Devri     |         13 | 2002-09-03 |        1 | Q    |
| Devri     |         13 | 2002-10-01 |        6 | T    |
| Will      |         17 | 2002-09-16 |        4 | Q    |
| Avery     |         20 | 2002-09-06 |        2 | Q    |
| Gregory   |         23 | 2002-10-01 |        6 | T    |
| Sarah     |         24 | 2002-09-23 |        5 | Q    |
| Carter    |         27 | 2002-09-16 |        4 | Q    |
| Carter    |         27 | 2002-09-23 |        5 | Q    |
| Gabrielle |         29 | 2002-09-16 |        4 | Q    |
| Grace     |         30 | 2002-09-23 |        5 | Q    |
+-----------+------------+------------+----------+------+
```

Here's a subtle point. The output displays the student IDs and the event IDs. The student_id column appears in both the student and score tables, so at first you might think that the selection list could name either student. student_id or score.student_id. That's not the case because the entire basis for being able to find the records we're interested in is that all the score table fields are returned as NULL. Selecting score.student_id would produce only a column of NULL values in the output. The same principle applies to deciding which event_id column to display. It appears in both the event and score tables, but the query selects event.event_id because the score.event_id values will always be NULL.

Using Subselects

One of the features that MySQL 4.1 introduces is subselect support, which is a long-awaited capability that allows one SELECT query to be nested inside other. The following is an example that looks up the IDs for event records corresponding to tests ('T') and uses them to select scores for those tests:

```
SELECT * FROM score
WHERE event_id IN (SELECT event_id FROM event WHERE type = 'T');
```

In some cases, subselects can be rewritten as joins. I'll show how to do that later in this section. You may find subselect rewriting techniques useful if your version of MySQL precedes 4.1.

A related feature that MySQL supports is the ability to delete or update records in one table based on the contents of another. For example, you might want to remove records in one table that aren't matched by any record in another, or copy values from columns in one table to columns in another. These types of operations are discussed in the "Multiple-Table Deletes and Updates" section later in this chapter.

There are several forms you can use to write subselects; this section surveys just a few of them.

- **Using a subselect to produce a reference value.** In this case, you want the inner SELECT to identify a single value to be used in comparisons with the outer SELECT. For example, to identify the scores for the quiz that took place on '2002-09-23', use an inner SELECT to determine the quiz event ID, and then match score records against it in the outer SELECT:

  ```
  SELECT * FROM score
  WHERE event_id =
  (SELECT event_id FROM event WHERE date = '2002-09-23' AND type = 'Q');
  ```

  With this form of subselect, where the inner query is preceded by a comparison operator, it's necessary that the inner join produce no more than a single value (that is, one row, one column). If it produces multiple values, the query will fail. (In some cases, it may be appropriate to satisfy this constraint by limiting the inner query result with LIMIT 1.)

  This form of subselect can be handy for situations where you'd be tempted to use an aggregate function in a WHERE clause. For example, to determine which president was born first, you might try the following:

  ```
  SELECT * FROM president WHERE birth = MIN(birth);
  ```

  That doesn't work because you can't use aggregates in WHERE clauses. (The WHERE clause determines which records to select, but the value of MIN() isn't known until after the records have already been selected.) However, you can use a subselect to produce the minimum birth date as follows:

  ```
  SELECT * FROM president
  WHERE birth = (SELECT MIN(birth) FROM president);
  ```

- **EXISTS and NOT EXISTS subselects.** These forms of subselects work by passing values from the outer query to the inner one to see whether they match the conditions specified in the inner query. For this reason, you'll need to qualify column names with table names if they are ambiguous (appear in more than one table). EXISTS and NOT EXISTS subselects are useful for finding records in one table that match or don't match records in another.

Refer once again to our t1 and t2 tables:

```
Table t1:      Table t2:
+----+----+    +----+----+
| i1 | c1 |    | i2 | c2 |
+----+----+    +----+----+
|  1 | a  |    |  2 | c  |
|  2 | b  |    |  3 | b  |
|  3 | c  |    |  4 | a  |
+----+----+    +----+----+
```

The following query identifies matches between the tables—that is, values that are present in both:

```
mysql> SELECT i1 FROM t1
    -> WHERE EXISTS (SELECT * FROM t2 WHERE t1.i1 = t2.i2);
+----+
| i1 |
+----+
|  2 |
|  3 |
+----+
```

NOT EXISTS identifies non-matches—values in one table that are not present in the other:

```
mysql> SELECT i1 FROM t1
    -> WHERE NOT EXISTS (SELECT * FROM t2 WHERE t1.i1 = t2.i2);
+----+
| i1 |
+----+
|  1 |
+----+
```

With these forms of subselect, the inner query uses * as the output column list. There's no need to name columns explicitly because the inner query is assessed as true or false based on whether or not it returns rows, not based on the particular values that the rows may contain. In MySQL, you can actually write pretty much anything for the column selection list, but if you want to make it explicit that you're returning a true value when the inner SELECT succeeds, you might write the queries like this:

```
SELECT i1 FROM t1
WHERE EXISTS (SELECT 1 FROM t2 WHERE t1.i1 = t2.i2);
SELECT i1 FROM t1
WHERE NOT EXISTS (SELECT 1 FROM t2 WHERE t1.i1 = t2.i2);
```

- **IN and NOT IN subselects.** The IN and NOT IN forms of subselect should return a single column of values from the inner SELECT to be evaluated in a comparison in the outer SELECT. For example, the preceding EXISTS and NOT EXISTS queries can be written using IN and NOT IN syntax as follows:

```
mysql> SELECT i1 FROM t1 WHERE i1 IN (SELECT i2 FROM t2);
+----+
| i1 |
+----+
|  2 |
|  3 |
+----+
mysql> SELECT i1 FROM t1 WHERE i1 NOT IN (SELECT i2 FROM t2);
+----+
| i1 |
+----+
|  1 |
+----+
```

Rewriting Subselects as Joins

For versions of MySQL prior to 4.1, subselects are not available. However, it's often possible to rephrase a query that uses a subselect in terms of a join. In fact, even if you have MySQL 4.1 or later, it's not a bad idea to examine queries that you might be inclined to write in terms of subselects; a join is sometimes more efficient than a subselect.

Rewriting Subselects That Select Matching Values

The following is an example query containing a subselect; it selects scores from the score table for all tests (that is, it ignores quiz scores):

```
SELECT * FROM score
WHERE event_id IN (SELECT event_id FROM event WHERE type = 'T');
```

The same query can be written without a subselect by converting it to a simple join:

```
SELECT score.* FROM score, event
WHERE score.event_id = event.event_id AND event.type = 'T';
```

As another example, the following query selects scores for female students:

```
SELECT * from score
WHERE student_id IN (SELECT student_id FROM student WHERE sex = 'F');
```

This can be converted to a join as follows:

```
SELECT score.* FROM score, student
WHERE score.student_id = student.student_id AND student.sex = 'F';
```

There is a pattern here. The subselect queries follow this form:

```
SELECT * FROM table1
WHERE column1 IN (SELECT column2a FROM table2 WHERE column2b = value);
```

Such queries can be converted to a join using the following form:

```
SELECT table1.* FROM table1, table2
WHERE table1.column1 = table2.column2a AND table2.column2b = value;
```

Rewriting Subselects That Select Non-Matching (Missing) Values

Another common type of subselect query searches for values in one table that are not present in another table. As we've seen before, the "which values are not present" type of problem is a clue that a LEFT JOIN may be helpful. The following is a query with a subselect that tests for students who are *not* listed in the absence table (it finds those students with perfect attendance):

```
SELECT * FROM student
WHERE student_id NOT IN (SELECT student_id FROM absence);
```

This query can be rewritten using a LEFT JOIN as follows:

```
SELECT student.*
FROM student LEFT JOIN absence ON student.student_id = absence.student_id
WHERE absence.student_id IS NULL;
```

In general terms, the subselect query form is as follows:

```
SELECT * FROM table1
WHERE column1 NOT IN (SELECT column2 FROM table2);
```

A query having that form can be rewritten like this:

```
SELECT table1.*
FROM table1 LEFT JOIN table2 ON table1.column1 = table2.column2
WHERE table2.column2 IS NULL;
```

This assumes that *table2.column2* is declared as NOT NULL.

Retrieving from Multiple Tables with UNION

If you want to create a result set by selecting records from multiple tables one after the other, you can do that using a UNION statement. UNION is available as of MySQL 4, although prior to that you can use a couple of workarounds (shown later).

For the following examples, assume you have three tables, t1, t2, and t3 that look like this:

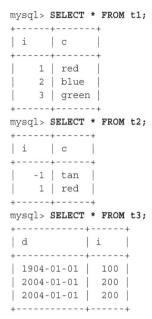

```
mysql> SELECT * FROM t1;
+------+-------+
| i    | c     |
+------+-------+
|    1 | red   |
|    2 | blue  |
|    3 | green |
+------+-------+
mysql> SELECT * FROM t2;
+------+------+
| i    | c    |
+------+------+
|   -1 | tan  |
|    1 | red  |
+------+------+
mysql> SELECT * FROM t3;
+------------+------+
| d          | i    |
+------------+------+
| 1904-01-01 |  100 |
| 2004-01-01 |  200 |
| 2004-01-01 |  200 |
+------------+------+
```

Tables t1 and t2 have integer and character columns, and t3 has date and inte-ger columns. To write a UNION statement that combines multiple retrievals, just write several SELECT statements and put the keyword UNION between them. For example, to select the integer column from each table, do this:

```
mysql> SELECT i FROM t1 UNION SELECT i FROM t2 UNION SELECT i FROM t3;
+------+
| i    |
+------+
|    1 |
|    2 |
|    3 |
|   -1 |
|  100 |
|  200 |
+------+
```

UNION has the following properties:

- The names and data types for the columns of the UNION result come from the names and types of the columns in the first SELECT. The second and subsequent SELECT statements in the UNION must select the same number of columns, but they need not have the same names or types.

Columns are matched by position (not by name), which is why these two queries return different results:

```
mysql> SELECT i, c FROM t1 UNION SELECT i, d FROM t3;
+------+------------+
| i    | c          |
+------+------------+
|    1 | red        |
|    2 | blue       |
|    3 | green      |
|  100 | 1904-01-01 |
|  200 | 2004-01-01 |
+------+------------+
mysql> SELECT i, c FROM t1 UNION SELECT d, i FROM t3;
+------+-------+
| i    | c     |
+------+-------+
|    1 | red   |
|    2 | blue  |
|    3 | green |
| 1904 | 100   |
| 2004 | 200   |
+------+-------+
```

In both cases, the columns selected from t1 (i and c) determine the types used in the UNION result. These columns have integer and string types, so type conversion takes place when selecting values from t3. For the first query, d is converted from date to string. That happens to result in no loss of information. For the second query, d is converted from date to integer (which *does* lose information), and i is converted from integer to string.

- By default, UNION eliminates duplicate rows from the result set:

```
mysql> SELECT * FROM t1 UNION SELECT * FROM t2 UNION SELECT * FROM t3;
+------+-------+
| i    | c     |
+------+-------+
|    1 | red   |
|    2 | blue  |
|    3 | green |
|   -1 | tan   |
| 1904 | 100   |
| 2004 | 200   |
+------+-------+
```

t1 and t2 both have a row containing values of 1 and 'red', but only one such row appears in the output. Also, t3 has two rows containing '2004-01-01' and 200, one of which has been eliminated.

If you want to preserve duplicates, follow the first UNION keyword with ALL:

```
mysql> SELECT * FROM t1 UNION ALL SELECT * FROM t2 UNION SELECT * FROM t3;
+------+-------+
| i    | c     |
+------+-------+
|    1 | red   |
|    2 | blue  |
|    3 | green |
|   -1 | tan   |
|    1 | red   |
| 1904 | 100   |
| 2004 | 200   |
| 2004 | 200   |
+------+-------+
```

- To sort a UNION result, add an ORDER BY clause after the last SELECT; it applies to the query result as a whole. However, because the UNION uses column names from the first SELECT, the ORDER BY should refer to those names, not the column names from the last SELECT, if they differ.

```
mysql> SELECT i, c FROM t1 UNION SELECT i, d FROM t3
    -> ORDER BY c;
+------+------------+
| i    | c          |
+------+------------+
|  100 | 1904-01-01 |
|  200 | 2004-01-01 |
|    2 | blue       |
|    3 | green      |
|    1 | red        |
+------+------------+
```

You can also specify an ORDER BY clause for an individual SELECT statement within the UNION. To do this, enclose the SELECT (including its ORDER BY) within parentheses:

```
mysql> (SELECT i, c FROM t1 ORDER BY i DESC)
    -> UNION (SELECT i, c FROM t2 ORDER BY i);
+------+-------+
| i    | c     |
+------+-------+
|    3 | green |
|    2 | blue  |
|    1 | red   |
|   -1 | tan   |
+------+-------+
```

- LIMIT can be used in a UNION in a manner similar to that for ORDER BY. If added to the end of the statement, it applies to the UNION result as a whole:

```
mysql> SELECT * FROM t1 UNION SELECT * FROM t2 UNION SELECT * FROM t3
    -> LIMIT 1;
+------+------+
| i    | c    |
+------+------+
|    1 | red  |
+------+------+
```

  If enclosed within parentheses as part of an individual SELECT statement, it applies only to that SELECT:

```
mysql> (SELECT * FROM t1 LIMIT 1)
    -> UNION (SELECT * FROM t2 LIMIT 1)
    -> UNION (SELECT * FROM t3 LIMIT 1);
+------+------+
| i    | c    |
+------+------+
|    1 | red  |
|   -1 | tan  |
| 1904 | 100  |
+------+------+
```

- You need not select from different tables. You can select different subsets of the same table using different conditions. This can be useful as an alternative to running several different SELECT queries, because you get all the rows in a single result set rather than as several result sets.

Prior to MySQL 4, UNION is unavailable, but you can work around this difficulty by selecting rows from each table into a temporary table and then selecting the contents of that table. In MySQL 3.23 and later, you can handle this problem easily by allowing the server to create the holding table for you. Also, you can make the table a temporary table so that it will be dropped automatically when your session with the server terminates. For quicker performance, use a HEAP (in-memory) table.

```
CREATE TEMPORARY TABLE tmp TYPE = HEAP SELECT ... FROM t1 WHERE ... ;
INSERT INTO tmp SELECT ... FROM t2 WHERE ... ;
INSERT INTO tmp SELECT ... FROM t3 WHERE ... ;
...
SELECT * FROM tmp ORDER BY ... ;
```

Because tmp is a TEMPORARY table, the server will drop it automatically when your client session ends. (Of course, you can drop the table explicitly as soon as you're done with it to allow the server to free resources associated with it. This is a good idea if you will continue to perform further queries, particularly for HEAP tables.)

For versions of MySQL older than 3.23, the concept is similar, but the details differ because the HEAP table type and TEMPORARY tables are unavailable, as is CREATE TABLE ... SELECT. To adapt the preceding procedure, it's necessary to explicitly create the table first before retrieving any rows into it. (The only table type available will be ISAM, so you cannot use a TYPE option.) Then retrieve the records into the table. When you're done with it, you must use DROP TABLE explicitly because the server will not drop it automatically.

```
CREATE TABLE tmp (column1, column2, ...);
INSERT INTO tmp SELECT ... FROM t1 WHERE ... ;
INSERT INTO tmp SELECT ... FROM t2 WHERE ... ;
INSERT INTO tmp SELECT ... FROM t3 WHERE ... ;
SELECT * FROM tmp ORDER BY ... ;
DROP TABLE tmp;
```

If you want to run a UNION-type query on MyISAM tables that have identical structure, you may be able to set up a MERGE table and query that as a workaround for lack of UNION. (In fact, this can be useful even if you do have UNION, because a query on a MERGE table will be simpler than the corresponding UNION query.) A query on the MERGE table is similar to a UNION that selects corresponding columns from the individual tables that make up the MERGE table. That is, SELECT on a MERGE table is like UNION ALL (duplicates are not removed), and SELECT DISTINCT is like UNION (duplicates are removed).

Multiple-Table Deletes and Updates

Prior to MySQL 4, one limitation of DELETE is that you can refer only to columns of the table from which you're deleting records. But sometimes it's useful to delete records based on whether they match or don't match records in another table. This capability has been added in MySQL 4.0.0. Similarly, it's often useful to update records in one table using the contents of records in another table, a feature introduced in MySQL 4.0.2. This section describes how to perform multiple-table DELETE and UPDATE operations. These types of statements draw heavily on the concepts used for joins, so be sure you're familiar with the material discussed earlier in the "Retrieving Records from Multiple Tables" section.

To perform a single-table DELETE or UPDATE, you refer only to the columns of one table and thus need not qualify the column names with the table name. For example, to delete all records in a table t that have id values greater than 100, you'd write a statement like this:

```
DELETE FROM t WHERE id > 100;
```

But what if you want to delete records based not on properties inherent in the records themselves but rather on their relationship to records in another table? For example, suppose you want to delete from t those records with id values that are found in another table t2?

To write a multiple-table DELETE, name all the tables in a FROM clause and specify the conditions used to match up records in the tables in the WHERE clause. The following statement deletes records from table t1 where there is a matching id value in table t2:

```
DELETE t1 FROM t1, t2 WHERE t1.id = t2.id;
```

Notice that the FROM clause names all the tables involved in the operation, just as when writing a join. In addition, if a column name appears in more than one of the tables, it becomes ambiguous and must be qualified with a table name. This too is similar to writing a join.

The syntax also allows for deleting records from multiple tables at once. To delete rows from *both* tables where there are matching id values, name them both after the DELETE keyword:

```
DELETE t1, t2 FROM t1, t2 WHERE t1.id = t2.id;
```

What if you want to delete non-matching records? Employ the same strategy that you'd use when writing a SELECT that identifies the non-matching records. That is, use a LEFT JOIN or RIGHT JOIN. For example, to identify records in t1 that have no match in t2, you'd write a SELECT as follows:

```
SELECT t1.* FROM t1 LEFT JOIN t2 ON t1.id = t2.id WHERE t2.id IS NULL;
```

The analogous DELETE statement to find and remove those records from t1 uses a LEFT JOIN as well:

```
DELETE t1 FROM t1 LEFT JOIN t2 ON t1.id = t2.id WHERE t2.id IS NULL;
```

A somewhat different multiple-table DELETE syntax is supported as of MySQL 4.0.2. With this syntax, use a FROM clause to indicate which tables records are to be deleted from and a USING clause to list the tables that determine which records to delete. The preceding multiple-table DELETE statements can be rewritten using this syntax as follows:

```
DELETE FROM t1 USING t1, t2 WHERE t1.id = t2.id;
DELETE FROM t1, t2 USING t1, t2 WHERE t1.id = t2.id;
DELETE FROM t1 USING t1 LEFT JOIN t2 ON t1.id = t2.id WHERE t2.id IS NULL;
```

Another type of multiple-table DELETE than is described here can be achieved by setting up a foreign key relationship between tables that includes an ON DELETE CASCADE constraint. See the "Foreign Keys and Referential Integrity" section later in this chapter for details.

The principles involved in writing multiple-table UPDATE statements are quite similar to those used for DELETE: Name all the tables that participate in the operation and qualify column references as necessary. Suppose that the quiz you gave on September 23, 2002 contained a question that everyone got wrong, and then you discover that the reason for this is that your answer key was incorrect. As a result, you must add a point to everyone's score. Without multiple-table UPDATE capability, you might accomplish this using two statements. First, look up the event ID corresponding to the quiz for the given date:

```
SELECT @id := event_id FROM event WHERE date = '2002-09-23' AND type = 'Q';
```

Then use the ID to identify the relevant score records:

```
UPDATE score SET score = score + 1 WHERE event_id = @id;
```

With a multiple-table UPDATE, you can do the same thing with a single statement:

```
UPDATE score, event SET score.score = score.score + 1
WHERE score.event_id = event.event_id
AND event.date = '2002-09-23' AND event.type = 'Q';
```

You not only can identify records to update based on the contents of another table, you can copy column values from one table to another. The following statement copies t1.a to t2.a for records that have a matching id column value:

```
UPDATE t1, t2 SET t2.a = t1.a WHERE t2.id = t1.id;
```

Performing Transactions

A transaction is a set of SQL statements that are executed as a unit without interruption. One use for transactions is to make sure that the records involved in an operation are not modified by other clients while you're working with them. MySQL automatically performs locking for single SQL statements to keep clients from interfering with each other. (For example, two clients cannot update the same record in a table simultaneously.) But automatic single-statement locking is not always sufficient to guarantee that a database operation achieves its intended result, because some operations are performed over the course of several statements. In this case, different operations may interfere with each other. A transaction groups statements into a single execution unit to prevent concurrency problems that might otherwise occur in a multiple-client environment.

Transaction support also includes commit and rollback capabilities, which allows you to require that the statements must execute as a unit or not at all.

That is, if the transaction succeeds, you know that all the statements within it executed successfully. If any part of the transaction fails, any statements executed up to that point within it are undone, leaving the database in the state it was in prior to the point at which the transaction began.

Transactional systems typically are characterized as providing ACID properties. ACID is an acronym for Atomic, Consistent, Isolated, and Durable, referring to four properties that transactions should have:

- **Atomicity**. The statements a transaction consists of form a logical unit. You can't have just some of them execute.
- **Consistency**. The database is consistent before and after the transaction executes. In other words, the transaction doesn't make a mess of your database.
- **Isolation**. One transaction has no effect on another.
- **Durability**. When a transaction executes successfully to completion, its effects are recorded permanently in the database.

Some of MySQL's table types are non-transactional (ISAM, MyISAM, and HEAP), and some are transactional (BDB and InnoDB). This section describes the types of problems that can occur if you don't pay attention to transactional issues, as well as how to address them using both non-transactional and transactional approaches.

Why Transactions Are Useful

The following example illustrates how concurrency problems can occur when multiple clients attempt to make changes to a database using operations that each require several statements. Suppose you're in the garment sales business and your cash register software automatically updates your inventory levels whenever one of your salesmen processes a sale. The sequence of events shown here outlines the operations that take place when multiple sales occur. For the example, assume that the initial shirt inventory level is 47.

1. Salesman A sells three shirts and registers the sale. The register software begins to update the database by selecting the current shirt count (47):

   ```
   SELECT quantity FROM inventory WHERE item = 'shirt';
   ```

2. In the meantime, Salesman B has sold two shirts and registered the sale. The software at the second register also begins to update the database:

   ```
   SELECT quantity FROM inventory WHERE item = 'shirt';
   ```

3. The first register computes the new inventory level to be 47–3 = 44 and updates the shirt count accordingly:

```
UPDATE inventory SET quantity = 44 WHERE item = 'shirt';
```

4. The second register computes the new inventory level to be 47–2 = 45 and updates the count:

```
UPDATE inventory SET quantity = 45 WHERE item = 'shirt';
```

At the end of this sequence of events, you've sold five shirts (that's good), but the inventory level says 45 (that's bad, because it should be 42). The problem is that if you look up the inventory level in one statement and update the value in another statement, you have a multiple-statement operation. The action taken in the second statement is dependent on the value retrieved in the first. If separate multiple-statement operations occur during overlapping time frames, the statements from each operation intertwine and interfere with each other. To solve this problem, it's necessary that the statements for a given operation execute without interference from other operations. A transactional system ensures this by executing each salesman's statements as a unit. As a result, Salesman B's statements won't execute until those for Salesman A have completed.

Another issue that occurs in database processing with multiple-statement operations is that, unless handled properly, an error occurring partway through the operation can leave your database in a halfway-updated (inconsistent) state. The typical example of this involves a financial transfer where money from one account is placed into another account. Suppose Bill writes a check to Bob for $100.00 and Bob cashes the check. Bill's account should be decremented by $100.00 and Bob's account incremented by the same amount:

```
UPDATE account SET balance = balance - 100 WHERE name = 'Bill';
UPDATE account SET balance = balance + 100 WHERE name = 'Bob';
```

If a crash occurs between the two statements, the operation is incomplete. If transactional capabilities are not available to you, you have to figure out the state of ongoing operations at crash time by examining the update log manually to determine how to undo them or complete them. The rollback capabilities of transaction support allow you to handle this situation properly by undoing the effect of the statements that executed before the error occurred. (You may still have to determine which transactions weren't entered and reissue them, but at least you don't have to worry about half-transactions making your database inconsistent.)

Non-Transactional Approaches to Transactional Problems

In a non-transactional environment, some transactional issues can be dealt with and some cannot. The following discussion covers what you can and cannot achieve without using transactions. Consider once again the shirt inventory scenario described earlier. To deal with the concurrency issues inherent in that situation, you can take a couple of approaches:

- **Lock the tables explicitly.** You can group statements and execute them as a unit by surrounding them with LOCK TABLES and UNLOCK TABLES statements. Lock all the tables that you need to use, issue your queries, and release the locks. This prevents anyone else from changing the tables while you have them locked. Using table locking, the inventory update scenario might be handled as follows:

  1. Salesman A sells three shirts and registers the sale. The register software begins the inventory process by acquiring a table lock and retrieving the current shirt count (47):

     ```
     LOCK TABLES inventory WRITE;
     SELECT quantity FROM inventory WHERE item = 'shirt';
     ```

     A WRITE lock is necessary here because the ultimate goal of the operation is to modify the inventory table, which involves writing to it.

  2. In the meantime, Salesman B has sold two shirts and registered the sale. The software at the second register also begins to update the database by acquiring a lock:

     ```
     LOCK TABLES inventory WRITE;
     ```

     In this case, this statement will block because Salesman A already holds a lock on the table.

  3. The first register computes the new inventory level to be 47−3 = 44, updates the shirt count, and releases the lock:

     ```
     UPDATE inventory SET quantity = 44 WHERE item = 'shirt';
     UNLOCK TABLES;
     ```

  4. When the first register releases the lock, the second register's lock request succeeds, and it can proceed to retrieve the current shirt count (44):

     ```
     SELECT quantity FROM inventory WHERE item = 'shirt';
     ```

5. The second register computes the new inventory level to be
   44–2 = 42, updates the shirt count, and releases the lock:

   ```
   UPDATE inventory SET quantity = 42 WHERE item = 'shirt';
   UNLOCK TABLES;
   ```

   Now the statements from the two operations don't get mixed up
   and the inventory level is set properly.

   If you're using multiple tables, you must lock all of them before you
   execute the grouped queries. If you only read from a particular
   table, however, you need only a read lock on it, not a write lock.
   (This lets other clients read the tables while you're using them,
   but prevents clients from writing to them.) Suppose you have a set
   of queries in which you want to make some changes to the inventory table, and you also need to read some data from a customer
   table. In this case, you need a write lock on the inventory table
   and a read lock on the customer table:

   ```
   LOCK TABLES inventory WRITE, customer READ;
   ... use the tables here ...
   UNLOCK TABLES;
   ```

- **Use relative updates, not absolute updates.** For the inventory
  updating method that uses explicit table locking, the operation involves
  looking up the current inventory level with one statement, computing
  the new value based on the number of shirts sold, and then updating the
  level to the new value with another statement. Another way to keep
  operations performed by multiple clients from interfering with each
  other is to reduce each operation to a single statement. This eliminates
  inter-statement dependencies that arise in multiple-statement operations.
  Not every operation can be handled by a single statement, but for the
  inventory update scenario, this strategy works well. It's possible to perform each inventory update in one step simply by modifying the shirt
  count relative to its current value:

  1. Salesman A sells three shirts and the register software decrements
     the shirt count by three:

     ```
     UPDATE inventory SET quantity = quantity - 3 WHERE item = 'shirt';
     ```

  2. Salesman B sells two shirts and the register software decrements the
     shirt count by two:

     ```
     UPDATE inventory SET quantity = quantity - 2 WHERE item = 'shirt';
     ```

With this method, each modification to the database no longer requires multiple statements and thus eliminates concurrency issues. This means there is no need to use explicit table locks. If an operation you want to perform is similar to this, there may be no need for transactions at all.

These non-transactional approaches can be applied successfully to many types of problems, but they have certain limitations:

- Not every operation can be written in terms of relative updates. Sometimes you *must* use multiple statements, in which case concurrency issues have to be considered and dealt with.

- You may be able to keep clients from interfering with each other by locking tables for the duration of a multiple-statement operation, but what happens if an error occurs in the middle of the operation? In this case, you'd want the effects of the earlier statements to be undone so that the database isn't left in a half-modified and inconsistent state. Unfortunately, although table locking can help you address concurrency issues, it provides no assistance in recovering from errors.

- The locking strategy requires you to lock and unlock your tables yourself. If you revise the operation to be performed in such a way that the set of tables affected changes, you must remember to modify the LOCK TABLES statement accordingly. A database system with transaction support would determine which locks are necessary and acquire them automatically.

Transactional capabilities help you deal with all these issues. A transaction handler executes a set of statements as a unit and manages concurrency issues by preventing clients from getting in the way of each other. It also allows rollback in the case of failure to keep half-executed operations from damaging your database, and it automatically acquires any locks that are necessary.

Using Transactions to Ensure Safe Statement Execution

To use transactions, you must use a transactional table type. The ISAM, MyISAM, and HEAP table types will not work; you must use either BDB or InnoDB tables. The BDB and InnoDB handlers first appeared in binary distributions in MySQL 3.23.17 and 3.23.29, respectively, and were added to source distributions as of MySQL 3.23.34. However, it's best to use more recent distributions if possible, to take advantage of the improvements that have been made since then. If you're not sure whether your server includes the BDB or InnoDB table handlers, see the "Determining Which Table Types Your Server Supports" section earlier in this chapter.

By default, MySQL runs in auto-commit mode, which means that changes made by individual statements are committed to the database immediately to make them permanent. In effect, each statement is its own transaction. To perform transactions explicitly, disable auto-commit mode and then tell MySQL when to commit or roll back changes.

One way to perform a transaction is to issue a BEGIN statement to disable auto-commit mode, execute the statements that make up the transaction, and end the transaction with a COMMIT statement to make the changes permanent. If an error occurs during the transaction, cancel it by issuing a ROLLBACK statement instead to undo the changes. BEGIN suspends the current auto-commit mode, so after the transaction has been committed or rolled back, the mode reverts to its state prior to the BEGIN. (If auto-commit was enabled beforehand, ending the transaction puts you back in auto-commit mode. If it was disabled, ending the current transaction causes you to begin the next one.)

The following example illustrates this approach. First, create a table to use:

```
mysql> CREATE TABLE t (name CHAR(20), UNIQUE (name)) TYPE = INNODB;
```

The statement creates an InnoDB table, but you can use BDB if you like. Next, initiate a transaction with BEGIN, add a couple of rows to the table, commit the transaction, and see what the table looks like:

```
mysql> BEGIN;
mysql> INSERT INTO t SET name = 'William';
mysql> INSERT INTO t SET name = 'Wallace';
mysql> COMMIT;
mysql> SELECT * FROM t;
+---------+
| name    |
+---------+
| Wallace |
| William |
+---------+
```

You can see that the rows have been recorded in the table. If you had started up another instance of mysql and selected the contents of t after the inserts but before the commit, the rows would not show up. They would not become visible to the other mysql process until the COMMIT statement had been issued by the first process.

If an error occurs during a transaction, you can cancel it with ROLLBACK. Using the t table again, you can see this by issuing the following statements:

```
mysql> BEGIN;
mysql> INSERT INTO t SET name = 'Gromit';
mysql> INSERT INTO t SET name = 'Wallace';
ERROR 1062: Duplicate entry 'Wallace' for key 1
mysql> ROLLBACK;
mysql> SELECT * FROM t;
+---------+
| name    |
+---------+
| Wallace |
| William |
+---------+
```

The second INSERT attempts to place a row into the table that duplicates an existing name value. The statement fails because name has a UNIQUE index. After issuing the ROLLBACK, the table has only the two rows that it contains prior to the failed transaction. In particular, the INSERT that was performed just prior to the point of the error has been undone and its effect is not recorded in the table.

Issuing a BEGIN statement while a transaction is in process commits the current transaction implicitly before beginning a new one.

Another way to perform transactions is to manipulate the auto-commit mode directly using SET statements:

```
SET AUTOCOMMIT = 0;
SET AUTOCOMMIT = 1;
```

Setting AUTOCOMMIT to zero disables auto-commit mode. The effect of any following statements become part of the current transaction, which you end by issuing a COMMIT or ROLLBACK statement to commit or cancel it. With this method, auto-commit mode remains off until you turn it back on, so ending one transaction also begins the next one. You can also commit a transaction by re-enabling auto-commit mode.

To see how this approach works, begin with the same table as for the previous examples:

```
mysql> DROP TABLE t;
mysql> CREATE TABLE t (name CHAR(20), UNIQUE (name)) TYPE = INNODB;
```

Then disable auto-commit mode, insert some records, and commit the transaction:

```
mysql> SET AUTOCOMMIT = 0;
mysql> INSERT INTO t SET name = 'William';
mysql> INSERT INTO t SET name = 'Wallace';
```

```
mysql> COMMIT;
mysql> SELECT * FROM t;
+---------+
| name    |
+---------+
| Wallace |
| William |
+---------+
```

At this point, the two records have been committed to the table, but auto-commit mode remains disabled. If you issue further statements, they become part of a new transaction, which may be committed or rolled back independently of the first transaction. To verify that auto-commit is still off and that ROLLBACK will cancel uncommitted statements, issue the following queries:

```
mysql> INSERT INTO t SET name = 'Gromit';
mysql> INSERT INTO t SET name = 'Wallace';
ERROR 1062: Duplicate entry 'Wallace' for key 1
mysql> ROLLBACK;
mysql> SELECT * FROM t;
+---------+
| name    |
+---------+
| Wallace |
| William |
+---------+
```

To restore auto-commit mode, use the following statement:

```
SET AUTOCOMMIT = 1;
```

Transactions also end under the following circumstances:

- In addition to statements like SET AUTOCOMMIT, BEGIN, COMMIT, and ROLLBACK that affect transactions explicitly, certain other statements do so implicitly because they cannot be part of a transaction. If you issue any of these while a transaction is in progress, the server commits the transaction first before executing the statement. Statements that cause a commit are as follows:

```
ALTER TABLE
CREATE INDEX
DROP DATABASE
DROP INDEX
DROP TABLE
LOAD MASTER DATA
LOCK TABLES
RENAME TABLE
TRUNCATE TABLE
UNLOCK TABLES (if tables currently are locked)
```

- If the client connection ends or is broken during a transaction before a commit occurs, the server rolls back the transaction automatically.

Transactions are useful in all kinds of situations. For example, suppose you're working with the `score` table that is part of the grade-keeping project and you discover that the grades for two students have gotten mixed up and need to be switched. The grades as entered incorrectly are as follows:

```
mysql> SELECT * FROM score WHERE event_id = 5 AND student_id IN (8,9);
+------------+----------+-------+
| student_id | event_id | score |
+------------+----------+-------+
|          8 |        5 |    18 |
|          9 |        5 |    13 |
+------------+----------+-------+
```

To fix this, student 8 should be given a score of 13 and student 9 a score of 18. That can be done easily with two statements:

```
UPDATE score SET score = 13 WHERE event_id = 5 AND student_id = 8;
UPDATE score SET score = 18 WHERE event_id = 5 AND student_id = 9;
```

However, it's necessary to ensure that both statements succeed as a unit—a problem to which transactional methods can be applied. To use BEGIN, do the following:

```
mysql> BEGIN;
mysql> UPDATE score SET score = 13 WHERE event_id = 5 AND student_id = 8;
mysql> UPDATE score SET score = 18 WHERE event_id = 5 AND student_id = 9;
mysql> COMMIT;
```

To accomplish the same thing by manipulating the auto-commit mode explicitly instead, do this:

```
mysql> SET AUTOCOMMIT = 0;
mysql> UPDATE score SET score = 13 WHERE event_id = 5 AND student_id = 8;
mysql> UPDATE score SET score = 18 WHERE event_id = 5 AND student_id = 9;
mysql> COMMIT;
mysql> SET AUTOCOMMIT = 1;
```

Either way, the result is that the scores are swapped properly:

```
mysql> SELECT * FROM score WHERE event_id = 5 AND student_id IN (8,9);
+------------+----------+-------+
| student_id | event_id | score |
+------------+----------+-------+
|          8 |        5 |    13 |
|          9 |        5 |    18 |
+------------+----------+-------+
```

Foreign Keys and Referential Integrity

A foreign key relationship allows you to declare that an index in one table is related to an index in another and allows you to place constraints on what may be done to the table containing the foreign key. The database enforces the rules of this relationship to maintain referential integrity. For example, the score table in the sampdb sample database contains a student_id column, which we use to relate score records to students in the student table. When we created these tables in Chapter 1, we did not set up any explicit relationship between them. Were we to do so, we would declare score.student_id to be a foreign key for the student.student_id column. That prevents a record from being entered into the score table unless it contains a student_id value that exists in the student table. (In other words, the foreign key prevents entry of scores for non-existent students.) We could also set up a constraint such that if a student is deleted from the student table, all corresponding records for the student in the score table should be deleted automatically as well. This is called *cascaded delete* because the effect of the delete cascades from one table to another.

Foreign keys help maintain the consistency of your data, and they provide a certain measure of convenience. Without foreign keys, you are responsible for keeping track of inter-table dependencies and maintaining their consistency from within your applications. In many cases, doing this isn't really that much work. It amounts to little more than adding a few extra DELETE statements to make sure that when you delete a record from one table, you also delete the corresponding records in any related tables. But if your tables have particularly complex relationships, you may not want to be responsible for implementing these dependencies in your applications. Besides, if the database engine will perform consistency checks for you, why not let it?

Foreign key support in MySQL is provided by the InnoDB table handler. This section describes how to set up InnoDB tables to define foreign keys, and how foreign keys affect the way you use tables. But first, it's necessary to define some terms:

- The parent is the table that contains the original key values.
- The child is the related table that refers to key values in the parent.
- Parent table key values are used to associate the two tables. Specifically, the index in the child table refers to the index in the parent. Its values must match those in the parent or else be set to NULL to indicate that there is no associated parent table record. The index in the child table is known as the foreign key—that is, the key that is foreign (external) to the parent table but contains values that point to the parent. A foreign key relationship can be set up to disallow NULL values, in which case all foreign key values must match a value in the parent table.

InnoDB enforces these rules to guarantee that the foreign key relationship stays intact with no mismatches. This is called *referential integrity*.

The syntax for declaring a foreign key in a child table is as follows, with optional parts shown in square brackets:

```
FOREIGN KEY [index_name] (index_columns)
    REFERENCES tbl_name (index_columns)
    [ON DELETE action]
    [ON UPDATE action]
    [MATCH FULL | MATCH PARTIAL]
```

Note that although all parts of this syntax are parsed, InnoDB does not implement the semantics for all the clauses. The ON UPDATE and MATCH clauses are not supported and are ignored if you specify them.[1]

The parts of the definition that InnoDB pays attention to are:

- FOREIGN KEY indicates the columns that make up the index in the child table that must match index values in the parent table. *index_name*, if given, is ignored.

- REFERENCES names the parent table and the index columns in that table that correspond to the foreign key in the child table. The *index_columns* part of the REFERENCES clause must have the same number of columns as the *index_columns* that follows the FOREIGN KEY keywords.

- ON DELETE allows you to specify what happens to the child table when parent table records are deleted. The possible actions are as follows:

  - ON DELETE CASCADE causes matching child records to be deleted when the corresponding parent record is deleted. In essence, the effect of the delete is cascaded from the parent to the child. This allows you to perform multiple-table deletions by deleting rows only from the parent table and letting InnoDB take care of deleting rows from the child table.

  - ON DELETE SET NULL causes index columns in matching child records to be set to NULL when the parent record is deleted. If you use this option, all the child table columns named in the foreign key definition must be declared to allow NULL values. (One implication of using this action is that you cannot declare the foreign key to be a PRIMARY KEY because primary keys do not allow NULL values.)

---

1. For table types other than InnoDB, the entire FOREIGN KEY definition is parsed and ignored.

To define a foreign key, adhere to the following guidelines:

- The child table must have an index where the foreign key columns are listed as its first columns. The parent table must also have an index in which the columns in the REFERENCES clause are listed as its first columns. (In other words, the columns in the key must be indexed in the tables on both ends of the foreign key relationship.) You must specify these indexes explicitly in the parent and child tables. InnoDB will not create them for you.

- Corresponding columns in the parent and child indexes must have compatible types. For example, you cannot match an INT column with a CHAR column. Corresponding character columns must be the same length. Corresponding integer columns must have the same size and must both be signed or both be UNSIGNED.

Let's see an example of how all this works. Begin by creating tables named parent and child, such that the child table contains a foreign key that references the par_id column in the parent table:

```
CREATE TABLE parent
(
    par_id      INT NOT NULL,
    PRIMARY KEY (par_id)
) TYPE = INNODB;

CREATE TABLE child
(
    par_id      INT NOT NULL,
    child_id    INT NOT NULL,
    PRIMARY KEY (par_id, child_id),
    FOREIGN KEY (par_id) REFERENCES parent (par_id) ON DELETE CASCADE
) TYPE = INNODB;
```

The foreign key in this case uses ON DELETE CASCADE to specify that when a record is deleted from the parent table, child records with a matching par_id value should be removed automatically as well.

Now insert a few records into the parent table and add some records that have related key values to the child table:

```
mysql> INSERT INTO parent (par_id) VALUES(1),(2),(3);
mysql> INSERT INTO child (par_id,child_id) VALUES(1,1),(1,2);
mysql> INSERT INTO child (par_id,child_id) VALUES(2,1),(2,2),(2,3);
mysql> INSERT INTO child (par_id,child_id) VALUES(3,1);
```

These statements result in the following table contents, where each par_id value in the child table matches a par_id value in the parent table:

```
mysql> SELECT * FROM parent;
+--------+
| par_id |
+--------+
|      1 |
|      2 |
|      3 |
+--------+
mysql> SELECT * FROM child;
+--------+----------+
| par_id | child_id |
+--------+----------+
|      1 |        1 |
|      1 |        2 |
|      2 |        1 |
|      2 |        2 |
|      2 |        3 |
|      3 |        1 |
+--------+----------+
```

To verify that InnoDB enforces the key relationship for insertion, try adding a record to the child table that has a par_id value not found in the parent table:

```
mysql> INSERT INTO child (par_id,child_id) VALUES(4,1);
ERROR 1216: Cannot add a child row: a foreign key constraint fails
```

Now see what happens when you delete a parent record:

```
mysql> DELETE FROM parent where par_id = 1;
```

MySQL deletes the record from the parent table:

```
mysql> SELECT * FROM parent;
+--------+
| par_id |
+--------+
|      2 |
|      3 |
+--------+
```

In addition, it cascades the effect of the DELETE statement to the child table:

```
mysql> SELECT * FROM child;
+--------+----------+
| par_id | child_id |
+--------+----------+
|      2 |        1 |
|      2 |        2 |
|      2 |        3 |
|      3 |        1 |
+--------+----------+
```

The preceding example shows how to arrange to have deletion of a parent record cause deletion of any corresponding child records. Another possibility is to let the child records remain in the table but have their foreign key columns set to NULL. To do this, it's necessary to make three changes to the definition of the child table:

- Use ON DELETE SET NULL rather than ON DELETE CASCADE. This tells InnoDB to set the foreign key column (par_id) to NULL instead of deleting the records.
- The original definition of child declares par_id as NOT NULL. That won't work with ON DELETE SET NULL, of course, so the column must be declared NULL instead.
- The original definition of child also declares par_id to be part of a PRIMARY KEY. However, a PRIMARY KEY cannot contain NULL values. Therefore, changing par_id to allow NULL also requires that the PRIMARY KEY be changed to a UNIQUE index. InnoDB UNIQUE indexes enforce uniqueness except for NULL values, which may occur multiple times in the index.

To see the effect of these changes, recreate the parent table using the original definition and load the same initial records into it. Then create the child table using the new definition shown here:

```
CREATE TABLE child
(
    par_id      INT NULL,
    child_id    INT NOT NULL,
    UNIQUE (par_id, child_id),
    FOREIGN KEY (par_id) REFERENCES parent (par_id) ON DELETE SET NULL
) TYPE = INNODB;
```

With respect to inserting new records, the child table behaves the same. That is, it allows insertion of records with par_id values found in the parent table, but disallows entry of values that aren't listed there:[2]

```
mysql> INSERT INTO child (par_id,child_id) VALUES(1,1),(1,2);
mysql> INSERT INTO child (par_id,child_id) VALUES(2,1),(2,2),(2,3);
mysql> INSERT INTO child (par_id,child_id) VALUES(3,1);
mysql> INSERT INTO child (par_id,child_id) VALUES(4,1);
ERROR 1216: Cannot add a child row: a foreign key constraint fails
```

2. Actually, there is one difference with respect to inserting records. Because the par_id column now is declared as NULL, you can explicitly insert records into the child table that contain NULL and no error will occur.

A difference in behavior occurs when you delete a parent record. Try removing a parent record and then check the contents of the `child` table to see what happens:

```
mysql> DELETE FROM parent where par_id = 1;
mysql> SELECT * FROM child;
+--------+----------+
| par_id | child_id |
+--------+----------+
|  NULL  |        1 |
|  NULL  |        2 |
|     2  |        1 |
|     2  |        2 |
|     2  |        3 |
|     3  |        1 |
+--------+----------+
```

In this case, the child records that had 1 in the `par_id` column are not deleted. Instead, the `par_id` column is set to NULL, as specified by the ON DELETE SET NULL constraint.

Foreign key capabilities did not all appear at the same time, as shown in the following table. The initial foreign key support prevents insertion or deletion of child records that violate key constraints. The other features were added later.

Feature	Version
Basic foreign key support	3.23.44
ON DELETE CASCADE	3.23.50
ON DELETE SET NULL	3.23.50

You can infer from the table that for the most complete foreign key feature support, it's best to use a version of MySQL at least as recent as 3.23.50 if at all possible. Another reason to use more recent versions is that the following problems were not rectified until MySQL 3.23.50:

- It is dangerous to use ALTER TABLE or CREATE INDEX to modify an InnoDB table that participates in foreign key relationships in either a parent or child role. The statement removes the foreign key constraints.

- SHOW CREATE TABLE does not show foreign key definitions. This also applies to `mysqldump`, which makes it problematic to properly restore tables that include foreign keys from backup files.

Living Without Foreign Keys

If you don't have InnoDB support (and thus cannot take advantage of foreign keys), what should you do to maintain the integrity of relationships between your tables?

The constraints that foreign keys enforce often are not difficult to implement through application logic. Sometimes, it's simply a matter of how you approach the data entry process. Consider the `student` and `score` tables from the grade-keeping project, which are related implicitly through the `student_id` values in each table. When you administer a test or quiz and have a new set of scores to add to the database, it's unlikely that you'd insert scores for non-existent students. Clearly, the way you'd enter a set of scores would be to start with a list of students from the `student` table, and then for each one, take the score and use the student's ID number to generate a new `score` table record. With this procedure, there isn't any possibility of entering a record for a student that doesn't exist, because you wouldn't just invent a score record to put in the `score` table.

What about the case where you delete a student record? Suppose you want to delete student number 13. This also implies you want to delete any score records for that student. With a foreign key relationship in place that specifies cascading delete, you'd simply delete the `student` table record with the following statement and let MySQL take care of removing the corresponding `score` table records automatically:

```
DELETE FROM student WHERE student_id = 13;
```

Without foreign key support, you must explicitly delete records for all relevant tables to achieve the same effect as cascading on `DELETE`:

```
DELETE FROM student WHERE student_id = 13;
DELETE FROM score WHERE student_id = 13;
```

Another way to do this, available as of MySQL 4, is to use a multiple-table delete that achieves the same effect as a cascaded delete with a single query. But watch out for a subtle trap. The following statement appears to do the trick, but it's actually not quite correct:

```
DELETE student, score FROM student, score
WHERE student.student_id = 13 AND student.student_id = score.student_id;
```

The problem with this statement is that it will fail in the case where the student doesn't have any scores; the `WHERE` clause will find no matches and thus will not delete anything from the `student` table. In this case, a `LEFT JOIN` is more appropriate, because it will identify the `student` table record even in the absence of any matching `score` table records:

```
DELETE student, score FROM student LEFT JOIN score USING (student_id)
WHERE student.student_id = 13;
```

Using FULLTEXT Searches

Versions of MySQL from 3.23.23 on include the capability for performing full text searches. The full text search engine allows you to look for words or phrases without using pattern-matching operations. This capability is enabled for a given table by creating a special kind of index and has the following characteristics:

- Full text searches are based on FULLTEXT indexes, which may be created only for MyISAM tables, and only for TEXT columns and non-BINARY CHAR and VARCHAR columns.

- FULLTEXT searches are not case sensitive. This follows as a consequence of the column types for which FULLTEXT indexes may be used.

- Common words are ignored for FULLTEXT searches, where "common" means "present in at least half the records." It's especially important to remember this when you're setting up a test table to experiment with the FULLTEXT capability. (Be sure to insert at least three records into your test table. If the table has just one or two records, every word in it will occur at least 50 percent of the time and you'll never get any results!) Certain very common words, such as "the," "after," and "other," are stop words that are always ignored. Words that are too short also are ignored. By default, "too short" is defined as less than four characters, but with a recent enough server may be set lower.

- Words are defined as sequences of characters that include letters, digits, apostrophes, and underscores. This means that a string like "full-blooded" is considered to contain two words—"full" and "blooded." Normally, a full text search matches whole words, not partial words, and the FULLTEXT engine considers a record to match a search string if it includes any of the words in the search string. A variant form of search called a boolean full text search allows you to impose the additional constraint that all the words must be present (either in any order, or, to perform a phrase search, in exactly the order listed in the search string). With a boolean search, it's also possible to match records that do *not* include certain words or to add a wildcard modifier to match all words that begin with a given prefix.

- A FULLTEXT index can be created for a single column or multiple columns. If it spans multiple columns, searches based on the index look through all the columns simultaneously. The flip side of this is that when you perform a search, you must specify a column list that corresponds exactly to the set of columns that matches some FULLTEXT index. For example, if you want to search col1 sometimes, col2 sometimes, and both col1 and col2 sometimes, you should have three indexes: one for each of the columns separately, and one that includes both columns.

Some of these features require more recent versions of MySQL than others. The following table shows the versions at which FULLTEXT features were introduced:

Feature	Version
Basic FULLTEXT searching	3.23.23
Configurable parameters	4.0.0
Boolean searches	4.0.1
Phrase searches	4.0.2

The following examples show how to use full text searching by creating FULL-TEXT indexes and then performing queries on them using the MATCH operator.

A FULLTEXT index is created the same way as other indexes. That is, you can define it with CREATE TABLE when creating the table initially or add it afterward with ALTER TABLE or CREATE INDEX. Because FULLTEXT indexes require you to use MyISAM tables, you can take advantage of one of the properties of the MyISAM handler if you're creating a new table to use for FULLTEXT searches: Table loading proceeds more quickly if you populate the table and then add the indexes afterward rather than loading data into an already indexed table. Suppose you have a data file named apothegm.txt containing famous sayings and the people to whom they're attributed:

```
Aeschylus              Time as he grows old teaches many lessons
Alexander Graham Bell  Mr. Watson, come here. I want you!
Benjamin Franklin      It is hard for an empty bag to stand upright
Benjamin Franklin      Little strokes fell great oaks
Benjamin Franklin      Remember that time is money
Miguel de Cervantes    Bell, book, and candle
Proverbs 15:1          A soft answer turneth away wrath
Theodore Roosevelt     Speak softly and carry a big stick
William Shakespeare    But, soft! what light through yonder window breaks?
```

If you want to search by phrase and attribution separately or together, you need to index the columns separately and also create an index that includes both columns. You can create, populate, and index a table named apothegm as follows:

```
CREATE TABLE apothegm (attribution VARCHAR(40), phrase TEXT);
LOAD DATA LOCAL INFILE 'apothegm.txt' INTO TABLE apothegm;
ALTER TABLE apothegm
    ADD FULLTEXT (phrase),
    ADD FULLTEXT (attribution),
    ADD FULLTEXT (phrase, attribution);
```

After setting up the table, perform searches on it using MATCH to name the column or columns to search and AGAINST() to specify the search string. For example:

```
mysql> SELECT * FROM apothegm WHERE MATCH(attribution) AGAINST('roosevelt');
+--------------------+-------------------------------------+
| attribution        | phrase                              |
+--------------------+-------------------------------------+
| Theodore Roosevelt | Speak softly and carry a big stick  |
+--------------------+-------------------------------------+
mysql> SELECT * FROM apothegm WHERE MATCH(phrase) AGAINST('time');
+--------------------+-----------------------------------------+
| attribution        | phrase                                  |
+--------------------+-----------------------------------------+
| Benjamin Franklin  | Remember that time is money             |
| Aeschylus          | Time as he grows old teaches many lessons |
+--------------------+-----------------------------------------+
mysql> SELECT * FROM apothegm WHERE MATCH(attribution,phrase)
    -> AGAINST('bell');
+----------------------+-----------------------------------+
| attribution          | phrase                            |
+----------------------+-----------------------------------+
| Alexander Graham Bell | Mr. Watson, come here. I want you! |
| Miguel de Cervantes  | Bell, book, and candle            |
+----------------------+-----------------------------------+
```

In the last example, note how the query finds records that contain the search word in different columns, which demonstrates the FULLTEXT capability of searching multiple columns at once. Also note that the order of the columns as named in the query is attribution, phrase. That differs from the order in which they were named when the index was created (phrase, attribution), which illustrates that order does not matter. What matters is that there must be some FULLTEXT index that consists of exactly the columns named.

If you just want to see how many records a search matches, use COUNT(*):

```
mysql> SELECT COUNT(*) FROM apothegm WHERE MATCH(phrase) AGAINST('time');
+----------+
| COUNT(*) |
+----------+
|        2 |
+----------+
```

By default, output rows for FULLTEXT searches are ordered by decreasing relevance when you use a MATCH expression in the WHERE clause. Relevance values are non-negative floating point values, with zero indicating "no relevance." To see these values, use a MATCH expression in the column output list:

```
mysql> SELECT phrase, MATCH(phrase) AGAINST('time') AS relevance
    -> FROM apothegm;
+----------------------------------------------------+----------------+
| phrase                                             | relevance      |
+----------------------------------------------------+----------------+
| Time as he grows old teaches many lessons          | 1.1976701021194 |
| Mr. Watson, come here. I want you!                 |              0 |
| It is hard for an empty bag to stand upright       |              0 |
| Little strokes fell great oaks                     |              0 |
| Remember that time is money                        | 1.2109839916229 |
| Bell, book, and candle                             |              0 |
| A soft answer turneth away wrath                   |              0 |
| Speak softly and carry a big stick                 |              0 |
| But, soft! what light through yonder window breaks? |              0 |
+----------------------------------------------------+----------------+
```

By default, a search finds records that contain any of the search words, so a query like the following will return records with either "hard" or "soft":

```
mysql> SELECT * FROM apothegm WHERE MATCH(phrase)
    -> AGAINST('hard soft');
+--------------------+-----------------------------------------------------+
| attribution        | phrase                                              |
+--------------------+-----------------------------------------------------+
| Benjamin Franklin  | It is hard for an empty bag to stand upright        |
| Proverbs 15:1      | A soft answer turneth away wrath                    |
| William Shakespeare | But, soft! what light through yonder window breaks? |
+--------------------+-----------------------------------------------------+
```

Greater control over multiple-word matching can be obtained as of MySQL 4.0.1, when support was added for boolean mode FULLTEXT searches. This type of search is performed by adding IN BOOLEAN MODE after the search string in the AGAINST() function. Boolean searches have the following characteristics:

- The 50% rule is ignored; searches will find words even if they occur in more than half of the records.
- Results are not sorted by relevance.
- Modifiers can be applied to words in the search string. A leading plus or minus sign requires a word to be present or not present in matching records. A search string of 'bell' matches records that contain "bell," but a search string of '+bell -candle' in boolean mode matches only records that contain "bell" and do not contain "candle."

```
mysql> SELECT * FROM apothegm
    -> WHERE MATCH(attribution,phrase)
    -> AGAINST('bell');
```

```
+----------------------+------------------------------------+
| attribution          | phrase                             |
+----------------------+------------------------------------+
| Alexander Graham Bell | Mr. Watson, come here. I want you! |
| Miguel de Cervantes  | Bell, book, and candle             |
+----------------------+------------------------------------+
mysql> SELECT * FROM apothegm
    -> WHERE MATCH(attribution,phrase)
    -> AGAINST('+bell -candle' IN BOOLEAN MODE);
+----------------------+------------------------------------+
| attribution          | phrase                             |
+----------------------+------------------------------------+
| Alexander Graham Bell | Mr. Watson, come here. I want you! |
+----------------------+------------------------------------+
```

A trailing asterisk acts as a wildcard so that any record containing words beginning with the search word match. For example, `'soft*'` matches "soft," "softly," "softness," and so on:

```
mysql> SELECT * FROM apothegm WHERE MATCH(phrase)
    -> AGAINST('soft*' IN BOOLEAN MODE);
+--------------------+--------------------------------------------------+
| attribution        | phrase                                           |
+--------------------+--------------------------------------------------+
| Proverbs 15:1      | A soft answer turneth away wrath                 |
| William Shakespeare | But, soft! what light through yonder window breaks? |
| Theodore Roosevelt | Speak softly and carry a big stick               |
+--------------------+--------------------------------------------------+
```

However, the wildcard feature cannot be used to match words shorter than the minimum index word length.

The full set of modifiers is listed in the entry for MATCH in Appendix C, "Operator and Function Reference."

- Stop words are ignored just as for non-boolean searches, even if marked as required. A search for `'+Alexander +the +great'` will find records containing "Alexander" and "great," but will ignore the stop word "the."

- A phrase search can be performed to require all words to be present in a particular order. Phrase searching requires MySQL 4.0.2. Enclose the search string in double quotes and include punctuation and whitespace as present in the phrase you want to match. In other words, you must specify the *exact* phrase:

```
mysql> SELECT * FROM apothegm
    -> WHERE MATCH(attribution,phrase)
    -> AGAINST('"bell book and candle"' IN BOOLEAN MODE);
Empty set (0.00 sec)
mysql> SELECT * FROM apothegm
    -> WHERE MATCH(attribution,phrase)
    -> AGAINST('"bell, book, and candle"' IN BOOLEAN MODE);
```

```
+---------------------+-----------------------+
| attribution         | phrase                |
+---------------------+-----------------------+
| Miguel de Cervantes | Bell, book, and candle |
+---------------------+-----------------------+
```

- It's possible to perform a boolean mode full text search on columns that are not part of a FULLTEXT index, although this will be much slower than using indexed columns.

Prior to MySQL 4, FULLTEXT search parameters can be modified only by making changes to the source code and recompiling the server. MySQL 4 provides several configurable parameters that can be modified by setting server variables. The two that are of most interest are ft_min_word_len and ft_max_word_len, which determine the shortest and longest words that will be indexed. The default values are 4 and 254; words with lengths outside that range are ignored when FULLTEXT indexes are built.

Suppose you want to change the minimum word length from 4 to 3. Do so like this:

1. Start the server with the ft_min_word_len variable set to 3. To ensure that this happens whenever the server starts, it's best to place the setting in an option file such as /etc/my.cnf:

   ```
   [mysqld]
   set-variable = ft_min_word_len=3
   ```

2. For any existing tables that already have FULLTEXT indexes, you must rebuild those indexes. You can drop and add the indexes, but it's easier just to do the following:

   ```
   REPAIR TABLE tbl_name USE_FRM;
   ```

3. Any new FULLTEXT indexes that you create after changing the parameter will use the new value automatically.

For more information on option files and setting server variables, see Appendix D.

Writing Comments

MySQL allows you to intersperse comments with your SQL code. This can be useful for documenting queries that you store in files. There are two recommended comment styles. First, anything from a '#' character to the end of a line is considered a comment. Second, C-style comments are allowed as well.

That is, anything between the '/*' and '*/' beginning and ending markers is considered a comment. C-style comments can span multiple lines:

```
# this is a single line comment
/* this is also a single line comment */
/* this, however,
   is a multiple line
   comment
*/
```

A third comment style is available as of MySQL 3.23.3: Begin the comment with two dashes and a space ('-- '); everything from the dashes to the end of the line is treated as a comment. Some other databases use the double dash to begin a comment. MySQL allows this but requires the space as an aid for disambiguation. Statements with expressions like 5--7 might be taken as containing a comment starting sequence otherwise. It's not likely you'd write such an expression as 5-- 7, so this is a useful heuristic. Still, it is only a heuristic, and it's probably better to use the '#' or '/*...*/' comment styles and resort to double dashes only when writing code that you may port to other databases that don't understand the other comment styles.

As of MySQL 3.22.7, you can "hide" MySQL-specific keywords in C-style comments by beginning the comment with '/*!' rather than with '/*'. MySQL looks inside this special type of comment and uses the keywords, but other database servers will ignore them as part of the comment. This has a portability benefit, at least for other servers that understand C-style comments. You can write code that takes advantage of MySQL-specific functions when executed by MySQL but that can be used with other database servers without modification. The following two statements are equivalent for database servers other than MySQL, but MySQL will perform an INSERT DELAYED operation for the second:

```
INSERT INTO absence (student_id,date) VALUES(13,'2002-09-28');
INSERT /*! DELAYED */ INTO absence (student_id,date) VALUES(13,'2002-09-28');
```

As of MySQL 3.22.26, C-style comments can be made version-specific. Follow the opening '/*!' sequence with a version number and the server will ignore the comment unless it is at least as recent as the version named. The comment in the following CREATE TABLE statement is ignored unless the server is version 3.23.0 or later:

```
CREATE TABLE t (i INT) /*!32300 TYPE = HEAP */;
```

Features That MySQL Does Not Support

This section describes features not supported by MySQL that are found in some other databases. Some of the items in this list are scheduled for implementation in the future.

- **Stored procedures and triggers.** A stored procedure is SQL code that is compiled and stored in the server. It can be executed later by the server without having to be sent from the client and parsed again. You can also make changes to a procedure to affect any client applications that use it. Trigger capability allows a stored procedure to be activated automatically when some event occurs, such as a record being deleted from a table. For example, you might do this if you wanted to regenerate some complex summary of which the record was a part, to keep the summary up to date. The current timetable is to implement stored procedures in MySQL 5.

- **Views.** A view is a logical entity that acts like a table but is not one. It provides a way to look at columns from different tables as though they're all part of the same table. Views are sometimes called *virtual tables*. The current timetable is to implement views in MySQL 5.

- **Record-level privileges.** MySQL supports various levels of privileges, from global privileges down to database, table, and column privileges. It does not support record-level privileges. However, you can use the GET_LOCK() and RELEASE_LOCK() functions in your applications to implement cooperative record locks. The procedure for this is described in the entry for GET_LOCK() in Appendix C.

- **'--' as a comment.** This comment style is not supported because it's an ambiguous construct, although as of MySQL 3.23.3, a comment beginning with two dashes and a space is accepted. See the "Writing Comments" section earlier in this chapter for more information.

4

Query Optimization

THE WORLD OF RELATIONAL DATABASE THEORY is a world dominated by tables and sets, and operations on tables and sets. A database is a set of tables, and a table is a set of rows and columns. When you issue a SELECT query to retrieve rows from a table, you get back another set of rows and columns. These are abstract notions that make no reference to the underlying representation a database system uses to operate on the data in your tables. Another abstraction is that operations on tables happen all at once; queries are conceptualized as set operations and there is no concept of time in set theory.

The real world, of course, is quite different. Database management systems implement abstract concepts but do so on real hardware bound by real physical constraints. As a result, queries take time—sometimes an annoyingly long time. And we, being impatient creatures, don't like to wait, so we leave the abstract world of instantaneous mathematical operations on sets and look around for ways to speed up our queries. Fortunately, there are several techniques for doing so. We index tables to allow the database server to look up rows more quickly. We consider how to write queries to take advantage of those indexes to the fullest extent. We write queries to affect the server's scheduling mechanism so that queries arriving from multiple clients cooperate better. We modify the server's operating parameters to get it to perform more efficiently. We think about what's going on with the underlying hardware and how we can work around its physical constraints to improve performance.

Those are the kinds of issues that this chapter focuses on, with the goal of assisting you in optimizing the performance of your database system so that it processes your queries as quickly as possible. MySQL is already quite fast, but even the fastest database can run queries more quickly if you help it do so.

Using Indexing

Indexing is the most important tool you have for speeding up queries. There are other techniques available to you, too, but generally the one thing that will make the most difference is the proper use of indexes. On the MySQL mailing list, people often ask for help in making a query run faster. In a surprisingly large number of cases, there are no indexes on the tables in question, and adding indexes often solves the problem immediately. It doesn't always work like that, because optimization isn't always simple. Nevertheless, if you don't use indexes, in many cases you're just wasting your time trying to improve performance by other means. Use indexing first to get the biggest performance boost and then see what other techniques might be helpful.

This section describes what an index is and how indexing improves query performance. It also discusses the circumstances under which indexes might degrade performance and provides guidelines for choosing indexes for your table wisely. In the next section, we'll discuss MySQL's query optimizer. It's good to have some understanding of the optimizer in addition to knowing how to create indexes because then you'll be better able to take advantage of the indexes you create. Certain ways of writing queries actually prevent your indexes from being useful, and generally you'll want to avoid having that happen. (Not always, though. Sometimes you'll want to override the optimizer's behavior. We'll cover some of those cases, too.)

Benefits of Indexing

Let's consider how an index works by beginning with a table that has no indexes. An unindexed table is simply an unordered collection of rows. For example, Figure 4.1 shows the ad table that we first saw in Chapter 1, "Getting Started with MySQL and SQL." There are no indexes on this table, so to find the rows for a particular company, it's necessary to examine each row in the table to see if it matches the desired value. This involves a full table scan, which is slow as well as tremendously inefficient if the table is large but contains only a few records matching the search criteria.

Figure 4.2 shows the same table but with the addition of an index on the company_num column in the ad table. The index contains an entry for each row in the ad table, but the index entries are sorted by company_num value. Now, instead of searching through the table row by row looking for items that match, we can use the index. Suppose we're looking for all rows for company 13. We begin scanning the index and find three rows for that company. Then we reach the row for company 14, a value higher than the one we're looking for. Index values are sorted, so when we read the record containing 14, we know we won't find any more matches and can quit looking. Thus, one efficiency gained by using the index is that we can tell where the matching rows end and can skip the rest. Another efficiency is that there are positioning algorithms for finding the first matching entry without doing a linear scan from the start of the index (for example, a binary search is much quicker than a scan). That way, we can quickly position to the first matching value and save a lot of time in the search. Databases use various techniques for positioning to index values quickly, but it's not so important here what those techniques are. What's important is that they work and that indexing is a good thing.

ad table

company_num	ad_num	hit_fee
14	48	0.01
23	49	0.02
17	52	0.01
13	55	0.03
23	62	0.02
23	63	0.01
23	64	0.02
13	77	0.03
23	99	0.03
14	101	0.01
13	102	0.01
17	119	0.02

Figure 4.1　Unindexed ad table.

ad table

index		company_num	ad_num	hit_fee
13		14	48	0.01
13		23	49	0.02
13		17	52	0.01
14		13	55	0.03
14		23	62	0.02
17		23	63	0.01
17		23	64	0.02
23		13	77	0.03
23		23	99	0.03
23		14	101	0.01
23		13	102	0.01
23		17	119	0.02

Figure 4.2　Indexed ad table.

You may be asking why we don't just sort the data file and dispense with the index file. Wouldn't that produce the same type of improvement in search speed? Yes, it would—if the table had a single index. But you might want to add a second index, and you can't sort the data file two different ways at once. (For example, you might want one index on customer names and another on customer ID numbers or phone numbers.) Using indexes as entities separate from the data file solves the problem and allows multiple indexes to be created. In addition, rows in the index are generally shorter than data rows. When you insert or delete new values, it's easier to move around shorter index values to maintain the sort order than to move around the longer data rows.

The example just described corresponds in general to the way MySQL indexes tables, although the particular details vary for different table types. For example, for a MyISAM or ISAM table, the table's data rows are kept in a data file, and index values are kept in an index file. You can have more than one index on a table; if you do, they're all stored in the same index file. Each index in the index file consists of a sorted array of key records that are used for fast access into the data file. By contrast, the BDB and InnoDB table handlers do not separate data rows and index values in the same way, although both maintain indexes as sets of sorted values. The BDB handler uses a single file per table to store both data and index values, and the InnoDB handler uses a single tablespace within which it manages data and index storage for all InnoDB tables.

The preceding discussion describes the benefit of an index in the context of single-table queries, where the use of an index speeds searches significantly by eliminating the need for full table scans. However, indexes are even more valuable when you're running queries involving joins on multiple tables. In a single-table query, the number of values you need to examine per column is the number of rows in the table. In a multiple-table query, the number of possible combinations skyrockets because it's the product of the number of rows in the tables.

Suppose you have three unindexed tables, t1, t2, and t3, each containing a column c1, c2, and c3, respectively, and each consisting of 1000 rows that contain the numbers 1 through 1000. A query to find all combinations of table rows in which the values are equal looks like this:

```
SELECT t1.c1, t2.c2, t3.c3
FROM t1, t2, t3
WHERE t1.c1 = t2.c2 AND t1.c1 = t3.c3;
```

The result of this query should be 1000 rows, each containing three equal values. If we process the query in the absence of indexes, we have no idea which rows contain which values. Consequently, we must try all combinations to find the ones that match the WHERE clause. The number of possible combinations is 1000×1000×1000 (1 billion!), which is a million times more than the number of matches. That's a lot of wasted effort, and this query is likely to be very slow, even for a database such as MySQL that is very fast. And that is with only 1000 rows per table. What happens when you have tables with millions of rows? As tables grow, the time to process joins on those tables grows even more if no indexes are used, leading to very poor performance. If we index each table, we can speed things up considerably because indexing allows the query to be processed as follows:

- Select the first row from table t1 and see what value the row contains.
- Using the index on table t2, go directly to the row that matches the value from t1. Similarly, using the index on table t3, go directly to the row that matches the value from t1.
- Proceed to the next row of table t1 and repeat the preceding procedure until all rows in t1 have been examined.

In this case, we're still performing a full scan of table t1, but we're able to do indexed lookups on t2 and t3 to pull out rows from those tables directly. The query runs about a million times faster this way—literally. (This example is contrived for the purpose of making a point, of course. Nevertheless, the problems it illustrates are real, and adding indexes to tables that have none often results in dramatic performance gains.)

MySQL uses indexes as just described to speed up searches for rows matching terms of a WHERE clause or rows that match rows in other tables when performing joins. It also uses indexes to improve the performance of other types of operations:

- For queries that use the MIN() or MAX() functions, the smallest or largest value in a column can be found quickly without examining every row if the column is indexed.
- MySQL can often use indexes to perform sorting and grouping operations quickly for ORDER BY and GROUP BY clauses.
- Sometimes MySQL can use an index to avoid reading data rows entirely. Suppose you're selecting values from an indexed numeric column in a MyISAM table and you're not selecting other columns from the table. In this case, by reading an index value from the index file, you've already got the value you'd get by reading the data file. There's no reason to read values twice, so the data file need not even be consulted.

Disadvantages of Indexing

In general, if MySQL can figure out how to use an index to process a query
more quickly, it will. This means that, for the most part, if you don't index
your tables, you're hurting yourself. You can see that I'm painting a rosy picture of the benefits of indexing. Are there disadvantages? Yes, there are. In practice, these drawbacks tend to be outweighed by the advantages, but you should
know what they are.

First, an index takes up disk space, and multiple indexes take up correspondingly more space. This may cause you to reach a table size limit more quickly
than if there are no indexes:

- For ISAM and MyISAM tables, indexing a table heavily may cause the
  index file to reach its maximum size more quickly than the data file.

- For BDB tables, which store data and index values together in the same
  file, adding indexes will certainly cause the table to reach the maximum
  file size more quickly.

- InnoDB tables all share space within the InnoDB tablespace. Adding
  indexes depletes storage within the tablespace more quickly. However, as
  long as you have additional disk space, you can expand the tablespace by
  adding new components to it. (Unlike files used for ISAM, MyISAM,
  and BDB tables, the InnoDB tablespace is not bound by your operating
  system's file size limit, because it can comprise multiple files.)

Second, indexes speed up retrievals but slow down inserts and deletes as well
as updates of values in indexed columns. That is, indexes slow down most
operations involving writing. This occurs because writing a record requires
writing not only the data row, it requires changes to any indexes as well. The
more indexes a table has, the more changes need to be made, and the greater
the average performance degradation. In the "Loading Data Efficiently" section
later in this chapter, we'll go into more detail about this phenomenon and
what you can do about it.

Choosing Indexes

The syntax for creating indexes was covered in the "Creating and Dropping
Indexes" section of Chapter 3, "MySQL SQL Syntax and Use." I assume
here that you've read that section. But knowing syntax doesn't in itself
help you determine how your tables should be indexed. That requires
some thought about the way you use your tables. This section gives some

guidelines on how to identify candidate columns for indexing and how best to set up indexes:

- **Index columns that you use for searching, sorting, or grouping, not columns you display as output.** In other words, the best candidate columns for indexing are the columns that appear in your WHERE clause, columns named in join clauses, or columns that appear in ORDER BY or GROUP BY clauses. Columns that appear only in the output column list following the SELECT keyword are not good candidates:

```
SELECT
    col_a                          ← not a candidate
FROM
    tbl1 LEFT JOIN tbl2
    ON tbl1.col_b = tbl2.col_c  ← candidates
WHERE
    col_d = expr;                  ← a candidate
```

  The columns that you display and the columns you use in the WHERE clause might be the same, of course. The point is that appearance of a column in the output column list is not in itself a good indicator that it should be indexed.

  Columns that appear in join clauses or in expressions of the form *col1 = col2* in WHERE clauses are especially good candidates for indexing. col_b and col_c in the query just shown are examples of this. If MySQL can optimize a query using joined columns, it cuts down the potential table-row combinations quite a bit by eliminating full table scans.

- **Use unique indexes.** Consider the spread of values in a column. Indexes work best for columns with unique values and most poorly with columns that have many duplicate values. For example, if a column contains many different age values, an index will differentiate rows readily. An index probably will not help much for a column that is used to record sex and contains only the two values 'M' and 'F'. If the values occur about equally, you'll get about half of the rows whichever value you search for. Under these circumstances, the index may never be used at all because the query optimizer generally skips an index in favor of a full table scan if it determines that a value occurs in more than about 30 percent of a table's rows.

- **Index short values.** If you're indexing a string column, specify a prefix length whenever it's reasonable to do so. For example, if you have a CHAR(200) column, don't index the entire column if most values are unique within the first 10 or 20 bytes. Indexing the first 10 or 20 bytes will save a lot of space in the index, and probably will make your queries faster as well. A smaller index involves less disk I/O, and shorter values can be compared more quickly. More importantly, with shorter key values, blocks in the index cache hold more key values, so MySQL can hold more keys in memory at once. This improves the likelihood of locating rows without reading additional index blocks from disk. (You want to use some common sense, of course. Indexing just the first character from a column isn't likely to be that helpful because there won't be very many distinct values in the index.)

- **Take advantage of leftmost prefixes.** When you create an *n*-column composite index, you actually create *n* indexes that MySQL can use. A composite index serves as several indexes because any leftmost set of columns in the index can be used to match rows. Such a set is called a *leftmost prefix*. (This is different than indexing a prefix of a column, which is using the first *n* bytes of the column for index values.)

  Suppose you have a table with a composite index on columns named state, city, and zip. Rows in the index are sorted in state/city/zip order, so they're automatically sorted in state/city order and in state order as well. This means that MySQL can take advantage of the index even if you specify only state values in a query or only state and city values. Thus, the index can be used to search the following combinations of columns:

  ```
  state, city, zip
  state, city
  state
  ```

  MySQL cannot use the index for searches that don't involve a leftmost prefix. For example, if you search by city or by zip, the index isn't used. If you're searching for a given state and a particular Zip code (columns 1 and 3 of the index), the index can't be used for the combination of values, although MySQL can narrow the search using the index to find rows that match the state.

- **Don't over-index.** Don't index everything in sight based on the assumption "the more, the better." That's a mistake. Every additional index takes extra disk space and hurts performance of write operations, as has already been mentioned. Indexes must be updated and possibly reorganized when you modify the contents of your tables, and the more indexes you have, the longer this takes. If you have an index that is rarely or never used, you'll slow down table modifications unnecessarily. In addition, MySQL considers indexes when generating an execution plan for retrievals. Creating extra indexes creates more work for the query optimizer. It's also possible (if unlikely) that MySQL will fail to choose the best index to use when you have too many indexes. Maintaining only the indexes you need helps the query optimizer avoid making such mistakes.

If you're thinking about adding an index to a table that is already indexed, consider whether the index you're thinking about adding is a leftmost prefix of an existing multiple-column index. If so, don't bother adding the index because, in effect, you already have it. (For example, if you already have an index on state, city, and zip, there is no point in adding an index on state.)

- **Consider the type of comparisons you perform on a column.** Generally, indexes are used for <, <=, =, >=, >, and BETWEEN operations. Indexes are also used for LIKE operations when the pattern has a literal prefix. If you use a column only for other kinds of operations, such as STRCMP(), there is no value in indexing it. For HEAP tables, indexes are hashed and are used only for equality comparisons. If you perform a range search (such as a < b) with a HEAP table, an index will not help.

- **Use the slow-query log to identify queries that may be performing badly.** This log can help you find queries that may benefit from indexing. Use the mysqldumpslow utility to view this log. (See Chapter 11, "General MySQL Administration" for a discussion of MySQL's log files.) If a given query shows up over and over in the slow-query log, that's a clue that you've found a query that may not be written optimally. You may be able to rewrite it to make it run more quickly. Keep the following points in mind when assessing your slow-query log:

  - "Slow" is measured in real time, so more queries will show up in the slow-query log on a heavily loaded server than on a lightly loaded one. You'll need to take this into account.

  - If you use the --log-long-format option in addition to enabling slow-query logging, the log also will include queries that execute without using any index. These queries aren't necessarily slow. (No index may be needed for small tables, for example.)

The MySQL Query Optimizer

When you issue a query that selects rows, MySQL analyzes it to see if any optimizations can be used to process the query more quickly. In this section, we'll look at how the query optimizer works. For additional information, consult the optimization chapter in the *MySQL Reference Manual*; it describes various optimization measures that MySQL takes.

The MySQL query optimizer takes advantage of indexes, of course, but it also uses other information. For example, if you issue the following query, MySQL will execute it very quickly, no matter how large the table is:

```
SELECT * FROM tbl_name WHERE 1 = 0;
```

In this case, MySQL looks at the WHERE clause, realizes that no rows can possibly satisfy the query, and doesn't even bother to search the table. You can see this by issuing an EXPLAIN statement, which tells MySQL to display some information about how it would execute a SELECT query without actually executing it. To use EXPLAIN, just put the word EXPLAIN in front of the SELECT statement:

```
mysql> EXPLAIN SELECT * FROM tbl_name WHERE 1 = 0;
+------------------+
| Comment          |
+------------------+
| Impossible WHERE |
+------------------+
```

Normally, EXPLAIN returns more information than that, including information about the indexes that will be used to scan tables, the types of joins that will be used, and estimates of the number of rows that will need to be scanned from each table.

How the Optimizer Works

The MySQL query optimizer has several goals, but its primary aims are to use indexes whenever possible and to use the most restrictive index to eliminate as many rows as possible as soon as possible. That last part may sound backward because it's non-intuitive. After all, because your goal in issuing a SELECT statement is to find rows, not to reject them. The reason the optimizer works this way is that the faster it can eliminate rows from consideration, the more quickly the rows that do match your criteria can be found. Queries can be processed more quickly if the most restrictive tests can be done first. Suppose you have a query that tests two columns, each of which has an index on it:

```
SELECT col3 FROM mytable
WHERE col1 = 'some value' AND col2 = 'some other value';
```

Suppose also that the test on col1 matches 900 rows, the test on col2 matches 300 rows, and that both tests succeed on 30 rows. Testing col1 first results in 900 rows that must be examined to find the 30 that also match the col2 value. That's 870 failed tests. Testing col2 first results in 300 rows that must be examined to find the 30 that also match the col1 value. That's only

270 failed tests, so less computation and disk I/O is required. As a result, the optimizer will attempt to test `col2` first.

You can help the optimizer take advantage of indexes by using the following guidelines.

Try to compare columns that have the same type. When you use indexed columns in comparisons, use columns that are of the same type. For example, `CHAR(10)` is considered the same as `CHAR(10)` or `VARCHAR(10)` but different than `CHAR(12)` or `VARCHAR(12)`. `INT` is different than `BIGINT`. Using columns of the same type is a requirement prior to MySQL 3.23, or indexes on the columns will not be used. From 3.23 on, this is not strictly necessary, but identical column types will still give you better performance than dissimilar types. If the columns you're comparing are of different types, you can use `ALTER TABLE` to modify one of them so that the types match.

Try to make indexed columns stand alone in comparison expressions. If you use a column in a function call or as part of a more complex term in an arithmetic expression, MySQL can't use the index because it must compute the value of the expression for every row. Sometimes this is unavoidable, but many times you can rewrite a query to get the indexed column to appear by itself.

The following `WHERE` clauses illustrate how this works. They are equivalent arithmetically, but quite different for optimization purposes. For the first line, the optimizer will simplify the expression 4/2 to the value 2 and then use an index on `mycol` to quickly find values less than 2. For the second expression, MySQL must retrieve the value of `mycol` for each row, multiply by 2, and then compare the result to 4. In this case, no index can be used, because each value in the column must be retrieved so that the expression on the left side of the comparison can be evaluated:

```
WHERE mycol < 4 / 2
WHERE mycol * 2 < 4
```

Let's consider another example. Suppose you have an indexed column `date_col`. If you issue a query such as the following, the index isn't used:

```
SELECT * FROM mytbl WHERE YEAR(date_col) < 1990;
```

The expression doesn't compare an indexed column to 1990; it compares a value calculated from the column value, and that value must be computed for each row. As a result, the index on `date_col` is not used because performing the query requires a full table scan. What's the fix? Just use a literal date, and the index on `date_col` can be used to find matching values in the columns:

```
WHERE date_col < '1990-01-01'
```

But suppose you don't have a specific date. You might be interested instead in finding records that have a date that lies within a certain number of days from today. There are several ways to express a comparison of this type—not all of which are equally good. Three possibilities are as follows:

```
WHERE TO_DAYS(date_col) - TO_DAYS(CURDATE()) < cutoff
WHERE TO_DAYS(date_col) < cutoff + TO_DAYS(CURDATE())
WHERE date_col < DATE_ADD(CURDATE(), INTERVAL cutoff DAY)
```

For the first line, no index is used because the column must be retrieved for each row so that the value of TO_DAYS(date_col) can be computed. The second line is better. Both cutoff and TO_DAYS(CURDATE()) are constants, so the right hand side of the comparison can be calculated by the optimizer once before processing the query, rather than once per row. But the date_col column still appears in a function call, so the index isn't used. The third line is best of all. Again, the right side of the comparison can be computed once as a constant before executing the query, but now the value is a date. That value can be compared directly to date_col values, which no longer need to be converted to days. In this case, the index can be used.

Don't use wildcards at the beginning of a LIKE pattern. Sometimes people search for strings using a WHERE clause of the following form:

```
WHERE col_name LIKE '%string%'
```

That's the correct thing to do if you want to find string no matter where it occurs in the column. But don't put '%' on both sides of the string simply out of habit. If you're really looking for the string only when it occurs at the beginning of the column, leave out the first '%'. Suppose you're looking in a column containing last names for names like MacGregor or MacDougall that begin with 'Mac'. In that case, write the WHERE clause like this:

```
WHERE last_name LIKE 'Mac%'
```

The optimizer looks at the literal initial part of the pattern and uses the index to find rows that match as though you'd written the following expression, which is in a form that allows an index on last_name to be used:

```
WHERE last_name >= 'Mac' AND last_name < 'Mad'
```

This optimization does not apply to pattern matches that use the REGEXP operator.

Help the optimizer make better estimates about index effectiveness. By default, when you are comparing values in indexed columns to a constant, the optimizer assumes that key values are distributed evenly within the index. The optimizer will also do a quick check of the index to estimate how many entries will be used when determining whether or not the index should be used for constant comparisons. For MyISAM and BDB tables, you can tell the server to perform an analysis of key values by using ANALYZE TABLE. This provides the optimizer with better information. Another option, for MyISAM tables, is to run myisamchk --analyze (or isamchk --analyze for ISAM tables). These utilities operate directly on the table files, so two conditions must be satisfied in order to use them for key analysis:

- You must have an account on the MySQL server host that allows you write access to the table files.
- You must cooperate with the server for access to the table files, because you don't want it to be accessing the table while you're working with its files. (Protocols for coordinating table access with the server are described in Chapter 13, "Database Backups, Maintenance, and Repair." Use the protocol that is appropriate for write access.)

Use EXPLAIN to verify optimizer operation. Check to see that indexes are being used in your query to reject rows quickly. If not, you might try using STRAIGHT_JOIN to force a join to be done using tables in a particular order. (Run the query both with and without STRAIGHT_JOIN; MySQL may have some good reason not to use indexes in the order you think is best.) As of MySQL 3.23.12, you can also try USE INDEX or IGNORE INDEX to give the server hints about which indexes to prefer.

Test alternate forms of queries, but run them more than once. When testing alternate forms of a query, run it several times each way. If you run a query only once each of two different ways, you'll often find that the second query is faster just because information from the first query is still in the disk cache and need not actually be read from the disk. You should also try to run queries when the system load is relatively stable to avoid effects due to other activities on your system.

Avoid overuse of MySQL's automatic type conversion. MySQL will perform automatic type conversion, but if you can avoid conversions, you may get better performance. For example, if num_col is an integer column, the following two queries both will return the same result:

```
SELECT * FROM mytbl WHERE num_col = 4;
SELECT * FROM mytbl WHERE num_col = '4';
```

But the second query involves a type conversion. The conversion operation itself involves a small performance penalty for converting the integer and string to double to perform the comparison. A more serious problem is that if num_col is indexed, a comparison that involves type conversion may prevent the index from being used.

Overriding Optimization

It sounds odd, but there may be times when you'll want to defeat MySQL's optimization behavior. Some of the reasons to do this are described in the following list:

To empty a table with minimal side effects. When you need to empty a table completely, it's fastest to have the server just drop the table and re-create it based on the description stored in its `.frm` file. To do this, use a TRUNCATE TABLE statement:

```
TRUNCATE TABLE tbl_name;
```

Prior to MySQL 4, you can achieve the same effect by using a DELETE statement with no WHERE clause:

```
DELETE FROM tbl_name;
```

The server's optimization of emptying a table by re-creating it from scratch makes the operation extremely fast because each row need not be deleted individually. However, there are some side effects that may be undesirable under certain circumstances:

- Prior to MySQL 4, DELETE with no WHERE clause may report the number of rows affected as zero, even when the table wasn't empty. TRUNCATE TABLE may do this for any version of MySQL, depending on the table type. Most of the time this doesn't matter, although it can be puzzling if you don't expect it. But for applications that require an accurate count of the number of deleted rows, a count of zero is not acceptable.

- For MyISAM tables, AUTO_INCREMENT values normally are not reused when rows are deleted. (See Chapter 2, "Working with Data in MySQL.") However, emptying a table by re-creating it may reset the sequence to begin over at 1.

If you encounter these side effects and want to avoid them, use an "unoptimized" full-table DELETE statement that includes a trivially true WHERE clause:

```
DELETE FROM tbl_name WHERE 1;
```

Adding the WHERE clause forces MySQL to do a row-by-row deletion, because it must evaluate the condition for each row to determine whether or not to delete it. The query executes much more slowly, but it will return the true number of rows deleted, and it will preserve the current AUTO_INCREMENT sequence number for MyISAM tables.

To override the optimizer's table join order. Use STRAIGHT_JOIN to force the optimizer to use tables in a particular order. If you do this, you should order the tables so that the first table is the one from which the smallest number of rows will be chosen. (If you are not sure which table this is, put the table with the most rows first.) In other words, try to order the tables to cause the most restrictive selection to come first. Queries perform better the earlier you can narrow the possible candidate rows. Make sure to try the query both ways; there may be some reason the optimizer isn't joining tables the way you think it should, and STRAIGHT_JOIN may not actually help.

Another possibility is to use the USE INDEX and IGNORE INDEX modifiers after a table name in the table list of a join to tell MySQL to use or ignore indexes. This may be helpful in cases where the optimizer doesn't make the correct choice.

To retrieve results in random order. As of MySQL 3.23.2, you can use ORDER BY RAND() to sort results randomly. Another technique, which is useful for older versions of MySQL, is to select a column of random numbers and sort on that column. However, if you try writing the query as follows, the optimizer defeats your intent:

```
SELECT ..., RAND() as rand_col FROM ... ORDER BY rand_col;
```

The problem here is that MySQL sees that the column is a function call, thinks that the value of the column will be a constant, and optimizes the ORDER BY clause right out of the query! You can fool the optimizer by referring to a table column in the expression. For example, if your table has a column named age, you can write the query as follows:

```
SELECT ..., age*0+RAND() as rand_col FROM ... ORDER BY rand_col;
```

In this case, the expression value is always equivalent to RAND(). But the optimizer doesn't know that, so it no longer guesses that the column contains a constant value in each row.

To avoid an endless update loop. Prior to MySQL 3.23.2, if you update a column that is indexed, it's possible for the rows that are updated to be updated endlessly if the column is used in the WHERE clause and the update moves the index value into the part of the range that hasn't been processed yet. Suppose the mytbl table has an integer column key_col that is indexed. Queries such as the following can cause problems:

```
UPDATE mytbl SET key_col = key_col+1 WHERE key_col > 0;
```

The solution for this is to use key_col in an expression term in the WHERE clause such that MySQL can't use the index:

```
UPDATE mytbl SET key_col = key_col+1 WHERE key_col+0 > 0;
```

Column Type Choices and Query Efficiency

This section provides some guidelines for choosing your columns that can help queries run more quickly.[1]

Don't use longer columns when shorter ones will do. If you are using fixed-length CHAR columns, don't make them unnecessarily long. If the longest value you store in a column is 40 bytes long, don't declare it as CHAR(255); declare it as CHAR(40). If you can use MEDIUMINT rather than BIGINT, your table will be smaller (less disk I/O), and values can be processed more quickly in computations. If the columns are indexed, using shorter values gives you even more of a performance boost. Not only will the index speed up queries, shorter index values can be processed more quickly than longer values.

If you have a choice about row storage format, use one that is optimal for your table type. For MyISAM and ISAM tables, use fixed-length columns rather than variable-length columns. This is especially true for tables that are modified often and therefore more subject to fragmentation. For example, make all character columns CHAR rather than VARCHAR. The tradeoff is that your table will use more space, but if you can afford the extra space, fixed-length rows can be processed more quickly than variable-length rows.

For InnoDB tables, the internal row storage format does not treat fixed-length and variable-length columns differently (all rows use a header containing pointers to the column values), so using CHAR is not in itself intrinsically better than using VARCHAR. In fact, because CHAR will on average take more space than VARCHAR, it's preferable to use VARCHAR to minimize the amount of storage and disk I/O needed to process rows.

For BDB tables, it usually doesn't make much difference either way. You can try a table both ways and run some empirical tests to check whether there's a significant difference for your particular system.

Declare columns to be NOT NULL. This gives you faster processing and requires less storage. It will also simplify queries sometimes because you don't need to check for NULL as a special case.

Consider using ENUM columns. If you have a string column that contains only a limited number of distinct values, consider converting it to an ENUM column. ENUM values can be processed quickly because they are represented as numeric values internally.

---

1. In this discussion, "BLOB types" should be read as meaning both BLOB and TEXT types.

Use PROCEDURE ANALYSE(). If you have MySQL 3.23 or newer, run PROCE-
DURE ANALYSE() to see what it tells you about the columns in your table:

```
SELECT * FROM tbl_name PROCEDURE ANALYSE();
SELECT * FROM tbl_name PROCEDURE ANALYSE(16,256);
```

One column of the output will be a suggestion for the optimal column type
for each of the columns in your table. The second example tells PROCEDURE
ANALYSE() not to suggest ENUM types that contain more than 16 values or that
take more than 256 bytes (you can change the values as you like). Without
such restrictions, the output may be very long; ENUM declarations are often difficult to read.

Based on the output from PROCEDURE ANALYSE(), you may find that your
table can be changed to take advantage of a more efficient type. Use ALTER
TABLE if you decide to change a column's type.

Use OPTIMIZE TABLE for tables that are subject to fragmentation. Tables
that are modified a great deal, particularly those that contain variable-length
columns, are subject to fragmentation. Fragmentation is bad because it leads to
unused space in the disk blocks used to store your table. Over time, you must
read more blocks to get the valid rows, and performance is reduced. This is true
for any table with variable-length rows, but is particularly acute for BLOB
columns because they can vary so much in size. The use of OPTIMIZE TABLE
on a regular basis helps keep performance on the table from degrading.

OPTIMIZE TABLE works with MyISAM and BDB tables, but defragments only
MyISAM tables. A defragmentation method that works for any table type is to
dump the table with mysqldump and then drop and recreate it using the dump
file:

```
% mysqldump --opt db_name tbl_name > dump.sql
% mysql db_name < dump.sql
```

Pack data into a BLOB column. Using a BLOB to store data that you pack
and unpack in your application may allow you to get everything with a single
retrieval operation rather than with several. This can also be helpful for data
that are not easy to represent in a standard table structure or that change over
time. In the discussion of the ALTER TABLE statement in Chapter 3, one of the
examples dealt with a table being used to hold results from the fields in a
Web-based questionnaire. That example discussed how you could use ALTER
TABLE to add columns to the table whenever you add questions to the questionnaire.

Another way to approach this problem is to have the application program that processes the Web form pack the data into some kind of data structure, and then insert it into a single BLOB column. For example, you could represent the questionnaire responses using XML and store the XML string in the BLOB column. This adds application overhead on the client side for encoding the data (and decoding it later when you retrieve records from the table), but simplifies the table structure and eliminates the need to change the table structure when you change your questionnaire.

On the other hand, BLOB values can cause their own problems, especially if you do a lot of DELETE or UPDATE operations. Deleting a BLOB may leave a large hole in the table that will be filled in later with a record or records of probably different sizes. (The preceding discussion of OPTIMIZE TABLE suggests how you might deal with this.)

Use a synthetic index. Synthetic index columns can sometimes be helpful. One method is to create a hash value based on other columns and store it in a separate column. Then you can find rows by searching for hash values. However, note that this technique is good only for exact-match queries. (Hash values are useless for range searches with operators such as < or >=). Hash values can be generated in MySQL 3.23 and up by using the MD5() function. Other options are to use SHA1() or CRC32(), which were introduced in MySQL 4.0.2 and 4.1, respectively.

A hash index can be particularly useful with BLOB columns. For one thing, you cannot index these types prior to MySQL 3.23.2. But even with 3.23.2 or later, it may be quicker to find BLOB values using a hash as an identifier value than by searching the BLOB column itself.

Avoid retrieving large BLOB values unless you must. For example, a SELECT * query isn't a good idea unless you're sure the WHERE clause is going to restrict the results to just the rows you want. Otherwise, you may be pulling potentially very large BLOB values over the network for no purpose. This is another case where BLOB identifier information stored in a synthetic index column can be useful. You can search that column to determine the row or rows you want and then retrieve the BLOB values from the qualifying rows.

Segregate BLOB values into a separate table. Under some circumstances, it may make sense to move BLOB columns out of a table into a secondary table if that allows you to convert the table to fixed-length row format for the remaining columns. This will reduce fragmentation in the primary table and allow you to take advantage of the performance benefits of having fixed-length rows. It also allows you to run SELECT * queries on the primary table without pulling large BLOB values over the network.

Loading Data Efficiently

Most of the time you'll probably be concerned about optimizing SELECT queries because they are the most common type of query and because it's not always straightforward to figure out how to optimize them. By comparison, loading data into your database is straightforward. Nevertheless, there are strategies you can use to improve the efficiency of data-loading operations. The basic principles are as follows:

- Bulk loading is more efficient than single-row loading because the index cache need not be flushed after each record is loaded; it can be flushed at the end of the batch of records. The more you can reduce index cache flushing, the faster data loading will be.

- Loading is faster when a table has no indexes than when it is indexed. If there are indexes, not only must the record be added to the data file, but each index must also be modified to reflect the addition of the new record.

- Shorter SQL statements are faster than longer statements because they involve less parsing on the part of the server and because they can be sent over the network from the client to the server more quickly.

Some of these factors may seem minor (the last one in particular), but if you're loading a lot of data, even small efficiencies make a difference. From the preceding general principles, several practical conclusions can be drawn about how to load data most quickly:

- LOAD DATA (all forms) is more efficient than INSERT because it loads rows in bulk. Index flushing takes place less often, and the server needs to parse and interpret one statement, not several.

- LOAD DATA is more efficient than LOAD DATA LOCAL. With LOAD DATA, the file must be located on the server and you must have the FILE privilege, but the server can read the file directly from disk. With LOAD DATA LOCAL, the client reads the file and sends it over the network to the server, which is slower.

- If you must use INSERT, use the form that allows multiple rows to be specified in a single statement:

  ```
  INSERT INTO tbl_name VALUES(...),(...),... ;
  ```

  The more rows you can specify in the statement, the better. This reduces the total number of statements you need and minimizes the amount of index flushing. This may seem to contradict the earlier remark that shorter statements can be processed faster than longer statements. But there is no contradiction. The principle here is that a single INSERT statement that inserts multiple rows is shorter overall than an equivalent set of individual single-row INSERT statements, and the multiple-row statement can be processed on the server with much less index flushing.

If you use mysqldump to generate database backup files, use the --extended-insert option so that the dump file contains multiple-row INSERT statements. You can also use --opt (optimize), which turns on the --extended-insert option automatically, as well as some other options that allow the dump file to be processed more efficiently when it is reloaded. Conversely, avoid using the --complete-insert option with mysqldump; the resulting INSERT statements will be for single rows and will be longer and require more parsing than will statements generated without --complete-insert.

- If you must use multiple INSERT statements, group them if possible to reduce index flushing. For transactional table types, do this by issuing the INSERT statements within a single transaction rather than in auto-commit mode:

```
BEGIN;
INSERT INTO tbl_name ... ;
INSERT INTO tbl_name ... ;
INSERT INTO tbl_name ... ;
COMMIT;
```

For non-transactional table types, obtain a write lock on the table and issue the INSERT statements while the table is locked:

```
LOCK TABLES tbl_name WRITE;
INSERT INTO tbl_name ... ;
INSERT INTO tbl_name ... ;
INSERT INTO tbl_name ... ;
UNLOCK TABLES;
```

You obtain the same benefit in both cases. The index is flushed once rather than once per INSERT statement, which is what happens in auto-commit mode or if the table has not been locked.

- Use the compressed client/server protocol to reduce the amount of data going over the network. For most MySQL clients, this can be specified using the --compress command line option. Generally, this should only be used on slow networks because compression uses quite a bit of processor time.

- Let MySQL insert default values for you. That is, don't specify columns in INSERT statements that will be assigned the default value anyway. On average, your statements will be shorter, reducing the number of characters sent over the network to the server. In addition, because the statements contain fewer values, the server does less parsing and value conversion.

- If a table is indexed, you can lessen indexing overhead by using batched inserts (LOAD DATA or multiple-row INSERT statements). These minimize the impact of index updating because the index needs flushing only after all rows have been processed, rather than after each row.

- For MyISAM and ISAM tables, if you need to load a lot of data into a new table to populate it, it's faster to create the table without indexes, load the data, and then create the indexes. It's faster to create the indexes all at once rather than to modify them for each row. For a table that already has indexes, data loading may be faster if you drop or deactivate the indexes beforehand and then rebuild or reactivate them afterward. These strategies do not apply to InnoDB or BDB tables, which do not have optimizations for separate index creation.

If you're considering using the strategy of dropping or deactivating indexes for loading data into MyISAM or ISAM tables, think about the overall circumstances of your situation in assessing whether any benefit is likely to be obtained. If you're loading a small amount of data into a large table, rebuilding the indexes probably will take longer than just loading the data without any special preparation.

To drop and rebuild indexes, use DROP INDEX and CREATE INDEX or the index-related forms of ALTER TABLE. To deactivate and reactivate indexes, you have two choices:

- You can use the DISABLE KEYS and ENABLE KEYS forms of ALTER TABLE:
  ```
  ALTER TABLE tbl_name DISABLE KEYS;
  ALTER TABLE tbl_name ENABLE KEYS;
  ```
  These statements turn off and on updating of any non-unique indexes in the table.

- The myisamchk or isamchk utilities can perform index manipulation. These utilities operate directly on the table files, so to use them you must have write access to the table files. You should also observe the precautions described in Chapter 13 for keeping the server from accessing a table while you're using its files.

The `DISABLE KEYS` and `ENABLE KEYS` statements are the preferred method for index deactivation and activation because the server does the work. However, they are available only as of MySQL 4. (Note that if you're using `LOAD DATA` to load data into an empty MyISAM table, the server performs this optimization automatically.)

To deactivate a MyISAM table's indexes "manually," make sure you've told the server to leave the table alone and then move into the appropriate database directory and run the following command:

```
% myisamchk --keys-used=0 tbl_name
```

After loading the table with data, reactivate the indexes:

```
% myisamchk --recover --quick --keys-used=n tbl_name
```

n is interpreted as a bitmask indicating which indexes to enable. Bit 0 corresponds to index 1. For example, if a table has three indexes, the value of n should be 7 (111 binary). You can determine index numbers with the `--description` option:

```
% myisamchk --description tbl_name
```

The commands for ISAM tables are similar except that you use `isamchk` rather than `myisamchk`, and the `--keys-used` value for `isamchk` indicates the highest-numbered index to use. (For a table with three indexes, n would be 3.)

The preceding data-loading principles also apply to mixed-query environments involving clients performing different kinds of operations. For example, you generally want to avoid long-running `SELECT` queries on tables that are changed (written to) frequently. This causes a lot of contention and poor performance for the writers. A possible way around this, if your writes are mostly `INSERT` operations, is to add new records to an auxiliary table and then add those records to the main table periodically. This is not a viable strategy if you need to be able to access new records immediately, but if you can afford to leave them inaccessible for a short time, use of the auxiliary table will help you two ways. First, it reduces contention with `SELECT` queries that are taking place on the main table, so they execute more quickly. Second, it takes less time overall to load a batch of records from the auxiliary table into the main table than it would to load the records individually; the index cache need be flushed only at the end of each batch rather than after each individual row.

One application for this strategy is when you're logging Web page accesses from your Web server into a MySQL database. In this case, it may not be a high priority to make sure the entries get into the main table right away.

For MyISAM tables, another strategy for reducing index flushing is to use the `DELAYED_KEY_WRITE` table creation option if your data are such that it's not absolutely essential that every single record be inserted in the event of abnormal system shutdown. (This might be the case if you're using MySQL for some sort of logging.) The option causes the index cache to be flushed only occasionally rather than after each insert. If you want to use delayed index flushing on a server-wide basis, start `mysqld` with the `--delay-key-write` option. In this case, index block writes for a table are delayed until blocks must be flushed to make room for other index values, until a flush-tables command has been executed, or until the table is closed.

For a replication slave server, you might want to use `--delay-key-write=ALL` to delay index flushing for all MyISAM tables, regardless of how they were created originally on the master server.

Scheduling and Locking Issues

The previous sections have focused primarily on making individual queries faster. MySQL also allows you to affect the scheduling priorities of statements, which may allow queries arriving from several clients to cooperate better so that individual clients aren't locked out for a long time. Changing the priorities can also ensure that particular kinds of queries are processed more quickly. This section looks at MySQL's default scheduling policy and the options that are available to you for influencing this policy. It also discusses the effect that table handler locking levels have on concurrency among clients. For the purposes of this discussion, a client performing a retrieval (a `SELECT`) is a reader. A client performing an operation that modifies a table (`DELETE`, `INSERT`, `REPLACE`, or `UPDATE`) is a writer.

MySQL's basic scheduling policy can be summed up as follows:

- Write requests should be processed in the order in which they arrive.
- Writes have higher priority than reads.

For MyISAM and ISAM tables, the scheduling policy is implemented with the aid of table locks. Whenever a client accesses a table, a lock for it must be acquired first. When the client is finished with a table, the lock on it can be released. It's possible to acquire and release locks explicitly by issuing `LOCK TABLES` and `UNLOCK TABLES` statements, but normally the server's lock manager automatically acquires locks as necessary and releases them when they no longer are needed.

A client performing a write operation must have a lock for exclusive access to the table. The table is in an inconsistent state while the operation is in progress because the data record is being deleted, added, or changed, and any indexes on the table may need to be updated to match. Allowing other clients to access the table while the table is in flux causes problems. It's clearly a bad thing to allow two clients to write to the table at the same time because that would quickly corrupt the table into an unusable mess. But it's not good to allow a client to read from an in-flux table, either, because the table might be changing right at the spot being read, and the results would be inaccurate.

A client performing a read operation must have a lock to prevent other clients from writing to the table so that the table doesn't change while the table is being read. However, the lock need not provide exclusive access for reading. The lock can allow other clients to read the table at the same time. Reading doesn't change the table, so there is no reason readers should prevent each other from accessing the table.

MySQL allows you to influence its scheduling policy by means of several query modifiers. One of these is the LOW_PRIORITY keyword for DELETE, INSERT, LOAD DATA, REPLACE, and UPDATE statements. Another is the HIGH_PRIORITY keyword for SELECT statements. The third is the DELAYED keyword for INSERT and REPLACE statements.

The LOW_PRIORITY keyword affects scheduling as follows. Normally, if a write operation for a table arrives while the table is being read, the writer blocks until the reader is done because once a query has begun it will not be interrupted. If another read request arrives while the writer is waiting, the reader blocks, too, because the default scheduling policy is that writers have higher priority than readers. When the first reader finishes, the writer proceeds, and when the writer finishes, the second reader proceeds.

If the write request is a LOW_PRIORITY request, the write is not considered to have a higher priority than reads. In this case, if a second read request arrives while the writer is waiting, the second reader is allowed to slip in ahead of the writer. Only when there are no more readers is the writer is allowed to proceed. One implication of this scheduling modification is that theoretically, it's possible for LOW_PRIORITY writes to be blocked forever. As long as additional read requests arrive while previous ones are still in progress, the new requests will be allowed to get in ahead of the LOW_PRIORITY write.

The HIGH_PRIORITY keyword for SELECT queries is similar. It allows a SELECT to slip in ahead of a waiting write, even if the write normally has higher priority.

The DELAYED modifier for INSERT acts as follows. When an INSERT DELAYED request arrives for a table, the server puts the rows in a queue and returns a status to the client immediately so that the client can proceed even before the rows have been inserted. If readers are reading from the table, the rows in the queue are held. When there are no readers, the server begins inserting the rows in the delayed-row queue. Every now and then, the server checks whether any new read requests have arrived and are waiting. If so, the delayed-row queue is suspended and the readers are allowed to proceed. When there are no readers left, the server begins inserting delayed rows again. This process continues until the queue is empty.

LOW_PRIORITY and DELAYED are similar in the sense that both allow row insertion to be deferred, but they are quite different in how they affect client operation. LOW_PRIORITY forces the client to wait until the rows can be inserted. DELAYED allows the client to continue and the server buffers the rows until it has time to process them.

INSERT DELAYED is useful if other clients may be running lengthy SELECT statements and you don't want to block waiting for completion of the insertion. The client issuing the INSERT DELAYED can proceed more quickly because the server simply queues the row to be inserted.

However, you should be aware of certain other differences between normal INSERT and INSERT DELAYED behavior. The client gets back an error if the INSERT DELAYED statement contains a syntax error, but other information that would normally be available is not. For example, you can't rely on getting the AUTO_INCREMENT value when the statement returns. You also won't get a count for the number of duplicates on unique indexes. This happens because the insert operation returns a status before the operation actually has been completed. Another implication is that if rows from INSERT DELAYED statements are queued while waiting to be inserted, and the server crashes or is killed with kill -9, the rows are lost. This is not true for a normal kill -TERM kill; in that case, the server inserts the rows before exiting.

The MyISAM handler does allow an exception to the general principle that readers block writers. This occurs under the condition that a MyISAM table has no holes in it (that is, it has no deleted rows), in which case, any INSERT statements must necessarily add rows at the end of the table rather than in the middle. Under such circumstances, clients are allowed to add rows to the table even while other clients are reading from it. These are known as *concurrent inserts* because they can proceed concurrently with retrievals without being blocked. If you use this feature, note the following:

- Do not use the LOW_PRIORITY modifier with your INSERT statements. It causes INSERT always to block for readers and thus prevents concurrent inserts from being performed.

- Readers that need to lock the table explicitly but still want to allow concurrent inserts should use LOCK TABLES ... READ LOCAL rather than LOCK TABLES ... READ. The LOCAL keyword allows you to acquire a lock that allows concurrent inserts to proceed, because it applies only to existing rows in the table and does not block new rows from being added to the end.

The scheduling modifiers did not appear in MySQL all at once. The following table lists the statements that allow modifiers and the version of MySQL in which each appeared. You can use the table to determine which capabilities your server has.

Statement Type	Version of Initial Appearance
DELETE LOW_PRIORITY	3.22.5
INSERT LOW_PRIORITY	3.22.5
INSERT DELAYED	3.22.15
LOAD DATA LOW_PRIORITY	3.23.0
LOAD DATA CONCURRENT	3.23.38
LOCK TABLES ... LOW_PRIORITY WRITE	3.22.8
LOCK TABLES ... READ LOCAL	3.23.11
REPLACE LOW_PRIORITY	3.22.5
REPLACE DELAYED	3.22.15
SELECT ... HIGH_PRIORITY	3.22.9
UPDATE LOW_PRIORITY	3.22.5
SET SQL_LOW_PRIORITY_UPDATES	3.22.5

Locking Levels and Concurrency

The scheduling modifiers just discussed allow you to influence the default scheduling policy. For the most part, they were introduced to deal with issues that arise from the use of table-level locks, which is what the MyISAM and ISAM handlers use to manage table contention.

MySQL now has BDB and InnoDB tables, which implement locking at different levels and thus have differing performance characteristics in terms of contention management. The BDB handler uses page-level locks. The InnoDB handler uses row-level locks, but only as necessary. (In many cases, such as when only reads are done, InnoDB may use no locks at all).

The locking level used by a table handler has a significant effect on concurrency among clients. Suppose two clients each want to update a row in a given table. To perform the update, each client requires a write lock. For a MyISAM table, the handler will acquire a table lock for the first client, which causes the second client to block until the first one has finished. With a BDB table, greater concurrency can be achieved because the updates can proceed simultaneously, as long as both rows are not located within the same page. With an InnoDB table, concurrency is even higher; both updates can happen at the same time as long as both clients aren't updating the same row.

The general principle is that table locking at a finer level allows better concurrency, because more clients can be using a table at the same time if they use different parts of it. The practical implication is that different table types will be better suited for different query mixes:

- ISAM and MyISAM are extremely fast for retrievals. However, the use of table-level locks can be a problem in environments with mixed retrievals and updates, especially if the retrievals tend to be long running. Under these conditions, updates may need to wait a long time before they can proceed.

- BDB and InnoDB tables can provide better performance when there are many updates. Because locking is done at the page or row level rather than at the table level, the extent of the table that is locked is smaller. This reduces lock contention and improves concurrency.

Table locking does have an advantage over finer levels of locking in terms of deadlock prevention. With table locks, deadlock never occurs. The server can determine which tables are needed by looking at the query and lock them all ahead of time. With InnoDB and BDB tables, deadlock can occur because the handlers do not acquire all necessary locks at the beginning of a transaction. Instead, locks are acquired as they are determined to be necessary during the course of processing the transaction. It's possible that two queries will acquire locks and then try to acquire further locks that each depend on already-held locks being released. As a result, each client holds a lock that the other needs before it can continue. This results in deadlock, and the server must abort one of the transactions. For BDB tables, you may be able to help prevent deadlock by using LOCK TABLES to acquire table locks explicitly because the BDB handler sees such locks. That doesn't work for InnoDB, because the handler is not aware of locks set by LOCK TABLES.

Optimization for Administrators

The previous sections have described optimizations that can be performed by unprivileged MySQL users. But there are also optimizations that can be performed only by administrators who have control of the MySQL server or the machine on which it runs. Some server parameters pertain to query processing and can be tuned, and certain hardware configuration issues have a direct effect on query processing speed. In general, the primary principles to keep in mind when performing administrative optimizations are as follows:

- Accessing data in memory is faster than accessing data from disk.
- Keeping data in memory as long as possible reduces the amount of disk activity.
- Retaining information from an index is more important than retaining contents of data records.

Specific ways you can apply these principles are discussed next.

Increase the size of the server's caches. The server has many parameters (variables) that you can change to affect its operation, several of which directly affect the speed of query processing. The most important parameters you can change are the sizes of the table cache and the caches used by the table handlers for indexing operations. If you have memory available, allocating it to the server's cache buffers will allow information to be held in memory longer and reduce disk activity. This is good, because it's much faster to access information from memory than to read it from disk.

- The table cache is used to hold information about open tables. Its size is controlled by the `table_cache` server variable. If the server accesses lots of tables, this cache fills up and the server must close tables that haven't been used for a while to make room for opening new tables.
  You can assess how effective the table cache is by checking the `Opened_tables` status indicator:

  ```
  SHOW STATUS LIKE 'Opened_tables';
  ```

  `Opened_tables` indicates the number of times a table had to be opened because it wasn't already open. (This value is also displayed as the `Opens` value in the output of the `mysqladmin status` command.) If the number remains stable or increases slowly, it's probably set to about the right value. If the number grows at a high rate, it means the cache is full a lot and that tables have to be closed to make room to open other tables. If you have file descriptors available, increasing the table cache size will reduce the number of table opening operations.

- The key buffer is used by the MyISAM and ISAM table handlers to hold index blocks for index-related operations. Its size is controlled by the `key_buffer_size` server variable. Larger values allow MySQL to hold more index blocks in memory at once, which increases the likelihood of finding key values in memory without having to read a new block from disk. The default size of the key buffer is 8MB. If you have lots of memory, that's a very conservative value and you should be able to increase it substantially and see a considerable improvement in performance for index-based retrievals and for index creation and modification operations.

- The InnoDB and BDB handlers have their own caches for buffering data and index values. The sizes are controlled by the `innodb_buffer_pool_size` and `bdb_cache_size` variables. The InnoDB handler also maintains a log buffer, the size of which is controlled by the `innodb_log_buffer_size` variable.

- Another special cache is the query cache, described later in its own section, "The Query Cache."

Instructions for setting server variables can be found in Chapter 11. When you change parameter values, adhere to the following guidelines:

- Change one parameter at a time. Otherwise, you're varying multiple independent variables and it becomes more difficult to assess the effect of each change.

- Increase server variable values incrementally. If you increase a variable by a huge amount on the theory that more is always better, you may run your system out of resources, causing it to thrash or slow to a crawl because you've set the value too high.

- To get an idea of the kinds of parameter variables that are likely to be appropriate for your system, take a look at the `my-small.cnf`, `my-medium.cnf`, `my-large.cnf`, and `my-huge.cnf` option files included with MySQL distributions. (You can find them under the `support-files` directory in source distributions and under the `share` directory in binary distributions.) These files will give you some idea of which parameters are best to change for servers that receive different levels of use and also some representative values to use for those parameters.

Other strategies you can adopt to help the server operate more efficiently include the following:

Disable table handlers that you don't need. The server won't allocate any memory for disabled handlers, allowing you to devote it elsewhere. The ISAM, InnoDB, and BDB handlers can be disabled entirely if you build the server from source, and the InnoDB and BDB handlers can be disabled at server startup time. See Chapter 11 for details.

Keep grant table permissions simple. Although the server caches grant table contents in memory, if you have any rows in the `tables_priv` or `columns_priv` tables, the server must check table- and column-level privileges for every query. If those tables are empty, the server can optimize its privilege checking to skip those levels.

If you build MySQL from source, configure it to use static libraries rather than shared libraries. Dynamic binaries that use shared libraries save on disk space, but static binaries are faster. (However, you cannot use static binaries if you want to load user-defined functions because the UDF mechanism relies on dynamic linking.)

The Query Cache

As of MySQL 4.0.1, the server can use a query cache to speed up processing of `SELECT` statements that are executed repeatedly. The resulting performance improvement often is dramatic. The query cache works as follows:

- The first time a given `SELECT` statement is executed, the server remembers the text of the query and the results that it returns.

- The next time the server sees that query, it doesn't bother to execute it again. Instead, the server pulls the query result directly from the cache and returns it to the client.

- Query caching is based on the literal text of query strings as they are received by the server. Queries are considered the same if the text of the queries is exactly the same. Queries are considered different if they differ in lettercase or come from clients that are using different character sets or communication protocols. They also are considered different if they are otherwise identical but do not actually refer to the same tables (for example, if they refer to identically named tables in different databases).

- When a table is updated, any cached queries that refer to it become invalid and are discarded. This prevents the server from returning out-of-date results.

Support for the query cache is built in by default. If you don't want to use the cache and want to avoid incurring even the minimal overhead that it involves, you can build the server without it by running the `configure` script with the `--without-query-cache` option.

For servers that include query cache support, cache operation is based on the values of three variables:

- query_cache_size determines the size of the query cache. A value of zero disables the cache, which is the default setting. (In other words, the cache is not used unless you turn it on explicitly.) To enable the cache, set query_cache_size value to the desired size of the cache, in bytes. For example, to allocate 16MB, use the following setting in an option file:

```
[mysqld]
set-variable = query_cache_size=16M
```

- query_cache_limit sets the maximum result set size that will be cached; query results larger than this value are never cached.

- query_cache_type determines the operating mode of the query cache. The possible mode values are as follows:

Mode	Meaning
0	Don't cache
1	Cache queries except those that begin with SELECT SQL_NO_CACHE
2	Cache on demand only those queries that begin with SELECT SQL_CACHE

Individual clients begin with query caching behavior in the state indicated by the server's default caching mode. A client may change how its queries are cached by the server by using the following statement:

```
SET SQL_QUERY_CACHE_TYPE = val;
```

val can be 0, 1, or 2, which have the same meaning as for the query_cache_type variable. The symbolic values OFF, ON, and DEMAND are synonyms for 0, 1, and 2.

A client can also control caching of individual queries by adding a modifier following the SELECT keyword. SELECT SQL_CACHE causes the query result to be cached if the cache is operating in demand mode. SELECT SQL_NO_CACHE causes the result not to be cached.

Suppression of caching can be useful for queries that retrieve information from a constantly changing table. In that case, the cache is unlikely to be of much use. Suppose you're logging Web server requests to a table in MySQL, and also that you periodically run a set of summary queries on the table. For a reasonably busy Web server, new rows will be inserted into the table frequently and thus any query results cached for the table become invalidated quickly. The implication is that although you might issue the summary queries repeatedly, it's unlikely that the query cache will be of any value for them. Under such circumstances, it makes sense to issue the queries using the SQL_NO_CACHE modifier to tell the server not to bother caching their results.

Hardware Issues

The earlier part of this chapter discusses techniques that help improve your server's performance regardless of your hardware configuration. You can of course get better hardware to make your server run faster. But not all hardware-related changes are equally valuable. When assessing what kinds of hardware improvements you might make, the most important principles are the same as those that apply to server parameter tuning. Put as much information in fast storage as possible, and keep it there as long as possible.

Several aspects of your hardware configuration can be modified to improve server performance:

- **Install more memory into your machine.** This enables you to increase the server's cache and buffer sizes, which allows it to keep data in memory longer and with less need to fetch information from disk.

- **Reconfigure your system to remove all disk swap devices if you have enough RAM to do all swapping into a memory file system.** Otherwise, some systems will continue to swap to disk even if you have sufficient RAM for swapping.

- **Add faster disks to improve I/O latency.** Seek time is typically the primary determinant of performance here. It's slow to move the heads laterally; when the heads are positioned, reading blocks off the track is fast by comparison. However, if you have a choice between adding more memory and getting faster disks, add more memory. Memory is always faster than your disks, and adding memory allows you to use larger caches, which reduces disk activity.

- **Take advantage of parallelism by redistributing disk activity across physical devices.** If you can split reading or writing across multiple physical devices, it will be quicker than reading and writing everything from the same device. For example, if you store databases on one device and logs on another, writing to both devices at once it will be faster than if databases and logs share the same device. Note that using different partitions on the same physical device isn't sufficient. That won't help because they'll still contend for the same physical resource (disk heads). The procedure for moving logs and databases is described in Chapter 10, "The MySQL Data Directory."

Before you relocate data to a different device, make sure you understand your system's load characteristics. If there's some other major activity already taking place on a particular physical device, putting a database there may actually make performance worse. For example, you may not realize any overall benefit if you process a lot of Web traffic and move a database onto the device where your Web server document tree is located. (If you have only a single drive, you can't perform much disk activity redistribution, of course.)

Use of RAID devices can give you some advantages of parallelism as well.

- **Use multi-processor hardware.** For a multi-threaded application like the MySQL server, multi-processor hardware can execute multiple threads at the same time.

II

Using MySQL Programming Interfaces

5

Introduction to MySQL Programming

THIS CHAPTER DESCRIBES SOME OF THE REASONS why you might want to write your own MySQL-based programs rather than just using the standard client programs included in the MySQL distribution. It also gives a conceptual overview of the interfaces we'll use for the three languages covered in the following chapters (C, Perl, and PHP) and discusses some factors to consider when choosing between languages.

Why Write Your Own MySQL Programs?

A MySQL distribution includes a set of utility programs. For example, `mysqldump` exports the structural definitions and contents of tables, `mysqlimport` loads data files into tables, `mysqladmin` performs administrative operations, and `mysql` enables you to interact with the server to execute arbitrary queries. Each of the standard MySQL utilities is designed to be a small, focused program with a specific, limited function. This is true even for `mysql`, which is more flexible than the other utilities in the sense that you can use it to execute any number of different queries. It's designed with the single purpose of allowing you to issue SQL queries directly to the server and view the results.

This limited nature of the MySQL clients is not a flaw—it's by design. The programs are general-purpose utilities that are not intended to anticipate all possible requirements you might have. The MySQL developers do not subscribe to the philosophy of writing huge, bloated programs that try to do everything you might possibly want to do (and thus end up including lots of code for many things you don't care about at all).

The standard client programs handle many of the most common tasks that MySQL users need to perform, but applications sometimes have requirements that are not addressed by the capabilities of those clients. In this part of the book, we'll discuss what you need to know to write your own MySQL-based programs for accessing your databases. To make this possible, MySQL includes a client-programming library that provides you with the flexibility to satisfy whatever specialized requirements your applications may have. By giving you access to the MySQL server, the client library opens up possibilities limited only by your own imagination.

To understand specifically what you gain by writing your own programs, consider what you can accomplish that way in comparison to using the capabilities of the `mysql` client and its no-frills interface to the MySQL server:

- **You can customize input handling.** With `mysql`, you enter raw SQL statements. With your own programs, you can provide input methods for the user that are more intuitive and easier to use. The program can eliminate the need for the user to know SQL—or even to be aware of the role of the database in the task being performed. Input collection can be something as rudimentary as a command-line style interface that prompts the user and reads a value or something as sophisticated as a screen-based entry form implemented using a screen management package, such as curses or S-Lang, an X window using Tcl/Tk, or a form in a Web page.

  For most people, it's a lot easier to specify search parameters by filling in a form rather than by issuing a `SELECT` statement. For example, a real estate agent looking for houses in a certain price range, style, or location just wants to enter search parameters into a form and get back the qualifying offerings with a minimum of fuss. For entering new records or updating existing records, similar considerations apply; a keyboard operator in a data entry department should need to know only the values to be entered into records, not the SQL syntax for `INSERT`, `REPLACE`, or `UPDATE`.

An additional reason to interpose an input-collection layer between the end user and the MySQL server is that you can validate input provided by the user. For example, you can check dates to make sure they conform to the format that MySQL expects, or you can require certain fields to be filled in.

Some applications might not even involve a user, such as when input for MySQL is generated by another program. You might configure your Web server to write log entries to MySQL rather than to a file. A system monitoring program can be set up to run periodically and record status information to a database.

- **You can customize your output.** `mysql` output is essentially unformatted; you have a choice of tab-delimited or tabular style. If you want nicer-looking output, you must format it yourself. This might range from something as simple as printing "Missing" rather than NULL to more complex report-generation requirements. Consider the following report:

```
State  City        Sales
------------------------------
AZ     Mesa          $94,384.24
       Phoenix       $17,328.28
              ----------------------
       subtotal     $117,712.52
------------------------------
CA     Los Angeles $118,198.18
       Oakland       $38,838.36
              ----------------------
       Subtotal     $157,036.54
==============================
       TOTAL        $274,749.06
```

This report includes several specialized elements:

- Customized headers
- Suppression of repeating values in the `State` column so that the values are printed only when they change
- Subtotal and total calculations
- Formatting of numbers, such as `94384.24`, to print as dollar amounts, such as `$94,384.24`

Another common type of task involving complex formatting is invoice production, where you need to associate each invoice header with information about the customer and about each item ordered. This kind of report can easily exceed `mysql`'s formatting capabilities.

For some types of tasks, you may not want to produce any output at all. Perhaps you're simply retrieving information to calculate a result that you insert back into another database table, or you may want the output to go somewhere other than to the user running the query. For example, if you're extracting names and email addresses to feed automatically into a process that generates form letters for bulk email, your program produces output. But the output consists of the messages that go to the mail recipients, not to the person running the program.

- **You can work around constraints imposed by the nature of SQL itself.** SQL is not a procedural language with a set of flow control structures, such as conditionals, loops, and subroutines. SQL scripts consist of a set of statements executed one at a time, from beginning to end, with minimal error checking.

If you execute a file of SQL queries using mysql in batch mode, mysql either quits after the first error, or, if you specify the --force option, executes all the queries indiscriminately, no matter how many errors occur. By writing your own program, it's possible to selectively adapt to the success or failure of queries by providing flow control around statement-execution operations. You can make execution of one query contingent on the success or failure of another, or make decisions about what to do next based on the result of a previous query.

SQL has very limited persistence across statements, and this carries into mysql. It's difficult to use the results from one query and apply them to another or to tie together the results of multiple queries. LAST_INSERT_ID() can be used to get the AUTO_INCREMENT value that was most recently generated by a prior statement, and SQL variables can be assigned values and referred to later. But that's about it.

This limitation makes certain common operations difficult to perform using SQL alone, such as retrieving a set of records and using each one as the basis for a complex series of subsequent operations. If you retrieve a list of customers and then look up a detailed credit history for each one, the process may involve several queries per customer. mysql is unsuitable for this kind of task because it may be necessary to issue several statements that depend on the results of previous queries.

In general, a tool other than mysql is needed for tasks that involve master-detail relationships and have complex output-formatting requirements. A program provides the "glue" that links queries together and enables you to use the output from one query as the input to another.

- **You can integrate MySQL into any application.** Many programs stand to benefit by exploiting the capability of a database to provide information. An application that needs to verify a customer number or check whether an item is present in inventory can do so by issuing a quick query. A Web application that enables a client to ask for all books by a certain author can look them up in a database and then send the results to the client's browser.

  It's possible to achieve a kind of rudimentary "integration" of MySQL into an application by using a shell script that invokes `mysql` with an input file containing SQL statements and then post-processing the output using other UNIX utilities. However, that can become ugly, especially as your task becomes more involved. It may also produce a sense of "it-works-but-feels-wrong" as the application grows by accretion into a messy patchwork. In addition, the process-creation overhead of a shell script that runs other commands may be more than you want to incur. It can be more effective to interact with the MySQL server directly, extracting exactly the information you want as you need it at each phase of your application's execution.

Chapter 1, "Getting Started with MySQL and SQL," enumerated several goals with respect to our `sampdb` sample database that require us to write programs to interact with the MySQL server. Some of these goals are shown in the following list:

- Format the Historical League member directory for printing
- Allow for online presentation and searching of the member directory
- Send membership renewal notices by email
- Easily enter scores into the grade book using a Web browser

One area that we'll consider in some detail is integrating MySQL's capabilities into a Web environment. MySQL provides no direct support for Web applications, but by combining MySQL with appropriate tools, you can issue queries from your Web server on behalf of a client user and report the results to the user's browser. This allows your databases to be accessed easily over the Web.

There are two complementary perspectives on the marriage of MySQL and the Web:

- **Using a Web server to provide enhanced access to MySQL.** In this case, your main interest is your database, and you want to use the Web as a tool to gain easier access to your data. This is the point of view a MySQL administrator probably would take. The place of a database in such a scenario is explicit and obvious because it's the focus of your interest. For example, you can write Web pages that enable you to see what tables your database contains, what each one's structure is, and what its contents are.

- **Using MySQL to enhance the capabilities of your Web server.** In this case, your primary interest is your Web site, and you may want to use MySQL as a tool for making your site's content more valuable to the people who visit it. This is the point of view a Web site developer probably would take. For example, if you run a message board or discussion list for visitors to the site, you can use a database to keep track of the messages. Here, the role of MySQL is more subtle, and visitors to the site may not even be aware that a database plays a part in the services the site offers.

These perspectives are not necessarily mutually exclusive. For example, in the Historical League scenario, we'll use the Web as a means for members to gain easy access to the contents of the membership directory by making entries available online. That is a use of the Web to provide access to the database. At the same time, adding directory content to the League's Web site increases the site's value to members. That is a use of the database to enhance the services provided at the site.

No matter how you view the integration of MySQL with the Web, the implementation is similar. You connect your Web site front end to your MySQL back end, using the Web server as an intermediary. The Web server collects information from a client user, sends it to the MySQL server in the form of a query, retrieves the result, and then returns it to the client's browser for viewing.

You don't have to put your data online, of course, but often there are benefits to doing so, particularly in comparison with accessing your data via the standard MySQL client programs:

- People accessing your data through the Web can use whichever browser they prefer, on whatever type of platform they prefer. They're not limited to systems on which the MySQL client programs run. No matter how widespread the MySQL clients are, Web browsers are more so.

- The interface for a Web application can be made simpler to use than that of a standalone command-line MySQL client.

- A Web interface can be customized to the requirements of a particular application. The MySQL clients are general-purpose tools with a fixed interface.

- Dynamic Web pages extend MySQL's capabilities to do things that are difficult or impossible to do using the MySQL clients. For example, you can't really put together an application that incorporates a shopping cart using just MySQL clients.

Any programming language can be used to write Web-based applications, but some are more suitable than others. We'll see this in the "Choosing an API" section later in this chapter.

APIs Available for MySQL

To facilitate application development, MySQL provides a client library written in the C programming language that enables you to access MySQL databases from within any C program. The client library implements an *application programming interface (API)* that defines how client programs establish and carry out communications with the server.

However, you are not limited to using C to write MySQL programs. You have several choices for writing applications that talk to the MySQL server. Many other language processors are either written in C themselves or have the capability of using C libraries, so the MySQL client library provides the means whereby MySQL bindings for these languages can be built on top of the C API. Examples of these are the client APIs for Perl, PHP, Python, Ruby, C++, Tcl, and others. There are also interfaces for Java (though these implement the client/server protocol directly rather than using the C library to handle communication.) Check the development portal at MySQL Web site for an up-to-date list because new language APIs become available from time to time:

```
http://www.mysql.com/portal/software/api/
```

Each language binding defines its own interface that specifies the rules for accessing MySQL. There is insufficient space here to discuss each of the APIs available for MySQL, so we'll concentrate on three of the most popular:

- **The C client library API.** This is the primary programming interface to MySQL. For example, it's used to implement the standard clients in the MySQL distribution, such as `mysql`, `mysqladmin`, and `mysqldump`.
- **The DBI (Database Interface) API for Perl.** DBI is implemented as a Perl module that interfaces with other modules at the DBD (Database Driver) level, each of which provides access to a specific type of database engine. (The particular DBD module on which we'll concentrate is the one that provides MySQL support, of course.) The most common uses of

DBI with MySQL are for writing standalone clients to be invoked from the command line and for scripts intended to be invoked by a Web server to provide Web access to MySQL.

- **The PHP API.** PHP is a server-side scripting language that provides a convenient way of embedding programs in Web pages. Such a page is processed by PHP on the server host before being sent to the client, which allows the script to generate dynamic content, such as including the result of a MySQL query in the page. "PHP" originally meant Personal Home Page, but PHP has grown far beyond its original humble beginnings. The PHP Web site now uses the name to stand for "PHP: Hypertext Preprocessor," which is self-referential in the same manner as GNU ("GNU's Not UNIX"). Like DBI, PHP includes support for accessing several database engines in addition to MySQL.

Each of these three APIs is described in detail in its own chapter. This chapter provides a comparative overview of the APIs to describe their general characteristics and to give you an idea why you might choose one over another for particular applications.

There's no reason to consider yourself locked into a single API, of course. Get to know each API and arm yourself with the knowledge that enables you to choose between them wisely. If you have a large project with several components, you might use multiple APIs and write some parts in one language and other parts in another language, depending on which one is most appropriate for each piece of the job. You may also find it instructive to implement an application several ways if you have time. This gives you direct experience with different APIs as they apply to your own applications.

If you need to get the software necessary for using any of the APIs, see Appendix A, "Obtaining and Installing Software."

Should you be interested in additional MySQL programming information beyond what is presented in the following chapters, other books are available. The two with which I am most familiar (because I wrote them!) are *MySQL and Perl for the Web* (New Riders, 2001) and *MySQL Cookbook* (O'Reilly, 2002). The first provides extensive coverage of the use of MySQL and DBI in Web environments. The second discusses Perl and PHP and also shows how to write MySQL programs using Python's DB-API interface and the Java JDBC interface.

> **Predecessors of DBI and PHP**
>
> The Perl predecessor to DBI is the Mysqlperl module, which is no longer supported and should not be used for new MySQL development. For one thing, Mysqlperl is MySQL-dependent, whereas DBI is not. If you write Perl applications for MySQL and then decide you want to use them with another database engine, it's easier to port DBI scripts than Mysqlperl scripts because they are less dependent on a particular database engine. (If you do happen to obtain a Perl script for accessing MySQL that is written for Mysqlperl, you can still use DBI because DBI can be built to include Mysqlperl emulation support.)
>
> The predecessor to PHP 3 and PHP 4 is PHP/FI 2.0 (FI stands for "form interpreter"). Like Mysqlperl, PHP/FI is obsolete and I won't discuss it further. At this point, PHP 3 is also declining in use in favor of PHP 4, which offers much-improved features and performance.

The C API

The C API is used within the context of compiled C programs. It's a client library that provides the lowest level interface available for talking to the MySQL server—giving you the capabilities you need for establishing a connection to and conversing with the server.

The C clients provided in the MySQL distribution are based on this API. The C client library also serves as the basis for the MySQL bindings for other languages, with the exception of the Java APIs. For example, the MySQL-specific driver for the Perl DBI module and the PHP processor are both made MySQL-aware by linking in the code for the MySQL C client library.

> **The Origin of the MySQL C API**
>
> If you have experience writing programs for the mSQL RDBMS, you'll notice that the MySQL C API is similar to the corresponding C API for mSQL. When the MySQL developers began implementing their SQL engine, a number of useful free utilities were available for mSQL. To make it possible to port those mSQL utilities to MySQL with minimum difficulty, the MySQL API was designed deliberately to be similar to the mSQL API. (MySQL even comes with a `msql2mysql` script that does simple textual substitution of mSQL API function names to the corresponding MySQL names. This operation is relatively trivial, but it actually takes care of much of the work involved in converting a mSQL program for use with MySQL.)

The Perl DBI API

The DBI API is used within the context of applications written for the Perl scripting language. This API is the most highly architected of the three APIs we're considering because it tries to work with as many databases as possible, while at the same time hiding as many database-specific details as possible from the script writer. DBI does this by using Perl modules that work together in a two-level architecture (see Figure 5.1):

- The DBI (database interface) level provides the general purpose interface for client scripts. This level provides an abstraction that does not refer to specific database engines.

- The DBD (database driver) level provides support for various database engines by means of drivers that are engine specific. The DBD-level module that implements DBI support for MySQL is named DBD::mysql. This module formerly went by the name Msql-Mysql-modules because it was originally written for mSQL and then extended for MySQL later. The current name of DBD::mysql reflects the fact that MySQL has pretty well eclipsed mSQL in popularity.

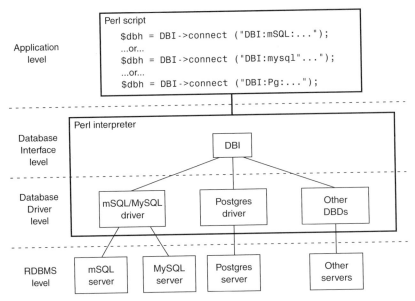

Figure 5.1   DBI architecture.

The DBI architecture enables you to write applications in relatively generic fashion. When you write a DBI script, you use a standard set of database-access calls. The DBI layer invokes the proper driver at the DBD level to handle your requests, and the driver handles the specific issues involved in communicating with the particular database server you want to use. The DBD level passes data returned from the server back up to the DBI layer, which presents the data to your application. The form of the data is consistent, no matter from which database the data originated.

The result is an interface that, from the application writer's point of view, hides differences between database engines but works with a wide variety of engines—as many for which there are drivers. DBI provides a consistent client interface that increases portability by allowing you to access each database in a uniform fashion.

The one aspect of script writing that is necessarily engine-specific occurs when you connect to a database server because you must indicate which driver to use to establish the connection. For example, to use a MySQL database, you connect as follows:

```
$dbh = DBI->connect ("DBI:mysql:...");
```

To use PostgreSQL or mSQL instead, connect as follows:

```
$dbh = DBI->connect ("DBI:Pg:...");

$dbh = DBI->connect ("DBI:mSQL:...");
```

After you've made the connection, you don't need to make any specific reference to the driver. DBI and the driver itself work out the database-specific details.

That's the theory, anyway. However, you should be aware of two factors that work against DBI script portability:

- SQL implementations differ between RDBMS engines, and it's perfectly possible to write SQL statements for one engine that another will not understand. If your SQL is reasonably generic, your scripts will be correspondingly portable between engines. But if your SQL is engine dependent, your scripts will be too. For example, if you use the MySQL-specific SHOW TABLES statement, your script won't work with other databases.

- DBD modules often provide engine-specific types of information to allow script writers to use particular features of particular database systems. As an example of this, the MySQL DBD provides a way to access properties of the columns in a query result, such as the maximum length of values in each column, whether or not columns are numeric, and so forth. These properties don't necessarily have any analog in other databases. DBD-specific features are antithetical to portability; by using them, you make it difficult to use a script written for MySQL with other database systems.

Despite the potential of these two factors for making your scripts database specific, the DBI mechanism for providing database access in an abstract fashion is a reasonable means of achieving portability. It's up to you to decide how much you want to take advantage of non-portable features. As you will discover in Chapter 7, "The Perl DBI API," I make little effort to avoid MySQL-specific constructs provided by the MySQL DBD, and all of them are listed in Appendix G, "Perl DBI API Reference." That's because you should know what those constructs are so that you can decide for yourself whether or not to use them.

> **The Meaning of DBI and DBD**
>
> Although the DBI level is database independent and the DBD level is database dependent, that isn't what "DBI" and "DBD" stand for. They mean "database interface" and "database driver."

The PHP API

Like Perl, PHP is a scripting language. Unlike Perl, PHP is designed less as a general-purpose language than as a language for writing Web applications. The PHP API is used primarily as a means of embedding executable scripts into Web pages. This makes it easy for Web developers to write pages with dynamically generated content. When a client browser sends a request for a PHP page to a Web server, PHP executes any script it finds in the page and replaces it with the script's output. The result is sent to the browser. This allows the page that actually appears in the browser to change according to the circumstances under which the page is requested. For example, when the following short PHP script is embedded in a Web page, it displays the IP address of the host that requested the page:

```
<?php echo $_SERVER["REMOTE_ADDR"]; ?>
```

As a less trivial and more interesting application, you can use a script to provide up-to-the-minute information to visitors based on the contents of your database. The following example shows a simple script that might be used at the Historical League Web site. The script issues a query to determine the current League membership count and reports it to the person visiting the site (if an error occurs, the script simply doesn't report any count):

```
<html>
<head>
<title>U.S. Historical League</title>
</head>
<body bgcolor="white">
<p>Welcome to the U.S. Historical League Web Site.</p>
<?php
# USHL home page
$conn_id = @mysql_connect ("cobra.snake.net", "sampadm", "secret")
    or exit ();
mysql_select_db ("sampdb")
```

```
    or exit ();
$result_id = mysql_query ("SELECT COUNT(*) FROM member")
    or exit ();
if ($row = mysql_fetch_row ($result_id))
    print ("<p>The League currently has " . $row[0] . " members.</p>");
mysql_free_result ($result_id);
?>
</body>
</html>
```

PHP scripts typically look like HTML pages with executable code embedded inside `<?php` and `?>` tags. A page can contain any number of code fragments. This provides an extremely flexible approach to script development. For example, you can write a PHP script as a normal HTML page initially—to set up the general page framework—and then add code later to generate the dynamic parts of the page.

PHP makes no effort to unify the interface to different database engines the way DBI does. Instead, the interface to each engine looks much like the interface for the corresponding C library implementing the low-level API for that engine. For example, the names of the PHP functions that you use to access MySQL from within PHP scripts are very similar to the names of the functions in the MySQL C client library. (If you prefer a more DBI-like approach, consider using PEAR, the PHP Extension and Add-on Repository. PEAR is an adjunct to PHP that includes a `PEAR::DB` module that provides a more abstract interface to database engines using a two-level architecture similar to that used by DBI. Visit `pear.php.net` for details.)

Choosing an API

This section provides general guidelines to help you choose an API for various types of applications. It compares the capabilities of the C, DBI, and PHP APIs to give you some idea of their relative strengths and weaknesses and to indicate when you might choose one over another.

I should probably point out first that I am not advocating any one of these languages over the others, although I do have my preferences. You will have your own preferences, too, as did the technical reviewers for this book. In fact, one reviewer felt that I should emphasize the importance of C for MySQL programming to a much greater extent, whereas another thought I should come down much harder on C programming and discourage its use! Weigh the factors discussed in this section and come to your own conclusions.

A number of considerations can enter in to your assessment of which API to choose for a particular task:

- **Intended execution environment.** The context in which you expect the application to be used.
- **Performance.** How efficiently applications perform when written in the API language.
- **Ease of development.** How convenient the API and its language make application writing.
- **Portability.** Whether or not the application will be used for database systems other than MySQL.

The following discussion examines each factor further. Be aware that some of the factors interact. For example, you may want an application that performs well, but it can be just as important to use a language that enables you to develop the application quickly, even if it doesn't perform quite as efficiently.

Execution Environment

When you write an application, you generally have some idea of the environment in which it will be used. For example, it might be a report generator program that you invoke from the shell or an accounts payable summary program that runs as a `cron` job at the end of each month. Commands run from the shell or from `cron` generally stand on their own and require little information from the execution environment. On the other hand, you might be writing an application intended to be invoked by a Web server. Such a program may expect to be able to extract very specific types of information from its execution environment: What browser is the client using? What parameters were entered into a mailing list subscription request form? Did the client supply the correct password for accessing personnel information?

Each API language varies in its suitability for writing applications in these differing environments:

- C is a general-purpose language, so in principle you can use it for anything. In practice, C tends to be used more often for standalone programs rather than for Web programming. One reason probably is that it's not as easy to perform text processing and memory management in C as it is in Perl or PHP, and those capabilities tend to be heavily used in Web applications.

- Perl, like C, is suitable for writing standalone programs. However, it also happens that Perl is quite useful for Web site development—for example, by using the CGI.pm module. This makes Perl a handy language for writing applications that link MySQL with the Web. Such an application can interface to the Web via the CGI.pm module and interact with MySQL using DBI.

- PHP is intended by design for writing Web applications, so that's obviously the environment to which it is best suited. Furthermore, database access is one of PHP's biggest strengths, so it's a natural choice for Web applications that perform MySQL-related tasks. It's possible to use PHP as a standalone interpreter (for example, to execute scripts from the shell), but it's not used that way very much.

Given these considerations, C and Perl are the most likely candidate languages if you're writing a standalone application. For Web applications, Perl and PHP are most suitable. If you need to write both types of applications but don't know any of these languages and want to learn as few as possible, Perl might be your best option.

Performance

All other things being equal, we generally prefer to have applications run as quickly as possible. However, the actual importance of performance tends to be related to the frequency with which a program is used. For a program that you run once a month as a cron job during the night, performance may not matter that much. If you run a program several times a second on a heavily used Web site, every bit of inefficiency you can eliminate can make a big difference. In the latter case, performance plays a significant role in the usefulness and appeal of your site. A slow site is annoying for users, no matter what the site is about, and if you depend on the site as a source of income, decreased performance translates directly into reduced revenue. You cannot service as many connections at a time, and visitors who tire of waiting simply give up and go elsewhere.

Performance assessment is a complex issue. The best indicator of how well your application will perform when written for a particular API is to write it under that API and try it. Additionally, the best comparative test is to implement it multiple times under different APIs to see how the versions stack up against each other. Of course, that's not how things usually work. More often, you just want to get your program written. After it's working, you can think about tuning it to see if it can run faster, use less memory, or if there is some other aspect that you can improve. But there are at least two general factors that you can count on to affect performance in a relatively consistent way:

- Compiled programs execute more quickly than interpreted scripts.
- For interpreted languages used in a Web context, performance is better when the interpreter is invoked as a module that is part of the Web server itself rather than as a separate process.

Compiled Versus Interpreted Languages

As a general principle, compiled applications are more efficient, use less memory, and execute more quickly than an equivalent version of the program written in a scripting language. This is due to the overhead involved with the language interpreter that executes the scripts. C is compiled and Perl and PHP are interpreted, so C programs generally will run faster than Perl or PHP scripts. Thus, C may be the best choice for a heavily used program.

There are, of course, factors that tend to diminish this clear distinction. For one thing, writing in C generally gives you a faster program, but it's quite possible to write inefficient C programs. Writing a program in a compiled language is no automatic passport to better performance; it's still necessary to think about what you're doing. In addition, the difference between compiled and interpreted programs is lessened if a scripted application spends most of its time executing code in the MySQL client library routines that are linked into the interpreter engine.

Standalone Versus Module Versions of Language Interpreters

For Web-based applications, script language interpreters are usually used in one of two forms—at least for Apache, the Web server used in this book for writing Web applications:

- You can arrange for Apache to invoke the script interpreter as a separate process. In this mode of operation, when Apache needs to run a Perl or PHP script, it starts up the corresponding interpreter and tells it to execute the script. In this case, Apache uses the interpreters as CGI programs—that is, it communicates with them using the Common Gateway Interface (CGI) protocol.
- The interpreter can be used as a module that is linked in directly to the Apache binary and that runs as part of the Apache process itself. In Apache terms, the Perl and PHP interpreters take the form of the `mod_perl` and `mod_php` modules.

Perl and PHP advocates will argue the speed advantages of their favorite inter-preter, but all agree that the form in which the interpreter runs is a much big-ger factor than the languages themselves. Either interpreter runs much faster as a module than as a standalone CGI application. With a standalone application, it's necessary to start up the interpreter each time a script is to be executed, so you incur a significant penalty in process-creation overhead. When used as a module within an already running Apache process, an interpreter's capabilities can be accessed from your Web pages instantly. This dramatically improves per-formance by reducing overhead and translates directly into an increased capac-ity to handle incoming requests and to dispatch them quickly.

The startup penalty for a standalone interpreter typically results in at least an order of magnitude poorer performance than the module interpreter. Interpreter startup cost is particularly significant when you consider that Web page serving typically involves quick transactions with light processing rather than substantial ones with a lot of processing. If you spend a lot of time just starting up and not very much actually executing the script, you're wasting most of your resources. It's like spending most of the day getting ready for work, arriving at 4 o'clock in the afternoon, and then going home at 5.

You might wonder why there is any benefit with the module versions of the interpreters—after all, you must still start up Apache itself, right? The savings comes from the fact that a given Apache process handles multiple requests. When Apache starts up, it immediately spawns a pool of child processes to be used to handle incoming requests. When a request arrives that involves execution of a script, there is already an Apache process ready and waiting to handle it. Also, each instance of Apache services multiple requests, so the process startup cost is incurred only once per set of requests, not once per request.

When Perl and PHP are installed in module form (as `mod_perl` and `mod_php`), which performs better? That is subject to debate, although the ques-tion became a lot less interesting when PHP 4 was released. PHP 3 had a sig-nificant disadvantage compared to Perl, which converts a script to an internally compiled form before running it. PHP 3 interprets each statement on-the-fly—a much slower approach, particularly for loops with a large number of iterations. PHP 4 incorporates Zend, a higher-performance interpreter engine that uses a compile-and-execute model similar to Perl. Thus, it's preferable to use PHP 4 rather than PHP 3 if possible. (This is true not just for PHP 4's improved performance, but also because it implements language features not available in PHP 3.)

If you're installing PHP yourself, I strongly recommend choosing PHP 4 over PHP 3. If you use PHP through an account with a service provider who hasn't upgraded, you may have to use PHP 3, but you probably should ask the provider to offer PHP 4 access as well.

One factor that remains a potentially significant difference between Perl and PHP is that the former has a bigger memory footprint; Apache processes are larger with `mod_perl` linked in than with `mod_php`. PHP was designed under the assumption that it must live cooperatively within another process and that it might be activated and deactivated multiple times within the life of that process. Perl was designed to be run from the command line as a standalone program, not as a language meant to be embedded in a Web server process. This probably contributes to its larger memory footprint; as a module, Perl simply isn't running in its natural environment. Other factors that contribute to the larger footprint are script caching and additional Perl modules that scripts use. In both cases, more code is brought into memory and remains there for the life of the Apache process. (To minimize this problem, there are techniques that allow you to designate only certain Apache processes as enabled for `mod_perl`. That way, you incur the extra memory overhead only for those processes that execute Perl scripts. The `mod_perl` area of the Apache Web site has a good discussion of various strategies from which to choose. Visit `http://perl.apache.org/docs/` for more information.)

The standalone version of a language interpreter does have one advantage over its module counterpart in that you can arrange for it to run scripts under a different user ID. The module versions run scripts under the same user ID as the Web server, which is typically an account with minimal privileges for security reasons. That doesn't work very well for scripts that require specific privileges (for example, if you need to be able to read or write protected files). You can combine the module and standalone approaches if you like. Use the module version by default and the standalone version for situations in which scripts need to run with the privileges of a particular user.

What this adds up to is that whether you choose Perl or PHP, you should try to use it as an Apache module rather than by invoking a separate interpreter process. Reserve use of the standalone interpreter only for those cases that cannot be handled by the module, such as scripts that require special privileges. For these instances, you can process your script by using Apache's suEXEC mechanism to start up the interpreter under a given user ID. (Another more recent option is to use Apache 2.x rather than 1.x. Apache 2.x allows groups of scripts to be run under specific user and group IDs.)

Development Time

The factors just described affect the performance of your applications, but raw execution efficiency may not be your only goal. Your own time is important, too, as is ease of programming, so another factor to consider in choosing an API for MySQL programming is how quickly you can develop your applications. If you can write a Perl or PHP script in half the time it takes to develop the equivalent C program, you may elect not to use the C API, even if the resulting application doesn't run quite as fast. It's often reasonable to be less concerned about a program's execution time than about the time you spend writing it, particularly for applications that aren't executed frequently. An hour of your time is worth a lot more than an hour of machine time!

Generally, scripting languages enable you to get a program going more quickly, especially for working out a prototype of the finished application. At least two factors contribute to this. First, scripting languages tend to provide more high-level constructs. This allows you to think at a higher level of abstraction so that you can think about what you want to do rather than about the details involved in doing it. For example, PHP associative arrays and Perl hashes are great time savers for maintaining data involving key/value relationships (such as student ID/student name pairs). C has no such construct. If you wanted to implement such a thing in C, you would need to write code to handle many low-level details involving issues, such as memory management and string manipulation, and you would need to debug it. This takes time.

Second, the development cycle has fewer steps for scripting languages. With C, you engage in an edit-compile-test cycle during application development. Every time you modify a program, you must recompile it before testing. With Perl and PHP, the development cycle is simply edit-test because you can run a script immediately after each modification with no compiling. On the other hand, the C compiler enforces more constraints on your program in the form of stricter type checking. The greater discipline imposed by the compiler can help you avoid bugs that you would not catch as easily in looser languages, such as Perl and PHP. If you misspell a variable name in C, the compiler will warn you. PHP and Perl won't do so unless you ask them to. These tighter constraints can be especially valuable as your applications become larger and more difficult to maintain.

In general, the tradeoff is the usual one between compiled and interpreted languages for development time versus performance: Do you want to develop the program using a compiled language so that it will execute more quickly when it runs, but spend more time writing it? Or do you want to write the program as a script so that you can get it running in the least amount of time, even at the cost of some execution speed?

It's also possible to combine the two approaches. Write a script as a "first draft" to quickly develop an application prototype to test out your logic and make sure the algorithms are appropriate. If the program proves useful and is executed frequently enough that performance becomes a concern, you can recode it as a compiled application. This gives you the best of both worlds—quick prototyping for initial development of the application and the best performance for the final product.

In a strict sense, the Perl DBI and PHP APIs give you no capabilities that are not already present in the C client library. This is because both of those APIs gain access to MySQL by having the MySQL C library linked into the Perl and PHP interpreters. However, the environment in which MySQL capabilities are embedded is very different for C than for Perl or PHP. Consider what tasks you'll need to perform as you interact with the MySQL server, and ask how much each API language will help you carry them out. The following are some examples:

- **Memory management.** In C, you find yourself working with `malloc()` and `free()` for any tasks involving dynamically allocated data structures. Perl and PHP handle that for you. For example, they allow arrays to grow in size automatically, and dynamic-length strings can be used without ever thinking about memory management.

- **Text manipulation.** Perl has the most highly developed capabilities in this area, and PHP runs a close second. C is very rudimentary by comparison, coming in a distant third.

Of course, in C you can write your own libraries to encapsulate tasks, such as memory management and text processing, into functions that make the job easier. But then you still have to debug them, and you also want your algorithms to be efficient. In these respects, it's a fair bet that the algorithms in Perl and PHP for these things have had the benefit of being examined by many pairs of eyes, so generally they should be both well debugged and reasonably efficient. You can save your own time by taking advantage of the time that others have already put into the job. (On the other hand, if an interpreter does happen to have a bug, you may simply have to live with it or try to find a workaround until the problem is fixed. When you write in C, you have a finer level of control over the behavior of your program.)

The languages differ in how "safe" they are. The C API provides the lowest-level interface to the server and enforces the least policy. In this sense, it provides the least amount of safety net. If you execute API functions out of order, you may be lucky and get an "out-of-sync" error, or you may be unlucky and have your program crash. Perl and PHP both protect you pretty well. A script will fail if you don't do things in the proper order, but the interpreter won't crash. Another fertile source of crashing bugs in C programs is the use of dynamically allocated memory and pointers associated with them. Perl and PHP handle memory management for you, so your scripts are much less likely to die from memory management bugs.

Development time is affected by the amount of external support that is available for a language. C external support is available in the form of wrapper libraries that encapsulate MySQL C API functions into routines that are easier to use. Libraries that do this are available for both C and C++. Perl undoubtedly has the largest number of add-ons, in the form of Perl modules (these are similar in concept to Apache modules). There is even an infrastructure in place designed to make it easy to locate and obtain these modules (the CPAN, or Comprehensive Perl Archive Network). Using Perl modules, you gain access to all kinds of functions without writing a line of code. Want to write a script that generates a report from a database and then mail it to someone as an attachment? Just visit `cpan.perl.org`, get one of the MIME modules, and you have instant attachment-generation capability. PHP doesn't have the same level of organized external support, although for PHP 4 the situation is changing with the development of PEAR.

Portability

The question of portability has to do with how easily a program written to use MySQL can be modified to use a different database engine. This may be something you don't care about. However, unless you can predict the future, it might be a little risky to say, "I'll never use this program with any database other than MySQL." Suppose you get a different job and want to use your old programs, but your new employer uses a different database system? What then? If portability is a priority, you should consider the clear differences between APIs:

- DBI provides the most portable API because database independence is an explicit DBI design goal.
- PHP is less portable because it doesn't provide the same sort of uniform interface to various database engines that DBI does. The PHP function calls for each supported database tend to resemble those in the corresponding underlying C API. There is some smoothing of differences, but at a minimum, you'll need to change the names of the database-related

functions you invoke. You may also have to revise your application's logic a bit as well because the interfaces for the various databases don't all work quite the same way. One way to minimize these issues for PHP scripts is to use the PEAR database abstraction module mentioned earlier.

- The C API provides the least portability between databases. By its very nature it is designed specifically for MySQL.

Portability in the form of database independence is especially important when you need to access multiple database systems within the same application. This can involve simple tasks, such as moving data from one RDBMS to another, or more complex undertakings, such as generating a report based on information combined from a number of database systems.

DBI and PHP both provide support for accessing multiple database engines, so you can easily connect simultaneously to servers for different databases, even on different hosts. However, DBI and PHP differ in their suitability for tasks that retrieve and process data from multiple disparate database systems. DBI is preferable because the set of access calls is the same, no matter which databases you're using. Suppose you want to transfer data between MySQL, mSQL, and PostgreSQL databases. With DBI, the only necessary difference in how you use the three databases is the DBI->connect() call used to connect to each server. With PHP's native database support functions, you'd have a more complicated script incorporating three sets of read calls and three sets of write calls. In this situation, you'd almost certainly want to use the PEAR module to minimize the differences between database access mechanisms.

6

The MySQL C API

MySQL PROVIDES A CLIENT LIBRARY WRITTEN in the C programming language that you can use to write client programs that access MySQL databases. This library defines an application-programming interface that includes the following facilities:

- Connection management routines that establish and terminate a session with a server
- Routines that construct queries, send them to the server, and process the results
- Status- and error-reporting functions for determining the exact reason for an error when an API call fails
- Routines that help you process options given in option files or on the command line

This chapter shows how to use the client library to write your own programs using conventions that are reasonably consistent with those used by the client programs included in the MySQL distribution. I assume you know something about programming in C, but I've tried not to assume you're an expert.

The chapter develops a series of client programs in a rough progression from very simple to more complex. The first part of this progression develops the framework for a client skeleton that does nothing but connect to and disconnect from the server. (The reason for this is that although MySQL client programs are written for different purposes, one thing they all have in common is that they must establish a connection to the server.) Development of the framework proceeds in the following stages:

- Begin with some bare-bones connection and disconnection code (`client1`).
- Add error checking (`client2`).
- Add the ability to get connection parameters at runtime, such as the hostname, username, and password (`client3`).

The resulting `client3` program is reasonably generic, so you can use it as the basis for any number of other client programs. After developing it, we'll pause to consider how to handle various kinds of queries. Initially, we'll discuss how to handle specific hard-coded SQL statements and then develop code that can be used to process arbitrary statements. After that, we'll add some query-processing code to `client3` to develop another program (`client4`) that's similar to the `mysql` client and can be used to issue queries interactively.

The chapter then shows how to take advantage of two capabilities that are new in MySQL 4:

- How to write client programs that communicate with the server over secure connections using the Secure Sockets Layer (SSL) protocol
- How to write applications that use `libmysqld`, the embedded server library

Finally, we'll consider (and solve) some common problems, such as, "How can I get information about the structure of my tables?" and "How can I insert images in my database?"

This chapter discusses functions and data types from the client library as they are needed. For a comprehensive listing of all functions and types, see Appendix F, "C API Reference." You can use that appendix as a reference for further background on any part of the client library you're trying to use.

The example programs are available online, so you can try them directly without typing them in yourself. They are part of the `sampdb` distribution; you can find them under the `capi` directory of the distribution. See Appendix A, "Obtaining and Installing Software," for downloading instructions.

Where to Find Example Programs

A common question on the MySQL mailing list is "Where can I find some examples of clients written in C?" The answer, of course, is "right here in this book!" But something many people seem not to consider is that the MySQL distribution itself includes several client programs that happen to be written in C (mysql, mysqladmin, and mysqldump, for example). Because the distribution is readily available in source form, it provides you with quite a bit of example client code. Therefore, if you haven't already done so, grab a source distribution sometime and take a look at the programs in its client directory.

General Procedure for Building Client Programs

This section describes the steps involved in compiling and linking a program that uses the MySQL client library. The commands to build clients vary somewhat from system to system, and you may need to modify the commands shown here a bit. However, the description is general and you should be able to apply it to most client programs you write.

Basic System Requirements

When you write a MySQL client program in C, you'll obviously need a C compiler. The examples shown here use gcc, which is probably the most common compiler used on UNIX. You'll also need the following in addition to the program's own source files:

- The MySQL header files
- The MySQL client library

The header files and client library constitute the basis of MySQL client programming support. If they are not installed on your system already, you'll need to obtain them. If MySQL was installed on your system from a source or binary distribution, client programming support should have been installed as part of that process. If RPM files were used, this support won't be present unless you installed the developer RPM. Should you need to obtain the MySQL header files and library, see Appendix A.

Compiling and Linking Client Programs

To compile and link a client program, you may need to specify where the MySQL header files and client library are located, because often they are not installed in locations that the compiler and linker search by default. For the following examples, suppose the header file and client library locations are /usr/local/include/mysql and /usr/local/lib/mysql.

To tell the compiler how to find the MySQL header files when you compile a source file into an object file, pass it an `-I` option that names the appropriate directory. For example, to compile `myclient.c` to produce `myclient.o`, you might use a command like this:

```
% gcc -c -I/usr/local/include/mysql myclient.c
```

To tell the linker where to find the client library and what its name is, pass `-L/usr/local/lib/mysql` and `-lmysqlclient` arguments when you link the object file to produce an executable binary, as follows:

```
% gcc -o myclient myclient.o -L/usr/local/lib/mysql -lmysqlclient
```

If your client consists of multiple files, name all the object files on the link command.

The link step may result in error messages having to do with functions that cannot be found. In such cases, you'll need to supply additional `-l` options to name the libraries containing the functions. If you see a message about `compress()` or `uncompress()`, try adding `-lz` or `-lgz` to tell the linker to search the `zlib` compression library:

```
% gcc -o myclient myclient.o -L/usr/local/lib/mysql -lmysqlclient -lz
```

If the message names the `floor()` function, add `-lm` to link in the math library. You might need to add other libraries as well. For example, you'll probably need `-lsocket` and `-lnsl` on Solaris.

As of MySQL 3.23.21, you can use the `mysql_config` utility to determine the proper flags for compiling and linking MySQL programs. For example, the utility might indicate that the following options are needed:

```
% mysql_config --cflags
-I'/usr/local/mysql/include/mysql'
% mysql_config --libs
-L'/usr/local/mysql/lib/mysql' -lmysqlclient -lz -lcrypt -lnsl -lm
```

To use `mysql_config` directly within your compile or link commands, invoke it within backticks:

```
% gcc -c `mysql_config --cflags` myclient.c
% gcc -o myclient myclient.o `mysql_config --libs`
```

The shell will execute `mysql_config` and substitute its output into the surrounding command, which automatically provides the appropriate flags for `gcc`.

If you don't use `make` to build programs, I suggest you learn how so that you won't have to type a lot of program–building commands manually. Suppose you have a client program, `myclient`, that comprises two source files, `main.c` and aux.c, and a header file, myclient.h. You might write a simple Makefile to build this program as follows. Note that indented lines are indented with tabs; if you use spaces, the Makefile will not work.

```
CC = gcc
INCLUDES = -I/usr/local/include/mysql
LIBS = -L/usr/local/lib/mysql -lmysqlclient
all: myclient
main.o: main.c myclient.h
    $(CC) -c $(INCLUDES) main.c
aux.o: aux.c myclient.h
    $(CC) -c $(INCLUDES) aux.c
myclient: main.o aux.o
    $(CC) -o myclient main.o aux.o $(LIBS)
clean:
    rm -f myclient main.o aux.o
```

Using the Makefile, you can rebuild your program whenever you modify any of the source files simply by running make, which displays and executes the necessary commands:

```
% make
gcc -c -I/usr/local/mysql/include/mysql myclient.c
gcc -o myclient myclient.o -L/usr/local/mysql/lib/mysql -lmysqlclient
```

That's easier and less error prone than typing long gcc commands. A Makefile also makes it easier to modify the build process. For example, if your system is one for which you need to link in additional libraries, such as the math and compression libraries, edit the LIBS line in the Makefile to add -lm and -lz:

```
LIBS = -L/usr/local/lib/mysql -lmysqlclient -lm -lz
```

If you need other libraries, add them to the LIBS line as well. Thereafter, when you run make, it will use the updated value of LIBS automatically.

Another way to change make variables other than editing the Makefile is to specify them on the command line. For example, if your C compiler is named cc rather than gcc (as is the case for Mac OS X, for example), you can say so as follows:

```
% make CC=cc
```

If mysql_config is available, you can use it to avoid writing literal include file and library directory pathnames in the Makefile. Write the INCLUDES and LIBS lines as follows instead:

```
INCLUDES = ${shell mysql_config --cflags}
LIBS = ${shell mysql_config --libs}
```

When make runs, it will execute each mysql_config command and use its output to set the corresponding variable value. The ${shell} construct shown here is supported by GNU make; you may need to use a somewhat different syntax if your version of make isn't based on GNU make.

If you're using an integrated development environment (IDE), you may not see or use a Makefile at all. The details will depend on your particular IDE.

Client 1—Connecting to the Server

Our first MySQL client program is about as simple as can be—it connects to a server, disconnects, and exits. That's not very useful in itself, but you have to know how to do it because you must be connected to a server before you can do anything with a MySQL database. Connecting to a MySQL server is such a common operation that the code you develop to establish the connection is code you'll use in every client program you write. Additionally, this task gives us something simple to start with. The client can be fleshed out later to do something more useful.

The code for our first client program, client1, consists of a single source file, client1.c:

```c
/* client1.c - connect to and disconnect from MySQL server */

#include <my_global.h>
#include <mysql.h>

static char *opt_host_name = NULL;      /* server host (default=localhost) */
static char *opt_user_name = NULL;      /* username (default=login name) */
static char *opt_password = NULL;       /* password (default=none) */
static unsigned int opt_port_num = 0;   /* port number (use built-in value) */
static char *opt_socket_name = NULL;    /* socket name (use built-in value) */
static char *opt_db_name = NULL;        /* database name (default=none) */
static unsigned int opt_flags = 0;      /* connection flags (none) */

static MYSQL *conn;                     /* pointer to connection handler */

int
main (int argc, char *argv[])
{
    /* initialize connection handler */
    conn = mysql_init (NULL);
    /* connect to server */
    mysql_real_connect (conn, opt_host_name, opt_user_name, opt_password,
                opt_db_name, opt_port_num, opt_socket_name, opt_flags);
    /* disconnect from server */
    mysql_close (conn);
    exit (0);
}
```

The source file begins by including the header files `my_global.h` and `mysql.h`. Depending on what a MySQL client does, it may need to include other header files as well, but usually these two are the bare minimum:

- `my_global.h` takes care of including several other header files that are likely to be generally useful, such as `stdio.h`. It also includes `windows.h` for Windows compatibility if you're compiling the program on Windows. (You may not intend to build the program under Windows yourself, but if you plan to distribute your code, having that file included will help anyone else who does compile under Windows.)
- `mysql.h` defines the primary MySQL-related constants and data structures.

The order of inclusion is important; `my_global.h` is intended to be included before any other MySQL-specific header files.

Next, the program declares a set of variables corresponding to the parameters that need to be specified when connecting to the server. For this client, the parameters are hardwired to have default values. Later, we'll develop a more flexible approach that allows the defaults to be overridden using values specified either in option files or on the command line. (That's why the names all begin with `opt_`; the intent is that eventually those variables will become settable through command options.) The program also declares a pointer to a `MYSQL` structure that will serve as a connection handler.

The `main()` function of the program establishes and terminates the connection to the server. Making a connection is a two-step process:

1. Call `mysql_init()` to obtain a connection handler. When you pass `NULL` to `mysql_init()`, it automatically allocates a `MYSQL` structure, initializes it, and returns a pointer to it. The `MYSQL` data type is a structure containing information about a connection. Variables of this type are called connection handlers.

2. Call `mysql_real_connect()` to establish a connection to the server. `mysql_real_connect()` takes about a zillion parameters:

    - *A pointer to the connection handler*—This should be the value returned by `mysql_init()`.
    - *The server host*—This value is interpreted in a platform-specific way. If you specify a string containing a hostname or IP address on UNIX, the client connects to the given host using a TCP/IP connection. If you specify `NULL` or the host `"localhost"`, the client connects to the server running on the local host using a UNIX socket.

On Windows, the behavior is similar, except that TCP/IP connections are used instead of UNIX sockets. Also, on Windows NT-based systems, the connection is attempted to the local server using a named pipe if the host is `"."` or `NULL`.

- *The username and password for the MySQL account to be used*—If the name is `NULL`, the client library sends your login name to the server. If the password is `NULL`, no password is sent.
- *The name of the database to select as the default database after the connection has been established*—If this value is `NULL`, no database is selected.
- *The port number and socket file*—The port number is used for TCP/IP connections. The socket name is used for UNIX socket connections (on UNIX) or named pipe connections (on Windows). The values `0` and `NULL` for the parameters tell the client library to use the default port number or socket (or pipe) name.
- *A flags value*—The program passes a value of `0` because it isn't using any special connection options.

You can find more information about `mysql_real_connect()` in Appendix F. For example, the description there discusses in more detail how the hostname parameter interacts with the port number and socket name parameters and lists the options that can be specified in the flags parameter. The appendix also describes `mysql_options()`, which you can use to specify other connection-related options prior to calling `mysql_real_connect()`.

To terminate the connection, invoke `mysql_close()` and pass it a pointer to the connection handler. If you allocated the handler automatically by passing `NULL` to `mysql_init()`, `mysql_close()` will automatically de-allocate the handler when you terminate the connection.

To try out `client1`, compile and link it using the instructions given earlier in the chapter for building client programs, and then run it. Under UNIX, run the program as follows:

```
% ./client1
```

The leading ". /" may be necessary on UNIX if your shell does not have the current directory (".") in its search path. If the directory is in your search path or you are using Windows, you can omit the ". /" from the command name:

```
% client1
```

The `client1` program connects to the server, disconnects, and exits. Not very exciting, but it's a start. However, it's *just* a start, because there are two significant shortcomings:

- The client does no error checking, so we don't really know whether or not it actually works!
- The connection parameters (hostname, username, and so forth) are hard-wired into the source code. It would be better to give the user the ability to override the parameters by specifying them in an option file or on the command line.

Neither of these problems is difficult to deal with. The next few sections address them both.

Client 2—Adding Error Checking

Our second client will be like the first one, but it will be modified to take into account the fact that errors may occur. It seems to be fairly common in programming texts to say "Error checking is left as an exercise for the reader," probably because checking for errors is—let's face it—such a bore. Nevertheless, it is much better for MySQL client programs to test for error conditions and respond to them appropriately. The client library functions that return status values do so for a reason, and you ignore them at your peril; you'll end up trying to track down obscure problems that occur in your programs due to failure to check for errors, or users of your programs will wonder why those programs behave erratically, or both.

Consider our first program, `client1`. How do you know whether it really connected to the server? You could find out by looking in the server log for `Connect` and `Quit` events corresponding to the time at which you ran the program:

```
020816 21:52:14      20 Connect     sampadm@localhost on
                     20 Quit
```

Alternatively, you might see an `Access denied` message instead, which indicates that no connection was established at all:

```
020816 22:01:47      21 Connect     Access denied for user: 'sampadm@localhost'
                                     (Using password: NO)
```

Unfortunately, `client1` doesn't tell us which of these outcomes occurred. In fact, it can't. It doesn't perform any error checking, so it doesn't even know itself what happened. That is unacceptable. You certainly shouldn't have to look in the server's log to find out whether you were able to connect to it! Let's fix this problem right away by adding some error checking.

Routines in the MySQL client library that return a value generally indicate success or failure in one of two ways:

- Pointer-valued functions return a non-NULL pointer for success and NULL for failure. (NULL in this context means "a C NULL pointer," not "a MySQL NULL column value.")

  Of the client library routines we've used so far, mysql_init() and mysql_real_connect() both return a pointer to the connection handler to indicate success and NULL to indicate failure.

- Integer-valued functions commonly return 0 for success and non-zero for failure. It's important not to test for specific non-zero values, such as −1. There is no guarantee that a client library function returns any particular value when it fails. On occasion, you may see code that tests a return value from a C API function mysql_XXX() incorrectly, like this:

```
if (mysql_XXX() == -1)        /* this test is incorrect */
    fprintf (stderr, "something bad happened\n");
```

  This test might work, and it might not. The MySQL API doesn't specify that any non-zero error return will be a particular value other than that it (obviously) isn't zero. The test should be written either like this:

```
if (mysql_XXX() != 0)        /* this test is correct */
    fprintf (stderr, "something bad happened\n");
```

  or like this, which is equivalent, and slightly simpler to write:

```
if (mysql_XXX())             /* this test is correct */
    fprintf (stderr, "something bad happened\n");
```

If you look through the source code for MySQL itself, you'll find that generally it uses the second form of the test.

Not every API call returns a value. The other client routine we've used, mysql_close(), is one that does not. (How could it fail? And if it did, so what? You were done with the connection, anyway.)

When a client library call does fail, two calls in the API are useful for finding out why. mysql_error() returns a string containing an error message, and mysql_errno() returns a numeric error code. The argument to both functions is a pointer to the connection handler. You should call them right after an error occurs; if you issue another API call that returns a status, any error information you get from mysql_error() or mysql_errno() will apply to the later call instead.

Generally, the user of a program will find the error string more enlightening than the error code, so if you report only one of the two values, I suggest it be the string. For completeness, the examples in this chapter report both values.

Taking the preceding discussion into account, we can write our second client program, `client2`, which is similar to `client1` but has proper error-checking code added. The source file, `client2.c`, is as follows:

```c
/*
 * client2.c - connect to and disconnect from MySQL server,
 * with error-checking
 */

#include <my_global.h>
#include <mysql.h>

static char *opt_host_name = NULL;      /* server host (default=localhost) */
static char *opt_user_name = NULL;      /* username (default=login name) */
static char *opt_password = NULL;       /* password (default=none) */
static unsigned int opt_port_num = 0;   /* port number (use built-in value) */
static char *opt_socket_name = NULL;    /* socket name (use built-in value) */
static char *opt_db_name = NULL;        /* database name (default=none) */
static unsigned int opt_flags = 0;      /* connection flags (none) */

static MYSQL *conn;                     /* pointer to connection handler */

int
main (int argc, char *argv[])
{
    /* initialize connection handler */
    conn = mysql_init (NULL);
    if (conn == NULL)
    {
        fprintf (stderr, "mysql_init() failed (probably out of memory)\n");
        exit (1);
    }
    /* connect to server */
    if (mysql_real_connect (conn, opt_host_name, opt_user_name, opt_password,
            opt_db_name, opt_port_num, opt_socket_name, opt_flags) == NULL)
    {
        fprintf (stderr, "mysql_real_connect() failed:\nError %u (%s)\n",
                        mysql_errno (conn), mysql_error (conn));
        mysql_close (conn);
        exit (1);
    }
    /* disconnect from server */
    mysql_close (conn);
    exit (0);
}
```

The error-checking logic is based on the fact that both `mysql_init()` and `mysql_real_connect()` return `NULL` if they fail. Note that although the program checks the return value of `mysql_init()`, no error-reporting function is called if it fails. That's because the connection handler cannot be assumed to contain any meaningful information when `mysql_init()` fails. By contrast, if `mysql_real_connect()` fails, the connection handler still won't contain information that corresponds to a valid connection, but it will contain diagnostic information that can be passed to the error-reporting functions. The handler can also be passed to `mysql_close()` to release any memory that may have been allocated automatically for it by `mysql_init()`. (Don't pass the handler to any other client routines, though! Because they generally assume a valid connection, your program may crash.)

Compile and link `client2`, and then try running it:

```
% ./client2
```

If `client2` produces no output (as just shown), it connected successfully. On the other hand, you might see something like this:

```
% ./client2
mysql_real_connect() failed:
Error 1045 (Access denied for user: 'sampadm@localhost' (Using password: NO))
```

This output indicates no connection was established, and it lets you know why. It also means that the first program, `client1`, never successfully connected to the server either. (After all, `client1` used the same connection parameters.) We didn't know it then because `client1` didn't bother to check for errors. `client2` does check, so it can tell us when something goes wrong.

Knowing about problems is better than not knowing, which is why you should test API function return values. Failure to do so is an unnecessary cause of programming difficulties. This phenomenon plays itself out frequently on the MySQL mailing list. Typical questions are "Why does my program crash when it issues this query?" or "How come my query doesn't return anything?" In many cases, the program in question didn't check whether or not the connection was established successfully before issuing the query or didn't check to make sure the server successfully executed the query before trying to retrieve the results. And when a program doesn't check for errors, the programmer ends up confused. Don't make the mistake of assuming that every client library call succeeds.

The rest of the programs in this chapter perform error checking, and your own programs should, too. It might seem like more work, but in the long run it's really less because you spend less time tracking down subtle problems. I'll also take this approach of checking for errors in Chapter 7, "The Perl DBI API," and Chapter 8, "The PHP API."

Now, suppose you do see an `Access denied` message when you run the `client2` program. How can you fix the problem? One possibility is to recompile the program after modifying the source code to change the initializers for the connection parameters to values that allow you to access your server. That might be beneficial in the sense that at least you'd be able to make a connection. But the values would still be hard-coded into your program. I recommend against that approach, especially for the password value. (You might think that the password becomes hidden when you compile your program into binary executable form, but it's not hidden at all if someone can run the `strings` utility on the binary. Not to mention the fact that anyone with read access to the source file can get the password with no work at all.)

In the next section, we'll develop more flexible methods of indicating how to connect to the server. But first I want to develop a simpler method for reporting errors, because that's something we'll need to be ready to do often. I will continue to use the style of reporting both the MySQL numeric error code and the descriptive error string when errors occur, but I prefer not to write out the calls to the error functions `mysql_errno()` and `mysql_error()` like this each time:

```
if (...some MySQL function fails...)
{
    fprintf (stderr, "...some error message...:\nError %u (%s)\n",
                    mysql_errno (conn), mysql_error (conn));
}
```

It's easier to report errors by using a utility function that can be called like this instead:

```
if (...some MySQL function fails...)
{
    print_error (conn, "...some error message...");
}
```

`print_error()` prints the error message and calls the MySQL error functions automatically. It's easier to write out the `print_error()` call than a long `fprintf()` call, and it also makes the program easier to read. Also, if `print_error()` is written to do something sensible even when conn is NULL, we can use it under circumstances such as when `mysql_init()` call fails. Then we won't have a mix of error-reporting calls—some to `fprintf()` and some to `print_error()`. A version of `print_error()` that satisfies this description can be written as follows:

```
void
print_error (MYSQL *conn, char *message)
{
```

```
        fprintf (stderr, "%s\n", message);
        if (conn != NULL)
        {
            fprintf (stderr, "Error %u (%s)\n",
                     mysql_errno (conn), mysql_error (conn));
        }
    }
}
```

I can hear someone in the back row objecting, "Well, you don't really have to call both error functions every time you want to report an error, so you're deliberately overstating the tedium of reporting errors that way just so your utility function looks more useful. And you wouldn't really write out all that error-printing code a bunch of times anyway; you'd write it once, and then use copy and paste when you need it again." Those are reasonable objections, but I would address them as follows:

- Even if you use copy and paste, it's easier to do so with shorter sections of code.

- Whether or not you prefer to invoke both error functions each time you report an error, writing out all the error-reporting code the long way leads to the temptation to take shortcuts and be inconsistent when you do report errors. Wrapping the error-reporting code in a utility function that's easy to invoke lessens this temptation and improves coding consistency.

- If you ever do decide to modify the format of your error messages, it's a lot easier if you only need to make the change one place rather than throughout your program. Or, if you decide to write error messages to a log file instead of (or in addition to) writing them to `stderr`, it's easier if you only have to change `print_error()`. This approach is less error prone and, again, lessens the temptation to do the job halfway and be inconsistent.

- If you use a debugger when testing your programs, putting a breakpoint in the error-reporting function is a convenient way to have the program break to the debugger when it detects an error condition.

For these reasons, programs in the rest of this chapter will use `print_error()` to report MySQL-related problems.

Client 3—Getting Connection Parameters at Runtime

Now we're ready to figure out how to do something smarter than using hard-wired default connection parameters—such as letting the user specify those values at runtime. The previous client programs have a significant shortcoming in that the connection parameters are written literally into the source code. To change any of those values, you have to edit the source file and recompile it. That's not very convenient, especially if you intend to make your program available for other people to use. One common way to specify connection parameters at runtime is by using command line options. For example, the programs in the MySQL distribution accept parameters in either of two forms, as shown in the following table.

Parameter	Long Option Form	Short Option Form
Hostname	`--host=host_name`	`-h host_name`
Username	`--user=user_name`	`-u user_name`
Password	`--password` or	`-p` or
	`--password=your_pass`	`-pyour_pass`
Port number	`--port=port_num`	`-P port_num`
Socket name	`--socket=socket_name`	`-S socket_name`

For consistency with the standard MySQL clients, our next client program, `client3`, will accept those same formats. It's easy to do this because the client library includes support for option processing. In addition, our client will have the ability to extract information from option files, which allows you to put connection parameters in `~/.my.cnf` (that is, the `.my.cnf` file in your home directory) or in any of the global option files. Then you don't have to specify the options on the command line each time you invoke the program. The client library makes it easy to check for MySQL option files and pull any relevant values from them. By adding only a few lines of code to your program, you can make it option file-aware, and you don't have to reinvent the wheel by writing your own code to do it. (Option file syntax is described in Appendix E, "MySQL Program Reference.")

Before writing `client3` itself, we'll develop a couple programs that illustrate how MySQL's option-processing support works. These show how option handling works fairly simply and without the added complication of connecting to the MySQL server and processing queries.

Accessing Option File Contents

To read option files for connection parameter values, use the `load_defaults()` function. `load_defaults()` looks for option files, parses their contents for any option groups in which you're interested, and rewrites your program's argument vector (the `argv[]` array) to put information from those groups in the form of command line options at the beginning of argv[]. That way, the options appear to have been specified on the command line so that when you parse the command options, you get the connection parameters as part of your normal option-processing code. The options are added to argv[] immediately after the command name and before any other arguments (rather than at the end), so that any connection parameters specified on the command line occur later than and thus override any options added by load_defaults().

The following is a little program, show_argv, that demonstrates how to use load_defaults() and illustrates how it modifies your argument vector:

```c
/* show_argv.c - show effect of load_defaults() on argument vector */

#include <my_global.h>
#include <mysql.h>

static const char *client_groups[] = { "client", NULL };

int
main (int argc, char *argv[])
{
int i;

    printf ("Original argument vector:\n");
    for (i = 0; i < argc; i++)
        printf ("arg %d: %s\n", i, argv[i]);

    my_init ();
    load_defaults ("my", client_groups, &argc, &argv);

    printf ("Modified argument vector:\n");
    for (i = 0; i < argc; i++)
        printf ("arg %d: %s\n", i, argv[i]);

    exit (0);
}
```

The option file-processing code involves several components:

- client_groups[] is an array of character strings indicating the names of the option file groups from which you want to obtain options. Client programs normally include at least "client" in the list (which represents the [client] group), but you can list as many groups as you want. The last element of the array must be NULL to indicate where the list ends.

- my_init() is an initialization routine that performs some setup operations required by load_defaults().

- `load_defaults()` reads the option files. It takes four arguments: the prefix used in the names of your option files (this should always be `"my"`), the array listing the names of the option groups in which you're interested, and the addresses of your program's argument count and vector. Don't pass the values of the count and vector. Pass their addresses instead because `load_defaults()` needs to change their values. Note in particular that even though `argv` is already a pointer, you still pass `&argv`, that pointer's address.

`show_argv` prints its arguments twice to show the effect that `load_defaults()` has on the argument array. First it prints the arguments as they were specified on the command line, and then it calls `load_defaults()` and prints the argument array again.

To see how `load_defaults()` works, make sure you have a `.my.cnf` file in your home directory with some settings specified for the `[client]` group. (On Windows, you can use the `C:\my.cnf` file.) Suppose the file looks like this:

```
[client]
user=sampadm
password=secret
host=some_host
```

If that is the case, executing `show_argv` should produce output like this:

```
% ./show_argv a b
Original argument vector:
arg 0: ./show_argv
arg 1: a
arg 2: b
Modified argument vector:
arg 0: ./show_argv
arg 1: --user=sampadm
arg 2: --password=secret
arg 3: --host=some_host
arg 4: a
arg 5: b
```

When `show_argv` prints the argument vector the second time, the values in the option file show up as part of the argument list. It's also possible that you'll see some options that were not specified on the command line or in your `~/.my.cnf` file. If this occurs, you will likely find that options for the `[client]` group are listed in a system-wide option file. This can happen because `load_defaults()` actually looks in several option files. On UNIX, it looks in `/etc/my.cnf` and in the `my.cnf` file in the MySQL data directory before reading `.my.cnf` in your home directory. On Windows, `load_defaults()` reads the my.ini file in your Windows system directory, C:\my.cnf, and the my.cnf file in the MySQL data directory.

Client programs that use load_defaults() almost always specify "client" in the list of option group names (so that they get any general client settings from option files), but you can set up your option file processing code to obtain options from other groups as well. Suppose you want show_argv to read options in both the [client] and [show_argv] groups. To accomplish this, find the following line in show_argv.c:

```
const char *client_groups[] = { "client", NULL };
```

Change the line to this:

```
const char *client_groups[] = { "show_argv", "client", NULL };
```

Then recompile show_argv, and the modified program will read options from both groups. To verify this, add a [show_argv] group to your ~/.my.cnf file:

```
[client]
user=sampadm
password=secret
host=some_host

[show_argv]
host=other_host
```

With these changes, invoking show_argv again will produce a different result than before:

```
% ./show_argv a b
Original argument vector:
arg 0: ./show_argv
arg 1: a
arg 2: b
Modified argument vector:
arg 0: ./show_argv
arg 1: --user=sampadm
arg 2: --password=secret
arg 3: --host=some_host
arg 4: --host=other_host
arg 5: a
arg 6: b
```

The order in which option values appear in the argument array is determined by the order in which they are listed in your option file, not the order in which option group names are listed in the client_groups[] array. This means you'll probably want to specify program-specific groups after the [client] group in your option file. That way, if you specify an option in both groups, the program-specific value will take precedence over the more general [client] group value. You can see this in the example just shown; the host option was specified in both the [client] and [show_argv] groups, but because the [show_argv] group appears last in the option file, its host setting appears later in the argument vector and takes precedence.

load_defaults() does not pick up values from your environment settings. If you want to use the values of environment variables, such as MYSQL_TCP_PORT or MYSQL_UNIX_PORT, you must arrange for that yourself by using getenv(). I'm not going to add that capability to our clients, but what follows is a short code fragment that shows how to check the values of a couple of the standard MySQL-related environment variables:

```
extern char *getenv ();
char *p;
int port_num = 0;
char *socket_name = NULL;

if ((p = getenv ("MYSQL_TCP_PORT")) != NULL)
    port_num = atoi (p);
if ((p = getenv ("MYSQL_UNIX_PORT")) != NULL)
    socket_name = p;
```

In the standard MySQL clients, environment variable values have lower precedence than values specified in option files or on the command line. If you check environment variables in your own programs and want to be consistent with that convention, check the environment before (not after) calling load_defaults() or processing command line options.

load_defaults() and Security

On multiple-user systems, utilities such as the ps program can display argument lists for arbitrary processes, including those being run by other users. Because of this, you may be wondering if there are any process-snooping implications of load_defaults() taking passwords that it finds in option files and putting them in your argument list. This actually is not a problem because ps displays the original argv[] contents. Any password argument created by load_defaults() points to an area of memory that it allocates for itself. That area is not part of the original vector, so ps never sees it.

On the other hand, a password that is given on the command line *does* show up in ps. This is one reason why it's not a good idea to specify passwords that way. One precaution a program can take to help reduce the risk is to remove the password from the argument list as soon as it starts executing. The next section, "Processing Command-Line Arguments," shows how to do that.

Processing Command-Line Arguments

Using `load_defaults()`, we can get all the connection parameters into the argument vector, but now we need a way to process the vector. The `handle_options()` function is designed for this. `handle_options()` is built into the MySQL client library, so you have access to it whenever you link in that library.

The option-processing methods described here were introduced in MySQL 4.0.2. Before that, the client library included option-handling code that was based on the `getopt_long()` function. If you're writing MySQL-based programs using the client library from a version of MySQL earlier than 4.0.2, you can use the version of this chapter from the first edition of this book, which describes how to process command options using `getopt_long()`. The first-edition chapter is available online in PDF format at the book's companion Web site at `http://www.kitebird.com/mysql-book/`.

The `getopt_long()`-based code has now been replaced with a new interface based on `handle_options()`. Some of the improvements offered by the new option-processing routines are:

- **More precise specification of the type and range of legal option values**. For example, you can indicate not only that an option must have integer values but that it must be positive and a multiple of 1024.

- **Integration of help text, to make it easy to print a help message by calling a standard library function**. There is no need to write your own special code to produce a help message.

- **Built in support for the standard `--no-defaults`, `--print-defaults`, `--defaults-file`, and `--defaults-extra-file` options**. These options are described in the "Option Files" section in Appendix E.

- **Support for a standard set of option prefixes, such as `--disable-` and `--enable-`, to make it easier to implement boolean (on/off) options**. These capabilities are not used in this chapter, but are described in the option-processing section of Appendix E.

Note: The new option-processing routines appeared in MySQL 4.0.2, but it's best to use 4.0.5 or later. Several problems were identified and fixed during the initial shaking-out period from 4.0.2 to 4.0.5.

To demonstrate how to use MySQL's option-handling facilities, this section describes a `show_opt` program that invokes `load_defaults()` to read option files and set up the argument vector and then processes the result using `handle_options()`.

show_opt allows you to experiment with various ways of specifying connection parameters (whether in option files or on the command line) and to see the result by showing you what values would be used to make a connection to the MySQL server. show_opt is useful for getting a feel for what will happen in our next client program, client3, which hooks up this option-processing code with code that actually does connect to the server.

show_opt illustrates what happens at each phase of argument processing by performing the following actions:

1. Set up default values for the hostname, username, password, and other connection parameters.

2. Print the original connection parameter and argument vector values.

3. Call load_defaults() to rewrite the argument vector to reflect option file contents and then print the resulting vector.

4. Call the option processing routine handle_options() to process the argument vector and then print the resulting connection parameter values and whatever is left in the argument vector.

The following discussion explains how show_opt works, but first take a look at its source file, show_opt.c:

```c
/*
 * show_opt.c - demonstrate option processing with load_defaults()
 * and handle_options()
 */

#include <my_global.h>
#include <mysql.h>
#include <my_getopt.h>

static char *opt_host_name = NULL;      /* server host (default=localhost) */
static char *opt_user_name = NULL;      /* username (default=login name) */
static char *opt_password = NULL;       /* password (default=none) */
static unsigned int opt_port_num = 0;   /* port number (use built-in value) */
static char *opt_socket_name = NULL;    /* socket name (use built-in value) */

static const char *client_groups[] = { "client", NULL };

static struct my_option my_opts[] =     /* option information structures */
{
    {"help", '?', "Display this help and exit",
    NULL, NULL, NULL,
    GET_NO_ARG, NO_ARG, 0, 0, 0, 0, 0, 0},
    {"host", 'h', "Host to connect to",
```

```
            (gptr *) &opt_host_name, NULL, NULL,
            GET_STR_ALLOC, REQUIRED_ARG, 0, 0, 0, 0, 0, 0},
            {"password", 'p', "Password",
            (gptr *) &opt_password, NULL, NULL,
            GET_STR_ALLOC, OPT_ARG, 0, 0, 0, 0, 0, 0},
            {"port", 'P', "Port number",
            (gptr *) &opt_port_num, NULL, NULL,
            GET_UINT, REQUIRED_ARG, 0, 0, 0, 0, 0, 0},
            {"socket", 'S', "Socket path",
            (gptr *) &opt_socket_name, NULL, NULL,
            GET_STR_ALLOC, REQUIRED_ARG, 0, 0, 0, 0, 0, 0},
            {"user", 'u', "User name",
            (gptr *) &opt_user_name, NULL, NULL,
            GET_STR_ALLOC, REQUIRED_ARG, 0, 0, 0, 0, 0, 0},
            { NULL, 0, NULL, NULL, NULL, NULL, GET_NO_ARG, NO_ARG, 0, 0, 0, 0, 0, 0 }
};

my_bool
get_one_option (int optid, const struct my_option *opt, char *argument)
{
    switch (optid)
    {
    case '?':
        my_print_help (my_opts);      /* print help message */
        exit (0);
    }
    return (0);
}

int
main (int argc, char *argv[])
{
int i;
int opt_err;

    printf ("Original connection parameters:\n");
    printf ("host name: %s\n", opt_host_name ? opt_host_name : "(null)");
    printf ("user name: %s\n", opt_user_name ? opt_user_name : "(null)");
    printf ("password: %s\n", opt_password ? opt_password : "(null)");
    printf ("port number: %u\n", opt_port_num);
    printf ("socket name: %s\n", opt_socket_name ? opt_socket_name : "(null)");

    printf ("Original argument vector:\n");
    for (i = 0; i < argc; i++)
        printf ("arg %d: %s\n", i, argv[i]);

    my_init ();
    load_defaults ("my", client_groups, &argc, &argv);
```

```
    printf ("Modified argument vector after load_defaults():\n");
    for (i = 0; i < argc; i++)
        printf ("arg %d: %s\n", i, argv[i]);

    if ((opt_err = handle_options (&argc, &argv, my_opts, get_one_option)))
        exit (opt_err);

    printf ("Connection parameters after handle_options():\n");
    printf ("host name: %s\n", opt_host_name ? opt_host_name : "(null)");
    printf ("user name: %s\n", opt_user_name ? opt_user_name : "(null)");
    printf ("password: %s\n", opt_password ? opt_password : "(null)");
    printf ("port number: %u\n", opt_port_num);
    printf ("socket name: %s\n", opt_socket_name ? opt_socket_name : "(null)");

    printf ("Argument vector after handle_options():\n");
    for (i = 0; i < argc; i++)
        printf ("arg %d: %s\n", i, argv[i]);

    exit (0);
}
```

The option-processing approach illustrated by `show_opt.c` involves the following aspects, which will be common to any program that uses the MySQL client library to handle command options:

1. In addition to the `my_global.h` and `mysql.h` header files, include `my_getopt.h` as well. `my_getopt.h` defines the interface to MySQL's option-processing facilities.

2. Define an array of `my_option` structures. In `show_opt.c`, this array is named `my_opts`. The array should have one structure per option that the program understands. Each structure provides information such as an option's short and long names, its default value, whether the value is a number or string, and so on. Details on members of the `my_option` structure are provided shortly.

3. After calling `load_defaults()` to read the option files and set up the argument vector, process the options by calling `handle_options()`. The first two arguments to `handle_options()` are the addresses of your program's argument count and vector. (Just as with `load_options()`, you pass the addresses of these variables, not their values.) The third argument points to the array of `my_option` structures. The fourth argument is a pointer to a helper function. The `handle_options()` routine and the `my_options` structures are designed to make it possible for most option-processing actions to be performed automatically for you by the client library. However, to allow for special actions that the library does not

handle, your program should also define a helper function for
`handle_options()` to call. In `show_opt.c`, this function is
named `get_one_option()`. The operation of the helper function
is described shortly.

The `my_option` structure defines the types of information that must be specified for each option that the program understands. It looks like this:

```
struct my_option
{
  const char *name;               /* option's long name */
  int        id;                  /* option's short name or code */
  const char *comment;            /* option description for help message */
  gptr       *value;              /* pointer to variable to store value in */
  gptr       *u_max_value;        /* The user defined max variable value */
  const char **str_values;        /* array of legal option values (unused) */
  enum get_opt_var_type var_type; /* option value's type */
  enum get_opt_arg_type arg_type; /* whether option value is required */
  longlong   def_value;           /* option's default value */
  longlong   min_value;           /* option's minimum allowable value */
  longlong   max_value;           /* option's maximum allowable value */
  longlong   sub_size;            /* amount to shift value by */
  long       block_size;          /* option value multiplier */
  int        app_type;            /* reserved for application-specific use */
};
```

The members of the `my_option` structure are used as follows:

- `name`

  The long option name. This is the `--name` form of the option, without
  the leading dashes. For example, if the long option is `--user`, list it as
  `"user"` in the `my_option` structure.

- `id`

  The short (single-letter) option name, or a code value associated with the
  option if it has no single-letter name. For example, if the short option is
  `-u`, list it as `'u'` in the `my_option` structure. For options that have only a
  long name and no corresponding single-character name, you should
  make up a set of option code values to be used internally for the short
  names. The values must be unique and different than all the single-character names. (To satisfy the latter constraint, make the codes greater than
  255, the largest possible single-character value. An example of this technique is shown in "Writing Clients That Include SSL Support"
  section later in this chapter.)

- comment

  An explanatory string that describes the purpose of the option. This is the text that you want displayed in a help message.

- value

  This is a gptr (generic pointer) value. It points to the variable where you want the option's argument to be stored. After the options have been processed, you can check that variable to see what the option's value has been set to. If the option takes no argument, value can be NULL. Otherwise, the data type of the variable that's pointed to must be consistent with the value of the var_type member.

- u_max_value

  This is another gptr value, but it's used only by the server. For client programs, set u_max_value to NULL.

- str_values

  This member currently is unused. In future MySQL releases, it might be used to allow a list of legal values to be specified, in which case any option value given will be required to match one of these values.

- var_type

  This member indicates what kind of value must follow the option name on the command line and can be any of the following:

var_type Value	Meaning
GET_NO_ARG	No value
GET_BOOL	Boolean value
GET_INT	Integer value
GET_UINT	Unsigned integer value
GET_LONG	Long integer value
GET_ULONG	Unsigned long integer value
GET_LL	Long long integer value
GET_ULL	Unsigned long long integer value
GET_STR	String value
GET_STR_ALLOC	String value

The difference between GET_STR and GET_STR_ALLOC is that for GET_STR, the option variable will be set to point directly at the value in the argument vector, whereas for GET_STR_ALLOC, a copy of the argument will be made and the option variable will be set to point to the copy.

- `arg_type`

  The `arg_type` value indicates whether a value follows the option name and can be any of the following:

`arg_type` Value	Meaning
`NO_ARG`	Option takes no following argument
`OPT_ARG`	Option may take a following argument
`REQUIRED_ARG`	Option requires a following argument

  If `arg_type` is `NO_ARG`, then `var_type` should be set to `GET_NO_ARG`.

- `def_value`

  For numeric-valued options, the option will be assigned this value by default if no explicit value is specified in the argument vector.

- `min_value`

  For numeric-valued options, this is the smallest value that can be specified. Smaller values are bumped up to this value automatically. Use 0 to indicate "no minimum."

- `max_value`

  For numeric-valued options, this is the largest value that can be specified. Larger values are bumped down to this value automatically. Use 0 to indicate "no maximum."

- `sub_size`

  For numeric-valued options, `sub_size` is an offset that is used to convert values from the range as given in the argument vector to the range that is used internally. For example, if values are given on the command line in the range from 1 to 256, but the program wants to use an internal range of 0 to 255, set `sub_size` to 1.

- `block_size`

  For numeric-valued options, if this value is non-zero, it indicates a block size. Option values will be rounded down to the nearest multiple of this size if necessary. For example, if values must be even, set the block size to 2; `handle_options()` will round odd values down to the nearest even number.

- `app_type`

  This is reserved for application-specific use.

The my_opts array should have a my_option structure for each valid option, followed by a terminating structure that is set up as follows to indicate the end of the array:

```
{ NULL, 0, NULL, NULL, NULL, NULL, GET_NO_ARG, NO_ARG, 0, 0, 0, 0, 0, 0 }
```

When you invoke handle_options() to process the argument vector, it skips over the first argument (the program name) and then processes option arguments—that is, arguments that begin with a dash. This continues until it reaches the end of the vector or encounters the special "end of options" argument ('--' by itself). As it moves through the argument vector, handle_options() calls the helper function once per option to allow that function to perform any special processing. handle_options() passes three arguments to the helper function— the short option value, a pointer to the option's my_option structure, and a pointer to the argument that follows the option in the argument vector (which will be NULL if the option is specified without a following value).

When handle_options() returns, the argument count and vector will have been reset appropriately to represent an argument list containing only the non-option arguments.

The following is a sample invocation of show_opt and the resulting output (assuming that ~/.my.cnf still has the same contents as for the final show_argv example in the "Accessing Option File Contents" section earlier in this chapter):

```
% ./show_opt -h yet_another_host --user=bill x
Original connection parameters:
host name: (null)
user name: (null)
password: (null)
port number: 0
socket name: (null)
Original argument vector:
arg 0: ./show_opt
arg 1: -h
arg 3: yet_another_host
arg 3: --user=bill
arg 4: x
Modified argument vector after load_defaults():
arg 0: ./show_opt
arg 1: --user=sampadm
arg 2: --password=secret
arg 3: --host=some_host
arg 4: -h
arg 5: yet_another_host
arg 6: --user=bill
arg 7: x
```

```
Connection parameters after handle_options():
host name: yet_another_host
user name: bill
password: secret
port number: 0
socket name: (null)
Argument vector after handle_options():
arg 0: x
```

The output shows that the hostname is picked up from the command line (overriding the value in the option file) and that the username and password come from the option file. handle_options() correctly parses options whether specified in short-option form (such as -h yet_another_host) or in long-option form (such as --user=bill).

The get_one_option() helper function is used in conjunction with handle_options(). For show_opt, it is fairly minimal and takes no action except for the --help or -? options (for which handle_options() passes an optid value of '?'):

```
my_bool
get_one_option (int optid, const struct my_option *opt, char *argument)
{
    switch (optid)
    {
    case '?':
        my_print_help (my_opts);    /* print help message */
        exit (0);
    }
    return (0);
}
```

my_print_help() is a client library routine that automatically produces a help message for you, based on the option names and comment strings in the my_opts array. To see how it works, try the following command; the final part of the output will be the help message:

```
% ./show_opt --help
```

You can add other cases to get_one_option() as necessary. For example, this function is useful for handling password options. When you specify such an option, the password value may or may not be given, as indicated by OPT_ARG in the option information structure. (That is, you can specify the option as --password or --password=your_pass if you use the long-option form or as -p or -pyour_pass if you use the short-option form.) MySQL clients typically allow you to omit the password value on the command line and then prompt you for it. This allows you to avoid giving the password on the command line, which keeps people from seeing your password. In later programs, we'll use get_one_option() to check whether or not a password value was given. We'll save the value if so, and,

otherwise, set a flag to indicate that the program should prompt the user for a password before attempting to connect to the server.

You may find it instructive to modify the option structures in show_opt.c to see how your changes affect the program's behavior. For example, if you set the minimum, maximum, and block size values for the --port option to 100, 1000, and 25, you'll find after recompiling the program that you cannot set the port number to a value outside the range from 100 to 1000 and that values get rounded down automatically to the nearest multiple of 25.

The option processing routines also handle the --no-defaults, --print-defaults, --defaults-file, and --defaults-extra-file options automatically. Try invoking show_opt with each of these options to see what happens.

Incorporating Option Processing into a MySQL Client Program

Now let's strip out from show_opt.c the stuff that's purely illustrative of how the option-handling routines work and use the remainder as a basis for a client that connects to a server according to any options that are provided in an option file or on the command line. The resulting source file, client3.c, is as follows:

```
/*
 * client3.c - connect to MySQL server, using connection parameters
 * specified in an option file or on the command line
 */

#include <string.h>      /* for strdup() */
#include <my_global.h>
#include <mysql.h>
#include <my_getopt.h>

static char *opt_host_name = NULL;      /* server host (default=localhost) */
static char *opt_user_name = NULL;      /* username (default=login name) */
static char *opt_password = NULL;       /* password (default=none) */
static unsigned int opt_port_num = 0;   /* port number (use built-in value) */
static char *opt_socket_name = NULL;    /* socket name (use built-in value) */
static char *opt_db_name = NULL;        /* database name (default=none) */
static unsigned int opt_flags = 0;      /* connection flags (none) */

static int ask_password = 0;            /* whether to solicit password */

static MYSQL *conn;                     /* pointer to connection handler */
```

```
static const char *client_groups[] = { "client", NULL };

static struct my_option my_opts[] =       /* option information structures */
{
    {"help", '?', "Display this help and exit",
    NULL, NULL, NULL,
    GET_NO_ARG, NO_ARG, 0, 0, 0, 0, 0, 0},
    {"host", 'h', "Host to connect to",
    (gptr *) &opt_host_name, NULL, NULL,
    GET_STR_ALLOC, REQUIRED_ARG, 0, 0, 0, 0, 0, 0},
    {"password", 'p', "Password",
    (gptr *) &opt_password, NULL, NULL,
    GET_STR_ALLOC, OPT_ARG, 0, 0, 0, 0, 0, 0},
    {"port", 'P', "Port number",
    (gptr *) &opt_port_num, NULL, NULL,
    GET_UINT, REQUIRED_ARG, 0, 0, 0, 0, 0, 0},
    {"socket", 'S', "Socket path",
    (gptr *) &opt_socket_name, NULL, NULL,
    GET_STR_ALLOC, REQUIRED_ARG, 0, 0, 0, 0, 0, 0},
    {"user", 'u', "User name",
    (gptr *) &opt_user_name, NULL, NULL,
    GET_STR_ALLOC, REQUIRED_ARG, 0, 0, 0, 0, 0, 0},
    { NULL, 0, NULL, NULL, NULL, NULL, GET_NO_ARG, NO_ARG, 0, 0, 0, 0, 0, 0 }
};

void
print_error (MYSQL *conn, char *message)
{
    fprintf (stderr, "%s\n", message);
    if (conn != NULL)
    {
        fprintf (stderr, "Error %u (%s)\n",
                mysql_errno (conn), mysql_error (conn));
    }
}

my_bool
get_one_option (int optid, const struct my_option *opt, char *argument)
{
    switch (optid)
    {
    case '?':
        my_print_help (my_opts);        /* print help message */
        exit (0);
    case 'p':                           /* password */
        if (!argument)                  /* no value given, so solicit it later */
            ask_password = 1;
        else                            /* copy password, wipe out original */
        {
            opt_password = strdup (argument);
            if (opt_password == NULL)
```

```
                  {
                      print_error (NULL, "could not allocate password buffer");
                      exit (1);
                  }
                  while (*argument)
                      *argument++ = 'x';
              }
              break;
      }
      return (0);
}

int
main (int argc, char *argv[])
{
int opt_err;

    my_init ();
    load_defaults ("my", client_groups, &argc, &argv);

    if ((opt_err = handle_options (&argc, &argv, my_opts, get_one_option)))
        exit (opt_err);

    /* solicit password if necessary */
    if (ask_password)
        opt_password = get_tty_password (NULL);

    /* get database name if present on command line */
    if (argc > 0)
    {
        opt_db_name = argv[0];
        --argc; ++argv;
    }

    /* initialize connection handler */
    conn = mysql_init (NULL);
    if (conn == NULL)
    {
        print_error (NULL, "mysql_init() failed (probably out of memory)");
        exit (1);
    }

    /* connect to server */
    if (mysql_real_connect (conn, opt_host_name, opt_user_name, opt_password,
            opt_db_name, opt_port_num, opt_socket_name, opt_flags) == NULL)
    {
        print_error (conn, "mysql_real_connect() failed");
        mysql_close (conn);
        exit (1);
    }
```

```
    /* ... issue queries and process results here ... */

    /* disconnect from server */
    mysql_close (conn);
    exit (0);
}
```

Compared to the `client1`, `client2`, and `show_opt` programs that we developed earlier, `client3` does a few new things:

- It allows a database to be selected on the command line; just specify the database after the other arguments. This is consistent with the behavior of the standard clients in the MySQL distribution.

- If a password value is present in the argument vector, `get_one_option()` makes a copy of it and then wipes out the original. This minimizes the time window during which a password specified on the command line is visible to `ps` or to other system status programs. (The window is only *minimized*, not eliminated. Specifying passwords on the command line still is a security risk.)

- If a password option was given without a value, `get_one_option()` sets a flag to indicate that the program should prompt the user for a password. That's done in `main()` after all options have been processed, using the `get_tty_password()` function. This is a utility routine in the client library that prompts for a password without echoing it on the screen. You may ask, "Why not just call `getpass()`?" The answer is that not all systems have that function—Windows, for example. `get_tty_password()` is portable across systems because it's configured to adjust to system idiosyncrasies.

`client3` connects to the MySQL server according to the options you specify. Assume there is no option file to complicate matters. If you invoke `client3` with no arguments, it connects to `localhost` and passes your UNIX login name and no password to the server. If instead you invoke `client3` as shown in the following command, it prompts for a password (because there is no password value immediately following `-p`), connects to `some_host`, and passes the username `some_user` to the server as well as the password you type:

```
% ./client3 -h some_host -p -u some_user some_db
```

`client3` also passes the database name `some_db` to `mysql_real_connect()` to make that the current database. If there is an option file, its contents are processed and used to modify the connection parameters accordingly.

The work we've done so far to produce client3 accomplishes something that's necessary for every MySQL client—connecting to the server using appropriate parameters. The process is implemented by the client skeleton, client3.c, which you can use as the basis for other programs. Copy it and add to it any application-specific details. That means you can concentrate more on what you're really interested in—being able to access the content of your databases. All the real action for your application will take place between the mysql_real_connect() and mysql_close() calls, but what we have now serves as a basic framework that you can use for many different clients. To write a new program, just do the following:

1. Make a copy of client3.c.
2. Modify the option-processing loop if you accept additional options other than the standard ones that client3.c knows about.
3. Add your own application-specific code between the connect and disconnect calls.

And you're done.

Processing Queries

The purpose of connecting to the server is to conduct a conversation with it while the connection is open. This section shows how to communicate with the server to process queries. Each query you run involves the following steps:

1. **Construct the query.** The way you do this depends on the contents of the query—in particular, whether it contains binary data.
2. **Issue the query by sending it to the server.** The server will execute the query and generate a result.
3. **Process the query result.** This depends on what type of query you issued. For example, a SELECT statement returns rows of data for you to process. An INSERT statement does not.

One factor to consider in constructing queries is which function to use for sending them to the server. The more general query-issuing routine is mysql_real_query(). With this routine, you provide the query as a counted string (a string plus a length). You must keep track of the length of your query string and pass that to mysql_real_query(), along with the string itself. Because the query is treated as a counted string rather than as a null-terminated string, it can contain anything, including binary data or null bytes.

The other query-issuing function, `mysql_query()`, is more restrictive in what it allows in the query string but often is easier to use. Any query passed to `mysql_query()` should be a null-terminated string, which means it cannot contain null bytes in the text of the query. (The presence of null bytes within the query string will cause it to be interpreted erroneously as shorter than it really is.) Generally speaking, if your query can contain arbitrary binary data, it might contain null bytes, so you shouldn't use `mysql_query()`.

On the other hand, when you are working with null-terminated strings, you have the luxury of constructing queries using standard C library string functions that you're probably already familiar with, such as `strcpy()` and `sprintf()`.

Another factor to consider in constructing queries is whether or not you need to perform any character-escaping operations. This is necessary if you want to construct queries using values that contain binary data or other troublesome characters, such as quotes or backslashes. This is discussed in the "Encoding Problematic Data in Queries" section later in this chapter.

A simple outline of query handling looks like this:

```
if (mysql_query (conn, query) != 0)
{
    /* failure; report error */
}
else
{
    /* success; find out what effect the query had */
}
```

`mysql_query()` and `mysql_real_query()` both return zero for queries that succeed and non-zero for failure. To say that a query "succeeded" means the server accepted it as legal and was able to execute it. It does not indicate anything about the effect of the query. For example, it does not indicate that a SELECT query selected any rows or that a DELETE statement deleted any rows. Checking what effect the query actually had involves additional processing.

A query may fail for a variety of reasons. Some common causes include the following:

- It contains a syntax error.
- It's semantically illegal—for example, a query that refers to a non-existent column of a table.
- You don't have sufficient privileges to access a table referred to by the query.

Queries can be grouped into two broad categories—those that do not return a result set (a set of rows) and those that do. Queries for statements such as INSERT, DELETE, and UPDATE fall into the "no result set returned" category. They don't return any rows, even for queries that modify your database. The only information you get back is a count of the number of rows affected.

Queries for statements such as SELECT and SHOW fall into the "result set returned" category; after all, the purpose of issuing those statements is to get something back. In the MySQL C API, the result set returned by such statements is represented by the MYSQL_RES data type. This is a structure that contains the data values for the rows and also metadata about the values (such as the column names and data value lengths). Is it legal for a result set to be empty (that is, to contain zero rows).

Handling Queries That Return No Result Set

To process a query that does not return a result set, issue it with mysql_query() or mysql_real_query(). If the query succeeds, you can determine out how many rows were inserted, deleted, or updated by calling mysql_affected_rows().

The following example shows how to handle a query that returns no result set:

```
if (mysql_query (conn, "INSERT INTO my_tbl SET name = 'My Name'") != 0)
{
    print_error (conn, "INSERT statement failed");
}
else
{
    printf ("INSERT statement succeeded: %lu rows affected\n",
            (unsigned long) mysql_affected_rows (conn));
}
```

Note how the result of mysql_affected_rows() is cast to unsigned long for printing. This function returns a value of type my_ulonglong, but attempting to print a value of that type directly does not work on some systems. (For example, I have observed it to work under FreeBSD but to fail under Solaris.) Casting the value to unsigned long and using a print format of %lu solves the problem. The same principle applies to any other functions that return my_ulonglong values, such as mysql_num_rows() and mysql_insert_id(). If you want your client programs to be portable across different systems, keep this in mind.

mysql_affected_rows() returns the number of rows affected by the query, but the meaning of "rows affected" depends on the type of query. For INSERT,

REPLACE, or DELETE, it is the number of rows inserted, replaced, or deleted. For UPDATE, it is the number of rows updated, which means the number of rows that MySQL actually modified. MySQL does not update a row if its contents are the same as what you're updating it to. This means that although a row might be selected for updating (by the WHERE clause of the UPDATE statement), it might not actually be changed.

This meaning of "rows affected" for UPDATE actually is something of a controversial point because some people want it to mean "rows matched"—that is, the number of rows selected for updating, even if the update operation doesn't actually change their values. If your application requires such a meaning, you can request that behavior when you connect to the server by passing a value of CLIENT_FOUND_ROWS in the flags parameter to mysql_real_connect().

Handling Queries That Return a Result Set

Queries that return data do so in the form of a result set that you deal with after issuing the query by calling mysql_query() or mysql_real_query(). It's important to realize that in MySQL, SELECT is not the only statement that returns rows. Statements such as SHOW, DESCRIBE, EXPLAIN, and CHECK TABLE do so as well. For all of these statements, you must perform additional row-handling processing after issuing the query.

Handling a result set involves the following steps:

1. **Generate the result set by calling `mysql_store_result()` or `mysql_use_result()`.** These functions return a MYSQL_RES pointer for success or NULL for failure. Later, we'll go over the differences between mysql_store_result() and mysql_use_result(), as well as the conditions under which you would choose one over the other. For now, our examples use mysql_store_result(), which retrieves the rows from the server immediately and stores them in the client.

2. **Call `mysql_fetch_row()` for each row of the result set.** This function returns a MYSQL_ROW value or NULL when there are no more rows. A MYSQL_ROW value is a pointer to an array of strings representing the values for each column in the row. What you do with the row depends on your application. You might simply print the column values, perform some statistical calculation on them, or do something else altogether.

3. **When you are done with the result set, call `mysql_free_result()` to de-allocate the memory it uses.**
If you neglect to do this, your application will leak memory. It's especially important to dispose of result sets properly for long-running applications; otherwise, you will notice your system slowly being taken over by processes that consume ever-increasing amounts of system resources.

The following example outlines how to process a query that returns a result set:

```
MYSQL_RES *res_set;

if (mysql_query (conn, "SHOW TABLES FROM sampdb") != 0)
    print_error (conn, "mysql_query() failed");
else
{
    res_set = mysql_store_result (conn);    /* generate result set */
    if (res_set == NULL)
            print_error (conn, "mysql_store_result() failed");
    else
    {
        /* process result set, then deallocate it */
        process_result_set (conn, res_set);
        mysql_free_result (res_set);
    }
}
```

The example hides the details of result set processing within another function, `process_result_set()`. We haven't defined that function yet, so we need to do so. Generally, operations that handle a result set are based on a loop that looks something like this:

```
MYSQL_ROW row;

while ((row = mysql_fetch_row (res_set)) != NULL)
{
    /* do something with row contents */
}
```

`mysql_fetch_row()` returns a `MYSQL_ROW` value, which is a pointer to an array of values. If the return value is assigned to a variable named `row`, each value within the row can be accessed as `row[i]`, where `i` ranges from 0 to the number of columns in the row minus one. There are several important points about the `MYSQL_ROW` data type to note:

- `MYSQL_ROW` is a pointer type, so you declare a variable of that type as `MYSQL_ROW row`, not as `MYSQL_ROW *row`.

- Values for all data types, even numeric types, are returned in the MYSQL_ROW array as strings. If you want to treat a value as a number, you must convert the string yourself.

- The strings in a MYSQL_ROW array are null-terminated. However, if a column may contain binary data, it can contain null bytes, so you should not treat the value as a null-terminated string. Get the column length to find out how long the column value is. (The "Using Result Set Metadata" section later in this chapter discusses how to determine column lengths.)

- NULL values are represented by NULL pointers in the MYSQL_ROW array. Unless you have declared a column NOT NULL, you should always check whether values for that column are NULL or your program may crash by attempting to dereference a NULL pointer.

What you do with each row will depend on the purpose of your application. For purposes of illustration, let's just print the rows with column values separated by tabs. To do that, it's necessary to know how many columns values rows contain. That information is returned by another client library function, mysql_num_fields().

The following is the code for process_result_set():

```c
void
process_result_set (MYSQL *conn, MYSQL_RES *res_set)
{
MYSQL_ROW       row;
unsigned int    i;

    while ((row = mysql_fetch_row (res_set)) != NULL)
    {
        for (i = 0; i < mysql_num_fields (res_set); i++)
        {
            if (i > 0)
                fputc ('\t', stdout);
            printf ("%s", row[i] != NULL ? row[i] : "NULL");
        }
        fputc ('\n', stdout);
    }
    if (mysql_errno (conn) != 0)
        print_error (conn, "mysql_fetch_row() failed");
    else
        printf ("%lu rows returned\n",
                (unsigned long) mysql_num_rows (res_set));
}
```

`process_result_set()` displays the contents of each row in tab-delimited format (displaying NULL values as the word "NULL"), and then prints a count of the number of rows retrieved. That count is available by calling `mysql_num_rows()`. Like `mysql_affected_rows()`, `mysql_num_rows()` returns a `my_ulonglong` value, so you should cast its value to `unsigned long` and use a `%lu` format to print it. But note that unlike `mysql_affected_rows()`, which takes a connection handler argument, `mysql_num_rows()` takes a result set pointer as its argument.

The code that follows the loop includes an error test. That's just a precaution-ary measure. If you create the result set with `mysql_store_result()`, a NULL return value from `mysql_fetch_row()` always means "no more rows." However, if you create the result set with `mysql_use_result()`, a NULL return value from `mysql_fetch_row()` can mean "no more rows" or that an error occurred. Because `process_result_set()` has no idea whether its caller used `mysql_store_result()` or `mysql_use_result()` to generate the result set, the error test allows it to detect errors properly either way.

The version of `process_result_set()` just shown takes a rather minimalist approach to printing column values—one that has certain shortcomings. For example, suppose you execute the following query:

```
SELECT last_name, first_name, city, state FROM president
ORDER BY last_name, first_name
```

You will receive the following output, which is not so easy to read:

```
Adams    John       Braintree    MA
Adams    John Quincy Braintree    MA
Arthur   Chester A.  Fairfield    VT
Buchanan    James   Mercersburg PA
Bush     George H.W. Milton   MA
Bush     George W.   New Haven    CT
Carter   James E.    Plains   GA
...
```

We could make the output prettier by providing information such as column labels and making the values line up vertically. To do that, we need the labels, and we need to know the widest value in each column. That information is available, but not as part of the column data values—it's part of the result set's metadata (data about the data). After we generalize our query handler a bit, we'll write a nicer display formatter in the "Using Result Set Metadata" section later in this chapter.

Printing Binary Data

Column values containing binary data that may include null bytes will not print properly using the `%s` `printf()` format specifier; `printf()` expects a null-terminated string and will print the column value only up to the first null byte. For binary data, it's best to use the column length so that you can print the full value. For example, you could use `fwrite()`.

A General Purpose Query Handler

The preceding query-handling examples were written using knowledge of whether or not the statement should return any data. That was possible because the queries were hardwired into the code; we used an `INSERT` statement, which does not return a result set, and a `SHOW TABLES` statement, which does.

However, you may not always know what kind of statement a given query represents. For example, if you execute a query that you read from the keyboard or from a file, it might be anything. You won't know ahead of time whether or not to expect it to return rows, or even whether it's legal. What then? You certainly don't want to try to parse the query to determine what kind of statement it is. That's not as simple as it might seem, anyway. It's not sufficient to see if the first word is `SELECT`, because the statement might begin with a comment, as follows:

```
/* comment */ SELECT ...
```

Fortunately, you don't have to know the query type in advance to be able to handle it properly. The MySQL C API makes it possible to write a general purpose query handler that correctly processes any kind of statement, whether or not it returns a result set, and whether or not it executes successfully. Before writing the code for this handler, let's outline the procedure that it implements:

1. Issue the query. If it fails, we're done.
2. If the query succeeds, call `mysql_store_result()` to retrieve the rows from the server and create a result set.
3. If `mysql_store_result()` succeeds, the query returned a result set. Process the rows by calling `mysql_fetch_row()` until it returns `NULL`, and then free the result set.
4. If `mysql_store_result()` fails, it could be that the query does not return a result set, or that it should have but an error occurred while trying to retrieve the set. You can distinguish between these outcomes by

passing the connection handler to `mysql_field_count()` and checking its return value:

- If `mysql_field_count()` returns 0, it means the query returned no columns, and thus no result set. (This indicates the query was a statement such as INSERT, DELETE, or UPDATE).

- If `mysql_field_count()` returns a non-zero value, it means that an error occurred, because the query should have returned a result set but didn't. This can happen for various reasons. For example, the result set may have been so large that memory allocation failed, or a network outage between the client and the server may have occurred while fetching rows.

The following listing shows a function that processes any query, given a connection handler and a null-terminated query string:

```
void
process_query (MYSQL *conn, char *query)
{
MYSQL_RES *res_set;
unsigned int field_count;

    if (mysql_query (conn, query) != 0) /* the query failed */
    {
        print_error (conn, "Could not execute query");
        return;
    }

    /* the query succeeded; determine whether or not it returns data */

    res_set = mysql_store_result (conn);
    if (res_set)                /* a result set was returned */
    {
        /* process rows, then free the result set */
        process_result_set (conn, res_set);
        mysql_free_result (res_set);
    }
    else                        /* no result set was returned */
    {
        /*
         * does the lack of a result set mean that the query didn't
         * return one, or that it should have but an error occurred?
         */
        if (mysql_field_count (conn) == 0)
        {
            /*
             * query generated no result set (it was not a SELECT, SHOW,
             * DESCRIBE, etc.), so just report number of rows affected
             */
```

```
        printf ("%lu rows affected\n",
                     (unsigned long) mysql_affected_rows (conn));
    }
    else    /* an error occurred */
    {
        print_error (conn, "Could not retrieve result set");
    }
  }
}
```

A slight complication to this procedure is that `mysql_field_count()` doesn't exist prior to MySQL 3.22.24. The workaround for earlier versions is to call `mysql_num_fields()` instead. To write programs that work with any version of MySQL, include the following code fragment in your source file after including `mysql.h` and before invoking `mysql_field_count()`:

```
#if !defined(MYSQL_VERSION_ID) || (MYSQL_VERSION_ID<32224)
#define mysql_field_count mysql_num_fields
#endif
```

The `#define` converts calls to `mysql_field_count()` into invocations of `mysql_num_fields()` for versions of MySQL earlier than 3.22.24.

Alternative Approaches to Query Processing

The version of `process_query()` just shown has the following three properties:

- It uses `mysql_query()` to issue the query.
- It uses `mysql_store_query()` to retrieve the result set.
- When no result set is obtained, it uses `mysql_field_count()` to distinguish occurrence of an error from a result set not being expected.

Alternative approaches are possible for all three of these aspects of query handling:

- You can use a counted query string and `mysql_real_query()` rather than a null-terminated query string and `mysql_query()`.
- You can create the result set by calling `mysql_use_result()` rather than `mysql_store_result()`.
- You can call `mysql_error()` or `mysql_errno()` rather than `mysql_field_count()` to determine whether result set retrieval failed or whether there was simply no set to retrieve.

Any or all of these approaches can be used instead of those used in
`process_query()`. The following is a `process_real_query()` function that
is analogous to `process_query()` but that uses all three alternatives:

```
void
process_real_query (MYSQL *conn, char *query, unsigned int len)
{
MYSQL_RES *res_set;
unsigned int field_count;

    if (mysql_real_query (conn, query, len) != 0)   /* the query failed */
    {
        print_error (conn, "Could not execute query");
        return;
    }

    /* the query succeeded; determine whether or not it returns data */

    res_set = mysql_use_result (conn);
    if (res_set)              /* a result set was returned */
    {
        /* process rows, then free the result set */
        process_result_set (conn, res_set);
        mysql_free_result (res_set);
    }
    else                      /* no result set was returned */
    {
        /*
         * does the lack of a result set mean that the query didn't
         * return one, or that it should have but an error occurred?
         */
        if (mysql_errno (conn) == 0)
        {
            /*
             * query generated no result set (it was not a SELECT, SHOW,
             * DESCRIBE, etc.), so just report number of rows affected
             */
            printf ("%lu rows affected\n",
                    (unsigned long) mysql_affected_rows (conn));
        }
        else    /* an error occurred */
        {
            print_error (conn, "Could not retrieve result set");
        }
    }
}
```

mysql_store_result() and mysql_use_result() Compared

The `mysql_store_result()` and `mysql_use_result()` functions are similar
in that both take a connection handler argument and return a result set.
However, the differences between them actually are quite extensive. The

primary difference between the two functions lies in the way rows of the result set are retrieved from the server. `mysql_store_result()` retrieves all the rows immediately when you call it. `mysql_use_result()` initiates the retrieval but doesn't actually get any of the rows. These differing approaches to row retrieval give rise to all other differences between the two functions. This section compares them so you'll know how to choose the one that's most appropriate for a given application.

When `mysql_store_result()` retrieves a result set from the server, it fetches the rows, allocates memory for them, and stores them in the client. Subsequent calls to `mysql_fetch_row()` never return an error because they simply pull a row out of a data structure that already holds the result set. Consequently, a NULL return from `mysql_fetch_row()` always means you've reached the end of the result set.

By contrast, `mysql_use_result()` doesn't retrieve any rows itself. Instead, it simply initiates a row-by-row retrieval, which you must complete yourself by calling `mysql_fetch_row()` for each row. In this case, although a NULL return from `mysql_fetch_row()` normally still means the end of the result set has been reached, it may mean instead that an error occurred while communicating with the server. You can distinguish the two outcomes by calling `mysql_errno()` or `mysql_error()`.

`mysql_store_result()` has higher memory and processing requirements than does `mysql_use_result()` because the entire result set is maintained in the client. The overhead for memory allocation and data structure setup is greater, and a client that retrieves large result sets runs the risk of running out of memory. If you're going to retrieve a lot of rows in a single result set, you may want to use `mysql_use_result()` instead.

`mysql_use_result()` has lower memory requirements because only enough space to handle a single row at a time need be allocated. This can be faster because you're not setting up as complex a data structure for the result set. On the other hand, `mysql_use_result()` places a greater burden on the server, which must hold rows of the result set until the client sees fit to retrieve all of them. This makes `mysql_use_result()` a poor choice for certain types of clients:

- Interactive clients that advance from row to row at the request of the user. (You don't want the server having to wait to send the next row just because the user decides to take a coffee break.)
- Clients that do a lot of processing between row retrievals.

In both of these types of situations, the client fails to retrieve all rows in the result set quickly. This ties up the server and can have a negative impact on other clients because tables from which you retrieve data are read-locked for the duration of the query. Any clients that are trying to update those tables or insert rows into them will be blocked.

Offsetting the additional memory requirements incurred by `mysql_store_result()` are certain benefits of having access to the entire result set at once. All rows of the set are available, so you have random access into them; the `mysql_data_seek()`, `mysql_row_seek()`, and `mysql_row_tell()` functions allow you to access rows in any order you want. With `mysql_use_result()`, you can access rows only in the order in which they are retrieved by `mysql_fetch_row()`. If you intend to process rows in any order other than sequentially as they are returned from the server, you must use `mysql_store_result()` instead. For example, if you have an application that allows the user to browse back and forth among the rows selected by a query, you'd be best served by using `mysql_store_result()`.

With `mysql_store_result()`, you have access to certain types of column information that are unavailable when you use `mysql_use_result()`. The number of rows in the result set is obtained by calling `mysql_num_rows()`. The maximum widths of the values in each column are stored in the `max_width` member of the `MYSQL_FIELD` column information structures. With `mysql_use_result()`, `mysql_num_rows()` doesn't return the correct value until you've fetched all the rows; similarly, `max_width` is unavailable because it can be calculated only after every row's data have been seen.

Because `mysql_use_result()` does less work than `mysql_store_result()`, it imposes a requirement that `mysql_store_result()` does not; the client must call `mysql_fetch_row()` for every row in the result set. If you fail to do this before issuing another query, any remaining records in the current result set become part of the next query's result set and an "out of sync" error occurs. (You can avoid this by calling `mysql_free_result()` before issuing the second query. `mysql_free_result()` will fetch and discard any pending rows for you.) One implication of this processing model is that with `mysql_use_result()` you can work only with a single result set at a time.

Sync errors do not happen with `mysql_store_result()` because when that function returns, there are no rows yet to be fetched from the server. In fact, with `mysql_store_result()`, you need not call `mysql_fetch_row()`

explicitly at all. This can sometimes be useful if all that you're interested in is whether you got a non-empty result rather than what the result contains. For example, to find out whether a table `mytbl` exists, you can execute the following query:

```
SHOW TABLES LIKE 'mytbl'
```

If, after calling `mysql_store_result()`, the value of `mysql_num_rows()` is non-zero, the table exists. `mysql_fetch_row()` need not be called.

Result sets generated with `mysql_store_result()` should be freed with `mysql_free_result()` at some point, but this need not necessarily be done before issuing another query. This means that you can generate multiple result sets and work with them simultaneously, in contrast to the "one result set at a time" constraint imposed when you're working with `mysql_use_result()`.

If you want to provide maximum flexibility, give users the option of selecting either result set processing method. `mysql` and `mysqldump` are two programs that do this. They use `mysql_store_result()` by default but switch to `mysql_use_result()` if you specify the `--quick` option.

Using Result Set Metadata

Result sets contain not only the column values for data rows but also information about the data. This information is called the result set metadata, which includes:

- The number of rows and columns in the result set, available by calling `mysql_num_rows()` and `mysql_num_fields()`.
- The length of each column value in the current row, available by calling `mysql_fetch_lengths()`.
- Information about each column, such as the column name and type, the maximum width of each column's values, and the table the column comes from. This information is stored in `MYSQL_FIELD` structures, which typically are obtained by calling `mysql_fetch_field()`. Appendix F describes the `MYSQL_FIELD` structure in detail and lists all functions that provide access to column information.

Metadata availability is partially dependent on your result set processing method. As indicated in the previous section, if you want to use the row count or maximum column length values, you must create the result set with `mysql_store_result()`, not with `mysql_use_result()`.

Result set metadata is helpful for making decisions about how to process result set data:

- Column names and widths are useful for producing nicely formatted output that has column titles and that lines up vertically.
- You use the column count to determine how many times to iterate through a loop that processes successive column values for data rows.
- You can use the row or column counts if you need to allocate data structures that depend on knowing the dimensions of the result set.
- You can determine the data type of a column. This allows you to tell whether a column represents a number, whether it contains binary data, and so forth.

Earlier, in the "Handling Queries That Return Data" section, we wrote a version of `process_result_set()` that printed columns from result set rows in tab-delimited format. That's good for certain purposes (such as when you want to import the data into a spreadsheet), but it's not a nice display format for visual inspection or for printouts. Recall that our earlier version of `process_result_set()` produced this output:

```
Adams    John       Braintree    MA
Adams    John Quincy Braintree    MA
Arthur   Chester A.  Fairfield    VT
Buchanan     James   Mercersburg PA
Bush     George H.W. Milton   MA
Bush     George W.   New Haven    CT
Carter   James E.    Plains  GA
...
```

Let's write a different version of `process_result_set()` that produces tabular output instead by titling and "boxing" each column. This version will display those same results in a format that's easier to look at:

```
+------------+--------------+--------------------+-------+
| last_name  | first_name   | city               | state |
+------------+--------------+--------------------+-------+
| Adams      | John         | Braintree          | MA    |
| Adams      | John Quincy  | Braintree          | MA    |
| Arthur     | Chester A.   | Fairfield          | VT    |
| Buchanan   | James        | Mercersburg        | PA    |
| Bush       | George H.W.  | Milton             | MA    |
| Bush       | George W.    | New Haven          | CT    |
| Carter     | James E.     | Plains             | GA    |
...

+------------+--------------+--------------------+-------+
```

The general outline of the display algorithm is as follows:

1. Determine the display width of each column.

2. Print a row of boxed column labels (delimited by vertical bars and preceded and followed by rows of dashes).

3. Print the values in each row of the result set, with each column boxed (delimited by vertical bars) and lined up vertically. In addition, print numbers right justified and print the word "NULL" for NULL values.

4. At the end, print a count of the number of rows retrieved.

This exercise provides a good demonstration of the use of result set metadata because it requires knowledge of quite a number of things about the result set other than just the values of the data contained in its rows.

You may be thinking to yourself, "Hmm, that description sounds suspiciously similar to the way mysql displays its output." Yes, it does, and you're welcome to compare the source for mysql to the code we end up with for process_result_set(). They're not the same, and you may find it instructive to compare the two approaches to the same problem.

First, it's necessary to determine the display width of each column. The following listing shows how to do this. Observe that the calculations are based entirely on the result set metadata and make no reference whatsoever to the row values:

```
MYSQL_FIELD     *field;
unsigned long   col_len;
unsigned int    i;

/* determine column display widths -- requires result set to be */
/* generated with mysql_store_result(), not mysql_use_result() */
mysql_field_seek (res_set, 0);
for (i = 0; i < mysql_num_fields (res_set); i++)
{
    field = mysql_fetch_field (res_set);
    col_len = strlen (field->name);
    if (col_len < field->max_length)
        col_len = field->max_length;
    if (col_len < 4 && !IS_NOT_NULL (field->flags))
        col_len = 4;    /* 4 = length of the word "NULL" */
    field->max_length = col_len;    /* reset column info */
}
```

This code calculates column widths by iterating through the MYSQL_FIELD structures for the columns in the result set. We position to the first structure by calling mysql_field_seek(). Subsequent calls to mysql_fetch_field()

return pointers to the structures for successive columns. The width of a column for display purposes is the maximum of three values, each of which depends on metadata in the column information structure:

- The length of `field->name`, the column title.
- `field->max_length`, the length of the longest data value in the column.
- The length of the string "NULL" if the column can contain NULL values. `field->flags` indicates whether or not the column can contain NULL.

Notice that after the display width for a column is known, we assign that value to `max_length`, which is a member of a structure that we obtain from the client library. Is that allowable, or should the contents of the MYSQL_FIELD structure be considered read-only? Normally, I would say "read-only," but some of the client programs in the MySQL distribution change the `max_length` value in a similar way, so I assume it's okay. (If you prefer an alternative approach that doesn't modify `max_length`, allocate an array of unsigned long values and store the calculated widths in that array.)

The display width calculations involve one caveat. Recall that `max_length` has no meaning when you create a result set using `mysql_use_result()`. Because we need `max_length` to determine the display width of the column values, proper operation of the algorithm requires that the result set be generated using `mysql_store_result()`. In programs that use `mysql_use_result()` rather than `mysql_store_result()`, one possible workaround is to use the length member of the MYSQL_FIELD structure, which tells you the maximum length that column values can be.

When we know the column widths, we're ready to print. Titles are easy to handle; for a given column, we simply use the column information structure pointed to by field and print the name member, using the width calculated earlier:

```
printf (" %-*s |", (int) field->max_length, field->name);
```

For the data, we loop through the rows in the result set, printing column values for the current row during each iteration. Printing column values from the row is a bit tricky because a value might be NULL, or it might represent a number (in which case we print it right justified). Column values are printed as follows, where `row[i]` holds the data value and field points to the column information:

```
if (row[i] == NULL)                 /* print the word "NULL" */
    printf (" %-*s |", (int) field->max_length, "NULL");
else if (IS_NUM (field->type))    /* print value right-justified */
    printf (" %*s |", (int) field->max_length, row[i]);
else                                /* print value left-justified */
    printf (" %-*s |", (int) field->max_length, row[i]);
```

The value of the IS_NUM() macro is true if the column type indicated by field->type is one of the numeric types, such as INT, FLOAT, or DECIMAL.

The final code to display the result set is as follows. Note that because we're printing lines of dashes multiple times, it's easier to write a print_dashes() function to do so rather than to repeat the dash-generation code several places:

```c
void
print_dashes (MYSQL_RES *res_set)
{
MYSQL_FIELD    *field;
unsigned int   i, j;

    mysql_field_seek (res_set, 0);
    fputc ('+', stdout);
    for (i = 0; i < mysql_num_fields (res_set); i++)
    {
        field = mysql_fetch_field (res_set);
        for (j = 0; j < field->max_length + 2; j++)
            fputc ('-', stdout);
        fputc ('+', stdout);
    }
    fputc ('\n', stdout);
}

void
process_result_set (MYSQL *conn, MYSQL_RES *res_set)
{
MYSQL_ROW      row;
MYSQL_FIELD    *field;
unsigned long  col_len;
unsigned int   i;

    /* determine column display widths -- requires result set to be */
    /* generated with mysql_store_result(), not mysql_use_result() */
    mysql_field_seek (res_set, 0);
    for (i = 0; i < mysql_num_fields (res_set); i++)
    {
        field = mysql_fetch_field (res_set);
        col_len = strlen (field->name);
        if (col_len < field->max_length)
            col_len = field->max_length;
        if (col_len < 4 && !IS_NOT_NULL (field->flags))
            col_len = 4;     /* 4 = length of the word "NULL" */
        field->max_length = col_len;     /* reset column info */
    }

    print_dashes (res_set);
    fputc ('|', stdout);
    mysql_field_seek (res_set, 0);
```

```
    for (i = 0; i < mysql_num_fields (res_set); i++)
    {
        field = mysql_fetch_field (res_set);
        printf (" %-*s |", (int) field->max_length, field->name);
    }
    fputc ('\n', stdout);
    print_dashes (res_set);

    while ((row = mysql_fetch_row (res_set)) != NULL)
    {
        mysql_field_seek (res_set, 0);
        fputc ('|', stdout);
        for (i = 0; i < mysql_num_fields (res_set); i++)
        {
            field = mysql_fetch_field (res_set);
            if (row[i] == NULL)                /* print the word "NULL" */
                printf (" %-*s |", (int) field->max_length, "NULL");
            else if (IS_NUM (field->type))  /* print value right-justified */
                printf (" %*s |", (int) field->max_length, row[i]);
            else                            /* print value left-justified */
                printf (" %-*s |", (int) field->max_length, row[i]);
        }
        fputc ('\n', stdout);
    }
    print_dashes (res_set);
    printf ("%lu rows returned\n", (unsigned long) mysql_num_rows (res_set));
}
```

The MySQL client library provides several ways of accessing the column information structures. For example, the code in the preceding example accesses these structures several times using loops of the following general form:

```
mysql_field_seek (res_set, 0);
for (i = 0; i < mysql_num_fields (res_set); i++)
{
    field = mysql_fetch_field (res_set);
    ...
}
```

However, the `mysql_field_seek()`/`mysql_fetch_field()` combination is only one way of getting MYSQL_FIELD structures. See the entries for the `mysql_fetch_fields()` and `mysql_fetch_field_direct()` functions in Appendix F for other ways of getting column information structures.

Client 4—An Interactive Query Program

Let's put together much of what we've developed so far and use it to write a simple interactive client, `client4`. This program lets you enter queries, executes them using our general purpose query handler `process_query()`, and displays the results using the `process_result_set()` display formatter developed in the preceding section.

client4 will be similar in some ways to mysql, although of course not with as many features. There are several restrictions on what client4 will allow as input:

- Each input line must contain a single complete statement.
- Statements should not be terminated by a semicolon or by \g.
- The only non-SQL commands that are recognized are quit and \q, which terminate the program. You can also use Ctrl-D to quit.

It turns out that client4 is almost completely trivial to write (about a dozen lines of new code). Almost everything we need is provided by our client program skeleton (client3.c) and by other functions that we have written already. The only thing we need to add is a loop that collects input lines and executes them.

To construct client4, begin by copying the client skeleton client3.c to client4.c. Then add to that the code for the process_query(), process_result_set(), and print_dashes() functions. Finally, in client4.c, look for the line in main() that says this:

```
/* ... issue queries and process results here ... */
```

Replace that line with the following while loop:

```
while (1)
{
    char    buf[10000];

    fprintf (stderr, "query> ");                    /* print prompt */
    if (fgets (buf, sizeof (buf), stdin) == NULL)   /* read query */
        break;
    if (strcmp (buf, "quit\n") == 0 || strcmp (buf, "\\q\n") == 0)
        break;
    process_query (conn, buf);                      /* execute query */
}
```

Compile client4.c to produce client4.o, link client4.o with the client library to produce client4, and you're done. You have an interactive MySQL client program that can execute any query and display the results. The following example shows how the program works, both for SELECT and non-SELECT queries, as well as for statements that are erroneous:

```
% ./client4
query> USE sampdb
```

```
0 rows affected
query> SELECT DATABASE(), USER()
+------------+--------------------+
| DATABASE() | USER()             |
+------------+--------------------+
| sampdb     | sampadm@localhost  |
+------------+--------------------+
1 rows returned
query> SELECT COUNT(*) FROM president
+----------+
| COUNT(*) |
+----------+
|       42 |
+----------+
1 rows returned
query> SELECT last_name, first_name FROM president ORDER BY last_name LIMIT 3
+-----------+-------------+
| last_name | first_name  |
+-----------+-------------+
| Adams     | John        |
| Adams     | John Quincy |
| Arthur    | Chester A.  |
+-----------+-------------+
3 rows returned
query> CREATE TABLE t (i INT)
0 rows affected
query> SELECT j FROM t
Could not execute query
Error 1054 (Unknown column 'j' in 'field list')
query> USE mysql
Could not execute query
Error 1044 (Access denied for user: 'sampadm@localhost' to database 'mysql')
```

Writing Clients That Include SSL Support

MySQL 4 includes SSL support, which you can use in your own programs to access the server over secure connections. To show how this is done, this section describes the process of modifying client4 to produce a similar client named sslclient that outwardly is much the same but allows encrypted connections to be established. For sslclient to work properly, MySQL must have been built with SSL support, and the server must be started with the proper options that identify its certificate and key files. You'll also need certificate and key files on the client end. For more information, see the "Setting Up Secure Connections" section in Chapter 12, "Security." In addition, you should use MySQL 4.0.5 or later. The SSL and option-handling routines for earlier 4.0.x releases will not behave quite as described here.

The `sampdb` distribution contains a source file, `sslclient.c`, from which the client program `sslclient` can be built. The following procedure describes how `sslclient.c` is created, beginning with `client4.c`:

1. Copy `client4.c` to `sslclient.c`. The remaining steps apply to `sslclient.c`.

2. To allow the compiler to detect whether SSL support is available, the MySQL header file `my_config.h` defines the symbol `HAVE_OPENSSL` appropriately. This means that when writing SSL-related code, you use the following construct so that the code will be ignored if SSL cannot be used:

   ```
   #ifdef HAVE_OPENSSL
       ...SSL-related code here...
   #endif
   ```

   `my_config.h` is included by `my_global.h`. `sslclient.c` already includes the latter file, so you need not include `my_config.h` explicitly.

3. Modify the `my_opts` array that contains option information structures to include entries for the standard SSL-related options as well (`--ssl-ca`, `--ssl-key`, and so on). The easiest way to do this is to include the contents of the `sslopt-longopts.h` file into the `my_opts` array with an `#include` directive. After making the change, `my_opts` looks like this:

   ```
   static struct my_option my_opts[] =      /* option information structures */
   {
       {"help", '?', "Display this help and exit",
       NULL, NULL, NULL,
       GET_NO_ARG, NO_ARG, 0, 0, 0, 0, 0, 0},
       {"host", 'h', "Host to connect to",
       (gptr *) &opt_host_name, NULL, NULL,
       GET_STR_ALLOC, REQUIRED_ARG, 0, 0, 0, 0, 0, 0},
       {"password", 'p', "Password",
       (gptr *) &opt_password, NULL, NULL,
       GET_STR_ALLOC, OPT_ARG, 0, 0, 0, 0, 0, 0},
       {"port", 'P', "Port number",
       (gptr *) &opt_port_num, NULL, NULL,
       GET_UINT, REQUIRED_ARG, 0, 0, 0, 0, 0, 0},
       {"socket", 'S', "Socket path",
       (gptr *) &opt_socket_name, NULL, NULL,
       GET_STR_ALLOC, REQUIRED_ARG, 0, 0, 0, 0, 0, 0},
       {"user", 'u', "User name",
       (gptr *) &opt_user_name, NULL, NULL,
       GET_STR_ALLOC, REQUIRED_ARG, 0, 0, 0, 0, 0, 0},

   #include <sslopt-longopts.h>
   ```

```
        { NULL, 0, NULL, NULL, NULL, NULL, GET_NO_ARG, NO_ARG, 0, 0, 0, 0, 0, 0
    }
    };
```

`sslopt-longopts.h` is a public MySQL header file. Its contents look like this (reformatted slightly):

```
#ifdef HAVE_OPENSSL
    {"ssl", OPT_SSL_SSL,
    "Enable SSL for connection. Disable with --skip-ssl",
    (gptr*) &opt_use_ssl, NULL, 0,
    GET_BOOL, NO_ARG, 0, 0, 0, 0, 0, 0},
    {"ssl-key", OPT_SSL_KEY, "X509 key in PEM format (implies --ssl)",
    (gptr*) &opt_ssl_key, NULL, 0,
    GET_STR, REQUIRED_ARG, 0, 0, 0, 0, 0, 0},
    {"ssl-cert", OPT_SSL_CERT, "X509 cert in PEM format (implies --ssl)",
    (gptr*) &opt_ssl_cert, NULL, 0,
    GET_STR, REQUIRED_ARG, 0, 0, 0, 0, 0, 0},
    {"ssl-ca", OPT_SSL_CA,
    "CA file in PEM format (check OpenSSL docs, implies --ssl)",
    (gptr*) &opt_ssl_ca, NULL, 0,
    GET_STR, REQUIRED_ARG, 0, 0, 0, 0, 0, 0},
    {"ssl-capath", OPT_SSL_CAPATH,
    "CA directory (check OpenSSL docs, implies --ssl)",
    (gptr*) &opt_ssl_capath, NULL, 0,
    GET_STR, REQUIRED_ARG, 0, 0, 0, 0, 0, 0},
    {"ssl-cipher", OPT_SSL_CIPHER, "SSL cipher to use (implies --ssl)",
    (gptr*) &opt_ssl_cipher, NULL, 0,
    GET_STR, REQUIRED_ARG, 0, 0, 0, 0, 0, 0},
#endif /* HAVE_OPENSSL */
```

4. The option structures defined by `sslopt-longopts.h` refer to the values `OPT_SSL_SSL`, `OPT_SSL_KEY`, and so on. These are used for the short option codes and must be defined by your program, which can be done by adding the following lines preceding the definition of the `my_opts` array:

```
#ifdef HAVE_OPENSSL
enum options
{
    OPT_SSL_SSL=256,
    OPT_SSL_KEY,
    OPT_SSL_CERT,
    OPT_SSL_CA,
    OPT_SSL_CAPATH,
    OPT_SSL_CIPHER
};
#endif
```

When writing your own applications, if a given program also defines codes for other options, make sure these OPT_SSL_*XXX* symbols have different values than those codes.

5. The SSL-related option structures in sslopt-longopts.h refer to a set of variables that are used to hold the option values. To declare these, use an #include directive to include the contents of the sslopt-vars.h file into your program preceding the definition of the my_opts array. sslopt-vars.h looks like this:

```
#ifdef HAVE_OPENSSL
static my_bool opt_use_ssl   = 0;
static char *opt_ssl_key     = 0;
static char *opt_ssl_cert    = 0;
static char *opt_ssl_ca      = 0;
static char *opt_ssl_capath = 0;
static char *opt_ssl_cipher = 0;
#endif
```

6. In the get_one_option() routine, add a line that includes the sslopt-case.h file:

```
my_bool
get_one_option (int optid, const struct my_option *opt, char *argument)
{
    switch (optid)
    {
    case '?':
        my_print_help (my_opts);     /* print help message */
        exit (0);
    case 'p':                        /* password */
        if (!argument)               /* no value given, so solicit it later */
            ask_password = 1;
        else                         /* copy password, wipe out original */
        {
            opt_password = strdup (argument);
            if (opt_password == NULL)
            {
                print_error (NULL, "could not allocate password buffer");
                exit (1);
            }
            while (*argument)
                *argument++ = 'x';
        }
        break;
```

```
#include <sslopt-case.h>
    }
    return (0);
}
```

`sslopt-case.h` includes cases for the `switch()` statement that detect when any of the SSL options were given and sets the `opt_use_ssl` variable if so. It looks like this:

```
#ifdef HAVE_OPENSSL
    case OPT_SSL_KEY:
    case OPT_SSL_CERT:
    case OPT_SSL_CA:
    case OPT_SSL_CAPATH:
    case OPT_SSL_CIPHER:
    /*
      Enable use of SSL if we are using any ssl option
      One can disable SSL later by using --skip-ssl or --ssl=0
    */
    opt_use_ssl= 1;
    break;
#endif
```

The effect of this is that after option processing has been done, it is possible to determine whether the user wants a secure connection by checking the value of `opt_use_ssl`.

If you follow the preceding procedure, the usual `load_defaults()` and `handle_options()` routines will take care of parsing the SSL-related options and setting their values for you automatically. The only other thing you need to do is pass SSL option information to the client library before connecting to the server if the options indicate that the user wants an SSL connection. Do this by invoking `mysql_ssl_set()` after calling `mysql_init()` and before calling `mysql_real_connect()`. The sequence looks like this:

```
/* initialize connection handler */
conn = mysql_init (NULL);
if (conn == NULL)
{
    print_error (NULL, "mysql_init() failed (probably out of memory)");
    exit (1);
}

#ifdef HAVE_OPENSSL
    /* pass SSL information to client library */
```

```
        if (opt_use_ssl)
            mysql_ssl_set (conn, opt_ssl_key, opt_ssl_cert, opt_ssl_ca,
                            opt_ssl_capath, opt_ssl_cipher);
    #endif

        /* connect to server */
        if (mysql_real_connect (conn, opt_host_name, opt_user_name, opt_password,
                opt_db_name, opt_port_num, opt_socket_name, opt_flags) == NULL)
        {
            print_error (conn, "mysql_real_connect() failed");
            mysql_close (conn);
            exit (1);
        }
```

Note that you don't test mysql_ssl_set() to see if it returns an error. Any problems with the information you supply to that function will result in an error when you call mysql_real_connect().

Produce sslclient by compiling sslclient.c and then run it. Assuming that the mysql_real_connect() call succeeds, you can proceed to issue queries. If you invoke sslclient with the appropriate SSL options, communication with the server should occur over an encrypted connection. To determine whether or not that is so, issue the following query:

```
    SHOW STATUS LIKE 'Ssl_cipher'
```

The value of Ssl_cipher will be non-blank if an encryption cipher is in use. (To make this easier, the version of sslclient included in the sampdb distribution actually issues the query for you and reports the result.)

Using the Embedded Server Library

MySQL 4 introduces an embedded server library, libmysqld, that contains the server in a form that can be linked (embedded) into applications. This allows you to produce MySQL-based applications that stand on their own, as opposed to applications that connect as a client over a network to a separate server program.

To write an embedded server application, two requirements must be satisfied. First, the embedded server library must be installed:

- If you're building from source, enable the library by using the --with-embedded-server option when you run configure.
- For binary distributions, use a Max distribution if the non-Max distribution doesn't include libmysqld.
- For RPM installs, make sure to install the embedded server RPM.

Second, you'll need to include a small amount of code in your application to start up and shut down the server.

After making sure that both requirements are met, it's necessary only to compile the application and link in the embedded server library (-lmysqld) rather than the regular client library (-lmysqlclient). In fact, the design of the server library is such that if you write an application to use it, you can easily produce either an embedded or a client/server version of the application simply by linking in the appropriate library. This works because the regular client library contains interface functions that have the same calling sequence as the embedded server calls but are stubs (dummy routines) that do nothing.

Writing an Embedded Server Application

Writing an application that uses the embedded server is little different than writing one that operates in a client/server context. In fact, if you begin with a program that is written as a client/server application, you can convert it easily to use the embedded server instead. For example, to modify client4 to produce an embedded application named embapp, copy client4.c to embapp.c and then perform the following steps to modify embapp.c:

1. Add mysql_embed.h to the set of MySQL header files used by the program:

   ```
   #include <my_global.h>
   #include <mysql.h>
   #include <mysql_embed.h>
   #include <my_getopt.h>
   ```

2. An embedded application includes both a client side and a server side, so it can process one group of options for the client and another group for the server. For example, an application named embapp might read the [client] and [embapp] groups from option files for the client part. To set that up, modify the definition of the client_groups array to look like this:

   ```
   static const char *client_groups[] =
   {
       "client", "embapp", NULL
   };
   ```

   Options in these groups can be processed by load_defaults() and handle_options() in the usual fashion. Then define another list of option groups for the server side to use. By convention, this list should include the [server] and [embedded] groups and also the [appname_SERVER] group, where *appname* is the name of your application. For a program named embapp, the application-specific group will be [embapp_SERVER], so you declare the list of group names as follows:

```
static const char *server_groups[] =
{
    "server", "embedded", "embapp_SERVER", NULL
};
```

3. Call mysql_server_init() before initiating communication with the server. A good place to do this is before you call mysql_init().

4. Call mysql_server_end() after you're done using the server. A good place to do this is after you call mysql_close().

After making these changes, the main() function in embapp.c will look like this:

```
int
main (int argc, char *argv[])
{
int opt_err;

    my_init ();
    load_defaults ("my", client_groups, &argc, &argv);

    if ((opt_err = handle_options (&argc, &argv, my_opts, get_one_option)))
        exit (opt_err);

    /* solicit password if necessary */
    if (ask_password)
        opt_password = get_tty_password (NULL);

    /* get database name if present on command line */
    if (argc > 0)
    {
        opt_db_name = argv[0];
        --argc; ++argv;
    }

    /* initialize embedded server */
    mysql_server_init (0, NULL, (char **) server_groups);

    /* initialize connection handler */
    conn = mysql_init (NULL);
    if (conn == NULL)
    {
        print_error (NULL, "mysql_init() failed (probably out of memory)");
        exit (1);
    }

    /* connect to server */
```

```
    if (mysql_real_connect (conn, opt_host_name, opt_user_name, opt_password,
            opt_db_name, opt_port_num, opt_socket_name, opt_flags) == NULL)
    {
        print_error (conn, "mysql_real_connect() failed");
        mysql_close (conn);
        exit (1);
    }

    while (1)
    {
        char    buf[10000];

        fprintf (stderr, "query> ");                    /* print prompt */
        if (fgets (buf, sizeof (buf), stdin) == NULL)   /* read query */
            break;
        if (strcmp (buf, "quit\n") == 0 || strcmp (buf, "\\q\n") == 0)
            break;
        process_query (conn, buf);                      /* execute query */
    }

    /* disconnect from server */
    mysql_close (conn);
    /* shut down embedded server */
    mysql_server_end ();
    exit (0);
}
```

Producing the Application Executable Binary

To produce the embedded-server executable binary for embapp, link in
the -lmysqld library rather than the -lmysqlclient library. The mysql_con-
fig utility is useful here. Just as it can show you the flags to use for linking in
the regular client library, it also can display the flags necessary
for the embedded server:

```
% mysql_config --libmysqld-libs
 -L'/usr/local/mysql/lib/mysql' -lmysqld -lz -lm
```

Thus, to produce an embedded version of embapp, use commands such as
these:

```
% gcc -c `mysql_config --cflags` embapp.c
% gcc -o embapp embapp.o `mysql_config --libmysqld-libs`
```

At this point, you have an embedded application that contains everything you
need to access your MySQL databases. However, be sure when you execute
embapp that it does not attempt to use the same data directory as any standalone
servers that may already be running on the same machine. Also, under UNIX,
the application must run with privileges that give it access to the data directory.
You can either run embapp while logged in as the user that owns the data

directory, or you can make it a setuid program that changes its user ID to that user when it starts up. For example, to set `embapp` to run with the privileges of a user named `mysqladm`, issue the following commands as `root`:

```
# chown mysqladm embapp
# chmod 4755 embapp
```

Should you decide that you want to produce a non-embedded version of the application that operates in a client/server context, link it against the regular client library. You can do so by building it as follows:

```
% gcc -c `mysql_config --cflags` embapp.c
% gcc -o embapp embapp.o `mysql_config --libs`
```

The regular client library includes dummy versions of `mysql_server_init()` and `mysql_server_end()` that do nothing, so no link errors will occur.

Miscellaneous Topics

This section covers several query-processing subjects that didn't fit very well into earlier sections of this chapter:

- How to use result set data to calculate a result after using result set metadata to help verify that the data are suitable for your calculations
- How to deal with data values that are troublesome to insert into queries
- How to work with binary data
- How to get information about the structure of your tables
- Common MySQL programming mistakes and how to avoid them

Performing Calculations on Result Sets

So far we've concentrated on using result set metadata primarily for printing query rows, but clearly there will be times when you need to do something with a result set besides print it. For example, you can compute statistical information based on the data values, using the metadata to make sure the data conform to requirements you want them to satisfy. What type of requirements? For starters, you'd probably want to verify that a column on which you're planning to perform numeric computations actually contains numbers.

The following listing shows a simple function, `summary_stats()`, that takes a result set and a column index and produces summary statistics for the values in the column. The function also reports the number of missing values, which it detects by checking for `NULL` values. These calculations involve two requirements that the data must satisfy, so `summary_stats()` verifies them using the result set metadata:

- The specified column must exist—that is, the column index must be within range of the number of columns in the result set. This range is from 0 to `mysql_num_fields()`−1.

- The column must contain numeric values.

If these conditions do not hold, `summary_stats()` simply prints an error message and returns. It is implemented as follows:

```
void
summary_stats (MYSQL_RES *res_set, unsigned int col_num)
{
MYSQL_FIELD     *field;
MYSQL_ROW       row;
unsigned int    n, missing;
double          val, sum, sum_squares, var;

    /* verify data requirements: column must be in range and numeric */
    if (col_num < 0 || col_num >= mysql_num_fields (res_set))
    {
        print_error (NULL, "illegal column number");
        return;
    }
    mysql_field_seek (res_set, col_num);
    field = mysql_fetch_field (res_set);
    if (!IS_NUM (field->type))
    {
        print_error (NULL, "column is not numeric");
        return;
    }

    /* calculate summary statistics */

    n = 0;
    missing = 0;
    sum = 0;
    sum_squares = 0;

    mysql_data_seek (res_set, 0);
    while ((row = mysql_fetch_row (res_set)) != NULL)
    {
        if (row[col_num] == NULL)
            missing++;
        else
        {
            n++;
            val = atof (row[col_num]);  /* convert string to number */
            sum += val;
            sum_squares += val * val;
        }
```

```
    }
    if (n == 0)
        printf ("No observations\n");
    else
    {
        printf ("Number of observations: %lu\n", n);
        printf ("Missing observations: %lu\n", missing);
        printf ("Sum: %g\n", sum);
        printf ("Mean: %g\n", sum / n);
        printf ("Sum of squares: %g\n", sum_squares);
        var = ((n * sum_squares) - (sum * sum)) / (n * (n - 1));
        printf ("Variance: %g\n", var);
        printf ("Standard deviation: %g\n", sqrt (var));
    }
}
```

Note the call to `mysql_data_seek()` that precedes the `mysql_fetch_row()` loop. It positions to the first row of the result set, which is useful in case you want to call `summary_stats()` multiple times for the same result set (for example, to calculate statistics on several different columns). The effect is that each time `summary_stats()` is invoked, it "rewinds" to the beginning of the result set. The use of `mysql_data_seek()` requires that you create the result set with `mysql_store_result()`. If you create it with `mysql_use_result()`, you can only process rows in order, and you can process them only once.

`summary_stats()` is a relatively simple function, but it should give you an idea of how you could program more complex calculations, such as a least-squares regression on two columns or standard statistics such as a *t*-test or an analysis of variance.

Encoding Problematic Data in Queries

If inserted literally into a query, data values containing quotes, nulls, or back-slashes can cause problems when you try to execute the query. The following discussion describes the nature of the difficulty and how to solve it.

Suppose you want to construct a SELECT query based on the contents of the null-terminated string pointed to by the name_val variable:

```
char query[1024];
```

```
sprintf (query, "SELECT * FROM mytbl WHERE name='%s'", name_val);
```

If the value of name_val is something like O'Malley, Brian, the resulting query is illegal because a quote appears inside a quoted string:

```
SELECT * FROM mytbl WHERE name='O'Malley, Brian'
```

You need to treat the quote specially so that the server doesn't interpret it as the end of the name. The ANSI SQL convention for doing this is to double the quote within the string. MySQL understands that convention and also allows the quote to be preceded by a backslash, so you can write the query using either of the following formats:

```
SELECT * FROM mytbl WHERE name='O''Malley, Brian'
SELECT * FROM mytbl WHERE name='O\'Malley, Brian'
```

Another problematic situation involves the use of arbitrary binary data in a query. This happens, for example, in applications that store images in a database. Because a binary value can contain any character (including quotes or backslashes), it cannot be considered safe to put into a query as is.

To deal with this problem, use `mysql_real_escape_string()`, which encodes special characters to make them usable in quoted strings. Characters that `mysql_real_escape_string()` considers special are the null character, single quote, double quote, backslash, newline, carriage return, and Ctrl-Z. (The last one is special on Windows, where it often signifies end-of-file.)

When should you use `mysql_real_escape_string()`? The safest answer is "always." However, if you're sure of the format of your data and know that it's okay—perhaps because you have performed some prior validation check on it—you need not encode it. For example, if you are working with strings that you know represent legal phone numbers consisting entirely of digits and dashes, you don't need to call `mysql_real_escape_string()`. Otherwise, you probably should.

`mysql_real_escape_string()` encodes problematic characters by turning them into 2-character sequences that begin with a backslash. For example, a null byte becomes '\0', where the '0' is a printable ASCII zero, not a null. Backslash, single quote, and double quote become '\\', '\ '', and '\"'.

To use `mysql_real_escape_string()`, invoke it as follows:

```
to_len = mysql_real_escape_string (conn, to_str, from_str, from_len);
```

`mysql_real_escape_string()` encodes `from_str` and writes the result into `to_str`. It also adds a terminating null, which is convenient because you can use the resulting string with functions such as `strcpy()`, `strlen()`, or `printf()`.

`from_str` points to a `char` buffer containing the string to be encoded. This string can contain anything, including binary data. `to_str` points to an existing `char` buffer where you want the encoded string to be written; do not pass an uninitialized or NULL pointer, expecting `mysql_real_escape_string()` to allocate space for you. The length of the buffer pointed to by `to_str` must be at least `(from_len*2)+1` bytes long. (It's possible that every character in `from_str` will need encoding with two characters; the extra byte is for the terminating null.)

`from_len` and `to_len` are unsigned `long` values. `from_len` indicates the length of the data in `from_str`; it's necessary to provide the length because `from_str` may contain null bytes and cannot be treated as a null-terminated string. `to_len`, the return value from `mysql_real_escape_string()`, is the actual length of the resulting encoded string, not counting the terminating null.

When `mysql_real_escape_string()` returns, the encoded result in `to_str` can be treated as a null-terminated string because any nulls in `from_str` are encoded as the printable '\0' sequence.

To rewrite the SELECT-constructing code so that it works even for name values that contain quotes, we could do something like the following:

```
char query[1024], *p;

p = strcpy (query, "SELECT * FROM mytbl WHERE name='");
p += strlen (p);
p += mysql_real_escape_string (conn, p, name, strlen (name));
*p++ = '\'';
*p = '\0';
```

Yes, that's ugly. If you want to simplify the code a bit, at the cost of using a second buffer, do the following instead:

```
char query[1024], buf[1024];

(void) mysql_real_escape_string (conn, buf, name, strlen (name));
sprintf (query, "SELECT * FROM mytbl WHERE name='%s'", buf);
```

`mysql_real_escape_string()` is unavailable prior to MySQL 3.23.14. As a workaround, you can use `mysql_escape_string()` instead:

```
to_len = mysql_escape_string (to_str, from_str, from_len);
```

The difference between them is that `mysql_real_escape_string()` uses the character set for the current connection to perform encoding. `mysql_escape_string()` uses the default character set (which is why it doesn't take a connection handler argument). To write source that will compile under any version of MySQL, include the following code fragment in your file:

```
#if !defined(MYSQL_VERSION_ID) || (MYSQL_VERSION_ID<32314)
#define mysql_real_escape_string(conn,to_str,from_str,len) \
        mysql_escape_string(to_str,from_str,len)
#endif
```

Then write your code in terms of `mysql_real_escape_string()`; if that function is unavailable, the `#define` causes it to be mapped to `mysql_escape_string()` instead.

Working with Image Data

One of the jobs for which `mysql_real_escape_string()` is essential involves loading image data into a table. This section shows how to do it. (The discussion applies to any other form of binary data as well.)

Suppose you want to read images from files and store them in a table named `picture` along with a unique identifier. The `BLOB` type is a good choice for binary data, so you could use a table specification like this:

```
CREATE TABLE picture
(
    pict_id     INT NOT NULL PRIMARY KEY,
    pict_data   BLOB
);
```

To actually get an image from a file into the `picture` table, the following function, `load_image()`, does the job, given an identifier number and a pointer to an open file containing the image data:

```
int
load_image (MYSQL *conn, int id, FILE *f)
{
char          query[1024*100], buf[1024*10], *p;
unsigned long from_len;
int           status;

    sprintf (query,
            "INSERT INTO picture (pict_id,pict_data) VALUES (%d,'",
            id);
    p = query + strlen (query);
    while ((from_len = fread (buf, 1, sizeof (buf), f)) > 0)
    {
        /* don't overrun end of query buffer! */
        if (p + (2*from_len) + 3 > query + sizeof (query))
        {
            print_error (NULL, "image too big");
            return (1);
        }
        p += mysql_real_escape_string (conn, p, buf, from_len);
    }
    *p++ = '\'';
    *p++ = ')';
    status = mysql_real_query (conn, query, (unsigned long) (p - query));
    return (status);
}
```

`load_image()` doesn't allocate a very large query buffer (100KB), so it works only for relatively small images. In a real-world application, you might allocate the buffer dynamically based on the size of the image file.

Getting an image value (or any binary value) back out of a database isn't nearly as much of a problem as putting it in to begin with because the data value is available in raw form in the `MYSQL_ROW` variable, and the length is available by calling `mysql_fetch_lengths()`. Just be sure to treat the value as a counted string, not as a null-terminated string.

Getting Table Information

MySQL allows you to get information about the structure of your tables, using any of the following queries (which are equivalent):

```
SHOW COLUMNS FROM tbl_name;
SHOW FIELDS FROM tbl_name;
DESCRIBE tbl_name;
EXPLAIN tbl_name;
```

Each statement is like `SELECT` in that it returns a result set. To find out about the columns in the table, all you need to do is process the rows in the result to pull out the information you want. For example, if you issue a `DESCRIBE president` statement using the `mysql` client, it returns the following information:

```
mysql> DESCRIBE president;
+------------+-------------+------+-----+------------+-------+
| Field      | Type        | Null | Key | Default    | Extra |
+------------+-------------+------+-----+------------+-------+
| last_name  | varchar(15) |      |     |            |       |
| first_name | varchar(15) |      |     |            |       |
| suffix     | varchar(5)  | YES  |     | NULL       |       |
| city       | varchar(20) |      |     |            |       |
| state      | char(2)     |      |     |            |       |
| birth      | date        |      |     | 0000-00-00 |       |
| death      | date        | YES  |     | NULL       |       |
+------------+-------------+------+-----+------------+-------+
```

If you execute the same query from your own client program, you get the same information (without the boxes).

If you want information only about a single column, add the column name:

```
mysql> DESCRIBE president birth;
+-------+------+------+-----+------------+-------+
| Field | Type | Null | Key | Default    | Extra |
+-------+------+------+-----+------------+-------+
| birth | date |      |     | 0000-00-00 |       |
+-------+------+------+-----+------------+-------+
```

Client Programming Mistakes to Avoid

This section discusses some common MySQL C API programming errors and how to avoid them. (These problems crop up periodically on the MySQL mailing list; I'm not making them up.)

Mistake 1—Using Uninitialized Connection Handler Pointers

The examples shown earlier in this chapter invoke `mysql_init()` with a NULL argument. That tells `mysql_init()` to allocate and initialize a MYSQL structure and return a pointer to it. Another approach is to pass a pointer to an existing MYSQL structure. In this case, `mysql_init()` will initialize that structure and return a pointer to it without allocating the structure itself. If you want to use this second approach, be aware that it can lead to certain subtle difficulties. The following discussion points out some problems to watch out for.

If you pass a pointer to `mysql_init()`, it must actually point to something. Consider the following piece of code:

```
main ()
{
MYSQL    *conn;

    mysql_init (conn);
    ...
}
```

The problem is that `mysql_init()` receives a pointer, but that pointer doesn't point anywhere sensible. `conn` is a local variable and thus is uninitialized storage that can point anywhere when `main()` begins execution. That means `mysql_init()` will use the pointer and scribble on some random area of memory. If you're lucky, `conn` will point outside your program's address space and the system will terminate it immediately so that you'll realize that the problem occurs early in your code. If you're not so lucky, `conn` will point into some data that you don't use until later in your program, and you won't notice a problem until your program actually tries to use that data. In that case, your problem will appear to occur much farther into the execution of your program than where it actually originates and may be much more difficult to track down.

Here's a similar piece of problematic code:

```
MYSQL    *conn;

main ()
{
```

```
mysql_init (conn);
mysql_real_connect (conn, ...)
mysql_query(conn, "SHOW DATABASES");
    ...
}
```

In this case, conn is a global variable, so it's initialized to 0 (that is, to NULL) before the program starts up. mysql_init() sees a NULL argument, so it initializes and allocates a new connection handler. Unfortunately, the value of conn remains NULL because no value is ever assigned to it. As soon as you pass conn to a MySQL C API function that requires a non-NULL connection handler, your program will crash. The fix for both pieces of code is to make sure conn has a sensible value. For example, you can initialize it to the address of an already-allocated MYSQL structure:

```
MYSQL conn_struct, *conn = &conn_struct;
    ...
mysql_init (conn);
```

However, the recommended (and easier!) solution is simply to pass NULL explicitly to mysql_init(), let that function allocate the MYSQL structure for you, and assign conn the return value:

```
MYSQL *conn;
    ...
conn = mysql_init (NULL);
```

In any case, don't forget to test the return value of mysql_init() to make sure it's not NULL (see Mistake 2).

Mistake 2—Failing to Check Return Values

Remember to check the status of calls that may fail. The following code doesn't do that:

```
MYSQL_RES *res_set;
MYSQL_ROW row;

res_set = mysql_store_result (conn);
while ((row = mysql_fetch_row (res_set)) != NULL)
{
    /* process row */
}
```

Unfortunately, if mysql_store_result() fails, res_set is NULL, in which case the while loop should never even be executed. (Passing NULL to mysql_fetch_row() likely will crash the program.) Test the return value of functions that return result sets to make sure you actually have something to work with.

The same principle applies to any function that may fail. When the code following a function depends on the success of the function, test its return value and take appropriate action if failure occurs. If you assume success, problems will occur.

Mistake 3—Failing to Account for NULL Column Values

Don't forget to check whether column values in the MYSQL_ROW array returned by mysql_fetch_row() are NULL pointers. The following code crashes on some machines if row[i] is NULL:

```
for (i = 0; i < mysql_num_fields (res_set); i++)
{
    if (i > 0)
        fputc ('\t', stdout);
    printf ("%s", row[i]);
}
fputc ('\n', stdout);
```

The worst part about this mistake is that some versions of printf() are forgiving and print "(null)" for NULL pointers, which allows you to get away with not fixing the problem. If you give your program to a friend who has a less-forgiving printf(), the program will crash and your friend will conclude that you're a lousy programmer. The loop should be written as follows instead:

```
for (i = 0; i < mysql_num_fields (res_set); i++)
{
    if (i > 0)
        fputc ('\t', stdout);
    printf ("%s", row[i] != NULL ? row[i] : "NULL");
}
fputc ('\n', stdout);
```

The only time you need not check whether a column value is NULL is when you have already determined from the column's information structure that IS_NOT_NULL() is true.

Mistake 4—Passing Nonsensical Result Buffers

Client library functions that expect you to supply buffers generally want them to really exist. Consider the following example, which violates that principle:

```
char *from_str = "some string";
char *to_str;
unsigned long len;

len = mysql_real_escape_string (conn, to_str, from_str, strlen (from_str));
```

What's the problem? `to_str` must point to an existing buffer, and it doesn't—it's not initialized and may point to some random location. Don't pass an uninitialized pointer as the `to_str` argument to `mysql_real_escape_string()` unless you want it to stomp merrily all over some random piece of memory.

## 7

The Perl DBI API

THIS CHAPTER DESCRIBES HOW TO USE the Perl DBI interface to MySQL. It does not discuss DBI philosophy or architecture. For information about those aspects of DBI (particularly in comparison with the C and PHP APIs), see Chapter 5, "Introduction to MySQL Programming."

The examples discussed here draw on our sample database, sampdb, using the tables created for the grade-keeping project and for the Historical League in Chapter 1, "Getting Started with MySQL and SQL." To get the most from this chapter, it's best if you know something about Perl. If you don't, you may be able to get along and write your own scripts simply by copying the sample code you see here, but you will probably find a good Perl book a worthwhile investment. One such book is *Programming Perl, Third Edition* by Wall, Christiansen, and Orwant (O'Reilly, 2000).

DBI is currently at version 1.32, although most of the discussion here applies to earlier 1.xx versions as well. Features described here that are not present in earlier versions are noted. DBI requires a version of Perl at least as recent as 5.005_03 (5.004_05 prior to DBI 1.21). You must also have the DBD::mysql Perl module installed, as well as the MySQL C client library and header files. If you plan to write Web-based DBI scripts in the manner discussed here, you should also obtain the CGI.pm module. In this chapter, CGI.pm is used in conjunction with the Apache Web server. If you need to obtain any of these packages, see Appendix A, "Obtaining and Installing Software." Instructions for obtaining the example scripts developed in this chapter are also given in that appendix. They are part of the `sampdb` distribution, which you can download to avoid typing in the scripts yourself. The scripts related to this chapter are found under the `perlapi` directory of the distribution.

For the most part, this chapter describes Perl DBI methods and variables only as they are needed for the discussion here. For a more comprehensive listing of all methods and variables, see Appendix G, "Perl DBI API Reference." You can use that appendix as a reference for further background on any part of DBI that you're trying to use. Online documentation is available by running the following commands:

```
% perldoc DBI
% perldoc DBI::FAQ
% perldoc DBD::mysql
```

At the database driver (DBD) level, the driver for MySQL is built on top of the MySQL C client library, and therefore shares some of its characteristics. See Chapter 6, "The MySQL C API," for more information about the client library.

Perl Script Characteristics

Perl scripts are just text files, so you can create them using any text editor. All Perl scripts in this chapter follow the UNIX convention that they begin with a #! (shebang) line that specifies the pathname of the program to use for executing the script. The line I use is as follows:

```
#! /usr/bin/perl -w
```

On UNIX, you'll need to modify the #! line if the pathname to Perl is different on your system, such as `/usr/local/bin/perl5` or `/opt/bin/perl`. Otherwise, Perl scripts won't run properly on your system.

I include a space after the #! because some systems interpret the sequence "#! /" as a 4-byte magic number, ignore the line if the space is missing, and thus treat the script as a shell script rather than as a Perl script.

The -w option tells Perl to issue a warning if it finds that you use questionable language constructs or perform operations such as printing uninitialized variables. This is useful because it can alert you to code that should be rewritten.

You can invoke a Perl script `myscript.pl` as follows on any system to run it:

```
% perl -w myscript.pl
```

However, you may also be able to execute the script without naming the `perl` program explicitly. On UNIX, do this by changing the file mode with `chmod` to make the script executable:

```
% chmod +x myscript.pl
```

Then you can run the script just by typing its name:

```
% ./myscript.pl
```

That is the invocation style that will be used for scripts written in this chapter. The leading `./` should be used if the script is located in your current directory ("`.`") and your shell does not have the current directory in its search path. Otherwise, you can omit the "`./`" from the command name:

```
% myscript.pl
```

Under Windows NT-based systems (NT, 2000, and XP), you can set up a filename association between Perl and filenames ending in `.pl`. For example, if you install ActiveState Perl, its installation program allows you to set up an association so that filenames ending with `.pl` are run by Perl. In that case, you can run Perl scripts just by naming them on the command line:

```
C:\> myscript.pl
```

Perl DBI Overview

This section provides background information for DBI—the information you'll need for writing your own scripts and for understanding scripts written by others. If you're already familiar with DBI, you may want to skip directly to the section "Putting DBI to Work."

DBI Data Types

In some ways, using the Perl DBI API is similar to using the C client library described in Chapter 6. When you use the C client library, you call functions and access MySQL-related data primarily by means of pointers to structures or arrays. When you use the DBI API, you also call functions and use pointers to structures, except that functions are called *methods*, pointers are called *references*, pointer variables are called *handles*, and the structures that handles point to are called *objects*.

DBI uses several kinds of handles. These tend to be referred to in DBI documentation by the conventional names shown in Table 7.1. The way you use these handles will become clear as we go along. Several conventional names for non-handle variables are used as well (see Table 7.2). This chapter doesn't actually use every one of these variable names, but it's useful to know them when you read DBI scripts written by other people.

Table 7.1 **Conventional Perl DBI Handle Variable Names**

Name	Meaning
$dbh	A handle to a database object
$sth	A handle to a statement (query) object
$fh	A handle to an open file
$h	A "generic" handle; the meaning depends on context

Table 7.2 **Conventional Perl DBI Non–Handle Variable Names**

Name	Meaning
$rc	The return code from operations that return true or false
$rv	The return value from operations that return an integer
$rows	The return value from operations that return a row count
@ary	An array (list) representing a row of values returned by a query

A Simple DBI Script

Let's start with a simple script, dump_members.pl, that illustrates several standard concepts in DBI programming, such as connecting to and disconnecting from the MySQL server, issuing queries, and retrieving data. This script produces output consisting of the Historical League's member list in tab-delimited format. The format is not so interesting in itself; at this point, it's more important see how to use DBI than to produce pretty output.

dump_members.pl looks like this:

```perl
#! /usr/bin/perl -w
# dump_members.pl - dump Historical League's membership list

use strict;
use DBI;

my $dsn = "DBI:mysql:sampdb:cobra.snake.net";   # data source name
my $user_name = "sampadm";                       # user name
my $password = "secret";                         # password
```

```
# connect to database
my $dbh = DBI->connect ($dsn, $user_name, $password,
                        { RaiseError => 1, PrintError => 0 });

# issue query
my $sth = $dbh->prepare ("SELECT last_name, first_name, suffix, email,"
    . "street, city, state, zip, phone FROM member ORDER BY last_name");
$sth->execute ();

# read results of query, then clean up
while (my @ary = $sth->fetchrow_array ())
{
    print join ("\t", @ary), "\n";
}
$sth->finish ();

$dbh->disconnect ();
exit (0);
```

To try out the script for yourself, either use the copy that's included in the sampdb distribution or create it using a text editor. (If you use a word processor, be sure to save the script as plain text. Don't save it in the word processor's native format, which is likely to be some proprietary binary format.) You'll probably need to change at least some of the connection parameters, such as the hostname, database name, username, or password. (That will be true for other scripts that name the connection parameters as well.) Later, in the "Specifying Connection Parameters" section, we'll see how to get parameters from an option file instead of putting them directly in the script.

Now let's go through the script a piece at a time. The first line contains the standard where-to-find-Perl indicator:

```
#! /usr/bin/perl -w
```

This line is part of every script we'll discuss in this chapter; I won't mention it further.

It's a good idea to include in a script at least a minimal description of its purpose, so the next line is a comment to give anyone who looks at the script a clue about what it does:

```
# dump_members.pl - dump Historical League's membership list
```

Text from a '#' character to the end of a line is considered a comment. It's a useful practice to sprinkle comments throughout your scripts to explain how they work.

Next we have a couple of use statements:

```
use strict;
use DBI;
```

use strict tells Perl to require you to declare variables before using them. You can write scripts without putting in a use strict line, but it's useful for catching mistakes, so I recommend you always include it. For example, if you declare a variable $my_var but then later refer to it erroneously as $mv_var, the following message will appear when you run the script in strict mode:

```
Global symbol "$mv_var" requires explicit package name at line n
```

When you see that, you think, "Huh? I never used any variable named $mv_var!" Then you look at line n of your script, see that you misspelled $my_var as $mv_var, and fix it. Without strict mode, Perl won't squawk about $mv_var; it simply creates a new variable by that name with a value of undef (undefined) and uses it without complaint. And you're left to wonder why your script doesn't work.

use DBI tells the Perl interpreter that it needs to pull in the DBI module. Without this line, an error occurs as soon as you try to do anything DBI-related in the script. You don't have to indicate which DBD-level driver module to use, though. DBI activates the right one for you when you connect to your database.

Because we're operating in strict mode, we must declare the variables the script uses by means of the my keyword (think of it as though the script is saying "I am explicitly indicating that these are my variables"). The next section of the script sets up the variables that specify connection parameters, and then uses them to connect to the database:

```
my $dsn = "DBI:mysql:sampdb:cobra.snake.net";    # data source name
my $user_name = "sampadm";                       # user name
my $password = "secret";                         # password

# connect to database
my $dbh = DBI->connect ($dsn, $user_name, $password,
                        { RaiseError => 1, PrintError => 0 });
```

The connect() call is invoked as DBI->connect() because it's a method of the DBI class. You don't really have to know what that means; it's just a little object-oriented jargon to make your head hurt. (If you do want to know, it means that connect() is a function that "belongs" to DBI.) connect() takes several arguments:

- **The data source.** (Also known as the data source name, or DSN.) Data source formats are determined by the requirements of the particular DBD module you want to use. For the MySQL driver, allowable formats include either of the following:

  ```
  DBI:mysql:db_name
  DBI:mysql:db_name:host_name
  ```

The capitalization of DBI doesn't matter, but mysql must be lowercase. *db_name* represents the name of the database you want to use, and *host_name* indicates the host where the server is running. If you omit the hostname, it defaults to localhost. (There actually are other allowable data source formats, which we'll discuss later in the "Specifying Connection Parameters" section.)

- **The username and password for your MySQL account.** This is self-explanatory.

- **An optional argument indicating additional connection attributes.** If it is given, this argument controls DBI's error-handling behavior. It should be passed as a reference to a hash that specifies connection attribute names and values. The weird-looking construct we've specified creates a reference to a hash that enables the RaiseError attribute and disables PrintError. These settings cause DBI to check for database-related errors and exit with an error message if it detects one. (That's why you don't see error-checking code anywhere in the dump_members.pl script; DBI handles it all.) The "Handling Errors" section later in this chapter covers alternate methods of responding to errors.

If the connect() call succeeds, it returns a database handle, which we assign to $dbh. By default, connect() returns undef if it fails. However, because the script enables RaiseError, DBI will exit after displaying an error message if something goes wrong in the connect() call. (This is true for other DBI methods, too; I'll describe what they return to indicate an error, but they won't return at all if RaiseError is enabled.)

After connecting to the database, dump_members.pl issues a SELECT query to retrieve the membership list, and then executes a loop to process each of the rows returned. These rows constitute the result set. To perform a SELECT, you prepare the query first, and then execute it:

```
# issue query
my $sth = $dbh->prepare ("SELECT last_name, first_name, suffix, email,"
   . "street, city, state, zip, phone FROM member ORDER BY last_name");
$sth->execute ();
```

prepare() is invoked using the database handle; it passes the SQL statement to the driver for preprocessing before execution. Some drivers actually do something with the statement at this point. Others just remember it until you invoke execute() to cause the statement to be performed. The return value from prepare() is a statement handle, here assigned to $sth. The statement handle is used for all further processing related to the statement.

Notice that the query string is specified with no terminating semicolon. You no doubt have developed the habit (through long hours of interaction with the mysql program) of terminating SQL statements with a '; ' character. However, it's best to break yourself of that habit when using DBI because semicolons often cause queries to fail with syntax errors. The same applies to adding \g to queries—don't. Those statement terminators are conventions of mysql and are not used when issuing queries in DBI scripts. The end of the query string implicitly terminates the query and no explicit terminator is necessary.

When you invoke a method without passing it any arguments, you can leave off the parentheses. The following two calls are equivalent:

```
$sth->execute ();
$sth->execute;
```

I prefer to include the parentheses because it makes the call look less like a variable reference to me. Your preference may be different.

After you call execute(), the rows of the membership list are available for processing. In the dump_members.pl script, the row-fetching loop simply prints the contents of each row as a tab-delimited set of values:

```
# read results of query, then clean up
while (my @ary = $sth->fetchrow_array ())
{
    print join ("\t", @ary), "\n";
}
$sth->finish ();
```

fetchrow_array() returns an array containing the column values of the current row, or an empty array when there are no more rows. Thus, the loop fetches successive rows returned by the SELECT statement and prints each one with tabs between column values. NULL values in the database are returned as undef values to the Perl script, but these print as empty strings, not as the word NULL. undef column values also have another effect when you run the script; they result in warnings like the following from the Perl interpreter:

```
Use of uninitialized value in join at dump_members.pl line n.
```

These warnings are triggered by the use of the -w option on the first line of the script. If you remove the option and run the script again, the warnings will go away. However, -w is useful for discovering problems (such as printing uninitialized variables!), so a better way to eliminate the warnings is to detect and deal with undef values. Some techniques for this are discussed in the "Handling Queries That Return a Result Set" section later in this chapter.

In the `print` statement, note that the tab and newline characters (represented as the \t and \n sequences) are enclosed in double quotes. In Perl, escape sequences are interpreted only when they occur within double quotes, not within single quotes. If single quotes had been used, the output would be full of literal instances of \t and \n.

After the row-fetching loop terminates, the call to `finish()` indicates that the statement handle is no longer needed and that any temporary resources allocated to it can be freed. In this script, the call to `finish()` is for illustrative purposes only. It's not actually necessary to invoke it here because the row-fetching call will do so automatically when it encounters the end of the result set. `finish()` is more useful in situations where you fetch only part of the result set and do not reach its end (for example, if for some reason you fetch only the first row). The examples from this point on will not use `finish()` unless it's necessary.

Having printed the membership list, we're done, so we can disconnect from the server and exit:

```
$dbh->disconnect ();
exit (0);
```

`dump_members.pl` illustrates a number of concepts that are common to most DBI programs, and at this point you could probably start writing your own DBI programs without knowing anything more. For example, to write out the contents of some other table, all you'd need to do is change the text of the SELECT statement that is passed to the `prepare()` method. In fact, if you want to see some applications of this technique, you can skip ahead immediately to the part of the "Putting DBI to Work" section that discusses how to generate the member list for the Historical League annual banquet program and the League's printed directory. However, DBI provides many other useful capabilities. The next sections cover some of these in more detail so that you can see how to do more than run simple SELECT statements in your Perl scripts.

Handling Errors

`dump_members.pl` turned on the `RaiseError` error-handling attribute when it invoked the `connect()` method so that errors would automatically terminate the script with an error message rather than just returning error codes. It's possible to handle errors in other ways. For example, you can check for errors yourself rather than having DBI do it.

To see how to control DBI's error-handling behavior, let's take a closer look at the connect() call's final argument. The two relevant attributes are RaiseError and PrintError:

- If RaiseError is enabled (set to a non-zero value), DBI calls die() to print a message and to exit if an error occurs in a DBI method.
- If PrintError is enabled, DBI calls warn() to print a message when a DBI error occurs, but the script continues executing.

By default, RaiseError is disabled and PrintError is enabled. In this case, if the connect() call fails, DBI prints a message but continues executing. Thus, with the default error-handling behavior that you get if you omit the fourth argument to connect(), you might check for errors as follows:

```
my $dbh = DBI->connect ($dsn, $user_name, $password)
    or exit (1);
```

If an error occurs, connect() returns undef to indicate failure, and that triggers the call to exit(). You don't have to print an error message because DBI already will have printed one.

If you were to explicitly specify the default values for the error-checking attributes, the call to connect() would look like this:

```
my $dbh = DBI->connect ($dsn, $user_name, $password,
                    { RaiseError => 0, PrintError => 1 })
    or exit (1);
```

That's more work to write out, but it's also more obvious to the casual reader what the error-handling behavior is.

If you want to check for errors yourself and print your own messages, disable both RaiseError and PrintError:

```
my $dbh = DBI->connect ($dsn, $user_name, $password,
                    { RaiseError => 0, PrintError => 0 })
    or die "Could not connect to server: $DBI::err ($DBI::errstr)\en";
```

The variables $DBI::err and $DBI::errstr used in the code just shown are useful for constructing error messages. They contain the MySQL error code and error string, much like the C API functions mysql_errno() and mysql_error(). If no error occurred, $DBI::err will be 0 or undef, and $DBI::errstr will be the empty string or undef. (In other words, both variables will be false.)

If you want DBI to handle errors for you so that you don't have to check for them yourself, enable RaiseError and disable PrintError:

```
my $dbh = DBI->connect ($dsn, $user_name, $password,
                    { RaiseError => 1, PrintError => 0 });
```

This is by far the easiest approach, and it is how almost all scripts presented in this chapter are written. The reason for disabling `PrintError` when enabling `RaiseError` is to prevent the possibility of having error messages being printed twice. (If both attributes are enabled, the DBI handlers for both may be called under some circumstances.)

Enabling `RaiseError` may not be appropriate if you want to execute some sort of cleanup code of your own when the script exits, although in this case you may be able to do what you want by redefining the `$SIG{__DIE__}` signal handler. Another reason you might want to avoid enabling the `RaiseError` attribute is that DBI prints technical information in its messages, like this:

```
disconnect(DBI::db=HASH(0x197aae4)) invalidates 1 active statement. Either
destroy statement handles or call finish on them before disconnecting.
```

That's useful information for a programmer, but it might not be the kind of thing you want to present to the everyday user. In that case, it can be better to check for errors yourself so that you can display messages that are more meaningful to the people you expect to be using the script. Or you might consider redefining the `$SIG{__DIE__}` handler here, too. That may be useful because it allows you to enable `RaiseError` to simplify error handling but replace the default error messages that DBI presents with your own messages. To provide your own __DIE__ handler, do something like the following before executing any DBI calls:

```
$SIG{__DIE__} = sub { die "Sorry, an error occurred\n"; };
```

You can also declare a subroutine in the usual fashion and set the signal handler value using a reference to the subroutine:

```
sub die_handler
{
    die "Sorry, an error occurred\n";
}

$SIG{__DIE__} = \&die_handler;
```

As an alternative to passing error-handling attributes literally in the `connect()` call, you can define them using a hash and pass a reference to the hash. Some people find that breaking out the attribute settings this way makes scripts easier to read and edit, but operationally both approaches are the same. The following example shows how to use an attribute hash:

```
my %attr =
(
    PrintError => 0,
    RaiseError => 0
);
my $dbh = DBI->connect ($dsn, $user_name, $password, \%attr)
    or die "Could not connect to server: $DBI::err ($DBI::errstr)\n";
```

The following script, dump_members2.pl, illustrates how you might write a script when you want to check for errors yourself and print your own messages. dump_members2.pl processes the same query as dump_members.pl but explicitly disables PrintError and RaiseError and then tests the result of every DBI call. When an error occurs, the script invokes the subroutine bail_out() to print a message and the contents of $DBI::err and $DBI::errstr before exiting:

```perl
#! /usr/bin/perl -w
# dump_members2.pl - dump Historical League's membership list

use strict;
use DBI;

my $dsn = "DBI:mysql:sampdb:cobra.snake.net";    # data source name
my $user_name = "sampadm";                       # user name
my $password = "secret";                         # password
my %attr =                                       # error-handling attributes
(
    PrintError => 0,
    RaiseError => 0
);

# connect to database
my $dbh = DBI->connect ($dsn, $user_name, $password, \%attr)
    or bail_out ("Cannot connect to database");

# issue query
my $sth = $dbh->prepare ("SELECT last_name, first_name, suffix, email,"
    . "street, city, state, zip, phone FROM member ORDER BY last_name")
    or bail_out ("Cannot prepare query");
$sth->execute ()
    or bail_out ("Cannot execute query");

# read results of query
while (my @ary = $sth->fetchrow_array ())
{
    print join ("\t", @ary), "\n";
}
!$DBI::err
    or bail_out ("Error during retrieval");

$dbh->disconnect ()
    or bail_out ("Cannot disconnect from database");
exit (0);

# bail_out() subroutine - print error code and string, then exit
```

```
sub bail_out
{
my $message = shift;

    die "$message\nError $DBI::err ($DBI::errstr)\n";
}
```

`bail_out()` is similar to the `print_error()` function we used for writing C programs in Chapter 6, except that `bail_out()` exits rather than returning to the caller. `bail_out()` saves you the trouble of writing out the values of `$DBI::err` and `$DBI::errstr` every time you want to print an error message. Also, by encapsulating error message printing into a subroutine, you can change the format of your error messages uniformly throughout your script simply by making a change to the subroutine.

The `dump_members2.pl` script has a test following the row-fetching loop. Because the script doesn't automatically exit if an error occurs in `fetchrow_array()`, it's prudent to determine whether the loop terminated because the result set was read completely (normal termination) or because an error occurred. The loop terminates either way, of course, but if an error occurs, output from the script will be truncated. Without an error check, the person running the script wouldn't have any idea that anything was wrong. If you're checking for errors yourself, be sure to test the result of your fetch loops.

Handling Queries That Return No Result Set

Statements that do not return rows, such as DELETE, INSERT, REPLACE, and UPDATE, are relatively easy to process compared to statements that do return rows, such as SELECT, DESCRIBE, EXPLAIN, and SHOW. To process a non–SELECT statement, pass it to `do()` by using the database handle. The `do()` method prepares and executes the query in one step. For example, to create a new member entry for Marcia Brown with an expiration date of June 3, 2005, you can do the following:

```
$rows = $dbh->do ("INSERT INTO member (last_name,first_name,expiration)"
                    . " VALUES('Brown','Marcia','2005-6-3')");
```

The `do()` method returns a count of the number of rows affected, `undef` if something goes wrong, and -1 if the number of rows is unknown for some reason. Errors can occur for various reasons. (For example, the query may be malformed or you may not have permission to access the table.) For a non-undef return, watch out for the case in which no rows are affected. When this happens, `do()` doesn't return the number 0; instead, it returns the string

"0E0" (Perl's scientific notation form of zero). "0E0" evaluates to 0 in a numeric context but is considered true in conditional tests so that it can be distinguished easily from undef. If do() returned 0, it would be more difficult to distinguish between the occurrence of an error (undef) and the "no rows affected" case. You can check for an error using either of the following tests:

```
if (!defined ($rows))
{
    print "An error occurred\n";
}
if (!$rows)
{
    print "An error occurred\n";
}
```

In numeric contexts, "0E0" evaluates as 0, so the following code will correctly print the number of rows for any non-undef value of $rows:

```
if (!$rows)
{
    print "An error occurred\n";
}
else
{
    $rows += 0; # force conversion to number if value is "0E0"
    print "$rows rows affected\n";
}
```

You could also print $rows using a %d format specifier with printf() to force an implicit conversion to a number:

```
if (!$rows)
{
    print "An error occurred\n";
}
else
{
    printf "%d rows affected\n", $rows;
}
```

The do() method is equivalent to using prepare() followed by execute(). This means that the preceding INSERT statement could be issued as follows rather than by invoking do():

```
$sth = $dbh->prepare ("INSERT INTO member (last_name,first_name,expiration)"
                . " VALUES('Brown','Marcia','2005-6-3')");
$rows = $sth->execute ();
```

Handling Queries That Return a Result Set

This section provides more information on several options that you have for executing row-fetching loops for SELECT queries (or for other SELECT-like queries that return rows, such as DESCRIBE, EXPLAIN, and SHOW). It also discusses how to get a count of the number of rows in a result, how to handle result sets for which no loop is necessary, and how to retrieve an entire result set all at once.

Writing Row-Fetching Loops

The dump_members.pl script retrieved data using a standard sequence of DBI methods: prepare() lets the driver preprocess the query, execute() begins executing the query, and fetchrow_array() fetches each row of the result set.

prepare() and execute() are fairly standard parts of processing any query that returns rows. However, for fetching the rows, fetchrow_array() is actually only one choice from among several available methods (see Table 7.3).

Table 7.3 **DBI Row-Fetching Methods**

Method Name	Return Value
fetchrow_array()	Array of row values
fetchrow_arrayref()	Reference to array of row values
fetch()	Same as fetchrow_arrayref()
fetchrow_hashref()	Reference to hash of row values, keyed by column name

The following examples show how to use each row-fetching method. The examples loop through the rows of a result set, and for each row, print the column values separated by commas. There are more efficient ways to write the code in some cases, but the examples are written the way they are for illustrative purposes (to show the syntax for accessing individual column values), not for efficiency.

fetchrow_array() is used as follows:

```
while (my @ary = $sth->fetchrow_array ())
{
    my $delim = "";
    for (my $i = 0; $i < @ary; $i++)
    {
        $ary[$i] = "" if !defined ($ary[$i]);    # NULL value?
        print $delim . $ary[$i];
        $delim = ",";
    }
    print "\n";
}
```

Each call to `fetchrow_array()` returns an array of row values, or an empty array when there are no more rows. The inner loop tests each column value to see if it's defined and sets it to the empty string if not. This converts NULL values (which are represented by DBI as undef) to empty strings.

It may seem that this is an entirely superfluous action; after all, Perl prints nothing for both undef and the empty string. The reason for the test is that if the script is run with the -w option, Perl will issue a Use of uninitialized value warning message if you attempt to print an undef value. Converting undef to the empty string eliminates the warnings. You'll see a similar construct used elsewhere throughout this chapter.

If you prefer to print another value for undef values, such as the string "NULL", just change the test a little bit:

```
while (my @ary = $sth->fetchrow_array ())
{
    my $delim = "";
    for (my $i = 0; $i < @ary; $i++)
    {
        $ary[$i] = "NULL" if !defined ($ary[$i]);    # NULL value?
        print $delim . $ary[$i];
        $delim = ",";
    }
    print "\n";
}
```

When working with an array of values, you can simplify the code a bit by using map to convert all the undef array elements at once:

```
while (my @ary = $sth->fetchrow_array ())
{
    @ary = map { defined ($_) ? $_ : "NULL" } @ary;
    print join (",", @ary) . "\n";
}
```

map processes each element of the array using the expression within the braces and returns an array of the resulting values.

An alternative to assigning the return value of `fetchrow_array()` to an array variable is to fetch column values into a set of scalar variables. This allows you to work with variable names that are more meaningful than $ary[0], $ary[1], and so forth. Suppose you want to retrieve member name and email values into variables. Using `fetchrow_array()`, you could select and fetch rows like this:

```
my $sth = $dbh->prepare ("SELECT last_name, first_name, suffix, email"
                    . " FROM member ORDER BY last_name");
$sth->execute ();
while (my ($last_name, $first_name, $suffix, $email) = $sth->fetchrow_array ())
{
    # do something with variables
}
```

When you use a list of variables this way, you must make sure that the order of the columns selected by the query matches the order of the variables into which you fetch the values. DBI has no idea of the order in which columns are named by your SELECT statement, so it's up to you to assign variables correctly. You can also cause column values to be assigned to individual variables automatically when you fetch a row, using a technique known as parameter binding. This is discussed further in the "Placeholders and Parameter Binding" section later in this chapter.

If you fetch a single value into a variable, be careful how you write the assignment. If you write the beginning of your loop as follows, it will work correctly:

```
while (my ($val) = $sth->fetchrow->array ()) ...
```

The value is fetched in list context, so the test will fail only when there are no more rows. But if instead you write the test like this, it will fail in mysterious ways:

```
while (my $val = $sth->fetchrow->array ()) ...
```

The difference here is that the value is fetched in scalar context, so if $val happens to be zero, undef, or the empty string, the test will evaluate as false and terminate the loop, even though you have not yet reached the end of the result set.

The second row-fetching method, fetchrow_arrayref (), is similar to fetchrow_array (), but instead of returning an array containing the column values for the current row, it returns a reference to the array, or undef when there are no more rows. Use it as follows:

```
while (my $ary_ref = $sth->fetchrow_arrayref ())
{
    my $delim = "";
    for (my $i = 0; $i < @{$ary_ref}; $i++)
    {
        $ary_ref->[$i] = "" if !defined ($ary_ref->[$i]);   # NULL value?
        print $delim . $ary_ref->[$i];
        $delim = ",";
    }
    print "\n";
}
```

You access array elements through the array reference $ary_ref. This is something like dereferencing a pointer, so you use $ary_ref->[$i] rather than $ary[$i]. To convert the reference to an array, use the @{$ary_ref} construct.

`fetchrow_arrayref()` is unsuitable for fetching variables into a list. For example, the following loop does not work:

```
while (my ($var1, $var2, $var3, $var4) = @{$sth->fetchrow_arrayref ()})
{
    # do something with variables
}
```

As long as `fetchrow_arrayref()` actually fetches a row, the loop functions properly. But when there are no more rows, `fetchrow_arrayref()` returns undef, and `@{undef}` isn't legal. (It's like trying to de-reference a NULL pointer in a C program.)

The third row-fetching method, `fetchrow_hashref()`, is used like this:

```
while (my $hash_ref = $sth->fetchrow_hashref ())
{
    my $delim = "";
    foreach my $key (keys (%{$hash_ref}))
    {
        $hash_ref->{$key} = "" if !defined ($hash_ref->{$key}); # NULL value?
        print $delim . $hash_ref->{$key};
        $delim = ",";
    }
    print "\n";
}
```

Each call to `fetchrow_hashref()` returns a reference to a hash of row values keyed on column names or undef when there are no more rows. In this case, column values don't come out in any particular order because members of Perl hashes are unordered. However, DBI keys the hash elements using the column names, so `$hash_ref` gives you a single variable through which you can access any column value by name. This means you can pull out the values (or any subset of them) in any order you want, and you don't have to know the order in which the columns were retrieved by the SELECT query. For example, to access the name and email fields, you can do the following:

```
while (my $hash_ref = $sth->fetchrow_hashref ())
{
    my $delim = "";
    foreach my $key ("last_name", "first_name", "suffix", "email")
    {
        $hash_ref->{$key} = "" if !defined ($hash_ref->{$key}); # NULL value?
        print $delim . $hash_ref->{$key};
        $delim = ",";
    }
    print "\n";
}
```

`fetchrow_hashref()` is especially useful when you want to pass a row of values to a function without requiring the function to know the order in which columns are named in the SELECT statement. In this case, you would call `fetchrow_hashref()` to retrieve rows and write a function that accesses values from the row hash using column names.

Keep in mind the following caveats when you use `fetchrow_hashref()`:

- If you need every bit of performance, `fetchrow_hashref()` is not the best choice because it's less efficient than `fetchrow_array()` or `fetchrow_arrayref()`.

- By default, the column names are used as key values with the same lettercase as the column names written in the SELECT statement. In MySQL, column names are not case sensitive, so the query will work the same way no matter what lettercase you use to write column names. But Perl hash key names *are* case sensitive, which may cause you problems. To avoid potential lettercase mismatch problems, you can tell `fetchrow_hashref()` to force column names into a particular lettercase by passing it a NAME_lc or NAME_uc attribute:

  ```
  $hash_ref = $sth->fetchrow_hashref ("NAME_lc"); # use lowercase names
  $hash_ref = $sth->fetchrow_hashref ("NAME_uc"); # use uppercase names
  ```

- The hash contains one element per unique column name. If you're performing a join that returns columns from multiple tables with overlapping names, you won't be able to access all the column values. For example, if you issue the following query, `fetchrow_hashref()` will return a hash having only one element, name:

  ```
  SELECT a.name, b.name FROM a, b WHERE a.name = b.name
  ```

  To avoid this problem, use aliases to make sure each column has a distinct name. For example, if you rewrite the query as follows, `fetchrow_hashref()` will return a reference to a hash with two elements, name and name2:

  ```
  SELECT a.name, b.name AS name2 FROM a, b WHERE a.name = b.name
  ```

Determining the Number of Rows Returned by a Query

How can you tell the number of rows returned by a SELECT or SELECT-like query? One way is to count the rows as you fetch them. In fact, this is the *only* portable way in DBI to know how many rows a SELECT query returned. Using the MySQL driver, you can call the rows() method using the statement handle after invoking execute(). But this is not portable to other database engines, and the DBI documentation explicitly discourages using `rows()` for `SELECT` statements. And even for MySQL, `rows()` doesn't return the correct result until you've fetched all the rows if you've set the `mysql_use_result` attribute. So you may as well just count the rows as you fetch them. (See Appendix G for more information about `mysql_use_result`.)

Fetching Single-Row Results

It's not necessary to run a loop to get your results if the result set consists of a single row. Suppose you want to write a script, `count_members.pl`, that tells you the current number of Historical League members. The code to perform the query looks like this:

```
# issue query
my $sth = $dbh->prepare ("SELECT COUNT(*) FROM member");
$sth->execute ();

# read results of query
my $count = $sth->fetchrow_array ();
$sth->finish ();
$count = "can't tell" if !defined ($count);
print "$count\n";
```

The `SELECT` statement will return only one row, so no loop is required; we call `fetchrow_array()` just once. In addition, because we're selecting only one column, it's not even necessary to assign the return value to an array. When `fetchrow_array()` is called in a scalar context (where a single value rather than a list is expected), it returns one column of the row or `undef` if no row is available. DBI does not define which element of the row `fetchrow_array()` returns in scalar context, but that's all right for the query just shown. It retrieves only a single value, so there is no ambiguity about what value is returned.

This code invokes `finish()` to free the result set, even though the set consists of just one row. (`fetchrow_array()` frees a result set implicitly when it reaches the end of the set, but that would happen here only if you called it a second time.)

Another type of query for which you expect at most a single record is one that contains `LIMIT 1` to restrict the number of rows returned. A common use for this is to return the row that contains the maximum or minimum value for a particular column. For example, the following query prints the name and birth date of the president who was born most recently:

```
my $query = "SELECT last_name, first_name, birth"
          . " FROM president ORDER BY birth DESC LIMIT 1";
```

```
my $sth = $dbh->prepare ($query);
$sth->execute ();

# read results of query
my ($last_name, $first_name, $birth) = $sth->fetchrow_array ();
$sth->finish ();
if (!defined ($last_name))
{
    print "Query returned no result\n";
}
else
{
    print "Most recently born president: $first_name $last_name ($birth)\n";
}
```

Other types of queries for which no fetch loop is necessary are those that use
MAX() or MIN() to select a single value. But in all these cases, an even
easier way to get a single-row result is to use the database handle method
selectrow_array(), which combines prepare(), execute(), and row fetching into a single call. It returns an array (not a reference) or an empty array if
the query returned no row or an error occurred. The previous example can be
rewritten as follows using selectrow_array():

```
my $query = "SELECT last_name, first_name, birth"
          . " FROM president ORDER BY birth DESC LIMIT 1";
my ($last_name, $first_name, $birth) = $dbh->selectrow_array ($query);
if (!defined ($last_name))
{
    print "Query returned no result\n";
}
else
{
    print "Most recently born president: $first_name $last_name ($birth)\n";
}
```

Working with Complete Result Sets

When you use a fetch loop, DBI doesn't provide any way to process the rows
in any order other than that in which they are returned by the loop. Also, after
you fetch a row, the previous row is lost unless you take steps to maintain it in
memory. These behaviors aren't always suitable. For example, they're undesirable if you need to make multiple passes through the rows to perform a statistical calculation. (You might go through the result set once to assess some
general numeric characteristics of your data, and then step through the rows
again performing a more specific analysis.)

It's possible to access your result set as a whole in a couple different ways. You
can perform the usual fetch loop and save each row as you fetch it, or you can
use a method that returns an entire result set all at once. Either way, you end up

with a matrix containing one row per row in the result set and as many columns as you selected. You can process elements of the matrix in any order you want, as many times as you want. The following discussion describes both approaches.

One way to use a fetch loop to capture the result set is to use `fetchrow_array()` and save an array of references to the rows. The following code does the same thing as the fetch-and-print loop in `dump_members.pl` except that it saves all the rows, and then prints the matrix. It illustrates how to determine the number of rows and columns in the matrix and how to access individual members of the matrix:

```perl
my @matrix = (); # array of array references

while (my @ary = $sth->fetchrow_array ())    # fetch each row
{
    push (@matrix, [ @ary ]); # save reference to just-fetched row
}

# determine dimensions of matrix
my $rows = scalar (@matrix);
my $cols = ($rows == 0 ? 0 : scalar (@{$matrix[0]}));

for (my $i = 0; $i < $rows; $i++)               # print each row
{
    my $delim = "";
    for (my $j = 0; $j < $cols; $j++)
    {
        $matrix[$i][$j] = "" if !defined ($matrix[$i][$j]); # NULL value?
        print $delim . $matrix[$i][$j];
        $delim = ",";
    }
    print "\n";
}
```

When determining the dimensions of the matrix, the number of rows must be determined first because calculation of the number of columns is contingent on whether or not the matrix is empty. If `$rows` is 0, the matrix is empty and `$cols` becomes 0 as well. Otherwise, the number of columns can be calculated as the number of elements in the first row by using the syntax `@{$matrix[0]}` to access the row as a whole.

The preceding example fetches each row as an array and then saves a reference to it. You might suppose that it would be more efficient to call `fetchrow_arrayref()` instead to retrieve row references directly:

```perl
my @matrix = (); # array of array references

while (my $ary_ref = $sth->fetchrow_arrayref ())
{
    push (@matrix, $ary_ref); # save reference to just-fetched row
}
```

That doesn't work because `fetchrow_arrayref()` reuses the array to which the reference points. The resulting matrix is an array of references, each of which points to the same row—the final row retrieved. Therefore, if you want to construct a matrix by fetching a row at a time, use `fetchrow_array()` rather than `fetchrow_arrayref()`.

As an alternative to using a fetch loop, you can use one of the DBI methods that return the entire result set. For example, `fetchall_arrayref()` returns a reference to an array of references, each of which points to the contents of one row of the result set. That's a mouthful, but in effect, the return value is a reference to a matrix. To use `fetchall_arrayref()`, call `prepare()` and `execute()`, and then retrieve the result as follows:

```
# fetch all rows into a reference to an array of references
my $matrix_ref = $sth->fetchall_arrayref ();
```

You can determine the dimensions of the array and access its elements as follows:

```
# determine dimensions of matrix
my $rows = (!defined ($matrix_ref) ? 0 : scalar (@{$matrix_ref}));
my $cols = ($rows == 0 ? 0 : scalar (@{$matrix_ref->[0]}));

for (my $i = 0; $i < $rows; $i++)            # print each row
{
    my $delim = "";
    for (my $j = 0; $j < $cols; $j++)
    {
        $matrix_ref->[$i][$j] = "" if !defined ($matrix_ref->[$i][$j]); # NULL?
        print $delim . $matrix_ref->[$i][$j];
        $delim = ",";
    }
    print "\n";
}
```

`fetchall_arrayref()` returns a reference to an empty array if the result set is empty. The result is `undef` if an error occurs, so if you don't have `RaiseError` enabled, be sure to check the return value before you start using it.

The number of rows and columns are determined by whether the matrix is empty. If you want to access an entire row `$i` of the matrix as an array, use the syntax `@{$matrix_ref->[$i]}`.

It's certainly simpler to use `fetchall_arrayref()` to retrieve a result set than to write a row-fetching loop, although the syntax for accessing array elements becomes a little trickier. A method that's similar to `fetchall_arrayref()` but that does even more work is `selectall_arrayref()`. This method performs the entire `prepare()`, `execute()`, fetch loop sequence for you. To use `selectall_arrayref()`, pass your query directly to it using the database handle:

```
# fetch all rows into a reference to an array of references
my $matrix_ref = $dbh->selectall_arrayref ($query);

# determine dimensions of matrix
my $rows = (!defined ($matrix_ref) ? 0 : scalar (@{$matrix_ref}));
my $cols = ($rows == 0 ? 0 : scalar (@{$matrix_ref->[0]}));

for (my $i = 0; $i < $rows; $i++)              # print each row
{
    my $delim = "";
    for (my $j = 0; $j < $cols; $j++)
    {
        $matrix_ref->[$i][$j] = "" if !defined ($matrix_ref->[$i][$j]); # NULL?
        print $delim . $matrix_ref->[$i][$j];
        $delim = ",";
    }
    print "\n";
}
```

Checking for NULL Values

When you retrieve information from a database, you may need to distinguish between column values that are NULL and those that are zero or empty strings. This is easy to do because DBI returns NULL column values as undef. However, you must be sure to use the correct test. If you try the following code fragment, it prints "false!" all three times:

```
$col_val = undef; if (!$col_val) { print "false!\n"; }
$col_val = 0;     if (!$col_val) { print "false!\n"; }
$col_val = "";    if (!$col_val) { print "false!\n"; }
```

What that demonstrates is that the form of the test is unable to distinguish between undef, 0, and the empty string. The next fragment prints "false!" for both tests, indicating that the test cannot distinguish undef from the empty string:

```
$col_val = undef; if ($col_val eq "") { print "false!\n"; }
$col_val = "";    if ($col_val eq "") { print "false!\n"; }
```

This fragment prints the same output, showing that the second test fails to distinguish 0 from the empty string:

```
$col_val = "";
if ($col_val eq "") { print "false!\n"; }
if ($col_val == 0)  { print "false!\n"; }
```

To distinguish between `undef` (`NULL`) column values and non-`undef` values, use `defined()`. After you know a value doesn't represent `NULL`, you can distinguish between other types of values using appropriate tests—for example:

```
if (!defined ($col_val))  { print "NULL\n"; }
elsif ($col_val eq "")    { print "empty string\n"; }
elsif ($col_val == 0)     { print "zero\n"; }
else                      { print "other\n"; }
```

It's important to perform the tests in the proper order because both the second and third comparisons are true if `$col_val` is an empty string. If you reverse the order of those comparisons, you'll incorrectly interpret empty strings as zero.

Quoting Issues

Thus far, we have constructed queries in the most basic way possible by using simple quoted strings. That causes a problem at the Perl lexical level when your quoted strings contain quoted values. You can also have problems at the SQL level when you want to insert or select values that contain quotes, backslashes, or binary data. If you specify a query as a Perl quoted string, you must escape any occurrences of the quoting character that occur within the query string itself:

```
$query = 'INSERT INTO absence VALUES(14,\'2002-9-16\')';
$query = "INSERT INTO absence VALUES(14,\"2002-9-16\")";
```

Both Perl and MySQL allow you to quote strings using either single or double quotes, so you can sometimes avoid escaping by mixing quote characters:

```
$query = 'INSERT INTO absence VALUES(14,"2002-9-16")';
$query = "INSERT INTO absence VALUES(14,'2002-9-16')";
```

However, the two types of quotes are not equivalent in Perl. Variable references are interpreted only within double quotes. Therefore, single quotes are not very useful when you want to construct queries by embedding variable references in the query string. For example, if the value of `$var` is `14`, the following two strings are not equivalent:

```
"SELECT * FROM member WHERE id = $var"
'SELECT * FROM member WHERE id = $var'
```

The strings are interpreted as follows; clearly, the first string is more like something you'd want to pass to the MySQL server:

```
"SELECT * FROM member WHERE id = 14"
'SELECT * FROM member WHERE id = $var'
```

An alternative to quoting strings with double quotes is to use the qq{} construct, which tells Perl to treat everything between qq{ and } as a double-quoted string. (Think of double-q as meaning "double-quote.") For example, the following two lines are equivalent:

```
$date = "2002-9-16";
$date = qq{2002-9-16};
```

You can construct queries without thinking so much about quoting issues when you use qq{} because you can use quotes (single or double) freely within the query string without having to escape them. In addition, variable references are interpreted. Both properties of qq{} are illustrated by the following INSERT statement:

```
$id = 14;
$date = "2002-9-16";
$query = qq{INSERT INTO absence VALUES($id,'$date')};
```

You don't have to use '{' and '}' as the qq delimiters. Other forms, such as qq() and qq//, will work, too, as long as the closing delimiter doesn't occur within the string. I prefer qq{} because the '}' character is less likely than ')' or '/' to occur within the text of the query and be mistaken for the end of the query string. For example, ')' occurs within the INSERT statement just shown, so qq() would not be a useful construct for quoting the query string.

The qq{} construct can cross line boundaries, which is useful if you want to make the query string stand out from the surrounding Perl code:

```
$id = 14;
$date = "2002-9-16";
$query = qq{
    INSERT INTO absence VALUES($id,'$date')
};
```

This is also useful if you simply want to format your query on multiple lines to make it more readable. For example, the SELECT statement in the dump_members.pl script looks like this:

```
$sth = $dbh->prepare ("SELECT last_name, first_name, suffix, email,"
    . "street, city, state, zip, phone FROM member ORDER BY last_name");
```

With qq{}, it could be written as follows instead:

```
$sth = $dbh->prepare (qq{
        SELECT
            last_name, first_name, suffix, email,
            street, city, state, zip, phone
        FROM member
        ORDER BY last_name
    });
```

It's true that double-quoted strings can cross line boundaries, too. But I find that qq{ and } stand out better than two lone '"' characters and make the statement easier to read. This book uses both forms; see which you prefer.

The qq{} construct takes care of quoting issues at the Perl lexical level so that you can get quotes into a string easily without having Perl complain about them. However, you must also think about SQL-level syntax. Consider the following attempt to insert a record into the member table:

```
$last = "O'Malley";
$first = "Brian";
$expiration = "2005-9-1";
$rows = $dbh->do (qq{
    INSERT INTO member (last_name,first_name,expiration)
    VALUES('$last','$first','$expiration')
});
```

The resulting string that do() sends to MySQL looks like this:

```
INSERT INTO member (last_name,first_name,expiration)
VALUES('O'Malley','Brian','2005-9-1')
```

That is not legal SQL because a single quote occurs within a single-quoted string. We encountered a similar quoting problem in Chapter 6. There we dealt with the issue by using mysql_real_escape_string(). DBI provides a similar mechanism—for each quoted value you want to use literally in a statement, call the quote() method and use its return value instead. The preceding example is more properly written as follows:

```
$last = $dbh->quote ("O'Malley");
$first = $dbh->quote ("Brian");
$expiration = $dbh->quote ("2005-9-1");
$rows = $dbh->do (qq{
    INSERT INTO member (last_name,first_name,expiration)
    VALUES($last,$first,$expiration)
});
```

Now the string that do() sends to MySQL looks like the following, with the quote that occurs within the quoted string properly escaped:

```
INSERT INTO member (last_name,first_name,expiration)
VALUES('O\'Malley','Brian','2005-9-1')
```

Note that when you refer to $last and $first in the query string, you do not add any surrounding quotes; the quote() method supplies them for you. If you add quotes yourself, your query will have too many of them, as shown by the following example:

```
$value = "paul";
$quoted_value = $dbh->quote ($value);

print "... WHERE name = $quoted_value\n";
print "... WHERE name = '$quoted_value'\n";
```

These statements produce the following output:

```
... WHERE name = 'paul'
... WHERE name = ''paul''
```

In the second case, the string contains too many quotes.

Placeholders and Parameter Binding

In the preceding sections, we've constructed queries by putting values to be inserted or used as selection criteria directly into the query string. It's not necessary to do this. DBI allows you to place special markers called placeholders into a query string, and then supply the values to be used in place of those markers when the query is executed. One reason for doing this is that you get the character-quoting benefits of the `quote()` method without having to invoke `quote()` explicitly. Another reason is for improved performance when you're executing a query over and over within a loop.

As an illustration of how placeholders work, suppose you're beginning a new semester at school and you want to clear out the student table for your grade book and then initialize it with the new students by using a list of student names contained in a file. Without placeholders, you can delete the existing table contents and load the new names as follows:

```
$dbh->do (qq{ DELETE FROM student } );  # delete existing rows
while (<>)                               # add new rows
{
    chomp;
    $_ = $dbh->quote ($_);
    $dbh->do (qq{ INSERT INTO student SET name = $_ });
}
```

This approach requires that you handle special characters in the data values yourself by calling `quote()`. It's also inefficient, because the basic form of the INSERT query is the same each time, and `do()` calls `prepare()` and `execute()` each time through the loop. It's more efficient to call `prepare()` a single time to set up the INSERT statement before entering the loop and invoke only `execute()` within the loop. That avoids all invocations of `prepare()` but one. DBI allows us to do this as follows:

```
$dbh->do (qq{ DELETE FROM student } );  # delete existing rows
my $sth = $dbh->prepare (qq{ INSERT INTO student SET name = ? });
while (<>)                               # add new rows
{
    chomp;
    $sth->execute ($_);
}
```

In general, if you find yourself calling do() inside a loop, it's better to invoke prepare() prior to the loop and execute() inside it. Note the '?' character in the INSERT query. That's the placeholder. When execute() is invoked, you pass the value to be substituted for the placeholder when the query is sent to the server. DBI will automatically quote special characters in the value, so there is no need to call quote().

Some things to note about placeholders:

- Do not enclose the placeholder character in quotes within the query string. If you do, it will not be recognized as a placeholder.
- Do not use the quote() method to specify placeholder values, or you will get extra quotes in the values you're inserting.
- You can have more than one placeholder in a query string, but be sure to pass as many values to execute() as there are placeholder markers.
- Each placeholder must specify a single value, not a list of values. For example, you cannot prepare and execute a statement like this:

```
my $sth = $dbh->prepare (qq{
            INSERT INTO member last_name, first_name VALUES(?)
});
$sth->execute ("Adams,Bill,2003-09-19");
```

  You must do it as follows:

```
my $sth = $dbh->prepare (qq{
            INSERT INTO member last_name, first_name VALUES(?,?,?)
});
$sth->execute ("Adams","Bill","2003-09-19");
```

- To specify NULL as a placeholder value, use undef.
- Placeholders and quote() are intended only for data values. Do not try to use a placeholder for keywords like SELECT or for identifiers like database, table, or column names. It won't work because the keyword or identifier will be placed into the query surrounded by quotes, and the query will fail with a syntax error.

For some database engines, you get another performance benefit by using placeholders in addition to improved efficiency in loops. Certain engines cache prepared queries as well as the plan they generate for executing the query efficiently. That way, if the same query is received by the server later, it can be reused without generating a new execution plan. Query caching is especially helpful for complex SELECT statements because it may take some time to generate a good execution plan. Placeholders give you a better chance of finding a query in the cache because they make queries more generic than queries constructed by embedding specific column values directly in the query string. MySQL does not cache queries this way, so placeholders don't improve performance in the manner just described. However, if you write your queries using placeholders, and then port the script for use with an engine that does cache execution plans, it will execute more efficiently than without placeholders. (MySQL has a query cache as of version 4.0.1, but it operates by caching result sets for lexically identical query strings, not by caching execution plans. The query cache is discussed in Chapter 4, "Query Optimization.")

The Phantom undef

Some DBI methods that execute a query string, such as do() and selectrow_array(), allow you to provide placeholder values to be bound to any '?' characters in the query. For example, you can update a record as follows:

```
my $rows = $dbh->do ("UPDATE member SET expiration = ? WHERE member_id = ?",
                     undef, "2005-01-01", 14);
```

Or fetch a record as follows:

```
my $ref = $dbh->selectrow_arrayref (
              "SELECT * FROM member WHERE member_id = ?",
                  undef, 14);
```

Observe that in both cases, the placeholder values are preceded by an undef argument that appears to do nothing. The reason it's there is that for query-execution methods that allow placeholder arguments, those arguments are preceded by another argument that can be used to specify query-processing attributes. Such attributes are rarely (if ever) used, but the argument still must be present, so just specify it as undef.

Binding Query Results to Script Variables

Placeholders allow you to substitute values into a query string at query execution time. In other words, you can parameterize the "input" to the query. DBI also provides a corresponding output operation called parameter binding that allows you to parameterize the "output" by retrieving column values into variables automatically when you fetch a row without having to assign values to the variables yourself.

Suppose you have a query to retrieve names from the member table. You can tell DBI to assign the values of the selected columns to Perl variables. When you fetch a row, the variables are automatically updated with the corresponding column values, which makes the retrieval very efficient. The following is an example that shows how to bind the columns to variables and then access them in the fetch loop:

```
my ($last_name, $first_name, $suffix);
my $sth = $dbh->prepare (qq{
            SELECT last_name, first_name, suffix
            FROM member ORDER BY last_name, first_name
});
$sth->execute ();
$sth->bind_col (1, \$last_name);
$sth->bind_col (2, \$first_name);
$sth->bind_col (3, \$suffix);
print "$last_name, $first_name, $suffix\n" while $sth->fetch ();
```

bind_col() should be called after execute() and before fetching rows. Each call should specify a column number and a reference to the variable you want to associate with the column. Column numbers begin with 1.

As an alternative to individual calls to bind_col(), you can pass all the variable references in a single call to bind_columns():

```
my ($last_name, $first_name, $suffix);
my $sth = $dbh->prepare (qq{
            SELECT last_name, first_name, suffix
            FROM member ORDER BY last_name, first_name
});
$sth->execute ();
$sth->bind_columns (\$last_name, \$first_name, \$suffix);
print "$last_name, $first_name, $suffix\n" while $sth->fetch ();
```

bind_columns() should be called after execute() and before fetching rows.

Specifying Connection Parameters

The most direct way to establish a server connection is to specify all the connection parameters as arguments to the connect() method:

```
my $dsn = "DBI:mysql:db_name:host_name";
my $dbh = DBI->connect ($dsn, user_name, password);
```

If you leave out connection parameters, DBI attempts to determine what values to use as follows:

- The DBI_DSN environment variable is used if set and the data source name (DSN) is undefined or is the empty string. The DBI_USER and DBI_PASS environment variables are used if set and the username and password are undefined (but not if they are the empty string). Under Windows, the USER variable is used if the username is undefined.

- If you leave out the hostname, DBI attempts to connect to the local host.
- If you specify `undef` or an empty string for the username, it defaults to your UNIX login name. Under Windows, the username defaults to ODBC.
- If you specify `undef` or an empty string for the password, no password is sent.

You can specify certain options in the DSN by appending them to the initial part of the string, each preceded by a semicolon. For example, you can use the `mysql_read_default_file` option to specify an option file pathname:

```
my $dsn = "DBI:mysql:sampdb;mysql_read_default_file=/u/paul/.my.cnf";
```

When the script executes, it will read the file for connection parameters. Suppose `/u/paul/.my.cnf` has the following contents:

```
[client]
host=cobra.snake.net
user=sampadm
password=secret
```

In this case, the `connect()` call will attempt to connect to the MySQL server on `cobra.snake.net` and will connect as user `sampadm` with password `secret`. Under UNIX, you can tell your script to use the option file that belongs to the person who happens to be running it by parameterizing the filename, as in the following:

```
my $dsn = "DBI:mysql:sampdb;mysql_read_default_file=$ENV{HOME}/.my.cnf";
```

`$ENV{HOME}` contains the pathname to the home directory of the user running the script, so the connection parameters that it uses will be pulled from that user's own option file. By writing a script in this way, you don't have to embed connection parameters literally in the script.

Using `mysql_read_default_file` causes the script to read only the named option file, which may be undesirable if you want it to look for parameters in system-wide option files as well (such as `/etc/my.cnf` under UNIX or `C:\my.cnf` under Windows). To have the script read all the standard option files for connection parameters, use `mysql_read_default_group` instead. This option causes parameters in the `[client]` group to be used, as well as in the group that you specify in the option's value. For example, if you have options that are specific to your `sampdb`-related scripts, you can list them in a `[sampdb]` group and then use a data source value like this:

```
my $dsn = "DBI:mysql:sampdb;mysql_read_default_group=sampdb";
```

If you want to read just the [client] group from the standard option files, specify the option like this:

```
my $dsn = "DBI:mysql:sampdb;mysql_read_default_group=client";
```

mysql_read_default_file and mysql_read_default_group require MySQL 3.22.10 or later, and DBD::mysql 1.21.06 or later. For more details on options for specifying the data source string, see Appendix G. For more information on the format of MySQL option files, see Appendix E, "MySQL Program Reference."

One difficulty with using mysql_read_default_file on Windows is that file pathnames typically begin with a drive letter and a colon. That's a problem because DBI interprets colons as the character that separates parts of the DSN string. It's possible to work around this, although the method is ugly:

1. Change location to the root directory of the drive where the option file is located, so that pathnames specified without a drive letter will be interpreted relative to that drive.

2. Specify the filename as the value of the mysql_read_default_file option in the DSN, but without the leading drive letter or colon.

3. If it's necessary to leave the current directory undisturbed by the connect operation, save the current directory pathname before calling connect() and then chdir() back to it after connecting.

The following code fragment shows how to do this if you want to use the option file C:\my.cnf. (Note that backslashes in Windows pathnames are specified as slashes in Perl strings.)

```
# save current directory pathname
use Cwd;
my $orig_dir = cwd ();
# change to root dir of drive where file is located
chdir ("C:/") or die "cannot chdir: $!\n";
# connect using parameters in C:\my.cnf
my $dsn = "DBI:mysql:sampdb:localhost;mysql_read_default_file=/my.cnf";
my $dbh = DBI->connect ($dsn, undef, undef,
                        { RaiseError => 1, PrintError => 0 });
# change back to original directory
chdir ($orig_dir) or die "cannot chdir: $!\n";
```

Using an option file doesn't prevent you from specifying connection parameters in the connect() call (for example, if you want the script to connect as a particular user). Any explicit hostname, username, and password values specified in the connect() call will override connection parameters found in the option file. For example, you might want your script to parse options such as

--host and --user from the command line and use those values, if they are given, in preference to any found in an option file. That would be useful because it's the way the standard MySQL clients behave. Your DBI scripts would therefore be consistent with that behavior.

For the remaining command-line scripts that we develop in this chapter, I'll use some standard connection setup and teardown code. I'll just show it once here so that we can concentrate on the main body of each script as we write it:

```perl
#! /usr/bin/perl -w

use DBI;
use strict;

# parse connection parameters from command line if given

use Getopt::Long;
$Getopt::Long::ignorecase = 0; # options are case sensitive
$Getopt::Long::bundling = 1;   # -uname = -u name, not -u -n -a -m -e

# default parameters - all undefined initially
my ($host_name, $password, $port_num, $socket_name, $user_name);

GetOptions (
    # =i means an integer argument is required after option
    # =s or :s means string argument is required or optional after option
    "host|h=s"      => \$host_name,
    "password|p:s"  => \$password,
    "port|P=i"      => \$port_num,
    "socket|S=s"    => \$socket_name,
    "user|u=s"      => \$user_name
) or exit (1);

# solicit password if option specified without option value
if (defined ($password) && !$password)
{
    # turn off echoing but don't interfere with STDIN
    open (TTY, "/dev/tty") or die "Cannot open terminal\n";
    system ("stty -echo < /dev/tty");
    print STDERR "Enter password: ";
    chomp ($password = <TTY>);
    system ("stty echo < /dev/tty");
    close (TTY);
    print STDERR "\n";
}

# construct data source
my $dsn = "DBI:mysql:sampdb";
$dsn .= ";host=$host_name" if $host_name;
```

```
$dsn .= ";port=$port_num" if $port_num;
$dsn .= ";mysql_socket=$socket_name" if $socket_name;
$dsn .= ";mysql_read_default_group=client";

# connect to server
my $dbh = DBI->connect ($dsn, $user_name, $password,
                        { RaiseError => 1, PrintError => 0 });
```

This code initializes DBI, looks for connection parameters on the command line, and then makes the connection to the MySQL server using parameters from the command line or found in the [client] group in the standard option files. If you have your connection parameters listed in your option file, you won't have to enter them when you run a script that uses this code.

The final part of each script will be similar, too; it simply terminates the connection and exits:

```
$dbh->disconnect ();
exit (0);
```

When we get to the Web programming section "Using DBI in Web Applications," we'll modify the connection setup code a bit, but the basic idea will be similar.

The password-prompting code works only under UNIX. For Windows, you'll probably want to put your MySQL password in the [client] group of one of the standard option files or else specify it directly on the command line.

There is one unfortunate difference between the way the standard MySQL clients and the Getopt module handle command-line options. With Getopt, you cannot specify a password option (--password or -p) without an argument unless it is either the last argument on the command line or is immediately followed by another option. Suppose you have a script that expects a table name argument to follow the options. If invoked as follows, Getopt will interpret mytbl as the password value rather than prompting for a password:

```
% ./myscript.pl -u paul -p mytbl
```

To get the script to prompt for a password, put the -p option before the -u option:

```
% ./myscript.pl -p -u paul mytbl
```

Debugging

When you want to debug a malfunctioning DBI script, two techniques are commonly used, either alone or in tandem. First, you can sprinkle print statements throughout your script. This allows you to tailor your debugging output the way you want it, but you must add the statements manually. Second, you can use DBI's built-in tracing capabilities. This is more general and more systematic, and it occurs automatically after you turn it on. DBI tracing also shows you information about the operation of the driver that you cannot get otherwise.

Debugging Using Print Statements

A common question on the MySQL mailing list runs like this: "I have a query that works fine when I execute it using the mysql program, but it doesn't work from my DBI script. How come?" It's not unusual to find that the DBI script really is issuing a different query than the questioner thinks. If you print a query before executing it, you may be surprised to see what you're actually sending to the server. Suppose a query as you type it into mysql looks like the following:

```
mysql> INSERT INTO member (last_name,first_name,expiration)
    -> VALUES('Brown','Marcia','2005-6-3');
```

Then you try the same thing in a DBI script (leaving out the terminating semicolon, of course):

```
$last = "Brown";
$first = "Marcia";
$expiration = "2005-6-3";
$query = qq{
    INSERT INTO member (last_name,first_name,expiration)
    VALUES($last,$first,$expiration)
};
$rows = $dbh->do ($query);
```

This doesn't work, even though it's the same query. Or is it? Try printing it:

```
print "$query\n";
```

Here is the result:

```
INSERT INTO member (last_name,first_name,expiration)
VALUES(Brown,Marcia,2005-6-3)
```

From this output, you can see that the query is not the same at all. There are no quotes around the column values in the VALUES() list. One way to specify the query properly is like this, using quote():

```
$last = $dbh->quote ("Brown");
$first = $dbh->quote ("Marcia");
$expiration = $dbh->quote ("2005-6-3");
$query = qq{
    INSERT INTO member (last_name,first_name,expiration)
    VALUES($last,$first,$expiration)
};
$rows = $dbh->do ($query);
```

Alternatively, you can specify the query using placeholders and pass the values to be inserted into it as arguments to the do() method:

```
$last = "Brown";
$first = "Marcia";
$expiration = "2005-6-3";
$query = qq{
    INSERT INTO member (last_name,first_name,expiration)
    VALUES(?,?,?)
};
$rows = $dbh->do ($query, undef, $last, $first, $expiration);
```

Unfortunately, when you do this, you cannot see what the complete query looks like by using a print statement because the placeholder values aren't evaluated until you invoke do(). When you use placeholders, tracing may be a more helpful debugging method.

Debugging Using Tracing

DBI offers a tracing mechanism that generates debugging information to help you figure out why a script doesn't work properly. Trace levels range from 0 (off) to 9 (maximum information). Generally, trace levels 1 and 2 are the most useful. A level 2 trace shows you the text of queries you're executing (including the result of placeholder substitutions), the result of calls to quote(), and so forth. This can be of immense help in tracking down a problem.

You can control tracing from within individual scripts by using the trace() method, or you can set the DBI_TRACE environment variable to affect tracing for all DBI scripts you run.

To use the trace() call, pass a trace level argument and optionally a filename. If you specify no filename, all trace output goes to STDERR; otherwise, it goes to the named file. The following call sets up a level 1 trace to STDERR:

```
DBI->trace (1);
```

This call sets up a level 2 trace to the trace.out file:

```
DBI->trace (2, "trace.out");
```

To disable tracing, specify a trace level of zero:

```
DBI->trace (0);
```

When invoked as DBI->trace(), all DBI operations are traced. For a more fine-grained approach, enable tracing at the individual handle level. This is useful when you have a good idea where a problem in your script lies and you don't want to wade through the trace output for everything that occurs up to that point. For example, if you're having problems with a particular SELECT query, you can trace the statement handle associated with the query

```
$sth = $dbh->prepare (qq{ SELECT ... }); # create the statement handle
$sth->trace (1);                         # enable tracing on the statement
$sth->execute ();
```

If you specify a filename argument to any trace() call, whether for DBI as a whole or for an individual handle, all trace output goes to that file.

As an alternative to the trace() method, you can use the TraceLevel attribute, available as of DBI 1.21. This attribute allows you to set or get the trace level for a given handle:

```
$dbh->{TraceLevel} = 3;                    # set database handle trace level
my $cur_level = $sth->{TraceLevel};   # get statement handle trace level
```

To turn on tracing globally so that it takes effect for all DBI scripts that you run, set the DBI_TRACE environment variable from your shell. The syntax for this depends on the shell you use:

- For csh or tcsh:
  ```
  % setenv DBI_TRACE value
  ```

- For sh, ksh, or bash:
  ```
  $ export DBI_TRACE=value
  ```

- For Windows:
  ```
  C:\> set DBI_TRACE=value
  ```

The format of value is the same for all shells: a number n to turn on tracing at level n to STDERR, a filename to turn on level 2 tracing to the named file, or n=file_name to turn on level n tracing to the named file. Here are some examples, using tcsh syntax:

- A level 1 trace to STDERR:
  ```
  % setenv DBI_TRACE 1
  ```

- A level 1 trace to the file trace.out:
  ```
  % setenv DBI_TRACE 1=trace.out
  ```

- A level 2 trace to the file trace.out:
  ```
  % setenv DBI_TRACE trace.out
  ```

Using DBI_TRACE is advantageous in that you can enable DBI script tracing without making any changes to your scripts. But if you turn on tracing to a file from your shell, be sure to turn it off after you resolve the problem. Debugging output is appended to the trace file without overwriting it, so the file can become quite large if you're not careful. It's a particularly bad idea to define `DBI_TRACE` in a shell startup file such as `.cshrc`, `.tcshrc`, `.login`, or `.profile`!

- For `csh` or `tcsh`, either of the following commands turn off tracing:

```
% setenv DBI_TRACE 0
% unsetenv DBI_TRACE
```

- For `sh`, `ksh`, or `bash`, do the following:

```
$ export DBI_TRACE=0
```

- On Windows, use either of the following commands:

```
C:\> unset DBI_TRACE
C:\> set DBI_TRACE=0
```

Using Result Set Metadata

You can use DBI to gain access to result set metadata—that is, descriptive information about the rows selected by a query. To get this information, access the attributes of the statement handle associated with the query that generated the result set. Some of these are standard DBI attributes that are available across all database drivers (such as `NUM_OF_FIELDS`, the number of columns in the result set). Others, which are MySQL-specific, are provided by `DBD::mysql`, the MySQL driver for DBI. These attributes, such as `mysql_max_length`, which tells you the maximum width of the values in each column, are not applicable to other database engines. To the extent that you use any of the MySQL-specific attributes, you risk making your scripts non-portable to other databases. On the other hand, they can make it easier to get the information you want.

You must ask for metadata at the right time. Generally, result set attributes are not available for a `SELECT` statement until after you've invoked `prepare()` and `execute()`. In addition, attributes may become invalid after you reach the end of the result set with a row-fetching function or after you invoke `finish()`.

The following example shows how to use one of the MySQL-specific metadata attributes, `mysql_max_length`, in conjunction with the more general attributes `NUM_OF_FIELDS`, which indicates the number of columns in the result set, and `NAME`, which holds their names. We can combine the information provided by these attributes to write a script, `box_out.pl`, that produces output from `SELECT` queries in the same boxed style that you get when you run the `mysql` client program in interactive mode. The main body of `box_out.pl` is as follows (you can replace the SELECT statement with any other; the output-writing routines are independent of the particular query):

```
my $sth = $dbh->prepare (qq{
    SELECT last_name, first_name, suffix, city, state
    FROM president ORDER BY last_name, first_name
});
$sth->execute (); # attributes should be available after this call

# actual maximum widths of column values in result set
my @wid = @{$sth->{mysql_max_length}};
# number of columns in result set
my $ncols = $sth->{NUM_OF_FIELDS};

# adjust column widths if data values are narrower than column headings
# or than the word "NULL"
for (my $i = 0; $i < $ncols; $i++)
{
    my $name_wid = length ($sth->{NAME}->[$i]);
    $wid[$i] = $name_wid if $wid[$i] < $name_wid;
    $wid[$i] = 4 if $wid[$i] < 4;
}

# print output
print_dashes (\@wid, $ncols);                 # row of dashes
print_row ($sth->{NAME}, \@wid, $ncols);      # column headings
print_dashes (\@wid, $ncols);                 # row of dashes
while (my $ary_ref = $sth->fetchrow_arrayref ())
{
    print_row ($ary_ref, \@wid, $ncols);      # row data values
}
print_dashes (\@wid, $ncols);                 # row of dashes
```

After the query has been initiated with execute(), we can grab the metadata we need. $sth->{NUM_OF_FIELDS} is a scalar value indicating how many columns are in the result set. $sth->{NAME} and $sth->{mysql_max_length} give us the column names and maximum width of each column's values. The value of each of these two attributes is a reference to an array that contains an element for each column of the result set, in the order that columns are named in the query.

The remaining calculations are very much like those used for the client4 program developed in Chapter 6. For example, to avoid misaligned output, we adjust the column width values upward if the name of a column is wider than any of the data values in the column.

The output functions print_dashes() and print_row() are written as follows. They too are similar to the corresponding code in client4:

```
sub print_dashes
{
```

```
my $wid_ary_ref = shift;      # reference to array of column widths
my $cols = shift;             # number of columns

    print "+";
    for (my $i = 0; $i < $cols; $i++)
    {
        print "-" x ($wid_ary_ref->[$i]+2) . "+";
    }
    print "\n";
}


# print row of data.  (doesn't right-align numeric columns)

sub print_row
{
my $val_ary_ref = shift;      # reference to array of column values
my $wid_ary_ref = shift;      # reference to array of column widths
my $cols = shift;             # number of columns

    print "|";
    for (my $i = 0; $i < $cols; $i++)
    {
        printf " %-*s |", $wid_ary_ref->[$i],
                defined ($val_ary_ref->[$i]) ? $val_ary_ref->[$i] : "NULL";
    }
    print "\n";
}
```

The output from `box_out.pl` looks like this:

```
+------------+---------------+--------+---------------------+-------+
| last_name  | first_name    | suffix | city                | state |
+------------+---------------+--------+---------------------+-------+
| Adams      | John          | NULL   | Braintree           | MA    |
| Adams      | John Quincy   | NULL   | Braintree           | MA    |
| Arthur     | Chester A.    | NULL   | Fairfield           | VT    |
| Buchanan   | James         | NULL   | Mercersburg         | PA    |
| Bush       | George H.W.   | NULL   | Milton              | MA    |
| Bush       | George W.     | NULL   | New Haven           | CT    |
| Carter     | James E.      | Jr.    | Plains              | GA    |
...
```

Our next script uses column metadata to produce output in a different format. This script, `show_member.pl`, allows you to take a quick look at Historical League member entries without entering any queries. Given a member's last name, it displays the selected entry as follows:

```
% ./show_member.pl artel
last_name:  Artel
first_name: Mike
suffix:
expiration: 2006-04-16
email:      mike_artel@venus.org
```

```
street:     4264 Lovering Rd.
city:       Miami
state:      FL
zip:        12777
phone:      075-961-0712
interests:  Civil Rights,Education,Revolutionary War
member_id:  63
```

You can also invoke show_member.pl using a membership number or using a pattern to match several last names. The following commands show the entry for member 23 or the entries for members with last names that start with "C":

```
% ./show_member.pl 23
% ./show_member.pl C%
```

The main body of the show_member.pl script is shown in the following code. It uses the NAME attribute to determine the labels to use for each row of output and the NUM_OF_FIELDS attribute to find out how many columns the result set contains:

```perl
my $count = 0;   # number of entries printed so far
my @label = ();  # column label array
my $label_wid = 0;

while (@ARGV)        # run query for each argument on command line
{
    my $arg = shift (@ARGV);

    # default is to do a search by last name...
    my $clause = "last_name LIKE " . $dbh->quote ($arg);
    # ...but do ID search instead if argument is numeric
    $clause = "member_id = " . $dbh->quote ($arg) if $arg =~ /^\d+$/;

    # issue query
    my $sth = $dbh->prepare (qq{
        SELECT * FROM member
        WHERE $clause
        ORDER BY last_name, first_name
    });
    $sth->execute ();

    # get column names to use for labels and
    # determine max column name width for formatting
    # (only do this the first time through the loop, though)
    if ($label_wid == 0)
    {
        @label = @{$sth->{NAME}};
        foreach my $label (@label)
        {
```

```
                    $label_wid = length ($label) if $label_wid < length ($label);
            }
        }

    # read and print query results
    my $matches = 0;
    while (my @ary = $sth->fetchrow_array ())
    {
        # print newline before 2nd and subsequent entries
        print "\n" if ++$count > 1;
        foreach (my $i = 0; $i < $sth->{NUM_OF_FIELDS}; $i++)
        {
            # print label
            printf "%-*s", $label_wid+1, $label[$i] . ":";
            # print value, if there is one
            print " " . $ary[$i] if defined ($ary[$i]);
            print "\n";
        }
        ++$matches;
    }
    print "\nNo match was found for \"$arg\"\n" if $matches == 0;
}
```

The purpose of show_member.pl is to show the entire contents of an entry, no matter what the fields are. By using SELECT * to retrieve all the columns and the NAME attribute to find out what they are, this script will work without modification, even if columns are added or dropped from the member table.

If you just want to know what columns a table contains without retrieving any rows, you can issue the following query:

```
SELECT * FROM tbl_name WHERE 1 = 0
```

After invoking prepare() and execute() in the usual way, you can get the column names from @{$sth->{NAME}}. Be aware, however, that although this little trick of using an "empty" query works for MySQL, it's not portable and doesn't work for all database engines.

For more information on the attributes provided by DBI and by DBD::mysql, see Appendix G. It's up to you to determine whether you want to strive for portability by avoiding MySQL-specific attributes or take advantage of them at the cost of portability.

Performing Transactions

One way to perform transactions in a DBI script is to issue explicit SET AUTOCOMMIT, BEGIN, COMMIT, and ROLLBACK statements. (These statements are described in Chapter 3, "MySQL SQL Syntax and Use.") However, DBI provides its own abstraction for performing transactional operations. This abstraction is expressed in terms of DBI methods and attributes and takes care of issuing the proper transaction-related SQL statements for you automatically. It's also portable to other database engines that support transactions, whereas the SQL statements may not be.

To use the DBI transaction mechanism, several requirements must be satisfied:

- You must have DBD::mysql 1.2216 or later.
- Your MySQL server must support table handlers for transaction-safe table types like InnoDB or BDB. Chapter 3 describes how to determine whether or not this is true.
- You application must use tables that have a transaction-safe type. If they are not, use ALTER TABLE to change their type. For example, to change a given table *tbl_name* to be an InnoDB table, use the following statement:

```
ALTER TABLE tbl_name TYPE = INNODB;
```

Assuming that these assumptions are satisfied, the general procedure for transactional processing in DBI is as follows:

1. Disable (or temporarily suspend) auto-commit mode so that SQL statements won't be committed until you commit them yourself.
2. Issue the queries that are part of a transaction, but do so within an eval block that executes with RaiseError enabled and PrintError disabled so that any errors will terminate the block without printing errors. If the block executes successfully, the last operation within it should be to commit the transaction.
3. When the eval block finishes, check its termination status. If an error occurred, invoke rollback() to cancel the transaction and report the error if that's appropriate.
4. Restore the auto-commit mode and error-handling attributes as necessary.

The following example shows how to implement this approach. It's based on a scenario from Chapter 3 that showed how to issue transaction-related statements manually from the mysql client. The scenario is one in which you discover that you've mistakenly mixed up two scores for students in the score table and need to switch them: Student 8 has been given a score of 18, student 9 has been given a score of 13, and the scores should be the other way around. The two UPDATE statements needed to correct this problem are as follows:

```
UPDATE score SET score = 13 WHERE event_id = 5 AND student_id = 8;
UPDATE score SET score = 18 WHERE event_id = 5 AND student_id = 9;
```

You want to update both records with the correct scores, but both updates should succeed as a unit. In the earlier chapter, the updates were surrounded by explicit SQL statements for setting the auto-commit mode, committing, and rolling back. Within a Perl script that uses the DBI transaction mechanism, the updates are performed as follows:

```
my $orig_re = $dbh->{RaiseError};      # save error-handling attributes
my $orig_pe = $dbh->{PrintError};
my $orig_ac = $dbh->{AutoCommit};      # save auto-commit mode

$dbh->{RaiseError} = 1;                # cause errors to raise exceptions
$dbh->{PrintError} = 0;                # but suppress error messages
$dbh->{AutoCommit} = 0;                # don't commit until we say so

eval
{
    # issue the statements that are part of the transaction
    my $sth = $dbh->prepare (qq{
            UPDATE score SET score = ?
            WHERE event_id = ? AND student_id = ?
        });
    $sth->execute (13, 5, 8);
    $sth->execute (18, 5, 9);
    $dbh->commit ();                   # commit the transaction
};
if ($@)                                # did the transaction fail?
{
    print "A transaction error occurred: $@\n";
    # roll back, but use eval to trap rollback failure
    eval { $dbh->rollback (); }
}

$dbh->{AutoCommit} = $orig_ac;         # restore auto-commit mode
$dbh->{RaiseError} = $orig_re;         # restore error-handling attributes
$dbh->{PrintError} = $orig_pe;
```

The eval block does the work of performing the transaction, and its termination status is available in the $@ variable. If the UPDATE statements execute without error, the commit() function is invoked to commit the transaction, and $@ will be empty. If an error occurs, the eval block fails and $@ holds the error message. In that case, the code prints the message, and then cancels the transaction by invoking rollback(). (The rollback operation is placed within its own eval block to prevent it from terminating the script if it fails.)

In this chapter, DBI scripts generally use an error-handling mode in which RaiseError is enabled and PrintError is disabled. This means that they already will have the values required for performing transactions, so it really wouldn't have been necessary to save, set, and restore those attributes as shown in the example. However, doing so is an approach that will work even for circumstances under which you're not sure in advance what the error-handling attributes might be set to.

Putting DBI to Work

At this point you've seen a number of the concepts involved in DBI programming, so let's move on to some of the things we wanted to be able to do with our sample database. Our goals were outlined initially in Chapter 1. Those that we'll tackle by writing DBI scripts in this chapter are listed here.

For the grade-keeping project, we want to be able to retrieve scores for any given quiz or test.

For the Historical League, we want to do the following:

- Produce the member directory in different formats. We want a names-only list for use in the program distributed at the League's annual banquet and in a format we can use for generating the printed directory.

- Find League members that need to renew their memberships soon, and then send email to let them know about it.

- Edit member entries. (We'll need to update their expiration dates when they renew their memberships, after all.)

- Find members that share a common interest.

- Put the directory online.

For some of these tasks, we'll write scripts that run from the command line. For the others, we'll create scripts in the next section, "Using DBI in Web Applications," that you can use in conjunction with your Web server. At the end of the chapter, we'll still have a number of goals left to accomplish, but we'll finish up those that remain in Chapter 8, "The PHP API."

Generating the Historical League Directory

One of our goals is to be able to produce information from the Historical League directory in different formats. The simplest format to be generated is a list of member names for the printed program distributed to guests at the annual League banquet. The format can be a simple plain text listing. It will become part of the larger document used to create the banquet program, so all we need is something that can be pasted into that document.

For the printable directory, a better representation than plain text is needed because we want something nicely formatted. A reasonable choice here is RTF

(Rich Text Format), a format developed by Microsoft that is understood by many word processors. Word is one such program, of course, but many others, such as WordPerfect and AppleWorks, understand it as well. Different word processors support RTF to varying degrees, but we'll use a basic subset of the full RTF specification that should be understandable by any word processor that is RTF-aware to even a minimal degree. (For example, the Mac OS X TextEdit application can read the RTF output we'll be generating in this section.)

The procedures for generating the banquet list and RTF directory formats are essentially the same—issue a query to retrieve the entries, and then run a loop that fetches and formats each entry. Given that basic similarity, it would be nice to avoid writing separate scripts for each format. To that end, let's write a single script (`gen_dir.pl`) that can generate different types of output. We can structure the script as follows:

1. Before writing out member entries, perform any initialization that might be necessary for the output format. No special initialization is necessary for the banquet program member list, but we'll need to write out some initial control language for the RTF version.

2. Fetch and print each entry, formatted appropriately for the type of output we want.

3. After all the entries have been processed, perform any necessary cleanup and termination. Again, no special handling is needed for the banquet list, but some closing control language is required for the RTF version.

It's possible that in the future we'll want to use this script to write output in other formats, so let's make it extensible by setting up a "switchbox," that is, a hash with an element for each output format. Each element specifies which functions to invoke to carry out each output generation phase for a given format—an initialization function, an entry-writing function, and a cleanup function:

```
# switchbox containing formatting functions for each output format
my %switchbox =
(
    "banquet" =>                         # functions for banquet list
    {
        "init"      => undef,            # no initialization needed
        "entry"     => \&format_banquet_entry,
        "cleanup"   => undef             # no cleanup needed
    },
    "rtf" =>                             # functions for RTF format
    {
```

```
         "init"      => \&rtf_init,
         "entry"     => \&format_rtf_entry,
         "cleanup"   => \&rtf_cleanup
     }
);
```

Each element of the switchbox is keyed by a format name ("banquet" or "rtf"). We'll write the script so that you just specify the format you want on the command line when you run it:

```
% ./gen_dir.pl banquet
% ./gen_dir.pl rtf
```

By setting up a switchbox this way, we'll be able to add the capability for a new format easily, should we want to do so:

1. Write three formatting functions for the output generation phases.

2. Add a new element to the switchbox that defines a format name and that points to the output functions.

3. To produce output in the new format, invoke gen_dir.pl and specify the format name on the command line.

The code for selecting the proper switchbox entry according to the first argument on the command line is shown next. If no format name or an invalid name is specified on the command line, the script produces an error message and displays a list of the allowable names. Otherwise, $func_hashref will point to the appropriate switchbox entry:

```
# make sure one argument was specified on the command line
@ARGV == 1
    or die "Usage: gen_dir format_type\nAllowable formats: "
           . join (" ", sort (keys (%switchbox))) . "\n";

# determine proper switchbox entry from argument on command line;
# if no entry is found, the format type is invalid
my $func_hashref = $switchbox{$ARGV[0]};

defined ($func_hashref)
    or die "Unknown format: $ARGV[0]\nAllowable formats: "
           . join (" ", sort (keys (%switchbox))) . "\n";
```

The format selection code is based on the fact that the output format names are the keys in the %switchbox hash. If a valid format name is given, the corresponding switchbox entry points to the output functions. If an invalid name is given, no entry will exist. This makes it unnecessary to hardwire any names into the format selection code. It also means that when you add a new entry to the switchbox, the code will detect it automatically with no change.

If a valid format name is specified on the command line, the preceding code sets $func_hashref. Its value will be a reference to the hash that points to the output writing functions for the selected format. We can invoke the initialization function, fetch and print the entries, and invoke the cleanup function:

```
# invoke the initialization function if there is one
&{$func_hashref->{init}} if defined ($func_hashref->{init});

# fetch and print entries if there is an entry formatting function
if (defined ($func_hashref->{entry}))
{
    my $sth = $dbh->prepare (qq{
        SELECT * FROM member ORDER BY last_name, first_name
    });
    $sth->execute ();
    while (my $entry_ref = $sth->fetchrow_hashref ("NAME_lc"))
    {
        # pass entry by reference to the formatting function
        &{$func_hashref->{entry}} ($entry_ref);
    }
}

# invoke the cleanup function if there is one
&{$func_hashref->{cleanup}} if defined ($func_hashref->{cleanup});
```

The entry-fetching loop uses `fetchrow_hashref()` for a reason. If the loop fetched an array, each formatting function would have to know the order of the columns. It's possible to figure that out by accessing the `$sth->{NAME}` attribute (which contains column names in the order in which they are returned), but why bother? By using a hash reference, formatting functions can just name the column values they want using `$entry_ref->{col_name}`. That technique is much easier than using the `NAME` attribute and it can be used for any format we want to generate because we know that any fields we need will be in the hash.

All that remains is to write the functions for each output format (that is, for the functions named by the switchbox entries).

Generating the Banquet Program Member List

For this output format, no initialization or cleanup calls are necessary; we only need an entry formatting function (`format_banquet_entry()`) that takes a reference to a member entry and prints the member's name. An outline of the function looks like this:

```
sub format_banquet_entry
{
    # print member name here, using first_name, last_name, and suffix
    elements of the hash printed to by the function argument
}
```

The tricky part of printing names is dealing with the suffix part. Suffixes such as Jr. or Sr. should be preceded by a comma and a space, whereas suffixes such as II or III should be preceded only by a space:

```
Michael Alvis IV
Clarence Elgar, Jr.
Bill Matthews, Sr.
Mark York II
```

The letters I, V, and X are the only ones used in the roman numerals for the 1st to the 39th generation. It's unlikely that we'll need any numerals beyond that range, so we can determine whether or not to add a comma by checking whether the suffix value matches the following pattern:

```
/^[IVX]+$/
```

The code in `format_banquet_entry()` that puts the parts of the name together in the proper order is something we'll need for the RTF version of the directory as well. So instead of duplicating that code in `format_rtf_entry()`, let's stuff it into a helper function:

```
sub format_name
{
my $entry_ref = shift;

    my $name = $entry_ref->{first_name} . " " . $entry_ref->{last_name};
    if (defined ($entry_ref->{suffix}))          # there is a name suffix
    {
        # no comma for suffixes of I, II, III, etc.
        $name .= "," unless $entry_ref->{suffix} =~ /^[IVX]+$/;
        $name .= " " . $entry_ref->{suffix}
    }
    return ($name);
}
```

With `format_name()` in place, the implementation of the `format_banquet_entry()` function that prints an entry becomes almost completely trivial:

```
sub format_banquet_entry
{
    printf "%s\n", format_name ($_[0]);
}
```

Generating the Print-Format Directory

Generating the RTF version of the directory is a little more involved than generating the member list for the banquet program. For one thing, we need to print more information from each entry. For another, we need to put out some RTF control language with each entry to achieve the effects that we want and some control language at the beginning and end of the document. A minimal framework for an RTF document looks like the following:

```
{\rtf0
{\fonttbl {\f0 Times;}}
\plain \f0 \fs24
    ...document content goes here...
}
```

The document begins and ends with curly braces '{' and '}'. RTF keywords begin with a backslash, and the first keyword of the document must be `\rtfn`, where n is the RTF specification version number the document corresponds to. Version 0 is fine for our purposes.

Within the document, we specify a font table to indicate the font to use for the entries. Font table information is listed in a group consisting of curly braces containing a leading `\fonttbl` keyword and some font information. The font table shown in the framework defines font number 0 to be in Times. (We only need one font, but you could use more if you wanted to be fancier.)

The next few directives set up the default formatting style: `\plain` selects plain format, `\f0` selects font 0 (which we've defined as Times in the font table), and `\fs24` sets the font size to 12 points (the number following `\fs` indicates the size in half-points). It's not necessary to set up margins because most word processors will supply reasonable defaults.

The framework is provided by the initialization and cleanup functions, which look like the following (note the double backslashes to get single backslashes in the output):

```
sub rtf_init
{
    print "{\\rtf0\n";
    print "{\\fonttbl {\\f0 Times;}}\n";
    print "\\plain \\f0 \\fs24\n";
}

sub rtf_cleanup
{
    print "}\n";
}
```

The content of the document is produced by the entry formatting function. To take a very simple approach, we can print each entry as a series of lines, with a label on each line. If the information corresponding to a particular output line is missing, the line is omitted. (For example, the Email: line does not need to be printed for members who have no email address.) Some lines (such as the Address: line) are composed of the information in multiple columns (street, city, state, zip), so the script must be able to deal with various combinations of missing values. The following is a sample of the output format we'll use:

```
Name: Mike Artel
Address: 4264 Lovering Rd., Miami, FL 12777
Telephone: 075-961-0712
Email: mike_artel@venus.org
Interests: Civil Rights,Education,Revolutionary War
```

For that entry, the RTF representation looks like this:

```
\b Name: Mike Artel\b0\par
Address: 4264 Lovering Rd., Miami, FL 12777\par
Telephone: 075-961-0712\par
Email: mike_artel@venus.org\par
Interests: Civil Rights,Education,Revolutionary War\par
```

To make the Name: line bold, it's surrounded by \b (with a space afterward) to turn boldface on and \b0 to turn boldface off. The member name is formatted by the format_name() function shown earlier in the "Generating the Banquet Program Member List" section. Each line has a paragraph marker (\par) at the end to tell the word processor to move to the next line—nothing too complicated. The primary difficulties lie in formatting the address string and determining which output lines should be printed:

```perl
sub format_rtf_entry
{
my $entry_ref = shift;

    printf "\\b Name: %s\\b0\\par\n", format_name ($entry_ref);
    my $address = "";
    $address .= $entry_ref->{street}
                            if defined ($entry_ref->{street});
    $address .= ", " . $entry_ref->{city}
                            if defined ($entry_ref->{city});
    $address .= ", " . $entry_ref->{state}
                            if defined ($entry_ref->{state});
    $address .= " " . $entry_ref->{zip}
                            if defined ($entry_ref->{zip});
    print "Address: $address\\par\n"
                            if $address ne "";
    print "Telephone: $entry_ref->{phone}\\par\n"
                            if defined ($entry_ref->{phone});
    print "Email: $entry_ref->{email}\\par\n"
                            if defined ($entry_ref->{email});
    print "Interests: $entry_ref->{interests}\\par\n"
                            if defined ($entry_ref->{interests});
    print "\\par\n";
}
```

You're not locked into this particular formatting style, of course. You can change how you print any of the fields, so you can change the style of your printed directory almost at will, simply by changing `format_rtf_entry()`. With the directory in its original form (a word processing document), that's something not so easily done.

The `gen_dir.pl` script is now complete, and you can generate the directory in either output format by running commands such as the following:

```
% ./gen_dir.pl banquet > names.txt
% ./gen_dir.pl rtf > directory.rtf
```

At this point, it's a simple step to read the name list and paste it into the annual banquet program document or to read the RTF file into any word processor that understands RTF.

DBI made it easy to extract the information we wanted from MySQL, and Perl's text-processing capabilities made it easy to put that information into the format we wanted to see. MySQL doesn't provide any particularly fancy way of formatting output, but it doesn't matter because of the ease with which you can integrate MySQL's database handling abilities into a language such as Perl, which has excellent text manipulation capabilities.

Sending Membership Renewal Notices

With the Historical League directory maintained in its original form (as a word processing document), it's a time-consuming and error-prone activity to determine which members need to be notified that their memberships should be renewed. Now that we have the information in a database, it's possible to automate the renewal-notification process a bit. We want to identify members who need to renew, and send them a message via email so that we don't have to contact them by phone or surface mail.

What we need to do is determine which members are due for renewal within a certain number of days. The query for this involves a date calculation that's relatively simple:

```
SELECT ... FROM member
WHERE expiration < DATE_ADD(CURDATE(), INTERVAL cutoff DAY)
```

cutoff signifies the number of days of leeway we want to grant. The query selects member entries that are due for renewal in fewer than that many days. To find memberships that have actually expired, a cutoff value of 0 identifies records with expiration dates in the past.

After we've identified the records that qualify for notification, what should we do with them? One option would be to send mail directly from the same script, but it might be useful first to be able to review the list without sending any messages. For this reason, we'll use a two-stage approach:

1. Run a script, need_renewal.pl, to identify members that need to renew. You can examine this list to verify it, and then use it as input to the second stage that sends the renewal notices.

2. Run a script, renewal_notify.pl, that sends members a "please renew" notice by email. The script should warn you about members without email addresses so that you can contact them by other means.

For the first part of this task, the need_renewal.pl script must identify which members need to renew. The main part of the script that does this is as follows:

```perl
# Use default cutoff of 30 days...
my $cutoff = 30;
# ...but reset if a numeric argument is given on the command line
$cutoff = shift (@ARGV) if @ARGV && $ARGV[0] =~ /^\d+$/;

warn "Using cutoff of $cutoff days\n";

my $sth = $dbh->prepare (qq{
        SELECT
            member_id, email, last_name, first_name, expiration,
            TO_DAYS(expiration) - TO_DAYS(CURDATE()) AS days
        FROM member
        WHERE expiration < DATE_ADD(CURDATE(), INTERVAL ? DAY)
        ORDER BY expiration, last_name, first_name
});
$sth->execute ($cutoff);      # pass cutoff as placeholder value

while (my $entry_ref = $sth->fetchrow_hashref ())
{
    # convert undef values to empty strings for printing
    foreach my $key (keys (%{$entry_ref}))
    {
        $entry_ref->{$key} = "" if !defined ($entry_ref->{$key});
    }
    print join ("\t",
                $entry_ref->{member_id},
                $entry_ref->{email},
                $entry_ref->{last_name},
                $entry_ref->{first_name},
                $entry_ref->{expiration},
                $entry_ref->{days} . " days")
        . "\n";
}
```

The output from the need_renewal.pl script looks something like the following (you'll get different output because the results are determined against the current date, which will be different for you while reading this book than for me while writing it):

```
89  g.steve@pluto.com         Garner  Steve   2002-08-03  -32 days
18  york_mark@earth.com       York    Mark    2002-08-24  -11 days
82  john_edwards@venus.org     Edwards John    2002-09-12  8 days
```

Observe that some memberships need to be renewed in a negative number of days. That means they've already expired! (This happens when you maintain records manually; people slip through the cracks. Now that we have the information in a database, we're finding out that we missed a few people before.)

The second part of the renewal notification task involves a script, renewal_notify.pl, that sends out the notices by email. To make renewal_notify.pl a little easier to use, we can make it understand three kinds of command-line arguments: membership ID numbers, email addresses, and filenames. Numeric arguments signify membership ID values, and arguments containing a '@' character signify email addresses. Anything else is interpreted as the name of a file that should be read to find ID numbers or email addresses. This method enables you to specify members by their ID number or email address, and you can do so either directly on the command line or by listing them in a file. (In particular, you can save the output of need_renewal.pl in a file, and then use the file as input to renewal_notify.pl.)

For each member who is to be sent a notice, the script looks up the relevant member table entry, extracts the email address, and sends a message to that address. If there is no address in the entry, renewal_notify.pl generates a warning message that you need to contact these members in some other way.

The main argument-processing loop operates as follows. If no arguments were specified on the command line, we read the standard input for input. Otherwise, we process each argument by passing it to interpret_argument() for classification as an ID number, an email address, or a filename:

```
if (@ARGV == 0)      # no arguments, read STDIN for values
{
    read_file (\*STDIN);
}
else
{
    while (my $arg = shift (@ARGV))
    {
        # interpret argument, with filename recursion
        interpret_argument ($arg, 1);
    }
}
```

The `read_file()` function reads the contents of a file (assumed to be open already) and looks at the first field of each line. (If we feed the output of `need_renewal.pl` to `renewal_notify.pl`, each line has several fields, but we want to look only at the first one, which will contain a member ID number.)

```
sub read_file
{
my $fh = shift;      # handle to open file
my $arg;

    while (defined ($arg = <$fh>))
    {
        # strip off everything past column 1, including newline
        $arg =~ s/\s.*//s;
        # interpret argument, without filename recursion
        interpret_argument ($arg, 0);
    }
}
```

The `interpret_argument()` function classifies each argument to determine whether it's an ID number, an email address, or a filename. For ID numbers and email addresses, it looks up the appropriate member entry and passes it to `notify_member()`. We have to be careful with members specified by email address. It's possible that two members have the same address (for example, a husband and wife), and we don't want to send a message to someone to whom it doesn't apply. To avoid this, we look up the member ID corresponding to an email address to make sure there is exactly one. If the address matches more than one ID number, it's ambiguous and we ignore it after printing a warning.

If an argument doesn't look like an ID number or email address, it's taken to be the name of a file to read for further input. We have to be careful here, too—we don't want to read a file if we're already reading a file in order to avoid the possibility of an infinite loop:

```
sub interpret_argument
{
my ($arg, $recurse) = @_;

    if ($arg =~ /^\d+$/)         # numeric membership ID
    {
        notify_member ($arg);
    }
    elsif ($arg =~ /@/)          # email address
    {
        # get member_id associated with address
        # (there should be exactly one)
        my $query = qq{ SELECT member_id FROM member WHERE email = ? };
```

```
        my $ary_ref = $dbh->selectcol_arrayref ($query, undef, $arg);
        if (scalar (@{$ary_ref}) == 0)
        {
            warn "Email address $arg matches no entry: ignored\n";
        }
        elsif (scalar (@{$ary_ref}) > 1)
        {
            warn "Email address $arg matches multiple entries: ignored\n";
        }
        else
        {
            notify_member ($ary_ref->[0]);
        }
    }
    else                            # filename
    {
        if (!$recurse)
        {
            warn "filename $arg inside file: ignored\n";
        }
        else
        {
            open (IN, $arg) or die "Cannot open $arg: $!\n";
            read_file (\*IN);
            close (IN);
        }
    }
}
```

The notify_member() function is responsible for actually sending the renewal notice. If it turns out that the member has no email address, notify_member() can't send any message, but it prints a warning so that you know you need to contact the member in some other way. (You can invoke show_member.pl with the membership ID number shown in the message to see the full entry, to find out what the member's phone number and address are, for example.) notify_member() looks like this:

```
sub notify_member
{
my $member_id = shift;

    warn "Notifying $member_id...\n";
    my $query = qq{ SELECT * FROM member WHERE member_id = ? };
    my $sth = $dbh->prepare ($query);
    $sth->execute ($member_id);
    my @col_name = @{$sth->{NAME}};
    my $entry_ref = $sth->fetchrow_hashref ();
    $sth->finish ();
    if (!$entry_ref)                            # no member found!
    {
        warn "NO ENTRY found for member $member_id!\n";
```

```
            return;
        }
        if (!defined ($entry_ref->{email}))      # no email address in entry
        {
            warn "Member $member_id has no email address; no message was sent\n";
            return;
        }
        open (OUT, "| $sendmail") or die "Cannot open mailer\n";
        print OUT <<EOF;
To: $entry_ref->{email}
Subject: Your USHL membership is in need of renewal

Greetings.  Your membership in the U.S. Historical League is
due to expire soon.  We hope that you'll take a few minutes to
contact the League office to renew your membership.  The
contents of your member entry are shown below.  Please note
particularly the expiration date.

Thank you.

EOF
        foreach my $col_name (@col_name)
        {
            printf OUT "$col_name:";
            printf OUT " $entry_ref->{$col_name}"
                            if defined ($entry_ref->{$col_name});
            printf OUT "\n";
        }
        close (OUT);
}
```

The `notify_member()` function sends mail by opening a pipe to the send-mail program and shoving the mail message into the pipe. The pathname to sendmail is set as a parameter near the beginning of the `renewal_notify.pl` script. You may need to change this path because the location of `sendmail` varies from system to system:

```
# change path to match your system
my $sendmail = "/usr/sbin/sendmail -t -oi";
```

If you don't have `sendmail`, the script will not work properly. (For example, Windows systems typically do not have `sendmail` installed.) To handle this case, the `sampdb` distribution contains a modified version of `renewal_notify.pl` that uses the `Mail::Sendmail` module that works without the `sendmail` program. If you install that module, you can use the modified version instead.

You could get fancier with this script—for example, by adding a column to the `member` table to record when the most recent renewal reminder was sent out and then having `renewal_notify.pl` update that column when it sends mail. Doing so would help you to not send out notices too frequently. As it is, we'll just assume you won't run this program more than once a month or so.

The two scripts are done now, so you can use them as follows. First, run `need_renewal.pl` to generate a list of memberships that have expired or will soon do so:

```
% ./need_renewal.pl > tmp
```

Then take a look at `tmp` to see if it looks reasonable. If so, use it as input to `renewal_notify.pl` to send renewal messages:

```
% ./renewal_notify.pl tmp
```

To notify individual members, you can specify them by ID number or email address. For example, the following command notifies member 18 and the member having the email address `g.steve@pluto.com`:

```
% ./renewal_notify.pl 18 g.steve@pluto.com
```

Historical League Member Entry Editing

After we start sending out renewal notices, it's safe to assume that some of the people we notify will renew their memberships. When that happens, we'll need a way to update their entries with new expiration dates. In the next chapter, we'll develop a way to edit member records over the Web, but here we'll develop a command-line script (`edit_member.pl`) that enables you to update entries using a simple approach of prompting for new values for each part of an entry. It works like this:

- If invoked with no argument on the command line, `edit_member.pl` assumes you want to enter a new member, prompts for the initial information to be placed in the member's entry, and creates a new entry.

- If invoked with a membership ID number on the command line, `edit_member.pl` looks up the existing contents of the entry, and then prompts for updates to each column. If you enter a value for a column, it replaces the current value. If you press Enter, the column is not changed. If you enter the word `none`, it clears the column's current value. (If you don't know a member's ID number, you can run `show_member.pl` *last_name* to see which entries match the given last name and from that determine the proper ID.)

It's probably overkill to allow an entire entry to be edited this way if all you want to do is update a member's expiration date. On the other hand, a script like this also provides a simple general-purpose way to update any part of an entry without knowing any SQL. (One special case is that edit_member.pl won't allow you to change the member_id field because that's automatically assigned when an entry is created and shouldn't change thereafter.)

The first thing edit_member.pl needs to know is the names of the columns in the member table:

```
# get member table column names
my $sth = $dbh->prepare (qq{ SELECT * FROM member WHERE 0 });
$sth->execute ();
my @col_name = @{$sth->{NAME}};
$sth->finish ();
Then we can enter the main loop:
if (@ARGV == 0) # if no arguments were given, create a new entry
{
    # pass reference to array of column names
    new_member (\@col_name);
}
else            # otherwise edit entries using arguments as member IDs
{
    # save @ARGV, then empty it so that when the script reads from
    # STDIN, it doesn't interpret @ARGV contents as input filenames
    my @id = @ARGV;
    @ARGV = ();
    # for each ID value, look up the entry, then edit it
    while (my $id = shift (@id))
    {
        $sth = $dbh->prepare (qq{
                SELECT * FROM member WHERE member_id = ?
            });
        $sth->execute ($id);
        my $entry_ref = $sth->fetchrow_hashref ();
        $sth->finish ();
        if (!$entry_ref)
        {
            warn "No member with member ID = $id\n";
            next;
        }
        # pass reference to array of column names and reference to entry
        edit_member (\@col_name, $entry_ref);
    }
}
```

The code for creating a new member entry is as follows. It solicits values for each member table column, and then issues an INSERT statement to add a new record:

```
sub new_member
{
my $col_name_ref = shift;    # reference to array of column names
my $entry_ref = { };         # create new entry as a hash

    return unless prompt ("Create new entry (y/n)? ") =~ /^y/i;
    # prompt for new values; user types in new value, or Enter
    # to leave value unchanged, "none" to clear the value, or
    # "exit" to exit without creating the record.
    foreach my $col_name (@{$col_name_ref})
    {
        next if $col_name eq "member_id";   # skip key field
        my $col_val = col_prompt ($col_name, undef);
        next if $col_val eq "";              # user pressed Enter
        return if lc ($col_val) eq "exit";  # early exit
        $col_val = undef if lc ($col_val) eq "none";
        $entry_ref->{$col_name} = $col_val;
    }
    # show values, ask for confirmation before inserting
    show_member ($col_name_ref, $entry_ref);
    return unless prompt ("\nInsert this entry (y/n)? ") =~ /^y/i;

    # construct an INSERT query, then issue it.
    my $query = "INSERT INTO member";
    my $delim = " SET "; # put "SET" before first column, "," before others
    foreach my $col_name (@{$col_name_ref})
    {
        # only specify values for columns that were given one
        next if !defined ($entry_ref->{$col_name});
        # quote() quotes undef as the word NULL (without quotes),
        # which is what we want.  Columns that are NOT NULL will
        # be assigned their default values.
        $query .= sprintf ("%s %s=%s", $delim, $col_name,
                            $dbh->quote ($entry_ref->{$col_name}));
        $delim = ",";
    }
    $dbh->do ($query) or warn "Warning: new entry not created?\n"
}
```

edit_member.pl uses two routines to prompt the user for information.
prompt() asks a question and returns the answer:

```
sub prompt
{
my $str = shift;

    print STDERR $str;
    chomp ($str = <STDIN>);
    return ($str);
}
```

`col_prompt()` takes a column name argument. It prints the name as a prompt to solicit a new column value and returns the value entered by the user:

```perl
sub col_prompt
{
my ($col_name, $entry_ref) = @_;

    my $prompt = $col_name;
    if (defined ($entry_ref))
    {
        my $cur_val = $entry_ref->{$col_name};
        $cur_val = "NULL" if !defined ($cur_val);
        $prompt .= " [$cur_val]";
    }
    $prompt .= ": ";
    print STDERR $prompt;
    my $str = <STDIN>;
    chomp ($str);
    return ($str);
}
```

The second argument to `col_prompt()` is a reference to the hash that represents the member entry. For creating a new entry, this value will be `undef`, but when editing existing records, it will point to the current contents of the entry. In that case, `col_prompt()` includes the current value of the column that it's prompting for in the prompt string so that the user can see what it is. The user can accept the value simply by pressing Enter.

The code for editing an existing member is similar to that for creating a new member. However, we have an entry to work with, so the prompt routine displays the current entry values, and the `edit_member()` function issues an UPDATE statement rather than an INSERT:

```perl
sub edit_member
{
# references to array of column names and to entry hash
my ($col_name_ref, $entry_ref) = @_;

    # show initial values, ask for okay to go ahead and edit
    show_member ($col_name_ref, $entry_ref);
    return unless prompt ("\nEdit this entry (y/n)? ") =~ /^y/i;
    # prompt for new values; user types in new value, or Enter
    # to leave value unchanged, "none" to clear the value, or
    # "exit" to exit without changing the record.
    foreach my $col_name (@{$col_name_ref})
    {
        next if $col_name eq "member_id";   # skip key field
        my $col_val = col_prompt ($col_name, $entry_ref);
```

```
        next if $col_val eq "";                # user pressed Enter
        return if lc ($col_val) eq "exit";   # early exit
        $col_val = undef if lc ($col_val) eq "none";
        $entry_ref->{$col_name} = $col_val;
    }
    # show new values, ask for confirmation before updating
    show_member ($col_name_ref, $entry_ref);
    return unless prompt ("\nUpdate this entry (y/n)? ") =~ /^y/i;

    # construct an UPDATE query, then issue it.
    my $query = "UPDATE member";
    my $delim = " SET "; # put "SET" before first column, "," before others
    foreach my $col_name (@{$col_name_ref})
    {
        next if $col_name eq "member_id";   # skip key field
        # quote() quotes undef as the word NULL (without quotes),
        # which is what we want.  Columns that are NOT NULL will
        # be assigned their default values.
        $query .= sprintf ("%s %s=%s", $delim, $col_name,
                           $dbh->quote ($entry_ref->{$col_name}));
        $delim = ",";
    }
    $query .= " WHERE member_id = " . $dbh->quote ($entry_ref->{member_id});
    $dbh->do ($query) or warn "Warning: entry not undated?\n"
}
```

A problem with `edit_member.pl` is that it doesn't do any input value validation. For most fields in the `member` table, there isn't much to validate—they're
just string fields. But for the expiration column, input values really should be
checked to make sure they look like dates. In a general-purpose data entry
application, you'd probably want to extract information about a table to determine the types of all its columns. Then you could base validation constraints
on those types. That's more involved than I want to go into here, so I'm just
going to add a quick hack to the `col_prompt()` function to check the format
of the input if the column is `expiration`. A minimal date value check can be
done as follows:

```
sub col_prompt
{
my ($col_name, $entry_ref) = @_;

loop:
    my $prompt = $col_name;
    if (defined ($entry_ref))
    {
        my $cur_val = $entry_ref->{$col_name};
        $cur_val = "NULL" if !defined ($cur_val);
        $prompt .= " [$cur_val]";
    }
```

```
$prompt .= ": ";
print STDERR $prompt;
my $str = <STDIN>;
chomp ($str);
# perform rudimentary check on the expiration date
if ($str && $col_name eq "expiration")  # check expiration date format
{
    if ($str !~ /^\d+\D\d+\D\d+$/)
    {
        warn "$str is not a legal date, try again\n";
        goto loop;
    }
}
return ($str);
}
```

The pattern tests for three sequences of digits separated by non-digit characters. This is only a partial check because it doesn't detect values such as "1999-14-92" as being illegal. To make the script better, you could give it more stringent date checks or add other checks, such as requiring the first and last name fields to be given non-empty values.

An improvement might be to skip the update operation for an existing entry if the user made no changes. You could do this by saving the original values of the member entry columns and then writing the UPDATE statement to update only those columns that have changed. If there were none, the statement need not even be issued. Another improvement would be to notify the user if the record was already changed by someone else while the user was editing it. To do this, write the WHERE clause to include AND col_name = col_val for each original column value. This will cause the UPDATE to fail if someone else had changed the record, which provides feedback that two people are trying to change the entry at the same time.

There's another shortcoming of the edit_member.pl script that you might consider how to address: As written, the script opens a connection to the database before executing the prompt loop and doesn't close it until writing out the record after the loop. If the user takes a long time to enter or update the record, or just happens to do something else for a while, the connection can remain open for a long time. How would you modify edit_member.pl to hold the connection open only as long as necessary?

Finding Historical League Members with Common Interests

One of the duties of the Historical League secretary is to process requests from members who'd like a list of other members who share a particular interest within the field of U.S. history, such as the Great Depression or the life of

Abraham Lincoln. It's easy enough to find such members when the directory is maintained in a word processor document by using the word processor's Find function. However, producing a list consisting *only* of the qualifying member entries is more difficult because it involves a lot of copy and paste. With MySQL, the job becomes much easier because we can just run a query like the following:

```
SELECT * FROM member WHERE interests LIKE '%lincoln%'
ORDER BY last_name, first_name
```

Unfortunately, the results don't look very nice if we run this query from the mysql client. Let's put together a little DBI script, interests.pl, that produces better-looking output. The script first checks to make sure there is at least one argument named on the command line, because there is nothing to search for otherwise. Then, for each argument, the script runs a search on the interests column of the member table:

```
@ARGV or die "Usage: interests.pl keyword\n";
search_members (shift (@ARGV)) while @ARGV;
```

To search for the keyword string, we put '%' wildcard characters on each side and perform a pattern match so that the string can be found anywhere in the interests column. Then we print the matching entries:

```
sub search_members
{
my $interest = shift;

    print "Search results for keyword: $interest\n\n";
    my $sth = $dbh->prepare (qq{
            SELECT * FROM member WHERE interests LIKE ?
            ORDER BY last_name, first_name
        });
    # look for string anywhere in interest field
    $sth->execute ("%" . $interest . "%");
    my $count = 0;
    while (my $hash_ref = $sth->fetchrow_hashref ())
    {
        format_entry ($hash_ref);
        ++$count;
    }
    print "Number of matching entries: $count\n\n";
}
```

The format_entry() function turns an entry into its printable representation. I won't show it here because it's essentially the same as the format_rtf_entry() function from the gen_dir.pl script, with the RTF control words stripped out. Take a look at the interests.pl script in the sampdb distribution to see the implementation.

Putting the Historical League Directory Online

In the next section, "Using DBI in Web Applications," we'll start writing scripts that connect to the MySQL server to extract information and write that information in the form of Web pages that appear in a client's Web browser. Those scripts generate HTML dynamically according to what the client requested. Before we reach that point, let's begin thinking about HTML by writing a DBI script that generates a static HTML document that can be loaded into a Web server's document tree. A good candidate for this task is to produce the Historical League directory in HTML format (after all, one of our goals was to put the directory online).

A simple HTML document has a structure something like the following:

```
<html>                          ← beginning of document
<head>                          ← beginning of document head
<title>My Page Title</title>    ← title of document
</head>                         ← end of document head
<body bgcolor="white">          ← beginning of document body
                                   (white background)
<h1>My Level 1 Heading</h1>     ← a level 1 heading

... content of document body ...

</body>                         ← end of document body
</html>                         ← end of document
```

It's not necessary to write a completely new script to generate the directory in HTML format. Recall that when we wrote the `gen_dir.pl` script, we used an extensible framework so that we'd be able to plug in code for producing the directory in additional formats. Let's take advantage of that extensibility now by adding code for generating HTML output. To do this, we need to make the following modifications to `gen_dir.pl`:

- Write document initialization and cleanup functions.
- Write a function to format individual entries.
- Add a switchbox element that identifies the format name and associates it with the functions that produce output in that format.

The HTML document outline just shown breaks down pretty easily into prolog and epilog sections that can be handled by the initialization and cleanup functions, as well as a middle part that can be generated by the entry-formatting function. The HTML initialization function generates everything up through the level 1 heading, and the cleanup function generates the closing `</body>` and `</html>` tags:

```
sub html_init
{
    print "<html>\n";
```

```
        print "<head>\n";
        print "<title>U.S. Historical League Member Directory</title>\n";
        print "</head>\n";
        print "<body bgcolor=\"white\">\n";
        print "<h1>U.S. Historical League Member Directory</h1>\n";
    }

    sub html_cleanup
    {
        print "</body>\n";
        print "</html>\n";
    }
```

The real work, as usual, lies in formatting the entries. But even this isn't very difficult. We can copy the format_rtf_entry() function, make sure any special characters in the entry are encoded, and replace the RTF control words with HTML markup tags:

```
    sub format_html_entry
    {
    my $entry_ref = shift;

        # Convert <, >, ", and & to the corresponding HTML entities
        # (&lt;, &gt;, &quot, &amp;)
        foreach my $key (keys (%{$entry_ref}))
        {
            next unless defined ($entry_ref->{$key});
            $entry_ref->{$key} =~ s/&/&amp;/g;
            $entry_ref->{$key} =~ s/\"/&quot;/g;
            $entry_ref->{$key} =~ s/>/&gt;/g;
            $entry_ref->{$key} =~ s/</&lt;/g;
        }
        printf "<strong>Name: %s</strong><br />\n", format_name ($entry_ref);
        my $address = "";
        $address .= $entry_ref->{street}
                                if defined ($entry_ref->{street});
        $address .= ", " . $entry_ref->{city}
                                if defined ($entry_ref->{city});
        $address .= ", " . $entry_ref->{state}
                                if defined ($entry_ref->{state});
        $address .= " " . $entry_ref->{zip}
                                if defined ($entry_ref->{zip});
        print "Address: $address<br />\n"
                                if $address ne "";
        print "Telephone: $entry_ref->{phone}<br />\n"
                                if defined ($entry_ref->{phone});
        print "Email: $entry_ref->{email}<br />\n"
                                if defined ($entry_ref->{email});
        print "Interests: $entry_ref->{interests}<br />\n"
                                if defined ($entry_ref->{interests});
        print "<br />\n";
    }
```

The function produces output that looks like this:

```
<strong>Name: Mike Artel</strong><br />
Address: 4264 Lovering Rd., Miami, FL 12777<br />
Telephone: 075-961-0712<br />
Email: mike_artel@venus.org<br />
Interests: Civil Rights,Education,Revolutionary War<br />
<br />
```

The reason for using `<br />` rather than `<br>` is to write the document as valid XHTML, which is more strict than HTML. Some distinctions between HTML and XHTML are discussed briefly in the "Writing Web Output" section later in this chapter.

The last modification needed for gen_dir.pl is to add to the switchbox another element that points to the HTML-writing functions. The modified switchbox looks like the following, where the final element defines a format named html that points to the functions that produce the various parts of an HTML-format document:

```
# switchbox containing formatting functions for each output format
my %switchbox =
(
    "banquet" =>                           # functions for banquet list
    {
        "init"      => undef,              # no initialization needed
        "entry"     => \&format_banquet_entry,
        "cleanup"   => undef              # no cleanup needed
    },
    "rtf" =>                               # functions for RTF format
    {
        "init"      => \&rtf_init,
        "entry"     => \&format_rtf_entry,
        "cleanup"   => \&rtf_cleanup
    },
    "html" =>                              # functions for HTML format
    {
        "init"      => \&html_init,
        "entry"     => \&format_html_entry,
        "cleanup"   => \&html_cleanup
    }
);
```

To make the directory available in HTML format, run the following command and install the resulting output file in your Web server's document tree:

```
% ./gen_dir.pl html > directory.html
```

When you update the member table in the database, you can run the command again to update the online version. If you want to avoid running the command manually, another strategy is to set up a cron job that executes periodically to update the online directory automatically. Suppose that the `gen_dir.pl` script is installed in `/u/paul/bin` and the Historical League directory in the Web server document tree is `/usr/local/apache/htdocs/ushl`. Then I might use a `crontab` entry like the following to update the directory every morning at 4 a.m.:

```
0 4 * * * /u/paul/bin/gen_dir.pl > /usr/local/apache/htdocs/ushl/directory.html
```

Note: The user that this `cron` job runs as must have permission both to execute scripts that are located in my `bin` directory and to write files into the document tree directory.

Using DBI in Web Applications

The DBI scripts developed thus far have been designed for use from the shell in a command-line environment, but DBI is useful in other contexts as well, such as in the development of Web-based applications. When you write DBI scripts that can be invoked from a Web browser, you open up new and interesting possibilities for interacting with your databases. For example, if you display data in tabular form, you can easily turn each column heading into a link that you can select to re-sort the data on that column. This allows you to view your data in a different way with a single click, without entering any queries. Or you can provide a form into which a user can enter criteria for a database search, and then display a page containing the results of the search. Simple capabilities like this can dramatically alter the level of interactivity you provide for accessing the contents of your databases. In addition, Web browser display capabilities typically are better than what you get with a terminal window, so you can create nicer-looking output as well.

In this section, we'll create the following Web-based scripts:

- **A general browser for the tables in the `sampdb` database.** This isn't related to any specific task we want to accomplish with the database, but it illustrates several Web programming concepts and provides a convenient means of seeing what information the tables contain.

- **A score browser allowing us to see the scores for any given quiz or test.** This is handy as a quick means of reviewing grade event results for the grade-keeping project, and it's useful when we need to establish the grading curve for a test so we can mark papers with letter grades.

- **A script to find Historical League members who share a common interest.** This is done by allowing the user to enter a search phrase, and then searching the `interests` column of the `member` table for that phrase. We already wrote a command-line script, `interests.pl`, to do this in the earlier section "Finding Historical League Members with Common Interests." But the command-line version can be executed only by people on the machine where it is installed. Providing a Web-based version opens up the directory to anyone who has a Web browser. Having another version also provides an instructive point of reference, allowing comparison of multiple approaches to the same task. (Actually, we'll develop two Web-based implementations. One is based on pattern matching, just like `interests.pl`. The other performs FULLTEXT searches.)

To write these scripts, we'll use the CGI.pm Perl module, which provides an easy way to link DBI to the Web. (For instructions on getting the CGI.pm module, see Appendix A.) CGI.pm is so called because it helps you write scripts that use the Common Gateway Interface protocol that defines how a Web server communicates with other programs. CGI.pm handles the details involved in a number of common housekeeping tasks, such as collecting the values of parameters passed as input to your script by the Web server. CGI.pm also provides convenient methods for generating HTML output, which reduces the chance of writing out malformed HTML compared to writing raw HTML tags yourself.

You'll learn enough about CGI.pm in this chapter to write your own Web applications, but of course not all of its capabilities are covered. To learn more about this module, see *Official Guide to Programming with CGI.pm*, by Lincoln Stein (John Wiley, 1998), or check the online documentation at `http://stein.cshl.org/WWW/software/CGI/`.

Another text covering CGI.pm that's specifically targeted to MySQL and DBI is my book *MySQL and Perl for the Web* (New Riders, 2000).

The Web-based scripts described in the remainder of this chapter are found under the `perlapi/web` directory of the `sampdb` distribution.

Setting up Apache for CGI Scripts

In addition to DBI and CGI.pm, there's one more component we need for writing Web-based scripts—a Web server. The instructions here are geared toward using scripts with the Apache server, but you should be able to use a different server if you like by adapting the instructions a bit.

I will assume here that the various parts of your Apache installation are located under `/usr/local/apache` for UNIX and under `C:\Apache` for Windows.

For our purposes, the most important subdirectories of the Apache top–level directory are `htdocs` (for the HTML document tree), `cgi-bin` (for executable scripts and programs to be invoked by the Web server), and `conf` (for configuration files). These directories may be located somewhere else on your system. If so, make the appropriate adjustments to the following notes.

You should verify that the `cgi-bin` directory is not located within the Apache document tree. This is a safety precaution that prevents clients from requesting the source code for your scripts as plain text. You don't want malicious clients to be able to examine your scripts for security holes by siphoning off the text of the scripts and studying them.

To install a CGI script for use with Apache, copy it to your `cgi-bin` directory. Under UNIX, the script must begin with a `#!` line and have its mode set to be executable, just as for a command line script. In addition, it's a good idea to set the script to be owned by the user that Apache runs as and to be accessible only to that user. For example, if Apache runs as a user named `www`, use the following commands to make a script named `myscript.pl` owned by and executable and readable only by that user:

```
# chown www myscript.pl
# chmod 500 myscript.pl
```

You may need to run these commands as `root`. If you don't have permission to install scripts in the `cgi-bin` directory, ask your system administrator to do so on your behalf.

Under Windows, the `chown` and `chmod` commands are unnecessary, but the script should still begin with a `#!` line. The line can list the full pathname to your Perl program. For example, if Perl is installed as `C:\Perl\bin\perl.exe`, the `#!` line can be written as follows:

```
#! C:/Perl/bin/perl -w
```

Alternatively, on Windows NT-based systems, you can write the line more simply as follows if your `PATH` environment variable is set to include the directory in which Perl is installed:

```
#! perl -w
```

The Perl scripts in the `sampdb` distribution all specify the pathname of Perl on the `#!` line as `/usr/bin/perl`. You'll need to modify each script as necessary for your own system.

After a script has been installed in the `cgi-bin` directory, you can request it from your browser by sending the appropriate URL to your Web server. For

example, if the Web server host is `www.snake.net`, you would request
`myscript.pl` from it using a URL like the following:

```
http://www.snake.net/cgi-bin/myscript.pl
```

Requesting a script with your browser causes it to be executed by the Web
server. The script's output is sent back to you, and the result appears as a page
in your browser.

When you run DBI scripts from the command line, warnings and error messages go to your terminal. In a Web environment, there is no terminal, so these
messages go to the Apache error log. You should determine where this log is
located because it can provide useful information to help debug your scripts.
On my system, it's the `error_log` file in the `logs` directory under the Apache
root, `/usr/local/apache`. It may be somewhere else on your system. The
location of the log is determined by the `ErrorLog` directive in the
`httpd.conf` configuration file, which is located in Apache's `conf` directory.

A Brief Introduction to CGI.pm

To write a Perl script that uses the CGI.pm module, put a `use CGI` statement
near the beginning of the script that imports the module's function names.
The standard set of the most commonly used functions can be imported as
follows:

```
use CGI qw(:standard);
```

Then you can invoke CGI.pm functions to produce various kinds of HTML
structures. In general, the function names are the same as the corresponding
HTML elements. For example, to produce a level 1 header and a paragraph,
invoke `h1()` and `p()`:

```
print h1 ("This is a header");
print p ("This is a paragraph");
```

CGI.pm also supports an object-oriented style of use that allows you to invoke
its functions without importing the names. To do this, include a `use` statement
and create a CGI object:

```
use CGI;
my $cgi = new CGI;
```

The object gives you access to CGI.pm functions, which you invoke as methods of the object:

```
print $cgi->h1 ("This is a header");
print $cgi->p ("This is a paragraph");
```

The object-oriented interface requires that you write the `$cgi->` prefix all the time; in this book I'll use the simpler function call interface. However, one disadvantage of the function call interface is that if a CGI.pm function has the same name as a Perl built-in function, you must invoke it in a non-conflicting way. For example, CGI.pm has a function named `tr()` that produces the `<tr>` and `</tr>` tags that surround the cells in a row of an HTML table. That function's name conflicts with the name of Perl's built-in `tr` transliteration function. To work around this problem when using the CGI.pm function call interface, invoke `tr()` as `Tr()` or as `TR()`. When you use the object-oriented interface, this problem does not occur because you invoke `tr()` as a method of your `$cgi` object (that is, as `$cgi->tr()`), which makes it clear that you're not referring to the built-in function.

Checking for Web Input Parameters

One of the things CGI.pm does for you is to take care of all the ugly details involved in collecting input information provided by the Web server to your script. All you need to do to get that information is invoke the `param()` function. You can get the names of all available parameters as follows:

```
my @param = param ();
```

To retrieve the value of a particular parameter, pass its name to `param()`. If the parameter is set, `param()` will return its value, or `undef` if it isn't set:

```
my $my_param = param ("my_param");
if (defined ($my_param))
{
    print "my_param value: $my_param\n";
}
else
{
    print "my_param is not set\n";
}
```

Writing Web Output

Many of CGI.pm's functions are used for generating output to be sent to the client browser. Consider the following HTML document:

```
<html>
<head>
<title>My Simple Page</title>
</head>
<body bgcolor="white">
<h1>Page Heading</h1>
<p>Paragraph 1.</p>
<p>Paragraph 2.</p>
</body>
</html>
```

The following script uses CGI.pm output functions to produce the equivalent document:

```
#! /usr/bin/perl -w
# simple_doc.pl - produce simple HTML page

use strict;
use CGI qw(:standard);

print header ();
print start_html (-title => "My Simple Page", -bgcolor => "white");
print h1 ("Page Heading");
print p ("Paragraph 1.");
print p ("Paragraph 2.");
print end_html ();
```

The `header()` function generates a `Content-Type:` header that precedes the page content. It's necessary to write this header when producing Web pages from scripts to let the browser know what kind of document to expect. (This differs from the way you write static HTML pages, for which it's not necessary to produce a header; the Web server sends one to the browser automatically.) By default, `header()` writes a header that looks like this:

```
Content-Type: text/html
```

Following the `header()` invocation are calls to functions that generate the page content. `start_html()` produces the tags from the opening `<html>` tag through the opening `<body>` tag, `h1()` and `p()` write the heading and paragraph elements, and `end_html()` adds the closing document tags.

As illustrated by the `start_html()` call, many CGI.pm functions allow you to specify named parameters, with each parameter given in *-name=>value* format. This is advantageous for functions that take many parameters that are optional, because you can specify just those parameters you need, and you can list them in any order.

Use of CGI.pm output-generating functions doesn't preclude you from writing out raw HTML yourself if you want. You can mix the two approaches, combining calls to CGI.pm functions with print statements that generate literal tags. However, one of the advantages of using CGI.pm to generate output instead of writing HTML yourself is that you can think in logical units rather than in terms of individual markup tags, and your HTML is less likely to contain errors. (The reason I say "less likely" is that CGI.pm won't prevent you from doing bizarre things, such as including a list inside of a heading.)

CGI.pm also provides some portability advantages that you don't get by writing your own HTML. For example, as of version 2.69, CGI.pm automatically writes

XHTML output. If you're using an older version of CGI.pm that writes plain HTML, you can upgrade your scripts to start writing XHTML instead; all you need to do is update CGI.pm itself.

XHTML is similar to HTML but has a more well-defined format. HTML is easy to learn and use, but one of its problems is that browser implementations tend to differ in how they interpret HTML. For example, they are forgiving of malformed HTML in different ways. This means that a not–quite–correct page may display properly in one browser but incorrectly in another. XHTML's requirements are stricter, to help ensure that documents are well formed. Some of the differences between HTML and XHTML are as follows:

- Unlike HTML, every opening tag in XHTML must have a closing tag. For example, paragraphs are written using `<p>` and `</p>` tags, but the closing `</p>` tag often is omitted in HTML documents. In XHTML, the `</p>` tag is required. For HTML tags that don't have any body, such as `<br>` and `<hr>`, the XHTML requirement that all tags be closed leads to ungainly constructs like `<br></br>` and `<hr></hr>`. To deal with this, XHTML allows single-tag shortcut forms (`<br/>`, `<hr/>`) that serve for both the opening and closing tags. However, older browsers that see tags like these will sometimes mistake the tag names as `br/` and `hr/`. Inserting a space before the slash and writing the tags as `<br />` and `<hr />` helps to minimize the occurrence of such problems.

- In HTML, tag and attribute names are not case sensitive. For example, `<tr>` and `<TR>` are the same. In XHTML, tag and attribute names should be lowercase, so only `<tr>` is allowable.

- HTML attribute values can be unquoted or even missing. For example, the following table data cell construct is legal in HTML:

    ```
    <td width=40 nowrap>Some text</td>
    ```

    In XHTML, attributes must have values, and they must be quoted. A common convention for HTML attributes that normally are used without a value is to use the attribute name as its value. The XHTML equivalent of the preceding `<tr>` element looks like the following:

    ```
    <td width="40" nowrap="nowrap">Some text</td>
    ```

All the Web scripts in this book generate output that conforms to XHTML rules. In this chapter, we'll rely on CGI.pm to generate properly-formatted XHTML markup. The scripts discussed in Chapter 8 will generate the markup tags for themselves, because PHP doesn't provide tag-generating functions the way CGI.pm does.

Escaping HTML and URL Text

If text that you write to a Web page may contain special characters, you should make sure they are escaped properly by processing the text with escapeHTML(). This is also true when you construct URLs that may contain special characters, although in that case you should use the escape() function instead. It's important to use the appropriate encoding function because each one treats different sets of characters as special and encodes special characters using formats that differ from one another. Consider the following short Perl script, escape_demo.pl:

```
#! /usr/bin/perl -w
# escape_demo.pl - demonstrate CGI.pm output-encoding functions

use CGI qw(escapeHTML escape);  # import escapeHTML() and escape()

$s = "x<=y, right?";
print escapeHTML ($s) . "\n";   # encode for use as HTML text
print escape ($s) . "\n";       # encode for use in a URL
```

The script encodes the string $s using each function and prints the result. When you run it, the script produces the following output, from which you can see that encoding conventions for HTML text are not the same as encoding for URLs:

```
x&lt;=y, right?
x%3C%3Dy%2C%20right%3F
```

The escape_demo.pl script imports the names of the encoding functions in the use CGI statement. They are not included in the standard set of functions, so you'll need to import them even if you also import the standard set, like this:

```
use CGI qw (:standard escapeHTML escape);
```

Writing Multiple-Purpose Pages

One of the primary reasons to write Web-based scripts that generate HTML instead of writing static HTML documents is that a script can produce different kinds of pages depending on the way it's invoked. All of the CGI scripts we're going to write have that property. Each one operates as follows:

- When you first request the script from your browser, it generates an initial page that allows you to select what kind of information you want.
- When you make a selection, your browser sends a request back to the Web server that causes the script to be re-invoked. The script then retrieves and displays in a second page the specific information you requested.

The primary problem here is that you want the selection that you make from the first page to determine the contents of the second page, but Web pages normally are independent of one another unless you make some sort of special arrangements. The solution is to have the script generate pages that set a parameter to a value that tells the next invocation of the script what you want. When you first invoke the script, the parameter will have no value; this tells the script to present its initial page. When you indicate what information you'd like to see, the script is invoked again, but this time the parameter will be set to a value that instructs the script what to do.

There are different ways for Web pages to pass instructions to a script. One way is for the page to include a form that the user fills in. When the user submits the form, its contents are submitted to the Web server. The server passes the information along to the script, which can find out what was submitted by invoking the `param()` function. This is what we'll do to implement keyword searches of the Historical League directory: The search page includes a form into which the user enters the word to search for.

Another way of specifying instructions for a script is to add parameter values to the end of the URL that you send to the Web server when you request the script. This is the approach we'll use for our `sampdb` table browser and score browser scripts. The way this works is that the script generates a page containing hyperlinks. When you select a link, it invokes the script again, but the link includes a parameter value that instructs the script what to do. In effect, the script invokes itself in different ways to provide different kinds of results, depending on which link you select.

A script can allow itself to be invoked by sending to the browser a page containing a self-referential hyperlink—that is, a link to its own URL. For example, if a script `myscript.pl` is installed in the Web server's `cgi-bin` directory, it can produce a page that contains the following link:

```
<a href="/cgi-bin/myscript.pl">Click Me!</a>
```

When the user clicks the text `Click Me!` in the page, the user's browser sends a request for `myscript.pl` back to the Web server. Of course, in and of itself, all that will do is cause the script to send out the same page again because no other information is supplied in the URL. However, if you add a parameter to it, that parameter is sent back to the Web server when the user selects the link. The server invokes the script and the script can call `param()` to detect that the parameter was set and take action according to its value.

To attach a parameter to the end of the URL, add a '?' character followed by a
name=value pair indicating the parameter name and its value. For example, to
add a `size` parameter with a value of `large`, write the URL as follows:

```
/cgi-bin/myscript.pl?size=large
```

To attach multiple parameters, separate them by ';' characters:[1]

```
/cgi-bin/myscript.pl?size=large;color=blue
```

To construct a self-referencing URL with attached parameters, a script should
begin by calling the `url()` function to obtain its own URL, and then append
parameters to it as follows:

```
$url = url ();          # get URL for script
$url .= "?size=large";  # add first parameter
$url .= ";color=blue";  # add second parameter
```

Using `url()` to get the script path allows you to avoid hardwiring the path
into the code.

To generate a hyperlink, pass the URL to CGI.pm's `a()` function:

```
print a ({-href => $url}, "Click Me!");
```

The `print` statement produces a hyperlink that looks like the following:

```
<a href="/cgi-bin/url.pl?size=large;color=blue">Click Me!</a>
```

The preceding example constructs the value of `$url` in somewhat cavalier
fashion, because it doesn't take into account the possibility that the parameter
values or the link label might contain special characters. Unless you're certain
that the values and the label don't require any encoding, it's best to use the
CGI.pm encoding functions. The `escape()` function encodes values to be
appended to a URL, and `escapeHTML()` encodes regular HTML text. For
example, if the value of the hyperlink label is stored in `$label`, and the values
for the `size` and `color` parameters are stored in the variables `$size` and
`$color`, you can perform the proper encoding as follows:

```
$url = sprintf ("%s?size=%s;color=%s",
                url (), escape ($size), escape ($color));
print a ({-href => $url}, escapeHTML ($label));
```

To see how self-referential URL construction works in the context of an
application, consider the following short CGI script, `flip_flop.pl`. When
first invoked, it presents a page called Page A that contains a single hyperlink.
Selecting the link invokes the script again, but the link also includes a `pageb`
parameter to tell `flip_flop.pl` to display Page B. (In this case, we don't care

---

1. CGI.pm also understands '&' as a parameter separator character. Other language APIs for
Web programming vary in their conventions, so you'll need to know whether they expect ';'
or '&' and construct URLs accordingly.

about the parameter's value, just whether or not it's set.) Page B will also contain a link to the script, but without a `pageb` parameter. This means that selecting the link in Page B causes the original page to be redisplayed. In other words, subsequent invocations of the script flip the page back and forth between Page A and Page B:

```perl
#! /usr/bin/perl -w
# flip_flop.pl - simple multiple-output-page CGI.pm script

use CGI qw(:standard);

my $url;

# determine which page to display based on absence or presence
# of the pageb parameter

if (!defined (param ("pageb"))) # display page A w/link to page B
{
    $this_page = "A";
    $next_page = "B";
    $url = url () . "?pageb=1";
}
else                           # display page B w/link to page A
{
    $this_page = "B";
    $next_page = "A";
    $url = url ();
}

print header ();
print start_html (-title => "Flip-Flop: Page $this_page",
                  -bgcolor => "white");
print p ("This is Page $this_page. To select Page $next_page, "
       . a ({-href => $url}, "click here"));
print end_html ();
```

Install the script in your `cgi-bin` directory, and then request it from your browser using the appropriate URL:

```
http://www.snake.net/cgi-bin/flip_flop.pl
```

Select the link in the page several times to see how the script alternates the pages that it generates.

Now, suppose another client comes along and starts requesting `flip_flop.pl`. What happens? Will the two of you interfere with each other? No, because the initial request from each of you will include no `pageb` parameter, and the script will respond with its initial page. Thereafter, the requests sent by each of you will include or omit the parameter according to which page you currently happen to be viewing. flip_flop.pl generates an alternating series of pages properly for each client, independent of the actions of any other client.

Connecting to the MySQL Server from Web Scripts

The command-line scripts developed in the earlier section "Putting DBI to Work" shared a common preamble for establishing a connection to the MySQL server. Most of our CGI scripts will share some code, too, but it's a little different:

```perl
#! /usr/bin/perl -w
use strict;
use DBI;
use CGI qw(:standard);

use Cwd;
# option file that should contain connection parameters for UNIX
my $option_file = "/usr/local/apache/conf/sampdb.cnf";
my $option_drive_root;
# override file values for Windows
if ($^O =~ /^MSWin/i || $^O =~ /^dos/)
{
    $option_drive_root = "C:/";
    $option_file = "/Apache/conf/sampdb.cnf";
}
# construct data source and connect to server (under Windows, save
# current working directory first, change location to option file
# drive, connect, then restore current directory)
my $orig_dir;
if (defined ($option_drive_root))
{
    $orig_dir = cwd ();
    chdir ($option_drive_root)
        or die "Cannot chdir to $option_drive_root: $!\n";
}
my $dsn = "DBI:mysql:sampdb;mysql_read_default_file=$option_file";
my $dbh = DBI->connect ($dsn, undef, undef,
                        { RaiseError => 1, PrintError => 0 });
if (defined ($option_drive_root))
{
    chdir ($orig_dir)
        or die "Cannot chdir to $orig_dir: $!\n";
}
```

This preamble differs from the one we used for command-line scripts in the following respects:

- The first section now contains use CGI and use Cwd statements. The first is for the CGI.pm module. The second is for the module that returns the pathname of the current working directory; it's used in case the script is running under Windows, as described shortly.

- No connection parameters are parsed from the command-line arguments. Instead, the code assumes they'll be listed in an option file.

- Instead of using mysql_read_default_group to read the standard option files, we use mysql_read_default_file to read a single file intended specifically for options to be used by Web scripts that access the sampdb database. As shown, the code looks for options stored in /usr/local/apache/conf/sampdb.cnf under UNIX or in C:\Apache\conf\sampdb.cnf under Windows. Note that under Windows the code changes location to the root directory of the drive where the option file is located before connecting and back to the original directory afterward. The rationale for this ugly hack is described in the "Specifying Connection Parameters" section earlier in this chapter.

The sampdb distribution contains a sampdb.cnf file that you can install for use by your DBI-based Web scripts. It looks like this:

```
[client]
host=cobra.snake.net
user=sampadm
password=secret
```

To use the Web-based scripts developed in this chapter on your own system, you should change the option filename in the preamble if you use a different name. You should also list in the option file those values that reflect the MySQL server host and the MySQL account name and password you want to use.

Under UNIX, you should set the option file to be owned by the account used to run Apache and set the file's mode to 400 or 600 so that no other user can read it. This keeps other users who have login accounts on the Web server host from reading the option file directly and prevents one form of security exploit.

Unfortunately, the option file can still be read by other users who can install a script for the Web server to execute. Scripts invoked by the Web server execute with the privileges of the account used for running the Web server. This means that another user who can install a Web script can write the script so that it opens the option file and displays its contents in a Web page. Because that script runs as the Web server user, it will have full permission to read the file, which exposes the connection parameters necessary to connect to MySQL and access the sampdb database. If you don't trust the other users on your machine, you may find it prudent to create a MySQL account that has read-only (SELECT) privileges on the sampdb database, and then list that account's name and password in the sampdb.cnf file, rather than your own name and password. That way you don't risk allowing scripts to connect to your database through a MySQL account that has permission to modify its tables. Chapter 11, "General MySQL Administration," discusses how to create a MySQL user account with restricted privileges. The downside of this strategy is that with a read-only MySQL account, you can write scripts only for data retrieval, not for data entry.

Alternatively, you can arrange to execute scripts under Apache's suEXEC mechanism. This allows you to execute a script as a specific trusted user, and then write the script to get the connection parameters from an option file that is readable only to that user. Another approach is available with Apache 2.x, which makes it possible to arrange for scripts located in particular directories to run with the privileges of a specific user—such as yourself. Then you can set the ownership and mode of sampdb.cnf and your scripts to be accessible only to you; other users won't be able to get at them.

Still another option for writing a script is to have it solicit a username and password from the client user, and then use those values to establish a connection to the MySQL server. This is more suitable for scripts that you create for administrative purposes than for scripts that you provide for general use. In any case, you should be aware that some methods of name and password solicitation are subject to attack by anyone who can put a sniffer on the network between the Web server and your browser, so you may want to set up a secure connection. That is beyond the scope of this book.

As you may gather from the preceding paragraphs, Web script security can be a tricky thing. It's definitely a topic about which you should read more for yourself, because it's a big subject that I really cannot do justice to here. The book *MySQL and Perl for the Web* mentioned earlier includes a chapter devoted specifically to Web security, including instructions for setting up secure connections using SSL. Other good sources of information are the security material in the Apache manual, and the WWW security FAQ available at http://www.w3.org/Security/Faq/.

A Web–Based Database Browser

Our first Web-based application is a simple script, db_browse.pl, that allows you to see what tables exist in the sampdb database and to examine the contents of any of these tables interactively from your Web browser. The script works like this:

- When you first request db_browse.pl from your browser, it connects to the MySQL server, retrieves a list of tables in the sampdb database, and sends your browser a page in which each table is presented as a hyperlink. When you select a table name link from this page, your browser sends a request to the Web server asking db_browse.pl to display the contents of that table.

- If db_browse.pl finds when it's invoked that you've selected a table name, it retrieves the contents of the table and presents the information to your Web browser. The heading for each column of data is the name of the column in the table. Headings are presented as hyperlinks; if you select one of them, your browser sends a request to the Web server to redisplay the same table, but this time sorted by the column you selected.

Before we go any further, you should be aware that although db_browse.pl is instructive in terms of illustrating several useful Web programming concepts, it also represents a security hole that can be exploited by unfriendly visitors to your site. The script is easily fooled into displaying any table that is accessible to the MySQL account named in the sampdb.cnf file. I'll describe how you can trick the script later, but for now what you should know is that you should install this script only if that account can access non-sensitive data. And it's a good idea to remove the script from your cgi-bin directory after you've tried it and understand how it works. (Alternatively, install it on a private server that is not accessible to untrusted users.) Here's a specific example of why db_browse.pl can be a problem. In Chapter 8, we'll write a script that Historical League members can use to edit their membership entries over the Web. Access to the entries is controlled through passwords that are stored in a member_pass table. Having db_browse.pl enabled at that point would allow anyone to look through the password table, and thus gain access to the information necessary to edit any member table entry.

Okay, assuming that you haven't been spooked by the preceding dire warnings, let's see how db_browse.pl works. The main body of the script puts out the initial part of the Web page and then checks the tbl_name parameter to see whether or not it's supposed to display some particular table:

```perl
#! /usr/bin/perl -w
# db_browse.pl - Allow sampdb database browsing over the Web

use strict;
use DBI;
use CGI qw (:standard escapeHTML escape);

# ... set up connection to database (not shown) ...

my $db_name = "sampdb";

# put out initial part of page
my $title = "$db_name Database Browser";
print header ();
print start_html (-title => $title, -bgcolor => "white");
print h1 ($title);

# parameters to look for in URL
my $tbl_name = param ("tbl_name");
my $sort_col = param ("sort_col");

# If $tbl_name has no value, display a clickable list of tables.
# Otherwise, display contents of the given table.  $sort_col, if
# set, indicates which column to sort by.

if (!defined ($tbl_name))
{
    display_table_names ($dbh, $db_name)
}
else
{
    display_table_contents ($dbh, $tbl_name, $sort_col);
}

print end_html ();
```

It's easy to find out what value a parameter has because CGI.pm does all the work of finding out what information the Web server passes to the script. We need only call param() with the name of the parameter in which we're interested. In the main body of db_browse.pl, that parameter is tbl_name. If it's not set, this is the initial invocation of the script and it displays the table list. Otherwise, it displays the contents of the table named by the tbl_name parameter, sorted by the column named in the sort_col parameter.

The `display_table_names()` function generates the initial page.
`display_table_names()` retrieves the table list and writes out a bullet list in
which each item is the name of a table in the sampdb database:

```
sub display_table_names
{
my ($dbh, $db_name) = @_;

    print p ("Select a table by clicking on its name:");

    # retrieve reference to single-column array of table names
    my $ary_ref = $dbh->selectcol_arrayref (qq{ SHOW TABLES FROM $db_name });

    # Construct a bullet list using the ul() (unordered list) and
    # li() (list item) functions.  Each item is a hyperlink that
    # re-invokes the script to display a particular table.
    my @item;
    foreach my $tbl_name (@{$ary_ref})
    {
        my $url = sprintf ("%s?tbl_name=%s", url (), escape ($tbl_name));
        my $link = a ({-href => $url}, escapeHTML ($tbl_name));
        push (@item, li ($link));
    }
    print ul (@item);
}
```

The `li()` function adds `<li>` and `</li>` tags around each list item and `ul()`
adds the `<ul>` and `</ul>` tags around the set of items. Each table name in the
list is presented as a hyperlink that reinvokes the script to display the contents
of the named table. The resulting list generated by `display_table_names()`
looks like this:

```
<ul>
<li><a href="/cgi-
bin/localhost/db_browse.pl?tbl_name=absence">absence</a></li>
<li><a href="/cgi-bin/localhost/db_browse.pl?tbl_name=event">event</a></li>
<li><a href="/cgi-bin/localhost/db_browse.pl?tbl_name=member">member</a></li>
...
</ul>
```

If the `tbl_name` parameter has a value when `db_browse.pl` is invoked, the
script passes that value to `display_table_contents()`, along with the name
of the column to sort the results by:

```
sub display_table_contents
{
my ($dbh, $tbl_name, $sort_col) = @_;
my @rows;
my @cells;
```

```perl
# if sort column not specified, use first column
$sort_col = "1" if !defined ($sort_col);

# present a link that returns user to table list page
print p (a ({-href => url ()}, "Show Table List"));

print p (strong ("Contents of $tbl_name table:"));

my $sth = $dbh->prepare (qq{
            SELECT * FROM $tbl_name ORDER BY $sort_col
            LIMIT 200
        });
$sth->execute ();

# Use the names of the columns in the database table as the
# headings in an HTML table.  Make each name a hyperlink that
# causes the script to be reinvoked to redisplay the table,
# sorted by the named column.

foreach my $col_name (@{$sth->{NAME}})
{
    my $url = sprintf ("%s?tbl_name=%s;sort_col=%s",
                        url (),
                        escape ($tbl_name),
                        escape ($col_name));
    my $link = a ({-href => $url}, escapeHTML ($col_name));
    push (@cells, th ($link));
}
push (@rows, Tr (@cells));

# display table rows
while (my @ary = $sth->fetchrow_array ())
{
    @cells = ();
    foreach my $val (@ary)
    {
        # display value if non-empty, else display non-breaking space
        if (defined ($val) && $val ne "")
        {
            $val = escapeHTML ($val);
        }
        else
        {
            $val = " ";
        }
        push (@cells, td ($val));
    }
    push (@rows, Tr (@cells));
}

# display table with a border
print table ({-border => "1"}, @rows);
}
```

If no column was named, `display_table_contents()` adds an ORDER BY 1 clause to the query to sort the results using the first column in the table. The query also includes a LIMIT 200 clause as a simple precaution against the script sending huge amounts of data to your browser. (That's not likely to happen for the tables in the `sampdb` database, but it might occur if you adapt the script to display the contents of tables in other databases.) `display_table_contents()` shows the rows from the table as an HTML table, using the `th()` and `td()` functions to produce table header and data cells, `Tr()` to group cells into rows, and `table()` to produce the `<table>` tags that surround the rows.

The HTML table presents column headings as hyperlinks that redisplay the database table; these links include a `sort_col` parameter that explicitly specifies the column to sort on. For example, for a page that displays the contents of the `event` table, the column heading links look like the following:

```
<a href="/cgi-bin/db_browse.pl?tbl_name=event&sort_col=date">date</a>
<a href="/cgi-bin/db_browse.pl?tbl_name=event&sort_col=type">type</a>
<a href="/cgi-bin/db_browse.pl?tbl_name=event&sort_col=event_id">event_id</a>
```

`display_table_contents()` uses a little trick of turning empty values into a non-breaking space (` `). In a bordered table, some browsers won't display borders for empty cells properly; putting a non-breaking space in the cell fixes that problem.

If you want to write a more general script, you could alter `db_browse.pl` to browse multiple databases. For example, you could have the script begin by displaying a list of databases on the server, rather than a list of tables within a particular database. Then you could pick a database to get a list of its tables and go from there.

Near the beginning of this section, I mentioned that the `db_browse.pl` script is easily fooled into displaying any table that is accessible to the `sampadm` account through which the script connects to the MySQL server. Suppose that account can access not only the `sampdb` database but also a database named `hr` that contains human resources information for a company, such as employment records. This can lead to a security breach. `db_browse.pl` does its work by constructing URLs containing the names of tables that are assumed to be in the `sampdb` database, but there's nothing to stop anyone from directly sending a request using a similar URL that names a table in the `hr` database:

```
http://www.snake.net/cgi-bin/db_browse.pl?tbl_name=hr.employee
```

In this case, the script will connect to MySQL and make `sampdb` the default database, but the SELECT statement that it constructs will refer explicitly to a table in the `hr` database:

```
SELECT * FROM hr.employee ORDER BY 1
```

The result is that the `db_browse.pl` script presents the contents of a sensitive table to anyone who can reach your Web server.

A Grade-Keeping Project Score Browser

Our next Web script, `score_browse.pl`, is designed to display scores that have been recorded for the grade-keeping project. Strictly speaking, we should have a way of entering the scores before we create a way of retrieving them. I'm saving the score entry script until the next chapter. In the meantime, we do have several sets of scores in the database already from the early part of the grading period. We can use the script to display those scores, even in the absence of a convenient score entry method. The script displays an ordered list of scores for any test or quiz, which is useful for determining the grading curve and assigning letter grades.

`score_browse.pl` has some similarities to `db_browse.pl` (both serve as information browsers), but is intended for the more specific purpose of looking at scores for a given quiz or test. The initial page presents a list of the possible grade events from which to choose and allows the user to select any of them to see the scores associated with the event. Scores for a given event are sorted by score with the highest scores first, so you can use the result to determine the grading curve.

The `score_browse.pl` script needs to examine only one parameter, `event_id`, to see whether or not a grade event was specified. If not, `score_browse.pl` displays the rows of the `event` table so that the user can select one. Otherwise, it displays the scores associated with the chosen event:

```
# ... set up connection to database (not shown) ...

# put out initial part of page
my $title = "Grade-Keeping Project -- Score Browser";
print header ();
print start_html (-title => $title, -bgcolor => "white");
print h1 ($title);

# parameter that tells us which event to display scores for
my $event_id = param ("event_id");
```

```
# if $event_id has no value, display the event list.
# otherwise display the scores for the given event.
if (!defined ($event_id))
{
    display_events ($dbh)
}
else
{
    display_scores ($dbh, $event_id);
}

print end_html ();
```

The `display_events()` function pulls out information from the `event` table and displays it in tabular form, using column names from the query for the table column headings. Within each row, the `event_id` value is displayed as a hyperlink that can be selected to trigger a query that retrieves the scores for the event. The URL for each event is simply the path to `score_browse.pl` with a parameter attached that specifies the event number:

```
/cgi-bin/score_browse.pl?event_id=n
```

`display_events()` is implemented as follows:

```
sub display_events
{
my $dbh = shift;
my @rows;
my @cells;

    print p ("Select an event by clicking on its number:");

    # get list of events
    my $sth = $dbh->prepare (qq{
        SELECT event_id, date, type
        FROM event
        ORDER BY event_id
    });
    $sth->execute ();

    # use column names for table column headings
    for (my $i = 0; $i < $sth->{NUM_OF_FIELDS}; $i++)
    {
        push (@cells, th (escapeHTML ($sth->{NAME}->[$i])));
    }
    push (@rows, Tr (@cells));

    # display information for each event as a row in a table
    while (my ($event_id, $date, $type) = $sth->fetchrow_array ())
    {
        @cells = ();
```

```
                # display event ID as a hyperlink that reinvokes the script
                # to show the event's scores
                my $url = sprintf ("%s?event_id=%s", url (), escape ($event_id));
                my $link = a ({-href => $url}, escapeHTML ($event_id));
                push (@cells, td ($link));
                # display event date and type
                push (@cells, td (escapeHTML ($date)));
                push (@cells, td (escapeHTML ($type)));
                push (@rows, Tr (@cells));
        }

        # display table with a border
        print table ({-border => "1"}, @rows);
    }
```

When the user selects an event, the browser sends a request for
score_browse.pl that has an event ID at the end. score_browse.pl finds
the event_id parameter set and calls the display_scores() function to list
all the scores for the specified event. This function also displays the text "Show
Event List" as a hyperlink back to the initial page so that the user can easily
return to the event list page and select a different event.
display_scores() looks like the following:

```
sub display_scores
{
my ($dbh, $event_id) = @_;
my @rows;
my @cells;

        # Generate a link to the script that does not include any event_id
        # parameter.  If the user selects this link, the script will display
        # the event list.
        print p (a ({-href => url ()}, "Show Event List"));

        # select scores for the given event
        my $sth = $dbh->prepare (qq{
            SELECT
                student.name, event.date, score.score, event.type
            FROM
                student, score, event
            WHERE
                student.student_id = score.student_id
                AND score.event_id = event.event_id
                AND event.event_id = ?
            ORDER BY
                event.date ASC, event.type ASC, score.score DESC
        });
        $sth->execute ($event_id);  # bind event ID to placeholder in query

        print p (strong ("Scores for event $event_id"));
```

```perl
    # use column names for table column headings
    for (my $i = 0; $i < $sth->{NUM_OF_FIELDS}; $i++)
    {
        push (@cells, th (escapeHTML ($sth->{NAME}->[$i])));
    }
    push (@rows, Tr (@cells));

    while (my @ary = $sth->fetchrow_array ())
    {
        @cells = ();
        foreach my $val (@ary)
        {
            # display value if non-empty, else display non-breaking space
            if (defined ($val) && $val ne "")
            {
                $val = escapeHTML ($val);
            }
            else
            {
                $val = " ";
            }
            push (@cells, td ($val));
        }
        push (@rows, Tr (@cells));
    }

    # display table with a border
    print table ({-border => "1"}, @rows);
}
```

The query that `display_scores()` runs is quite similar to one that we developed way back in Chapter 1 in the "Retrieving Information From Multiple Tables" section that describes how to write joins. In that chapter, we asked for scores for a given date because dates are more meaningful than event ID values. In contrast, when we use `score_browse.pl`, we know the exact event ID. That's not because we think in terms of event IDs (we don't) but because the script presents a list of them from which to choose, along with their dates and types. You can see that this type of interface reduces the need to know particular details. You don't need to know an event ID; it's necessary only to be able to recognize the date of the event you want and the script will provide the ID for you.

Historical League Common-Interest Searching

The `db_browse.pl` and `score_browse.pl` scripts allow the user to make a selection from a list of choices in an initial page where the choices are presented as hyperlinks that re-invoke the script with particular parameter values. Another way to allow users to provide information is to present a form that the user fills in. This is more appropriate when the range of possible choices isn't constrained to some easily determined set of values. Our next script demonstrates this method of soliciting user input.

In the earlier section "Putting DBI to Work," we constructed a command-line script, `interests.pl`, for finding Historical League members who share a particular interest. However, that script isn't something that League members have access to; the League secretary must run the script from the command prompt and then mail the result to the member who requested the list. It'd be nice to make this search capability more widely available so that members could use it themselves. Writing a Web-based script is one way to do that. The rest of this section discusses two approaches to table searching. The first is based on pattern matching, and the second uses MySQL `FULLTEXT` search capabilities.

Performing Searches Using Pattern Matching

The first search script, `ushl_browse.pl`, displays a form into which the user can enter a keyword. When the user submits the form, the script is re-invoked to search the `member` table for qualifying members and display the results. The search is done by adding the '`%`' wildcard character to both ends of the keyword and performing a `LIKE` pattern match, which finds records that have the keyword anywhere in the `interests` column value.

The main part of the script displays the keyword form. It also checks to see if a keyword was just submitted and, if so, performs a search:

```
my $title = "U.S. Historical League Interest Search";
print header ();
print start_html (-title => $title, -bgcolor => "white");
print h1 ($title);

# parameter to look for
my $keyword = param ("keyword");

# Display a keyword entry form.  In addition, if $keyword is defined,
# search for and display a list of members who have that interest.

print start_form (-method => "POST");
print p ("Enter a keyword to search for:");
print textfield (-name => "keyword", -value => "", -size => 40);
print submit (-name => "button", -value => "Search");
print end_form ();

# connect to server and run a search if a keyword was specified
if (defined ($keyword) && $keyword !~ /^\s*$/)
{
    # ... set up connection to database (not shown) ...
    search_members ($dbh, $keyword);
    # ... disconnect (not shown) ...
}
```

The script communicates information to itself a little differently than db_browse.pl or score_browse.pl. The keyword parameter is not added to the end of a URL. Instead, the information in the form is encoded by the browser and sent as part of a POST request. However, CGI.pm makes it irrelevant how the information is sent because param() returns the parameter value no matter how it was sent—just one more thing that CGI.pm does to make Web programming easier.

Keyword searches are performed by the search_members() function. It takes a database handle and the keyword as arguments, and then runs the search query and displays the list of matching member records:

```
sub search_members
{
my ($dbh, $interest) = @_;

    print p ("Search results for keyword: " . escapeHTML ($interest));
    my $sth = $dbh->prepare (qq{
            SELECT * FROM member WHERE interests LIKE ?
            ORDER BY last_name, first_name
        });
    # look for string anywhere in interest field
    $sth->execute ("%" . $interest . "%");
    my $count = 0;
    while (my $ref = $sth->fetchrow_hashref ())
    {
        format_html_entry ($ref);
        ++$count;
    }
    print p ("Number of matching entries: $count");
}
```

When you run the ush1_browse.pl script, you'll notice that each time you submit a keyword value, it's redisplayed in the form on the next page. This happens even though the script specifies an empty string as the value of the keyword field when it generates the form. The reason is that CGI.pm automatically fills in form fields with values from the script execution environment if they are present. If you want to defeat this behavior and make the field blank every time, include an override parameter in the textfield() call:

```
print textfield (-name => "keyword",
                        -value => "",
                        -override => 1,
                        -size => 40);
```

search_members() uses a helper function format_html_entry() to display individual entries. That function is much like the one of the same name that we wrote earlier for the `gen_dir.pl` script. (See the "Generating the Historical League Directory" section earlier in this chapter.) However, whereas the earlier version of the function generated HTML by printing markup tags directly, the version used by `ushl_browse.pl` uses CGI.pm functions to produce the tags:

```
sub format_html_entry
{
my $entry_ref = shift;

    # encode characters that are special in HTML
    foreach my $key (keys (%{$entry_ref}))
    {
        next unless defined ($entry_ref->{$key});
        $entry_ref->{$key} = escapeHTML ($entry_ref->{$key});
    }
    print strong ("Name: " . format_name ($entry_ref)) . br ();
    my $address = "";
    $address .= $entry_ref->{street}
                            if defined ($entry_ref->{street});
    $address .= ", " . $entry_ref->{city}
                            if defined ($entry_ref->{city});
    $address .= ", " . $entry_ref->{state}
                            if defined ($entry_ref->{state});
    $address .= " " . $entry_ref->{zip}
                            if defined ($entry_ref->{zip});
    print "Address: $address" . br ()
                            if $address ne "";
    print "Telephone: $entry_ref->{phone}" . br ()
                            if defined ($entry_ref->{phone});
    print "Email: $entry_ref->{email}" . br ()
                            if defined ($entry_ref->{email});
    print "Interests: $entry_ref->{interests}" . br ()
                            if defined ($entry_ref->{interests});
    print br ();
}
```

`format_html_entry()` uses the `format_name()` function to glue the `first_name`, `last_name`, and `suffix` column values together. It's identical to the function of the same name in `gen_dir.pl`.

Performing Searches Using a FULLTEXT Index

Historical League members may have multiple interests. If so, they are separated by commas in the `interests` column of the `member` table. For example

```
Revolutionary War,Spanish-American War,Colonial period,Gold rush,Lincoln
```

Can you use `ushl_browse.pl` to search for records that match multiple interests? Sort of, but not really. You can enter several words into the search form,

but records won't match unless you separate the words by commas
and unless the interests in the records occur in the same order you list
them. A more flexible way to approach the interest-searching task is to use a
FULLTEXT index.[2] This section describes a script ushl_ft_browse.pl that
does so. It requires very little work.

The requirements for using ushl_ft_browse.pl are that you must have
MySQL 3.23.23 or later and that the member table must be a MyISAM table.
If you created member as some other table type, you can convert it to a
MyISAM table with ALTER TABLE:

```
mysql> ALTER TABLE member TYPE = MYISAM;
```

Next, it's necessary to index the member table properly. To do that, use the following statement:

```
mysql> ALTER TABLE member ADD FULLTEXT (interests);
```

That allows the interests column to be used for FULLTEXT searches. The
ushl_ft_browse.pl script in the sampdb distribution is based on
ushl_browse.pl and differs from it only in the search_members() function
that constructs the search query. The modified version of the function looks
like this:

```
sub search_members
{
my ($dbh, $interest) = @_;

    print p ("Search results for keyword: " . escapeHTML ($interest));
    my $sth = $dbh->prepare (qq{
            SELECT * FROM member WHERE MATCH(interests) AGAINST(?)
            ORDER BY last_name, first_name
        });
    # look for string anywhere in interest field
    $sth->execute ($interest);
    my $count = 0;
    while (my $ref = $sth->fetchrow_hashref ())
    {
        format_html_entry ($ref);
        ++$count;
    }
    print p ("Number of matching entries: $count");
}
```

2. MySQL's FULLTEXT capabilities are described in Chapter 3.

This version of `search_members()` has the following changes relative to the earlier one:

- The query uses `MATCH()...AGAINST()` rather than `LIKE`.
- No "`%`" wildcard characters are added to the keyword string to convert it to a pattern.

With these changes, you can invoke `ush1_ft_browse.pl` from your Web browser and enter multiple keywords into the search form (with or without commas). The script will find member entries that match any of them.

You could of course get a lot fancier with this script. One possibility would be to take advantage of the fact that `FULLTEXT` searches can search multiple columns at once by setting up the index to span several columns and then modifying `ush1_ft_browse.pl` to search them all. For example, you could drop the original `FULLTEXT` index and add another that uses the `last_name` and `full_name` columns in addition to the `interests` column:

```
mysql> ALTER TABLE member DROP INDEX interests;
mysql> ALTER TABLE member ADD FULLTEXT (interests,last_name,first_name);
```

To use the new index, modify the `SELECT` query in the `search_members()` function to change `MATCH(interests)` to `MATCH(interests,last_name,first_name)`.

Another change you might make to `ush1_ft_browse.pl` would be to add a couple of radio buttons to the form to allow the user to choose between Match Any Keyword and Match All Keywords modes. The Match Any mode is the one the script uses currently. To implement a Match All mode, change the query to use an `IN BOOLEAN MODE` type of `FULLTEXT` search, and precede each keyword by a '+' character to require that it be present in matching records. See Chapter 3 for details.

The PHP API

PHP IS A SCRIPTING LANGUAGE FOR WRITING Web pages containing embedded code that is executed whenever a page is accessed and that can generate dynamic content to be included as part of the output sent to a client's Web browser. This chapter describes how to write PHP-based Web applications that use MySQL. For a comparison of PHP with the C and Perl DBI APIs for MySQL programming, see Chapter 5, "Introduction to MySQL Programming."

The examples in this chapter draw on our sampdb sample database, using the tables created for the grade-keeping project and for the Historical League in Chapter 1, "Getting Started with MySQL and SQL." The applications described here should run under either PHP 3 or PHP 4, although I recommend PHP 4 for performance and security reasons.

This chapter was written under the assumption that you'll use PHP in conjunction with the Apache Web server. In addition, PHP must be built with the MySQL C client library linked in, or it will not know how to access MySQL databases. If you need to obtain any of this software, see Appendix A, "Obtaining and Installing Software." That appendix also provides instructions for obtaining the sampdb distribution that contains the example scripts developed in this chapter. You can download the scripts to avoid typing them in yourself. You'll find the scripts pertaining to the chapter under the phpapi directory of that distribution.

Under UNIX, PHP can be used as an Apache module or as a standalone interpreter used as a traditional CGI program. Under Windows, PHP can run only as a standalone program unless you use Apache 2.x and PHP 4. In that case, you have the option of running PHP as an Apache module. On either platform, running PHP as a module is preferable for performance reasons.

For the most part, this chapter describes only those MySQL–related PHP functions that are needed for the discussion here. For a more comprehensive listing of PHP's MySQL functions, see Appendix H, "PHP API Reference." You'll likely also want to consult the PHP manual, which describes all the functions that PHP provides, including those for using databases other than MySQL (PHP is not limited to working with MySQL any more than DBI is). The manual is available from the PHP Web site at `http://www.php.net/`. Another helpful source of information is *PHP Functions Essential Reference* by Greant et al. (New Riders, 2002).

Filenames for PHP scripts generally end with an extension that allows your Web server to recognize that they should be executed by invoking the PHP interpreter. If you use an extension that isn't recognized, your PHP scripts will be served as plain text. The extension used in this chapter is `.php`. Another common extension is `.phtml`. For instructions on configuring Apache to recognize the extension you want to use, see Appendix A. (If you are not in control of the Apache installation on your machine, check with the system administrator to find out the proper extension to use.) The appendix also describes how to set up Apache to treat any script named `index.php` as the default page for the directory in which it is located, similar to the way Apache uses files named `index.html`.

To use the scripts developed in this chapter, you'll need to install them where your Web server can access them. I'll adopt the convention in this chapter that the U.S. Historical League and grade-keeping projects have their own directories called `ushl` and `gp` at the top level of the Apache document tree. To set up your Web server that way, you should create those directories now. If the Web site host is `www.snake.net`, pages in those two directories will have URLs that begin as follows:

```
http://www.snake.net/ushl/...
http://www.snake.net/gp/...
```

For example, the home pages in each directory can be called `index.php` and are accessed as follows:

```
http://www.snake.net/ushl/index.php
http://www.snake.net/gp/index.php
```

If you have Apache configured to use `index.php` as the default page for a directory, the following URLs are equivalent to the preceding ones:

```
http://www.snake.net/ushl/
http://www.snake.net/gp/
```

PHP Overview

The basic function of PHP is to interpret a script to produce a Web page that is sent to a client. The script typically contains a mix of HTML and executable code. The HTML is sent literally to the client, whereas the PHP code is executed and replaced by whatever output it produces. Consequently, the client never sees the code; it sees only the resulting HTML page.[1]

When PHP begins reading a file, it simply copies whatever it finds there to the output, under the assumption that the contents of the file represent literal text, such as HTML content. When the PHP interpreter encounters a special opening tag, it switches from HTML mode to PHP code mode and starts interpreting the file as PHP code to be executed. The interpreter switches from code mode back to HTML mode when it sees another special tag that signals the end of the code. This allows you to mix static text (the HTML part) with dynamically generated results (output from the PHP code part) to produce a page that varies depending on the circumstances under which it is called. For example, you might use a PHP script to process the result of a form into which a user has entered parameters for a database search. Depending on what the user types, the search parameters may be different each time the form is submitted, so when the script searches for and displays the information the user requested, each resulting page will be different.

Let's see how PHP works beginning with an extremely simple script:

```
<html>
<body>
<p>hello, world</p>
</body>
</html>
```

This script is in fact *so* simple that it contains no PHP code! "What good is that?," you ask. That's a reasonable question. The answer is that it's sometimes useful to set up a script containing just the HTML framework for the page you want to produce and then add the PHP code later. This is perfectly legal, and the PHP interpreter has no problem with it.

---

1. PHP scripts developed in this chapter generate pages that are valid as XHTML, not just as HTML. See "Writing Web Output" in Chapter 7, "The Perl DBI API," for a brief description of XHTML.

To include PHP code in a script, distinguish it from the surrounding text with the special opening and closing tags, `<?php` and `?>`. When the PHP interpreter encounters the opening `<?php` tag, it switches from HTML mode to PHP code mode and treats whatever it finds as executable code until it sees the closing `?>` tag. The code between the tags is interpreted and replaced by its output. The previous example could be rewritten to include a small section of PHP code like the following:

```
<html>
<body>
<p><?php print ("hello, world"); ?></p>
</body>
</html>
```

In this case, the code part is minimal, consisting of a single line. When the code executes, it produces the output `hello, world`, which becomes part of the output sent to the client's browser. Thus, the Web page produced by this script is equivalent to the one produced by the preceding example where the script consisted entirely of HTML.

You can use PHP code to generate any part of a Web page. We've already seen one extreme, in which the entire script consists of literal HTML and contains no PHP code. The other extreme is for the HTML to be produced completely from within code mode:

```
<?php
print ("<html>\n");
print ("<body>\n");
print ("<p>hello, world</p>\n");
print ("</body>\n");
print ("</html>\n");
?>
```

These three examples demonstrate that PHP gives you a lot of flexibility in how you produce output. PHP leaves it up to you to decide whatever combination of HTML and PHP code is appropriate. PHP is also flexible in that you don't need to put all your code in one place. You can switch between HTML and PHP code mode throughout the script however you please, as often as you want.

PHP allows tag styles other than the `<?php` and `?>` style that is used for examples in this chapter. See Appendix H for a description of the tag styles that are available and instructions on enabling them.

Standalone PHP Scripts

The example scripts in this chapter are written with the expectation that they will be invoked by a Web server to generate a Web page. However, if you have a standalone version of PHP, you can use it to execute PHP scripts from the command line. For example, suppose you have a script named `hello.php` that looks like this:

```
<?php print ("hello, world\n"); ?>
```

To execute the script from the command line yourself, use the following command:

```
% php -q hello.php
hello, world
```

This is sometimes useful when you're working on a script, because you can see right away whether it has syntax errors or other problems without having to request the script from a browser each time you make a change. (For this reason, you may want to build a standalone version of PHP, even if normally you use it as a module from within Apache.)

You can make the script directly executable (just like a shell or Perl script) by adding to it a `#!` line at the beginning that names the pathname to PHP. Suppose that PHP is installed in the `/usr/local/bin` directory. You can modify the script to look like this:

```
#! /usr/local/bin/php -q
<?php print ("hello, world\n"); ?>
```

Make it executable with `chmod +x`, and you can invoke it as follows:

```
% chmod +x hello.php
% ./hello.php
hello, world
```

If all that PHP provided was the ability to produce what is essentially static HTML by means of print statements, it wouldn't be very useful. Where PHP's power comes in is through its ability to generate dynamic output that can vary from one invocation of a script to the next. The next script demonstrates this. It's still relatively short, but a bit more substantial than the previous examples. It shows how easily you can access a MySQL database from PHP and use the results of a query in a Web page. The following script was presented very briefly in Chapter 5. It forms a simple basis for a home page for the Historical League Web site. As we go on, we'll make the script a bit more elaborate, but for now all it does is display a short welcome message and a count of the current League membership:

```
<html>
<head>
<title>U.S. Historical League</title>
</head>
<body bgcolor="white">
<p>Welcome to the U.S. Historical League Web Site.</p>
```

```php
<?php
# USHL home page

$conn_id = @mysql_connect ("cobra.snake.net", "sampadm", "secret")
    or exit ();
mysql_select_db ("sampdb")
    or exit ();
$result_id = mysql_query ("SELECT COUNT(*) FROM member")
    or exit ();
if ($row = mysql_fetch_row ($result_id))
    print ("<p>The League currently has " . $row[0] . " members.</p>");
mysql_free_result ($result_id);
?>
</body>
</html>
```

The welcome message is just static text, so it's easiest to write it as literal HTML. The membership count, on the other hand, is dynamic and changes from time to time, so it must be determined on-the-fly by querying the member table in the sampdb database.

The text of the code within the opening and closing script tags performs a simple task:

1. It opens a connection to the MySQL server and makes the sampdb database the default database.

2. It sends a query to the server to determine how many members the Historical League has at the moment (assessed as the number of rows in the member table).

3. The script constructs from the query result a message containing the membership count and then disposes of the result set.

If an error occurs at any point during this process, the script simply exits without producing any further output. It doesn't display any error message because that's likely simply to be confusing to people visiting the Web site.[2]

You can find this script as a file named index.php in the phpapi/ushl directory of the sampdb distribution. Change the connection parameters as necessary, install a copy of it as index.php in the ushl directory of your Web server's document tree, and request it from your browser using either of the following URLs:

```
http://www.snake.net/ushl/
http://www.snake.net/ushl/index.php
```

2. If you generate an entire Web page by means of PHP code, exiting on an error without producing any output at all is likely to annoy visitors to your site, because some browsers will display a "This page contained no data" dialog box that must be dismissed. It's better in this case to display a page containing at least a message indicating that the request could not be satisfied.

Let's break down the script into pieces to see how it works. The first step is to connect to the server using `mysql_connect()`:

```
$conn_id = @mysql_connect ("cobra.snake.net", "sampadm", "secret")
   or exit ();
```

This function takes three arguments that indicate the name of the MySQL server host and the name and password for your MySQL account. `mysql_connect()` returns a connection identifier if it successfully established a connection or `FALSE` if an error occurs. If the connection attempt fails, the script calls `exit()` to terminate immediately.

Perhaps it makes you nervous that the name and password are embedded in the script for all to see. Well, it should. It's true that the name and password don't appear in the resulting Web page that is sent to the client because the script's contents are replaced by its output. Nevertheless, if the Web server becomes misconfigured somehow and fails to recognize that your script needs to be processed by PHP, it will send your script as plain text, and your connection parameters will be exposed. We'll deal with this problem in the "Using Functions and Include Files" section later in this chapter.

What about the '@' character that appears in front of the `mysql_connect()` call? That is the "Shut up, please" operator. Some PHP functions write an error message when they fail, in addition to returning a status code. In the case of `mysql_connect()`, a failed connection attempt would cause a message like the following to appear in the Web page that is sent to the client's browser:

```
Warning: MySQL Connection Failed: Access denied for user:
 'sampadm@cobra.snake.net' (Using password: YES)
```

That's ugly, and the person visiting our site may not know what to make of it or what to do about it. Putting '@' in front of the `mysql_connect()` call suppresses this error message so that we can choose how to deal with errors ourselves on the basis of the return value. For the script at hand, the best thing to do if an error occurs is to produce no output at all pertaining to the membership count. In that case, the page will contain only the welcome message.

You can precede any PHP expression with the `@` operator, but, in my experience, the most likely cause of failure is the initial connection call; hence, the example scripts in this chapter suppress messages only from `mysql_connect()`. (If some explicit error indicator is necessary, the scripts print their own message.)

mysql_connect( ) Versus mysql_pconnect( )

A function similar to mysql_connect () is mysql_pconnect (). Both take hostname, username, and password arguments and return a connection identifier or FALSE to indicate success or failure of the connection attempt. The difference between the two calls is that mysql_connect () establishes a non-persistent connection, whereas mysql_pconnect () establishes a persistent connection. A persistent connection differs from a non-persistent one in that it is not closed when the script terminates. Suppose an Apache process executes a PHP script that calls mysql_pconnect () to open a persistent connection. If the same process later executes another PHP script that calls mysql_pconnect () with the same arguments, the connection is reused. For many database engines, using persistent connections is much more efficient than establishing each connection from scratch. However, there is little advantage for MySQL because the connection-establishment process is extremely efficient. In fact, it may even be disadvantageous to use persistent connections. On a busy Web site with many PHP scripts, you may end up with Apache processes that hold open so many connections to the MySQL server that all available connection slots get used up. You may be able to deal with this issue by increasing the value of the max_connections server variable (see the "Tuning the Server" section in Chapter 11, "General MySQL Administration"), but another option is to use non-persistent connections.

The connection identifier returned by mysql_connect () can be passed to several other MySQL-related calls in the PHP API. However, for such calls, the identifier is always optional. For example, you can call mysql_select_db () using either of the following forms:

```
mysql_select_db ($db_name, $conn_id);
mysql_select_db ($db_name);
```

If you omit the connection identifier argument from a call to any MySQL-related PHP function that takes one, the function uses the most recently opened connection. Thus, if your script opens only a single connection, that connection will be the default and you never need to specify a connection argument explicitly in any of your MySQL calls. This is quite different than MySQL programming with the C or DBI APIs, for which there is no such default.

The connection code in our simple home page script was written as follows using the $conn_id variable to make it clearer what kind of value mysql_connect () returns:

```
$conn_id = @mysql_connect ("cobra.snake.net", "sampadm", "secret")
    or exit ();
```

However, the script doesn't actually use $conn_id anywhere else, so that statement actually could have been written more simply as follows:

```
@mysql_connect ("cobra.snake.net", "sampadm", "secret")
    or exit ();
```

Assuming the connection is established successfully, the next step is to select a database:

```
mysql_select_db ("sampdb")
    or exit ();
```

If `mysql_select_db()` fails, we exit silently. An error is unlikely to occur at this point if we've been able to connect to the server and the database exists, but it's still prudent to check for problems and take appropriate action.

After selecting the database, the script sends a member-counting query to the server, extracts the result, displays it, and frees the result set:

```
$result_id = mysql_query ("SELECT COUNT(*) FROM member")
    or exit ();
if ($row = mysql_fetch_row ($result_id))
    print ("<p>The League currently has " . $row[0] . " members.</p>");
mysql_free_result ($result_id);
```

The `mysql_query()` function sends the query to the server to be executed. (Note that the query string contains no terminating semicolon character or `\g` sequence, in contrast to the way you issue queries from within the `mysql` program.) `mysql_query()` returns FALSE if the query was illegal or couldn't be executed for some reason; otherwise, it returns a result identifier. This identifier is a value that we can use to obtain information about the result set. For the query shown, the result set consists of a single row with a single column value representing the membership count. To get this value, we pass the result identifier to `mysql_fetch_row()` to fetch the row, assign the row to the variable `$row`, and access its first element, `$row[0]`, which also happens to be its only element.

After processing the result set, we free it by passing the result identifier to `mysql_free_result()`. This call is included for completeness. It actually isn't necessary here because PHP automatically releases any active result sets when a script terminates. `mysql_free_result()` is useful primarily in scripts that execute very large queries or a large number of queries, where it helps prevents an excessive amount of memory from being used.

Variables in PHP

In PHP, you can make variables spring into existence simply by using them. Our home page script uses three variables, `$conn_id`, `$result_id`, and `$row`, none of which are declared anywhere. (There are contexts in which you do declare variables, such as when you reference a global variable inside a function, but we'll get to that later.)

Variables are signified by an identifier preceded by a dollar sign ($). This is true no matter what kind of value the variable represents, although for arrays and objects you tack on some extra stuff to access individual

continues

elements of the value. If a variable $x represents a single scalar value, such as a number or a string, you access it as just $x. If $x represents an array with numeric indices, you access its elements as $x[0], $x[1], and so on. If $x represents an array with associative indices such as "yellow" or "large", you access its elements as $x["yellow"] or $x["large"]. (PHP arrays can even have both numeric and associative elements. For example, $x[1] and $x["large"] both can be elements of the same array.) If $x represents an object, it has properties that you access as $x->*property_name*. For example, $x->yellow and $x->large may be properties of $x. Numbers are not legal as property names, so $x->1 is not a valid construct in PHP.

PHP's Linguistic Influences

If you have experience with C programming, you've probably noticed that many of the syntactic constructs in our PHP script are very similar to what you use for C programming. PHP syntax is in fact largely drawn from C, so the similarity is not coincidental. If you have some background in C, you'll be able to transfer much of it to PHP. In fact, if you're not sure how to write an expression or control structure in PHP, just try it the way you'd write it in C and it'll often be correct.

Although PHP has its roots mainly in C, elements of Java and Perl are present, too. You can certainly see this in the comment syntax, where any of the following forms are allowed:

- #   Perl-style comment from '#' to end of line
- //   C++- or Java-style comment from // to end of line
- /*   C-style comment from slash-star to star-slash */

Other similarities with Perl include the '.' string concatenation operator (including '.=' as additive concatenation) and the way that variable references and escape sequences are interpreted within double quotes but not within single quotes.

Using Functions and Include Files

PHP scripts differ from DBI scripts in that PHP scripts are located within your Web server document tree, whereas DBI scripts typically are located in a cgi-bin directory that's located outside of the document tree. This brings up a security issue; A server misconfiguration error can cause pages located within the document tree to leak out as plain text to clients. This means that usernames and passwords for establishing connections to the MySQL server are at a higher risk of being exposed to the outside world if they are used in a PHP script than in a DBI script.

Our initial Historical League home page script is subject to this problem because it contains the literal values of the MySQL username and password. Let's move these connection parameters out of the script using two of PHP's capabilities—functions and include files. We'll write a function sampdb_connect() to establish the connection and put the function in an include file—a file that is not part of our main script but that can be referenced from it. Some advantages of this approach are as follows:

- **It's easier to write connection establishment code.** We can write out the connection parameters once in the sampdb_connect() helper function, not in every individual script that needs to connect. Also, because the scripts we develop here will always use the sampdb database, the helper function can select it after connecting. This way it handles the work of two MySQL operations. Hiding details like this tends to make scripts more understandable because you can concentrate on the unique aspects of each script without being distracted by the connection setup code.

- **The include file can be used by multiple scripts.** This promotes code reusability and makes code more maintainable. It also allows global changes to be made easily to every script that accesses the file. For example, if we move the sampdb database from cobra to boa, we don't need to change a bunch of individual scripts, we just change the hostname argument of the mysql_connect() call in the include file where the sampdb_connect() function is defined.

- **The include file can be moved outside of the Apache document tree.** This means that clients cannot request the include file directly from their browsers, so that its contents cannot be exposed to them, even if the Web server becomes misconfigured. Using an include file is a good strategy for hiding any kind of sensitive information that you don't want to be sent offsite by your Web server. However, although this is a security improvement, don't be lulled into thinking that it makes the name and password secure in all senses. Other users that have login accounts on the Web server host may be able to read the include file directly unless you take some precautions. The "Connecting to the MySQL Server from Web Scripts" section in Chapter 7, "The Perl DBI API," has some notes that pertain to installing DBI configuration files so as to protect them from other users. Similar precautions apply to the use of PHP include files.

To use include files, you need to have a place to put them, and you need to tell PHP to look for them. If your system already has such a location, you can use that. If not, use the following procedure to establish an include file location:

1. Create a directory outside of the Web server document tree in which to store PHP include files. I use /usr/local/apache/lib/php, which is outside my document tree (/usr/local/apache/htdocs), not within it.

2. Include files can be accessed from scripts by full pathname or, if you set up PHP's search path, by just their basenames (the last component of the pathname).[3] The latter approach is more convenient because PHP will find the file for us. The search path used by PHP when searching for include files is controlled by the value of the `include_path` configuration setting in the PHP initialization file, `php.ini`. Find this file on your system (mine is installed in `/usr/local/lib`), and locate the `include_path` line. If it has no value, set it to the full pathname of your new include directory:

   ```
   include_path = "/usr/local/apache/lib/php"
   ```

   If `include_path` already has a value, add the new directory to that value:

   ```
   include_path = "current_value:/usr/local/apache/lib/php"
   ```

   For UNIX, directories listed in `include_path` should be separated by colon characters, as shown. For Windows, use semicolons instead.

3. Create the include file that you want to use and put it into the include directory. The file should have some distinctive name; we'll use `sampdb.php`. This file eventually will contain several functions, but to start with, it need contain only the `sampdb_connect()` function, as shown in the following listing:

   ```php
   <?php
   # sampdb.php - sampdb sample database common functions

   # Connect to the MySQL server using our top-secret name and password

   function sampdb_connect ()
   {
       $conn_id = @mysql_connect ("cobra.snake.net", "sampadm", "secret");
       if ($conn_id && mysql_select_db ("sampdb"))
           return ($conn_id);
       return (FALSE);
   }
   ?>
   ```

   If the `sampdb_connect()` function successfully connects and selects the database, it returns a connection identifier. If an error occurs, it returns FALSE. Because `sampdb_connect()` prints no message when an error occurs, the caller can exit silently or print a message as circumstances warrant.

---

3. The use of PHP include files is somewhat analogous to the use of C header files. For example, the way that PHP will look for them in several directories is similar to the way the C preprocessor looks in multiple directories for C header files.

Observe that the PHP code in the `sampdb.php` file is bracketed within `<?php` and `?>` script tags. That's because PHP begins reading include files in HTML mode. If you omit the tags, PHP will send out the file as plain text rather than interpreting it as PHP code. (That's just fine if you intend the file to produce literal HTML, but if you want its contents to be executed, you must enclose the PHP code within script tags.)

4. To reference the include file from a script, use a line like the following:

```
include "sampdb.php";
```

When PHP sees that line, it searches for the file and reads its contents. Anything in the file becomes accessible to the following parts of the script.

A version of `sampdb.php` is included in the `phpapi` directory of the `sampdb` distribution. Copy it into the include directory you want to use and then set the file's mode and ownership so that it's readable by your Web server. You should also modify the connection parameters to reflect those that you use for connecting to MySQL.

After setting up `sampdb.php`, we can modify the Historical League home page to reference it and connect to the MySQL server by calling the `sampdb_connect()` function:

```
<html>
<head>
<title>U.S. Historical League</title>
</head>
<body bgcolor="white">
<p>Welcome to the U.S. Historical League Web Site.</p>
<?php
# USHL home page - version 2

include "sampdb.php";

sampdb_connect ()
    or exit ();
$result_id = mysql_query ("SELECT COUNT(*) FROM member")
    or exit ();
if ($row = mysql_fetch_row ($result_id))
    print ("<p>The League currently has " . $row[0] . " members.</p>");
mysql_free_result ($result_id);
?>
</body>
</html>
```

You can find the script just shown as `index2.php` in the `phpapi/ush1` directory of the `sampdb` distribution. Copy it to the `ush1` directory in your Web server's document tree, naming it `index.php` to replace the file of that name that is there now. This replaces the less secure version with a more secure one because the new file contains no literal MySQL name or password.

---

include Versus require

PHP has a `require` statement that is similar to `include`. For `include`, the file is read and evaluated each time the `include` statement is executed during the course of the script's execution. For `require`, the contents of the file replace the `require` statement, whether or not it falls into the script's execution path. This means that if you have code containing one of these directives and the code may be executed several times, it's more efficient to use `require`. On the other hand, if you want to read a different file each time you execute your code or you have a loop that iterates through a set of files, you want `include` because you can set a variable to the name of the file you want to include and use the variable as the argument to `include`.

PHP 4 adds two related statements—`include_once` and `require_once`. These are similar to `include` and `require` except that if the named file has already been read earlier, it will not be read again. This can be useful when include files include other files to avoid the possibility of including a file multiple times and perhaps triggering function redefinition errors.

You may be thinking that we haven't really saved all that much coding in the home page by using an include file, but just wait. The `sampdb.php` file can be used for other functions as well, and can serve as a convenient repository for any routine that we expect to be useful in multiple scripts. In fact, we can create two more such functions to put in that file right now. Every Web script we write in the remainder of the chapter will generate a fairly stereotypical set of HTML tags at the beginning of a page and another set at the end. Rather than writing out those tags in each script, we can write functions `html_begin()` and `html_end()` to generate them for us. The `html_begin()` function can take a couple arguments that specify a page title and header. The code for the two functions is as follows:

```php
function html_begin ($title, $header)
{
    print ("<html>\n");
    print ("<head>\n");
    if ($title != "")
        print ("<title>$title</title>\n");
    print ("</head>\n");
    print ("<body bgcolor=\"white\">\n");
    if ($header != "")
        print ("<h2>$header</h2>\n");
}
```

```php
function html_end ()
{
    print ("</body></html>\n");
}
```

After putting `html_begin()` and `html_end()` in `sampdb.php`, the Historical League home page can be modified to use them. The resulting script looks as follows:

```php
<?php
# USHL home page - version 3

include "sampdb.php";

$title = "U.S. Historical League";
html_begin ($title, $title);
?>

<p>Welcome to the U.S. Historical League Web Site.</p>

<?php
sampdb_connect ()
    or exit ();
$result_id = mysql_query ("SELECT COUNT(*) FROM member")
    or exit ();
if ($row = mysql_fetch_row ($result_id))
    print ("<p>The League currently has " . $row[0] . " members.</p>");
mysql_free_result ($result_id);

html_end ();
?>
```

Notice that the PHP code has been split into two pieces, with the literal HTML text of the welcome message appearing between the pieces.

The use of functions for generating the initial and final part of the page provides an important capability. If you want to change the look of your page headers or footers, just modify the functions appropriately, and every script that uses them will be affected automatically. For example, you might want to put a message "Copyright USHL" at the bottom of each Historical League page. Adding the message to a page-trailer function, such as `html_end()`, is an easy way to do that.

A Simple Data-Retrieval Page

The script that we've embedded in the Historical League home page runs a query that returns just a single row (the membership count). Our next script shows how to process a multiple-row result set (the full contents of the `member` table). This is the PHP equivalent of the DBI script `dump_members.pl` developed in Chapter 7, so we'll call it `dump_members.php`. The PHP version differs from the DBI version in that it's intended to be used in a Web environment rather than from the command line. For this reason, it needs to produce HTML output rather than simply writing tab-delimited text. To make rows and columns line up nicely, `dump_members.php` writes the member records as an HTML table. The script looks like the following:

```php
<?php
# dump_members.php - dump Historical League membership list as HTML table

include "sampdb.php";

$title = "U.S. Historical League Member List";
html_begin ($title, $title);

sampdb_connect ()
    or die ("Cannot connect to server");

# issue query
$query = "SELECT last_name, first_name, suffix, email,"
    . "street, city, state, zip, phone FROM member ORDER BY last_name";
$result_id = mysql_query ($query)
    or die ("Cannot execute query");

print ("<table>\n");                    # begin table
# read results of query, then clean up
while ($row = mysql_fetch_row ($result_id))
{
    print ("<tr>\n");                   # begin table row
    for ($i = 0; $i < mysql_num_fields ($result_id); $i++)
    {
        # escape any special characters and print table cell
        printf ("<td>%s</td>\n", htmlspecialchars ($row[$i]));
    }
    print ("</tr>\n");                   # end table row
}
mysql_free_result ($result_id);
print ("</table>\n");                   # end table

html_end ();
?>
```

This script uses the `die()` function to print a message and to exit if an error occurs.[4] This is a different approach to error handling than we used in the Historical League home page. There, printing the membership count was just a

---

4. The `die()` function is similar to `exit()`, but it prints a message before exiting.

little addition to the script's main purpose presenting a greeting to the visitor. For `dump_members.php`, showing the query result is the entire reason for the script's existence, so if a problem occurs that prevents the result from being displayed, it's reasonable to print an error message indicating what the problem was.

To try out the `dump_members.php` script, install it in the `ushl` directory of your Web server document tree and access it as follows:

```
http://www.snake.net/ushl/dump_members.php
```

To let people know about `dump_members.php`, place a link to it in the Historical League home page script. The modified script then looks like this:

```php
<?php
# USHL home page - version 4

include "sampdb.php";

$title = "U.S. Historical League";
html_begin ($title, $title);
?>

<p>Welcome to the U.S. Historical League Web Site.</p>

<?php
sampdb_connect ()
    or exit ();
$result_id = mysql_query ("SELECT COUNT(*) FROM member")
    or exit ();
if ($row = mysql_fetch_row ($result_id))
    print ("<p>The League currently has " . $row[0] . " members.</p>");
mysql_free_result ($result_id);
?>

<p>
You can view the directory of members <a href="dump_members.php">here</a>.
</p>

<?php
html_end ();
?>
```

The `dump_members.php` script serves the purpose of demonstrating how a PHP script can retrieve information from MySQL and convert it into Web page content. If you like, you can modify the script to produce more elaborate results. One such modification is to display the values from the email column as live hyperlinks rather than as static text to make it easier for site visitors to send mail to League members. The `sampdb` distribution contains a `dump_members2.php` script that does this. It differs from `dump_members.php` only slightly in the loop that fetches and displays member entries. The original loop looks as follows:

```
while ($row = mysql_fetch_row ($result_id))
{
    print ("<tr>\n");                     # begin table row
    for ($i = 0; $i < mysql_num_fields ($result_id); $i++)
    {
        # escape any special characters and print table cell
        printf ("<td>%s</td>\n", htmlspecialchars ($row[$i]));
    }
    print ("</tr>\n");                     # end table row
}
```

The email addresses are in the fourth column of the query result, so `dump_members2.php` treats that column differently than the rest, printing a hyperlink if the value is not empty:

```
while ($row = mysql_fetch_row ($result_id))
{
    print ("<tr>\n");                     # begin table row
    for ($i = 0; $i < mysql_num_fields ($result_id); $i++)
    {
        print ("<td>");
        if ($i == 3 && $row[$i] != "")  # email is in 4th column of result
        {
            printf ("<a href=\"mailto:%s\">%s</a>",
                        $row[$i],
                        htmlspecialchars ($row[$i]));
        }
        else
        {
            # escape any special characters and print table cell
            print (htmlspecialchars ($row[$i]));
        }
        print ("</td>\n");
    }
    print ("</tr>\n");                     # end table row
}
```

Processing Query Results

This section examines in more detail PHP's facilities for executing MySQL queries and handling result sets. In PHP, queries are issued by calling the mysql_query() function, which takes a query string and a connection identifier as arguments. The connection identifier is optional, so you can invoke mysql_query() using either of the following forms:

```
$result_id = mysql_query ($query, $conn_id);   # use explicit connection
$result_id = mysql_query ($query);             # use default connection
```

mysql_query() returns a result identifier, which must be interpreted according to the type of statement you issue. For non-SELECT statements such as DELETE, INSERT, REPLACE, and UPDATE that don't return rows, mysql_query() returns TRUE or FALSE to indicate the success or failure of the query. For a successful query, you can call mysql_affected_rows() to find out how many rows were changed (deleted, inserted, replaced, or updated, as the case may be).

For SELECT statements, mysql_query() returns either a result identifier or FALSE to indicate the success or failure of the query. For a successful query, you use the result identifier to obtain further information about the result set. For example, you can determine how many rows or columns the result set has by calling mysql_num_rows() or mysql_num_fields(). To access the records in the result, you can call any of several row-fetching functions.

If mysql_query() returns FALSE, it means the statement failed—in other words, some error occurred and the query couldn't even be executed. A statement can fail for any number of reasons:

- It may be malformed and contain a syntax error.
- The query may be syntactically correct but semantically meaningless, such as when you try to select a column from a table containing no such column.
- You may not have sufficient privileges to perform the query.
- The MySQL server host may have become unreachable due to network problems.

If mysql_query() returns FALSE and you want to know the particular reason for the error, call mysql_error() or mysql_errno() to obtain the error message string or numeric error code (see the "Handling Errors" section later in this chapter).

> **Don't Assume That mysql_query( ) Will Succeed**
>
> On the PHP mailing list, it's common for new PHP users to ask why a script prints the following error message:
>
> ```
> Warning: 0 is not a MySQL result index in file on line n
> ```
>
> This message indicates that a result identifier value of zero (that is, FALSE) was passed to some function (such as a row-fetching routine) that expects a valid result identifier. This means that an earlier call to mysql_query() returned FALSE (in other words, mysql_query() failed), and the script passed the return value to another function without bothering to check it first. That is a mistake. When you use mysql_query(), always test its return value if the code that follows it depends on the success of the query.

When mysql_query() does not return FALSE, the result identifier must be properly interpreted to be useful. For example, two common mistakes are to think that the return value is a row count or that it contains the data returned by your query. Neither is true, as the following sections demonstrate.

Handling Queries That Return No Result Set

For statements that modify rows, the return value from mysql_query() is not a row count. It is simply an indicator of success or failure, nothing more. To get a row count, call mysql_affected_rows(). Suppose you want to delete the record for member 149 in the member table and report the result. An incorrect way of doing so is as follows:

```
$result_id = mysql_query ("DELETE FROM member WHERE member_id = 149");
if (!$result_id)
    print ("member 149 was not deleted\n");
else
    print ("member 149 was deleted\n");
```

This code is incorrect because it treats $result_id as a row count and assumes that a value of 0 (FALSE) means the query executed successfully but deleted no rows. But what it really means is that the query failed to execute. Another incorrect way to interpret the result from mysql_query() is as follows:

```
$result_id = mysql_query ("DELETE FROM member WHERE member_id = 149");
if (!$result_id)
    print ("query failed\n");
else
    print ("member 149 was deleted\n");
```

This code properly distinguishes query failure from query success, but is still incorrect because it assumes that if the query succeeded it actually deleted a record. Why is that wrong? Because a DELETE statement need not actually delete anything to execute successfully. If there does happen to be a member with an ID of 149, MySQL deletes the record and `mysql_query()` returns TRUE. But if no such member exists, `mysql_query()` still returns TRUE, because the query is legal. To determine whether or not a successful query actually deleted any rows, call `mysql_affected_rows()`. The following example shows the proper way to interpret the result identifier:

```
$result_id = mysql_query ("DELETE FROM member WHERE member_id = 149");
if (!$result_id)
    print ("query failed\n");
else if (mysql_affected_rows () < 1)
    print ("no record for member 149 was found\n");
else
    print ("member 149 was deleted\n");
```

Handling Queries That Return a Result Set

To process a query that returns rows, you must first execute the query and then, if it succeeds, fetch the contents of the result set. It's easy to forget that this process has two stages, especially if the query returns only a single value. Consider the following attempt to determine how many records are in the `member` table:

```
$result_id = mysql_query ("SELECT COUNT(*) FROM member");
print ("The member table has $result_id records\n");
```

This code is incorrect. It assumes that because the result set consists of only a single data value, that value must be what `mysql_query()` returns. That is untrue. `$result_id` allows you to access the result set, but is never itself the result. Even if the result consists of a single value, you must still fetch it after executing the query. The following code illustrates one way to do this. It makes sure that `mysql_query()` succeeds and then fetches the record into `$row` with `mysql_fetch_row()`. Only if both operations succeed does the code print the value of COUNT(*):

```
$result_id = mysql_query ("SELECT COUNT(*) FROM member");
if (!$result_id || !($row = mysql_fetch_row ($result_id)))
    print ("query failed\n");
else
    print ("The member table has $row[0] records\n");
```

A similar approach can be used when you expect to get back several records, although in this case you'll usually use a loop to fetch the rows. The following example illustrates one way to do this:

```
$result_id = mysql_query ("SELECT * FROM member");
if (!$result_id)
    print ("query failed\n");
```

```
    else
    {
        printf ("number of rows returned: %d\n", mysql_num_rows ($result_id));
        # fetch each row in result set
        while ($row = mysql_fetch_row ($result_id))
        {
            # print values in row, separated by commas
            for ($i = 0; $i < mysql_num_fields ($result_id); $i++)
            {
                if ($i > 0)
                    print (",");
                print ($row[$i]);
            }
            print ("\n");
        }
        mysql_free_result ($result_id);
    }
}
```

If the query fails, the result is FALSE, and the script simply prints a message to that effect. If the query succeeds, mysql_query() returns a valid result identifier that is useful in a number of ways (though not as a row count!). The result identifier can be used for any of the following purposes:

- Pass it to mysql_num_rows() to determine the number of rows in the result set.
- Pass it to mysql_num_fields() to determine the number of columns in the result set.
- Pass it to a row-fetching routine to fetch successive rows of the result set. The example uses mysql_fetch_row(), but there are other choices, which we'll see shortly.
- Pass it to mysql_free_result() to allow PHP to free the result set and dispose of any resources associated with it.

PHP provides several row-fetching functions for retrieving a result set after mysql_query() successfully executes a SELECT query (see Table 8.1). Each of these functions takes a result identifier as the argument and returns FALSE when there are no more rows.

Table 8.1 **PHP Row-Fetching Functions**

Function Name	Return Value
mysql_fetch_row()	An array; elements are accessed by numeric indices
mysql_fetch_assoc()	An array; elements are accessed by associative indices
mysql_fetch_array()	An array; elements are accessed by numeric or associative indices
mysql_fetch_object()	An object; elements are accessed as properties

The most basic call is `mysql_fetch_row()`, which returns the next row of the result set as an array. Elements of the array are accessed by numeric indices in the range from 0 to `mysql_num_fields()−1`. The following example shows how to use `mysql_fetch_row()` in a simple loop that fetches and prints the values in each row in tab-delimited format:

```
$query = "SELECT * FROM president";
$result_id = mysql_query ($query)
    or die ("Query failed");
while ($row = mysql_fetch_row ($result_id))
{
    for ($i = 0; $i < mysql_num_fields ($result_id); $i++)
    {
        if ($i > 0)
            print ("\t");
        print ($row[$i]);
    }
    print ("\n");
}
mysql_free_result ($result_id);
```

For each row in the result set that is available, the value assigned to `$row` is an array. You access its elements as `$row[$i]`, where `$i` is the numeric column index. To determine the number of elements in each row, pass the result identifier to `mysql_num_fields()`. You might be tempted to count the number of values by passing `$row` to PHP's `count()` function, which counts the number of values in an array. That is problematic if the result set contains NULL values, which PHP represents using unset values. `count()` doesn't count unset values in PHP 3, which makes it an unreliable measure of the number of columns. Use `mysql_num_fields()` to do so; that's what it's for.

Another way to fetch an array is to assign the result to a list of variables. For example, to fetch the `last_name` and `first_name` columns directly into variables named `$ln` and `$fn` and print the names in first name, last name order, do the following:

```
$query = "SELECT last_name, first_name FROM president";
$result_id = mysql_query ($query)
    or die ("Query failed");
while (list ($ln, $fn) = mysql_fetch_row ($result_id))
    printf ("%s %s\n", $fn, $ln);
mysql_free_result ($result_id);
```

The variables can have any legal names you like, but their order in the `list()` must correspond to the order of the columns selected by the query.

`mysql_fetch_assoc()`, the second row-fetching function listed in
Table 8.1, returns a row with elements that are accessed by associative index.
The element names are the names of the columns selected by the query:

```
$query = "SELECT last_name, first_name FROM president";
$result_id = mysql_query ($query)
    or die ("Query failed");
while ($row = mysql_fetch_assoc ($result_id))
    printf ("%s %s\n", $row["first_name"], $row["last_name"]);
mysql_free_result ($result_id);
```

`mysql_fetch_assoc()` is newer than the other row-fetching functions; it's
available only as of PHP 4.0.3.

The third row-fetching function, `mysql_fetch_array()`, returns a row with
elements that can be accessed both by numeric index and associative index. In
other words, you can access elements by number or by name:

```
$query = "SELECT last_name, first_name FROM president";
$result_id = mysql_query ($query)
    or die ("Query failed");
while ($row = mysql_fetch_array ($result_id))
{
    printf ("%s %s\n", $row[1], $row[0]);
    printf ("%s %s\n", $row["first_name"], $row["last_name"]);
}
mysql_free_result ($result_id);
```

The information returned by `mysql_fetch_array()` is a combination of the
information returned by `mysql_fetch_row()` and `mysql_fetch_assoc()`.
Despite that, performance differences between the functions are negligible, and
you can call `mysql_fetch_array()` with no particular penalty.

The final row-fetching function, `mysql_fetch_object()`, returns the next
row of the result set as an object. This means you access elements of the row
using $row->*col_name* syntax. For example, if you retrieve the last_name
and first_name values from the president table, the columns can be
accessed as follows:

```
$query = "SELECT last_name, first_name FROM president";
$result_id = mysql_query ($query)
    or die ("Query failed");
while ($row = mysql_fetch_object ($result_id))
    printf ("%s %s\n", $row->first_name, $row->last_name);
mysql_free_result ($result_id);
```

What if your query contains calculated columns? For example, you might issue
a query that returns values that are calculated as the result of an expression:

```
SELECT CONCAT(first_name, ' ', last_name) FROM president
```

A query that is written like that is unsuitable for use with
`mysql_fetch_object()`. The name of the selected column is the expression
itself, which isn't a legal property name. However, you can supply a legal
name by giving the column an alias. The following query aliases the column
as `full_name`:

```
SELECT CONCAT(first_name, ' ', last_name) AS full_name FROM president
```

If you fetch the results of this query with `mysql_fetch_object()`, the alias
allows the column to be accessed as `$row->full_name`.

Testing for NULL Values in Query Results

PHP represents NULL values in result sets as unset values. One way to check for
NULL in a column value returned from a SELECT query is to use the `isset()`
function. The following example selects and prints names and email addresses from
the member table, printing "No email address available" if the address is NULL:

```
$query = "SELECT last_name, first_name, email FROM member";
$result_id = mysql_query ($query)
    or die ("Query failed");
while (list ($last_name, $first_name, $email) = mysql_fetch_row ($result_id))
{
    printf ("Name: %s %s, Email: ", $first_name, $last_name);
    if (!isset ($email))
        print ("no email address available");
    else
        print ($email);
    print ("\n");
}
mysql_free_result ($result_id);
```

A related function is `empty()`, but `empty()` returns the same result for NULL
and empty strings, so it's not useful as a NULL value test.

In PHP 4, you can test for NULL values using the PHP NULL constant by using
the `===` identically-equal-to operator:

```
$query = "SELECT last_name, first_name, email FROM member";
$result_id = mysql_query ($query)
    or die ("Query failed");
while (list ($last_name, $first_name, $email) = mysql_fetch_row ($result_id))
{
    printf ("Name: %s %s, Email: ", $first_name, $last_name);
    if ($email === NULL)
        print ("no email address available");
    else
        print ($email);
    print ("\n");
}
mysql_free_result ($result_id);
```

Handling Errors

PHP puts three means at your disposal for dealing with errors in MySQL-based scripts. The two are generally applicable to many kinds of errors, and one is specific to MySQL operations. First, you can use the @ operator to suppress any error message a function might emit. We've been doing this in calls to `mysql_connect()` to prevent error messages from that function from appearing in the page sent to the client:

```
$conn_id = @mysql_connect ("cobra.snake.net", "sampadm", "secret");
```

Second, the `error_reporting()` function can be used to turn error reporting on or off at any of the following levels shown in Table 8.2.

Table 8.2 **PHP Error-Handling Levels**

Error Level	Types of Errors Reported
E_ERROR	Normal function errors
E_WARNING	Normal warnings
E_PARSE	Parser errors
E_NOTICE	Notices
E_CORE_ERROR	Errors from core engine
E_CORE_WARNING	Warnings from core engine
E_COMPILE_ERROR	Errors from compiler
E_COMPILE_WARNING	Warnings from compiler
E_USER_ERROR	User-generated error
E_USER_WARNING	User-generated warning
E_USER_NOTICE	User-generated notice
E_ALL	All errors

To control error reporting with `error_reporting()`, call it with an argument equal to the bitwise OR of the levels you want enabled. Turning off the E_ERROR and level E_WARNING levels should be sufficient to suppress messages from MySQL functions:

```
error_reporting (E_PARSE | E_NOTICE);
```

You probably don't want to turn off level E_PARSE warnings about parse errors; if you do, you may have a difficult time debugging any changes you make to your scripts. Level E_NOTICE warnings often can be ignored but sometimes indicate a problem with your script that you should pay attention to, so you may want to leave that level enabled as well. Normally, you need not be concerned about the other error levels, except perhaps E_ALL to enable all messages.

In PHP 3, only four error levels are available, and they must be referred to by literal values, not symbolic constants (see Table 8.3).

Table 8.3 **PHP 3 Error-Handling Levels**

Error Level	Types of Errors Reported
1	Normal function errors
2	Normal warnings
4	Parser errors
8	Notices

The third error-handling technique is to use `mysql_error()` and `mysql_errno()`. These functions report error information that is returned by the MySQL server. They are similar to the calls with the same names in the C API. `mysql_error()` returns an error message in string form (an empty string if no error occurred). `mysql_errno()` returns an error number (0 if no error occurred). Both functions take a connection identifier argument specifying a connection to the MySQL server, and both return error information for the most recently invoked MySQL function on that connection that returns a status. The connection identifier is optional; if it's missing, the most recently opened connection is used. For example, you could report an error from `mysql_query()` as follows:

```
$result_id = mysql_query ($query);
if (!$result_id)
{
    print ("errno: " . mysql_errno() . "\n");
    print ("error: " . mysql_error() . "\n");
}
```

With the C API, you can get error information from `mysql_error()` and `mysql_errno()`, even when an attempt to connect to the server fails. That's also true for PHP, but only as of PHP 4.0.6. Prior to 4.0.6, the PHP versions of `mysql_error()` and `mysql_errno()` do not return useful error information for a connection until the connection has been established successfully. (In other words, if a connection attempt fails, you cannot use `mysql_error()` or `mysql_errno()` to report the reason why.) Under these circumstances, if you want to report a specific reason for connection failure rather than some generic message, you must take special measures. See Appendix H for instructions on how to do this.

The scripts in this chapter print fairly generic error messages, such as "Query failed" as they detect an error. However, while you're developing a script, you'll often find it useful to add a call to `mysql_error()` to help you discover the particular reason for an error.

Quoting Issues

It's necessary to be aware of quoting issues when you're constructing query strings in PHP, just as it is in other languages, such as C and Perl. The way to deal with quoting problems is similar, too, although the function names are different in the various languages. Suppose you're constructing a query to insert a new record into a table. In the query string, you might put quotes around each value to be inserted into a string column:

```
$last = "O'Malley";
$first = "Brian";
$expiration = "2002-9-1";
$query = "INSERT INTO member (last_name,first_name,expiration)"
        . " VALUES('$last','$first','$expiration')";
```

The problem here is that one of the quoted values itself contains a quote (O'Malley) that results in a syntax error if you send the query to the MySQL server. To deal with this in C, we could call mysql_real_escape_string() or mysql_escape_string(), and in a Perl DBI script, we could use quote(). PHP has an addslashes() function that accomplishes much the same objective. For example, a call to addslashes("O'Malley") returns the value O\'Malley. The previous example should be written as follows to prevent quoting problems:

```
$last = addslashes ("O'Malley");
$first = addslashes ("Brian");
$expiration = addslashes ("2002-9-1");
$query = "INSERT INTO member (last_name,first_name,expiration)"
        . " VALUES('$last','$first','$expiration')";
```

In DBI, quote() adds surrounding quotes to the string, but in PHP, addslashes() does not, so it's still necessary to specify quotes explicitly in the query string around the values to be inserted. This technique works well for all except unset values, for which you'd want to insert the word NULL into the query string without any surrounding quotes. This problem does have a solution, which we'll consider shortly.

Alternatives to addslashes() include mysql_escape_string() as of PHP 4.0.3, and mysql_real_escape_string() as of PHP 4.3.0:

```
$escaped_str = mysql_escape_string ($str);
```

```
$escaped_str = mysql_real_escape_string ($str, $conn_id);
```

Each of these is based a function of the same name in the MySQL C API. mysql_real_escape_string() takes into account the character set of the connection when performing encoding, which is why it takes a connection identifier argument. If you omit that argument, the function uses the character set of the current connection.

Given that it's possible to choose from up to three functions when handling string escaping, it can become very messy to pick one each time a string is to be encoded for insertion into a query string. So let's write a `quote_value()` utility routine to be placed into the `sampdb.php` library file. `quote_value()` will do the work of escaping a string with the most recent of the available encoding functions, using `function_exists()` to check which functions are available:

```
function quote_value ($str)
{
    if (!isset ($str))
        return ("NULL");
    if (function_exists ("mysql_real_escape_string"))
        return ("'" . mysql_real_escape_string ($str) . "'");
    if (function_exists ("mysql_escape_string"))
        return ("'" . mysql_escape_string ($str) . "'");
    return ("'" . addslashes ($str) . "'");
}
```

In addition to choosing from among the available encoding functions, `quote_value()` also solves the problem of handling unset (NULL) values that was mentioned a short while back. If the argument is an unset value, `quote_value()` returns the word NULL with no surrounding quotes; otherwise, it escapes the argument and returns the resulting value, including surrounding single quotes. Thus, to use `quote_value()` for query construction, you insert the value that it returns directly into the query string, without adding any extra quotes yourself:

```
$last = quote_value ("O'Malley");
$first = quote_value ("Brian");
$expiration = quote_value ("2002-9-1");
$query = "INSERT INTO member (last_name,first_name,expiration)"
        . " VALUES($last,$first,$expiration)";
```

The preceding discussion covers quoting issues that occur when constructing query strings to be sent to the MySQL server. Quoting issues also occur when generating output to be presented in Web pages. If you're writing a string that should appear as HTML or as part of a URL, it's best to encode it if the string may contain characters that are special within HTML or URLs. The PHP functions `htmlspecialchars()` and `urlencode()` can be used for this. They're similar to the CGI.pm `escapeHTML()` and `escape()` methods discussed in Chapter 7.

Putting PHP to Work

The remaining part of this chapter tackles the goals set out in Chapter 1 that we have yet to accomplish:

- For the grade-keeping project, we need to write a script that allows us to enter and edit test and quiz scores.
- For visitors to the Historical League Web site, we want to develop an online quiz about U.S. presidents and to make it interactive so that the questions can be generated on-the-fly.
- We also want to allow Historical League members to edit their directory entries online. This will keep the information up to date and reduce the amount of entry editing that must be done by the League secretary.

Each of these scripts generates multiple Web pages and communicates from one invocation of the script to the next by means of information embedded in the pages it creates. If you're not familiar with the concept of inter-page communication, you might want to read the "Writing Multiple-Purpose Pages" section in Chapter 7.

Entering Student Scores

In this section, we'll turn our attention to the grade-keeping project and write a `score_entry.php` script for managing test and quiz scores. The Web directory for the project is named `gp` under the Apache document tree root, which corresponds to this URL for our site:

```
http://www.snake.net/gp/
```

The directory is thus far unpopulated, so visitors requesting that URL may receive only a "Page not found" error or an empty directory listing page. To rectify that problem, create a short script named `index.php` and place it in the `gp` directory to serve as the project's home page. The following script suffices for now. It contains two links. One is to the `score_browse.pl` script we wrote in Chapter 7 that pertains to the grade-keeping project. The other is to the `score_entry.php` script that we're about to write:

```php
<?php
# Grade-Keeping Project home page

include "sampdb.php";

$title = "Grade-Keeping Project";
html_begin ($title, $title);
?>
```

```
<p>
<a href="/cgi-bin/score_browse.pl">View</a> test and quiz scores
</p>
<p>
<a href="score_entry.pl">Enter or edit</a> test and quiz scores
</p>

<?php
html_end ();
?>
```

Let's consider how to design and implement the `score_entry.php` script that will let us enter a set of test or quiz scores or edit existing sets of scores. Entry capability will be useful whenever we have a new set of scores to add to the database. Editing capability is necessary for changing scores later, for example, to handle scores of students who take a test or quiz later than the rest of the class due to absence for illness or other reason (or, perish the thought, to correct errors should we happen to enter a score incorrectly). The conceptual outline of the score entry script is as follows:

- The initial page presents a list of known grade events and allows you to choose one or to indicate that you want to create a new event.

- If you choose to create a new event, the script presents a page that allows you to specify the date and type of event (test or quiz). After it adds the event to the database, the script redisplays the event list page, which at that point will include the new event.

- If you choose an existing event from the list, the script presents a score-entry page showing the event ID, date, and type, a table that lists each student in the class, and a Submit button. Each row in the table shows one student's name and current score for the event. For new events, all scores will be blank. For existing events, the scores will be those you entered at some earlier time. You can fill in or change the scores and then select the Submit button. The script will then enter the scores into the `score` table or revise existing scores.

Before implementing the `score_entry.php` script, we must take a slight detour to discuss how input parameters work in PHP. The script needs to perform several different actions, which means that it must pass a status value from page to page so that the script can tell what it's supposed to do each time it's invoked. One way to do this is to pass parameters at the end of the URL. For example, we can add a parameter named `action` to the script URL as follows:

```
http://www.snake.net/gp/score_entry.php?action=value
```

Parameter values may also come from the contents of a form submitted by the user. Each field in the form that is returned by the user's browser as part of a form submission will have a name and a value.

PHP makes input parameters available to scripts through special arrays. Parameters encoded at the end of a URL and sent as a GET request are placed in the $HTTP_GET_VARS global array. For parameters received in a POST request (such as the contents of a form that has a method attribute value of POST), the parameters are placed in the $HTTP_POST_VARS global array. These arrays are associative, with elements keyed to the parameter names. For example, an action parameter sent in the URL becomes available to a PHP script as the value of $HTTP_GET_VARS["action"]. If a form contains a field named address and the form is submitted via a POST request, the value becomes available as $HTTP_POST_VARS["address"].

Parameter values are available for fields in forms, too. Suppose a form contains fields named name and address. When a user submits the form, the Web server invokes a script to process the form's contents. If the form is submitted as a GET request, the script can determine what values were entered into the form by checking the values of the $HTTP_GET_VARS["name"] and $HTTP_GET_VARS["address"] variables. If the form is submitted as a POST request, the variables will be in $HTTP_POST_VARS["name"] and $HTTP_POST_VARS["address"]. For forms that contain a lot of fields, it can be inconvenient to give them all unique names. PHP makes it easy to pass arrays in and out of forms. If you use field names such as x[0], x[1], and so on, PHP will store them in $HTTP_GET_VARS["x"] or $HTTP_POST_VARS["x"], which will be an array. If you assign the array value to a variable $x, the array elements are available as $x[0], $x[1], and so on.

In most cases, you won't care whether a parameter was submitted via GET or POST, so we can write a utility routine (script_param()), that takes a parameter name and checks both arrays to find the parameter value. If the parameter is not present, the routine returns an unset value:

```php
function script_param ($name)
{
global $HTTP_GET_VARS, $HTTP_POST_VARS;

    unset ($val);
    if (isset ($HTTP_GET_VARS[$name]))
        $val = $HTTP_GET_VARS[$name];
    else if (isset ($HTTP_POST_VARS[$name]))
        $val = $HTTP_POST_VARS[$name];
    # return @$val rather than $val to prevent "undefined value"
    # messages in case $val is unset and warnings are enabled
    return (@$val);
}
```

Note that the `script_param()` function explicitly declares the arrays to be global using the `global` keyword. PHP global variables are accessible without `global` only in global scope, such as when you use them in the main body of a script. In non-global scope, such as within a function, `global` indicates to PHP that you mean to access a global variable rather than a variable that is local to the function and just happens to have the same name. The function also uses the `@` operator in the `return()` statement to suppress error messages. (If a parameter is not available, `script_param()` returns an unset value, and if the script happens to have modified the error reporting level to include warnings, returning an unset value would otherwise cause a warning to be printed.)

PHP 4.1 introduced two new parameter arrays: `$_GET` and `$_PUT`. These are similar to `$HTTP_GET_VARS` and `$HTTP_POST_VARS`, but are superglobal arrays. This means they are accessible in any scope without a `global` declaration. To modify `script_param()` to use the newer superglobal arrays if they are available, write the function as follows:

```
function script_param ($name)
{
global $HTTP_GET_VARS, $HTTP_POST_VARS;

    unset ($val);
    if (isset ($_GET[$name]))
        $val = $_GET[$name];
    else if (isset ($_POST[$name]))
        $val = $_POST[$name];
    else if (isset ($HTTP_GET_VARS[$name]))
        $val = $HTTP_GET_VARS[$name];
    else if (isset ($HTTP_POST_VARS[$name]))
        $val = $HTTP_POST_VARS[$name];
    if (isset ($val) && get_magic_quotes_gpc ())
        $val = remove_backslashes ($val);
    # return @$val rather than $val to prevent "undefined value"
    # messages in case $val is unset and warnings are enabled
    return (@$val);
}
```

This modified version of `script_param()` is the one that you'll find in the `sampdb.php` library file in the `sampdb` distribution. It allows a script to easily access by name the value of input parameters without being concerned which array they might be stored in. You'll notice that this revised version also contains another change in addition to checking the `$_GET` and `$_PUT` arrays; after extracting the parameter value, it passes the value to `remove_backslashes()`. The purpose of this is to adapt to configurations that have the `magic_quotes_gpc` setting enabled with a line like the following in the PHP initialization file:

```
magic_quotes_gpc = On;
```

If that setting is turned on, PHP adds backslashes to parameter values to quote special characters such as quotes or backslashes. The extra backslashes make it more difficult to check parameter values to see if they're valid, so `remove_backslashes()` strips them out. It's implemented as follows. The algorithm is recursive because in PHP 4 it's possible to create parameters that take the form of nested arrays:

```
function remove_backslashes ($val)
{
    if (!is_array ($val))
        $val = stripslashes ($val);
    else
    {
        reset ($val);
        while (list ($k, $v) = each ($val))
            $val[$k] = remove_backslashes ($v);
    }
    return ($val);
}
```

Web Input Parameters and register_globals

You may be familiar with PHP's `register_globals` configuration setting that causes Web input parameters to be registered directly into script variables. For example, a form field or URL parameter named x would be stored directly into a variable named $x in your script. Unfortunately, enabling this capability means that clients can set variables in your scripts in ways you may not intend. This is a security risk, so the PHP developers now recommend that `register_globals` be disabled. The `script_param()` routine deliberately uses only the arrays provided specifically for input parameters, which is more secure and also works regardless of the `register_globals` setting.

Now that we have support in place for extracting Web input parameters conveniently, we can use that support for writing `score_entry.php`. That script needs to be able to communicate information from one invocation of itself to the next. We'll use a parameter called `action` for this, which can be obtained when the script executes as follows:

```
$action = script_param ("action");
```

If the parameter isn't set, that means the script is being invoked for the first time; otherwise, it can test the value of $action to find out what to do. The general framework for `script_entry.php` looks as follows:

```
<?php
# score_entry.php - Score Entry script for grade-keeping project

include "sampdb.php";
```

```
# define action constants
define ("SHOW_INITIAL_PAGE", 0);
define ("SOLICIT_EVENT", 1);
define ("ADD_EVENT", 2);
define ("DISPLAY_SCORES", 3);
define ("ENTER_SCORES", 4);

# ... put input-handling functions here ...

$title = "Grade-Keeping Project -- Score Entry";
html_begin ($title, $title);

sampdb_connect ()
    or die ("Cannot connect to database server");

# determine what action to perform (the default if
# none is specified is to present the initial page)

$action = script_param ("action");
if (!isset ($action))
    $action = SHOW_INITIAL_PAGE;

switch ($action)
{
case SHOW_INITIAL_PAGE:     # present initial page
    display_events ();
    break;
case SOLICIT_EVENT:         # ask for new event information
    solicit_event_info ();
    break;
case ADD_EVENT:             # add new event to database
    add_new_event ();
    display_events ();
    break;
case DISPLAY_SCORES:        # display scores for selected event
    display_scores ();
    break;
case ENTER_SCORES:          # enter new or edited scores
    enter_scores ();
    display_events ();
    break;
default:
    die ("Unknown action code ($action)");
}

html_end ();
?>
```

The $action variable can take on several values, which we test in the switch
statement. In PHP, switch is much like its C counterpart; it's used here to
determine which action to take and to call the functions that implement the

action. To avoid having to use literal action values, the switch statement refers to symbolic action names that are set up earlier in the script using PHP's define() construct.

Let's examine the functions that handle these actions one at a time. The first one, display_events(), presents a list of allowable events by retrieving rows of the event table from MySQL and displaying them. Each row of the table lists the event ID, date, and event type (test or quiz). The event ID appears in the page as a hyperlink that you can select to edit the scores for that event. Following the event rows, the function adds one more row containing a link that allows a new event to be created:

```
function display_events ()
{
    print ("Select an event by clicking on its number, or select\n");
    print ("New Event to create a new grade event:<br /><br />\n");
    $query = "SELECT event_id, date, type FROM event ORDER BY event_id";
    $result_id = mysql_query ($query)
        or die ("Cannot execute query");
    print ("<table border=\"1\">\n");

    # Print a row of table column headers

    print ("<tr>\n");
    display_cell ("th", "Event ID");
    display_cell ("th", "Date");
    display_cell ("th", "Type");
    print ("</tr>\n");

    # Present list of existing events.  Associate each event id with a
    # link that will show the scores for the event; use mysql_fetch_array()
    # to fetch each row so that its columns can be referred to by name.

    while ($row = mysql_fetch_array ($result_id))
    {
        print ("<tr>\n");
        $url = sprintf ("%s?action=%s&event_id=%s",
                        script_name (),
                        urlencode (DISPLAY_SCORES),
                        urlencode ($row["event_id"]));
        display_cell ("td",
                    "<a href=\"$url\">"
                        . htmlspecialchars ($row["event_id"])
                        . "</a>",
                    FALSE);
        display_cell ("td", $row["date"]);
        display_cell ("td", $row["type"]);
        print ("</tr>\n");
    }
```

```
        # Add one more link for creating a new event

        print ("<tr align=\"center\">\n");
        $url = sprintf ("%s?action=%s",
                        script_name (),
                        urlencode (SOLICIT_EVENT));
        display_cell ("td colspan=\"3\"",
                        "<a href=\"$url\">" . "Create New Event" . "</a>",
                        FALSE);
        print ("</tr>\n");

        print ("</table>\n");
    }
```

The URLs for the hyperlinks that re-invoke score_entry.php are constructed using script_name(), a function that determines the script's own pathname. (It can be found in the sampdb.php file.) script_name() is useful because it allows you to avoid hardwiring the name of the script into the code; if you write the name literally into the script and then rename it, the script breaks.

script_name() is somewhat similar to script_param() in that it accesses PHP global arrays. However, it uses different arrays because the script name is part of the information supplied by the Web server, not as part of the input parameters:

```
function script_name ()
{
global $HTTP_SERVER_VARS, $PHP_SELF;

    if (isset ($_SERVER["PHP_SELF"]))
        return ($_SERVER["PHP_SELF"]);
    if (isset ($HTTP_SERVER_VARS["PHP_SELF"]))
        return ($HTTP_SERVER_VARS["PHP_SELF"]);
    return ($PHP_SELF);
}
```

The display_cell() function used by display_events() generates cells in the event table:

```
# Display a cell of an HTML table.  $tag is the tag name ("th" or "td"
# for a header or data cell), $value is the value to display, and
# $encode should be true or false, indicating whether or not to perform
# HTML-encoding of the value before displaying it.  $encode is optional,
# and is true by default.

function display_cell ($tag, $value, $encode = TRUE)
{
    if ($value == "")    # is the value empty or unset?
        $value = " ";
    else if ($encode)    # perform HTML-encoding if requested
        $value = htmlspecialchars ($value);
    print ("<$tag>$value</$tag>\n");
}
```

If you select the "Create New Event" link in the table that display_events() presents, score_entry.php is re-invoked with an action of SOLICIT_EVENT. That triggers a call to solicit_event_info(), which displays a form that allows you to enter the date and type for the new event:

```
function solicit_event_info ()
{
    printf ("<form method=\"POST\" action=\"%s?action=%s\">\n",
                script_name (),
                urlencode (ADD_EVENT));
    print ("Enter information for new grade event:<br /><br />\n");
    print ("Date: ");
    print ("<input type=\"text\" name=\"date\" value=\"\" size=\"10\" />\n");
    print ("<br />\n");
    print ("Type: ");
    print ("<input type=\"radio\" name=\"type\" value=\"T\"");
    print (" checked=\"checked\" />Test\n");
    print ("<input type=\"radio\" name=\"type\" value=\"Q\" />Quiz\n");
    print ("<br /><br />\n");
    print ("<input type=\"submit\" name=\"button\" value=\"Submit\" />\n");
    print ("</form>\n");
}
```

The form generated by solicit_event_info() contains an edit field for entering the date, a pair of radio buttons for specifying whether the new event is a test or a quiz, and a Submit button. The default event type is 'T' (test). When you fill in this form and submit it, score_entry.php is invoked again, this time with an action value equal to ADD_EVENT. Then the add_new_event() function is called to enter a new row into the event table, which is the first point at which MySQL actually enters into the operation of the script:

```
function add_new_event ()
{
    $date = script_param ("date");  # get date and event type
    $type = script_param ("type");  # entered by user

    if (empty ($date))  # make sure a date was entered, and in ISO format
        die ("No date specified");
    if (!preg_match ('/^\d+\D\d+\D\d+$/', $date))
        die ("Please enter the date in ISO format (CCYY-MM-DD)");
    if ($type != "T" && $type != "Q")
        die ("Bad event type");

    $date = quote_value ($date);
    $type = quote_value ($type);
    if (!mysql_query ("INSERT INTO event (date,type) VALUES($date,$type)"))
        die ("Could not add event to database");
}
```

add_new_event() uses the `script_param()` library routine to access the parameter values that correspond to the date and type fields in the new-event entry form. Then it performs some minimal safety checks:

- The date should not be empty, and it should have been entered in ISO format. The `preg_match()` function performs a pattern match for ISO format:

```
preg_match ('/^\d+\D\d+\D\d+$/', $date)
```

  Single quotes are used here to prevent interpretation of the dollar sign and the backslashes as special characters. The test is true if the date consists of three sequences of digits separated by non–digit characters. That's not bullet-proof, but it's easy to add to the script, and it will catch many common errors.

- The event type must be one of those allowed in the type column of the event table ('T' or 'Q').

If the parameter values look okay, add_new_event() enters a new record into the event table. The query construction code uses quote_value() to make sure the data values are quoted properly for insertion into the query string. After executing the statement, add_new_event() returns to the main part of the script (the switch statement), which displays the event list again so that you can select the new event and begin entering scores for it.

When you select an item from the event list shown by the display_events() function, the score_entry.php script invokes the display_scores() function. Each event link contains an event number encoded as an event_id parameter, so display_scores() gets the parameter value, checks it to make sure it's an integer, and uses it in a query to retrieve a row for each student and any current scores the students may have for the event:

```
function display_scores ()
{
    # Get event ID number, which must look like an integer
    $event_id = script_param ("event_id");
    if (!preg_match ('/^\d+$/', $event_id))
        die ("Bad event ID");

    # select scores for the given event
    $query = sprintf ("
        SELECT
            student.student_id, student.name, event.date,
            score.score AS score, event.type
        FROM student, event
```

```
                LEFT JOIN score ON student.student_id = score.student_id
                     AND event.event_id = score.event_id
        WHERE event.event_id = %s
        ORDER BY student.name
    ", quote_value ($event_id));
    $result_id = mysql_query ($query)
        or die ("Cannot execute query");
    if (mysql_num_rows ($result_id) < 1)
        die ("No information was found for the selected event");

    printf ("<form method=\"POST\" action=\"%s?action=%s&event_id=%s\">\n",
                script_name (),
                urlencode (ENTER_SCORES),
                urlencode ($event_id));

    # print scores as an HTML table

    $row_num = 0;
    while ($row = mysql_fetch_array ($result_id))
    {
        # print event info and table heading preceding the first row
        if ($row_num == 0)
        {
            printf ("Event ID: %s, Event date: %s, Event type: %s\n",
                        htmlspecialchars ($event_id),
                        htmlspecialchars ($row["date"]),
                        htmlspecialchars ($row["type"]));
            print ("<br /><br />\n");
            print ("<table border=\"1\">\n");
            print ("<tr>\n");
            display_cell ("th", "Name");
            display_cell ("th", "Score");
            print "</tr>\n";
        }
        ++$row_num;
        print ("<tr>\n");
        display_cell ("td", $row["name"]);
        $col_val = sprintf ("<input type=\"text\" name=\"score[%s]\"",
                            htmlspecialchars ($row["student_id"]));
        $col_val .= sprintf (" value=\"%s\" size=\"5\" /><br />\n",
                            htmlspecialchars ($row["score"]));
        display_cell ("td", $col_val, FALSE);
        print ("</tr>\n");
    }

    print ("</table>\n");
    print ("<br />\n");
    print ("<input type=\"submit\" name=\"button\" value=\"Submit\" />\n");
    print "</form>\n";
}
```

The query that display_scores() uses to retrieve score information for the selected event is not just a simple join between tables, because that wouldn't select a row for any student who has no score for the event. In particular, for a new event, the join would select no records, and we'd have an empty entry form. We need to use a LEFT JOIN to force a row to be retrieved for each student, whether or not the student already has a score in the score table. If the student has no score for the given event, the value retrieved by the query will be NULL. (Background for a query similar to the one that display_scores() uses to retrieve score records from MySQL was given in Chapter 3, "MySQL SQL Syntax and Use," in the "Checking for Values Not Present in a Table" section.)

The scores retrieved by the query are placed in the form as input fields having names like score[n], where n is a student_id value. You can enter or edit the scores and then submit the form to have them stored in the database. When your browser sends the form back to the Web server, PHP will convert these fields into elements of an array associated with the name score that can be retrieved as follows:

```
$score = script_param ("score");
```

Elements of the array will be keyed by student ID, so we can easily associate each student with the corresponding score submitted in the form. The form contents are handled by the enter_scores() function, which looks like the following:

```
function enter_scores ()
{
    # Get event ID number and array of scores for the event

    $event_id = script_param ("event_id");
    $score = script_param ("score");

    if (!preg_match ('/^\d+$/', $event_id)) # must look like integer
        die ("Bad event ID");

    $invalid_count = 0;
    $blank_count = 0;
    $nonblank_count = 0;
    reset ($score);
    while (list ($student_id, $newscore) = each ($score))
    {
        $newscore = trim ($newscore);
        if (empty ($newscore))
        {
            # if no score is provided for student in the form, delete any
            # score the student may have had in the database previously
```

```
                    ++$blank_count;
                    $query = sprintf ("
                                    DELETE FROM score
                                    WHERE event_id = %s AND student_id = %s
                                ",
                                    quote_value ($event_id),
                                    quote_value ($student_id));
                }
                else if (!preg_match ('/^\d+$/', $newscore)) # must look like integer
                {
                    ++$nonblank_count;
                    $query = sprintf ("
                                    REPLACE INTO score (event_id,student_id,score)
                                    VALUES(%s,%s,%s)
                                ",
                                    quote_value ($event_id),
                                    quote_value ($student_id),
                                    quote_value ($newscore));
                }
                else
                {
                    ++$invalid_count;
                    continue;
                }
                if (!mysql_query ($query))
                    die ("score entry failed, event_id $event_id,"
                            ."student_id $student_id");
            }
        printf ("Number of scores entered: %d<br />\n", $nonblank_count);
        printf ("Number of scores missing: %d<br />\n", $blank_count);
        printf ("Number of invalid scores: %d<br />\n", $invalid_count);
        print ("<br />\n");
    }
```

The student ID values and scores associated with them are obtained by iterating through the $score array with PHP's each() function. The loop processes each score as follows:

- If the score is blank after any whitespace is trimmed from its ends, there is nothing to be entered. But just in case there was a score before, the script tries to delete it. (Perhaps we mistakenly entered a score earlier for a student who actually was absent, and now we need to remove it.) If the student had no score, DELETE will find no record to remove, but that's harmless.

- If the score is not blank, the function performs some rudimentary validation of the value and accepts it if it looks like an integer. Note that integer testing is done using a pattern match rather than PHP's is_int()

function. The latter is for testing whether a variable's type is integer, but form values are encoded as strings. is_int() will return FALSE for any string, even if it contains only digit characters. What we need here is a content check to verify the string, so a pattern match serves our purposes better. The following test is TRUE if every character from the beginning to the end of the string $str is a digit:

```
preg_match ('/^\d+$/', $str)
```

If the score looks okay, we add it to the score table. The query uses REPLACE rather than INSERT because we may be replacing an existing score rather than entering a new one. If the student had no score for the grade event, REPLACE adds a new record, just like INSERT; otherwise, REPLACE replaces the old score with the new one.

That takes care of the score_entry.php script. All score entry and editing can be done from your Web browser now. One obvious shortcoming is that the script provides no security; anyone who can connect to the Web server can edit scores. The script that we'll write later for Historical League member entry editing shows a simple authentication scheme that could be adapted for this script. For more serious security, you'd set up an SSL connection to protect the traffic between your browser and the Web server. But that's beyond the scope of this book.

Some other modifications you could make to the score_entry.php script are as follows:

- Display information about which scores were bad.
- Enter the scores within a transaction and roll back the transaction if any bad scores are found. To do this, you must make sure the score table uses a transactional type, such as InnoDB. Then you'd precede the score entry loop with a BEGIN statement and follow it with a COMMIT or ROLLBACK statement, depending on the value of $invalid_count.

If you decide to modify the script to use a transactional approach, it's important to use a non-persistent connection. Should the script die in the middle of the transaction, you'd want the transaction to be rolled back, which is what will happen with a non-persistent connection. PHP will close the connection, and the MySQL server automatically will roll back any transaction in progress if the client exits abnormally. With a persistent connection, PHP will keep the connection open, so it's possible that the incomplete transaction might not be rolled back.

U.S. President Quiz

One of the goals for the Historical League Web site was to use it for presenting an online version of a quiz, similar to some of the quizzes that the League publishes in the children's section of its newsletter, *Chronicles of U.S. Past.* We created the `president` table, in fact, so that we could use it as a source of questions for a history-based quiz. Let's do this now, using a script called `pres_quiz.php`.

The basic idea is to pick a president at random, ask a question about him, and then solicit an answer from the user and see whether or not the answer is correct. The types of questions the script might present could be based on any part of the `president` table records, but for simplicity, we'll constrain it to asking only where presidents were born. Another simplifying measure is to present the questions in multiple-choice format. That's easier for the user, who only needs to pick from among a set of choices rather than typing in a response. It's also easier for us because we don't have to do any pattern matching to check whatever the user might have typed. We need only a simple comparison of the user's choice and the value that we're looking for.

The `pres_quiz.php` script must perform two functions. First, when initially invoked, it should generate and display a new question by looking up information from the `president` table. Second, if the user has submitted a response, the script must check it and provide feedback to indicate whether it was correct. If the response was incorrect, the script should redisplay the same question; otherwise, it should generate and display a new question.

The outline for the script is quite simple. If the user isn't submitting a response, it presents the initial question page; otherwise, it checks the answer:

```php
<?php
# pres_quiz.php - script to quiz user on presidential birthplaces

include "sampdb.php";

# ... put quiz-handling functions here ...

$title = "U.S. President Quiz";
html_begin ($title, $title);
sampdb_connect ()
    or die ("Sorry, could not connect to database; no quiz available");

$response = script_param ("response");
if (!isset ($response))      # invoked for first time
    present_question ();
else                         # user submitted response to form
    check_response ();

html_end ();
?>
```

To create the questions, we'll use ORDER BY RAND(), a feature introduced in MySQL 3.23.2. Using the RAND() function, we can select rows at random from the president table. For example, to pick a president name and birthplace randomly, the following query does the job:

```
SELECT CONCAT(first_name, ' ', last_name) AS name,
CONCAT(city, ', ', state) AS place
FROM president ORDER BY RAND() LIMIT 1;
```

The name will be the president about whom we ask the question, and the birthplace will be the correct answer to the question "Where was this president born?" We'll also need to present some incorrect choices, which we can select using a similar query:

```
SELECT DISTINCT CONCAT(city, ', ', state) AS place
FROM president ORDER BY RAND();
```

From the result of this query, we'll select the first four values that differ from the correct response. The reason for using DISTINCT in this query is to avoid the possibility of selecting the same birthplace for the choice list more than once. DISTINCT would be unnecessary if birthplaces were unique, but they are not, as you can discover by issuing the following statement:

```
mysql> SELECT city, state, COUNT(*) AS count FROM president
    -> GROUP BY city, state HAVING count > 1;
+-----------+-------+-------+
| city      | state | count |
+-----------+-------+-------+
| Braintree | MA    |     2 |
+-----------+-------+-------+
```

The function that generates the question and the set of possible responses looks like this:

```
function present_question ()
{
    # issue query to pick a president and get birthplace
    $query = "SELECT CONCAT(first_name, ' ', last_name) AS name,"
            . " CONCAT(city, ', ', state) AS place"
            . " FROM president ORDER BY RAND() LIMIT 1";
    $result_id = mysql_query ($query)
        or die ("Cannot execute query");
    $row = mysql_fetch_array ($result_id)
        or die ("Cannot fetch result");
    $name = $row["name"];
    $place = $row["place"];
    # Construct the set of birthplace choices to present.
    # Set up the $choices array containing five birthplaces, one
    # of which is the correct response.
    $query = "SELECT DISTINCT CONCAT(city, ', ', state) AS place"
            . " FROM president ORDER BY RAND()";
    $result_id = mysql_query ($query)
        or die ("Cannot execute query");
```

```
    $choices[] = $place;    # initialize array with correct choice
    while (count ($choices) < 5 && $row = mysql_fetch_array ($result_id))
    {
        if ($row["place"] == $place)
            continue;
        $choices[] = $row["place"]; # add another choice
    }
    # seed random number generator, randomize choices, then display form
    srand ((float) microtime () * 10000000);
    shuffle ($choices);
    display_form ($name, $place, $choices);
}
```

present_question() as shown will not work if your version of MySQL precedes 3.23.2, because older versions don't allow functions in the ORDER BY
clause. Check the comments in the source code of the pres_quiz.php script
for a description of some modifications you can use to work around this limitation.

The display_form() function called by present_question() generates the
quiz question using a form that displays the name of the president, a set of
radio buttons that lists the possible choices, and a Submit button. This form
serves the obvious purpose of presenting quiz information to the user, but it
also needs to do something else: It must present the quiz information to the
client and arrange that when the user submits a response, the information sent
back to the Web server allows the script to check whether the response is correct and redisplay the question if not.

Presenting the quiz question is a matter of displaying the president's name and
the possible birthplace choices, which is straightforward enough. Arranging to
be able to check the response and possibly redisplay the question is a little
trickier. It requires that we have access to the correct answer and also to all the
information needed to regenerate the question. One way to do this is to use a
set of hidden fields to include all the necessary information in the form. These
fields become part of the form and will be returned when the user submits a
response, but they are not displayed for the user to see.

We'll call the hidden fields name, place, and choices to represent the president's name, correct birthplace, and the set of possible choices. The choices can
be encoded as a single string easily by using implode() to concatenate the
values with a special delimiter character in between. (The delimiter allows us
to properly break apart the string later with explode() if it becomes necessary
to redisplay the question.) The display_form() function takes care of producing the form:

```
    function display_form ($name, $place, $choices)
    {
```

```
    printf ("<form method=\"POST\" action=\"%s\">\n", script_name ());
    hidden_field ("name", $name);
    hidden_field ("place", $place);
    hidden_field ("choices", implode ("#", $choices));
    printf ("Where was %s born?<br /><br />\n", htmlspecialchars ($name));
    for ($i = 0; $i < 5; $i++)
    {
        radio_button ("response", $choices[$i], $choices[$i], FALSE);
        print ("<br />\n");
    }
    print ("<br />\n");
    submit_button ("submit", "Submit");
    print ("</form>\n");
}
```

`display_form()` uses several helper functions to generate the form fields. The first is `hidden_field()` that generates the `<input>` tag for a hidden field:

```
function hidden_field ($name, $value)
{
    printf ("<input type=\"%s\" name=\"%s\" value=\"%s\" />\n",
            "hidden",
            htmlspecialchars ($name),
            htmlspecialchars ($value));
}
```

Because `hidden_field()` is a general-purpose routine likely to be useful in many scripts, the logical place to put it is in our library file, `sampdb.php`. Note that it uses `htmlspecialchars()` to encode both the `name` and `value` attributes of the `<input>` tag in case the `$name` or `$value` variables contain special characters, such as quotes.

Two other helper functions, `radio_button()` and `submit_button()`, are implemented as follows:

```
function radio_button ($name, $value, $label, $checked)
{
    printf ("<input type=\"%s\" name=\"%s\" value=\"%s\"%s />%s\n",
            "radio",
            htmlspecialchars ($name),
            htmlspecialchars ($value),
            ($checked ? " checked=\"checked\"" : ""),
            htmlspecialchars ($label));
}

function submit_button ($name, $value)
{
    printf ("<input type=\"%s\" name=\"%s\" value=\"%s\" />\n",
            "submit",
            htmlspecialchars ($name),
            htmlspecialchars ($value));
}
```

When the user chooses a birthplace from among the available options and submits the form, the response is returned to the Web server as the value of the `response` parameter. We can discover the value of `response` by calling `script_param()`, which also gives us a way to figure out whether the script is being called for the first time or if the user is submitting a response to a previously displayed form. The parameter will not be set if this is a first-time invocation, so the main body of the script can determine what it should do based on the parameter's presence or absence:

```
$response = script_param ("response");
if (!isset ($response))      # invoked for first time
    present_question ();
else                         # user submitted response to form
    check_response ();
```

We still need to write the `check_response()` function that compares the user's response to the correct answer. For this, the values present in the `name`, `place`, and `choices` hidden fields are needed. We encoded the correct answer in the `place` field of the form, and the user's response will be in the `response` field, so to check the answer all we need to do is compare the two. Based on the result of the comparison, `check_response()` provides some feedback and then either generates and displays a new question or redisplays the same question:

```
function check_response ()
{
    $name = script_param ("name");
    $place = script_param ("place");
    $choices = script_param ("choices");
    $response = script_param ("response");

    # Is the user's response the correct birthplace?

    if ($response == $place)
    {
        print ("That is correct!<br />\n");
        printf ("%s was born in %s.<br />\n",
                htmlspecialchars ($name),
                htmlspecialchars ($place));
        print ("Try the next question:<br /><br />\n");
        present_question();
    }
    else
    {
        printf ("\"%s\" is not correct.  Please try again.<br /><br />\n",
                htmlspecialchars ($response));
        $choices = explode ("#", $choices);
        display_form ($name, $place, $choices);
    }
}
```

We're done. Add a link for `pres_quiz.php` to the Historical League home page, and visitors can try out the quiz to test their knowledge.

> **Hidden Fields Are Not Secure**
>
> `pres_quiz.php` relies on hidden fields as a means of transmitting information that is needed for the next invocation of the script but that the user should not see. That's fine for a script like this, which is intended only for fun. But hidden fields should *not* be used for any information that the user must not ever be allowed to examine directly, because they are not secure in any sense. To see why not, install `pres_quiz.php` in the `ushl` directory of your Web server document tree and request it from your browser. Then use the browser's View Source command to see the raw HTML for the quiz page. There you'll find the contents of the `place` hidden field that contains the correct answer for the current quiz question, exposed for anyone to see. This means it's very easy to cheat on the quiz. That's no big deal for this particular application, but the example does illustrate that hidden fields are not secure in the least. Do not use them for information that really must be kept secure from the user.

Historical League Online Member Entry Editing

Our final PHP script, `edit_member.php`, is intended to allow the Historical League members to edit their own directory entries online. Using this script, members will be able to correct or update their membership information whenever they want without having to contact the League office to submit the changes. Providing this capability should help keep the member directory more up to date, and, not incidentally, reduce the workload of the League secretary.

One precaution we need to take is to make sure each entry can be modified only by the member the entry is for or by the League secretary. This means we need some form of security. As a demonstration of a simple form of authentication, we'll use MySQL to store passwords for each member and require that a member supply the correct password to gain access to the editing form that our script presents. The script works as follows:

- When initially invoked, `edit_script.php` presents a login form containing fields for the member ID and a password.
- When the login form is submitted, the script looks in a password table that associates member IDs and passwords. If the password matches, the script looks up the member entry from the `member` table and displays it for editing.
- When the edited form is submitted, we update the entry in the database using the contents of the form.

For any of this to work, of course, we'll need to assign passwords. An easy way to do this is to generate them randomly. The following statements set up a table named `member_pass` and then create a password for each member by generating an MD5 checksum from a random number and using the first eight characters of the result. In a real situation, you might let members pick their own passwords, but this technique provides a quick and easy way to set something up initially:

```
mysql> CREATE TABLE member_pass (
    -> member_id INT UNSIGNED NOT NULL PRIMARY KEY,
    -> password CHAR(8));
mysql> INSERT INTO member_pass (member_id, password)
    -> SELECT member_id, LEFT(MD5(RAND()), 8) AS password FROM member;
```

The `MD5()` function is unavailable prior to MySQL 3.23.2. Another way to generate eight-character random values that works in any version of MySQL is as follows:

```
mysql> INSERT INTO member_pass (member_id, password)
    -> SELECT member_id, FLOOR(RAND()*99999999) AS password FROM member;
```

These values are less varied than those based on `MD5()` because they are composed entirely of digits.

In addition to a password for each person listed in the `member` table, we'll add a special entry to the `member_pass` table for member 0, with a password that will serve as the administrative (superuser) password. The League secretary can use this password to gain access to any entry:

```
mysql> INSERT INTO member_pass (member_id, password) VALUES(0, 'bigshot');
```

Note: Before creating the `member_pass` table, you might want to remove the `samp_browse.pl` script from your Web server's script directory. (That script, written in Chapter 7 allows anyone to browse the contents of any table in the sampdb database—including the `member_pass` table. Thus, it could be used to see any League member's password or the administrative password.)

When the `member_pass` table has been set up, we're ready to begin building `edit_member.php`. The framework for the script is as follows:

```php
<?php
# edit_member.php - Edit Historical League member entries via the Web

include "sampdb.php";

# define action constants
define ("SHOW_INITIAL_PAGE", 0);
define ("DISPLAY_ENTRY", 1);
define ("UPDATE_ENTRY", 2);

# ... put input-handling functions here ...
```

```
$title = "U.S. Historical League -- Member Editing Form";
html_begin ($title, $title);

sampdb_connect ()
    or die ("Cannot connect to server");

# determine what action to perform (the default if
# none is specified is to present the initial page)

$action = script_param ("action");
if (!isset ($action))
    $action = SHOW_INITIAL_PAGE;

switch ($action)
{
case SHOW_INITIAL_PAGE:     # present initial page
    display_login_page ();
    break;
case DISPLAY_ENTRY:         # display entry for editing
    display_entry ();
    break;
case UPDATE_ENTRY:          # store updated entry in database
    update_entry ();
    break;
default:
    die ("Unknown action code ($action)");
}

html_end ();
?>
```

The initial page is presented by display_login_page(), which generates a form that asks for a member ID and password:

```
function display_login_page ()
{
    printf ("<form method=\"POST\" action=\"%s?action=%s\">\n",
                script_name (),
                urlencode (DISPLAY_ENTRY));
    print ("Enter your membership ID number and password,\n");
    print ("then select Submit.\n<br /><br />\n");
    print ("<table>\n");
    print ("<tr>");
    print ("<td>Member ID</td><td>");
    text_field ("member_id", "", 10);
    print ("</td></tr>");
    print ("<tr>");
    print ("<td>Password</td><td>");
    password_field ("password", "", 10);
    print ("</td></tr>");
    print ("</table>\n");
    submit_button ("button", "Submit");
    print ("</form>\n");
}
```

The captions and the value entry fields in the form are presented within the framework of an HTML table to make them line up nicely. With only two fields, this is a minor touch, but it's a generally useful technique, especially when you create forms with captions of very dissimilar lengths, because it eliminates vertical raggedness. Lining up the form components can make the form easier for the user to read and understand.

`display_login_form()` uses two more helper functions that can be found in the `sampdb.php` library file. `text_field()` presents an editable text input field:

```
function text_field ($name, $value, $size)
{
    printf ("<input type=\"%s\" name=\"%s\" value=\"%s\" size=\"%s\" />\n",
            "text",
            htmlspecialchars ($name),
            htmlspecialchars ($value),
            htmlspecialchars ($size));
}
```

`password_field()` is the same, except that the `type` attribute is `password` (so I won't show it).

When the user enters a member ID and password and submits the form, the `action` parameter will be equal to `DISPLAY_ENTRY`, and the `switch` statement in the next invocation of `edit_member.php` will invoke the `display_entry()` function to check the password and display the member entry if the password matches:

```
function display_entry ()
{
    # Get script parameters; trim whitespace from ID, but
    # not from password, because password must match exactly.

    $member_id = trim (script_param ("member_id"));
    $password = script_param ("password");

    if (empty ($member_id))
        die ("No member ID was specified");
    if (!preg_match ('/^\d+$/', $member_id))     # must look like integer
        die ("Invalid member ID was specified (must be an integer)");
    if (empty ($password))
        die ("No password was specified");
    if (check_pass ($member_id, $password)) # regular member
        $admin = FALSE;
    else if (check_pass (0, $password))     # administrator
        $admin = TRUE;
    else
        die ("Invalid password");
```

```php
$query = sprintf ("
                SELECT
                    last_name, first_name, suffix, email, street, city,
                    state, zip, phone, interests, member_id, expiration
                FROM member WHERE member_id = %s
                ORDER BY last_name
            ", quote_value ($member_id));
$result_id = mysql_query ($query);
if (!$result_id)
    die ("Cannot execute query");
if (mysql_num_rows ($result_id) == 0)
    die ("No user with member_id = $member_id was found");
if (mysql_num_rows ($result_id) > 1)
    die ("More than one user with member_id = $member_id was found");

printf ("<form method=\"POST\" action=\"%s?action=%s\">\n",
            script_name (),
            urlencode (UPDATE_ENTRY));

# Add member ID and password as hidden values so that next invocation
# of script can tell which record the form corresponds to and so that
# the user need not re-enter the password.

hidden_field ("member_id", $member_id);
hidden_field ("password", $password);

# Read results of query and format for editing

$row = mysql_fetch_array ($result_id);

print ("<table>\n");

# Display member ID as static text

display_column ("Member ID", $row, "member_id", FALSE);

# $admin is true if the user provided the administrative password,
# false otherwise. Administrative users can edit the expiration
# date, regular users cannot.

display_column ("Expiration", $row, "expiration", $admin);

# Display other values as editable text

display_column ("Last name", $row, "last_name");
display_column ("First name", $row, "first_name");
display_column ("Suffix", $row, "suffix");
display_column ("Email", $row, "email");
display_column ("Street", $row, "street");
display_column ("City", $row, "city");
display_column ("State", $row, "state");
display_column ("Zip", $row, "zip");
```

```
        display_column ("Phone", $row, "phone");
        display_column ("Interests", $row, "interests");

        print ("</table>\n");

        submit_button ("button", "Submit");
        print "</form>\n";

    }
```

The first thing `display_entry()` does is to verify the password. If the password supplied by the user matches the password stored in the `member_pass`
table for the given member ID, or if it matches the administrative password
(that is, the password for the special member ID 0), `edit_member.php` displays
the entry in a form so that its contents can be edited. The password-checking
function `check_pass()` runs a simple query to yank a record from the mem-
ber_pass table and compare its `password` column value to the password supplied by the user in the login form:

```
    function check_pass ($id, $pass)
    {
        $query = sprintf ("SELECT password FROM member_pass WHERE member_id = %s",
                          quote_value ($id));
        $result_id = mysql_query ($query);
        if (!$result_id)
            die ("Error reading password table");
        if ($row = mysql_fetch_array ($result_id))
            return ($row["password"] == $pass); # TRUE if password matches
        return (FALSE);                          # no record found
    }
```

Assuming that the password matches, `display_entry()` looks up the record
from the `member` table corresponding to the given member ID and then goes
on to generate an editing form initialized with the values from the record.
Most of the fields are presented as editable text fields so that the user can
change them, but there are two exceptions. First, the `member_id` value is displayed as static text. This is the key value that uniquely identifies the record, so
it should not be changed. Second, the expiration date is not something that we
want League members to be able to change. (They'd be able to push the date
farther into the future, in effect renewing their memberships without paying
the yearly dues.) On the other hand, if the administrative password was given
at login time, the script does present the expiration date in an editable field.
Assuming the League secretary knows this password, the secretary can then
update the expiration date for members who renew their memberships.

Display of field labels and values is handled by the `display_column()` function. Its arguments are the label to display next to the field value, the array that contains the record to be edited, the name of the column within the record that contains the field value, and a boolean value that indicates whether to present the value in editable or static form. The last value is optional, with a default value of TRUE:

```
function display_column ($label, $row, $col_name, $editable = TRUE)
{
    print ("<tr>\n");
    printf ("<td>%s</td>\n", htmlspecialchars ($label));
    print ("<td>");
    if ($editable)  # display as edit field
        text_field ("row[$col_name]", $row[$col_name], 80);
    else            # display as read-only text
        print (htmlspecialchars ($row[$col_name]));
    print ("</td>\n");
    print ("</tr>\n");
}
```

For editable values, `display_column()` generates text fields using names that have the format `row[col_name]`. That way, when the user submits the form, PHP will place all the field values into an array variable with elements keyed by column name. This makes it easy to extract the form contents and to associate each field value with its corresponding `member` table column when we update the record in the database. For example, by fetching the array into a `$row` variable, we can access the telephone number as `$row["phone"]`.

The `display_entry()` function also embeds the `member_id` and `password` values as hidden fields in the form so that they will carry over to the next invocation of `edit_script.php` when the user submits the edited entry. The ID allows the script to determine which `member` table record to update, and the password allows it to verify that the user logged in before. (Notice that this simple authentication method involves passing the password back and forth in clear text, which isn't generally such a great idea. But the Historical League is not a high-security organization, so this method suffices for our purposes. Were you performing operations like financial transactions, you'd want to use a more secure form of authentication.)

The function that updates the membership entry when the form is submitted looks like this:

```
function update_entry ()
{
    # Get script parameters; trim whitespace from ID, but
    # not from password, because it must match exactly, or
    # from row, because it is an array.
```

```
$member_id = trim (script_param ("member_id"));
$password = script_param ("password");
$row = script_param ("row");

$member_id = trim ($member_id);
if (empty ($member_id))
    die ("No member ID was specified");
if (!preg_match ('/^\d+$/', $member_id))    # must look like integer
    die ("Invalid member ID was specified (must be an integer)");
if (!check_pass ($member_id, $password) && !check_pass (0, $password))
    die ("Invalid password");

# We'll need a result set to use for assessing nullability of
# member table columns.  The following query provides one without
# selecting any rows.  Use the query result to construct an
# associative array that maps column names to true/false values
# indicating whether columns allow NULL values.

$result_id = mysql_query ("SELECT * FROM member WHERE 1 = 0");
if (!$result_id)
    die ("Cannot query member table");
$nullable = array ();
for ($i = 0; $i < mysql_num_fields ($result_id); $i++)
{
    $fld = mysql_fetch_field ($result_id, $i);
    $nullable[$fld->name] = !$fld->not_null;    # TRUE if nullable
}
mysql_free_result ($result_id);

# Iterate through each field in the form, using the values to
# construct the UPDATE statement.

$query = "UPDATE member ";
$delim = "SET";
reset ($row);
while (list ($col_name, $val) = each ($row))
{
    $query .= "$delim $col_name=";
    $delim = ",";
    # if a form value is empty, update the corresponding column value
    # with NULL if the column is nullable.  This prevents trying to
    # put an empty string into the expiration date column when it
    # should be NULL, for example.
    $val = trim ($val);
    if (empty ($val))
    {
        if ($nullable[$col_name])
            $query .= "NULL";    # enter NULL
        else
            $query .= "\'";    # enter empty string
    }
```

```
        }
        else
            $query .= quote_value ($val);
    }
    $query .= sprintf (" WHERE member_id = %s", quote_value ($member_id));
    if (mysql_query ($query))
        print ("Member entry was updated successfully.\n");
    else
        print ("Member entry was not updated.\n");
}
```

First we re-verify the password to make sure someone isn't attempting to hoax us by sending a faked form, and then the entry is updated. The update requires some care because if a field in the form is blank, it may need to be entered as NULL rather than as an empty string. The expiration column is an example of this. Suppose the League secretary logs in with the administrative password (so that the expiration field is editable) and clears the field to indicate "lifetime membership." This should correspond to a NULL membership expiration date in the database. If the script inserts an empty string into the expiration column when the form is submitted, MySQL will convert the value to '0000-00-00', which is incorrect. So it's necessary to be able to tell which columns can take NULL values and insert NULL (rather than an empty string) when such a column is left blank in the form.

To handle this problem, update_entry() looks up the metadata for the member table and constructs an associative array keyed on column name that indicates which columns can have NULL values and which cannot. This information is returned by the mysql_fetch_field() function, which requires a result identifier for the table whose columns we're checking. We get that by executing a trivial SELECT query that returns no rows:

```
SELECT * FROM member WHERE 1 = 0
```

The query returns an empty result set, but also produces the metadata that we need for assessing the nullability of the member table columns.

At this point, the edit_member.php script is finished. Install it in the ushl directory of the Web document tree and let the members know their passwords; they'll be able to update their own membership information over the Web.

MySQL Administration

9

Introduction to MySQL Administration

AS DATABASE SYSTEMS GO, MySQL IS relatively simple to use, and the effort required to bring up a MySQL installation and use it is modest as well. MySQL's simplicity probably accounts for much of its popularity, especially among people who aren't, and don't want to be, system administrators. It helps to be a trained computer professional, of course, but that's certainly not a requirement for running a successful MySQL installation.

Nevertheless, MySQL won't run itself, regardless of your level of expertise. Someone must watch over it to make sure it operates smoothly and efficiently, and someone must know what to do when problems occur. If the job falls on you to make sure MySQL is happy at your site, keep reading.

Part III of this book, "MySQL Administration," examines the various aspects of MySQL administration. This chapter provides a brief description of the responsibilities involved in administrating a MySQL installation, and the following chapters provide instructions for carrying them out.

If you are a new or inexperienced MySQL administrator, don't let the long list of responsibilities presented in this chapter scare you. Each task listed in the following sections is important, but you need not learn them all at once. If you like, you can use the chapters in this part of the book as a reference, looking up topics as you discover that you need to know about them.

If you have experience administrating other database systems, you will find that running a MySQL installation is similar in some ways and that your experience is a valuable resource. But MySQL administration has its own unique requirements; this part of the book will help you become familiar with them.

Overview of Administrative Duties

The MySQL database system consists of several components. You should be familiar with what these components are and the purpose of each to understand both the nature of the system you're administrating and the tools available to help you do your job. If you take the time to understand what you're overseeing, your work will be much easier. To that end, you should acquaint yourself with the following aspects of MySQL:

- **The MySQL server.** The server, `mysqld`, is the hub of a MySQL installation; it performs all manipulation of databases and tables. `mysqld_safe` is a related program used to start up the server, monitor it, and restart it in case it goes down. (Prior to MySQL 4, `mysqld_safe` is named `safe_mysqld`.) If you run multiple servers on a single host, `mysqld_multi` can help you manage them more easily.

- **The MySQL clients and utilities.** Several MySQL programs are available to help you communicate with the server. For administrative tasks, the most important of these are:
  - `mysql`—An interactive program that allows you to send SQL statements to the server and to view the results
  - `mysqladmin`—An administrative program that lets you perform tasks such as shutting down the server or checking its status if it appears not to be functioning properly
  - `mysqlcheck`, `isamchk`, and `myisamchk`—Utilities that help you perform table analysis and optimization, as well as crash recovery if tables become damaged
  - `mysqldump` and `mysqlhotcopy`—Tools for backing up your databases or copying databases to another server

- **The server's language, SQL.** Some administrative duties can be performed using only the `mysqladmin` command-line utility, but you're better off if you're also able to talk to the server in its own language. As a simple example, you may need to find out why a user's privileges aren't working the way you expect them to work. There is no substitute for being able to go in and communicate with the server directly, which you can do by using the `mysql` client program to issue SQL queries that let you examine the grant tables. And if your version of MySQL predates the introduction of the GRANT statement, mysql can be used to set up each user's privileges by manipulating the grant tables directly.

If you don't know any SQL, be sure to acquire at least a basic understanding of it. A lack of SQL fluency will only hinder you, whereas the time you take to learn will be repaid many times over. A real mastery of SQL takes some time, but the basic skills can be attained quickly. For instruction in SQL and the use of the mysql command-line client, see Chapter 1, "Getting Started with MySQL and SQL."

- **The MySQL data directory.** The data directory is where the server stores its databases and status files. It's important to understand the structure and contents of the data directory so that you know how the server uses the file system to represent databases and tables, as well as where files, such as the logs, are located and what's in them. You should also know your options for managing allocation of disk space across file systems should you find that the file system on which the data directory is located is becoming too full.

General Administration

General administration deals primarily with the operation of mysqld, the MySQL server, and with providing your users access to the server. The following duties are most important in carrying out this responsibility:

- **Server startup and shutdown.** You should know how to start and stop the server manually from the command line and how to arrange for automatic startup and shutdown when your system starts up and shuts down. It's also important to know what to do to get the server going again if it crashes or will not start properly.

- **User account maintenance.** You should understand the difference between MySQL user accounts and UNIX or Windows login accounts. You should know how to set up MySQL accounts by specifying which users can connect to the server and from where they can connect. New users should also be advised on the proper connection parameters that they will need to use to connect to the server successfully. It's not their job to figure out how you've set up their accounts! You'll also need to know how to reset forgotten passwords.

- **Log file maintenance.** You should understand what types of log files you can maintain, as well as when and how to perform log file maintenance. Log rotation and expiration are essential to prevent the logs from filling up your file system.

- **Database backup and copying.** Database backups are of crucial importance in the event of a severe system crash. You want to be able to restore your databases to the state they were in at the time of the crash with as little data loss as possible. Note that backing up your databases is not the same thing as performing general system backups (as is done, for example, by using the UNIX `dump` program). The files corresponding to your database tables may be in flux due to server activity when system backups take place, so restoring those files will not give you internally consistent tables. The `mysqldump` program generates backup files that are more useful for database restoration, and it allows you to create backups without taking down the server. You may also need to move databases in the event of a full disk.

  If you decide to run a database on a faster host, you'll need to copy its contents to a different machine. You should understand the procedure for doing this, should the need arise. Database files may be system dependent, so you can't necessarily just copy the files.

- **Database replication.** Making a backup or a copy of a database takes a snapshot of its state at one point in time. Another option available to you is to use replication, which involves setting up two servers in cooperative fashion such that changes to databases managed by one server are propagated on a continuing basis to the corresponding databases managed by the other server.

- **Server configuration and tuning.** Your users want the server to perform at its best. The quick-and-dirty method for improving how well your server runs is to buy more memory or to get faster disks. But those brute-force techniques are no substitute for understanding how the server works. You should know what parameters are available for tuning the server's operation and how they apply to your situation. At some sites, queries tend to be mostly retrievals. At others, inserts and updates dominate. The choice of which parameters to change will be influenced by the query mix that you observe at your own site.

  Configuration issues also include localizing the server (for example, to make sure that it uses the proper character set and time zone).

- **Multiple servers.** It's useful to run multiple servers under some circumstances. You can test a new MySQL release while leaving your current production installation in place, or provide better privacy for different groups of users by giving each group its own server. (The latter scenario is particularly relevant to ISPs.) For such situations, you should know how to set up multiple simultaneous installations.

- **MySQL software updates.** New MySQL releases appear frequently. You should know how to keep up to date with these releases to take advantage of bug fixes and new features. Understand the circumstances under which it's more reasonable to hold off on upgrading, and know how to choose between the stable and development releases.

Security

When you run a MySQL installation, it's important to make sure that the information your users entrust to their databases is kept secure. The MySQL administrator is responsible for controlling access to the data directory and the server and should understand the following issues:

- **File system security.** A UNIX machine may host several user accounts that have no MySQL-related administrative duties. It's important to ensure that these accounts have no access to the data directory. This prevents them from compromising data on a file system level by copying database tables or removing them, or by being able to read log files that may contain sensitive information. You should know how to set up a UNIX user account to be used for running the MySQL server, how to set up the data directory so that it is owned by that user, and how to start up the server to run with that user's privileges.

- **Server security.** You must understand how the MySQL security system works so that when you set up user accounts, you grant the proper privileges. Users connecting to the server over the network should have permission to do only what they are supposed to be able to do. You don't want to inadvertently grant superuser access to anonymous users due to faulty understanding of the security system!

Database Repair and Maintenance

Every MySQL administrator hopes to avoid having to deal with corrupted or destroyed database tables. But hope alone won't keep problems from occurring. You should take steps to minimize your risks and learn what to do if bad things do happen:

- **Crash recovery.** Should disaster strike in spite of your best efforts, you should know how to repair or restore your tables. Crash recovery should be necessary only rarely, but when it is, it's an unpleasant, high-stress business (especially with the phone ringing and people knocking on the door while you're scrambling to fix things). Nevertheless, you must know how to do it because your users will be quite unhappy otherwise. Be familiar with MySQL's table-checking and repair utilities. Know how to recover data using your backup files and how to use the update logs to recover changes that were made after your most recent backup.

- **Preventive maintenance.** A regular program of preventive maintenance should be put in place to minimize the likelihood of database corruption or damage. You should also be making backups, of course, but preventive maintenance reduces the chance that you'll need to use them.

The preceding outline summarizes the responsibilities you undertake by becoming a MySQL administrator. The next few chapters discuss them in more detail and describe procedures to follow so that you can carry out these responsibilities effectively. We'll discuss the MySQL data directory first; that's the primary resource you're maintaining, and you should understand its layout and contents. From there we move on to general administrative duties, a discussion of MySQL's security system, and maintenance and troubleshooting.

10

The MySQL Data Directory

Conceptually, most relational database systems are broadly similar; they manage a set of databases, and each database includes a set of tables. But every system has its own way of organizing the data it manages, and MySQL is no exception. By default, all information managed by the MySQL server mysqld is stored under a location called the MySQL data directory. All databases are stored here, as well as the status and log files that provide information about the server's operation. If you have any administrative responsibilities for a MySQL installation, familiarity with the layout and use of the data directory is fundamental to carrying out your duties. You can also benefit from reading this chapter even if you don't perform any MySQL administration; it never hurts to have a better idea of how the server operates.

This chapter covers the following topics:

- **How to determine the location of the data directory.** You need to know this so that you can administer its contents effectively.

- **How the server organizes and provides access to the databases and tables it manages.** This is important for setting up preventive maintenance schedules and for performing crash recovery should table corruption ever occur.

- **What status and log files the server generates and what they contain.** Their contents provide useful information about how the server is running, which is useful if you encounter problems.

- **How to change the default location or organization of the data directory.** This can be important for managing the allocation of disk resources on your system—for example, by balancing disk activity across drives or by relocating data to file systems with more free space. You can also use this knowledge in planning placement of new databases.

For UNIX systems, the chapter assumes the existence of a login account that is used for performing MySQL administrative tasks and for running the server. In this book, the user and group names for that account are `mysqladm` and `mysqlgrp`. The reasons for using a designated login account for MySQL administration are discussed in Chapter 11, "General MySQL Administration."

Location of the Data Directory

A default data directory location is compiled into the server. Under UNIX, typical defaults are `/usr/local/mysql/var` if you install MySQL from a source distribution, `/usr/local/mysql/data` if you install from a binary distribution, and `/var/lib/mysql` if you install from an RPM file. Under Windows, the default data directory is `C:\mysql\data`.

The data directory location can be specified explicitly when you start up the server by using a `--datadir=dir_name` option. This is useful if you want to place the directory somewhere other than its default location. Another way to specify the location is to list it in an option file that the server reads at startup time. Then you don't need to include it on the command line each time you start the server. Data directory relocation is covered later in the chapter.

As a MySQL administrator, you should know where your server's data directory is located. If you run multiple servers, you should know where each one's data directory is. But if you don't know the location (perhaps you are taking over for a previous administrator who left poor notes), there are several ways to find out:

- Ask the server for the location. The server maintains a number of variables pertaining to its operation, and it can report any of their values. The data directory location is indicated by the `datadir` variable, which you can obtain using a `mysqladmin variables` command or a `SHOW`

VARIABLES statement. From the command line, use `mysqladmin`. On UNIX, the output might look like this:

```
% mysqladmin variables
+--------------+----------------------+
| Variable_name | Value               |
+--------------+----------------------+
...
| datadir       | /usr/local/mysql/var/ |
...
```

On Windows, the output might look like the following instead:

```
C:\> mysqladmin variables
+--------------+----------------------------+
| Variable_name | Value                     |
+--------------+----------------------------+
...
| datadir       | c:\mysql\data\            |
...
```

From within `mysql`, check the variable's value like this:

```
mysql> SHOW VARIABLES LIKE 'datadir';
+--------------+----------------------+
| Variable_name | Value               |
+--------------+----------------------+
| datadir       | /usr/local/mysql/var/ |
+--------------+----------------------+
```

If you have multiple servers running, they will be listening on different TCP/IP port numbers, sockets, or named pipes. You can get data directory information from each of them in turn by supplying appropriate `--port` or `--socket` options to connect to the port or socket on which each server is listening. Specifying a host of 127.0.0.1 explicitly tells `mysqladmin` to connect to the server on the local host using a TCP/IP connection:

```
% mysqladmin --host=127.0.0.1 --port=port_num variables
```

Under UNIX, specifying a value of `localhost` causes a UNIX socket connection to be used. You can also specify a `--socket` option if necessary to indicate the socket file pathname:

```
% mysqladmin --host=localhost --socket=/path/to/socket variables
```

Under Windows NT-based systems, a named pipe connection can be specified by giving '.' as a hostname, perhaps with a `--socket` option to indicate the pipe name:

```
C:\> mysqladmin --host=. --socket=pipe_name variables
```

For any platform, to connect via TCP/IP to a remote server running on another host, specify a --host option that indicates the name of the server host:

```
% mysqladmin --host=host_name variables
```

Specify a --port option as well if you need to connect to a port number other than the default.

- Under UNIX, use the ps command to see the command line of any currently executing mysqld process or processes. By looking for a --datadir option, you may be able to determine the data directory location. If you have a BSD-style ps, try the following command:

```
% ps axww | grep mysqld
```

For a System V-style ps, try this instead:

```
% ps -ef | grep mysqld
```

The ps command can be especially useful if your system runs multiple servers because you can discover multiple data directory locations at once. The drawbacks are that ps must be run on the server host and that no useful information is produced unless the --datadir option was specified explicitly on the mysqld command line. (On the other hand, some of the startup scripts that invoke mysqld for you attempt to determine the data directory pathname and put it in the mysqld command line, which makes that information available to ps.)

- Look in an option file that the server reads when it starts up. For example, if you look in /etc/my.cnf under UNIX or C:\my.cnf under Windows, you may find a datadir line in the [mysqld] option group:

```
[mysqld]
datadir=/path/to/data/directory
```

The pathname indicates the location of the data directory.

- The server's help message includes an indication of the default data directory location that is compiled in. This will tell you the directory that the server actually uses when it runs, if the location is not overridden at startup time. To see this output, issue the following command:

```
% mysqld --help
...
datadir       /usr/local/mysql/var/
...
```

- If you installed MySQL from a source distribution, you can examine its configuration information to determine the data directory location. For example, the location is available in the top-level `Makefile`. But be careful: The location is the value of the `localstatedir` variable in the `Makefile`, not the value of the `datadir` variable, as you might expect. Also, if the distribution is located on an NFS-mounted file system that is used to build MySQL for several hosts, the configuration information will be accurate only for the host for which the distribution was most recently built. That may not show you the data directory for the server in which you're interested.

- Failing any of the previous methods, you can use `find` to search for database files. The following command searches for `.frm` (description) files:

  ```
  % find / -name "*.frm" -print
  ```

The `.frm` files store the definitions of the tables managed by the server, so they are part of any MySQL installation. These files normally will be found in directories that all have a common parent directory; that parent should be the data directory.

In the examples that follow throughout this chapter where I denote the location of the MySQL data directory as *DATADIR*, you should interpret that as the location of the data directory for the server on your own machine.

Structure of the Data Directory

The MySQL data directory contains all of the databases and tables managed by the server. In general, these are organized into a tree structure that is implemented in straightforward fashion by taking advantage of the hierarchical structure of the UNIX or Windows file systems:

- Each database corresponds to a directory under the data directory.
- Tables within a database correspond to files in the database directory.

The exception to this hierarchical implementation of databases and tables as directories and files is that the InnoDB table handler stores all InnoDB tables from all databases within a single common tablespace. This tablespace is implemented using one or more large files that are treated as a single unified data structure within which tables and indexes are represented. The InnoDB tablespace files are stored in the data directory by default.

The data directory also may contain other files:

- An option file, my.cnf.
- The server's process ID (PID) file. When it starts up, the server writes its process ID to this file so that other programs can discover the value if they need to send signals to it. (This file is not used on Windows or by the embedded server.)
- Status and log files that are generated by the server. These files provide important information about the server's operation and are valuable for administrators, especially when something goes wrong and you're trying to determine the cause of the problem. If some particular query kills the server, for example, you may be able to identify the offending query by examining the log files.
- It's common to store files in the data directory such as the DES key file or the server's SSL certificate and key files.

How the MySQL Server Provides Access to Data

When MySQL is used in the usual client/server setup, all databases under the data directory are managed by a single entity—the MySQL server mysqld. Client programs never manipulate data directly. Instead, the server provides the sole point of contact though which databases are accessed, acting as the intermediary between client programs and the data they want to use. Figure 10.1 illustrates this architecture.

When the server starts up, it opens any log files that you request it to maintain and then presents a network interface to the data directory by listening for various types of network connections. (Details of how the server listens are presented in Chapter 11.) To access data, client programs establish a connection to the server and then communicate requests as SQL queries to perform the desired operations—for example, creating a table, selecting records, or updating records. The server performs each operation and sends back the result to the client. The server is multi-threaded and can service multiple simultaneous client connections. However, because update operations are performed one at a time, the practical effect is to serialize requests so that two clients can never change a given record at exactly the same time.

If you're running an application that uses the embedded server, a slightly different architecture applies, because there is only one "client"—that is, the application into which the server is linked. In this case, the server listens to an internal communication channel rather than to network interfaces. Nevertheless, it's still the embedded server part of the application that manages access to the data directory, and it's still necessary to coordinate query activity arriving over multiple connections if the application happens to open several connections to the server.

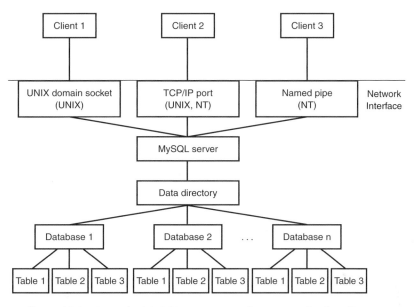

Figure 10.1   How the MySQL server controls access to the data directory.

Under normal conditions, having the server act as the sole arbiter of database access provides assurance against the kinds of corruption that can result from multiple processes accessing the database tables at the same time. Nevertheless, administrators should be aware that there are times when the server does not have exclusive control of the data directory:

- **When you run multiple servers on a single data directory.**
  Normally you run a single server to manage all databases on a host, but it's possible to run multiple servers. If each server manages its own independent data directory, there is no problem of interaction. But it's possible to start multiple servers and point them at the same data directory. In general, this is not a good idea. If you try it, you'd better make sure your system provides good file locking or the servers will not cooperate properly. You also risk having your log files become a source of confusion (rather than a source of helpful information) if you have multiple servers writing to them at the same time.

- **When you run table repair utilities.** Programs such as `myisamchk` and `isamchk` are used for table maintenance, troubleshooting, and repair operations, and they operate directly on the files that correspond to the tables. As you might guess, because these utilities can change table contents, allowing them to operate on tables at the same time the server is doing so can cause table damage. The best way to avoid problems of this sort is to bring down the server before running any repair utilities. If that is not possible, it's very important to understand how to tell the server not to access a table while you're operating on it with a repair utility. See Chapter 13, "Database Backups, Maintenance, and Repair," for instructions on the proper use of these programs. (Another alternative is to use the `CHECK TABLE` and `REPAIR TABLE` statements, which eliminate the interaction by instructing the server itself to perform the table maintenance operations.)

How MySQL Represents Databases in the File System

Each database managed by the MySQL server has its own database directory. This exists as a subdirectory of the data directory, with the same name as the database it represents. For example, a database `mydb` corresponds to the database directory *DATADIR*/`mydb`. This representation allows several database-level statements to be almost trivial in their implementation.

`SHOW DATABASES` is essentially nothing more than a list of the names of the directories located within the data directory. Some database systems keep a master table that lists all the databases maintained, but there is no such construct in MySQL. Given the simplicity of the data directory structure, the list of databases is implicit in the contents of the data directory, and such a table would be unnecessary overhead.

`CREATE DATABASE` *db_name* creates an empty directory *db_name* in the data directory. Under UNIX, the directory is owned by and accessible only to the login account that is used for running the server. This means that the `CREATE DATABASE` operation is equivalent to executing the following shell commands on the server host while logged in under that account:

```
% cd DATADIR
% mkdir db_name
% chmod u=rwx,go-rwx db_name
```

The minimal approach of representing a new database by an empty directory contrasts with other database systems that create a number of control or system files even for an "empty" database.

The DROP DATABASE statement is implemented nearly as easily. DROP DATA-BASE *db_name* removes the *db_name* directory in the data directory, along with any table files contained within it. This is almost the same as executing the following commands on UNIX:

```
% cd DATADIR
% rm -rf db_name
```

or the following commands on Windows:

```
C:\> cd DATADIR
C:\> del /S db_name
```

The differences between a DROP DATABASE statement and the shell commands are as follows:

- For DROP DATABASE, the server removes only files with extensions known to be used for tables. If you've created other files in the database directory, the server leaves them intact, and the directory itself is not removed. (One implication of this is that the database name continues to be displayed by SHOW DATABASES.)

- InnoDB table and index contents are maintained in the InnoDB table-space, not as files in the database directory. If a database contains InnoDB tables, you must use DROP DATABASE so that the InnoDB handler can remove the tables from the tablespace; *do not* remove the database directory by using an rm or del command.

How MySQL Represents Tables in the File System

MySQL supports handlers for several types of database tables: ISAM, MyISAM, MERGE, BDB, InnoDB, and HEAP. Every table in MySQL is represented on disk by at least one file, which is the .frm file that contains a description of the table's structure. For most table types, there are also other files that contain the data rows and index information. These vary according to the table type, as outlined in the following discussion. (The descriptions here focus primarily on the characteristics of the table types as they are stored on disk. For information about how these types differ in features and behavior, see Chapter 3, "MySQL SQL Syntax and Use.")

ISAM Tables

The original table type in MySQL is the ISAM type. MySQL represents each ISAM table by three files in the database directory of the database that contains the table. The files all have a basename that is the same as the table name and an extension that indicates the purpose of the file. For example, a table named `mytbl` is represented by three files:

- `mytbl.frm` is the description file that stores the format (structure) of the table.
- `mytbl.ISD` is the ISAM data file that stores the contents of the table's rows.
- `mytbl.ISM` contains index information for any indexes the table has.

MyISAM Tables

MySQL 3.23 introduced the MyISAM table type as the successor to the ISAM type, which now is considered pretty much obsolete. Like the ISAM handler, the MyISAM handler represents each table by three files, using the extensions `.frm`, `.MYD`, and `.MYI` for the description, data, and index files, respectively.

MERGE Tables

A MERGE table is a logical construct. It represents a collection of identically structured MyISAM tables that are treated for query purposes as a single larger table. Within a database directory, a MERGE table is represented by its `.frm` file and a `.MRG` file that is nothing more than a list of the names of the table's constituent MyISAM tables, one name per line.

One implication of this representation is that it's possible to change the definition of a MERGE table by flushing the table cache with FLUSH TABLES and then directly editing the `.MRG` file to change the list of MyISAM tables named there. (I'm not sure I'd recommend actually doing this, though.)

BDB Tables

The BDB handler represents each table by two files, the `.frm` description file and a `.db` file that contains the table's data and index information.

InnoDB Tables

The preceding table types all are represented using files that each are uniquely associated with a single table. InnoDB tables are handled in a somewhat different way. The only file that corresponds directly to a given InnoDB table is the `.frm` table description file, which is located in the directory for the database to which the table belongs. The data and indexes for all InnoDB tables are managed together within a single unified tablespace. Typically, the tablespace itself is represented by one or more large files in the data directory. These components of the tablespace form a logically contiguous storage area equal in size to the sum of the sizes of the individual files.

HEAP Tables

HEAP tables are in-memory tables. Because the server stores a HEAP table's data and indexes in memory rather than on disk, the table is not represented in the file system at all, other than by its `.frm` file.

How SQL Statements Map onto Table File Operations

Every table type uses a `.frm` file to store the table description, so the output from SHOW TABLES FROM *db_name* is the same as a listing of the basenames of the `.frm` files in the database directory for *db_name*. Some database systems maintain a registry that lists all tables contained in a database. MySQL does not because it is unnecessary; the "registry" is implicit in the structure of the data directory.

To create a table of any of the types supported by MySQL, you issue a CREATE TABLE statement that defines the table's structure. For all table types, the server creates a `.frm` file that contains the internal encoding of that structure. The server also creates any other files that are associated with tables of the given type. For example, it creates `.MYD` and `.MYI` data and index files for a MyISAM table or a `.db` data/index file for a BDB table. For InnoDB tables, the handler initializes data and index information for the table within the InnoDB tablespace. Under UNIX, the ownership and mode of any files created to represent the table are set to allow access only to the account that the server runs as.

When you issue an ALTER TABLE statement, the server re-encodes the table's `.frm` file to reflect the structural change indicated by the statement and modifies the contents of the data and index files likewise. This happens for CREATE INDEX and DROP INDEX as well because they are handled by the server as equivalent ALTER TABLE statements. Altering an InnoDB table causes the handler to modify the table's data and indexes within the InnoDB tablespace.

DROP TABLE is implemented by removing the files that represent the table. Dropping an InnoDB table also causes any space associated with the table in the InnoDB tablespace to be marked as free.

For some table types, you can remove a table manually by removing the files in the database directory to which the table corresponds. For example, if mydb is the current database and mytbl is an ISAM, MyISAM, BDB, or MERGE table, DROP TABLE mytbl is roughly equivalent to the following commands on UNIX:

```
% cd DATADIR
% rm -f mydb/mytbl.*
```

or to the following commands on Windows:

```
C:\> cd DATADIR
C:\> del mydb\mytbl.*
```

For an InnoDB or HEAP table, parts of the table are not represented within the file system in discrete files, so DROP TABLE does not have a file system command equivalent. For example, the .frm file is the only file uniquely associated with an InnoDB table. Removing that file will leave the table data and indexes "stranded" within the InnoDB tablespace.

Operating System Constraints on Database and Table Naming

MySQL has general rules for naming databases and tables. The rules are listed in detail in Chapter 3 but can be summarized briefly as follows:

- Names can be constructed from the alphanumeric characters in the current character set, as well as the underscore and dollar characters ('_' and '$').
- Names can be up to 64 characters long.
- From MySQL 3.23.6 on, other characters can be used in a name by quoting the name in backticks (for example, `odd@name`). Quoting is often necessary if you use reserved words as column names.

However, because names of databases and tables correspond to names of directories and files, the operating system on which a server runs may impose additional constraints that stem from file system naming conventions:

- You are limited in database and table names to the characters that are legal in filenames. This is true for every table type, because every type is represented in the file system by at least a .frm file. For example, '$' is allowed in a name by MySQL's rules, but if your operating system doesn't allow it in filenames, you can't use it in directory or table names either. In practice, this is not a concern for either UNIX or Windows. The greatest difficulty you might have is referring to names directly from the shell when performing database administration. For example, the '$' dollar sign character is special to UNIX shells. If you give a database a name such as $mydb that includes that character, any reference to the name from the command line may be interpreted by the shell as a variable reference:

```
% ls $mydb
mydb: Undefined variable.
```

If this happens, you must escape the '$' character or use quoting to suppress its special meaning:

```
% ls \$mydb
% ls '$mydb'
```

If you use quotes, use single quotes. Double quotes do not suppress variable interpretation.

- A database or table name cannot include the pathname separator character, even if quoted. For example, on UNIX and Windows, pathname components are separated by '/' and '\', respectively, and neither character can be used. The reason that both are disallowed regardless of platform is to make it easier to move databases and tables from one platform to another. (For example, if you were allowed to use '/' in the name of a table on Windows, you could not move the table to UNIX.)

- Although MySQL allows database and table names to be up to 64 characters long, the length of names is also bound by the length allowed by your operating system. Normally this is not a problem, although under UNIX, some older System V-ish systems may enforce a 14-character limit. In that case, the effective limit on database names is 14 characters. The limit for table names is 10 characters because names of files representing tables end with a period and an extension of up to three characters.

- Case sensitivity of the underlying file system affects how you name and refer to databases and tables. If the file system is case sensitive (as is typical for UNIX), the two names mytbl and MYTBL refer to different tables. If the file system is not case sensitive (as for Windows or for HFS+ file systems under Mac OS X), mytbl and MYTBL refer to the same table. You should keep this issue in mind if you develop a database on a server that uses case sensitive filenames and there is a possibility you might move the database to a server where filenames are not case sensitive.

One way to deal with the issue of case sensitivity is to always name your databases and tables with a given lettercase. Another is to set the lower_case_table_names server variable to 1, which has two effects:

- The server converts a table's name to lowercase before creating the corresponding disk files.

- When the table is referenced later in a query, the server converts its name to lowercase before attempting to find the table on disk.

The result of these actions is that names are not treated as case sensitive. However, there are two caveats you should keep in mind with respect to use of the `lower_case_table_names` variable. First, it does not apply to database names until MySQL 4.0.2; prior to that it applies only to table names. Second, you should enable this variable before you start creating databases or tables, not after. If you create names that include uppercase characters and then set the variable, it will not have the desired effect because then you will already have names stored on disk that are not entirely lowercase. To avoid this problem, rename any databases or tables with names that contain uppercase characters to names that are entirely lowercase before enabling the variable.

Factors That Affect Maximum Table Size

Table sizes in MySQL are bounded, but sizes are limited by a combination of factors, so it is not always a simple matter to determine precisely what the bounds are. Factors that affect table size are as follows:

- MySQL has its own internal limits on table sizes. These vary by table type:
  - For ISAM tables, the `.ISD` and `.ISM` files are limited to 4GB apiece.
  - For MyISAM tables, the `.MYD` and `.MYI` files also are limited to 4GB apiece by default. However, by using the `AVG_ROW_LENGTH` and `MAX_ROWS` options when you create the table, the files can be approximately 8 million terabytes apiece. (See the description for `CREATE TABLE` in Appendix D, "SQL Syntax Reference.")
  - The maximum size of a MERGE table is a function of the combined maximum sizes of its constituent MyISAM tables.
  - BDB table sizes are bound by the `.db` file size allowed by the handler. This varies according to the table page size (which is determined at server build time), but for even the smallest page size (512 bytes), the maximum file size is 2 terabytes.
  - For InnoDB, the maximum size of the InnoDB tablespace is 4 billion pages, where the default page size is 16KB. (MySQL can be recompiled from source to use an InnoDB page size ranging from 8KB to 64KB.) The maximum tablespace size also is the bound on the size of any individual InnoDB table.
- The operating system imposes a maximum file size limit. In general, the trend has been for operating systems to relax file size constraints over time, but limits as low as 2GB are still relatively common. This size limit applies to files used to represent tables, such as the `.MYD` and `.MYI` files

for a MyISAM table. It also applies to the component files that make up the InnoDB tablespace. However, the InnoDB tablespace size can easily exceed the maximum file size; just configure a tablespace that consists of multiple files, each of which is the maximum file size. Another way to circumvent the file size limit is to use raw partitions in the InnoDB tablespace, which can be done as of MySQL 3.23.41. Tablespace components that are on raw partitions can be as large as the partition itself.

- For table types that represent data and indexes in separate files (such as ISAM and MyISAM), a table's size limit is reached when any of its individual files hits its own size limit. The table's indexing characteristics will affect which file this will be. For a table with no or few indexes, it is likely that the data file will reach its size limit first. For a heavily indexed table, the index file may hit the limit first.

- The presence of an `AUTO_INCREMENT` column implicitly limits the number of rows a table may have. For example, if the column is `TINYINT UNSIGNED`, the maximum value it may hold is 255, so that also becomes the maximum number of rows the table may hold. Larger integer types allow more rows. More generally, placing any unique index on a table limits its row count to the maximum number of unique values in the index.

To determine the actual table size you can achieve, you must consider all applicable factors. The effective maximum table size likely will be determined by the smallest of those factors. Suppose you want to create a ISAM table. MySQL will allow the data and index files to reach 4GB. But if your operating system imposes a size limit on files of 2GB, that will be the effective limit for the table files. On the other hand, if your system has large file support, files can be bigger than 4GB and then the determining factor on table size will be MySQL's internal 4GB limit.

With respect to InnoDB tables, one point to keep in mind is that all such tables must fit within the InnoDB tablespace. If you have a single InnoDB table, it can be as large as the tablespace. But if, as is more likely, you have many InnoDB tables, they all share the same space and thus each is constrained in size not only by the size of the tablespace but also by how much of the tablespace is allocated to other tables. Any individual InnoDB table can grow as long as the tablespace is not full. Conversely, when the tablespace fills up, no InnoDB table can grow any larger until you add another component to the tablespace to make it bigger. (As of MySQL 3.23.50, you can make the last tablespace component auto-extending, so that it will grow as long as it does not exceed the file size limit of your system and disk space is available. See Chapter 11 for details on tablespace configuration.)

Implications of Data Directory Structure for System Performance

The structure of the MySQL data directory is easy to understand because it uses the hierarchical structure of the file system in such a natural way. At the same time, this structure has certain performance implications, particularly regarding operations that open the files that represent database tables.

One consequence of the data directory structure is that for table handlers that represent each table using multiple files, an open table can require multiple file descriptors, not just one. The server caches descriptors intelligently, but a busy server can easily use up lots of them while servicing many simultaneous client connections or executing complex queries that reference several tables. This can be a problem, because file descriptors are a scarce resource on many systems, particularly those that set the default per-process descriptor limit fairly low.

Another effect of representing each table by its own files is that table-opening time increases with the number of tables. Operations that open tables map onto the file-opening operations provided by the operating system and, as such, are bound by the efficiency of the system's directory-lookup routines. Normally this isn't much of an issue, but it is something to consider if you'll need large numbers of tables in a database. For example, a MyISAM table is represented by three files. If you want to have 10,000 MyISAM tables, your database directory will contain 30,000 files. With that many files, you may notice a slowdown due to the time taken by file-opening operations. (Linux ext2 and Solaris file systems are subject to this problem.) If this is cause for concern, you might want to think about using a type of file system that is highly efficient at dealing with large numbers of files. For example, ReiserFS exhibits good performance even with large numbers of small files. If that is not possible, it may be necessary to reconsider the structure of your tables in relation to the needs of your applications and reorganize your tables accordingly. Ask whether or not you really require so many tables; sometimes applications multiply tables needlessly. An application that creates a separate table per user results in many tables, all of which have identical structures. If you wanted to combine the tables into a single table, you might be able to do so by adding another column identifying the user to which each row applies. If this significantly reduces the number of tables, the application's performance improves.

As always in database design, you must consider whether this particular strategy is worthwhile for a given application. Reasons not to combine tables in the manner just described are as follows:

- **Increased disk space requirements**. Combining tables reduces the number of tables required (decreasing table-opening times) but adds another column (increasing disk space requirements). This is a typical time versus space tradeoff, and you'd need to decide which factor is most important. If speed is paramount, you'd probably be willing to sacrifice a little extra disk space. If space is tight, it might be more acceptable to use multiple tables and live with a slight delay.

- **Security considerations**. These may constrain your ability or desire to combine tables. One reason to use a separate table per user is to allow access to each table only to that user by means of table-level privileges. If you combine tables, data for all users will be in the same table.

    MySQL has no provision for restricting access to particular rows to a given user; thus, you might not be able to combine tables without compromising access control. On the other hand, if all access to the data is controlled by your application (users never connect directly to the database), you can combine the tables and use application logic to enforce row-level access to the combined result.

Another way to create many tables without requiring so many individual files is to use InnoDB tables. The InnoDB handler associates only a `.frm` file uniquely with each table and stores the data and index information for all InnoDB tables together in the InnoDB tablespace. This minimizes the number of disk files needed to represent the tables, and it also substantially reduces the number of file descriptors required for open tables. InnoDB needs only one descriptor per component file of the tablespace (which is constant during the life of the server process) and briefly a descriptor for any table that it opens while it reads the table's `.frm` file.

MySQL Status and Log Files

In addition to database directories, the MySQL data directory contains a number of status and log files, as summarized in Table 10.1. The default location for these files is the server's data directory, and the default name for each of them is derived using the server host name, denoted as *HOSTNAME* in the table.

Table 10.1 **MySQL Status and Log Files**

File Type	Default Name	File Contents
Process ID file	`HOSTNAME.pid`	The server process ID
General query log	`HOSTNAME.log`	Connect/disconnect events and query information
Slow-query log	`HOSTNAME-slow.log`	Text of queries that take a long time to process
Update log	`HOSTNAME.nnn`	Text of queries that modify data
Binary update log	`HOSTNAME-bin.nnn`	Binary representation of queries that modify data
Binary update log index	`HOSTNAME-bin.index`	List of current binary update log files
Error log	`HOSTNAME.err`	Startup and shutdown events and error conditions

The Process ID File

The server writes its process ID (PID) into the PID file when it starts up and removes the file when it shuts down. The PID file is the means by which a server allows itself to be found by other processes. For example, if the operating system runs the `mysql.server` script at system shutdown time to shut down the MySQL server, that script examines the PID file to determine which process it needs to send a termination signal to.

The MySQL Log Files

MySQL can maintain a number of different log files. Most logging is optional; you can use server startup options to enable just the logs you need and also to specify their names if you don't like the defaults. This section describes the log files briefly. For more information about the logs and the options that control the server's logging behavior, see Chapter 11.

The general log provides general information about server operation: who is connecting from where and what queries they are issuing. The update log provides query information, too, but only for queries that modify database contents. The contents of the update log are written as SQL statements that can be executed by providing them as input to the `mysql` client. The binary update log is similar to the update log but is represented in a more efficient binary format. The accompanying binary log index file lists which binary log files the server currently is maintaining.

Update and binary update logs are useful if you have a crash and must revert to backup files because you can repeat the updates performed after the backup was made by feeding the logs to the server. This allows you to bring your databases up to the state they were in when the crash occurred. This procedure is described in more detail in Chapter 13. The binary logs are also used if you set up replication servers because they serve as a record of the updates that must be transmitted from a master server to slave servers.

Here is a sample of the kind of information that appears in the general log as the result of a short client session that creates a table in the `test` database, inserts a row into the table, and then drops the table:

```
020727 15:00:17      1 Connect     sampadm@localhost on test
                     2 Query       CREATE TABLE mytbl (val INT)
                     2 Query       INSERT INTO mytbl VALUES(1)
                     2 Query       DROP TABLE mytbl
                     2 Quit
```

The general log contains columns for date and time, server thread (connection) ID, event type, and event-specific information. For any line that is missing the date and time fields, the values are the same as for the previous line that does have them. (In other words, the server logs the date and time only when they change from the previously logged date and time.)

The same session appears in the update log as follows. The statements include terminating semicolons, allowing them to be given as input to the `mysql` program should the updates need to be repeated for a recovery operation.

```
use test;
CREATE TABLE mytbl (val INT);
INSERT INTO mytbl VALUES(1);
DROP TABLE mytbl;
```

For the update log, an extended form of logging is available by using the `--log-long-format` option. Extended logging provides information about who issued each query and when. This uses more disk space, of course, but may be useful if you want to know who is doing what without trying to correlate update log contents with the connection events in the general log.

For the session just shown, extended update logging produces the following information:

```
# Time: 020727 15:00:17
# User@Host: sampadm[sampadm] @ localhost []
use test;
CREATE TABLE mytbl (val INT);
# User@Host: sampadm[sampadm] @ localhost []
INSERT INTO mytbl VALUES(1);
# User@Host: sampadm[sampadm] @ localhost []
DROP TABLE mytbl;
```

The extra information is written using lines that begin with '#' so that they are interpreted as comments if you feed the log to mysql for execution by the server.

The error log contains a record of diagnostic information produced by the server when exceptional conditions occur. It's useful if the server fails to start up or exits unexpectedly because it often will contain the reason why.

Logs can grow quite large, so it's important to make sure they don't fill up your file system. You can expire the logs periodically to keep the amount of space that use within bounds. For information on log file maintenance, see Chapter 11.

It's a good idea to make sure your log files are secure and not readable by arbitrary users because they may contain the text of queries that include sensitive information, such as passwords. For example, the following log entry displays the password for the root user; it's certainly not the kind of information you want just anyone to have access to:

```
020727 15:47:24      4 Query      UPDATE user SET
                                   Password=PASSWORD('secret')
                                   WHERE user='root'
```

The logs are written to the data directory by default, so securing your logs is a matter of securing the data directory against being accessed through login accounts other than that of the MySQL administrator. A detailed procedure for this is presented in Chapter 12, "Security."

Relocating Data Directory Contents

The preceding part of this chapter discusses the data directory structure in its default configuration, which is that all databases, status, and log files are located within it. However, you have some latitude in determining the placement of the data directory's contents. MySQL allows you to relocate the data directory itself or certain elements within it. There are several reasons why you might want to do this:

- You can put the data directory on a file system that has a capacity greater than the file system where it's located by default.
- If your data directory is on a busy disk, you can put it on a less active drive to balance disk activity across physical devices. You can put databases and log files on different drives or distribute databases across drives for the same reasons. Similarly, the InnoDB tablespace is conceptually a single large block of storage, but you can put its individual component files on different drives to improve performance.

- Putting databases and logs on different disks helps minimize the damage that can be caused by a failure of a single disk.

- You might want to run multiple servers, each with its own data directory. This is one way to work around problems with per-process file descriptor limits, especially if you cannot reconfigure the kernel for your system to allow higher limits.

- Some systems keep server PID files in a specific directory, such as /var/run. You might want to put the MySQL PID file there, too, for consistency of system operation. In similar fashion, if your system uses /var/log for log files, you can also put the MySQL logs there. (However, many systems allow only root to write to these directories. That means you'd need to run the server as root, which for security reasons is not a good idea.)

The rest of this section discusses which parts of the data directory can be moved and how you go about making such changes.

Relocation Methods

There are two ways to relocate the data directory or elements within it:

- You can specify an option at server startup time, either on the command line or in an option file. For example, if you want to specify the data directory location, you can start the server with a --datadir=*dir_name* option on the command line or you can put the following lines in an option file:

```
[mysqld]
datadir=dir_name
```

Typically, the option file group name for server options is [mysqld], as shown in the example. However, depending on your circumstances, other option group names may be more appropriate. For example, the [embedded] group applies to the embedded server. Or if you're running multiple servers using mysqld_multi, the group names will be of the form [mysqld*n*], where *n* is some integer associated with a particular server instance. Chapter 11 discusses which option groups apply to different server startup methods and also provides instructions for running multiple servers.

- You can move the thing to be relocated, and then make a symlink (symbolic link) in the original location that points to the new location.

Neither of these methods works universally for everything that you can relocate. Table 10.2 summarizes what can be relocated and which relocation methods can be used. If you use an option file, it is possible to specify options in the global option file (such as /etc/my.cnf under UNIX or C:\my.cnf or my.ini in the system directory under Windows).

It's also possible to use the option file my.cnf in the default data directory (the directory compiled into the server). This is a good option file to use for server-specific options if you run multiple servers, but because the server looks for it only in the compiled-in data directory location, the file won't be found if you relocate that directory. (One workaround for this problem is to move the data directory and then make its original location a symlink that points to the new location.)

Table 10.2 **Relocation Method Summary**

Entity to Relocate	Applicable Relocation Methods
Entire data directory	Startup option or symlink
Individual database directories	Symlink
Individual database tables	Symlink
InnoDB tablespace files	Startup option
PID file	Startup option
Log files	Startup option

Assessing the Effect of Relocation

Before attempting to relocate anything, it's a good idea to verify that the operation will have the desired effect. I tend to favor the du, df, and ls -l commands for obtaining disk space information, but all of these depend on correctly understanding the layout of your file system.

The following example illustrates a subtle trap to watch out for when assessing a data directory relocation. Suppose your data directory is /usr/local/mysql/data and you want to move it to /var/mysql because df indicates the /var file system has more free space (as shown by the following example):

```
% df /usr /var
Filesystem   1K-blocks     Used    Avail Capacity  Mounted on
/dev/wd0s3e     396895   292126    73018     80%    /usr
/dev/wd0s3f    1189359  1111924   162287     15%    /var
```

How much space will relocating the data directory free up on the /usr file system? To find out, use du -s to see how much space that directory uses:

```
% cd /usr/local/mysql/data
% du -s
133426   .
```

That's about 130MB, which should make quite a difference on /usr. But will it really? Try df in the data directory:

```
% df /usr/local/mysql/data
Filesystem   1K-blocks     Used    Avail Capacity  Mounted on
/dev/wd0s3f    1189359  1111924   162287    15%     /var
```

That's odd. If we're requesting the free space for the file system containing the data directory (that is, /usr), why does df report the space on the /var file system? The following ls -l command provides the answer:

```
% ls -l /usr/local/mysql/data
...
lrwxrwxr-x  1 mysqladm  mysqlgrp  10 Dec 11 23:46 data -> /var/mysql
...
```

This output shows that /usr/local/mysql/data is a symlink to /var/mysql. In other words, the data directory *already* has been relocated to the /var file system and replaced with a symlink that points there. So much for freeing up a lot of space on /usr by moving the data directory to /var!

Moral: A few minutes spent assessing the effect of relocation is a worthwhile investment. It doesn't take long, and it can keep you from wasting a lot of time moving things around only to find that you've failed to achieve your objective.

Relocation Precautions

You should bring down the server before performing any relocation operation and then restart it afterward. For some types of relocations, such as moving a database directory, it is *possible* to keep the server running, but not recommended. If you do that, you must make sure the server is not accessing the database you're moving. You should also be sure to issue a FLUSH TABLES statement before moving the database to make sure the server closes all open table files. Failure to observe these precautions can result in damaged tables.

Relocating the Entire Data Directory

To relocate the data directory, bring down the server and move the data directory to its new location. Then you should either remove the original data directory and replace it with a symlink that points to the new location or restart the server with a --datadir option that explicitly indicates the new location. The symlink method is preferable if the data directory contains a my.cnf file and you want the server to continue to find it.

Relocating Individual Databases

The server wants to find database directories in the data directory, so the only way to relocate a database is by the symlink method. Under UNIX, do so as follows:

1. Shut down the server if it is running.
2. Copy or move the database directory to its new location.
3. Remove the original database directory.
4. Create a symlink in the data directory that has the name of the original database and that points to the new database location.
5. Restart the server.

The following example shows how you might use this procedure to move a database bigdb to a different location:

```
% mysqladmin -p -u root shutdown
Enter password: ******
% cd DATADIR
% tar cf - bigdb | (cd /var/db; tar xf -)
% mv bigdb bigdb.orig
% ln -s /var/db/bigdb .
% mysqld_safe &
```

You should execute these commands while logged in as the MySQL administrator. The procedure shown here renames the original database directory to bigdb.orig as a precaution. After you verify that the server works properly with the relocated database, you can remove the original one:

```
% rm -rf bigdb.orig
```

Under Windows, database relocation is handled somewhat differently:

1. Shut down the server if it is running.
2. Move the database directory to where you want it.
3. Create a .sym file in the MySQL data directory that points to the new database location. For example, if you move the sampdb database from C:\mysql\data\sampdb to E:\mysql-book\sampdb, you should create a file named sampdb.sym in C:\mysql\data that contains the following line:

```
E:\mysql-book\sampdb\
```

The .sym file acts as a symbolic link to let the MySQL server know where to find the relocated database directory.

4. Make sure that symbolic link support is enabled when you start the server. You can do this with the --use-symbolic-links option on the command line or by placing the following lines in an option file:

```
[mysqld]
use-symbolic-links
```

For Windows database relocation to work properly as just described, you must be running a -max server (mysqld-max or mysqld-max-nt) from MySQL 3.23.16 or later.

If you're moving a database to another file system as an attempt to redistribute database storage, remember that InnoDB table contents are stored within the InnoDB tablespace, not in the database directory. For a database composed primarily of InnoDB tables, relocating the database directory may have little effect on storage distribution.

> **Removing a Relocated Database**
>
> You can remove a database with the DROP DATABASE statement, but servers from versions of MySQL older than 3.23 have trouble removing a database that has been relocated. The tables in the database are removed correctly, but an error occurs when the server attempts to remove the database directory because the directory is a symlink and not a real directory. If you encounter this problem, you must complete the DROP DATABASE operation by manually removing the database directory and the symlink that points to it.

Relocating Individual Tables

Relocation of an individual table is supported only under certain limited circumstances:

- You must be using MySQL 4.0 or later.
- Your operating system must have a working realpath() call.
- The table to be relocated must be a MyISAM table.

If those conditions are all true, you can move the table's .MYD data and .MYI index files to their new locations and then create symlinks to them in the database directory under the original data and index filenames. (Leave the .frm file in the database directory.)

You should not try to relocate a table if any of the preceding conditions are not satisfied. If you do so anyway and then refer to the table with an ALTER TABLE, OPTIMIZE TABLE, or REPAIR TABLE statement, your changes may be undone. Each of those statements operates by creating in the database directory a temporary table that implements your alteration or optimization, and then deleting the original table and renaming the temporary table to the original name. The result is that your symlinks are removed and the new table ends up right back in the database directory where your original table was before you moved it. Furthermore, the old table files that you moved out of the database directory are still in the location where you moved them—and you might not even realize they are there, continuing to take up space. Also, the symlinks have been destroyed, so when you realize later what has happened, you may not have any good way of tracking down the files if you've forgotten where you moved them. Because it's difficult to guarantee that no one with access to the table will ever alter or optimize it (and thus undo any attempted relocation), it's best to leave tables in the database directory.

Relocating the InnoDB Tablespace

You configure the InnoDB tablespace initially by listing the locations of its component files in an option file, using the `innodb_data_home_dir` and `innodb_data_file_path` options. (For details on configuring the tablespace, see Chapter 11.) If you have already created the tablespace, it's possible to relocate regular files that are part of it, for example, to distribute them across different file systems. Because you list the file locations using startup options, the way to relocate some or all of the tablespace files is like this:

1. Shut down the server if it is running.
2. Move the tablespace file or files that you want to relocate.
3. Update the option file where the InnoDB configuration is defined to reflect the new locations of any files that you moved.
4. Restart the server.

Strictly speaking, it's possible to relocate a tablespace component by moving it and then creating a symlink to it at the original location. But there's no point in doing so; you have to list a location for component in the option file anyway, so you may as well list the real location rather than that of a symlink.

Relocating Status and Log Files

To relocate the PID file, bring down the server and then restart it with the appropriate option to specify the file's new location. For example, to create the

PID file as `/tmp/mysql.pid`, use `--pid-file=/tmp/mysql.pid` on the command line or include the following lines in an option file:

```
[mysqld]
pid-file=/tmp/mysql.pid
```

If you specify the filename as an absolute pathname, the server creates the file using that pathname. Otherwise, the file is created under the data directory. For example, if you specify `--pid-file=mysqld.pid`, the PID file will be `mysqld.pid` in the data directory.

To relocate log files, use server startup options. For a description of these options and how to use them, see Chapter 11.

11

General MySQL Administration

I F YOU'RE ACTING AS YOUR SITE'S MySQL administrator, this chapter discusses what you'll need to do to keep MySQL running smoothly. These responsibilities include making sure the server is up and running as much of the time as possible, setting up user accounts so that clients can access the server, and maintaining log files. You may also want to modify the server's operating parameters for better performance, run multiple servers, or set up replication between servers. Finally, because MySQL is under active development, an administrator must be able to determine when to upgrade MySQL by installing new releases. Other significant administrative concerns are covered in Chapter 12, "Security," and Chapter 13, "Database Backups, Maintenance, and Repair."

Several programs are covered in these chapters that are essential for MySQL administrators to know about:

- `mysqld`, the MySQL server.
- Scripts for starting up the server. These include `mysqld_safe`, `mysql.server`, and `mysqld_multi`. (Prior to MySQL 4, `mysqld_safe` is named `safe_mysqld`.)

- `mysqladmin` performs miscellaneous administrative operations.
- `mysqldump` and `mysqlhotcopy` are used for database backup and copying operations.
- `mysqlcheck`, `myisamchk`, and `isamchk` are utilities that perform table integrity checking and repair operations.

Much of the information in this chapter can be better appreciated if you have an understanding of MySQL's data directory, which is where the server stores databases, log files, and other information. For more information, see Chapter 10, "The MySQL Data Directory." Additional information specific to the SQL statements and programs discussed here is provided in Appendix D, "SQL Syntax Reference," and Appendix E, "MySQL Program Reference."

Securing a New MySQL Installation

The MySQL installation procedure sets up the server's data directory and populates it with two databases:

- A `mysql` database that contains the grant tables
- A `test` database that can be used for testing purposes

If you've just installed MySQL for the first time (for example, using the instructions in Appendix A, "Obtaining and Installing Software"), the grant tables in the `mysql` database will be in their initial state that allows anyone to connect to the server without a password. This is insecure, so you should set up some passwords. If you're setting up a second installation on a machine that already has MySQL installed in another location, you'll need to set up passwords for the new server. However, in this case, you may run into the complication noted in the "Setting Up Passwords for a Second Server" section later in this chapter. If you're upgrading MySQL by installing a newer version on top of an existing installation for which the grant tables are already set up, you can skip this section.

The examples in the following discussion use a MySQL server hostname of `cobra.snake.net`; change the instructions to use your own hostname. The examples also assume that your server is running, because you'll need to connect to it.

How the Grant Tables Are Set Up Initially

The grant tables in the `mysql` database are set up during the MySQL installation procedure with two kinds of accounts:

- Accounts that have a username of `root`. These are superuser accounts intended for administrative purposes. They have all privileges and can do anything, including deleting all your databases. (By the way, the fact that the MySQL and UNIX superuser accounts each have the name `root` is coincidental. Each has exceptional privileges, but they have nothing to do with each other.)

- Accounts that are associated with no username at all. These are "anonymous" accounts; they're useful for testing because they allow people to connect to the server without having accounts explicitly set up for them in advance. Anonymous users usually are given very few privileges to limit the scope of what they can do. However, for Windows, there is an important exception that you may want to take action on, as described later.

Every account known to a MySQL server is listed in the `user` table of its `mysql` database, so that's where you'll find the initial `root` and anonymous accounts. None of these accounts have passwords initially because it's expected that you'll supply your own. Therefore, one of your first acts in administering a MySQL installation should be to establish passwords, at least for the privileged accounts. Otherwise, unauthorized users can gain `root` access to your server easily. After you secure the initial accounts, you can proceed to set up other accounts to allow the members of your user community to connect to the server under names that you specify and with privileges appropriate for what those users should be allowed to do. (Instructions for setting up new accounts are given in the "Managing MySQL User Accounts" section later in this chapter.)

Entries in the `user` table contain a `Host` value indicating where a user can connect from, and `User` and `Password` values indicating the name and password the user must give when connecting from that host. The `user` table also has a number of columns indicating what superuser privileges the account has, if any.

Under UNIX, the data directory is initialized during the installation procedure by running `mysql_install_db`, a script that sets up the grant tables in the `mysql` database. `mysql_install_db` initializes the `user` table as follows:

Host	User	Password	Superuser Privileges
localhost	root		All
cobra.snake.net	root		All
localhost			None
cobra.snake.net			None

These entries allow connections as follows:

- The `root` entries allow you to connect to the local MySQL server, using a hostname of `localhost` or `cobra.snake.net`. For example, from `cobra.snake.net` you can connect as `root` with the `mysql` program using either of the following commands:

```
% mysql -h localhost -u root
% mysql -h cobra.snake.net -u root
```

  As `root`, you have all privileges and can perform any operation.

- The entries with blank `User` values are the anonymous accounts. They allow connections to the local server without any username:

```
% mysql -h localhost
% mysql -h cobra.snake.net
```

  Anonymous users have no superuser privileges, but another grant table (the `db` table, not shown) specifies that anonymous users can use the `test` database or any database having a name that begins with `test_`.

Under Windows, the data directory and the `mysql` database are included pre-initialized with the MySQL distribution with accounts that are set up somewhat differently than those on UNIX systems. The Windows `user` table entries look like this:

Host	User	Password	Superuser Privileges
localhost	root		All
%	root		All
localhost			All
%			None

In these entries, the `Host` value of `%` acts as a wildcard, meaning that the user named by the `User` value can connect from any host. Thus, the initial Windows `user` table entries specify accounts as follows:

- You can connect as `root` from the local host *or* from any remote host. As `root`, you have all privileges and can perform any operation.

- You can connect anonymously with no username. If you connect from the local host, you will have the same superuser privileges as `root` and can do anything. If you connect remotely from another host, you will have no superuser privileges. On Windows, the `db` table allows anonymous users access to the `test` database or any database having a name that begins with `test`.

For Windows, an important implication of the fact that one of the `root` accounts has % for a `Host` value is that *anyone, anywhere* can connect as `root` with no password. This leaves your server completely vulnerable, so you'll certainly want to lock down that account by giving it a password. In addition, the fact that the `localhost` anonymous account has the same privileges as `root` means that it's not sufficient to assign passwords just to the `root` accounts. It's also a good idea to establish a password for the local anonymous account to revoke its superuser privileges or perhaps to delete it entirely. The following discussion covers all three options.

Establishing Passwords for the Initial MySQL Accounts

This section describes the various methods for setting passwords for the `root` accounts. Depending on the method you use, you may also need to tell the server to reload the grant tables so that it notices the change. (The server performs access control using in-memory copies of the grant tables. For some methods of changing passwords in the `user` table, the server may not recognize that you've changed anything, so you must tell it explicitly to reread the tables.) This section also suggests some options for dealing with the anonymous superuser account that is present initially in the `user` table on Windows.

One way to establish passwords is to use the `mysqladmin` program:

```
% mysqladmin -h localhost -u root password "rootpass"
% mysqladmin -h cobra.snake.net -u root password "rootpass"
```

This works for both UNIX and Windows. The word "password" in these commands is a literal word that indicates what you want `mysqladmin` to do (set a password), and *rootpass* represents the value to which you want to set the password. Both `mysqladmin` commands are necessary. The first sets the password for the `root` account associated with `localhost` and the second for the account associated with `cobra.snake.net`. (On Windows, the second command sets the password for the `root` account associated with the `Host` value of %.)

A second way to set the passwords is to issue SET PASSWORD statements. Each statement names the `User` and `Host` values of the `user` table entry that you want to modify, in `'user_name'`@`'host_name'` format. For UNIX, change the passwords like this:

```
% mysql -u root
mysql> SET PASSWORD FOR 'root'@'localhost' = PASSWORD('rootpass');
mysql> SET PASSWORD FOR 'root'@'cobra.snake.net' = PASSWORD('rootpass');
```

For Windows, use a slightly different second statement because one of the root accounts has a different Host value:

```
C:\> mysql -u root
mysql> SET PASSWORD FOR 'root'@'localhost' = PASSWORD('rootpass');
mysql> SET PASSWORD FOR 'root'@'%' = PASSWORD('rootpass');
```

Another way to assign passwords is to modify the user table directly. This works for any version of MySQL, and actually may be your only recourse if you have a *really* old version of MySQL that predates both mysqladmin password and SET PASSWORD. To set the password for both root entries at the same time, do the following:

```
% mysql -u root
mysql> USE mysql;
mysql> UPDATE user SET Password=PASSWORD('rootpass') WHERE User='root';
mysql> FLUSH PRIVILEGES;
```

If you use mysqladmin password or SET PASSWORD to change passwords, the server notices that you've made a change to the grant tables and automatically rereads them to refresh its in-memory copy of the tables. If you use UPDATE to modify the user table directly, it's necessary to tell the server to reload the tables explicitly. One way to do so, if you have MySQL 3.22.9 or later, is to issue a FLUSH PRIVILEGES statement, as shown in the preceding example. You can also use mysqladmin to reload the grant tables:

```
% mysqladmin -u root reload
% mysqladmin -u root flush-privileges
```

reload should work for any version of MySQL; flush-privileges is available as of MySQL 3.22.12. From now on, whenever I say "reload the grant tables," I mean you should use one of the three methods just shown; it doesn't matter which one. (Examples in the remaining part of this chapter generally use FLUSH PRIVILEGES.)

After you have set the root password (and reloaded the grant tables if necessary), you'll need to specify your new password whenever you connect to the server as root:

```
% mysql -p -u root
Enter password: rootpass
mysql>
```

Another effect of setting the root password is that no one else will be able to connect as root without knowing the password, which is really the point of the exercise.

The need to specify a password when connecting as root from this point on will be true not just for mysql but also for programs like mysqladmin, `mysqldump`, and so on. For brevity, many of the examples in the rest of this chapter do not show the `-u` or `-p` options; I assume you'll add them as necessary whenever you connect to the server as `root`.

The `user` table at this stage still contains anonymous user entries that have no password. If you have no need for these entries, consider deleting them entirely. To do this, connect to the server as `root` (using your new password, of course), delete any rows from the `user` and `db` tables that have a blank `User` value, and reload the grant tables:

```
% mysql -p -u root
Enter password: rootpass
mysql> USE mysql;
mysql> DELETE FROM user WHERE User = '';
mysql> DELETE FROM db WHERE User = '';
mysql> FLUSH PRIVILEGES;
```

If you leave the anonymous user accounts in place, remember that the local anonymous user has the same privileges as `root` on Windows, which may be more access than you care to allow. To weaken that account to the same strength as the one for the remote anonymous user, revoke its superuser privileges by connecting to the server as `root` and issuing these statements:

```
mysql> REVOKE ALL ON *.* FROM ''@'localhost';
mysql> REVOKE GRANT OPTION ON *.* FROM ''@'localhost';
```

Another option for dealing with this account is to assign it a password; for example:

```
mysql> SET PASSWORD FOR ''@'localhost' = PASSWORD('anonpass');
```

An implication of leaving the anonymous users in place is that they result in the curious phenomenon described in the "A Privilege Puzzle" section in Chapter 12. But you can read that section another time, after you have read the more general background material later in this chapter that describes how to set up new accounts.

Setting Up Passwords for a Second Server

The preceding instructions assume that you want to establish passwords on a system that hasn't had MySQL installed on it before. However, if MySQL is already installed in one location and you're setting the passwords for a new server installed in a second location on the same machine, you may find that when you attempt to connect to the new server without a password, it rejects the attempt with the following error:

```
% mysql -u root
ERROR 1045: Access denied for user: 'root@localhost' (Using password: YES)
```

Hm! Why did the server say it received a password when you didn't specify one? What this usually indicates is that you have an option file set up that lists the password for accessing the previously installed server. `mysql` finds the option file and automatically uses the password listed there. To override that and explicitly specify "no password," use a `-p` option and press Enter when `mysql` prompts for the password:

```
% mysql -p -u root
Enter password:            ← just press Enter
```

You can use this strategy for `mysqladmin` and for other MySQL programs as well.

Additional discussion on using several servers can be found in the "Running Multiple Servers" section later in this chapter.

Arranging for MySQL Server Startup and Shutdown

One general goal that you will have as a MySQL administrator is to make sure the server is running as much of the time as possible so that your users can access it. Occasionally, however, it's necessary to bring down the server. For example, if you're relocating a database, you don't want the server updating tables in that database at the same time. The tension between the desire to keep the server running and the need to shut it down occasionally is something this book can't resolve for you. But we can at least discuss how to get the server started and stopped so that you have the ability to perform either operation as you see fit. Many aspects of the procedures for this are different for UNIX and Windows, so the following discussion covers them separately.

Running the MySQL Server on UNIX

On UNIX, the MySQL server can be started either manually or automatically at system startup time. It's also possible to arrange for the server to run automatically at system boot time as part of the standard startup procedure. (In fact, this is probably how you'll start the server under normal operating conditions after you get everything set up the way you want.) But before discussing how to start the server, let's consider which login account it should be run under when it does start. On a multiuser operating system such as UNIX, you have a choice about which login account to use for running the server. For example, if you start it manually, the server runs as the UNIX user you happen to be logged in as. That is, if I log in as `paul` and start the server, it runs as `paul`. If instead I use the `su` command to switch user to `root` and then start the server, it runs as `root`.

You should keep in mind two goals for your MySQL server startup procedures under UNIX:

- **You want the server to run as some user other than `root`.** To say the server runs "as" a given user means that the server process is associated with the user ID of that user's login account, and that it has that user's privileges for reading and writing files in the file system. This has certain security implications, particularly for processes that run as the `root` user, because `root` is allowed to do anything, however dangerous. (Some of the problems that can arise are described in Chapter 12.) One way to avoid these dangers is to have the server relinquish its special privileges. Processes that start as `root` have the capability to change their user ID to that of another account and thus give up `root`'s privileges in exchange for those of a regular unprivileged user. This makes the process less dangerous. In general, you should limit the power of any process unless it really needs `root` access, and `mysqld` in particular does not. The server needs to access and manage the contents of the MySQL data directory, but little else. This means that if the server starts as `root`, you should tell it to change during its startup procedure to run as an unprivileged user. (An exception occurs on Solaris if you have trouble with the server being swapped out a lot and you want to force it to remain locked in memory by using the `--memlock` option. This option requires running the server as `root`.)

- **You want the server to run as the same user all the time.** It's inconsistent for the server to run as one user sometimes and as another user other times. That leads to files and directories being created under the data directory with different ownerships and can even result in the server not being able to access certain databases or tables. Consistently running the server as the same user enables you to avoid this problem.

Running the Server Using an Unprivileged Login Account

To set up for running the server as an unprivileged non-`root` user, follow this procedure:

1. Shut down the server if it's running:

   ```
   % mysqladmin -p -u root shutdown
   ```

2. Choose a login account to use for running `mysqld`. You can use any account, but it's cleaner conceptually and administratively to create a separate account that is devoted exclusively to MySQL activity. You can also designate a group name specifically for use with MySQL. I'll call these user and group names `mysqladm` and `mysqlgrp`. If you use different names, substitute them anywhere you see `mysqladm` and `mysqlgrp` throughout this book. For example, if you have installed MySQL under your own account and have no special administrative privileges on your system, you'll probably run the server under your own user ID. In this case, substitute your own login name and group name for `mysqladm` and `mysqlgrp`. If you installed MySQL on Linux using an RPM file, the installation procedure may have created an account automatically, using `mysql` for both the user and group names. Substitute that name for `mysqladm` and `mysqlgrp`.

3. If necessary, create the login account for the name you've chosen using your system's usual account-creation procedure. You'll need to do this as `root`.

4. Modify the user and group ownership of the data directory and any subdirectories and files under it so that the `mysqladm` user owns them. For example, if the data directory is `/usr/local/mysql/data`, you can set up ownership for that directory and its contents as follows (you'll need to run this command as `root`):

   ```
   # chown -R mysqladm.mysqlgrp /usr/local/mysql/data
   ```

5. It's a good security precaution to set the access mode of the data directory to keep other people out of it. To do this, modify its permissions so that only `mysqladm` can use it. If the data directory is `/usr/local/mysql/data`, you can set up everything in and under it to be accessible only to `mysqladm` by turning off all the "group" and "other" permissions as follows:

   ```
   # chmod -R go-rwx /usr/local/mysql/data
   ```

The last couple of steps actually are part of a more comprehensive lockdown procedure that is detailed in Chapter 12. Be sure to check that chapter for additional instructions on making ownership and mode assignments, particularly if your MySQL installation has a non-standard organization.

After completing the preceding procedure, you should make sure to always start the server with an option of `--user=mysqladm` so that if it's invoked by `root`, it will switch its user ID to `mysqladm`. (This is true both for when you run the server manually as `root` and for setting up the server to be invoked during your system's startup procedure. UNIX systems perform startup operations as the UNIX `root` user, so any processes initiated as part of that procedure execute by default with `root` privileges.) The best way to ensure that the user is specified consistently is to list it in an option file. For example, put the following lines in `/etc/my.cnf`:

```
[mysqld]
user=mysqladm
```

For more information on option files, see the "Specifying Startup Options" section later in this chapter.

If you start the server while logged in as `mysqladm`, the presence of the `user` line in your option file will result in a warning to the effect that the option can be used only by `root`. This means the server does not have not have the ability to change its user ID and will run as `mysqladm`. That's what you want anyway, so just ignore the warning.

The `--user` option was added to `mysqld` in MySQL 3.22. If you have an older version, use the `su` command to tell the system to run the server under a particular account when you start it while running as `root`. You'll need to read your system's manual page for `su` because different versions of `su` vary in their invocation syntax.

Methods for Starting the Server

After you've decided what account to use for running the server, you have several choices about how to start it up. It's possible to run the server manually from the command line or automatically during the system startup procedure. Methods for doing this include the following:

- **Invoke `mysqld` directly**

  This is probably the least-common method. I won't discuss it further except to say that `mysqld --help` is a useful command for finding out what startup options the server supports.

- **Invoke the `mysqld_safe` script**

  `mysqld_safe` invokes the server and then monitors it and restarts it if it dies. `mysqld_safe` is commonly used on BSD-style versions of UNIX, and it is also used by `mysql.server` on non-BSD systems. (`mysqld_safe` is called `safe_mysqld` prior to MySQL 4, which you'll need to take into account for any instructions given in this chapter relating to `mysqld_safe`.)

`mysqld_safe` redirects error messages and other diagnostic output from the server into a file in the data directory to produce an error log. `mysqld_safe` sets the ownership of the error log so that it is owned by the user named with the `--user` option. This can lead to trouble if you to use different `--user` values at different times. The symptom is that `mysqld_safe`'s attempt to write to the error log will fail with a "permission denied" error. This can be especially problematic because if you examine the error log to see what the difficulty is, it will contain no useful information related to the cause. If this problem occurs, remove the error log and invoke `mysqld_safe` again.

■ **Invoke the `mysql.server` script**

`mysql.server` starts up the server by executing `mysqld_safe`. This script can be invoked with an argument of `start` or `stop` to indicate whether you want the server to start up or shut down. It serves as a wrapper around `mysqld_safe` for use on systems that use the System V method of arranging startup and shutdown scripts into several directories. Each directory corresponds to a particular run level and contains scripts to be invoked when the machine enters or exits that run level.

■ **To coordinate several servers, use the `mysqld_multi` script**

This startup method is more complicated than the others, so I'll defer discussion to the "Running Multiple Servers" section later in this chapter.

The `mysqld_safe` and `mysqld_multi` scripts are installed in the `bin` directory under the MySQL installation directory or can be found in the `scripts` directory of the MySQL source distribution. The `mysql.server` script is installed under the `share/mysql` directory under the MySQL installation directory or can be found in the `support-files` directory of the MySQL source distribution. You'll need to copy it to the proper startup directory and make it executable if you want to use it. If you install MySQL using an RPM file obtained from the MySQL Web site, the `mysql.server` script is installed under the name `mysql`; you'll find it in the `/etc/rc.d/init.d` directory. If you use a MySQL RPM obtained from RedHat, a similar startup script is installed under the name `mysqld`.

The arrangements that you'll need to make to have a startup script execute at system boot time depend on the type of system you have. Read through the following examples and use or adapt the instructions that most closely match the startup procedures for your system.

For BSD-style systems, it's common to have a few files in the `/etc` directory that initiate services at boot time. These files often have names that begin with rc, and it's likely that there will be a file named `rc.local` (or something similar) intended specifically for starting locally installed services. On such a system, you might add lines like the following to `rc.local` to start up the server:

```
if [ -x /usr/local/bin/mysqld_safe ]; then
    /usr/local/bin/mysqld_safe &
fi
```

Modify the lines appropriately if the pathname to your MySQL `bin` directory is different on your system.

For System V-style systems, you can install `mysql.server`. Copy it to the appropriate startup directory under `/etc`. This may have been done for you already if you run Linux and installed MySQL from an RPM file. Otherwise, install the script in the main startup script directory with the name you want to use, make sure the script is executable, and place links to it in the appropriate run level directory.

Note: I'll assume here that `mysql.server` gets installed into the startup directory under the name `mysql`, but I'll generally continue to discuss it as `mysql.server` to make it clear what I'm referring to.

The layout for startup file directories varies from system to system, so you'll need to check around to see how your system organizes them. For example, under Solaris, the general multiuser run level is 2. The main script directory is `/etc/init.d`, and the run level directory is `/etc/rc2.d`, so the commands would look like this:

```
# cp mysql.server /etc/init.d/mysql
# cd /etc/init.d
# chmod +x mysql
# cd /etc/rc2.d
# ln -s ../init.d/mysql S99mysql
```

At system startup time, the boot procedure automatically will invoke the `S99mysql` script with an argument of `start`.

Linux has a similar set of directories, but they are organized under `/etc/rc.d` (for example, `/etc/rc.d/init.d` and `/etc/rc.d/rc3.d`). Linux systems typically have a `chkconfig` command that is intended for startup script management. You can use it to help you install the `mysql.server` script instead of manually running commands like those just shown. The following instructions show how to install `mysql.server` into the startup directories using a name of `mysql`:

1. Copy the `mysql.server` script from wherever it's located into the `init.d` directory and make it executable:

   ```
   # cp mysql.server /etc/rc.d/init.d/mysql
   # chmod +x /etc/rc.d/init.d/mysql
   ```

2. Register the script and enable it:
```
# chkconfig --add mysql
# chkconfig mysql on
```

To verify that the script has been properly enabled, run `chkconfig` with the `--list` option:
```
# chkconfig --list mysql
mysql              0:off   1:off   2:on    3:on    4:on    5:on    6:off
```

That output indicates that the script will execute during startup for run levels 3, 4, and 5.

If you don't have `chkconfig`, you can use a procedure similar to that used for Solaris, although the pathnames are slightly different. To enable the script for run level 3, use the following commands:
```
# cp mysql.server /etc/rc.d/init.d/mysql
# cd /etc/rc.d/init.d
# chmod +x mysql
# cd /etc/rc.d/rc3.d
# ln -s ../init.d/mysql S99mysql
```

Under Mac OS X, the startup procedure is different yet. The `/Library/StartupItems` and `/System/Library/StartupItems` directories contain subdirectories for the services that are initiated at system boot time. You can set up MySQL using existing services as a model, or, more simply, you can just visit `http://www.entropy.ch/software/macosx/mysql/` for a startup item package. After installing the package, you may need to modify its main script a bit to match the location where you have your server installed.

Running the MySQL Server On Windows

MySQL distributions for Windows include several servers, each of which is built with different options. You can find a summary of the different servers in Appendix A. For this discussion, I'll use `mysqld` for examples that apply to any version of Windows on which MySQL runs and `mysqld-nt` for examples that are more applicable to NT-based versions of Windows (NT, 2000, and XP).

You can start the server manually from the command line under any version of Windows. In addition, for NT-based systems, it's possible to install any server as a service. You can set the MySQL service to run automatically when Windows starts up, and control it from the command line or by using the Windows Services Manager. If you use one of the servers built specifically for NT, you can set it up so that clients can connect using named pipes.

Running the Server Manually

To start a server manually, invoke it from the command line:

```
C:\> mysqld
```

If you want error messages to go to the console window rather than to the error log (the mysql.err file in the data directory), use the --console option:

```
C:\> mysqld --console
```

Use mysqld-nt on NT-based systems if you want to allow connections via named pipes. Named pipe support is enabled by default for mysqld-nt up through MySQL 3.23.49. This has now been changed; to take advantage of named pipe support for MySQL 3.23.50 and up, add the --enable-named-pipe option to the startup command. (It's not necessarily a good idea to do this! The reason named pipes now are disabled by default is that they were found to cause problems at server shutdown time on many machines. If you use this option, be sure to check whether or not your server shuts down properly.)

To stop the server, use mysqladmin:

```
C:\> mysqladmin -p -u root shutdown
```

Running the Server as a Service

On NT-based versions of Windows, the MySQL server can be installed as a service using the following command:

```
C:\> mysqld-nt --install
```

This will cause the server to run automatically whenever Windows starts. If you prefer to use a service that does not run automatically, install the server as a "manual" service:

```
C:\> mysqld-nt --install-manual
```

These examples use mysqld-nt, but you can actually install any server as a service. You might install mysqld instead if you don't care about named pipe support, for example.

As a general rule, when you install a server as a service, you give no other options on the command line and list them in an option file instead. (See the "Specifying Startup Options" section later in this chapter.) An exception to this rule occurs if you install several Windows servers as services. For details, see the "Running Multiple Servers" section later in this chapter.

After the server has been installed as a service, you can control it using the service name, which is MySql. This can be done from the command line or from the Windows Services Manager if you prefer a graphical interface. The Services Manager can be found as a Services item in the Windows Control Panel or in the Administrative Tools item in the Control Panel, depending on your version of Windows.

To start or stop the service from the command line, use the following commands (the service name actually can be given in any lettercase because it is not case sensitive):

```
C:\> net start MySql
C:\> net stop MySql
```

If you use the Services Manager, it presents a window that displays a list of the services it knows about, along with additional information such as whether each service is running and whether it is automatic or manual. To start or stop the MySQL server, select its entry in the services list and then choose the appropriate button or menu item.

You can also shut down the server from the command line with mysqladmin shutdown.

To remove the server from the list of services, shut it down if it is running, and then issue the following command:

```
C:\> mysqld-nt --remove
```

Note: Although you can control services using either the Services Manager or commands at the DOS prompt, you should try to avoid interactions between the two approaches. Make sure to close the Services Manager whenever you invoke service-related commands from the prompt.

Specifying Startup Options

On any platform, there are two primary methods for specifying startup options when you invoke the server:

- You can list them on the command line, in which case it's possible to use either the long or short forms of any option for which both forms are available. For example, you can use either --user=mysqladm or -u mysqladm.
- You can list the options in an option file. When specifying an option this way, only its long option form can be used, and it's given without the leading dashes:

```
user=mysqladm
```

It's generally easiest to use an option file. You can do so for any startup method, and once you put the options there, they'll take effect each time the server starts. Listing options on the command line works only when starting up the server manually or by using `mysqld_safe`. It does not work for `mysql.server`, which is intended to support only `start` and `stop` options on the command line. Also, with limited exceptions, you cannot specify startup options on the command line if you use `--install` or `--install-manual` to install a Windows server as a service. (The exceptions are discussed in the "Running Multiple Servers" section later in this chapter.)

The usual files used for specifying server options under UNIX are the `/etc/my.cnf` file and the `my.cnf` file in the data directory. Under Windows, you can use the `my.ini` file in the Windows system directory, `C:\my.cnf`, and the `my.cnf` file in the data directory. If the file you want to use it doesn't exist, create it.

Generally, server startup options are placed in the `[mysqld]` option group. For example, to indicate that you want the server to run as `mysqladm` and to use a base directory location of `/usr/local/mysql`, you can put following group in the option file:

```
[mysqld]
user=mysqladm
basedir=/usr/local/mysql
```

That is equivalent to launching the server as follows with the options on the command line:

```
% mysqld --user=mysqladm --basedir=/usr/local/mysql
```

The complete list of option groups used by servers and the server startup programs is shown in the following table:

Program	Option Groups Used By Program
mysqld	[mysqld], [server]
mysqld_safe	[mysqld], [server], [mysqld_safe], [safe_mysqld]
safe_mysqld	[mysqld], [server], [safe_mysqld]
mysql.server	[mysqld], [mysql_server]
libmysqld	[embedded], [server]

The line for `libmysqld` refers to the embedded server that can be linked into programs to produce MySQL-based applications that do not require a separate standalone server. (Chapter 6, "The MySQL C API," describes how to write applications that use the embedded server.)

The [server] group can be used for options that apply to any server, whether standalone or embedded. The [mysqld] or [embedded] groups can be used for options that apply only to standalone servers or to embedded servers. Similarly, the [mysqld_safe] or [mysql_server] groups allow you to specify options that are used only when you invoke one startup script or the other.

Prior to MySQL 4, mysqld_safe was called safe_mysqld. Instructions in this book that refer to the [mysqld_safe] option group that is used by mysqld_safe should be read as references to the [safe_mysqld] group if you're using safe_mysqld instead.

See Appendix E for more information on the format and syntax of option files.

If you launch the server by using a startup script, a third way to specify options is to modify the script to pass those options directly to the server. I don't recommend this except as a last resort. It has the significant disadvantage that you'll have to remember to redo your changes each time you install a new version of MySQL, which will wipe out your modified script with the new version.

Shutting Down the Server

To shut down the server manually, use mysqladmin:

```
% mysqladmin -p -u root shutdown
```

This works for both UNIX and Windows. If you installed the server as a service under Windows, it's also possible to stop the server manually from the command line:

```
C:\> net stop MySql
```

Or you can use the graphical interface offered by the Services Manager to select and stop the server.

If you have set the server to start up automatically when your system boots, you shouldn't need to do anything special to stop it automatically at system shutdown time. BSD UNIX systems normally shut down services by sending processes a TERM signal. They either respond to the signal appropriately or are killed unceremoniously. mysqld responds by terminating when it receives this signal.

For System V-style UNIX systems that start the server with mysql.server, the shutdown process will invoke that script with an argument of stop to tell the server to shut down. You can also invoke the script yourself to shut down the server manually. For example, if you've installed the `mysql.server` script as `/etc/rc.d/init.d/mysql`, you can invoke it as follows (you'll need to be root to do this):

```
# /etc/rc.d/init.d/mysql stop
```

If you run the MySQL server as a service on a Windows NT-based system, the service manager automatically will tell the server to stop at system shutdown time. Under other versions of Windows, or if you do not run the server as a service, you should bring down the server manually with `mysqladmin shutdown` at the command line before shutting down Windows.

Regaining Control of the Server When You Can't Connect to It

Under certain circumstances, you may need to restart the server manually due to an inability to connect to it. Of course, this is somewhat paradoxical because typically when you manually shut down the server, you do so by connecting to it with `mysqladmin shutdown`, which tells it to terminate. How then can this situation arise?

First, the MySQL `root` password might have gotten set to a value that you don't know. This can happen when you change the password—for example, if you accidentally type an invisible control character when you enter the new password value. Or you may simply have forgotten the password.

Second, under UNIX, connections to `localhost` are made through a UNIX domain socket file (for example, `/tmp/mysql.sock`). If the socket file gets removed, local clients won't be able to use it to connect. This might happen if your system runs a `cron` job that removes temporary files in `/tmp` now and then.

If the reason you can't connect is that the socket file has been removed, you can get it back simply by restarting the server. The server will re-create the socket file when it comes back up. The trick here is that because the socket file is gone, you can't use it to establish a connection for telling the server to shut down. You must establish a TCP/IP connection instead. To do this, connect to the local server by specifying a host value of `127.0.0.1` rather than `localhost`:

```
% mysqladmin -p -u root -h 127.0.0.1 shutdown
```

`127.0.0.1` is an IP number (it refers to the local host's loopback interface), so it explicitly forces a TCP/IP connection to be used rather than a socket connection.

If it is the case that the socket file is being removed by a `cron` job, the missing-socket problem will recur until you change the `cron` job or use a socket file located somewhere else. You can specify a different socket by naming it in a global option file. For example, if the MySQL base directory is `/usr/local/mysql`, you can move the socket file there by adding the following lines to `/etc/my.cnf`:

```
[mysqld]
socket=/usr/local/mysql/mysql.sock

[client]
socket=/usr/local/mysql/mysql.sock
```

It's necessary to specify the pathname both for the server and for client programs so that they all use the same socket file. If you set the pathname only for the server, client programs will still expect to find the socket at the old location. Restart the server after making the change so that it creates the socket in the new location. Unfortunately, this method works only for clients that read the option file; many do, but some may not. If you recompile MySQL from source, you can reconfigure the distribution to use a different pathname by default for the server and clients both. This will also automatically affect third-party programs that use the client library.

If you can't connect because you can't remember or don't know the `root` password, you need to regain control of the server so that you can set the password again. To do this, perform the following procedure:

1. Shut down the server. Under UNIX, if you can log in as `root` on the server host, you can terminate the server using the `kill` command. Find out the server's process ID by looking in the server's PID file (which is usually located in the data directory) or by using the `ps` command. Then try telling the server process to shut down normally by sending it a TERM signal:

   ```
   # kill -TERM PID
   ```

   That way, tables and logs will be flushed properly. If the server is jammed and unresponsive to a normal termination signal, you can use `kill -9` to forcibly terminate it.

   ```
   # kill -9 PID
   ```

   That is a last resort because there may be unflushed modifications, and you risk leaving tables in an inconsistent state.

   Under Linux, `ps` may show several `mysqld` "processes." These are really threads of the same process, so you can kill any of them to kill them all.

If you start the server using `mysqld_safe`, it will be monitoring the server and will immediately restart it after you kill it. To avoid this, determine the PID of the `mysqld_safe` process and kill it first before killing `mysqld`.

If you run the server as a service under Windows, you can bring it down normally without knowing any passwords by using the Services Manager or by issuing this command:

```
C:\> net stop MySql
```

To forcibly terminate the server on Windows, use the Task Manager (Alt-Ctrl-Del). Like `kill -9` on UNIX, this is a last resort.

2. Restart the server with the `--skip-grant-tables` option to disable use of the grant tables for verifying connections. That allows you to connect with no password and with all privileges. However, it also leaves your server wide open so that other people can connect the same way, so issue a `FLUSH PRIVILEGES` statement as soon as you connect:

```
% mysql
mysql> FLUSH PRIVILEGES;
```

The `FLUSH` statement tells the server to reread the grant tables, causing it to start using them again. You will remain connected, but the server will require any subsequent connection attempts by other clients to be validated with the tables as usual. The `FLUSH` statement also re-enables the `GRANT` statement, which is disabled when the server is not using the grant tables. After reloading the tables, you can change the `root` password, as shown in the "Securing a New MySQL Installation" section earlier in this chapter.

3. After changing the `root` password, you may want to shut down the server again and bring it back up using your normal startup procedure.

Should you be forced to terminate the server with `kill -9` under UNIX or with the Task Manager under Windows, the abrupt nature of the shutdown gives the server no chance to flush any unsaved changes to disk. It's possible that this may result in table corruption. To help deal with problems that may occur due to this kind of shutdown, it's a good idea to have the server's auto-recovery capabilities enabled. For details, see Chapter 13.

Managing MySQL User Accounts

The MySQL administrator should know how to set up MySQL user accounts by specifying which users can connect to the server, where they can connect from, and what they can do while connected. This information is stored in the grant tables in the `mysql` database and is managed primarily by means of two statements:

- `GRANT` creates MySQL accounts and specifies their privileges.
- `REVOKE` removes privileges from existing MySQL accounts.

These statements were introduced in MySQL 3.22.11 to make it easier to manage user accounts. Prior to 3.22.11, it was necessary to manipulate the contents of the grant tables directly by issuing SQL statements such as `INSERT` and `UPDATE`. `GRANT` and `REVOKE` act as a front end to the grant tables. They are more convenient to work with conceptually because you describe the permissions you want to allow, and the server maps your requests onto the proper grant table modifications automatically. Nevertheless, although it's much easier to use `GRANT` and `REVOKE` than to modify the grant tables directly, I advise that you supplement the material in this chapter by reading Chapter 12. That chapter discusses the grant tables in more detail, to help you understand how they work beyond the level of the `GRANT` and `REVOKE` statements. It also contains a section on setting up accounts without using `GRANT`, which is how you'll need to set up privileges if your server is older than 3.22.11.

You may also want to consider using the `mysqlaccess` and `mysql_setpermission` scripts, which are part of the MySQL distribution. These are Perl scripts that provide an alternative to the `GRANT` statement for setting up user accounts. `mysql_setpermission` requires that you have DBI support installed.

The `GRANT` and `REVOKE` statements affect four tables:

Grant Table	Contents
`user`	Users who can connect to the server and their global privileges
`db`	Database-level privileges
`tables_priv`	Table-level privileges
`columns_priv`	Column-level privileges

There is a fifth grant table named `host`, but it is not affected by `GRANT` or `REVOKE` and is not discussed here. For information on how it works, see Chapter 12.

When you issue a `GRANT` statement for an account, an entry is created for that account in the `user` table. If the statement specifies any global privileges (administrative privileges or privileges that apply to all databases), those are recorded in the `user` table, too. If you specify privileges that are specific to a given database, table, or table column, they are recorded in the `db`, `tables_priv`, and `columns_priv` tables.

The rest of this section describes how to set up MySQL user accounts and grant privileges, how to revoke privileges and remove users from the grant tables entirely, and how to change passwords or reset lost passwords.

Creating New Users and Granting Privileges

The syntax for the GRANT statement looks like this:

```
GRANT privileges (columns)
    ON what
    TO account IDENTIFIED BY 'password'
    REQUIRE encryption requirements
    WITH grant or resource management options;
```

Several of these clauses are optional and need not be specified at all. In general, you'll most commonly fill in the following parts:

- *privileges*

  The privileges to assign to the account. For example, the SELECT privilege allows a user to issue SELECT statements and the SHUTDOWN privilege allows the user to shut down the server.

- *columns*

  The columns the privileges apply to. This is optional, and you use it only to set up column-specific privileges. If you want to list more than one column, separate their names by commas.

- *what*

  The level at which the privileges apply. The most powerful level is the global level for which any given privilege applies to all databases and all tables. Global privileges can be thought of as superuser privileges. Privileges also can be made database-specific, table-specific, or (if you specify a *columns* clause) column-specific.

- *account*

  The account that is being granted the privileges. The *account* value consists of a username and a hostname in '*user_name*'@'*host_name*' format because in MySQL, you specify not only who can connect but from where. This allows you to set up separate accounts for two users who have the same name but who connect from different locations. MySQL lets you distinguish between them and assign privileges to each independently of the other. The *user_name* and *host_name* values are recorded in the User and Host columns of the user table entry for the account and in any other grant table records that the GRANT statement creates.

Your username in MySQL is just a name that you use to identify yourself when you connect to the server. The name has no necessary connection to your UNIX login name or Windows name. By default, client programs will use your login name as your MySQL username if you don't specify a name explicitly, but that's just a convention. There is also nothing special about the name `root` that is used for the MySQL superuser that can do anything. It's just a convention. You could just as well change this name to `nobody` in the grant tables and then connect as `nobody` to perform operations that require superuser privileges.

- *password*

  The password to assign to the account. This is optional. If you specify no `IDENTIFIED BY` clause for a new user, that user is assigned no password (which is insecure). If you use `GRANT` to modify the privileges of an existing account, the account's password is either replaced or left unchanged, depending on whether you include or omit an `IDENTIFIED BY` clause. When you do use `IDENTIFIED BY`, the *password* value should be the literal text of the password; `GRANT` will encode the password for you. Don't use the `PASSWORD()` function as you do with the `SET PASSWORD` statement.

The `REQUIRE` and `WITH` clauses are optional. `REQUIRE` is available as of MySQL 4.0.0 and is used for setting up accounts that must connect over secure connections using SSL. `WITH` is used to grant the `GRANT OPTION` privilege that allows the account to give its own privileges to other users. As of MySQL 4.0.2, `WITH` is also used to specify resource management options that allow you to place limits on how many connections or queries an account can use per hour. These options help you prevent the account from hogging the server.

Usernames, passwords, and database and table names are case sensitive in grant table entries. Hostnames and column names are not.

When you want to set up an account, it's generally possible to figure out the kind of `GRANT` statement to issue by asking some simple questions:

- Who can connect, and from where? What is the user's name, and where will that user connect from?
- What type of access should the account be given? That is, what level of privileges should the user have, and what should they apply to?
- Are secure connections required?
- Should the user be allowed to administer privileges?
- Should the user's resource consumption be limited?

The following discussion asks these questions and provides some examples showing how to use the GRANT statement to set up MySQL user accounts.

Who Can Connect, and from Where?

The *account* part of the GRANT statement specifies the user's name and where that user can connect from. You can allow a user to connect from as specific or broad a set of hosts as you like. At the one extreme, you can limit access to a single host if you know users will be connecting only from that host. For example, to grant access to all the tables in the sampdb database for host-specific accounts, you can use statements like these:

```
GRANT ALL ON sampdb.* TO 'boris'@'localhost' IDENTIFIED BY 'ruby';
GRANT ALL ON sampdb.* TO 'fred'@'ares.mars.net' IDENTIFIED BY 'quartz';
```

If the username or hostname parts of the *account* value do not contain any special characters such as '-' or '%', you may not need to quote them (for example, boris@localhost is legal without quotes). However, it should always be safe to use quotes, and the examples in this book do so as a rule. But note that the username and hostname are quoted separately; use 'boris'@'local-host', not 'boris@localhost'.

Allowing a user to connect from a single host is the strictest form of access you can allow. At the other extreme, you may have a user who travels a lot and needs to be able to connect from hosts all over the world. If the user's name is max, you can allow him to connect from anywhere, as follows:

```
GRANT ALL ON sampdb.* TO 'max'@'%' IDENTIFIED BY 'diamond';
```

The '%' character functions as a wildcard with the same meaning as in a LIKE pattern match. Thus, as a hostname specifier, % means "any host." This is the easiest way to set up a user, but it's also the least secure. (Using it also may result in occasional head-scratching on your part, for reasons described in the "A Privilege Puzzle" in Chapter 12.)

To take a middle ground, you can allow a user to connect from a limited set of hosts. For example, to allow mary to connect from any host in the snake.net domain, use a host specifier of %.snake.net:

```
GRANT ALL ON sampdb.* TO 'mary'@'%.snake.net' IDENTIFIED BY 'topaz';
```

The other LIKE wildcard character ('_') can be used in host values to match any single character.

The host part of the *account* value can be given using an IP address rather than a hostname, if you want. You can specify a literal IP address or an address that contains pattern characters. Also, as of MySQL 3.23, you can specify IP numbers with a netmask indicating which bits to use for the network number:

```
GRANT ALL ON sampdb.* TO 'joe'@'192.168.128.3' IDENTIFIED BY 'water';
GRANT ALL ON sampdb.* TO 'ardis'@'192.168.128.%' IDENTIFIED BY 'snow';
GRANT ALL ON sampdb.* TO 'rex'@'192.168.128.0/255.255.128.0'
    IDENTIFIED BY 'ice';
```

The first of these statements indicates a specific host from which the user can connect. The second specifies an IP pattern for the `192.168.128` Class C subnet. In the third statement, `192.168.128.0/255.255.128.0` specifies a netmask that has the first 17 bits turned on. It matches any host with `192.168.128` in the first 17 bits of its IP address.

Using a host value of `localhost` in a `GRANT` statement allows the user to connect to the server from the local host by specifying a host value of `localhost` or `127.0.0.1` (the local host's loopback IP address). A `localhost` account also matches on Windows when the user connects by specifying a hostname of '.' (period) if the server supports named pipes. On UNIX, connections to `localhost` are made via the UNIX socket file. On Windows, connections to '.' are made via a named pipe if named pipes are available. All other connections are made via TCP/IP, including connections to `127.0.0.1`, the loopback address.

If you give no hostname part at all in an account specifier, it's the same as using host part of `%`. Thus, `'max'` and `'max'@'%'` are equivalent *account* values in `GRANT` statements. This means that if you intend to specify an account of `'boris'@'localhost'` but mistakenly write `'boris@localhost'` instead, MySQL will accept it as legal. What happens is that MySQL interprets `'boris@localhost'` as containing only a user part and adds the default host part of `%` to it, resulting in an effective account name of `'boris@localhost'@'%'`. To avoid this, be sure always to quote the user and host parts of account specifiers separately.

How to Specify Your Local Hostname in Grant Table Entries

It's common to have problems connecting from the server host if you use the server's hostname rather than `localhost`. This can occur due to a mismatch between the way the name is specified in the grant tables and the way your name resolver reports the name to programs. Suppose the server host's fully qualified name is `cobra.snake.net`. If the resolver reports an unqualified name, such as `cobra`, but the grant tables contain entries with the fully qualified name (or vice versa), this mismatch will occur.

To determine if this is happening on your system, try connecting to the local server using a `-h` option that specifies the name of your host:

```
% mysql -h cobra.snake.net
```

continues

Then look in the server's general log file. How does it write the hostname when it reports the connection attempt? Is the name in unqualified or fully qualified form? Whichever form it's in, that tells you how you'll need to specify the hostname part of account name specifiers when you issue GRANT statements.

What Type of Access Should the User Be Given?

You can grant several types of privileges. These are summarized in Table 11.1 and described in more detail in Chapter 12. That chapter discusses the privileges in terms of both their purpose and their relationship to the underlying grant tables.

Table 11.1   **MySQL Privilege Types**

Privilege Specifier	Operation Allowed by Privilege
CREATE TEMPORARY TABLES	Create temporary tables
EXECUTE	Execute stored procedures (reserved for future use)
FILE	Read and write files on the server host
GRANT OPTION	Grant the account's privileges to other accounts
LOCK TABLES	Explicitly lock tables with LOCK TABLES statements
PROCESS	View information about the threads executing within the server
RELOAD	Reload the grant tables or flush the logs or caches
REPLICATION CLIENT	Ask about master and slave server locations
REPLICATION SLAVE	Act as a replication slave server
SHOW DATABASES	Issue SHOW DATABASES statements
SHUTDOWN	Shut down the server
SUPER	Kill threads and perform other supervisory operations
ALTER	Alter tables and indexes
CREATE	Create databases and tables
DELETE	Delete existing rows from tables
DROP	Drop (remove) databases and tables
INDEX	Create or drop indexes
INSERT	Insert new rows into tables
REFERENCES	Unused (reserved for future use)
SELECT	Retrieve existing rows from tables
UPDATE	Modify existing table rows
ALL	All operations (except GRANT); ALL PRIVILEGES is a synonym
USAGE	A special "no privileges" privilege

The privilege specifiers in the first group shown in the table are administrative privileges. Normally, these are granted relatively sparingly because they allow users to affect the operation of the server. (The SHUTDOWN privilege is not one you hand out on an everyday basis, for example.) The privileges in the second group apply to databases, tables, and columns, and control access to data managed by the server. The specifiers in the third group are special. ALL means "all privileges" (except that it does not include the GRANT OPTION privilege). USAGE means "no privileges"—that is, "create the account, but don't grant it any privileges." USAGE also can be used to modify non-privilege-related aspects of an account without changing its current privileges.

Some of the privileges are new in MySQL 4.0.2, so you can't grant them if you have an earlier version. These are CREATE TEMPORARY TABLES, EXECUTE, LOCK TABLES, REPLICATION CLIENT, REPLICATION SLAVE, SHOW DATABASES, and SUPER. The introduction of these privileges changes how some operations are controlled. For example, the ability to kill any thread running within the server is granted through the PROCESS privilege prior to MySQL 4.0.2, and through the SUPER privilege from 4.0.2 on. Normally, this is not a problem, as long as you upgrade your grant tables when updating from a pre-4.0.2 server to 4.0.2 or later; MySQL distributions contain a mysql_fix_privilege_tables script that installs columns for the newer privileges, and each account's SUPER privilege is initialized from its PROCESS privilege. Thus, any user who can kill threads prior to 4.0.2 can continue to do so from 4.0.2 on. (The specific rules that are used to migrate privileges when you upgrade to 4.0.2 or later are described in Chapter 12 in the "Dealing with Changes to Grant Table Structure" sidebar.)

Be aware that you cannot grant the CREATE TEMPORARY TABLES or LOCK TABLES privileges on a database-specific basis in MySQL 4.0.2 or 4.0.3, so you should avoid using those versions if possible. This problem was corrected in MySQL 4.0.4.

You can grant privileges at different levels all the way from global down to column-specific. This is controlled by the ON clause specifier, as shown in the following table:

Privilege Specifier	Level At Which Privileges Apply
ON *.*	Global privileges; all databases, all tables
ON *	Global privileges if no default database has been selected, database-level privileges for the current database otherwise
ON db_name.*	Database-level privileges; all tables in the named database
ON db_name.tbl_name	Table-level privileges; all columns in the named table
ON tbl_name	Table-level privileges; all columns in the named table in the default database

Global privileges are the most powerful because they apply to any database. To make `ethel` a superuser who can do anything, including being able to grant privileges to other users, issue this statement:

```
GRANT ALL ON *.* TO 'ethel'@'localhost' IDENTIFIED BY 'coffee'
    WITH GRANT OPTION;
```

The `ON *.*` clause means "all databases, all tables." As a safety precaution, the statement specifies that `ethel` can connect only from the local host. Limiting the hosts from which a superuser can connect is usually wise because it limits the hosts from which password-cracking attempts can be mounted.

Some privileges are administrative in nature and can be granted using only the `ON *.*` global-privilege specifier. These include FILE, PROCESS, RELOAD, SHUT-DOWN, and the other privileges in the first section of Table 11.1. For example, the RELOAD privilege allows use of FLUSH, so the following statement sets up a user named `flush` that can do nothing but issue FLUSH statements:

```
GRANT RELOAD ON *.* TO 'flush'@'localhost' IDENTIFIED BY 'flushpass';
```

This type of MySQL account can be useful for writing administrative scripts in which you need to perform operations such as flushing the logs during log file rotation. (See the "Log File Expiration" section later in this chapter.)

Database-level privileges apply to all tables in a particular database. These are granted by using an ON *db_name*.* clause:

```
GRANT ALL ON sampdb.* TO 'bill'@'racer.snake.net' IDENTIFIED BY 'rock';
GRANT SELECT ON menagerie.* TO 'reader'@'%' IDENTIFIED BY 'dirt';
```

The first of these statements grants `bill` full privileges for any table in the `sampdb` database. The second creates a restricted-access user named `reader` who can access any table in the `menagerie` database, but only with SELECT statements. That is, `reader` is a "read-only" user.

You can list multiple privileges to be granted at the same time by naming them separated by commas. For example, to give a user the ability to read and modify the contents of existing tables in the `sampdb` database but not to create new tables or drop tables, you would not grant the ALL privilege for the database. Instead, you grant several more-specific privileges:

```
GRANT SELECT,INSERT,DELETE,UPDATE ON sampdb.* TO 'jennie'@'%'
    IDENTIFIED BY 'boron';
```

For more fine-grained access control below the database level, you can grant privileges on individual tables, or even on individual columns in tables. Column-specific privileges are useful when there are parts of a table you want to hide from a user or when you want a user to be able to modify only particular columns. Suppose someone volunteers to help you at the Historical

League office with the duties that you perform as the League secretary. That's good news, but you decide to begin by granting your new assistant read-only access to the `member` table that contains membership information, plus a column-specific `UPDATE` privilege on the `expiration` column of that table. That way, your assistant will have write access only for the rather modest task of updating expiration dates as people renew their memberships. The statements to set up this MySQL account are as follows:

```
GRANT SELECT ON sampdb.member
    TO 'assistant'@'localhost' IDENTIFIED BY 'officehelp';
GRANT UPDATE (expiration) ON sampdb.member
    TO 'assistant'@'localhost';
```

The first statement grants read access to the entire `member` table and sets up a password. The second statement adds the `UPDATE` privilege, but only for the `expiration` column. It's not necessary to specify the password again because that was done by the first statement.

If you want to grant column-specific privileges for more than one column, specify a list of column names separated by commas. For example, to add `UPDATE` privileges for the address fields of the `member` table for the `assistant` user, issue the following statement. The new privileges will be added to any that already exist for the user:

```
GRANT UPDATE (street,city,state,zip) ON sampdb.member
    TO 'assistant'@'localhost';
```

Records in the grant tables do not "follow" renaming operations. For example, any privileges tied specifically to a given table will no longer apply if the table is renamed. This principle is true at the database, table, and column levels.

Why the "No Privileges" USAGE Privilege is Useful

The special privilege specifier USAGE means "no privileges." At first glance, this may not seem very useful, but it is. It allows you to change characteristics of an account other than those that pertain to privileges, while leaving the existing privileges alone. To use it, grant the USAGE privilege at the global level, specify the account name, and provide the new non-privilege characteristics of the account. For example, if you want to change an account password, require that the user connect using SSL, or impose a connection limit on an account without affecting the privileges held by the account, use statements like the following:

```
GRANT USAGE ON *.* TO account IDENTIFIED BY 'new_password';
GRANT USAGE ON *.* TO account REQUIRE SSL;
GRANT USAGE ON *.* TO account WITH MAX_CONNECTIONS_PER_HOUR 10;
```

Are Secure Connections Required?

As of MySQL 4, secure connections can be made using the SSL (Secure Sockets Layer) protocol, which encrypts the data stream between the client and the server so that it is not sent in the clear. In addition, X509 can be used as a means for the client to provide identification information over SSL connections. Secure connections provide an extra measure of protection, but this comes at the price of the extra CPU horsepower required to perform encryption and decryption. SSL is supported only on UNIX at the moment.

To specify options for secure connections, use a REQUIRE clause. To require that a user connect via SSL without being more specific about the type of secure connection the user must make, use REQUIRE SSL:

```
GRANT ALL ON sampdb.* TO 'eladio'@'%.snake.net' IDENTIFIED BY 'flint'
    REQUIRE SSL;
```

To be more specific, you can require that the client present a valid X509 certificate:

```
GRANT ALL ON sampdb.* TO 'eladio'@'%.snake.net' IDENTIFIED BY 'flint'
    REQUIRE X509;
```

To be more specific yet, REQUIRE allows you to indicate that the client's X509 certificate must have certain characteristics or that the connection must be encrypted using a particular cipher type. These characteristics are given with ISSUER, SUBJECT, or CIPHER options in the REQUIRE clause. (ISSUER and SUBJECT refer to the certificate issuer and recipient.) For example, the ssl directory of the sampdb distribution includes a client certificate file, client-cert.pem, that you can use for testing SSL connections. The issuer and subject values in the certificate can be displayed like this:

```
% openssl x509 -subject -noout -in client-cert.pem
issuer= /C=US/ST=WI/L=Madison/O=sampdb/OU=CA/CN=sampdb
subject= /C=US/ST=WI/L=Madison/O=sampdb/OU=client/CN=sampdb
```

The following GRANT statement creates an account for which the client must present a certificate that matches both of those values:

```
GRANT ALL ON sampdb.* TO 'eladio'@'%.snake.net' IDENTIFIED BY 'flint'
    REQUIRE ISSUER '/C=US/ST=WI/L=Madison/O=sampdb/OU=CA/CN=sampdb'
    AND SUBJECT '/C=US/ST=WI/L=Madison/O=sampdb/OU=client/CN=sampdb';
```

To indicate explicitly that secure connections are not required, use REQUIRE NONE. The NONE option is available as of MySQL 4.0.4.

Some additional points to be aware of when using a REQUIRE clause:

- Issuing a GRANT statement that requires an account to use secure connections only sets up a constraint on the account. It doesn't actually provide the means for a client to connect securely with that account. For that to happen, MySQL must be configured to include SSL support, and you must start the server and clients in a particular way. Instructions for doing so are given in Chapter 12.

- If the server and client programs are configured with SSL support, any user will be *able* to use secure connections. REQUIRE is used only to indicate that an account *must* connect using secure connections.

- There is little point in using a REQUIRE clause for accounts that don't connect to the server over an external network. Such connections can't be snooped, so making them secure gains you nothing and incurs the increased computational load without benefit. Accounts like this include those that connect to the server only through a UNIX socket file or a named pipe or to the IP address 127.0.0.1 (the host's loopback interface). These connections use interfaces that are handled entirely internally to the host and for which no traffic crosses an external network.

Should the User Be Allowed to Administer Privileges?

You can allow the owner of a database to control access to the database by granting the owner all privileges on the database and specifying the WITH GRANT OPTION when you do. For example, if you want alicia to be able to connect from any host in the big-corp.com domain and administer privileges for all tables in the sales database, you could use the following GRANT statement:

```
GRANT ALL ON sales.*
    TO 'alicia'@'%.big-corp.com' IDENTIFIED BY 'shale'
    WITH GRANT OPTION;
```

In effect, the WITH GRANT OPTION clause allows you to delegate access-granting rights to another user. Be aware that two users with the GRANT OPTION privilege can grant each other their own privileges. If you've given one user only the SELECT privilege but another user has GRANT OPTION plus other privileges in addition to SELECT, the second user can make the first one "stronger."

Another way to grant the GRANT OPTION privilege is simply to list it in the beginning part of the GRANT statement:

```
GRANT GRANT OPTION ON sales.* TO 'alicia'@'%.big-corp.com';
```

However, a statement such as this one will not work:

```
GRANT ALL,GRANT OPTION ON sales.* TO 'alicia'@'%.big-corp.com';
```

ALL can be used only by itself, not in a list that names other privilege specifiers.

Should the User's Resource Consumption Be Limited?

As of MySQL 4.0.2, you can place limits on the number of times per hour that a user can connect to the server and the number of queries or updates per hour the user can issue. These limits are specified in the WITH clause. The following statement sets up a user spike that has full access to the sampdb database, but can connect only ten times per hour and issue 200 queries per hour (of which at most 50 can be updates):

```
GRANT ALL ON sampdb.* TO 'spike'@'localhost' IDENTIFIED BY 'pyrite'
    WITH MAX_CONNECTIONS_PER_HOUR 10 MAX_QUERIES_PER_HOUR 200
    MAX_UPDATES_PER_HOUR 50;
```

The order of the resource management options within the WITH clause does not matter. The default value for each option is zero, which means "no limit."

An administrative user who has the RELOAD privilege can reset the current counter values by issuing a FLUSH USER_RESOURCES statement. FLUSH PRIVILEGES does this as well. After the counters have been reset, accounts that have reached their hourly limits can once again connect and issue queries.

Revoking Privileges and Removing Users

To take away a user's privileges, use the REVOKE statement. The syntax for REVOKE is somewhat similar to that for the GRANT statement, except that TO is replaced by FROM; and there are no IDENTIFIED BY, REQUIRE, or WITH clauses:

```
REVOKE privileges (columns) ON what FROM account;
```

The account part must match the account part of the original GRANT statement for the user whose privileges you want to revoke. The privileges part need not match; you can grant privileges with a GRANT statement and then revoke only some of them with REVOKE. For example, the following GRANT statement grants all privileges on the sampdb database, and the REVOKE statement removes the account's privileges for making changes to existing records:

```
GRANT ALL ON sampdb.* TO 'boris'@'localhost' IDENTIFIED BY 'ruby';
REVOKE DELETE,UPDATE ON sampdb.* FROM 'boris'@'localhost';
```

The GRANT OPTION privilege is not included in ALL, so if you have granted it, you can revoke it only by naming it explicitly in the *privileges* part of a REVOKE statement:

```
REVOKE GRANT OPTION ON sales.* FROM 'alicia'@'%.big-corp.com';
```

REVOKE removes privileges from an account, but it will not delete the account entirely. An entry for the account will remain in the user table, even if you revoke all of its privileges. This means the user can still connect to the server. To remove an account entirely, you must explicitly delete its record from the user table with a DELETE statement. For example, to delete the account for mary@%.snake.net, do this:

```
% mysql -u root
mysql> USE mysql;
mysql> DELETE FROM user
    -> WHERE User = 'mary' and Host = '%.snake.net';
mysql> FLUSH PRIVILEGES;
```

The DELETE statement removes the account's entry from the user table, and the FLUSH statement tells the server to reload the grant tables. FLUSH is necessary because the server reloads the grant tables automatically when you use GRANT or REVOKE, but not when you modify them directly. (To be complete, check the other grant tables for any records relating to the account, and delete any that may be present before flushing the privileges.)

Somewhat paradoxically, there are a few revocation operations that are done with GRANT. For example, if you specify that an account must connect using SSL, there is no REVOKE syntax for rescinding that requirement. Instead, issue a GRANT statement grants the USAGE privilege at the global level (to leave existing privileges unchanged) and include a REQUIRE NONE clause to indicate that SSL is not required:

```
GRANT USAGE ON *.* TO account REQUIRE NONE;
```

Similarly, if you set up resource limits on a user, you don't remove those limits with REVOKE. Instead, use GRANT with USAGE to set the limit values to zero ("no limit"):

```
GRANT USAGE ON *.* TO account
    WITH MAX_CONNECTIONS_PER_HOUR 0 MAX_QUERIES_PER_HOUR 0
    MAX_UPDATES_PER_HOUR 0;
```

Changing Passwords or Resetting Lost Passwords

One way to change or reset an account's password is to use an UPDATE statement that identifies the User and Host values for the account's user table record:

```
mysql> UPDATE user SET Password=PASSWORD('silicon')
    -> WHERE User='boris' AND Host='localhost';
mysql> FLUSH PRIVILEGES;
```

However, it's a lot easier to use SET PASSWORD because you name the account using the same format as for GRANT, and it's unnecessary to flush the privileges explicitly:

```
mysql> SET PASSWORD FOR 'boris'@'localhost' = PASSWORD('silicon');
```

SET PASSWORD also is safer than UPDATE; with UPDATE, it's easier to make a mistake and change the wrong user table entry.

Another way to change a password is to use GRANT USAGE with an IDENTIFIED BY clause, in which case you specify the password literally rather than by using the PASSWORD() function:

```
mysql> GRANT USAGE ON *.* TO 'boris'@'localhost' IDENTIFIED BY 'silicon';
```

If you need to reset the root password because you've forgotten it and can't connect to the server, you have something of a conundrum because normally you have to connect as root to change the root password. If you don't know the password, you'll need to force down the server and restart it without grant table validation. The procedure for this is described in the "Regaining Control of the Server When You Can't Connect to It" section earlier in this chapter.

Maintaining Log Files

When the MySQL server begins executing, it examines its startup options to see whether or not it should perform logging and opens the appropriate log files if it should. There are several types of logs you can tell the server to generate:

- **The general query log**

    This log contains a record of client connections, queries, and various other miscellaneous events. It is useful for monitoring server activity— who is connecting, from where, and what they are doing. It's the most convenient log to use when you want to determine what queries clients are sending to the server, which can be very useful for troubleshooting or debugging.

- **The slow-query log**

  This log's purpose is to help you identify statements that may be in need of being rewritten for better performance. The server maintains a `long_query_time` variable that defines "slow" queries. If a query takes more than that many seconds of real time, it is considered slow and is recorded in the slow-query log. The slow-query log is also used to log queries for which no indexes were used.

- **The update log**

  This log records queries that modify the database. The term "update" in this context refers not just to UPDATE statements, but to any statement that modifies data. For this reason, it contains a record of queries such as DELETE, INSERT, REPLACE, CREATE TABLE, DROP TABLE, GRANT, and REVOKE. Update log contents are written as SQL statements in a form that can be used as input to the `mysql` program. Originally, the purpose of this log was to create a record to be used in conjunction with backups to restore tables after a crash. (You can restore a database from your backup files and then rerun any queries that modified the database subsequent to the backup by using the update logs as input to `mysql`. That way you can bring the tables to the state they were in at the time of the crash.) But as of MySQL 3.23.14, when the binary update log was introduced, the update log should be considered deprecated.

- **The binary update log and the binary log index file**

  The binary update log contents are similar to the contents of the update log, but it's stored in a more efficient format and with additional information. It is used for recovery operations and for transmitting updates to replication slave servers. The binary logs are accompanied by an index file that lists which binary log files exist on the server.

The default location for each of these log files is the data directory, although the server won't create any of them unless you ask for them. Each log can be enabled by specifying a startup option for `mysqld`. Other than the binary log, these logs are written in ASCII format and can be viewed directly. To see the contents of a binary log, use the `mysqlbinlog` utility.

Another log file, the error log, is a special case that is handled somewhat differently. (For example, on UNIX it's created by the `mysqld_safe` script rather than by the server.) It's described in detail later in the section "The Error Log." The server also manages some special-purpose logs that are associated with particular table handlers. The ISAM log is used for debugging purposes to record changes to ISAM and MyISAM tables; I won't mention it further. The BDB and InnoDB table handlers maintain logs of their own for internal purposes (such as for performing auto-recovery after a crash).

Of all the logs, the general query log is most useful for monitoring the server, so when you first start using MySQL, I recommend that you enable the general log in addition to whatever other logs you want. After you have gained some experience with MySQL, you may want to turn off the general log to reduce your disk-space requirements.

To enable logging, use the options shown in the following table. If the log file-name is optional (as indicated by square brackets) and you don't provide one, the server uses a default name and writes the log file in the data directory. The default name for each of the log files is derived from the name of your server host, represented by *HOSTNAME* in the following discussion. If you specify a log name that is a relative pathname, the name is interpreted with respect to the data directory. A full pathname can be specified to place the log in some other directory. The server will create any log file that does not exist, but will not create the directory in which the file is to be written. If necessary, create the directory before starting the server.

Logging Option	Log Enabled by Option
`--log[=file_name]`	General log file
`--log-bin[=file_name]`	Binary update log file
`--log-bin-index=file_name`	Binary update log index file
`--log-update[=file_name]`	Update log file
`--log-slow-queries[=file_name]`	Slow-query log file
`--log-isam[=file_name]`	ISAM/MyISAM log file
`--log-long-format`	Affects slow-query and update log format

If the BDB or InnoDB table handlers are enabled, they create their own logs (by default, in the data directory). You cannot control whether or not the logs are generated, but you can specify where they are written by using the following options:

Logging Option	Purpose
`--bdb-logdir=dir_name`	BDB log file directory
`--innodb_log_arch_dir=dir_name`	InnoDB log archive directory
`--innodb_log_group_home_dir=dir_name`	InnoDB log file directory

If you specify either of the InnoDB options, you should specify both, and you must give both the same value.

You can specify logging options on the command line for `mysqld` or `mysqld_safe`. However, because you usually specify log options the same way each time you start the server, it's most common to list them in an appropriate group of an option file. Typically, options are listed in the `[mysqld]` group, but they need not always be. The "Specifying Startup Options" section earlier in this chapter details the option groups applicable to the server and to the server startup programs.

Flushing the Logs

Flushing the logs causes the server to close and reopen the log files. This can be done by executing `mysqladmin flush-logs` or (as of MySQL 3.22.9) with a `FLUSH LOGS` statement. Sending a `SIGHUP` signal to the server also flushes the logs. (Another way to flush the logs is to use `mysqladmin refresh`, but that does other things as well, so it's overkill if you just want to flush the logs.)

Log flushing applies to the general log, update log, binary update log and index file, and slow-query log; but not to the error log or table handler-specific logs. For the binary log, flushing the logs causes the server to close the current log file and open a new one with the next number in the sequence. This also happens with the update log if you're generating a numbered series of update log files.

Log flushing can be useful for log expiration or rotation purposes, as discussed in the "Log File Expiration" section later in this chapter.

The General Query Log

This log contains a record of when clients connect to the server, each query that is sent to it by clients, and various other events that are not represented as queries (such as server startup and shutdown). If you enable the general log by specifying the `--log` option without a filename, the default name is *HOSTNAME*.`log` in the data directory.

Queries are written to this log in the order that the server receives them. This may well be different than the order in which they finish executing, particularly for a mix of short and long queries.

The Slow-Query Log

The slow-query log provides a record of which queries took a long time to execute, where "long" is defined by the value of the `long_query_time` server variable in seconds. Slow queries also cause the server to increment its `Slow_queries` status counter. The slow-query log can be useful for identifying queries that you might be able to improve if you rewrite them. However, you'll need to take general load into account when interpreting the contents of this log. Query time is measured in real time (not CPU time), so if your server is bogged down, it's more likely that a query will be assessed as being slow, even if at some other time it runs under the limit.

If you enable the slow-query log by specifying `--log-slow-queries` without a filename, the default name is *HOSTNAME*`-slow.log` in the data directory. If the `--log-long-format` option is given in conjunction with `--log-slow-queries`, MySQL also logs queries that execute without benefit of any index.

Because the time a query takes is not known until it finishes, queries are written to the slow-query log after they execute, not when they are received.

Use the `mysqldumpslow` utility to see what queries are contained in the slow-query log.

The Update Log

The update log is used to record statements that modify data, such as `INSERT`, `DELETE`, or `UPDATE`. `SELECT` statements are not written to this log. An `UPDATE` statement such as the following is not written to the update log, either, because it doesn't actually change any values:

```
UPDATE t SET i = i;
```

MySQL must execute a statement first to determine whether it modifies data, so queries are written to the update log when they finish executing rather than when they are received.

Prior to MySQL 3.23.14 (when the binary update log was introduced), the update log can be used for database backup and recovery. However, the update log now is deprecated in favor of the binary log, which serves the same purposes and supports replication operations as well.

Update logging is enabled with the `--log-update` option. The MySQL server names update log files using the following rules:

- If you enable the update log by specifying `--log-update` without a filename, the server generates a numbered series of log files in the data directory using your server's hostname as the file basename: *HOST-NAME*`.001`, *HOSTNAME*`.002`, and so forth.[1]

---

1. There are plans to change numbered log names to use six digits rather than three. This will help make log names sort better. Currently, they sort out of order when you cross the threshold from `.999` to `.1000`. Using six digits will make out-of-order sorting much less likely.

- If you specify a log name that contains no extension, the server uses that name rather than the hostname as the basename and generates a numbered series of log files. For example, if you specify `--log-update=update`, it generates update logs named `update.001`, `update.002`, and so forth.

- If you enable update logging and specify a log name that contains an extension, the server always uses exactly that name for the log and does not generate a numbered series of log files.

For update logs that are generated in numbered sequence, the server creates the next file in the series whenever it starts up or the logs are flushed.

If the `--log-long-format` option is given in conjunction with `--log-update`, MySQL writes additional information to the log, indicating which user issued each statement and at what time.

The Binary Update Log and the Binary Log Index File

Like the update log, the binary update log is used for recording queries that modify data, but its contents are written in a more efficient binary format rather than in ASCII. The binary log also contains additional information, such as query execution timestamps. The binary nature of this log means that it is not directly viewable, but you can use the `mysqlbinlog` utility to produce readable binary log output.

The binary update log can be used for database backup and recovery, and you must enable it if you want to set up a server as a master server that is replicated to a slave server.

If you enable the binary log by specifying `--log-bin` without a filename, binary logs are generated in numbered sequence, using *HOSTNAME*-bin as the basename—*HOSTNAME*-bin.001, *HOSTNAME*-bin.002, and so on. Otherwise, the name that you specify is used as the basename (with the exception that if the name includes an extension, the extension is stripped). The next file in the sequence is generated each time you start the server, flush the logs, or when the current log reaches its maximum size. This size is determined by the value of the `max_binlog_size` server variable. (Note that these rules for generating binary log file names are similar to but are not quite the same as the rules used for update log naming.)

Queries are written to the binary update log in order of execution. That is, they're logged in the order they finish, not the order in which they are received, which is an important property for making replication work properly.

Queries that are part of a transaction are cached until the transaction is committed, at which time all queries in the transaction are logged. If the transaction is rolled back, the transaction is not written to the binary log because it results in no changes to the database. (This is similar to the way individual queries are not written to the update log unless they actually change data; for the binary update log, the same principle applies, but extends across multiple statements in transactional context.)

If you enable binary logging, the server also creates an accompanying binary log index file that lists the names of the existing binary log files. The default index filename is the same as the basename of the binary logs, with an `.index` extension. To specify a name explicitly, use the `--log-bin-index` option. If the name includes no extension, `.index` will be added to the name automatically. For example, if you specify `--log-bin-index=binlog`, the index filename becomes `binlog.index`.

If you are using the binary logs for replication purposes, be sure not to delete any binary log file until you are sure that its contents have been replicated to all applicable slave servers and it is no longer needed. The "Expiring Replication-Related Log Files" section, later in this chapter, describes how to check this.

> ### Log Files and System Backups
>
> Your update or binary update logs won't be any good for database recovery or replication if a disk crash causes you to lose them. Make sure you're performing regular file system backups. It's also a good idea to write these logs to a disk different from the one on which your databases are stored, which requires that you relocate them from the data directory where the server writes them by default. See Chapter 10 for instructions on relocating log files.

The Error Log

The error log is used for recording diagnostic and error information. This log is handled differently on UNIX and Windows, as described in the following discussion.

The Error Log on UNIX

On UNIX, the error log is not created by the server, unlike the other logs, but rather by the `mysqld_safe` script that is used to start up the server.

`mysqld_safe` creates the error log by redirecting the server's standard output and standard error output (the output streams known as `stdout` and `stderr`

in the C programming language). The default error log name is
HOSTNAME.err. You can specify a different error log name by passing an
--err-log option to mysqld_safe on the command line or by including an
err-log line in the [mysqld_safe] group of an option file. (Prior to MySQL
4, mysqld_safe is named safe_mysqld. The safe_mysqld script supports --
err-log back to version 3.23.22 . Before that, safe_mysqld always writes the
log using the default name, and there is no way to change it other than by
editing the script.)

If you specify a relative pathname for the error log, the name is interpreted
with respect to the directory from which mysqld_safe is invoked. This is in
contrast to the other log files, which are created by mysqld and for which relative pathnames are interpreted with respect to the data directory. Because you
won't necessarily always invoke mysqld_safe from the same directory (for
example, if you execute it manually on different occasions), it's best to specify
an absolute pathname to ensure that the error log is always created in the same
location.

Note that if the error log file already exists but is not writable to the login
account used for running the server, startup will fail with no output being
written to the error log. This can happen if you start up the server with different --user values at different times. It's best to use the same account consistently, as discussed in the "Running the Server Using an Unprivileged Login
Account" section earlier in this chapter.

The error log is created if you start the server using the mysql.server script
because mysql.server invokes mysqld_safe. However, mysql.server
doesn't recognize --err-log on the command line or in its [mysql_server]
option group, so if you want to give a specific error log name in this case, you
must do so in the [mysqld_safe] group of an option file.

If you start mysqld directly, error messages go to your terminal and there is no
error log. You can redirect the output yourself to capture a record of diagnostic
output. For example, to write error information to a file named
/tmp/mysql.err, invoke the server like this for csh or tcsh:

```
% mysqld >& /tmp/mysql.err &
```

or like this for sh and similar shells:

```
% mysqld > /tmp/mysql.err 2>&1 &
```

The Error Log on Windows

On Windows, the server writes diagnostic information to the file `mysql.err` in the data directory by default. No alternative filename can be given. If you start the server with the `--console` option, it writes diagnostic output to the console window and does not create an error log. (The `--console` option has no effect if you run the server as a service because there is no console to write to in that case.)

Log File Expiration

One danger of enabling logging is that it has the potential to generate huge amounts of information, possibly filling up your disks. This is especially true if you have a busy server that processes lots of queries. To keep the last few logs available online while preventing log files from growing without bound, you can use log file expiration techniques. Some of the methods available for keeping logs manageable include the following:

- **Log rotation**. This applies to logs that have a fixed filename, such as the general query log and the slow-query log.

- **Age-based expiration**. This method removes log files that are older than a certain age. It can be applied to numbered log files that are created in numbered sequence, such as the update logs and the binary update logs.

- **Replication-related expiration**. If you use the binary update log files for replication, it's better not to expire them based on age. Instead, you should consider a binary log file eligible for expiration only after its contents have been replicated to all slave servers. This form of expiration therefore is based on determining which binary logs are still in use.

Log rotation is often used in conjunction with log flushing to make sure that any buffered log information has been written to disk. Logs can be flushed by executing a `mysqladmin flush-logs` command or by issuing a `FLUSH LOGS` statement.

The rest of this section describes how to use these expiration techniques. For any that you put into practice, you should also consider how the log files fit into your database-backup methods. (It's a good idea to back up any log files that may be needed for recovery operations, so you don't want to expire such files before you've backed them up!) The example scripts discussed here can be found in the `admin` directory of the `sampdb` distribution.

Rotating Fixed-Name Log Files

The MySQL server writes some types of log information to files that have fixed names. This is true for the general query log and the slow-query log. It's also true for the update log if you're not logging updates to a numbered series of files. To expire fixed-name logs, use log rotation. This allows you to maintain the last few logs online, but limit the number to as many as you choose to prevent them from overrunning your disk.

Log file rotation works as follows. Suppose the log file is named log. At the first rotation, you rename log to log.1 and tell the server to begin writing a new log file. At the second rotation, rename log.1 to log.2, log to log.1, and tell the server to begin writing another new log file. In this way, each file rotates through the names log.1, log.2, and so forth. When the file reaches a certain point in the rotation, you expire it by letting the previous file overwrite it. For example, if you rotate the logs daily and you want to keep a week's work of logs, you would keep log.1 through log.7. At each rotation, you would expire log.7 by letting log.6 overwrite it to become the new log.7.

The frequency of log rotation and the number of old logs you keep will depend on how busy your server is (active servers generate more log information) and how much disk space you're willing to devote to old logs.

On UNIX, you can rename the current log file while the server has it open. Flushing the logs causes the server to close that file and open a new one, thereby creating a new log file with the original name. The following shell script can be used to perform rotation of fixed-name log files:

```sh
#! /bin/sh
# rotate_fixed_logs.sh - rotate MySQL log file that has a fixed name

# Argument 1: log file name

if [ $# -ne 1 ]; then
    echo "Usage: $0 logname" 1>&2
    exit 1
fi

logfile=$1

mv $logfile.6 $logfile.7
mv $logfile.5 $logfile.6
mv $logfile.4 $logfile.5
mv $logfile.3 $logfile.4
mv $logfile.2 $logfile.3
mv $logfile.1 $logfile.2
mv $logfile $logfile.1
mysqladmin flush-logs
```

The script takes the log file name as its argument. You can either specify the full pathname of the file or change directory into the log directory and specify the file's name in that directory. For example, to rotate a log named `log` in `/usr/mysql/data`, you can use the following command:

```
% rotate_fixed_logs.sh /usr/mysql/data/log
```

or the following commands:

```
% cd /usr/mysql/data
% rotate_fixed_logs.sh log
```

It's best to run the script while logged in as `mysqladm`, to make sure that you have permission to rename the log files. Note that the `mysqladmin` command in the script includes no connection parameter arguments, such as `-u` or `-p`. If the relevant connection parameters for invoking `mysql` are stored in `mysqladm`'s `.my.cnf` option file, you don't need to specify them on the `mysqladmin` command in the script. If you don't use an option file, the `mysqladmin` command needs to know how to connect to the server using a MySQL account that has sufficient privileges to flush the logs. To handle this, you might want to set up a limited-privilege account that can't do anything but issue flush commands. Then you can put that account's password in the script with minimal risk if you make the script accessible only to `mysqladm`. If you want to do this, the MySQL account should have only the RELOAD privilege. For example, to call the user `flush` and assign a password of `flushpass`, use the following GRANT statement:

```
GRANT RELOAD ON *.* TO 'flush'@'localhost' IDENTIFIED BY 'flushpass';
```

After creating this account, change the `mysqladmin` command in the `rotate_fixed_logs.sh` script to look like this:

```
mysqladmin -u flush -pflushpass flush-logs
```

To rotate and flush the logs periodically, see the "Automating the Log Expiration Procedure" section later in this chapter.

Under Linux, you may prefer to use the `logrotate` utility to install the `mysql-log-rotate` script that comes with the MySQL distribution rather than using `rotate_fixed_logs.sh` or writing your own script. Look for `mysql-log-rotate` in `/usr/share/mysql` for RPM distributions, in the `support-files` directory of your MySQL installation for binary distributions, or under the `share/mysql` directory of MySQL source distributions.

On Windows, log rotation doesn't work quite the same way as on UNIX. If you attempt to rename a log file while the server has it open, a "file in use" error occurs. To rotate the logs, shut down the server first and then rename the files and restart the server. I'll leave it to you to stop and restart the server as you want, but the log file renaming can be performed using the following batch script:

```
@echo off
REM rotate_fixed_logs.bat - rotate MySQL log file that has a fixed name

if not "%1" == "" goto ROTATE
    @echo Usage: rotate_fixed_logs logname
    goto DONE

:ROTATE
set logfile=%1
erase %logfile%.7
rename %logfile%.6 %logfile%.7
rename %logfile%.5 %logfile%.6
rename %logfile%.4 %logfile%.5
rename %logfile%.3 %logfile%.4
rename %logfile%.2 %logfile%.3
rename %logfile%.1 %logfile%.2
rename %logfile% %logfile%.1
:DONE
```

`rotate_fixed_logs.bat` is invoked much like the `rotate_fixed_logs.sh` shell script, with a single argument that names the log file to be rotated. For example, like this:

```
C:\> rotate_fixed_logs C:\mysql\data\log
```

or like this:

```
C:\> cd \mysql\data
C:\> rotate_fixed_logs log
```

The first few times a log rotation script executes, you won't have a full set of log files in the rotation and the script may complain that it can't find all the files to be rotated. That's normal.

Expiring Numbered Log Files

Fixed-name log files can be expired using filename rotation, as just discussed. For numbered log files, such as those you can generate for the update log and the binary update log, log expiration needs to be handled a bit differently. In this case, you can expire files based on age (assessed as time of last modification) rather than by rotating them through a given set of names. The reason for doing this is that numbered logs are not necessarily created on a fixed schedule, so you can't assume that it's okay to retain just the last *n* files. If the server happens to receive several log flushing commands in a short time span, you can easily have that many logs, none of which are old enough to need expiring.

For logs generated by the server with sequenced filenames, an expiration script based on age might look like this:

```
#! /usr/bin/perl -w
# expire_numbered_logs.pl - Look through a set of numbered MySQL
# log files and delete those that are more than a week old.

# Usage: expire_numbered_logs.pl logfile ...

use strict;
die "Usage: $0 logfile ...\n" if @ARGV == 0;
my $max_allowed_age = 7;     # max allowed age in days
foreach my $file (@ARGV)     # check each argument
{
    unlink ($file) if -e $file && -M $file >= $max_allowed_age;
}
exit (0);
```

expire_numbered_logs.pl is written in Perl. It works on both UNIX and Windows because Perl is a cross-platform scripting language. To use the script, invoke it with the names of the log files that are candidates for expiration. For example, on UNIX, you can do this:

```
% expire_numbered_logs.pl /usr/mysql/data/update.[0-9]*
```

or this:

```
% cd /usr/mysql/data
% expire_numbered_logs.pl update.[0-9]*
```

Note that the expire_numbered_logs.pl script is *dangerous* if you don't pass it appropriate arguments! For example, you definitely don't want to invoke it as follows:

```
% cd /usr/mysql/data
% expire_numbered_logs.pl *
```

That will remove all files in the data directory that are more than a week old, not just log files.

Expiring Replication-Related Log Files

The server generates binary update logs in numbered sequence. One way to manage them is to expire them based on age, as described in the previous section. However, if you're using the binary logs for replication, age is not necessarily an indicator of whether a log can be removed. Instead, you should expire a binary log only after its contents have been replicated to all the slave servers.

Unfortunately, the master server itself doesn't know how many slaves there are or which files have been propagated to them. The master won't purge binary logs that have not yet been sent to connected slaves, but there is no guarantee that a given slave is connected at any particular time. This means that you yourself must know which servers are acting as slaves and then connect to each one and issue a `SHOW SLAVE STATUS` statement to determine which of the master's binary log files the slave currently is processing. (The file's name is the value in the `Master_Log_File` column.) Any binary log that is no longer used by any of the slaves can be removed. Suppose you have the following scenario:

- The local server is the master and it has two slaves, S1 and S2.
- The binary log files that exist on the master have names from `binlog.038` through `binlog.042`.
- `SHOW SLAVE STATUS` produces the following result on S1:

  ```
  mysql> SHOW SLAVE STATUS\G
  ...
  Master_Log_File: binlog.41
  ...
  ```

And this result on S2:

```
mysql> SHOW SLAVE STATUS\G
...
Master_Log_File: binlog.40
...
```

In this case, the lowest-numbered binary log still required by the slaves is `binlog.40`, so any log with a lower number can be removed. To do that, connect to the master server and issue the following statement:

```
mysql> PURGE MASTER LOGS TO 'binlog.040';
```

That causes the server to delete all binary logs with numbers lower than the named file, which for the situation just described, includes `binlog.038` and `binlog.039`.

`SHOW SLAVE STATUS` is available as of MySQL 3.23.22, and `PURGE MASTER LOGS` is available as of MySQL 3.23.28. Both statements require the `SUPER` privilege (`PROCESS` prior to MySQL 4.0.2).

Automating the Log Expiration Procedure

It's possible to invoke log expiration scripts on a manual basis, but if you have a way to schedule the commands to execute automatically, you don't have to remember to run them yourself. One way to do this is to use the `cron` utility and set up a `crontab` file that defines the expiration schedule. If you're not familiar with `cron`, check the relevant UNIX manual pages using the following commands:

```
% man cron
% man crontab
```

You may need to use another command to read about the `crontab` file format:

```
% man 5 crontab
```

Suppose that you want to rotate the general query logs and expire numbered update logs using the `rotate_fixed_logs.sh` and `expire_num-bered_logs.pl` scripts, and that these scripts are installed in `/u/mysqladm/bin`. Log in as `mysqladm` and then edit the `mysqladm` user's `crontab` file using the following command:

```
% crontab -e
```

This command will allow you to edit a copy of your current `crontab` file (which may be empty if no `cron` jobs have yet been set up). Add lines to the file that look like the following:

```
0 4 * * * /u/mysqladm/bin/rotate_fixed_logs.sh /usr/mysql/data/log
0 4 * * * /u/mysqladm/bin/expire_numbered_logs.pl /usr/mysql/data/update.[0-9]*
```

These entries tell `cron` to run both scripts at 4 a.m. each morning. You can vary the time or scheduling as desired; check the `crontab` manual page for the format of the entries. You'll probably want to expire the logs more frequently for a busy server that generates lots of log information than for one that is less active.

If you want to make sure the logs are flushed regularly (for example, to generate the next numbered update log or binary update log), you can schedule a `mysqladmin flush-logs` command to execute periodically by adding another `crontab` entry. You may need to list the full pathname to `mysqladmin` to make sure that `cron` can find it.

Additional Server Configuration Topics

This section discusses several topics that can help you configure the server more specifically to the way you want to run it or that can help you achieve higher server performance:

- Controlling how the server listens to network interfaces for client connections
- Enabling or disabling LOCAL capability for LOAD DATA
- Internationalization and localization issues, such as the server's time zone setting and the character sets that it supports
- Enabling or disabling handlers for specific table types
- Configuring the InnoDB table handler
- Tuning the server by setting its internal variables

Controlling How the Server Listens for Connections

The MySQL server listens for connections on several network interfaces, which you can control as follows:

- On all platforms, the server listens on a network port for TCP/IP connections, unless started with the `--skip-networking` option. The default port number is 3306; to specify a different number, use the `--port` option. If the server host has more than one IP address, you can specify which one the MySQL server should use when listening for connections by specifying a `--bind-address` option.

- Under UNIX, the server listens on a UNIX domain socket file for connections from local clients that connect to the special host-name `local-host`. The default socket file is `/tmp/mysql.sock`; to specify a different name, use the `--socket` option.

- When run on Windows NT-based systems, servers with `-nt` in their names include named pipe support. By default, the pipe name is `MySql`; to specify a different name, use the `--socket` option. Prior to 3.23.50, named pipe support is always enabled. After that, it is off by default and you must enable it explicitly with the `--enable-named-pipe` option.

If you run a single server, it's typical to let the server use its default network settings. If you run more than one server, it's necessary to make sure each one uses unique networking parameters. See the "Running Multiple Servers" section later in this chapter for more information.

The preceding discussion applies only to standalone servers that operate in a client/server environment. It does not apply to the embedded server, which communicates with the client program that it's linked into by means of an internal channel and does not listen to any external network interfaces at all.

Enabling or Disabling LOCAL Capability for LOAD DATA

As of MySQL 3.23.49, the `LOCAL` capability for the `LOAD DATA` statement can be controlled at build time and at runtime:

- At build time, `LOCAL` can be enabled or disabled by default by using the `--enable-local-infile` or `--disable-local-infile` option when you run `configure`.

- At runtime, the server can be started with the `--local-infile` or `--disable-local-infile` options to enable or disable `LOCAL` capability on the server side. (Prior to MySQL 4.0.2, disable it with `--local-infile=0`.)

If LOCAL is disabled in the server, clients cannot use this capability at all. If it is enabled, the client library may still have LOCAL disabled by default on the client side, but certain programs may allow it to be enabled on demand. For example, mysql supports a --local-infile option to allow LOCAL.

Internationalization and Localization Issues

Internationalization refers to the ability of software to be used according to local convention for any of a variety of locations. Localization refers to selecting a particular set of local conventions from among those sets that are supported. The following aspects of MySQL configuration relate to internationalization and localization:

- The server time zone
- The language used for displaying diagnostic and error messages
- The available character sets and the default character set

Selecting the Server Time Zone

If your server doesn't determine the local time zone properly, it will report times incorrectly (in GMT, for example). To correct this on UNIX, you can set the zone explicitly. But note that you indicate the time zone to the safe_mysqld or mysqld_safe startup script, not to the mysqld server itself.

To specify a time zone, use the --timezone option. It's probably best to specify this option in an option file, especially if you invoke safe_mysqld or mysqld_safe through mysql.server, which does not support command line options. For example, to specify the U.S. Central time zone for mysqld_safe, add the following to your option file:

```
[mysqld_safe]
timezone=US/Central
```

The example shows one widely used syntax (it works on Solaris, Linux, or Mac OS X, for example). Another common syntax is as follows:

```
[mysqld_safe]
timezone=CST6CDT
```

Use whatever syntax is appropriate for your system.

Prior to MySQL 4, mysqld_safe is called safe_mysqld, which also supports --timezone back to version 3.23.28. The command-line syntax is the same as for mysqld_safe, but if you use an option file, put the time zone setting in the [safe_mysqld] group. Prior to MySQL 3.23.28, mysqld_safe has no

--timezone option, so unfortunately it's necessary to modify safe_mysqld itself. Do so by inserting a couple of lines that set the TZ environment variable somewhere prior to the line that starts the server. For example, add lines that look like this:

```
TZ=U.S./Central
export TZ
```

or like this:

```
TZ=CST6CDT
export TZ
```

Selecting the Error Message Language

The server has the ability to produce diagnostic and error messages in any of several languages. The default is english, but you can specify others. To see which are available, look under the share/mysql directory of your MySQL installation. The directories that have language names correspond to the available languages. To change the message language, use the --language startup option with an argument of either the language name or the pathname to the language directory. For example, to use French if your installation is located under /usr/local/mysql, you might use either --language=french or --language=/usr/local/mysql/share/mysql/french.

Configuring Character Set Support

MySQL can support any of a number of character sets. The choice of character set obviously affects which characters are allowed in string values, but it also affects operational characteristics such as the sort order used in string comparisons and the characters that are legal in table and column names. This section describes how to configure the MySQL's character set support. For information on using character sets from the client perspective, see Chapter 2, "Working with Data in MySQL."

To find out which character sets are available to your server as it is currently configured, look under the MySQL installation directory, for example, in the share/mysql/charsets directory. The Index file there lists which sets you can use. You can also find out the names by issuing the following query:

```
mysql> SHOW VARIABLES LIKE 'character_sets';
```

Or, as of MySQL 4.1, you can issue a SHOW CHARACTER SET statement to get the list of character set names and some additional information about each set.

To specify the default character set and the sets that are available to choose from, you can configure the server at build time using options to the `configure` script:

- The default character set is `latin1`. To select a different default, use the `--with-charset` option.

- To specify which character sets to include support for, use the `--with-extra-charsets` option. The argument to this option is a comma-separated list of character set names. For example, you can include support for the `latin1`, `big5`, and `hebrew` character sets as follows:

    ```
    % ./configure --with-extra-charsets=latin1,big5,hebrew
    ```

Two special character set names can be used with the `--with-extra-charsets` option to select groups of character sets—`all` includes all available character sets, and `complex` includes all complex character sets. A set is complex if it is either a multi-byte character set or if it requires special rules for sorting.

At runtime, the server uses its default built-in character set unless you specify otherwise. To select a different set, use the `--default-character-set` option when you start the server.

Although the server can use different character sets, it supports only a single set at a time prior to MySQL 4.1. As of 4.1, the configuration-time and runtime options for controlling which sets are available or used by default are the same as before, but support also is available at the SQL level for on-the-fly selection of character sets at the server, database, table, column, and string constant level. In other words, the server can support multiple character sets simultaneously. The availability of improved character set support makes it more likely that your users will want to use alternate character sets, so it's also more likely that you'll need to consider building in support for a larger number of sets. (For example, the availability of Unicode support is something for which many users have been waiting, so you may want to enable it when you build the server.)

Prior to MySQL 4.1, if you change your server's default character set after you've already created tables, the order in which key values are stored in the indexes may need to be updated to be correct for sort order of the new character set. To fix this for MyISAM tables, reorder the indexes by using `myisam-chk` with the `--recover` and `--quick` options, together with a `--set-character-set` option that specifies the character set to use. To do this, the server must be down when you run `myisamchk`. You can also leave the server running and reorder indexes with a REPAIR TABLE ... QUICK statement or a mysqlcheck --repair --quick command. Another option, which is not specific to MyISAM tables, is to dump the tables, drop them, and reload them. As of MySQL 4.1, the improved character set support makes index rebuilding no longer necessary when you change sets. However, you should update older tables to 4.1 format to take advantage of this capability, as described in the next section, "Converting Older Tables to Enable MySQL 4.1 Character Set Support."

On the client side, you can specify the character set that you want a client program to use by giving the --default-character-set option. If the character set you want isn't available as part of your MySQL installation, but you do have the necessary character set files installed under another directory, you can use them by specifying the --character-sets-dir option to the client program.

Converting Older Tables to Enable MySQL 4.1 Character Set Support

When upgrading from a version of MySQL older than 4.1 to version 4.1 or later, the best thing to do is convert your tables to 4.1 format so that you can make full use of the improved character set support:

1. Make a backup of your databases using mysqldump:

   ```
   % mysqldump -p -u root --all-databases --opt > dumpfile.sql
   ```

   --all-databases causes all databases to be dumped, and --opt optimizes the dump file to be smaller so that it can be processed more quickly when reloaded. (mysqldump is discussed further in Chapter 13.)

2. Bring down the server.

3. Upgrade your MySQL installation and restart the server, but do not change the server's default character set.

4. Convert your tables to 4.1 format by reloading them from the backup file:
   ```
   % mysql -p -u root < dumpfile.sql
   ```

This procedure allows the server to install new character set support information into the tables, which has two important effects:

- Each column is assigned the server's character set as its own. This means you can change the server character set later and each column will retain its character set, unaffected by the change. (That is, the column becomes "insulated" from modifications to the server character set, so indexes on the column don't go out of whack.)

- If you subsequently modify the column's character set, the server will automatically reorder any indexes of which it is a part to reflect the collating sequence of the new character set.

It's also possible to upgrade and then convert your tables after upgrading the server by using ALTER TABLE, but the process is laborious, tedious, and error-prone. Suppose a table is defined like this:

```
CREATE TABLE t
(
    c1 CHAR(10),
    c2 CHAR(10),
    c3 CHAR(10)
);
```

To convert the columns to have explicit character set information, use the following statement:

```
ALTER TABLE t
    MODIFY c1 CHAR(10) CHARACTER SET latin1,
    MODIFY c2 CHAR(10) CHARACTER SET latin1,
    MODIFY c3 CHAR(10) CHARACTER SET latin1;
```

That's a lot of work, especially because it must be done for each table. It's easier to use the dump-and-reload method.

Selecting Table Handlers

MySQL supports multiple table handlers. Some of these can be built-in or omitted at configuration time, and some of those that are built in can be disabled at server startup time:

- Up until MySQL 4, the ISAM handler is always built-in. As of MySQL 4, the ISAM handler can be omitted with the --without-isam option to configure.

  For the embedded server, the ISAM handler is omitted by default. To include it, you must edit the mysql_embed.h file in the source distribution and rebuild the server. But, in general, it's better to convert ISAM tables to MyISAM tables and avoid continued reliance on the ISAM storage format. ISAM support will be phased out in the future.

- The BDB handler can be built-in with the --with-berkeley-db option to configure. If built in, it can be disabled at server startup time with the --skip-bdb option.

- Up until MySQL 4, the InnoDB handler can be built-in with the --with-innodb option to configure. As of MySQL 4, InnoDB is built-in by default but can be omitted with the `--without-innodb` option to `configure`. If built-in, the InnoDB handler can be disabled at server startup time with the `--skip-innodb` option.

- The MyISAM handler is always built-in as of MySQL 3.23, and can be neither omitted at configuration time nor disabled at server startup time.

Configuring the InnoDB Tablespace

The InnoDB table handler does not use separate files for each table the way that other table handlers do. Instead, it manages all InnoDB tables within a single tablespace, which is a logically unified block of storage that the handler treats as a giant data structure. (In a sense, the tablespace is something like a virtual file system.) The only file uniquely associated with an individual InnoDB table is the `.frm` description file that is stored in the database directory of the database that the table belongs to.

The InnoDB tablespace, although logically a single storage area, comprises one or more files on disk. Each component can be a regular file or a raw partition. This section describes the configuration options that you use to set up and manage the InnoDB tablespace. It's possible to specify these options on the server command line, but this is rarely done in practice. Instead, you should configure the tablespace using an appropriate server group in an option file (for example, the `[mysqld]` or `[server]` group) so that the same configuration gets used consistently each time the server starts up. Two options are the most important:

- `innodb_data_home_dir` specifies the parent directory of all the component files that make up the tablespace. If you don't specify this option, its default value is the data directory.
- `innodb_data_file_path` indicates the specifications for the component files of the tablespace under the InnoDB home directory. The value of this option is a list of one or more file specifications, separated by semicolons. Each specification consists of a filename, a size, and possibly other options, separated by colons. The combined size of the tablespace components must be at least 10MB.

In MySQL 3.23, you must provide a value for `innodb_data_file_path` or the InnoDB handler will not start up properly. (One consequence of this is that the server will not start up, either. You can see if startup failure is InnoDB-related by checking the error log.) In MySQL 4, the server will create a default tablespace consisting of a single file named `ibdata1`. This tablespace is a 64MB non-auto-extending file in MySQL 4.0.0 and 4.0.1, and a 10MB auto-extending file thereafter.

As a simple example, suppose you want to create a tablespace consisting of two 10MB files named `innodata1` and `innodata2` in the data directory. Configure the files as follows:

```
innodb_data_file_path = innodata1:10M;innodata2:10M
```

No `innodb_data_home_dir` setting is required in this case because its default value is the server's data directory, the desired location for the files.

The following rules describe how the InnoDB handler combines the values of `innodb_data_home_dir` and `innodb_data_file_path` to determine the pathnames of the tablespace files:

- If `innodb_data_home_dir` is empty, all the file specifications in `innodb_data_file_path` are treated as absolute pathnames.

- If `innodb_data_home_dir` is not empty, it should name the directory under which all the file specifications in `innodb_data_file_path` should be found. In this case, those filenames are interpreted relative to the `innodb_data_home_dir` value.

- If `innodb_data_home_dir` is not specified, its default value is the pathname to the MySQL data directory, and the filenames in `innodb_data_file_path` are interpreted relative to the data directory.

Based on the preceding rules, if the data directory is `/var/mysql/data`, the following three configurations all specify the same set of tablespace files:

```
innodb_data_home_dir=
innodb_data_file_path=/var/mysql/data/ibdata1:10M;/var/mysql/data/ibdata2:10M

innodb_data_home_dir=/var/mysql/data
innodb_data_file_path=ibdata1:10M;ibdata2:10M

innodb_data_file_path=ibdata1:10M;ibdata2:10M
```

The `innodb_data_file_path` value consists of file specifications that are separated by semicolons, and the parts of each specification are separated by colons. The simplest file specification syntax consists of a filename and a size, but other syntaxes are legal:

```
path:size
path:size:autoextend
path:size:autoextend:max:maxsize
```

The first format specifies a file with a fixed size of `size`. A `size` value should be a positive integer followed by M or G to indicate units of megabytes or gigabytes. The second format specifies an auto-extending file; if the file fills up, InnoDB extends it by 8MB at a time. The third format is similar, but includes a value indicating the maximum size to which the auto-extending file is allowed to grow. Auto-extending tablespace components can be used as of MySQL 3.23.50, but only the final component of the tablespace can be listed as auto-extending.

To set up the tablespace initially, add the appropriate lines to the option file (making sure that none of the component files already exist) and then start the server. InnoDB will notice that the files do not exist and will proceed to create and initialize them.

As of MySQL 3.23.41, it is possible to use raw partitions as components of the InnoDB tablespace. One reason to do this is that you can easily create very large tablespaces. A partition component can span the entire extent of the partition, whereas regular file components are limited in size to the maximum file size allowed by your operating system. In addition, raw partition files are guaranteed to be composed of entirely contiguous space on disk, whereas regular files are subject to file system fragmentation. When it initializes the tablespace, InnoDB tries to minimize fragmentation of regular files by writing enough zeros to the files to force space for them to be allocated all at once rather than incrementally. But this can only reduce fragmentation; it cannot guarantee that it will not occur.

Including a raw partition in the tablespace is a two-step procedure. Suppose you want to use a 2GB partition that has a pathname of /dev/rdsk8. In this case, it's necessary to specify a value for innodb_data_home_dir because the partition doesn't lie under the data directory. Configure the partition as follows:

1. Configure the partition initially with a size value that has a newraw suffix. This indicates that the file is a raw partition that needs to be initialized:

   ```
   innodb_data_home_dir =
   innodb_data_file_path = /dev/rdsk8:2Gnewraw
   ```

   After adding these lines to your [mysqld] option group, start the server. InnoDB will see the suffix and initialize the partition. (It will also treat the tablespace as read-only because it knows that you have not completed the second step.) After the partition has been initialized, shut down the server.

2. Modify the configuration information to change the suffix from `newraw` to `raw`:

```
innodb_data_home_dir =
innodb_data_file_path = /dev/rdsk8:2Graw
```

Then start the server again. InnoDB will see that `new` is not present, so it knows that the partition has been initialized and that it can use the tablespace in read/write fashion.

If you specify a raw partition as part of the InnoDB tablespace, make sure its permissions are set so that the server has read/write access to it. Also, make sure the partition is being used for no other purpose. Otherwise, you will have competing processes, each thinking that they own the partition and can use it as they please, with the result that they'll stomp all over each other's data. For example, if you mistakenly specify a swap partition for use by InnoDB, your system will behave quite erratically!

When configuring the InnoDB tablespace on Windows systems, backslashes in pathnames can be specified using either single forward slashes ('/') or doubled backslashes ('\\'). Also, you should still separate the parts of each file specification with colons, even though colons may also appear in filenames (full Windows pathnames begin with a drive letter and a colon). When it encounters a colon, InnoDB resolves this ambiguity by looking at the following character. If it is a digit, the next part of the specification is taken to be a size. Otherwise, it's taken as part of a pathname. For example, the following configuration sets up a tablespace consisting of files on the C and D drives with sizes of 50MB and 60MB:

```
innodb_data_home_dir =
innodb_data_file_path = C:/ibdata1:50M;D:/ibdata2:60M
```

Each time InnoDB starts up, it creates the tablespace data files if necessary. It also creates log files if they do not exist. By default, these logs are created in the data directory and have names that begin with `ib_`. Note that InnoDB will create only files, not directories. Any directories that will be needed by InnoDB must be created prior to starting the server. (You can indicate where to create the log files using the options described earlier in this chapter in the "Maintaining Log Files" section.)

When you're setting up the initial tablespace, if startup fails because InnoDB cannot create some necessary file, check the error log to see what the problem was. Then remove all the files that InnoDB created (excluding any raw partitions you may be using), correct the configuration error, and start the server again.

Once a tablespace has been initialized, you cannot change the size of its component files. However, you can add another file to the list of existing files, which may be helpful if the tablespace fills up. A symptom of a full tablespace is that InnoDB transactions that should succeed will begin rolling back. You can also check the free space explicitly with the following statement, where `tbl_name` is the name of any InnoDB table:

```
mysql> SHOW TABLE STATUS LIKE 'tbl_name';
```

To make the tablespace larger by adding another component, use the following procedure:

1. Shut down the server if it is running.
2. If the final component of the tablespace is an auto-extending file, you must change its specification to that of a fixed-size file before adding another file after it. To do this, determine the current actual size of the file. Then round the size down to the nearest multiple of 1 megabyte (measured as 1,048,576 bytes rather than as 1,000,000 bytes) and use that size in the file's specification. Suppose you have a file currently listed like this:

   ```
   innodb_data_file_path = ibdata1:100M:autoextend
   ```

   If the file's actual size now is 121,634,816 bytes, that is 121,634,816 / 1,048,576 = 116 megabytes. Change the specification as follows:

   ```
   innodb_data_file_path = ibdata1:116M
   ```

3. Add the specification for the new component to the end of the current file list. If the new component is a regular file, make sure that it does not already exist. If the component is a raw partition, add it using the two-step procedure described earlier for specifying a partition as part of the tablespace.
4. Restart the server.

If you want to reconfigure the tablespace in some way other than adding a new file to the end, you must dump and reconstruct it using the new configuration:

1. Use `mysqldump` to dump all your InnoDB tables.
2. Shut down the server, and delete your existing InnoDB tablespace and log files and the `.frm` files that correspond to InnoDB tables.
3. Reinitialize the tablespace according to the new configuration you want to use.
4. Reload the dump file into the server to re-create the InnoDB tables.

Tuning the Server

The MySQL server has several parameters (variables) that affect how it operates. If the default parameter values are not appropriate, you can change them to values that are better for the environment in which your server runs. For example, if you have plenty of memory, you can tell the server to use larger buffers for disk and index operations. This will hold more information in memory and decrease the number of disk accesses that need to be made. If your system is more modest, you can tell the server to use smaller buffers. This will likely make the server run more slowly, but may improve overall system performance by preventing the server from hogging system resources to the detriment of other processes.

The following sections discuss how to set or examine server variables and describe some of the variables that have application to the operation of the server as a whole or more specifically to the InnoDB table handler. A complete list of server variables is given in Appendix D under the description for the SHOW VARIABLES statement. You can also find additional discussion of server tuning in the optimization chapter of the *MySQL Reference Manual*.

Setting and Checking Server Variable Values

Server variables can be set at server startup time. Also, as of MySQL 4.0.3, many of these variables can be modified dynamically while the server is running.

The allowable syntax for setting a server variable at startup time depends on your version of MySQL. As of MySQL 4.0.2, you can treat a variable name as an option name and set it directly. For example, the size of the table cache is controlled by the table_cache variable. To set the table cache size to 128, you can do so using the following option on the command line:

```
--table_cache=128
```

You can also set the variable in an option file using the following syntax:

```
[mysqld]
table_cache=128
```

Another feature of the variable-as-option syntax is that underscores can be given as dashes so that the option looks more like other options:

```
--table-cache=128
```

You can also set the variable in an option file using the following syntax:

```
[mysqld]
table-cache=128
```

The other way to set a variable is by using the `--set-variable` or `-O` option, which can be used on the command line like this:

```
--set-variable=table_cache=128
-O table_cache=128
```

In option files, only the long-option form is allowable:

```
[mysqld]
set-variable=table_cache=128
```

If you need to set several variables, use one option for each.

Prior to MySQL 4.0.2, variable names cannot be treated as options, so only the `--set-variable` or `-O` option formats can be used. From 4.0.2 on, `--set-variable` and `-O` are still supported, but are deprecated.

Whichever syntax you use to set variables, it's usually easier to do so in an option file because you don't have to remember to set the variables each time you start the server.

Server variables can be set only at startup time prior to MySQL 4.0.3, and their values remain fixed for the duration of the server process. MySQL 4.0.3 introduces two changes with respect to server variable handling:

- Many variables can be set dynamically while the server is running. This gives you better control over its operation and can help you avoid bringing down the server under circumstances when that might otherwise be necessary. (For example, you can experiment with buffer sizes to see how that affects server performance without having to stop and restart the server for each change.) Changes made this way do not last beyond server exit time, but should you determine a value for a variable that is better than its current default, you can set the variable in an option file to cause the value to be used whenever the server starts in the future.

- Variables can exist at two levels—global and session-specific. Global variables affect the operation of the server as a whole. Session-level variables affect only the behavior of a given client connection. For variables that exist at both levels, the global values are used to initialize the corresponding session variables. This happens only when a new connection begins; changing a global variable during a connection does not affect the current value of the connection's corresponding session variable.

To set a global variable named *var_name*, use a SET statement having one of the following formats:

```
SET GLOBAL var_name = value;
SET @@GLOBAL.var_name = value;
```

To set a session variable, similar formats apply:

```
SET SESSION var_name = value;
SET @@SESSION.var_name = value;
```

If no level indicator is present at all, the SET statement modifies the session level variable:

```
SET var_name = value;
SET @@var_name = value;
```

You can set several variables in a single SET statement by separating the assignments with commas:

```
SET SESSION sql_warnings = 0, GLOBAL table_type = InnoDB;
```

In all cases in which SESSION is allowed, you can substitute LOCAL as a synonym (this includes use of @@LOCAL for @@SESSION).

You must have the SUPER privilege to set a global variable. The setting persists until changed again or the server exits. No special privileges are needed to set a session variable. The setting persists until changed again or the current connection terminates.

To see the current values of server variables, use a SHOW VARIABLES statement. This statement allows you to display all variables or just those with names that match a given SQL pattern:

```
SHOW VARIABLES;
SHOW VARIABLES LIKE 'pat';
```

As of 4.0.3, additional formats are allowed so that you can specifically request the values of global or session variables:

```
SHOW GLOBAL VARIABLES;
SHOW GLOBAL VARIABLES LIKE 'pat';
SHOW SESSION VARIABLES;
SHOW SESSION VARIABLES LIKE 'pat';
```

When no GLOBAL or SESSION keyword is used, the statement returns a variable's session value, if one exists at that level, and the global value if not.

From the command line, mysqladmin variables displays the current values of the server's global variables.

The entry for SHOW VARIABLES in Appendix D lists server variables, including which of them can be modified dynamically and at which levels.

General Purpose Server Variables

Several of the variables that are most likely to be useful for general performance tuning are described in the following list.

- `back_log`

  The number of incoming client connection requests that can be queued
  while processing requests from the current clients. If you have a very
  busy site, you may want to increase the value of this variable.

- `delayed_queue_size`

  This variable determines the number of rows from INSERT DELAYED
  statements that can be queued before clients performing additional
  INSERT DELAYED statements get blocked. If you have many clients that
  perform this kind of INSERT and you find that they are blocking, increasing this variable will allow more of them to continue more quickly.
  (INSERT DELAYED is discussed in the "Scheduling and Locking Issues"
  section of Chapter 4, "Query Optimization.")

- `flush_time`

  If your system has problems and tends to lock up or reboot often, setting
  this variable to a non-zero value causes the server to flush the table cache
  every `flush_time` seconds. Writing out table changes in this way
  degrades performance, but can reduce the chance of table corruption or
  data loss.

  You can start the server with the `--flush` option on the command line
  to force table changes to be flushed after every update.

- `key_buffer_size`

  The size of the buffer used to hold index blocks. Index-based retrievals
  and sorts are faster if you increase the value of this variable, as are operations that create or modify indexes. A larger key buffer makes it more
  likely that MySQL will find key values in memory, which reduces the
  number of disk accesses needed for index processing.

  This variable is called `key_buffer` in versions of MySQL prior to 3.23.
  The server recognizes both names as of 3.23.

- `max_allowed_packet`

  The maximum size to which the buffer used for client communications
  can grow. The largest value to which this variable can be set is 16MB
  prior to MySQL 4 and 1GB for MySQL 4 and later.

If you have clients that send large BLOB or TEXT values, this server variable may need to be increased, and you'll also need to increase it on the client end. Clients currently use a default buffer size of 16MB. For example, to invoke mysql with a 64MB packet limit, do so as follows:

```
% mysql --set-variable=max_allowed_packet=64M
```

- max_connections

  The maximum number of simultaneous client connections the server will allow. If your server is busy, you may need to increase this value. For example, if your MySQL server is used by an active Web server to process lots of queries generated by DBI or PHP scripts, visitors to your site may find requests being refused if this variable is set too low.

- table_cache

  The size of the table cache. Increasing this value allows mysqld to keep more tables open simultaneously, and reduces the number of file open-and-close operations that must be done.

If you increase the values of max_connections or table_cache, the server will require a larger number of file descriptors. That may cause problems with operating system limits on the per-process number of file descriptors, in which case you'll need to increase the limit or work around it. Procedures vary for increasing the limit on the number of file descriptors. You may be able to do this at runtime using the --open-files-limit option to mysqld_safe, if you use that script to start up the server. Otherwise, you may need to reconfigure your system. Some systems can be configured simply by editing a system description file and rebooting. For others, you must edit a kernel description file and rebuild the kernel. Consult the documentation for your system to see how to proceed.

One way to work around per-process file descriptor limits is to split your data directory into multiple data directories and run multiple servers. This effectively multiplies the number of file descriptors available by the number of servers you run. On the other hand, other complications can cause you problems. To name two, you cannot access databases in different data directories from a single server, and you might need to replicate privileges in the grant tables across different servers for users that need access to more than one server.

Some variables pertain to resources that are allocated to each client, and increasing them has the potential to dramatically increase the server's resource requirements if you have many simultaneous clients. For example, two values that administrators sometimes increase in hopes of improving performance are those of the `read_buffer_size` and `sort_buffer_size` variables. (Prior to MySQL 4.0.3, these variables are called `record_buffer` and `sort_buffer`.) The values of these variables determine the size of the buffers that are used during join and sort operations. However, these buffers are allocated for each connection, so if you make the values of the corresponding variables quite large, performance may actually suffer due to exorbitant system resource consumption. Be cautious about changing the sizes of per-connection buffers. Increase them incrementally and then test your changes rather than bumping them up by a large amount all at once. This will allow you to assess the effect of each change with less likelihood of serious performance degradation. Be sure to use realistic test conditions as well. These buffers are allocated only as needed rather than as soon as a client connects. (For example, a client that runs no joins needs no join buffer.) Your test conditions should use clients that connect at the same time and run complex queries so that you can see the real effect on the server's memory requirements.

InnoDB Handler Variables

In addition to the general-purpose server variables, the server has several InnoDB-related variables when InnoDB support is enabled. The following list describes a few that commonly are used to affect the operation of the InnoDB handler.

- `innodb_buffer_pool_size`

  If you have the memory, making the InnoDB buffer pool larger can reduce disk usage for accessing table data and indexes.

- `innodb_log_buffer_size`

  Increasing the size of this buffer allows larger transactions to be buffered through to commit time without having to flush to disk partway through.

- `innodb_log_file_size, innodb_log_files_in_group`

  When its logs fill up, InnoDB checkpoints the buffer pool by flushing it to disk. Using larger InnoDB log files reduces the frequency with which the logs fill up, and thus reduces the number of times this flushing occurs. (The tradeoff is that with larger logs, the time for recovery after a crash will increase.) You can modify `innodb_log_file_size` to change the size of the log files or `innodb_log_files_in_group` to change the number of files. The important characteristic is the total size of the logs, which is the product of the two values. Note that the total size of the logs must not exceed 4GB.

Running Multiple Servers

Most people run a single MySQL server on a given machine, but there are circumstances under which it can be useful to run multiple servers:

- You may want to test a new version of the server while leaving your production server running. In this case, you'll be running different server binaries.

- Operating systems typically impose per-process limitations on the number of open file descriptors. If your system makes it difficult to raise the limit, running multiple instances of the server binary is one way to work around that limitation. (For example, raising the limit may require recompiling the kernel, and you may not be able to do that if you're not in charge of administering the machine.)

- Internet service providers often provide individual customers with their own MySQL installation, which necessarily requires multiple servers. This may involve running multiple instances of the same binary if all customers run the same version of MySQL, or different binaries if some customers run different versions than others.

Those are some of the more common reasons to run multiple servers, but there are others. For example, if you write MySQL documentation, it's often necessary to test various server versions empirically to see how their behavior differs. I fall into this category, for which reason I have lots of servers installed (more than 30 at the moment). However, I run just a couple of them all the time. The others I run only on occasion for testing purposes, so I need to be able to start and stop them easily on demand.

General Multiple Server Issues

Running several servers is more complicated than running just one because you need to keep them from interfering with each other. Some of the issues that arise occur when you install MySQL. If you use different versions, they must each be placed into a different location. For precompiled binary distributions, you can accomplish this by unpacking them into different directories. For source distributions that you compile yourself, you can use the `--prefix` option for `configure` to specify a different installation location for each distribution.

Other issues occur at runtime when you start up the servers. Each server process must have unique values for several parameters. For example, every server must listen to a different TCP/IP port for incoming connections or else they will collide with each other. This is true whether you run different server binaries or multiple instances of the same binary. A similar problem occurs if you enable logging. Each server should write to its own set of log files because having different servers write to the same files is sure to cause problems.

You can specify a server's options at runtime when you start it, typically in an option file. Alternatively, if you run several server binaries that you compile from source yourself, you can specify during the build process a different set of parameter values for each server to use. These become its built-in defaults, and you need not specify them explicitly at runtime.

When you run multiple servers, be sure to keep good notes on the parameters you're using so that you don't lose track of what's happening. One way to do this is to use option files to specify the parameters. (This can be useful even for servers that have unique parameter values compiled in because the option files serve as a form of explicit documentation.)

The following discussion enumerates several types of options that have the potential for causing conflicts if they're not set on a per-server basis. Note that some options will influence others, and thus you may not need to set each one explicitly for every server. For example, every server must use a unique process ID file when it runs. But the data directory is the default location for the PID file, so if each server has a different data directory, that will implicitly result in different default PID files.

- If you're running different server versions, it's typical for each distribution to be installed under a different base directory. It's also best if each server uses a separate data directory.[2] To specify these values explicitly, use the following options:

Option	Purpose
`--basedir=dir_name`	Pathname to root directory of MySQL installation
`--datadir=dir_name`	Pathname to data directory

  In many cases, the data directory will be a subdirectory of the base directory, but not always. For example, an ISP may provide a common MySQL installation for its customers (that is, the same set of client and server binaries) but run different instances of the server, each of which manages a given customer's data directory. In this case, the base directory may be the same for all servers, but individual data directories may be located elsewhere, perhaps under customer home directories.

---

2. It's sometimes *possible* to have different servers share the same directory, but I don't recommend it.

- The following options must have different values for each server, to keep servers from stepping on each other:

Option	Purpose
`--port=port_num`	Port number for TCP/IP connections
`--socket=file_name`	Pathname to UNIX domain socket file
`--pid-file=file_name`	Pathname to file in which server writes its process ID

- If you enable logging, any log names that you use must be different for each server. Otherwise, you'll have multiple servers contending to log to the same files. That is at best confusing, and at worst it prevents things like replication from working correctly. Log files named by the options in the following table are created under the server's data directory if you specify relative filenames. If each server uses a different data directory, you need not specify absolute pathnames to get each one to log to a distinct set of files. (See the "Maintaining Log Files" section earlier in this chapter for more information about naming log files.)

Logging Option	Log Enabled by Option
`--log[=file_name]`	General log file
`--log-bin[=file_name]`	Binary update log file
`--log-bin-index=file_name`	Binary update log index file
`--log-update[=file_name]`	Update log file
`--log-slow-queries[=file_name]`	Slow-query log file
`--log-isam[=file_name]`	ISAM/MyISAM log file

- If the BDB or InnoDB table handlers are enabled, the directories in which they write their logs must be unique per server. By default, the server writes these logs in the data directory. To change the location, use the following options:

Logging Option	Purpose
`--bdb-logdir=dir_name`	BDB log file directory
`--innodb_log_arch_dir=dir_name`	InnoDB log archive directory
`--innodb_log_group_home_dir=dir_name`	InnoDB log file directory

If you specify either of the InnoDB options, you should specify both, and you must give both the same value.

- Under UNIX, if you use `mysql_safe` to start your servers, it creates an error log (by default in the data directory). You can specify the error log name explicitly with `--err-log=file_name`. Note that this option must be given to `mysqld_safe` rather than to `mysqld`, and that relative path-names are interpreted with respect to the directory from which `mysqld_safe` is invoked, not with respect to the data directory as for the other log files. If you use this option, specify an absolute pathname to make sure you always create the error log in the same location.

- Under UNIX, it may also be necessary to specify a `--user` option on a per-server basis to indicate the login account to use for running each server. This is very likely if you're providing individual MySQL server instances for different users, each of whom "owns" a separate data directory.

- Under Windows, different servers that are installed as services must each use a unique service name.

Configuring and Compiling Different Servers

If you're going to build different versions of the server, you should install them in different locations. The easiest way to keep different distributions separate is to indicate a different installation base directory for each one by using the `--prefix` option when you run `configure`. If you incorporate the version number into the base directory name, it's easy to tell which directory corresponds to which version of MySQL. This section illustrates one way to accomplish that, by describing the particular configuration conventions that I use to keep my own MySQL installations separate.

The layout I use places all MySQL installations under a common directory: `/var/mysql`. To install a given distribution, I put it in a subdirectory of `/var/mysql` named using the distribution's version number. For example, I use `/var/mysql/40005` as the installation base directory for MySQL 4.0.5, which can be accomplished by running `configure` with a `--prefix=/var/mysql/40005` option. I also use other options for additional server-specific values, such as the TCP/IP port number and socket pathname. The configuration I use makes the TCP/IP port number equal to the version number, puts the socket file directly in the base directory, and names the data directory as `data` there.

To set up these configuration options, I use a shell script named `config-ver` that looks like the following (note that the data directory option for `configure` is `--localstatedir`, not `--datadir`):

```
VERSION="40005"
PREFIX="/var/mysql/$VERSION"
# InnoDB is included by default as of MySQL 4:
# - prior to 4.x, include InnoDB with --with-innodb
```

```
# - from 4.x on, exclude InnoDB with --without-innodb
HANDLERS="--with-berkeley-db"
OTHER="--enable-local-infile --with-embedded-server"
rm -f config.cache
./configure \
    --prefix=$PREFIX \
    --localstatedir=$PREFIX/data \
    --with-unix-socket-path=$PREFIX/mysql.sock \
    --with-tcp-port=$VERSION \
    $HANDLERS $OTHER
```

I make sure the first line is set to the proper version number and modify the
other values as necessary, according to whether or not I want the InnoDB and
BDB table handlers, LOCAL support for LOAD DATA, and so forth. That done,
the following commands configure, build, and install the distribution:

```
% sh config-ver
% make
% make install
```

Next, I change location into the installation base directory and initialize its
data directory and grant tables:

```
% cd /var/mysql/40005
% ./bin/mysql_install_db
```

At this point, I perform the MySQL installation lockdown procedure
described briefly in the "Arranging for MySQL Server Startup and
Shutdown" section earlier in this chapter and in more detail in Chapter 12.

After that, all that remains is to set up any options that I want to use in option
files and to arrange for starting up the server. One way to do this is discussed
in the "Using mysqld_multi for Server Management" section later in this
chapter.

Strategies for Specifying Startup Options

After you have your servers installed, how do you get them started up with the
proper set of runtime options that each one needs? You have several choices:

- If you run different servers that you build yourself, you can compile in a
  different set of defaults for each one, and no options need to be given at
  runtime. This has the disadvantage that it's not necessarily obvious what
  parameters any given server is using.

- To specify options at runtime, you can list them on the command line or
  in option files. If you need to specify lots of options, writing them on
  the command line is likely to be impractical. Putting them in option files

is more convenient, although then the trick is to get each server to read the proper set of options. Strategies for accomplishing this include the following:

- Use a `--defaults-file` option to specify the file that the server should read to find all of its options, and specify a different file for each server. This way, you can put all the options needed by a given server into one file to fully specify its setup in a single place. (Note that when you use this option, none of the usual option files, such as `/etc/my.cnf`, will be read.)

- Put any options that are common to all servers in a global option file such as `/etc/my.cnf` and use a `--defaults-extra-file` option on the command line to specify a file that contains additional options that are specific to a given server. For example, use the `[mysqld]` group in `/etc/my.cnf` for options that should apply to all servers. These need not be replicated in individual per-server option files.

  Be sure that any options placed into a common option group are understood by all servers that you run. For example, you can't use `local-infile` to enable the use of `LOAD DATA LOCAL` if any of your servers are older than version 3.23.49 because that is when that option was introduced. Its presence in a common option group will cause startup failure for older servers.

- Servers look for an option file named `my.cnf` in the compiled-in data directory location. If each server has a different data directory pathname compiled in, you can use these `my.cnf` files to list options specific to the corresponding servers. In other words, use `/etc/my.cnf` for any common settings that you want all servers to use, and use `DATADIR/my.cnf` for server-specific settings where `DATADIR` varies per server. (Note that this strategy does not work if you need to specify the data directory location at runtime. Nor will it work if you're running multiple instances of a given server binary.)

- Use the `mysqld_multi` script to manage startup for multiple servers. This script allows you to list the options for all servers in a single file, but associate each server with its own particular option group in the file.

- Under Windows, you can run multiple services, using special option file group-naming conventions specific to this style of server setup.

The following sections show some ways to apply these strategies by demonstrating how to use `mysqld_multi` and how to run multiple servers under Windows.

Using mysqld_multi For Server Management

On UNIX, the `mysqld_safe` and `mysql.server` scripts that are commonly used to start up servers both work best in a single-server setting. To make it easier to handle several servers, the `mysqld_multi` script can be used instead.

`mysqld_multi` works on the basis that you assign a specific number to each server setup you want to create and then list that server's options in an option file group `[mysqldn]`, where *n* is the number. The option file can also contain a group `[mysqld_multi]` that lists options specifically for `mysqld_multi` itself. For example, if I have servers installed for MySQL 3.23.51, 4.0.5, and 4.1.0, I might designate their option groups as `[mysqld32351]`, `[mysqld40005]`, and `[mysqld40100]` and set up the options in the `/etc/my.cnf` file as follows:

```
[mysqld32351]
basedir=/var/mysql/32351
datadir=/var/mysql/32351/data
mysqld=/var/mysql/32351/bin/mysqld_safe
socket=/var/mysql/32351/mysql.sock
port=32351
local-infile=1
user=mysqladm
log=log
log-update=update-log
innodb_data_file_path = ibdata1:10M

[mysqld40005]
basedir=/var/mysql/40005
datadir=/var/mysql/40005/data
mysqld=/var/mysql/40005/bin/mysqld_safe
socket=/var/mysql/40005/mysql.sock
port=40005
local-infile=1
user=mysqladm
log=log
log-bin=binlog
innodb_data_file_path = ibdata1:10M:autoextend

[mysqld40100]
basedir=/var/mysql/40100
datadir=/var/mysql/40100/data
mysqld=/var/mysql/40100/bin/mysqld_safe
socket=/var/mysql/40100/mysql.sock
port=40100
local-infile=1
user=mysqladm
```

```
log=log
log-bin=binlog
skip-innodb
skip-bdb
language=french
default-character-set=utf8
```

The layout parameters that I've set up here for each server correspond to the directory configuration described earlier in this chapter in the "Configuring and Compiling Different Servers" section. I've also specified additional server-specific parameters that correspond to variations in types of logs, tables handlers, and so forth.

To start a given server, invoke `mysqld_multi` with a command word of `start` and the server's option group number on the command line:

```
% mysqld_multi --no-log start 32351
```

The `--no-log` option causes status messages to be sent to the terminal rather than to a log file. This allows you to see what's going on more easily. You can specify more than one server by giving the group numbers as a comma-separated list. A range of server numbers can be specified by separating the numbers with a dash. However, there must be no whitespace in the server list:

```
% mysqld_multi --no-log start 32351,40005-40100
```

To stop servers or obtain a status report indicating whether or not they are running, use a command word of `stop` or `report` followed by the server list. For these commands, `mysqld_multi` will invoke `mysqladmin` to communicate with the servers, so you'll also need to specify a username and password for an administrative account:

```
% mysqld_multi --nolog --user=root --password=rootpass stop 32351
% mysqld_multi --nolog --user=root --password=rootpass report 32351,40100
```

The username and password must be applicable to all servers that you want to control with a given command. `mysqld_multi` attempts to determine the location of `mysqladmin` automatically, or you can specify the path explicitly in the `[mysqld_multi]` group of an option file. You can also list a default administrative username and password in that option group to be used for the `stop` and `report` commands—for example:

```
[mysqld_multi]
mysqladmin=/usr/local/mysql/bin/mysqladmin
user=leeloo
password=multipass
```

If you put the administrative username and password in the file, make sure that it isn't publicly readable!

Running Multiple Servers on Windows

There are a couple ways to run multiple servers on Windows. One method is based on starting the servers manually, and the other is to use multiple services.

To start multiple servers manually, create an option file for each one that lists its parameters. For example, to run two servers that use the same program binaries but different data directories, you might create two option files that look like the following:

`C:\my.cnf1` file:

```
[mysqld]
basedir=C:/mysql
datadir=C:/mysql/data
port=3306
```

`C:\my.cnf2` file:

```
[mysqld]
basedir=C:/mysql
datadir=C:/mysql/data2
port=3307
```

Then start the servers from the command line, using `--defaults-file` to tell each one to read a specific option file:

```
C:\> mysqld --defaults-file=C:\my.cnf1
C:\> mysqld --defaults-file=C:\my.cnf2
```

Clients should connect by specifying the port number appropriate for the server they wish to access. This includes the use of `mysqladmin` for shutting down the servers. The first of the following commands uses the default port (3306) and the second specifies port 3307 explicitly:

```
C:\> mysqladmin -p -u root shutdown
C:\> mysqladmin -P 3307 -p -u root shutdown
```

Windows NT-based systems have service support, and it's possible as of MySQL 4.0.2 to specify the service name when you install a server:[3]

```
C:\> mysql-nt --install service_name
```

This allows you to run multiple MySQL servers by choosing different service names. The rules that govern this capability are as follows:

- With no *service_name* argument, the server uses the default service name (`MySql`) and reads the `[mysqld]` group from option files.
- With a *service_name* argument, the server uses that name as the service name and reads the `[service_name]` group from option files.

3. It's now also possible to specify a service name argument in the 3.23 series as of MySQL 3.23.54.

- The server that runs using the default service name will support named pipes using the pipe name MySql. Any server for which you specify a service name explicitly will not support named pipes and listens only for TCP/IP connections, unless you specify a --socket option to indicate a different pipe name.
- Each server must manage a different data directory.

Suppose you want to run two instances of mysqld-nt, using service and named pipe names of MySql and mysqlsvc2, and the same data directories shown in the previous example. Set up the options for each server in one of the standard option files (such as C:\my.cnf) as follows:

```
# group for default (MySql) service
[mysqld]
basedir=C:/mysql
datadir=C:/mysql/data
port=3306
enable-named-pipe

# group for mysqlsvc2 service
[mysqlsvc2]
basedir=C:/mysql
datadir=C:/mysql/data2
port=3307
enable-named-pipe
socket=mysqlsvc2
```

To install and start up the services, use the following commands:

```
C:\> mysql-nt --install
C:\> net start MySql
C:\> mysql-nt --install mysqlsvc2
C:\> net start mysqlsvc2
```

Clients can connect to the default server using the default port or pipe name. To connect to the second server, specify its port number or pipe name explicitly:

```
C:\> mysql --port=3307
C:\> mysql --host=. --socket=mysqlsvc2
```

To shut down the servers, use mysqladmin shutdown, net stop, or the Services Manager. To uninstall the servers, shut them down if they are running and then remove them by specifying --remove and the same service name that you used at server installation time:

```
C:\> mysql-nt --remove
C:\> mysql-nt --remove mysqlsvc2
```

As of MySQL 4.0.3, you can specify a --defaults-file option as the final option on the command line when you install the server:

```
C:\> mysqld-nt --install service_name --defaults-file=file_name
```

This gives you an alternative means of providing server-specific options. The name of the file will be remembered and used by the server whenever it starts up, and it will read options from the `[mysqld]` group of the file. To use this service installation syntax, you *must* specify a service name; to use the default service, use the name `MySql` explicitly.

Setting Up Replication Servers

One form of database "replication" involves copying a database to another server. But then you have to repeat the operation later if the original changes and you want to keep the copy up to date. To achieve continual updating of a secondary database as changes are made to the contents of a master database, use MySQL's live replication capabilities. This gives you a means of keeping a copy of a database and making sure that changes to the original database propagate on a timely basis to the copy automatically.

Replication Concepts

Database replication in MySQL is based on the following principles:

- In a replication relationship, one server acts as the master and another server acts as the slave. Each server must be assigned a unique replication ID.

- The master and the slave must begin in a synchronized state with identical copies of the databases to be replicated. After that, updates are made on the master server and propagate to the slave. Updates are not made directly to the replicated databases on the slave.

- The means of communication of updates is based on the master server's binary update logs, which is where updates that are to be sent to the slave are recorded. Consequently, binary logging must be enabled on the master server.

- The slave server must have permission to connect to the master and request updates. The slave's progress is tracked based on replication coordinates, which consist of the name of the binary log file from which the slave currently is reading and its position within the file.

- You can have multiple slaves per master, but not multiple masters per slave. However, a slave can serve as a master to another slave, thus creating a chain of replication servers.

Replication support is relatively new in MySQL and still under active development, so it's sometimes difficult to keep track of just which replication-related feature was added when. Replication capabilities were added beginning with MySQL 3.23.15 but, in general, it's best to run the most recent server that you can. You'll also need to consider replication compatibility constraints between different versions of the server. The general compatibility rules are as follows:

- 3.23.x slaves cannot communicate with 4.x masters.
- 4.0.0 slaves can communicate only with 4.0.0 masters.
- 4.0.1 and later slaves can communicate with 3.23.x masters or with 4.x masters from a version equal to or greater than the slave.

In general, I recommend that you adhere to the following guidelines:

- Try to match MySQL versions for your master and slave servers. For example, try to match 3.23.x masters with 3.23.x slaves, not 4.x masters with 3.23.x slaves—or vice versa.
- Within a given 3.23.x or 4.x version series, try to use the most recent versions possible. This will give you the benefit of the richest feature set and the greatest number of restrictions removed and problems eliminated.

Assuming that your servers are version-compatible, they must also be feature-compatible. For example, if the master server replicates InnoDB tables that use foreign keys and MyISAM tables that require RAID features, the slave server must include the InnoDB handler and RAID support.

Establishing a Master–Slave Replication Relationship

The following procedure describes how to set up a master-slave replication relationship between two servers:

1. Determine what ID value you want to assign to each server. These IDs must be different and should be positive integer values that fit into 64 bits. The ID values will be needed for the `server-id` startup option used with each server.

2. The slave server needs an account on the master server so that it can connect and request updates. On the master server, set up an account like this:

   ```
   GRANT REPLICATION SLAVE ON *.*
   TO 'slave_user'@'slave_host'
   IDENTIFIED BY 'slave_pass';
   ```

Use the REPLICATION SLAVE privilege for MySQL 4.0.2 and up and the FILE privilege for earlier versions. (The required privilege changed as part of the grant table modifications that were introduced in MySQL 4.0.2.) You'll need the *slave_user* and *slave_pass* values later when you set up the slave server. No other privileges are needed if the account is used only for the single, limited purpose of replication. However, you may want to grant additional privileges to the account if you plan to use it connect to the master from the slave "manually" with mysql for testing. Then you won't be so limited in what you can do. (For example, if REPLICATION SLAVE is the only privilege the account has, you may not even be able to see database names on the master server with SHOW DATABASES.)

3. Perform the initial synchronization of the slave server to the master server by copying the master's databases to the slave. One way to do this is to make a backup on the master host and then move it to the slave host and load it into the slave server. Another method is to copy all the databases over the network from the master to the slave. See Chapter 13 for database backup and copying techniques.

   Another way to set up the slave is to use LOAD DATA FROM MASTER, available as of MySQL 4.0.0. Use of this statement is subject to the following conditions:

   - All tables to be replicated must be MyISAM tables.

   - You must issue the statement while connected to the slave server using an account that has the SUPER privilege.

   - The account used by the slave server to connect to the master server must have the RELOAD and SUPER privileges. To grant these privileges at the same time as REPLICATION SLAVE when you set up the account, modify the GRANT statement shown earlier to look like this:

     ```
     GRANT REPLICATION SLAVE,RELOAD,SUPER ON *.*
     TO 'slave_user'@'slave_host'
     IDENTIFIED BY 'slave_pass';
     ```

     Note that this is an account on the master server and differs from the one just mentioned in the previous item, which is an account on the slave.

   - The operation performed by LOAD DATA FROM MASTER acquires a global read lock. This blocks all updates on the master server for the duration of the transfer to the slave.

Some of these restrictions may be lifted in the future.

Whatever method you use to copy databases from the master to the slave, you'll need to make sure that no updates occur on the master between the time when you make the backup and the time that you reconfigure the master to enable binary logging.

4. Shut down the master server if it is running.

5. Modify the master's configuration to tell the server its replication ID and to enable binary logging. To do this, add lines like the following to an option file that the master server reads when it starts up:

```
[mysqld]
server-id=master_server_id
log-bin=binlog_name
```

6. Restart the master server; from this point on, it will log updates by writing them to the binary log. (If you already had binary logging enabled, back up your existing binary logs before restarting the server. Then, after it comes up, connect to it and issue a RESET MASTER statement to clear the existing binary logs.)

7. Shut down the slave server if it is running.

8. Configure the slave server to know its replication ID, where to find the master server, and how to connect to it. In the simplest case, the two servers will be running on separate hosts and using the default TCP/IP port, and you'll need only four lines in the [mysqld] group of an option file that the slave server reads when it starts up:

```
[mysqld]
server-id=slave_server_id
master-host=master_host
master-user=slave_user
master-password=slave_pass
```

slave_server_id is the replication ID of the slave server. It must be different from the master's ID. master_host is the name of the host where the master server is running. On UNIX, if the master host is the same as the slave host, use 127.0.0.1 rather than localhost to make sure that the slave uses a TCP/IP connection. (A socket file is used for connections to localhost, and replication through a socket file is not supported.) The slave_user and slave_pass values should be the name and password of the account that you set up on the master server earlier for the slave server to use when it connects to the master to request updates. Be sure to put these lines in an option file that is accessible only to the MySQL administrator's login account on the slave server because you should keep the username and password confidential. Don't use `/etc/my.cnf`, for example, which normally is world-readable. One possibility is to use `my.cnf` in the server's data directory and make sure the data directory contents are locked down, as described in Chapter 12.

If it's necessary to be more specific about how to establish the connection to the master server, you can include a `master-port` line in the option group to indicate a port number if the master isn't listening on the default port.

If the connection between the master and slave is intermittent or unreliable, you may want to change the defaults for the connection attempt interval or the number of retries before giving up (60 seconds and 86,400 times, respectively). The `master-connect-retry` and `master-retry-count` options can be used for this.

9. Restart the slave server. A slave uses two sources of information to figure out where it is in the replication process. One is the `master.info` file in the data directory, and the other is the configuration information specified by the server's startup options. The first time you start a slave server, it finds no `master.info` file and uses the values of the `master-xxx` options in the option file to determine how to connect. Then it creates a new `master.info` file in which to record that information and its replication status. Thereafter, when the slave server starts, it uses the information in the `master.info` file in preference to the option file. (This means that if you later change the master host information in the option file, you'll need to remove the `master.info` file and restart the slave server or it will ignore your changes.)

The procedure just described is based on the assumption that you want to replicate all databases from one server to another, including the `mysql` database that contains the grant tables. If you don't want to have the same accounts on both hosts, you can exclude replication of the `mysql` database. (For example, you might want to set up a private replication slave that people cannot connect to even if they have an account on the master.) To exclude the `mysql` database, add the following line to the `[mysqld]` group in the master's option file when you enable binary logging:

```
binlog-ignore-db=mysql
```

To exclude multiple databases, use this option multiple times, once per database.

After you have replication set up and running, there are several statements that you may find useful for monitoring or controlling the master and the slave. Details about these statements are available in Appendix D. A brief summary follows:

- `SLAVE STOP` and `SLAVE START` suspend and resume a slave server's replication-related activity. These statements can be useful for telling the slave to be quiescent while you're making a backup, for example.

- `SHOW SLAVE STATUS` on the slave shows its replication coordinates. This information can be used to determine which binary logs are no longer needed.

- `PURGE MASTER` on the master expires binary logs. You can use this after using `SHOW SLAVE STATUS` on each of the slaves.

- `CHANGE MASTER` on the slave lets you alter several of the slave's current replication parameters, such as which binary update log it reads from the master or which relay log file it writes to.

As of MySQL 4.0.2, replication slaves use two threads internally. The I/O thread talks to the master server, requests updates from it, and writes updates to a relay log file. The SQL thread reads the relay logs and executes the updates it finds there. (The relay logs serve as the means by which the I/O thread communicates changes to the SQL thread.) For slave servers that operate using this two-thread model, you can use `SLAVE STOP` and `SLAVE START` to suspend or resume each thread individually by adding `IO_THREAD` or `SQL_THREAD` to the end of the statement. For example, `SLAVE STOP SQL_THREAD` stops execution by the slave of the updates in the relay logs, but allows the slave to continue to read updates from the master and record them in the relay logs.

Relay logs are generated in numbered sequence, much like the binary update logs. There is also a relay log index file analogous to the binary update log index. The default relay log and index filenames are *HOSTNAME-*`relay-bin.`*nnn* and *HOSTNAME-*`relay-bin.index`. The defaults can be changed with the `--relay-log` and `--relay-log-index` server startup options. Another related status file is the relay information file, which has a default name of `relay-log.info` and can be changed with the `--relay-log-info-file` option.

Updating MySQL

When MySQL was first released publicly, it was at version 3.11.1. It's currently in the version 4.0.x series for stable releases and the 4.1.x series for development releases. Updates appear fairly often and are issued for both the stable and development series. The pace of ongoing development raises the question for the MySQL administrator as to whether you should upgrade your existing MySQL installation when new releases appear. This section provides some guidelines to help you make this decision.

The first thing you should do when a new release appears is to find out how it differs from previous releases. To make sure you're aware of new releases, subscribe to the `announce@lists.mysql.com` mailing list. Each announcement includes the new change notes, so this is a good way to remain apprised of new developments. (Alternatively, check the "Change Notes" appendix in the *MySQL Reference Manual* to familiarize yourself with what's new.) Then ask yourself the following questions:

- Are you experiencing problems with your current version that the new version fixes?

- Does the new version have additional features that you want or need?

- Is performance improved for certain types of operations that you use?

If the answer to all of these questions is No, you don't have any compelling reason to upgrade. If the answer to any of them is Yes, you may want to go ahead. At this point, it's often useful to wait a few days and watch the MySQL mailing list to see what other people report about the release. Was the upgrade helpful? Were bugs or other problems found?

Some other factors to consider that may help you make your decision are as follows:

- Releases in the stable series are most often for bug fixes, not new features. There is generally less risk for upgrades within the stable series than within the development series. (Of course, if you're running a development series server, you may not be that concerned about risk anyway!)

- It's possible that if you upgrade MySQL, you'll need to upgrade other programs that are built with the MySQL C client library linked in. For example, after a MySQL upgrade, you may also need to rebuild the Perl `DBD::mysql` module and PHP to link the new client library into them. (An obvious symptom that you need to do this is when all your MySQL-related DBI and PHP scripts start dumping core after you upgrade MySQL.) It's not generally a big deal to rebuild these programs, but if you prefer to avoid it, you may be better off not upgrading MySQL. If you use statically linked rather than dynamically linked programs, the likelihood of this problem is much reduced. However, your system memory requirements then increase.

If you're still not sure whether to upgrade, you can always test the new server independently of your current server. You can do this either by running it in parallel with your production server or by installing it on a different machine. It's easier to maintain independence between servers if you use a different machine because you have greater freedom to configure it as you want. If you elect to run the new server in parallel with an existing server on the same host, be sure to configure it with unique values for parameters such as the installation location, the data directory, and the network port and socket on which the server listens for connections. See the "Running Multiple Servers" section earlier in this chapter.

In either case, you'll probably want to test the new server using a copy of the data in your existing databases. See the "Backing Up and Copying Databases" section earlier in this chapter for instructions on copying databases.

If you do decide to upgrade, see if there are any remarks in the "Change Notes" appendix in the MySQL Reference Manual about any special steps you must take when upgrading. Usually there aren't any, but check anyway. This is particularly important if the new release introduces a behavior that is incompatible with earlier releases.

If you upgrade to a version that is not backward-compatible with older versions and then decide to revert to the earlier version, it may not be so easy to downgrade. For example, if you upgrade from MySQL 4.0.x to 4.1.x and convert your tables to 4.1 format, they'll be incompatible with 4.0.x servers. Downgrading can be difficult in this case.

Don't Be Afraid to Try Development Releases

It's not a wise idea to use a development release for production purposes, such as managing your business assets. On the other hand, I do encourage you to test new releases, perhaps with a copy of your production data. The greater the number of people who try new releases, the more thoroughly they are exercised. This improves the likelihood of finding any bugs that may exist, which is a good thing. Bug reports are a significant factor in helping MySQL development move forward because the developers actually fix problems that the user community reports.

If you want an ongoing source of queries for a test server, consider using a production server as a replication master and set up the test server as a replication slave. That way, queries executed by the master server will be sent to the slave server, providing it with a continual stream of queries. This also gives you a chance to see how the test server performs under conditions that mirror production use.

12

Security

As a MySQL administrator, you are responsible for maintaining the security and integrity of your MySQL installation. Chapter 11, "General MySQL Administration," already touched on a few security-related topics, such as the importance of setting up the initial MySQL `root` password and how to set up user accounts. Those topics were dealt with as part of the process of getting your installation up and running. In this chapter, we'll look more closely at security-related issues:

- Why security is important and what kind of attacks you should guard against
- Risks you face from other users with login accounts on the server host (internal security) and what you can do about them
- Risks you face from clients connecting to the server over the network (external security) and what you can do about them

The MySQL administrator is responsible for keeping the contents of databases secure so that only those who have the proper authorization can access records. This involves both internal and external security. Internal security concerns the issues that arise in relation to other users who have direct access to the MySQL server host—that is, other users who have login accounts on that host. Generally, internal security exploits involve file system access, so you'll want to protect the contents of your MySQL installation from being attacked by people who have accounts on the machine on which the server runs. In particular, the data directory should be owned and controlled by the administrative MySQL login account used for running the server. If you don't do this, your other security-related efforts may be compromised. For example, you'll want to make sure you've properly set up the accounts listed in the grant tables that control client connections over the network. But if the access mode for the data directory contents is too permissive, someone might be able to put in place an entirely different client access policy by replacing the files that correspond to the grant tables.

External security concerns the issues involved with clients connecting from outside. It's necessary to protect the MySQL server from being attacked through connections coming in over the network asking for access to database contents. You should set up the MySQL grant tables so they don't allow access to the databases managed by the server unless a valid name and password are supplied. Another danger is that it may be possible for a third party to monitor the network and capture traffic between the server and a client. If this is a concern, you may want to configure your MySQL installation to support connections that use the Secure Sockets Layer (SSL) protocol.

This chapter provides a guide to the issues you should be aware of and gives instructions showing how to prevent unauthorized access at both the internal and external levels. The chapter often refers to the login account used for running the MySQL server and for performing other MySQL-related administrative tasks. The user and group names used here for this account are `mysqladm` and `mysqlgrp`. Change the names in the examples if you use other user and group names.

Internal Security: Preventing Unauthorized File System Access

This section shows how to lock down your MySQL installation to keep it from being tampered with by unauthorized users on the server host. The section applies only to UNIX systems; I assume that if you're running a server on Windows, you have complete control of the machine and that there are no other local users. (In other words, it's best to keep a Windows-based server out of the reach of other users and restricted from general access.)

The MySQL installation procedure creates several directories, some of which need to be protected differently than others. For example, there is no need for the server binary to be accessible to anyone other than the MySQL administrative account. By contrast, the client programs normally should be publicly accessible so that other users can run them—but not so accessible that other users can modify or replace them.

Other files to be protected are created after the initial installation, either by yourself as part of your post-installation configuration procedure or by the server as it runs. Files created by you include option files or SSL-related files. Directories and files that the server creates during its operation include database directories, the files under those directories that correspond to tables in the databases, log files, and the UNIX socket file.

Clearly you want to maintain the privacy of the databases maintained by the server. Database owners usually, and rightly, consider database contents private. Even if they don't, it should be their choice to make the contents of a database public, not to have its contents be exposed through insufficient protection of the database directory.

The log files must be kept secure because they contain the text of queries. This is a general concern in that anyone with log file access can monitor changes to the contents of databases. A more specific security issue relating to log files is that queries such as GRANT and SET PASSWORD are logged. The log files thus contain the text of sensitive queries, including passwords. MySQL uses password encryption, but this applies to connection establishment after passwords already have been set up. The process of setting up a password involves a query such as GRANT, INSERT, or SET PASSWORD, and such queries are logged in plain text form in some of the logs. An attacker who has read access to the logs may be able to discover sensitive information through an act as simple as running grep on the log files to look for words such as GRANT or PASSWORD.

Other files must be accessible to client programs, such as the UNIX socket file. But normally you'll want to allow only use of the file, not control of it. For example, if a user can delete the socket file, that can cripple the ability of clients to connect to the local server.

How to Steal Data

The following description provides a brief example that illustrates why security is important. It underscores the fact that you don't want other users to have direct access to the MySQL data directory.

The MySQL server provides a flexible privilege system implemented through the grant tables in the mysql database. You can set up the contents of these tables to allow or deny database access to clients any way you want. This provides you with security against unauthorized network access to your data. However, setting up good security for network access to your databases is an exercise in futility if other users on the server host have direct access to the contents of the data directory. Unless you know you are the only person who ever logs in on the machine where the MySQL server is running, you need to be concerned about the possibility of other people on that machine gaining access to the data directory.

Obviously you don't want other users on the server host to have direct write access to data directory files because then they can stomp all over your status files or database tables. But direct read access is just as dangerous. If a table's files can be read, it is trivial to steal the files and to get MySQL itself to show you the contents of the table. How? Like this:

1. Install your own rogue MySQL server on the server host, but with a port, socket, and data directory that are different from those used by the official server.

2. Run `mysql_install_db` to initialize your data directory. This action gives you full access to your server as the MySQL `root` user and sets up a `test` database that can serve as a convenient repository for stolen tables.

3. Access the data directory of the server you want to attack, copying the files corresponding to the table or tables that you want to steal into the `test` directory under your own server's data directory. This action requires only read access to the targeted data directory.

4. Start your rogue server. Presto! Its `test` database now contains copies of the stolen tables, which you can access at will. `SHOW TABLES FROM test` shows which tables you have a copy of, and `SELECT *` shows the entire contents of any of them.

5. If you want to be really nasty, open up the permissions on the anonymous user accounts for your server so that anyone can connect to the server from any host to access your `test` database. That effectively publishes the stolen tables to the world.

Think about this scenario for a moment, and then reverse the perspective. Do you want someone to do that to you? Of course not. So protect yourself using the instructions in the following discussion.

Securing Your MySQL Installation

The procedure described here shows how to set up ownerships and access modes for the directories and files that make up your MySQL installation. The instructions here use `mysqladm` and `mysqlgrp` for the user and group names that are to be given ownership of the installation. The instructions also assume initially a standard layout such that all parts of your MySQL installation are located under a single base directory, rather than having different parts of it installed in various places throughout your file system. The installation base directory is `/usr/local/mysql` and the data directory is under that with a pathname of `/usr/local/mysql/data`. After going through the procedure, I'll describe how to handle some non-standard types of installation layouts. Your system layout may vary from any of those described here, but you should be able to adapt the general principles appropriately. Change the names and pathnames as necessary for your own system. If you run multiple servers, you should perform the procedure for each one.

You can determine whether your data directory contains insecure files or directories by executing `ls -l`. Look for files or directories that have the "group" or "other" permissions turned on. The following is a listing of a data directory that is insecure, as are some of the database directories within it:

```
% ls -la /usr/local/mysql/data
total 10148
drwxrwxr-x   11 mysqladm  wheel         1024 May  8 12:20 .
drwxr-xr-x   22 root      wheel          512 May  8 13:31 ..
drwx------    2 mysqladm  mysqlgrp       512 Apr 16 15:57 menagerie
drwxrwxr-x    2 mysqladm  wheel          512 Jun 25  1998 mysql
drwx------    7 mysqladm  mysqlgrp      1024 May  7 10:45 sampdb
drwxrwxr-x    2 mysqladm  wheel         1536 Jun 25  1998 test
drwx------    2 mysqladm  mysqlgrp      1024 May  8 18:43 tmp
```

Some of those database directories have proper permissions: `drwx------` allows read, write, and execute access to the owner, but no access to anyone else. But other directories have an overly-permissive access mode: `drwxrwxr-x` allows read and execute access to all other users, even those outside of the `mysqlgrp` group. The situation shown in this example is one that resulted over time, starting with an older MySQL installation that was progressively upgraded to successive newer versions. The less-restrictive permissions were created by older MySQL servers that were less stringent than more recent servers about setting permissions. (Notice that the more restrictive database directories, `menagerie`, `sampdb`, and `tmp`, all have more recent dates.) The behavior of a MySQL server now is to set the permissions on database directories that it creates to be accessible only to the account it runs as.

You can also use `ls -l` to check the base directory of the MySQL installation. For example, you might get a result something like this:

```
% ls -la /usr/local/mysql
total 44
drwxrwxr-x   13 mysqladm  mysqlgrp      1024 May  7 10:45 .
drwxr-xr-x   24 root      wheel         1024 May  1 12:54 ..
drwxr-xr-x    2 mysqladm  mysqlgrp      1024 Jul 16 20:58 bin
drwxrwxr-x   12 mysqladm  wheel         1024 May  8 12:20 data
drwxr-xr-x    3 mysqladm  mysqlgrp       512 May  7 10:45 include
drwxr-xr-x    2 mysqladm  mysqlgrp       512 May  7 10:45 info
```

```
drwxr-xr-x    3 mysqladm mysqlgrp       512 May   7 10:45 lib
drwxr--r-x    2 mysqladm mysqlgrp       512 Jul 16 20:58 libexec
drwxr-xr-x    3 mysqladm mysqlgrp       512 May   7 10:45 man
drwxr-xr-x    6 mysqladm mysqlgrp      1024 May   7 10:45 mysql-test
drwxr-xr-x    3 mysqladm mysqlgrp       512 May   7 10:45 share
drwxr-xr-x    7 mysqladm mysqlgrp      1024 May   7 10:45 sql-bench
```

The `data` directory permissions and ownership need to be changed, as already indicated. One other change you might make is to restrict access to the `libexec` directory, which is where the `mysqld` server lives. Nobody but the MySQL administrator needs access to the server, so you can make that directory private to `mysqladm`.

To correct problems such as those just described, use the following procedure. The general idea is to lock down everything to be accessible only to `mysqladm` except for those parts of the installation that other users have a legitimate need to access:

1. If the MySQL server is running, shut it down:

   ```
   % mysqladmin -p -u root shutdown
   ```

2. Set the owner and group name assignments of the entire MySQL installation to those of the MySQL administrative account using the following command, which you must execute as `root`:

   ```
   # chown -R mysqladm.mysqlgrp /usr/local/mysql
   ```

   Another popular approach is to make everything owned by `root` except the data directory, which you can accomplish like this:

   ```
   # chown -R root.mysqlgrp /usr/local/mysql
   # chown -R mysqladm.mysqlgrp /usr/local/mysql/data
   ```

   If you set the general ownership to `root`, you'll need to perform most of the following steps as `root`. Otherwise, you can perform them as `mysqladm`.

3. For the base directory and any of its subdirectories that clients should be able to access, change their mode so that `mysqladm` has full access and everyone else has only read and execute permission. That may be how they are set already, but if not, change them. For example, the base directory can be set using either of the following commands:

   ```
   % chmod 755 /usr/local/mysql
   % chmod u=rwx,go=rx /usr/local/mysql
   ```

   Similarly, the `bin` directory that contains the client programs can be set with either of the following commands:

   ```
   % chmod 755 /usr/local/mysql/bin
   % chmod u=rwx,go=rx /usr/local/mysql/bin
   ```

Directories that clients need not have access to can be made private to
mysqladm. The libexec directory that contains the server is an example.
Either of the following commands will set its mode appropriately:

```
% chmod 700 /usr/local/mysql/libexec
% chmod u=rwx,go-rwx /usr/local/mysql/libexec
```

4. Change the mode of your data directory and all files and directories
   under it so that they are private to mysqladm. This prevents accounts
   other than the one used for running the server from directly accessing
   the contents of your data directory. You can do this with the following
   command:

```
% chmod -R go-rwx /usr/local/mysql/data
```

After following the preceding instructions, your MySQL installation base
directory will have ownerships and permissions that look something like this:

```
% ls -la /usr/local/mysql
total 44
drwxr-xr-x    13 mysqladm mysqlgrp      1024 May   7 10:45 .
drwxr-xr-x    24 root     wheel         1024 May   1 12:54 ..
drwxr-xr-x     2 mysqladm mysqlgrp      1024 Jul 16 20:58 bin
drwx------    12 mysqladm mysqlgrp      1024 May   8 12:20 data
drwxr-xr-x     3 mysqladm mysqlgrp       512 May   7 10:45 include
drwxr-xr-x     2 mysqladm mysqlgrp       512 May   7 10:45 info
drwxr-xr-x     3 mysqladm mysqlgrp       512 May   7 10:45 lib
drwx------     2 mysqladm mysqlgrp       512 Jul 16 20:58 libexec
drwxr-xr-x     3 mysqladm mysqlgrp       512 May   7 10:45 man
drwxr-xr-x     6 mysqladm mysqlgrp      1024 May   7 10:45 mysql-test
drwxr-xr-x     3 mysqladm mysqlgrp       512 May   7 10:45 share
drwxr-xr-x     7 mysqladm mysqlgrp      1024 May   7 10:45 sql-bench
```

As shown, everything now is owned by mysqladm, with a group membership
of mysqlgrp. (The listing for '. .' refers to the parent directory of
/usr/local/mysql. That directory is owned by and modifiable only by root,
which is good. You don't want unprivileged users to be able to mess with the
directory containing your installation.)

The data directory under the base directory will have even more restrictive
permissions:

```
% ls -la /usr/local/mysql/data
total 10148
drwx------    11 mysqladm mysqlgrp      1024 May   8 12:20 .
drwxr-xr-x    22 mysqladm mysqlgrp       512 May   8 13:31 ..
drwx------     2 mysqladm mysqlgrp       512 Apr 16 15:57 menagerie
drwx------     2 mysqladm mysqlgrp       512 Jun 25  1998 mysql
drwx------     7 mysqladm mysqlgrp      1024 May   7 10:45 sampdb
drwx------     2 mysqladm mysqlgrp      1536 Jun 25  1998 test
drwx------     2 mysqladm mysqlgrp      1024 May   8 18:43 tmp
```

Here, the '. .' line refers to the parent of the data directory, that is, the MySQL base directory.

An exception to the `mysqladm`-only policy of access to the data directory may be necessary for particular files. For example, if you create a `my.cnf` option file in the data directory, it will be necessary to open up access to the directory a little if you want to place client options in the file. (Otherwise, client programs won't be able to read the file.) The same applies if you place the UNIX socket file in the data directory. To allow client programs to access these files without providing full read access to the data directory, use the following command:

```
% chmod go+x /usr/local/mysql/data
```

As stated earlier, the preceding procedure assumes that all MySQL-related files are located under a single base directory. If that's not true, you'll need to locate each MySQL-related directory and perform the appropriate operations on each of them. For example, if your data directory is located at `/var/mysql/data` rather than under `/usr/local/mysql`, you'll need to issue two commands to change the ownership of your installation properly:

```
# chown -R mysqladm.mysqlgrp /usr/local/mysql
# chown -R mysqladm.mysqlgrp /var/mysql/data
```

Or suppose you create an `innodb` directory under the MySQL installation directory under which to keep all InnoDB-related files. By default, these files are placed in the data directory. If you put them in an `innodb` directory instead, you'll want to set that directory to have the same access mode as the data directory. This principle also applies if you relocate other files that normally would be placed in the data directory, such as log files.

Another complication occurs if some of the directories under the installation root are really symbolic links that point elsewhere. If your version of `chown` doesn't follow symlinks, you'll need to track them down and apply the ownership changes where the links point to. One way to do this is to use `find`:

```
# find /usr/local/mysql -follow -print | xargs chown mysqladm.mysqlgrp
```

Similar considerations apply to changing access modes. For example, if there are symbolic links under your data directory and `chmod` doesn't follow them, use the following command instead:

```
% find /usr/local/mysql/data -follow -print | xargs chmod go-rwx
```

Note that parts of these instructions *do not apply* if your installation is such that the MySQL server and client programs are installed in general system directories along with other non-MySQL programs. (For example, the server may be in `/usr/sbin` and the clients in `/usr/bin`.) In that case, the ownership and mode of the MySQL programs should be set the same as other binaries in those directories.

Because the ownership and mode of data directory contents at this point are set to allow access only to the `mysqladm` user, you should make sure the server always runs as `mysqladm` from now on. An easy way to ensure this is to specify the user in the `[mysqld]` group of the `/etc/my.cnf` file or the `my.cnf` file in the data directory:

```
[mysqld]
user=mysqladm
```

That way, the server will run as `mysqladm` whether you start it while logged in as `root` or as `mysqladm`. Additional information on running the server using a particular login account is given in Chapter 11.

After securing your MySQL installation, you can restart the server.

Securing the Socket File

The server uses a UNIX domain socket file for connections by clients to `localhost`. The socket file normally is publicly accessible so that client programs can use it. However, it should not be located in a directory where arbitrary clients have delete permission. For example, it's common for the socket file to be created in the `/tmp` directory, but on some UNIX systems, that directory has permissions that allow users to delete files other than their own. That means any user can remove the socket file and, as a result, prevent client programs from establishing `localhost` connections to the server until the server is restarted to re-create the socket file. It's better if the `/tmp` directory has its "sticky bit" set, so that even if anyone can create files in the directory, users can remove only their own files.

Some installations place the socket file in the data directory, which leads to a problem if you make the data directory private to `mysqladm`—no client can access the socket file unless it is run by `root` or `mysqladm`. In this case, one option is to open up the data directory slightly so that clients can see the socket file:

```
% chmod go+x /usr/local/mysql/data
```

Otherwise, you can change the location in which the server creates the socket file. Either specify a different location in a global option file or recompile from source to build in a different default location. If you elect to use an option file, be sure to specify the location both for the server and for clients. For example, you can place the socket file in the base directory as follows:

```
[mysqld]
socket=/usr/local/mysql/mysql.sock
[client]
socket=/usr/local/mysql/mysql.sock
```

Recompiling is more work, but is a more complete solution because using an option file will not work for clients that do not check option files. (All the standard MySQL clients do, but third-party programs may not.) By recompiling, the new socket location will become the default known by the client library; any program that uses the client library thus gets the new location as its own default, whether or not it uses option files.

Securing Option Files

Option files represent a potential point of compromise to the extent that they contain options that should not be exposed. As a general principle, you shouldn't make an option file publicly readable if it contains sensitive information, such as MySQL account names or passwords. /etc/my.cnf normally is publicly readable because it's a common location in which to specify global client options. (This means you should not use it for server options, such as replication passwords.) Each user-specific .my.cnf option file should be owned by and readable only by the user in whose home directory the file appears. The option file in the server's data directory can go either way, depending on what you use it for.

One way to ensure that user-specific option files have the proper mode and ownership is to run a program that looks for such files and corrects any problems. The following Perl script, chk_mysql_opt_files.pl, will do this:

```perl
#! /usr/bin/perl -w
# chk_mysql_opt_files.pl - check user-specific .my.cnf files and make sure
# the ownership and mode is correct. Each file should be owned by the
# user in whose home directory the file is found. The mode should
# have the "group" and "other" permissions turned off.

# This script must be run as root.  Execute it with your password file as
# input.  If you have an /etc/passwd file, run it like this:
#  chk_mysql_opt_file.pl /etc/passwd
# For Mac OS X, use the netinfo database:
#  nidump passwd . | chk_mysql_opt_file.pl

use strict;
while (<>)
{
    my ($uid, $home) = (split (/:/, $_)) [2,5];
    my $cnf_file = "$home/.my.cnf";
    next unless -f $cnf_file;                 # is there a .my.cnf file?
    if ((stat ($cnf_file)) [4] != $uid)    # test ownership
    {
        warn "Changing ownership of $cnf_file to $uid\n";
        chown ($uid, (stat ($cnf_file)) [5], $cnf_file);
    }
}
```

```
    my $mode = (stat ($cnf_file))[2];
    if ($mode & 077)                    # test group/other access bits
    {
        warn sprintf ("Changing mode of %s from %o to %o\n",
                        $cnf_file, $mode, $mode & ~077);
        chmod ($mode & ~077, $cnf_file);
    }
}
exit (0);
```

You can find `chk_mysql_opt_files.pl` in the `admin` directory of the `sampdb` distribution. You must run this script as `root` because it needs to be able to change mode and ownership of files owned by other users. To execute the script automatically, set it up as a nightly `cron` job run by `root`.

One of the standard option files that MySQL programs look for is the `my.cnf` file in the compiled-in location of the data directory. If you make the data directory private to `mysqladm`, client programs cannot read that file. This means that if you want to put client parameters in the file, you'll have to open up access to the data directory a bit. To do this, turn on "execute" permission for the directory, and also make sure that the `my.cnf` file itself is publicly readable:

```
% chmod go+x /usr/local/mysql/data
% chmod +r /usr/local/mysql/data/my.cnf
```

However, if you do this, the file becomes unsuitable for listing options that must be private to the server, such as replication passwords.

External Security: Preventing Unauthorized Network Access

The MySQL security system is flexible. It allows you to set up user access privileges in many different ways. Normally, you do this by using the GRANT and REVOKE statements, which modify on your behalf the grant tables that control client access. However, you may have an older version of MySQL that does not support these statements (they were not functional prior to MySQL 3.22.11), or you may find that user privileges don't seem to be working the way you want. For such situations, it's helpful to understand the structure of the MySQL grant tables and how the server uses them to determine access permissions. Such an understanding allows you to add, remove, or modify user privileges by modifying the grant tables directly. It also allows you to diagnose privilege problems when you examine the tables.

I assume that you've read the "Managing MySQL User Accounts" section in Chapter 11 and that you understand how the GRANT and REVOKE statements work. GRANT and REVOKE provide a convenient way for you to set up MySQL user accounts and associate privileges with them, but they are just a front end. All the real action takes place in the MySQL grant tables. (In fact, the "Setting Up MySQL Accounts Without GRANT Statements" section later in this chapter discusses how to modify the grant tables directly to achieve the same results that you get by issuing GRANT statements.)

Structure and Contents of the MySQL Grant Tables

Access to MySQL databases by clients who connect to the server over the network is controlled by the contents of the grant tables. These tables are located in the mysql database and are initialized during the process of installing MySQL on a machine for the first time (as described in Appendix A, "Obtaining and Installing Software," for example). These tables are named user, db, tables_priv, columns_priv, and host. They are used as follows:

- The user table lists accounts for users that may connect to the server, their passwords, and which global (superuser) privileges each user has, if any. It's important to recognize that any privileges that are enabled in the user table are global privileges that apply to *all databases.* For example, if you enable the DELETE privilege in a user table entry, the account associated with the entry can delete records from any table in any database. Think carefully before you do this.

  Because of the superuser nature of privileges specified in the user table, it's generally best to leave all the privileges turned off for entries in this table and list more specific privileges in other tables that are more restrictive. There are two types of exceptions to this principle:

  - Superusers, such as root and other administrative accounts, need global privileges to operate the server. These accounts tend to be few.
  - A few specific global privileges usually can be granted safely. These pertain to creating temporary tables, locking tables, and being able to use the SHOW DATABASES statement. Most installations probably will grant these, but others where tighter control is necessary will not.

  The user table also has columns for SSL options that pertain to the establishment of secure connections with SSL and columns for resource management that can be used to prevent a given account from monopolizing the server.

- The db table lists which accounts have privileges for which databases. If you grant a privilege here, it applies to all tables in a database.

- The `tables_priv` table specifies table-level privileges. A privilege specified here applies to all columns in a table.

- The `columns_priv` table specifies column-level privileges. A privilege specified here applies to a particular column in a table.

- The `host` table is used in combination with the `db` table to control database access privileges to particular hosts at a finer level than is possible with the `db` table alone. This table is unaffected by the GRANT and REVOKE statements, so it's likely that you will never use it at all.

The structure of each grant table is shown in Tables 12.1, 12.2, and 12.3, broken down by type of column. All grant tables contain two primary kinds of columns—scope-of-access columns that determine when an entry applies and privilege columns that determine which privileges an entry grants. The privilege columns can be subdivided further into columns for administrative operations and those that are related to database and table operations. The `user` table has additional columns for SSL connections and resource management; these are present only in the `user` table because they apply globally. Some of the grant tables contain other miscellaneous columns, but they don't concern us here because they have no bearing on account management.

Table 12.1 Grant Table Scope-of-Access Columns

Scope-of-Access Columns

user Table	db Table	tables_priv Table	columns_priv Table	host Table
Host	Host	Host	Host	Host
User	User	User	User	
Password	Db	Db	Db	Db
		Table_name	Table_name	
			Column_name	

Table 12.2 Grant Table Privilege Columns

Administrative Privilege Columns

user Table	db Table	host Table
Create_tmp_table_priv	Create_tmp_table_priv	Create_tmp_table_priv
Execute_priv		
File_priv		
Grant_priv	Grant_priv	Grant_priv
Lock_tables_priv	Lock_tables_priv	Lock_tables_priv

continues

Table 12.2 **Continued**

Administrative Privilege Columns

user Table	**db Table**	**host Table**
Process_priv		
Reload_priv		
Repl_client_priv		
Repl_slave_priv		
Show_db_priv		
Shutdown_priv		
Super_priv		

Database/Table Privilege Columns

user Table	**db Table**	**host Table**
Alter_priv	Alter_priv	Alter_priv
Create_priv	Create_priv	Create_priv
Delete_priv	Delete_priv	Delete_priv
Drop_priv	Drop_priv	Drop_priv
Index_priv	Index_priv	Index_priv
Insert_priv	Insert_priv	Insert_priv
References_priv	References_priv	References_priv
Select_priv	Select_priv	Select_priv
Update_priv	Update_priv	Update_priv

tables_priv Table	**columns_priv Table**
Table_priv	Column_priv

Table 12.3 **Grant Table SSL and Resource Management Columns (user Table Only)**

SSL Columns	**Resource Management Columns**
ssl_type	max_connections
ssl_cipher	max_questions
x509_issuer	max_updates
x509_subject	

The grant table system includes `tables_priv` and `columns_priv` tables for setting up table-specific and column-specific privileges. However, there is no analogous `rows_priv` table because MySQL doesn't provide record-level privileges. For example, you cannot restrict a user's access to just those rows in a table that contain a particular value in some column. If you need this capability, you must provide it using application programming. (One way to perform advisory record-level locking is to use the `GET_LOCK()` function described in Appendix C, "Operator and Function Reference.")

Dealing with Changes to Grant Table Structure

The structure of the grant tables has changed occasionally over time, so if you examine the tables in your server's mysql database, you may find that certain tables or columns are not present:

- The tables_priv and columns_priv tables were introduced in MySQL 3.22.11 (at the same time as the GRANT statement). If you have an older version of MySQL, your mysql database will have only the user, db, and host tables.
- The SSL columns in the user table were added in MySQL 4.0.0.
- The resource-management columns in the user table were added in MySQL 4.0.2.
- Several privilege columns were added to the user table in MySQL 4.0.2: Create_tmp_table_priv, Execute_priv, Lock_tables_priv, Repl_client_priv, Repl_slave_priv, Show_db_priv, and Super_priv. In MySQL 4.0.4, the Create_tmp_table_priv and Lock_tables_priv privileges were added to the db and hosts tables as well.

If your grant table structure doesn't match what you expect based on the description just given, you can bring the tables up to date by running the mysql_fix_privilege_tables script. It needs to connect to the local server as the MySQL root user, so invoke it with the appropriate password:

```
% mysql_fix_privilege_tables root-password
```

If you upgrade to MySQL 4.0.2 or later from an earlier version, the new privilege columns added to the user table by the mysql_fix_privilege_tables script are initialized for existing non-anonymous user table entries as follows:

- Show_db_priv is set to the existing Select_priv value.
- Execute_priv and Super_priv are set to the existing Process_priv value. Repl_client_priv and Repl_slave_priv are set to the existing File_priv value.
- Create_tmp_table_priv and Lock_tables_priv are set to 'Y'.

It's actually best to upgrade to 4.0.4 or later if possible rather than to 4.0.2 or 4.0.3. The lack of the Create_tmp_table_priv and Lock_tables_priv privileges in the db table for those two releases results in the inability to grant them on a database-specific basis and causes some administrative difficulties.

Grant Table Scope-of-Access Columns

The grant table scope columns are used to determine which rows to use when a given account attempts to perform a given operation. Each grant table entry contains Host and User columns to indicate that the entry applies to connections from a given host by a particular user. For example, a user table record with localhost and bill in the Host and User columns would be used for connections from the local host by bill, but not for connections by betty. (The host table is an exception; it's used in a special way that we won't get into just yet.) The other tables contain additional scope columns. The db table contains a Db column to indicate which database the entry applies to. Similarly, rows in the `tables_priv` and `columns_priv` tables contain scope fields that further narrow their scope to a particular table in a database or column in a table.

Grant Table Privilege Columns

The grant tables also contain privilege columns. These indicate which privileges are held by the user who matches the values listed in the scope columns. The privileges supported by MySQL are shown in the following lists, which show the administrative privileges and the privileges that control database and table access. Each list uses the privilege names that are used for the GRANT statement. For the most part, these privilege names bear an obvious resemblance to the names of privilege columns in the user, db, and host tables. For example, the SELECT privilege corresponds to the Select_priv column.

Administrative Privileges

The following privileges apply to administrative operations that control the operation of the server or a user's ability to grant privileges:

- CREATE TEMPORARY TABLES

  Allows you to create temporary tables with the CREATE TEMPORARY TABLE statement.

- EXECUTE

  Allows you to execute stored procedures. This privilege is currently unimplemented. It will come into effect when stored procedures are implemented in a future version of MySQL (currently scheduled for MySQL 5).

- FILE

  Allows you to tell the server to read or write files on the server host. To keep the use of this privilege within certain bounds, the server takes certain precautions:

  - You can access only files that are world-readable, and thus likely not to be considered protected in any way.

  - Any file that you want to write must not already exist. This prevents you from coercing the server into overwriting important files, such as /etc/passwd or database files in a database belonging to someone else. (If this constraint were not enforced, you could completely replace the contents of the grant tables in the mysql database, for example.)

Despite these precautions, this privilege should not be granted without just cause; it can be extremely dangerous, as discussed in the "Grant Table Risks to Avoid" section later in this chapter. If you do grant the FILE privilege, be sure not to run the server as the UNIX root user, because root can create new files anywhere in the file system. By running the server from an ordinary login account, the server can create files only in directories accessible to that account.

- GRANT OPTION

  Allows you to grant other users the privileges you have yourself, including the GRANT OPTION privilege.

- LOCK TABLES

  Allows you to lock tables by issuing explicit LOCK TABLES statements. This privilege applies only to tables for which you also have the SELECT privilege, but allows you to place read or write locks, not just read locks. The privilege does not apply to locks that are acquired implicitly on your behalf by the server during the process of query execution. Such locks are set and released automatically regardless of your LOCK TABLES privilege setting.

- PROCESS

  The MySQL server is multi-threaded such that each client connection is serviced by a separate thread. These threads can be thought of as processes running within the server. Prior to MySQL 4.0.2, the PROCESS privilege allows you to view information about threads that are currently executing using the SHOW PROCESSLIST statement or the mysqladmin processlist command. It also allows you to kill threads with the KILL statement or the mysqladmin kill command. (You can always see or kill your own threads, even without the PROCESS privilege. What this privilege adds is the global ability to see or kill any thread, even those associated with other users.) The PROCESS privilege also allows mysqladmin debug, and it overrides any max_connections setting when connecting to the server, so that you can access the connection slot that the server reserves for administrative connections even when all the regular slots are taken.

  In MySQL 4.0.2 or later, PROCESS controls only the ability to see threads; the ability to kill them is controlled by the SUPER privilege, as is the ability to use mysqladmin debug and the reserved connection slot.

- RELOAD

  Allows you to perform a variety of server administration operations. This privilege gives you the ability to issue statements such as FLUSH and RESET. It also lets you perform the following mysqladmin commands: reload, refresh, flush-hosts, flush-logs, flush-privileges, flush-status, flush-tables, and flush-threads.

- REPLICATION CLIENT

  Allows you to inquire about the location of master and slave servers.

- REPLICATION SLAVE

  Allows a client to connect to a master server and request slave server updates. It's granted to accounts used by slave servers. Prior to MySQL 4.0.2, replication slaves are set up using the FILE privilege instead.

- SHOW DATABASES

  Controls the ability to use the SHOW DATABASES statement.

- SHUTDOWN

  Allows you to shut down the server with mysqladmin shutdown.

- SUPER

  Allows you to kill server threads, use mysqladmin debug, and access the reserved connection slot, as discussed in the description for the PROCESS privilege. Other statements allowed by this privilege are CHANGE MASTER, PURGE MASTER LOGS, and SET for modifying global server variables and the global transaction isolation level. SUPER also allows you to perform DES decryption based on the keys stored in the DES key file.

Database and Table Privileges

The following privileges apply to operations on databases and tables:

- ALTER

  Allows you to use the ALTER TABLE statement, although you may also need additional privileges, depending on what you want to do with the table.

- CREATE

  Allows you to create databases and tables. This privilege does not allow you to create indexes on a table, except those declared initially in the CREATE TABLE statement.

- DELETE

  Allows you to remove existing records from tables.

- DROP

  Allows you to drop databases and tables. This privilege does not allow you to drop indexes.

- INDEX

  Allows you to create or drop indexes from tables.

- INSERT

  Allows you to insert new records in tables.

- REFERENCES

  This is currently unused. Eventually it may be used to define who can set up foreign key constraints.

- SELECT

  Allows you to retrieve data from tables using SELECT statements. This privilege is unnecessary for SELECT statements such as SELECT NOW() or SELECT 4/2 that do nothing more than evaluate expressions and involve no tables.

- UPDATE

  Allows you to modify existing records in tables.

Some operations require a combination of privileges. For example, REPLACE may implicitly cause a DELETE followed by an INSERT, so it requires both the DELETE and INSERT privileges.

Privilege Column Storage Structure

In the user, db, and host tables, each privilege is specified as a separate column. These columns are all declared to have a type of ENUM('N','Y'), with a default value of 'N' (off). For example, the Select_priv column is defined as follows:

```
Select_priv ENUM('N','Y') NOT NULL DEFAULT 'N'
```

Privileges in the tables_priv and columns_priv tables are represented by a SET, which allows any combination of privileges to be stored in a single column. The Table_priv column in the tables_priv table is defined as follows:

```
SET('Select','Insert','Update','Delete','Create','Drop',
    'Grant','References','Index','Alter')
```

The `Column_priv` column in the `columns_priv` table is defined as follows:

```
SET('Select','Insert','Update','References')
```

The reason there are fewer column privileges than table privileges is that fewer operations make sense at the column level. For example, you can delete a row from a table to remove it, but you can't delete individual columns of a row.

The `tables_priv` and `columns_priv` tables are newer than the other three, which is why they use the more efficient `SET` representation. (It's possible that the `user`, `db`, and `host` tables may be reorganized in the future to represent privileges by `SET` columns as well.)

The `user` table contains several administrative privilege columns that are not present in any of the other grant tables, such as `File_priv`, `Process_priv`, `Reload_priv`, and `Shutdown_priv`. Such privileges are present only in the `user` table because they are global privileges that are not associated with any particular database or table. For example, it doesn't make sense to allow or not allow a user to shut down the server based on what the current database is.

Grant Table SSL-Related Columns

Several columns in the `user` table apply to authentication of secure connections over SSL. The primary column is `ssl_type`, which indicates whether and what type of secure connection is required. It is represented as an `ENUM` with four possible values:

- `'NONE'` indicates that secure connections are not required. This is the default value; it's used when you set up an account but do not specify any `REQUIRE` clause or when you specify `REQUIRE NONE` explicitly.
- `'ANY'` indicates that a secure connection is required, but that it can be any kind of secure connection; it's a kind of "generic" requirement. The column is set to this value when you specify `REQUIRE SSL` in a `GRANT` statement.
- `'X509'` indicates that a secure connection is required and that the client must supply a valid X509 certificate. The contents of the certificate are not otherwise relevant. The column is set to this value when you specify `REQUIRE X509`.
- `'SPECIFIED'` indicates that the secure connection must meet specific requirements. The column is set to this value when you specify any combination of `ISSUER`, `SUBJECT`, or `CIPHER` values in the `REQUIRE` clause.

For all `ssl_type` values except `'SPECIFIED'`, the server ignores the values in the other SSL-related columns when validating client connection attempts. For `'SPECIFIED'`, the server checks the other columns and, for any that have non-empty values, the client must supply matching information. These columns are:

- `ssl_cipher`

  If non-empty, this column indicates the cipher method that the client must use when connecting.

- `x509_issuer`

  If non-empty, this column indicates the issuer value that must be found in the X509 certificate presented by the client.

- `x509_subject`

  If non-empty, this column indicates the subject value that must be found in the X509 certificate presented by the client.

`ssl_cipher`, `x509_issuer`, and `x509_subject` all are represented in the user table as BLOB columns.

Grant Table Resource Management Columns

The following columns in the `user` table allow you to limit the extent to which any given MySQL account can consume server resources:

- `max_connections`

  The number of times per hour the account can connect to the server.

- `max_questions`

  The number of queries per hour the account can issue.

- `max_updates`

  Like `max_questions`, but applies more specifically to queries that modify data.

For each of these columns, a value of zero means "no limit."

If the server restarts, the current counters are reset to zero. A reset also occurs if you reload the grant tables or issue a FLUSH USER_RESOURCES statement.

How the Server Controls Client Access

There are two stages of client access control when you use MySQL. The first stage occurs when you attempt to connect to the server. The server looks at the user table to see if it can find an entry that matches the host you're connecting from, your name, and the password you supplied. If there is no match, you can't connect. If there is a match and your `user` table is recent enough to include the SSL or resource management columns, the server also checks those columns:

- If you've exceeded your connections-per-hour limit, the connection is rejected.
- If the `user` table entry indicates that secure connections are required, the server determines whether the credentials you supply match those required in the SSL-related columns. If not, the connection is rejected.

If everything checks out okay, the server establishes the connection and you proceed to the second stage. For secure connections, encryption is used.

In the second stage, for each query you issue, the server checks the grant tables to see whether or not you have sufficient privileges to perform the query. (If the resource management columns are present in the `user` table, the server also checks your queries-per-hour and updates-per-hour limits. It does this prior to checking your access privileges—after all, if you've exceeded those limits, there is little point in checking your privileges.) The second stage continues until you disconnect from the server.

The following discussion describes in some detail the rules that the MySQL server uses to match grant table entries to incoming client connection requests and to queries. This includes the types of values that are legal in the grant table scope columns, how privilege values from different grant tables are combined, and the order in which table entries within a given grant table are searched.

Scope Column Contents

Each scope column is governed by rules that define what kinds of values are legal and how the server interprets those values. Some of the scope columns require literal values, but most of them allow wildcard or other special values.

- `Host`

  A `Host` column value can be a hostname or an IP number. The value `localhost` means the local host. It matches if you connect using a host value of `localhost` or `127.0.0.1` or if you connect using a named pipe on Windows NT-based systems using a '`.`' host value. However, `localhost` does not match if you connect using the host's actual name or IP number. Suppose the name of the local host is `cobra.snake.net` and there are two entries for a user named `bob` in the `user` table, one with a `Host` value of `localhost` and the other with a value of cobra.snake.net. The entry with localhost will match if bob connects either of the following ways, on either UNIX or Windows:

```
% mysql -p -u bob -h localhost
% mysql -p -u bob -h 127.0.0.1
```

In addition, on Windows, the entry matches if bob connects like this:

```
C:\> mysql -p -u bob -h .
```

The localhost connection will use a UNIX socket on UNIX, and TCP/IP on Windows. The 127.0.0.1 connection will use TCP/IP on both platforms. The '.' connection will use a named pipe on Windows.

The entry with a Host value of cobra.snake.net will match if bob connects from cobra.snake.net using the server's name or IP number. In both cases, the connection will use TCP/IP.

You can also specify Host values using wildcards. The '%' and '_' SQL pattern characters can be used and have the same meaning as when you use the LIKE operator in a query. (Regular expressions of the type used with REGEXP are not allowed.) The SQL pattern characters work both for names and for IP numbers. For example, %.kitebird.com matches any host in the kitebird.com domain, and %.edu matches any host at any educational institution. Similarly, 192.168.% matches any host in the 192.168 class B subnet, whereas 192.168.3.% matches any host in the 192.168.3 class C subnet.

A Host value of % matches any host at all, and can be used to allow a user to connect from anywhere. With one exception, a blank Host value in a grant table is the same as %. (The exception is the db table, for which a blank Host value means "check the host table for further information." This process is described in the "Query Access Verification" section later in this chapter.)

As of MySQL 3.23, you can also specify a network number with a netmask indicating which bits of the client IP address must match the network number. For example, 192.168.128.0/255.255.255.0 specifies a 24-bit network number and matches any client host for which the first 24 bits of its IP address have a value equal to 192.168.128.

- User

Usernames must be either literal values or blank (empty). A blank value matches any name and thus means "anonymous." Otherwise, the value matches exactly the name specified. In particular, % as a User value does not mean blank; instead, it matches a user with a literal name of %, which is probably not what you want.

When an incoming connection is verified against the `user` table, if the first matching entry contains a blank `User` value, the client is considered to be an anonymous user.

- `Password`

  `Password` values are either blank (empty) or non-blank, and wildcards are not allowed. A blank password doesn't mean that any password matches; it means that the user must specify no password.

  Passwords are stored as encrypted values, not literal text. If you store a literal password in the `Password` column, the user will not be able to connect! The `GRANT` statement and the `mysqladmin password` command encrypt the password for you automatically, but if you use statements such as `INSERT`, `REPLACE`, `UPDATE`, or `SET PASSWORD` to modify the grant tables directly, be sure to specify the password using `PASSWORD('new_password')` rather than just `'new_password'`.

- `Db`

  In the `db` and `host` tables, `Db` values can be specified literally or by using the '`%`' or '`_`' SQL pattern characters to specify a wildcard. A value of `%` or blank matches any database. In the `columns_priv` and `tables_priv` tables, `Db` values must be literal database names and match exactly the name specified; patterns and empty values are not allowed.

- `Table_name`, `Column_name`

  Values in these columns must be literal table or column names and match exactly the name specified; patterns and empty values are not allowed.

Some scope columns are treated by the server as case sensitive, whereas others are not, as summarized in Table 12.4. Note in particular that `Db` and `Table_name` values are always treated as case sensitive, even though treatment of database and table names in queries depends on the case sensitivity of the file system on which the server runs (typically case sensitive under UNIX, and not case sensitive under Windows).

Table 12.4 **Case Sensitivity in Grant Table Scope Columns**

Column	Case Sensitive
Host	No
User	Yes
Password	Yes
Db	Yes
Table_name	Yes
Column_name	No

How Passwords Are Stored in the user Table

The MySQL server encrypts passwords with the PASSWORD() function before storing them in the user table, to prevent them from being exposed as plain text even to users who have read access to the table. It seems to be a common assumption that PASSWORD() implements the same kind of encryption as is used for UNIX passwords, but it doesn't. The two kinds of encryption are similar in that both are one-way and not reversible, but MySQL doesn't use the same encryption algorithm that UNIX does. This means that even if you use your UNIX password as your MySQL password, you shouldn't expect the encrypted password strings to match. If you want to perform UNIX encryption for an application, use the CRYPT() function rather than PASSWORD(). (If you're curious about what other encryption options are available for use in your applications, see the "Security-Related Functions" section in Appendix C.)

Query Access Verification

Each time you issue a query, the server determines whether you've exceeded your resource limits and, if not, checks whether you have sufficient privileges to execute the query. The resource limits are given by the max_questions and max_updates values stored in the user table, if your version of MySQL is recent enough to have those columns. The server examines your access privileges by checking, in order, the user, db, tables_priv, and columns_priv tables, until it either determines you have proper access or it has searched all the tables in vain. More specifically:

1. The server checks the user table entry that matched when you connected initially, to see what global privileges you have. If you have any and they are sufficient for the query, the server executes it.

2. If your global privileges are insufficient, the server looks for an entry for you in the db table. If it finds one, it adds the privileges in that entry to your global privileges. If the result is sufficient for the query, the server executes it.

3. If the combination of your global and database-level privileges is insufficient, the server keeps looking, first in the tables_priv table and then in the columns_priv table.

4. If you don't have permission after all the tables have been checked, the server rejects your attempt to execute the query.

In boolean terms, the privileges in the grant tables are combined by the server as follows:

```
user OR db OR tables_priv OR columns_priv
```

I see that you're wondering why the preceding description refers to only four grant tables when there are five grant tables. Okay, you caught me. The server really checks access permissions like this:

```
user OR (db AND host) OR tables_priv OR columns_priv
```

I showed the simpler expression first because the more complex expression will never come into play for most MySQL installations. That's because the host table that appears in the more complex expression is not affected at all by the GRANT and REVOKE statements. It's affected only if you manipulate it directly with INSERT, UPDATE, and so forth. This means that if you adopt the usual administrative policy of managing user accounts with GRANT and REVOKE, your host table will never be used and you can forget about it entirely.

However, if you do want to use the host table, here's how it works:

1. When the server checks for database-level privileges, it looks at the db table entry for the client. If the Host column value is blank, it means "Look in the host table to find out which hosts can access the database."

2. To check the host table, the server looks for entries with the same Db column value as the entry from the db table. If no host table entry matches the client host, no database-level privileges are granted. If an entry does have a Host column value that matches the host from which the client is connecting, the db table entry and the host table entry are combined to produce the client's database-level privileges.

However, the privileges are combined using a logical AND, which means that the client doesn't have a given privilege unless it's present in both the db table and host table entries. In this way, you can grant a basic set of privileges in the db table entry, and then selectively disable them for particular hosts using host table entries. For example, you might allow access to a database from all hosts in your domain, but turn off database privileges for hosts that are located in less secure areas.

The preceding description no doubt makes access checking sound like a rather complicated process, especially when you consider that the server checks privileges for every single query that clients issue. However, the process is quite fast because the server doesn't actually look up information from the grant tables for every query. Instead, it reads the contents of the tables into memory when it starts up and then verifies queries using the in-memory copies. This gives a performance boost to access-checking operations, but has a rather important side effect: If you change the contents of the grant tables directly, the server won't notice the privilege change.

For example, if you add a new MySQL user by using an INSERT statement to add a new record to the user table, the user named in the entry won't be able to connect to the server. This is something that often confuses new administrators (and sometimes more-experienced ones!), but the solution is quite simple.

Tell the server to reload the contents of the grant tables after you change them. You can do this by issuing a FLUSH PRIVILEGES statement or by executing mysqladmin flush-privileges or mysqladmin reload.

There is no need to tell the server to reload the grant tables when you use GRANT, REVOKE, or SET PASSWORD to set up or modify a user's account. The server maps those statements onto operations that modify the grant tables and then refreshes the in-memory copies of the tables automatically.

Scope Column Matching Order

The MySQL server sorts entries in the grant tables in a particular way and then tries to match incoming connections by looking through the entries in order. The first match found determines the entry that is used. It's important to understand the sorting order that MySQL uses, especially for the user table. This seems to trip up a lot of people in their attempts to understand MySQL security.

When the server reads the contents of the user table, it sorts entries according to the values in the Host and User columns. The Host column is dominant, so entries with the same Host value are sorted together and then ordered according to the User value. However, sorting is not lexical, or rather, it's only partially so. The principle to keep in mind is that literal values are preferred over patterns, and more-specific patterns are preferred over less-specific patterns. This means that if you're connecting from boa.snake.net and there are entries with Host values of boa.snake.net and %.snake.net, the first entry will be preferred. Similarly, %.snake.net is preferred over %.net, which in turn is preferred over %. Matching for IP numbers works that way, too. For a client connecting from a host with an IP number of 192.168.3.14, entries with the following Host values all match, but are preferred in the order shown:

```
192.168.3.14
192.168.3.%
192.168.%
192.%
%
```

A Privilege Puzzle

This section describes a particular scenario that demonstrates why it's useful to understand the order in which the server sorts user table entries when validating connection attempts. It also shows how to solve a problem that seems to be fairly common with new MySQL installations, at least judged by the frequency with which it comes up on the MySQL mailing list—a MySQL administrator sets up a new installation, including the default `root` and anonymous-user entries in the `user` table. A good administrator will assign passwords for the `root` accounts, but it's common to leave the anonymous users as is, with no passwords. Now, suppose the administrator wants to set up a new account for a user who will be connecting from several different hosts. The easiest way to allow this is by creating the account with `%` as the host part of the account name in the `GRANT` statement, so that the user can connect from anywhere:

```
GRANT ALL ON sampdb.* TO 'fred'@'%' IDENTIFIED BY 'cocoa';
```

The intent here is to grant the user `fred` all privileges for the `sampdb` database and allow him to connect from any host he likes. Unfortunately, the probable result is that `fred` will be able to connect from any host *except* the server host itself! For example, when `fred` connects from `boa.snake.net`, the attempt succeeds:

```
% mysql -p -u fred -h cobra.snake.net sampdb
Enter password: cocoa
mysql>
```

But if `fred` logs in on the server host `cobra.snake.net` and tries to connect, the attempt fails, even though `fred` supplies his password correctly:

```
% mysql -p -u fred sampdb
Enter password: cocoa
ERROR 1045: Access denied for user: 'fred@localhost' (Using password: YES)
```

This situation occurs if your `user` table contains the default anonymous-user entries (the entries with blank usernames). These entries are created by the `mysql_install_db` initialization script under UNIX and are present in the pre-initialized `user` table included with Windows distributions. The reason the connection fails is that when the server attempts to validate `fred`, one of the anonymous-user entries takes precedence over `fred`'s entry in the matching order. The anonymous-user entry requires the user to connect with no password (not the password `cocoa`), so a password mismatch results.

Why does this happen? To understand what's going on, it's necessary to consider both how MySQL's grant tables are set up initially and how the server uses `user` table entries to validate client connections. For example, under UNIX, when you run the `mysql_install_db` script on `cobra.snake.net` to initialize the grant tables, the resulting `user` table contains rows with `Host` and `User` values that look like this:[1]

---

1. A detailed description of the initial `user` table entries is given in the "Securing a New MySQL Installation" section in Chapter 11.

```
+-------------------+------+
| Host              | User |
+-------------------+------+
| localhost         | root |
| cobra.snake.net   | root |
| localhost         |      |
| cobra.snake.net   |      |
+-------------------+------+
```

The first two entries allow `root` to connect to the server on the local host by specifying either `localhost` or the host's actual name. The second two entries allow users to connect anonymously to the local server. After the administrator sets up the account for `fred` with the `GRANT` statement shown earlier, the user table contains the following entries:

```
+-------------------+------+
| Host              | User |
+-------------------+------+
| localhost         | root |
| cobra.snake.net   | root |
| localhost         |      |
| cobra.snake.net   |      |
| %                 | fred |
+-------------------+------+
```

But the order of the entries as shown is not the order the server uses when validating connection requests. Instead, it sorts entries by host first and then by user within host, putting more-specific values first and less-specific values last:

```
+-------------------+------+
| Host              | User |
+-------------------+------+
| localhost         | root |
| localhost         |      |
| cobra.snake.net   | root |
| cobra.snake.net   |      |
| %                 | fred |
+-------------------+------+
```

The two entries with `localhost` in the `Host` column sort together, with the entry for `root` first because that's a more specific username than the blank value. The entries with `cobra.snake.net` sort together in a similar way. Furthermore, all four of these entries have a literal `Host` value without any wildcard characters, so they all sort ahead of the entry for `fred`, which does use a wildcard character in its `Host` value. In particular, both of the anonymous user entries take precedence over `fred`'s entry in the sorting order.

The result is that when `fred` attempts to connect from the local host, one of the entries with a blank username matches before the entry containing `%` in the `Host` column. The blank password in the anonymous user entry doesn't match fred's password of cocoa, so the connection fails. One implication of this phenomenon is that it is possible for fred to connect from the local host *if he specifies no password.* But then he will be validated as an anonymous user and won't have the privileges associated with the fred@% account.

What all this means is that although it's very convenient to use wildcards when you set up an account for a user who will connect from multiple hosts, the user may have problems connecting from the local host due to the anonymous entries in the user table.

What is the solution to this problem? Actually, there are two. First, you can set up another account for fred that explicitly lists localhost as the host value:

```
GRANT ALL ON sampdb.* TO 'fred'@'localhost' IDENTIFIED BY 'cocoa';
```

If you do that, the entries in the user table will sort as follows:

```
+-----------------+------+
| Host            | User |
+-----------------+------+
| localhost       | fred |
| localhost       | root |
| localhost       |      |
| cobra.snake.net | root |
| cobra.snake.net |      |
| %               | fred |
+-----------------+------+
```

Now when fred connects from the local host, the entry with localhost and fred will match ahead of the anonymous user entries. When he connects from any other host, the entry with % and fred will match. The downside of having two entries for fred is that whenever you want to make a privilege or password change for him, you'll have to make the change twice.

The second solution is to delete the anonymous entries from the user table entirely. To do this, you cannot use REVOKE, because that only revokes privileges; it won't remove account entries from the user table. It's necessary to use DELETE instead:

```
% mysql -u root mysql
mysql> DELETE FROM user WHERE User = '';
mysql> FLUSH PRIVILEGES;
```

The sort order of the remaining entries becomes:

```
+-----------------+------+
| Host            | User |
+-----------------+------+
| localhost       | root |
| cobra.snake.net | root |
| %               | fred |
+-----------------+------+
```

Now when `fred` attempts to connect from the local host, he'll succeed, because there won't be any `user` table entries that will match ahead of his.

In general, I recommend that if you want to make your life easier as an administrator, you should delete the anonymous-user entries that are present in the initial grant tables. (In my view, these entries are generally not very useful, and they tend to cause more problems than they're worth.)

The puzzle presented in this section addresses a specific situation, but contains a more general lesson. If privileges for a given account don't work the way you expect, look in the grant tables to see if there's some entry containing `Host` values that are more specific than the entry for the user in question and that will match connection attempts by that user. If so, that may explain the problem. You may need to make the user's entry more specific or add another entry to cover the more specific case.

Grant Table Risks to Avoid

This section describes some precautions to observe when you grant privileges and the attendant risks of unwise choices.

Avoid creating anonymous user accounts. Even if they don't have privileges to cause damage directly, allowing a user to connect still may provide access to that user to look around and gather information, such as what databases and tables you have.

Find accounts that have no passwords and either remove them or assign passwords. To find such accounts, use the following query in the `mysql` database:

```
mysql> SELECT Host, User FROM user WHERE Password = '';
```

If it's not necessary, don't use patterns in hostname specifiers when setting up accounts. Broadening the range of hosts from which a given user can connect also broadens the range from which an imposter claiming to be that user can try to break in.

Grant superuser privileges sparingly. That is, don't enable privileges in `user` table entries. Those privileges are global and allow the user to affect the operation of your server or to access any table in any database. Instead, use the other grant tables to restrict user privileges to particular databases, tables, or columns.

Don't grant privileges for the `mysql` database because it contains the grant tables. A user with privileges on that database may be able to modify its tables to acquire privileges on any other database as well. In effect, granting privileges that allow a user to modify the `mysql` database tables gives that user a global `GRANT OPTION` privilege. (After all, if the user can modify the tables directly, that's pretty much equivalent to being able to issue any `GRANT` statement you can think of.)

Be careful with the GRANT OPTION privilege. Two users with different privileges that both have the GRANT OPTION privilege can make each other's access rights more powerful.

The FILE privilege is particularly dangerous; don't grant it lightly. The following is an example of something a user with the FILE privilege can do:

```
CREATE TABLE etc_passwd (pwd_entry TEXT);
LOAD DATA INFILE '/etc/passwd' INTO TABLE etc_passwd;
```

After executing those statements, the user has access to contents of your server host's password file just by issuing a SELECT:

```
SELECT * FROM etc_passwd;
```

The name of any publicly readable file on the server host can be substituted for /etc/passwd in the LOAD DATA statement. If the user has connected from a remote host, the effect is that granting the FILE privilege gives that user network access to potentially a large portion of your server host's file system.

The FILE privilege also can be exploited to compromise databases on systems that aren't set up with sufficiently restrictive data directory permissions. This is a reason why you should set the data directory contents to be readable only by the server. If files corresponding to database tables are world readable, not only can any user with an account on the server host read them, but any client user with the FILE privilege can connect over the network and read them, too! The following procedure demonstrates how:

1. Create a table with a LONGBLOB column:

   ```
   USE test;
   CREATE TABLE tmp (b LONGBLOB);
   ```

2. Use the table to read in the contents of each of the files that correspond to the table you want to steal. For example, if a user has a MyISAM table named x in a database other_db, the table is represented by three files, x.frm, x.MYD, and x.MYI. You can read those files and copy them into corresponding files in the test database as follows:

   ```
   LOAD DATA INFILE './other_db/x.frm' INTO TABLE tmp
       FIELDS ESCAPED BY '' LINES TERMINATED BY '';
   SELECT * FROM tmp INTO OUTFILE 'x.frm'
       FIELDS ESCAPED BY '' LINES TERMINATED BY '';
   DELETE FROM tmp;
   LOAD DATA INFILE './other_db/x.MYD' INTO TABLE tmp
       FIELDS ESCAPED BY '' LINES TERMINATED BY '';
   SELECT * FROM tmp INTO OUTFILE 'x.MYD'
       FIELDS ESCAPED BY '' LINES TERMINATED BY '';
   DELETE FROM tmp;
   LOAD DATA INFILE './other_db/x.MYI' INTO TABLE tmp
   ```

```
    FIELDS ESCAPED BY '' LINES TERMINATED BY '';
SELECT * FROM tmp INTO OUTFILE 'x.MYI'
    FIELDS ESCAPED BY '' LINES TERMINATED BY '';
```

3. After executing those statements, the `test` database directory also will contain files named `x.frm`, `x.MYD`, and `x.MYI`. In other words, the `test` database will contain a table x that is a stolen duplicate of the table in the `other_db` database.

To avoid having someone attack your users' tables in the same way, set the permissions on your data directory contents according to the instructions given earlier in this chapter in the "Securing Your MySQL Installation" section. As an additional measure, you can also use the `--skip-show-database` option when you start the server to limit users from using SHOW DATABASES and from using SHOW TABLES for databases to which they have no access. This helps prevent users from finding out about databases and tables they shouldn't be accessing.

The dangers of the FILE privilege are amplified if you run the MySQL server as `root`. That's inadvisable in the first place, and is particularly so when combined with FILE. Because `root` can create files anywhere in the file system, a user with the FILE privilege can do so as well, even a user who has connected from a remote host. The server won't create a file that already exists, but it's sometimes possible to create new files that will alter the operation of the server host or compromise its security. For example, if any of the `/etc/resolv.conf`, `/etc/hosts.equiv`, `/etc/hosts.lpd`, or `/etc/sudoers` files do not exist, a user who can use the MySQL server to create them can drastically change the way your server host behaves. To avoid these problems, don't run `mysqld` as `root`. (See the "Running the Server Using an Unprivileged Login Account" section in Chapter 11.)

The PROCESS privilege should be granted only to trusted MySQL accounts. With PROCESS, a user can use SHOW PROCESSLIST to see the text of queries being executed by the server. This allows a user to snoop on other users and possibly see information that should remain private.

Don't give people the RELOAD privilege who don't need it. RELOAD allows a user to issue FLUSH and RESET statements, which can be abused in several ways:

- If you have configured the server to perform update or binary update logging using a numbered sequence of files, each FLUSH LOGS statement creates a new update or binary update log file. A user with the RELOAD privilege who performs many log flushing operations can cause the server to create large numbers of files.

- A user with the RELOAD privilege can defeat the resource management mechanism by reloading the grant tables with FLUSH PRIVILEGES or with FLUSH USER_RESOURCES. Both statements reset all resource management counters to zero.

- FLUSH TABLES can be used repeatedly to cause the server to flush its open-table cache, which degrades performance by preventing the server from taking advantage of the cache. RESET QUERY CACHE has the same effect on performance by negating the benefits of the query cache.

- RESET MASTER LOGS causes a replication master server to delete all of its binary update logs whether or not they are still in use, which removes the information necessary to maintain replication integrity.

The ALTER privilege can be used in ways you may not intend. Suppose you want user1 to be able to access table1 but not table2. A user with the ALTER privilege may be able to subvert your intent by using ALTER TABLE to rename table2 to table1.

Setting Up MySQL Accounts Without GRANT Statements

If you have a version of MySQL older than 3.22.11, you can't use the GRANT (or REVOKE) statements to manage MySQL accounts and access privileges. However, you can modify the contents of the grant tables directly using statements like INSERT. It's easier to do that if you understand how the GRANT statement modifies the grant tables because you'll know what kind of INSERT statements correspond to various GRANT statements.

GRANT acts to modify the grant tables as follows:

- When you issue a GRANT statement, you specify a username and hostname and possibly a password. A user table entry is created for the user, and these values are recorded in the User, Host, and Password columns of the entry. In addition, if you specify global privileges in the GRANT statement, those privileges are recorded in the privilege columns of the user table entry.

- If you specify database-level privileges in the GRANT statement, the username and hostname are recorded in the User and Host columns of a db table entry. The database you granted privileges for is recorded in the Db column, and the privileges you granted are recorded in the privilege columns.

- For table-level and column-level privileges, the effects are similar. Entries are created in the tables_priv and columns_priv tables to record the username, hostname, and database, as well as the table or table and column as necessary. The privileges granted are recorded in the privilege columns.

If you keep the preceding description in mind, you should be able to do anything GRANT does without using GRANT itself. But remember that when you modify the grant tables directly, you'll need to tell the server to reload the grant tables or it won't notice your changes. You can force a reload by executing a mysqladmin reload command.[2] If you forget to do that, you'll be wondering why the server isn't doing what you want.

The following GRANT statement uses ON *.* to specify global privileges. It creates an account for a superuser who has all privileges, including the ability to grant privileges to other users:

```
GRANT ALL ON *.* TO 'ethel'@'localhost' IDENTIFIED BY 'coffee'
    WITH GRANT OPTION;
```

The statement will create an entry for ethel@localhost in the user table. It also will turn on all the privileges there because that's where superuser (global) privileges are stored. To do the same thing with INSERT, the statement is as follows:

```
INSERT INTO user VALUES('localhost','ethel',PASSWORD('coffee'),
    'Y','Y','Y','Y','Y','Y','Y','Y','Y','Y','Y','Y','Y','Y');
```

That's one ugly INSERT statement! You may even find that it doesn't work, depending on your version of MySQL. This statement assumes that the user table has 14 privilege columns, which is the number present at the point when GRANT was implemented. Because the structure of the grant tables has changed on occasion, you may have a different number. Use SHOW COLUMNS to find out just what privilege columns your user table contains, and adjust the INSERT statement accordingly. Note too that although the GRANT statement encrypts the password for you, INSERT does not; it's necessary to use the PASSWORD() function to encrypt passwords in your INSERT statements.

The following GRANT statement creates another account with superuser status, but for only a single privilege:

```
GRANT RELOAD ON *.* TO 'flush'@'localhost' IDENTIFIED BY 'flushpass';
```

You may remember this statement from Chapter 11 where we created an account for log file maintenance purposes that has privileges for flushing the server logs. The equivalent INSERT statement for this GRANT statement is a bit simpler than for the preceding one, so it's easier to list the column names and

---

2. The mysqladmin flush-privileges command and the FLUSH PRIVILEGES statement also tell the server to reload the grant tables, but of course if the reason you're not using GRANT is that your server is too old to support it, it's also too old to support mysqladmin flush-privileges or FLUSH PRIVILEGES.

specify only the one privilege column. Each of the other privilege columns will be set to its default value (`'N'`):

```
INSERT INTO user (Host,User,Password,Reload_priv)
    VALUES('localhost','flush',PASSWORD('flushpass'),'Y');
```

Database-level privileges are granted with an `ON` *db_name*.`*` clause rather than `ON *.*`:

```
GRANT ALL ON sampdb.* TO 'boris'@'localhost' IDENTIFIED BY 'ruby';
```

These privileges are not global, so they won't be stored in the `user` table. However, to duplicate the effect of this `GRANT` statement, it's necessary to create an entry in the `user` table so that the user can connect. This means that a `user` table entry is needed along with a `db` table entry that records the database-level privileges:

```
INSERT INTO user (Host,User,Password)
    VALUES('localhost','boris',PASSWORD('ruby'));
INSERT INTO db VALUES('localhost','sampdb','boris',
    'Y','Y','Y','Y','Y','Y','N','Y','Y','Y');
```

The `'N'` value in the second statement is for the `GRANT OPTION` privilege. Setting the column to `'Y'` instead would duplicate the effect of a database-level `GRANT` statement that has `WITH GRANT OPTION` at the end.

To set table-level or column-level privileges, use `INSERT` statements for the `tables_priv` or `columns_priv` tables. Of course, if you don't have the `GRANT` statement, you won't have those two tables, either, because they appeared in MySQL at the same time. If you do have the tables and want to manipulate them manually for some reason, be aware that you don't enable privileges using individual columns. You set either the `tables_priv.Table_priv` or `columns_priv.Column_priv` column to a `SET` value consisting of the privileges you want to enable. For example, to enable `SELECT` and `INSERT` privileges for a table, you'd set the `Table_priv` column to a value of `'Select,Insert'` in the relevant `tables_priv` entry.

If you want to modify privileges for a MySQL account that already exists, use `UPDATE` rather than `INSERT`. This is true whether you are adding or revoking privileges.

To remove an account entirely, use `DELETE` to remove entries from each grant table in which the account appears. For example, to remove an account for `mike@%.snake.net`, issue the following statements:

```
DELETE FROM user WHERE User = 'mike' AND Host = '%.snake.net';
DELETE FROM db WHERE User = 'mike' AND Host = '%.snake.net';
DELETE FROM host WHERE User = 'mike' AND Host = '%.snake.net';
```

If you also happen to have the `tables_priv` or `columns_priv` tables, issue the following statements as well:

```
DELETE FROM tables_priv WHERE User = 'mike' AND Host = '%.snake.net';
DELETE FROM columns_priv WHERE User = 'mike' AND Host = '%.snake.net';
```

If you prefer to avoid issuing queries that modify the grant tables directly, you may want to take a look at the `mysqlaccess` and `mysql_setpermissions` scripts that come with the MySQL distribution.

Setting Up Secure Connections

On UNIX, MySQL 4 provides support for secure, encrypted connections over SSL. By default, an SSL-enabled MySQL installation allows a client to ask for secure connections on an optional basis. (The tradeoff is that a normal unencrypted connection has higher performance, whereas an encrypted connection is secure but somewhat slower due to the additional computational burden that encryption imposes.) It's also possible for administrators to specify using a GRANT statement that a given account is *required* to connect securely.

Note that there is little point in using SSL for connections to the local host that are made using a UNIX socket file, a named pipe, or to the IP address `127.0.0.1` (the network loopback interface). The real benefit of SSL comes when the information that you're transmitting goes over a network that may be susceptible to snooping.

To take advantage of SSL support for encrypted connections between the server and client programs, use the following general procedure:

- Make sure the `user` table contains the SSL-related columns.
- Make sure the server and client programs have been compiled with OpenSSL support.
- Start the server with options that tell it where to find its certificate and key files; these are necessary to set up secure connections.
- To connect securely with a client program, invoke it with options that tell it where to find your certificate and key files.

The following discussion describes this process in more detail.

To use SSL for secure connections, the `user` table of the `mysql` database must contain the SSL columns described in the "Grant Table SSL-Related Columns" section in this chapter. If you have installed MySQL using version 4.0.0 or later, your `user` table should contain these columns already. If you have upgraded to MySQL 4.x from an earlier version, the columns may not be present, in which case you should run the `mysql_fix_privilege_tables` script to update the tables.

Your MySQL distribution must be built with OpenSSL included. Either get a binary distribution that has OpenSSL compiled in or build MySQL from source. In the latter case, you must have OpenSSL installed; if you need to get it, visit www.openssl.org. Then build MySQL by running `configure` with the `--with-vio` and `--with-openssl` options. After you start your OpenSSL-enabled server, verify that it supports SSL by connecting with `mysql` and issuing the following query:

```
mysql> SHOW VARIABLES LIKE 'have_openssl';
+---------------+-------+
| Variable_name | Value |
+---------------+-------+
| have_openssl  | YES   |
+---------------+-------+
```

If you don't see YES, SSL support was not enabled correctly.

When your MySQL installation has been enabled to support SSL, the server and its clients can communicate securely. Each end of a connection uses three files to set up secure communications. Briefly summarized, these files are:

- A Certificate Authority (CA) certificate. A CA is a trusted third party; its certificate is used to verify the authenticity of the client and server certificates. It's common to purchase a CA certificate from a commercial entity, but you can generate your own.
- A certificate file that authenticates one side of the connection to the other.
- A key file, used to encrypt and decrypt traffic over the connection.

The server's certificate and key files must be installed first. The `ssl` directory of the `sampdb` distribution contains some boilerplate files that you can use for this:

- `ca-cert.pem`—The Certificate Authority certificate
- `server-cert.pem`—The server's certificate
- `server-key.pem`—The server's public key

Copy these files to your server's data directory and then add some lines to the [mysqld] group of an option file that the server reads when it starts up, such as /etc/my.cnf on UNIX. The options should indicate the pathnames to the certificate and key files. For example, if the data directory is /usr/local/mysql/data, the options will be listed as follows:

```
[mysqld]
ssl-ca=/usr/local/mysql/data/ca-cert.pem
ssl-cert=/usr/local/mysql/data/server-cert.pem
ssl-key=/usr/local/mysql/data/server-key.pem
```

You can put the certificate and key files elsewhere if you like, but the location should be one that only the server has access to. After modifying the option file, restart the server.

At this point, client programs can still connect to the server only over unencrypted connections. To set up a client program to use secure connections, it's necessary to use certificate and key files on the client side as well. The `ssl` directory of the `sampdb` distribution contains files for this. You can use the same CA certificate file (`ca-cert.pem`), and the client certificate and key files are named `client-cert.pem` and `client-key.pem`. Copy these files to some directory under your own account and then add some lines to the `.my.cnf` file in your home directory to let the client program know where they are. Suppose I want to use encrypted connections for `mysql`. To do this, I'd copy the SSL files to my home directory, `/u/paul`, and then put the following lines in my `.my.cnf` file:

```
[mysql]
ssl-ca=/u/paul/ca-cert.pem
ssl-cert=/u/paul/client-cert.pem
ssl-key=/u/paul/client-key.pem
```

You can set up your own account similarly. (It's also a good precaution to make sure your certificate and key files are accessible only to yourself.) After modifying `.my.cnf` to indicate where the SSL files are located, invoke `mysql` and issue a `\s` or STATUS command. The SSL line in the output should indicate that the connection is encrypted:

```
mysql> \s
--------------
./mysql  Ver 12.10 Distrib 4.1.0-alpha, for apple-darwin5.5 (powerpc)
Connection id:          1
Current database:
Current user:           root@localhost
SSL:                    Cipher in use is EDH-RSA-DES-CBC3-SHA
...
```

You can also issue the following query to see what the SSL-related server status variables are set to:

```
SHOW STATUS LIKE 'Ssl%';
```

The presence of the SSL-related options in the [mysql] group causes `mysql` to use SSL connections by default. If you comment out those lines or remove them from your option file, `mysql` will use a regular non-encrypted connection. It's also possible to ignore the options by invoking `mysql` like this:

```
% mysql --skip-ssl
```

The SSL options in the `[mysql]` group can be copied to other program-specific groups as well if you want to use SSL for other programs. However, note that if you put the options in the general `[client]` group, that will cause any client program that doesn't understand about SSL to fail—so that may not be such a good idea.

As an alternative to listing SSL options in the option file, you can specify them on the command line. For example, in my home directory I might invoke `mysql` like this (type the command all on one line):

```
% mysql --ssl-ca=ca-cert.pem --ssl-cert=client-cert.pem
    --ssl-key=client-key.pem
```

However, that becomes burdensome if you have to do it often.

The discussion thus far describes how any account can use SSL on an optional basis. You can also disallow unencrypted connections for an account and require it to use SSL. This can be done both for new accounts and for existing accounts.

To set up a new account, use a `GRANT` statement as you normally would but add a `REQUIRE` clause that specifies the constraints that connections must satisfy. Suppose you want to set up a user named `laura` who will be connecting to the server on `cobra.snake.net` from the host `rat.snake.net` to access the `finance` database. If you want to require only that connections be encrypted, use the following statement:

```
GRANT ALL ON finance.* TO 'laura'@'rat.snake.net'
IDENTIFIED BY 'moneymoneymoney'
REQUIRE SSL;
```

For more security, use `REQUIRE X509` instead. Then `laura` must supply a valid X509 client certificate when connecting. (This will be the file named by the `ssl-cert` option.) As long as the certificate is valid, its contents don't otherwise matter. To specify more constrained requirements, use some combination of `CIPHER`, `ISSUER`, and `SUBJECT` in the `REQUIRE` clause. `CIPHER` indicates the type of encryption cipher on which you want the connection to be based. `ISSUER` or `SUBJECT` indicate that the client certificate must have been issued by a particular source or for a particular recipient. These clauses narrow the scope of otherwise-valid certificates to include only those with specific content. The following GRANT statement requires a particular issuer in the client certificate and specifies the use of EXP1024-RC4-SHA encryption:

```
GRANT ALL ON finance.* TO 'laura'@'rat.snake.net'
IDENTIFIED BY 'moneymoneymoney'
REQUIRE ISSUER '/C=US/ST=WI/L=Madison/O=sampdb/OU=CA/CN=sampdb'
CIPHER 'EXP1024-RC4-SHA';
```

To modify an existing account to require SSL connections, use a GRANT USAGE statement of the following form, where *require_options* specifies the SSL characteristics you want to enforce:

```
GRANT USAGE ON *.* TO 'user_name'@'host_name' REQUIRE require_options;
```

GRANT USAGE ON *.* leaves the account's privileges unchanged, so the statement modifies only its SSL-related attributes.

If an account currently is set to require SSL and you want to rescind the requirement, use GRANT USAGE in conjunction with REQUIRE NONE:

```
GRANT USAGE ON *.* TO 'user_name'@'host_name' REQUIRE NONE;
```

The certificate and key files in the sampdb distribution suffice to allow you to establish encrypted connections. However, they're publicly available, so connections thus established cannot truly be said to be secure. After you use these files to verify that SSL is working properly, you should replace them with ones that you generate yourself. For instructions on making your own certificate and key files, see the ssl/README file in the sampdb distribution. You may also want to consider purchasing a commercial certificate.

13

Database Backups, Maintenance, and Repair

IDEALLY, MySQL RUNS SMOOTHLY FROM THE TIME that you first install it. But problems sometimes do occur for a variety of reasons, ranging from power outages to hardware failure to improper shutdown of the MySQL server (such as when you terminate it with `kill -9` or the machine crashes). Events such as these, many of which are beyond your control, can result in damage to database tables, typically caused by incomplete writes in the middle of a change to a table. This chapter describes what you can do to minimize your risks and to be ready in case disaster strikes anyway. The techniques covered here include making database backups, performing table checking and repair operations, and how to use recovery procedures in case you do lose data. The chapter also covers database copying procedures for transferring a database to another server, because these are often are quite similar to backup techniques.

To prepare in advance for problems, take the following actions:

- Use the MySQL server's auto-recovery capabilities.
- Set up a database backup schedule. Should the worst occur and you be faced with catastrophic system failure, you'll need the backups in order to perform recovery operations. Enable your binary log, too, so that you have a record of updates that were made after the backup. The overhead associated with binary logging is negligible (perhaps 1%), so there is little reason not to enable it.

- Set up scheduled preventive maintenance that performs table checking periodically. Routine table-checking procedures can help you detect and correct minor problems before they become worse.

If table damage or data loss does occur despite your efforts, exercise your options for dealing with such problems:

- Check your tables and then fix any that are found to be corrupt if possible. Minor damage often can be taken care of with MySQL's table repair capabilities.
- For circumstances under which table checking and repair isn't sufficient to get you up and running again, perform data recovery using your backups and your binary update logs. First, use the backups to restore your tables to their state at the time of the backup. After that, use the logs to re-apply any updates that were made after the backup, to bring your tables to their state when the crash occurred.

The tools at your disposal for carrying out these tasks include the capabilities of the MySQL server itself and also several other utilities included in the MySQL distribution:

- When the server starts up, it has the ability to check tables for problems and correct many of them. This is useful when you restart the server after a crash. Some of the checks are automatic and others can be enabled at your option.
- The `mysqldump` and `mysqlhotcopy` programs help you make backups of your databases to be used should you need to recover them later.
- You can tell the server to perform several types of table maintenance and repair operations by means of SQL statements such as CHECK TABLE and REPAIR TABLE. The `mysqlcheck` utility provides a command line interface to these statements.
- Another way to check tables for problems and perform various corrective actions on them is to use the `myisamchk` and `isamchk` utilities.

Some of these programs work in cooperation with the server, such as `mysqlcheck` and `mysqldump`. They connect to the server and issue SQL statements to tell the server what kind of table checking or backup operation to perform. Others, like `myisamchk` and `isamchk`, operate directly on the files used to represent tables. However, because the server also accesses those files while it runs, such utilities act in effect as competitors to the server, and you must take steps to prevent them from interfering with each other. For example, if you're repairing a table with `myisamchk`, it's necessary to keep the server from trying to access the table at the same time. Failure to do so can result in much worse problems than those you're trying to correct!

The need to cooperate with the server arises in connection with several of the administrative tasks discussed in this chapter, from making backups to performing table repair. Therefore, the chapter begins by describing how to keep the server at bay when necessary. After that it discusses how to prepare for problems, and then how to use repair and recovery techniques if necessary.

Under UNIX, operations that require you to directly access table files or other files under the data directory should be performed while logged in as the MySQL administrator, so that you have permission to use the files. In this book, the name of that account is `mysqladm`. It's also possible to access the files as `root`, but in that case, make sure when you're done that any files you work with have the same mode and ownership as when you began.

For a full listing of the options supported by the statements and programs discussed in this chapter, see Appendix D, "SQL Syntax Reference," and Appendix E, "MySQL Program Reference."

The relationship of isamchk to myisamchk

The `myisamchk` utility that is used for MyISAM table checking and repair is discussed extensively in this chapter. Another related utility is `isamchk`, which is much like `myisamchk` but is used for ISAM tables. Direct discussion of `isamchk` is at a minimum here because, given the superior performance and features offered by MyISAM tables, ISAM tables are not used much any more. However, if you do need to work with ISAM tables, the two programs are so similar that most of the instructions in this chapter pertaining to `myisamchk` can be adapted easily for `isamchk`. Just keep the following points in mind:

- Read any `myisamchk`-related references to `.MYD` and `.MYI` data and index files that are used for MyISAM tables as references to `.ISD` and `.ISM` data and index files that are used for ISAM tables.

- You won't damage a table by telling the wrong program to check it, but the program won't do anything except issue a warning message. For example, the following command tells `isamchk` to check all the MyISAM tables in the current directory:

  ```
  % isamchk *.MYI
  ```

  But `isamchk` operates on ISAM tables, not on MyISAM tables, so the result will just be warning messages.

- `myisamchk` supports a few options that `isamchk` does not. Check Appendix E to see what they are.

Coordinating with the Server

Some types of administrative operations are performed by connecting to the server and telling it what to do. Suppose you want to perform some consistency checks or table repairs on a MyISAM table. One way to do this is to issue a CHECK TABLE or REPAIR TABLE statement and let the server do the work. In this case, the server will access the .frm, .MYD, and .MYI files that represent the table. In general, this is the best approach to take if possible. By having the server perform the requested operations, you can let it handle any issues involved in coordinating access to the table. This means that they become non-issues as far as you're concerned and you need not think about them.

Another way to check or repair the table is to invoke the myisamchk utility, which also accesses the table files. In this case, however, the table operations are done not by the server, but by a program external to it. This raises the issue of table access coordination. While myisamchk is working with the table, it's necessary to prevent the server from trying to change it at the same time. If you don't do that, it's possible that the competing efforts to access the table will damage it and make it unusable. It's obviously a bad thing for the server and myisamchk both to be writing to the table at the same time, but even having one of them read while the other program is writing isn't good, either. The program doing the reading can become confused if the table is being changed by the other program at the same time.

The same issue comes up in other contexts as well. For example, some backup techniques involve making copies of the table files. It's necessary to keep the server from changing the tables during the backup procedure to ensure consistent backup files. Some recovery methods are based on replacing damaged tables with good backup copies, in which case, you have to keep the server from accessing the table at all.

One way to keep the server from interfering with you is to bring it down; clearly, if it's not running, it can't access the tables you're working with. But administrators are understandably reluctant to take the server completely offline—after all, that makes all your other databases and tables unavailable as well. The procedures described in this section will help you avoid interaction between a running server and operations that you're performing external to the server.

To coordinate with the server, use a locking protocol. The server has two kinds of locking:

- It uses internal locking to keep requests from different clients from getting mixed up with each other—for example, to keep one client's SELECT query from being interrupted by another client's UPDATE query.

- The server also can use external locking to keep other programs from modifying table files while it's using them. This is based on the locking capabilities available for your operating system at the file system level. Normally, the reason the server uses external locking is for cooperation with programs like myisamchk during table checking operations. However, external locking doesn't work reliably on some systems, in which case you can't depend on it and should use an internal locking protocol instead. Also, external locking is useful only for operations that require read-only access to table files. You should not use it if you require read/write access. (For example, if you want to repair a table and not just check it, you should use internal locking.)

The information in this section applies when working with table types for which each table is represented by its own files, such as MyISAM, BDB, and ISAM tables. It does not apply to the InnoDB handler, which represents all InnoDB tables together within the files that make up the InnoDB tablespace.

Preventing Interactions Using Internal Locking

The locking protocols described here use the server's internal locking mechanism to prevent it from accessing a table while you work on it. The general idea is that you connect to the server with mysql and issue a LOCK TABLE statement for the table you want to use. Then, with mysql idle (that is, sitting there not doing anything with the table except keeping it locked), you do whatever you need to do with the table files. When you're done, switch back to your mysql session and release the lock to tell the server it's okay to use the table again.

The locking protocol to use depends on whether you need only read access to the table's files or read/write access. For operations that just check or copy the files, read-only access is sufficient. For operations that modify the files, such as table repair or replacing damaged files with good ones, you'll need read/write access.

The locking protocols use the LOCK TABLE and UNLOCK TABLE statements to acquire and release locks. They also use FLUSH TABLE to tell the server to flush any pending changes to disk and as a means of informing the server that it will need to reopen the table when next it accesses it. The examples use the named-table form of FLUSH TABLE that takes a table name argument and flushes just a specific table. If your version of MySQL is older than 3.23.23, you'll need to use FLUSH TABLES, which does not take a table name and flushes the entire table cache.

You *must* perform all the LOCK, FLUSH, and UNLOCK statements from within a single mysql session. If you lock a table and then quit mysql, the lock will be released. At that point, the server will consider itself free to use the table again, with the result that it is no longer safe for you to work with the table files.

It's easiest to perform the locking procedures if you keep two windows open—one for running mysql and the other for working with the table files. This allows you to leave mysql running while you do your work. If you're not using a windowing environment, you'll need to suspend and resume mysql using your shell's job control facilities while you work with the table.

Locking a Table for Read-Only Access

This protocol is appropriate for operations in which you only need to read a table's files, such as making copies of the files or checking them for inconsistencies. It's sufficient to acquire a read lock in this case; the server will prevent other clients from modifying the table but will allow them to read from it. This protocol should *not* be used when you need to modify a table.

1. In window A, invoke mysql and issue the following statements to obtain a read lock and flush the table:

   ```
   % mysql db_name
   mysql> LOCK TABLE tbl_name READ;
   mysql> FLUSH TABLE tbl_name;
   ```

   The lock prevents other clients from writing to the table and modifying it while you're checking it. The FLUSH statement causes the server to close the table files, which flushes out any unwritten changes that may still be cached.

2. With mysql sitting idle, switch to window B so you can work with the table files. For example, you can check a MyISAM table as follows:

   ```
   % myisamchk tbl_name
   ```

3. When you're done working with the table, switch back to the mysql session in window A and release the table lock:

   ```
   mysql> UNLOCK TABLE;
   ```

It's possible that your work with the table will indicate that further action is necessary. For example, if you check a table with myisamchk, it may find problems that need correction. The corrective procedure will require read/write access, which you can obtain safely using the protocol described next.

Locking a Table for Read/Write Access

This protocol is appropriate for operations such as table repair in which you actually need to modify a table's files. To do this, you must acquire a write lock to completely prevent all server access to the table while you're working on it.

The locking procedure for repairing a table is similar to procedure for checking it, with two differences. First, you must obtain a write lock rather than a read lock. You'll be modifying the table, so you can't let the server access it at all. Second, you should issue another FLUSH TABLE statement after working with the table. Some operations, such as repairing a table with myisamchk, build a new index file, and the server won't notice that unless you flush the table cache again. To lock a table for read/write access, use this procedure:

1. Invoke mysql in window A and issue the following statements to obtain a write lock and flush the table:

   ```
   % mysql db_name
   mysql> LOCK TABLE tbl_name WRITE;
   mysql> FLUSH TABLE tbl_name;
   ```

2. With mysql sitting idle, switch to window B so you can work directly with the table files. For example, you can repair a MyISAM table as follows:

   ```
   % myisamchk --recover tbl_name
   ```

   This example is for illustration only. The particular commands you issue will depend on what you're doing. (Note that it may be prudent to make copies of the table files first, in case something goes wrong.)

3. When you're done working with the table, switch back to the mysql session in window A, flush the table again, and release the table lock:

   ```
   mysql> FLUSH TABLE tbl_name;
   mysql> UNLOCK TABLE;
   ```

Locking All Databases for Read Access

A convenient way to prevent clients from making any changes to any table is to place a read lock on all tables in all databases at once. To do this, issue the following statement:

```
mysql> FLUSH TABLES WITH READ LOCK;
```

To release the lock, do this:

```
mysql> UNLOCK TABLES;
```

While the tables are locked this way, other clients can read from them but cannot make changes. This is a good way to make the server quiescent for operations such as making copies of all your database directories. On the other hand, it's unfriendly to clients that need to make updates, so you should hold the server lock no longer than necessary.

Preventing Interactions Using External Locking

In some cases, you can use external locking to coordinate with the server while you're working directly with table files. For example, if external locking is supported by your system, `myisamchk` and `isamchk` know how to use it to cooperate with the server. However, this should be used only for activities that require read-only access, such as table checking. External locking should not be relied on for operations, such as table repair, that require read/write access. External locking is based on file locking, but repair operations performed by `myisamchk` and `isamchk` copy table files to new files as they work and then use them to replace the originals. The server knows nothing of the new files, which renders useless any attempt at coordinating access by means of file locks.

External locking is disabled by default on all systems as of MySQL 4. You can enable it if you're certain that it works correctly on your system, but in general, it's better to avoid it and use internal locking instead.

To determine whether or not the server is able to use external locking, check the appropriate server variable. The variable is named `skip_external_locking` as of MySQL 4 and `skip_locking` before that, but you can check for whichever of these your server uses by issuing the following query:

```
mysql> SHOW VARIABLES LIKE 'skip%locking';
+-----------------------+-------+
| Variable_name         | Value |
+-----------------------+-------+
| skip_external_locking | ON    |
+-----------------------+-------+
```

Depending on the value of the `skip_external_locking` (or `skip_locking`) variable, proceed as follows:

- If `skip_external_locking` is `ON`, external locking is suppressed, and the server won't know when `myisamchk` or `isamchk` are accessing a table. If you need to leave the server up while working directly with the table files, it will be necessary to use internal locking to tell the server to leave the table alone. Use the protocol for read-only or read/write access as appropriate for what you're doing.

- If `skip_external_locking` is `OFF`, external locking is enabled and you can use `myisamchk` or `isamchk` for read-only operations, such as checking tables. The server and the utility will cooperate for table access. However, before running either utility, you should flush the table cache with `mysqladmin flush-tables` and you must make sure that no one attempts to update the tables until you're done with them. To repair tables, you may need to modify them, so you can't use external locking. Use the internal locking protocol for read/write access instead.

Preparing for Disaster

This section covers some general strategies that MySQL administrators can use to keep their databases intact:

- Take advantage of any auto-recovery capabilities that the server offers.
- Have a policy of making regular database backups, so that you have something to fall back on if your databases are irretrievably lost.

Another step you can take is to schedule regular preventive maintenance. Techniques for this are discussed in the "Table Repair and Data Recovery" section later in this chapter because they use the table maintenance utilities described in that section.

Using the Server's Auto-Recovery Capabilities

One of your first lines of defense in maintaining database integrity is the MySQL server's ability to perform automatic recovery at startup time. When the server begins executing, it can perform certain types of table checking to help deal with problems resulting from an earlier server or machine crash. MySQL is designed to recover from a variety of problems, so if you do nothing more than restart the server normally, it will make the necessary corrections for you in most cases. The possible actions taken by the server include the following:

- If the InnoDB table handler is enabled, it can check for a variety of problems automatically. Committed transactions that are present in the redo logs but not yet flushed to tables are rolled forward (redone). Uncommitted transactions in progress at the time of the crash are rolled back (discarded) using the undo logs. The result is to leave your InnoDB tables in a consistent state, so that their contents reflect all transactions that had been committed up to the point of the crash.

- The BDB table handler, if enabled, also attempts auto-recovery based on the contents of its log files.
- The MyISAM handler can perform automatic checking and repair operations. This is controlled by the server's `--myisam-recover=level` option, where `level` can be empty to disable checking or a comma-separated list of one or more of the following values: `DEFAULT` (same as specifying no option), `BACKUP` (create a backup of the table if it is changed), `FORCE` (force recovery even if more than a row of data will be lost), or `QUICK` (quick recovery). The `--myisam-recover` option is available as of MySQL 3.23.25.

If InnoDB or BDB auto-recovery fails due to a non-recoverable problem, the server exits after writing a message to the error log. To force the server to start up anyway so that you can attempt a manual recovery procedure, see the "Recovering the InnoDB Tablespace or BDB Tables" section later in the chapter.

No automatic table startup timetable checking is available for ISAM tables. Nor is it likely there ever will be; ISAM support in MySQL is essentially frozen because MyISAM tables are preferable. I encourage you to consider converting your ISAM tables to MyISAM tables. To convert a table to MyISAM format, use an `ALTER TABLE` statement:

```
ALTER TABLE tbl_name TYPE = MYISAM;
```

You can also use the `mysql_convert_table_format` utility to convert all tables in a database with a single command. This script is written in Perl and requires that you have DBI installed. To see how to use it, invoke it with the `--help` option.

If you don't want to convert your ISAM tables, you can arrange to check them by invoking `isamchk` before the server starts up. Also, if your server is older than 3.23.25 (prior to the introduction of `--myisam-recover`), you can check your MyISAM tables by invoking `myisamchk` before the server starts up. The "Scheduling Preventive Maintenance" section later in this chapter discusses how to arrange for table checking with these utilities before the server starts up.

Backing Up and Copying Databases

It's important to back up your databases in case tables are lost or damaged. If a serious system crash occurs, you want to be able to restore your tables to the state they were in at the time of the crash with as little data loss as possible. Likewise, a user who issues an unwise `DROP DATABASE` or `DROP TABLE` will likely show up at your door requesting that you perform data recovery. Sometimes it's even the MySQL administrator who inadvertently causes the damage, for example, by trying to edit a table file directly using an editor, such as `vi` or `emacs`. This is certain to do bad things to the table!

The techniques that are used for creating backups are also useful for copying databases to another server. Most commonly, a database is transferred to a server running on another host, but you can also transfer data to another server running on the same host. You might do this if you're running a server for a new release of MySQL and want to test it with some real data from your production server.

Another use for backups is to set up a replication server, because one of the first steps in setting up a slave server is to take a snapshot of the master server at a specific point in time. The backup serves as this snapshot, and loading it into the slave server brings it up to date with respect to the master server. Thereafter, updates made on the master server are replicated to the slave server through the standard replication protocol. The procedure for setting up replication is discussed in Chapter 11, "General MySQL Administration."

The two main methods for backing up databases are to use the `mysqldump` program or to directly copy database files (for example, with `mysqlhotcopy`, `cp`, `tar`, or `cpio`). Each method has its own advantages and disadvantages:

- `mysqldump` operates in cooperation with the MySQL server. Direct-copy methods involve file copy operations that are done external to the server, and you must take steps to ensure that the server does not modify the tables while you copy them. This is the same problem that occurs if you try to use file system backups to back up databases: If a database table is being updated during the file system backup, the table files that go into the backup may be in an inconsistent state momentarily and will be worthless for restoring the table later. However, whereas with file system backups you may have no control over the backup schedule, when you use direct-copy methods to copy tables, you can take steps to make sure the server leaves the tables alone.

- `mysqldump` is slower than direct-copy techniques because the dump operation involves transferring the information over the network. Direct-copy backup methods operate at the file system level and require no network traffic.

- `mysqldump` generates text files that are portable to other machines, even those with a different hardware architecture. Such files are therefore usable for copying databases. Files generated by direct-copy methods may or may not be portable to other machines. This depends on whether or not they correspond to tables that use a machine independent storage format.

ISAM tables do not satisfy this constraint. For example, copying files from Solaris on SPARC to Solaris on SPARC will work, but copying files from Solaris on SPARC to Solaris on Intel or to Mac OS X will not work. MyISAM and InnoDB tables normally are machine independent. For those table types, directly copied files can be moved to a server running on a machine with a different hardware architecture. For further discussion of the characteristics of various table types, including whether they are portable, see Chapter 3, "MySQL SQL Syntax and Use."

Whichever backup method you choose, there are certain principles to which you should adhere to assure the best results if you ever need to restore database contents:

- Perform backups regularly. Set a schedule and stick to it.
- Tell the server to perform binary update logging (see the "Maintaining Log Files" section in Chapter 11). The binary logs can help when you need to restore databases after a crash. After you use your backup files to restore the databases to the state they were in at the time of the backup, you can re-apply the changes that occurred after the backup was made by running the queries contained in the logs. This restores the tables in the databases to their state at the time the crash occurred.
- Use a consistent and understandable naming scheme for your backup files. Names like `backup1`, `backup2`, and so forth are not particularly meaningful; when it comes time to perform a restore operation, you'll waste time figuring out what's in the files. You may find it useful to construct backup filenames using database names and dates—for example:

```
% mysqldump sampdb > /archive/mysql/sampdb.2002-10-02
% mysqldump menagerie > /archive/mysql/menagerie.2002-10-02
```

- Expire your backup files periodically to keep them from filling your disk. One way to do this is use the log file rotation techniques discussed in Chapter 11. You can apply the same principles to backup file expiration as well.
- Back up your backup files using file system backups. If you have a complete crash that wipes out not only your data directory but also the disk drive containing your database backups, you'll be in real trouble. Back up your logs, too.
- Put your backup files on a different file system than the one you use for your databases. This reduces the likelihood of filling up the file system containing the data directory as a result of generating backups. Also, if this file system is on another drive, you further reduce the extent of damage that can be caused by drive failure, because loss of any one drive cannot destroy both your data directory and your backups.

Using mysqldump to Back Up and Copy Databases

When you use the `mysqldump` program to generate database backup files, the file is written in SQL format by default, consisting of CREATE TABLE statements that create the tables being dumped and INSERT statements containing the data for the rows in the tables. To re-create the database later, you can take the `mysqldump` output file and use it as input to `mysql` to reload it into MySQL. (Note that you do *not* use `mysqlimport` to read SQL-format `mysqldump` output!)

You can dump an entire database into a single text file as follows:

```
% mysqldump sampdb > /archive/mysql/sampdb.2002-10-02
```

The beginning of the output file will look something like this:

```
-- MySQL dump 9.06
--
-- Host: localhost    Database: sampdb
-------------------------------------------------------------
-- Server version    4.0.3-beta-log
--
-- Table structure for table 'absence'
--
CREATE TABLE absence (
  student_id int(10) unsigned NOT NULL default '0',
  date date NOT NULL default '0000-00-00',
  PRIMARY KEY  (student_id,date)
) TYPE=MyISAM;
--
-- Dumping data for table 'absence'
--
INSERT INTO absence VALUES (3,'2002-09-03');
INSERT INTO absence VALUES (5,'2002-09-03');
INSERT INTO absence VALUES (10,'2002-09-06');
...
```

The rest of the file consists of more CREATE TABLE and INSERT statements.

Backup files often are large, so you'll likely want to do what you can to make them smaller. One way to do this is to use the `--opt` option, which optimizes the dump process to generate a smaller file:

```
% mysqldump --opt sampdb > /archive/mysql/sampdb.2002-10-02
```

You can also compress the dump file. For example, to compress the backup as you generate it, use a command like the following:

```
% mysqldump --opt sampdb | gzip > /archive/mysql/sampdb.2002-10-02.gz
```

If you find large dump files difficult to manage, it's possible to dump the contents of individual tables by naming them after the database name on the `mysqldump` command line. Then `mysqldump` will dump just the named tables rather than all the tables in the database. This partitions the dump into smaller, more manageable files. The following example shows how to dump some of the `sampdb` tables into separate files:

```
% mysqldump --opt sampdb student score event absence > gradebook.sql
% mysqldump --opt sampdb member president > hist-league.sql
```

`--opt` is useful when you're generating backup files that are intended to be used to periodically refresh the contents of another database. That's because it automatically enables the `--add-drop-table` option, which tells `mysqldump` to precede each CREATE TABLE statement in the file with a DROP TABLE IF EXISTS statement for the same table. Then, when you take the backup file and load it into the second database, you won't get an error if the tables already exist. If you're running a second test server that's not a replication slave, you can use this technique to periodically reload it with a copy of the data from the databases on your production server.

If you want to transfer a database to another server, you may not even need to create backup files. Make sure that the database exists on the other host and then dump the database over the network using a pipe so that `mysql` reads the output of `mysqldump` directly. For example, to copy the `sampdb` database from the local host to the server on `boa.snake.net`, do so like this:

```
% mysqladmin -h boa.snake.net create sampdb
% mysqldump --opt sampdb | mysql -h boa.snake.net sampdb
```

If you don't have a MySQL account on the local host that allows you to access the `boa.snake.net` server, but you do have such an account on `boa.snake.net` itself, use `ssh` to remotely invoke MySQL commands on that host:

```
% ssh boa.snake.net mysqladmin create sampdb
% mysqldump --opt sampdb | ssh boa.snake.net mysql sampdb
```

Later, if you want to refresh the `sampdb` database on `boa.snake.net`, repeat the `mysqldump` command.

Other `mysqldump` options you may find useful include the following:

- The combination of `--flush-logs` and `--lock-tables` is helpful for checkpointing your database. `--lock-tables` locks all the tables that you're dumping, and `--flush-logs` closes and reopens the log files. If you're generating sequenced update or binary update logs, the new log will contain only those queries that modify databases subsequent to the checkpoint. This synchronizes your log to the time of the backup. (Locking all the tables is not so good for client access during the backups if you have clients that need to perform updates, however.)

If you use `--flush-logs` to checkpoint the logs to the time of the backup, it's probably best to dump the entire database. During restore operations, it's common to extract log contents on a per-database basis. If you dump individual tables, it's much more difficult to synchronize log checkpoints against your backup files. (There is no option for extracting updates for individual tables, so you'll have to extract them yourself.)

- By default, `mysqldump` reads the entire contents of a table into memory before writing it out. This isn't really necessary and, in fact, is almost a recipe for failure if you have really large tables. You can use the `--quick` option to tell `mysqldump` to write each row as soon as it has been retrieved. To further optimize the dump process, use `--opt` instead of `--quick`. The `--opt` option turns on other options that speed up dumping the data. In addition, the dump file is written in such a way that it can be processed more quickly later when loaded back into the server.

  Performing backups using `--opt` is probably the most common method because of the benefits for backup speed. Be warned, however, that the `--opt` option does have a price; what `--opt` optimizes is your backup procedure, not access by other clients to the database. The `--opt` option prevents anyone from updating any of the tables that you're dumping by locking all the tables at once. You can easily see for yourself the effect of this on general database access. Just try making a backup at the time of day when your database is normally most heavily used. It won't take long for your phone to start ringing with people calling to find out what's going on. (I'd appreciate it if you would refrain from asking how it is that I happen to know this.)

- An option that has something of the opposite effect of `--opt` is `--delayed`. This option causes `mysqldump` to write INSERT DELAYED statements rather than INSERT statements. If you are loading a dump file into another database and you want to minimize the impact of the operation on other queries that may be taking place in that database, `--delayed` is helpful for achieving that end.

- Normally you name a database on the `mysqldump` command line, optionally followed by specific table names. To dump several databases at once, use the `--databases` option. Then `mysqldump` will interpret all names as database names and dump all the tables in each of them. To dump all of a server's databases, use `--all-databases`. In this case, you supply no database or table name arguments. Be careful with the `--all-databases` option if you intend to load the dump output into another server; the dump will include the grant tables in the `mysql` database, and you may not really want to replace the other server's grant tables.

- The `--compress` option is helpful when copying a database to another machine because it reduces the number of bytes traveling over the network:

```
% mysqldump --opt sampdb | mysql --compress -h boa.snake.net sampdb
```

Notice that the `--compress` option is given for the program that communicates with the server on the remote host, not the one that communicates with the local host. Compression applies only to network traffic; it does not cause compressed tables to be created in the destination database.

- By default, `mysqldump` dumps both table structure (the CREATE TABLE statements) and table contents (the INSERT statements). To dump just one or the other, use the `--no-create-info` or `--no-data` options.

`mysqldump` has many other options as well. Consult Appendix E for more information.

Using Direct-Copy Database Backup and Copying Methods

Another way to back up a database or tables that doesn't involve `mysqldump` is to copy table files directly. Typically, this is done using utilities such as cp, tar, or cpio. When you use a direct-copy backup method, you must make sure the tables aren't being used. If the server is changing a table while you're copying it, the copies will be worthless. The best way to ensure the integrity of your copies is to bring down the server, copy the files, and restart the server. If you don't want to bring down the server, use the read-access locking protocol described in the "Coordinating with the Server" section earlier in this chapter. That will prevent the server from changing the tables while you're copying them.

Assuming that the server is either down or that you've read-locked the tables you want to copy, the following example shows how to back up the entire `sampdb` database to a backup directory. If the data directory is `/usr/local/mysql/data`, the commands look like this:

```
% cd /usr/local/mysql/data
% cp -r sampdb /archive/mysql
```

Individual tables can be backed up as follows:

```
% cd /usr/local/mysql/data/sampdb
% cp member.* /archive/mysql/sampdb
% cp score.* /archive/mysql/sampdb
...
```

When you're done backing up, you can restart the server if you brought it down. If you left the server running and locked the tables, you can release the locks.

Direct-copy methods apply to copying a database from one machine to another, too. For example, you can use scp rather than cp. If the data directory on boa.snake.net is /var/mysql/data, the following commands copy the sampdb database directory to that host:

```
% cd /usr/local/mysql/data
% scp -r sampdb boa.snake.net:/var/mysql/data
```

Note that copying databases to another host this way involves some additional constraints:

- Both machines must have the same hardware architecture, or the tables you're copying must all be of a portable table type. The resulting tables on the second host may appear to have very strange contents otherwise.

- You must prevent the servers on *both* hosts from attempting to change the files while you're copying them. The safest approach is to bring down both servers while you're working with the tables.

- Direct-copy methods, such as those just described, work best for table types like MyISAM and ISAM that represent a given table with a unique set of files in the database directory. For types such as InnoDB, you must observe additional precautions. See the "Backing Up the InnoDB Tablespace or BDB Tables" section later in this chapter.

Making Backups with mysqlhotcopy

As of version 3.23.11, MySQL distributions include mysqlhotcopy, a Perl DBI script that helps you make database backups. The "hot" in the name refers to the fact that the backups are made while the server is running; you need not take it offline.

mysqlhotcopy has the following principal benefits:

- It's faster than mysqldump because it directly copies the files rather than requesting them through the server the way mysqldump does. (This means that you must run it on the server host; it does not work with remote servers.)

- It's convenient because it automatically manages for you the locking protocol necessary to keep the server from changing the tables while they're being copied. mysqlhotcopy does this using internal locking (described earlier in the "Coordinating with the Server" section).

- It can flush the logs, which synchronizes the checkpoints for the backup files and the logs and makes it easier to use the backups for recovery, should that be necessary later.

There are several ways to invoke mysqlhotcopy. Suppose you want to copy the sampdb database. The following command will create a directory sampdb_copy in the server's data directory and copy the files in the sampdb database directory into it:

```
% mysqlhotcopy sampdb
```

To copy the database into a directory named sampdb under a directory you specify, specify that directory after the database name. For example, to copy the sampdb database to a directory /archive/2002-09-12/sampdb, use the following command:

```
% mysqlhotcopy sampdb /archive/2002-09-12
```

To find out what mysqlhotcopy will do for any given command, include the -n option in your invocation syntax. This runs mysqlhotcopy in "no execution" mode, such that it just prints commands rather than executing them.

Making Backups with BACKUP TABLE

The BACKUP TABLE statement, available as of MySQL 3.23.25, provides a way to back up individual tables by having the server itself copy the table's files. It works for MyISAM tables only. To use this statement, name the files you want to back up and a path to the directory *on the server host* where you want the files copied. For example,

```
BACKUP TABLE tbl1, tbl2, tbl3 TO '/archive/sampdb';
```

The directory must exist and be writable to the server, you must have the FILE privilege and also the SELECT privilege for the tables. BACKUP TABLE flushes each table to cause any pending changes to be written to disk and then copies each table's .frm and .MYD description and data files from the database directory. It does not copy the .MYI index file, because that can be rebuilt from the other two files.

BACKUP TABLE locks the tables one at a time. This means that for a multiple-table backup, it's possible for the backup files to be different than the actual state of the tables when the statement finishes. Suppose you're backing up tbl1 and tbl2. BACKUP TABLE will lock tbl1 only while backing it up, so it might be modified while tbl2 is being backed up. This means that when BACKUP TABLE finishes, the contents of tbl1 will differ from the contents of the backup files. To make sure that the backup files as a group match the contents of the corresponding tables, disable modifications to any of the tables for the duration of the BACKUP TABLE statement by read-locking them all. Issue an UNLOCK TABLES statement afterward to release the locks—for example:

```
LOCK TABLES tbl1 READ, tbl2 READ;
BACKUP TABLE tbl1, tbl2 TO 'backup_dir_path';
UNLOCK TABLES;
```

A table that has been backed up with BACKUP TABLE can be reloaded into the server with RESTORE TABLE, as described in the "Table Repair and Data Recovery" section later in this chapter.

Backing Up the InnoDB Tablespace or BDB Tables

InnoDB and BDB tables can be dumped using mysqldump, just like any other kind of tables. You can also use direct-copy methods, but take care to observe the following special requirements:

- InnoDB tables are not represented using separate files (except that each has a .frm description file). Instead, they are all represented together within the InnoDB tablespace, which is a set of one or more large files. To directly copy the InnoDB tablespace, copy all of its component files. You should do this after the server has been shut down to make sure that the InnoDB handler has committed any pending transactions. For completeness, you should also copy all the .frm files corresponding to InnoDB tables, the InnoDB log files, and the option file in which the tablespace configuration is specified. (Make a copy of the option file because you'll want it for reinitializing the tablespace should you suffer loss of the current option file.)

  Another method is to use InnoDB Hot Backup, available from innodb.com. This is a commercial tool that allows you to make InnoDB backups with the server running.

- To directly copy BDB tables, you should copy all BDB tables managed by the server, and you must also copy the BDB log files. Do this when the server has been shut down. The BDB handler requires the logs to be present when the server starts up, which means that should it be necessary to restore BDB tables, you'll need to provide the logs as well. BDB log files are created in the data directory by default and have names of the form log.nnnnnnnnnn with a 10-digit suffix.

Using Replication to Help Make Backups

Making backups is important, but it introduces a conflict of interest into your duties as a MySQL administrator. On the one hand, you want to maximize the availability of your server to the members of your user community, which includes allowing them to make database updates. On the other hand, for recovery purposes, backups are most useful if you make sure your backup file and log file checkpoints are synchronized. These goals conflict because the best way to synchronize backup and log checkpoints is by flushing the logs when you make the backup, combined with making sure no updates occur by either bringing the server down or locking all the tables at once (for example, with the `--opt` option to `mysqldump`). Unfortunately, disallowing updates reduces client access to the tables for the duration of the backup.

If you have a replication slave server set up, it can help you resolve this conflict. Rather than making backups on the master server, use the slave server instead. Then you need not bring down the master or otherwise make it unavailable to clients during the backup. Instead, suspend replication on the slave server with `SLAVE STOP` and make a backup from the slave. (If you are using a direct-copy backup method, issue a `FLUSH TABLES` statement as well.) Afterward, re-enable replication with `SLAVE START` and the slave will catch up on any updates made by the master server during the backup period. Depending on your backup method, you may not even need to suspend replication. For example, if you're backing up only a single database, you can use `mysqlhotcopy` or `mysqldump` with the appropriate options to lock all the tables at once. In that case, the slave server can stay up, but it won't attempt any updates to the locked tables during the backup. When the backup is done and the locks are released, the slave resumes update processing automatically.

Using a Backup to Rename a Database

MySQL has no command for renaming a database, but you can still do so. Dump the database with `mysqldump`, create a new empty database with the new name, and then reload the dump file into the new database. After that you can drop the old database. The following example shows how to rename `db1` to `db2`:

```
% mysqldump db1 > db1.sql
% mysqladmin create db2
% mysql db2 < db1.sql
% mysqladmin drop db1
```

An easier way to rename a database is to bring down the server, rename the database directory, and restart the server. However, this strategy can be used only if you have no BDB or InnoDB tables in the database. It doesn't work for BDB tables because the pathname to each table is encoded in its .db file. Nor does it work for InnoDB tables because the database name for each table is stored in the InnoDB tablespace, which is unaffected by renaming the database directory.

Whichever method you use for renaming a database, remember that access rights to it are controlled through the grant tables in the mysql database. If any of the grant tables have entries that refer specifically to the database that was renamed, you'll need to adjust the entries appropriately to refer to the new name. For a database renamed from db1 to db2, the statements to use look like this:

```
mysql> UPDATE db SET Db = 'db2' WHERE Db = 'db1';
mysql> UPDATE tables_priv SET Db = 'db2' WHERE Db = 'db1';
mysql> UPDATE columns_priv SET Db = 'db2' WHERE Db = 'db1';
mysql> UPDATE host SET Db = 'db2' WHERE Db = 'db1';
```

No such statement is needed for the user table, because it has no Db column.

Table Repair and Data Recovery

Database damage occurs for a number of reasons and varies in extent. If you're lucky, you may simply have minor damage to a table or two (for example, if your machine goes down briefly due to a power outage). In this case, it's likely that the server can repair the damage when it comes back up. If you're not so lucky, you may have to replace your entire data directory (for example, if a disk died and took your data directory with it). Recovery is also needed under other circumstances, such as when users mistakenly drop databases or tables or delete a table's contents. Whatever the reason for these unfortunate events, you'll need to perform some sort of recovery:

- If tables are damaged but not lost, try to repair them using the CHECK TABLE statement or with the mysqlcheck or myisamchk utilities. You may not need to resort to using backup files at all if the damage is such that a repair operation can fix it.

- If tables are lost or irreparable, you'll need to restore them.

The first part of this section describes table checking and repair procedures you can use to deal with more minor forms of damage. This includes interactive procedures to be used as needed and non-interactive procedures to be used for setting up scheduled preventive maintenance. The second part of the section discusses how to recover tables and databases if you lose them entirely or they are damaged beyond repair.

Checking and Repairing Database Tables

If you suspect that table corruption has occurred, the general procedure for damage detection and correction is as follows:

1. Check the table for errors. If the table checks okay, you're done. If not, you must repair it.

2. Make copies of the table files before beginning repair, just in case something goes wrong. That is unlikely, but if it happens, you can make a new copy of the table from the copied files and try a different recovery method.

3. Try to repair the table. If the repair operation succeeds, you're done. If not, restore the table from your database backups and update logs.

The final step of this procedure assumes that you've been performing database backups and have binary update logging enabled. If that's not true, you're living dangerously. Read the discussion earlier in this chapter that describes how to make backups. Also, read Chapter 11 to find out how to enable the log. You don't ever want to be in the position of having irretrievably lost a table because you were lax about saving the information necessary to restore it.

You can check or repair tables by using `myisamchk`, which operates on the table files directly. Or you can tell the server to check or repair tables using the `CHECK TABLE` or `REPAIR TABLE` statements (or by using `mysqlcheck`, which .connects to the server and issues these statements for you). An advantage of using the SQL statements or `mysqlcheck` is that the server does the work for you. If you run `myisamchk`, you must ensure that the server stays away from the table files while you're working on them.

As mentioned earlier in the chapter, if you have a choice between letting the server do the work and running an external utility, let the server do the work. Then you don't have to worry about issues of table access coordination. The primary reasons you might decide to use an external program, such as `myisamchk`, are as follows:

- You can use it when the server is down. `CREATE TABLE` and `REPAIR TABLE` require that the server be running.

- You can tell `myisamchk` to use larger buffers to make checking and repair operations run faster. This can be helpful if you have very large tables.

- `myisamchk` can be used with older servers. `CHECK TABLE` and `REPAIR TABLE` were introduced in MySQL 3.23.13 and 3.23.14, respectively, whereas `myisamchk` is available back to 3.23.0. (Of course, this particular distinction becomes less relevant as time passes and servers older than 3.23.13 become less common.)

Note: The information given here for `myisamchk` can be adapted for use with `isamchk`. See the "The relationship of `isamchk` to `myisamchk`" section near the beginning of this chapter.

Checking and Repairing Tables Using myisamchk

Before you use `myisamchk` to check or repair tables, you may want to bring down the server so that it doesn't access the table files while you're using them. If you want to leave the server running, make sure you read the "Coordinating with the Server" section earlier in this chapter. That section discusses the appropriate locking protocols to use to prevent the server from using a table at the same time you're performing checking or repair procedures on it.

Invoking myisamchk

`myisamchk` makes no assumptions about where tables are located; to run it, you specify the pathnames to the table files you want to use. It's most convenient to do this if you're in the directory that contains the tables, so typically you change location into the relevant database directory first before invoking `myisamchk`. Then tell it which tables you want to check or repair, along with the options that indicate what type of operation to perform:

```
% myisamchk options tbl_name ...
```

A `tbl_name` argument can be either a table name or the name of the table's index file. This means you can use a filename pattern based on the index file extension to name pick up all the relevant files in the current directory:

```
% myisamchk options *.MYI
```

If you don't want to use the original table files, you can copy them to another directory and then work with the copies in that directory.

Checking Tables with myisamchk

`myisamchk` provides table-checking methods that vary in how thoroughly they examine a table. To perform a normal table check, use either of the following commands:

```
% myisamchk tbl_name
% myisamchk --check tbl_name
```

`myisamchk`'s default action with no options is `--check`, so those commands are equivalent.

The normal check method is usually sufficient to identify problems. If it reports no errors but you still suspect damage (perhaps because queries do not seem to be working properly), you can perform a more extensive check by specifying the --extend-check option. This can be very slow, but it is extremely thorough; for each record in the table's data file, the associated key for every index in the index file is checked to make sure it really points to the correct record. (myisamchk also supports a --medium-check option to perform an intermediate check that is less thorough but faster than extended checking.)

If no errors are reported for a check with --extend-check, you can be sure your table is okay. If you still have problems with the table, the cause must lie elsewhere. Re-examine any queries that seem to yield problematic results to verify that they are written correctly. If you believe the problem may be with the MySQL server, consider filing a bug report or upgrading to a newer version.

If myisamchk reports that a table has errors, you should try to repair it.

Repairing Tables with myisamchk

Table repair is an ugly business, made more so by the fact that the details tend to be very incident-specific. Nevertheless, there are general guidelines and procedures you can follow to significantly increase your chances of being able to fix the tables. Generally, you begin with the fastest repair method to see if that will correct the damage. If you find that it is not sufficient, you can escalate to more thorough (but slower) repair methods until either the damage has been repaired or you cannot escalate further. (In practice, most problems are fixable without going to more extensive and slower repair modes.) If the table cannot be repaired, you'll need to restore the table from your backups. Instructions for recovery using backup files and log files are given later in this chapter.

To perform a standard repair operation on a table, use the following procedure:

1. Try to fix the table using the --recover option, and use the --quick option as well to attempt recovery based only on the contents of the index file. This will repair the table without touching the data file:

   ```
   % myisamchk --recover --quick tbl_name
   ```

2. If problems remain, rerun the command without the --quick option to allow myisamchk to go ahead and modify the data file, too:

   ```
   % myisamchk --recover tbl_name
   ```

3. If that doesn't work, try the --safe-recover repair mode. This is slower than regular recovery mode, but is capable of fixing a few problems that --recover mode will not:

   ```
   % myisamchk --safe-recover tbl_name
   ```

It's possible when you run these commands that `myisamchk` will stop with an error message of the form `Can't create new temp file:` *file_name*. If that happens, repeat the command and add the `--force` option to force removal of the temporary file that may have been left around from a previous failed repair attempt.

If the standard repair procedure fails to repair the table, your index file may be missing or damaged beyond repair. It's also possible, though unlikely, that the table description file is missing. In either of these cases, you'll need to replace the affected files and then try the standard repair procedure again.

To regenerate the index file for a table `t`, use this procedure:

1. Move into the database directory that contains the crashed table.
2. Move the table's data file, `t.MYD`, to a safe place.
3. Invoke `mysql` and re-create a new empty table by executing the following statement, which uses the table description file, `t.frm`, to regenerate new data and index files from scratch:

   ```
   mysql> TRUNCATE TABLE t;
   ```

   Prior to MySQL 4.0, use `DELETE` instead:

   ```
   mysql> DELETE FROM t;
   ```

4. Exit `mysql` and move the original data file back into the database directory, replacing the new empty data file you just created. The data file and the index file now will be out of sync, but the index file now has a legal internal structure that the server can be interpret and rebuild based on the contents of the data file and table description file.
5. Attempt a standard table repair again.

To recover the table description file, `t.frm`, restore it from your backup files and then attempt a standard repair again. If for some reason you have no backup but you know the `CREATE TABLE` statement that must be issued to create the table, you still may be able to repair it:

1. Move into the database directory that contains the crashed table.
2. Move the table's data file, `t.MYD`, to a safe place. If you want to try to use the index file, `t.MYI`, move that, too.
3. Invoke `mysql` and issue the `CREATE TABLE` statement that creates the table.
4. Exit `mysql` and move the original data file back into the database directory, replacing the new data file you just created. If you moved the index file in step 2, move it back into the database directory, too.
5. Attempt a standard table repair again.

Getting myisamchk to Run Faster

myisamchk can take a long time to run, especially if you're working with a big table or using one of the more-extensive checking or repair methods. You can speed up this process by telling myisamchk to use more memory when it runs. myisamchk has several operating parameters that can be set. The most important of these variables control the sizes of the buffers that it uses:

Variable	Meaning
key_buffer_size	Size of buffer used to hold index blocks
read_buffer_size	Size of buffer used for read operations
sort_buffer_size	Size of buffer used for sorting
write_buffer_size	Size of buffer used for write operations

To find out what values myisamchk uses for these variables by default, run it with the --help option. To specify a different value, use --set-variable *variable=value* or -O *variable=value* on the command line. You can abbreviate the variable names as key, read, sort, and write. For example, if you have lots of memory, you can tell myisamchk to use a 512MB sort buffer and 1MB read and write buffers by invoking it like this:

```
% myisamchk -O sort=512M -O read=1M -O write=1M other-options tbl_name
```

sort_buffer_size is used only with the --recover option (not with --safe_recover), and in that case, key_buffer_size is not used.

Checking and Repairing Tables Using the Server

The CHECK TABLE and REPAIR TABLE statements provide a SQL interface to the server's table checking and repair capabilities. They work for MyISAM tables. As of MySQL 3.23.39, CHECK TABLE also works for InnoDB tables.

For each statement, you provide a list of one or more table names followed by options to indicate what type of check or repair mode to use. For example, the following statement performs a medium level check on three tables, but only if they have not been properly closed:

```
CHECK TABLE tbl1, tbl2, tbl3 FAST MEDIUM;
```

The following statement tries to repair the same tables in quick repair mode:

```
REPAIR TABLE tbl1, tbl2, tbl3 QUICK;
```

CHECK TABLE allows the following options to specify what type of check to perform:

- CHANGED

  Don't check tables unless they were not properly closed or have been changed since the last time they were checked.

- EXTENDED

  Perform an extensive check. This is the most thorough check available and consequently the slowest. It attempts to verify that the data rows and the indexes are fully consistent.

- FAST

  Don't check tables unless they were not properly closed.

- MEDIUM

  Perform a medium-level check. This is the default if you specify no options.

- QUICK

  Perform a quick check that scans only the index rows. It does not check the data rows.

It's possible that CHECK TABLE will actually modify a table in some cases. For example, if a table was marked as corrupt or as not having been closed properly but the check finds no problems, CHECK TABLE will mark the table as okay. This change involves only modifying an internal flag.

REPAIR TABLE allows the following options to specify the repair mode:

- EXTENDED

  Attempt a repair by recreating the indexes. (This is like using the --safe-recover option with myisamchk.)

- QUICK

  Attempt a quick repair of just the indexes.

- USE_FRM

  Attempt a repair using the table's .frm description file. The repair recreates the index based on the table description. Essentially, it automates the procedure described earlier that uses the .frm file to rebuild the index from the table description under circumstances when the index file is missing or unusable, and this can be useful if the index has been lost or corrupted. This option was introduced in MySQL 4.0.2.

With no options, REPAIR TABLE performs a standard repair operation like that done by myisamchk --recover.

The mysqlcheck utility provides a command line interface to the CHECK TABLE and REPAIR TABLE statements. This program connects to the server and issues the appropriate statements for you based on the options you specify. It is available as of MySQL 3.23.38. It can check MyISAM tables (and InnoDB tables, as of MySQL 3.23.39).

Typically, you invoke mysqlcheck with a database name, optionally followed by one or more table names. With just a database name, mysqlcheck checks all the tables in the database:

```
% mysqlcheck sampdb
```

With table names following the database name, it checks only those tables:

```
% mysqlcheck sampdb president member
```

If you specify the --databases option, all following names are interpreted as database names and mysqlcheck checks all the tables in each one:

```
% mysqlcheck --databases sampdb test
```

If you specify --all-databases, mysqlcheck checks all tables in all databases. In this case, you supply no database or table name arguments:

```
% mysqlcheck --all-databases
```

By default, mysqlcheck checks tables using a standard check but supports options that allow you to be more specific about the type of operation to perform. The following table shows some mysqlcheck options and the CHECK TABLE options to which they correspond:

mysqlcheck Option	**CHECK TABLE Option**
--check-only-changed	CHANGED
--extended	EXTENDED
--fast	FAST
--medium-check	MEDIUM
--quick	QUICK

mysqlcheck can also perform table repair operations. The following table shows some mysqlcheck options and the REPAIR TABLE options to which they correspond:

mysqlcheck Option	**REPAIR TABLE Option**
--repair	No options (performs a standard repair operation)
--repair --quick	QUICK
--repair --extended	EXTENDED

mysqlcheck provides a convenience over issuing the CHECK TABLE and REPAIR TABLE statements directly because those statements require that you explicitly name each table to be checked or repaired. mysqlcheck looks up the table names and constructs for you statements that name the appropriate tables.

Scheduling Preventive Maintenance

In addition to enabling auto-recovery and instituting backup procedures, as described earlier in this chapter, you should consider setting up a schedule of preventive maintenance. This helps detect problems automatically so that you can take steps to correct them. By arranging to check your tables on a regular basis, you'll reduce the likelihood of having to resort to your backups. This is most easily accomplished by using a cron job, typically invoked from the crontab file of the account used to run the server. For example, if you run the server as the mysqladm user, you can set up periodic check from the crontab file for mysqladm. (See Chapter 11 for information about setting up cron jobs.)

To check MyISAM and InnoDB tables automatically on a periodic basis while the server is online, use the mysqlcheck utility. Suppose you want to invoke mysqlcheck from the crontab file for the mysqladm user. Add an entry to that file that looks something like the following:

```
0 3 * * 0 /usr/local/mysql/bin/mysqlcheck --all-databases
    --check-only-changed --silent
```

(The command as shown here takes two lines, but you should write it all on a single line.) This entry tells cron to run mysqlcheck at 3 a.m. every Sunday. You can vary the time or scheduling as desired.

The --all-databases option causes mysqlcheck to check all tables in all databases. This gives you an easy way to use it for maximum effect.

The --check-only-changed option tells mysqlcheck to skip any table that hasn't been modified since it was last checked successfully, and the --silent option suppresses output unless there are errors in the tables. (cron jobs typically generate a mail message if a job produces any output at all, and there's little reason to receive mail for table-checking jobs that find no problems.) But note that even with --silent you may get some diagnostic output from mysqlcheck if your databases have tables of types that it doesn't know how to check.

If you have ISAM tables or if you have MyISAM tables but an older version of MySQL that doesn't include mysqlcheck, you can use isamchk and myisamchk to check tables. To perform an automatic table check, write a simple script that runs those utilities on all the MyISAM and ISAM tables under a given directory. The following script illustrates one way to do this:

```
#! /bin/sh
# chk_mysql_tables.sh - check all MyISAM/ISAM tables under a given directory

# Argument 1: directory pathname

if [ $# -ne 1 ]; then
    echo "Usage: $0 dirname" 1>&2
    exit 1
fi

# Change location to directory, check tables under it.
# Notes:
# - Prior to MySQL 3.23.22, change --check-only-changed to --fast
# - isamchk does not support --check-only-changed or --fast

cd $1
if [ $? -ne 0 ]; then
    echo "Cannot cd to $1" 1>&2
    exit 1
fi
find . -name "*.MYI" -follow -print \
    | xargs myisamchk --silent --check-only-changed
find . -name "*.ISM" -follow -print \
    | xargs isamchk --silent
```

To use only one of the table checking utilities in this script, just omit the commands for the other. For example, if you have no ISAM tables, you can omit the isamchk command because in that case, find will provide it with no filenames and isamchk will display a usage message indicating that you need to specify some arguments.

Make the script executable with chmod +x and then invoke it with the pathname of your data directory to check all your MyISAM and ISAM tables:

```
% chk_mysql_tables.sh /usr/local/mysql/data
```

To check just the tables in a given database, invoke the script with the pathname to the corresponding database directory:

```
% chk_mysql_tables.sh /usr/local/mysql/data/sampdb
```

To invoke the script automatically, set it up as a cron job. If you run multiple servers on your system, you can run chk_mysql_tables.sh multiple times, each time with a different data directory argument.

Ideally, there will be no output from `chk_mysql_tables.sh`. However, if external locking is disabled (which it is by default as of MySQL 4), it's possible that the server will change a table while you're checking it. The script just checks the tables without attempting to repair them, so this won't cause any damage, but the `myisamchk` or `isamchk` utilities may falsely report problems for tables that are actually okay. (That is somewhat unfortunate, but it's better than the opposite problem of having the utilities report no damage when there actually is some.) If your system supports external locking, this problem won't occur. See the "Coordinating with the Server" section earlier in this chapter for information about external locking.

You can also run the `chk_mysql_tables.sh` script at machine boot time by invoking it from one of your system startup scripts. If you're using a BSD-style system and your MySQL server startup command is located in `/etc/rc.local` or the equivalent, you can simply invoke `chk_mysql_tables.sh` from that same file before starting up the server. For a System-V style system, look in the `/etc/rc.d` directory. You may be able to use `rc.sysinit` or a similar script to run `chk_mysql_tables.sh` before the MySQL server starts up.

Using Backups for Data Recovery

Recovery procedures involve two sources of information—your backup files and your binary logs. The backup files restore tables to the state they were in at the time the backup was performed. However, tables typically will have been modified between the time of the dump and the time at which problems occurred. The binary logs contain the queries used to make those changes, so you can repeat the queries by using the logs as input to `mysql`. (This is why you should enable binary logging. If you haven't yet done so, you should do so right now and generate a new backup before reading further.)

The recovery procedure varies depending on how much information you must restore. In fact, it may be easier to restore an entire database than a single table because it's easier to apply the update logs for a database than for a table.

What Logs Should You Use for Recovery Operations?

The possible logs that you can use in conjunction with your backup files for recovery operations are the update logs and the binary update logs. The binary update logs are better for recovery purposes, so you should use them in preference to the update logs if possible. The discussion in this section is written under the assumption that you'll use the binary logs. However, binary logging is available only as of MySQL 3.23.14. If you don't have that capability, you can use the update logs instead. Adjust the instructions accordingly.

Recovering an Entire Database

First of all, if the database you want to recover is the `mysql` database that contains the grant tables, you'll need to run the server using the `--skip-grant-tables` option. Otherwise, it will complain about not being able to find the grant tables. It's also a good idea to use `--skip-networking` to cause the server to reject all remote connection attempts while you're performing the restoration. After you've restored the tables, bring down the server and restart it normally so that it uses the grant tables and listens to the network interfaces as usual.

The general recovery procedure involves the following steps:

1. Copy the contents of the database directory somewhere else. You may want them later—or example, to perform post-mortem examination of the corpses of crashed tables.

2. Reload the database using your most recent backup files. If you're using backups generated by `mysqldump` as files that contain SQL statements, use them as input to `mysql`. If you're using files that were directly copied from the database (for example, with `mysqlhotcopy`, `tar`, or `cp`), bring down the server, copy the files directly into the database directory, and restart the server. (The reason for bringing down the server is that you don't want it trying to access the files during the copy operation.)

3. Use the binary update logs to repeat the queries that modified database tables subsequent to the time at which the backup was made. For any applicable log, convert it to ASCII format with `mysqlbinlog` and use the result as input to `mysql`. Specify the `--one-database` option so that `mysql` executes queries only for the database you're interested in recovering.

If you know you need to apply all the log files, normally you can use the following command in the directory where they are located:

```
% ls -t -r -1 binlog.[0-9]* | xargs mysqlbinlog | mysql --one-database db_name
```

The `ls` command produces a single-column list of update log files, sorted by name, which normally should be the order in which they were generated by the server. However, if the numeric extensions of the filenames don't all have the same number of digits, that won't work. For example, if you have logs named `binlog.998`, `binlog.999`, and `binlog.1000`, `ls` will sort them with `binlog.1000` first. Piping the names through `sort` won't work, either, because it sorts the names the same way. It's necessary to perform a numeric sort based only on the extension values. The following short Perl script does this:

```
#! /usr/bin/perl -w
# ext_num_sort.pl - sort filenames based on numeric extension value.

use strict;

my @files = <>;          # read all input lines
@files = sort {          # sort them by numeric extension
            my $anum = $1 if $a =~ /\.(\d+)$/;
            my $bnum = $1 if $b =~ /\.(\d+)$/;
            $anum <=> $bnum;
        } @files;
print @files;            # print them
exit (0);
```

Use the script as follows:

```
% ls -1 binlog.[0-9]* | ext_num_sort.pl | xargs mysqlbinlog \
    | mysql --one-database db_name
```

The preceding discussion assumes that you want to apply all the update logs, but it's often the case that you'll have to apply just some of them—those that were written after some particular backup, for example. If the logs made since the time of your backup are named binlog.1392, binlog.1393, and so on, you can rerun the statements in them as follows:

```
% mysqlbinlog binlog.1392 | mysql --one-database db_name
% mysqlbinlog binlog.1393 | mysql --one-database db_name
...
```

If the reason that you're performing recovery and using the logs to restore information is because someone issued an ill-advised DROP DATABASE, DROP TABLE, or DELETE statement, be sure to remove that statement from the log file in which it appears before applying the log! To do this, convert the log to ASCII format and save it in a file. Then edit the file and feed the result to mysql:

```
% mysqlbinlog logfile > textfile
% vi textfile
% mysql --one-database db_name < textfile
```

If you don't have binary update logs but you do have the text update logs, you don't need to use mysqlbinlog; the logs will already be in ASCII format. In this case, to apply the updates for a given database from all the logs at once, do the following:

```
% ls -1 update.[0-9]* | ext_num_sort.pl | xargs cat \
    | mysql --one-database db_name
```

To apply individual logs, do the following:

```
% mysql --one-database db_name < update.1392
% mysql --one-database db_name < update.1393
 . . .
```

The problem of logs not sorting properly due to having different extension lengths should occur less frequently in the future. At some point (perhaps in the 4.1 series), the server will be changed to use extensions with a minimum of six digits rather than three. That change should make `ext_num_sort.pl` unnecessary.

Recovering Individual Tables

Recovering individual tables can be more difficult than recovering a database. If you have a backup file generated by `mysqldump` and it contains data for many tables, not just the one you're interested in (which is likely), you'll need to extract the relevant part of the file and use it as input to `mysql`. And that's the easy part! The hard part is pulling out the pieces of the logs that apply to just that table. You may find the `mysql_find_rows` utility helpful for this; it can extract multiple-line queries from update logs or from binary update logs that have been converted to ASCII with `mysqlbinlog`.

Another possibility is to restore the entire database into a second, empty database. From that database, dump the table you want to restore by using `mysql-dump --add-drop-table` and then load it back into the original database. (`--add-drop-table` makes sure that the restore operation begins with a clean slate.) This procedure may actually be easier than trying to restore a single table by extracting the relevant lines from update logs. Another possibility (for table types other than BDB or InnoDB) is to copy the table files from the second database back to the database directory of the original database. Make sure the server for both databases are down when you copy the files back into the database directory.

Recovering Tables Using RESTORE TABLE

RESTORE TABLE is the counterpart to BACKUP TABLE and thus works to restore MyISAM tables that have been copied using the latter statement. It is available as of MySQL 3.23.25 and requires the FILE and INSERT privileges. To use RESTORE TABLE, name the table or tables that you want to restore, along with the directory on the server host where the backup files are located. Suppose you previously backed up three tables using BACKUP TABLE as follows:

```
BACKUP TABLE tbl1, tbl2, tbl3 TO '/archive/sampdb';
```

To restore any or all of those tables, name the ones you want in a RESTORE TABLE statement. For example, restore tbl1 and tbl3 as follows:

```
RESTORE TABLE tbl1, tbl3 FROM '/archive/sampdb';
```

RESTORE TABLE reloads a table's .frm and .MYD description and data files into the database directory and then uses them to rebuild the .MYI index file.

Recovering Tables That Have Foreign Key Relationships

If you have trouble using a dump file to restore tables that have foreign key relationships because the tables are not listed in the file in the order required by those relationships, you can temporarily turn off key checking with the following statement:

```
SET FOREIGN_KEY_CHECKS = 0;
```

FOREIGN_KEY_CHECKS is available as of MySQL 3.23.52. After the tables have been imported, enable key checking again:

```
SET FOREIGN_KEY_CHECKS = 1;
```

Turning key checking off allows you to create and load the tables in any order. It also speeds up loading.

It's necessary to turn off key checking within the same connection as that used to reload the dump file because the setting affects the current connection only. You can accomplish this by loading the file with the source command rather than by naming it on the command line. Suppose you have a dump file named dump.sql containing tables from a database named mydata. Load it as follows:

```
% mysql mydata
mysql> SET FOREIGN_KEY_CHECKS = 0;
mysql> source dump.sql;
mysql> SET FOREIGN_KEY_CHECKS = 1;
mysql> ...
```

The second SET statement is necessary only if you plan to issue further statements within the mysql session after loading the dump file. If you exit after loading the file, it is unneeded.

Recovering the InnoDB Tablespace or BDB Tables

The InnoDB table handler attempts to perform any necessary auto-recovery when the server restarts after a crash. However, in the event that InnoDB detects a non-recoverable problem, startup will fail. In this case, set the innodb_force_recovery server variable to a non-zero value between 1 and

6 to cause the server to start up even if InnoDB recovery after a crash otherwise fails. To set the variable, put a line like the following in your `[mysqld]` option group:

```
set-variable = innodb_force_recovery=level
```

The InnoDB handler attempts more conservative strategies for lower numbers. A typical recommended starting value of `level` is 4. After the server starts up, dump your InnoDB tables with `mysqldump` to get back as much information as possible, drop the tables, and restore them from the `mysqldump` output file. This procedure will recreate the tables in a form that is internally consistent and may be sufficient to achieve a satisfactory recovery. After performing the recovery, remove the line that sets `innodb_force_recovery` from the option line.

If you need to restore the entire InnoDB tablespace, the approach to use depends on how you made your backup. (I assume that you have created one, using the instructions in the "Backing Up the InnoDB Tablespace or BDB Tables" section earlier in this chapter.)

- If you used a direct-copy method, you should have copies of the tablespace files, the log files, the `.frm` file for each table, and the server option file that defines your InnoDB configuration. After making sure the server is down, delete any existing InnoDB files and replace them with your backup copies. Then make sure your current server option file lists the InnoDB configuration the same way as your saved option file and restart the server.

- If you backed up the InnoDB tablespace by running `mysqldump` to generate a SQL file containing the CREATE TABLE and INSERT statements necessary to recreate the tables from scratch, and then you should reinitialize the tablespace and reload the dump file into it. With the server down, throw away any existing InnoDB-related files: The tablespace files (other than raw partitions), log files, and the `.frm` files for all InnoDB tables. Reconfigure the tablespace the same way you did initially. (See the "Configuring the InnoDB Tablespace" section in Chapter 11. A saved copy of the server option file may be helpful as a record of what that configuration should look like. Also, remember that initializing the tablespace is a two-step process if you're using any raw partitions.) When the server finishes creating the new tablespace, reload the backup file that contains the SQL statements for recreating the InnoDB tables by using it as input to `mysql`.

After restoring the tablespace from the backups, re-apply any updates from your binary logs that occurred after the backup was made. This is easiest if you're restoring your tablespace as part of restoring your entire set of databases, because in that case you can apply all the updates. If you're restoring only the InnoDB tablespace, applying the logs will be trickier because you want to use only updates for InnoDB tables.

The BDB handler, like the InnoDB handler, attempts auto-recovery when you start the server after a crash. If startup fails because of a non-recoverable BDB problem, move any BDB log files from the data directory to some other directory (or remove them if you don't plan to examine them further). Then start the server with the `--bdb-no-recover` option. If the log files were corrupted, this may allow the server to start up and create a new BDB log. If the server still won't start up, you can try to replace your BDB files from backups:

- If you directly copied the relevant files, you should have the BDB table files and the BDB log files. With the server down, remove the existing BDB files from your data directory and replace them with your backups.

- If you used `mysqldump` to generate a backup consisting of SQL statements to recreate the tables, bring down the server and remove the existing BDB table and log files. Then restart the server and load the backup file by using it as input to `mysql`.

After restoring the backup, re-apply any post-backup updates from the binary logs (observing the same caveat noted earlier with regard to InnoDB recovery).

IV

Appendixes

A

Obtaining and Installing Software

THIS APPENDIX DESCRIBES HOW TO OBTAIN the sampdb distribution that is used for setting up the sample database that serves for examples throughout this book. To use the distribution, you'll also need to have MySQL running; to that end, the appendix also discusses how to obtain and install MySQL and related software, such as the Perl DBI and CGI.pm modules, PHP, and Apache. It provides information for both UNIX and Windows. For these packages, the purpose of this appendix is to bring together summary installation instructions for each of them in one place, not to replace the instructions that come with them. In fact, I encourage you to read those instructions. This appendix provides general information that should suffice for many situations, but each package also contains instructions to help you troubleshoot problems when a standard installation procedure fails. For example, the MySQL manual contains an extensive chapter dealing with installation procedures and includes solutions for many system-specific problems.

Obtaining the sampdb Sample Database Distribution

The sampdb distribution contains the files that are used to set up and access the sampdb sample database. It is available at the following address:

```
http://www.kitebird.com/mysql-book/
```

The sampdb distribution is available as either a compressed tar file or as a ZIP file. To unpack a distribution in tar format, use one of the following commands (use the second command if your version of tar doesn't understand the z option):

```
% tar zxf sampdb.tar.gz
% gunzip < sampdb.tar.gz | tar xf -
```

To unpack a ZIP-format distribution, use a utility such as WinZip, pkunzip, or unzip.

When you unpack the distribution, it will create a directory named sampdb that contains several files and subdirectories:

- A README file containing additional general instructions for using the distribution. This is the first file you should read. Individual subdirectories of the distribution may also contain README files with more specific information.
- Files for creating and loading the sampdb database. These are used in Chapter 1, "Getting Started with MySQL and SQL."
- A capi directory containing the C programs from Chapter 6, "The MySQL C API."
- A perlapi directory containing the Perl DBI scripts from Chapter 7, "The Perl DBI API."
- A phpapi directory containing the PHP scripts from Chapter 8, "The PHP API."

The sampdb directory also will include a few other directories containing files that are referenced at various other points in the book.

Obtaining MySQL and Related Software

You must install MySQL if you haven't already done so, but you need to install only those third-party tools that you plan to use:

- To write Perl scripts that access MySQL databases, you must install the DBI and DBD::mysql modules. If you plan to write Web-based DBI scripts, you'll probably want to install the CGI.pm module as well, and you'll need a Web server. The Apache server is used in this book, but others may work, too.

- If you want to write PHP scripts, you must install PHP. Normally, PHP is used for Web scripting, which means you also need a Web server. The Apache server is used in this book for PHP.

Precompiled binaries are available for many of the installation packages. Various RPM files are available for Linux. If you prefer to compile software from source or if a binary distribution isn't available for your platform, you'll need a C compiler (C++ for MySQL).

If you have an account with an Internet Service Provider that offers MySQL services, it's very likely that all these packages have been installed already. In that case, you can go ahead and use them and skip the rest of this appendix. Otherwise, the primary distribution points for each of the packages you'll need are shown in the following table. Several of these sites offer mirror sites that provide the same software, but that may be closer to you and result in better download times.

Package	Location
MySQL	`http://www.mysql.com/`
Perl modules	`http://cpan.perl.org/`
PHP	`http://www.php.net/`
Apache	`http://www.apache.org/`

The version of a package you install depends on your needs:

- If you need maximum stability, you probably should be conservative and use the most recent stable version of a package. That gives you the benefit of the newest features and the greatest number of bug fixes without exposing you to experimental code in development versions.

- If you're interested in being on the cutting edge or you require a feature that's available only in the newest version, you should use the latest development release.

- For MySQL, pre-built binary and RPM distributions often are built using optimization flags that are better than what the configuration script in the source distribution might figure out by itself. The MySQL developers recommend that you use a binary distribution of MySQL obtained from `www.mysql.com` if possible. They build distributions using some commercial optimizing compilers to make MySQL even faster.

Consequently, programs in these distributions may run faster than those you'd compile yourself. In addition, they have extensive experience in avoiding or working around bugs in various compilers that result in generation of incorrect code that prevents MySQL from working properly.

The Web sites for each package indicate which versions are the latest stable releases and which are development releases. They also provide per-version feature change lists to help you decide which release is best for you.

If you are working with binary or RPM distributions, unpacking a distribution is equivalent to installing it because the files are unpacked into the directories where you want them to end up. You may need to be `root` to unpack a distribution if it installs files in protected directories.

For a source distribution, you can unpack it into the area that you want to use for compiling and then install the software into the desired installation location. You may need to be `root` to perform the install step, but that should not be necessary for any configuration or compilation steps.

If you are installing from source on UNIX, several of the packages discussed here are configured with the `configure` utility, which makes it easy to set up and build software on a variety of systems. If a build fails, you may need to rerun `configure` with different options than those you originally specified. Before doing so, you should prevent `configure` from picking up information that it saved from the previous time you ran it. Clean out stored the configuration like this:

```
% make distclean
```

or like this:

```
% rm config.cache
% make clean
```

Subscribing to Mailing Lists for Help

When you install a package, it's a good idea to subscribe to the general discussion list for that package so that you can ask questions and receive helpful answers. If you install development releases, you definitely should join and read the mailing list associated with the software to stay abreast of bug reports and fixes. If you don't join a general discussion list, you should at least subscribe to the announcement list so that you receive notices of new releases. Instructions for subscribing to mailing lists and using them are provided in the Introduction. The Web sites for each package also provide subscription information.

Installing MySQL on UNIX

Distributions are available for several versions of MySQL. Currently, stable releases have version numbers in the 4.0 series and development releases are in the 4.1 series. Generally, you should use the highest-numbered version in the series you want to use that is available in the distribution format you want to work with.

MySQL distributions come in binary, RPM, and source formats. Binary and RPM distributions are easier to install, but you must accept the installation layout and configuration defaults that are built into the distribution. Source distributions are more difficult to install because you must compile the software, but you also get more control over configuration parameters. For example, you can compile the distribution for client support only without building the server, and you can install the software wherever you want.

MySQL distributions contain one or more of the following components:

- The `mysqld` server
- Client programs (`mysql`, `mysqladmin`, and so forth) and client programming support (C libraries and header files)
- Documentation
- The benchmark database
- Language support

Source and binary distributions contain all of these items. RPM files contain only some of them, so you may need to install multiple RPMs to get everything you need.

If you plan to connect to a server that's running on another machine, you don't need to install a server. But you should always install client software for the following reasons:

- If you don't run a server, you'll need the clients so that you can connect to a server on another machine.
- If you do run a server, you'll want to be able to connect to it from the server host, not be forced to log in on another machine that has the client software just to test your server.
- The C client library is required for writing programs using any API that incorporates that library. For example, you'll need it for DBI if you plan to write MySQL-based Perl scripts.

Overview of UNIX MySQL Installation

Installing MySQL on UNIX involves the following steps:

1. If you are going to install a server, create a login account for the user and group that you'll use for running it. (This is for a first-time installation only, not for an upgrade to a newer version.)

2. Obtain and unpack any distributions you want to install. If you are using a source distribution, compile it and install it.

3. Run the `mysql_install_db` script to initialize the data directory and grant tables. (This is for a first-time installation only, not for an upgrade to a newer version.)

4. Start the server.

5. Read Chapter 11, "General MySQL Administration," to become familiar with general administrative procedures. In particular, you should read the sections on server startup and shutdown and on running the server using an unprivileged user account.

Creating a Login Account for the MySQL User

This step is necessary only for a first-time installation and only if you're going to run a MySQL server. You can skip it for an upgrade or if you're running MySQL client software only.

The MySQL server can be run as any UNIX user on your system, but for security and administrative reasons, you should not run the server as `root`. I recommend that you create a separate account to use for MySQL administration and that you run the server as that user. That way, you can log in as that user and have full privileges in the data directory for performing maintenance and troubleshooting. Procedures for creating user accounts vary from system to system. Consult your local documentation for specific details.

This book uses `mysqladm` and `mysqlgrp` for the UNIX user and group names of the MySQL administrative account. If you plan to install MySQL only for your own use, you can run it as yourself, in which case you'll use your own login and group names wherever you see `mysqladm` and `mysqlgrp` in this book. If you use RPM files, the RPM installation procedure will create a login account for a user named `mysql` automatically for you. In that case, you will want to substitute `mysql` for `mysqladm`.

Advantages of using a separate, unprivileged account rather than `root` for running MySQL are as follows:

- If you do not run MySQL as `root`, no one can exploit the server as a security hole to gain `root` access.

- It's safer to perform MySQL administrative tasks as an unprivileged user than as `root`.

- The server will create files owned by `mysqladm` rather than by `root`. The fewer `root`-owned files on your system, the better.

- It's cleaner conceptually to separate MySQL activity into its own account, and it's easier to see what things on your system are MySQL-related. For example, in the directory where `crontab` files are kept, you'll have a separate file for the MySQL user, `mysqladm`. Otherwise, the MySQL `cron` jobs will be listed in `root`'s `crontab` file, along with everything else done as `root` on a periodic basis.

Obtaining and Installing a MySQL Distribution on UNIX

The following instructions use *version* to stand for the version number of the MySQL distribution you're working with and *platform* to stand for the name of the platform on which you're installing it. These are used in distribution filenames so that distributions can be identified easily and distinguished from one another. A version number is something like 3.23.52 or 4.0.5-beta. A platform name is something like `sun-solaris2.8-sparc` or `pc-linux-gnu-i686`.

Binary distribution files that have `-max` in the filename include a server built with additional features that the standard server does not have. The particular features change occasionally, so you should check the MySQL Web site to see how the standard and max distributions currently differ. If you're compiling from source, you enable or disable features by running the `configure` script with the appropriate options.

Installing a Binary Distribution

Binary distribution files have names such as `mysql-version-platform.tar.gz`. Obtain the distribution file for the version and platform you want and put it in the directory under which you want to install MySQL—for example, `/usr/local`.

Unpack the distribution using one of the following commands (use the second command if your version of `tar` doesn't understand the `z` option):

```
% tar zxf mysql-version-platform.tar.gz
% gunzip < mysql-version-platform.tar.gz | tar xf -
```

Unpacking a distribution file creates a directory named `mysql-version-platform` that contains the distribution's contents. To make it easier to refer to this directory, create a symbolic link to it named `mysql`:

```
% ln -s mysql-version-platform mysql
```

Now you can refer to the installation directory as `/usr/local/mysql` if you installed MySQL under `/usr/local`.

To allow invocation of MySQL client programs from the command line without typing their full pathnames, set your `PATH` environment variable to include the `bin` directory located under the MySQL installation directory. Your path is set in one of your shell's startup files.

If you are going to use only the client support provided by the distribution and are not running a server, you're done installing MySQL. If you are installing MySQL for the first time, go to the "Initializing the Data Directory and Grant Tables" section later in this appendix. If you are updating an existing installation, go to the "Starting the Server" section later in this appendix.

Installing an RPM Distribution

RPM files are available for installing MySQL on Linux systems. These have filenames like the following:

- `MySQL-client-version-platform.rpm`—The client programs.
- `MySQL-version-platform.rpm`—The server software.
- `MySQL-Max-version-platform.rpm`—Additional server software to add extra features. Before installing this, you *must* install the corresponding MySQL-*version-platform*.rpm file first.
- `MySQL-embedded-version-platform.rpm`—The embedded server, `libmysqld`.
- `MySQL-devel-version-platform.rpm`—Development support (client libraries and header files) for writing client programs. You'll need this if you want to use or write Perl DBI scripts for accessing MySQL databases.
- `MySQL-shared-version-platform.rpm`—Shared client libraries.

- MySQL-bench-*version-platform*.rpm—Benchmarks and tests. These require Perl DBI support. (See "Installing Perl DBI Support on UNIX" later in this appendix.)
- MySQL-*version*.src.rpm—The source for the server, clients, benchmarks, and tests.

You don't need to be in any particular directory when you install from an RPM file because RPMs include information indicating where their contents should be installed. For any RPM file *rpm_file*, you can determine where it will be installed with the following command:

```
% rpm -qpl rpm_file
```

To install an RPM file, use the following command (you'll probably need to do this as root):

```
# rpm -i rpm_file
```

Various parts of MySQL are divided into different RPM files, so you may need to install more than one RPM. To install client support, use the following command:

```
# rpm -i MySQL-client-version-platform.rpm
```

For server support, use the following commands (skip the second one if you don't want the additional features provided by the Max server):

```
# rpm -i MySQL-version-platform.rpm
# rpm -i MySQL-Max-version-platform.rpm
```

If you plan to write your own programs using the client programming support, make sure to install the development RPM file:

```
# rpm -i MySQL-devel-version-platform.rpm
```

If you want to install from the source RPM file, the following command should be sufficient:

```
# rpm —recompile MySQL-version.src.rpm
```

To allow invocation of MySQL client programs from the command line without typing their full pathnames, set your PATH environment variable to include the bin directory located under the MySQL installation directory. Your path is set in one of your shell's startup files.

If you plan to use only the client support provided by the distribution and are not running a server, you're done installing MySQL. If you are installing MySQL for the first time, go to the "Initializing the Data Directory and Grant Tables" section later in this appendix. If you are updating an existing installation, go to the "Starting the Server" section later in this appendix.

Installing a Source Distribution

MySQL source distributions have names such as `mysql-`*`version`*`.tar.gz`, where *version* is the MySQL version number. Pick the directory under which you want to unpack the distribution and move into it. Obtain the distribution file and unpack it using one of the following commands (use the second command if your version of `tar` doesn't understand the `z` option):

```
% tar zxf mysql-version.tar.gz
% gunzip < mysql-version.tar.gz | tar xf -
```

Unpacking a distribution file creates a directory named `mysql-`*`version`* that contains the distribution's contents; change the location into that directory:

```
% cd mysql-version
```

Now you need to configure and compile the distribution before you can install it. If the following steps fail, check the installation chapter in the *MySQL Reference Manual*, particularly any system-specific notes it may contain about your type of machine.

Use the `configure` command to configure the distribution:

```
% ./configure
```

You may want to specify options for `configure`. To obtain a list of available options, run the following command:

```
% ./configure --help
```

The following list shows some configuration options many people find helpful:

- `--with-innodb`, `--without-innodb`—Include or exclude support for InnoDB tables. Prior to MySQL 4, use `--with-innodb` to include the InnoDB handler. As of MySQL 4, InnoDB is included by default; use `--without-innodb` to exclude it.

- `--with-berkeley-db`—Include support for BDB tables.

- `--without-server`—Configure for building client support only (client programs or client libraries). You might do this if you're planning to access a server that's already running on another machine.

- `--with-embedded-server`—Build the embedded server library, `lib-mysqld`.

- `--prefix=`*`path_name`*—By default, the installation root directory is `/usr/local`. The data directory, clients, the server, client libraries, header files, manual pages, and language files are installed in the `var`, `bin`, `libexec`, lib, include, man, and share directories under this directory. If you want to change the installation root, use the --prefix option. For example, to install everything under the /usr/local/mysql directory, use --prefix=/usr/local/mysql.

- --localstatedir=*path_name*—This option changes the location of the data directory. You can use this if you don't want to put your databases under the installation root directory.

- --with-low-memory—The sql/sql_yacc.cc source file requires a lot of memory to compile, which sometimes causes the build process to fail, even on systems with generous amounts of RAM and swap space. Symptoms of this problem include error messages about "Fatal Signal 11" or exhaustion of virtual memory. The --with-low-memory option causes the compiler to be invoked with options that result in lower memory use.

After you run configure, compile the distribution and then install it:

```
% make
% make install
```

You may need to be root to run the install command if you didn't run configure with a --prefix option that specifies an installation directory in which you have write permission.

To allow invocation of MySQL client programs from the command line without typing their full pathnames, set your PATH environment variable to include the bin directory located under the MySQL installation directory. Your path is set in one of your shell's startup files.

If you are going to use only the client support provided by the distribution and are not running a server, you're done installing MySQL. If you are installing MySQL for the first time, go to the "Initializing the Data Directory and Grant Tables" later in this appendix. If you are updating an existing installation, go to the "Starting the Server" section later in this appendix.

Initializing the Data Directory and Grant Tables

Before you can use your MySQL installation, you need to initialize the mysql database that contains the grant tables controlling network access to your server. This step is needed only for a first-time installation and only if you will run a server. It is not needed for client-only installations.

In the following instructions, DATADIR represents the pathname to your data directory. Normally, you run the commands shown here as root. If you're logged in as the MySQL user (that is, `mysqladm`) or you've installed MySQL under your own account because you intend to run it for yourself, you can execute the commands without being `root`. In that case, you can skip the `chown` and `chmod` commands.

To initialize the data directory, the `mysql` database, and the default grant tables, change location into the MySQL installation directory and run the `mysql_install_db` script. (You need not do this if you are installing from RPM files because `mysql_install_db` will be run for you automatically.) For example, if you installed MySQL into `/usr/local/mysql`, the commands look like this:

```
# cd /usr/local/mysql
# ./bin/mysql_install_db
```

If `mysql_install_db` fails, consult the installation chapter in the *MySQL Reference Manual* to see if it says anything about the problem you're encountering, and then try again. Note that if `mysql_install_db` doesn't run to completion successfully, any grant tables it creates are likely incomplete. You should remove them because `mysql_install_db` may not try to re-create any tables that it finds already existing. You can remove the entire `mysql` database as follows:

```
# rm -rf DATADIR/mysql
```

After running `mysql_install_db`, change the user and group ownership and the mode of all files under the data directory. Assuming that the user and group are `mysqladm` and `mysqlgrp`, the commands are as follows:

```
# chown -R mysqladm.mysqlgrp DATADIR
# chmod -R go-rwx DATADIR
```

The `chown` command changes the ownership to the MySQL user, and `chmod` changes the mode to keep everybody out of the data directory except that user.

Starting the Server

This step is needed only if you plan to run a server. Skip it for a client-only installation. Run the commands in this section from the MySQL installation directory (just as for the commands in the previous section). Normally, you run the commands as `root`. If you're logged in as the MySQL user (that is, `mysqladm`) or you've installed MySQL under your own account, you can execute the commands without being `root` and should omit the `--user` option.

Change location into the MySQL installation directory (for example, `/usr/local/mysql`) and then use the following command to start the server:

```
# cd /usr/local/mysql
# ./bin/mysqld_safe --user=mysqladm &
```

The `--user` option tells the server to run as `mysqladm`. (Note that prior to MySQL 4, `mysqld_safe` is named `safe_mysql`.)

There are other actions that you'll probably want to perform at this point:

- The default installation allows the MySQL `root` user to connect without a password. It's a good idea to establish a password for security reasons.

- You can arrange for the server to start up and shut down automatically as part of your system's normal startup and shutdown procedures.

- You can put the `--user` option in an option file to avoid having to specify it each time you start the server.

- Various kinds of logging can be enabled. These are useful for monitoring the server and for data-recovery procedures.

- For a server that supports InnoDB tables, you can configure the InnoDB table handler.

Instructions for performing these actions are given in Chapter 11.

Installing Perl DBI Support on UNIX

Install the DBI software if you want to write Perl scripts that access MySQL databases. You must install the DBI module that provides the general DBI driver, and the `DBD::mysql` module that provides the MySQL-specific driver. DBI requires Perl 5.005_003 or later. (If you don't have Perl installed, visit `http://www.perl.com/`, download a Perl distribution, and install it before you install DBI support.) The MySQL C client library must be available as well because `DBD::mysql` uses it. (The C library should have been installed as part of the MySQL installation procedure.) You also can install the CGI.pm module if you want to write Web-based DBI scripts.

To find out if a given Perl module is already installed, use the `perldoc` command; if a module is installed, `perldoc` will display its documentation:

```
% perldoc DBI
% perldoc DBD::mysql
% perldoc CGI
```

The easiest way to install Perl modules under UNIX is to use the CPAN shell. Issue the following commands as `root`:

```
# perl -MCPAN -e shell
cpan> install DBI
cpan> install DBD::mysql
cpan> install CGI
```

You also can download source distributions from cpan.perl.org as compressed tar files. Unpack a distribution file *dist_file*.tar.gz using one of the following commands (use the second command if your version of tar doesn't understand the z option):

```
% tar zxf dist_file.tar.gz
% gunzip < dist_file.tar.gz | tar xf -
```

Then change location into the distribution directory created by the tar command and run the following commands (you may need to be root to run the installation step):

```
% perl Makefile.PL
% make
% make test
# make install
```

Whichever installation method you choose, Perl will ask you some questions when you install the DBD::mysql module:

- **Which drivers do you want to install?**   There are choices for various combinations of MySQL and mSQL. Unless you also run mSQL, select only MySQL to keep things simple.

- **Do you want to install the MysqlPerl emulation?**   MysqlPerl is the old Perl interface for MySQL. It is obsolete, so answer No to this question unless you have old MysqlPerl scripts and want to enable emulation support for them in the DBI module.

- **Where is your MySQL installed?**   This should be the grandparent of the directory containing your MySQL header files. The location is likely something like /usr/local or /usr/local/mysql unless you installed MySQL in a non-standard place.

- **Which database should I use for testing the MySQL drivers?** The default is test, which should be okay unless you've removed the anonymous-user entries from the MySQL grant tables. In that case, you'll need to give the name of a database to which you have access and then specify a valid MySQL username and password for the final two questions.

- **On which host is the database running?** `localhost` should be sufficient if you're running a local server. If not, name a host that is running a server to which you have access. The MySQL server must be running on the host that you name when you run the `make test` command or the tests will fail.

- **Username for connecting to the database? Password for connecting to the database?** The name and password to use for connecting to the MySQL server for testing. The default is `undef` for both questions, which causes the driver to connect as the anonymous user. Specify non-blank values if you need to connect non-anonymously.

If you have problems installing the Perl modules, consult the README file for the relevant distribution as well as the mail archives for the DBI mailing list. The answers for most installation problems can be found there.

Installing Apache and PHP on UNIX

The following instructions assume that you'll run PHP as a DSO (dynamic shared object) module using the Apache `httpd` server. This means that Apache should be installed first, and then you can build and install PHP. If Apache is not installed on your system already, you can either install a binary distribution that has DSO support enabled or compile a source distribution to include DSO support. After Apache has been installed, configure your PHP distribution by using one of the following commands:

```
% ./configure --with-mysql --with-apxs
% ./configure --with-mysql --with-apxs=/path/to/apxs
```

The `--with-mysql` option indicates that you want to build PHP to include MySQL client support. This option must be included for MySQL-based PHP scripts to work correctly. If the first command fails because `configure` cannot tell where the `apxs` script is located, use the second command to indicate its location explicitly. (The `apxs` Apache Extension Tool is a helper script that provides other modules with information about your Apache configuration.) After configuring PHP, build and install it as follows (you may need to be `root` to perform the installation commands):

```
% make
# make install
# cp php.ini-dist /usr/local/lib/php.ini
```

The `cp` command installs a baseline PHP initialization file where PHP can find it. You can substitute `php.ini-recommended` for `php.ini-dist` if you like; take a look at both and choose the one you prefer.

After PHP is installed, edit the Apache configuration file, `httpd.conf`. You'll need to instruct Apache to load the PHP module when it starts up and also how to recognize PHP scripts.

To tell Apache to load the PHP module, `httpd.conf` will need to include `LoadModule` and `AddModule` directives in the appropriate sections (look for other similar directives). The directives may be added for you during the installation step. If not, they should look something like the following:

```
LoadModule php4_module libexec/libphp4.so
AddModule mod_php4.c
```

Next, edit `httpd.conf` to tell Apache how to recognize PHP scripts. PHP recognition is based on the filename extension that you use for PHP scripts. `.php` is the most common extension and is the one used for examples in this book. Another popular extension is `.phtml`. You can simply enable them both if you want; that may be best anyway if you're going to be installing pages that you obtain from other people that use one or another of these extensions. To do so, include the following lines in the configuration file:

```
AddType application/x-httpd-php3 .php
AddType application/x-httpd-php3 .phtml
```

You can also tell Apache to recognize `index.php` and `index.phtml` as allowable default files for a directory when no filename is specified at the end of a URL. You'll probably find a line in `httpd.conf` that looks like the following:

```
DirectoryIndex index.html
```

Change it to

```
DirectoryIndex index.php index.phtml index.html
```

After editing the Apache configuration file, bring down the httpd server, if one was already running, and then restart it. On many systems, the following commands (executed as root) accomplish this:

```
# /usr/local/apache/bin/apachectl stop
# /usr/local/apache/bin/apachectl start
```

You can also set up Apache to start up and shut down at system startup and shutdown time. See the Apache documentation for instructions. Normally, this involves running `apachectl start` at boot time and `apachectl stop` at shutdown time.

If you encounter problems setting up PHP, check the "VERBOSE INSTALL" section of the INSTALL file included with the PHP distribution. (It's not a bad idea to read that file anyway. It contains lots of useful information.)

Installing MySQL on Windows

You can run MySQL on NT-based systems, such as Windows NT, 2000, and XP, or on non–NT systems, such as Windows 95, 98, and Me. To do so, you must have TCP/IP support installed. On Windows NT 4, make sure your system is at service pack 3 or later. On Windows 95, make sure your Winsock software is at least version 2.

I recommend that you use an NT-based version of Windows if possible. Then you'll have the option of running the MySQL server as a service that Windows starts and stops automatically at system startup and shutdown time. The NT servers also support the option of allowing clients to connect over named pipes.

In addition to the MySQL server and client programs, you may also want to install MyODBC, the MySQL driver for the ODBC (Open Database Connectivity) standard developed by Microsoft. MyODBC allows ODBC-compliant programs to access MySQL databases. For example, you can install MyODBC and then use ODBC programs such as Microsoft Access to connect to a MySQL server.

Windows MySQL distributions are available from the MySQL Web site as ZIP files, with filenames in the form `mysql-version-win.zip`. To unpack a ZIP file, just double-click it. If that does not work, use a program such as WinZip, `pkunzip`, or `unzip`. The result will be a folder that contains a `Setup.exe` application that you should launch to install MySQL. The default installation location is `C:\mysql`, but you can select a different directory.

After installing MySQL on Windows, it is unnecessary to initialize the data directory or the grant tables because they are included pre-initialized in the distribution. However, if you install MySQL in any location other than the default of `C:\mysql`, you *must* place a `[mysqld]` option group in an option file that the server reads when it starts up so that it can determine where the installation base directory and the data directory are located. (The option file can be either `C:\my.cnf` or the `my.ini` file in your Windows system directory.) For example, if you install MySQL in `E:\mysql`, the option group should look like the following (note the use of forward slashes in the pathnames rather than backslashes):

```
[mysqld]
basedir=E:/mysql
datadir=E:/mysql/data
```

You'll also need to change the pathnames in the commands shown in the following instructions if you select an installation directory other than the default.

On Windows, you can choose from the following servers:

Server	Description
mysqld	Standard server
mysqld-nt	Optimized server with named pipe support
mysqld-max	Optimized server with transaction and symbolic link support
mysqld-max-nt	Like mysqld-max but with named pipe support

The servers with -nt in their name support connections over named pipes when run on NT-based systems. However, named pipe support is enabled by default only prior to MySQL 3.23.50. To use this capability from 3.23.50 on, you should add a line to the [mysqld] group in your option file:

```
[mysqld]
enable-named-pipe
```

On Windows NT-based systems, the mysqld-nt server can be installed to run as a service that starts automatically whenever Windows starts (you can substitute mysqld-max-nt in the following command):

```
C:\> C:\mysql\bin\mysqld-nt --install
```

If you use --install-manual rather than --install, the server is installed as a manual service that does not run automatically when Windows starts up.

If you install mysqld-nt as a service, you can specify other options by putting them in the [mysqld] group of an option file.

For a server that is installed as a service, you can start it manually using the Windows Services Manager. You should be able to find this as a Services item in the Windows Control Panel or in the Administrative Tools item in the Control Panel. The service also can be started using the following command:

```
C:\> net start MySQL
```

To stop the server, use the Services Manager or one of the following commands:

```
C:\> net stop MySQL
C:\> C:\mysql\bin\mysqladmin -u root shutdown
```

To remove MySQL as a service, shut down the server if it is running, and then invoke the following command:

```
C:\> C:\mysql\bin\mysqld-nt --remove
```

To avoid interactions between the Services Manager and commands issued from the DOS prompt, it is best to close the Services Manager whenever you invoke service-related commands from the prompt.

On non-NT-based systems (or on NT systems if you do not install the server as a service), you must start and stop the server manually from the command line. To run `mysqld`, start it as follows (you can substitute `mysqld-max` in this command):

```
C:\> C:\mysql\bin\mysqld
```

You can specify other options on the command line if you want. To shut down the server, use `mysqladmin`:

```
C:\> C:\mysql\bin\mysqladmin -u root shutdown
```

To run a server in console mode (so that it displays error messages in a console window), invoke it as follows:

```
C:\> C:\mysql\bin\mysqld --console
```

Any of the servers can be run in console mode. In this case, you can specify other options on the command line after the `--console` option or in an option file. To shut down the server, use `mysqladmin`.

If you have problems getting the server to run, check the Windows notes in the installation chapter in the *MySQL Reference Manual*.

To allow invocation of MySQL client programs from the command line without typing their full pathnames, set your PATH environment variable to include the `C:\mysql\bin` directory. (If you installed MySQL somewhere else, adjust the pathname appropriately.) You can set your path in the `AUTOEXEC.BAT` file or (on NT-based systems) by using the System item in the Control Panel.

The default installation allows anyone to connect to MySQL as `root` without a password, so you should set up passwords as described in Chapter 11, "General MySQL Administration." That chapter also contains instructions for other actions such as enabling logging or configuring the InnoDB table handler.

Installing Perl DBI Support on Windows

The easiest way to install Perl modules under Windows is to get the ActiveState Perl distribution from `www.activestate.com` and install it. Then fetch and install the additional Perl modules that you need. The `ppm` (Perl Package Manager) program is used for this. To find out what modules are already installed, use this command:

```
C:\> ppm info
```

Then install the modules you need using the appropriate commands from the following list. It's likely that CGI.pm will already be installed, but you'll probably need to install the DBI-related packages:

```
C:\> ppm
ppm> install DBI
ppm> install DBD::mysql
ppm> install CGI
```

Installing Apache and PHP on Windows

Apache and PHP are available as Windows binaries from the Apache and PHP Web sites listed near the beginning of this appendix. Under Apache 1.3.x, PHP can be run only as a standalone CGI program. Under Apache 2.x, you can run PHP either as a standalone program or as an Apache module.

Installing MyODBC on Windows

Distributions of MyODBC 3 are packaged as executable files with filenames of the form MyODBC-*version*.exe. Download a distribution file and then launch it to install it. For versions prior to MyODBC 3, distributions are packaged as ZIP files. There are separate distributions for NT- and non-NT–based systems (distinguished by -nt and -win95 in the filenames). To install a ZIP-format distribution, double-click it to unpack it and then run the Setup.exe application inside the resulting folder. If you encounter an error such as "Problems while copying MFC30.DLL" while installing MyODBC with Setup.exe, MFC30.DLL is being used by some application. In this case, try selecting the Ignore option that is presented with the error message. MySQL should finish installing and most likely will work despite the error. If it doesn't, try restarting Windows in safe mode and running Setup.exe again.

After installing a MyODBC distribution, configure the driver using the ODBC item in the Control Panel. (It should be located in the Control Panel or in the Administrative Tools item in the Control Panel, with a name like Data Sources (ODBC) or ODBC Data Sources.) When you run the ODBC item, you'll see a window that allows you to set up a data source name (DSN). Click the User DSN tab and then click the Add button to bring up a window that lists the available data source drivers. Select the MySQL driver from the list and click the Finish button. Another window will appear that allows you to enter connection parameters for the data source. Fill in parameters that are appropriate for the connection that you want to establish and then click OK.

The following example shows how to fill in the fields to set up a data source for connecting to the local server to access the sampdb database with a user-name and password of sampadm and secret:

Field Name	Field Value
Data Source Name:	sampdb-dsn
Host Name (or IP):	localhost
Database Name:	sampdb
User:	sampadm
Password:	secret
Port:	3306

After configuring MyODBC, you should be able to use ODBC-aware programs to access MySQL databases. For example, one common use for MyODBC is to connect to a MySQL server from Microsoft Access. After ODBC has been set up, use the following steps to connect to the MySQL server from within Access:

1. Start the Access program.
2. Open your database or create a new database.
3. From the File menu, select Get External Data and then select Link Tables.
4. In the window that appears, click the Files of Type pop-up menu and select ODBC Databases.
5. Select the DSN that you configured in the Control Panel ODBC item for connecting to MySQL.
6. Select the MySQL tables you want to use.

After performing this procedure, the selected tables will be available through Access. Note that the MYSQL tables must already exist; this procedure does not create them.

B

Column Type Reference

THIS APPENDIX DESCRIBES EACH COLUMN TYPE provided by MySQL. More information on the use of each type is available in Chapter 2, "Working with Data in MySQL." All types listed here have been present in MySQL at least as far back as MySQL 3.22.0. Some types have undergone changes in behavior since then, as indicated in the type descriptions.

Type name specifications are written using the following conventions:

- **Square brackets ([ ]).** Optional information.
- **M.** The maximum display width; unless otherwise specified, M should be an integer from 1 to 255.
- **D.** The number of digits following the decimal point for types that have a fractional part; D should be an integer from 0 to 30. D should also be no greater than M-2. Otherwise, the value of M is adjusted to be D +2.

In ODBC terminology, M and D correspond to "precision" and "scale."

For each type description, one or more of the following kinds of information are provided:

- **Meaning.** A short description of the type.
- **Allowable attributes.** Optional attribute keywords that may be associated with the column type in CREATE TABLE or ALTER TABLE statements. Attributes are listed in alphabetical order, but this does not necessarily correspond to the order imposed by the syntax of CREATE TABLE or ALTER TABLE. See Appendix D, "SQL Syntax Reference," for the syntax of those statements. The attributes listed in each column type description are in addition to the global attributes listed shortly.
- **Allowable length.** For string types, the maximum allowable length of column values.
- **Range.** For numeric or date and time types, the range of values the type can represent. For integer numeric types, two ranges are given because integer columns can be signed or unsigned, and the ranges are different for each case.
- **Zero value.** For date and time types, the "zero" value that is stored if an illegal value is inserted into the column.
- **Default value.** The default value if no explicit DEFAULT attribute is given in the type specification.
- **Storage required.** The number of bytes required to store values of the type. For some types, this value is fixed. The amount varies for other types, depending on the length of the value stored in the column.
- **Comparisons.** Whether comparisons are case sensitive for string types. This applies to sorting and indexing as well because those operations are based on comparisons.
- **Synonyms.** Any synonyms for the type name.
- **Notes.** Any miscellaneous observations about the type.

Certain global attributes apply to all or almost all column types. They are listed here rather than in each type description:

- NULL or NOT NULL can be specified for every type.
- DEFAULT default_value can be specified for most types. Default values must be constants. For example, you cannot specify DEFAULT NOW() for a DATETIME column. A default value specification is ineffective for TIMESTAMP columns and columns with the AUTO_INCREMENT attribute, and is

illegal for BLOB and TEXT columns. (Capabilities for non-constant default values and default values for BLOB and TEXT columns are scheduled for inclusion in MySQL 4.1, but are not yet present as of this writing.)

Numeric Types

MySQL provides numeric types for integer and floating point values. Types can be chosen according to the range of values you need to represent.

Values for numeric types are padded with leading zeroes to the column's display width if the ZEROFILL attribute is specified.

For integer types, a column must be a PRIMARY KEY or a UNIQUE index if the AUTO_INCREMENT attribute is specified. Inserting NULL into an AUTO_INCREMENT column inserts the next sequence value for the column (typically a value that is one greater than the column's current maximum value). More information on the precise behavior of AUTO_INCREMENT columns is given in Chapter 2.

If the UNSIGNED attribute is specified for a numeric type, negative values are disallowed, except that UNSIGNED for FLOAT or DOUBLE columns is unsupported prior to MySQL 4.0.2. (UNSIGNED can be given in the definition for such a column prior to 4.0.2, but is ineffective in preventing negative values from being stored, and may result in negative values being displayed incorrectly if the column also is declared with the ZEROFILL attribute.)

In some cases, specifying one attribute causes another to be enabled as well. Specifying ZEROFILL for a numeric type automatically causes the column to be UNSIGNED. As of MySQL 3.23, specifying AUTO_INCREMENT automatically causes the column to be NOT NULL.

Note that DESCRIBE and SHOW COLUMNS report the default value for an AUTO_INCREMENT column as NULL, although you cannot insert a literal NULL into such a column. This indicates that you produce the default column value (the next sequence number) by setting the column to NULL when you create a new record.

TINYINT[(M)]

Meaning: A very small integer

Allowable attributes: AUTO_INCREMENT, UNSIGNED, ZEROFILL

Range: −128 to 127 (-2^7 to 2^7-1) or 0 to 255 (0 to 2^8-1) if UNSIGNED

Default value: NULL if column can be NULL, 0 if NOT NULL.

Storage required: 1 byte

Synonyms: INT1[(M)]. BIT and BOOL are synonyms for TINYINT(1)

SMALLINT[(M)]

Meaning: A small integer

Allowable attributes: AUTO_INCREMENT, UNSIGNED, ZEROFILL

Range: –32768 to 32767 (-2^{15} to $2^{15}-1$) or 0 to 65535 (0 to $2^{16}-1$) if UNSIGNED

Default value: NULL if column can be NULL, 0 if NOT NULL

Storage required: 2 bytes

Synonyms: INT2[(M)]

MEDIUMINT[(M)]

Meaning: A medium-sized integer

Allowable attributes: AUTO_INCREMENT, UNSIGNED, ZEROFILL

Range: –8388608 to 8388607 (-2^{23} to $2^{23}-1$) or 0 to 16777215 (0 to $2^{24}-1$) if UNSIGNED

Default value: NULL if column can be NULL, 0 if NOT NULL

Storage required: 3 bytes

Synonyms: INT3[(M)] and MIDDLEINT[(M)]

INT[(M)]

Meaning: A normal-sized integer

Allowable attributes: AUTO_INCREMENT, UNSIGNED, ZEROFILL

Range: –2147483648 to 2147483647 (-2^{31} to $2^{31}-1$) or 0 to 4294967295 (0 to $2^{32}-1$) if UNSIGNED

Default value: NULL if column can be NULL, 0 if NOT NULL

Storage required: 4 bytes

Synonyms: INTEGER[(M)] and INT4[(M)]

BIGINT [(*M*)]

Meaning: A large integer

Allowable attributes: AUTO_INCREMENT, UNSIGNED, ZEROFILL

Range: −9223372036854775808 to 9223372036854775807 (-2^{63} to $2^{63}-1$) or 0 to 18446744073709551615 (0 to $2^{64}-1$) if UNSIGNED

Default value: NULL if column can be NULL, 0 if NOT NULL

Storage required: 8 bytes

Synonyms: INT8 [(*M*)]

FLOAT (*p*)

Meaning: A floating-point number, with the minimum required bits of precision given by *p*. For *p* values from 0 to 24, the type is treated as a single-precision column, equivalent to FLOAT with no *M* or *D* specifiers. For values from 25 to 53, the type is treated as a double-precision column, equivalent to DOUBLE with no *M* or *D* specifiers.

Allowable attributes: UNSIGNED (as of MySQL 4.0.2), ZEROFILL.

Range: See the FLOAT and DOUBLE type descriptions in the following sections.

Default value: NULL if column can be NULL, 0 if NOT NULL.

Storage required: 4 bytes for single precision, 8 bytes for double precision.

Note: Prior to MySQL 3.23.6, the allowable *p* values are 4 and 8. From MySQL 3.23.0 to 3.23.5, FLOAT(4) and FLOAT(8) are treated as single-precision and double-precision columns stored to full hardware precision. Prior to MySQL 3.23, FLOAT(4) and FLOAT(8) are equivalent to FLOAT(10,2) and DOUBLE(16,4) and have values rounded to 2 and 4 decimals, not stored to the hardware precision.

FLOAT [(*M,D*)]

Meaning: A small floating-point number; single-precision (less precise than DOUBLE). *M* is the display width, *D* is the minimum required number of decimals precision. If *D* is 0, column values have no decimal point or fractional part. If *M* and *D* are omitted, the display size and number of decimals are undefined.

Allowable attributes: UNSIGNED (as of MySQL 4.0.2), ZEROFILL.

Range: Minimum non-zero values are ±1.175494351E−38; maximum non-zero values are ±3.402823466E+38. Negative values are disallowed if the column is UNSIGNED.

Default value: NULL if column can be NULL, 0 if NOT NULL.

Storage required: 4 bytes.

Synonyms: Prior to MySQL 3.23.6, FLOAT and FLOAT4 are synonyms for FLOAT(10,2).

Note: Prior to MySQL 3.23.6, FLOAT(*M*, *D*) column values are rounded to *D* decimals, not stored to the full precision allowed by your hardware.

DOUBLE[(*M*, *D*)]

Meaning: A large floating-point number; double-precision (more precise than FLOAT). *M* is the display width, *D* is the minimum required number of decimals precision. If *D* is 0, column values have no decimal point or fractional part. If *M* and *D* are omitted, the display size and number of decimals are undefined.

Allowable attributes: UNSIGNED (as of MySQL 4.0.2), ZEROFILL.

Range: Minimum non-zero values are ±2.2250738585072014E−308, maximum non-zero values are ±1.7976931348623157E+308. Negative values are disallowed if the column is UNSIGNED.

Default value: NULL if column can be NULL, 0 if NOT NULL.

Storage required: 8 bytes.

Synonyms: DOUBLE PRECISION[(*M*, *D*)] and REAL[(*M*, *D*)] are synonyms for DOUBLE[(*M*, *D*)]. Prior to MySQL 3.23.6, DOUBLE and FLOAT8 are synonyms for DOUBLE(16,4).

Note: Prior to MySQL 3.23.6, DOUBLE(*M*, *D*) column values are rounded to *D* decimals, not stored to the full precision allowed by your hardware.

DECIMAL[(*M*, [*D*])]

Meaning: A floating-point number, stored as a string (1 byte per digit, decimal point, or − sign). *M* is the display width, *D* is the minimum required number of decimals precision. If *D* is 0, column values have no decimal point or fractional part. *M* and *D* default to 10 and 0 if omitted. (Prior to MySQL 3.23.6, *M* and *D* are required, not optional.)

Allowable attributes: UNSIGNED (as of MySQL 4.0.2), ZEROFILL.

Range: Maximum range is the same as for DOUBLE; effective range for a given DECIMAL type is determined by M and D.

Default value: NULL if column can be NULL, 0 if NOT NULL.

Storage required: M+2 bytes normally (the extra two bytes are for the sign and decimal point characters). If the column is UNSIGNED, no sign character need be stored, which reduces the storage required by one byte. If D is 0, no decimal point need be stored, which also reduces the storage required by one byte. Prior to MySQL 3.23, DECIMAL requires M bytes, and the sign and decimal characters are stored within the M bytes allocated to each column value. This means that any given DECIMAL(M, D) specification has a larger range as of MySQL 3.23 than before, but also requires more storage.

Synonyms: NUMERIC[(M, [D])] and DEC[(M, [D])].

Note: In conformance with ANSI SQL, the value of M does not include the bytes needed for the sign character or decimal point as of MySQL 3.23.

String Types

The MySQL string types are commonly used to store text, but are general-purpose types and may hold arbitrary data. Types are available to hold values of varying maximum lengths and can be chosen according to whether or not you want values to be treated in case sensitive fashion.

As of MySQL 4.1, you can specify character sets on a column-specific basis for the CHAR, VARCHAR, and TEXT types. The syntax is CHARACTER SET charset, where charset is a character set identifier such as latin1, greek, or utf8. The allowable character sets supported by the server can be determined by issuing a SHOW CHARACTER SET statement. Note that specifying a character set for CHAR or VARCHAR columns precludes use of the BINARY attribute that normally is allowable for those types.

CHAR [(M)]

Meaning: A fixed-length character string 0 to M bytes long. M should be an integer from 0 to 255 prior (1 to 255 prior to MySQL 3.23). If M is omitted, it defaults to 1. Strings longer than M characters are chopped to length M when stored. Strings shorter than M characters are right-padded with spaces when stored. Trailing spaces are removed when values are retrieved.

Allowable attributes: BINARY, CHARACTER SET (as of MySQL 4.1).

Allowable length: 0 to M bytes.

Default value: NULL if column can be NULL, ' ' (empty string) if NOT NULL.

Storage required: *M* bytes.

Comparisons: Not case sensitive, unless the BINARY attribute is specified.

Synonyms: CHAR with no argument is a synonym for CHAR(1). BINARY(*M*) is a synonym for CHAR(*M*) BINARY. As of MySQL 3.23.5, NCHAR(*M*) and NATIONAL CHAR(*M*) are synonyms for CHAR(*M*).

VARCHAR(*M*)

Meaning: A variable-length character string 0 to *M* bytes long. *M* should be an integer from 0 to 255 prior (1 to 255 prior to MySQL 4.0.2). Strings longer than *M* characters are chopped to length *M* when stored. Trailing spaces are removed from values when stored. (Trailing space removal is scheduled to become optional in MySQL 4.1, but that has not been implemented as of this writing.)

Allowable attributes: BINARY, CHARACTER SET (as of MySQL 4.1).

Allowable length: 0 to *M* bytes.

Default value: NULL if column can be NULL, ' ' (empty string) if NOT NULL.

Storage required: Length of value, plus 1 byte to record the length.

Comparisons: Not case sensitive, unless the BINARY attribute is specified.

Synonyms: CHAR VARYING(*M*). As of MySQL 3.23.5, NCHAR VARYING(*M*) and NATIONAL CHAR VARYING(*M*) are synonyms for VARCHAR(*M*).

TINYBLOB

Meaning: A small BLOB value

Allowable attributes: None, other than the global attributes

Allowable length: 0 to 255 (0 to 2^8-1) bytes

Default value: NULL if column can be NULL, ' ' (empty string) if NOT NULL

Storage required: Length of value plus 1 byte to record the length

Comparisons: Case sensitive

BLOB

Meaning: A normal-sized BLOB value

Allowable attributes: None, other than the global attributes

Allowable length: 0 to 65535 (0 to $2^{16}-1$) bytes

Default value: NULL if column can be NULL, ' ' (empty string) if NOT NULL

Storage required: Length of value plus 2 bytes to record the length

Comparisons: Case sensitive

MEDIUMBLOB

Meaning: A medium-sized BLOB value

Allowable attributes: None, other than the global attributes

Allowable length: 0 to 16777215 (0 to $2^{24}-1$) bytes

Default value: NULL if column can be NULL, ' ' (empty string) if NOT NULL

Storage required: Length of value plus 3 bytes to record the length

Comparisons: Case sensitive

Synonyms: LONG VARBINARY

LONGBLOB

Meaning: A large BLOB value

Allowable attributes: None, other than the global attributes

Allowable length: 0 to 4294967295 (0 to $2^{32}-1$) bytes

Default value: NULL if column can be NULL, ' ' (empty string) if NOT NULL

Storage required: Length of value plus 4 bytes to record the length

Comparisons: Case sensitive

TINYTEXT

Meaning: A small TEXT value

Allowable attributes: CHARACTER SET (as of MySQL 4.1)

Allowable length: 0 to 255 (0 to $2^{8}-1$) bytes

Default value: NULL if column can be NULL, ' ' (empty string) if NOT NULL

Storage required: Length of value plus 1 byte to record the length

Comparisons: Not case sensitive

TEXT

Meaning: A normal-sized TEXT value

Allowable attributes: CHARACTER SET (as of MySQL 4.1)

Allowable length: 0 to 65535 (0 to $2^{16}-1$) bytes

Default value: NULL if column can be NULL, ' ' (empty string) if NOT NULL

Storage required: Length of value plus 2 bytes to record the length

Comparisons: Not case sensitive

MEDIUMTEXT

Meaning: A medium-sized TEXT value

Allowable attributes: CHARACTER SET (as of MySQL 4.1)

Allowable length: 0 to 16777215 (0 to $2^{24}-1$) bytes

Default value: NULL if column can be NULL, ' ' (empty string) if NOT NULL

Storage required: Length of value plus 3 bytes to record the length

Comparisons: Not case sensitive

Synonyms: LONG VARCHAR

LONGTEXT

Meaning: A large TEXT value

Allowable attributes: CHARACTER SET (as of MySQL 4.1)

Allowable length: 0 to 4294967295 (0 to $2^{32}-1$) bytes

Default value: NULL if column can be NULL, ' ' (empty string) if NOT NULL

Storage required: Length of value plus 4 bytes to record the length

Comparisons: Not case sensitive

ENUM('*value1*','*value2*',...)

Meaning: An enumeration; column values may be assigned exactly one member of the value list

Allowable attributes: None, other than the global attributes listed in the chapter introduction

Default value: NULL if column can be NULL, first enumeration value if NOT NULL

Storage required: 1 byte for enumerations with 1 to 255 members, 2 bytes for enumerations with 256 to 65535 members

Comparisons: Not case sensitive (case sensitive prior to MySQL 3.22.1)

SET('*value1*','*value2*',...)

Meaning: A set; column values may be assigned zero or more members of the value list

Allowable attributes: None, other than the global attributes listed in the chapter introduction

Default value: NULL if column can be NULL, ' ' (empty set) if NOT NULL

Storage required: 1 byte (for sets with 1 to 8 members), 2 bytes (9 to 16 members), 3 bytes (17 to 24 members), 4 bytes (25 to 32 members), or 8 bytes (33 to 64 members)

Comparisons: Not case sensitive (case sensitive prior to MySQL 3.22.1)

Date and Time Types

MySQL provides types to represent temporal data in various forms. Date and time types are available, either together or in combination. There is a special timestamp type that is updated automatically when a record changes and a type for storing years if you don't need a complete date.

The terms *CC*, *YY*, *MM*, and *DD* in date formats represent century, year, month, and day. The terms *hh*, *mm*, and *ss* in time formats represent hour, minute, and second.

DATE

Meaning: A date, in '*CCYY-MM-DD*' format

Allowable attributes: None, other than the global attributes

Range: `'1000-01-01'` to `'9999-12-31'`

Zero value: `'0000-00-00'`

Default value: NULL if column can be NULL, `'0000-00-00'` if NOT NULL

Storage required: 3 bytes (4 bytes prior to MySQL 3.22)

TIME

Meaning: A time, in `'hh:mm:ss'` format (`'-hh:mm:ss'` for negative values); represents elapsed time but can be treated as time of day.

Allowable attributes: None, other than the global attributes.

Range: `'-838:59:59'` to `'838:59:59'`.

Zero value: `'00:00:00'`.

Default value: NULL if column can be NULL, `'00:00:00'` if NOT NULL.

Storage required: 3 bytes.

Note: Although `'00:00:00'` is used as the zero value when illegal values are inserted into a TIME column, that is also a legal value that lies within the normal column range.

DATETIME

Meaning: A date and time value, in `'CCYY-MM-DD hh:mm:ss'` format

Allowable attributes: None, other than the global attributes

Range: `'1000-01-01 00:00:00'` to `'9999-12-31 23:59:59'`

Zero value: `'0000-00-00 00:00:00'`

Default value: NULL if column can be NULL, `'0000-00-00 00:00:00'` if NOT NULL

Storage required: 8 bytes

TIMESTAMP [(M)]

Meaning: A timestamp (date and time), in `CCYYMMDDhhmmss` format. Inserting a NULL into any TIMESTAMP column of a table inserts the current date and time. In addition, changing the value of any other column in the row causes the *first* TIMESTAMP column to be updated to the date and time at which the modification occurs. Values are stored and used in calculations internally to full 14-character precision, regardless of the display width.

Allowable attributes: None, other than the global attributes.

Range: 19700101000000 to sometime in the year 2037.

Zero value: 00000000000000.

Default value: The current date and time for the first TIMESTAMP column in a table, 0 for any others. Note that DESCRIBE and SHOW COLUMNS report the default value for TIMESTAMP columns as NULL, though you cannot insert a literal NULL into such a column. This indicates that you set a TIMESTAMP to the current date and time when you create a new record by setting it to NULL.

Storage required: 4 bytes.

Note: If NOT NULL is specified as an attribute, it is ignored.

YEAR [(*M*)]

Meaning: A year value. If given, *M* must be 2 or 4 for formats of YY or CCYY. If omitted, *M* defaults to 4.

Allowable attributes: None, other than the global attributes.

Range: 1901 to 2155, and 0000 for YEAR(4). 1970 to 2069 for YEAR(2), but only the last two digits are displayed.

Zero value: 0000 for YEAR(4), 00 for YEAR(2).

Default value: NULL if column can be NULL, 0000 or 00 if NOT NULL.

Storage required: 1 byte.

C

Operator and Function Reference

THIS APPENDIX LISTS THE OPERATORS AND FUNCTIONS you can use to construct expressions in SQL statements. Unless otherwise indicated, the operators and functions listed here have been present in MySQL at least as far back as MySQL 3.22.0. If an operator or function appears to act differently than described here, check the change notes in the *MySQL Reference Manual* to see if its behavior has been modified.

Operator and function examples are written in the following format:

```
expression                                    → result
```

The `expression` demonstrates how to use an operator or function, and the `result` shows the value that results from evaluating the expression. For example

```
LOWER('ABC')                                  → 'abc'
```

This means that the function call LOWER('ABC') produces the string result 'abc'. You can try the examples shown in this appendix for yourself using the mysql program. To try the preceding example, invoke mysql, type in the example expression with SELECT in front of it and a semicolon after it and press Enter:

```
mysql> SELECT LOWER('ABC');
+--------------+
| LOWER('ABC') |
+--------------+
| abc          |
+--------------+
```

MySQL does not require a SELECT statement to have a FROM clause, which makes it easy to experiment with operators and functions by entering arbitrary expressions in this way. (Some database systems don't let you issue a SELECT without a FROM—an unfortunate restriction.)

Examples include complete SELECT statements for functions that cannot be demonstrated otherwise. The "Summary Functions" section is written that way because those functions make no sense except in reference to a particular table.

Function names, as well as operators that are words, such as BETWEEN, can be specified in any lettercase.

Certain types of function arguments occur repeatedly and are represented by names with the following conventional meanings:

- *expr* represents an expression; depending on the context, this can be a numeric, string, date, or time expression, and can incorporate constants, references to table columns, or other expressions.
- *str* represents a string; it can be a literal string, a reference to a string-valued table column, or an expression that produces a string.
- *n* represents an integer (as do letters near to *n* in the alphabet).
- *x* represents a floating-point number (as do letters near to *x* in the alphabet).

Other argument names are used less often and are defined where used. Optional parts of operator or function call sequences are indicated by square brackets ([]).

Evaluating an expression often involves type conversion of the values in that expression. See Chapter 2, "Working with Data in MySQL," for details on the circumstances under which type conversion occurs and the rules that MySQL uses to convert values from one type to another.

Operators

Operators are used to combine terms in expressions to perform arithmetic, compare values, perform bitwise or logical operations, and match patterns.

Operator Precedence

Operators have varying levels of precedence. The levels are shown in the following list, from highest to lowest. Operators on the same line have the same precedence. Operators at a given precedence level are evaluated left to right. Operators at a higher precedence level are evaluated before operators at a lower precedence level.

```
BINARY   COLLATE
NOT   !
^
XOR
- (unary minus)   ~ (unary bit negation)
*   /   %
+   -
<<   >>
&
|
<   <=   =   <=>   !=   <>   >=   >   IN   IS   LIKE   REGEXP   RLIKE
BETWEEN   CASE   WHEN   THEN   ELSE
AND   &&
OR   ||
:=
```

The unary operators (unary minus, unary bit negation, NOT, and BINARY) bind more tightly than the binary operators. That is, they group with the immediately following term in an expression, not with the rest of the expression as a whole.

```
-2+3                                    → 1
-(2+3)                                  → -5
```

Grouping Operators

Parentheses can be used to group parts of an expression. They override the default operator precedence that determines the order in which terms of an expression are evaluated (see "Operator Precedence" earlier in this appendix). Parentheses can also be used simply for visual clarity, to make an expression more readable.

```
1 + 2 * 3 / 4                           → 2.50
(((1 + 2) * 3) / 4)                     → 2.25
```

Arithmetic Operators

These operators perform standard arithmetic. The arithmetic operators work on numbers, not strings (although strings that look like numbers are converted automatically to the corresponding numeric value). Arithmetic involving NULL values produces a NULL result.

- +

  Addition; evaluates to the sum of the arguments.

  ```
  2 + 2                                        → 4
  3.2 + 4.7                                    → 7.9
  '43bc' + '21d'                               → 64
  'abc' + 'def'                                → 0
  ```

  The final example in this listing shows that + does not serve as the string concatenation operator the way it does in some languages. Instead, the strings are converted to numbers before the arithmetic operation takes place. Strings that don't look like numbers are converted to 0. Use the CONCAT() function to concatenate strings.

- -

  Subtraction; evaluates to the difference of the operands when used between two terms of an expression. Evaluates to the negative of the operand when used in front of a single term (that is, it flips the sign of the term).

  ```
  10 - 7                                       → 3
  -(10 - 7)                                    → -3
  ```

- *

  Multiplication; evaluates to the product of the operands.

  ```
  2 * 3                                        → 6
  2.3 * -4.5                                   → -10.3
  ```

- /

  Division; evaluates to the quotient of the operands. Division by zero produces a NULL result.

  ```
  3 / 1                                        → 3.00
  1 / 3                                        → 0.33
  1 / 0                                        → NULL
  ```

- %

  The modulo operator; evaluates to the remainder of m divided by n. m % n is the same as MOD(m,n). As with division, the modulo operator with a divisor of zero returns NULL.

  ```
  12 % 4                                       → 0
  12 % 5                                       → 2
  12 % 0                                       → NULL
  ```

Arithmetic for the +, -, and * operators is performed with BIGINT values (64-bit integers) if both arguments are integers. This means expressions involving large values might exceed the range of 64-bit integer calculations, with unpredictable results:

```
999999999999999999 * 999999999999999999       → -7527149226598858751
99999999999 * 99999999999 * 99999999999         → -1504485813132150785
18014398509481984 * 18014398509481984            → 0
```

For / and %, BIGINT values are used only when the division is performed in a context where the result is converted to an integer.

Comparison Operators

Comparison operators return 1 if the comparison is true and 0 if the comparison is false. You can compare numbers or strings. Operands are converted as necessary according to the following rules:

- Other than for the <=> operator, comparisons involving NULL values evaluate as NULL. (<=> is like =, except that the value of the expression NULL <=> NULL is true.)

- If both operands are strings, they are compared lexically as strings. Binary strings are compared on a byte-by-byte basis using the numeric value of each byte. Comparisons for non-binary strings are performed character by character, using the collating sequence of the character set in which the strings are expressed. If the strings have different character sets (as is possible as of MySQL 4.1), the comparison might not yield meaningful results. A comparison between a binary and a non-binary string is treated as a comparison of binary strings.

- If both operands are integers, they are compared numerically as integers.

- As of MySQL 3.23.22, hexadecimal constants are compared as numbers. Before that, hex constants that are not compared to a number are compared as binary strings.

- If either operand is a TIMESTAMP or DATETIME value and the other is a constant, the operands are compared as TIMESTAMP values. This is done to make comparisons work better for ODBC applications.

- If none of the preceding rules apply, the operands are compared numerically as floating-point values. Note that this includes the case of comparing a string and a number. The string is converted to a number, which results in a value of 0 if the string doesn't look like a number. For example, '14.3' converts to 14.3, but 'L4.3' converts to 0.

The following comparisons illustrate these rules:

```
2 < 12                                          → 1
'2' < '12'                                      → 0
'2' < 12                                        → 1
```

The first comparison involves two integers, which are compared numerically. The second comparison involves two strings, which are compared lexically. The third comparison involves a string and a number, so they are compared as floating-point values.

String comparisons are not case sensitive unless the comparison involves a binary string. Thus, a case-sensitive comparison is performed if you use the BINARY keyword or are comparing values from CHAR BINARY, VARCHAR BINARY, or BLOB columns.

- =

    Evaluates to 1 if the operands are equal; 0 otherwise.

    ```
    1 = 1                                       → 1
    1 = 2                                       → 0
    'abc' = 'abc'                               → 1
    'abc' = 'def'                               → 0
    'abc' = 'ABC'                               → 1
    BINARY 'abc' = 'ABC'                        → 0
    BINARY 'abc' = 'abc'                        → 1
    'abc' = 0                                   → 1
    ```

    'abc' is equal to both 'abc' and 'ABC' because string comparisons are not case sensitive by default. String comparisons can be made case sensitive by using the BINARY operator. 'abc' is equal to 0 because it's converted to a number in accordance to the comparison rules. Because 'abc' doesn't look like a number, it's converted to 0 for purposes of the comparison.

    The current character set determines the comparison value of characters that are similar but differ in accent or diacritical marks.

- <=>

    The NULL-safe equality operator; it's similar to =, except that it evaluates to 1 when the operands are equal, even when they are NULL.

    ```
    1 <=> 1                                     → 1
    1 <=> 2                                     → 0
    NULL <=> NULL                               → 1
    NULL = NULL                                 → NULL
    ```

    The final two examples show how = and <=> handle NULL comparisons differently.

    <=> was introduced in MySQL 3.23.0.

- `!= or <>`

  Evaluates to `1` if the operands are unequal; `0` otherwise.

  ```
  3.4 != 3.4                              → 0
  'abc' <> 'ABC'                          → 0
  BINARY 'abc' <> 'ABC'                   → 1
  'abc' != 'def'                          → 1
  ```

- `<`

  Evaluates to `1` if the left operand is less than the right operand; `0` otherwise.

  ```
  3 < 10                                  → 1
  105.4 < 10e+1                           → 0
  'abc' < 'ABC'                           → 0
  'abc' < 'def'                           → 1
  ```

- `<=`

  Evaluates to `1` if the left operand is less than or equal to the right operand; otherwise, evaluates to `0`.

  ```
  'abc' <= 'a'                            → 0
  'a' <= 'abc'                            → 1
  13.5 <= 14                              → 1
  (3 * 4) - (6 * 2) <= 0                  → 1
  ```

- `>=`

  Evaluates to `1` if the left operand is greater than or equal to the right operand; otherwise, evaluates to `0`.

  ```
  'abc' >= 'a'                            → 1
  'a' >= 'abc'                            → 0
  13.5 >= 14                              → 0
  (3 * 4) - (6 * 2) >= 0                  → 1
  ```

- `>`

  Evaluates to `1` if the left operand is greater than the right operand; otherwise, evaluates to `0`.

  ```
  PI() > 3                                → 1
  'abc' > 'a'                             → 1
  SIN(0) > COS(0)                         → 0
  ```

- `expr BETWEEN min AND max`
  `expr NOT BETWEEN min AND max`

  BETWEEN evaluates to `1` if `expr` lies within the range of values spanned by `min` and `max` (inclusive); otherwise, it evaluates to `0`. For NOT BETWEEN, the opposite is true. If the operands `expr`, `min`, and `max` are all of the same type, these expressions are equivalent:

  ```
  expr BETWEEN min AND max
  (min <= expr AND expr <= max)
  ```

If the operands are not of the same type, type conversion occurs and the two expressions may not be equivalent. BETWEEN is evaluated using comparisons determined depending on the type of *expr*:

- If *expr* is a string, the operands are compared lexically as strings. The comparisons are case sensitive or not, depending on whether or not *expr* is a binary string.
- If *expr* is an integer, the operands are compared numerically as integers.
- If neither of the preceding rules is true, the operands are compared numerically as floating-point numbers.

```
'def' BETWEEN 'abc' and 'ghi'        → 1
'def' BETWEEN 'abc' and 'def'        → 1
13.3 BETWEEN 10 and 20               → 1
13.3 BETWEEN 10 and 13               → 0
2 BETWEEN 2 and 2                    → 1
'B' BETWEEN 'A' and 'a'              → 0
BINARY 'B' BETWEEN 'A' and 'a'       → 1
```

- CASE *expr* WHEN *expr1* THEN *result1* ...
     [ELSE *default*] END
  CASE WHEN *expr1* THEN *result1* ...
     [ELSE *default*] END

The first form of CASE compares the initial expression *expr* to the expression following each WHEN. For the first one that is equal, the corresponding THEN value becomes the result. This is useful for comparing a given value to a set of values.

```
CASE 0 WHEN 1 THEN 'T' WHEN 0 THEN 'F' END      → 'F'
CASE 'F' WHEN 'T' THEN 1 WHEN 'F' THEN 0 END    → 0
```

The second form of CASE evaluates WHEN expressions until one is found that is true (not zero and not NULL). The corresponding THEN value becomes the result. This is useful for performing non-equality tests or testing arbitrary conditions.

```
CASE WHEN 1=0 THEN 'absurd' WHEN 1=1 THEN 'obvious' END
                                            → 'obvious'
```

If no WHEN expression matches, the ELSE value is the result. If there is no ELSE clause, CASE evaluates to NULL.

```
CASE 0 WHEN 1 THEN 'true' ELSE 'false' END      → 'false'
CASE 0 WHEN 1 THEN 'true' END                   → NULL
CASE WHEN 1=0 THEN 'true' ELSE 'false' END      → 'false'
CASE WHEN 1/0 THEN 'true' END                   → NULL
```

The type of the value following the first THEN determines the type of the entire CASE expression.

```
CASE 1 WHEN 0 THEN 0 ELSE 1 END          → 1
CASE 1 WHEN 0 THEN '0' ELSE 1 END        → '1'
```

CASE was introduced in MySQL 3.23.3.

- expr IN (*value1,value2,...*)

  expr NOT IN (*value1,value2,...*)

  IN() evaluates to 1 if *expr* is one of the values in the list; otherwise, it evaluates to 0. For NOT IN(), the opposite is true. The following expressions are equivalent:

  ```
  expr NOT IN (value1,value2,...)
  NOT (expr IN (value1,value2,...))
  ```

  If all values in the list are constants, MySQL sorts them and evaluates the IN() test using a binary search, which is very fast.

  ```
  3 IN (1,2,3,4,5)                        → 1
  'd' IN ('a','b','c','d','e')            → 1
  'f' IN ('a','b','c','d','e')            → 0
  3 NOT IN (1,2,3,4,5)                    → 0
  'd' NOT IN ('a','b','c','d','e')        → 0
  'f' NOT IN ('a','b','c','d','e')        → 1
  ```

- *expr* IS NULL

  expr IS NOT NULL

  IS NULL evaluates to 1 if the value of expr is NULL; otherwise it evaluates to 0. IS NOT NULL is the opposite. The following expressions are equivalent:

  ```
  expr IS NOT NULL
  NOT (expr IS NULL)
  ```

  IS NULL and IS NOT NULL should be used to determine whether or not the value of expr is NULL. You cannot use the regular comparison operators = and != for this purpose. (As of MySQL 3.23, you can also use <=> to test for equality with NULL.)

  ```
  NULL IS NULL                            → 1
  0 IS NULL                               → 0
  NULL IS NOT NULL                        → 0
  0 IS NOT NULL                           → 1
  NOT (0 IS NULL)                         → 1
  NOT (NULL IS NULL)                      → 0
  NOT NULL IS NULL                        → 1
  ```

The last example returns the result shown because NOT binds more tightly than IS (see the "Operator Precedence" section earlier in this appendix).

Bit Operators

This section describes operators that perform bitwise calculations. Bit operations are performed using BIGINT values (64-bit integers), which limits the maximum range of the operations. Bit operations involving NULL values produce a NULL result.

- &

  Evaluates to the bitwise AND (intersection) of the operands.

  ```
  1 & 1                                             → 1
  1 & 2                                             → 0
  7 & 5                                             → 5
  ```

- |

  Evaluates to the bitwise OR (union) of the operands.

  ```
  1 | 1                                             → 1
  1 | 2                                             → 3
  1 | 2 | 4 | 8                                     → 15
  1 | 2 | 4 | 8 | 15                                → 15
  ```

- ^

  Evaluates to the bitwise XOR (exclusive-Or) of the operands.

  ```
  1 ^ 1                                             → 0
  1 ^ 0                                             → 1
  255 ^ 127                                         → 128
  ```

  This operator was introduced in MySQL 4.0.2. Prior to that, you can produce the same result for two values m and n using the following expression:

  ```
  (m & (~n)) | ((~m) & n)
  ```

- <<

  Shifts the leftmost operand left the number of bit positions indicated by the right operand. Shifting by a negative amount results in a value of 0.

  ```
  1 << 2                                            → 4
  2 << 2                                            → 8
  1 << 62                                           → 4611686018427387904
  1 << 63                                           → -9223372036854775808
  1 << 64                                           → 0
  ```

The last two examples demonstrate the limits of 64-bit calculations.

<< was introduced in MySQL 3.22.2.

- `>>`

  Shifts the leftmost operand right the number of bit positions indicated by the right operand. Shifting by a negative amount results in a value of 0.

`16 >> 3`	→ 2
`16 >> 4`	→ 1
`16 >> 5`	→ 0

  `>>` was introduced in MySQL 3.22.2.

- `~`

  Performs bitwise negation of the following expression. That is, all 0 bits become 1 and vice versa.

`~0`	→ -1
`~(-1)`	→ 0
`~~(-1)`	→ -1

  `~` was introduced in MySQL 3.23.5.

Logical Operators

Logical operators (also known as boolean operators, after the mathematician George Boole, who formalized their use) test the truth or falseness of expressions. All logical operations return 1 for true and 0 for false. Logical operators interpret non-zero operands as true and operands of 0 as false. NULL values are handled as indicated in the operator descriptions.

Logical operators expect operands to be numbers, so string operands are converted to numbers before the operator is evaluated.

- NOT or !

  Logical negation; evaluates to 1 if the following operand is false and 0 if the operand is true, except that NOT NULL is NULL.

`NOT 0`	→ 1
`NOT 1`	→ 0
`NOT NULL`	→ NULL
`NOT 3`	→ 0
`NOT NOT 1`	→ 1
`NOT '1'`	→ 0
`NOT '0'`	→ 1
`NOT ''`	→ 1
`NOT 'abc'`	→ 1

- AND or &&

  Logical AND; evaluates to 1 if both operands are true (not 0 and not NULL); 0 otherwise.

  ```
  0 AND 0                                    → 0
  0 AND 3                                    → 0
  4 AND 2                                    → 1
  ```

  The behavior of AND is version-dependent with respect to NULL operands (that is, operands of unknown value). As of MySQL 3.23.9, AND evaluates to 0 if the result can be known to be false, NULL if the result cannot be determined.

  ```
  1 AND NULL                                 → NULL
  0 AND NULL                                 → 0
  NULL AND NULL                              → NULL
  ```

  Prior to MySQL 3.23.9, AND evaluates to 0 with NULL operands. In effect, NULL is treated as 0.

  ```
  1 AND NULL                                 → 0
  0 AND NULL                                 → 0
  NULL AND NULL                              → 0
  ```

- OR or ||

  Logical OR; evaluates to 1 if either operand is true (not zero and not NULL); 0 otherwise.

  ```
  0 OR 0                                     → 0
  0 OR 3                                     → 1
  4 OR 2                                     → 1
  ```

  The behavior of OR is version-dependent with respect to NULL operands (that is, operands of unknown value). As of MySQL 3.23.9, OR evaluates to 1 if the result can be known to be true; NULL if the result cannot be determined.

  ```
  1 OR NULL                                  → 1
  0 OR NULL                                  → NULL
  NULL OR NULL                               → NULL
  ```

  Prior to MySQL 3.23.9, OR evaluates to 1 if the result can be known to be true; 0 otherwise. In effect, NULL is treated as 0.

  ```
  1 OR NULL                                  → 1
  0 OR NULL                                  → 0
  NULL OR NULL                               → 0
  ```

- XOR

  Logical exclusive-XOR; evaluates to 1 if exactly one operand is true (not zero and not NULL), and 0 otherwise. Evaluates to NULL if either operand is NULL.

  ```
  0 XOR 0                                              → 0
  0 XOR 9                                              → 1
  7 XOR 0                                              → 1
  5 XOR 2                                              → 0
  ```

  XOR was introduced in MySQL 4.0.2. Prior to that, you can produce the same result for two values *m* and *n* using the following expression:

  ```
  (m AND (NOT n)) OR ((NOT m) AND n)
  ```

In MySQL, !, ||, and && indicate logical operations, as they do in C. Note in particular that || does not perform string concatenation as it does in some versions of SQL. Use the CONCAT() function instead to concatenate strings. (You can start the server in ANSI mode with the --ansi option if you want || to be treated as the string concatenation operator.)

Cast Operators

Cast operators convert values from one type to another.

- _charset str

  To treat a string constant or column value as though it has a given character set, precede it with a _charset operator, where charset is the name of a character set supported by the server. For example, the following expressions treat the string 'abc' as having a character set of cp1256, utf8, or ucs2:

  ```
  _cp1256 'abc'
  _utf8 'abc'
  _ucs2 'abc'
  ```

  The _charset operator was introduced in MySQL 4.1.0.

- BINARY str

  BINARY causes the following operand to be treated as a binary string so that comparisons involving the string are case sensitive. If the following operand is a number, it is converted to string form:

  ```
  'abc' = 'ABC'                                        → 1
  'abc' = BINARY 'ABC'                                 → 0
  BINARY 'abc' = 'ABC'                                 → 0
  '2' < 12                                             → 1
  '2' < BINARY 12                                      → 0
  ```

In the last example, BINARY causes a number-to-string conversion. The comparison is then performed lexically because both operands are strings.

BINARY was introduced in MySQL 3.23.0.

- *str* COLLATE *charset*

The COLLATE operator causes the given string *str* to be compared using the collating order for the character set *charset*. This affects operations such as comparisons, sorting, grouping, and DISTINCT.

```
SELECT ... WHERE col_name COLLATE utf8 > 'M';
SELECT MAX(col_name COLLATE greek) FROM ... ;
SELECT ... GROUP BY col_name COLLATE latin1;
SELECT ... ORDER BY col_name COLLATE czech;
SELECT DISTINCT col_name COLLATE latin1_de FROM ...;
```

The COLLATE operator was introduced in MySQL 4.1.0.

Pattern-Matching Operators

MySQL provides SQL pattern matching using LIKE and regular expression pattern matching using REGEXP. SQL pattern matches are not case sensitive unless the string to be matched or the pattern string are binary strings. The same is true for regular expression pattern matches, with the exception that regular expressions are always case sensitive prior to MySQL 3.23.4. SQL pattern matching succeeds only if the pattern matches the entire string to be matched. Regular expression pattern matching succeeds if the pattern is found anywhere in the string.

- *str* LIKE *pat* [ESCAPE '*c*']
  str NOT LIKE *pat* [ESCAPE '*c*']

LIKE performs a SQL pattern match and evaluates to 1 if the pattern string *pat* matches the entire string expression *str*. If the pattern does not match, LIKE evaluates to 0. For NOT LIKE, the opposite is true. These two expressions are equivalent:

```
str NOT LIKE pat [ESCAPE 'c']
NOT (str LIKE pat [ESCAPE 'c'])
```

The result is NULL if either string is NULL.

Two characters have special meaning in SQL patterns and serve as wild-cards:

- '%' matches any sequence of characters (including an empty string) other than NULL.
- '_' (underscore) matches any single character.

Patterns can contain either or both wildcard characters:

```
'catnip' LIKE 'cat%'                        → 1
'dogwood' LIKE '%wood'                       → 1
'bird' LIKE '____'                           → 1
'bird' LIKE '___'                            → 0
'dogwood' LIKE '%wo__'                       → 1
```

Case sensitivity of SQL pattern matching using LIKE is determined by the strings being compared. Normally, comparisons are not case sensitive. If either string is a binary string, the comparison is case sensitive:

```
'abc' LIKE 'ABC'                             → 1
BINARY 'abc' LIKE 'ABC'                      → 0
'abc' LIKE BINARY 'ABC'                      → 0
```

Because '%' matches any sequence of characters, it even matches no characters:

```
'' LIKE '%'                                  → 1
'cat' LIKE 'cat%'                            → 1
```

In MySQL, you can use LIKE with numeric expressions:

```
50 + 50 LIKE '1%'                            → 1
200 LIKE '2__'                               → 1
```

To match a wildcard character literally, turn off its special meaning in the pattern string by preceding it with the escape character, '\':

```
'100% pure' LIKE '100%'                      → 1
'100% pure' LIKE '100\%'                     → 0
'100% pure' LIKE '100\% pure'                → 1
```

If you want to use an escape character other than '\', specify it using an ESCAPE clause:

```
'100% pure' LIKE '100^%' ESCAPE '^'          → 0
'100% pure' LIKE '100^% pure' ESCAPE '^'     → 1
```

- *str* REGEXP *pat*

  str NOT REGEXP *pat*

  REGEXP performs a regular expression pattern match. It evaluates to 1 if the pattern string *pat* matches the string expression *str*; 0 otherwise. NOT REGEXP is the opposite of REGEXP, so these two expressions are equivalent:

  ```
  str NOT REGEXP pat
  NOT (str REGEXP pat)
  ```

  Regular expressions are similar to the patterns used by the UNIX utilities grep and sed. The pattern sequences you can use are shown in Table C.1.

Table C.1 **Regular Expression Elements**

Element	Meaning
^	Match the beginning of the string
$	Match the end of the string
.	Match any single character, including newline
[...]	Match any character appearing between the brackets
[^...]	Match any character not appearing between the brackets
e*	Match zero or more instances of pattern element e
e+	Match one or more instances of pattern element e
e?	Match zero or one instances of pattern element e
e1|e2	Match pattern element $e1$ or $e2$
e{m}	Match m instances of pattern element e
e{m,}	Match m or more instances of pattern element e
e{,n}	Match zero to n instances of pattern element e
e{m,n}	Match m to n instances of pattern element e
(...)	Group pattern elements into a single element
Other	Non-special characters match themselves

The result of a regular expression match is NULL if either string is NULL.

A regular expression pattern need not match the entire string, it just needs to be found somewhere in the string.

```
'cats and dogs' REGEXP 'dogs'            → 1
'cats and dogs' REGEXP 'cats'            → 1
'cats and dogs' REGEXP 'c.*a.*d'         → 1
'cats and dogs' REGEXP 'o'               → 1
'cats and dogs' REGEXP 'x'               → 0
```

You can use '^' or '$' to force a pattern to match only at the beginning or end of the string.

```
'abcde' REGEXP 'b'                       → 1
'abcde' REGEXP '^b'                      → 0
'abcde' REGEXP 'b$'                      → 0
'abcde' REGEXP '^a'                      → 1
'abcde' REGEXP 'e$'                      → 1
'abcde' REGEXP '^a.*e$'                  → 1
```

The [...] and [^...] constructs specify character classes. Within a class, a range of characters can be indicated using a dash between the two endpoint characters of the range. For example, [a-z] matches any lowercase letter, and [0-9] matches any digit.

```
'bin' REGEXP '^b[aeiou]n$'               → 1
'bxn' REGEXP '^b[aeiou]n$'               → 0
'oboeist' REGEXP '^ob[aeiou]+st$'        → 1
```

```
'wolf359' REGEXP '[a-z]+[0-9]+'                    → 1
'wolf359' REGEXP '[0-9a-z]+'                       → 1
'wolf359' REGEXP '[0-9]+[a-z]+'                    → 0
```

To indicate a literal ']' within a class, it must be the first character of the class. To indicate a literal '-', it must be the first or last character of the class. To indicate a literal '^', it must not be the first character after the '['.

Several special POSIX character class constructions having to do with collating sequences and equivalence classes are available as well, as shown in Table C.2.

Table C.2 **Regular Expression POSIX Character Classes**

Element	Meaning
[:alnum:]	Alphabetic and numeric characters
[:alpha:]	Alphabetic characters
[:blank:]	Whitespace (space or tab characters)
[:cntrl:]	Control characters
[:digit:]	Decimal digits (0–9)
[:graph:]	Graphic (non-blank) characters
[:lower:]	Lowercase alphabetic characters
[:print:]	Graphic or space characters
[:punct:]	Punctuation characters
[:space:]	Space, tab, newline, or carriage return
[:upper:]	Uppercase alphabetic characters
[:xdigit:]	Hexadecimal digits (0–9, a–f, A–F)

The POSIX constructors are used within character classes:

```
'abc' REGEXP '[[:space:]]'                         → 0
'a c' REGEXP '[[:space:]]'                         → 1
'abc' REGEXP '[[:digit:][:punct:]]'                → 0
'a0c' REGEXP '[[:digit:][:punct:]]'                → 1
'a,c' REGEXP '[[:digit:][:punct:]]'                → 1
```

MySQL uses syntax similar to C for escape sequences within regular expression strings. For example, \n, \t, and \\ are interpreted as newline, tab, and backslash. To specify such characters in a pattern, double the backslashes (\\n, \\t, and \\\\). One backslash is stripped off when the query is parsed, and the remaining escape sequence is interpreted when the pattern match is performed.

- *str* RLIKE *pat*

  str NOT RLIKE *pat*

  RLIKE and NOT RLIKE are synonyms for REGEXP and NOT REGEXP.

Functions

Functions are called to perform a calculation and return a value. By default, functions must be invoked with no space between the function name and the parentheses following it:

```
NOW()                    Correct
NOW ()                   Incorrect
```

If you start the server in ANSI mode with the --ansi option, it will allow spaces after function names, although a side-effect is that all function names become reserved words. You may also be able to select this behavior on a connection-specific basis, depending on the client program. For example, you can start mysql with the --ignore-space option; in C programs, you can call mysql_real_connect() with the CLIENT_IGNORE_SPACE option.

In most cases, multiple arguments to a function are separated by commas. Spaces are allowed around function arguments:

```
CONCAT('abc','def')      This is okay
CONCAT( 'abc' , 'def' )  This is okay, too
```

There are a few exceptions to this syntax, such as TRIM() or EXTRACT():

```
TRIM(' ' FROM ' x ')                      → 'x'
EXTRACT(YEAR FROM '2003-01-01')           → 2003
```

Each function entry describes its allowable syntax.

Comparison Functions

- GREATEST(*expr1*,*expr2*,...)

  Returns the largest argument, where "largest" is defined according to the following rules:

  - If the function is called in an integer context or all its arguments are integers, the arguments are compared as integers.
  - If the function is called in a floating-point context or all its arguments are floating-point values, the arguments are compared as floating-point values.
  - If neither of the preceding two rules applies, the arguments are compared as strings. The comparisons are not case sensitive unless some argument is a binary string.

    ```
    GREATEST(2,3,1)                → 3
    GREATEST(38.5,94.2,-1)         → 94.2
    GREATEST('a','ab','abc')       → 'abc'
    GREATEST(1,3,5)                → 5
    GREATEST('A','b','C')          → 'c'
    GREATEST(BINARY 'A','b','C')   → 'b'
    ```

GREATEST() was introduced in MySQL 3.22.5. In earlier versions, you can use MAX() instead.

- IF(*expr1*,*expr2*,*expr3*)

If *expr1* is true (not 0 or NULL), returns *expr2*; otherwise, it returns *expr3*. IF() returns a number or string according to the context in which it is used.

```
IF(1,'true','false')                → 'true'
IF(0,'true','false')                → 'false'
IF(NULL,'true','false')             → 'false'
IF(1.3,'non-zero','zero')           → 'non-zero'
IF(0.3,'non-zero','zero')           → 'zero'
IF(0.3 != 0,'non-zero','zero')      → 'non-zero'
```

expr1 is evaluated as an integer value, and the last three examples indicate how this behavior can catch you unaware if you're not careful. 1.3 converts to the integer value 1, which is true. But 0.3 converts to the integer value 0, which is false. The last example shows the proper way to use a floating-point number: Test the number using a comparison expression. The comparison treats the number correctly as a floating-point value and produces a true or false comparison result as an integer 1 or 0, as required by IF().

- IFNULL(*expr1*,*expr2*)

Returns *expr2* if the value of the expression *expr1* is NULL; otherwise, it returns *expr1*. IFNULL() returns a number or string depending on the context in which it is used.

```
IFNULL(NULL,'null')                 → 'null'
IFNULL('not null','null')           → 'not null'
```

- INTERVAL(*n*,*n1*,*n2*,...)

Returns 0 if *n* < *n1*, 1 if *n* < *n2*, and so on or –1 if *n* is NULL. The values *n1*, *n2*, ... must be in strictly increasing order (*n1* < *n2* < ...) because a fast binary search is used. Otherwise, INTERVAL() will behave unpredictably.

```
INTERVAL(1.1,0,1,2)                 → 2
INTERVAL(7,1,3,5,7,9)               → 4
```

- ISNULL(*expr*)

Returns 1 if the value of the expression *expr* is NULL; otherwise, it returns 0.

```
ISNULL(NULL)                        → 1
ISNULL(0)                           → 0
ISNULL(1)                           → 0
```

- LEAST(*expr1,expr2,...*)

  Returns the smallest argument, where "smallest" is defined using the
  same comparison rules as for the GREATEST() function.

  ```
  LEAST(2,3,1)                              → 1
  LEAST(38.5,94.2,-1)                       → -1.0
  LEAST('a','ab','abc')                     → 'a'
  ```

  LEAST() was introduced in MySQL 3.22.5. In earlier versions, you can
  use MIN() instead.

- NULLIF(*expr1,expr2*)

  Returns *expr1* if the two expression values differ, NULL if they are the
  same.

  ```
  NULLIF(3,4)                               → 3
  NULLIF(3,3)                               → NULL
  ```

  NULLIF() was introduced in MySQL 3.23.19.

- STRCMP(*str1,str2*)

  This function returns 1, 0, or -1, depending on whether the first argument is lexically greater than, equal to, or less than the second argument.
  If either argument is NULL, the function returns NULL. As of MySQL
  4.0.0, the comparison is not case sensitive unless either argument is a
  binary string:

  ```
  STRCMP('a','a')                           → 0
  STRCMP('a','A')                           → 0
  STRCMP('A','a')                           → 0
  STRCMP(BINARY 'a','A')                    → 1
  STRCMP(BINARY 'A','a')                    → -1
  ```

  Prior to MySQL 4.0.0, the comparison is case sensitive:

  ```
  STRCMP('a','a')                           → 0
  STRCMP('a','A')                           → 1
  STRCMP('A','a')                           → -1
  ```

Cast Functions

These functions convert values from one type to another.

- CAST(*expr* AS *type*)

  Cast an expression value *expr* to a given type. The *type* value can be
  BINARY (binary string), DATE, DATETIME, TIME, SIGNED, SIGNED INTEGER,
  UNSIGNED, or UNSIGNED INTEGER.

  ```
  CAST(304 AS BINARY)                       → '304'
  CAST(-1 AS UNSIGNED)                       →
  18446744073709551615
  ```

CAST() can be useful for forcing columns to have a particular type when creating a new table with CREATE TABLE ... SELECT.

```
mysql> CREATE TABLE t SELECT CAST(20020101 AS DATE) AS date_val;
mysql> SHOW COLUMNS FROM t;
+----------+------+------+-----+------------+-------+
| Field    | Type | Null | Key | Default    | Extra |
+----------+------+------+-----+------------+-------+
| date_val | date |      |     | 0000-00-00 |       |
+----------+------+------+-----+------------+-------+
mysql> SELECT * FROM t;
+------------+
| date_val   |
+------------+
| 2002-01-01 |
+------------+
```

CAST() was introduced in MySQL 4.0.2. It is similar to CONVERT(), but CAST() has ANSI SQL syntax, whereas CONVERT() has ODBC syntax.

- CONVERT(*expr*, *type*)

  CONVERT(*expr* USING *charset*)

  The first form of CONVERT() serves the same purpose as CAST(), but has slightly different syntax. The *expr* and *type* arguments have the same meaning. The USING form converts the value to use a given character set.

  ```
  CONVERT(304,BINARY)              → '304'
  CONVERT(-1,UNSIGNED)             → 18446744073709551615
  CONVERT('abc' USING utf8);       → 'abc'
  ```

  CONVERT() was introduced in MySQL 4.0.2. The form that has USING syntax was introduced in MySQL 4.1.0.

Numeric Functions

Numeric functions return NULL if an error occurs. For example, if you pass arguments to the function that are out of range or otherwise invalid, the function will return NULL.

- ABS(*x*)

  Returns the absolute value of *x*.

  ```
  ABS(13.5)                        → 13.5
  ABS(-13.5)                       → 13.5
  ```

- ACOS(*x*)

  Returns the arccosine of *x* or NULL if *x* is not in the range from
  −1 to 1.

  ```
  ACOS(1)                                 → 0.000000
  ACOS(0)                                 → 1.570796
  ACOS(-1)                                → 3.141593
  ```

- ASIN(*x*)

  Returns the arcsine of *x* or NULL if *x* is not in the range from −1 to 1.

  ```
  ASIN(1)                                 → 1.570796
  ASIN(0)                                 → 0.000000
  ASIN(-1)                                → -1.570796
  ```

- ATAN(*x*)

  ATAN(*y*,*x*)

  The one–argument form of ATAN() returns the arctangent of *x*. The two–
  argument form is a synonym for ATAN2().

  ```
  ATAN(1)                                 → 0.785398
  ATAN(0)                                 → 0.000000
  ATAN(-1)                                → -0.785398
  ```

- ATAN2(*y*,*x*)

  This is like ATAN(y/x), but it uses the signs of both arguments to determine the quadrant of the return value.

  ```
  ATAN2(1,1)                              → 0.785398
  ATAN2(1,-1)                             → 2.356194
  ATAN2(-1,1)                             → -0.785398
  ATAN2(-1,-1)                            → -2.356194
  ```

- CEILING(*x*)

  Returns the smallest integer not less than *x*. The return type is always a
  BIGINT value.

  ```
  CEILING(3.8)                            → 4
  CEILING(-3.8)                           → -3
  ```

- COS(*x*)

  Returns the cosine of *x*, where *x* is measured in radians.

  ```
  COS(0)                                  → 1.000000
  COS(PI())                               → -1.000000
  COS(PI()/2)                             → 0.000000
  ```

- COT(*x*)

  Returns the cotangent of *x*, where *x* is measured in radians.

  ```
  COT(PI()/2)                             → 0.00000000
  COT(PI()/4)                             → 1.00000000
  ```

- CRC32(*str*)

  Computes a cyclic redundancy check value from the argument, which is treated as a string. The return value is a 32-bit unsigned value in the range from 0 to $2^{32}-1$ or NULL if the argument is NULL.

CRC32('xyz')	→ 3951999591
CRC32('0')	→ 4108050209
CRC32(0)	→ 4108050209
CRC32(NULL)	→ NULL

  CRC32() was introduced in MySQL 4.1.0.

- DEGREES(*x*)

  Returns the value of *x*, converted from radians to degrees.

DEGREES(PI())	→ 180
DEGREES(PI()*2)	→ 360
DEGREES(PI()/2)	→ 90
DEGREES(-PI())	→ -180

- EXP(*x*)

  Returns e^x, where e is the base of natural logarithms.

EXP(1)	→ 2.718282
EXP(2)	→ 7.389056
EXP(-1)	→ 0.367879
1/EXP(1)	→ 0.36787944

- FLOOR(*x*)

  Returns the largest integer not greater than *x*. The return type is always a BIGINT value.

FLOOR(3.8)	→ 3
FLOOR(-3.8)	→ -4

- LN(*x*)

  This is a synonym for LOG(); it was introduced in MySQL 4.0.3.

- LOG(*x*)

  LOG(*b*,*x*)

  The one-argument form of LOG() returns the natural (base e) logarithm of *x*.

LOG(0)	→ NULL
LOG(1)	→ 0.000000
LOG(2)	→ 0.693147
LOG(EXP(1))	→ 1.000000

  The two-argument form returns the logarithm of *x* to the base *b*.

LOG(10,100)	→ 2.000000
LOG(2,256)	→ 8.000000

The two-argument form was introduced in MySQL 4.0.3. For earlier versions, you can compute the logarithm of x to the base b using `LOG(x)/LOG(b)`.

```
LOG(100)/LOG(10)                              → 2.00000000
LOG10(100)                                    → 2.000000
```

- `LOG10(x)`

Returns the logarithm of x to the base 10.

```
LOG10(0)                                      → NULL
LOG10(10)                                     → 1.000000
LOG10(100)                                    → 2.000000
```

- `LOG2(x)`

Returns the logarithm of x to the base 2.

```
LOG2(0)                                       → NULL
LOG2(255)                                     → 7.994353
LOG2(32767)                                   → 14.999956
```

`LOG2()` tells you the "width" of a value in bits. One use for this is to assess the amount of storage required for the value.

`LOG2()` was introduced in MySQL 4.0.3.

- `MOD(m, n)`

`MOD()` performs a modulo operation. `MOD(m, n )` is the same as m `%` n. See the "Arithmetic Operators" section earlier in this appendix.

- `PI()`

Returns the value of π.

```
PI()                                          → 3.141593
```

- `POW(x, y )`

Returns x^y; that is, x raised to the power y.

```
POW(2,3)                                      → 8.000000
POW(2,-3)                                     → 0.125000
POW(4,.5)                                      → 2.000000
POW(16,.25)                                    → 2.000000
```

- `POWER(x, y )`

This function is a synonym for `POW()`.

- `RADIANS(x)`

Returns the value of x, converted from degrees to radians.

```
RADIANS(0)                                    → 0
RADIANS(360)                                   → 6.2831853071796
RADIANS(-360)                                  → -6.2831853071796
```

- RAND()

  RAND(*n*)

  RAND() returns a random floating-point value in the range from 0.0 to 1.0. RAND(*n*) does the same thing, using *n* as the seed value for the randomizer. All calls to RAND() with the same value of *n* return the same result. You can use this property when you need a repeatable sequence of numbers. (Call RAND() the first time with an argument of *n*, and then call it successively with no argument to get the next numbers in the sequence.)

RAND(10)	→ 0.18109053110805
RAND(10)	→ 0.18109053110805
RAND()	→ 0.7502322306393
RAND()	→ 0.20788959060599
RAND(10)	→ 0.18109053110805
RAND()	→ 0.7502322306393
RAND()	→ 0.20788959060599

  In the examples, notice how sequential calls to RAND() behave when you supply an argument compared to when you do not.

  Seeding operations are client-specific. If one client invokes RAND(*n*) to seed the random number generator, that does not affect the numbers returned for other clients.

- ROUND(*x*)

  ROUND(*x*, *d*)

  ROUND(*x*) returns the value of *x*, rounded to an integer. ROUND(*x*, *d*) returns the value of *x*, rounded to a number with *d* decimal places. If *d* is 0, the result has no decimal point or fractional part.

ROUND(15.3)	→ 15
ROUND(15.5)	→ 16
ROUND(-33.27834,2)	→ -33.28
ROUND(1,4)	→ 1.0000

  The precise behavior of ROUND() depends on the rounding behavior of your underlying math library. This means the results from ROUND() may vary from system to system.

- SIGN(*x*)

  Returns -1, 0, or 1, depending on whether the value of *x* is negative, zero, or positive.

SIGN(15.803)	→ 1
SIGN(0)	→ 0
SIGN(-99)	→ -1

- SIN(*x*)

  Returns the sine of *x*, where *x* is measured in radians.
  ```
  SIN(0)                                    → 0.000000
  SIN(PI())                                 → 0.000000
  SIN(PI()/2)                               → 1.000000
  ```

- SQRT(*x*)

  Returns the non-negative square root of *x*.
  ```
  SQRT(625)                                 → 25.000000
  SQRT(2.25)                                → 1.500000
  SQRT(-1)                                  → NULL
  ```

- TAN(*x*)

  Returns the tangent of *x*, where *x* is measured in radians.
  ```
  TAN(0)                                    → 0.000000
  TAN(PI()/4)                               → 1.000000
  ```

- TRUNCATE(*x*, *d*)

  Returns the value *x*, with the fractional part truncated to *d* decimal places. If *d* is 0, the result has no decimal point or fractional part. If *d* is greater than the number of decimal places in *x*, the fractional part is right-padded with trailing zeros to the desired width.

  ```
  TRUNCATE(1.23,1)                          → 1.2
  TRUNCATE(1.23,0)                          → 1
  TRUNCATE(1.23,4)                          → 1.2300
  ```

String Functions

Most of the functions in this section return a string result. Some of them, such as LENGTH(), take strings as arguments and return a number. For functions that operate on strings based on string positions, the position of the first (leftmost) character is 1 (not 0).

Several string functions are multi-byte safe as of MySQL 3.23.7: INSERT(), INSTR(), LCASE(), LEFT(), LOCATE(), LOWER(), MID(), POSITION(), REPLACE(), REVERSE(), RIGHT(), RTRIM(), SUBSTRING(), SUBSTRING_INDEX(), TRIM(), UCASE(), and UPPER().

- ASCII(*str*)

  Returns the ASCII code of the leftmost character of the string *str*. It returns 0 if *str* is empty or NULL if *str* is NULL.
  ```
  ASCII('abc')                              → 97
  ASCII('')                                 → 0
  ASCII(NULL)                               → NULL
  ```

- `BIN(n)`

  Returns the value of n in binary form as a string. The following two expressions are equivalent:

  ```
  BIN(n)
  CONV(n,10,2)
  ```

  See the description of `CONV()` for more information.

  `BIN()` was introduced in MySQL 3.22.4.

- `CHAR(n1,n2,...)`

  Interprets the arguments as ASCII codes and returns a string consisting of the concatenation of the corresponding character values. `NULL` arguments are ignored.

  ```
  CHAR(65)                          → 'A'
  CHAR(97)                          → 'a'
  CHAR(89,105,107,101,115,33)       → 'Yikes!'
  ```

- `CHARACTER_LENGTH(str)`

  This function is a synonym for `CHAR_LENGTH()`.

- `CHAR_LENGTH(str)`

  This function is similar to `LENGTH()`, except that as of MySQL 3.23.6, multi-byte characters are each counted as having a length of 1.

- `CHARSET(str)`

  Returns the name of the character set in which the string `str` is represented.

  ```
  CHARSET('abc')                    → 'latin1'
  CHARSET(CONVERT('abc' USING utf8)) → 'utf8'
  ```

  `CHARSET()` was introduced in MySQL 4.1.0.

- `COALESCE(expr1,expr2,...)`

  Returns the first non-`NULL` element in the list or `NULL` if no argument is non-`NULL`.

  ```
  COALESCE(NULL,1/0,2,'a',45+97)    → '2'
  COALESCE(NULL,1/0)                → NULL
  ```

  `COALESCE()` was introduced in MySQL 3.23.3.

- `CONCAT(str1,str2,...)`

  Returns a string consisting of the concatenation of all of its arguments. Returns `NULL` if any argument is `NULL`. `CONCAT()` can be called with a single argument.

  ```
  CONCAT('abc','def')               → 'abcdef'
  CONCAT('abc')                     → 'abc'
  CONCAT('abc',NULL)                → NULL
  CONCAT('Hello',', ','goodbye')    → 'Hello, goodbye'
  ```

If the arguments to CONCAT() have different character sets (as is possible as of MySQL 4.1), the result has the character set of the first argument.

Another way to concatenate strings is to just specify them next to each other.

```
'three' 'blind' 'mice'                                  → 'threeblindmice'
'abc' 'def' = 'abcdef'                                   → 1
```

- CONCAT_WS(*delim*, *str1*, *str2*, ...)

  Returns a string consisting of the concatenation of its second and following arguments, with the *delim* string used as the separator between strings. Returns NULL if *delim* is NULL, but ignores any NULL values or empty strings in the list of strings to be concatenated.

```
CONCAT_WS(',','a','b','c','d')                          → 'a,b,c,d'
CONCAT_WS('*-*','lemon','','lime',NULL,'grape')         → 'lemon*-*lime*-*grape'
```

- CONV(*n*, *from_base*, *to_base*)

  Given a number *n* represented in base *from_base*, returns a string representation of *n* in base *to_base*. The result is NULL if any argument is NULL. *from_base* and *to_base* should be integers in the range from 2 to 36. *n* is treated as a BIGINT value (64-bit integer), but can be specified as a string because numbers in bases higher than 10 can contain non-decimal digits. (This is also the reason that CONV() returns a string; the result may contain characters from A to Z for bases 11 to 36.) The result is 0 if *n* is not a legal number in base *from_base*. (For example, if *from_base* is 16 and *n* is 'abcdefg', the result is 0 because g is not a legal hexadecimal digit.)

  Non-decimal characters in *n* can be specified in either uppercase or lowercase. Non-decimal characters in the result will be uppercase.

  Convert 14 specified as a hexadecimal number to binary:

```
CONV('e',16,2)                                          → '1110'
```

  Convert 255 specified in binary to octal:

```
CONV(11111111,2,8)                                      → '377'
CONV('11111111',2,8)                                    → '377'
```

  n is treated as an unsigned number by default. If you specify *to_base* as a negative number, *n* is treated as a signed number.

```
CONV(-10,10,16)                                         → 'FFFFFFFFFFFFFFF6'
CONV(-10,10,-16)                                        → '-A'
```

  CONV() was introduced in MySQL 3.22.4.

- ELT(*n*,*str1*,*str2*,...)

Returns the *n*-th string from the list of strings *str1*, *str2*,.... Returns NULL if *n* is NULL, the *n*th string is NULL, or there is no *n*th string. The index of the first string is 1. ELT() is complementary to FIELD().

```
ELT(3,'a','b','c','d','e')                → 'c'
ELT(0,'a','b','c','d','e')                → NULL
ELT(6,'a','b','c','d','e')                → NULL
ELT(FIELD('b','a','b','c'),'a','b','c')   → 'b'
```

- EXPORT_SET(*n*,*on*,*off*,[*delim*,[*bit_count*]])

Returns a string consisting of the strings *on* and *off*, separated by the delimiter string *delim*. *on* is used to represent each bit that is set in *n*, and *off* is used to represent each bit that is not set. *bit_count* indicates the maximum number of bits in *n* to examine. The default delimiter is a comma, and the default *bit_count* value is 64. Returns NULL if any argument is NULL.

```
EXPORT_SET(7,'+','-','',5)                → '+++--'
EXPORT_SET(0xa,'1','0','',6)              → '010100'
EXPORT_SET(97,'Y','N',',',8)             → 'Y,N,N,N,N,Y,Y,N'
```

EXPORT_SET() was introduced in MySQL 3.23.2.

- FIELD(*str*,*str1*,*str2*,...)

Finds *str* in the list of strings *str1*, *str2*, ... and returns the index of the matching string. Returns 0 if there is no match or if *str* is NULL. The index of the first string is 1. FIELD() is complementary to ELT().

```
FIELD('b','a','b','c')                    → 2
FIELD('d','a','b','c')                    → 0
FIELD(NULL,'a','b','c')                   → 0
FIELD(ELT(2,'a','b','c'),'a','b','c')     → 2
```

- FIND_IN_SET(*str*,*str_list*)

str_list is a string consisting of substrings separated by commas (that is, it is like a SET value). FIND_IN_SET() returns the index of *str* within *str_list*. Returns 0 if *str* is not present in *str_list* or NULL if either argument is NULL. The index of the first substring is 1.

```
FIND_IN_SET('cow','moose,cow,pig')        → 2
FIND_IN_SET('dog','moose,cow,pig')        → 0
```

- FORMAT(*x*, *d*)

  Formats the number *x* to *d* decimals using a format like '*nn*,*nnn*.*nnn*' and returns the result as a string. If *d* is 0, the result has no decimal point or fractional part.

  ```
  FORMAT(1234.56789,3)                    → '1,234.568'
  FORMAT(999999.99,2)                     → '999,999.99'
  FORMAT(999999.99,0)                     → '1,000,000'
  ```

  Note the rounding behavior exhibited by the final example.

- HEX(*n*)

  HEX(*str*)

  With a numeric argument *n*, HEX() returns the value of the argument in hexadecimal form, as a string. The following two expressions are equivalent:

  ```
  HEX(n)
  CONV(n,10,16)
  ```

  See the description of CONV() for more information.

  Prior to MySQL 4.0.1, HEX() always interprets its argument as a string.

  ```
  HEX(255)                                → 'FF'
  HEX('255')                              → 'FF'
  ```

  As of MySQL 4.0.1, HEX() can accept a string argument and returns a string consisting of each character in the argument represented as two hex digits:

  ```
  HEX('255')                              → '323535'
  HEX('abc')                              → '616263'
  ```

  HEX() was introduced in MySQL 3.22.4.

- INSERT(*str*,*pos*,*len*,*ins_str*)

  Returns the string *str*, with the substring beginning at position *pos* and *len* characters long replaced by the string *ins_str*. Returns the original string if *pos* is out of range or NULL if any argument is NULL.

  ```
  INSERT('nighttime',6,4,'fall')         → 'nightfall'
  INSERT('sunshine',1,3,'rain or ')      → 'rain or shine'
  INSERT('sunshine',0,3,'rain or ')      → 'sunshine'
  ```

- INSTR(*str*,*substr*)

  INSTR() is like the two-argument form of LOCATE(), but with the arguments reversed. The following two expressions are equivalent:

  ```
  INSTR(str,substr)
  LOCATE(substr,str)
  ```

- LCASE(*str*)

This function is a synonym for LOWER().

- LEFT(*str*, *len*)

Returns the leftmost *len* characters from the string *str* or the entire string if there aren't that many characters. Returns NULL if *str* is NULL. Returns the empty string if *len* is NULL or less than 1.

```
LEFT('my left foot', 2)                    → 'my'
LEFT(NULL,10)                              → NULL
LEFT('abc',NULL)                           → ''
LEFT('abc',0)                              → ''
```

- LENGTH(*str*)

Returns the length of the string *str*.

```
LENGTH('abc')                              → 3
LENGTH('')                                 → 0
LENGTH(NULL)                               → NULL
```

- LOCATE(*substr*, *str*)

  LOCATE(*substr*, *str*, *pos*)

The two-argument form of LOCATE() returns the position of the first occurrence of the string *substr* within the string *str* or 0 if *substr* does not occur within *str*. Returns NULL if any argument is NULL. If the position argument *pos* is given, LOCATE() starts looking for *substr* at that position. As of MySQL 4.0.1, the test is not case sensitive unless either argument is a binary string:

```
LOCATE('b','abc')                          → 2
LOCATE('b','ABC')                          → 2
LOCATE(BINARY 'b','ABC')                   → 0
```

Prior to MySQL 4.0.1, the test is case sensitive:

```
LOCATE('b','abc')                          → 2
LOCATE('b','ABC')                          → 0
```

- LOWER(*str*)

Returns the string *str* with all the characters converted to lowercase or NULL if *str* is NULL.

```
LOWER('New York, NY')                      → 'new york, ny'
LOWER(NULL)                                → NULL
```

- LPAD(*str*, *len*, *pad_str*)

  Returns a string consisting of the value of the string *str*, left-padded with the string *pad_str* to a length of *len* characters. Returns NULL if any argument is NULL.

  ```
  LPAD('abc',12,'def')          → 'defdefdefabc'
  LPAD('abc',10,'.')            → '.......abc'
  ```

  As of MySQL 3.23.29, LPAD() shortens the result to *len* characters:

  ```
  LPAD('abc',2,'.')             → 'ab'
  ```

  Prior to MySQL 3.23.29, LPAD() returns *str* if *str* is already *len* characters long:

  ```
  LPAD('abc',2,'.')             → 'abc'
  ```

  LPAD() was introduced in MySQL 3.22.2.

- LTRIM(*str*)

  Returns the string *str* with leftmost (leading) spaces removed or NULL if *str* is NULL.

  ```
  LTRIM('  abc  ')             → 'abc  '
  ```

- MAKE_SET(*n*, *bit0_str*, *bit1_str*, ...)

  Constructs a SET value (a string consisting of substrings separated by commas) based on the value of the integer *n* and the strings *bit0_str*, *bit1_str*, ... For each bit that is set in the value of *n*, the corresponding string is included in the result. (If bit 0 is set, the result includes *bit0_str*, and so on.) If *n* is 0, the result is the empty string. If *n* is NULL, the result is NULL. If any string in the list is NULL, it is ignored when constructing the result string.

  ```
  MAKE_SET(8,'a','b','c','d','e')       → 'd'
  MAKE_SET(7,'a','b','c','d','e')       → 'a,b,c'
  MAKE_SET(2+16,'a','b','c','d','e')    → 'b,e'
  MAKE_SET(2|16,'a','b','c','d','e')    → 'b,e'
  MAKE_SET(-1,'a','b','c','d','e')      → 'a,b,c,d,e'
  ```

  The last example selects every string because the value –1 has all bits turned on.

  MAKE_SET() was introduced in MySQL 3.22.2.

- MATCH(*column_list*) AGAINST(*str*)
  MATCH(*column_list*) AGAINST(*str* IN BOOLEAN MODE)

MATCH performs a search operation using a FULLTEXT index. The MATCH list consists of one or more column names separated by commas. These must be the columns that make up a FULLTEXT index on the table you are searching. The *str* argument to AGAINST() indicates the word or words to search for in the given columns. Words are sequences of characters made up of letters, digits, single quotes, or underscores. The parentheses are optional for MATCH, but not for AGAINST.

MATCH produces a relevance ranking for each row. Ranks are non-negative floating-point numbers, with a rank of zero indicating that the search words were not found. Positive values indicate that at least one search word was found. Words that are present in the more than half the rows of the table are considered to have zero relevance because they are so common. In addition, MySQL has an internal list of stop words (such as "the" and "but") that are never considered relevant.

If the search string is followed by IN BOOLEAN MODE, the search results are based purely on absence or presence of the search words without regard to how often they occur in the table. For boolean searches, words in the search string can be modified with the following operators to affect how the search is done:

- + or -

  A leading + or - indicates that the word must be present or absent.

- < or >

  A leading < or > decreases or increases a word's contribution to the relevance value calculation.

- ~

  A leading ~ negates a word's contribution to the relevance value calculation, but does not exclude rows containing the word entirely, as - would.

- *

  A trailing * acts as a wildcard operator. For example, act* matches act, acts, action, and so on.

- "*phrase*"

  A phrase search can be performed by surrounding the phrase within double quotes. Each word must be present in the order given in the phrase.

- ()

  Parentheses group words into expressions.

Words with no modifiers are treated as optional in a boolean search, just as for non-boolean searches.

It's possible to perform a boolean-mode search in the absence of a FULL-TEXT index, but this can be quite slow.

FULLTEXT searching was introduced in MySQL 3.23.23, boolean mode searches in MySQL 4.0.1 and phrase searching in MySQL 4.0.2.

More information on FULLTEXT searching can be found in Chapter 3, "MySQL SQL Syntax and Use."

- MID(*str,pos,len*)

  MID(*str,pos*)

  The three-argument form returns a substring of the string *str*, beginning at position *pos* and *len* characters long. The two-argument form returns the substring beginning at *pos* to the end of the string. Returns NULL if any argument is NULL.

  ```
  MID('what a dull example',8,4)          → 'dull'
  MID('what a dull example',8)            → 'dull example'
  ```

  MID() is actually a synonym for SUBSTRING() and can be used with any of the forms of syntax that SUBSTRING() allows.

- OCT(*n*)

  Returns the value of *n* in octal form, as a string. The following two expressions are equivalent:

  ```
  OCT(n)
  CONV(n,10,8)
  ```

  See the description of CONV() for more information.

  OCT() was introduced in MySQL 3.22.4.

- OCTET_LENGTH(*str*)

  This function is a synonym for LENGTH().

- POSITION(*substr* IN *str*)

  This is like the two-argument form of LOCATE(). The following expressions are equivalent:

  ```
  POSITION(substr IN str)
  LOCATE(substr,str)
  ```

- ORD(`str`)

Returns the ordinal value of the first character of the string `str` or NULL if `str` is NULL. If the first character is not a multi-byte character, ORD() is the same as ASCII().

```
ORD('abc')                                      → 97
ASCII('abc')                                    → 97
```

For a multi-byte character, ORD() returns a value determined from the ASCII values of the character's individual bytes $b1$ through bn. The formula is as follows:

```
( ... ((ASCII(b1)*256 + ASCII(b2)))*256 + ...) + ASCII(bn)
```

ORD() was introduced in MySQL 3.23.6.

- QUOTE(`str`)

Processes its argument to return a string that is properly quoted for use in an SQL statement. This is useful for writing queries that produce other queries as their result. For non-NULL values, the return value has each single quote, ASCII NUL, backslash, and Ctrl-Z character escaped with a leading backslash, and the result is surrounded by single quotes. For NULL values, the return value is the word "NULL" without surrounding single quotes.

```
QUOTE('X')                                      → 'X'
QUOTE("'")                                      → '\''
QUOTE(NULL)                                      → NULL
```

QUOTE() was introduced in MySQL 4.0.3.

- REPEAT(`str`,`n`)

Returns a string consisting of n repetitions of the string `str`. Returns the empty string if n is non-positive or NULL if either argument is NULL.

```
REPEAT('x',10)                                  → 'xxxxxxxxxx'
REPEAT('abc',3)                                  → 'abcabcabc'
```

- REPLACE(`str`, `from_str`, `to_str`)

Returns a string consisting of the string `str` with all occurrences of the string `from_str` replaced by the string `to_str`. If `to_str` is empty, the effect is to delete occurrences of `from_str`. If `from_str` is empty, REPLACE() returns `str` unchanged. Returns NULL if any argument is NULL.

```
REPLACE('abracadabra','a','oh')                  → 'ohbrohcohdohbroh'
REPLACE('abracadabra','a','')                    → 'brcdbr'
REPLACE('abracadabra','','x')                    → 'abracadabra'
```

- REVERSE(*str*)

  Returns a string consisting of the string *str* with the characters reversed.
  Returns NULL if *str* is NULL.

  ```
  REVERSE('abracadabra')                  → 'arbadacarba'
  REVERSE('tararA ta tar a raT')          → 'Tar a rat at Ararat'
  ```

- RIGHT(*str*, *len*)

  Returns the rightmost *len* characters from the string *str* or the entire
  string if there aren't that many characters. Returns NULL if *str* is NULL.
  Returns the empty string if *len* is NULL or less than 1.

  ```
  RIGHT('rightmost',4)                    → 'most'
  ```

- RPAD(*str*, *len*, *pad_str*)

  Returns a string consisting of the value of the string *str*, right-padded
  with the string *pad_str* to a length of *len* characters. Returns NULL if
  any argument is NULL.

  ```
  RPAD('abc',12,'def')                    → 'abcdefdefdef'
  RPAD('abc',10,'.')                      → 'abc.......'
  ```

  As of MySQL 3.23.29, RPAD() shortens the result to *len* characters:

  ```
  RPAD('abc',2,'.')                       → 'ab'
  ```

  Prior to MySQL 3.23.29, RPAD() returns *str* if *str* is already *len* characters long:

  ```
  RPAD('abc',2,'.')                       → 'abc'
  ```

  RPAD() was introduced in MySQL 3.22.2.

- RTRIM(*str*)

  Returns the string *str* with rightmost (trailing) spaces removed or NULL
  if *str* is NULL.

  ```
  RTRIM('  abc  ')                        → '  abc'
  ```

- SOUNDEX(*str*)

  Returns a soundex string calculated from the string *str* or NULL if *str* is
  NULL. Non-alphanumeric characters in *str* are ignored. International
  non-alphabetic characters outside the range from A to Z are treated as
  vowels.

  ```
  SOUNDEX('Cow')                          → 'C000'
  SOUNDEX('Cowl')                         → 'C400'
  SOUNDEX('Howl')                         → 'H400'
  SOUNDEX('Hello')                        → 'H400'
  ```

- SPACE(*n*)

  Returns a string consisting of *n* spaces, the empty set if *n* is non-positive, or NULL if *n* is NULL.

  ```
  SPACE(6)                                    → '      '
  SPACE(0)                                    → ''
  SPACE(NULL)                                 → NULL
  ```

- SUBSTRING(*str*,*pos*)

  SUBSTRING(*str*,*pos*,*len*)

  SUBSTRING(*str* FROM *pos*)

  SUBSTRING(*str* FROM *pos* FOR *len*)

  Returns a substring from the string *str*, beginning at position *pos*, or NULL if any argument is NULL. If a *len* argument is given, returns a substring that many characters long; otherwise, it returns the entire rightmost part of *str*, beginning at position *pos*.

  ```
  SUBSTRING('abcdef',3)                       → 'cdef'
  SUBSTRING('abcdef',3,2)                     → 'cd'
  ```

  The following expressions are equivalent:

  ```
  SUBSTRING(str,pos,len)
  SUBSTRING(str FROM pos FOR len)
  MID(str,pos,len)
  ```

- SUBSTRING_INDEX(*str*,*delim*,*n*)

  Returns a substring from the string *str*. If *n* is positive, SUBSTRING_INDEX() finds the *n*th occurrence of the delimiter string *delim* and then returns everything to the left of that delimiter. If *n* is negative, SUBSTRING_INDEX() finds the *n*th occurrence of *delim*, counting back from the right end of *str*, and then returns everything to the right of that delimiter. If *delim* is not found in *str*, the entire string is returned. Returns NULL if any argument is NULL.

  ```
  SUBSTRING_INDEX('jar-jar','j',-2)           → 'ar-jar'
  SUBSTRING_INDEX('sampadm@localhost','@',1)  → 'sampadm'
  SUBSTRING_INDEX('sampadm@localhost','@',-1) → 'localhost'
  ```

- TRIM([[LEADING | TRAILING | BOTH] [*trim_str*] FROM] *str*)

  Returns the string *str* with leading and/or trailing instances of the string *trim_str* trimmed off. If LEADING is specified, TRIM() strips leading occurrences of *trim_str*. If TRAILING is specified, TRIM() strips trailing occurrences of *trim_str*. If BOTH is specified, TRIM() strips leading and trailing occurrences of *trim_str*. The default is BOTH if none of

LEADING, TRAILING, or BOTH is specified. TRIM() strips spaces if
trim_str is not specified.

```
TRIM('^' FROM '^^^xyz^^')                          → 'xyz'
TRIM(LEADING '^' FROM '^^^xyz^^')                  → 'xyz^^'
TRIM(TRAILING '^' FROM '^^^xyz^^')                 → '^^^xyz'
TRIM(BOTH '^' FROM '^^^xyz^^')                     → 'xyz'
TRIM(BOTH FROM '   abc   ')                        → 'abc'
TRIM('   abc   ')                                  → 'abc'
```

- UCASE(*str*)

  This function is a synonym for UPPER().

- UPPER(*str*)

  Returns the string *str* with all the characters converted to uppercase, or
  NULL if *str* is NULL.

  ```
  UPPER('New York, NY')                            → 'NEW YORK, NY'
  UPPER(NULL)                                       → NULL
  ```

Date and Time Functions

The date and time functions take various types of arguments. In general, a
function that expects a DATE argument will also accept a DATETIME or TIME-
STAMP argument, and will ignore the time part of the value. Some functions
that expect a TIME value accept DATETIME or TIMESTAMP
arguments and ignore the date part.

Many of the functions in this section are able to interpret numeric arguments
as temporal values:

```
MONTH('2004-07-25')                                → 7
MONTH(20040725)                                    → 7
```

Similarly, many functions that normally return temporal values return numbers
when used in numeric context:

```
CURDATE()                                          → '2002-05-14'
CURDATE() + 0                                      → 20020514
```

If you don't supply legal date or time values to date and time functions, you
can't expect a reasonable result. Verify your arguments first.

- ADDDATE(*date*, INTERVAL *expr interval*)

  This function is a synonym for DATE_ADD().

- CURDATE()

  Returns the current date as a string in `'CCYY-MM-DD'` format or as a number in `CCYYMMDD` format, depending on the context in which it is used.

  ```
  CURDATE()                                          →  '2002-05-14'
  CURDATE() + 0                                      →  20020514
  ```

- CURRENT_DATE()

  This function is a synonym for CURDATE(); the parentheses are optional.

- CURRENT_TIME()

  This function is a synonym for CURTIME(); the parentheses are optional.

- CURRENT_TIMESTAMP()

  This function is a synonym for NOW(); the parentheses are optional.

- CURTIME()

  Returns the current time of day as a string in `'hh:mm:ss'` format or as a number in `hhmmss` format, depending on the context in which it is used.

  ```
  CURTIME()                                          →  '09:51:36'
  CURTIME() + 0                                      →  95136
  ```

- DATE_ADD(`date`, INTERVAL `expr interval`)

  Takes a date or date and time value `date`, adds a time interval to it, and returns the result. `expr` specifies the time value to be added to `date` (or subtracted, if `expr` begins with '-'), and `interval` specifies how to interpret the interval. The result is a DATE value if `date` is a DATE value and no time-related values are involved in calculating the result. Otherwise, the result is a DATETIME value. The result is NULL if `date` is not a legal date.

  ```
  DATE_ADD('2002-12-01',INTERVAL 1 YEAR)          →  '2003-12-01'
  DATE_ADD('2002-12-01',INTERVAL 60 DAY)          →  '2003-01-30'
  DATE_ADD('2002-12-01',INTERVAL -3 MONTH)        →  '2002-09-01'
  DATE_ADD('2002-12-01 08:30:00',INTERVAL 12 HOUR) →  '2002-12-01 20:30:00'
  ```

  Table C.3 shows the allowable `interval` values, their meanings, and the format in which values for each interval type should be specified. The keyword INTERVAL and the `interval` specifiers can be given in any lettercase.

Table C.3 **DATE_ADD() Interval Types**

Type	Meaning	Value Format
SECOND	Seconds	*ss*
MINUTE	Minutes	*mm*
HOUR	Hours	*hh*
DAY	Days	*DD*
MONTH	Months	*MM*
YEAR	Years	*YY*
MINUTE_SECOND	Minutes and seconds	'*mm:ss*'
HOUR_MINUTE	Hours and minutes	'*hh:mm*'
HOUR_SECOND	Hours, minutes, and seconds	'*hh:mm:ss*'
DAY_HOUR	Days and hours	'*DD hh*'
DAY_MINUTE	Days, hours, and minutes	'*DD hh:mm*'
DAY_SECOND	Days, hours, minutes, and seconds	'*DD hh:mm:ss*'
YEAR_MONTH	Years and months	'*YY-MM*'

The expression *expr* that is added to the date can be specified as a number or as a string, unless it contains non-digit characters, in which case, it must be a string. The delimiter characters can be any-punctuation character:

```
DATE_ADD('2002-12-01',INTERVAL '2:3' YEAR_MONTH)  → '2005-03-01'
DATE_ADD('2002-12-01',INTERVAL '2-3' YEAR_MONTH)  → '2005-03-01'
```

The parts of the value of *expr* are matched from right to left against the parts to be expected based on the *interval* specifier. For example, the expected format for HOUR_SECOND is '*hh:mm:ss*'. An *expr* value of '15:21' is interpreted as '00:15:21', not as '15:21:00'.

```
DATE_ADD('2002-12-01 12:00:00',INTERVAL '15:21' HOUR_SECOND)
                                          → '2002-12-01 12:15:21'
```

If *interval* is YEAR, MONTH, or YEAR_MONTH and the day part of the result is larger than the number of days in the result month, the day is set to the maximum number of days in that month.

```
DATE_ADD('2002-12-31',INTERVAL 2 MONTH)           → '2003-02-28'
```

DATE_ADD() was introduced in MySQL 3.22.4. In addition, an alternate syntax is supported as of MySQL 3.23.4:

```
'2002-12-31' + INTERVAL 2 MONTH                   → '2003-02-28'
INTERVAL 2 MONTH + '2002-12-31'                   → '2003-02-28'
```

- DATE_FORMAT(*date*, *format*)

Formats a date or date and time value *date* depending on the formatting string *format* and returns the resulting string. DATE_FORMAT() can be used to reformat DATE or DATETIME values from the form MySQL uses to provide any format you want.

```
DATE_FORMAT('2002-12-01','%M %e, %Y')        → 'December 1, 2002'
DATE_FORMAT('2002-12-01','The %D of %M')     → 'The 1st of December'
```

Table C.4 shows the available specifiers that can be used in the formatting string.

The '%' character preceding each format code is required. (Prior to MySQL 3.23, the '%' is allowed but is optional.) Characters present in the formatting string that are not listed in the table are copied to the result string literally.

If you refer to time specifiers for a DATE value, the time part of the value is treated as '00:00:00'.

```
DATE_FORMAT('2002-12-01','%i')               → '00'
```

The %v, %V, %x, and %X format specifiers were introduced in MySQL 3.23.8.

Table C.4 **DATE_FORMAT() Formatting Specifiers**

Specifier	Meaning
%S, %s	Second in two-digit form (00, 01, ..., 59)
%i	Minute in two-digit form (00, 01, ..., 59)
%H	Hour in two-digit form, 24-hour time (00, 01, ..., 23)
%h, %I	Hour in two-digit form, 12-hour time (01, 02, ..., 12)
%k	Hour in numeric form, 24-hour time (0, 1, ..., 23)
%l	Hour in numeric form, 12-hour time (1, 2, ..., 12)
%T	Time in 24-hour form (*hh:mm:ss*)
%r	Time in 12-hour form (*hh:mm:ss* AM or *hh:mm:ss* PM)
%p	AM or PM
%W	Weekday name (Sunday, Monday, ..., Saturday)
%a	Weekday name in abbreviated form (Sun, Mon, ..., Sat)
%d	Day of the month in two-digit form (00, 01, ..., 31)
%e	Day of the month in numeric form (1, 2, ..., 31)
%D	Day of the month with English suffix (1st, 2nd, 3rd, ...)
%w	Day of the week in numeric form (0=Sunday, 1=Monday, ..., 6=Saturday)
%j	Day of the year in three-digit form (001, 002, ..., 366)
%U	Week (00, ..., 53), where Sunday is the first day of the week

continues

Table C.4 **Continued**

Specifier	Meaning
%u	Week (00, ..., 53), where Monday is the first day of the week
%V	Week (01, ..., 53), where Sunday is the first day of the week
%v	Week (01, ..., 53), where Monday is the first day of the week
%M	Month name (January, February, ..., December)
%b	Month name in abbreviated form (Jan, Feb, ..., Dec)
%m	Month in two-digit form (01, 02, ..., 12)
%c	Month in numeric form (1, 2, ..., 12)
%Y	Year in 4-digit form
%y	Year in 2-digit form
%X	Year for the week in which Sunday is the first day, 4-digit form
%x	Year for the week in which Monday is the first day, 4-digit form
%%	A literal '%' character

- DATE_SUB(*date*, INTERVAL *expr interval*)

  Performs date arithmetic in the same manner as DATE_ADD(), except that *expr* is subtracted from the date value *date*. See DATE_ADD() for more information.

  ```
  DATE_SUB('2002-12-01',INTERVAL 1 MONTH)          → '2002-11-01'
  DATE_SUB('2002-12-01',INTERVAL '13-2' YEAR_MONTH) → '1989-10-01'
  DATE_SUB('2002-12-01 04:53:12',INTERVAL '13-2' MINUTE_SECOND)
                                                   → '2002-12-01 04:40:10'
  DATE_SUB('2002-12-01 04:53:12',INTERVAL '13-2' HOUR_MINUTE)
                                                   → '2002-11-30 15:51:12'
  ```

  DATE_SUB() was introduced in MySQL 3.22.4. In addition, an alternate syntax is supported as of MySQL 3.23.4:

  ```
  '2002-12-01' - INTERVAL 1 MONTH          → '2002-11-01'
  ```

- DAYNAME(*date*)

  Returns a string containing the weekday name for the date value *date*.

  ```
  DAYNAME('2002-12-01')                    → 'Sunday'
  DAYNAME('1900-12-01')                    → 'Saturday'
  ```

- DAYOFMONTH(*date*)

  Returns the numeric value of the day of the month for the date value *date* in the range from 1 to 31.

  ```
  DAYOFMONTH('2002-12-01')                 → 1
  DAYOFMONTH('2002-12-25')                 → 25
  ```

- DAYOFWEEK(*date*)

  Returns the numeric value of the weekday for the date value *date*.
  Weekday values are in the range from 1 for Sunday to 7 for Saturday, per
  the ODBC standard. See also the WEEKDAY() function.

DAYOFWEEK('2002-12-08')	→ 1
DAYNAME('2002-12-08')	→ 'Sunday'
DAYOFWEEK('2002-12-14')	→ 7
DAYNAME('2002-12-14')	→ 'Saturday'

- DAYOFYEAR(*date*)

  Returns the numeric value of the day of the year for the date value *date*
  in the range from 1 to 366.

DAYOFYEAR('2002-12-01')	→ 335
DAYOFYEAR('2004-12-31')	→ 366

- EXTRACT(*interval* FROM *datetime*)

  Returns the part of the date and time value *datetime* indicated by
  interval, which can be any of the interval specifiers that are allowed for
  DATE_ADD().

EXTRACT(YEAR FROM '2002-12-01 13:42:19')	→ 2002
EXTRACT(MONTH FROM '2002-12-01 13:42:19')	→ 12
EXTRACT(DAY FROM '2002-12-01 13:42:19')	→ 1
EXTRACT(HOUR_MINUTE FROM '2002-12-01 13:42:19')	→ 1342
EXTRACT(SECOND FROM '2002-12-01 13:42:19')	→ 19

  As of MySQL 3.23.39, EXTRACT() can be used with dates that have
  "missing" parts.

EXTRACT(YEAR FROM '2004-00-12')	→ 2004
EXTRACT(MONTH FROM '2004-00-12')	→ 0
EXTRACT(DAY FROM '2004-00-12')	→ 12

  EXTRACT() was introduced in MySQL 3.23.0.

- FROM_DAYS(*n*)

  Given a numeric value *n* representing the number of days since the year
  0 (typically obtained by calling TO_DAYS()), returns the corresponding
  date.

TO_DAYS('2009-12-01')	→ 734107
FROM_DAYS(734107 + 3)	→ '2009-12-04'

  FROM_DAYS() is intended only for dates covered by the Gregorian
  calendar (1582 on).

- FROM_UNIXTIME(*unix_timestamp*)

  FROM_UNIXTIME(*unix_timestamp,format*)

  Given a UNIX timestamp value *unix_timestamp* such as is returned by
  UNIX_TIMESTAMP(), returns a date and time value as a string in '*CCYY-
  MM-DD hh:mm:ss*' format or as a number in *CCYYMMDDhhmmss* format,
  depending on the context in which it is used. If the *format* argument is
  given, the return value is formatted as a string, just as it would be by the
  DATE_FORMAT() function.

UNIX_TIMESTAMP()	→ 1021389416
FROM_UNIXTIME(1021389416)	→ '2002-05-14 10:16:56'
FROM_UNIXTIME(1021389416,'%Y')	→ '2002'

- HOUR(*time*)

  Returns the numeric value of the hour for the time value *time* in the
  range from 0 to 23.

HOUR('12:31:58')	→ 12
HOUR(123158)	→ 12

- MINUTE(*time*)

  Returns the numeric value of the minute for the time value *time* in the
  range from 0 to 59.

MINUTE('12:31:58')	→ 31
MINUTE(123158)	→ 31

- MONTH(*date*)

  Returns the numeric value of the month of the year for the date value
  date in the range from 1 to 12.

MONTH('2002-12-01')	→ 12
MONTH(20021201)	→ 12

- MONTHNAME(*date*)

  Returns a string containing the month name for the date value *date*.

MONTHNAME('2002-12-01')	→ 'December'
MONTHNAME(20021201)	→ 'December'

- NOW()

  Returns the current date and time as a string in '*CCYY-MM-DD
  hh:mm:ss*' format or as a number in *CCYYMMDDhhmmss* format, depending on the context in which it is used.

NOW()	→ '2002-05-14 10:19:20'
NOW() + 0	→ 20020514101920

- PERIOD_ADD(*period*,*n*)

  Adds *n* months to the period value *period* and returns the result. The return value format is *CCYYMM*. The *period* argument format can be *CCYYMM* or *YYMM* (neither is a date value).

PERIOD_ADD(200202,12)	→ 200302
PERIOD_ADD(0202,-3)	→ 200111

- PERIOD_DIFF(*period1*,*period2*)

  Takes the difference of the period-valued arguments and returns the number of months between them. The arguments can be in the format *CCYYMM* or *YYMM* (neither is a date value).

PERIOD_DIFF(200302,200202)	→ 12
PERIOD_DIFF(200111,0202)	→ -3

- QUARTER(*date*)

  Returns the numeric value of the quarter of the year for the date value *date* in the range from 1 to 4.

QUARTER('2002-12-01')	→ 4
QUARTER('2003-01-01')	→ 1

- SECOND(*time*)

  Returns the numeric value of the second for the time value *time* in the range from 0 to 59.

SECOND('12:31:58')	→ 58
SECOND(123158)	→ 58

- SEC_TO_TIME(*seconds*)

  Given a number of seconds *seconds*, returns the corresponding time value as a string in '*hh:mm:ss*' format or as a number in *hhmmss* format, depending on the context in which it is used.

SEC_TO_TIME(29834)	→ '08:17:14'
SEC_TO_TIME(29834) + 0	→ 81714

- SUBDATE(*date*,INTERVAL *expr interval*)

  This function is a synonym for DATE_SUB().

- SYSDATE()

  This function is a synonym for NOW().

- TIME_FORMAT(*time*,*format*)

  Formats the time value *time* according to the formatting string format and returns the resulting string. This function also accepts DATETIME or

TIMESTAMP arguments. The formatting string is like that used by
DATE_FORMAT(), but the only specifiers that can be used are those that
are time-related. Other specifiers result in a NULL value or 0.

```
TIME_FORMAT('12:31:58','%H %i')                → '12 31'
TIME_FORMAT(123158,'%H %i')                    → '12 31'
```

- TIME_TO_SEC(*time*)

Given a value *time* representing elapsed time, returns a number representing the corresponding number of seconds. The return value can be
passed to SEC_TO_TIME() to convert it back to a time.

```
TIME_TO_SEC('08:17:14')                        → 29834
SEC_TO_TIME(29834)                             → '08:17:14'
```

If given a DATETIME or TIMESTAMP value, TIME_TO_SEC() ignores the
date part.

```
TIME_TO_SEC('2002-03-26 08:17:14')             → 29834
```

- TO_DAYS(*date*)

Returns a numeric value representing the date value *date* converted to
the number of days since the year 0. The return value can be passed to
FROM_DAYS() to convert it back to a date.

```
TO_DAYS('2002-12-01')                          → 731550
FROM_DAYS(731550 - 365)                        → '2001-12-01'
```

If given a DATETIME or TIMESTAMP value, TO_DAYS() ignores the time
part.

```
TO_DAYS('2002-12-01 12:14:37')                 → 731550
```

TO_DAYS() is intended only for dates covered by the Gregorian
calendar (1582 on).

- UNIX_TIMESTAMP()
UNIX_TIMESTAMP(*date*)

When called with no arguments, returns the number of seconds since
the UNIX epoch ('1970-01-01 00:00:00' GMT). When called with a
date-valued argument *date*, returns the number of seconds between the
epoch and that date. *date* can be specified several ways: as a DATE, DATE-
TIME, or TIMESTAMP value; or as a number in the format *CCYYMMDD* or
YYMMDD in local time.

```
UNIX_TIMESTAMP()                               → 1021389578
UNIX_TIMESTAMP('2002-12-01')                   → 1038722400
UNIX_TIMESTAMP(20021201)                       → 1038722400
```

- WEEK(*date*)

  WEEK(*date*, *first_day*)

  When called with a single argument, returns a number representing the week of the year for the date value *date* in the range from 0 to 53. The week is assumed to start on Sunday. When called with two arguments, WEEK() returns the same kind of value, but the *first_day* argument indicates the day on which the week starts. If *first_day* is 0, the week starts on Sunday. If *first_day* is 1, the week starts on Monday.

  ```
  WEEK('2002-12-08')                                    → 50
  WEEK('2002-12-08',0)                                  → 50
  WEEK('2002-12-08',1)                                  → 49
  ```

  A WEEK() value of 0 indicates that the date occurs prior to the first Sunday of the year (or prior to the first Monday, if the second argument is 1).

  ```
  WEEK('2005-01-01')                                    → 0
  DAYNAME('2005-01-01')                                 → 'Saturday'
  WEEK('2006-01-01',1)                                  → 0
  DAYNAME('2006-01-01')                                 → 'Sunday'
  ```

  The two-argument form of WEEK() was introduced in MySQL 3.22.1.

- WEEKDAY(*date*)

  Returns the numeric value of the weekday for the date value *date*. Weekday values are in the range from 0 for Monday to 6 for Sunday; see also the DAYOFWEEK() function.

  ```
  WEEKDAY('2002-12-08')                                 → 6
  DAYNAME('2002-12-08')                                 → 'Sunday'
  WEEKDAY('2002-12-16')                                 → 0
  DAYNAME('2002-12-16')                                 → 'Monday'
  ```

- YEAR(*date*)

  Returns the numeric value of the year for the date value *date* in the range from 1000 to 9999.

  ```
  YEAR('2002-12-01')                                    → 2002
  YEAR(20021201)                                        → 2002
  ```

- YEARWEEK(*date*)

  YEARWEEK(*date*, *first_day*)

  When called with a single argument, returns a number in the format *CCYYWW* representing the year and week of the year for the date value *date*. The week value ranges from 01 to 53. The week is assumed to start on Sunday. When called with two arguments, YEARWEEK() returns the same kind of value, but the *first_day* argument indicates the day on which the week starts. If *first_day* is 0, the week starts on Sunday. If *first_day* is 1, the week starts on Monday.

```
YEARWEEK('2006-01-01')                       → 200601
YEARWEEK('2006-01-01',0)                      → 200601
YEARWEEK('2006-01-01',1)                      → 200552
```

Note that it is possible for the year part in the result to differ from the year in the *date* argument. This occurs in cases where WEEK() would return a week value of 0. YEARWEEK() never returns a week value of 0. Instead, it returns a value consisting of the previous year and the final week number from that year.

```
WEEK('2005-01-01')                           → 0
YEARWEEK('2005-01-01')                        → 200452
```

YEARWEEK() was introduced in MySQL 3.23.8.

Summary Functions

Summary functions are also known as aggregate functions. They calculate a single value based on a group of values. However, the resulting value is based only on non-NULL values from the selected rows (with the exception that COUNT(*) counts all rows). Summary functions can be used to summarize an entire set of values or to produce summaries for each subgroup of a set of values when the query includes a GROUP BY clause. See the "Generating Summaries" section in Chapter 1, "Getting Started with MySQL and SQL."

For the examples in this section, assume the existence of a table mytbl with an integer column mycol that contains eight rows with the values 1, 3, 5, 5, 7, 9, 9, and NULL.

```
mysql> SELECT mycol FROM mytbl;
+-------+
| mycol |
+-------+
|     1 |
|     3 |
|     5 |
|     5 |
|     7 |
|     9 |
|     9 |
|  NULL |
+-------+
```

- AVG(*expr*)

  Returns the average value of *expr* for all non-NULL values in the selected rows.

  ```
  SELECT AVG(mycol) FROM mytbl              → 5.5714
  SELECT AVG(mycol)*2 FROM mytbl            → 11.1429
  SELECT AVG(mycol*2) FROM mytbl            → 11.1429
  ```

- BIT_AND(*expr*)

  Returns the bitwise AND value of *expr* for all non-NULL values in the selected rows.

  ```
  SELECT BIT_AND(mycol) FROM mytbl              → 1
  ```

- BIT_OR(*expr*)

  Returns the bitwise OR value of *expr* for all non-NULL values in the selected rows.

  ```
  SELECT BIT_OR(mycol) FROM mytbl              → 15
  ```

- COUNT(*expr*)

  COUNT(*)

  COUNT(DISTINCT *expr1*, *expr2*,...)

  With an expression argument, returns a count of the number of non-NULL values in the result set. With an argument of *, returns a count of all rows in the result set, regardless of their contents.

  ```
  SELECT COUNT(mycol) FROM mytbl            → 7
  SELECT COUNT(*) FROM mytbl                → 8
  ```

  For ISAM and MyISAM tables, COUNT(*) with no WHERE clause is optimized to return the number of records in the table named in the FROM clause very quickly. When more than one table is named, COUNT(*) returns the product of the number of rows in the individual tables:

  ```
  SELECT COUNT(*) FROM mytbl AS m1, mytbl AS m2      → 64
  ```

  As of MySQL 3.23.2, COUNT(DISTINCT) can be used to count the number of distinct non-NULL values.

  ```
  SELECT COUNT(DISTINCT mycol) FROM mytbl           → 5
  SELECT COUNT(DISTINCT MOD(mycol,3)) FROM mytbl    → 3
  ```

  If multiple expressions are given, COUNT(DISTINCT) counts the number of distinct combinations of non-NULL values.

- MAX(*expr*)

  Returns the maximum value of *expr* for all non-NULL values in the selected rows. MAX() can also be used with strings or temporal values, in which case it returns the lexically or temporally greatest value.

  ```
  SELECT MAX(mycol) FROM mytbl                        → 9
  ```

- MIN(*expr*)

  Returns the minimum value of *expr* for all non-NULL values in the selected rows. MIN() can also be used with strings or temporal values, in which case it returns the lexically or temporally least value.

  ```
  SELECT MIN(mycol) FROM mytbl                        → 1
  ```

- STD(*expr*)

  Returns the standard deviation of *expr* for all non-NULL values in the selected rows.

  ```
  SELECT STD(mycol) FROM mytbl                        → 2.7701
  ```

- STDDEV(*expr*)

  This function is a synonym for STD().

- SUM(*expr*)

  Returns the sum of *expr* for all non-NULL values in the selected rows.

  ```
  SELECT SUM(mycol) FROM mytbl                        → 39
  ```

Security-Related Functions

These functions perform various security-related operations, such as encrypting or decrypting strings. Several of these functions come in pairs, with one function producing an encrypted value and the other performing decryption. Such pairs of functions typically use a string as a key or password value. You must decrypt a value with the same key used to encrypt it if you want to get back the original value. Otherwise, the decrypted result will be meaningless.

When using encryption functions that return a binary string, if you want to save the result in a database, it's conventional to use a column that is one of the BLOB types.

- AES_DECRYPT(*str*,*key_str*)

  Given an encrypted string *str* obtained as a result of a call to AES_ENCRYPT(), decrypts it using the key string *key_str* and returns the resulting string. Returns NULL if either argument is NULL.

  ```
  AES_DECRYPT(AES_ENCRYPT('secret','scramble'),'scramble')
                                                → 'secret'
  ```

`AES_DECRYPT()` was introduced in MySQL 4.0.2.

- `AES_ENCRYPT(str,key_str)`

Encrypts the string `str` with the key string `key_str` using the Advanced Encryption Standard (AES) and a 128-bit key length. Returns the result as a binary string or NULL if either argument is NULL. The string can be decoded with `AES_DECRYPT()` using the same key string.

`AES_ENCRYPT()` was introduced in MySQL 4.0.2.

- `DECODE(str,key_str)`

Given an encrypted string `str` obtained as a result of a call to `ENCODE()`, decrypts it using the key string `key_str`. Returns the resulting string or NULL if `str` is NULL.

```
DECODE(ENCODE('secret','scramble'),'scramble')    → 'secret'
```

- `DES_DECRYPT(str)`
  `DES_DECRYPT(str,key_str)`

Decrypts a string `str`, which should be an encrypted value produced by `DES_ENCRYPT()`. If SSL support has not been enabled or decryption fails, `DES_DECRYPT()` returns NULL.

If a `key_str` argument is given, it is used as the decryption key. If no `key_str` argument is given, `DES_DECRYPT()` uses a key from the server's DES key file to decrypt the string. The key number is determined from bits 0–6 of the first byte of the encrypted string. The location of the key file is specified at server startup time by means of the `--des-key-file` option. If different keys are used to encrypt and decrypt the string, the result will not be meaningful.

If `str` does not look like an encrypted string, `DES_DECRYPT()` returns the string unchanged. (This will occur, for example, if the first byte does not have bit 7 set.)

Use of the single-argument form of `DES_DECRYPT()` requires the SUPER privilege.

`DES_DECRYPT()` was introduced in MySQL 4.0.1.

- `DES_ENCRYPT(str)`
  `DES_ENCRYPT(str,key_num)`
  `DES_ENCRYPT(str,key_str)`

Performs DES encryption on the string *str* and returns the encrypted result as a binary string. The encrypted string can be decrypted with DES_DECRYPT(). If SSL support has not been enabled or encryption fails, DES_ENCRYPT() returns NULL.

If a *key_str* argument is given, it is used as the encryption key. If a *key_num* argument is given, it should be a value from 0 to 9, indicating the key number of an entry in the server's DES key file. In this case, the encryption key is taken from that entry. If no *key_str* or *key_num* argument is given, the first key from the DES key file is used to perform encryption. (This is not necessarily the same as specifying a *key_num* value of 0.)

The first byte of the resulting string indicates how the string was encrypted. This byte will have bit 7 set, and bits 0–6 indicate the key number. The number is 0 to 9 to specify which key in the DES key file was used to encrypt the string, or 127 if a *key_str* argument was used. For example, if you encrypt a string using key 3, the first byte of the result will be 131 (that is, 128+3). If you encrypt a string with a *key_str* value, the first byte will be 255 (that is, 128+127).

For encryption performed on the basis of a key number, the server reads the DES key file to find the corresponding key string. The location of the key file is specified at server startup time by means of the --des-key-file option. The key file contains lines of the following format:

    key_num key_str

Each *key_num* value should be a number from 0 to 9, and the *key_str* value is the corresponding encryption key. *key_num* and *key_str* should be separated by at least one whitespace character. Lines in the key file can be arranged in any order.

Unlike DES_DECRYPT(), DES_ENCRYPT() does not require the SUPER privilege to use keys from the DES key file. (Anyone is allowed to encrypt information based on the key file; only privileged users are allowed to decrypt it.)

DES_ENCRYPT() was introduced in MySQL 4.0.1.

- ENCODE(*str*,*key_str*)

  Encrypts the string *str* using the key string *key_str* and returns the result as a binary string. The string can be decoded with DECODE() using the same key string.

- ENCRYPT(*str*)

  ENCRYPT(*str,salt*)

  Encrypts the string *str* and returns the resulting string or NULL if either argument is NULL. This is a non-reversible encryption. The *salt* argument, if given, should be a string with two characters. (As of MySQL 3.22.16, *salt* can be longer than two characters.) By specifying a *salt* value, the encrypted result for *str* will be the same each time. With no *salt* argument, identical calls to ENCRYPT() yield different results over time.

  ```
  ENCRYPT('secret','AB')              → 'ABS5SGh1EL6bk'
  ENCRYPT('secret','AB')              → 'ABS5SGh1EL6bk'
  ENCRYPT('secret')                   → '9u0hlzMKCx9N2'
  ENCRYPT('secret')                   → 'avGJcOP2vakBE'
  ```

  ENCRYPT() uses the UNIX crypt() system call, so if crypt() is unavailable on your system, ENCRYPT() always returns NULL. ENCRYPT() is subject to the way crypt() operates for those systems on which it is present. In particular, on some systems, crypt() looks only at the first eight characters of the string to be encrypted.

- MD5(*str*)

  Calculates a 128-bit checksum from the string *str* based on the RSA Data Security, Inc. MD5 Message-Digest algorithm. The return value is a string consisting of 32 hexadecimal digits or NULL if the argument is NULL.

  ```
  MD5('secret')              → '5ebe2294ecd0e0f08eab7690d2a6ee69'
  ```

  MD5() was introduced in MySQL 3.23.2. See also the SHA1() function.

- PASSWORD(*str*)

  Given a string *str*, calculates and returns an encrypted password string of the form used in the MySQL grant tables. This is a non-reversible encryption.

  ```
  PASSWORD('secret')              → '428567f408994404'
  ```

  Note that PASSWORD() does *not* use the same algorithm as the one used on UNIX to encrypt user account passwords. For that type of encryption, use ENCRYPT().

- SHA(*str*)

  This function is a synonym for SHA1().

- SHA1(*str*)

Calculates a 160-bit checksum from the string *str* using the Secure Hash Algorithm. The return value is a string consisting of 40 hexadecimal digits or NULL if the argument is NULL.

```
SHA1('secret')              → 'e5e9fa1ba31ecd1ae84f75caaa474f3a663f05f4'
```

SHA1() was introduced in MySQL 4.0.2. See also the MD5() function.

Miscellaneous Functions

The functions in this section do not fall into any of the other categories.

- BENCHMARK(*n*, *expr*)

Evaluates the expression *expr* repetitively *n* times. BENCHMARK() is something of an unusual function in that it is intended for use within the mysql client program. Its return value is always 0, and thus is of no use. The value of interest is the elapsed time that mysql prints after displaying the result of the query:

```
mysql> SELECT BENCHMARK(1000000,PASSWORD('secret'));
+---------------------------------------+
| BENCHMARK(1000000,PASSWORD('secret')) |
+---------------------------------------+
|                                     0 |
+---------------------------------------+
1 row in set (2.35 sec)
```

The time is only an approximate indicator of how quickly the server evaluates the expression because it represents wall-clock time on the client, not CPU time on the server. The time can be influenced by factors such as the load on the server, whether the server is in a runnable state or swapped out when the query arrives, and so forth. You may want to execute it several times to see what a representative value is.

BENCHMARK() was introduced in MySQL 3.22.15.

- BIT_COUNT(*n*)

Returns the number of bits that are set in the argument, which is treated as a BIGINT value (a 64-bit integer).

```
BIT_COUNT(0)                           → 0
BIT_COUNT(1)                           → 1
BIT_COUNT(2)                           → 1
BIT_COUNT(7)                           → 3
BIT_COUNT(-1)                          → 64
BIT_COUNT(NULL)                        → NULL
```

- BIT_LENGTH(*str*)

  Returns the length of the string *str* in bits or NULL if the argument is NULL.

  ```
  BIT_LENGTH('abc')                              → 24
  BIT_LENGTH('a long string')                    → 104
  ```

  BIT_LENGTH() was introduced in MySQL 4.0.2 for ODBC compatibility.

- CONNECTION_ID()

  Returns the connection identifier for the current connection. This is the thread identifier that the server associates with the client connection.

  ```
  CONNECTION_ID()                                → 10146
  ```

  CONNECTION_ID() was introduced in MySQL 3.23.14.

- DATABASE()

  Returns a string containing the current database name or the empty string if there is no current database.

  ```
  DATABASE()                                     → 'sampdb'
  ```

- FOUND_ROWS()

  Returns the number of rows that a preceding SELECT statement would have returned without a LIMIT clause. For example, the following statement would return a maximum of 10 rows:

  ```
  mysql> SELECT * FROM mytbl LIMIT 10;
  ```

  To determine how many rows the statement would have returned without the LIMIT clause, do the following:

  ```
  mysql> SELECT SQL_CALC_FOUND_ROWS * FROM mytbl LIMIT 10;
  mysql> SELECT FOUND_ROWS();
  ```

  FOUND_ROWS() was introduced in MySQL 4.0.0.

- GET_LOCK(*str*, *timeout*)

  GET_LOCK() is used in conjunction with RELEASE_LOCK() and IS_FREE_LOCK() to perform advisory (cooperative) locking. You can use the two functions to write applications that cooperate based on the status of an agreed-upon lock name.

  GET_LOCK() is called with a lock name indicated by the string *str* and a timeout value of *timeout* seconds. It returns 1 if the lock was obtained successfully within the timeout period, 0 if the lock attempt failed due to timing out, or NULL if an error occurred. The *timeout* value determines how long to wait while attempting to obtain the lock, not the duration of the lock. After it is obtained, the lock remains in force until released.

The following call acquires a lock named 'Nellie', waiting up to 10 seconds for it:

```
GET_LOCK('Nellie',10)
```

The lock applies only to the string name itself. It does not lock a database, a table, or any rows or columns within a table. In other words, the lock does not prevent any other client from doing anything to database tables, which is why GET_LOCK() locking is advisory only—it simply allows other cooperating clients to determine whether or not the lock is in force.

A client that has a lock on a name blocks attempts by other clients to lock the name (or attempts by other threads within a multi-threaded client that maintains multiple connections to the server). Suppose client 1 locks the string 'Nellie'. If client 2 attempts to lock the same string, it will block until client 1 releases the lock or until the timeout period expires. In the former case, client 2 will acquire the lock successfully; in the latter case, it will fail.

Because two clients cannot lock a given string at the same time, applications that agree on a name can use the lock status of that name as an indicator of when it is safe to perform operations related to the name. For example, you can construct a lock name based on a unique key value for a row in a table to allow cooperative locking of that row.

To release a lock explicitly, call RELEASE_LOCK() with the lock name:

```
RELEASE_LOCK('Nellie')
```

RELEASE_LOCK() returns 1 if the lock was released successfully, 0 if the lock was held by another connection (you can only release your own locks), or NULL if no such lock exists.

Any lock held by a client is automatically released if the client issues another GET_LOCK() call because only one string at a time can be locked per client connection. In this case, the lock being held is released before the new lock is obtained, even if the lock name is the same. A lock also is released when the client's connection to the server terminates. Note that if you have a very long-running client and its connection times out due to inactivity, any lock held by the client is released.

GETLOCK(*str*,0) can be used as a simple poll to determine without waiting whether or not a lock on *str* is in force. (Of course, this will lock the string if it is not currently locked, so remember to call RELEASE_LOCK() as appropriate.)

To test the status of a lock name, invoke IS_FREE_LOCK(*str*), which returns 1 if the name is available (not currently being used as a lock), 0 if the name is in use, or NULL if an error occurred.

All three functions return NULL if the lock name argument is NULL.

- INET_ATON(*str*)

Given an IP address represented as a string in dotted-quad notation, returns the integer representation of the address or NULL if the argument is not a valid IP address.

```
INET_ATON('64.28.67.70')                    → 1075594054
INET_ATON('255.255.255.255')                → 4294967295
INET_ATON('256.255.255.255')                → NULL
INET_ATON('www.mysql.com')                  → NULL
```

INET_ATON() was introduced in MySQL 3.23.15.

- INET_NTOA(*n*)

Given the integer representation of an IP address, returns the corresponding dotted-quad representation as a string or NULL if the value is illegal.

```
INET_NTOA(1075594054)                       → '64.28.67.70'
INET_NTOA(2130706433)                       → '127.0.0.1'
```

INET_NTOA() was introduced in MySQL 3.23.15.

- IS_FREE_LOCK(*str*)

Checks the status of the advisory lock named by *str*. IS_FREE_LOCK() is used in conjunction with GET_LOCK(). See the description of GET_LOCK() for details.

IS_FREE_LOCK() was introduced in MySQL 4.0.2.

- LAST_INSERT_ID()
LAST_INSERT_ID(*expr*)

With no argument, returns the AUTO_INCREMENT value that was most recently generated during the current server session or 0 if no such value has been generated. With an argument, LAST_INSERT_ID() is intended to be used in an UPDATE statement. The result is treated the same way as an automatically generated value, which is useful for generating sequences.

More details can be found in Chapter 2. For both forms of
`LAST_INSERT_ID()`, the value is maintained by the server on a per-connection basis and cannot be changed by other clients, even by those that
cause new automatically generated values to be created.

The form of `LAST_INSERT_ID()` that takes an argument was introduced
in MySQL 3.22.9.

- `LOAD_FILE(file_name)`

Reads the file `file_name` and returns its contents as a string. The file
must be located on the server, must be specified as an absolute (full)
pathname, and must be world-readable to ensure that you're not trying to
read a protected file. Because the file must be on the server, you must
have the `FILE` privilege. If any of these conditions fail, `LOAD_FILE()`
returns `NULL`.

`LOAD_FILE()` was introduced in MySQL 3.23.0.

- `MASTER_POS_WAIT(log_file,pos)`

This function is used when testing master replication servers. It causes
the master to block until the slave server reaches the given position in
the log file. If the slave has already reached that position, the function
returns immediately. If the slave isn't running, the master blocks until the
slave is started and reaches the given position.

`MASTER_POS_WAIT()` returns the number of log file events it had to wait
for until the slave reached the position, or `NULL` if an error occurred or
the master server information has not been initialized.

`MASTER_POS_WAIT()` was introduced in MySQL 3.23.32.

- `RELEASE_LOCK(str)`

Releases the advisory lock named by `str`. `RELEASE_LOCK()` is used in
conjunction with `GET_LOCK()`. See the description of `GET_LOCK()` for
details.

- `SESSION_USER()`

This function is a synonym for `USER()`.

- `SYSTEM_USER()`

This function is a synonym for `USER()`.

- USER()

  Returns a string representing the current client user, as a string of t
  form `'user@host'`, where *user* is the user name and *host* is the na
  of the host from which the client connection was established.

  ```
  USER()                                            → 'sampadm@localho
  SUBSTRING_INDEX(USER(),'@',1)                     → 'sampadm'
  SUBSTRING_INDEX(USER(),'@',-1)                    → 'localhost'
  ```

  Prior to MySQL 3.22.1, the return value from USER() consists only of
  the user name.

- VERSION()

  Returns a string describing the server version.

  ```
  VERSION()                                         → '4.0.3-beta-log'
  ```

  The value consists of a version number, possibly followed by one or
  more suffixes. The suffixes may include the following:

  - -alpha, -beta, or -gamma indicate the stability of the MySQL
    release.
  - -debug means that the server is running in debug mode.
  - -demo indicates that the server is running in demo mode (used in
    MySQL 3.23.30 and earlier only).
  - -embedded indicates the embedded server, libmysqld.
  - -log means logging is enabled.
  - -max indicates a server compiled with additional features.
  - -nt indicates a server built for Windows NT-based systems.

SQL Syntax Reference

T HIS APPENDIX DESCRIBES

- Each of the SQL statements provided by MySQL
- How to set and use user-defined variables within SQL statements
- The syntax for writing comments in SQL code. Comments are used to write descriptive text that is ignored by the server and to hide MySQL-specific keywords (these keywords will be executed by MySQL but ignored by other database servers).

MySQL development is ongoing, so enhancements to its SQL implementation are made on a continuing basis. You will find it useful to consult the online *MySQL Reference Manual* at http://www.mysql.com/ occasionally to see what new capabilities are being added.

The syntax descriptions use the following conventions:

- Optional information is enclosed in square brackets ([]).
- Vertical bars (|) separate alternative items in a list. If a list is enclosed in square brackets, one alternative may be chosen. If a list is enclosed in curly brackets ({}), one alternative must be chosen.

- Ellipsis notation (...) indicates that the term preceding the ellipsis can be repeated.
- *n* indicates an integer.
- `'string'` indicates a string value. A single-quoted value such as `'file_name'` or `'pattern'` indicates a more specific kind of value, such as a filename or a pattern.

Unless otherwise indicated, the statements listed here have been present in MySQL at least as far back as MySQL 3.22.0.

SQL Statements

This section describes the syntax and meaning of each of MySQL's SQL statements. A statement will fail if you do not have the necessary privileges to perform it. For example, USE *db_name* fails if you have no permission to access the database *db_name*.

ALTER DATABASE

```
ALTER DATABASE db_name action_list
```

This statement changes global database characteristics. The *action_list* specifies one or more actions separated by commas. However, there is currently only one possible action:

```
[DEFAULT] CHARACTER SET charset
```

charset may be a character set name or DEFAULT to have the database use the current server character set by default.

ALTER DATABASE requires the ALTER privilege for the database.

This statement was introduced in MySQL 4.1.

ALTER TABLE

```
ALTER [IGNORE] TABLE tbl_name action_list
```

ALTER TABLE allows you to rename tables or modify their structure. To use it, specify the table name *tbl_name* then give the specifications for one or more actions to be performed on the table. The IGNORE keyword comes into play if the action could produce duplicate key values in a unique index in the new table. Without IGNORE, the effect of the ALTER TABLE statement is canceled. With IGNORE, the rows that duplicate values for unique key values are deleted.

Except for table renaming operations, ALTER TABLE works by creating from the original table a new one that incorporates the changes to be made. If an error occurs, the new table is discarded and the original remains unchanged. If the operation completes successfully, the original table is discarded and replaced by the new one. During the operation, other clients may read from the original table. Any clients that try to update the table are blocked until the ALTER TABLE statement completes, at which point the updates are applied to the new table.

action_list specifies one or more actions separated by commas. Each action is performed in turn. An action may be any of the following:

- ADD [COLUMN] *col_declaration*
  [FIRST | AFTER *col_name*]

  Adds a column to the table. *col_declaration* is the column declaration; it has the same format as that used for the CREATE TABLE statement. The column becomes the first column in the table if the FIRST keyword is given or is placed after the named column if AFTER *col_name* is given. If the column placement is not specified, the column becomes the last column of the table.

  ```
  ALTER TABLE t ADD id INT UNSIGNED NOT NULL AUTO_INCREMENT PRIMARY KEY;
  ALTER TABLE t ADD id INT UNSIGNED NOT NULL AUTO_INCREMENT PRIMARY KEY FIRST;
  ALTER TABLE t ADD id INT UNSIGNED NOT NULL AUTO_INCREMENT PRIMARY KEY
      AFTER suffix;
  ```

- ADD [COLUMN] (*create_definition*,...)

  Adds columns or indexes to the table. Each *create_definition* is a column or index definition, in the same format as for CREATE TABLE. This syntax was introduced in MYSQL 3.23.11.

- ADD [CONSTRAINT *name*]
  FOREIGN KEY [*index_name*] (*index_columns*)
  reference_definition

  Adds a foreign key definition to a table. This is supported only for InnoDB tables. The foreign key is based on the columns named in *index_columns*, which is a list of one or more columns in the table separated by commas. Any CONSTRAINT or *index_name*, if given, are ignored. *reference_definition* defines how the foreign key relates to the parent table. The syntax is as described in the entry for CREATE TABLE. ADD FOREIGN KEY was introduced in MySQL 3.23.50. (There is a corresponding DROP FOREIGN KEY clause, but currently it is just parsed and ignored.)

  ```
  ALTER TABLE child
      ADD FOREIGN KEY (par_id) REFERENCES parent (par_id) ON DELETE CASCADE;
  ```

- ADD FULLTEXT [KEY | INDEX] [*index_name*] (*index_columns*)

  Adds a FULLTEXT index to a MyISAM table. The index is based on the columns named in *index_columns*, which is a list of one or more columns in the table separated by commas. ADD FULLTEXT was introduced in MySQL 3.23.23.

  ```
  ALTER TABLE poetry ADD FULLTEXT (author,title,stanza);
  ```

- ADD INDEX [*index_name*] (*index_columns*)

  Adds an index to the table. The index is based on the columns named in *index_columns*, which is a list of one or more columns in the table separated by commas. For CHAR and VARCHAR columns, you can index a prefix of the column, using *col_name*(*n*) syntax to index the first *n* bytes of column values. For BLOB and TEXT columns, you *must* specify a prefix value; you cannot index the entire column. If the index name *index_name* is not specified, a name is chosen automatically based on the name of the first indexed column.

- ADD PRIMARY KEY (*index_columns*)

  Adds a primary key on the given columns. The key is given the name PRIMARY. *index_columns* is specified as for the ADD INDEX clause. An error occurs if a primary key already exists or if any of the columns are defined to allow NULL values.

  ```
  ALTER TABLE president ADD PRIMARY KEY (last_name, first_name);
  ```

- ADD UNIQUE [*index_name*] (*index_columns*)

  Adds a unique-valued index to *tbl_name*. *index_name* and *index_columns* are specified as for the ADD INDEX clause.

  ```
  ALTER TABLE absence ADD UNIQUE id_date (student_id, date);
  ```

- ALTER [COLUMN] *col_name*
  {SET DEFAULT *value* | DROP DEFAULT}

  Modifies the given column's default value, either to the specified value or by dropping the current default value. In the latter case, a new default value is assigned, as described in the entry for the CREATE TABLE statement.

  ```
  ALTER TABLE event ALTER type SET DEFAULT 'Q';
  ALTER TABLE event ALTER type DROP DEFAULT;
  ```

- CHANGE [COLUMN] *col_name col_declaration*
  [FIRST | AFTER *col_name*]

  Changes a column's name and definition. *col_name* is the column's current name, and *col_declaration* is the declaration to which the column should be changed. *col_declaration* is in the same format as that used for the CREATE TABLE statement. Note that the declaration must include the new column name, so if you want to leave the name unchanged, it's necessary to specify the same name twice. FIRST or AFTER may be used as of MySQL 4.0.1 and have the same effect as for ADD COLUMN.

  ```
  ALTER TABLE student CHANGE name name VARCHAR(40);
  ALTER TABLE student CHANGE name student_name CHAR(30) NOT NULL;
  ```

- DISABLE KEYS

  For a MyISAM table, this disables the updating of non-unique indexes that normally occurs when the table is changed. ENABLE KEYS may be used to re-enable index updating. DISABLE KEYS was introduced in MySQL 4.0.

  ```
  ALTER TABLE score DISABLE KEYS;
  ```

- DROP [COLUMN] *col_name* [RESTRICT | CASCADE]

  Removes the given column from the table. If the column is part of any indexes, it is removed from those indexes. If all columns from an index are removed, the index is removed as well.

  ```
  ALTER TABLE president DROP suffix;
  ```

  The RESTRICT and CASCADE keywords have no effect. They are parsed for compatibility with code ported from other databases, but ignored.

- DROP INDEX *index_name*

  Removes the given index from the table.

  ```
  ALTER TABLE member DROP INDEX name;
  ```

- DROP PRIMARY KEY

  Removes the primary key from the table. If a table has no unique index that was created as a PRIMARY KEY but has one or more UNIQUE indexes, the first one of those is dropped.

  ```
  ALTER TABLE president DROP PRIMARY KEY;
  ```

- ENABLE KEYS

  For a MyISAM table, re-enables updating for non-unique indexes that have been disabled with DISABLE KEYS. ENABLE KEYS was introduced in MySQL 4.0.

  ```
  ALTER TABLE score ENABLE KEYS;
  ```

- MODIFY [COLUMN] col_declaration
  [FIRST | AFTER col_name]

  Changes the declaration of a column. The column declaration col_declaration is given, using the same format for column descriptions as is shown in the entry for the CREATE TABLE statement. The declaration begins with a column name, which is how the column that is to be modified is identified. MODIFY was introduced in MySQL 3.22.16. FIRST or AFTER may be used as of MySQL 4.0.1 and have the same effect as for ADD COLUMN.

  ```
  ALTER TABLE student MODIFY name VARCHAR(40) DEFAULT '' NOT NULL;
  ```

- ORDER BY col_list

  Sorts the rows in the table according to the columns named in col_list, which should be a list of one or more columns in the table separated by columns. The default sort order is ascending. A column name can be followed by ASC or DESC to specify ascending or descending order explicitly. Sorting a table this way may improve performance of subsequent queries that retrieve records in the same order. This is mostly useful for a table that will not be modified afterward, because rows will not remain in order if the table is modified after performing the ORDER BY operation. This option was introduced in MySQL 3.23.28.

  ```
  ALTER TABLE score ORDER BY event_id, student_id;
  ```

- RENAME [TO | AS] new_tbl_name

  Renames the table tbl_name to new_tbl_name.

  ```
  ALTER TABLE president RENAME TO prez;
  ```

  Prior to MySQL 3.23.17, there is no keyword between RENAME and the new table name. From 3.23.17 on, TO is optional there, and from 3.23.23 on, TO or AS are optional there.

- *table_options*

  Specifies table options of the sort that may be given in the *table_options* part of a CREATE TABLE statement.

  ```
  ALTER TABLE score TYPE = MYISAM CHECKSUM = 1;
  ALTER TABLE sayings CHARACTER SET utf8;
  ```

  Any version-specific constraints on the availability of a given table option are as described in the entry for the CREATE TABLE statement.

ANALYZE TABLE

```
ANALYZE {TABLE | TABLES} tbl_name [, tbl_name] ...
```

This statement causes MySQL to analyze each of the named tables, storing the distribution of key values present in each table's indexes. It works for MyISAM and BDB tables and requires SELECT and INSERT privileges on each table. After analysis, the Cardinality column of the output from SHOW INDEX indicates the number of distinct values in the indexes. Information from the analysis can be used by the optimizer during subsequent queries to perform certain types of joins more quickly.

Analyzing a table requires a read lock, which prevents that table from being updated during the operation. If you run ANALYZE TABLE on a table that has already been analyzed and that has not been changed since, no analysis is performed.

ANALYZE TABLE produces output in the format described under the entry for CHECK TABLE.

ANALYZE TABLE was introduced in MySQL 3.23.14.

BACKUP TABLE

```
BACKUP {TABLE | TABLES} tbl_name [, tbl_name] ... TO 'dir_name'
```

Copies the named table or tables to the directory named by '*dir_name*', which should be the full pathname to a directory on the server host where the backup files should be written. BACKUP TABLE works only for MyISAM tables and requires the SELECT and FILE privileges. It copies the table definition and data files (the .frm and .MYD files), which are the minimum required to restore the table. Index files are not copied because they can be re-created as necessary (using RESTORE TABLE) from the definition and data files.

Tables are read-locked individually as they are backed up. If you are backing up a set of tables, it's possible that tables named later in the table list will be modified while earlier tables are being backed up, or vice versa. If you want to ensure that all the tables are backed up as a group with the contents they have when BACKUP TABLE begins executing, use LOCK TABLE to lock them first and then unlock them after backing up with UNLOCK TABLE. Of course, this will cause the tables to be unavailable for a longer time to other clients that want to update the tables.

The files created by BACKUP TABLE will be owned by the account used to run the server. Any existing backup files for a table are overwritten.

BACKUP TABLE was introduced in MySQL 3.23.25.

Back up table t by creating files t.frm and t.MYD in the directory /var/mysql/bkup:

```
BACKUP TABLE t TO '/var/mysql/bkup';
```

BEGIN

```
BEGIN [WORK]
```

Begins a transaction by disabling auto-commit mode until the next COMMIT or ROLLBACK statement. Statements executed while auto-commit mode is disabled will be committed or rolled back as a unit.

After the transaction has been committed or rolled back, auto-commit mode is restored to the state it was in prior to BEGIN. To manipulate auto-commit mode explicitly, use SET AUTOCOMMIT. (See the description for the SET statement.)

Issuing a BEGIN while a transaction is in progress causes the transaction to be committed implicitly.

BEGIN was introduced in MySQL 3.23.17. BEGIN WORK was introduced as a synonym in MySQL 3.23.19.

CHANGE MASTER

```
CHANGE MASTER TO master_defs
```

For use on replication slave servers to change the parameters that indicate which master host to use, how to connect to it, or which logs to use. *master_defs* is a comma-separated list of one or more parameter definitions in *param = value* format. The allowable definitions are as follows:

- MASTER_CONNECT_RETRY = *n*

  The number of seconds to wait between attempts to connect to the master

- MASTER_HOST = '*host_name*'

  The host on which the master server is running

- MASTER_LOG_FILE = '*file_name*'

  The name of the master's binary update log file to use for replication

- MASTER_LOG_POS = *n*

  The position within the master log file from which to begin or resume replication

- MASTER_PASSWORD = '*pass_val*'

  The password to use for connecting to the master server

- MASTER_PORT = *n*

  The port number to use for connecting to the master server

- MASTER_USER = '*user_name*'

  The username to use for connecting to the master server

- RELAY_LOG_FILE = '*file_name*'

  The slave relay log file name

- RELAY_LOG_POS = *n*

  The current position within the slave relay log

With the exception of the hostname or port number, only those parameters that you specify explicitly are changed. Changes to the host or port normally indicate that you're switching to a different master server, so in those cases, the binary update log filename and position are reset to the empty string and zero.

CHANGE MASTER was introduced in MySQL 3.23.23. The RELAY_LOG_FILE and RELAY_LOG_POS options were introduced in MySQL 4.0.2 (replication relay logs were not instituted until then).

CHECK TABLE

```
CHECK {TABLE | TABLES} tbl_name [, tbl_name] ... [options]
```

This statement checks tables for errors. It works with MyISAM tables and also with InnoDB tables as of MySQL 3.23.39. It requires the SELECT privilege on each table.

options, if given, is a list naming one or more of the following options (not separated by commas):

- CHANGED

  Check only those tables that have been changed since they were last checked or that have not been closed properly.

- EXTENDED

  Perform an extended check that attempts to ensure that the table is fully consistent. For example, it verifies that each key in each index points to a data row. This option can be slow.

- FAST

  Check only those tables that have not been closed properly.

- MEDIUM

  Check the index, scan the data rows for problems, and perform a check-sum verification. This is the default if no options are given.

- QUICK

  Don't scan the data rows, just the index.

CHECK TABLE returns information about the result of the operation—for example:

```
mysql> CHECK TABLE t;
+---------+-------+----------+----------+
| Table   | Op    | Msg_type | Msg_text |
+---------+-------+----------+----------+
| test.t  | check | status   | OK       |
+---------+-------+----------+----------+
```

ANALYZE TABLE, OPTIMIZE TABLE, and REPAIR TABLE also return information in this format. Table indicates the table on which the operation was performed. Op indicates the type of operation and has a value of check, analyze, optimize, or repair. The Msg_type and Msg_text columns provide information about the result of the operation.

CHECK TABLE was introduced in MySQL 3.23.13, but it does not work under Windows prior to 3.23.25. The QUICK, FAST, and MEDIUM options were added in MySQL 3.23.16, 3.23.23, and 3.23.31, respectively. From 3.23.15 to 3.23.25, only a single option is allowed and TYPE = must precede it; after that, TYPE = is deprecated, and multiple options are allowed.

COMMIT

```
COMMIT
```

Commits changes made by statements that are part of the current transaction to record those changes permanently in the database. COMMIT works only for transaction-safe table types. (For non-transactional table types, statements are committed as they are executed.)

COMMIT has no effect if auto-commit mode has not been disabled with BEGIN or by setting AUTOCOMMIT to 0.

Some statements implicitly end any current transaction, as if a COMMIT had been performed:

```
ALTER TABLE
BEGIN
CREATE INDEX
DROP DATABASE
DROP INDEX
DROP TABLE
LOAD MASTER DATA
LOCK TABLES
RENAME TABLE
SET AUTOCOMMIT = 1
TRUNCATE TABLE
UNLOCK TABLES (if tables currently are locked)
```

COMMIT was introduced in MySQL 3.23.14.

CREATE DATABASE

```
CREATE DATABASE [IF NOT EXISTS] db_name
    [[DEFAULT] CHARACTER SET charset]
```

Creates a database with the given name. The statement fails if you don't have the proper privilege to create it. Attempts to create a database with a name that already exists normally result in an error; if the IF NOT EXISTS clause is specified, the database is not created but no error occurs. This clause was introduced in MySQL 3.23.12.

As of MySQL 4.1, the DEFAULT CHARACTER SET clause can be used to specify a default character set attribute for the database. charset can be a character set name or DEFAULT to have tables in the database use the current server character set by default. Database attributes are stored in the db.opt file in the database directory.

CREATE FUNCTION

```
CREATE [AGGREGATE] FUNCTION function_name
    RETURNS {STRING | REAL | INTEGER}
    SONAME 'shared_library_name'
```

Specifies a user-defined function (UDF) to be loaded into the func table in the mysql database. function_name is the name by which you want to refer to the function in SQL statements. The keyword following RETURNS indicates the return type of the function. The `'shared_library_name'` string names the pathname of the file that contains the executable code for the function.

The AGGREGATE keyword, if given, indicates that the function is an aggregate (group) function like SUM() or MAX(). AGGREGATE was introduced in MySQL 3.23.5.

CREATE FUNCTION requires that the server be built as a dynamically linked binary (not as a static binary) because the UDF mechanism requires dynamic linking. For instructions on writing user-defined functions, refer to the *MySQL Reference Manual*.

CREATE INDEX

```
CREATE [UNIQUE | FULLTEXT] INDEX index_name
    ON tbl_name (index_columns)
```

Adds an index named *index_name* to the table *tbl_name*. This statement is handled as an ALTER TABLE ADD INDEX, ALTER TABLE ADD UNIQUE, or ALTER TABLE ADD FULLTEXT statement, according to the absence or presence of the UNIQUE or FULLTEXT keywords. See the entry for ALTER TABLE for details. CREATE INDEX cannot be used to create a PRIMARY KEY; use ALTER TABLE instead.

If you want to create several indexes on a table, it's preferable to use ALTER TABLE directly; you can add them all with a single statement, which is faster than adding them individually.

CREATE INDEX is functional only as of MySQL 3.22. The option of creating FULLTEXT indexes was introduced in MySQL 3.23.23.

CREATE TABLE

```
CREATE [TEMPORARY] TABLE [IF NOT EXISTS] tbl_name
    (create_definition,...)
    [table_options]
    [[IGNORE | REPLACE] [AS] select_statement]

create_definition:
    {   col_declaration [reference_definition]
      | [CONSTRAINT symbol] PRIMARY KEY (index_columns)
      | [CONSTRAINT symbol] UNIQUE [INDEX | KEY] [index_name] (index_columns)
      | {INDEX | KEY} [index_name] (index_columns)
      | FULLTEXT [INDEX | KEY] [index_name] (index_columns)
      | [CONSTRAINT symbol] FOREIGN KEY [index_name] (index_columns)
            [reference_definition]
      | [CONSTRAINT symbol] CHECK (expr)
    }
```

```
col_declaration:
    col_name col_type
        [NOT NULL | NULL] [DEFAULT default_value]
        [AUTO_INCREMENT] [PRIMARY KEY] [UNIQUE [KEY]]
        [COMMENT 'string']

reference_definition:
    REFERENCES tbl_name (index_columns)
        [ON DELETE reference_action]
        [ON UPDATE reference_action]
        [MATCH FULL | MATCH PARTIAL]

reference_action:
    {RESTRICT | CASCADE | SET NULL | NO ACTION | SET DEFAULT}
```

The CREATE TABLE statement creates a new table named *tbl_name* in the current database. If the name is specified as *db_name.tbl_name*, the table is created in the named database.

If the TEMPORARY keyword is given, the table exists only until the current client connection ends (either normally or abnormally) or until a DROP TABLE statement is issued. A temporary table is visible only to the client that created it.

Normally, attempts to create a table with a name that already exists result in an error. No error occurs under two conditions. First, if the IF NOT EXISTS clause is specified, the table is not created but no error occurs. Second, if TEMPORARY is specified and the original table is not a temporary table, the new temporary table is created, but the original table named *tbl_name* becomes hidden to the client while the temporary table exists. The original table remains visible to other clients. The original table becomes visible again either at the next client session, if an explicit DROP TABLE is issued for the temporary table, or if the temporary table is renamed to some other name.

The *create_definition* list names the columns and indexes that you want to create. The list is optional if you create the table by means of a trailing SELECT statement. The *table_options* clause allows you to specify various properties for the table. If a trailing *select_statement* is specified (in the form of an arbitrary SELECT statement), the table is created using the result set returned by the SELECT statement. These clauses are described more fully in the following sections.

The IF NOT EXISTS clause, the *table_options* clause, and the ability to create a table from the result of a SELECT statement were introduced in MySQL 3.23. TEMPORARY tables were introduced in MySQL 3.23.2.

Column and index definitions. A `create_definition` can be a column or index definition, a `FOREIGN KEY` clause, or a `CHECK` clause. `CHECK` is parsed for compatibility with other database systems, but otherwise ignored. `FOREIGN KEY` is treated similarly, except for InnoDB tables.

A column declaration `col_declaration` begins with a column name `col_name` and a type `col_type` and may be followed by several optional keywords. The column type may be any of the types listed in Appendix B, Column Type Reference. See that appendix for type-specific attributes that apply to the columns you want to declare. Other optional keywords that may follow the column type are as follows:

- `NULL` or `NOT NULL`

  Specifies that the column may or may not contain `NULL` values. If neither is specified, `NULL` is the default.

- `DEFAULT` `default_value`

  Specifies the default value for the column. This cannot be used for `BLOB` or `TEXT` types. A default value must be a constant, specified as a number, a string, or `NULL`.

  If no default is specified, a default value is assigned. For columns that may take `NULL` values, the default is `NULL`. For columns that may not be `NULL`, the default is assigned as follows:

  - For numeric columns, the default is 0, except for `AUTO_INCREMENT` columns. For `AUTO_INCREMENT`, the default is the next number in the column sequence.

  - For date and time types other than `TIMESTAMP`, the default is the "zero" value for the type (for example, `'0000-00-00'` for `DATE`). For `TIMESTAMP`, the default is the current date and time for the first `TIMESTAMP` column in a table, and the "zero" value for any following `TIMESTAMP` columns.

  - For string types other than `ENUM`, the default is the empty string. For `ENUM`, the default is the first enumeration element.

- `AUTO_INCREMENT`

  This keyword applies only to integer column types. An `AUTO_INCREMENT` column is special in that when you insert `NULL` into it, the value actually inserted is the next value in the column sequence. (Typically, this is one greater than the current maximum value in the column.)
  `AUTO_INCREMENT` values start at 1 by default. For MyISAM tables (and for

HEAP tables as of MySQL 4.1), the first value may be specified explicitly with the AUTO_INCREMENT = n table option. The column must also be specified as a UNIQUE index or PRIMARY KEY and should be NOT NULL. There may be at most one AUTO_INCREMENT column per table.

- PRIMARY KEY

  Specifies that the column is a PRIMARY KEY. A PRIMARY KEY must be NOT NULL.

- UNIQUE [KEY]

  Specifies that the column is a UNIQUE index. This attribute may be specified as of MySQL 3.23.

- COMMENT 'string'

  Specifies a descriptive comment to be associated with the column. Prior to MySQL 4.1, this attribute is parsed but ignored. As of 4.1, it is remembered and displayed by SHOW CREATE TABLE and SHOW FULL COLUMNS.

The PRIMARY KEY, UNIQUE, INDEX, KEY, and FULLTEXT clauses specify indexes. PRIMARY KEY and UNIQUE specify indexes that must contain unique values. INDEX and KEY are synonymous; they specify indexes that may contain duplicate values. The index is based on the columns named in index_columns, each of which must be a column in tbl_name. If there are multiple columns, they should be separated by commas. For CHAR and VARCHAR columns, you can index a prefix of the column, using col_name(n) syntax to index the first n bytes of column values. (The exception is that InnoDB tables do not allow index prefixes.) For BLOB and TEXT columns, you *must* specify a prefix value; you cannot index the entire column. Prefixes for columns named in a FULLTEXT index are ignored if given. If the index name index_name is not specified, a name is chosen automatically based on the name of the first indexed column.

FULLTEXT indexes are allowed only for MyISAM tables and only for TEXT columns and non-BINARY CHAR and VARCHAR columns.

Indexed columns must be declared NOT NULL for ISAM tables, and for HEAP tables prior to MySQL 4.0.2. PRIMARY KEY columns must always be declared NOT NULL.

Table options. The table_options clause is available as of MySQL 3.23 (some of the options appeared later, as indicated in the descriptions). Table options can include one or more of the options in the following list. If multiple options are present, they should not be separated by commas. Each specifier applies to all table types unless otherwise noted. As of MySQL 4.1, the = sign following the option name is optional.

- `AUTO_INCREMENT = n`

  The first `AUTO_INCREMENT` value to be generated for the table. This option is effective only for MyISAM tables, and for HEAP tables as of MYSQL 4.1.

- `AVG_ROW_LENGTH = n`

  The approximate average row length of your table. For MyISAM tables, MySQL uses the product of the `AVG_ROW_LENGTH` and `MAX_ROWS` values to determine the maximum data file size. The MyISAM handler can use internal row pointers with a table from 2 to 8 bytes wide. The default pointer width is wide enough to allow tables up to 4GB. If you require a larger table (and your operating system supports larger files), the `MAX_ROWS` and `AVG_ROW_LENGTH` table options allow the MyISAM handler to adjust the internal pointer width. A large product of these values causes the handler to use wider pointers. (Conversely, a small product allows the handler to use smaller pointers. This won't save you much space if the table is small anyway, but if you have many small tables, the cumulative savings may be significant.)

- `[DEFAULT] CHARACTER SET charset`

  Specifies the table's default character set. `charset` can be a character set name or `DEFAULT` to use the database character set if it is defined or the server character set if not. This option determines which character set is used for character columns that are declared without an explicit character set. In the following example, `c1` will be assigned the `sjis` character set and `c2` the `ujis` character set:

  ```
  CREATE TABLE t
  (
      c1 CHAR(50) CHARACTER SET sjis,
      c2 CHAR(50)
  ) CHARACTER SET ujis;
  ```

  This option also applies to subsequent table modifications made with `ALTER TABLE` for character column changes that do not name a character set explicitly.

CHARACTER SET was introduced in MySQL 4.1. It can be given in any of several variant synonymous forms. The following are all equivalent:

```
CHARACTER SET charset
CHARSET = charset
CHARSET charset
```

These synonymous forms can also be used in other places where character sets can be specified, such as in column definitions or in the CREATE DATABASE and ALTER DATABASE statements.

- CHECKSUM = {0 | 1}

  If this is set to 1, MySQL maintains a checksum for each table row. There is a slight penalty for updates to the table, but the presence of checksums improves the table checking process. (MyISAM tables only.)

- COMMENT = 'string'

  A comment for the table. The maximum length is 60 characters. This comment is shown by SHOW CREATE TABLE and SHOW TABLE STATUS.

- DATA DIRECTORY = 'dir_name'

  This option is used for MyISAM tables only, and indicates the directory where the data (.MYD) file should be written. 'dir_name' must be a full pathname. This option was introduced in MySQL 4.0, and works only if the server is started without the --skip-symlink option. On some operating systems, such as Mac OS X, FreeBSD, and BSDI, symlinks are not thread-safe and are disabled by default.

- DELAY_KEY_WRITE = {0 | 1}

  If this is set to 1, the index cache is flushed only occasionally for the table, rather than after each insert operation. (MyISAM tables only.)

- INDEX DIRECTORY = 'dir_name'

  This option is used for MyISAM tables only and indicates the directory where the index (.MYI) file should be written. 'dir_name' must be a full pathname. This option was introduced in MySQL 4.0, and is subject to the same constraints as the DATA DIRECTORY option.

- INSERT_METHOD = {NO | FIRST | LAST}

  This is used for MERGE tables to specify how to insert rows. A value of NO disallows inserts entirely. Values of FIRST or LAST indicate that rows should be inserted into the first or last of the MyISAM tables that make up the MERGE table. This option was introduced in MySQL 4.0.

- MAX_ROWS = *n*

  The maximum number of rows you plan to store in the table. The description of the AVG_ROW_LENGTH option indicates how this value is used. (MyISAM tables only.)

- MIN_ROWS = *n*

  The minimum number of rows you plan to store in the table. This option can be used for HEAP tables to give the HEAP handler a hint about how to optimize memory usage.

- PACK_KEYS = {0 | 1 | DEFAULT}

  This option controls index compression for MyISAM and ISAM tables, which allows runs of similar index values to be compressed. The usual effect is an update penalty and an improvement in retrieval performance. A value of 0 specifies no index compression. A value of 1 specifies compression for string (CHAR and VARCHAR) values and (for MyISAM tables) numeric index values. As of MySQL 4.0, a value of DEFAULT can be used, which specifies compression only for long string columns.

- PASSWORD = '*string*'

  Specifies a password for encrypting the table's description file. This option normally has no effect; it enabled only for certain support contract customers.

- RAID_TYPE = {1 | STRIPED | RAID0}
  RAID_CHUNKS = *n*
  RAID_CHUNKSIZE = *n*

  These options are used together and are available as of MySQL 3.23.12 for use with MyISAM to achieve larger effective table sizes. The options are ineffective unless MySQL was configured with the --with-raid option at build time.

  The default RAID_TYPE value is STRIPED; the other two types actually are just aliases for STRIPED. RAID_CHUNKS and RAID_CHUNKSIZE control the allocation of space to be used for the table's data. The server creates several directories under the database directory (the number is determined by the RAID_CHUNKS value) and creates a data file named *tbl_name*.MYD in each. As rows are added to the table, the server writes to the file in the first directory until it fills up and then proceeds to the next directory. The size of the file in each directory is controlled by the value of RAID_CHUNKSIZE, which is measured in KB (1024 bytes). Directories are named using hexadecimal digits in the sequence 00, 01, and so forth. For example, if RAID_CHUNKS is 256 and

RAID_CHUNKSIZE is 1000, the server creates 256 directories named 00 through ff, and writes up to 1000KB of data to the file in each directory.

- ROW_FORMAT =
  {DEFAULT | FIXED | DYNAMIC | COMPRESSED}

  This option applies only to MyISAM tables and specifies the row storage type. The option can be used as of MySQL 3.23.6.

- TYPE =
  {ISAM | MYISAM | MERGE | HEAP | BDB | INNODB}

  Specifies the table storage format. The characteristics of these storage formats are described in the "Table Types" section in Chapter 3, "MySQL SQL Syntax and Use." The default format for MySQL as of version 3.23 is MyISAM unless the server has been configured otherwise (either at build time or if the server was started with a --default-table-type option). MRG_MYISAM, BERKELEYDB, and INNOBASE are synonyms for MERGE, BDB, and INNODB, respectively. If you specify a table type that is legal but for which no table handler is available, MySQL uses the default storage format. If you give an invalid value for the option, an error results. This option was introduced in MySQL 3.23. Prior to that, CREATE TABLE always creates tables in ISAM format.

- UNION = (tbl_list)

  This option is used for MERGE tables. It specifies the list of MyISAM tables that make up the MERGE table.

Trailing SELECT statement. If a select_statement clause is specified (as a trailing SELECT query), the table is created using the contents of the result set returned by the query. Rows that duplicate values on a unique index are either ignored or they replace existing rows according to whether IGNORE or REPLACE is specified. If neither is specified, the statement aborts with an error.

Foreign key support. The InnoDB table handler provides foreign key support. A foreign key in a child table is indicated by FOREIGN KEY, an optional index name, a list of the columns that make up the foreign key, and a REFERENCES definition. The index name, if given, is ignored. The REF-ERENCES definition names the parent table and columns to which the foreign key refers and indicates what to do when a parent table record is deleted. The actions that InnoDB implements are CASCADE (delete the corresponding child table records) and SET NULL (set the foreign key columns in the corresponding child table records to NULL). The RESTRICT, NO ACTION, and SET DEFAULT actions are parsed but ignored.

ON UPDATE and MATCH clauses in REFERENCE definitions are parsed but ignored. (If you specify a foreign key definition for a table type other than InnoDB, the entire definition is ignored.)

The following statements demonstrate some ways in which CREATE TABLE can be used.

Create a table with three columns. The id column is a PRIMARY KEY, and the last_name and first_name columns are indexed together:

```
CREATE TABLE customer
(
    id          SMALLINT UNSIGNED NOT NULL AUTO_INCREMENT,
    last_name   CHAR(30) NOT NULL,
    first_name  CHAR(20) NOT NULL,
    PRIMARY KEY (id),
    INDEX (last_name, first_name)
);
```

Create a temporary table and make it a HEAP (in-memory) table for greater speed:

```
CREATE TEMPORARY TABLE tmp_table
    (id MEDIUMINT NOT NULL UNIQUE, name CHAR(40))
    TYPE = HEAP;
```

Create a table as a copy of another table:

```
CREATE TABLE prez_copy SELECT * FROM president;
```

Create a table using only part of another table:

```
CREATE TABLE prez_alive SELECT last_name, first_name, birth
    FROM president WHERE death IS NULL;
```

If creation declarations are specified for a table created and populated by means of a trailing SELECT statement, the declarations are applied after the table contents have been inserted into the table. For example, you can declare that a selected column should be made into a PRIMARY KEY:

```
CREATE TABLE new_tbl (PRIMARY KEY (a)) SELECT a, b, c FROM old_tbl;
```

As of MySQL 4.1, you can specify declarations for the columns in the new table to override the definitions that would be used by default based on the characteristics of the result set:

```
CREATE TABLE new_tbl (a INT NOT NULL AUTO_INCREMENT, b DATE, PRIMARY KEY (a))
    SELECT a, b, c FROM old_tbl;
```

DELETE

```
DELETE [LOW_PRIORITY] [QUICK] FROM tbl_name
    [WHERE where_expr] [ORDER BY ...] [LIMIT n]
```

```
DELETE [LOW_PRIORITY] [QUICK] tbl_name [, tbl_name] ...
    FROM tbl_name [, tbl_name] ...
    [WHERE where_expr]

DELETE [LOW_PRIORITY] [QUICK] FROM tbl_name [, tbl_name] ...
    USING tbl_name [, tbl_name] ...
    [WHERE where_expr]
```

The first form of the DELETE statement deletes rows from the table *tbl_name*. The rows deleted are those that match the conditions specified in the WHERE clause:

```
DELETE FROM score WHERE event_id = 14;
DELETE FROM member WHERE expiration < CURDATE();
```

If the WHERE clause is omitted, *all records in the table are deleted.*

Specifying LOW_PRIORITY causes the statement to be deferred until no clients are reading from the table. LOW_PRIORITY was introduced in MySQL 3.22.5.

For MyISAM tables, specifying QUICK can make the statement quicker; the MyISAM handler will not perform its usual index tree leaf merging. QUICK was introduced in MySQL 3.23.25.

If the LIMIT clause is given, the value *n* specifies the maximum number of rows that will be deleted. LIMIT was introduced in MySQL 3.22.7.

With ORDER BY, rows are deleted in the resulting sort order. Combined with LIMIT, this provides more precise control over which rows are deleted. ORDER BY was introduced in MySQL 4.0.0 and has same syntax as for SELECT.

Normally, DELETE returns the number of records deleted. DELETE with no WHERE clause will empty the table, and you may find that, prior to MySQL 4, the server optimizes this special case by dropping and recreating the table from scratch rather than deleting records on a row-by-row basis. This is extremely fast, but a row count of zero may be returned. To obtain a true count, specify a WHERE clause that matches all records—for example:

```
DELETE FROM tbl_name WHERE 1;
```

There is a significant performance penalty for row-by-row deletion, however.

If you don't need a row count, another way to empty a table is to use TRUNCATE TABLE.

The second and third forms of DELETE allow rows to be deleted from multiple tables at once. They also allow you to identify the rows to delete based on joins between tables. These forms are available as of MySQL 4.0.0 and 4.0.2, respectively. Names in the list of tables from which rows are to be deleted can be given as *tbl_name* or *tbl_name*.*; the latter form is supported for ODBC compatibility.

To delete rows in `t1` having `id` values that match those in `t2`, use the first multiple-table syntax like this:

```
DELETE t1 FROM t1, t2 WHERE t1.id = t2.id;
```

or the second syntax like this:

```
DELETE FROM t1 USING t1, t2 WHERE t1.id = t2.id;
```

DESCRIBE

```
{DESCRIBE | DESC} tbl_name [col_name | 'pattern']
```

```
{DESCRIBE | DESC} select_statement
```

DESCRIBE with a table name produces the same kind of output as SHOW COLUMNS. See the SHOW entry for more information. With this syntax, a trailing column name or string is interpreted as a pattern, as for the LIKE operator, and restricts output to those columns having names that match the pattern.

Display output for the `last_name` column of the `president` table:

```
DESCRIBE president last_name;
```

Display output for both the `last_name` and `first_name` columns of the `president` table:

```
DESCRIBE president '%name';
```

DESCRIBE with a SELECT statement is a synonym for EXPLAIN. See the EXPLAIN entry for more information. (DESCRIBE and EXPLAIN actually are completely synonymous in MySQL, but DESCRIBE is more often used to obtain table descriptions and EXPLAIN to obtain SELECT statement execution information.)

DO

```
DO expr [, expr] ...
```

Evaluates the expressions without returning any results. This makes DO more convenient than SELECT for expression evaluation, because you need not deal with a result set. For example, DO can be used for setting variables or for invoking functions that you are interested in primarily for their side effects rather than for their return values.

```
DO @sidea := 3, @sideb := 4, @sidec := SQRT(@sidea*@sidea+@sideb*@sideb);
DO RELEASE_LOCK('mylock');
```

DO was introduced in MySQL 3.23.47.

DROP DATABASE

```
DROP DATABASE [IF EXISTS] db_name
```

Drops (removes) the given database. After you drop a database, it's gone, so be careful. The statement fails if the database does not exist (unless you specify IF EXISTS) or if you don't have the proper privilege. The IF EXISTS clause can be specified to suppress the error message that normally results if the database does not exist. IF EXISTS was introduced in MySQL 3.22.2.

A database is represented by a directory under the data directory. If you have put non-table files in that directory, those files are not deleted by the DROP DATABASE statement. In that case, the database directory itself is not removed, either, and its name will continue to be listed by SHOW DATABASES.

DROP FUNCTION

```
DROP FUNCTION function_name
```

Removes a user-defined function that was previously loaded with CREATE FUNCTION.

DROP INDEX

```
DROP INDEX index_name ON tbl_name
```

Drops the index index_name from the table tbl_name. This statement is handled as an ALTER TABLE DROP INDEX statement. See the entry for ALTER TABLE for details. DROP INDEX cannot be used to drop a PRIMARY KEY; use ALTER TABLE instead.

DROP INDEX is functional only as of MySQL 3.22.

DROP TABLE

```
DROP TABLE [IF EXISTS] tbl_name [, tbl_name] ... [RESTRICT | CASCADE]
```

Drops the named table or tables from the database they belong to. If the IF EXISTS clause is given, dropping a non-existent table is not an error. IF EXISTS was introduced in MySQL 3.22.2.

The RESTRICT and CASCADE keywords have no effect. They are parsed for compatibility with code ported from other databases, but ignored. These keywords can be used as of MySQL 3.23.29.

EXPLAIN

```
EXPLAIN tbl_name [col_name | 'pattern']
```

```
EXPLAIN select_statement
```

The first form of this statement is equivalent to DESCRIBE tbl_name. See the description of the DESCRIBE statement for more information.

The second form of the EXPLAIN statement provides information about how MySQL would execute the SELECT statement following the EXPLAIN keyword.

```
EXPLAIN SELECT score.* FROM score, event
    WHERE score.event_id = event.event_id AND event.event_id = 14;
```

Output from EXPLAIN consists of one or more rows containing the following columns:

- table

  The table to which the output row refers.

- type

  The type of join that MySQL will perform. The possible types are, from best to worst: system, const, eq_ref, ref, range, index, and ALL. The better types are more restrictive, meaning that MySQL has to look at fewer rows from the table when performing the retrieval.

- possible_keys

  The indexes that MySQL considers candidates for finding rows in the table named in the table column. A value of NULL means that no indexes were found.

- key

  The index that MySQL actually will use for finding rows in the table. A value of NULL indicates that no index will be used.

- key_len

  How much of the index will be used. This can be less than the full index row length if MySQL will use a leftmost prefix of the index.

- ref

  The values to which MySQL will compare index values. The word const or '???' means the comparison is against a constant; a column name indicates a column-to-column comparison.

- rows

  An estimate of the number of rows from the table that MySQL must examine to perform the query. The product of the values in this column is an estimate of the total number of row combinations that must be examined from all tables.

- Extra

  Using index indicates that MySQL can retrieve information for the table using only information in the index without examining the data file (this used to appear as Only index). Using where indicates the use of the information in the WHERE clause of the SELECT statement (this used to appear as where used).

FLUSH

```
FLUSH option [, option] ...
```

Flushes various internal caches used by the server. Each *option* value should be one of the following items:

- DES_KEY_FILE

  Reload the DES key file used for encryption and decryption by the DES_ENCRYPT() and DES_DECRYPT() functions. This option was introduced in MySQL 4.0.1.

- HOSTS

  Flushes the host cache.

- LOGS

  Flushes the log files by closing and reopening them.

- MASTER

  This has been renamed to RESET MASTER, which should be used instead.

- PRIVILEGES

  Reloads the grant tables. If you modify the tables with GRANT or REVOKE, the server reloads its in-memory copies of the tables automatically. If you modify the tables directly using statements such as INSERT or UPDATE, it's necessary to tell the server to reload them explicitly. This statement also resets the resource management limits to zero, like the USER_RESOURCES option.

- QUERY CACHE

  Flush the query cache to defragment it, without removing statements from the cache. (To clear the cache entirely, use RESET QUERY CACHE.) This option was introduced in MySQL 4.0.1.

- SLAVE

  This has been renamed to RESET SLAVE, which should be used instead.

- STATUS

  Reinitializes the status variables. This option was introduced in MySQL 3.22.11.

- TABLES [tbl_name [, tbl_name] ...]

  Without any table names, closes any open tables in the table cache. As of MySQL 3.23.23, you can specify an optional comma-separated list of one or more table names to flush specific tables rather than the entire table cache. Also as of that version, FLUSH TABLE is a synonym for FLUSH TABLES.

  If the query cache is operational, FLUSH TABLES also flushes the query cache.

- TABLES WITH READ LOCK

  Flushes all tables in all databases and then places a read lock on them, which is held until you issue an UNLOCK TABLES statement. This statement allows clients to read tables but prohibits any changes from being made, which is useful for getting a backup for your entire server with the guarantee that no tables will change during the backup period. Of course, from the client point of view, this means that the period during which updates are disallowed is greater. This option was introduced in MySQL 3.23.18.

- USER_RESOURCES

  Reset the counters for account resource management limits (such as MAX_QUERIES_PER_HOUR). Accounts that have reached their limits will once again be able to proceed in their activities. This option was introduced in MySQL 4.0.2.

The FLUSH statement requires the RELOAD privilege. It was introduced in MySQL 3.22.9; some of its options were introduced later, as noted in the preceding descriptions.

GRANT

```
GRANT priv_type [(column_list)] [, priv_type [(column_list)] ] ...
    ON {*.* | * | db_name.* | db_name.tbl_name | tbl_name}
    TO account [IDENTIFIED BY 'password']
        [, account [IDENTIFIED BY 'password'] ] ...
    [REQUIRE security_options]
    [WITH grant_or_resource_options]
```

The GRANT statement grants access privileges to one or more MySQL users. The *priv_type* value specifies the privileges to be granted. It consists of privilege types chosen from the following list. ALL is used by itself. For the other privileges, you can specify one or more of them as a comma-separated list. ALL signifies the combination of all the other privileges, except for GRANT OPTION, which must be granted separately or by adding a WITH GRANT OPTION clause.

Privilege Specifier	Operation Allowed by Privilege
ALTER	Alter tables and indexes
CREATE	Create databases and tables
CREATE TEMPORARY TABLES	Create temporary tables
DELETE	Delete existing rows from tables
DROP	Drop (remove) databases and tables
EXECUTE	Execute stored procedures (reserved for future use)
FILE	Read and write files on the server host
GRANT OPTION	Grant the account's privileges to other accounts
INDEX	Create or drop indexes
INSERT	Insert new rows into tables
LOCK TABLES	Explicitly lock tables with LOCK TABLES statements
PROCESS	View information about the threads executing within the server
REFERENCES	Unused (reserved for future use)
RELOAD	Reload the grant tables or flush the logs or caches
REPLICATION CLIENT	Ask about master and slave server locations
REPLICATION SLAVE	Act as a replication slave server
SELECT	Retrieve existing rows from tables
SHOW DATABASES	Issue SHOW DATABASES statements
SHUTDOWN	Shut down the server
SUPER	Kill threads and perform other supervisory operations
UPDATE	Modify existing table rows
ALL	All operations (except GRANT); ALL PRIVILEGES is a synonym
USAGE	A special "no privileges" privilege

The LOCK TABLES privilege can be exercised only over tables for which you also have the SELECT privilege, but it allows you to place any kind of lock, not just read locks.

You can always view or kill your own threads. The SUPER privilege allows you to view or kill any threads.

The CREATE TEMPORARY TABLES, EXECUTE, LOCK TABLES, REPLICATION CLIENT, REPLICATION SLAVE, SHOW DATABASES, and SUPER privileges were added in MySQL 4.0.2. Prior to 4.0.2, operations that require SHOW DATABASES, the replication privileges, or SUPER were controlled by the SELECT, FILE, and PROCESS privileges, respectively.

The ON clause specifies how widely the privileges should be granted, as shown in the following table:

Privilege Specifier	Level at Which Privileges Apply
ON *.*	Global privileges; all databases, all tables
ON *	Global privileges if no default database has been selected, database-level privileges for the current database otherwise
ON *db_name*.*	Database-level privileges; all tables in the named database
ON *db_name*.*tbl_name*	Table-level privileges; all columns in the named table
ON *tbl_name*	Table-level privileges; all columns in the named table in the default database

When a table is named in the ON clause, privileges can be made column-specific by naming one or more comma-separated columns in the *column_list* clause. (This applies only for the INSERT, REFERENCES, SELECT, and UPDATE privileges, which are the only ones that can be granted on a column-specific basis.)

The TO clause specifies one or more accounts to which the privileges should be granted. Each account name consists of a specifier in '*user_name*'@'*host_name*' format and can be followed by an optional IDENTIFIED BY clause to specify a password. The *user_name* and *host_name* parts need not be quoted if they contain no special characters. However, if quoted, they must be quoted separately. (For example, bill@%.com should be quoted as 'bill'@'%.com', not as 'bill@%.com'.) The *user_name* can be a name or an empty string (' '); the latter specifies an anonymous user. *host_name* can be given as localhost, a hostname, an IP address, or a pattern matching a domain name or network number. The pattern characters are '%' and '_', with the same meaning as for the LIKE operator. A *user_name* specified alone with no hostname is equivalent to '*user_name*'@'%'. As of MySQL 3.23, it's also possible for *host_name* to be an IP number/netmask pair in *n.n.n.n/m.m.m.m* notation, where *n.n.n.n* indicates the IP address and *m.m.m.m* indicates the netmask to use for the network number.

The IDENTIFIED BY clause, if given, assigns a password to the user. The password should be specified in plain text, without using the PASSWORD() function, in contrast to the way passwords are specified for the SET PASSWORD statement. If the account already exists and IDENTIFIED BY is specified, the new password replaces the old one. The existing password remains unchanged otherwise.

The REQUIRE clause, if given, allows you to specify that secure connections are to be used and what kinds of information the client is required to supply. The REQUIRE keyword may be followed by:

- NONE to indicate that secure connections are not required.
- A generic connection type of SSL to require that connections for the account use SSL.
- X509 to require that the user supply a valid X509 certificate. In this case, the client can present any X509 certificate; it doesn't matter what its contents are other than that it is valid.
- One or more of the following options to require that the connection be established with certain characteristics:
    - CIPHER '*str*' requires the connection to be established with '*str*' as its encryption cipher.
    - ISSUER '*str*' requires the client certificate to have '*str*' as the certificate issuer value.
    - SUBJECT '*str*' requires the client certificate to have '*str*' as the certificate subject value.

    If you give more than one of these options, they can optionally be separated by AND. The order of the options doesn't matter.

The WITH clause, if given, can specify that the account is able to grant other accounts the privileges that it holds itself. As of MySQL 4.0.2, it can also be used to place limits on the account's resource consumption. The allowable options are shown next. You can specify more than one option; their order does not matter.

- GRANT OPTION

    This account is allowed to grant its own privileges to other accounts, including the right to grant privileges.

- MAX_CONNECTIONS_PER_HOUR *n*

  The account is allowed to make *n* connections to the server per hour.

- MAX_QUERIES_PER_HOUR *n*

  The account is allowed to issue *n* queries per hour.

- MAX_UPDATES_PER_HOUR *n*

  The account is allowed to issue *n* queries that modify data per hour.

For the options that set numeric limits, a value of 0 means "no limit."

The GRANT statement was introduced in MySQL 3.22.11. The REQUIRE clause was introduced in MySQL 4.0.0; its NONE option was introduced in 4.0.4, at which time the AND option separator between REQUIRE options also was made optional. The resource management options were introduced in 4.0.2.

The following statements demonstrate some ways in which the GRANT statement can be used. See Chapter 11, "General MySQL Administration," for other examples. See Chapter 12, "Security," for information on setting up secure connections using SSL.

Create an account for paul who can access all tables in the sampdb database from any host. The following two statements are equivalent because a missing hostname part in the account identifier is equivalent to %:

```
GRANT ALL ON sampdb.* TO 'paul' IDENTIFIED BY 'secret';
GRANT ALL ON sampdb.* TO 'paul'@'%' IDENTIFIED BY 'secret';
```

Create an account with read-only privileges for the tables in the menagerie database. The lookonly user can connect from any host in the xyz.com domain:

```
GRANT SELECT ON menagerie.* TO 'lookonly'@'%.xyz.com'
    IDENTIFIED BY 'ragweed';
```

Create an account with full privileges, but only for the member table in the sampdb database. The member_mgr user can connect from a single host:

```
GRANT ALL ON sampdb.member TO 'member_mgr'@'boa.snake.net'
    IDENTIFIED BY 'doughnut';
```

Create a superuser who can do anything, including granting privileges to other users, but who must connect from the local host:

```
GRANT ALL ON *.* TO 'superduper'@'localhost' IDENTIFIED BY 'homer'
    WITH GRANT OPTION;
```

Create an anonymous user of the menagerie database who can connect from the local host with no password:

```
GRANT ALL ON menagerie.* TO ''@'localhost';
```

Create an account for a remote user who must connect via SSL and present a valid X509 certificate:

```
GRANT ALL ON privatedb.*
TO 'paranoid'@'%.mydom.com' IDENTIFIED BY 'keepout'
REQUIRE X509;
```

Create an account for a limited-access user who can issue only 100 queries per hour, of which at most 10 can be updates:

```
GRANT ALL ON test.*
TO 'caleb'@'localhost' IDENTIFIED BY 'rosepetal'
WITH MAX_QUERIES_PER_HOUR 100 MAX_UPDATES_PER_HOUR 10;
```

HANDLER

```
HANDLER tbl_name OPEN [AS alias_name]

HANDLER tbl_name READ
    [FIRST | NEXT]
    [where_clause] [limit_clause]

HANDLER tbl_name READ index_name
    [FIRST | NEXT | PREV | LAST | [< | <= | = | => | >] (expr_list)]
    [where_clause] [limit_clause]

HANDLER tbl_name CLOSE
```

HANDLER provides a low-level interface to the MyISAM and InnoDB table handlers that bypasses the optimizer and accesses table contents directly. To access a table through the HANDLER interface, first use HANDLER ... OPEN to open it. The table remains available for use until you issue a HANDLER ... CLOSE statement to close it explicitly or until or the connection terminates. While the table is open, use HANDLER ... READ to access the table's contents.

HANDLER provides no protection against concurrent updates. It does not lock the table, so it's possible for the table to be modified while HANDLER has it open, and there is no guarantee that the modifications will be reflected in the records that you read from the file.

HANDLER was introduced for MyISAM tables in MySQL 4.0.0 and extended to work with InnoDB tables in 4.0.3.

INSERT

```
INSERT [LOW_PRIORITY | DELAYED] [IGNORE] [INTO]
    tbl_name [(column_list)]
    VALUES (expr [, expr] ...) [, (...)] ...
```

```
INSERT [LOW_PRIORITY | DELAYED] [IGNORE] [INTO]
    tbl_name [(column_list)]
    SELECT ...

INSERT [LOW_PRIORITY | DELAYED] [IGNORE] [INTO]
    tbl_name SET col_name=expr [, col_name=expr] ...
```

Inserts rows into an existing table `tbl_name` and returns the number of rows inserted. The `INTO` keyword is optional as of MySQL 3.22.5.

`LOW_PRIORITY` causes the statement to be deferred until no clients are reading from the table. `LOW_PRIORITY` was introduced in MySQL 3.22.5.

`DELAYED` causes the rows to be placed into a queue for later insertion, and the statement returns immediately so that the client can continue on without waiting. However, in this case, `LAST_INSERT_ID()` will not return the `AUTO_INCREMENT` value for any `AUTO_INCREMENT` column in the table. `DELAYED` inserts were introduced in MySQL 3.22.15; they work only for ISAM and MyISAM tables.

If `IGNORE` is specified, rows that duplicate values for unique keys in existing rows are discarded. If duplicate values occur without `IGNORE`, an error occurs and no more rows are inserted. `IGNORE` was introduced in MySQL 3.22.10.

The first form of `INSERT` requires a `VALUES()` list that specifies all values to be inserted. If no `column_list` is given, the `VALUES()` list must specify one value for each column in the table. If a `column_list` is given consisting of one or more comma-separated column names, one value per column must be specified in the `VALUES()` list. Columns not named in the column list are set to their default values. As of MySQL 3.22.5, multiple value lists can be specified, allowing multiple rows to be inserted using a single `INSERT` statement. As of MySQL 3.23.3, the `column_list` and `VALUES()` list can be empty, which can be used as follows to create a record for which all columns are set to their default values:

```
INSERT INTO t () VALUES();
```

As of MySQL 4.0.3, the word `DEFAULT` can be used in a `VALUES()` list to set a column to its default value explicitly without knowing what the default value is.

The second form of `INSERT` retrieves records according to the `SELECT` statement and inserts them into `tbl_name`. The `SELECT` statement must select as many columns as are in `tbl_name` or as many columns as are named in `column_list` if a column list is specified. When a column list is specified, any columns not named in the list are set to their default values. You cannot select records from the same table into which you are inserting them.

The third form of INSERT, available as of MySQL 3.22.10, inserts columns named in the SET clause to the values given by the corresponding expressions. Columns not named are set to their default values.

```
INSERT INTO absence (student_id, date) VALUES(14,'1999-11-03'),(34,NOW());
INSERT INTO absence SET student_id = 14, date = '1999-11-03';
INSERT INTO absence SET student_id = 34, date = NOW();
INSERT INTO score (student_id, score, event_id)
    SELECT student_id, 100 AS score, 15 AS event_id FROM student;
```

KILL

```
KILL thread_id
```

Kills the server thread with the given *thread_id*. You must have the SUPER privilege (PROCESS prior to MySQL 4.0.2) to kill the thread unless it is one of your own. The KILL statement allows only a single ID. The mysqladmin kill command performs the same operation but allows multiple thread ID values to be specified on the command line.

This statement was introduced in MySQL 3.22.9.

LOAD DATA

```
LOAD DATA [LOW_PRIORITY | CONCURRENT ] [LOCAL] INFILE 'file_name'
    [IGNORE | REPLACE]
    INTO TABLE tbl_name
    import_options
    [IGNORE n LINES]
    [(column_list)]
```

LOAD DATA reads records from the file *file_name* and loads them in bulk into the table *tbl_name*. This is faster than using a set of INSERT statements.

LOW_PRIORITY causes the statement to be deferred until no clients are reading from the table. LOW_PRIORITY was introduced in MySQL 3.23.0.

CONCURRENT is used only for MyISAM tables. It allows other clients to retrieve from the table while rows are being loaded into it. CONCURRENT was introduced in MySQL 3.23.38.

Without the LOCAL keyword, the file is read directly by the server on the server host. In this case, you must have the FILE privilege and the file must either be located in the database directory of the default database or world readable. If LOCAL is specified, the client reads the file on the client host and sends its contents over the network to the server. In this case, the FILE privilege is not required. LOCAL became functional in MySQL 3.22.15. However, as of 3.23.49, LOCAL can be disabled or enabled selectively. If it is disabled on the server side, you cannot use it from the client side. If it is enabled on the server side but disabled by default on the client side, you'll need to enable it explicitly. For example, with the mysql program, you can use the --local-infile flag to enable the LOCAL capability.

When LOCAL is not specified in the LOAD DATA statement, the server locates the file as follows:

- If 'file_name' is an absolute pathname, the server looks for the file starting from the root directory.
- If 'file_name' is a relative pathname, interpretation depends on whether or not the name contains a single component. If so, the server looks for the file in the database directory of the default database. If the filename contains multiple components, the server looks for the file beginning in the server's data directory.

If LOCAL is given, the filename is interpreted as follows:

- If 'file_name' is an absolute pathname, the client looks for the file starting from the root directory.
- If 'file_name' is a relative pathname, the client looks for the file beginning with your current directory.

For Windows, backslashes in filenames can be written either as slashes ('/') or as doubled backslashes ('\\').

Rows that duplicate values in a unique index are either ignored or replace existing rows according to whether IGNORE or REPLACE is specified. If neither is specified, an error occurs, and any remaining records are ignored. If LOCAL is specified, transmission of the file cannot be interrupted, so the default behavior is like that of IGNORE if neither duplicate-handling option is given.

The import_options clause indicates the format of the data. The options available in this clause also apply to the export_options clause for the SELECT ... INTO OUTFILE statement. The syntax for import_options is as follows:

```
[FIELDS
    [TERMINATED BY 'string']
    [[OPTIONALLY] ENCLOSED BY 'char']
    [ESCAPED BY 'char' ] ]
[LINES
    [STARTING BY 'string']
    [TERMINATED BY 'string'] ]
```

The `'string'` and `'char'` values can include the following escape sequences to indicate special characters:

Sequence	Meaning
\0	ASCII 0
\b	Backspace
\n	Newline (linefeed)
\r	Carriage return
\s	Space
\t	Tab
\'	Single quote
\"	Double quote
\\	Backslash

As of MySQL 3.22.10, you can also use hexadecimal constants to indicate arbitrary characters. For example, LINES TERMINATED BY 0x02 indicates that lines are terminated by Ctrl-B (ASCII 2) characters.

If FIELDS is given, at least one of the TERMINATED BY, ENCLOSED BY, or ESCAPED BY clauses must be given, but if multiple clauses are present, they can appear in any order. Similarly, if LINES is given, at least one of the STARTING BY or TERMINATED BY clauses must be given, but if both are present, they can appear in any order. If both FIELDS and LINES are given, FIELDS must precede LINES.

The parts of the FIELDS clause are used as follows:

- TERMINATED BY specifies the character or characters that delimit values within a line.

- ENCLOSED BY specifies a quote character that is stripped from the ends of field values if it is present. This occurs whether or not OPTIONALLY is present. For output (SELECT ... INTO OUTFILE), the ENCLOSED BY character is used to enclose field values in output lines. If OPTIONALLY is given, values are quoted only for CHAR and VARCHAR columns.

  To include an instance of the ENCLOSED BY character within an input field value, it should either be doubled or preceded by the ESCAPED BY character. Otherwise, it will be interpreted as signifying the end of the field. For output, instances of the ENCLOSED BY character within field values are preceded by the ESCAPED BY character.

- The ESCAPED BY character is used to specify escaping of special characters. In the following examples, assume that the escape character is backslash ('\'). For input, the unquoted sequence \N (backslash-N) is interpreted as NULL. The \0 sequence (backslash-ASCII '0') is interpreted as a zero-valued byte. For other escaped characters, the escape character is stripped off, and the following character is used literally. For example, \" is interpreted as a double quote, even if field values are enclosed within double quotes.

For output, the escape character is used to encode NULL as an unquoted \N sequence, and zero-valued bytes as \0. In addition, instances of the ESCAPED BY and ENCLOSED BY characters are preceded by the escape character, as are the first characters of the field and line termination strings. If the ESCAPED BY character is empty (ESCAPED BY ''), no escaping is done. To specify an escape character of '\', double it (ESCAPED BY '\\').

The parts of the LINES clause are used as follows:

- The LINES STARTING BY value specifies a character or characters that begin lines.
- The LINES TERMINATED BY value specifies a character or characters that signify the ends of lines.

If neither FIELDS nor LINES is given, the defaults are as if you had specified them like this:

```
FIELDS
    TERMINATED BY '\t'
    ENCLOSED BY ''
    ESCAPED BY '\\'
LINES
    STARTING BY ''
    TERMINATED BY '\n'
```

In other words, fields within a line are tab-delimited without being quoted, backslash is treated as the escape character, and lines are terminated by newline characters.

If the TERMINATED BY and ENCLOSED BY values for the FIELDS clause are both empty, a fixed-width row format is used with no delimiters between fields. Column values are read (or written, for output) using the display widths of the columns. For example, VARCHAR(15) and MEDIUMINT(5) columns are read as 15-character and 5-character fields for input. For output, the columns are written using 15 characters and 5 characters. NULL values are written as strings of spaces.

NULL values in an input data file are indicated by the unquoted sequence \N. If the FIELDS ENCLOSED BY character is not empty, all non-NULL input values must be quoted with the enclosed-by character and the unquoted word NULL also will be interpreted as a NULL value.

If the `IGNORE` *n* `LINES` clause is given, the first *n* lines of the input are discarded. For example, if your data file has a row of column headers that you don't want to put into the database table, you can use `IGNORE 1 LINES`:

```
LOAD DATA LOCAL INFILE 'mytbl.txt' INTO TABLE mytbl IGNORE 1 LINES;
```

If no `column_list` is specified, input lines are assumed to contain one value per column in the table. If a list consisting of one or more comma-separated column names is given, input lines should contain a value for each named column. Columns not named in the list are set to their default values. If an input line is short of the expected number of values, columns for which values are missing are set to their default values.

If you have a tab-delimited text file that you created on Windows, you can use the default column separator, but the lines are probably terminated by carriage return/newline pairs. To load the file, specify a different line terminator ('\r' indicates a carriage return, and '\n' indicates a newline):

```
LOAD DATA LOCAL INFILE 'mytbl.txt' INTO TABLE mytbl
    LINES TERMINATED BY '\r\n';
```

Unfortunately, for files created on Windows, you may end up with a malformed record in the database if the program that created the data file uses the odd MS-DOS convention of putting the Ctrl-Z character at the end of the file to indicate end-of-file. Either write the file using a program that doesn't do this, or delete the record after loading the file.

Files in comma-separated values (CSV) format have commas between fields, and fields can be quoted with double quotes. Assuming lines have newlines at the end, the `LOAD DATA` statement to load such a file looks like this:

```
LOAD DATA LOCAL INFILE 'mytbl.txt' INTO TABLE mytbl
    FIELDS TERMINATED BY ',' ENCLOSED BY '"';
```

The following statement reads a file for which fields are separated by Ctrl-A (ASCII 1) characters, and lines are terminated by Ctrl-B (ASCII 2) characters:

```
LOAD DATA LOCAL INFILE 'mytbl.txt' INTO TABLE mytbl
    FIELDS TERMINATED BY 0x01 LINES TERMINATED BY 0x02;
```

LOAD ... FROM MASTER

```
LOAD DATA FROM MASTER
```

```
LOAD TABLE tbl_name FROM MASTER
```

These statements are used on replication slave servers to request data from the master server. `LOAD DATA FROM MASTER` requests all tables from the master. It also updates the slave's replication coordinates so that the slave will replicate only updates on the master that were made after completion of the `LOAD DATA` operation.

The tables to transfer are subject to any restrictions specified by any `--replicate-xxx` options with which the slave server may have been started. The statement itself also has a number of constraints that must be satisfied, as detailed in the "Establishing a Master-Slave Replication Relationship" section in Chapter 11. If these conditions are acceptable, this statement provides a convenient way to initialize a slave server.

`LOAD TABLE ... FROM MASTER` transfers a copy of just the named table from the master to the slave. This is used primarily for replication debugging.

`LOAD TABLE ... FROM MASTER` was introduced in MySQL 3.23.19, and `LOAD DATA FROM MASTER` in MySQL 4.0.0.

LOCK TABLE

```
LOCK {TABLE | TABLES}
    tbl_name [AS alias_name] lock_type
    [, tbl_name [AS alias_name] lock_type] ...
```

Obtains a lock on the named tables, waiting if necessary until all locks are acquired. Each `lock_type` value must be one of the following:

- READ

  Acquire a read lock. This blocks other clients that want to write to the table, but allows other clients to read the table.

- READ LOCAL

  This is a variation on a READ lock, designed for concurrent insert situations. It applies only to MyISAM tables that do not have any holes in them resulting from deleted record. READ LOCAL allows you to lock a table explicitly but still allow concurrent inserts for a MyISAM table that has no holes in it. (If the table does have holes in it, the lock is treated as a regular READ lock.)

- WRITE

  Acquire a write lock. This blocks all other clients, whether they want to read from or write to the table.

- LOW_PRIORITY WRITE

  This type of lock allows other readers to read the table if the request is waiting for another client that is already reading the table. The lock is not acquired until there are no more readers.

LOCK TABLE allows an alias to be specified so that you can lock a table under an alias that you are going to use when referring to the table in a subsequent query. (If you use a table multiple times in a query, you must obtain a lock for each instance of the table, locking aliases as necessary.)

LOCK TABLE releases any existing locks that you currently hold. Thus, to lock multiple tables, you must lock them all using a single LOCK TABLE statement. Any locks that are held by a client when it terminates are released automatically.

LOW_PRIORITY write locks were introduced in MySQL 3.22.8 and READ LOCAL locks in MySQL 3.23.11.

```
LOCK TABLES student READ, score WRITE, event READ;
LOCK TABLE member READ;
LOCK TABLES t AS t1 READ, t AS t2 READ;
```

OPTIMIZE TABLE

```
OPTIMIZE {TABLE | TABLES} tbl_name [, tbl_name] ...
```

DELETE, REPLACE, and UPDATE statements can result in areas of unused space in a table, particularly for tables that have variable-length rows. To counter this, OPTIMIZE TABLE performs the following actions:

- Defragments the table to eliminate wasted space and reduce the table size.
- Coalesces the contents of variable-rows that have become fragmented into non-contiguous pieces, so that each row is stored contiguously.
- Sorts the index pages if necessary.
- Updates the internal table statistics.

OPTIMIZE TABLE can be used only with MyISAM and BDB tables (and for BDB tables, it actually maps onto ANALYZE TABLE). It requires SELECT and INSERT privileges on each table.

Issuing an OPTIMIZE TABLE statement is like executing myisamchk with the --check-only-changed, --quick, --sort-index, and --analyze options. However, with myisamchk, you must arrange to prevent the server from accessing the table at the same time. With OPTIMIZE TABLE, you let the server do the work, and it takes care of making sure that other clients do not modify a table while it's being optimized.

OPTIMIZE TABLE produces output in the format described under the entry for CHECK TABLE.

OPTIMIZE TABLE was introduced in MySQL 3.22.7.

PURGE MASTER LOGS

```
PURGE MASTER LOGS TO 'log_name'
```

Deletes all the binary update logs on the server that were generated earlier than the named log file and resets the binary update log index file to list only those logs that remain. Normally, you use this after running SHOW SLAVE STA-TUS on each of the master's slaves to determine which log files are still in use. This statement requires the SUPER privilege (PROCESS prior to MySQL 4.0.2).

Remove `binlog.001` through `binlog.009` (or whichever of them exist) and cause `binlog.010` to become the first of the remaining log files:

```
PURGE MASTER LOGS TO 'binlog.010';
```

PURGE MASTER LOGS was introduced in MySQL 3.23.28.

RENAME TABLE

```
RENAME {TABLE | TABLES} tbl_name TO new_tbl_name [, ...]
```

Renames one or more tables. RENAME TABLE is similar to ALTER TABLE ... RENAME, except that it can rename multiple tables at once and locks them all during the rename operation. This is advantageous if you need to prevent any of the tables from being accessed during the operation.

RENAME TABLE was introduced in MySQL 3.23.23.

REPAIR TABLE

```
REPAIR {TABLE | TABLES} tbl_name [, tbl_name] ... [options]
```

This statement performs table repair operations. It works only for MyISAM tables and requires SELECT and INSERT privileges on each table. `options`, if given, is a list naming one or more of the following options (not separated by commas):

- EXTENDED

  Perform an extended repair that recreates the indexes. This is similar to running `myisamchk --safe-recover` on the tables, except that the repair is performed by the server rather than by an external utility.

- QUICK

  Repair only the index; leave the data file alone.

- USE_FRM

  Uses the table's `.frm` file to figure out how to interpret the contents of the data file and then uses the data file to rebuild the index file. This can be useful if the index has become lost or irrecoverably corrupted.

REPAIR TABLE with no options performs a table repair option like that done by `myisamchk --recover`.

REPAIR TABLE produces output in the format described under the entry for CHECK TABLE.

REPAIR TABLE was introduced in MySQL 3.23.14. The QUICK and USE_FRM options were added in MySQL 3.23.16 and 4.0.2. From 3.23.14 to 3.23.25, only a single option is allowed and TYPE = must precede it; after that, TYPE = is deprecated, and multiple options are allowed.

REPLACE

```
REPLACE [LOW_PRIORITY | DELAYED] [INTO]
    tbl_name [(column_list)]
    VALUES (expr [, expr] ...) [, (...)] ...

REPLACE [LOW_PRIORITY | DELAYED] [INTO]
    tbl_name [(column_list)]
    SELECT ...

REPLACE [LOW_PRIORITY | DELAYED] [INTO]
    tbl_name SET col_name=expr [, col_name=expr] ...
```

The REPLACE statement is like INSERT, with the exception that if a row to be inserted has a value for a unique index that duplicates the value in a row already present in the table, the old row is deleted before the new one is inserted. For this reason, there is no IGNORE clause option in the syntax of REPLACE. See the INSERT entry for more information.

It's possible for a REPLACE to delete more than one row if the table contains multiple unique indexes. This can happen if a new row matches values in several of the unique indexes, in which case, all the matching rows are deleted before the new row is inserted.

REPLACE requires the INSERT and DELETE privileges. Prior to MySQL 4.0.5, it also requires the UPDATE privilege.

RESET

```
RESET option [, option] ...
```

The RESET statement is similar to FLUSH in that it affects log or cache information. (In fact, RESET began life as part of the FLUSH statement.) Each option value should be one of the following items:

- MASTER

  Delete the existing binary update logs for a replication master server, create a new log file with the numbering sequence set to 001, and reset the binary update log index to name just the new file.

- QUERY CACHE

    Clear the query cache and remove any queries currently registered in it. (To defragment the cache without clearing it, use FLUSH QUERY CACHE.)

- SLAVE

    If the server is acting as a replication slave, this option tells it to forget its replication coordinates (that is, its current replication binary log filename and position within that file).

RESET requires the RELOAD privilege.

RESET was introduced in MySQL 3.23.26. The QUERY CACHE option was introduced in MySQL 4.0.1. From 3.23.19 to 3.23.25, RESET MASTER and RESET SLAVE are available as FLUSH MASTER and FLUSH SLAVE.

RESTORE TABLE

```
RESTORE {TABLE | TABLES} tbl_name [, tbl_name] ... FROM 'dir_name'
```

Restores the named table or tables using files located in the backup directory that were created with BACKUP TABLE. 'dir_name' should be the full pathname to the directory on the server host that contains the backup files. The tables to be restored must not already exist.

RESTORE TABLE works only for MyISAM tables and requires the INSERT and FILE privileges. The restore operation for each table uses only the table definition and data files (the .frm and .MYD files). Indexes are rebuilt using the information contained in those two files.

RESTORE TABLE was introduced in MySQL 3.23.25.

REVOKE

```
REVOKE priv_type [(column_list)] [, priv_type [(column_list)] ...]
    ON {*.* | * | db_name.* | db_name.tbl_name | tbl_name}
    FROM account [, account ] ...
```

This statement revokes privileges from the named account or accounts. The priv_type, column_list, and account clauses are specified the same way as for the GRANT statement. The same kind of specifiers as for GRANT are allowed in the ON clause as well.

REVOKE does not remove the account from the user grant table. This means that the account can still be used to connect to the MySQL server. To remove the account entirely, you must manually delete its entry from the user table. (However, look for the capability of removing the entry automatically in the future.)

The REVOKE statement was introduced in MySQL 3.22.11.

Revoke all privileges for superduper@localhost:

```
REVOKE ALL ON *.* FROM 'superduper'@'localhost';
```

Revoke privileges that allow the member_mgr user to modify the member table in the sampdb database:

```
REVOKE INSERT,DELETE,UPDATE ON sampdb.member
    FROM 'member_mgr'@'boa.snake.net';
```

Revoke all privileges for a single table in the menagerie database from the anonymous user on the local host:

```
REVOKE ALL ON menagerie.pet FROM ''@'localhost';
```

Note that ALL revokes all but the GRANT OPTION privilege. If you want to revoke that privilege as well, you must do so explicitly:

```
REVOKE GRANT OPTION ON menagerie.pet FROM ''@'localhost';
```

ROLLBACK

```
ROLLBACK
```

Rolls back changes made by statements that are part of the current transaction so that those changes are forgotten. This works only for transaction-safe table types. (For non-transactional table types, statements are committed as they are executed and thus cannot be rolled back.)

ROLLBACK does nothing if auto-commit mode has not been disabled with BEGIN or by setting AUTOCOMMIT to 0.

ROLLBACK was introduced in MySQL 3.23.14.

SELECT

```
SELECT
    [select_options]
    select_list
    [
        INTO OUTFILE 'file_name' export_options
      | INTO DUMPFILE 'file_name'
      | INTO @var_name [, @var_name ] ...
    ]
    [FROM tbl_list
    [WHERE where_expr]
    [GROUP BY {unsigned_integer | col_name | formula} [ASC | DESC] , ...]
    [HAVING where_expr]
    [ORDER BY {unsigned_integer | col_name | formula} [ASC | DESC] , ...]
    [LIMIT [skip_count,] show_count]
    [PROCEDURE procedure_name(arg_list)]
    [FOR UPDATE | LOCK IN SHARE MODE] ]
```

SELECT normally is used to retrieve rows from one or more tables. However, because everything in the statement is optional except the SELECT keyword and the *select_list* clause, it's also possible to write statements that simply evaluate expressions:

```
SELECT 'one plus one =', 1+1;
```

The *select_options* clause, if present, can contain the following options:

- ALL
  DISTINCT
  DISTINCTROW

  These keywords control whether or not duplicate rows are returned. ALL causes all rows to be returned, which is the default. DISTINCT and DIS-TINCTROW specify that duplicate rows should be eliminated from the result set.

- HIGH_PRIORITY

  Specifying HIGH_PRIORITY gives the statement a higher priority if it normally would have to wait. If other statements, such as INSERT or UPDATE, are waiting to write to tables named in the SELECT because some other client is reading the tables, HIGH_PRIORITY causes a SELECT statement to be given priority over those write statements. This should be done only for SELECT statements that you know will execute quickly and that must be done immediately because it slows down execution of the write statements. HIGH_PRIORITY was introduced in MySQL 3.22.9.

- SQL_BUFFER_RESULT

  Tell the server to buffer the query result in a separate temporary table rather than keeping the table or tables named in the SELECT locked while waiting for the entire query result to be sent to the client. This helps the server release the locks sooner, which gives other clients access to the tables more quickly. (However, using this option also requires more disk space and memory.) SQL_BUFFER_RESULT was introduced in MySQL 3.23.13.

- SQL_CACHE
  SQL_NO_CACHE

  If the query cache is operating in demand mode, SQL_CACHE causes the query result to be cached. SQL_NO_CACHE suppresses any caching of the query result. These options were introduced in MySQL 4.0.1.

- SQL_CALC_FOUND_ROWS

  Normally, the row count from a query that includes a LIMIT clause is the number of rows actually returned. SQL_CALC_FOUND_ROWS tells the server to determine how large the query result would be without the LIMIT. This row count can be obtained by issuing a SELECT FOUND_ROWS() statement following the initial SELECT.

- SQL_SMALL_RESULT
  SQL_BIG_RESULT

  These keywords provide a hint that the result set will be small or large, which gives the optimizer information that it can use to process the query more effectively. SQL_SMALL_RESULT and SQL_BIG_RESULT were introduced in MySQL 3.22.12 and 3.23.0, respectively.

- STRAIGHT_JOIN

  Forces tables to be joined in the order named in the FROM clause. This option can be useful if you believe that the optimizer is not making the best choice.

The *select_list* clause names the output columns to be returned. Multiple columns should be separated by commas. Columns can be references to table columns or expressions. Any column can be assigned a column alias using the AS *alias_name* syntax. The alias then becomes the column name in the output and can also be referred to in GROUP BY, ORDER BY, and HAVING clauses. However, you cannot refer to the alias in a WHERE clause.

The special notation * means "all columns from the tables named in the FROM clause," and *tbl_name*.* means "all columns from the named table."

The result of a SELECT statement can be written into a file *file_name* using an INTO OUTFILE '*file_name*' clause. The syntax of the *export_options* clause is the same as for the *import_options* clause of the LOAD DATA statement. See the LOAD DATA entry for more information.

INTO DUMPFILE '*file_name*' is similar to INTO OUTFILE but writes only a single row and writes the output entirely without interpretation. That is, it writes raw values without delimiters, quotes, or terminators. This can be useful if you want to write BLOB data to a file, such as an image or other binary data. INTO DUMPFILE was introduced in MySQL 3.23.5.

For both INTO OUTFILE and INTO DUMPFILE, the filename is interpreted using the same rules that apply when reading non-LOCAL files with LOAD DATA. You must have the FILE privilege, the output file must not already exist, and the file is created by the server on the server host. Its ownership will be set to the account used to run the server.

As of MySQL 4.1, the results of a SELECT can be stored into a set of user-defined variables of the form @var_name. The query must select a single row of values, and must name one variable per output column, separated by commas.

The FROM clause names one or more tables from which rows should be selected. MySQL supports the following join types for use in SELECT statements:

```
tbl_list:
    tbl_name
    tbl_list, tbl_name
    tbl_list [CROSS] JOIN tbl_name
    tbl_list INNER JOIN tbl_name ON conditional_expr
    tbl_list INNER JOIN tbl_name USING (column_list)
    tbl_list STRAIGHT_JOIN tbl_name
    tbl_list LEFT [OUTER] JOIN tbl_name ON conditional_expr
    tbl_list LEFT [OUTER] JOIN tbl_name USING (column_list)
    tbl_list NATURAL [LEFT [OUTER]] JOIN tbl_name
    { OJ tbl_list LEFT OUTER JOIN tbl_name ON conditional_expr }
    tbl_list RIGHT [OUTER] JOIN tbl_name ON conditional_expr
    tbl_list RIGHT [OUTER] JOIN tbl_name USING (column_list)
    tbl_list NATURAL [RIGHT [OUTER]] JOIN tbl_name
    (tbl_list)
```

Each table name can be accompanied by an alias or index hints. That is, the full syntax for referring to a table actually looks like this:

```
tbl_name
    [[AS] alias_name]
    [USE INDEX (index_list) | IGNORE INDEX (index_list)]
```

Tables can be assigned aliases in the FROM clause using either tbl_name alias_name or tbl_name AS alias_name syntax. An alias provides an alternate name by which to refer to the table columns elsewhere in the query.

The USE INDEX or IGNORE INDEX clauses can be used as of MySQL 3.23.12 to provide index hints to the optimizer. This can be helpful in cases where the optimizer doesn't make the correct choice about which index to use in a join. (USE KEY and IGNORE KEY are synonyms for USE INDEX and IGNORE INDEX.) index_list should name one or more indexes separated by commas. Each index in index_list should be the name of an index from the table, or the keyword PRIMARY to indicate the table's PRIMARY KEY.

The join types select rows from the named tables as indicated in the following descriptions. The rows actually returned to the client may be limited by WHERE, HAVING, or LIMIT clauses.

- For a single table named by itself, SELECT retrieves rows from that table.

- If multiple tables are named and separated by commas, SELECT returns all possible combinations of rows from the tables. Using JOIN or CROSS JOIN is equivalent to using commas. STRAIGHT_JOIN is similar, but forces the optimizer to join the tables in the order that the tables are named. It can be used if you believe that the optimizer is not making the best choice.

- INNER JOIN is like the comma operator but requires an ON or USING() clause to constrain matches between tables, similar to a LEFT JOIN. (However, note that prior to MySQL 3.23.17, INNER JOIN is exactly like the comma operator and does not allow ON or USING() clauses.)

- LEFT JOIN retrieves rows from the joined tables, but forces a row to be generated for every row in the left table, even if there is no matching row in the right table. When there is no match, columns from the right table are returned as NULL values. Matching rows are determined according to the condition specified in the ON *conditional_expr* clause or the USING *(column_list)* clause. *conditional_expr* is an expression of the form that can be used in the WHERE clause. *column_list* consists of one or more comma-
separated column names, each of which must be a column that occurs in both of the joined tables. LEFT OUTER JOIN is equivalent to LEFT JOIN. So is the syntax that begins with OJ, which is included for ODBC compatibility. (The curly braces shown for the OJ syntax are not metacharacters; they are literal characters that must be present in the statement.)

- NATURAL LEFT JOIN is equivalent to LEFT JOIN USING *(column_list)*, where *column_list* names all the columns that are common to both tables.

- The RIGHT JOIN types are like the corresponding LEFT JOIN types but with the table roles reversed. RIGHT JOIN is allowed as of MySQL 3.23.25.

The WHERE clause specifies an expression that is applied to rows selected from the tables named in the FROM clause. (Column aliases cannot be referred to in the WHERE clause.) Rows that do not satisfy the criteria given by the expression are rejected. The result set can be further limited by HAVING and LIMIT clauses.

The GROUP BY *column_list* clause groups rows of the result set according to the columns named in the list. This clause is used when you specify summary functions such as COUNT() or MAX() in the *select_list* clause. Columns can be referred to by column names, aliases, or by position within *select_list*. Column positions are numbered beginning with 1. As of 3.23.2, you can use expressions in GROUP BY clauses to group by expression results.

In MySQL, GROUP BY not only groups rows, it sorts the results. As of MySQL 3.23.47, you can also use ASC and DESC after GROUP BY column specifiers to specify an explicit grouping order (and thus affect the output order). The output order resulting from GROUP BY is overridden by any ORDER BY clause that is present.

The HAVING clause specifies a secondary expression that is used to limit rows after they have satisfied the conditions named by the WHERE clause. Rows that do not satisfy the HAVING condition are rejected. HAVING is useful for expressions involving summary functions that cannot be tested in the WHERE clause. However, if a condition is legal in either the WHERE clause or the HAVING clause, it is preferable to place it in the WHERE clause where it will be subject to analysis by the optimizer.

ORDER BY indicates how to sort the result set. Like GROUP BY, columns can be referred to by column names, aliases, or by position at which columns appear in the output column list. Output columns are sorted in ascending order by default. To specify a sort order for a column explicitly, follow the column indicator by ASC (ascending) or DESC (descending). As of 3.23.2, you can use expressions in ORDER BY clauses. For example, ORDER BY RAND() returns rows in random order. However, unlike GROUP BY, expressions in an ORDER BY clause cannot refer to summary (aggregate) functions.

The LIMIT clause can be used to select a section of rows from the result set. It takes either one or two arguments, which must be integer constants. LIMIT *n* returns the first *n* rows. LIMIT *m, n* skips the first *m* rows and then returns the next *n* rows. The two-argument form also allows LIMIT *m,* -1 to skip the first *m* rows and then retrieve all the remaining rows, however many that may be.

PROCEDURE names a procedure to which the data in the result set will be sent before a result set is returned to the client. The argument list, *arg_list*, can be empty or a comma-separated list of arguments to pass to the procedure. As of MySQL 3.23, you can use PROCEDURE ANALYSE() to obtain information about the characteristics of the data in the columns named in the column selection list.

The FOR UPDATE and LOCK IN SHARE MODE clauses place locks on the selected rows until the current transaction is committed or rolled back. This can be useful in multiple-statement transactions. If you use FOR UPDATE with a table for which the handler uses page-level or row-level locks (BDB or InnoDB), the selected rows are write-locked for exclusive use. Using LOCK IN SHARE MODE sets read locks on the rows, allowing other clients to read but not modify them. These locking clauses were introduced in MySQL 3.23.35.

The following statements demonstrate some ways in which the SELECT statement can be used. See Chapter 1, "Getting Started with MySQL and SQL," and Chapter 3 for many other examples.

Select the entire contents of a table:

```
SELECT * FROM president;
```

Select entire contents, but sort by name:

```
SELECT * FROM president ORDER BY last_name, first_name;
```

Select records for presidents born on or after '1900-01-01':

```
SELECT * FROM president WHERE birth >= '1900-01-01';
```

Do the same, but sort in birth order:

```
SELECT * FROM president WHERE birth >= '1900-01-01' ORDER BY birth;
```

Determine which states are represented by rows in the member table:

```
SELECT DISTINCT state FROM member;
```

Select rows from member table and write columns as comma-separated values into a file:

```
SELECT * INTO OUTFILE '/tmp/member.txt'
    FIELDS TERMINATED BY ',' FROM member;
```

Select the top five scores for a particular grade event:

```
SELECT * FROM score WHERE event_id = 9 ORDER BY score DESC LIMIT 5;
```

Subselect support. MySQL 4.1 adds subselect support, allowing one SELECT to be nested within another. Several forms of subselect are available:

- A subselect can be introduced by a comparison operator, in which case it must produce a single value.

  Select the president record having the earliest birth value:

  ```
  SELECT * FROM president
  WHERE birth = (SELECT MIN(birth) FROM president);
  ```

  Select scores from a given grade event that are higher than the event's average score:

  ```
  SELECT * FROM score WHERE event_id = 5
  AND score > (SELECT AVG(score) FROM score WHERE event_id = 5);
  ```

- A subselect can be introduced by `EXISTS` or `NOT EXISTS`. In this case, the inner `SELECT` may refer to columns from the outer `SELECT` and thus column references may need to be qualified with table names to avoid ambiguity.

  Select students who have at least one absence:

  ```
  SELECT student_id, name FROM student WHERE EXISTS
  (SELECT * FROM absence WHERE absence.student_id = student.student_id);
  ```

  Select students who have no absences:

  ```
  SELECT student_id, name FROM student WHERE NOT EXISTS
  (SELECT * FROM absence WHERE absence.student_id = student.student_id);
  ```

  `SELECT *` is used in the subselect because the inner query is evaluated to produce a true or false value, not particular column values.

- A subselect can be introduced by `IN` or `NOT IN`, in which case it should return a single column of values. The preceding `EXISTS` and `NOT EXISTS` queries can be rewritten to use `IN` and `NOT IN` as follows:

  ```
  SELECT student_id, name FROM student
  WHERE student_id IN (SELECT student_id FROM absence);

  SELECT student_id, name FROM student
  WHERE student_id NOT IN (SELECT student_id FROM absence);
  ```

SET

```
SET [OPTION] option_setting [, option_setting ] ...
```

The `SET` statement is used to assign values to a variety of options, user-defined variables, global or session variables, or the transaction isolation level. `SET TRANSACTION ISOLATION LEVEL` is described in a separate entry, and information about user-defined variables is provided in the "SQL Variables" section later in this appendix.

The word `OPTION` in the `SET` statement is allowed but deprecated; it may be removed in a future version of MySQL.

The syntax for each value assignment is *name op val*, where *name* is the SQL option or variable to be assigned a value, *op* is the assignment operator, and *val* is the value to assign. Prior to MySQL 3.23.6, only = can be used as the assignment operator; from 3.23.6 on, either = or := can be used.

`SET` can be used to assign values to any of several SQL options:

```
SET SQL_LOG_BIN = 1;
SET AUTOCOMMIT = 0;
```

or to set user-defined variables:

```
SET @day = CURDATE(), @time = CURTIME();
```

In addition, as of MySQL 4.0.3, the server supports several dynamic system variables that can be changed while the server is running, and SET is used to modify these values, too. (Prior to 4.0.3, system variables can be set only at server startup time, necessitating a restart to change values.) Dynamic variables exist at two levels. Global variables are server-wide and affect all clients. Session variables (also called local variables) are specific to a given client connection only. For variables that exist at both levels, the session variables are initialized for each new client connection from the values of the corresponding global variables. Any client can modify its own session variables. To modify a global variable, it is necessary to have the SUPER privilege.

To set a global variable (for example, table_type), use a statement having either of the following forms:

```
SET GLOBAL table_type = InnoDB;
SET @@GLOBAL.table_type = InnoDB;
```

To set a session variable, substitute the word SESSION for GLOBAL:

```
SET SESSION table_type = InnoDB;
SET @@SESSION.table_type = InnoDB;
```

You can also use LOCAL as a synonym for SESSION:

```
SET LOCAL table_type = InnoDB;
SET @@LOCAL.table_type = InnoDB;
```

If none of GLOBAL, SESSION, or LOCAL are present, the SET statement modifies the session-level variable:

```
SET table_type = InnoDB;
SET @@table_type = InnoDB;
```

To check the value of system variables, use SHOW VARIABLES. The entry in this appendix for that statement lists the variables that are available and indicates which of them can be modified dynamically.

The following list describes SQL options that can be controlled with SET. Several of the option descriptions here indicate that you need the SUPER privilege to set the option; prior to MySQL 4.0.2, you need the PROCESS privilege instead.

- AUTOCOMMIT = {0 | 1}

  Sets the auto-commit level for transaction processing. Setting the value to 0 disables auto-commit mode so that subsequent statements do not take effect until a commit is performed (either with a COMMIT statement or by setting AUTOCOMMIT to 1). Statements in the transaction can be canceled with ROLLBACK if a commit has not occurred. Setting AUTOCOMMIT to 1 re-enables auto-commit mode (and commits the pending transaction, if any). With auto-commit mode enabled, statements take effect immediately; essentially, each statement is its own transaction.

- CHARACTER SET [=] {*charset* | DEFAULT}

Specifies the character set used by the client. Strings sent to and from the client are mapped using this character set. The only character set name currently allowable for this option is cp1251_koi8. The character set name DEFAULT restores the default character set. The = is optional as of MySQL 4.0.3; prior to that, it must be omitted.

- FOREIGN_KEY_CHECKS = {0 | 1}

Setting this option to 0 or 1 disables or enables foreign key checking. The default is to perform checking. Disabling key checks can be useful, for example, when restoring a dump file that creates and loads tables in a different order than that required by their foreign key relationships. You can re-enable key checking after loading the tables. This option was introduced in MySQL 3.23.52. It has no effect except for InnoDB tables.

- INSERT_ID = *n*

Specifies the value to be used by the next INSERT statement when inserting an AUTO_INCREMENT column. This is used for update log processing.

- LAST_INSERT_ID = *n*

Specifies the value to be returned by LAST_INSERT_ID(). This is used for update log processing.

- PASSWORD [FOR *account*] = PASSWORD('*pass_val*')

With no FOR clause, sets the password for the current account to '*pass_val*'. With a FOR clause, sets the password for the given account. You must have privileges for modifying the mysql database to be able to set another account's password. *account* is specified in '*user_name*'@'*host_name*' format using the same types of values for *user_name* and *host_name* that are acceptable for the GRANT statement.

```
SET PASSWORD = PASSWORD('secret');
SET PASSWORD FOR 'paul' = PASSWORD('secret');
SET PASSWORD FOR 'paul'@'localhost' = PASSWORD('secret');
SET PASSWORD FOR 'bill'@'%.bigcorp.com' = PASSWORD('old-sneep');
```

- SQL_AUTO_IS_NULL = {0 | 1}

  If this is set to 1, the most recently generated AUTO_INCREMENT value can be selected using a WHERE clause of the form WHERE *col_name* IS NULL, where *col_name* is the name of the AUTO_INCREMENT column. This feature is used by some ODBC programs, such as Access. The default is 1. This option was introduced in MySQL 3.23.5.

- SQL_BIG_SELECTS = {0 | 1}

  This option is used in conjunction with MAX_JOIN_SIZE as follows:

  - If SQL_BIG_SELECTS is set to 1 (the default), queries that return result sets of any size are allowed.

  - If SQL_BIG_SELECTS is set to 0, queries that are likely to return a large number of rows are disallowed. In this case, the value of MAX_JOIN_SIZE is used when executing a join. The server makes an estimate of the number of row combinations it will need to examine. If the value exceeds the MAX_JOIN_SIZE value, the server returns an error rather than executing the query.

  Setting MAX_JOIN_SIZE to a value other than DEFAULT automatically sets SQL_BIG_SELECTS to 0.

- SQL_BIG_TABLES = {0 | 1}
  BIG_TABLES = {0 | 1}

  All internal temporary tables are stored on disk rather than in memory if this is option is set to 1. Performance is slower, but SELECT statements that require large temporary tables will not generate "table full" errors. The default is 0 (hold temporary tables in memory). This option normally is not needed for MySQL 3.23 and up. BIG_TABLES is the preferred name for this option as of MySQL 4.

- SQL_BUFFER_RESULT = *n*

  Setting this option to 1 causes the server to use temporary tables to hold results from SELECT queries. The effect is that the server can more quickly release locks held on the tables from which the results are produced. This option was introduced in MySQL 3.23.13.

- SQL_LOG_BIN = {0 | 1}

  Setting this option to 1 enables binary update logging for the current client. Setting the option to 0 turns the log off. The client must have the SUPER privilege for this statement to have any effect. This option was introduced in MySQL 3.23.16.

- SQL_LOG_OFF = {0 | 1}

  If this option is set to 1, the current client's queries are not logged in the general log file. If set to 0, logging for the client is enabled. The client must have the SUPER privilege for this statement to have any effect.

- SQL_LOG_UPDATE = {0 | 1}

  If this option is set to 1, the current client's queries are logged in the update log file. If set to 0, logging for the client is enabled. The client must have the SUPER privilege for this statement to have any effect. SQL_LOG_UPDATE was introduced in MySQL 3.22.5.

- SQL_LOW_PRIORITY_UPDATES = {0 | 1}
  LOW_PRIORITY_UPDATES = {0 | 1}

  If this option is set to 1, statements that modify table contents (DELETE, INSERT, REPLACE, UPDATE) wait until no SELECT is active or pending for the table. SELECT statements that arrive while another is active begin executing immediately rather than waiting for low-priority modification statements. This option was introduced in MySQL 3.22.5. LOW_PRIOR-ITY_UPDATES is the preferred name as of MySQL 4.

- SQL_MAX_JOIN_SIZE = {*n* | DEFAULT}
  MAX_JOIN_SIZE = {*n* | DEFAULT}

  This option is used in combination with SQL_BIG_SELECTS, as discussed in the description for that option.

  MAX_JOIN_SIZE is the preferred name for this option as of MySQL 4.

- SQL_QUERY_CACHE_TYPE =
  {0 | 1 | 2 | OFF | ON | DEMAND}
  QUERY_CACHE_TYPE =
  {0 | 1 | 2 | OFF | ON | DEMAND}

  Sets the query cache mode for the current client.

Mode	Meaning
0, OFF	Don't cache
1, ON	Cache queries except those that begin with SELECT SQL_NO_CACHE
2, DEMAND	Cache on demand only those queries that begin with SELECT SQL_CACHE

  This option was introduced in MySQL 4.0.1. QUERY_CACHE_TYPE is the preferred name.

- SQL_QUOTE_SHOW_CREATE = {0 | 1}

  This option controls whether to use backticks to quote table, column, and index names in the output from SHOW CREATE TABLE statements. The default is 1 (use quoting). Turning quoting off by setting the option to 0 can be useful when producing CREATE TABLE statements for use with other database servers or with MySQL servers older than version 3.23.6 that do not understand backtick quoting. However, if you turn quoting off, you should make sure that your tables do not use names that are reserved words or that contain special characters. This option was introduced in MySQL 3.23.26.

- SQL_SAFE_UPDATES = {0 | 1}

  If this option is set to 1, UPDATE and DELETE statements are allowed only if the records to be modified are identified by key values or if a LIMIT clause is used. This option was introduced in MySQL 3.22.32.

- SQL_SELECT_LIMIT = {n | DEFAULT}

  Specifies the maximum number of records to return from a SELECT statement. The presence of an explicit LIMIT clause in a statement takes precedence over this option. The default value is "no limit." A value of DEFAULT restores the default if you have changed it.

- SQL_SLAVE_SKIP_COUNTER = n

  Tells a slave server to skip the next n events from the master server. The slave thread must not be running. This option was introduced in MySQL 3.23.33. As of MySQL 4.0.3, it is necessary to use SET GLOBAL rather than just SET to modify this option.

- SQL_WARNINGS = {0 | 1}

  If set to 1, MySQL reports warning counts even for single-row inserts. The default is 0, so warning counts normally are reported only for INSERT statements that insert multiple rows. This option was introduced in MySQL 3.22.11.

- TIMESTAMP = {timestamp_value | DEFAULT}

  Specifies a TIMESTAMP value. This is used for update log processing.

- UNIQUE_CHECKS = {0 | 1}

  Setting this option to 0 or 1 disables or enables uniqueness checks for secondary unique indexes in InnoDB tables. This option was introduced in MySQL 3.23.52.

SET TRANSACTION ISOLATION LEVEL

```
SET [GLOBAL | SESSION] TRANSACTION ISOLATION LEVEL level
```

This statement sets the global (server-wide) or session (client-specific) transaction isolation level or the level for just the next transaction within the current session. If neither GLOBAL nor SESSION is specified, the statement sets the level for the next transaction. The SUPER privilege (PROCESS prior to 4.0.2) is required to set the global isolation level. A global change affects clients that connect after the change is made, not those clients that are already connected.

The transaction level indicated by level should be one of the following values: READ UNCOMMITTED, READ COMMITTED, REPEATABLE READ, or SERIALIZABLE.

This statement was introduced in MySQL 3.23.36. It has an effect for InnoDB tables only as of MySQL 3.23.50; prior to that, InnoDB always operates in REPEATABLE READ mode. Until MySQL 4.0.5, the other allowable value for InnoDB is SERIALIZABLE, and setting the level to any other value causes REPEATABLE READ to be used. As of MySQL 4.0.5, InnoDB also supports the READ COMMITTED and READ UNCOMMITTED isolation levels.

The BDB handler is unaffected by this statement, because BDB always runs at the SERIALIZABLE level.

SHOW

```
SHOW BINLOG EVENTS [IN 'file_name'] [FROM n]
    [LIMIT [skip_count,] show_count]
SHOW CHARACTER SET
SHOW COLUMN TYPES
SHOW [FULL] COLUMNS FROM tbl_name [FROM db_name] [LIKE 'pattern']
SHOW CREATE DATABASE db_name
SHOW CREATE TABLE tbl_name
SHOW DATABASES [LIKE 'pattern']
SHOW GRANTS FOR account
SHOW INDEX FROM tbl_name [FROM db_name]
SHOW INNODB STATUS
SHOW LOGS
SHOW MASTER LOGS
SHOW MASTER STATUS
SHOW PRIVILEGES
SHOW [FULL] PROCESSLIST
SHOW SLAVE HOSTS
SHOW SLAVE STATUS
SHOW STATUS [LIKE 'pattern']
SHOW TABLE STATUS [FROM db_name] [LIKE 'pattern']
SHOW TABLE TYPES
SHOW [OPEN] TABLES [FROM db_name] [LIKE 'pattern']
SHOW [GLOBAL | SESSION ] VARIABLES [LIKE 'pattern']
```

The various forms of the SHOW statement provide information about databases, tables, columns, and indexes, or information about server operation. Several of the forms take an optional FROM *db_name* clause, allowing you to specify the database for which information should be shown. If the clause is not present, the default database is used. (As of MySQL 4.0, IN is a synonym for FROM in each of these statements.)

Some forms allow an optional LIKE '*pattern*' clause to limit output to values that match the pattern. '*pattern*' is interpreted as a SQL pattern and may contain the '%' or '_' wildcard characters.

SHOW BINLOG EVENTS

This statement is used on replication master servers to display events in a binary update log file. Its output includes the following columns:

- Log_name

  The binary log file name

- Pos

  The position of the event within the log file

- Event_type

  The type of event, such as Query for a statement that is to be executed

- Server_id

  The ID of the server that logged the event

- Orig_log_pos

  The position of the event in the original log file on the master server

- Info

  Event information, such as the statement text for a Query event

SHOW BINLOG EVENTS was introduced in MySQL 4.0.

SHOW CHARACTER SET

Displays a list of the character sets supported by the server.

The output from SHOW CHARACTER SET currently includes the following types of information about each character set, although it's likely that this format will undergo some change in the future to include additional information.

- Name

  The character set name.

- Id

  The internal character set ID number.

- strx_maxlen

  A cost factor relating to the amount of memory that must be allocated for internal string conversion operations when sorting values in the character set.

- mb_maxlen

  Indicates the length of the "widest" character in the character set, in bytes. For multi-byte character sets, this value will be greater than one. For non-multi-byte sets, all characters take a single byte, so the value is one.

SHOW CHARACTER SET was introduced in MySQL 4.1.

SHOW COLUMN TYPES

This statement lists information about the column types that can be used when creating MySQL tables.

The output from SHOW COLUMN TYPES includes the following columns:

- Type

  The column type.

- Size

  The type's storage size in bytes.

- Min_Value

  The minimum value of the type's range.

- Max_Value

  The maximum value of the type's range.

- Prec

  The type's precision.

- Scale

  The type's scale factor.

- Nullable

  Whether or not the type allows NULL values.

- Auto_Increment

  Whether or not the type can be used for AUTO_INCREMENT sequences.

- Unsigned

  Whether or not the type has the UNSIGNED attribute.

- Zerofill

  Whether or not the type has the ZEROFILL attribute.

- Searchable

  Whether or not the type is searchable.

- Case_Sensitive

  Whether or not the type is case sensitive.

- Default

  The type's default value. There may be more than one value listed, because the default value may depend on whether the column is declared to allow NULL values.

- Comment

  A descriptive comment about the column type.

SHOW COLUMN TYPES was introduced in MySQL 4.1.

SHOW [FULL] COLUMNS

The SHOW COLUMNS statement lists the columns for the given table. SHOW FIELDS is a synonym for SHOW COLUMNS.

```
SHOW COLUMNS FROM president;
SHOW FIELDS FROM president;
SHOW COLUMNS FROM president FROM sampdb;
SHOW FULL COLUMNS FROM tables_priv FROM mysql LIKE '%priv';
```

The output from SHOW COLUMNS provides the following types of information about each column in the table:

- Field

  The column name.

- Type

  The column type. This can include type attributes following the type name.

- Null

  YES if the column can contain NULL values, blank otherwise.

- Key

  Whether or not the column is indexed.

- `Default`

  The column's default value.

- `Extra`

  Extra information about the column.

- `Privileges`

  The privileges that you hold for the column. This information is available only as of MySQL 3.23.0. It is always displayed from 3.23.0 to 3.23.32 and from 3.23.32 on is displayed only if you specify the `FULL` keyword.

- `Comment`

  The value of any `COMMENT` clause that was specified in the column declaration. This information is displayed only as of MySQL 4.1, and only if you specify the `FULL` keyword.

SHOW CREATE DATABASE

This statement displays the `CREATE DATABASE` statement necessary to create the named database.

```
SHOW CREATE DATABASE sampdb;
```

This statement was introduced in MySQL 4.1.

SHOW CREATE TABLE

This statement displays the `CREATE TABLE` statement that corresponds to the structure of the named table.

```
SHOW CREATE TABLE absence;
```

Table, column, and index names in the statement produced by `SHOW CREATE TABLE` are quoted by default. Quoting can be controlled by setting the `SQL_QUOTE_SHOW_CREATE` option. (This option is described in the entry for the `SET` statement.)

`SHOW CREATE TABLE` was introduced in MySQL 3.23.20.

SHOW DATABASES

The `SHOW DATABASES` statement lists the databases available on the server host.

```
SHOW DATABASES;
SHOW DATABASES LIKE 'test%';
```

If you don't have the `SHOW DATABASES` privilege, you'll see only the databases for which you have some kind of access privilege.

SHOW GRANTS

The SHOW GRANTS statement displays grant information about the specified user, which should be given in 'user_name'@'host_name' form, using the same types of values for user_name and host_name that are acceptable for the GRANT statement.

```
SHOW GRANTS FOR 'root'@'localhost';
SHOW GRANTS FOR ''@'cobra.snake.net';
```

The output is in the form of the GRANT statements that would need to be issued to recreate the account privileges.

SHOW GRANTS was introduced in MySQL 3.23.4.

SHOW INDEX

The SHOW INDEX statement displays information about a table's indexes. SHOW KEYS is a synonym for SHOW INDEX.

```
SHOW INDEX FROM score;
SHOW KEYS FROM score;
SHOW INDEX FROM sampdb.score;
SHOW INDEX FROM score FROM sampdb;
```

The output from SHOW INDEX contains the following columns:

- Table

  The name of the table containing the index.

- Non_unique

  This value is 1 if the index can contain duplicate values and 0 if it cannot.

- Key_name

  The index name.

- Seq_in_index

  The number of the column within the index. Index columns are numbered beginning with 1.

- Column_name

  The column name.

- Collation

  The column sorting order within the index. The values may be A (ascending), D (descending), or NULL (not sorted). Descending keys are not yet available, but will be implemented in the future.

- Cardinality

  The number of unique values in the index. `myisamchk` or `isamchk` update this value for MyISAM or ISAM tables when run with the `--analyze` option. The `ANALYZE TABLE` statement updates this value for MyISAM or BDB tables.

- Sub_part

  The prefix length in bytes, if only a prefix of the column is indexed. This is `NULL` if the entire column is indexed.

- Packed

  How the key is packed, or `NULL` if it is not packed.

- Null

  `YES` if the column can contain `NULL` values, blank otherwise.

- Index_type

  The method used to index the column, such as `BTREE` or `FULLTEXT`.

- Comment

  Reserved for internal comments about the index.

The `Packed` and `Comment` columns were added in MySQL 3.23.0. The `Null` and `Index_type` columns were added in 4.0.2.

SHOW INNODB STATUS

This statement displays information about the internal operation of the InnoDB table handler. It was introduced in MySQL 3.23.52.

SHOW LOGS

This statement displays information about the server's log files. Currently, it is used only for the BDB logs.

The output from `SHOW LOGS` includes the following columns:

- File

  The log file name

- Type

  The log type

- Status

  The log status, for example, `IN USE`

`SHOW LOGS` was introduced in MySQL 3.23.29.

SHOW MASTER LOGS

This statement is used on replication master servers. It displays the names of the binary logs currently available on the master. It can be useful before issuing a PURGE MASTER LOGS statement after running SHOW SLAVE STATUS on each of the slaves to determine the binary logs to which they currently are positioned.

This statement was introduced in MySQL 3.23.28.

SHOW MASTER STATUS

This statement is used on replication master servers. It provides information about the status of the master's binary update logs.

The output from SHOW MASTER STATUS includes the following columns:

- File

  The name of the binary update log file

- Position

  The current position at which the server is writing to the file

- Binlog_do_db

  A comma-separated list of databases that are explicitly replicated to the binary log with --binlog-do-db options, blank if no such options were given

- Binlog_ignore_db

  A comma-separated list of databases that are explicitly excluded from the binary log with --binlog-ignore-db options, blank if no such options were given

SHOW MASTER STATUS was introduced in MySQL 3.23.22.

SHOW PRIVILEGES

SHOW PRIVILEGES displays the privileges that can be granted and information about the purpose of each one.

The output from SHOW PRIVILEGES includes the following columns:

- Privilege

  The privilege name

- Context

  The applicability of the privilege, such as `Server Admin` (server administration), `Databases`, or `Tables`

- Comment

  A description of the purpose of the privilege

`SHOW PRIVILEGES` was introduced in MySQL 4.1.

SHOW [FULL] PROCESSLIST

`SHOW PROCESSLIST` displays information about the threads executing within the server. The output contains the following columns:

- Id

  The thread ID number for the client.

- User

  The client name associated with the thread.

- Host

  The host from which the client is connected.

- db

  The default database for the thread.

- Command

  The statement being executed by the thread.

- Time

  The amount of time used by the statement currently executing in the thread, in seconds.

- State

  Information about what MySQL is doing while processing a SQL statement. The value can be useful for reporting a problem with MySQL or when asking a question on the MySQL mailing list about why a thread stays in some state for a long time.

- Info

  The query being executed. As of MySQL 3.23.7, the `FULL` option can be added to see the full text of queries in the `Info` field. Without it, only the first 100 characters are displayed.

SHOW SLAVE HOSTS

This statement is used on replication master servers. It displays information about the slave servers that are currently registered with the master.

The output from SHOW SLAVE HOSTS includes the following columns:

- Server_id

  The slave server ID

- Host

  The slave host

- User

  The account name the slave used to connect

- Password

  The account password the slave used to connect

- Port

  The port to which the slave is connected

- Rpl_recovery_rank

  The replication recovery rank

- Master_id

  The master server ID

The User and Password columns are shown only if the master server was started with the --show-slave-auth-info option.

SHOW SLAVE HOSTS was introduced in MySQL 4.0.

SHOW SLAVE STATUS

This statement is used on slave servers and provides information about the replication status of the server.

The output from SHOW SLAVE STATUS includes the following columns:

- Master_Host

  The master host name or IP address

- Master_User

  The user name for connecting to the master

- Master_Port

  The port number for connecting to the master

- `Connect_retry`

  The number of times to attempt connections to the master before giving up

- `Master_Log_File`

  The name of the current master binary update log file

- `Read_Master_Log_Pos`

  The current position within the master binary update log file where the slave I/O thread is reading

- `Relay_Log_File`

  The name of the current relay log file

- `Relay_Log_Pos`

  The current position within the relay log file

- `Relay_Master_Log_File`

  The name of the current master relay log file

- `Slave_IO_Running`

  Whether the slave I/O thread is running

- `Slave_SQL_Running`

  Whether the slave SQL thread is running

- `Replicate_do_db`

  A comma-separated list of databases that are explicitly replicated with `--replicate-do-db` options, blank if no such options were given

- `Replicate_ignore_db`

  A comma-separated list of databases that are explicitly excluded from replication with `--replicate-ignore-db` options, blank if no such options were given

- `Last_errno`

  The most recent error number or 0 if none

- `Last_error`

  The most recent error message or blank if none

- `Skip_counter`

  The number of events from the master that the slave should skip

- `Exec_master_log_pos`

  The current position within the master binary update log file where the slave SQL thread is executing

- `Relay_log_space`

  The combined size of the relay log files

`SHOW SLAVE STATUS` was introduced in MySQL 3.23.22.

SHOW STATUS

The `SHOW STATUS` statement displays the server's status variables and their values. As of MySQL 3.23.0, a `LIKE` `'pattern'` clause can be added to display only variables having names that match the pattern.

The more general variables are listed next. Variables for statement counters, the query cache, and SSL are listed in separate groups after that.

- `Aborted_clients`

  The number of client connections aborted due to clients not closing the connection properly.

- `Aborted_connects`

  The number of failed attempts to connect to the server.

- `Bytes_received`

  The total number of bytes received from all clients. This variable was introduced in MySQL 3.23.7.

- `Bytes_sent`

  The total number of bytes sent to all clients. This variable was introduced in MySQL 3.23.7.

- `Connections`

  The number of attempts to connect to the server (both successful and unsuccessful). If this number is quite high, you may want to look into using persistent connections in your clients if possible.

- `Created_tmp_disk_tables`

  The number of on-disk temporary tables created while processing queries. This variable was introduced in MySQL 3.23.24.

- `Created_tmp_files`

  The number of temporary files created by the server. This variable was introduced in MySQL 3.23.28.

- `Created_tmp_tables`

  The number of in-memory temporary tables created while processing queries.

- Delayed_errors

  The number of errors occurring while processing INSERT DELAYED rows.

- Delayed_insert_threads

  The current number of INSERT DELAYED handlers.

- Delayed_writes

  The number of INSERT DELAYED rows that have been written.

- Flush_commands

  The number of FLUSH statements that have been executed.

- Handler_commit

  The number of requests to commit a transaction. This variable was introduced in MySQL 4.0.2.

- Handler_delete

  The number of requests to delete a row from a table.

- Handler_read_first

  The number of requests to read the first row from an index.

- Handler_read_key

  The number of requests to read a row based on an index value.

- Handler_read_next

  The number of requests to read the next row in index order.

- Handler_read_prev

  The number of requests to read the previous row in descending index order. This variable was introduced in MySQL 3.23.6.

- Handler_read_rnd

  The number of requests to read a row based on its position.

- Handler_read_rnd_next

  The number of requests to read the next row. If this number is high, you are likely performing many queries that require full table scans or that are not using indexes properly. This variable was introduced in MySQL 3.23.6.

- Handler_rollback

  The number of requests to roll back a transaction. This variable was introduced in MySQL 4.0.2.

- Handler_update

  The number of requests to update a row in a table.

- Handler_write

  The number of requests to insert a row in a table.

- Key_blocks_used

  The number of blocks in use in the index cache.

- Key_read_requests

  The number of requests to read a block from the index cache.

- Key_reads

  The number of physical reads of index blocks from disk.

- Key_write_requests

  The number of requests to write a block to the index cache.

- Key_writes

  The number of physical writes of index blocks to disk.

- Max_used_connections

  The maximum number of connections that have been open simultaneously.

- Not_flushed_delayed_rows

  The number of rows waiting to be written for INSERT DELAYED queries.

- Not_flushed_key_blocks

  The number of blocks in the key cache that have been modified but not yet flushed to disk.

- Opened_tables

  The total number of tables that have been opened. If this number is high, it may be a good idea to increase your table cache size.

- Open_files

  The number of open files.

- Open_streams

  The number of open streams. A stream is a file opened with fopen(); this applies only to log files.

- Open_tables

  The number of open tables.

- Questions

  The number of queries that have been received by the server (this includes both successful and unsuccessful queries). The ratio of Questions to Update yields the number of queries per second.

- Rpl_status

  Failsafe replication status. This variable was introduced in MySQL 4.0.0, but is not yet used.

- Select_full_join

  The number of joins performed without using indexes. This variable was introduced in MySQL 3.23.25.

- Select_full_range_join

  The number of joins performed using a range search on a reference table. This variable was introduced in MySQL 3.23.25.

- Select_range

  The number of joins performed using a range on the first table. This variable was introduced in MySQL 3.23.25.

- Select_range_check

  The number of joins performed such that a range search must be used to fetch rows on a secondary table. This variable was introduced in MySQL 3.23.25.

- Select_scan

  The number of joins performed that used a full scan of the first table. This variable was introduced in MySQL 3.23.25.

- Slave_open_temp_tables

  The number of temporary tables the slave thread has open. This variable was introduced in MySQL 3.23.29.

- Slave_running

  Whether this server is acting as a slave that is currently connected to a server. This variable was introduced in MySQL 3.23.16.

- Slow_launch_threads

  The number of threads that took longer than slow_launch_time seconds to create. This variable was introduced in MySQL 3.23.15.

- Slow_queries

  The number of queries that look longer than long_query_time seconds to execute.

- Sort_merge_passes

  The number of merge passes performed by the sort algorithm. This variable was introduced in MySQL 3.23.28.

- `Sort_range`

  The number of sort operations performed using a range. This variable was introduced in MySQL 3.23.25.

- `Sort_rows`

  The number of rows sorted. This variable was introduced in MySQL 3.23.25.

- `Sort_scan`

  The number of sort operations performed using a full table scan. This variable was introduced in MySQL 3.23.25.

- `Table_locks_immediate`

  The number of requests for a table lock that could be satisfied immediately with no waiting. This variable was introduced in MySQL 3.23.33.

- `Table_locks_waited`

  The number of requests for a table lock that could be satisfied only after waiting. If this value is high, it indicates performance problems. This variable was introduced in MySQL 3.23.33.

- `Threads_cached`

  The number of threads currently in the thread cache. This variable was introduced in MySQL 3.23.17.

- `Threads_connected`

  The number of currently open connections.

- `Threads_created`

  The total number of threads that have been created to handle client connections. This variable was introduced in MySQL 3.23.31.

- `Threads_running`

  The number of threads that are not sleeping.

- `Uptime`

  The number of seconds since the server started running.

Statement Counter Status Variables

As of MySQL 3.23.47, the server maintains a set of status variables that serve as counters to indicate the number of times particular types of statements (commands) have been executed. There are dozens of such variables, and they all have similar names, so they are not listed individually here. Each statement counter variable name begins with `Com_`, and has a suffix that indicates the type of statement to which the counter corresponds. For example, `Com_select` and `Com_drop_table` indicate how many SELECT and DROP TABLE statements the server has executed.

Query Cache Status Variables

The following variables display information about the operation of the query cache. They were introduced in MySQL 4.0.1, when the query cache itself was added.

- `Qcache_free_blocks`

  The number of free memory blocks in the query cache

- `Qcache_free_memory`

  The amount of free memory for the query cache

- `Qcache_hits`

  The number of hits in the query cache, that is, the number of query requests satisfied by queries held in the cache

- `Qcache_inserts`

  The number of queries that have ever been registered in the query cache

- `Qcache_not_cached`

  The number of queries that were uncacheable or for which caching was suppressed with the `SQL_NO_CACHE` keyword

- `Qcache_queries_in_cache`

  The number of queries currently registered in the cache

- `Qcache_total_blocks`

  The total number of memory blocks in the query cache

Note that SHOW VARIABLES also lists a few query cache-related variables; they all have names that begin with `query_cache`.

SSL Status Variables

The following variables provide information about the SSL management code. Many of them reflect the state of the current connection and will be blank unless the connection actually is secure. These variables were introduced in MySQL 4.0, when SSL support was added. However, they are unavailable unless SSL support actually has been built into the server.

- `Ssl_accept_renegotiates`

  The number of start renegotiations in server mode.

- `Ssl_accepts`

  The number of started SSL/TLS handshakes in server mode.

- `Ssl_callback_cache_hits`

  The number of sessions successfully retrieved from the external session cache in server mode.

- `Ssl_cipher`

  The SSL cipher (protocol) for the current connection (blank if no cipher is in effect). You can use this variable to determine whether or not the current connection is encrypted.

- `Ssl_cipher_list`

  The list of available SSL ciphers

- `Ssl_client_connects`

  The number of started SSL/TLS handshakes in client mode

- `Ssl_connect_renegotiates`

  The number of start renegotiations in client mode

- `Ssl_ctx_verify_depth`

  The SSL context verification depth

- `Ssl_ctx_verify_mode`

  The SSL context verification mode

- `Ssl_default_timeout`

  The default SSL session timeout

- `Ssl_finished_accepts`

  The number of successfully established SSL/TLS sessions in server mode

- `Ssl_finished_connects`

  The number of successfully established SSL/TLS sessions in client mode

- `Ssl_session_cache_hits`

  The number of SSL sessions found in the session cache

- `Ssl_session_cache_misses`

  The number of SSL sessions not found in the session cache

- `Ssl_session_cache_mode`

  The type of SSL caching used by the server

- `Ssl_session_cache_overflows`

  The number of sessions removed from the cache because it was full

- `Ssl_session_cache_size`

  The number of sessions that can be stored in the SSL session cache.

- `Ssl_session_cache_timeouts`

  The number of sessions that have timed out

- `Ssl_sessions_reused`

  Whether or not the session was reused from an earlier session

- `Ssl_used_session_cache_entries`

  The number of sessions currently in the session cache

- `Ssl_verify_depth`

  The SSL verification depth

- `Ssl_verify_mode`

  The SSL verification mode

- `Ssl_version`

  The protocol version of the connection

SHOW TABLE STATUS

The `SHOW TABLE STATUS` statement displays descriptive information about the tables in a database.

```
SHOW TABLE STATUS;
SHOW TABLE STATUS FROM sampdb;
SHOW TABLE STATUS FROM mysql LIKE '%priv';
```

The output from `SHOW TABLE STATUS` includes the following columns:

- `Name`

  The table name.

- `Type`

  The table type; this is a value like `NISAM` (ISAM), `MyISAM`, `HEAP`, or `InnoDB`.

- `Row_format`

  The row storage format; this can be `Fixed` (fixed-length rows), `Dynamic` (variable-length rows), or `Compressed`.

- `Rows`

  The number of rows in the table. For some table types, such as BDB and InnoDB, this is only an approximate count.

- `Avg_row_length`

  The average number of bytes used by table rows.

- `Data_length`

  The actual size in bytes of the table data file.

- `Max_data_length`

  The maximum size in bytes that the table data file can grow to.

- `Index_length`

  The actual size in bytes of the index file.

- `Data_free`

  The number of unused bytes in the data file. If this number is very high, it may be a good idea to issue an `OPTIMIZE TABLE` statement for the table.

- `Auto_increment`

  The next value that will be generated for an `AUTO_INCREMENT` column.

- `Create_time`

  The time when the table was created.

- `Update_time`

  The time when the table was most recently modified.

- `Check_time`

  For MyISAM tables, the time at which the table was last checked or repaired by `myisamchk`; the value is `NULL` if the table has never been checked or repaired.

- `Charset`

  The table's character set.

- `Create_options`

  Extra options that were specified in the *table_options* clause of the `CREATE TABLE` statement that created the table.

- `Comment`

  The text of any comment specified when the table was created. For an InnoDB table, this column shows foreign key definitions; it also displays the amount of free space in the InnoDB tablespace.

`SHOW TABLE STATUS` was introduced in MySQL 3.23.0. The `Charset` column was added in MySQL 4.1.

SHOW TABLE TYPES

SHOW TABLE TYPES lists the table handlers that the server supports.

The output from this statement includes the following columns:

- Type

  The table type (MyISAM, InnoDB, and so on)

- Support

  The level of support: YES for supported, NO for not supported, DISABLED for supported but disabled at runtime, or DEFAULT to indicate that the table type is the default type

- Comment

  Descriptive text about the table type

SHOW TABLE TYPES was introduced in MySQL 4.1.

SHOW [OPEN] TABLES

The SHOW TABLES statement displays the names of the non-TEMPORARY tables in a database.

```
SHOW TABLES;
SHOW TABLES FROM sampdb;
SHOW TABLES FROM mysql LIKE '%priv';
```

As of MySQL 3.23.33, SHOW OPEN TABLES can be used, which displays the list of open tables that are registered in the table cache. The FROM and LIKE clauses are ignored for this form of the statement.

```
SHOW OPEN TABLES;
```

SHOW [GLOBAL | SESSION] VARIABLES

The SHOW VARIABLES statement displays a list of server variables and their values.

```
SHOW VARIABLES;
SHOW VARIABLES LIKE '%thread%';
```

As of MySQL 4.0.3, the server can display the values of variables at both the global (server-wide) or session (client-specific) level. By default, SHOW displays the session-level value for any given variable or the global value if no session value exists. To display global or session values explicitly, specify a level indicator:

```
SHOW GLOBAL VARIABLES [LIKE 'pattern'];
SHOW SESSION VARIABLES [LIKE 'pattern'];
```

LOCAL is a synonym for SESSION. It is also possible to retrieve the values of dynamic variables using SELECT:

```
SELECT @@GLOBAL.table_type, @@SESSION.table_type, @@LOCAL.table_type;
```

Using SELECT has the advantage that you can more easily manipulate the query result in certain contexts.

SHOW VARIABLES output includes the variables in the following list. Unless otherwise indicated, the variables listed have been present in MySQL at least as far back as MySQL 3.22.0. (Many of the InnoDB variables were introduced in MySQL 3.23.29 under names beginning with innobase_ and renamed in 3.23.37 to begin with innodb_.) Some of the variables are present only under certain configurations. For example, many of those that begin with bdb_ are shown only if the BDB table handler is present.

As of MySQL 4.0.3, several server variables can be modified dynamically while the server is running. (The entry for the SET statement describes how to do this.) For variables that can be modified this way, the variable name is followed by the words *global* or *session* in parentheses to indicate the levels at which the variable can be modified. (Prior to MySQL 4.0.3, these parenthetical indicators have no meaning.)

- back_log

  The maximum number of pending connection requests that can be queued while current connections are being processed.

- ansi_mode

  Whether the server was started with the --ansi option. This variable was introduced in MySQL 3.23.6, and removed in 3.23.41 when the sql_mode variable was added.

- basedir

  The pathname to the root directory of the MySQL installation.

- bdb_cache_size

  The size of the buffer used by the BDB table handler to cache data and index rows. Starting MySQL with --skip-bdb to disable the BDB handler causes this to be set to zero, which reduces memory use. This variable was introduced in MySQL 3.23.14.

- bdb_home

  The BDB home directory; normally has the same value as datadir. This variable was introduced in MySQL 3.23.14.

- `bdb_log_buffer_size`

  The size of the buffer used for the BDB transaction log. This variable was introduced in MySQL 3.23.21.

- `bdb_logdir`

  The pathname to the directory in which the BDB handler writes log files. This variable was introduced in MySQL 3.23.14.

- `bdb_max_lock`

  The maximum number of simultaneous locks that can be placed on a BDB table. This variable was introduced in MySQL 3.23.29.

- `bdb_shared_data`

  Indicates whether or not BDB was started in multi-process mode. This variable was introduced in MySQL 3.23.29.

- `bdb_tmpdir`

  The directory where the BDB handler creates temporary files. This variable was introduced in MySQL 3.23.14.

- `bdb_version`

  Version number of the BDB handler. This variable was introduced in MySQL 3.23.31.

- `binlog_cache_size` *(global)*

  The size of the cache that is used to store SQL statements that are part of a transaction before they are flushed to the binary log. (This occurs only if the transaction is committed. If the transaction is rolled back, the statements are discarded.) This variable was introduced in MySQL 3.23.29.

- `bulk_insert_buffer_size` *(global, session)*

  The size of the cache used to help optimize bulk inserts into MyISAM tables. This includes LOAD DATA statements, multiple-row INSERT statements, and INSERT INTO ... SELECT statements. Setting the value to zero disables the optimization.

  This variable was introduced as `myisam_bulk_insert_tree_size` in MySQL 4.0.0 and renamed to `bulk_insert_buffer_size` in 4.0.3.

- `character_set`

  The name of the default character set. This variable was introduced in MySQL 3.23.3.

- `character_sets`

  The list of supported character sets. The value is a set of space-separated character set names. This variable was introduced in MySQL 3.23.15.

- `concurrent_insert`   (*global*)

  Whether or not the server allows `INSERT` queries on MyISAM tables while `SELECT` queries are active. Enabled by default, but it can be disabled with `--skip-concurrent-insert`. This variable was introduced in MySQL 3.23.7.

- `connect_timeout`   (*global*)

  The number of seconds that `mysqld` will wait for packets during the initial connection handshake.

- `convert_character_set`   (*session*)

  The character set to use for mapping strings sent to and from the client. This variable was introduced in MySQL 4.0.3.

- `datadir`

  The pathname to the MySQL data directory.

- `delayed_insert_limit`   (*global*)

  The number of rows from `INSERT DELAYED` statements that will be inserted into a table before checking whether any new `SELECT` statements for the table have arrived. If any have, the insert operation is suspended to allow retrievals to execute.

- `delayed_insert_timeout`   (*global*)

  When the handler for `INSERT DELAYED` operations finishes inserting queued rows, it waits this many seconds to see if any new `INSERT DELAYED` rows arrive. If so, it handles them; otherwise, it terminates.

- `delayed_queue_size`   (*global*)

  The number of rows that may be queued for `INSERT DELAYED` statements. If the queue is full, further `INSERT DELAYED` statements block until there is room in the queue.

- `delay_key_write`   (*global*)

  Whether or not the server respects delayed key writes for MyISAM tables created with the `DELAY_KEY_WRITE` option. This variable can have three values. `ON` (the default value) tells the server to honor the `DELAY_KEY_WRITE` option for tables declared with that option. (Key writes are delayed for tables declared with `DELAY_KEY_WRITE=1` but not for tables declared with `DELAY_KEY_WRITE=0`.) A value of `OFF` means that key writes are never delayed for any table, no matter how it was declared. A value of `ALL` forces key writes always to be delayed for every table, no matter how it was declared.

  This variable was introduced as `delayed_key_write` in MySQL 3.23.5 and renamed to `delay_key_write` in 3.23.8.

- `flush` (*global*)

  Indicates whether or not the server flushes tables after each update.

  This variable was introduced in MySQL 3.22.9, but was used only on Windows from 3.22.9 to 3.22.11.

- `flush_time` (*global*)

  If this variable has a non-zero value, tables are closed to flush pending changes to disk every `flush_time` seconds. The default value is 0 for UNIX and 1800 (30 minutes) for Windows; use the `--flush` option to change the value. This variable was introduced in MySQL 3.22.18.

- `ft_boolean_syntax`

  The list of operators that are supported for `FULLTEXT` searches that use `IN BOOLEAN MODE`. This variable was introduced in MySQL 4.0.1.

- `ft_max_word_len`

  The maximum length of words that can be included in a `FULLTEXT` index. Longer words are ignored. If you change the value of this variable, you should rebuild any `FULLTEXT` indexes that are present in tables managed by the server. This variable was introduced in MySQL 4.0.0.

- `ft_max_word_len_for_sort`

  The maximum length of words that are considered short enough for the fast index-creation method used by `ALTER TABLE`, `CREATE INDEX`, and `REPAIR TABLE` to build `FULLTEXT` indexes. Words that exceed this length are inserted using a slower method. This variable was introduced in MySQL 4.0.0.

- `ft_min_word_len`

  The minimum length of words that can be included in a `FULLTEXT` index. Shorter words are ignored. If you change the value of this variable, you should rebuild any `FULLTEXT` indexes that are present in tables managed by the server. This variable was introduced in MySQL 4.0.0.

- `have_bdb`

  `YES` if the BDB table handler is present and enabled, `DISABLED` if the handler is present but disabled, `NO` if the handler is not present. This variable was introduced in MySQL 3.23.30.

- `have_innodb`

  `YES` if the InnoDB table handler is present and enabled, `DISABLED` if the handler is present but disabled, `NO` if the handler is not present.

  This variable was introduced as `have_innobase` in MySQL 3.23.30 and renamed to `have_innodb` in MySQL 3.23.37.

- have_isam

  YES if the ISAM table handler is present and enabled, DISABLED if the handler is present but disabled, NO if the handler is not present. This variable was introduced in MySQL 3.23.30.

- have_openssl

  YES or NO to indicate whether the server supports encrypted client connections using SSL. This variable was introduced in MySQL 3.23.43 but is not meaningful until 4.0.0 when SSL support was implemented.

- have_query_cache

  Whether or not the query cache is available. This variable was introduced in MySQL 4.0.2.

- have_raid

  Indicates whether or not the RAID-related CREATE TABLE options are supported. This variable was introduced in MySQL 3.23.30.

- have_symlink

  Whether or not symbolic linking support is enabled. This variable was introduced in MySQL 4.0.0.

- init_file

  The name of the file containing SQL statements to be executed by the server when it starts (blank if none). This file is specified using the --init-file option. This variable was introduced in MySQL 3.23.2.

- innodb_additional_mem_pool_size

  The size of the InnoDB memory pool for storing internal data structures. This variable was introduced in MySQL 3.23.37.

- innodb_buffer_pool_size

  The size of the InnoDB cache for buffering table data and indexes. This variable was introduced in MySQL 3.23.37.

- innodb_data_file_path

  The specifications for the InnoDB tablespace component files. This variable was introduced in MySQL 3.23.37.

- innodb_data_home_dir

  The pathname to the directory under which the InnoDB tablespace components are located. This variable was introduced in MySQL 3.23.37.

- innodb_fast_shutdown

  Whether or not InnoDB will use its quicker shutdown method that skips some of the operations that it performs normally. This variable was introduced in MySQL 3.23.44.

- `innodb_file_io_threads`

  The number of file I/O threads used by InnoDB. This variable was introduced in MySQL 3.23.37.

- `innodb_flush_log_at_trx_commit`

  This option controls InnoDB log flushing when transactions are committed.

Value	Meaning
0	Write to log once per second and flush to disk
1	Write to log at each commit and flush to disk
2	Write to log at each commit, but flush to disk only once per second

  This variable was introduced in MySQL 3.23.37.

- `innodb_flush_method`

  The method InnoDB uses for log flushing. This variable was introduced in MySQL 3.23.39.

- `innodb_force_recovery`

  Normally 0, but can be set to a value from 1 to 6 to cause the server to start up after a crash even if InnoDB recovery fails. For a description of how this variable is used, see Chapter 13, "Database Backups, Maintenance, and Repair." This variable was introduced in MySQL 3.23.44.

- `innodb_lock_wait_timeout`

  The number of seconds InnoDB waits for a lock for a transaction. If the lock cannot be acquired, InnoDB rolls back the transaction. This variable was introduced in MySQL 3.23.37.

- `innodb_log_arch_dir`

  This variable is unused. It was introduced in MySQL 3.23.37.

- `innodb_log_archive`

  This variable is unused. It was introduced in MySQL 3.23.37.

- `innodb_log_buffer_size`

  The size of the InnoDB transaction log buffer. This variable was introduced in MySQL 3.23.37.

- `innodb_log_files_in_group`

  The number of log files InnoDB maintains. The product of `innodb_log_files_in_group` and `innodb_log_file_size` determines the total InnoDB log size. This variable was introduced in MySQL 3.23.37.

- innodb_log_file_size

  The size of each InnoDB log file. The product of innodb_log_files_in_group and innodb_log_file_size determines the total InnoDB log size. This variable was introduced in MySQL 3.23.37.

- innodb_log_group_home_dir

  The directory in which InnoDB log files are written. This variable was introduced in MySQL 3.23.37.

- innodb_mirrored_log_groups

  The number of InnoDB log file groups to maintain. The value should always be 1. This variable was introduced in MySQL 3.23.37.

- innodb_thread_concurrency

  The limit on the number of threads that InnoDB tries to maintain. This variable was introduced in MySQL 3.23.44.

- interactive_timeout (*global, session*)

  The number of seconds an interactive client connection can remain idle before the server considers itself free to close it. For non-interactive clients, the value of the wait_timeout variable is used instead. This variable was introduced in MySQL 3.23.7.

- join_buffer_size (*global, session*)

  The size of the full-join buffer (that is, the buffer for joins that are performed without use of indexes).

  This variable was called join_buffer prior to MySQL 3.23.

- key_buffer_size (*global*)

  The size of the buffer used for index blocks. This buffer is shared among connection-handler threads.

  This variable was called key_buffer prior to MySQL 3.23.

- language

  The language used to display error messages. The value can be either the language name or the pathname of the directory containing the language files.

- large_files_support

  Whether or not the server was built with support for handling large files. This variable was introduced in MySQL 3.23.28.

- `local_infile` *(global)*

  Whether or not LOCAL is allowed for LOAD DATA statements. This variable was introduced in MySQL 4.0.3.

- `locked_in_memory`

  Whether or not the server is locked in memory. This variable was introduced in MySQL 3.23.25.

- `log`

  Whether or not query logging is enabled.

- `log_bin`

  Whether or not the binary update log is enabled. This variable was introduced in MySQL 3.23.14.

- `log_slave_updates`

  Whether or not a replication slave server is logging updates that it receives from the master. Slave update logging can be enabled to allow a slave server to act as a master to another slave in a chained replication configuration. This variable was introduced in MySQL 3.23.17.

- `log_slow_queries`

  Whether or not the slow-query log is enabled. This variable was introduced in MySQL 4.0.2.

- `log_update`

  Whether or not update logging is enabled. This variable was introduced in MySQL 3.22.18.

- `log_warnings` *(global, session)*

  Whether or not to log non-critical warnings to the error log. This variable was introduced in MySQL 4.0.3.

- `long_query_time` *(global, session)*

  The number of seconds that defines a "slow" query. Any query taking longer than this causes the Slow_queries counter to be incremented. In addition, if the slow-query log is enabled, the query is written to the log.

- `lower_case_table_names`

  Whether or not to force table names as stored on disk to lowercase (and also database names as of MySQL 4.0.2). This variable was introduced in MySQL 3.23.6.

- low_priority_updates (*global, session*)

Whether the server was started with the --low-priority-updates option to give updates a lower priority than retrievals. This variable was introduced in MySQL 3.22.5.

- max_allowed_packet (*global, session*)

The maximum size of the buffer used for communication between the server and the client. The buffer is initially allocated to be net_buffer_length bytes long but can grow up to max_allowed_packet bytes as necessary. The maximum value for max_allowed_packet is 1GB from MySQL 4 and later, 16MB prior to MySQL 4.

- max_binlog_cache_size (*global*)

The maximum binary log cache size. This restricts the total combined size of the statements that make up a transaction. This variable was introduced in MySQL 3.23.29.

- max_binlog_size (*global*)

The maximum size of a binary log. If the log reaches this size, the log is rotated. The allowable range of values is 1KB to 1GB. This variable was introduced in MySQL 3.23.33.

- max_connections (*global*)

The maximum number of simultaneous client connections allowed.

- max_connect_errors (*global*)

The number of failed connections from a host that are allowed before the host is blocked from further connection attempts. This is done on the basis that someone may be attempting to break in from that host. The FLUSH HOSTS statement or mysqladmin flush-hosts command can be used to clear the host cache to re-enable blocked hosts.

- max_delayed_threads (*global*)

The maximum number of threads that will be created to handle INSERT DELAYED statements. Any such statements that are received while the maximum number of handlers is already in use will be treated as non-DELAYED statements.

This option was introduced as max_delayed_insert_threads in MySQL 3.22.15 and renamed to max_delayed_threads in 3.23.0.

- max_heap_table_size (*global, session*)

The maximum allowed size of HEAP tables. This variable can be used to help prevent the server from using excessive amounts of memory. It was introduced in MySQL 3.23.0.

- `max_join_size` *(global, session)*

  When executing a join, the MySQL optimizer estimates how many row combinations it will need to examine. If the estimate exceeds `max_join_size` rows, an error is returned. This can be used if users tend to write indiscriminate `SELECT` queries that return an inordinate number of rows.

- `max_sort_length` *(global, session)*

  `BLOB` or `TEXT` values are sorted using the first `max_sort_length` bytes of each value.

- `max_tmp_tables` *(global, session)*

  The maximum number of temporary tables a client can have open simultaneously. This variable was introduced in MySQL 3.23.0 but currently is unused.

- `max_user_connections` *(global)*

  The maximum number of simultaneous client connections allowed to any single account. The default value is zero, which means "no limit." The number of per-account connections is bound in any case by the value of `max_connections`. This variable was introduced in MySQL 3.23.34.

  To specify connection limits for specific accounts, use the `GRANT` statement.

- `max_write_lock_count` *(global)*

  After this many write locks, the server starts allowing queries that require read locks a higher priority than normal. This variable was introduced in MySQL 3.23.7.

- `myisam_bulk_insert_tree_size`

  See the description for `bulk_insert_buffer_size`.

- `myisam_max_extra_sort_file_size` *(global, session)*

  This value is used by the MyISAM handler to help decide when to use a slower but safer key cache index creation method.

  This variable was introduced in MySQL 3.23.37. The value is measured in bytes as of MySQL 4.0.3 and in MB before that.

- `myisam_max_sort_file_size` *(global, session)*

  MyISAM table index rebuilding for statements such as `REPAIR TABLE`, `ALTER TABLE`, or `LOAD DATA` can use a temporary file or the key cache. The value of this variable determines which method is used; if the temporary file would be larger than this value, the key cache is used instead.

This variable was introduced in MySQL 3.23.37. The value is measured in bytes as of MySQL 4.0.3 and in MB before that.

- `myisam_recover_options`

  The value of the `--myisam-recover` option that the server was started with to specify the MyISAM auto-checking mode. This variable was introduced in MySQL 3.23.36.

- `myisam_sort_buffer_size` *(global, session)*

  The size of the buffer that is allocated to sort an index for MyISAM tables during ALTER TABLE, CREATE INDEX, and REPAIR TABLE operations. This variable was introduced in MySQL 3.23.16.

- `named_pipe`

  Whether or not named pipe support is enabled. This is used for Windows NT-based servers. This variable was introduced in MySQL 3.23.50. (Prior to 3.23.50, named pipe support is enabled by default for servers that support named pipes.)

- `net_buffer_length` *(global, session)*

  The initial size of the buffer used for communication between the server and the client. This buffer can be expanded up to `max_allowed_packet` bytes long.

- `net_read_timeout` *(global, session)*

  The number of seconds to wait for data from a client connection before timing out. This variable was introduced in MySQL 3.23.20.

- `net_retry_count` *(global, session)*

  The number of times to retry an interrupted read. This variable was introduced in MySQL 3.23.7.

- `net_write_timeout` *(global, session)*

  The number of seconds to wait before timing out while writing a block to a client connection. This variable was introduced in MySQL 3.23.20.

- `open_files_limit`

  If non-zero, this variable is the number of file descriptors the server will attempt to reserve. If zero, the server uses the larger of `max_connections*5` and `max_connections + table_cache*2` as the number of descriptors to reserve. This variable was introduced in MySQL 3.23.30.

- `pid_file`

  The pathname of the file where the server writes its process ID number. This variable was introduced in MySQL 3.22.23.

- `port`

  The number of the TCP/IP port to which the server listens for client connections.

- `protocol_version`

  The version number of the client/server protocol the server is using. This variable was introduced in MySQL 3.22.18.

- `query_cache_limit`   (*global*)

  The maximum size of cached query results; larger results are not cached. This variable was introduced in MySQL 4.0.1.

- `query_cache_size`   (*global*)

  The amount of memory to use for query result caching. Set this variable to zero to disable the query cache. This variable was introduced in MySQL 4.0.1.

- `query_cache_type`   (*global, session*)

  The mode of operation of the query cache.

Mode	Meaning
OFF	Don't cache
ON	Cache queries except those that begin with `SELECT SQL_NO_CACHE`
DEMAND	Cache on demand only those queries that begin with `SELECT SQL_CACHE`

  This variable was introduced as `query_cache_startup_type` in MySQL 4.0.1 and renamed to `query_cache_type` in 4.0.3.

- `read_buffer_size`   (*global, session*)

  The size of the buffer used by threads that perform sequential table scans. A buffer is allocated as necessary per client.

  Prior to MySQL 4.0.3, this variable is called `record_buffer`.

- `read_rnd_buffer_size`   (*global, session*)

  The size of the buffer used for reading rows in order after a sort. A buffer is allocated as necessary per client.

  This variable was introduced as `record_rnd_buffer` in MySQL 3.23.41 and renamed to `read_rnd_buffer_size` in 4.0.3.

- `record_buffer`

  See the description for `read_buffer_size`.

- `record_rnd_buffer`

  See the description for `read_rnd_buffer_size`.

- `rpl_recovery_rank`   (*global*)

  The server's replication recovery rank. This is unused currently; its purpose in the future will be to allow a slave server that has lost its master to select a new master from among communicating replication servers. This variable was introduced in MySQL 4.0.0.

- `safe_show_database`

  Whether or not to show databases names unconditionally. If the value is ON, users can see names only for databases for which they have database or table privileges. If OFF, all database names are shown to all users. This variable was introduced in MySQL 3.23.30. As of 4.0.3, you should instead grant the SHOW DATABASES privilege to users that need to see all databases. This variable has been removed as of MySQL 4.0.5.

- `server_id`   (*global*)

  The server's replication ID number. This variable was introduced in MySQL 3.23.26.

- `skip_external_locking`

  Whether or not use of external locking (file system locking) is suppressed.

  This variable as called `skip_locking` prior to MySQL 4.0.3.

- `skip_locking`

  See the description for `skip_external_locking`.

- `skip_networking`

  OFF to allow TCP/IP connections, ON to disable them. In the latter case clients can connect from the local host only, using UNIX socket connections under UNIX or named pipes under Windows. This variable was introduced in MySQL 3.22.23.

- `skip_show_database`

  ON to show database names only to users who have the SHOW DATABASES privilege (PROCESS prior to MySQL 4.0.2). OFF for no such requirement. This variable was introduced in MySQL 3.23.4.

- `slave_net_timeout` *(global)*

  The number of seconds to wait for data from a master server before timing out. This variable was introduced in MySQL 3.23.40.

- `slow_launch_time` *(global)*

  The number of seconds that defines "slow" thread creation. Any thread taking longer to create causes the `Slow_launch_threads` status counter to be incremented. This variable was introduced in MySQL 3.23.15.

- `socket`

  The pathname to the UNIX domain socket, or the name of the named pipe under Windows.

- `sort_buffer_size` *(global, session)*

  The size of the buffer used by threads for performing sort operations (GROUP BY or ORDER BY). This buffer is allocated as necessary per client. Normally, if you may have many clients that do sorting at the same time, it is unwise to make this value very large (more than 1MB).

  Prior to MySQL 4.0.3, this variable is called `sort_buffer`.

- `sql_mode`

  The value of the `--sql-mode` option. This variable was introduced in MySQL 3.23.41; it replaces `ansi_mode`.

- `table_cache` *(global)*

  The maximum number of tables that can be open. This cache is shared between threads.

- `table_type` *(global, session)*

  The default table type, used for tables that are created without a TYPE = *type_name* option or with an unsupported *type_name* value. This variable was introduced in MySQL 3.23.0.

- `thread_cache_size` *(global)*

  The maximum number of threads to maintain in the thread cache. This variable was introduced in MySQL 3.23.16.

- `thread_concurrency`

  This variable applies only to Solaris. The value is passed to `thr_concurrency()` to provide a hint to the thread manager about how many threads to run simultaneously. This variable was introduced in MySQL 3.23.7.

- `thread_stack`

  The stack size for each thread.

- `timezone`

  The server's time zone setting. This variable was introduced in MySQL 3.23.15.

- `tmpdir`

  The pathname to the directory where the server creates temporary files. This option was introduced in MySQL 3.22.4. It was called `tmp_dir` from 3.22.0 to 3.22.3.

- `tmp_table_size` *(global, session)*

  The maximum number of bytes allowed for temporary tables. Prior to MySQL 3.23, if a table exceeds this size, `mysqld` returns an error to the client. From 3.23 on, if a table exceeds this size, the server converts that table to a MyISAM table on disk and increments the `Created_tmp_disk_tables` status variable. If you have memory to spare, higher values of this variable allow the server to maintain larger temporary tables.

- `transaction_isolation`

  See the description for `tx_isolation`.

- `tx_isolation` *(global, session)*

  The default transaction isolation level.

  This variable was introduced as `transaction_isolation` in MySQL 3.23.36 and renamed to `tx_isolation` in 4.0.3.

- `version`

  The server version. The value consists of a version number, possibly followed by one or more suffixes. The suffix values are listed in the description of the `VERSION()` function in Appendix C, "Operator and Function Reference."

- `wait_timeout` *(global, session)*

  The number of seconds a non-interactive client connection can remain idle before the server considers itself free to close it. For interactive clients, the value of the `interactive_timeout` variable is used instead.

SLAVE

```
SLAVE {START | STOP} [slave_options]
```

This statement controls the operation of a replication slave server. SLAVE
START initiates a slave thread and SLAVE STOP terminates it.

SLAVE was introduced in MySQL 3.23.16. As of MySQL 4.0.2, an optional
`slave_options` clause can be specified. It should consist of one or more of
the following options, separated by commas:

- IO_THREAD

  Start or stop the I/O thread that gets queries from the master server and
  stores them in the relay log.

- SQL_THREAD

  Start or stop the SQL thread that reads the relay log and executes them.

TRUNCATE

```
TRUNCATE [TABLE] tbl_name
```

TRUNCATE TABLE performs a fast truncation of table contents by dropping and
recreating the table. This is much faster than deleting each row individually.

This statement is not transaction-safe; an error will occur should you issue a
TRUNCATE TABLE statement in the middle of an active transaction or while
you are holding any explicit table locks.

TRUNCATE TABLE was introduced in MySQL 3.23.28, but prior to 3.23.33, the
TABLE keyword must be omitted.

UNION

```
select_statement
    UNION [ALL] select_statement
    [UNION select_statement] ...
```

UNION isn't really a separate statement, it's a way of combining SELECT statements such that their results are concatenated one after the other. Each SELECT
statement must produce the same number of columns in its result set. The
names and types of the columns in the final result are determined by the column names in the first SELECT. If the types of corresponding columns do not
match, implicit type conversion will take place for rows from the second and
following tables.

By default, UNION eliminates duplicates. This is like the effect of DISTINCT but
extended over all the result sets. UNION ALL preserves duplicates so that all
rows are returned.

ORDER BY or LIMIT clauses can be applied to an individual SELECT statement within a UNION by placing the statement within parentheses. ORDER BY or LIMIT clauses that occur at the end of the entire UNION and not within parentheses apply to the UNION result as a whole. In this case, any columns named in an ORDER BY should refer to the names of the columns in the first SELECT.

UNION was introduced in MySQL 4.0.0.

UNLOCK TABLE

```
UNLOCK {TABLE | TABLES}
```

This statement releases any table locks being held by the current client.

UPDATE

```
UPDATE [LOW_PRIORITY] [IGNORE] tbl_name
    SET col_name=expr [, col_name=expr ] ...
    [WHERE where_expr] [ORDER BY ... ] [LIMIT n]

UPDATE [LOW_PRIORITY] [IGNORE] tbl_name , tbl_name ...
    SET col_name=expr [, col_name=expr ] ...
    [WHERE where_expr]
```

For the first syntax, UPDATE modifies the contents of existing rows in the table *tbl_name*. The rows to be modified are those selected by the expression specified in the WHERE clause. For those rows that are selected, each column named in the SET clause is set to value of the corresponding expression.

```
UPDATE member SET expiration = NULL, phone = '197-602-4832'
    WHERE member_id = 14;
```

If no WHERE clause is given, *all records in the table are updated*.

UPDATE returns the number of rows that were updated. However, a row is not considered as having been updated unless some column value actually changed. Setting a column to the value it already contains is not considered to affect the row. If your application really needs to know how many rows matched the WHERE clause regardless of whether or not the UPDATE actually changed any values, you should specify the CLIENT_FOUND_ROWS flag when you establish a connection to the server. See the entry for the mysql_real_connect() function in Appendix F, "C API Reference."

LOW_PRIORITY causes the statement to be deferred until no clients are reading from the table. LOW_PRIORITY was introduced in MySQL 3.22.5.

If updating a record would result in a duplicate key value in a unique index, UPDATE will terminate in error. Adding IGNORE causes such records not to be updated and no error occurs. IGNORE was introduced in MySQL 3.23.16.

ORDER BY causes rows to be updated according to the resulting sort order. This clause was introduced in MySQL 4.0.0 and has same syntax as for SELECT.

If the LIMIT clause is given, the value *n* specifies the maximum number of rows that will be updated. LIMIT was introduced in MySQL 3.23.3.

The second UPDATE syntax is like the first but allows multiple tables to be named to perform a multiple-table update. In this case, the WHERE clause can specify conditions based on a join between tables, and the SET clause can update columns in multiple tables. For example, the following statement updates rows in t1 having id values that match those in t2, copying the quantity values from t2 to t1:

```
UPDATE t, t2 SET t.quantity = t2.quantity WHERE t.id = t2.id;
```

Multiple-table updates were introduced in MySQL 4.0.2.

USE

```
USE db_name
```

Selects *db_name* to make it the current database (the default database for table references that include no explicit database name). The USE statement fails if the database doesn't exist or if you have no privileges for accessing it.

SQL Variables

As of MySQL 3.23.6, user-defined SQL variables can be assigned values, and you can refer to those variables in other statements later.

User-defined variable names begin with '@' and can consist of alphanumeric characters from the current character set, and the '_', '$', and '.' characters. Variable names are case sensitive.

Variables can be assigned with the = or := operators in SET statements or with the := operator in other statements, such as SELECT. Multiple assignments can be performed in a single statement.

```
mysql> SET @x = 0, @y = 2;
mysql> SET @color := 'red', @size := 'large';
mysql> SELECT @x, @y, @color, @size;
```

```
+------+------+--------+-------+
| @x   | @y   | @color | @size |
+------+------+--------+-------+
|    0 |    2 | red    | large |
+------+------+--------+-------+
mysql> SELECT @count := COUNT(*) FROM president;
+--------------------+
| @count := COUNT(*) |
+--------------------+
|                 42 |
+--------------------+
```

Variables can be assigned numeric, string, or NULL values, and can be assigned from arbitrary expressions, including those that refer to other variables.

Variables have a value of NULL until explicitly assigned a value. The values do not persist across sessions with the server. That is, values are lost when a connection terminates.

In SELECT statements that return multiple rows, variable assignments are performed for each row. The final value is the value assigned for the last row.

In MySQL 4.1 and later, variables have the same character set as that for the value they are assigned:

```
mysql> SET @s = _pclatin2 'abc'; SELECT CHARSET(@s);
+-------------+
| CHARSET(@s) |
+-------------+
| pclatin2    |
+-------------+
```

Comment Syntax

This section describes how to write comments in your SQL code. It also points out a shortcoming of the mysql client program with respect to comment interpretation. Comments are often used in query files that are executed using mysql in batch mode, so you should be particularly aware of this limitation when you're writing such files.

The MySQL server understands three types of comments:

- Anything from '#' to the end of the line is treated as a comment. This syntax is the same as is used in most shells and Perl.

- Anything between '/*' and '*/' is treated as a comment. This form of comment may span multiple lines. This syntax is the same as is used in the C language.

- As of MySQL 3.23.3, you can begin a comment with '`--` ' (that is, two dashes and a space); everything from the dashes to the end of the line is treated as a comment. This comment style is used by some other databases, except that the space is not required. MySQL requires the space as a disambiguation character so that expressions such as *value1-value2*, where *value2* is negative, will not be treated as comments.

Comments are ignored by the server when executing queries, with the exception that C-style comments that begin with '`/*!`' are given special treatment. The text of the comment should contain SQL keywords, and the keywords will be treated by the MySQL server as part of the statement in which the comment appears. For example, the following lines are considered equivalent by the server:

```
INSERT LOW_PRIORITY INTO mytbl SET ... ;
INSERT /*! LOW_PRIORITY */ INTO mytbl SET ... ;
```

This form of comment is intended to be used for MySQL-specific extensions and keywords. MySQL will recognize the keywords, and other SQL servers will ignore them. This makes it easier to write queries that take advantage of MySQL-specific features but that still work with other database systems. The '`/*!`' comment style was introduced in MySQL 3.22.7.

As of MySQL 3.22.26, you can follow the '`/*!`' sequence with a version number to tell MySQL to ignore the comment unless the server version number is at least as recent as that version. The comment in the following UPDATE statement is ignored unless the server is version 3.23.3 or later:

```
UPDATE mytbl SET mycol = 100 WHERE mycol < 100 /*!32303 LIMIT 100 */;
```

The mysql client is more limited than the MySQL server in its ability to understand comments. mysql gets confused if certain constructs appear in C-style comments because it uses a less sophisticated parser than the server. For example, a quote character appearing inside of a C-style comment will fool mysql into thinking it's parsing a string, and it continues looking for the end of the string until a matching quote is seen. The following statements demonstrate this behavior:

```
mysql> SELECT /* I have no quote */ 1;
+---+
| 1 |
+---+
| 1 |
+---+
mysql> SELECT /* I've got a quote */ 1;
    '>
```

`mysql` parses the first statement without problems, sends it to the server for execution, and prints another `mysql>` prompt. The second statement contains a comment with an unmatched quote. As a result, `mysql` goes into string-parsing mode. It's still in that mode after you enter the line, as indicated by the `'>` prompt. To escape from this, type a matching quote followed by a `\c` command to cancel the query. (See Appendix E, "MySQL Program Reference," for more information on the meaning of `mysql`'s prompts.)

Semicolon is another character that will confuse `mysql` if it occurs within a C-style comment.

E

MySQL Program Reference

THIS APPENDIX DESCRIBES THE MySQL PROGRAMS named in the following list. Later in the appendix, each program is described in more detail, including a description of its purpose, its invocation syntax, the options it supports, and a description of any internal variables it has. (Note that programs are ordered without regard to any '_' or '.' characters in their names.) Unless otherwise indicated, the program options and variables listed here have been present in MySQL at least as far back as MySQL 3.22.0.

- `libmysqld`

  The embedded MySQL server. This isn't really a program; it's a library that you link into other programs to produce standalone applications that include a server.

- `myisamchk` and `isamchk`

  Utilities for checking and repairing tables, performing key distribution analysis, and de-activating and re-activating indexes.

- `myisampack` and `pack_isam`

  Utilities to produce compressed read-only tables.

- `mysql`

  Interactive program with line–editing capabilities for sending queries to the MySQL server; can also be used in batch mode to execute queries stored in a file.

- `mysqlaccess`

  Script for testing access privileges.

- `mysqladmin`

  Utility for performing administrative operations.

- `mysqlbinlog`

  Utility for displaying binary update logs in ASCII format.

- `mysqlbug`

  Script for generating bug reports.

- `mysqlcheck`

  Table checking, repair, optimization, and analysis utility.

- `mysql_config`

  Utility that displays proper flags for compiling MySQL–based programs.

- `mysqld`

  The MySQL server; this program must be running so that clients have access to the databases administered by the server.

- `mysqld_multi`

  Script for starting and stopping multiple servers.

- `mysqld_safe`

  Script for starting up and monitoring the MySQL server. (Prior to MySQL 4, this script is named `safe_mysqld`.)

- `mysqldump`

  Utility for dumping the contents of database tables.

- `mysqlhotcopy`

  Database backup utility.

- `mysqlimport`

  Utility for bulk loading of data into tables.

- `mysql_install_db`

  Script for initializing the server's data directory and grant tables.

- `mysql.server`

  Script for starting up and shutting down the MySQL server.

- `mysqlshow`

  Utility that provides information about databases or tables.

In the syntax descriptions, optional information is indicated by square brackets (`[]`).

Specifying Program Options

Most MySQL programs understand several options that affect their operation. Options can be specified on the command line or in option files. In addition, some options can be specified by setting environment variables. Options specified on the command line take precedence over options specified any other way, and options in option files take precedence over environment variable values.

Most MySQL programs understand the `--help` option, which provides a quick way to get online help about a program from the program itself. For example, if you're not sure how to use `mysqlimport`, invoke it like this for instructions:

```
% mysqlimport --help
```

The `-?` option is the same as `--help`, although your shell may interpret the '?' character as a filename wildcard character:

```
% mysqlimport -?
mysqlimport: No match.
```

If that happens to you, try the following instead:

```
% mysqlimport -\?
```

Some options show up in help messages only under certain circumstances. For example, the `--debug` or SSL-related options appear only if MySQL has been compiled with debugging or SSL support, and Windows-only options, such as `-pipe`, are displayed only on Windows systems.

Most options have both a long (full-word) form and a short (single-letter) form. The `--help` and `-?` options just described are an example of this. Long-form options that are followed by a value should be given in `--name=val` format, where *name* is the option name and *val* is its value. In most cases, if a short-form option is followed by a value, the option and the value can be separated by whitespace. For example, when you specify a username, `-usampadm` is equivalent to `-u sampadm`. The `-p` (password) option is an exception; any password value must follow the `-p` with no intervening space.

Each program description lists all options a program currently understands. If a program doesn't seem to recognize an option listed in its description, you may have an older version of the program that precedes the addition of the option. (But double-check the syntax just to make sure you simply haven't specified the option incorrectly.)

The MySQL 4.0.2 "Great Divide" in Option Processing

A significant change occurred in MySQL 4.0.2, when option handling was revised to provide a more uniform format for specifying boolean options that have on/off values. Such options now have a base form, and a standard set of related forms are recognized, as shown in the following table.

Option	Meaning
`--name`	Base option form; enable option
`--enable-name`	`--enable-` prefix; enable option
`--disable-name`	`--disable-` prefix; do not enable option
`--skip-name`	`--skip-` prefix; do not enable option
`--name=1`	`=1` suffix; enable option
`--name=0`	`=0` suffix; do not enable option

For example, many MySQL commands support a `--compress` option to turn on compression in the client/server protocol. Prior to MySQL 4.0.2, you either specify this option to enable compression or omit it to not use compression. That is still possible, but as of MySQL 4.0.2, `--enable-compress` and `--compress=1` are also recognized to enable compression, and `--disable-compress`, `--skip-compress`, and `--compress=0` are recognized as meaning compression should not be used.

The program descriptions later in this appendix use the marker "(*boolean*)" to signify which options are subject to this kind of interpretation—that is, options for which the prefixes and suffixes shown in the table are supported. The presence of this marker indicates that it's now preferable to use the `--enable-`, `--disable-`, and `--skip-` prefixes. However, when running programs from versions older than 4.0.2, you may need to use the `=0` or `=1` suffixes or perhaps even a different syntax. For example, older versions of `mysql` support a `--no-named-columns` option to suppress column names in query results. As of MySQL 4.0.2, the base option is `--named-columns` (which is also the default setting), and you suppress column headings using `--disable-named-columns` or `--skip-named-columns`.

Given that the installed base of MySQL currently includes a large percentage of pre–4.0.2 installations, what this means is that it may sometimes not be clear which options to use when running a given MySQL program. (Most options are the same no matter your version of MySQL, but boolean option syntax has changed in some cases.) This problem should diminish over time as the installed base shifts toward MySQL 4 and older installations are phased out. When in doubt, invoke a program with the `--help` option to find out which option forms it supports.

Other 4.0.2-related changes in option processing include:

- Option names can be shortened to unambiguous prefixes, which can make it easier to specify options that have very long names.

- You can set program variables from the command line or in option files by treating variable names as option names. It is no longer necessary to use the `--set-variable` or `-O` options. See the "Setting Program Variables" section later in this appendix for more information.

- `mysqld` supports a `--maximum-` prefix for specifying a maximum value to which user-modifiable variables can be set. For example, the server allows users to set the sort buffer size by changing the `sort_buffer_size` variable. If you want to place a maximum
limit of 64MB on the value of this variable, start the server with a `--maximum-sort_buffer_size=64M` option.

- A `--loose-` prefix is supported to help make it easier to use differing versions of a program that may not all understand quite the same set of options. For example, servers from version 4.1 and later understand the `--old-passwords` option, but older servers do not. If you specify the option as `--loose-old-passwords`, any server from 4.0.2 on will use or ignore the option according to whether or not it understands `--old-passwords`.

Standard MySQL Program Options

Several options have a standard meaning across multiple MySQL programs. Rather than writing out their meanings repeatedly in program descriptions, they are shown here once, and the "Standard Options Supported" section for each program entry indicates which of these options a program understands. (That section lists only long-format names, but programs also understand the corresponding short-format options unless otherwise specified.)

The standard options are as follows:

- `--character-sets-dir=dir_name`

  The directory where character set files are stored.

- `--compress, -C` (*boolean*)

  Use compression for the protocol used for communication between the client and the server if the server supports it. This option is used only by client programs. It was introduced in MySQL 3.22.3.

- `--debug=debug_options, -# debug_options`

  Turn on debugging output. This option is unavailable unless MySQL was built with debugging support enabled. The `debug_options` string consists of colon-separated options. A typical value is `d:t:o,file_name`, which enables debugging, turns on function call entry and exit tracing, and sends output to the file `file_name`.

  If you expect to do much debugging, you should examine the file `dbug/dbug.c` in the MySQL source distribution for a description of all the options you can use.

- `--default-character-set=charset`

  The name of the default character set.

- `--help, -?`

  Print a help message and exit.

- `--host=host_name, -h host_name`

  The host to connect to (that is, the host where the server is running). This option is used only by client programs.

- `--password[=pass_val], -p[pass_val]`

  The password to use when connecting to the server. If `pass_val` is not specified after the option name, the program will ask you to enter one. If `pass_val` is given, it must immediately follow the option name with no space in between. (This means that the short form is given as `-ppass_val`, not as `-p pass_val`.) This option is used only by client programs.

- `--pipe, -W`

  Use a named pipe to connect to the server. This option is used only for client programs running under Windows, and only for connecting to Windows NT-based servers that support named pipes.

- `--port=port_num`, `-P port_num`

  For client programs, this is the port number to use when connecting to the server. This is used for TCP/IP connections (connections where the host is not `localhost` on UNIX or '.' on Windows). For `mysqld`, this option specifies the port on which to listen for TCP/IP connections.

- `--set-variable var=value`, `-O var=value`

  This option allows you to set values for program operating parameters. `var` is the variable name, and `value` is the value to assign to it.

  The option is unnecessary as of MySQL 4.0.2 because you can set a variable directly using just its name. The old and new syntaxes are both described in the "Setting Program Variables" section later in this appendix.

- `--silent`, `-s`

  Run in silent mode. This doesn't necessarily mean the program is completely silent, simply that it produces less output than usual. Several programs allow this option to be specified multiple times to cause the program to become increasingly silent. (This works in option files, too.)

- `--socket=file_name`, `-S file_name`

  For client programs on UNIX, this is the full pathname of the socket file to use when connecting to the server with a hostname of `localhost`. For client programs on Windows, this is the name of the named pipe to use when '.' is specified as the hostname.

- `--user=user_name`, `-u user_name`

  For client programs, this is the MySQL username to use when connecting to the server. The default if this option is not specified is your login name under UNIX and ODBC under Windows. For `mysqld`, this option indicates the name of the UNIX account to be used for running the server. For this option to be effective, the server must be started as `root` so that it can change its user ID.

- `--verbose`, `-v`

  Run in verbose mode; the program produces more output than usual. Several programs allow this option to be specified multiple times to cause the program to be increasingly verbose. (This works in option files, too.)

- `--version`, `-V`

  This option tells the program to print its version information string and exit.

Standard SSL Options

The following options are used for establishing secure connections. They are available as of MySQL 4.0.0, but only if MySQL is compiled with SSL support. See Chapter 12, "Security," for information on setting up secure connections.

- `--ssl`

  Allow SSL connections (or disallow them if `--disable-ssl` is used). `--ssl` is implied by each of the other SSL options.

- `--ssl-ca=file_name`

  The pathname to the certificate authority file.

- `--ssl-capath=dir_name`

  The pathname to a directory of trusted certificates, to be used for certificate verification.

- `--ssl-cert=file_name`

  The pathname to the certificate file.

- `--ssl-cipher=str`

  A string listing the SSL ciphers that can be used to encrypt traffic sent over the connection. The value should name one or more cipher types separated by commas.

- `--ssl-key=file_name`

  The pathname to the key file.

Setting Program Variables

Several MySQL programs have variables (operating parameters) that you can set. As of MySQL 4.0.2, you can set a variable by treating its name as an option. For example, to invoke `mysql` with the `connect_timeout` variable set to 10, use the following command:

```
% mysql --connect_timeout=10
```

This syntax also allows underscores in variable names to be given as dashes to make variable options look more like other options:

```
% mysql --connect-timeout=10
```

Prior to MySQL 4.0.2, use the `--set-variable` option to set variables (or its short-form equivalent, `-O`). To set the `connect_timeout` variable, do so like this:

```
% mysql --set-variable=connect_timeout=10
% mysql -O connect_timeout=10
```

`--set-variable` and `-O` are still supported in MySQL 4.0.2 and later, but are deprecated.

For variables that represent buffer sizes or lengths, values are in bytes if specified as a number with no suffix or can be specified with a suffix of 'K' or 'M' to indicate kilobytes or megabytes. Suffixes are not case sensitive; 'k' and 'm' are equivalent to 'K' and 'M'. From MySQL 4.0.2 on, you can also use 'G' or 'g' to indicate gigabytes.

Each program's variables are listed in the program's description in this appendix and are also displayed when you invoke the program with the `--help` option.

Option Files

Option files were introduced in MySQL 3.22.10 and are supported by most MySQL programs. They provide a means for storing program options so that you don't have to type them on the command line each time you invoke a program. You can find example option files in the `share/mysql` directory under the MySQL installation directory or in the `support-files` directory of a source distribution.

Any option specified in an option file can be overridden by specifying a different value for the option explicitly on the command line.

MySQL programs that support option files look for them in several locations; however, it is not an error for an option file to be missing. Under UNIX, the following files are checked for options, in the order shown:

Filename	Contents
`/etc/my.cnf`	Global options
`DATADIR/my.cnf`	Server-specific options
`~/.my.cnf`	User-specific options

Under Windows, the following option files are read in order:

Filename	Contents
`SYSTEMDIR\my.ini`	Global options
`C:\my.cnf`	Global options
`DATADIR\my.cnf`	Server-specific options

`DATADIR` represents the pathname to the data directory on your machine. (This is the pathname compiled into the server; it cannot be changed with the `--datadir` option.) Under Windows, `DATADIR` is `C:\mysql\data`. `SYSTEMDIR` represents the pathname to the Windows system directory (usually something like `C:\Windows` or `C:\WinNT`).

Global option files are used by all MySQL programs that are option file-aware. An option file in a server's data directory is used only by programs from a distribution that was built with that directory as the default data directory location. User-specific files are used by programs run by that user.

Windows users should be especially careful about the following issues when using option files:

- Windows pathnames often contain backslash ('`\`') characters, which are treated as escape characters by MySQL. For options that take pathname values, backslashes should be written as slashes ('`/`') or as doubled backslashes ('`\\`').

- Windows likes to hide filename extensions. If you create an option file named `my.cnf`, Windows may display it as just `my`. Should you observe that and attempt to change the name to `my.cnf` in Windows Explorer, you may find that the option file no longer works. The reason is that you will actually have renamed the file from `my.cnf` to `my.cnf.cnf`!

- Option files must be plain text files. You can create an option file in a word processor, but if you do, be sure to save it in text format, not in the word processor's native document format.

Four options related to option-file processing are standard across most MySQL programs and have the following meanings; if you use any of them, it must be the first option on the command line.

- `--defaults-extra-file=file_name`

  Read options from this file in addition to the regular option files. It is read after the global and server-specific option files and before the user-specific file. This option was introduced in MySQL 3.23.26, except for `safe_mysqld` (3.23.27) and `mysql_install_db` (3.23.29).

- `--defaults-file=file_name`

  Read options from this file only. Normally, programs search for option files in several locations, but if `--defaults-file` is specified, only the named file is read. This option was introduced in MySQL 3.22.23.

- `--no-defaults`

  Suppress the use of any option files. In addition, this option causes other option-file related options such as `--defaults-file` to be unrecognized.

- `--print-defaults`

   Print the option values that will be used if you invoke the program with no options on the command line. This shows the values that will be picked up from option files (and environment variables). `--print-defaults` is useful for verifying proper setup of an option file. It's also useful if MySQL programs seem to be using options that you never specified. You can use `--print-defaults` to determine if options are being picked up from some option file.

If you invoke a program with the `--help` option, one part of the help message will show the option files that the program normally attempts to read. (The set of files read will be affected by use of the `--defaults-file`, `--defaults-extra-file`, or `--no-defaults` options.)

Options are specified in groups. The following is an example:

```
[client]
user=sampadm
password=secret

[mysql]
no-auto-rehash

[mysqlshow]
status
```

Group names are given inside square brackets. The special group name `[client]` allows you to specify options that apply to all client programs. Otherwise, group names usually correspond to a specific program name. In the preceding example, `[mysql]` indicates the option group for the `mysql` client, and `[mysqlshow]` indicates the option group for `mysqlshow`. The standard MySQL client programs look at both the `[client]` group and the group with the same name as the client name. For example, `mysql` looks at the `[client]` and `[mysql]` groups, and `mysqlshow` looks at the `[client]` and `[mysqlshow]` groups.

Any options following a group name are associated with that group. An option file can contain any number of groups, and groups listed later take precedence over groups listed earlier. If a given option is found multiple times in the groups a program looks at, the value listed last is used.

Each option should be specified on a separate line. The first word on the line is the option name, which must be specified in long-name format without the leading dashes. (For example, to specify compression on the command line, you can use either `-C` or `--compress`, but in an option file, you can only use compress.) Any long-format option supported by a program can be listed in an option file. If the option requires a value, list the name and value separated by an '=' character.

Consider the following command line:

```
% mysql --compress --user=sampadm --set-variable=max_allowed_packet=16M
```

To specify the same information in an option file using the [mysql] group, you'd do so as follows:

```
[mysql]
compress
user=sampadm
set-variable=max_allowed_packet=16M
```

Observe that in an option file, set-variable is followed by a '=' character in addition to the '=' character between the variable name and its value. (On a command line, you can actually use either a '=' character or a space.)

As of MySQL 4.0.2, which allows variable names to be treated directly as options, you can use:

```
% mysql --compress --user=sampadm --max_allowed_packet=16M
```

or:

```
[mysql]
compress
user=sampadm
max_allowed_packet=16M
```

Option file lines that are empty or that begin with '#' or ';' are treated as comments and ignored. Leading spaces in option group lines are ignored.

Certain escape sequences can be used in option file values to indicate special characters:

Sequence	Meaning
\b	Backspace
\n	Newline (linefeed)
\r	Carriage return
\s	Space
\t	Tab
\\	Backslash

Be careful not to put options in the [client] group that really are understood only by a single client. For example, if you put the mysql-specific skip-line-numbers option in the [client] group, you will suddenly find that other client programs, such as `mysqlimport`, no longer work. (You'll get an error message, followed by the help message.) Move `skip-line-numbers` to the `[mysql]` group instead and you will be all right.

Options understood by all or most MySQL programs that read the `[client]` group are as follows:

```
character-sets-dir=charset_directory_path
compress
connect-timeout=seconds
database=db_name
debug
default-character-set=charset_name
disable-local-infile
host=host_name
init-command=query
interactive-timeout=seconds
local-infile
password=your_pass
pipe
port=port_num
return-found-rows
socket=socket_name
ssl-ca=ssl_certificate_authority file
ssl-capath=ssl_certificate_authority_directory_path
ssl-cert=ssl_certificate_file
ssl-key=ssl_key_file
timeout=seconds
user=user_name
```

Option file support was introduced in MySQL 3.22.10, but some of the allowable option values were introduced later:

- `debug` was introduced in MySQL 3.22.11.

- `return-found-rows` was introduced in MySQL 3.22.15.

- `character-sets-dir` and `default-character-set` were introduced in MySQL 3.23.14.

- `interactive-timeout` was introduced in MySQL 3.23.28.

- `connect-timeout` was introduced in MySQL 3.23.49. `connect-timeout` is a synonym for `timeout`, which now is deprecated.

- `disable-local-infile` and `local-infile` were introduced in MySQL 3.23.49.

- `ssl-ca`, `ssl-capath`, `ssl-cert`, and `ssl-key` were introduced in MySQL 4.0.0.

Using my_print_defaults to Check Options

The `my_print_defaults` utility is useful for determining what options a given program will find in option files. It reads option files and shows which options are found there for one or more option groups. For example, the `mysql` program uses options from the `[client]` and `[mysql]` option groups. To find out which options in your option files apply to `mysql`, invoke `my_print_defaults` like this:

```
% my_print_defaults client mysql
```

Similarly, the server `mysqld` uses options in the `[mysqld]` and `[server]` groups. To find out what options are present in option files, use the following command:

```
% my_print_defaults mysqld server
```

`my_print_defaults` is available as of MySQL 3.23.19 under UNIX and 4.0.4 under Windows.

Keep User-Specific Option Files Private

Under UNIX, make sure that each user-specific option file is owned by the proper user and that the mode is set to 600 or 400 so that other users cannot read it. You don't want MySQL username and password information exposed to anyone other than the user to whom the file applies. You can make your own option file accessible only to yourself by issuing either of the following commands in your home directory:

```
% chmod 600 .my.cnf
% chmod go-rwx .my.cnf
```

Environment Variables

MySQL programs look at the values of the several environment variables to obtain option settings. Environment variables have low precedence; options specified using environment variables can be overridden by options specified in an option file or on the command line.

MySQL programs check the following environment variables:

- MYSQL_DEBUG

  The options to use when debugging. This variable has no effect unless MySQL was built with debugging support enabled. Setting MYSQL_DEBUG is like using the --debug option.

- MYSQL_PWD

  The password to use when establishing connections to the MySQL server. Setting MYSQL_PWD is like using the --password option.

  Using the MYSQL_PWD variable to store a password constitutes a security risk because other users on your system can easily discover its value. For example, the ps utility will show environment variable settings for other users.

- MYSQL_TCP_PORT

  For clients, this is the port number to use when establishing a TCP/IP connection to the server. For mysqld, this is the port on which to listen for TCP/IP connections. Setting MYSQL_TCP_PORT is like using the --port option.

- MYSQL_UNIX_PORT

  For clients, this is the pathname of the socket file to use when establishing UNIX domain socket connections to the server running on localhost. For mysqld, this is the socket on which to listen for local connections. Setting MYSQL_UNIX_PORT is like using the --socket option.

- TMPDIR

  The pathname of the directory in which to create temporary files. Setting this variable is like using the --tmpdir option.

- USER

  This is the MySQL username to use when connecting to the server. This variable is used only by client programs running under Windows; setting it is like using the --user option.

The mysql client checks the value of three additional environment variables:

- MYSQL_HISTFILE

  The name of the file to use for storing command-line history. The default value if this variable is not set is $HOME/.mysql_history, where $HOME is the location of your home directory.

- MYSQL_HOST

  The host to connect to when establishing a connection to the server. Setting this variable is like using the --host option.

- MYSQL_PS1

  The string to use instead of mysql> for the primary prompt. The string may contain the special sequences described in the entry for mysql.

libmysqld

libmysqld is the MySQL embedded server. It is a library that you link into a host program to produce a standalone application that includes a MySQL server. libmysqld does not include support for several features that are part of mysqld. For example, ISAM support is disabled to save space, SSL support is not included because communication with the host program does not use networking, and the server neither connects to nor can be connected to by other programs. The latter restriction rules out using an embedded server for replication.

However, because the embedded server requires no networking capabilities, and because it need not produce any output files at all, one use for libmysqld is to create applications that are suitable for execution directly from read-only media, such as CD-ROM, and by machines that are used in standalone fashion (for example, to run an information kiosk).

libmysqld does not read options from the command line itself, but you can arrange to pass it options and it will interpret them like any other MySQL program. For the most part, libmysqld understands the same options as mysqld; consult the entry for that program for more information. Options related to server functions that libmysqld does not support (for example, replication options) are ignored.

For more information about using the embedded server, see:

- Chapter 6, "The MySQL C API," describes how to write host programs that include the embedded server.
- Chapter 11, "General MySQL Administration," discusses administrative concerns common to all servers.
- Appendix F, "C API Reference" describes the C API functions that are specific to the embedded server.

myisamchk and isamchk

These utilities allow you to check and repair damaged tables, display table information, perform index key value distribution analysis, and disable or enable indexes. Chapter 4, "Query Optimization," provides more information on key analysis and index disabling. Chapter 13, "Database Backups, Maintenance, and Repair," provides more information on table checking and repair.

myisamchk is used for tables that use the MyISAM storage format. These tables have data and index filenames with .MYD and .MYI suffixes. Use isamchk for tables that use the older ISAM storage format. These have data and index filenames with .ISD and .ISM suffixes. If you tell either utility to operate on a table of the wrong type, it will print a warning message and ignore the table.

Do not allow the MySQL server to access a table while you're performing checking or repair operations. Chapter 13 discusses how to prevent the server from using a table while myisamchk or isamchk are working on it.

Usage

```
myisamchk [options] tbl_name[.MYI] ...
isamchk [options] tbl_name[.ISM] ...
```

With no options, these utilities check the named tables for errors. Otherwise, the tables are processed according to the meaning of the specified options. If you perform an operation that may modify a table, it's a good idea to make a copy of it first.

A *tbl_name* argument can be either the name of a table or the name of the index file for the table. (Index files have an extension of .MYI for MyISAM tables or .ISM for ISAM tables.) Using index filenames is convenient because you can use filename wildcards to operate on all tables for a given storage type in a single command. For example, you can check all the MyISAM and ISAM tables in a directory as follows:

```
% myisamchk *.MYI
% isamchk *.ISM
```

These utilities make no assumptions about where table files are located. You must specify the pathname to the files you want to use if they are not in the current directory. Because table files are not assumed to be located under the server's data directory, you can copy table files into another directory and operate on the copies rather than the originals.

Some of the options refer to index numbers. Indexes are numbered beginning with 1. You can issue a SHOW INDEX query or use the mysqlshow --keys command to find out the index numbering for a particular table. The Key_name column lists indexes in the same order that myisamchk and isamchk see them.

Standard Options Supported by isamchk and myisamchk

--character-sets-dir	--help	--verbose
--debug	--set-variable	--version
--default-character-set	--silent	

--default-character-set is available only for isamchk. The --silent option means that only error messages are printed. The --verbose option prints more information when given with the --description or --extend-check options for either program, or when given with the --check option for myisamchk. The --silent and --verbose options can be specified multiple times for increased effect.

Options Common to `myisamchk` and `isamchk`

`isamchk` and `myisamchk` have many options in common:

- `--analyze, -a`

  Perform key distribution analysis. This can help the server perform index-based lookups and joins more quickly. You can obtain information about key distribution after the analysis by running `isamchk` or `myisamchk` again with the `--description` and `--verbose` options.

- `--block-search=n, -b n`

  Print out the start of the table row that contains a block starting at block *n*. This is for debugging only.

- `--description, -d`

  Prints descriptive information about the table.

- `--extend-check, -e`

  Perform an extended table check. It should rarely be necessary to use this option because `myisamchk` and `isamchk` normally find any errors with one of the less extensive checking modes.

- `--force, -f`

  Force a table to be checked or repaired even if a temporary file for the table already exists. Normally, `myisamchk` and `isamchk` simply exit after printing an error message if they find a file named *tbl_name*.TMD because that may indicate another instance of the program is already running. However, the file may also exist if you killed a previous invocation of the program while it was running, in which case the file can be removed safely. If you know that to be the case, use `--force` to tell either utility to run even if the temporary file exists. (Alternatively, you can remove the temporary file manually.)

  If you use `--force` when checking tables, the program automatically restarts with `--recover` for any table found to have problems. In addition, as of MySQL 4.0.2, `myisamchk` will update the table state the same way the `--update-state` option does.

- `--information, -i`

  Print statistical information about table contents.

- `--keys-used=n, -k n`

  Used with `--recover`. For `isamchk`, tells MySQL to update only the first *n* indexes. In other words, this de-activates indexes numbered higher than *n*. For myisamchk, *n* is a bitmask that indicates which indexes to use. The first index is bit zero. In either case, specifying a value of 0 turns off all indexes. This can be used to improve the performance of INSERT, DELETE, and UPDATE operations. Turning the indexes back on restores normal indexing behavior. (For isamchk, specify an index number equal to the highest-numbered index; for myisamchk, specify a bitmask that includes a bit for each index.)

- --no-symlinks, -l

If a table argument is a symbolic link, normally the table the symlink points to is repaired. When this option is specified, symlinks are not followed. Instead the symlink is replaced with the new (repaired) version of the file.

For myisamchk, this option is unavailable as of MySQL 4 because it will not remove symlinks during repair operations.

- --quick, -q *(boolean)*

This option is used in conjunction with --recover for faster repair than when --recover is used alone. The data file is not touched when both options are given. To force the program to modify the data file if duplicate key values are found, specify the --quick option twice.

- --recover, -r

Perform a normal recovery operation. This can fix most problems except the occurrence of duplicate values in an index that should be unique.

- --safe-recover, -o

Use a recovery method that is slower than the --recover method, but that can fix a few problems that --recover cannot. --safe-recover also uses less disk space than --recover.

- --sort-index, -S

Sort the index blocks to speed up sequential block reads for subsequent retrievals.

- --sort-records=*n*, -R *n*

Sort data records according to the order in which records are listed in index *n*. Subsequent retrievals based on the given index should be faster. The first time you perform this operation on a table, it may be very slow because your records will be unordered. If you have MySQL 3.23.28 or later, ALTER TABLE ... ORDER BY accomplishes the same thing as --sort-records, and normally will be faster.

- --unpack, -u

  Unpack a packed file. myisamchk can unpack MyISAM files packed with myisampack; isamchk can unpack ISAM files packed with pack_isam. This option can be used to convert a compressed read-only table to modifiable form. It cannot be used with --quick or with --sort-records.

- --wait, -w

  If a table is locked, wait until it is available. Without --wait, the program will wait 10 seconds for a lock and then print an error message if no lock can be obtained.

Options Specific to `myisamchk`

Although there are no options specific to isamchk, there are several specific to myisamchk.

- --backup, -B

  For options that modify the data (.MYD) file, make a backup using a file-name of the form *tbl_name-time*.BAK. *time* is a number representing a timestamp. The backup file is written to the directory where the table files are located. This option was introduced in MySQL 3.23.25, the same version in which the BACKUP TABLE statement appeared, but the option does not have the same function as that statement.

- --check, -c

  Check tables for errors. This is the default action if no options are specified.

- --check-only-changed, -C

  Check tables only if they have not been changed since the last check. This option was introduced in MySQL 3.23.22. Prior to that, use --fast instead.

- --correct-checksum

  For tables created with the CHECKSUM = 1 option, ensure that the checksum information in the table is correct. This option was introduced in MySQL 4.0.0.

- --data-file-length=*n*, -D *n*

  The maximum length to which the data file should be allowed to grow when rebuilding a data file that has become full. (This occurs when a file reaches the size limit imposed by MySQL or by the file size constraints of your operating system. It also occurs when the number of rows reaches the limit imposed by internal table data structures.) The value is specified in bytes. This option is effective only when used with `--recover` or `--safe-recover`.

- `--fast, -F`

  Check tables only if they have not been closed properly. Prior to MySQL 3.23.22, this option acts like `--check-only-changed`; that is, tables are checked only if they have been modified since they were last checked.

- `--medium-check, -m`

  Check a table using a method that is faster than `--extend-check`, but slightly less thorough. (The `myisamchk` help message says that this method finds "only" 99.99% of all errors.) This checking mode should be sufficient for most circumstances. Medium check mode works by calculating CRC values for the keys in the index and comparing them with the CRC values calculated from the indexed columns in the data file.

- `--parallel-recover, -p`

  Perform recovery as for `--recover`, but rebuild the indexes in parallel using multiple threads. This can be faster than a non-parallel rebuild, but this option should be considered experimental. This option was introduced in MySQL 4.0.2.

- `--read-only, -T`

  Do not mark the table as having been checked.

- `--set-auto-increment[=n], -A[n]`

  Set the AUTO_INCREMENT counter so that subsequent sequence values start at n (or at a higher value if the table already contains records with AUTO_INCREMENT values as large as n). If no value is specified, this option sets the next AUTO_INCREMENT value to one greater than the current maximum value stored in the table.

  If n is specified after `-A`, there must be no intervening space or the value will not be interpreted correctly.

- `--set-character-set=charset`

  When rebuilding indexes, use the collating order of the given character set to determine the order of index entries. This is useful for reordering indexes of MyISAM tables after changing the server's default character set and normally is used in conjunction with `--recover` and `--quick`. This option was introduced in MySQL 3.23.14.

- `--sort-recover, -n`

  Force sorted recovery even if the temporary file necessary to perform the operation would become quite large. This option was introduced in MySQL 3.23.22.

- `--start-check-pos=n`

  Begin reading the data file at position *n*. This option was introduced in MySQL 3.23.25. It is used only for debugging.

- `--tmpdir=dir_name, -t dir_name`

  The pathname of the directory to use for temporary files. The default is the value of the `TMPDIR` environment variable or `/tmp` if that variable is not set. As of MySQL 4.1, the option value can be given as a list of directories to be used in round-robin fashion. Under UNIX, separate directory names by colons; under Windows, separate them by semicolons.

- `--update-state, -U`

  Update the internal flag that is stored in the table to indicate its state. Tables that are okay are marked as such, and tables for which an error occurs are marked as in need of repair. Using this option makes subsequent invocations of `myisamchk` with the `--check-only-changed` option more efficient for tables that are okay. This option was introduced in MySQL 3.23.14.

Variables for `myisamchk` and `isamchk`

The following `isamchk` and `myisamchk` variables can be set using the instructions in the "Setting Program Variables" section earlier in this appendix.

- `key_buffer_size`

  The size of the buffer used for index blocks.

- `read_buffer_size`

  The read buffer size.

- `write_buffer_size`

  The write buffer size.

- `sort_buffer_size`

  The size of the buffer used for key value sorting operations. (This is used for `--recover`, but not for `--safe-recover`.)

- `sort_key_blocks`

  This variable is related to the depth of the B-tree structure used for the index. You should not need to change it.

- decode_bits

  The number of bits to use when decoding compressed tables. Larger values may result in faster operation but will require more memory. Generally, the default value is sufficient.

The following variables can be set for `myisamchk` only. They were added in MySQL 4.0.0.

- ft_max_word_len

  The maximum length of words that can be included in a FULLTEXT index. Longer words are ignored.

- ft_max_word_len_for_sort

  The length of words that are considered short enough to be inserted into a FULLTEXT index using a more efficient optimized algorithm. Longer words are inserted more slowly.

- ft_min_word_len

  The minimum length of words that can be included in a FULLTEXT index. Shorter words are ignored.

- myisam_block_size

  The block size used for index blocks.

myisampack and pack_isam

The `myisampack` and `pack_isam` utilities produce compressed, read-only tables. They achieve typical storage requirement reductions of 40 to 70 percent while maintaining fast record access. `myisampack` packs MyISAM tables and works with all column types. `pack_isam` packs ISAM tables and works only with tables that contain no BLOB or TEXT columns.

`myisampack` and `pack_isam` are generally available as of MySQL 3.23.19, the first version released under the GNU General Public License (GPL). Prior to that, they are available to support customers only, so it's to your advantage to use a version of MySQL at least as recent as 3.23.19.

No special version of MySQL is needed to read tables that have been packed with these utilities. This makes them especially applicable for applications for which you want to distribute a table containing archival or encyclopedic information that is read-only and need not be updated. For example, if you are setting up a CD-ROM for an application that uses the embedded server, you'll be able to pack more data on the disk by using compressed MyISAM tables.

If you want to convert a packed file back to unpacked and modifiable form, you can do so by using `myisamchk --unpack` (for MyISAM tables) or `isam-chk --unpack` (for ISAM tables).

`myisampack` and `pack_isam` pack data files, but do not touch index files. You must update the indexes by running `myisamchk --recover --quick` after running `myisampack` or `isamchk --recover --quick` after running `pack_isam`.

Usage

```
myisampack [options] tbl_name ...
pack_isam [options] tbl_name ...
```

A `tbl_name` argument can be either the name of a table or the name of the index file for the table (a `.MYI` file for MyISAM tables or an `.ISM` file for ISAM tables). The name must include the pathname to the directory in which the table is located if you are not in that directory.

Standard Options Supported by `myisampack` and `pack_isam`

```
--character-sets-dir    --help          --verbose
--debug                 --silent        --version
```

`--character-sets-dir` is supported only by `myisampack`, and only as of MySQL 3.23.33.

Options Common to `myisampack` and `pack_isam`

- `--backup, -b`

  Make a backup of the data file for each `tbl_name` argument as `tbl_name.OLD` before packing it.

- `--force, -f`

  Force a table to be packed even if the resulting packed file is larger than the original or if a temporary file for the table already exists. Normally, `myisampack` or `pack_isam` simply exit after printing an error message if they find a file named `tbl_name.TMD`, because that may indicate another instance of the program is already running. However, the file may also exist if you killed a previous invocation of the program while it was running, in which case the file can be removed safely. If you know that to be the case, use `--force` to tell either utility to pack the table even if the temporary file exists. (Alternatively, you can remove the temporary file manually.)

- `--join=join_tbl, -j join_tbl`

  Join (merges) all the tables named on the command line into a single packed table named *join_tbl*. All the tables to be merged must have the same structure. (Column names, types, and indexes must be identical.)

- `--test, -t`

  Run in test mode. A packing test is run, and information is printed about the results you would obtain if you actually packed the table.

- `--tmpdir=dir_name, -T dir_name`

  The pathname of the directory to use for temporary files.

- `--wait, -w` (*boolean*)

  Wait and retry if a table is in use. (You should not pack a table if it might be updated while you're packing it.)

Options Specific to `pack_isam`

Although there are no options specific to `myisampack`, there is one specific to `pack_isam`.

- `--packlength=n, -p n`

  Use a record length storage size of *n* bytes, where *n* is an integer from 1 to 3. `pack_isam` automatically attempts to determine the number of bytes needed to record the length of each record in the packed table. In some cases, it may determine that a smaller length could have been used. If so, `pack_isam` issues a message to that effect. You can run `pack_isam` again and explicitly specify the smaller length with a `--packlength` option to achieve some additional space savings.

`mysql`

The `mysql` client is an interactive program that allows you to connect to the server, issue queries, and view the results. `mysql` can also be used in batch mode to execute queries that are stored in a file if you redirect the input of the command to read from that file—for example:

```
% mysql -u sampadm -p -h cobra.snake.net sampdb < my_query_file
```

In interactive mode, when `mysql` starts up, it displays a `mysql>` prompt to indicate that it's waiting for input. To issue a query, type it in (using multiple lines if necessary) and then indicate the end of the query by typing '`;`' (semicolon) or `\g`. `mysql` sends the query to the server, displays the results, and then prints another prompt to indicate that it's ready for another query. \G also terminates a query but causes query results to be displayed vertically, that is, with one column value per output line.

mysql varies the prompt to indicate what it's waiting for as you enter input lines. The mysql> prompt is the primary prompt, displayed at the beginning of each query. The other prompts are secondary prompts, displayed to obtain additional lines for the current query.

Prompt	Meaning
mysql>	Waiting for the first line of a new query
->	Waiting for the next line of the current query
'>	Waiting for completion of a single-quoted string in current query
">	Waiting for completion of a double-quoted string in current query

The '> and "> prompts indicate that you've begun a single-quoted or double-quoted string on a previous line and have not yet entered the terminating quote. Usually, this happens when you've forgotten to terminate a string. If that's the case, to escape from string-collection mode, enter the appropriate matching quote that is indicated by the prompt, followed by \c to cancel the current query.

When mysql is used in interactive mode, it saves queries in a history file. This file is $HOME/.mysql_history by default or can be specified explicitly by setting the MYSQL_HISTORY environment variable. Queries can be recalled from the command history and re-issued, either with or without further editing. The following list shows some of these editing commands:

Key Sequence	Meaning
Up arrow or Ctrl-P	Recall previous line
Down arrow or Ctrl-N	Recall next line
Left arrow or Ctrl-B	Move cursor left (backward)
Right arrow or Ctrl-F	Move cursor right (forward)
Escape B	Move backward one word
Escape F	Move forward one word
Ctrl-A	Move cursor to beginning of line
Ctrl-E	Move cursor to end of line
Ctrl-D	Delete character under cursor
Delete	Delete character to left of cursor
Escape D	Delete word
Escape Backspace	Delete word to left of cursor
Ctrl-K	Erase everything from cursor to end of line
Ctrl-_	Undo last change; may be repeated

Some options suppress use of the history file. Generally, these are options that indicate non-interactive use of `mysql`, such as `--batch`, `--html`, and `--quick`.

On Windows, command-line editing in `mysql` might not work. In this case, you can try the `mysqlc` client, which is similar to `mysql` but has command editing compiled in specially. (That's an advantage, but the corresponding disadvantage is that `mysqlc` hasn't been updated for a while, so it doesn't understand newer options or internal commands.)

`mysqlc` requires the `cygwinb19.dll` library. If that library is not already installed in the same directory where `mysqlc` is installed (the `bin` directory of your MySQL distribution), look in the distribution's `lib` directory and copy the library to the MySQL `bin` directory or to your Windows system directory.

Usage

```
mysql [options] [db_name]
```

If you specify a *db_name* argument, that database becomes the current (default) database for your session. If you specify no *db_name* argument, `mysql` starts with no current database and you'll need to either qualify all table references with a database name or issue a USE *db_name* statement to specify a default database.

Standard Options Supported by `mysql`

`--character-sets-dir`	`--host`	`--silent`
`--compress`	`--password`	`--socket`
`--debug`	`--pipe`	`--user`
`--default-character-set`	`--port`	`--verbose`
`--help`	`--set-variable`	`--version`

`--character-sets-dir` and `--default-character-set` can be used as of MySQL 3.23.15. As of MySQL 4, `mysql` also supports the standard SSL options.

`--silent` and `--verbose` can be given multiple times for increased effect.

Options Specific to `mysql`

- `--auto-rehash`   (*boolean*)

  When `mysql` starts up, it can hash database, table, and column names to construct a data structure that allows for fast completion of names. (You can type the initial part of a name when entering a query and then press

Tab; mysql will complete the name unless it's ambiguous.) Name hashing is on by default; --skip-auto-hash suppresses hash calculation, which allows mysql to start up more quickly, particularly if you have many tables.

If hashing has been disabled and you want to use name completion after starting mysql, you can use the rehash command at the mysql> prompt. This option was introduced in MySQL 4.0.2. Prior to 4.0.2, use --no-auto-rehash to disable name hashing.

- --batch, -B

  Run in batch mode. Query results are displayed in tab-delimited format (each row on a separate line with tabs between column values). This is especially convenient for generating output that you want to import into another program, such as a spreadsheet. Query results include an initial row of column headings by default. To suppress these headings, use the --skip-column-names option.

- --column-names *(boolean)*

  Display column names with query results. This option was introduced in MySQL 4.0.2.

- --database=*db_name*, -D *db_name*

  The default database. This option was introduced in MySQL 3.22.29.

- --debug-info, -T *(boolean)*

  Print debugging information when the program terminates.

- --execute=*query*, -e *query*

  Execute the query and quit. You should enclose the query in quotes to prevent your shell from interpreting it as multiple command-line arguments. Multiple queries can be given; separate them by semicolons in the *query* string.

- --force, -f *(boolean)*

  Normally when mysql reads queries from a file, it exits if an error occurs. This option causes mysql to keep processing queries, regardless of errors.

- --html, -H *(boolean)*

  Produce HTML output. This option became functional in MySQL 3.22.26.

- `--i-am-a-dummy`   *(boolean)*

  This option is synonymous with `--safe-updates`. It was introduced in MySQL 3.23.11.

- `--ignore-spaces, -i`

  Cause the server to ignore spaces between function names and the '(' character that introduces the argument list. Normally, function names must be followed immediately by the parenthesis with no intervening spaces. This option causes function names to be treated as reserved words. This option was introduced in MySQL 3.22.21.

- `--line-numbers`   *(boolean)*

  Display line numbers in error messages. This is the default; to suppress line numbers, use `--skip-line-numbers`. This option was introduced in MySQL 4.0.2. From 3.22.5 to 4.0.2, line numbers can be disabled with either `--skip-line-numbers` or `-L`.

- `--local-infile`   *(boolean)*

  Allow or disallow LOAD DATA LOCAL. As of MySQL 3.23.49, LOCAL capabilities may be present but disabled by default. If LOAD DATA LOCAL results in an error, try again after invoking `mysql` with the `--local-infile` option. This option can also be used to disable LOCAL if it is enabled: Use `--disable-local-infile` as of MySQL 4.0.2, `--local-infile=0` before that.

  This option has no effect if the server has been configured to disallow use of LOCAL.

- `--named-commands, -G`   *(boolean)*

  Allow long forms of `mysql`'s internal commands at the beginning of any input line. If this capability is disabled with `--disable-named-commands`, long commands are allowed only at the primary prompt and disallowed at the secondary prompts. (That is, they are disallowed on second and subsequent lines of a multiple-line statements.)

  This option has a complicated history. Named commands are enabled by default up through MySQL 3.23.22 and disabled by default thereafter. They can be disabled using `--no-named-commands` from MySQL 3.23.11 to 3.23.22, enabled with `--enable-named-commands` from 3.23.23 to 4.0.1, and controlled either way with the boolean option `--named-commands` thereafter.

- `--no-auto-rehash, -A`

  See the description for `--auto-rehash`; `--no-auto-rehash` is depre-cated as of MySQL 4.0.2.

- `--no-beep, -b` (*boolean*)

  Don't emit a beep when an error occurs.

  This option was introduced in MySQL 4.0.2.

- `--no-named-commands, -g`

  See the description for `--named-commands`; `--no-named-commands` is deprecated as of MySQL 4.0.2.

- `--no-pager`

  See the description for `--pager`; this option was introduced in MySQL 3.23.28 but is deprecated in favor of `--disable-pager` as of MySQL 4.0.2.

- `--no-tee`

  See the description for `--tee`; this option was introduced in MySQL 3.23.28 but is deprecated in favor of `--disable-tee` as of MySQL 4.0.2.

- `--one-database, -o`

  This option is used when updating databases from the contents of an update log file. It tells `mysql` to update only the default database (the database named on the command line). Updates to other databases are ignored. If no database is named on the command line, no updates are performed.

- `--pager[=program]`

  Use a paging program (for example, `/bin/more` or `/bin/less`) to display long query results one page at a time. If *program* is missing, the paging program is determined from the value of the `PAGER` environ-ment variable. Output paging is unavailable in batch mode, and does not work under Windows. Paging can be disabled with `--disable-pager`.

  `--pager` was introduced in MySQL 3.23.28. Prior to 4.0.2, disable pag-ing with `--no-pager` rather than `--disable-pager`.

- `--prompt=str`

  Change the primary prompt from `mysql>` to the string defined by `str`. The string can contain special sequences, as described in the "`mysql` Prompt Definition Sequences" section" later in this appendix. This option was introduced in MySQL 4.0.2.

- `--quick, -q`

  Normally, `mysql` retrieves the entire result of a query from the server before displaying it. This option causes each row to be displayed as it is retrieved, which uses much less memory and can allow some large queries to be performed successfully that would fail otherwise. However, this option should not be specified for interactive use; if the user pauses the output or suspends `mysql`, the server continues to wait, which can interfere with other clients.

- `--raw, -r`   (*boolean*)

  Write column values without escaping any special characters. This option is used in conjunction with the `--batch` option.

- `--safe-updates, -U`   (*boolean*)

  This option places some limits on what you can do and can be beneficial for new MySQL users. Updates (statements that modify data) are allowed only if the records to be modified are identified by key values or if a `LIMIT` clause is used. This helps prevent queries that mistakenly change or wipe out all or large parts of a table. In addition, result sets produced by non-join and join retrievals are limited to one thousand and one million rows, respectively. These limits can be changed by setting the `select_limit` and `max_join_size` variables. This option was introduced in MySQL 3.23.11.

- `--skip-column-names, -N`

  Suppress display of column names as column headers in query results. You can also achieve this effect by specifying the `--silent` option twice. This option was introduced in MySQL 3.22.20. The `-N` form is deprecated as of MySQL 4.0.2. See the description for `--column-names`.

- `--skip-line-numbers, -L`

  Suppress line numbers in error messages. This option was introduced in MySQL 3.22.5. The `-L` form is deprecated as of MySQL 4.0.2. See the description for `--line-numbers`.

- `--table, -t`   (*boolean*)

  Produce output in tabular format with values in each row delimited by bars and lined up vertically. This is the default output format when `mysql` is not run in batch mode.

- `--tee=file_name`

  Append a copy of all output to the named file. Output copying can be disabled with `--disable-tee`. This option does not work in batch mode. It was introduced in MySQL 3.23.28. Prior to 4.0.2, disable the tee file with `--no-tee` rather than `--disable-tee`.

- `--unbuffered, -n` (*boolean*)

  Flush the buffer used for communication with the server after each query.

- `--vertical, -E`

  Print query results vertically—that is, with each row of a query result displayed as a set of output lines, one column per line. (Each line consists of a column name and value.) The display for each row is preceded by a line indicating the row number within the result set. Vertical display format can be useful when a query produces very long lines.

  If this option is not specified, you can turn on vertical display format for individual queries by terminating them with `\G` rather than with ';' or `\g`.

  This option was introduced in MySQL 3.22.5.

- `--wait, -w`

  If a connection to the server cannot be established, wait and retry.

- `--xml, -X` (*boolean*)

  Produce XML output. This option was introduced in MySQL 4.0.0.

Variables for `mysql`

The following `mysql` variables can be set using the instructions in the "Setting Program Variables" section earlier in this appendix.

- `connect_timeout`

  The number of seconds to wait before timing out when attempting to connect to the server. This variable was introduced in MySQL 3.23.28.

- `max_allowed_packet`

  The maximum size of the buffer used for communication between the server and the client.

- `max_join_size`

  Limits the number of rows returned by SELECT statements that involve joins if the `--safe-updates` option is given. This variable was introduced in MySQL 3.23.11.

- net_buffer_length

    The initial size of the buffer used for communication between the server and the client. This buffer can be expanded up to max_allowed_packet bytes long.

- select_limit

    Limits the number of rows returned by SELECT statements if the --safe-updates option is given. This variable was introduced in MySQL 3.23.11.

mysql Commands

In addition to allowing you to send SQL statements to the MySQL server, mysql understands several of its own internal commands. Each command must be given on a single line; a semicolon at the end of the line is unnecessary but allowed. Most of the commands have a long form, consisting of a word, and a short form, consisting of a backslash followed by a single letter. Commands in long form are not case sensitive. Commands in short form must be specified using the lettercase shown in the following list.

Note that if you have disabled named commands (for example, with the --disable-named-commands option), long command names are recognized only at the primary mysql> prompt.

- clear, \c

    Clear (cancel) the current query. The current query is the query that you are in the process of typing; this command does not cancel a query that has already been sent to the server and for which mysql is displaying output.

- connect [*db_name* [*host_name*]],
    \r [*db_name* [*host_name*]]

    Connect (or reconnect) to the given database on the given host. If the database name or hostname is missing, the most recently used values from the current mysql session are used.

- edit, \e

    Edit the current query. mysql attempts to determine what editor to use by examining the EDITOR and VISUAL environment variables. If neither variable is set, mysql uses vi. This option is unavailable under Windows.

- ego, \G

  Send the current query to the server and display the result vertically. This command was introduced in MySQL 3.22.11.

- exit

  Same as quit.

- go, \g, ;

  Send the current query to the server and display the result.

- help, \h, ?

  Display a help message describing the available mysql commands.

- nopager, \n

  Disable the pager and send output to the standard output. This command was introduced in MySQL 3.23.28. It is unavailable under Windows.

- notee, \t

  Stop writing to the tee file. This command was introduced in MySQL 3.23.28.

- pager [program], \P [program]

  Send output through the paging program specified by program or through the program specified in the PAGER environment variable. This command was introduced in MySQL 3.23.28. It is unavailable under Windows.

- print, \p

  Print the current query (the text of the query itself, not the results obtained by executing the query).

- prompt arguments, \R arguments

  Redefine the primary mysql prompt. Everything following the first space after the prompt keyword becomes part of the prompt string, including other spaces. The string can contain special sequences, as described in the "mysql Prompt Definition Sequences" section later in this appendix. To revert the prompt to the default, specify prompt or \R with no argument. This command was introduced in MySQL 4.0.2.

- quit, \q

  Quit mysql.

- rehash, \#

  Recalculate the information needed for database, table, and column name completion. See the description for the --auto-rehash option.

- source *file_name*, \. *file_name*

  Read and execute the queries contained in the named file. For Windows filenames that include backslash ('\') pathname separators, specify them using slash ('/') instead. This command was introduced in MySQL 3.23.9.

- status, \s

  Retrieve and display status information from the server. This is useful if you want to check the server version, current database, whether the connection is secure, and so forth.

- system *command*, \! *command*

  Execute *command* using your default shell. This option was introduced in MySQL 4.0.1. It is unavailable under Windows.

- tee *file_name*, \T *file_name*

  Copy output to the end of the named file.

  This command was introduced in MySQL 3.23.28.

- use *db_name*, \u *db_name*

  Select the given database to make it the current database.

mysql Prompt Definition Sequences

The MYSQL_PS1 environment variable, the --prompt option, or the prompt command can be used to redefine the primary mysql> query prompt that mysql prints. Within the prompt definition, the special escape sequences shown in the following table can be used.

Sequence	Meaning
\c	Current input line
\d	Current database name, or "(none)" if no database is selected
\D	Full date and time
\h	Current host
\m	Minute
\o	Month number
\O	Month name, three letters
\p	Current port number, socket name, or named pipe name
\P	a.m./p.m. indicator
\r	Hour (12-hour time)
\R	Hour (24-hour time)
\s	Second
\S	Semicolon
\t	Tab
\u	Current username, without hostname

continues

Sequence	Meaning
\U	Current username, including hostname
\v	Server version
\y	Year (2-digit)
\Y	Year (4-digit)
\w	Weekday name, three letters
\'	Single quote
\"	Double quote
_	Space character
\	Space character (the sequence is backslash-space)
\\	Literal '\'
\n	Newline (linefeed)
\x	Literal '*x*' for any '*x*' not listed above

mysqlaccess

This script allows you to connect to a server, retrieve access privilege information, and test the result of specifying user privileges. It does this using copies of the user, db, and host tables from the mysql database. (mysqlaccess cannot be used to experiment with table or column privileges, however.) You can also commit changes you make to the temporary tables back into the actual tables in the mysql database.

To use mysqlaccess, you must have sufficient privileges to access the grant tables yourself.

Usage

```
mysqlaccess [host_name [user_name [db_name]]] options
```

Standard Options Supported by mysqlaccess

```
--host        --password     --user       --version
```

Options Specific to mysqlaccess

- --brief, -b

  Display results in single-line format.

- --commit

  Copy the temporary grant tables back to the mysql database. Be sure to execute a mysqladmin flush-privileges command afterward so that the server notices the changes.

- `--copy`

  Load the grant tables into the temporary tables.

- `--db=`*`db_name`*, `-d `*`db_name`*

  The database name.

- `--debug=`*`n`*

  Specify the debugging level. *n* should be an integer from 0 to 3, with higher values producing greater amounts of diagnostic output.

- `--howto`

  Display some examples demonstrating how to use `mysqlaccess`.

- `--old_server`

  Use this option when the server is older than MySQL 3.21; it causes `mysqlaccess` to make certain adjustments to the queries that it sends to the server.

- `--plan`

  Display a list of enhancements planned for future releases of `mysqlaccess`.

- `--preview`

  Display the privilege differences between the actual and temporary grant tables.

- `--relnotes`

  Print the `mysqlaccess` release notes.

- `--rhost=`*`host_name`*, `-H `*`host_name`*

  The remote server host to connect to.

- `--rollback`

  Undo the changes made to the temporary grant tables.

- `--spassword=`*`pass_val`*, `-P `*`pass_val`*

  The password for the MySQL superuser (a user with sufficient privileges to modify the grant tables).

- `--superuser=`*`user_name`*, `-U `*`user_name`*

  The username for the MySQL superuser.

- `--table`, `-t`

  Display results in tabular format.

mysqladmin

The `mysqladmin` utility communicates with the MySQL server to perform a variety of administrative operations. You can use `mysqladmin` to obtain information from or control the operation of the server, set passwords, and create or drop databases.

Usage

```
mysqladmin [options] command ...
```

Standard Options Supported by `mysqladmin`

`--character-sets-dir`	`--password`	`--socket`
`--compress`	`--pipe`	`--user`
`--debug`	`--port`	`--verbose`
`--help`	`--set-variable`	`--version`
`--host`	`--silent`	

`--silent` causes `mysqladmin` to exit silently if it cannot connect to the server. `--verbose` was added in MySQL 3.22.30. It causes `mysqladmin` to print more information for a few commands. `--character-sets-dir` was added in 3.23.21. As of MySQL 4, `mysqladmin` also supports the standard SSL options.

Options Specific to `mysqladmin`

- `--count=n, -c n`

  The number of iterations to make when `--sleep` is given. This option was introduced in MySQL 4.0.3.

- `--force, -f` (*boolean*)

  This option has two effects. First, it causes `mysqladmin` not to ask for confirmation of the `drop db_name` command. Second, when multiple commands are specified on the command line, `mysqladmin` attempts to execute each command even if errors occur. Normally, `mysqladmin` will exit after the first error.

- `--relative, -r` (*boolean*)

  Show the difference between the current and previous values when used with `--sleep`. Currently, this option works only with the `extended-status` command.

- `--sleep=`*n*`, -i` *n*

  Execute the commands named on the command line repeatedly with a delay of *n* seconds between each repetition.

- `--timeout=`*n*`, -t` *n*

  Wait *n* seconds before timing out when attempting to connect to the server. This option was introduced in MySQL 3.22.1 and removed in 3.23.29 when the `connect_timeout` variable was introduced.

- `--vertical, -E`   (*boolean*)

  This option is like `--relative` but displays output vertically. It was introduced in MySQL 3.23.14.

- `--wait[=`*n*`], -w[`*n*`]`

  The number of times to wait and retry if a connection to the server cannot be established. The default value of *n* is 1 if no value is given. If *n* is specified after `-w`, there must be no intervening space or the value will not be interpreted correctly.

Variables for `mysqladmin`

The following `mysqladmin` variables can be set using the instructions in the "Setting Program Variables" section earlier in this appendix.

- `connect_timeout`

  The number of seconds to wait before timing out when attempting to connect to the server. This variable was introduced in MySQL 3.23.29 when the `--timeout` option was removed.

- `shutdown_timeout`

  For `shutdown` commands, the number of seconds to wait for a successful shutdown. This variable was introduced in MySQL 3.23.34.

`mysqladmin` Commands

Following any options on the command line, you can specify one or more of the following commands. Each command name can be shortened to a prefix, as long as the prefix is unambiguous. For example, `processlist` can be shortened to `process` or `proc`, but not to `p`.

Several of these commands have an equivalent SQL statement, as noted in the descriptions. For more information about the meaning of the SQL statements, see Appendix D, "SQL Syntax Reference."

- create *db_name*

  Create a new database with the given name. This command is like the CREATE DATABASE *db_name* statement.

- drop *db_name*

  Delete the database with the given name and any tables that may be in the database. Be careful with this command; you can't get the database back. mysqladmin asks for confirmation of this command unless the --force option was given. This command is like the DROP DATABASE *db_name* statement.

- debug

  Instruct the server to dump debugging information.

- extended-status

  Display the names and values of the server's status variables. This command is like the SHOW STATUS statement. It was introduced in MySQL 3.22.10.

- flush-hosts

  Flush the host cache. This command is like the FLUSH HOSTS statement.

- flush-logs

  Flush (close and reopen) the log files. This command is like the FLUSH LOGS statement.

- flush-privileges

  Reload the grant tables. This command is like the FLUSH PRIVILEGES statement. It was introduced in MySQL 3.22.12.

- flush-status

  Clear the status variables. (This resets several counters to zero.) This command is like the FLUSH STATUS statement.

- flush-tables

  Flush the table cache. This command is like the FLUSH TABLES statement.

- flush-threads

  Flush the thread cache.

- `kill` *id*, *id*, ...

  Kill the server threads specified by the given identifier numbers. If you specify multiple numbers, the ID list should contain no spaces so that it will not be confused for another command following the `kill` command. To find out what threads are currently running, use `mysqladmin processlist`. This command is like issuing a `KILL` statement for each thread ID.

- `password` *new_password*

  Change the password for account that you use when invoking `mysqladmin`. (Being able to connect to the server using this account serves as verification that you know the current password.) The password will be set to *new_password*. This command is like the `SET PASSWORD` statement.

- `ping`

  Check whether the MySQL server is running.

- `processlist`

  Display a list of the currently executing server threads. This command is like the `SHOW PROCESSLIST` statement. With the `--verbose` option, this command is like `SHOW FULL PROCESSLIST`.

- `refresh`

  This command flushes the table cache and the grant tables and closes and reopens the log files. If the server is a replication master server, the command tells it to delete the binary update logs listed in the binary log index file and to truncate the index. If the server is a slave server, the command tells it to forget its position in the master logs.

- `reload`

  Reload the grant tables. This command is like the `FLUSH PRIVILEGES` statement.

- `shutdown`

  Shut down the server.

- `start-slave`

  Start a replication slave server. This command is like the `SLAVE START` statement. It was introduced in MySQL 3.23.16.

- `status`

  Display a short status message from the server.

- `stop-slave`

  Stop a replication slave server. This command is like the `SLAVE STOP` statement. It was introduced in MySQL 3.23.16.

- `variables`

  Display the names and values of the server's variables. This command is like the `SHOW VARIABLES` statement. As of MySQL 4.0.3, which supports the notion of both global and session variables, this command is like `SHOW GLOBAL VARIABLES`. (There is no support for `SHOW SESSION VARIABLES` because that wouldn't make any sense.)

- `version`

  Retrieve and display the server version information string. This is the same information that is returned by the `VERSION()` function (see Appendix C, "Operator and Function Reference").

`mysqlbinlog`

The `mysqlbinlog` utility displays the contents of a binary update log file in readable format. This program can read log files on the local host directly or connect to a remote server to read remote logs.

The format of binary update logs has changed from time to time. You may find it necessary to use a version of `mysqlbinlog` that is at least as recent as your server version to avoid compatibility problems.

Usage

```
mysqlbinlog [options] file_name ...
```

Standard Options Supported by `mysqlbinlog`

`--debug`	`--host`	`--port`	`--version`
`--help`	`--password`	`--user`	

The `--host`, `--password`, `--port`, and `--user` options are used when you want to connect to a remote server to access its binary logs. Otherwise, `mysqlbinlog` reads local log files directly without connecting to a server.

Options Specific to `mysqlbinlog`

- `--database=`*db_name*`, -d `*db_name*,

  Extract statements from the log file only for the named database. This option works only when reading local logs.

- `--offset=`*n*`, -o `*n*

  Skip the first *n* entries in the log file.

- `--position=`*n*`, -j `*n*

  Start reading the log file at position *n*.

- `--result-file=`*file_name*`, -r `*file_name*

  Write output to the named file.

- `--short-form, -s`

  Show only the statements in the log; omit any extra information in the log that is associated with the statements.

- `--table=`*tbl_name*`, -t `*tbl_name*

  Obtain a raw dump of the named table.

mysqlbug

The *MySQL Reference Manual* contains a detailed procedure for filing a bug report. Following that procedure helps ensure that your report will be helpful and will contain sufficient information to resolve the problem you're reporting. A key part of this procedure is to use the `mysqlbug` script. It's used to create and send a bug report to the MySQL mailing list when you discover a problem with MySQL. `mysqlbug` gathers information about your system and MySQL configuration and then drops you into an editor containing the contents of the mail message to be sent. (`mysqlbug` attempts to determine what editor to use by examining the `VISUAL` and `EDITOR` environment variables. If neither variable is set, `mysqlbug` uses `emacs`.)

Edit the message to add as much information as you can about the problem you are reporting, and then write out the message to save your changes and exit the editor. `mysqlbug` will ask you whether to send the report and then mails it if you confirm.

Please use `mysqlbug` to report bugs, but don't use it lightly. In many cases, a "bug" isn't a bug at all or is a report of something that has already been documented in the *MySQL Reference Manual*. The MySQL mailing list archives are another useful source of information for checking whether behavior that you observe actually is erroneous. Links to the manual and to the archives can be found at `http://www.mysql.com/documentation/`.

`mysqlbug` is a shell script and does not run on Windows. If you use the `WinMySQLAdmin` or `MySQLCC` Windows applications, you can use their error-reporting facilities. Alternatively, the `mysqlbug.txt` file in the top directory of the MySQL distribution can be used as a template. Fill it in and email it to `bugs@lists.mysql.com`.

Usage

```
mysqlbug [address]
```

The bug report is sent to the MySQL mailing list by default. If you specify an email address on the command line, the report is sent to that address instead. You can specify your own address to try out `mysqlbug` without sending the report to the mailing list; that's not a bad idea when you're first using the script and are perhaps not quite sure how it works.

mysqlcheck

`mysqlcheck` is a utility for checking and repairing tables. It presents a command-line interface to the CHECK TABLE, ANALYZE TABLE, OPTIMIZE TABLE, and REPAIR TABLE statements. It's somewhat similar to `myisamchk` but is used while the server is running. `mysqlcheck` works by sending administrative queries to the server to be executed. This contrasts with `myisamchk`, which operates directly on table files and thus requires either that you coordinate table access with the server or bring down the server.

`mysqlcheck` was introduced in MySQL 3.23.38. All `mysqlcheck` options are supported for MyISAM tables. `mysqlcheck` can also analyze BDB tables, and, as of MySQL 3.23.40, can check InnoDB tables.

Usage

`mysqlcheck` can be run in any of three modes:

```
mysqlcheck [options] db_name [tbl_name] ...
mysqlcheck [options] --databases db_name ...
mysqlcheck [options] --all-databases
```

In the first case, the named tables in the given database are checked. If no tables are named, `mysqlcheck` checks all tables in the database. In the second case, all arguments are taken as database names and `mysqlcheck` checks all tables in each one. In the third case, `mysqlcheck` checks all tables in all databases.

Standard Options Supported by `mysqlcheck`

`--character-sets-dir`	`--host`	`--socket`
`--compress`	`--password`	`--user`
`--debug`	`--pipe`	`--verbose`
`--default-character-set`	`--port`	`--version`
`--help`	`--silent`	

As of MySQL 4, `mysqlcheck` also supports the standard SSL options.

Options Specific to `mysqlcheck`

`mysqlcheck` supports the following options to control how it processes tables. Following this list is a description of the equivalences between these options and the SQL statements to which they correspond.

- `--all-databases, -A`   (*boolean*)

  Check all tables in all databases.

- `--analyze, -a`

  Perform table analysis by issuing an `ANALYZE TABLE` statement. (For example, this analyzes the distribution of key values.) The results of the analysis can help the server perform index-based lookups and joins more quickly.

- `--all-in-1, -1`   (*boolean*)

  Without this option, `mysqlcheck` issues separate queries for each table. This option causes `mysqlcheck` to group tables by database and name all tables within each database in a single query.

- `--auto-repair`   (*boolean*)

  If any tables to be checked are found to have problems, run a second phase to repair them automatically after the check phase has finished.

- `--check, -c`

  Issue a `CHECK TABLE` statement to check for errors. This is the default action if no action is specified explicitly.

- `--check-only-changed, -C`

  Check only tables that have changed since they were last checked or that have not been closed properly.

- `--databases, -B`   (*boolean*)

  Interpret all arguments as database names and check all tables in each database.

- `--extended, -e` *(boolean)*

  Perform an extended table check. If used with `--repair`, use a more extensive but slower repair method than is used for `--repair` by itself.

- `--fast, -F` *(boolean)*

  Check only tables that have not been closed properly.

- `--force, -f` *(boolean)*

  Continue executing even if errors occur.

- `--medium-check, -m`

  Perform table checking using a method that is faster than `--extended` but slightly less thorough. This checking mode should be sufficient for most circumstances.

- `--optimize, -o`

  Perform table optimization by issuing an OPTIMIZE TABLE statement.

- `--quick, -q` *(boolean)*

  For table checking, this option skips checking links in the data rows. Used with `--repair`, this option repairs only the index file and leaves the data file untouched. Giving this option twice is no different than giving it once, in contrast to `myisamchk`, which does behave differently when the option is specified twice.

- `--repair, -r`

  Perform table repair by issuing a REPAIR TABLE statement. This repair mode should correct most problems except the occurrence of duplicate values in an index that should be unique.

- `--tables`

  Override `--databases`.

- `--use-frm` *(boolean)*

  Used with `--repair` to perform a table repair operation that uses the `.frm` file to interpret the data file and rebuild the index file. This option can be used when the index file has been lost or corrupted. It was introduced in MySQL 4.0.5.

The relationship between `mysqlcheck`'s options and the SQL statements that it issues is described by the following tables, which show the statements that correspond to `mysqlcheck`'s options.

Table checking options (MyISAM and InnoDB tables only):

Option	Corresponding Statement	
`--check`	`CHECK TABLE` *tbl_list*	
`--check-only-changed`	`CHECK TABLE` *tbl_list* `CHANGED`	
`--extended`	`CHECK TABLE` *tbl_list* `EXTENDED`	
`--fast`	`CHECK TABLE` *tbl_list* `FAST`	
`--medium-check`	`CHECK TABLE` *tbl_list* `MEDIUM`	
`--quick`	`CHECK TABLE` *tbl_list* `QUICK`	

Table analysis options (MyISAM and BDB tables only);

Option	Corresponding Statement
`--analyze`	`ANALYZE TABLE` *tbl_list*

Table repair options (MyISAM tables only):

Option(s)	Corresponding Statement	
`--repair`	`REPAIR TABLE` *tbl_list*	
`--repair --quick`	`REPAIR TABLE` *tbl_list* `QUICK`	
`--repair --extended`	`REPAIR TABLE` *tbl_list* `EXTENDED`	
`--repair --use-frm`	`REPAIR TABLE` *tbl_list* `USE_FRM`	

Table optimization options (MyISAM tables only):

Option	Corresponding Statement
`--optimize`	`OPTIMIZE TABLE` *tbl_list*

mysql_config

The `mysql_config` utility is an aid to developing MySQL-based programs written in C. It can be used to obtain the proper flags needed to compile C source files or link in MySQL libraries.

`mysql_config` is available as of MySQL 3.23.21.

Usage

```
mysql_config [options]
```

Options Specific to `mysql_config`

- `--cflags`

  Display the include directory flags needed to access MySQL header files.

- `--embedded, --embedded-libs`

  These options are synonyms for `--libmysqld-libs`.

- `--libs`

  Display the library flags needed to link in the client library.

- `--socket`

  Display the default MySQL socket file pathname.

- `--port`

  Display the default MySQL TCP/IP port number.

- `--version`

  Display the MySQL version string.

- `--libmysqld-libs`

  Display the library flags needed to link in `libmysqld`, the embedded server library.

`mysqld`

`mysqld` is the MySQL server. It provides database access to client programs, so it must be running or clients cannot use databases administered by the server. When `mysqld` starts up, it opens network ports to listen on and then waits for client connections. `mysqld` is multi-threaded and processes each client connection using a separate thread to provide concurrency among clients. Queries that write to the database are executed atomically; when the server begins executing such a query, it will execute no other query for the data involved until the current query has finished. For example, no two clients can ever modify the same row in a table at the same time.

Usage

The usual invocation sequence is simply the server name followed by any desired options:

```
mysqld [options]
```

On Windows NT-based systems, a server can be installed to run as a service. For example, the `mysqld-nt` server might be installed to run automatically at system startup time or removed as a service as follows:

```
C:\> mysqld-nt --install
C:\> mysqld-nt --remove
```

The default service name is `MySql`. As of MySQL 4.0.2, you can provide a service name following the option:

```
C:\> mysqld-nt --install service_name
C:\> mysqld-nt --remove service_name
```

This allows multiple servers to be run under different service names. With no *service_name* argument, `MySql` is used as the service name and the server reads the `[mysqld]` group from option files at startup time. With a *service_name* argument, that name becomes the service name and the server reads the `[service_name]` group from option files at startup time.

As of MySQL 4.0.3, you can also provide a `--defaults-file` option following the service name to specify an additional file of options for the server to read at startup time:

```
C:\> mysqld-nt --install service_name --defaults-file=file_name
```

In this case, the *service_name* argument is not optional.

The preceding remarks about `--install` apply to `--install-manual` as well. (In addition, the modifications allowing you to specify arguments after `--install` have been backported into the 3.23 series beginning with MySQL 3.23.54.)

Standard Options Supported by `mysqld`

```
--character-sets-dir      --help           --socket
--debug                   --port           --user
--default-character-set   --set-variable   --version
```

`--character-sets-dir` and `--default-character-set` are available as of MySQL 3.23.14. As of MySQL 4, `mysqld` also supports the standard SSL options.

Note that although `--socket` is supported, the corresponding short form (`-S`) is not.

On UNIX, if the `--user` option is given, it specifies the username of the account to use for running the server. In this case, when the server starts up, it looks up the user and group ID values of the account from the password file and then changes its user and group IDs to match. In this way, the server runs with the privileges associated with that user, not `root` privileges. (The server must be started as `root` for the `--user` option to be effective; it will not be able to change its user ID otherwise.) As of MySQL 4.0.2, the `--user` option value can be the numeric user ID.

Options Specific to `mysqld`

The first section of options listed here are general options. It is followed by sections that list options specific to Windows, to particular table handlers, and to replication.

- `--ansi, -a`

  Tell the server to use ANSI behavior for certain types of SQL syntax, rather than MySQL-specific syntax. This option can be used to make the server more ANSI compliant.

  This option was introduced in MySQL 3.23.6. It is equivalent to using the `--sql-mode` option with the `REAL_AS_FLOAT`, `PIPES_AS_CONCAT`, `ANSI_QUOTES`, `IGNORE_SPACE`, `SERIALIZE`, and `ONLY_FULL_GROUP_BY` flags.

- `--basedir=dir_name, -b dir_name`

  The pathname to the MySQL installation directory. Many other path-names are resolved beginning at this directory if they are given as relative pathnames.

- `--big-tables`

  Allow large result sets to be processed by saving all temporary results to disk rather than by holding them in memory. This avoids most "table full" messages that occur as a result of having insufficient memory to hold large result sets. This option is unnecessary as of MySQL 3.23.

- `--bind-address=ip_addr`

  Bind to the given IP address. Normally, `mysqld` binds to the default IP address for the host on which the server is running. This option can be used to select an alternative address to bind to if the host has multiple addresses.

- `--bootstrap`

  This option is used by installation scripts when you first install MySQL. It was introduced in MySQL 3.22.10.

- `--chroot=dir_name, -r dir_name`

  Run the MySQL server anchored to the given directory as its root directory. See the `chroot()` UNIX manual page for more information on running in a `chroot()`-ed environment. This option was introduced in MySQL 3.22.2.

- `--concurrent-insert` (*boolean*)

  Allow concurrent inserts on MyISAM tables or disallow them with `--skip-concurrent-insert`. If a MyISAM table has no holes, concurrent inserts add new records at the end of the table while retrievals are being performed on the existing rows. This option was introduced as a boolean option in MySQL 4.0.2. From 3.23.25 to 4.0.1, only `--skip-concurrent-insert` may be used.

- `--core-file`

  Cause a core file to be generated before exiting when a fatal error occurs. This option was introduced in MySQL 3.23.23.

- `--datadir=dir_name, -h dir_name`

  The pathname to the MySQL data directory.

- `--default-table-type=type`

  The default table storage type to use. The `type` value should be the name of one of the table handlers that the server supports, such as ISAM, MyISAM, HEAP, BDB, or InnoDB. (The value is not case sensitive.) If this option is not specified, the server uses whatever default type was compiled into it at build time (usually MyISAM). This option was introduced in MySQL 3.23.

- `--delay-key-write=val`

  Set the mode used by the server for handling delayed key writes for MyISAM files. `val` can be `ON` (delay key writes on a per-table basis, according to any `DELAY_KEY_WRITE` value specified when tables were created; this is the default), `OFF` (never delay key writes for any MyISAM table), or `ALL` (delay key writes for all MyISAM tables). `OFF` and `ALL` enforce a policy that is applied regardless of how tables were declared when they were created.

  It's common to run replication slave servers with `--delay-key-write=ALL` to obtain increased performance for MyISAM tables by delaying key writes no matter how the tables were created originally.

This option was introduced in MySQL 3.23.3 and renamed to
`--delay-key-write-for-all-tables` in 3.23.11. As of MySQL 4.0.3,
it can be used again. In the interim, you can use
`--skip-delay-key-write` to achieve the same effect as `OFF`.

- `--des-key-file=`*file_name*

The name of the file that holds DES keys for the `DES_ENCRYPT()` and
`DES_DECRYPT()` functions. For a description of the format of this file, see
the entry for `DES_ENCRYPT()` in Appendix C. This option was introduced in MySQL 4.0.1.

- `--enable-locking`

See the description for `--external-locking`. This option is deprecated
as of MySQL 4.0.3.

- `--enable-pstack`   (*boolean*)

Enable symbolic stack printing when an error occurs. This option was
introduced in MySQL 4.0.0.

- `--exit-info[=`*n*`]`, `-T[`*n*`]`

Cause the server to debugging information when it terminates. If *n* is
specified after `-T`, there must be no intervening space or the value will
not be interpreted correctly. This option was introduced in MySQL 3.22.

- `--external-locking`   (*boolean*)

Enable external locking (file system locking) for systems such as
Linux where external locking is off by default. This option was
introduced in MySQL 4.0.3 as a boolean option. Prior to that, use
`--enable-locking` or `--skip-locking` to enable or disable external
locking.

External locking is effective only for operations such as table checking that
just read tables. For operations that modify tables, such as repairs, you should
bring down the server while running `isamchk` or `myisamchk` to avoid the
risk of table damage. (See Chapter 13 for details.) In general, it is preferable
to use `mysqlcheck` rather than `myisamchk` if possible. `mysqlcheck` tells the
server to do the work, so there is no need to coordinate with the server
explicitly or to know anything about external locking.

- `--flush`

Flush all tables to disk after each update. This reduces the risk of table
corruption in the event of a crash but seriously degrades performance.
Thus, it is useful only if you have an unstable system. This option was
introduced in MySQL 3.22.9. It applies only to MyISAM and ISAM
tables.

- `--init-file=file_name`

Name a file of SQL statements to be executed at startup time. A relative filename is interpreted starting at the data directory. The file should contain one statement per line.

- `--language=lang_name`, `-L lang_name`

Display error messages to clients in the specified language. Normally, `lang_name` will be a value such as `english` or `german`, but it can also be the full pathname to the directory containing the language files.

- `--local-infile` (*boolean*)

Allow or disallow LOAD DATA LOCAL. As of MySQL 3.23.49, LOCAL capabilities may be present but disabled by default. Invoke the server with the `--local-infile` option to enable LOCAL on the server side. This option can also be used to disable LOCAL from the server side if it is enabled by default: Use `--disable-local-infile` as of MySQL 4.0.2, `--local-infile=0` before that.

- `--log[=file_name]`, `-l[file_name]`

Turn on logging to the general log file. The general log contains information about client connections and queries. If `file_name` is not given, the log filename is `HOSTNAME.log` in the data directory, where `HOSTNAME` is the name of the server host. If `file_name` is given as a relative path, it is interpreted starting at the data directory. If `file_name` is specified after `-l`, there must be no intervening space or the value will not be interpreted correctly.

- `--log-bin[=file_name]`

Enable the binary update log. If `file_name` is not given, the log filename is `HOSTNAME-bin.nnn` in the data directory, where `HOSTNAME` is the name of the server host and `nnn` is a sequence of numbers incremented by one each time a new log is created. If `file_name` is given as a relative path, it is interpreted starting at the data directory. This option was introduced in MySQL 3.23.14.

- `--log-bin-index=file_name`

Enable the binary update log index file. If `file_name` is given as a relative path, it is interpreted starting at the data directory. This option was introduced in MySQL 3.23.15.

- `--log-slow-queries[=file_name]`

Turn on slow-query logging to the named file. If no file is named, the default name is `HOSTNAME-slow.log` in the data directory, where

HOSTNAME is the name of the server host. If *file_name* is given as a relative path, it is interpreted starting at the data directory. This option was introduced in MySQL 3.23.9.

- `--log-isam[=file_name]`

Enable index file logging. This is used only for debugging ISAM/MyISAM operations. If you specify no name, the default is `myisam.log` in the data directory.

- `--log-long-format`

Write additional information to the update log and to the slow-query log. This option was introduced in MySQL 3.22.7.

- `--log-update[=file_name]`

Turn on logging to the update log file. The update log contains the text of any query that modifies database tables. If *file_name* is not given, the update log filename is *HOSTNAME*.nnn in the data directory, where *HOSTNAME* is the name of the server host and *nnn* is a sequence number one greater than that of the previous update log.

If *file_name* is given and the final component contains no extension, the server adds a numeric extension of the form *nnn* with a value as previously described. If the final component of the pathname includes an extension, that name is used without modification as the update log filename. If *file_name* is given as a relative path, it is interpreted starting at the data directory.

The update log is deprecated as of MySQL 3.23.14, the version in which the binary update log was introduced.

- `--log-warnings` (*boolean*)

Write certain non-critical warning messages to the log file. This option was introduced as `--warnings` in MySQL 3.23.40 and renamed to `--log-warnings` in 4.0.3.

- `--low-priority-updates`

Give updates lower priority than retrievals. This option was introduced in MySQL 3.23. (It was called `--low-priority-inserts` from MySQL 3.22.5 until MySQL 3.23.)

- `--memlock` (*boolean*)

Lock the server in memory if possible. This option was introduced in MySQL 3.23.25. It is effective only on Solaris, and only if the server is run as `root`.

- `--myisam-recover=level`

  Control the type of automatic MyISAM table checking that the server performs at startup time. `level` can be empty to disable checking or a comma-separated list of one or more of the following values: `DEFAULT` (same as specifying no option), `BACKUP` (create a backup of the table if it is changed), `FORCE` (force recovery even if more than a row of data will be lost), or `QUICK` (quick recovery). This option was introduced in MySQL 3.23.25.

- `--new, -n`

  Use new, possibly unsafe routines. These are features in MySQL that are not yet declared stable. This option should be used only if you are feeling adventurous.

- `--old-protocol, -o`

  Use the protocol that was used for client/server communications prior to MySQL 3.21. This option may be needed if the server communicates with very old client programs.

- `--old-passwords`

  As of MySQL 4.1, the server supports a new password encryption method. Existing accounts that have passwords encrypted the old way are still supported, but new passwords will be encrypted using the new method. Use this option to force the old method to be used even for new passwords. (This can be useful if you want to be able to downgrade the server or move the accounts to an older server.) This option was introduced in MySQL 4.1.

- `--one-thread`

  Run using a single thread; used for debugging under Linux, which normally uses three threads at a minimum. This option was introduced in MySQL 3.22.2.

- `--pid-file=file_name`

  When `mysqld` starts up, it writes its process ID (PID) into a file. This option specifies the pathname of the PID file. The file can be used by other processes to determine the server's process number, typically for purposes of sending a signal to it. For example, `mysql.server` reads the file when it sends a signal to the server to shut down. This option has no effect on Windows or for the embedded server. If `file_name` is given as a relative path, it is interpreted starting at the data directory.

- `--safe-mode`

  This option is like `--skip-new` but disables even more things. You can try it if MySQL appears to be unstable or if complex queries seem to yield incorrect results. If using this option improves server operation, please note that fact when you use `mysqlbug` to report the problems you encounter.

- `--safe-show-database`   (*boolean*)

  Don't show the names of databases to users who have no privileges for accessing them. This option was introduced in MySQL 3.23.30. However, it is deprecated as of MySQL 4.0.2 when the SHOW DATABASES privilege was introduced to allow control over the ability to see database names.

- `--safe-user-create`   (*boolean*)

  Disallow account creation by users who do not have write access to the user grant table. This option was introduced in MySQL 3.23.41.

- `--safemalloc-mem-limit=n`

  Simulate a memory shortage. The value represents the limit on the amount of memory available for allocation. This option can be used only if the server was built with the `--with-debug=full` option at configuration time. This option was introduced in MySQL 3.23.28.

- `--skip-concurrent-insert`

  See the description for `--concurrent-insert`.

- `--skip-grant-tables, -Sg`   (*boolean*)

  Disable use of the grant tables for verifying client connections. This gives any client full access to do anything. It also disables the GRANT and REVOKE statements. You can tell the server to begin using the grant tables again by issuing a FLUSH PRIVILEGES statement or a `mysqladmin flush-privileges` command.

  The `-Sg` form of this option is unavailable as of MySQL 4.0.0.

- `--skip-host-cache`

  Disable use of the hostname cache.

- `--skip-locking`

  See the description for `--external-locking`. This option is deprecated as of MySQL 4.0.3.

- `--skip-name-resolve`

  Do not try to resolve hostnames. If this option is specified, the grant tables must specify hosts by IP number or as `localhost`.

- `--skip-networking`

  Do not allow TCP/IP connections. Only local clients can connect and must do so using the UNIX socket by specifying a hostname of `local-host`.

- `--skip-new`

  Do not use new, possibly unsafe routines. See the description for `--new`.

- `--skip-safemalloc`

  Do not perform memory allocation checking. This option can be used only if the server was built with the `--with-debug=full` option at configuration time. This option was introduced in MySQL 3.23.37.

- `--skip-show-database`

  Do not allow unprivileged users to issue `SHOW DATABASES` queries or to use `SHOW TABLES` on databases for which they have no access. This option was introduced in MySQL 3.23.

- `--skip-stack-trace`

  Don't print a stack trace when failure occurs. This option was introduced in MySQL 3.23.38.

- `--skip-symlink`

  Disallow table symlinking. This option was introduced in MySQL 3.23.39.

- `--skip-thread-priority`

  Normally, updates (queries that modify tables) run at a higher priority than those that retrieve data. If that is undesirable, this option causes the server not to give different priorities to different types of queries.

- `--sql-bin-update-same` *(boolean)*

  Yoke together `SQL_LOG_BIN` and `SQL_LOG_UPDATE` so that setting one (with the `SET` statement) sets the other as well. This option was introduced in MySQL 3.23.16.

- `--sql-mode=flags`

  This option modifies certain aspects of the server's behavior to cause it to act according to ANSI SQL or to be compatible with older servers. `flags` should be a comma-separated list of one or more of the following options:

  - `ANSI_QUOTES`

    Treat double quote as the quote character for identifiers, such as database, table, and column names, and not as a string quote character. (Backticks are still allowed for name quoting.)

- IGNORE_SPACE

  Allow spaces between function names and the following opening parenthesis. This results in function names being treated as reserved words.

- NO_UNSIGNED_SUBTRACTION

  As of MySQL 4, subtraction between integer operands results in an unsigned result if either operand is unsigned. This option allows signed results, which is compatible with the behavior of MySQL prior to version 4.

- ONLY_FULL_GROUP_BY

  Normally, MySQL allows SELECT statements with columns in the output column list that are not named in the GROUP BY clause:

  ```
  SELECT a, b, COUNT(*) FROM t GROUP BY a;
  ```

  The ONLY_FULL_GROUP_BY flag requires output columns to be named in the GROUP BY:

  ```
  SELECT a, b, COUNT(*) FROM t GROUP BY a, b;
  ```

- PIPES_AS_CONCAT

  Treat || as a string concatenation operator rather than as logical OR.

- REAL_AS_FLOAT

  The REAL column type becomes a synonym for FLOAT rather than for DOUBLE.

- SERIALIZE

  Use SERIALIZABLE as the default transaction isolation level.

--sql-mode is similar to --ansi in that it allows ANSI behaviors to be enabled, but is more flexible because features can be selected on an individual basis. Note also that NO_UNSIGNED_SUBTRACTION behavior can be selected only with --sql-mode.

The --sql-mode option was introduced in MySQL 3.23.41. The NO_UNSIGNED_SUBTRACTION flag value was introduced in MySQL 4.0.0.

- --temp-pool   (*boolean*)

  With this option, the server uses a small set of names for temporary files rather than creating a unique name for each file. This avoids some caching problems on Linux. This option was introduced in MySQL 3.23.33; it is enabled by default as of MySQL 4.0.3.

- `--transaction-isolation=level`

  Set the default transaction isolation level. The allowable `level` values are READ-UNCOMMITTED, READ-COMMITTED, REPEATABLE-READ, and SERIALIZ-ABLE. This option was introduced in MySQL 3.23.26.

- `--tmpdir=dir_name, -t dir_name`

  The pathname of the directory to use for temporary files. This option was introduced in MySQL 3.22.4. As of MySQL 4.1, the option value can be given as a list of directories to be used in round-robin fashion. Under UNIX, separate directory names by colons; under Windows, separate them by semicolons.

- `--warnings`

  See the description for `--log-warnings`.

Windows Options

The options in this section are available only for servers running under Windows. Several of them are service-related and apply only to Windows NT-based systems.

- `--console` (*boolean*)

  Display a console window for error messages. This option was introduced in MySQL 3.22.4.

- `--enable-named-pipe` (*boolean*)

  Prior MySQL 3.23.50 named piped are enabled by default for NT servers that support them (that is, servers with `-nt` in their name). As of 3.23.50, named pipes are disabled by default; this option can be used to turn named pipe support on.

  Note that enabling named pipes may cause problems at server shutdown time, for which reason you should avoid doing so if possible.

- `--install`

  Install the server as a service that runs automatically when Windows starts up. (Windows NT systems only.)

- `--install-manual`

  Install the server as a service that does not run automatically when Windows starts up. You must explicitly start the service yourself. This option was introduced in MySQL 3.23.44. (Windows NT systems only.)

- `--remove`

  Remove the server as a service. (Windows NT systems only.)

- `--standalone`

  Run the server as a standalone program rather than as a service. (Windows NT systems only.)

- `--use-symbolic-links` (*boolean*)

  Support symbolic linking of database directories. This option was introduced in MySQL 3.23.17. As of MySQL 4.0, database symlinking support is enabled by default; use `--skip-symlink` to disable it.

BDB Options

The options in this section are specific to the BDB table handler.

- `--bdb-home=dir_name`

  The BDB home directory. If specified explicitly, the value should be the same as for `--datadir`. This option was introduced in MySQL 3.23.14.

- `--bdb-lock-detect=val`

  Set the BDB deadlock detection/resolution mode. `val` should be one of the following values indicating how to choose a transaction to abort when it becomes necessary to break a deadlock: YOUNGEST (most recently started transaction), OLDEST (longest-lived transaction), RANDOM (a randomly chosen transaction), or DEFAULT (transaction chosen using the default policy, which currently is the same as RANDOM). This option was introduced in MySQL 3.23.15.

- `--bdb-logdir=dir_name`

  The pathname to the directory where the BDB handler writes log files. This option was introduced in MySQL 3.23.14.

- `--bdb-no-recover`

  Tell the BDB handler not to attempt auto-recovery of BDB files at startup time. It can be useful for getting the server running in some cases when it exits at startup due to auto-recovery failure. This option was introduced in MySQL 3.23.30. (The `--bdb-recover` option is used from 3.23.16 to 3.23.29, but with the opposite meaning.)

- `--bdb-no-sync`

  Don't flush BDB logs synchronously. This option was introduced in MySQL 3.23.14.

- `--bdb-shared-data`

  Start the BDB handler in multi-process mode. This option was introduced in MySQL 3.23.29.

- `--bdb-tempdir=dir_name`

  The pathname to the directory where the BDB handler writes temporary files. This option was introduced in MySQL 3.23.14.

- `--skip-bdb`

  Disable the BDB table handler. If you don't use BDB tables, this option saves memory. It was introduced in MySQL 3.23.15.

InnoDB Options

The options in this section are specific to the InnoDB table handler. Many of the InnoDB options were introduced in MySQL 3.23.29 under names beginning with `--innobase` and renamed in 3.23.37 to begin with `--innodb`.

- `--innodb_data_file_path=filespec_list`

  The specifications for the InnoDB tablespace component files. The format of the option value is discussed in the InnoDB configuration instructions in Chapter 11. This option was introduced in MySQL 3.23.37.

- `--innodb_data_home_dir=dir_name`

  The pathname to the directory under which the InnoDB tablespace components are located. This option was introduced in MySQL 3.23.37.

- `--innodb_fast_shutdown`   (*boolean*)

  Speed up the server shutdown process; the InnoDB handler skips some of the operations that it performs normally. This option was introduced in MySQL 3.23.44.

- `--innodb_flush_log_at_trx_commit=n`

  This option has a value of 1 by default, which causes InnoDB log flushing when transactions are committed. Setting the option to zero will reduce the amount of flushing to disk that InnoDB performs. However, this comes at a somewhat increased potential for losing a few of the most recent committed transactions if a crash occurs. The possible values are as follows:

Value	Meaning
0	Write to log once per second and flush to disk
1	Write to log at each commit and flush to disk
2	Write to log at each commit, but flush to disk only once per second

  This option was introduced in MySQL 3.23.37. An option value of 2 is allowed as of MySQL 3.23.52.

- `--innodb_flush_method=val`

  This option applies only on UNIX. It specifies the method used to flush data to the InnoDB logs. The allowable values are `fdatasync` (the default) and `O_DSYNC`. This option was introduced in MySQL 3.23.39.

- `--innodb_log_group_home_dir=dir_name`

  The pathname to the directory where the InnoDB handler should write its log files. This option was introduced in MySQL 3.23.37.

- `--innodb_log_arch_dir=dir_name`

  This option is not currently used. It was introduced in MySQL 3.23.37.

- `--innodb_log_archive=n`

  This option is not currently used. It was introduced in MySQL 3.23.37.

- `--skip-innodb`

  Disable the InnoDB table handler. If you don't use InnoDB tables, this option saves memory. This option was introduced as `--skip-innobase` in MySQL 3.23.26 and renamed to `--skip-innodb` in 3.23.37.

Replication Options

The options in this section pertain to MySQL's replication capabilities.

For a replication slave server, several options are used in conjunction with the master information file (named `master.info` in the data directory by default). When the server starts up, if no `master.info` file exists, it uses the values of the `--master-host`, `--master-user`, `--master-password`, `--master-port`, and `--master-connect-retry` options when establishing the connection to the master server. It also saves the values in the `master.info` file. If the file does exist when the slave starts up, it uses the contents of the file and ignores the options. You must remove the file and restart the server for the options to take effect. The name of the file itself can be changed with the `--master-info-file` option.

- `--abort-slave-event-count=n`

  This option is used by `mysql-test-run` for replication testing. It was introduced in MySQL 3.23.28.

- `--binlog-do-db=db_name`

  For a replication master, log updates only for the named database. No other databases will be replicated. To log updates for multiple databases, repeat the option once for each database name. This option was introduced in MySQL 3.23.23.

- `--binlog-ignore-db=db_name`

  For a replication master, do not log updates for the named database. To ignore updates for multiple databases, repeat the option once for each database name. This option was introduced in MySQL 3.23.23.

- `--disconnect-slave-event-count=n`

  This option is used by `mysql-test-run` for replication testing. It was introduced in MySQL 3.23.28.

- `--init-rpl-role=val`

  Indicate the replication role; `val` can be `master` or `slave`. This option is used by the `mysql-test-run` script for replication testing. It was introduced in MySQL 4.0.0.

- `--log-slave-updates` (*boolean*)

  This option causes a replication slave to log updates that it receives from the master server to its own binary update log. It's necessary to do this if the slave acts as a master to another server (that is, if you chain slave servers). This option was introduced in MySQL 3.23.17.

- `--master-connect-retry=n`

  For a replication slave, the number of seconds between attempts to connect to the master if the master is unavailable. This option was introduced in MySQL 3.23.15.

- `--master-host=host_name`

  For a replication slave, the host where the master server is running. `host_name` can be given as a name or IP number. This option was introduced in MySQL 3.23.15.

- `--master-info-file=file_name`

  For a replication slave, the name of the file that stores information about the current replication state. The contents of this file are the replication coordinates (master binary update log name and position), master host, username, password, port number, and connection retry interval. The default name for this file is `master.info` in the data directory. This option was introduced in MySQL 3.23.15.

- `--master-password=pass_val`

  For a replication slave, the password of the account it uses for connecting to the master server. If no password is given, the default is the empty password. This option was introduced in MySQL 3.23.15.

- `--master-port=port_num`

  For a replication slave, the TCP/IP port to use for connecting to the master server. If no port is given, the default port number compiled into the server is used (usually 3306). This option was introduced in MySQL 3.23.15.

- `--master-retry-count=n`

  For a replication slave, the number of times to attempt a connection to a master server before giving up. This option was introduced in MySQL 3.23.43.

- `--master-ssl` (*boolean*)

  `--master-ssl-cert=file_name`

  `--master-ssl-key=file_name`

  These options were introduced in MySQL 4.0.0, but are unimplemented. They are reserved for future use to allow replication over secure connections. (This set of options is incomplete at the moment, anyway. `--master-ssl-ca` and `--master-ssl-cipher` need to be implemented as well.)

- `--master-user=user_name`

  For a replication slave, the username of the account it uses for connecting to the master server. If no username is given, the default is `test`. This option was introduced in MySQL 3.23.15.

- `--max-binlog-dump-events=n`

  This option is used by `mysql-test-run` for replication testing. This option was introduced in MySQL 3.23.40.

- `--old-rpl-compat` (*boolean*)

  Tells the server to use the old replication binary update log format for LOAD DATA statements that does not store the data in the log. This option was introduced in MySQL 4.0.0.

- `--reckless-slave`

  This option is used for replication debugging. This option was introduced in MySQL 4.0.2.

- `--relay-log=file_name`

  For a replication slave, the name of the relay log. (In MySQL 4, the slave I/O thread stores updates read from the master in the relay log, and the SQL thread reads the relay log for queries and updates them.) The default relay log name is `HOSTNAME-relay-bin.nnn` in the data directory, where `HOSTNAME` is the name of the server host and `nnn` is a sequence of numbers incremented by one each time a new log is created. This option was introduced in MySQL 4.0.2.

- `--relay-log-index=file_name`

  For a replication slave, the name of the relay log index file. The default name is `HOSTNAME-relay-bin.index` in the data directory, where `HOSTNAME` is the name of the server host. This option was introduced in MySQL 4.0.2.

- `--relay-log-info-file=file_name`

  For a replication slave, the name of the relay log information file. The default name is `relay-log.info` in the data directory. This option was introduced in MySQL 4.0.2.

- `--replicate-do-db=db_name`

  For a replication slave, replicate only the named database. To restrict replication to a set of databases, repeat the option once for each database name. This option was introduced in MySQL 3.23.16.

- `--replicate-do-table=db_name.tbl_name`

  For a replication slave, replicate only the named table. To restrict replication to a set of tables, repeat the option once for each table name. This option was introduced in MySQL 3.23.28.

- `--replicate-ignore-db=db_name`

  For a replication slave, do not replicate the named database. To ignore multiple databases, repeat the option once for each database name. This option was introduced in MySQL 3.23.16.

- `--replicate-ignore-table=tbl_name`

  For a replication slave, do not replicate the named table. To ignore multiple tables, repeat the option once for each table name. This option was introduced in MySQL 3.23.28.

- `--replicate-rewrite-db=master_db->slave_db`

  This option tells a replication slave to treat one database as another. Updates made to the original database `master_db` on the master server are replicated as updates to the database `slave_db` on the slave server. This option was introduced in MySQL 3.23.26. When given on the command line, the option value should be enclosed within quotes to prevent the command interpreter from treating the '>' character as an output redirection operator.

- `--replicate-wild-do-table=pattern`

  For a replication slave, replicate only tables with names that match the given pattern. To restrict replication to a set of patterns, repeat the option once for each pattern. This option was introduced in MySQL 3.23.28.

- `--replicate-wild-ignore-table=pattern`

  For a replication slave, do not replicate tables with names that match the given pattern. To ignore multiple patterns, repeat the option once for each pattern. This option was introduced in MySQL 3.23.28.

- `--server-id=n`

  The replication server ID value. The value must be unique among communicating replication servers. This option was introduced in MySQL 3.23.26.

- `--show-slave-auth-info`   (*boolean*)

  Display the slave server username and password in the output of the SHOW SLAVE STATUS statement. This option was introduced in MySQL 4.0.0.

- `--skip-slave-start`

  Do not start the slave automatically. It must be started manually by issuing a SLAVE START statement. This option was introduced in MySQL 3.23.26.

- `--slave-load-tmpdir=dir_name`

  The pathname to the directory used by a slave server for processing LOAD DATA statements. This option was introduced in MySQL 4.0.0.

- `--slave-skip-errors=error_list`

  The list of errors that a slave server should ignore rather than suspending replication if they occur. A value of `all` means all errors should be ignored, which is essentially the behavior obtained by using the `--reckless-slave` option. Otherwise, the value should be a list of one or more error numbers separated by commas. This option was introduced in MySQL 3.23.47.

- `--sporadic-binlog-dump-fail`   (*boolean*)

  This option is used by `mysql-test-run` for replication testing. This option was introduced in MySQL 3.23.40.

Variables for `mysqld`

To see what values `mysqld` will use by default, use the following command:

```
% mysqld --help
```

To see what values the currently executing `mysqld` is using, use this command:

```
% mysqladmin variables
```

You can also check the current variable values by issuing a SHOW VARIABLES statement. The variables shown by that statement are described in the entry for SHOW in Appendix D. Any mysqld variable can be set at startup time using the instructions in the "Setting Program Variables" section earlier in this appendix. In addition, as of MySQL 4.0.3, several variables can be modified dynamically; for more information, see the entry for the SET statement in Appendix D.

mysqld_multi

The mysqld_multi script makes it easier to run several mysqld servers on a single host. It allows you to start or stop servers or determine whether they are running.

Usage

```
mysqld_multi [options] command server_list
```

Command is one of start, stop, or report. The server_list argument indicates which servers you want to manipulate. For further instructions on using mysqld_multi, see Chapter 11.

Standard Options Supported by mysqld_multi

```
--help        --password      --user        --version
```

mysqld_multi passes the --user and --password option values to mysqladmin when it needs to stop servers or determine if they are running.

Options Specific to mysqld_multi

- --config-file=file_name

  The option file to read to obtain options for the servers that mysqld_multi manipulates. Without --config-file, /etc/my.cnf and the .my.cnf file in your home directory are read to obtain server options. (mysqld_multi reads the standard option files for its own options. This option does not change that behavior.)

- --example

  Display a sample option file that demonstrates option file groups suitable for use with mysqld_multi.

- --log=file_name

  The name of the log file where mysqld_multi should log its actions. Output is appended to the log if it already exists. The default log file is /tmp/mysqld_multi.log. To disable logging, use --no-log.

- --mysqladmin=*file_name*

  The pathname to the `mysqladmin` binary you want to use. This can be useful if `mysqld_multi` cannot find `mysqladmin` by itself or if you want to use a different version.

- --mysqld=*file_name*

  The pathname to the `mysqld` binary you want to use. This can be useful if `mysqld_multi` cannot find `mysqld` by itself or if you want to use a different version. (It's allowable to specify a pathname to `mysqld`, `mysqld_safe`, or `safe_mysqld` here.)

- --no-log

  Display log output rather than writing it to a log file. (If you want to see output, you must use this option because the default is to log to a file.)

- --tcp-ip

  By default, `mysqld_multi` attempts to connect to a server using a UNIX socket file. This option causes the connection attempt to use TCP/IP instead. It can be useful when a server is running but its socket file has been removed, in which case the server will be accessible only via TCP/IP.

mysqld_safe

`mysqld_safe` is a shell script that starts up the `mysqld` server and monitors it. If the server dies, `mysqld_safe` restarts it. Prior to MySQL 4, `mysqld_safe` was known as `safe_mysqld`.

`mysqld_safe` is a shell script and is unavailable on Windows.

Usage

```
mysqld_safe [options]
```

Options Specific to `mysld_safe`

Options that can be used with `mysqld` can also be used with `mysqld_safe`, which simply passes them to `mysqld`. In addition, `mysqld_safe` understands the following options of its own:

- --core-file-size=*n*

  Limit the size of core files to *n* bytes if the server crashes. This option was introduced in MySQL 3.23.28.

- `--err-log=file_name`

  Use this file for the error log. Relative names are interpreted with respect to the directory from which `mysqld_safe` was invoked. If this option is not specified, the default error log is *HOSTNAME*.err in the data directory, where *HOSTNAME* is the name of the current host. This option was introduced in MySQL 3.23.22.

- `--ledir=dir_name`

  Look for the server in this directory. (It's taken to be the location of the "libexec" directory.) This option was introduced in MySQL 3.23.22.

- `--open-files-limit=n`

  Set the number of available open file descriptors to *n*. This option was introduced in MySQL 3.23.41.

- `--mysqld=file_name`

  Use *file_name* as the path to the `mysqld` program. This option was introduced in MySQL 3.23.30.

- `--timezone=tzspec`

  Set the timezone to *tzspec*. This can be useful if the server doesn't determine the system timezone automatically. This option was introduced in MySQL 3.23.28.

Upgrading Tips

If you're upgrading to MySQL 4.x from MySQL 3.x, when `mysqld_safe` was known as `safe_mysqld`, watch out for the following things:

- Any startup scripts that invoke `safe_mysqld` should be modified to invoke `mysqld_safe`. The `mysql.server` script is one example. However, if you replace your older version with a 4.x version, that will update it automatically to invoke `mysqld_safe`. If you're using your own startup scripts, make the necessary adjustments.

- `[safe_mysqld]` groups in option files should be renamed to `[mysqld_safe]`.

mysqldump

The `mysqldump` program writes the contents of database tables into text files. These files can be used for a variety of purposes, such as database backups, moving databases to another server, or setting up a test database based on the contents of an existing database.

By default, output for each dumped table consists of a CREATE TABLE statement that creates the table, followed by a set of INSERT statements that load the contents of the table. If the --tab option is given, table contents are written to a data file in raw format and the table creation SQL statement is written to a separate file.

Usage

mysqldump can be run in any of three modes:

```
mysqldump [options] db_name [tbl_name] ...
mysqldump [options] --databases db_name ...
mysqldump [options] --all-databases
```

In the first case, the named tables in the given database are dumped. If no tables are named, mysqldump dumps all tables in the database. In the second case, all arguments are taken as database names and mysqldump dumps all tables in each one. In the third case, mysqldump dumps all tables in all databases.

The most common way to use mysqldump is as follows:

```
% mysqldump --opt db_name > backup_file
```

Note that this backup file should be imported back into MySQL with mysql rather than with mysqlimport:

```
% mysql db_name < backup_file
```

Standard Options Supported by mysqldump

--character-sets-dir	--host	--socket
--compress	--password	--user
--debug	--pipe	--verbose
--default-character-set	--port	--version
--help	--set-variable	

The --character-sets-dir and --default-character-set options were added in MySQL 3.23.15. As of MySQL 4, mysqldump also supports the standard SSL options.

Options Specific to mysqldump

The following options control how mysqldump operates. The next section, "Data Format Options for mysqldump," describes options that can be used in conjunction with the --tab option to indicate the format of data files.

- --add-drop-table (*boolean*)

  Add a DROP TABLE IF EXISTS statement before each CREATE TABLE statement. This option was introduced in MySQL 3.22.4.

- `--add-locks` (*boolean*)

  Add `LOCK TABLE` and `UNLOCK TABLE` statements around the set of `INSERT` statements that load the data for each table. This option was introduced in MySQL 3.22.3.

- `--all, -a` (*boolean*)

  Add additional information to the `CREATE TABLE` statements that mysqldump generates, such as the table type, the beginning `AUTO_INCREMENT` value, and so forth. This is the information that you can specify in the *table_options* part of the `CREATE TABLE` syntax. (See Appendix D.) This option was introduced in MySQL 3.22.23.

- `--all-databases, -A` (*boolean*)

  Dump all tables in all databases. This option was introduced in MySQL 3.23.12.

- `--allow-keywords` (*boolean*)

  Allow for the creation of column names that are keywords. This option was introduced in MySQL 3.22.3.

- `--complete-insert, -c` (*boolean*)

  Use `INSERT` statements that name each column to be inserted.

- `--databases, -B` (*boolean*)

  Interpret all arguments as database names and dump all tables in each database. This option was introduced in MySQL 3.23.12.

- `--delayed-insert` (*boolean*)

  Write `INSERT DELAYED` statements. This option was introduced in MySQL 3.22.15.

- `--disable-keys, -K` (*boolean*)

  Add `ALTER TABLE ... DISABLE KEYS` and `ALTER TABLE ... ENABLE KEYS` statements to the output to disable key updating while `INSERT` statements are being processed. This speeds up index creation for MyISAM tables. This option was introduced in MySQL 3.23.48.

- `--extended-insert, -e` (*boolean*)

  Write multiple-row `INSERT` statements. These can be loaded more efficiently than single-row statements. This option was introduced in MySQL 3.22.15.

- `--first-slave, -x` (*boolean*)

  Lock all tables across all databases using `FLUSH TABLES WITH READ LOCK`. (Note that this type of lock is ineffective for obtaining a consistent backup of InnoDB tables; use `--single-transaction` instead.) This option was introduced in MySQL 3.23.22.

- `--flush-logs, -F` (*boolean*)

Flush the server log files before starting the dump.

- `--force, -f` (*boolean*)

Continue execution even if errors occur.

- `--lock-tables, -l` (*boolean*)

Obtain locks for all tables being dumped before dumping them. Cannot be used with `--single-transaction`.

- `--master-data`

This option helps make a backup that can be used with a slave server. It writes the master server filename and position at the end of the output. Use of `--master-data` automatically enables `--first-slave`. This option was introduced in MySQL 3.23.48.

- `--no-autocommit` (*boolean*)

Write the `INSERT` statements for each table within a transaction. The resulting output can be loaded more efficiently than executing each statement in auto-commit mode. This option was introduced in MySQL 3.23.48.

- `--no-create-db, -n` (*boolean*)

Do not write `CREATE DATABASE` statements. (Normally, these are added to the output automatically when `--databases` or `--all-databases` are used.) This option was introduced in MySQL 3.23.12.

- `--no-create-info, -t` (*boolean*)

Do not write `CREATE TABLE` statements. This is useful if you want to dump just table data.

- `--no-data, -d` (*boolean*)

Do not write table data. This is useful if you want to dump just the `CREATE TABLE` statements.

- `--opt`

Optimize table dumping speed and write a dump file that is optimal for reloading speed. This option turns on whichever of the following options are present in your version of `mysqldump`: `--add-drop-table`, `--add-locks`, `--all`, `--disable-keys`, `--extended-insert`, `--lock-tables`, and `--quick`. This option was introduced in MySQL 3.22.3.

- --quick, -q (*boolean*)

  By default, mysqldump reads the entire contents of a table into memory and then writes it out. This option causes each row to be written to the output as soon as it has been read from the server, which is much less memory intensive. However, if you use this option, you should not suspend mysqldump; doing so causes the server to wait, which can interfere with other clients.

- --quote-names, -Q (*boolean*)

  Quote table and column names by enclosing them within backtick ('`') characters. This is useful if names are reserved words or contain special characters. This option was introduced in MySQL 3.23.6.

- --result-file=*file_name*, -r *file_name*

  Write output to the named file. This option is intended for Windows, where it prevents conversion of linefeeds to carriage return/linefeed pairs. This option was introduced in MySQL 3.23.28.

- --single-transaction (*boolean*)

  This option allows consistent dumps of InnoDB tables. The idea is that all the tables are dumped within a single transaction, which has the effect of read-locking them all at once. This option was introduced in MySQL 4.0.2. It cannot be used with --lock-tables.

- --tab=*dump_dir*, -T *dump_dir*

  This option causes mysqldump to write two files per table, using *dump_dir* as the location for the files. The directory must already exist. For each table *tbl_name*, a file *dump_dir*/*tbl_name*.txt is written containing the data from the table, and a file *dump_dir*/*tbl_name*.sql is written containing the CREATE TABLE statement for the table. You must have the FILE privilege to use this option.

  By default, data files are written as newline-terminated lines consisting of tab-separated column values. This format can be changed using the options described under the "Data Format Options for mysqldump" section later in this appendix.

  The effect of the --tab option can be confusing unless you understand exactly how it works:

  - Some of the files are written on the server and some are written on the client. *dump_dir* is used on the server host for the *.txt files and on the client host for the *.sql files. If the two hosts are different, the output files are created on different machines. To avoid any uncertainty about where files will be written, it is best to run mysqldump on the server host when you use this option.

- The `*.txt` files will be owned by the account used to run the server, and the `*.sql` files will be owned by you. This is a consequence of the fact that the server itself writes the `*.txt` files, whereas the `CREATE TABLE` statements are sent by the server to mysqldump, which writes the `*.sql` files.

- `--tables`

  Override `--databases`. This option was introduced in MySQL 3.23.12.

- `--where=`*`where_clause`*`, -w `*`where_clause`*

  Only dump records selected by the `WHERE` clause given by *where_clause*. You should enclose the clause in quotes to prevent the shell from interpreting it as multiple command-line arguments. This option was introduced in MySQL 3.22.7.

- `--xml, -X`

  Generate XML output. This option can be used as of MySQL 3.23.51 (it was introduced in 3.23.48, but output was not well-formed).

Data Format Options for `mysqldump`

If you specify the `--tab` or `-T` option to generate a separate data file for each table, several additional options apply. You may need to enclose the option value in appropriate quoting characters. These options are analogous to the data format options for the `LOAD DATA` statement. See the entry for `LOAD DATA` in Appendix D.

- `--fields-enclosed-by=`*`char`*

  Specifies that column values should be enclosed within the given character, usually a quote character. The default is not to enclose column values within anything. This option precludes the use of `--fields-optionally-enclosed-by`.

- `--fields-escaped-by=`*`char`*

  Specifies the escape character for escaping special characters. The default is no escape character.

- `--fields-optionally-enclosed-by=`*`char`*

  Specifies that column values should be enclosed within the given character, usually a quote character. The character is used for non–numeric columns. The default is not to enclose column values within anything. This option precludes the use of `--fields-enclosed-by`.

- `--fields-terminated-by=`*`str`*

  Specifies the column value separation character or characters to use for data files. By default, values are separated by tab characters.

- `--lines-terminated-by=`*`str`*

  Specifies the character or characters to write at the end of output lines. The default is to write newlines. This option was introduced in MySQL 3.22.4.

Variables for `mysqldump`

The following `mysqldump` variables can be set using the instructions in the "Setting Program Variables" section earlier in this appendix.

- `max_allowed_packet`

  The maximum size of the buffer used for communication between the server and the client.

- `net_buffer_length`

  The initial size of the buffer used for communication between the server and the client. This buffer can be expanded up to `max_allowed_packet` bytes long.

`mysqlhotcopy`

The `mysqlhotcopy` performs efficient backups of databases and tables. It works only for MyISAM and ISAM tables. `mysqlhotcopy` is a Perl script and requires that you have DBI support installed. It does not currently work on Windows.

`mysqlhotcopy` connects to the server on the local host and sends table flushing and locking statements to the server for each table to be copied and then copies the table files to another location to make a backup. This ensures that outstanding table modifications have been flushed to disk and that the server won't try to further modify the table while it is being copied. (Essentially, `mysqlhotcopy` implements the protocol described in Chapter 13 for telling the server to leave the designated tables alone while you're working directly with the table files.)

`mysqlhotcopy` was introduced in MySQL 3.23.11.

Usage

This program can be invoked in a number of ways. The general invocation syntax is as follows:

```
mysqlhotcopy [options] db_name[./regex/] [new_db_name | dir_name]
```

For example, to make a copy of the database *db_name* named *db_name_copy* under the data directory, use the following command:

```
% mysqlhotcopy [options] db_name
```

To copy the *db_name* database to a directory named *db_name* under the /tmp directory instead, do this:

```
% mysqlhotcopy [options] db_name /tmp
```

More examples are provided in the online documentation, available with the following command:

```
% perldoc mysqlhotcopy
```

Standard Options Supported by `mysqlhotcopy`

--debug	--host	--port	--user
--help	--password	--socket	

The `--host` option, if given, is intended *only* for specifying the name of the local host. Normally, `mysqlhotcopy` tries to connect to the local server using a UNIX socket file. It will connect over TCP/IP instead if you specify the actual name of the server using the `--host` option. The `--port` option can be used in this case to specify a port number other than the default. The `--host` option was introduced in MySQL 3.23.52.

Options Specific to `mysqlhotcopy`

- `--allowold`

  If the target directory already exists, rename it using an `_old` suffix. If the copy fails, the renamed directory is restored to the original name. If the copy operation succeeds, the renamed directory is deleted, unless the `--keepold` option is also given.

- `--checkpoint=db_name.tbl_name`

  Write a checkpoint record to the given table, which should have been created in advance with the following structure:

  ```
  CREATE TABLE tbl_name
  (
      time_stamp TIMESTAMP NOT NULL,
  ```

```
        src         VARCHAR(32),
        dest        VARCHAR(60),
        msg         VARCHAR(255)
    );
```

src and dest are the source and destination database names, and msg indicates success or failure of the copy operation.

- --dryrun, -n

"No execution" mode. mysqlhotcopy reports what actions it would take to perform the command, without actually doing them. This is useful for checking whether mysqlhotcopy will do what you expect, particularly when you're learning how to use it.

- --flushlog

Flush the logs after all the tables have been locked and before copying them. This has the effect of checkpointing them to the time of the copy operation.

- --keepold

If the previous target directory exists, rename it with an _old suffix prior to making a new copy. This option implies --allowold.

- --method=*copy_method*

The method to use for copying files. A value of cp uses the cp program. Experimental support for an scp method is also available. In this case, the *copy_method* value should be the entire scp command to use, and the destination directory must already exist. The scp method may result in your tables being locked for a much longer time than a local copy due to the extra time required to copy the files over the network.

- --noindices

Don't copy index files. (If you need to use the backup files later to recover the tables, you can recreate the indexes by using the files with myisamchk --recover for MyISAM tables or isamchk --recover for ISAM tables.

- --quiet, -q

Produce no output except when errors occur.

- --record_log_pos=*db_name.tbl_name*

Before copying tables, issue SHOW MASTER STATUS and SHOW SLAVE STATUS statements and record the results in the given table, which should have been created in advance with the following structure:

```
CREATE TABLE tbl_name
(
    host             VARCHAR(60) NOT NULL,
    time_stamp       TIMESTAMP NOT NULL,
    log_file         VARCHAR(32) NULL,
    log_pos          INT NULL,
    master_host      VARCHAR(60) NULL,
    master_log_file  VARCHAR(32) NULL,
    master_log_pos   INT NULL,
    PRIMARY KEY (host)
);
```

The results from SHOW MASTER STATUS are recorded in the log_file and log_pos columns. This information provides replication coordinates for the binary logs; if the backup host is a replication master server, a slave should begin from these coordinates if it is initialized from the backup files as a slave of the master. The results from SHOW SLAVE STATUS are recorded in the master_host, master_log_file, and master_log_pos columns; they can be used if the backup host is a replication slave server and you want to initialize another slave of the same master from the backup files.

- --regexp=pattern

  Copy all databases having names that match the given regular expression. The final argument of the command should be the directory where you want to copy the databases.

- --resetmaster

  Reset the binary update logs by issuing a RESET MASTER statement after all the tables have been locked and before they are copied.

- --resetslave

  Reset the information in the master.info file by issuing a RESET SLAVE statement after all the tables have been locked and before they are copied.

- --suffix=str

  This option is used when making a copy of databases into the database directory. Each new database directory name is the same as the original with the given suffix added.

- --tmpdir=dir_name

  The pathname of the directory in which to create temporary files. The default is to use the directory named by the TMPDIR environment variable or /tmp if the variable is not set.

mysqlimport

The mysqlimport utility is a bulk loader for reading the contents of text files into existing tables. It functions as a command-line interface to the LOAD DATA SQL statement and is an efficient way to enter rows into tables.

mysqlimport reads data files only. It does *not* read SQL-format dump files produced by mysqldump. Use mysql to read such files instead.

Usage

```
mysqlimport [options] db_name file_name ...
```

The *db_name* argument specifies the database that contains the tables into which you want to load data. The tables to load are determined from the filename arguments. For each filename, any extension from the first period in the name is stripped off and the remaining basename is used as the name of the table into which the file should be loaded. For example, mysqlimport will load the contents of a file named president.txt into the president table.

Standard Options Supported by mysqlimport

--character-sets-dir	--host	--socket
--compress	--password	--user
--debug	--pipe	--verbose
--default-character-set	--port	--version
--help	--silent	

The --character-sets-dir and --default-character-set options were added as of MySQL 3.23.21 and 3.23.41, respectively. As of MySQL 4, mysqlimport also supports the standard SSL options.

Options Specific to mysqlimport

The following options control how mysqlimport processes input files. The next section, "Data Format Options for mysqlimport," describes options that can be used to indicate the format of the data in the input files.

- --columns=*col_list*

  List the columns in the table to which columns in the data file correspond. Values in input rows will be loaded into the named columns, and other columns will be set to their default values. *col_list* is a list of one or more column names separated by commas. This option was introduced in MySQL 3.23.17.

- `--delete, -d` *(boolean)*

Empty each table before loading any data into it.

- `--force, -f` *(boolean)*

Continue loading rows even if errors occur.

- `--ignore, -i`

When an input row contains a value for a unique key that already exists in the table, keep the existing row and discard the input row. The `--ignore` and `--replace` options are mutually exclusive.

- `--ignore-lines=n`

Ignore the first *n* lines of the data file. This can be used to skip an initial row of column labels, for example. This option was introduced in MySQL 4.0.2.

- `--local, -L` *(boolean)*

By default, `mysqlimport` lets the server read the data file, which means that the file must be located on the server host and that you must have the `FILE` privilege. Specifying the `--local` option tells `mysqlimport` to read the data file itself and send it to the server. This is slower but works when you're running `mysqlimport` on a different machine than the server host, as well as on the server host even if you don't have the `FILE` privilege.

The `--local` option was introduced in MySQL 3.22.15. As of MySQL 3.23.49, it will be ineffective if the server has been configured to disallow use of `LOAD DATA LOCAL`.

- `--lock-tables, -l` *(boolean)*

Lock each table before loading data into it.

- `--low-priority` *(boolean)*

Use the `LOW_PRIORITY` scheduling modifier to load data into the table. This option was introduced in MySQL 3.22.27.

- `--replace, -r` *(boolean)*

  When an input row contains a value for a unique key that already exists in the table, replace the existing row with the input row. The `--ignore` and `--replace` options are mutually exclusive.

Data Format Options for `mysqlimport`

By default, `mysqlimport` assumes that data files contain newline-terminated lines consisting of tab-separated values. The expected format can be altered using the following options. You may need to enclose the option value in appropriate quoting characters. These options are analogous to the data format options for the LOAD DATA statement. See the entry for LOAD DATA in Appendix D.

- `--fields-enclosed-by=char`

  Specifies that column values are enclosed within the given character, usually a quote character. By default, values are assumed not to be enclosed by any character. This option precludes the use of `--fields-optionally-enclosed-by`.

- `--fields-escaped-by=char`

  Specifies the escape character used to escape special characters. The default is no escape character.

- `--fields-optionally-enclosed-by=char`

  Specifies that column values can be enclosed within the given character, usually a quote character. This option precludes the use of `--fields-enclosed-by`.

- `--fields-terminated-by=str`

  Specifies the character or characters that separate column values. By default, values are assumed to be separated by tab characters.

- `--lines-terminated-by=str`

  Specifies the character or characters that terminate input lines. By default, lines are assumed to be terminated by newline characters.

mysql_install_db

The mysql_install_db script creates the server's data directory, initializes the mysql database that contains the grant tables, and creates an empty test database. mysql_install_db populates the grant tables with initial accounts for the root and anonymous users. See Chapter 11 for details on these accounts and how to secure your installation by establishing passwords.

mysql_install_db is a shell script and is unavailable on Windows. However, it is unnecessary on Windows, because distributions include the mysql and test databases preinitialized.

Usage

```
mysql_install_db [options]
```

Options Specific to mysql_install_db

The version numbers mentioned in this section indicate when you can first use the options on the command line, but you can set the values for many of them in earlier versions by placing appropriate entries in the [mysqld] group of the global option file. As of MySQL 3.23.39, the script also reads the [mysql_install_db] option group, which is more useful for options, such as --ldata and --force, that are understood only by mysql_install_db and not mysqld.

- --basedir=*dir_name*

  Use this directory as the MySQL base directory.

- --datadir=*dir_name*, --ldata=*dir_name*

  Use this directory as the MySQL data directory. The --datadir option was introduced in MySQL 3.23.17 and --ldata in MySQL 3.23.24.

- --force

  Run even if the current hostname cannot be determined. (The IP number of the host will be used to create grant table entries instead, which means you'll need to use the IP number rather than the hostname except for connections to localhost.) This option was introduced in MySQL 3.22.17.

- --user=*user_name*

Run the server as the named user. This is useful for making sure that any directories and files created by the server are owned by this user if you run the script as the UNIX `root` user. This option was introduced in MySQL 3.23.17.

mysql.server

`mysql.server` is a script that starts and stops the `mysqld` server by invoking `mysqld_safe` (or `safe_mysqld`, depending on your version of MySQL). `mysql.server` is a shell script and is unavailable on Windows. It was introduced in MySQL 3.22.7.

Usage

```
mysql.server start
mysql.server stop
```

Normally, `mysql.server` is used on a System V-style system and is installed in one of the runtime directories under the `/etc` directory. The system starts the server by invoking the script with an argument of `start` at system boot time. The system shuts down the server by invoking the script with an argument of `stop` at system shutdown time. The script can also be invoked by hand with the appropriate argument to start or stop the server.

mysqlshow

`mysqlshow` lists databases, tables within a database, or information about columns or indexes within a table. It acts as a command-line interface to the SHOW SQL statement.

Usage

```
mysqlshow [options] [db_name [tbl_name [col_name]]]
```

If no database name is specified, `mysqlshow` lists all databases on the server host. If a database name but no table name is specified, all tables in the database are listed. If database and table names are specified but no column name is specified, it lists the columns in the table. If all the names are specified, `mysql-`

`show` shows information about the given column.

If the final argument contains a shell wildcard ('`*`' or '`?`'), output is limited to values that match the wildcard. '`*`' and '`?`' are treated as the '`%`' and '`_`' SQL wildcard characters for the `LIKE` operator. As of MySQL 3.22.26, `mysqlshow` also interprets '`%`' and '`_`' as wildcard characters.

Standard Options Supported by `mysqlshow`

`--character-sets-dir`	`--host`	`--socket`
`--compress`	`--password`	`--user`
`--debug`	`--pipe`	`--verbose`
`--help`	`--port`	`--version`

`--character-sets-dir` was added in MySQL 3.23.21. As of MySQL 4, `mysqlshow` also supports the standard SSL options.

Options Specific to `mysqlshow`

- `--status, -i` (*boolean*)

  Display the same kind of table information displayed by the `SHOW TABLE STATUS` statement. This option was introduced in MySQL 3.23.

- `--keys, -k` (*boolean*)

  Show information about table indexes in addition to information about table columns. This option is meaningful only if you specify a table name.

`safe_mysqld`

`safe_mysqld` is the name that the `mysqld_safe` script had prior to MySQL 4. For information on usage, see the description for `mysqld_safe`. That description also includes tips on what to do when upgrading from MySQL 3.x to MySQL 4.x.

F

C API Reference

THIS APPENDIX DESCRIBES THE C LANGUAGE APPLICATION-PROGRAMMING interface for the MySQL client library. The API consists of a set of functions for communicating with MySQL servers and accessing databases and a set of data types used by those functions. The client library functions can be classified into the following categories:

- Connection management routines to establish and terminate connections to the server
- Error-reporting routines to get error codes and messages
- Query construction and execution routines to construct queries and send them to the server
- Result set processing routines to handle results from queries that return data
- Information routines that provide information about the client, server, protocol version, and the current connection
- Administrative routines for controlling server operation
- Thread routines for writing threaded clients

- Routines for communicating with the embedded MySQL server, `libmysqld`
- Debugging routines to generate debugging information
- Deprecated routines that now are considered obsolete

Unless otherwise indicated, you can assume a function is present in the client library at least as far back as MySQL 3.22.0.

This appendix serves as a reference, so it includes only brief code fragments illustrating use of the client library. For complete client programs and instructions for writing them, see Chapter 6, "The MySQL C API."

Compiling and Linking

At the source level, the interface to the client library is defined in the `mysql.h` header file, which your own source files can include:

```
#include <mysql.h>
```

To tell the compiler where to find this file, you may need to specify an `-Ipath` option, where *path* is the pathname to the directory where the MySQL header files are installed. For example, if your MySQL header files are installed in `/usr/include/mysql` or `/usr/local/mysql/include`, you can compile a source file `my_func.c` by using commands that look something like the following:

```
% gcc -I/usr/include/mysql -c my_func.c
% gcc -I/usr/local/mysql/include -c my_func.c
```

If you need to access other MySQL header files, they can be found in the same directory as `mysql.h`. For example, `mysql_com.h` contains constants and macros for interpreting query result metadata. The header files `errmsg.h` and `mysqld_error.h` contain constants for error codes. (Note that although you might want to look at `mysql_com.h` to see what's in it, you don't actually need to include this file explicitly because `mysql.h` does so. Including `mysql.h` thus gives your program access to `mysql_com.h` as well.)

At the object level, the client library is provided as the `mysqlclient` library. To link this library into your program, specify `-lmysqlclient` on the link command. You'll probably also need to tell the linker where to find the library using a `-Lpath` option, where *path* is the directory where the library is installed. For example:

```
% gcc -o myprog my_main.o my_func.o -L/usr/lib/mysql -lmysqlclient
% gcc -o myprog _main.o my_func.o -L/usr/local/mysql/lib -lmysqlclient
```

If a link command fails with "unresolved symbol" errors, you'll need to specify additional libraries for the linker to search. Common examples include the math library (-lm) and the zlib library (-lz or -lgz).

An easy way to determine the proper header file directories for compiling or library flags for linking is to use the mysql_config utility, available as of MySQL 3.23.21. Invoke it as follows to find out which flags are appropriate for your system:

```
% mysql_config --cflags
-I'/usr/local/mysql/include/mysql'
% mysql_config --libs
-L'/usr/local/mysql/lib/mysql' -lmysqlclient -lz -lcrypt -lnsl -lm
```

The output shown is illustrative, and likely will be different on your system.

C API Data Types

Data types for the MySQL client library are designed to represent the entities you deal with in the course of a session with the server. There are types for the connection itself, for results from a query, for a row within a result, and for metadata (descriptive information about the columns making up a result). The terms "column" and "field" are synonymous in the following discussion.

Scalar Data Types

MySQL's scalar data types represent values such as very large integers, boolean values, and field or row offsets.

- my_bool

  A boolean type, used for the return value of mysql_change_user(), mysql_eof(), and mysql_thread_init().

- my_ulonglong

  A long integer type, used for the return value of functions that return row counts or other potentially large numbers, such as mysql_affected_rows(), mysql_num_rows(), and mysql_insert_id(). To print a my_ulonglong value, cast it to unsigned long and use a format of %lu. For example:

  ```
  printf ("Row count = %lu\n", (unsigned long) mysql_affected_rows (conn));
  ```

  The value will not print correctly on some systems if you don't do this, because there is no standard for printing long long values with printf(). However, if the value to be printed might actually exceed the maximum allowed by unsigned long ($2^{32}-1$), %lu won't work, either. You'll need to check your printf() documentation to see if there is some implementation-specific means of printing the value. For example, a %llu format specifier might be available.

- MYSQL_FIELD_OFFSET

  This data type is used by the mysql_field_seek() and mysql_field_tell() functions to represent offsets within the set of MYSQL_FIELD structures for the current result set.

- MYSQL_ROW_OFFSET

  This data type is used by the mysql_row_seek() and mysql_row_tell() functions to represent offsets within the set of rows for the current result set.

Non-Scalar Data Types

MySQL's non-scalar types represent structures or arrays. Any instance of a MYSQL or MYSQL_RES structure should be considered as a "black box"—that is, you should refer only to the structure itself, not to elements within the structure. The MYSQL_ROW and MYSQL_FIELD types have no such restriction. You access elements of these structures freely to obtain data and metadata returned as a result of a query.

- MYSQL

  The primary client library type is the MYSQL structure, which is used for connection handlers. A handler contains information about the state of a connection with a server. To open a session with the server, initialize a MYSQL structure with mysql_init() and then pass it to mysql_real_connect(). After you've established the connection, use the handler to issue queries, generate result sets, get error information, and so on. When you're done with the connection, pass the handler to mysql_close(), after which the handler should no longer be used.

- MYSQL_FIELD

  The client library uses MYSQL_FIELD structures to represent metadata about the columns in the result set, one structure per column. The number of MYSQL_FIELD structures in the set can be determined by calling mysql_num_fields(). You can access successive field structures by calling mysql_fetch_field() or move back and forth among structures with mysql_field_tell() and mysql_field_seek().

The MYSQL_FIELD structure is useful for presenting or interpreting the contents of data rows. It looks like this:

```
typedef struct st_mysql_field {
    char *name;
    char *org_name;
    char *table;
    char *org_table;
    char *db;
    char *def;
    unsigned long length;
    unsigned long max_length;
    unsigned int flags;
    unsigned int decimals;
    enum enum_field_types type;
} MYSQL_FIELD;
```

MYSQL_FIELD structure members have the following meanings:

- name

  The column name, as a null-terminated string. For a column that is calculated as the result of an expression, name is that expression in string form. If a column or expression is given an alias, name is the alias name. For example, the following query results in name values of `"mycol"`, `"4*(mycol+1)"`, `"mc"`, and `"myexpr"`:

  ```
  SELECT mycol, 4*(mycol+1), mycol AS mc, 4*(mycol+1) AS myexpr ...
  ```

- org_name

  This member is like name, except that column aliases are ignored. That is, org_name represents the original column name. For a column that is calculated as the result of an expression, org_name is an empty string. This member is unused prior to MySQL 4.1.

- table

  The name of the table that the column comes from, as a null-terminated string. If the table was given an alias, table is the alias name. For a column that is calculated as the result of an expression, table is an empty string. For example, if you issue a query like the following, the table name for the first column is mytbl, whereas the table name for the second column is the empty string:

  ```
  SELECT mycol, mycol+0 FROM mytbl ...
  ```

- org_table

  This member is like table, except that table aliases are ignored; that is, org_table represents the original table name. For a column that is calculated as the result of an expression, org_table is an empty string. This member is unused prior to MySQL 4.1.

- db

  The database in which the table containing the column is located as a null-terminated string. For a column that is calculated as the result of an expression, db is an empty string. This member is unused prior to MySQL 4.1.

- def

  The default value for the column, as a null-terminated string. This member of the MYSQL_FIELD structure is set only for result sets obtained by calling mysql_list_fields() and is NULL otherwise.

  Default values for table columns also can be obtained by issuing a DESCRIBE *tbl_name* or SHOW COLUMNS FROM *tbl_name* query and examining the result set.

- length

  The length of the column, as specified in the CREATE TABLE statement used to create the table. For a column that is calculated as the result of an expression, the length is determined from the elements in the expression.

- max_length

  The length of the longest column value actually present in the result set. For example, if a string column in a result set contains the values "Bill", "Jack", and "Belvidere", the value of max_length for the column will be 9.

  Because the max_length value can be determined only after all the rows have been seen, it is meaningful only for result sets created with mysql_store_result(). max_length is 0 for result sets created with mysql_use_result().

- flags

  The flags member specifies attributes for the columns. Within the flags value, attributes are represented by individual bits, which can be tested via the bitmask constants shown in Table F.1. For example, to determine whether or not a column's values are UNSIGNED, test the flags value as follows:

  ```
  if (field->flags & UNSIGNED_FLAG)
      printf ("%s values are UNSIGNED\n", field->name);
  ```

Table F.1 **MYSQL_FIELD flags Member Values**

flags Value	Meaning
AUTO_INCREMENT_FLAG	Column has the AUTO_INCREMENT attribute
BINARY_FLAG	Column has the BINARY attribute
MULTIPLE_KEY_FLAG	Column is a part of a non-unique index
NOT_NULL_FLAG	Column cannot contain NULL values
PRI_KEY_FLAG	Column is a part of a PRIMARY KEY
UNIQUE_KEY_FLAG	Column is a part of a UNIQUE index
UNSIGNED_FLAG	Column has the UNSIGNED attribute
ZEROFILL_FLAG	Column has the ZEROFILL attribute

BINARY_FLAG is set for case-sensitive string columns. This includes columns for which the BINARY keyword is specified explicitly (such as CHAR BINARY), as well as BLOB columns.

A few flags constants indicate column types rather than column attributes; they are now deprecated because you should use field->type to determine the column type. Table F.2 lists these deprecated constants.

Table F.2 **Deprecated MYSQL_FIELD flags Member Values**

flags Value	Meaning
BLOB_FLAG	Column contains BLOB or TEXT values
ENUM_FLAG	Column contains ENUM values
SET_FLAG	Column contains SET values
TIMESTAMP_FLAG	Column contains TIMESTAMP values

- decimals

  The number of decimals for numeric columns, zero for non-numeric columns. For example, the decimals value is 3 for a DECIMAL(8,3) column but 0 for a BLOB column.

- type

  The column type. For a column that is calculated as the result of an expression, type is determined from the types of the elements in the expression. For example, if mycol is a VARCHAR(20) column, type is FIELD_TYPE_VAR_STRING, whereas type for LENGTH(mycol) is FIELD_TYPE_LONGLONG. The possible type values are listed in mysql_com.h and shown in Table F.3.

Table F.3 **MYSQL_FIELD type Member Values**

type Value	Column Type
FIELD_TYPE_BLOB	BLOB or TEXT
FIELD_TYPE_DATE	DATE
FIELD_TYPE_DATETIME	DATETIME
FIELD_TYPE_DECIMAL	DECIMAL or NUMERIC
FIELD_TYPE_DOUBLE	DOUBLE or REAL
FIELD_TYPE_ENUM	ENUM
FIELD_TYPE_FLOAT	FLOAT
FIELD_TYPE_INT24	MEDIUMINT
FIELD_TYPE_LONG	INT
FIELD_TYPE_LONGLONG	BIGINT
FIELD_TYPE_NULL	NULL
FIELD_TYPE_SET	SET
FIELD_TYPE_SHORT	SMALLINT
FIELD_TYPE_STRING	CHAR
FIELD_TYPE_TIME	TIME
FIELD_TYPE_TIMESTAMP	TIMESTAMP
FIELD_TYPE_TINY	TINYINT
FIELD_TYPE_VAR_STRING	VARCHAR
FIELD_TYPE_YEAR	YEAR

You might see references to FIELD_TYPE_CHAR in older source files; that was a one-byte type that is now called FIELD_TYPE_TINY. Similarly, FIELD_TYPE_INTERVAL is now called FIELD_TYPE_ENUM.

- MYSQL_RES

  Queries such as SELECT or SHOW that return data to the client do so by means of a result set, represented as a MYSQL_RES structure. This structure contains information about the rows returned by the query.

  After you have a result set, you can call API functions to get result set data (the data values in each row of the set) or metadata (information about the result, such as how many columns there are, their types, their lengths, and so on).

- MYSQL_ROW

  The MYSQL_ROW type contains the values for one row of data, represented as an array of strings. All values are returned in string form (even numbers), except that if a value in a row is NULL, it is represented in the MYSQL_ROW structure by a C NULL pointer.

The number of values in a row is given by `mysql_num_fields()`. The i-th column value in a row is given by `row[i]`. Values of i range from `0` to `mysql_num_fields(res_set)-1`, where `res_set` is a pointer to a `MYSQL_RES` result set.

Note that the `MYSQL_ROW` type is already a pointer, so you should declare a row variable as follows:

```
MYSQL_ROW row;        /* correct */
```

Not like the following:

```
MYSQL_ROW *row;       /* incorrect */
```

Values in a `MYSQL_ROW` array have terminating nulls, so non-binary values can be treated as null-terminated strings. However, data values that may contain binary data might contain null bytes internally and should be treated as counted strings. To get a pointer to an array that contains the lengths of the values in the row, call `mysql_fetch_lengths()` as follows:

```
unsigned long *length;
length = mysql_fetch_lengths (res_set);
```

The length of the i-th column value in a row is given by `length[i]`. If the column value is `NULL`, the length will be zero.

Accessor Macros

`mysql.h` contains a few macros that allow you to test `MYSQL_FIELD` members more conveniently. `IS_NUM()` tests the `type` member; the others listed here test the `flags` member.

- `IS_NUM()` is true (non-zero) if values in the column have a numeric type:
  ```
  if (IS_NUM (field->type))
      printf ("Field %s is numeric\n", field->name);
  ```

- `IS_PRI_KEY()` is true if the column is part of a `PRIMARY KEY`:
  ```
  if (IS_PRI_KEY (field->flags))
      printf ("Field %s is part of primary key\n", field->name);
  ```

- `IS_NOT_NULL()` is true if the column cannot contain `NULL` values:
  ```
  if (IS_NOT_NULL (field->flags))
      printf ("Field %s values cannot be NULL\n", field->name);
  ```

- `IS_BLOB()` is true if the column is a `BLOB` or `TEXT`. However, this macro tests the deprecated `BLOB_FLAG` bit of the `flags` member, so `IS_BLOB()` is deprecated as well.

C API Functions

Client library functions for the C API are described in detail in the following sections, grouped by category, and listed alphabetically within category. Certain parameter names recur throughout the function descriptions and have the following conventional meanings:

- conn is a pointer to the MYSQL connection handler for a server connection.
- res_set is a pointer to a MYSQL_RES result set structure.
- field is a pointer to a MYSQL_FIELD column information structure.
- row is a MYSQL_ROW data row from a result set.
- row_num is a row number within a result set, from 0 to one less than the number of rows.
- col_num is a column number within a row of a result set, from 0 to one less than the number of columns.

For brevity, where these parameters are not mentioned in the descriptions of functions in which they occur, you can assume the meanings just given.

Connection Management Routines

These functions allow you to establish and terminate connections to a server, to set options affecting the way connection establishment occurs, to re-establish connections that have timed out, and to change the current username.

A typical sequence involves calling mysql_init() to initialize a connection handler, mysql_real_connect() to establish the connection, and mysql_close() to terminate the connection when you are done with it. If it's necessary to indicate special options or set up an encrypted SSL connection, call mysql_options() or mysql_ssl_set() after mysql_init() and before mysql_real_connect().

- my_bool

```
mysql_change_user (MYSQL *conn,
                   const char *user_name,
                   const char *password,
                   const char *db_name);
```

Changes the user and the default database for the connection specified by conn. The database becomes the default for table references that do not include a database specifier. If db_name is NULL, no default database is selected.

mysql_change_user() returns true if the user is allowed to connect to the server and, if a database was specified, has permission to access the database. Otherwise, the function fails and the current user and database remain unchanged.

If is faster to use this function to change the current user than to close the connection and open it again with different parameters. It can also be used to implement persistent connections for programs that serve different users during the course of their execution.

mysql_change_user() was introduced in MySQL 3.23.3.

- void

mysql_close (MYSQL *conn);

Closes the connection specified by conn. Call this routine when you are done with a server session. If the connection handler was allocated automatically by mysql_init(), mysql_close() de-allocates it.

Do not call mysql_close() if the attempt to open a connection failed.

- MYSQL *

mysql_init (MYSQL *conn);

Initializes a connection handler and returns a pointer to it. If the parameter points to an existing MYSQL handler structure, mysql_init() initializes it and returns its address:

```
MYSQL conn_struct, *conn;
conn = mysql_init (&conn_struct);
```

If the parameter is NULL, mysql_init() allocates a new handler, initializes it, and returns its address:

```
MYSQL *conn;
conn = mysql_init (NULL);
```

The second approach is preferable over the first; letting the client library allocate and initialize the handler itself avoids problems that may arise with shared libraries if you upgrade MySQL to a newer version that uses a different internal organization for the MYSQL structure.

If `mysql_init()` fails, it returns NULL. This can happen if `mysql_init()` cannot allocate a new handler.

If `mysql_init()` allocates the handler, `mysql_close()` deallocates it automatically when you close the connection.

`mysql_init()` was introduced in MySQL 3.22.1.

- `int`
  `mysql_options` `(MYSQL *conn,`

                   `enum mysql_option option,`

                   `const char *arg);`

  This function allows you to tailor connection behavior more precisely than is possible with `mysql_real_connect()` alone. Call it after `mysql_init()` and before `mysql_real_connect()`. You can call `mysql_options()` multiple times if you want to set several options. (If you call `mysql_options()` multiple times to set a given option, `mysql_real_connect()` uses the most recently specified value for that option.)

  The `option` argument specifies which connection option you want to set. Additional information needed to set the option, if any, is specified by the `arg` argument. (Note that `arg` is always interpreted as a pointer.) You can pass an `arg` value of NULL for options that require no additional information.

  `mysql_options()` returns zero for success or non-zero if the `option` value is unknown.

  `mysql_options()` itself was introduced in MySQL 3.22.1, but some of the allowable option values were introduced later, as indicated in the option descriptions. The following options are available:

  - `MYSQL_INIT_COMMAND`

    Specifies a query to execute after connecting to the server. `arg` points to a null-terminated string containing the query. The query will be executed after reconnecting as well (for example, if you call `mysql_ping()`). Any result set returned by the query is discarded.

    `MYSQL_INIT_COMMAND` was introduced in MySQL 3.22.10.

  - `MYSQL_OPT_COMPRESS`

    Specifies that the connection should use the compressed client/server protocol if the server supports it. `arg` is NULL.

    It is also possible to specify compression when you call `mysql_real_connect()`.

- MYSQL_OPT_CONNECT_TIMEOUT

  Specifies the connection timeout in seconds. arg is a pointer to an unsigned int containing the timeout value.

- MYSQL_OPT_LOCAL_INFILE

  Enables or disables the use of LOAD DATA LOCAL. arg is a pointer to an unsigned int that should be non-zero to enable this capability or zero to disable it. This option will be ineffective if the server has been configured to always disallow LOAD DATA LOCAL.

  MYSQL_OPT_LOCAL_INFILE was introduced in MySQL 3.23.49. (From MySQL 3.22.15 to 3.23.48, LOAD DATA LOCAL is always enabled, and prior to 3.22.15, it is unavailable.)

- MYSQL_OPT_NAMED_PIPE

  Specifies that the connection to the server should use a named pipe. arg is NULL. This option is for Windows clients only and only for connections to Windows NT-based servers.

  MYSQL_OPT_NAMED_PIPE was introduced in MySQL 3.22.5.

- MYSQL_READ_DEFAULT_FILE

  Specifies an option file to read for connection parameters, rather than the usual option files that are searched by default if option files are read. arg points to a null-terminated string containing the filename. Options will be read from the [client] group in the file. If you use MYSQL_READ_DEFAULT_GROUP to specify a group name, options from that group will be read from option files, too.

  MYSQL_READ_DEFAULT_FILE was introduced in MySQL 3.22.10.

- MYSQL_READ_DEFAULT_GROUP

  Specifies an option file group in which to look for option values. arg points to a null-terminated string containing the group name. (Specify the group name without the surrounding '[' and ']' characters.) The named group will be read in addition to the [client] group. If you also name a particular option file with MYSQL_READ_DEFAULT_FILE, options are read from that file only. Otherwise, the client library looks for the options in the standard option files.

  Note that if you specify neither MYSQL_READ_DEFAULT_FILE nor MYSQL_READ_DEFAULT_GROUP, no option files are read.

  MYSQL_READ_DEFAULT_GROUP was introduced in MySQL 3.22.10.

- MYSQL_SET_CHARSET_DIR

  Specifies the pathname of the directory where character set files are located. `arg` points to a null-terminated string containing the directory pathname. The directory is on the client host; this option is used when the client needs to access character sets that aren't compiled into the client library but for which definition files are available.

  MYSQL_SET_CHARSET_DIR was introduced in MySQL 3.23.14.

- MYSQL_SET_CHARSET_NAME

  Indicates the name of the default character set to use. `arg` points to a null-terminated string containing the character set name.

  MYSQL_SET_CHARSET_NAME was introduced in MySQL 3.23.14.

  Certain options can also be specified by means of an option file in either the `[client]` group or in a group that you specify with the MYSQL_READ_DEFAULT_GROUP option. The list of options that pertain to client programs is given in the "Option Files" section of Appendix E, "MySQL Program Reference."

  For Windows pathnames specified with the MYSQL_READ_DEFAULT_FILE or MYSQL_SET_CHARSET_DIR options, '\' characters can be given either as '/' or as '\\', although '/' is preferable.

  The `mysql_options()` calls in the following example have the effect of setting connection options so that `mysql_real_connect()` reads `C:\my.cnf.extra` for information from the `[client]` and `[mygroup]` groups, connects using a named pipe and a timeout of 10 seconds, and executes a `SET SQL_BIG_TABLES=1` statement after the connection has been established. Communication over the connection will use the compressed protocol.

```
MYSQL *conn;
unsigned int timeout;

if ((conn = mysql_init (NULL)) == NULL)
    ... deal with error ...
mysql_options (conn, MYSQL_READ_DEFAULT_FILE, "C:/my.cnf.extra");
mysql_options (conn, MYSQL_READ_DEFAULT_GROUP, "mygroup");
mysql_options (conn, MYSQL_OPT_NAMED_PIPE, NULL);
timeout = 10;
mysql_options (conn, MYSQL_OPT_CONNECT_TIMEOUT,
                (char *) &timeout);
mysql_options (conn, MYSQL_INIT_COMMAND, "SET SQL_BIG_TABLES=1");
mysql_options (conn, MYSQL_OPT_COMPRESS, NULL);
if (mysql_real_connect (conn, ...) == NULL)
    ... deal with error ...
```

- `int`

  `mysql_ping` `(MYSQL *conn);`

  Checks whether the connection indicated by `conn` is still up. If not, `mysql_ping()` reconnects using the same parameters that were used initially to make the connection. Thus, you should not call `mysql_ping()` without first successfully having called `mysql_real_connect()`. Returns zero if the connection was up or was successfully re-established; returns non-zero if an error occurred.

  `mysql_ping()` was introduced in MySQL 3.22.1.

- `MYSQL *`

  `mysql_real_connect` `(MYSQL *conn,`
                               `const char *host_name,`
                               `const char *user_name,`
                               `const char *password,`
                               `const char *db_name,`
                               `unsigned int port_num,`
                               `const char *socket_name,`
                               `unsigned int flags);`

  Connects to a server and returns a pointer to the connection handler. `conn` should be a pointer to an existing connection handler that has been initialized by `mysql_init()`. The return value is the address of the handler for a successful connection or `NULL` if an error occurred.

  If the connection attempt fails, you can pass the `conn` handler value to `mysql_errno()` and `mysql_error()` to obtain error information. However, you should not pass the `conn` value to any other client library routines that assume a connection has been established successfully.

  `host_name` indicates the name of the MySQL server host. Table F.4 shows how the client attempts to connect for various `host_name` values for UNIX and Windows clients. Note that the name `"localhost"` is special for UNIX systems. It indicates that you want to connect using a UNIX socket rather than a TCP/IP connection. To connect to a server running on the local host using TCP/IP, pass `"127.0.0.1"` (a string containing the IP address of the local host's loopback interface) for the `host_name` value, rather than passing the string `"localhost"`.

Table F.4 **Client Connection Types by Server Hostname Type**

Hostname Value	UNIX Connection Type	Windows Connection Type
`hostname`	TCP/IP connection to the named host	TCP/IP connection to the named host
`IP number`	TCP/IP connection to the named host	TCP/IP connection to the named host
`localhost`	UNIX socket connection to the local host	TCP/IP connection to the local host
`127.0.0.1`	TCP/IP connection to the named host	TCP/IP connection to the named host
`. (period)`	Does not apply	Named pipe connection to the local host
`NULL`	UNIX socket connection to the local host	TCP/IP connection to the local host; on Windows NT-based systems, a named pipe connection is attempted first before falling back to TCP/IP

`user_name` is your MySQL username. If this is `NULL`, the client library sends a default name. Under UNIX, the default is your login name. Under Windows, the default is your name as specified in the `USER` environment variable if that variable is set and `"ODBC"` otherwise.

`password` is your password. If this is `NULL`, you will only be able to connect if the password is blank in the `user` grant table entry that matches your username and the host from which you are connecting.

`db_name` is the database to use. If this is `NULL`, no initial database is selected.

`port_num` is the port number to use for TCP/IP connections. If this is `0`, the default port number is used.

`socket_name` is the UNIX socket name to use for connections to `"localhost"` under UNIX or the pipe name for named pipe connections under Windows. If this is `NULL`, the default socket or pipe name is used.

The port number and socket name are used according to the value of `host_name`. Under UNIX, `mysql_real_connect()` connects using a UNIX domain socket if you connect to `"localhost"`. Under Windows, `mysql_real_connect()` connects using a named pipe if you connect to `"."`; otherwise, the function connects using TCP/IP.

The `flags` value can be one or more of the values shown in the following list or can be `0` to specify no options. These options affect the operation of the server:

- `CLIENT_COMPRESS`

  Specifies that the connection should use the compressed client/server protocol if the server supports it.

- `CLIENT_FOUND_ROWS`

  Specifies that for `UPDATE` queries, the server should return the number of rows matched rather than the number of rows changed. Use of this option can hinder the MySQL optimizer and make updates slower.

- `CLIENT_IGNORE_SPACE`

  Normally, function names must be followed immediately by the parenthesis that begins the argument list with no intervening spaces. This option tells the server to ignore all spaces between the function name and the argument list, which also has the side effect of making all function names reserved words.

  This option was introduced in MySQL 3.22.7.

- `CLIENT_INTERACTIVE`

  Identifies the client as an interactive client. This tells the server that it can close the connection after a number of seconds of client inactivity equal to the server's `interactive_timeout` variable value. Normally, the value of the `wait_timeout` variable is used.

  This option was introduced in MySQL 3.23.28.

- `CLIENT_NO_SCHEMA`

  Disallows `db_name.tbl_name.col_name` syntax. If you specify this option, the server allows only references of the forms `tbl_name.col_name`, `tbl_name`, or `col_name` in queries.

- `CLIENT_ODBC`

  Identifies the client as an ODBC client.

  This option was introduced in MySQL 3.22.4.

- `CLIENT_SSL`

  This is used internally for SSL connections; client programs should not use it.

- CLIENT_TRANSACTIONS

  Indicates to the server that the client knows about transactions. That is, the client understands that the server will have rolled back an active transaction if the connection drops during the transaction when not running in auto-commit mode.

  This option was introduced in MySQL 3.23.17.

The flag values are bit values, so you can combine them in additive fashion using either the | or the + operator. For example, the following expressions are equivalent:

```
CLIENT_COMPRESS | CLIENT_ODBC
CLIENT_COMPRESS + CLIENT_ODBC
```

The mysql_real_connect() db_name parameter was added in 3.22.0. The use of mysql_init() to initialize the MYSQL connection handler argument began in 3.22.1.

- int
  mysql_ssl_set (MYSQL *conn,
                     const char *key,
                     const char *cert,
                     const char *ca,
                     const char *capath,
                     const char *cipher);

This function is used for setting up a secure connection over SSL to the MySQL server. If OpenSSL support is not compiled into the client library, mysql_ssl_set() does nothing. Otherwise, it sets up the information required to establish an encrypted connection when you call mysql_real_connect(). (In other words, to set up a secure connection, call mysql_ssl_set() first and then mysql_real_connect().)

mysql_ssl_set() always returns 0; any SSL setup errors will result in an error at the time you call mysql_real_connect().

key is the path to the key file. cert is the path to the certificate file. ca is the path to the certificate authority file. capath is the path to a directory of trusted certificates to be used for certificate verification. cipher is a string listing the cipher or ciphers to use. Any parameter that is unused can be passed as NULL.

mysql_ssl_set() was introduced in MySQL 4.0.0. It requires some additional MySQL configuration ahead of time. (See Chapter 12 for information on using secure connections.)

Error-Reporting Routines

The functions in this section allow you to determine and report the causes of errors.

- unsigned int
  mysql_errno (MYSQL *conn);

  Returns an error code for the most recently invoked client library routine that returned a status. The error code is zero if no error occurred or non-zero otherwise. The possible error codes are listed in the errmsg.h and mysqld_error.h MySQL header files.
  ```
  if (mysql_errno (conn) == 0)
      printf ("Everything is okay\n");
  else
      printf ("Something is wrong!\n");
  ```

- const char *
  mysql_error (MYSQL *conn);

  Returns a null-terminated string containing an error message for the most recently invoked client library routine that returned a status. The return value is the empty string if no error occurred (this is, the zero-length string " ", not a NULL pointer). Although normally you call mysql_error() after you already know an error occurred, the return value itself can be used to detect the occurrence of an error:
  ```
  char *err = mysql_error (conn);
  if (err[0] == '\0')                     /* empty string? */
      printf ("Everything is okay\n");
  else
      printf ("Something is wrong!\n");
  ```

Query Construction and Execution Routines

The functions in this section allow you to send queries to the server. mysql_real_escape_string() helps you construct queries by escaping characters that need special treatment. Each query string must consist of a single SQL statement and should not end with a semicolon character (';') or a \g sequence. ';' and \g are conventions of the mysql client program, not of the C client library.

- int
  mysql_query (MYSQL *conn, const char *query_str);

Given a query specified as a null-terminated string, `mysql_query()` sends the query to the server to be executed. The string should not contain binary data; in particular, it should not contain null bytes because `mysql_query()` will interpret the first one as the end of the query. If your query does contain binary data, use `mysql_real_query()` instead. `mysql_real_query()` is slightly faster than `mysql_query()`.

`mysql_query()` returns zero for success or non-zero for failure. A successful query is one that the server accepts as legal and executes without error. Success does not imply anything about the number of rows affected or returned.

▪ unsigned long
`mysql_real_escape_string` `(MYSQL *conn,`
　　　　　　　　　　　　　　`char *to_str,`
　　　　　　　　　　　　　　`const char *from_str,`
　　　　　　　　　　　　　　`unsigned long from_len);`

Encodes a string that can contain special characters so that it can be used in an SQL statement, taking into account the current character set when performing encoding. Table F.5 lists the characters that are considered special and how they are encoded. (Note that the list does not include the SQL pattern characters, '%' and '_'.)

Table F.5 **mysql_real_escape_string() Character Encodings**

Special Character	Encoding
NUL (ASCII 0)	\0 (backslash–zero)
Backslash	\\ (backslash–backslash)
Single quote	\' (backslash–single quote)
Double quote	\" (backslash–double quote)
Newline	\n (backslash–'n')
Carriage return	\r (backslash–'r')
Ctrl-Z	\Z (backslash–'Z')

The only characters that MySQL itself requires to be escaped within a string are backslash and the quote character that surrounds the string (either ' ' or ' " '). `mysql_real_escape_string()` escapes the others to produce strings that are easier to read and to process in log files.

The buffer to be encoded is specified as a counted string. `from_str` points to the buffer, and `from_len` indicates the number of bytes in it. `mysql_real_escape_string()` writes the encoded result into the buffer pointed to by `to_str` and adds a null byte. `to_str` must point to an existing buffer that is at least `(from_len*2)+1` bytes long. (In the worst case scenario, every character in `from_str` might need to be encoded as a two-character sequence, and you also need room for the terminating null byte.)

`mysql_real_escape_string()` returns the length of the encoded string, not counting the terminating null byte.

The resulting encoded string contains no internal nulls but is null-terminated, so you can use it with functions such as `strlen()` or `strcat()`.

When you write literal strings in your program, take care not to confuse the lexical escape conventions of the C programming language with the encoding done by `mysql_real_escape_string()`. Consider the following example source code and the output produced by it:

```
to_len = mysql_real_escape_string (conn, to_str, "\0\\\'\"\n\r\032", 7);
printf ("to_len = %d, to_str = %s\n", to_len, to_str);
```

The output is:

```
to_len = 14, to_str = \0\\\'\"\n\r\Z
```

The printed value of `to_str` in the output looks very much like the string specified as the third argument of the `mysql_real_escape_string()` call in the original source code, but is in fact quite different.

`mysql_real_escape_string()` was introduced in MySQL 3.23.14 as a replacement for `mysql_escape_string()`, which does not take into account the current character set and is now deprecated. To write code that will work with any version of MySQL, include the following fragment in any source file that uses `mysql_real_escape_string()`:

```
#if !defined(MYSQL_VERSION_ID) || (MYSQL_VERSION_ID<32314)
#define mysql_real_escape_string(conn,to_str,from_str,len) \
        mysql_escape_string(to_str,from_str,len)
#endif
```

This maps `mysql_real_escape_string()` to `mysql_escape_string()` when the source is compiled under older versions of MySQL.

- int
  mysql_real_query (MYSQL *conn,
                        const char *query_str,
                        unsigned long length);

  Given a query specified as a counted string, mysql_real_query() sends the query to the server to be executed. The string can contain binary data (including null bytes). The query text is given by query_str, and the length is indicated by length.

  mysql_real_query() returns zero for success, and it returns non-zero for failure. A successful query is one that the server accepts as legal and executes without error. Success does not imply anything about the number of rows affected or returned.

  Prior to MySQL 4, the length argument is an unsigned int.

- int
  mysql_select_db (MYSQL *conn, const char *db_name);

  Selects the database named by db_name as the current database, which becomes the default for table references that contain no explicit database specifier. If you do not have permission to access the database, mysql_select_db() fails.

  mysql_select_db() is most useful for changing databases within the course of a connection. Normally you will specify the initial database to use when you call mysql_real_connect(), which is faster than calling mysql_select_db() after connecting.

  mysql_select_db() returns zero for success, non-zero for failure.

Result Set Processing Routines

When a query produces a result set, the functions in this section allow you to retrieve the set and access its contents. The mysql_store_result() and mysql_use_result() functions create the result set, and one or the other must be called before using any other functions in this section. Table F.6 compares the two functions.

Table F.6 **Comparison of mysql_store_result() and mysql_use_result()**

mysql_store_result()	mysql_use_result()
All rows in the result set are fetched by mysql_store_result() itself.	mysql_use_result() initializes the result set but defers row retrieval to mysql_fetch_row().
Uses more memory; all rows are stored in the client.	Uses less memory; one row is stored at a time.
Slower due to overhead involved in allocating memory for the entire result set.	Faster because memory need be allocated only for the current row.
A NULL return from mysql_fetch_row() indicates the end of the result set, not an error.	A NULL return from mysql_fetch_row() indicates the end of the result set or an error because a communications failure can disrupt retrieval of the current record.
mysql_num_rows() can be called anytime after mysql_store_result() has been called.	mysql_num_rows() returns a correct row count only after all rows have been fetched.
mysql_affected_rows() is a synonym for mysql_num_rows().	mysql_affected_rows() cannot be used.
Random access to result set rows is possible with mysql_data_seek(), mysql_row_seek(), and mysql_row_tell().	No random access into result set; rows must be processed in order as returned by the server. mysql_data_seek(), mysql_row_seek(), and mysql_row_tell() should not be used.
Tables are read-locked for no longer than necessary to fetch the data rows.	Tables can stay read-locked if the client pauses in mid-retrieval, locking out other clients attempting to modify the tables.
The max_length member of result set MYSQL_FIELD structures is set to the longest value actually present in the result set for the columns in the set.	max_length is not set to any meaningful value, because it cannot be known until all rows are retrieved.

- my_ulonglong
mysql_affected_rows (MYSQL *conn);

Returns the number of rows changed by the most recent DELETE, INSERT, REPLACE, or UPDATE query. For such queries, mysql_affected_rows() can be called immediately after a successful call to mysql_query(). You can also call this function after issuing a statement that returns rows. In this case, the function acts the same way as mysql_num_rows() and is subject to the same constraints as that function on when the value is meaningful, as well as the additional constraint that if you use mysql_use_result() to generate the result set, mysql_affected_rows() is never meaningful.

mysql_affected_rows() returns zero if no query has been issued, or if the query was of a type that can return rows but selects none. A return value greater than zero indicates the number of rows changed (for DELETE, INSERT, REPLACE, UPDATE) or returned (for queries that return rows). A return value of –1 indicates either an error or that you (erroneously) called mysql_affected_rows() after issuing a query that returns rows but before actually retrieving the result set. However, because mysql_affected_rows() returns an unsigned value, you can detect a negative return value only by casting the result to a signed value before performing the comparison:

```
if ((long) mysql_affected_rows (conn) == -1)
    fprintf (stderr, "Error!\n");
```

If you have specified that the client should return the number of rows matched for UPDATE queries, mysql_affected_rows() returns that value rather than the number of rows actually modified. (MySQL does not update a row if the columns to be modified are the same as the new values.) This behavior can be selected by passing CLIENT_FOUND_ROWS in the flags parameter to mysql_real_connect().

mysql_real_connect() returns a my_ulonglong value; see the note about printing values of this type in the "Scalar Data Types" section earlier in this appendix.

- void
  mysql_data_seek (MYSQL_RES *res_set,
                       my_ulonglong row_num);

Seeks to a particular row of the result set. The value of row_num can range from 0 to mysql_num_rows(res_set)–1. The results are unpredictable if row_num is out of range.

mysql_data_seek() requires that the entire result set has been retrieved, so you can use it only if the result set was created by mysql_store_result(), not by mysql_use_result().

mysql_data_seek() differs from mysql_row_seek(), which takes a row offset value as returned by mysql_row_tell() rather than a row number.

Prior to MySQL 3.23.7, the row_num argument was of type unsigned int.

- MYSQL_FIELD *

  mysql_fetch_field (MYSQL_RES *res_set);

  Returns a structure containing information (metadata) about a column in the result set. After you successfully execute a query that returns rows, the first call to mysql_fetch_field() returns information about the first column. Subsequent calls return information about successive columns following the first or NULL when no more columns are left.

  Related functions are mysql_field_tell() to determine the current column position or mysql_field_seek() to select a particular column to be returned by the next call to mysql_fetch_field().

  The following example seeks to the first MYSQL_FIELD, and then fetches successive column information structures:

  ```
  MYSQL_FIELD    *field;
  unsigned int   i;

  mysql_field_seek (res_set, 0);
  for (i = 0; i < mysql_num_fields (res_set); i++)
  {
      field = mysql_fetch_field (res_set);
      printf ("column %u: name = %s max_length = %lu\n",
              i, field->name, field->max_length);
  }
  ```

- MYSQL_FIELD *

  mysql_fetch_fields (MYSQL_RES *res_set);

  Returns an array of all column information structures for the result set. These can be accessed as follows:

  ```
  MYSQL_FIELD    *field;
  unsigned int   i;

  field = mysql_fetch_fields (res_set);
  for (i = 0; i < mysql_num_fields (res_set); i++)
  {
      printf ("column %u: name = %s max_length = %lu\n",
              i, field[i].name, field[i].max_length);
  }
  ```

  Compare this to the example shown for mysql_fetch_field(). Note that although both functions return values of the same type, those values are accessed using slightly different syntax for each function. mysql_fetch_field() returns a pointer to a single field structure; mysql_fetch_fields() returns a pointer to an array of field structures.

- MYSQL_FIELD *

  mysql_fetch_field_direct (MYSQL_RES *res_set, unsigned int
                            col_num);

  Given a column index, returns the information structure for that column. The value of col_num can range from 0 to
  mysql_num_fields (res_set)-1. The results are unpredictable if
  col_num is out of range.

  The following example accesses MYSQL_FIELD structures directly:

  ```
  MYSQL_FIELD    *field;
  unsigned int   i;

  for (i = 0; i < mysql_num_fields (res_set); i++)
  {
      field = mysql_fetch_field_direct (res_set, i);
      printf ("column %u: name = %s max_length = %lu\n",
              i, field->name, field->max_length);
  }
  ```

  mysql_fetch_field_direct () does not work properly prior to
  MySQL 3.23.

- unsigned long *

  mysql_fetch_lengths (MYSQL_RES *res_set);

  Returns a pointer to an array of unsigned long values representing the
  lengths of the column values in the current row of the result set.
  You must call mysql_fetch_lengths () each time you call
  mysql_fetch_row () or your lengths will be out of sync with your data
  values.

  The length for NULL values is zero, but a zero length does not by itself
  indicate a NULL data value. An empty string also has a length of zero, so
  you must check whether the data value is a NULL pointer to distinguish
  between the two cases.

  The following example displays lengths and values for the current row,
  printing the word "NULL" if the value is NULL:

  ```
  unsigned long *length;

  length = mysql_fetch_lengths (res_set);
  for (i = 0; i < mysql_num_fields (res_set); i++)
  {
      printf ("length is %lu, value is %s\n",
              length[i], (row[i] != NULL ? row[i] : "NULL"));
  }
  ```

Prior to MySQL 3.22.5, the return type of `mysql_fetch_lengths()` was `unsigned int`.

- `MYSQL_ROW`

  `mysql_fetch_row` `(MYSQL_RES *res_set);`

  Returns a pointer to the next row of the result set, represented as an array of strings (except that `NULL` column values are represented as `NULL` pointers). The *i*-th value in the row is the *i*-th member of the value array. Values of *i* range from 0 to `mysql_num_fields(res_set)-1`.

  Values for all data types, even numeric types, are returned as strings. If you want to perform a numeric calculation with a value, you must convert it yourself—for example, with `atoi()`, `atof()`, or `sscanf()`.

  `mysql_fetch_row()` returns `NULL` when there are no more rows in the data set. (If you use `mysql_use_result()` to initiate a row-by-row result set retrieval, `mysql_fetch_row()` also returns `NULL` if a communications error occurred.)

  Data values are null-terminated, but you should not treat values that can contain binary data as null-terminated strings. Treat them as counted strings instead. To do this, you will need the column value lengths, which can be obtained by calling `mysql_fetch_lengths()`.

  The following code shows how to loop through a row of data values and determine whether each value is `NULL`:

  ```
  MYSQL_ROW      row;
  unsigned int   i;

  while ((row = mysql_fetch_row (res_set)) != NULL)
  {
      for (i = 0; i < mysql_num_fields (res_set); i++)
      {
          printf ("column %u: value is %s\n",
                  i, (row[i] == NULL ? "NULL" : "not NULL"));
      }
  }
  ```

  To determine the types of the column values, use the column metadata stored in the `MYSQL_FIELD` column information structures, obtained by calling `mysql_fetch_field()`, `mysql_fetch_fields()`, or `mysql_fetch_field_direct()`.

- unsigned int

  mysql_field_count (MYSQL *conn);

  Returns the number of columns for the most recent query on the given connection. This function is usually used when mysql_store_result() or mysql_use_result() return NULL. mysql_field_count() tells you whether or not a result set should have been returned. A return value of zero indicates no result set and no error. A non-zero value indicates that columns were expected and that, because none were returned, an error occurred.

  The following example illustrates how to use mysql_field_count() for error-detection purposes:

```
res_set = mysql_store_result (conn);
if (res_set == NULL)     /* no result set was returned */
{
    /*
     * does the lack of a result set mean that an error
     * occurred or that no result set should be expected?
     */
    if (mysql_field_count (conn) > 0)
    {
        /*
         * a result set was expected, but mysql_store_result()
         * did not return one; this means an error occurred
         */
        printf ("Problem processing the result set\n");
    }
    else
    {
        /*
         * a result set was not expected; query returned no data
         * (it was not a SELECT, SHOW, DESCRIBE, or EXPLAIN),
         * so just report number of rows affected by query
         */
        printf ("%lu rows affected\n",
                    (unsigned long) mysql_affected_rows (conn));
    }
}
else    /* a result set was returned */
{
    /* ... process rows here, then free result set ... */
    mysql_free_result (res_set);
}
```

`mysql_field_count()` was introduced in MySQL 3.22.24. Prior to that version, `mysql_num_fields()` was used for the same purpose. To write code that will work with any version of MySQL, include the following fragment in any source file that uses `mysql_field_count()`:

```
#if !defined(MYSQL_VERSION_ID) || (MYSQL_VERSION_ID<32224)
#define mysql_field_count mysql_num_fields
#endif
```

This maps `mysql_field_count()` to `mysql_num_fields()` when the source is compiled under older versions of MySQL.

- MYSQL_FIELD_OFFSET

  mysql_field_seek (MYSQL_RES *res_set, MYSQL_FIELD_OFFSET
                 offset);

  Seeks to the column information structure specified by `offset`. The next call to `mysql_fetch_field()` will return the information structure for that column. `offset` is *not* a column index; it is a MYSQL_FIELD_OFFSET value obtained from an earlier call to `mysql_field_tell()` or from `mysql_field_seek()`.

  To reset to the first column, the `offset` value should be zero.

- MYSQL_FIELD_OFFSET

  mysql_field_tell (MYSQL_RES *res_set);

  Returns the current column information structure offset. This value can be passed to `mysql_field_seek()`.

- void

  mysql_free_result (MYSQL_RES *res_set);

  De-allocates the memory used by the result set. You must call `mysql_free_result()` for each result set you work with. Typically, result sets are generated by calling `mysql_store_result()` or `mysql_use_result()`. However, some client library functions generate result sets implicitly, and you are responsible for freeing those sets, too. These functions are `mysql_list_dbs()`, `mysql_list_fields()`, `mysql_list_processes()`, and `mysql_list_tables()`.

  As of MySQL 3.22.3, `mysql_free_result()` automatically fetches and discards any unfetched rows for result sets generated by calling `mysql_use_result()`.

- my_ulonglong
mysql_insert_id (MYSQL conn);

Returns the AUTO_INCREMENT value generated by the most recently executed query on the given connection. Returns zero if no query has been
executed or if the previous query did not generate an AUTO_INCREMENT
value. (A zero return value is distinct from any valid AUTO_INCREMENT
value because such values are positive.)

You should call mysql_insert_id() immediately after issuing the query
that you expect to generate a new value. If you issue another query
before calling mysql_insert_id(), its value will be reset. Note that this
behavior differs from that of the SQL function LAST_INSERT_ID().
mysql_insert_id() is maintained in the client and is set for each query.
The value of LAST_INSERT_ID() is maintained in the server and persists
from query to query until you generate another AUTO_INCREMENT value.

The values returned by mysql_insert_id() are connection-specific and
are not affected by AUTO_INCREMENT activity on other connections.

mysql_insert_id() returns a my_ulonglong value; see the note about
printing values of this type in the "Scalar Data Types" section earlier in
this appendix.

- unsigned int
mysql_num_fields (MYSQL_RES *res_set);

Returns the number of columns in the result set. mysql_num_fields()
is often used to iterate through the columns of the current row of the
set, as illustrated by the following example:

```
MYSQL_ROW       row;
unsigned int    i;

while ((row = mysql_fetch_row (res_set)) != NULL)
{
    for (i = 0; i < mysql_num_fields (res_set); i++)
    {
        /* do something with row[i] here ... */
    }
}
```

Prior to MySQL 3.22.24, mysql_num_fields() was also used to perform
the function now performed by mysql_field_count(), that is, to test
whether or not a NULL return from mysql_store_result() or

`mysql_use_result()` indicates an error. This is why in older source code you will sometimes see `mysql_num_fields()` being called with a pointer to a connection handler rather than with a pointer to a result set. `mysql_num_fields()` used to be callable either way, but invoking it with a connection handler argument now is deprecated. You should always retrieve a column count with `mysql_field_count()` instead; see the description of that function for an example that shows how to use it even for older versions of MySQL.

- `my_ulonglong`

  mysql_num_rows `(MYSQL_RES *res_set);`

  Returns the number of rows in the result set. If you generate the result set with `mysql_store_result()`, you can call `mysql_num_rows()` anytime thereafter:

  ```
  if ((res_set = mysql_store_result (conn)) != NULL)
  {
      /* mysql_num_rows() can be called now */
  }
  ```

  If you generate the result set with `mysql_use_result()`, `mysql_num_rows()` doesn't return the correct value until you have fetched all the rows:

  ```
  if ((res_set = mysql_use_result (conn)) != NULL)
  {
      /* mysql_num_rows() cannot be called yet */
      while ((row = mysql_fetch_row (res_set)) != NULL)
      {
          /* mysql_num_rows() still cannot be called */
      }
      /* mysql_num_rows() can be called now */
  }
  ```

  `mysql_num_rows()` returns a `my_ulonglong` value; see the note about printing values of this type in the "Scalar Data Types" section earlier in this appendix.

- `MYSQL_ROW_OFFSET`

  mysql_row_seek `(MYSQL_RES *res_set, MYSQL_ROW_OFFSET off-`
  `                    set);`

  Seeks to a particular row of the result set. `mysql_row_seek()` is similar to `mysql_data_seek()`, but the `offset` value is not a row number. `offset` is a `MYSQL_ROW_OFFSET` value that must be obtained from a call to `mysql_row_tell()` or `mysql_row_seek()` or zero to seek to the first row.

mysql_row_seek() returns the previous row offset.

mysql_row_seek() requires that the entire result set has been retrieved, so you can use it only if the result set was created by mysql_store_result(), not by mysql_use_result().

- MYSQL_ROW_OFFSET

  mysql_row_tell (MYSQL_RES *res_set);

  Returns an offset representing the current row position in the result set. This is not a row number; the value can be passed only to mysql_row_seek(), not to mysql_data_seek().

  mysql_row_tell() requires that the entire result set has been retrieved, so you can use it only if the result set was created by mysql_store_result(), not by mysql_use_result().

- MYSQL_RES *

  mysql_store_result (MYSQL *conn);

  Following a successful query, returns the result set and stores it in the client. Returns NULL if the query returns no data or an error occurred. When mysql_store_result() returns NULL, call mysql_field_count() or one of the error-reporting functions to determine whether a result set was not expected or whether an error occurred.

  When you are done with the result set, pass it to mysql_free_result() to de-allocate it.

  See the comparison of mysql_store_result() and mysql_use_result() in Table F.6.

- MYSQL_RES *

  mysql_use_result (MYSQL *conn);

  Following a successful query, initiates a result set retrieval but does not retrieve any data rows itself. You must call mysql_fetch_row() to fetch the rows one by one. Returns NULL if the query returns no data or an error occurred. When mysql_use_result() returns NULL, call mysql_field_count() or one of the error-reporting functions to determine whether a result set was not expected or whether an error occurred.

When you are done with the result set, pass it to
`mysql_free_result()` to de-allocate it. As of MySQL 3.22.3, that is
all that is necessary to finish query processing because
`mysql_free_result()` automatically retrieves and discards any
unfetched rows before releasing the result set. (Prior to MySQL 3.22.3,
you should fetch the rows yourself until none are left and then call
`mysql_free_result()`. If you fail to do so before issuing another
query, an "out of sync" error will occur.)

See the comparison of `mysql_store_result()` and
`mysql_use_result()` in Table F.6. `mysql_store_result()` and
`mysql_use_result()` are both used to retrieve result sets, but they affect
the way you can use other result set-handling functions.

Information Routines

These functions provide information about the client, server, protocol version,
and the current connection. The values returned by most of these are retrieved
from the server at connect time and stored within the client library.

- `const char *`
  `mysql_character_set_name` `(MYSQL *conn);`

  Returns the name of the default character set for the given connection,
  for example, `"latin1"`.

  `mysql_character_set_name()` was introduced in MySQL 3.23.21.

- `const char *`
  `mysql_get_client_info` `(void);`

  Returns a null-terminated string describing the client library version, for
  example, `"3.23.51"`.

- `const char *`
  `mysql_get_host_info` `(MYSQL *conn);`

  Returns a null-terminated string describing the given connection, such
  as `"Localhost via UNIX socket"`, `"cobra.snake.net via
  TCP/IP"`, or `". via named pipe"`.

- `unsigned int`
  `mysql_get_proto_info` `(MYSQL *conn);`

  Returns a number indicating the client/server protocol version used for
  the given connection.

- `const char *`
  `mysql_get_server_info` (MYSQL *conn);

  Returns a null-terminated string describing the server version, for example, `"4.0.2-alpha-log"`. The value consists of a version number, possibly followed by one or more suffixes. The suffix values are listed in the description of the `VERSION()` function in Appendix C, "Operator and Function Reference."

- `const char *`
  `mysql_info` (MYSQL *conn);

  Returns a string containing information about the effect of the most recently executed query of the following types. The string format is given immediately following each query:

  ```
  ALTER TABLE ...
      Records: 0 Duplicates: 0 Warnings: 0
  INSERT INTO ... SELECT ...
      Records: 0 Duplicates: 0 Warnings: 0
  INSERT INTO ... VALUES (...),(...),...
      Records: 0 Duplicates: 0 Warnings: 0
  LOAD DATA ...
      Records: 0 Deleted: 0 Skipped: 0 Warnings: 0
  UPDATE ...
      Rows matched: 0 Changed: 0 Warnings: 0
  ```

  The numbers will vary according to the particular query you've executed.

  `mysql_info()` returns non-`NULL` for `INSERT INTO ... VALUES` only if the statement contains more than one value list. For statements not shown in the preceding list, `mysql_info()` always returns `NULL`.

  The string returned by `mysql_info()` is in the language used by the server, so you can't necessarily count on being able to parse it by looking for certain words.

- `const char *`
  `mysql_stat` (MYSQL *conn);

  Returns a null-terminated string containing server status information or `NULL` if an error occurred. The format of the string is subject to change. Currently it looks something like the following:

  ```
  Uptime: 1189474  Threads: 4  Questions: 331869  Slow queries: 50  Opens: 1424
  Flush tables: 1  Open tables: 64 Queries per second avg: 0.279
  ```

These values may be interpreted as follows:

- Uptime is the number of seconds the server has been up.
- Threads is the number of threads currently running in the server.
- Questions is the number of queries the server has executed.
- Slow queries is the number of queries that took longer to process than the time indicated by the server's long_query_time variable.
- Opens is the number of tables the server has opened.
- Flush tables is the number of FLUSH, REFRESH, and RELOAD statements that have been executed.
- Open tables is the number of tables the server currently has open.
- Queries per second is the ratio of Questions to Uptime.

Not coincidentally, the information returned by the mysql_stat() function is the same as that reported by the mysqladmin status command. (mysqladmin itself invokes this function to get the information.)

- unsigned long
mysql_thread_id (MYSQL *conn);

Returns the thread number that the server associates with the current connection. You can use this number as an identifier for mysql_kill().

Do not invoke mysql_thread_id() until just before you need the value. If you retrieve the value and store it, the value may be incorrect when you use it later. This can happen if your connection goes down and then is re-established (for example, with mysql_ping()) because the server will assign the new connection a different thread identifier.

Administrative Routines

The functions in this section allow you to control aspects of server operation.

- int
mysql_shutdown (MYSQL *conn);

Instructs the server to shut down. You must have the SHUTDOWN privilege to do this.

mysql_shutdown() returns zero for success or non-zero for failure.

Threaded Client Routines

The routines in this section are used for writing multi-threaded clients.

- void
  mysql_thread_end (void);

  Frees any thread-specific variables initialized by `mysql_thread_init()`. To avoid memory leaks, you should call this function explicitly to terminate any threads that you create.

  `mysql_thread_end()` was introduced in MySQL 4.0.0.

- my_bool
  mysql_thread_init (void);

  Initializes thread-specific variables. This function should be called for any thread you create that will call MySQL functions. In addition, you should call `mysql_thread_end()` before terminating the thread.

  `mysql_thread_init()` was introduced in MySQL 4.0.0.

- unsigned int
  mysql_thread_safe (void);

  Returns `1` if the client library is thread-safe, `0` otherwise. The value of this function reflects whether MySQL was configured with the `--enable-thread-safe-client` option.

  `mysql_thread_safe()` was introduced in MySQL 3.23.14

Embedded Server Communication Routines

This section describes routines that are used to communicate with `libmysqld`, the embedded MySQL server. To write a program that uses the embedded server, you should specify `-lmysqld` rather than `-lmysqlclient` when you link your program to produce an executable image. To find out the particular library flags that are appropriate for linking in the embedded server on your system, use the following command:

```
% mysql_config --libmysqld-libs
```

The regular client library, `-lmysqlclient`, contains dummy versions of these routines that do nothing. This means that if you call these routines within your program, it is possible to produce a standalone client or one that uses the embedded server from the same source code, depending on which library you select at link time.

- void

  mysql_server_end (void);

  Shuts down the embedded server. You should call this function after you're done using the server.

- int

  mysql_server_init (int argc,
                         char **argv,
                         char **groups);

  Initializes the embedded server. This function must be called before calling any other mysql_xxx() functions.

  The argc and argv arguments are like the standard arguments passed to main() in C programs: argc is the argument count; if there are none, argc should be zero. Otherwise, argc should be the number of arguments passed to the server. argv is a vector of null-terminated strings containing the arguments. Note that argv[0] will be ignored.

  The groups argument is a vector of null-terminated strings indicating which option file groups the embedded server should read. The final element of the vector should be NULL. If group itself is NULL, the server reads the [server] and [embedded] option file groups by default. Group names in the groups vector should be given without the surrounding '[' and ']' characters.

Debugging Routines

Thee following functions allow you to generate debugging information on either the client or server end of the connection. This requires MySQL to be compiled to support debugging. (Use the --with-debug option when you configure the MySQL distribution, or --with-debug=full for more information. The latter option enables safemalloc, a library that performs extensive memory allocation checking.)

- void

  mysql_debug (const char *debug_str);

  Performs a DBUG_PUSH operation using the string debug_str. The format of the string is described in the MySQL Reference Manual.

  To use mysql_debug(), the client library must be compiled with debugging support.

- `int`
  mysql_dump_debug_info `(MYSQL *conn);`

  Instructs the server to write debugging information to the log. You must have the PROCESS privilege to do this prior to MySQL 4.0.2 and the SUPER privilege from 4.0.2 on.

  `mysql_dump_debug_info()` returns zero for success, non-zero for failure.

Deprecated Routines

The MySQL client library includes a number of functions that now are deprecated because there are alternative preferred ways to do the same thing. Most of these functions can be replaced by issuing an equivalent query with `mysql_query()`. For example, `mysql_create_db("`*db_name*`")` can be replaced with the following call:

```
mysql_query (conn, "CREATE DATABASE db_name")
```

Over time, more functions have become deprecated as MySQL understands more SQL statements. For example, when the SQL FLUSH PRIVILEGES statement was added, `mysql_reload()` became deprecated. As FLUSH has been extended to perform a wider variety of flush operations, `mysql_refresh()` became deprecated, too. The following descriptions indicate the version of MySQL at which each function became deprecated and the preferred way to perform each function now. If your client library is older than the MySQL version listed, you must still use the deprecated function. (But you should consider upgrading. In general, it is safe to upgrade to newer MySQL client libraries because they will work with both old and new servers.)

A few functions, such as `mysql_connect()`, `mysql_eof()`, and `mysql_escape_string()` are deprecated because they have been replaced by other functions that do more or that provide more information.

To plan for the future, it's best to avoid all functions listed in this section because some or all of them may disappear eventually.

- `MYSQL *`
  mysql_connect `(MYSQL *conn,`
  `                  const char *host_name,`
  `                  const char *user_name,`
  `                  const char *password);`

This is the predecessor of `mysql_real_connect()`. It is in fact now implemented as a call to `mysql_real_connect()`.

This function is deprecated as of MySQL 3.22.0.

- `int`
  `mysql_create_db` `(MYSQL *conn,`
  `const char *db_name);`

Creates a database with the name given by `db_name`. This can be done now by issuing a CREATE DATABASE statement with `mysql_query()`.

`mysql_create_db()` returns zero for success or non-zero for failure.

This function is deprecated as of MySQL 3.21.15.

- `int`
  `mysql_drop_db` `(MYSQL *conn,`
  `const char *db_name);`

Drops the database named by `db_name`. This can be done now by issuing a DROP DATABASE statement with `mysql_query()`.

`mysql_drop_db()` returns zero for success or non-zero for failure.

This function is deprecated as of MySQL 3.21.15.

- `my_bool`
  `mysql_eof` `(MYSQL_RES *res_set);`

Returns non-zero if the end of a result set has been reached and zero if an error occurred. `mysql_eof()` is used when you use the combination of `mysql_use_result()` to initiate a result set retrieval and `mysql_fetch_row()` to fetch the data rows one at a time. With `mysql_use_result()`, a NULL return from `mysql_fetch_row()` can mean either that the end of the set has been reached or that an error occurred. `mysql_eof()` distinguishes between the two outcomes.

`mysql_errno()` and `mysql_error()` can be used now to achieve the same effect, although actually they return more information. (They indicate the reason for any error that may have occurred, rather than simply whether or not it did occur.)

This function is deprecated as of MySQL 3.21.17.

- unsigned long
  mysql_escape_string (char *to_str,
                               const char *from_str,
                               unsigned long from_len);

  Encodes a string that can contain special characters so that it can be used in an SQL statement. mysql_escape_string() is like mysql_real_escape_string() except that it does not take a conn argument indicating the current connection and does not take into account the current character set when performing encoding. See the description of mysql_real_escape_string() for more information.

  As of MySQL 3.23.14, mysql_escape_string() is deprecated and mysql_real_escape_string() should be used in preference to it.

  Prior to MySQL 3.23.6, the from_len argument is an unsigned int.

- int
  mysql_kill (MYSQL *conn, unsigned long thread_id);

  Kills the server thread identified by thread_id and returns zero for success or non-zero for failure. You can always kill your own threads. To kill other threads, you must have PROCESS privilege prior to MySQL 4.0.2, and the SUPER privilege from 4.0.2 on.

  The effect of this function can be achieved by issuing a KILL statement with mysql_query().

  mysql_kill() is deprecated as of MySQL 3.22.9.

- MYSQL_RES *
  mysql_list_dbs (MYSQL *conn, const char *wild);

  Returns a result set listing database names on the server or NULL if an error occurred. The list contains all databases matching the SQL pattern indicated by wild (which can contain the '%' and '_' wildcard pattern characters) or all databases if wild is NULL. You are responsible for calling mysql_free_result() to free the result set.

  The list produced by mysql_list_dbs() can be obtained by executing a SHOW DATABASES statement with mysql_query() and then processing the result set.

  This function is deprecated as of MySQL 3.22.0.

- MYSQL_RES *
  mysql_list_fields (MYSQL *conn,
                       const char *tbl_name,
                       const char *wild);

  Returns a result set that contains metadata about the columns in the given table, or NULL if an error occurred. The result set includes information for all column names matching the SQL pattern indicated by wild (which can contain the '%' and '_' wildcard pattern characters) or all columns if wild is NULL. You are responsible for calling mysql_free_result() to free the result set.

  The information produced by mysql_list_fields() can be obtained by executing a SELECT*FROM t WHERE 0 query (where t is the table name) and then accessing the result set metadata.

  This function is deprecated as of MySQL 3.22.0.

- MYSQL_RES *
  mysql_list_processes (MYSQL *conn);

  Returns a result set containing a list of the processes currently running in the server or NULL if an error occurred. If you have the PROCESS privilege, the list contains all server processes. If you do not, the list contains only your own processes. You are responsible for calling mysql_free_result() to free the result set.

  The list produced by mysql_list_fields() can be obtained by executing a SHOW PROCESSLIST query with mysql_query() and then processing the result set.

  This function is deprecated as of MySQL 3.22.0.

- MYSQL_RES *
  mysql_list_tables (MYSQL *conn, char *wild);

  Returns a result set listing tables in the current database or NULL if an error occurred. The list contains all table names matching the SQL pattern indicated by wild (which can contain the '%' and '_' wildcard pattern characters) or all tables if wild is NULL. You are responsible for calling mysql_free_result() to free the result set.

  The list produced by mysql_list_tables() can be obtained by executing a SHOW TABLES statement with mysql_query() and then processing the result set.

  This function is deprecated as of MySQL 3.22.0.

- `int`
`mysql_refresh` `(MYSQL *conn,`
                      `unsigned int options);`

This function is similar in effect to the SQL `FLUSH` and `RESET` statements except that you can tell the server to flush several kinds of things at once. `mysql_refresh()` returns zero for success or non-zero for failure.

The `options` value should be composed from one or more of the values shown in the following list. You must have the `RELOAD` privilege to perform these operations.

- `REFRESH_GRANT`

  Reloads the grant table contents. This is equivalent to issuing a `FLUSH PRIVILEGES` statement.

- `REFRESH_HOSTS`

  Flushes the host cache. This is equivalent to issuing a `FLUSH HOSTS` statement.

- `REFRESH_LOG`

  Flushes the log files by closing and reopening them. This applies to whatever logs the server has open and is equivalent to issuing a `FLUSH LOGS` statement.

- `REFRESH_MASTER`

  Tells a replication master server to delete the binary logs listed in the binary log index file and to truncate the index. This is equivalent to issuing a `RESET MASTER` statement.

  This option was introduced in MySQL 3.23.19.

- `REFRESH_SLAVE`

  Tells a replication slave server to forget its position in the master logs. This is equivalent to issuing a `RESET SLAVE` statement.

  This option was introduced in MySQL 3.23.19.

- `REFRESH_STATUS`

  Reinitializes the status variables to zero. This is equivalent to issuing a `FLUSH STATUS` statement.

  This option was introduced in MySQL 3.22.11.

- `REFRESH_TABLES`

  Closes all open tables. This is equivalent to issuing a `FLUSH TABLES` statement.

- REFRESH_THREADS

  Flushes the thread cache.

  This option was introduced in MySQL 3.23.16.

The option flags are bit values, so you can combine them in additive fashion using either the | or the + operator. For example, the following expressions are equivalent:

```
REFRESH_LOG | REFRESH_TABLES
REFRESH_LOG + REFRESH_TABLES
```

mysql_refresh() is deprecated because you can perform the same actions by issuing FLUSH or RESET statements. See the descriptions of those statements in Appendix D, "SQL Syntax Reference."

- int

mysql_reload (MYSQL *conn);

Instructs the server to reload the grant tables. This can be done now by issuing a FLUSH PRIVILEGES query with mysql_query(). You must have the RELOAD privilege to use mysql_reload().

mysql_reload() returns zero for success, non-zero for failure.

This function is deprecated as of MySQL 3.21.9.

G

Perl DBI API
Reference

THIS APPENDIX DESCRIBES THE PERL DBI application programming interface. The API consists of a set of methods and attributes for communicating with database servers and accessing databases from Perl scripts. The appendix also describes MySQL-specific extensions to DBI provided by `DBD::mysql`, the MySQL database driver. It does not describe the older Mysqlperl interface, which is obsolete.

Some DBI methods and attributes are not discussed here, either because they do not apply to MySQL or because they are new, experimental methods that may change as they are developed or may even be dropped. Some MySQL-specific DBD methods are not discussed because they are obsolete. If you want more information about new or obsolete methods, see the DBI documentation or the MySQL DBD documentation, which you can get by running the following commands:

```
% perldoc DBI
% perldoc DBI::FAQ
% perldoc DBD::mysql
```

This appendix serves as a reference, so it includes only brief code fragments illustrating use of the Perl DBI API. For complete client scripts and instructions for writing them, see Chapter 7, "The Perl DBI API."

Writing Scripts

Every Perl script that uses the DBI module must include the following line:

```
use DBI;
```

It's not necessary to include a use line for a particular DBD-level module because DBI will take care of activating the proper module when you connect to the server.

Normally, a DBI script opens a connection to a MySQL server using the connect() method and closes the connection with disconnect(). While the connection is open, queries can be issued. The methods used to execute queries vary, depending on the type of statement. Non-SELECT queries typically are performed with the do() method. SELECT queries typically are performed by passing the query to prepare(), calling execute(), and finally retrieving query results a row at a time in a loop that repeatedly invokes a row-fetching method, such as fetchrow_array() or fetchrow_hashref().

When you issue queries from within a DBI script, each query string must consist of a single SQL statement and should not end with a semicolon character (';') or a \g sequence. ';' and \g are conventions of the mysql client program and are not used for DBI.

DBI Methods

The method descriptions here are written in a somewhat different format than is used for the C functions in Appendix F, "C API Reference," and for the PHP functions in Appendix H, "PHP API Reference." Functions in those appendixes are written in prototype form, with return value types and parameter types listed explicitly. The descriptions here indicate parameter and return value types using variables, where the leading character of each variable indicates its type: '$' for a scalar, '@' for an array, and '%' for a hash (associative array). In addition, any parameter listed with a leading '\' signifies a reference to a variable of the given type, not the variable itself. A variable name suffix of ref indicates that the variable's value is a reference.

Certain variable names recur throughout this appendix and have the conventional meanings shown in Table G.1.

Table G.1   **Conventional Perl DBI Variable Names**

Name	Meaning
$drh	A handle to a driver object
$dbh	A handle to a database object
$sth	A handle to a statement (query) object
$fh	A handle to an open file
$h	A "generic" handle; the meaning depends on context
$rc	The return code from operations that return true or false
$rv	The return value from operations that return an integer
$rows	The return value from operations that return a row count
$str	The return value from operations that return a string
@ary	An array representing a list of values
@row_ary	An array representing a row of values returned by a query

Many methods accept a hash argument %attr containing attributes that affect the way the method works. This hash should be passed by reference, which you can do two ways:

- Set up the contents of the hash value %attr before invoking the method and then pass it to the method:

```
my %attr = (AttrName1 => value1, AttrName2 => value2);
$ret_val = $h->method (..., \%attr);
```

- Supply an anonymous hash directly in the method invocation:

```
$ret_val = $h->method (..., {AttrName1 => value1, AttrName2 => value2});
```

The way in which a method or function is used is indicated by the calling sequence. DBI-> indicates a DBI class method, DBI:: indicates a DBI function, and $DBI:: indicates a DBI variable. For methods that are called using handles, the handle name indicates the scope of the method. $dbh-> indicates a database handle method, $sth-> indicates a statement handle method, and $h-> indicates a method that can be called with different kinds of handles. Optional information is indicated by square brackets ([]). The following is an example calling sequence:

```
@row_ary = $dbh->selectrow_array ($statement, [\%attr [, @bind_values]]);
```

This indicates that the selectrow_array() method is called as a database handle method because it's invoked using $dbh->. The parameters are $statement (a scalar value), %attr (a hash that should be passed as a reference, as indicated by the leading '\'), and @bind_values (an array). The second and third parameters are optional. The return value, @row_ary, is an array representing the row of values returned by the method.

Each method description indicates what the return value is when an error occurs, but that value is returned on error only if the `RaiseError` attribute is disabled. If `RaiseError` is enabled, the method raises an exception rather than returning and the script automatically terminates.

In the descriptions that follow, the term "`SELECT` query" should be taken to mean a `SELECT` query or any other query that returns rows, such as `DESCRIBE`, `EXPLAIN`, or `SHOW`.

DBI Class Methods

The `%attr` parameter for methods in this section can be used to specify method-processing attributes. (An attribute parameter that is missing or `undef` means "no attributes.") For MySQL, the most important attributes are `PrintError`, `RaiseError`, and `AutoCommit`. Attributes passed to `connect()` or `connect_cached()` become part of the resulting database handle returned by those methods. For example, to turn on automatic script termination when a DBI error occurs within any method associated with a given database handle, enable `RaiseError` when you create the handle:

```
$dbh = DBI->connect ($data_source, $user_name, $password, {RaiseError => 1});
```

`PrintError`, `RaiseError`, and `AutoCommit` are discussed in the "DBI Attributes" section later in this appendix.

- `@ary = DBI->`**`available_drivers`** `([$quiet]);`

  Returns a list of available DBI drivers. The default value of the optional `$quiet` parameter is `0`, which causes a warning to be issued if multiple drivers with the same name are found. To suppress the warning, pass a `$quiet` value of `1`.

- `$dbh = DBI->`**`connect`** `($data_source,`
  `$user_name,`
  `$password`
  `[, \%attr]);`

  `connect()` establishes a connection to a database server and returns a database handle or `undef` if the connection attempt fails. To terminate a successfully established connection, invoke `disconnect()` using the database handle returned by `connect()`.

  ```
  $dbh = DBI->connect ("DBI:mysql:sampdb:cobra.snake.net",
                       "sampadm", "secret", \%attr)
      or die "Could not connect\n";
  $dbh->disconnect ();
  ```

  The data source can be given in several forms. The first part is always `DBI:mysql:`, where `DBI` can be given in any lettercase and the driver name, mysql, must be lowercase. Everything after the second colon (which must be present) is interpreted by the driver, so the syntax described in the following discussion does not necessarily apply to any driver other than DBD::mysql.

Following the second colon, you can also specify a database name and hostname in the initial part of the data source string:

```
$data_source = "DBI:mysql:db_name";
$data_source = "DBI:mysql:db_name:host_name";
```

The database can be specified as *db_name* or as database=*db_name*. The hostname can be specified as *host_name* or as host=*host_name*.

Following the initial part of the data source string, you can specify several options in *attribute*=*value* format. Each option setting should be preceded by a semicolon. For example

```
DBI:mysql:sampdb:localhost;mysql_socket=/tmp/mysql.sock;mysql_compression=1
```

The MySQL driver understands the following options:

- host=*host_name*

  The host to which to connect. For TCP/IP connections, a port number can also be specified by using *host_name*:*port_num* format or by using the port attribute.

  On UNIX systems, connections to the host localhost use UNIX domain sockets by default. (In this case, you can use mysql_socket to specify the socket name.) Use host=127.0.0.1 if you want to connect to the local host using TCP/IP.

  On Windows NT-based systems, connections to the host '.' connect to the local server using a named pipe or TCP/IP if that doesn't work. (In this case, you can use mysql_socket to specify the pipe name.)

- port=*port_num*

  The port number to which to connect. This option is ignored for non-TCP/IP connections (for example, connections to localhost under UNIX).

- mysql_client_found_rows=*val*

  For UPDATE queries, the MySQL server by default returns the number of rows affected (changed) rather than the number of rows matched. Passing a value of 1 for the mysql_client_found_rows option tells the server to return the number of rows matched instead. A value of 0 leaves the default behavior unchanged.

mysql_client_found_rows was introduced in DBD::mysql 1.2208.

- mysql_compression=1

  This option enables compressed communication between the client and the MySQL server.

  mysql_compression was introduced in DBD::mysql 1.1920 and requires MySQL 3.22.3 or later.

- mysql_connect_timeout=*seconds*

  The number of seconds to wait during the connection attempt before timing out and returning failure.

  mysql_connect_timeout was introduced in DBD::mysql 1.2207.

- mysql_local_infile=*val*

  This option may be used as of MySQL 3.23.49 to control availability of the LOCAL capability for the LOAD DATA statement. Setting the option to 1 enables LOCAL if it is disabled in the MySQL client library by default (as long as the server has not also been configured to disallow it). Setting the option to 0 disables LOCAL if it is enabled in the client library.

  mysql_local_infile was introduced in DBD::mysql 2.1020.

- mysql_read_default_file=*file_name*

  By default, DBI scripts do not check any MySQL option files for connection parameters. mysql_read_default_file allows you to specify an option file to read. The filename should be a full pathname. (Otherwise, it will be interpreted relative to the current directory, and you will get inconsistent results depending on where the script is run.)

  If you expect that a script will be used by multiple users and you want each of them to connect using parameters specified in their own option file (rather than using parameters that you hardwire into the script), specify the filename as $ENV{HOME}/.my.cnf. The script then will use the .my.cnf file in the home directory of whatever user happens to be running the script.

  Specifying an option filename that includes a drive letter doesn't work under Windows because the ':' character that separates the drive letter and the following pathname is also used by DBI as a separator within the data source string. An ugly way to work around this is to specify the filename without the drive letter and `chdir()` to that drive before invoking `connect()`. To leave the current directory undisturbed by the operation, you should save the current directory before calling `connect()` and then `chdir()` back to it after connecting.

`mysql_read_default_file` was introduced in `DBD::mysql` 1.2106, and requires MySQL 3.22.10 or later.

- `mysql_read_default_group=group_name`

  Specify an option file group in which to look for connection parameters. If `mysql_read_default_group` is used without `mysql_read_default_file`, the standard option files are read. If both `mysql_read_default_group` and `mysql_read_default_file` are used, only the file named by the latter is read.

  The `[client]` option file group is always read from option files. `mysql_read_default_group` allows you to specify a group to be read in addition to the `[client]` group. For example, `mysql_read_default_group=dbi` specifies that both the `[dbi]` and `[client]` groups should be used. If you only want the `[client]` group to be read, use `mysql_read_default_group=client`.

  The format of option files is described in Appendix E, "MySQL Program Reference."

  `mysql_read_default_group` was introduced in `DBD::mysql` 1.2106 and requires MySQL 3.22.10 or later.

- `mysql_socket=socket_name`

  Under UNIX, this option specifies the pathname of the UNIX domain socket to use for connections to `localhost`. Under Windows, it indicates a named pipe name. This option is ignored for TCP/IP connections (for example, connections to hosts other than `localhost` on UNIX).

  `mysql_socket` requires MySQL 3.21.15 or later.

- `mysql_ssl=1`
  `mysql_ssl_ca_file=file_name`
  `mysql_ssl_ca_path=dir_name`
  `mysql_ssl_cipher=str`
  `mysql_ssl_client_cert=file_name`
  `mysql_ssl_client_key=file_name`

  These options are used to establish a secure connection to the server using SSL. Setting `mysql_ssl` to 1 enables use of SSL.

The other options then may be used to specify the other characteristics of the connection; their meanings are the same as the corresponding arguments of the `mysql_ssl_set()` function in the C API. For details, see the entry for that function in Appendix F. If you enable `mysql_ssl`, you should also specify values for at least the `mysql_ssl_ca_file`, `mysql_ssl_client_cert`, and `mysql_ssl_client_key` options.

These options require MySQL 4 or later and may be used as of `DBD::mysql` 2.1013.

If connection parameters are not specified explicitly in the arguments to `connect()`, DBI examines several environment variables to determine which parameters to use:

- If the data source is undefined or empty, the value of the `DBI_DSN` variable is used.

- If the driver name is missing from the data source, the value of the `DBI_DRIVER` variable is used.

- If the *user_name* or *password* parameters of the `connect()` call are undefined, the values of the `DBI_USER` and `DBI_PASS` variables are used. This does not occur if the parameters are empty strings. (Use of `DBI_PASS` is a security risk, so you shouldn't use it on multiple-user systems where environment variable values may be visible to other users by means of system-monitoring commands.)

DBI uses default values for any connection parameters that remain unknown after all information sources have been consulted. If the hostname is unspecified, it defaults to `localhost`. If the username is unspecified, it defaults to your login name under UNIX and to `ODBC` under Windows. If the password is unspecified, there is no default; instead, no password is sent.

- `$dbh = DBI->`**`connect_cached`**` ($data_source,`
  `                          $user_name,`
  `                          $password`
  `                          [, \%attr]);`

This method is like `connect()` except that DBI caches the database handle internally. If a subsequent call is made to `connect_cached()` with the same connection parameters while the connection is still active, DBI returns the cached handle rather than opening a new connection. If the cached handle is no longer valid, DBI establishes a new connection and then caches and returns the new handle.

- @ary = DBI->**data_sources** ($driver [, \%attr]);

  Returns a list of databases available through the named driver. For MySQL, $driver should be mysql (lowercase). If $driver is undef or the empty string, DBI checks the value of the DBI_DRIVER environment variable to get the driver name.

  For many DBI drivers, data_sources() returns an empty or incomplete list. For MySQL in particular, this function returns nothing unless the driver can connect to the server on the local host with no name or password. This is unlikely to be true except for insecure server configurations.

- $drh = DBI->**install_driver** ($driver_name);

  Activates a DBD-level driver and returns a driver handle for it or dies with an error message if the driver cannot be found. For MySQL, the driver name is mysql (it must be lowercase). Normally, it is not necessary to use this method because DBI activates the proper driver automatically when you invoke the connect() method. However, install_driver() can be helpful if you're using the func() method to perform administrative operations. (See the "MySQL-Specific Administrative Methods" section later in this appendix.)

Database Handle Methods

The methods in this section are invoked through a database handle and can be used after you have obtained such a handle by calling the connect() or connect_cached() method.

The %attr parameter for methods in this section can be used to specify method-processing attributes. (An attribute parameter of undef means "no attributes.") For MySQL, the most important of these are PrintError and RaiseError. For example, if RaiseError currently is disabled, you can enable it while processing a particular statement to cause automatic script termination if a DBI error occurs:

```
$rows = $dbh->do ($statement, {RaiseError => 1});
```

PrintError and RaiseError are discussed in the "DBI Attributes" section later in this appendix.

- $rc = $dbh->**begin_work** ();

  Turns off auto-commit mode by disabling the AutoCommit database handle attribute. This allows a multiple-statement transaction to be performed. AutoCommit remains disabled until the next call to commit() or rollback(), after which it becomes enabled again. Use of begin_work() differs from disabling the AutoCommit attribute manually; in the latter case, you must also re-enable AutoCommit manually after committing or rolling back.

begin_work() returns true if AutoCommit was disabled successfully, and it returns false if it was already disabled. If MySQL does not support transactions, attempting to disable AutoCommit results in a fatal error.

begin_work() was introduced in DBI 1.20. Transaction support requires DBD::mysql 1.2216 or later and MySQL 3.23.17 or later.

- $rc = $dbh->**commit** ();

  Commits the current transaction if MySQL supports transactions and AutoCommit is disabled. If AutoCommit is enabled, invoking commit() has no effect and results in a warning.

  Transaction support requires DBD::mysql 1.2216 or later and MySQL 3.23.17 or later.

- $rc = $dbh->**disconnect** ();

  Terminates the connection associated with the database handle. If the connection is still active when the script exits, DBI terminates it automatically but issues a warning.

  The behavior of disconnect() is undefined with respect to active transactions. If a transaction is active, you should terminate it explicitly by invoking commit() or rollback() before calling disconnect().

- $rows = $dbh->**do** ($statement
                       [, \%attr
                       [, @bind_values]]);

  Prepares and executes the query indicated by $statement. The return value is the number of rows affected, -1 if the number of rows is unknown, and undef if an error occurred. If the number of rows affected is zero, the return value is the string "0E0", which evaluates as zero in numeric contexts but is considered true in boolean contexts.

  do() is used primarily for statements that do not retrieve rows, such as DELETE, INSERT, REPLACE, or UPDATE. Trying to use do() for a SELECT statement is ineffective; you don't get back a statement handle, so you won't be able to fetch any rows.

  Normally, no attributes are passed to do(), so the %attr parameter can be specified as undef. @bind_values represents a list of values to be bound to placeholders, which are indicated by '?' characters within the query string.

If a query includes no placeholders, you can omit both the `%attr` parameter and the value list:

```
$rows = $dbh->do ("UPDATE member SET expiration = NOW() WHERE member_id = 39");
```

If the query does contain placeholders, the list must contain as many values as there are placeholders and must be preceded by the `%attr` argument. In the following example, the attribute argument is `undef` and is followed by two data values to be bound to the two placeholders in the query string:

```
$rows = $dbh->do ("UPDATE member SET expiration = ? WHERE member_id = ?",
                  undef,
                  "2005-11-30", 39);
```

- `$rc = $dbh->`**`ping`**` ();`

  Re-establishes the connection to the server if the connection has timed out. Returns true if the connection was still active or was re-established successfully and false otherwise.

- `$sth = $dbh->`**`prepare`**` ($statement [, \%attr]);`

  Prepares the query indicated by `$statement` for later execution and returns a statement handle or `undef` if an error occurs. The statement handle returned from a successful invocation of `prepare()` can be used with `execute()` to execute the query.

- `$sth = $dbh->`**`prepare_cached`**` ($statement`
  `                              [, \%attr`
  `                              [, $allow_active]]);`

  This method is like `prepare()` except that DBI caches the statement handle internally. If a subsequent call is made to `prepare_cached()` with the same `$statement` and `%attr` arguments, DBI returns the cached handle rather than creating a new one. If the cached handle is active, DBI calls `finish()` and issues a warning before returning the handle. To suppress the warning, pass a true value for `$allow_active`.

- `$str = $dbh->`**`quote`**` ($value [, $data_type]);`

  Processes a string to perform quoting and escaping of characters that are special in SQL. The resulting string can be used as a data value in a statement without causing a syntax error when you execute the statement. For example, the string `I'm happy` is returned as `'I\'m happy'`. If `$value` is `undef`, it is returned as the literal word `NULL`. Note that the return value includes surrounding quote characters as necessary, so you should not add extra quotes around it when you insert the value into a query string.

Do not use quote() with values that you are going to insert into a query using placeholders. DBI quotes such values automatically.

The $data_type parameter is usually unnecessary because MySQL converts string values in queries to other data types as necessary. $data_type can be specified as a hint that a value is of a particular type—for example, DBI::SQL_INTEGER to indicate the $value represents an integer.

- $rc = $dbh->**rollback** ();

  Rolls back the current transaction if MySQL supports transactions and AutoCommit is disabled. If AutoCommit is enabled, invoking rollback() has no effect and results in a warning.

  Transaction support requires DBD::mysql 1.2216 or later and MySQL 3.23.17 or later.

- $ary_ref =
  $dbh->**selectall_arrayref** ($statement
                               [, \%attr
                               [, @bind_values]]);

  Combines the effect of prepare(), execute(), and fetchall_arrayref() to execute the query specified by $statement. If $statement is a handle to a previously prepared statement, the prepare() step is omitted. The %attr and @bind_values parameters have the same meaning as for the do() method.

  The return value is a reference to an array. Each array element is a reference to an array containing the values for one row of the result set. The array will be empty if the result set contains no rows.

  If an error occurred, selectall_arrayref() returns undef unless a partial result set already has been fetched. In that case, it returns the rows retrieved to that point. To determine whether a non-undef return value represents success or failure, check $dbh->err() or $DBI::err.

- $hash_ref =
  $dbh->**selectall_hashref** ($statement, $key_col
                              [, \%attr
                              [, @bind_values]]);

  Combines the effect of prepare(), execute(), and fetchall_hashref() to execute the query specified by

$statement. If $statement is a handle to a previously prepared state-ment, the prepare() step is omitted. The %attr and @bind_values parameters have the same meaning as for the do() method.

The return value is a reference to a hash that contains one element for each row of the result set. Hash keys are the values of the column indi-cated by $key_col, which should be either the name of a column selected by the query, or a column number (beginning with 1). Values in the key column should be unique to avoid loss of rows due to key colli-sions in the hash. The hash will be empty if the result set contains no rows. Otherwise, the value of each hash element is a reference to a hash containing one row of the result set, keyed by the names of the columns selected by the query.

If an error occurred, selectall_hashref() returns undef unless a par-tial result set already has been fetched. In that case, it returns the rows retrieved to that point. To determine whether a non-undef return value represents success or failure, check $dbh->err() or $DBI::err.

selectall_hashref() was introduced in DBI 1.20. (It actually appeared in 1.15, but with different behavior than it currently has.)

- $ary_ref =
$dbh->**selectcol_arrayref** ($statement,
                      [\%attr
                      [, @bind_values]]);

Combines the effect of prepare(), execute(), and a row-fetching oper-ation to execute the query specified by $statement. If $statement is a handle to a previously prepared statement, the prepare() step is omitted. The %attr and @bind_values parameters have the same meaning as for the do() method.

The return value is a reference to an array containing the first column from each row.

If an error occurred, selectcol_arrayref() returns undef unless a partial result set already has been fetched. In that case, it returns the rows retrieved to that point. To determine whether a non-undef return value represents success or failure, check $dbh->err() or $DBI::err.

selectcol_arrayref() was introduced in DBI 1.09.

- `@row_ary =`
`$dbh->`**`selectrow_array`** `($statement`
`[, \%attr`
`[, @bind_values]]);`

Combines the effect of `prepare()`, `execute()`, and `fetchrow_array()` to execute the query specified by `$statement`. If `$statement` is a handle to a previously prepared statement, the `prepare()` step is omitted. The `%attr` and `@bind_values` parameters have the same meaning as for the `do()` method.

When called in a list context, `selectrow_array()` returns an array representing the values in the first row of the result set or an empty array if no row was returned or an error occurred. In a scalar context, `selectrow_array()` returns one element of the array or `undef` if no row was returned or if an error occurred. Which element is returned is undefined; see the note on this behavior in the entry for `fetchrow_array()`.

To distinguish between no row and an error in list context, check `$sth->err()` or `$DBI::err`. A value of zero indicates that no row was returned. However, in the absence of an error, an `undef` return value in scalar context may represent either a `NULL` column value or that no row was returned.

- `$ary_ref =`
`$dbh->`**`selectrow_arrayref`** `($statement`
`[, \%attr`
`[, @bind_values]]);`

Combines the effect of `prepare()`, `execute()`, and `fetchrow_arrayref()` to execute the query specified by `$statement`. If `$statement` is a handle to a previously prepared statement, the `prepare()` step is omitted. The `%attr` and `@bind_values` parameters have the same meaning as for the `do()` method.

The return value is a reference to an array containing the values in the first row of the result set or `undef` if an error occurred.

`selectrow_arrayref()` was introduced in DBI 1.15.

- `$hash_ref =`
`$dbh->`**`selectrow_hashref`** `($statement`
`[, \%attr`
`[, @bind_values]]);`

Combines the effect of `prepare()`, `execute()`, and
`fetchrow_hashref()` to execute the query specified by `$statement`.
If `$statement` is a handle to a previously prepared statement, the
`prepare()` step is omitted. The `%attr` and `@bind_values` parameters
have the same meaning as for the `do()` method.

The return value is a reference to a hash containing the first row of the
result set or `undef` if an error occurred. The hash elements are keyed by
the names of the columns selected by the query.

`selectrow_hashref()` was introduced in DBI 1.16.

Other Database Handle Methods

A number of additional database handle methods for getting database and table
metadata have appeared in recent versions of DBI. However, some of them are
still experimental, and most haven't been implemented for MySQL yet. These
include `column_info()`, `foreign_key_info()`, `get_info()`, `primary_key()`,
`primary_key_info()`, `table_info()`, `tables()`, `type_info()`, and
`type_info_all()`. For more information about them, consult the DBI documentation:

```
% perldoc DBI
```

Statement Handle Methods

The methods in this section are invoked through a statement handle that you
obtain by calling a method such as `prepare()` or `prepare_cached()`.

- `$rc = $sth->`**`bind_col`** `($col_num, \$var);`

  Binds a given output column from a SELECT query to a Perl variable,
  which should be passed as a reference. `$col_num` should be in the range
  from 1 to the number of columns selected by the query. Each time a row
  is fetched, the variable is updated automatically with the column value.

  `bind_col()` should be called after `execute()` and before fetching rows.

  `bind_col()` returns false if the column number is not in the range from
  1 to the number of columns selected by the query.

- `$rc = $sth->`**`bind_columns`** `(\$var1, \$var2, ...);`

  Binds a list of variables to columns returned by a prepared SELECT statement. See the description of the `bind_col()` method. Like `bind_col()`,
  `bind_columns()` should be called after
  `execute()` and before fetching rows.

`bind_columns()` returns false if the number of arguments doesn't match the number of columns selected by the query.

- `$rv = $sth->`**`bind_param`**` ($n, $value [, \%attr]);`
  `$rv = $sth->`**`bind_param`**` ($n, $value [, $bind_type]);`

Binds a value to a placeholder in a query string so that the value will be included in the statement when it is sent to the server. Placeholders are represented by '?' characters in the query string. This method should be called after `prepare()` and before `execute()`.

`$n` specifies the number of the placeholder to which the value `$value` should be bound and should be in the range from 1 to the number of placeholders. To bind a NULL value, `$value` should be `undef`.

The `%attr` or `$bind_type` parameter can be supplied as a hint about the type of the value to be bound. For example, to specify that the value represents an integer, you can invoke `bind_param()` in either of the following ways:

```
$rv = $sth->bind_param ($n, $value, { TYPE => DBI::SQL_INTEGER });
$rv = $sth->bind_param ($n, $value, DBI::SQL_INTEGER);
```

The default is to treat the variable as a VARCHAR. This is normally sufficient because MySQL converts string values in queries to other data types as necessary.

- `$rows = $sth->`**`dump_results`**` ([$maxlen`
  `                                   [, $line_sep`
  `                                   [, $field_sep`
  `                                   [, $fh]]]]);`

Fetches all rows from the statement handle `$sth`, formats them by calling the utility function `DBI::neat_list()`, and prints them to the given file handle. Returns the number of rows fetched.

The defaults for the `$maxlen`, `$line_sep`, `$field_sep`, and `$fh` parameters are 35, `"\n"`, `", "`, and STDOUT.

- `$rv = $sth->`**`execute`**` ([@bind_values]);`

Executes a prepared statement. For SELECT statements, `execute()` returns true if the statement executed successfully or `undef` if an error occurred. For non-SELECT statements, the return value is the number of rows affected: -1 if the number of rows is unknown, and `undef` if an error occurred. If the number of rows affected is zero, the return value is the string `"0E0"`, which evaluates as zero in numeric contexts but is considered true in boolean contexts.

The @bind_values parameter has the same meaning as for the do()
method.

- $ary_ref = $sth->**fetch** ();

  fetch() is an alias for fetchrow_arrayref().

- $ary_ref =
  $sth->**fetchall_arrayref** ([$slice_array_ref]);

  $ary_ref =
  $sth->**fetchall_arrayref** ([$slice_hash_ref]);

  Fetches all rows from the statement handle $sth and returns a reference
  to an array that contains one reference for each row fetched. This array
  will be empty if the result set contains no rows. Otherwise, each element
  of $ary_ref is a reference to one row of the result set. The meaning of
  the row references depends on the type of argument you pass. With no
  argument or an array slice argument, each row reference points to an
  array of column values. Array slice values begin at 0 because they are Perl
  array indices. Negative values count back from the end of the row. Thus,
  to fetch the first and last columns of each row, do the following:

  ```
  $ary_ref = $sth->fetchall_arrayref ([0, -1]);
  ```

  With a hash slice argument, each row reference points to a hash of column values, indexed by the names of the columns you want to retrieve.
  To specify a hash slice, column names should be given as hash keys and
  each key should have a value of 1:

  ```
  $ary_ref = $sth->fetchall_arrayref ({id => 1, name => 1});
  ```

  To fetch all columns as a hash, pass an empty hash reference:

  ```
  $ary_ref = $sth->fetchall_arrayref ({});
  ```

  If an error occurred, fetchall_arrayref() returns the rows fetched up
  to the point of the error. Check $sth->err() or $DBI::err to
  determine whether or not an error occurred.

- $hash_ref = $sth->**fetchall_hashref** ($key_col);

  Fetches the result set and returns a reference to a hash that contains one
  element for each row of the result set. Hash keys are the values of the
  column indicated by $key_col, which should be either the name of a
  column selected by the query, or a column number (beginning with 1).
  Values in the key column should be unique to avoid loss of rows due
  to key collisions in the hash. The hash will be empty if the result set

contains no rows. Otherwise, the value of each hash element is a reference to a hash containing one row of the result set, keyed by the names
of the columns selected by the query.

If an error occurred due to an invalid key column argument,
`fetchall_hashref()` returns `undef`. Otherwise, it returns the rows
fetched up to the point of the error. To determine whether a non-`undef`
return value represents success or failure, check `$sth->err()` or
`$DBI::err`.

- `@ary = $sth->`**`fetchrow_array`**` ();`

    When called in a list context, `fetchrow_array()` returns an array con-
    taining column values for the next row of the result set or an empty
    array if there are no more rows or an error occurred. In a scalar context,
    `fetchrow_array()` returns one element of the array or `undef` if there
    are no more rows or an error occurred. Prior to version 1.29, the DBI
    documentation stated that `fetchrow_array()` returned the first column
    value in scalar context. Applications should no longer rely on this behav-
    ior because which element is returned now is undefined; you can tell for
    sure only for queries that select a single column.

    To distinguish between normal exhaustion of the result set and an error
    in list context, check `$sth->err()` or `$DBI::err`. A value of zero indi-
    cates you've reached the end of the result set without error. However, in
    the absence of an error, an `undef` return value in scalar context can rep-
    resent either a NULL column value or the end of the result set.

- `$ary_ref = $sth->`**`fetchrow_arrayref`**` ();`

    Returns a reference to an array containing column values for the next
    row of the result set or `undef` if there are no more rows or an error
    occurred.

    To distinguish between normal exhaustion of the result set and an error,
    check `$sth->err()` or `$DBI::err`. A value of zero indicates you've
    reached the end of the result set without error.

- `$hash_ref = $sth->`**`fetchrow_hashref`**` ([$name]);`

    Returns a reference to a hash containing column values for the next row
    of the result set or `undef` if there are no more rows or an error occurred.
    Hash index values are the column names, and elements of the hash are
    the column values.

The $name argument can be specified to control hash key lettercase. It defaults to "NAME" (use column names as specified in the query). To force hash keys to be lowercase or uppercase, you can specify a $name value of "NAME_lc" or "NAME_uc" instead. (Another way to control hash key letter case is with the FetchHashKeyName attribute, which is discussed in the "DBI Attributes" section later in this appendix.)

To distinguish between normal exhaustion of the result set and an error, check $sth->err() or $DBI::err. A value of zero indicates you've reached the end of the result set without error.

- $rc = $sth->**finish** ();

Frees any resources associated with the statement handle. Normally, you need not invoke this method yourself because row-fetching methods invoke it implicitly when they reach the end of the result set. If you fetch only part of a result set, calling finish() explicitly lets DBI know that you are done fetching data from the handle.

Calling finish() invalidates statement attributes, and because this method can be invoked implicitly by row-fetching methods when they detect the end of the result set, it's best to access any attributes you need immediately after invoking execute(), rather than waiting until later.

- $rv = $sth->**rows** ();

Returns the number of rows affected by the statement associated with $sth, or -1 if an error occurred. This method is used primarily for statements such as UPDATE or DELETE that do not return rows. For SELECT statements, you should not rely on the rows() method; count the rows as you fetch them instead.

General Handle Methods

The methods in this section are not specific to particular types of handles. They can be invoked using driver, database, or statement handles.

- $rv = $h->**err** ();

Returns the numeric error code for the most recently invoked driver operation. For MySQL, this is the error number returned by the MySQL server. A return value of 0 or undef indicates that no error occurred.

- $str = $h->**errstr** ();

Returns the string error message for the most recently invoked driver operation. For MySQL, this is the error message returned by the MySQL server. A return value of the empty string or undef indicates that no error occurred.

- DBI->**trace** ($trace_level [, $trace_filename]);
  $h->**trace** ($trace_level [, $trace_filename]);

  Sets a trace level. Tracing provides information about DBI operation. The trace level can be in the range from 0 (off) to 9 (maximum information). Tracing can be enabled for all DBI operations within a script by invoking trace as a DBI class method or for an individual handle:

  ```
  DBI->trace (2);      # Turn on global script tracing
  $sth->trace (2);     # Turn on per-handle tracing
  ```

  Tracing can also be enabled on a global level for all DBI scripts you run by setting the DBI_TRACE environment variable.

  Trace output goes to STDERR by default. The $filename parameter can be supplied to direct output to a different file. Output is appended to any existing contents of the file; the file is not overwritten.

  Each trace call causes output from *all* traced handles to go to the same file. If a file is named, all trace output goes there. If no file is named, all trace output goes to STDERR.

- DBI->**trace_msg** ($str [, $min_level]);
  $h->**trace_msg** ($str [, $min_level]);

  When called as a class method (DBI->trace_msg()), writes the message in $str to the trace output if tracing has been enabled at the DBI level. When called as a handle method ($h->trace_msg()), writes the message if the handle is being traced or if tracing has been enabled at the DBI level.

  The $min_level parameter can be supplied to specify that the message should be written only if the trace level is at least at that level.

MySQL–Specific Administrative Methods

This section describes the func() method that DBI provides as a means of accessing driver-specific operations directly. Note that func() is not related to the use of stored procedures. Stored procedure methods currently are not defined by DBI.

- $rc = $drh->func ("**createdb**",
                   $db_name, $host_name, $user_name, $password, "admin");

```
$rc = $drh->func ("dropdb",
                  $db_name, $host_name, $user_name, $pass-
                  word, "admin");
$rc = $drh->func ("reload",
                  $host_name, $user_name,
                  $password, "admin");
$rc = $drh->func ("shutdown",
                  $host_name, $user_name,
                  $password, "admin");
$rc = $dbh->func ("createdb", $db_name, "admin");
$rc = $dbh->func ("dropdb", $db_name, "admin");
$rc = $dbh->func ("reload", "admin");
$rc = $dbh->func ("shutdown", "admin");
```

The func() method is accessed either through a driver handle or through a database handle. A driver handle is not associated with an open connection, so if you access func() that way, you must supply arguments for the hostname, username, and password to allow the method to establish a connection. If you access func() with a database handle, those arguments are unnecessary. A driver handle can be obtained, if necessary, as follows:

```
$drh = DBI->install_driver ("mysql");    # note: "mysql" must be lowercase
```

The actions understood by func() are as follows:

- createdb

  Creates the database named by $db_name. You must have the CREATE privilege for the database to do this.

- dropdb

  Drops (removes) the database named by $db_name. You must have the DROP privilege for the database to do this.

  Be careful; if you drop a database, it's gone. You can't get it back.

- reload

  Tells the server to reload the grant tables. This is necessary if you modify the contents of the grant tables directly using DELETE, INSERT, or UPDATE rather than using GRANT or REVOKE. You must have the RELOAD privilege to use reload.

- shutdown

  Shuts down the server. You must have the SHUTDOWN privilege to do this.

Note that the only func() action that cannot be performed through the usual DBI query-processing mechanism is shutdown. For the other actions, it is preferable to issue a CREATE DATABASE, DROP DATABASE, or FLUSH PRIVILEGES statement rather than invoking func().

DBI Utility Functions

DBI provides a few utility routines that can be used for testing or printing values. These functions are invoked as DBI::func_name(), rather than as DBI->func_name().

- @bool = DBI::**looks_like_number** (@ary);

  Takes a list of values and returns an array with one member for each element of the list. Each member indicates whether the corresponding argument looks like a number: true if it does, false if it doesn't, and undef if the argument is undefined or empty.

- $str = DBI::**neat** ($value [, $maxlen]);

  Returns a string containing a nicely formatted representation of the $value argument. Strings are returned with surrounding quotes; numbers are not. (But note that quoted numbers are considered to be strings.) Undefined values are reported as undef, and unprintable characters are reported as '.' characters. For example, if you execute the following loop:

  ```
  for my $val ("a", "3", 3, undef, "\x01\x02")
  {
      print DBI::neat ($val) . "\n";
  }
  ```

  The results will look like this:

  ```
  'a'
  '3'
  3
  undef
  '..'
  ```

  The $maxlen argument controls the maximum length of the result. If the result is longer than $maxlen, it is shortened to $maxlen–4 characters and "...'" is added. If $maxlen is 0, undef, or missing, it defaults to the current value of $DBI::neat_maxlen, which itself has a default value of 400.

Don't use `neat()` for query construction; if you need to perform quoting or escaping of data values to be placed into a query string, use placeholders or the `quote()` method instead.

- `$str = DBI::`**`neat_list`** `(\@ary`

  `[, $maxlen`

  `[, $sep]]);`

  Calls `neat()` for each element of the list pointed to by the first argument, joins them with the separator string `$sep` and returns the result as a single string.

  The `$maxlen` argument is passed to `neat()` and thus applies to individual arguments, not to the combined result of the `neat()` calls.

  If `$sep` is missing, the default is `", "`.

DBI Attributes

DBI provides attribute information at several levels. Most attributes are associated with database handles or statement handles, but not with both. Some attributes, such as `PrintError` and `RaiseError`, can be associated with either database handles or statement handles. In general, each handle has its own attributes, but some attributes that hold error information, such as `err` and `errstr`, are dynamic in that they associate with the most recently used handle.

Attributes passed to `connect()` or `connect_cached()` become part of the resulting database handle returned by those methods.

Database Handle Attributes

The attributes in this section are associated with database handles.

- `$dbh->{`**`AutoCommit`**`};`

  This attribute can be set to true or false to enable or disable transaction auto-commit mode. The default is true. Setting `AutoCommit` to false allows multiple-statement transactions to be performed, each of which is terminated by calling `commit()` for a successful transaction or `rollback()` to abort an unsuccessful transaction. See also the description of the `begin_work()` database handle method.

  If MySQL does not support transactions, attempting to disable `AutoCommit` results in a fatal error.

  Transaction support requires `DBD::mysql` 1.2216 or later and MySQL 3.23.17 or later.

- $dbh->{**Statement**};

  Holds the query string most recently passed to prepare() through the given database handle.

General Handle Attributes

The following attributes can be applied to individual handles or specified in the %attr parameter to methods that take such a parameter to affect the operation of the method.

- $h->{**ChopBlanks**};

  This attribute can be set to true or false to determine whether or not row-fetching methods will chop trailing spaces from character column values. ChopBlanks is false by default for most database drivers. This attribute has no effect for CHAR or VARCHAR columns, because the MySQL server does not return trailing spaces for those types anyway. However, for BLOB and TEXT columns, setting ChopBlanks to true will cause removal of trailing spaces.

- $h->{**FetchHashKeyName**};

  Controls the lettercase used for hash keys in result set rows that are returned by fetchrow_hashref() or other methods that invoke fetchrow_hashref(). The default value is "NAME" (use column names as specified in the SELECT statement). Other allowable values are "NAME_lc" or "NAME_uc", which cause column name hash keys to be forced to lowercase or uppercase. This attribute applies only to database and driver handles.

  FetchHashKeyName was introduced in DBI 1.19.

- $h->{**HandleError**};

  This attribute is used for error processing. It can be set to a reference to a subroutine to be invoked when an error occurs prior to the usual RaiseError and PrintError processing. If the subroutine returns true, RaiseError and PrintError processing is skipped; otherwise, it is performed as usual. (Of course, the error routine can terminate the script rather than returning.)

  DBI passes three arguments to the error routine—the text of the error message, the DBI handle being used at the point of occurrence of the error, and the first value returned by the method that failed.

  HandleError was introduced in DBI 1.21.

- $h->{**PrintError**};

  If set true, the occurrence of a DBI-related error causes a warning message to be printed. PrintError is false by default. This attribute does not affect the value returned by DBI methods when they fail. It determines only whether they print a message before returning.

- $h->{**RaiseError**};

  If set true, the occurrence of a DBI-related error causes automatic script termination. RaiseError is false by default.

- $h->{**ShowErrorStatement**};

  When set true, messages produced as a result of errors have the relevant query text appended to them. ShowErrorStatement is false by default. The effect of this attribute is limited to statement handles and to the prepare() and do() methods.

  ShowErrorStatement was introduced in DBI 1.19.

- $h->{**TraceLevel**};

  Sets or gets the trace level for the given handle. This attribute provides an alternative to the trace() method.

  TraceLevel was introduced in DBI 1.21.

MySQL-Specific Database Handle Attributes

The attributes in this section are specific to the DBI MySQL driver, DBD::mysql. As indicated in the attribute descriptions, each of them corresponds to a function in the MySQL C API. For more information, see Appendix F.

- $rv = $dbh->{**mysql_errno**};

  Returns the most recent error number, like the C API function mysql_errno().

- $str = $dbh->{**mysql_error**};

  Returns the most recent error string, like the C API function mysql_error().

- $str = $dbh->{**mysql_hostinfo**};

  Returns a string describing the given connection, like the C API function mysql_get_host_info().

- $str = $dbh->{**mysql_info**};

  Returns information about queries that affect multiple rows, like the C API function mysql_info().

- `$rv = $dbh->{`**`mysql_insertid`**`};`

  Returns the AUTO_INCREMENT value that was most recently generated on the connection associated with `$dbh`, like the C API function `mysql_insert_id()`.

  This attribute can also be used with statement handles.

- `$rv = $dbh->{`**`mysql_protoinfo`**`};`

  Returns a number indicating the client/server protocol version used for the given connection, like the C API function `mysql_get_proto_info()`.

- `$str = $dbh->{`**`mysql_serverinfo`**`};`

  Returns a string describing the server version, for example, `"4.0.2-alpha-log"`. The value consists of a version number, possibly followed by one or more suffixes. This attribute returns the same information as the C API function `mysql_get_server_info()`. The suffix values are listed in the description of the VERSION() function in Appendix C, "Operator and Function Reference."

- `$str = $dbh->{`**`mysql_stat`**`};`

  Returns a string containing server status information, like the C API function `mysql_stat()`.

- `$rv = $dbh->{`**`mysql_thread_id`**`};`

  Returns the thread number of the connection associated with `$dbh`, like the C API function `mysql_thread_id()`.

  As of DBD::mysql 2.0900, several MySQL-specific database handle attributes have been designated obsolete and should no longer be used. Table G.2 lists these together with the corresponding preferred attributes. If your version of DBD::mysql does not support the preferred attributes, try the deprecated forms instead or upgrade to a newer version. It's also possible to write code that uses the newer version of an attribute if it's available and falls back to the older version otherwise. For example:

  ```
  my $info = $dbh->{mysql_info};
  # use old form if new form unavailable
  $info = $dbh->{info} unless defined ($info);
  ```

Table G.2 **Deprecated MySQL-Specific Database Handle Attributes**

Deprecated Attribute	Preferred Attribute
errno	mysql_errno
error	mysql_error
hostinfo	mysql_hostinfo

Deprecated Attribute	Preferred Attribute
info	mysql_info
protoinfo	mysql_protoinfo
serverinfo	mysql_serverinfo
stats	mysql_stat
thread_id	mysql_thread_id

Statement Handle Attributes

Statement handle attributes generally apply to SELECT (or SELECT-like) queries and are not valid until the query has been passed to prepare() to obtain a statement handle and execute() has been called for that handle. In addition, finish() may invalidate statement attributes; in general, it is not safe to access them after finish() has been invoked (or after reaching the end of a result set, which causes finish() to be invoked implicitly).

Many statement handle attributes have values that are a reference to an array of values, one value per column of the query. The number of elements in the array is given by the $sth->{NUM_OF_FIELDS} attribute. For a statement attribute *stmt_attr* that is a reference to an array, you can refer to the entire array as @{$sth->{*stmt_attr*}} or loop through the elements in the array as follows:

```
for (my $i = 0; $i < $sth->{NUM_OF_FIELDS}; $i++)
{
    my $value = $sth->{stmt_attr}->[$i];
}
```

The NAME_hash, NAME_lc_hash, and NAME_uc_hash attributes return a reference to a hash. You can loop through the hash elements as follows:

```
foreach my $key (keys (%{$sth->{stmt_attr}}))
{
    my $value = $sth->{stmt_attr}->{$key};
}
```

- $ary_ref = $sth->{**NAME**};

  A reference to an array of strings indicating the name of each column. The lettercase of the names is as specified in the SELECT statement.

- $ary_ref = $sth->{**NAME_hash**};

  A reference to a hash of strings indicating the name of each column. The lettercase of the names is as specified in the SELECT statement. The value of each hash element indicates the position of the corresponding column within result set rows (beginning with 0).

  NAME_hash was introduced in DBI 1.20.

- `$ary_ref = $sth->{NAME_lc};`

  Like NAME, but the names are returned as lowercase strings.

- `$ary_ref = $sth->{NAME_lc_hash};`

  Like NAME_hash, but the names are returned as lowercase strings.
  NAME_lc_hash was introduced in DBI 1.20.

- `$ary_ref = $sth->{NAME_uc};`

  Like NAME, but the names are returned as uppercase strings.

- `$ary_ref = $sth->{NAME_uc_hash};`

  Like NAME_hash, but the names are returned as uppercase strings.
  NAME_uc_hash was introduced in DBI 1.20.

- `$ary_ref = $sth->{NULLABLE};`

  A reference to an array of values indicating whether each column can be
  NULL. Values for each element can be 0 or an empty string (no), 1 (yes),
  or 2 (unknown).

- `$rv = $sth->{NUM_OF_FIELDS};`

  The number of columns in a result set or zero for a non-SELECT statement.

- `$rv = $sth->{NUM_OF_PARAMS};`

  The number of placeholders in a prepared statement.

- `$ary_ref = $sth->{PRECISION};`

  A reference to an array of values indicating the precision of each column. DBI uses "precision" in the ODBC sense, which for MySQL
  means the maximum width of the column. For numeric columns, this is
  the display width. For string columns, it's the maximum length of the
  column as defined in the CREATE TABLE statement.

- `$ary_ref = $sth->{SCALE};`

  A reference to an array of values indicating the scale of each column. DBI
  uses "scale" in the ODBC sense, which for MySQL means the number of
  decimal places for floating-point columns. For other columns, the scale is 0.

- `$str = $sth->{Statement};`

  The text of the statement associated with $sth as seen by prepare()
  before any placeholder substitution takes place.

- `$ary_ref = $sth->{TYPE};`

  A reference to an array of values indicating the numeric type of each
  column. Prior to DBD::mysql 1.1919, this attribute is like mysql_type.
  As of 1.1919, it contains portable type numbers, and mysql_type can be
  accessed to obtain MySQL-specific type numbers.

MySQL–Specific Statement Handle Attributes

These attributes are specific to the DBI MySQL driver, DBD::mysql. Most of them should be considered read–only and should be accessed after invoking execute(). Exceptions are the mysql_store_result and mysql_use_result attributes. DBD::mysql provides the capability for controlling the result set processing style used by your script. The statement handle attributes mysql_store_result and mysql_use_result select the result set processing behavior of the C API functions mysql_store_result() and mysql_use_result(). See Appendix F for a discussion of these two functions and how they differ. By default, DBI uses mysql_store_result(), but you can enable the mysql_use_result attribute, which tells DBI to use mysql_use_result() instead. Do the following after prepare() but before execute():

```
$sth = $dbh->prepare (...);
$sth->{mysql_use_result} = 1;
$sth->execute();
```

- $rv = $sth->{**mysql_insertid**};

  The AUTO_INCREMENT value that was most recently generated on the connection associated with $sth.

  This attribute can also be used with database handles.

- $ary_ref = $sth->{**mysql_is_auto_increment**};

  A reference to an array of values indicating whether or not each column is an AUTO_INCREMENT column.

  This attribute can be used as of DBD::mysql 2.1014.

- $ary_ref = $sth->{**mysql_is_blob**};

  A reference to an array of values indicating whether or not each column is a BLOB or TEXT type.

- $ary_ref = $sth->{**mysql_is_key**};

  A reference to an array of values indicating whether each column is part of a key.

- $ary_ref = $sth->{**mysql_is_num**};

  A reference to an array of values indicating whether each column is a numeric type.

- $ary_ref = $sth->{**mysql_is_pri_key**};

  A reference to an array of values indicating whether each column is part of a PRIMARY KEY.

- `$ary_ref = $sth->{mysql_length};`

  This is like the PRECISION attribute.

- `$ary_ref = $sth->{mysql_max_length};`

  A reference to an array of values indicating the actual maximum length of the column values in the result set.

- `$sth->{mysql_store_result};`

  If mysql_store_result is enabled (set to 1), result sets are retrieved from the MySQL server using the mysql_store_result() C API function rather than by using mysql_use_result(). See Appendix F for a discussion of these two functions and how they differ.

  If you set the mysql_store_result attribute, do so after invoking prepare() and before invoking execute().

- `$ary_ref = $sth->{mysql_table};`

  A reference to an array of values indicating the name of the table from which each column comes. The table name for a calculated column is the empty string.

- `$ary_ref = $sth->{mysql_type};`

  A reference to an array of values indicating the MySQL-specific type number for each column in the result set.

- `$ary_ref = $sth->{mysql_type_name};`

  A reference to an array of values indicating the MySQL-specific type name for each column in the result set.

- `$sth->{mysql_use_result};`

  If mysql_use_result is enabled (set to 1), result sets are retrieved from the MySQL server using the mysql_use_result() C API function rather than by using mysql_store_result(). See Appendix F for a discussion of these two functions and how they differ.

  Note that use of this attribute causes some attributes, such as mysql_max_length, to become invalid. It also invalidates the use of the rows() method, although it's better to count rows when you fetch them anyway.

  If you set the mysql_use_result attribute, do so after invoking prepare() and before invoking execute().

Several MySQL–specific attributes that were available in older versions of DBD::mysql are now deprecated and have been replaced by newer preferred forms, as indicated in Table G.3. If your version of DBD::mysql does not support the preferred attributes, try the deprecated forms instead or upgrade to a newer version. It's also possible to write code that uses the newer version of an attribute if it's available and falls back to the older version otherwise—for example:

```
my $lengths = $sth->{PRECISION};
# use old form if new form unavailable
$lengths = $sth->{length} unless defined ($lengths);
```

Note that insertid is a statement handle attribute, whereas its preferred form, mysql_insertid, can be used as either a database or statement handle attribute.

Table G.3   **Deprecated MySQL–Specific Statement Handle Attributes**

Deprecated Attribute	Preferred Attribute
insertid	mysql_insertid
is_blob	mysql_is_blob
is_key	mysql_is_key
is_not_null	NULLABLE
is_num	mysql_is_num
is_pri_key	mysql_is_pri_key
length	PRECISION
max_length	mysql_max_length
table	mysql_table

Dynamic Attributes

The following attributes are associated with the most recently used handle, represented by $h in the following descriptions. They should be used immediately after invoking whatever handle method sets them and before invoking another method that resets them.

- $rv = **$DBI::err;**

  This is the same as calling $h->err().

- $str = **$DBI::errstr;**

  This is the same as calling $h->errstr().

- $rows = **$DBI::rows;**

  This is the same as calling $h->rows().

DBI Environment Variables

DBI consults several environment variables, listed in Table G.4. All of them, except DBI_TRACE, are used by the connect() method. DBI_DRIVER is used by the data_sources() method, and DBI_TRACE is used by trace().

Table G.4 **DBI Environment Variables**

Name	Meaning
DBI_DRIVER	DBD-level driver name ("mysql" for MySQL)
DBI_DSN	Data source name
DBI_PASS	Password
DBI_TRACE	Trace level and/or trace output file
DBI_USER	Username

H

PHP API Reference

THIS APPENDIX DESCRIBES THE PHP APPLICATION programming interface for MySQL. The API consists of a set of functions for communicating with MySQL servers and accessing databases. These functions fall into the following categories:

- Connection management routines
- Error-reporting routines
- Query construction and execution routines
- Result set processing routines
- Information routines
- Deprecated routines

This appendix serves as a reference, so it includes only brief code fragments illustrating use of the PHP API. For complete client scripts and instructions for writing them, see Chapter 8, "The PHP API." The functions described here are those that pertain directly to MySQL. The PHP manual contains many hundreds of pages of reference material, so this appendix summarizes no more than a small part of PHP's capabilities. To obtain the complete PHP manual, visit the PHP Web site at http://www.php.net/.

Writing PHP Scripts

PHP scripts are plain text files that can contain a mixture of HTML and PHP code. The script is interpreted to produce a Web page as output that is sent to the client. The HTML is copied to the output without interpretation. PHP code is interpreted and replaced by whatever output the code produces.

PHP begins interpreting a file in HTML mode. You can switch into and out of PHP code mode using special tags that signify the beginning and end of PHP code. You can switch between modes any number of times within a file. PHP understands four types of tags, although some of them must be explicitly enabled if you want to use them. One way to do this is by turning them on in the PHP initialization file, `php.ini` (`php3.ini` in PHP 3). The location of this file is system dependent; on many UNIX systems, it's found in `/usr/lib` or `/usr/local/lib`. On Windows, look in the Windows system directory.

PHP understands the following tag styles:

- The default style uses `<?php` and `?>` tags:

    ```
    <?php print ("Hello, world."); ?>
    ```

- Short-open-tag style uses `<?` and `?>` tags:

    ```
    <? print ("Hello, world."); ?>
    ```

    In PHP 4, this style also allows `<?=` and `?>` tags as a shortcut for displaying the result of an expression without using a print statement:

    ```
    <?= "Hello, world." ?>
    ```

    Short tags can be enabled with a directive in the PHP initialization file:

    ```
    short_open_tag = On;
    ```

- Active Server Page-compatible style uses `<%` and `%>` tags:

    ```
    <% print ("Hello, world."); %>
    ```

    In PHP 4, this style also allows `<%=` and `%>` tags as a shortcut for displaying the result of an expression without using a print statement:

    ```
    <%= "Hello, world." %>
    ```

    ASP-style tags can be enabled with a directive in the PHP initialization file:

    ```
    asp_tags = On;
    ```

    Support for ASP tags was introduced in PHP 3.0.4.

- If you use an HTML editor that doesn't understand the other tags, you can use `<script>` and `</script>` tags:

```
<script language="php"> print ("Hello, world."); </script>
```

The examples in this appendix use `<?php` and `?>` for the opening and closing tags.

Functions

The following descriptions discuss each of PHP's MySQL-related functions. Certain parameter names recur throughout the function descriptions and have the following conventional meanings:

- Most functions take a `conn_id` (connection identifier) parameter. This is a resource that indicates a connection to a MySQL server, typically obtained by calling `mysql_connect()` or `mysql_pconnect()`. If the connection identifier is optional and is missing from a function call, PHP uses the most recently opened connection. In this case, many functions will try to establish a connection if no connection is specified and there isn't one open.

- A `result_id` parameter indicates a result set identifier. This is a resource containing information about the rows in a query result. Result sets typically are obtained by calling `mysql_query()`, although other functions create them as well.

- `row_num` and `col_num` indicate row and column numbers within a result set. Both are numbered starting from 0.

- Optional parameters are indicated by square brackets (`[]`).

Some functions produce an error message if an error occurs, in addition to returning a status value. In Web contexts, this message appears in the output sent to the client browser, which may not be what you want. To suppress the (possibly cryptic) error message a function normally would produce, precede the function name by the `@` operator. For example, to suppress the error message from a `mysql_connect()` call so that you can report failure in a more suitable manner, you might do something like the following:

```
<?php
    $conn_id = @mysql_connect ("cobra.snake.net", "sampadm", "secret")
        or die ("Could not connect\n");
    print ("Connected successfully\n");
?>
```

The examples in this appendix use the @ operator for connect calls and print their own message if a connection error occurs.

Another way to suppress error messages is to use the error_reporting() function:

```
<?php
    error_reporting (0); # suppress all error messages
    $conn_id = mysql_connect ("cobra.snake.net", "sampadm", "secret")
        or die ("Could not connect\n");
    print ("Connected successfully\n");
?>
```

Many of the example scripts in this appendix print "Connected success-fully" after establishing a connection to the MySQL server. The reason they do this is to make sure the script prints some output, in case you try the script for yourself. (A PHP script that runs successfully but produces no output can trigger a "page contains no data" warning in some browsers, which gives the misleading impression that the script failed somehow.)

The examples also print messages and query results as plain text for the most part. This is done to make the scripts easier to read. However, for scripts intended for execution in a Web environment, you generally should encode output with htmlspecialchars() if it may contain characters that are special in HTML, such as '<', '>', or '&'.

In the descriptions that follow, the term "SELECT query" should be taken to mean a SELECT query or any other query that returns rows, such as DESCRIBE, EXPLAIN, or SHOW.

Connection Management Routines

The routines in this section allow you to open and close connections to the MySQL server or to change the current MySQL username.

- int

  mysql_change_user (string user_name,
                          string password
                          [, string db_name
                          [, resource conn_id]]);

  Changes the user and the default database for the connection specified by conn_id or for the current connection if no conn_id parameter is specified. The database becomes the default for table references that do not include a database specifier. If db_name is not specified, no default database is selected.

`mysql_change_user()` returns `true` if the user is allowed to connect to the server and, if a database was specified, has permission to access the database. Otherwise, the function fails and the current user and database remain unchanged.

`mysql_change_user()` requires MySQL 3.23.3 or later. It was introduced in PHP 3.0.13 but is unavailable in PHP 4.

```php
<?php
    $conn_id = @mysql_connect ("cobra.snake.net", "sampadm", "secret")
        or die ("Could not connect\n");
    mysql_change_user ("unknown", "public")
        or die ("Could not change user\n");
    print ("User changed successfully\n");
?>
```

- bool

  mysql_close ([resource conn_id]);

Closes the connection to the MySQL server identified by conn_id. If no connection is specified, `mysql_close()` closes the most recently opened connection.

`mysql_close()` returns `true` for success or `false` for an error. For persistent connections opened with `mysql_pconnect()`, `mysql_close()` returns `true` but ignores the close request and leaves the connection open. If you are going to close a connection, you should open it using `mysql_connect()` rather than `mysql_pconnect()`.

```php
<?php
    $conn_id = @mysql_connect ("cobra.snake.net", "sampadm", "secret")
        or die ("Could not connect\n");
    print ("Connected successfully\n");
    mysql_close ($conn_id);
?>
```

It's not required that you close a non-persistent connection explicitly; PHP will close it automatically when the script terminates. On the other hand, if a script will execute for a while after it has finished accessing the MySQL server, closing the connection when you no longer need it is friendlier to the server, which then can reuse the connection for another client more quickly.

- resource

  mysql_connect ([string host_name]
                    [, string user_name]
                    [, string password]
                    [, new_conn]]]);

Opens a connection to the MySQL server on host host_name for user user_name with the given password. Returns the connection identifier associated with the new connection or returns false if an error occurred.

As of PHP 3.0B4, the hostname parameter can be specified with an optional port number in "host_name:port_num" format. As of PHP 3.0.10, if the hostname is "localhost", the hostname parameter can be specified with an optional pathname to specify the UNIX domain socket path, in "localhost:socket_name" form. The socket should be specified as a full pathname. To connect to the local host but use a TCP/IP connection rather than a UNIX socket, specify a hostname value of "127.0.0.1".

If the hostname parameter is missing, the default is "localhost". If the username parameter is missing or empty, the default is the username that PHP is running as. (If PHP is running as an Apache module, this is the username for the account the Web server is running as. If PHP is executing as a standalone program, this is the name of the user running the PHP script.) If the password parameter is missing or empty, the empty password is sent.

In PHP 4, you can change the default values that are used for missing connection parameter arguments by specifying configuration directives in the PHP initialization file, php.ini. The directives are listed in Table H.1.

Table H.1 **PHP 4 Configuration Directives for Setting Default Connection Parameters**

Connection Parameter	Configuration Directive
Hostname	mysql.default_host
Username	mysql.default_user
Password	mysql.default_password
Port number	mysql.default_port
Socket pathname	mysql.default_socket

While the connection is open, if mysql_connect() is called with the same connection parameters (hostname, username, password), no new connection is generated; mysql_connect() returns the existing connection identifier instead. As of PHP 4.2.0, you can override this behavior and force mysql_connect() to open a new connection by passing a true value for the new_conn parameter.

The connection can be closed by calling `mysql_close()`. If the connection is open when the script terminates, the connection is closed automatically.

PHP functions that take an optional connection identifier argument use the most recently open connection if the argument is omitted. If no connection is open, several functions will attempt to open one. These include functions that issue queries, functions that select, create, or drop databases, and functions that retrieve information about the connection. In all such cases, the result is as though `mysql_connect()` is called with no arguments, thus using the default connection parameters. Should the implicit connection attempt fail, the calling function fails as well.

```php
<?php
    $conn_id = @mysql_connect ("cobra.snake.net", "sampadm", "secret")
        or die ("Could not connect\n");
    print ("Connected successfully\n");
    mysql_close ($conn_id);
?>
```

- resource

mysql_pconnect ([string host_name]
                    [, string user_name
                    [, string password]]);

`mysql_pconnect()` is similar to `mysql_connect()` except that it opens a persistent connection. That is, the connection stays open when the script terminates. If another call is made to `mysql_pconnect()` with the same connection parameters (hostname, username, password) while the connection is open, the connection will be reused. This avoids the overhead of tearing down and reopening connections and is more efficient than non–persistent connections.

Persistent connections only make sense when PHP is executing as a module within a Web server process that continues to run after the PHP script terminates. (The connection can be reused when the server receives another request for a PHP script that connects to MySQL with the same parameters.) In a script executed by a standalone version of PHP, the connection is closed when the script terminates because the PHP process terminates as well.

Calling `mysql_close()` on a persistent connection is nonsensical; if you do this, `mysql_close()` returns `true` but leaves the connection open.

```php
<?php
    $conn_id = @mysql_pconnect ("cobra.snake.net", "sampadm", "secret")
        or die ("Could not connect\n");
    print ("Connected successfully\n");
?>
```

- `bool`

  mysql_ping (`[resource conn_id]`);

  Re-establishes the connection to the server if the connection has timed out. Returns `true` if the connection was still active or was re-established successfully, `false` otherwise.

  `mysql_ping()` was introduced in PHP 4.3.0.

Error-Reporting Routines

The `mysql_errno()` and `mysql_error()` functions return error number and message information for MySQL-related PHP functions. However, prior to PHP 4.0.6, no error information is available from either function without a valid connection identifier. This means that they are not useful for reporting the result of failed `mysql_connect()` or `mysql_pconnect()` calls because no such identifier is available until a connection has been established successfully. If you want to get the MySQL error message for failed connection attempts under these circumstances, enable the `track_errors` variable with a directive in the PHP initialization file:

```
track_errors = On;
```

Then restart your Web server if you're running PHP as an Apache module. After you've done that, you can obtain an error string for failed connection attempts by referring to the `$php_errormsg` variable:

```php
<?php
    $conn_id = @mysql_connect("badhost", "baduser", "badpass")
        or die ("Could not connect: $php_errormsg\n");
    print ("Connected successfully\n");
?>
```

You can adopt a combined approach that uses the error functions if they return information for a failed connection attempt and falls back to $php_errormsg if they do not. The following example shows one way to do this. If mysql_error() returns non-zero, that means the error routines can be used. Otherwise, the code uses $php_errormsg to get the error message:

```php
<?php
    if (!($conn_id = @mysql_connect("badhost", "baduser", "badpass")))
    {
        # mysql_errno() returns non-zero if it works for connect errors
        if (mysql_errno ())
        {
            $msg = sprintf ("Could not connect: %s (%d)\n",
                            mysql_error (), mysql_errno ());
        }
        else                    # fall back to $php_errormsg
        {
            $msg = "Could not connect: $php_errormsg\n";
        }
        die ($msg);
    }
    print ("Connected successfully\n");
?>
```

- int

  mysql_errno ([resource conn_id]);

  For the given connection (or the current connection if none is specified), returns the error number for the MySQL-related function that most recently returned a status. A value of zero means no error occurred.

```php
<?php
    $conn_id = @mysql_connect ("cobra.snake.net", "sampadm", "secret")
        or die ("Could not connect, error=" . mysql_errno () . "\n");
    print ("Connected successfully\n");
    mysql_select_db ("sampdb")
        or die ("Could not select database, error=" . mysql_errno () . "\n");
    $query = "SELECT * FROM president";
    $result_id = mysql_query ($query)
        or die ("query failed, error=" . mysql_errno () . "\n");
    mysql_free_result ($result_id);
?>
```

- string

  mysql_error ([resource conn_id]);

  For the given connection (or the current connection if none is specified), returns a string containing the error message for the MySQL-related function that most recently returned a status. An empty string means no error occurred.

  ```php
  <?php
      $conn_id = @mysql_connect ("cobra.snake.net", "sampadm", "secret")
          or die ("Could not connect, error=" . mysql_error () . "\n");
      print ("Connected successfully\n");
      mysql_select_db ("sampdb")
          or die ("Could not select database, error=" . mysql_error () . "\n");
      $query = "SELECT * FROM president";
      $result_id = mysql_query ($query)
          or die ("query failed, error=" . mysql_error () . "\n");
      mysql_free_result ($result_id);
  ?>
  ```

Query Construction and Execution Routines

The routines in this section are used to issue queries to the MySQL server. Each query string must consist of a single SQL statement, and should not end with a semicolon character (';') or a \g sequence. ';' and \g are conventions of the mysql client program and are not used when issuing queries through PHP.

- string

  mysql_escape_string (string str);

  Escapes any quotes and other special characters in the str argument by preceding each with a backslash, returning the result as a new string. This is used to make data values safe for insertion into SQL queries. PHP 4.3.0 and later supports a mysql_real_escape_string() function as well, which is similar to mysql_escape_string() but takes a connection identifier argument and takes into account the current character set when performing encoding. See the entry for mysql_real_escape_string() elsewhere in this appendix.

  The list of the characters escaped by these functions is given in the description for the mysql_real_escape_string() function described in Appendix F, "C API Reference."

`mysql_escape_string()` was introduced in PHP 4.0.3. Prior to that, you can use `addslashes()` to achieve much the same result.

```php
<?php
    $conn_id = @mysql_connect ("cobra.snake.net", "sampadm", "secret")
        or die ("Could not connect\n");
    mysql_select_db ("sampdb")
        or die ("Could not select database\n");
    $last_name = mysql_escape_string ("O'Malley");
    $first_name = mysql_escape_string ("Brian");
    $query = "INSERT INTO member (last_name,first_name,expiration)"
        . " VALUES('$last_name','$first_name','2002-6-3')";
    $result_id = mysql_query ($query)
        or die ("Query failed\n");
    printf ("membership number for new member: %d\n",
            mysql_insert_id());
?>
```

- resource

  mysql_list_dbs (`[resource conn_id]`);

  Returns a result identifier for a result set consisting of the names of the databases the server knows about, one database name per row of the result set. Returns `false` if an error occurred. No default database need be selected before calling this routine. The result set can be processed by any of the usual row-fetching functions or by `mysql_db_name()`. For any such function that takes a row number parameter, the number should be in the range from `0` to `mysql_num_rows()-1`. The result identifier can be passed to `mysql_free_result()` to free any resources associated with it.

```php
<?php
    $conn_id = @mysql_connect ("cobra.snake.net", "sampadm", "secret")
        or die ("Could not connect\n");
    $result_id = mysql_list_dbs ()
        or die ("Query failed\n");
    print ("Databases (using mysql_fetch_row()):<br />\n");
    while ($row = mysql_fetch_row ($result_id))
        printf ("%s<br />\n", $row[0]);
    mysql_free_result ($result_id);
    $result_id = mysql_list_dbs ()
        or die ("Query failed\n");
    print ("Databases (using mysql_db_name()):<br />\n");
    for ($i = 0; $i < mysql_num_rows ($result_id); $i++)
        printf ("%s<br />\n", mysql_db_name ($result_id, $i));
    mysql_free_result ($result_id);
?>
```

- resource
mysql_list_fields (string db_name,
                          string tbl_name
                          [, resource conn_id]);

Returns a result identifier for a result set containing information about the columns in a table or `false` if an error occurred. No default database need be selected before calling this routine. The db_name and tbl_name parameters identify the database and table in which you're interested. The result identifier can be used with the functions mysql_field_flags(), mysql_field_len(), mysql_field_name(), and mysql_field_type(). The result identifier can be passed to mysql_free_result() to free any resources associated with it.

```php
<?php
    $conn_id = @mysql_connect ("cobra.snake.net", "sampadm", "secret")
        or die ("Could not connect\n");
    $result_id = mysql_list_fields ("sampdb", "member")
        or die ("Query failed\n");
    print ("member table column information:<br />\n");
    for ($i = 0; $i < mysql_num_fields ($result_id); $i++)
    {
        printf ("column %d:", $i);
        printf (" name %s,", mysql_field_name ($result_id, $i));
        printf (" len %d,", mysql_field_len ($result_id, $i));
        printf (" type %s,", mysql_field_type ($result_id, $i));
        printf (" flags %s\n", mysql_field_flags ($result_id, $i));
        print ("<br />\n");
    }
    mysql_free_result ($result_id);
?>
```

- resource
mysql_list_processes ([resource conn_id]);

Returns a result identifier for a result set containing information about the processes currently running in the server or `false` if an error occurred. If you have the PROCESS privilege, the list contains all server processes. If you do not, the list contains only your own processes.

The result set identifier can be passed to any of the usual row-fetching functions and to mysql_free_result() to free any resources associated with the result set.

mysql_list_processes() was introduced in PHP 4.3.0.

- resource

mysql_list_tables (string db_name

[, resource conn_id]);

Returns a result identifier for a result set consisting of the names of the tables in the given database name, one table name per row of the result set. Returns `false` if an error occurred. No default database need be selected before calling this routine. The result set can be processed by any of the usual row-fetching functions or by `mysql_tablename()`. For any such function that takes a row number parameter, the number should be in the range from `0` to `mysql_num_rows()`-1. The result identifier can be passed to `mysql_free_result()` to free any resources associated with it.

```php
<?php
    $conn_id = @mysql_connect ("cobra.snake.net", "sampadm", "secret")
        or die ("Could not connect\n");
    $result_id = mysql_list_tables ("sampdb")
        or die ("Query failed\n");
    print ("sampdb tables (using mysql_fetch_row()):<br />\n");
    while ($row = mysql_fetch_row ($result_id))
        printf ("%s<br />\n", $row[0]);
    mysql_free_result ($result_id);
    $result_id = mysql_list_tables ("sampdb")
        or die ("Query failed\n");
    print ("sampdb tables (using mysql_tablename()):<br />\n");
    for ($i = 0; $i < mysql_num_rows ($result_id); $i++)
        printf ("%s<br />\n", mysql_tablename ($result_id, $i));
    mysql_free_result ($result_id);
?>
```

- int

mysql_query (string query

[, resource conn_id

[, int fetch_mode]]);

Sends the query string to the MySQL server to be executed. For DELETE, INSERT, REPLACE, and UPDATE statements, `mysql_query()` returns `true` for success and `false` if an error occurred. For a successful query, you can call `mysql_affected_rows()` to find out how many rows were modified.

As of PHP 4.2.0, an optional `fetch_mode` parameter can be given to indicate whether `mysql_query()` should fetch and buffer the result set immediately or defer row fetching until later. The possible `fetch_mode` values are MYSQL_STORE_RESULT (buffered) and MYSQL_USE_RESULT (unbuffered), with the default being MYSQL_STORE_RESULT. Using

MYSQL_USE_RESULT causes `mysql_query()` to act like `mysql_unbuffered_query()`; see the description of that function for more information.

For SELECT statements, `mysql_query()` returns a positive result set identifier for success and `false` if an error occurred. For a successful query, the result identifier can be used with the various result set processing functions that take a `result_id` argument. The identifier can be passed to `mysql_free_result()` to free any resources associated with the result set.

A "successful" query is one that executes without error, but success implies nothing about whether the query returns any rows. The following query is perfectly legal but returns no rows:

```
SELECT * FROM president WHERE 1 = 0
```

A query can fail for any of several reasons. For example, it may be syntactically malformed, semantically invalid, or illegal because you don't have permission to access the tables named in the query.

```php
<?php
    $conn_id = @mysql_connect ("cobra.snake.net", "sampadm", "secret")
        or die ("Could not connect\n");
    print ("Connected successfully\n");
    mysql_select_db ("sampdb")
        or die ("Could not select database\n");
    $query = "SELECT * FROM president";
    $result_id = mysql_query ($query)
        or die ("Query failed\n");
    mysql_free_result ($result_id);
?>
```

- string
  mysql_real_escape_string (string str
                               [, resource conn_id]);

Escapes any quotes and other special characters in the str argument by preceding each with a backslash, returning the result as a new string. This is used to make data values safe for insertion into SQL queries. `mysql_real_escape_string()` differs from the `mysql_escape_string()` function in that it takes a connection identifier argument and takes into account the current character set when performing encoding. `mysql_escape_string()` does not. See the entry for `mysql_escape_string()` elsewhere in this appendix.

The list of the characters escaped by these functions is given in the description for the `mysql_real_escape_string()` function described in Appendix F.

`mysql_real_escape_string()` requires MySQL 3.23.14 or later. It was introduced in PHP 4.3.0. Prior to that, you can use `mysql_escape_string()` or `addslashes()` to achieve much the same result.

```php
<?php
    $conn_id = @mysql_connect ("cobra.snake.net", "sampadm", "secret")
        or die ("Could not connect\n");
    mysql_select_db ("sampdb")
        or die ("Could not select database\n");
    $last_name = mysql_real_escape_string ("O'Malley");
    $first_name = mysql_real_escape_string ("Brian");
    $query = "INSERT INTO member (last_name,first_name,expiration)"
        . " VALUES('$last_name','$first_name','2002-6-3')";
    $result_id = mysql_query ($query)
        or die ("Query failed\n");
    printf ("membership number for new member: %d\n", mysql_insert_id());
?>
```

- bool

mysql_select_db (string db_name
                    [, resource conn_id]);

Selects the given database to make it the default database for the given connection. Tables referenced in subsequent queries are assumed to be in that database unless they are explicitly qualified with a database name. Returns `true` for success and `false` if an error occurred.

```php
<?php
    $conn_id = @mysql_connect ("cobra.snake.net", "sampadm", "secret")
        or die ("Could not connect\n");
    mysql_select_db ("sampdb")
        or die ("Could not select database\n");
    print ("Database selected successfully\n");
?>
```

- int
mysql_unbuffered_query (string query
         [, resource conn_id
         [, int fetch_mode]]);

mysql_unbuffered_query() is similar to mysql_query() except that by default it does not immediately fetch the rows of the result set into memory. The differences between the two functions correspond to the differences between the C API functions mysql_store_result() and mysql_use_result(). See Appendix F for a comparison of the tradeoffs between those two functions and a description of when each is appropriate. The same considerations apply to the PHP functions mysql_query() and mysql_unbuffered_query(). In particular, some PHP functions work properly only for queries issued in buffered mode. These include mysql_data_seek(), mysql_num_rows(), and mysql_result() and its aliases.

As of PHP 4.2.0, an optional fetch_mode parameter can be given to indicate whether mysql_unbuffered_query() should fetch and buffer the result set immediately or defer row fetching until later. The possible fetch_mode values are MYSQL_STORE_RESULT (buffered) and MYSQL_USE_RESULT (unbuffered), with the default being MYSQL_USE_RESULT. In unbuffered fetch mode, you must fetch all the rows returned by the query before issuing another query. The result identifier can be passed to mysql_free_result() to free any resources associated with the result set. This will automatically retrieve and discard any unfetched rows for you.

mysql_unbuffered_query() is available as of PHP 4.0.6.

```php
<?php
    $conn_id = @mysql_connect ("cobra.snake.net", "sampadm", "secret")
        or die ("Could not connect\n");
    mysql_select_db ("sampdb")
        or die ("Could not select database\n");
    $query = "SELECT first_name, last_name FROM member";
    $result_id = mysql_unbuffered_query ($query)
        or die ("Query failed\n");
    while (list ($first_name, $last_name)
                            = mysql_fetch_row ($result_id))
        print ("$first_name $last_name\n");
    mysql_free_result ($result_id);
?>
```

Result Set Processing Routines

The routines in this section are used to retrieve the results of queries. They also provide access to information about the result, such as how many rows were affected or the metadata for result set columns.

- int
  mysql_affected_rows ([resource conn_id]);

  Returns the number of rows affected (modified) by the most recent DELETE, INSERT, REPLACE, or UPDATE statement on the given connection. mysql_affected_rows() returns 0 if no rows were changed and -1 if an error occurred.

  After a SELECT query, mysql_affected_rows() returns the number of rows selected. However, normally you should use mysql_num_rows() with SELECT statements.

  ```php
  <?php
      $conn_id = @mysql_connect ("cobra.snake.net", "sampadm", "secret")
          or die ("Could not connect\n");
      mysql_select_db ("sampdb")
          or die ("Could not select database\n");
      $query = "INSERT INTO member (last_name,first_name,expiration)"
          . " VALUES('Brown','Marcia','2002-6-3')";
      $result_id = mysql_query ($query)
          or die ("Query failed\n");
      $count = mysql_affected_rows ();
      printf ("%d row%s inserted\n", $count, $count == 1 ? "" : "s");
  ?>
  ```

- bool
  mysql_data_seek (resource result_id, int row_num);

  Each result set returned by a SELECT query has an internal row cursor to indicate which row should be returned by the next call to the row–fetching functions mysql_fetch_array(), mysql_fetch_assoc(), mysql_fetch_object(), or mysql_fetch_row(). Call mysql_data_seek() to set the cursor for a result set to the given row. The row number should be in the range from 0 to mysql_num_rows()-1. mysql_data_seek() returns true if the row number is legal and false otherwise.

  ```php
  <?php
      $conn_id = @mysql_connect ("cobra.snake.net", "sampadm", "secret")
          or die ("Could not connect\n");
  ```

```
        mysql_select_db ("sampdb")
            or die ("Could not select database\n");
        $query = "SELECT last_name, first_name FROM president";
        $result_id = mysql_query ($query)
            or die ("Query failed\n");
        # fetch rows in reverse order
        for ($i = mysql_num_rows ($result_id) - 1; $i >= 0; $i--)
        {
            if (!mysql_data_seek ($result_id, $i))
            {
                printf ("Cannot seek to row %d\n", $i);
                continue;
            }
            if(!($row = mysql_fetch_object ($result_id)))
                continue;
            printf ("%s %s<br />\n", $row->last_name, $row->first_name);
        }
        mysql_free_result ($result_id);
    ?>
```

- string
  mysql_db_name (resource result_id,
                    int row_num
                    [, mixed field]);

Given a result identifier returned by mysql_list_dbs() and a row number within the result, mysql_db_name() returns the database name stored in the given row of the set, or it returns false if an error occurred. The row number should be in the range from 0 to mysql_num_rows()-1.

mysql_db_name() was introduced in PHP 3.0.6. It is actually an alias for mysql_result().

```
    <?php
        $conn_id = @mysql_connect ("cobra.snake.net", "sampadm", "secret")
            or die ("Could not connect\n");
        $result_id = mysql_list_dbs ()
            or die ("Query failed\n");
        print ("Databases:<br />\n");
        for ($i = 0; $i < mysql_num_rows ($result_id); $i++)
            printf ("%s<br />\n", mysql_db_name ($result_id, $i));
        mysql_free_result ($result_id);
    ?>
```

- array

mysql_fetch_array (resource result_id
 [, int result_type]);

Returns the next row of the given result set as an array or `false` if there are no more rows. The array contains values stored both by numeric column indices (beginning at 0) and associatively keyed by column names. In other words, each column value can be accessed using either its numeric column index or its name. Associative indices are case sensitive and must be given in the same case that was used to name columns in the query. Suppose you issue the following query:

```
SELECT last_name, first_name FROM president
```

If you fetch rows from the result set into an array named `$row`, array elements can be accessed as follows:

```
$row[0]                    Holds last_name value
$row[1]                    Holds first_name value
$row["last_name"]          Holds last_name value
$row["first_name"]         Holds first_name value
```

Keys are not qualified by the table names of the corresponding columns, so if you select columns with the same name from different tables, a name clash results. Precedence is given to the column named last in the list of columns selected by the query. To access the hidden column, use its numeric index or rewrite the query to provide a unique alias for the column.

Prior to PHP 3.0.7, `mysql_fetch_array()` always returns values both by numeric and associative indices. As of PHP 3.0.7, a `result_type` parameter can be given to indicate what kinds of values to return. `result_type` should be `MYSQL_ASSOC` (return values by name indices only), `MYSQL_NUM` (return values by numeric indices only), or `MYSQL_BOTH` (return values by both types of indices). The default if `result_type` is missing is `MYSQL_BOTH`. Note that calling `mysql_fetch_array()` with a `result_type` of `MYSQL_ASSOC` or `MYSQL_NUM` is equivalent to calling `mysql_fetch_assoc()` or `mysql_fetch_row()`.

```php
<?php
    $conn_id = @mysql_connect ("cobra.snake.net", "sampadm", "secret")
        or die ("Could not connect\n");
    mysql_select_db ("sampdb")
        or die ("Could not select database\n");
```

```
        $query = "SELECT last_name, first_name FROM president";
        $result_id = mysql_query ($query)
            or die ("Query failed\n");
        while ($row = mysql_fetch_array ($result_id))
        {
            # print each name twice, once using numeric indices,
            # once using associative (name) indices
            printf ("%s %s<br />\n", $row[0], $row[1]);
            printf ("%s %s<br />\n", $row["last_name"], $row["first_name"]);
        }
        mysql_free_result ($result_id);
    ?>
```

- array

  mysql_fetch_assoc (resource result_id);

  Returns the next row of the given result set as an associative array or false if there are no more rows. Column values can be accessed using associative indices corresponding to the names of the columns selected by the query from which the result set was generated.

  Calling mysql_fetch_assoc() is the same as calling mysql_fetch_array() with a second argument of MYSQL_ASSOC. Column values with numeric indices are not returned.

  mysql_fetch_assoc() was introduced in PHP 4.0.3.

```
    <?php
        $conn_id = @mysql_connect ("cobra.snake.net", "sampadm", "secret")
            or die ("Could not connect\n");
        mysql_select_db ("sampdb")
            or die ("Could not select database\n");
        $query = "SELECT last_name, first_name FROM president";
        $result_id = mysql_query ($query)
            or die ("Query failed\n");
        while ($row = mysql_fetch_assoc ($result_id))
        {
            printf ("%s %s<br />\n", $row["last_name"], $row["first_name"]);
        }
        mysql_free_result ($result_id);
    ?>
```

- object

  mysql_fetch_field (resource result_id
                         [, int col_num]);

Returns metadata information about the given column in the result set or `false` if there is no such column. If col_num is omitted, successive calls to `mysql_fetch_field()` return information about successive columns of the result set. The return value is `false` if no more columns remain. If col_num is specified, it should be in the range from 0 to `mysql_num_fields()-1`. In this case, `mysql_fetch_field()` returns information about the given column, or it returns `false` if col_num is out of range.

The information is returned as an object that has the properties shown in Table H.2.

```php
<?php
    $conn_id = @mysql_connect ("cobra.snake.net", "sampadm", "secret")
        or die ("Could not connect\n");
    $result_id = mysql_list_fields ("sampdb", "president")
        or die ("Query failed\n");
    print ("Table: sampdb.president<br />\n");
    # get column metadata
    for ($i = 0; $i < mysql_num_fields ($result_id); $i++)
    {
        printf ("Information for column %d:<br />\n", $i);
        $meta = mysql_fetch_field ($result_id);
        if (!$meta)
        {
            print ("No information available<br />\n");
            continue;
        }
        print ("<pre>\n");
        printf ("blob:         %s\n", $meta->blob);
        printf ("def:          %s\n", $meta->def);
        printf ("max_length:   %s\n", $meta->max_length);
        printf ("multiple_key: %s\n", $meta->multiple_key);
        printf ("name:         %s\n", $meta->name);
        printf ("not_null:     %s\n", $meta->not_null);
        printf ("numeric:      %s\n", $meta->numeric);
        printf ("primary_key:  %s\n", $meta->primary_key);
        printf ("table:        %s\n", $meta->table);
        printf ("type:         %s\n", $meta->type);
        printf ("unique_key:   %s\n", $meta->unique_key);
        printf ("unsigned:     %s\n", $meta->unsigned);
        printf ("zerofill:     %s\n", $meta->zerofill);
        print ("</pre>\n");
    }
    mysql_free_result ($result_id);
?>
```

Table H.2 **mysql_fetch_field( ) Properties**

Property	Meaning
blob	1 if the column is a BLOB (or TEXT) type, 0 otherwise
def	Default value of column
max_length	The length of the largest column value in the result set
multiple_key	1 if the column is a part of a non-unique index, 0 otherwise
name	The column name
not_null	1 if the column cannot contain NULL values, 0 otherwise
numeric	1 if the column has a numeric type, 0 otherwise
primary_key	1 if the column is a part of a PRIMARY KEY, 0 otherwise
table	The name of the table containing the column (empty for calculated columns)
type	The name of the type of the column
unique_key	1 if the column is a part of a UNIQUE index, 0 otherwise
unsigned	1 if the column has the UNSIGNED attribute, 0 otherwise
zerofill	1 if the column has the ZEROFILL attribute, 0 otherwise

The def member of the object returned by mysql_fetch_field() is valid only if the result set was obtained by calling the mysql_list_fields() function. Otherwise, it will be the empty string.

The type member will have one of the values listed in Table H.3. For a column calculated from an expression, the type value will reflect the expression type. A type value of "unknown" most likely indicates that the MySQL server is newer than the version of the MySQL client library PHP is using and that the server knows about a new type the library doesn't recognize.

Table H.3 **mysql_fetch_field( ) type Member Values**

Value	Type of Column
blob	BLOB (or TEXT) column
date	DATE column
datetime	DATETIME column
int	Integer numeric column
null	Column containing only NULL values
real	Floating-point numeric column
string	String column other than BLOB or TEXT
time	TIME columns
timestamp	TIMESTAMP column
unknown	Unknown column type
year	YEAR column

- array

mysql_fetch_lengths (resource result_id);

Returns an array containing the lengths of the column values in the row
most recently fetched by any of the functions mysql_fetch_array(),
mysql_fetch_assoc(), mysql_fetch_object(), or
mysql_fetch_row(). Array element indices range from 0 to
mysql_num_fields()-1. Returns false if no row has yet been fetched
or if an error occurred.

```php
<?php
    $conn_id = @mysql_connect ("cobra.snake.net", "sampadm", "secret")
        or die ("Could not connect\n");
    mysql_select_db ("sampdb")
        or die ("Could not select database\n");
    $query = "SELECT * FROM president";
    $result_id = mysql_query ($query)
        or die ("Query failed\n");
    $row_num = 0;
    while (mysql_fetch_row ($result_id))
    {
        ++$row_num;
        # get lengths of column values
        printf ("Lengths of values in row %d:<br />\n", $row_num);
        $len = mysql_fetch_lengths ($result_id);
        if (!$len)
        {
            print ("No information available<br />\n");
            break;
        }
        print ("<pre>\n");
        for ($i = 0; $i < mysql_num_fields ($result_id); $i++)
            printf ("column %d: %s\n", $i, $len[$i]);
        print ("</pre>\n");
    }
    mysql_free_result ($result_id);
?>
```

- object

mysql_fetch_object (resource result_id
                        [, int result_type]);

Returns the next row of the given result set as an object or false
if there are no more rows. Column values can be accessed as properties
of the object. The property names are the names of the columns
selected by the query from which the result set was generated.

The `result_type` parameter can be `MYSQL_ASSOC` (return values by name indices only), `MYSQL_NUM` (return values by numeric indices only), or `MYSQL_BOTH` (return values by both types of indices). The default if `result_type` is missing is `MYSQL_BOTH`. Numbers are not legal property names, so you can access values by the numeric indices only by playing tricks, such as treating the object as an array.

```php
<?php
    $conn_id = @mysql_connect ("cobra.snake.net", "sampadm", "secret")
        or die ("Could not connect\n");
    mysql_select_db ("sampdb")
        or die ("Could not select database\n");
    $query = "SELECT last_name, first_name FROM president";
    $result_id = mysql_query ($query)
        or die ("Query failed\n");
    while ($row = mysql_fetch_object ($result_id))
        printf ("%s %s<br />\n", $row->last_name, $row->first_name);
    mysql_free_result ($result_id);
?>
```

- array

`mysql_fetch_row` `(resource result_id);`

Returns the next row of the given result set as an array or `false` if there are no more rows. Column values can be accessed as array elements, using column indices in the range from `0` to `mysql_num_fields()-1`.

Calling `mysql_fetch_row()` is the same as calling `mysql_fetch_array()` with a second argument of `MYSQL_NUM`. Column values with associative indices are not returned.

```php
<?php
    $conn_id = @mysql_connect ("cobra.snake.net", "sampadm", "secret")
        or die ("Could not connect\n");
    mysql_select_db ("sampdb")
        or die ("Could not select database\n");
    $query = "SELECT last_name, first_name FROM president";
    $result_id = mysql_query ($query)
        or die ("Query failed\n");
    while ($row = mysql_fetch_row ($result_id))
        printf ("%s %s<br />\n", $row[0], $row[1]);
    mysql_free_result ($result_id);
?>
```

- string
mysql_field_flags (resource result_id,
                          int col_num);

Returns metadata information about the given column in the result set
as a string or false if an error occurred. The string consists of space-separated words indicating which of a column's flag values are true. For
flags that are false, the corresponding word is not present in the string.
Table H.4 lists the words that can be present in the string. col_num
should be in the range from 0 to mysql_num_fields()-1.

```php
<?php
    $conn_id = @mysql_connect ("cobra.snake.net", "sampadm", "secret")
        or die ("Could not connect\n");
    mysql_select_db ("sampdb")
        or die ("Could not select database\n");
    $query = "SELECT * FROM member";
    $result_id = mysql_query ($query)
        or die ("Query failed\n");
    for ($i = 0; $i < mysql_num_fields ($result_id); $i++)
    {
        printf ("column %d:", $i);
        printf (" name %s,", mysql_field_name ($result_id, $i));
        printf (" flags %s\n", mysql_field_flags ($result_id, $i));
        print ("<br />\n");
    }
    mysql_free_result ($result_id);
?>
```

Table H.4   **mysql_field_flags() Values**

Property	Meaning
auto_increment	Column has the AUTO_INCREMENT attribute
binary	Column has the BINARY attribute
blob	Column is a BLOB or TEXT type
enum	Column is an ENUM
multiple_key	Column is a part of a non-unique index
not_null	Column cannot contain NULL values
primary_key	Column is a part of a PRIMARY KEY
timestamp	Column is a TIMESTAMP
unique_key	Column is a part of a UNIQUE index
unsigned	Column has the UNSIGNED attribute
zerofill	Column has the ZEROFILL attribute

The "binary" property is set for case sensitive string columns. This includes columns for which the BINARY keyword is specified explicitly (such as CHAR BINARY), as well as BLOB columns.

To access the individual words of a string returned by mysql_field_flags(), split it with explode():

```
$words = explode (" ", mysql_field_flags ($result_id, $i));
```

- int
mysql_field_len (resource result_id,
                    int col_num);

Returns the maximum possible length of values in the given column of the result set. col_num should be in the range from 0 to mysql_num_fields()-1.

```
<?php
    $conn_id = @mysql_connect ("cobra.snake.net", "sampadm", "secret")
        or die ("Could not connect\n");
    mysql_select_db ("sampdb")
        or die ("Could not select database\n");
    $query = "SELECT * FROM member";
    $result_id = mysql_query ($query)
        or die ("Query failed\n");
    for ($i = 0; $i < mysql_num_fields ($result_id); $i++)
    {
        printf ("column %d:", $i);
        printf (" name %s,", mysql_field_name ($result_id, $i));
        printf (" len %d\n", mysql_field_len ($result_id, $i));
        print ("<br />\n");
    }
    mysql_free_result ($result_id);
?>
```

- string
mysql_field_name (resource result_id,
                     int col_num);

Returns the name of the given column of the result set. col_num should be in the range from 0 to mysql_num_fields()-1.

```
<?php
    $conn_id = @mysql_connect ("cobra.snake.net", "sampadm", "secret")
        or die ("Could not connect\n");
    mysql_select_db ("sampdb")
        or die ("Could not select database\n");
    $query = "SELECT * FROM president";
    $result_id = mysql_query ($query)
        or die ("Query failed\n");
```

```
        # get column names
        for ($i = 0; $i < mysql_num_fields ($result_id); $i++)
        {
            printf ("Name of column %d: ", $i);
            $name = mysql_field_name ($result_id, $i);
            if (!$name)
                print ("No name available<br />\n");
            else
                print ("$name<br />\n");
        }
        mysql_free_result ($result_id);
    ?>
```

- int

  mysql_field_seek (resource result_id,
                      int col_num);

  Sets the index for subsequent calls to mysql_fetch_field(). The next
  call to mysql_fetch_field() that is issued without an explicit column
  number will return information for column col_num. Returns true if
  the seek succeeds and false otherwise. col_num should be in the range
  from 0 to mysql_num_fields()-1.

```
    <?php
        $conn_id = @mysql_connect ("cobra.snake.net", "sampadm", "secret")
            or die ("Could not connect\n");
        mysql_select_db ("sampdb")
            or die ("Could not select database\n");
        $query = "SELECT * FROM president";
        $result_id = mysql_query ($query)
            or die ("Query failed\n");
        # get column metadata
        for ($i = 0; $i < mysql_num_fields ($result_id); $i++)
        {
            printf ("Information for column %d:<br />\n", $i);
            if (!mysql_field_seek ($result_id, $i))
            {
                print ("Cannot seek to column<br />\n");
                continue;
            }
            $meta = mysql_fetch_field ($result_id, $i);
            if (!$meta)
            {
                print ("No information available<br />\n");
                continue;
            }
            print ("<pre>\n");
            printf ("blob:        %s\n", $meta->blob);
            printf ("max_length:  %s\n", $meta->max_length);
            printf ("multiple_key: %s\n", $meta->multiple_key);
```

```
        printf ("name:          %s\n", $meta->name);
        printf ("not_null:       %s\n", $meta->not_null);
        printf ("numeric:        %s\n", $meta->numeric);
        printf ("primary_key:    %s\n", $meta->primary_key);
        printf ("table:          %s\n", $meta->table);
        printf ("type:           %s\n", $meta->type);
        printf ("unique_key:     %s\n", $meta->unique_key);
        printf ("unsigned:       %s\n", $meta->unsigned);
        printf ("zerofill:       %s\n", $meta->zerofill);
        print ("</pre>\n");
    }
    mysql_free_result ($result_id);
?>
```

- string
  mysql_field_table (resource result_id,
                        int col_num);

Returns the name of the table that contains the given column of the
result set. For columns that are calculated as the result of an expression,
the name is empty. col_num should be in the range from 0 to
mysql_num_fields()-1.

```
<?php
    $conn_id = @mysql_connect ("cobra.snake.net", "sampadm", "secret")
        or die ("Could not connect\n");
    mysql_select_db ("sampdb")
        or die ("Could not select database\n");
    $query = "SELECT * FROM president";
    $result_id = mysql_query ($query)
        or die ("Query failed\n");
    for ($i = 0; $i < mysql_num_fields ($result_id); $i++)
    {
        printf ("column %d:", $i);
        printf (" name %s,", mysql_field_name ($result_id, $i));
        printf (" table %s\n", mysql_field_table ($result_id, $i));
        print ("<br />\n");
    }
    mysql_free_result ($result_id);
?>
```

- string
  mysql_field_type (resource result_id,
                        int col_num);

Returns the type name for the given column of the result set. The return
value will be one of those described for the type value returned by
the mysql_field_flags() function; see the description of that function

for a list of these values. `col_num` should be in the range from `0` to `mysql_num_fields()-1`.

```php
<?php
    $conn_id = @mysql_connect ("cobra.snake.net", "sampadm", "secret")
        or die ("Could not connect\n");
    mysql_select_db ("sampdb")
        or die ("Could not select database\n");
    $query = "SELECT * FROM president";
    $result_id = mysql_query ($query)
        or die ("Query failed\n");
    for ($i = 0; $i < mysql_num_fields ($result_id); $i++)
    {
        printf ("column %d:", $i);
        printf (" name %s,", mysql_field_name ($result_id, $i));
        printf (" type %s\n", mysql_field_type ($result_id, $i));
        print ("<br />\n");
    }
    mysql_free_result ($result_id);
?>
```

- bool
  mysql_free_result (resource result_id);

  Frees any resources associated with the given result set. Result sets are returned by `mysql_query()`, `mysql_unbuffered_query()`, `mysql_list_dbs()`, `mysql_list_fields()`, `mysql_list_processes()`, and `mysql_list_tables()`.

  Result sets are freed automatically when a script terminates, but you may want to call this function explicitly in a script that generates many result sets. For example, executing the following loop in a PHP script will use a considerable amount of memory:

```php
<?php
    for ($i = 0; $i < 10000; $i++)
    {
        $result_id = mysql_query ("SELECT * from president");
    }
?>
```

  Adding a `mysql_free_result()` call after the `mysql_query()` call will reduce the amount of result set memory used to almost nothing:

```php
<?php
    for ($i = 0; $i < 10000; $i++)
    {
        $result_id = mysql_query ("SELECT * from president");
        mysql_free_result ($result_id);
    }
?>
```

You should also call `mysql_free_result()` explicitly if you terminate your fetch loop early after issuing a query with `mysql_unbuffered_query()`. `mysql_free_result()` will take care of fetching and discarding the remaining rows automatically. If you fail to do this, an "out of sync" error will occur when you issue the next query.

- int
mysql_insert_id ([resource conn_id]);

Returns the `AUTO_INCREMENT` value generated by the most recently executed query on the given connection. Returns zero if no such value has been generated during the life of the connection. Generally, you should call `mysql_insert_id()` immediately after issuing a query that you expect to generate a new value. If you issue another query before calling `mysql_insert_id()`, its value will be reset.

Note that the behavior of `mysql_insert_id()` differs from that of the SQL function `LAST_INSERT_ID()`. `mysql_insert_id()` is maintained in the client and is set for each query. The value of `LAST_INSERT_ID()` is maintained in the server and persists from query to query.

The values returned by `mysql_insert_id()` are connection-specific and are not affected by `AUTO_INCREMENT` activity on other connections.

Be careful when using this function to get `AUTO_INCREMENT` values from `BIGINT` columns. The range of `BIGINT` exceeds that of the type PHP uses internally to hold the `mysql_insert_id()` return value. Be careful, too, if you try the PHP manual's suggested workaround of getting the value by issuing a `SELECT LAST_INSERT_ID()` query instead. You may find that using the result in numeric context results in conversion to a floating-point value.

```php
<?php
    $conn_id = @mysql_connect ("cobra.snake.net", "sampadm", "secret")
        or die ("Could not connect\n");
    mysql_select_db ("sampdb")
        or die ("Could not select database\n");
    $query = "INSERT INTO member (last_name,first_name,expiration)"
        . " VALUES('Brown','Marcia','2002-6-3')";
    $result_id = mysql_query ($query)
        or die ("Query failed\n");
    printf ("membership number for new member: %d\n", mysql_insert_id());
?>
```

- int

mysql_num_fields (resource result_id);

Returns the number of columns in the given result set.

```php
<?php
    $conn_id = @mysql_connect ("cobra.snake.net", "sampadm", "secret")
        or die ("Could not connect\n");
    mysql_select_db ("sampdb")
        or die ("Could not select database\n");
    $query = "SELECT * FROM president";
    $result_id = mysql_query ($query)
        or die ("Query failed\n");
    printf ("Number of columns: %d\n", mysql_num_fields ($result_id));
    mysql_free_result ($result_id);
?>
```

- int

mysql_num_rows (resource result_id);

Returns the number of rows in the given result set.

```php
<?php
    $conn_id = @mysql_connect ("cobra.snake.net", "sampadm", "secret")
        or die ("Could not connect\n");
    mysql_select_db ("sampdb")
        or die ("Could not select database\n");
    $query = "SELECT * FROM president";
    $result_id = mysql_query ($query)
        or die ("Query failed\n");
    printf ("Number of rows: %d\n", mysql_num_rows ($result_id));
    mysql_free_result ($result_id);
?>
```

- mixed

mysql_result (resource result_id, int row_num
                    [, mixed column]);

Returns a value from the given row row_num of a result set. The column is identified by the column parameter, which can be either a numeric column index, the name of a column specified in the query, or the column name specified as tbl_name.col_name, where tbl_name is the name of the table containing the column. (For the latter case, if you refer to the table using an alias in the query, you can refer to the column as alias_name.col_name.)

This function is slow; it's preferable to use mysql_fetch_array(), mysql_fetch_assoc(), mysql_fetch_object(), or `mysql_fetch_row()` instead. If you do use `mysql_result()`, it's faster to specify a numeric column index than a column name for the `column` value.

```php
<?php
    $conn_id = @mysql_connect ("cobra.snake.net", "sampadm", "secret")
        or die ("Could not connect\n");
    mysql_select_db ("sampdb")
        or die ("Could not select database\n");
    $query = "SELECT last_name, first_name FROM president";
    $result_id = mysql_query ($query)
        or die ("Query failed\n");
    for ($i = 0; $i < mysql_num_rows ($result_id); $i++)
    {
        for ($j = 0; $j < mysql_num_fields ($result_id); $j++)
        {
            if ($j > 0)
                print (" ");
            print (mysql_result ($result_id, $i, $j));
        }
        print ("<br />\n");
    }
    mysql_free_result ($result_id);
?>
```

- string
  mysql_tablename (resource result_id, int row_num);

  Given a result identifier returned by `mysql_list_tables()` and a row number within the result, `mysql_tablename()` returns the table name stored in the given row of the set or `false` if an error occurred. `row_num` should be in the range from 0 to `mysql_num_rows()-1`.

  `mysql_tablename()` is actually an alias for `mysql_result()`.

```php
<?php
    $conn_id = @mysql_connect ("cobra.snake.net", "sampadm", "secret")
        or die ("Could not connect\n");
    $result_id = mysql_list_tables ("sampdb")
        or die ("Query failed\n");
    print ("sampdb tables:<br />\n");
    for ($i = 0; $i < mysql_num_rows ($result_id); $i++)
        printf ("%s<br />\n", mysql_tablename ($result_id, $i));
    mysql_free_result ($result_id);
?>
```

Information Routines

The routines in this section return information about the client, server, protocol version, and the current connection. The following example demonstrates how to call these routines.

```php
<?php
    $conn_id = @mysql_connect ("cobra.snake.net", "sampadm", "secret")
        or die ("Could not connect\n");
    $info = mysql_character_set_name ()
        or die ("Could not get character set name\n");
    print ("Character set name: $info\n");
    $info = mysql_get_client_info ()
        or die ("Could not get client info\n");
    print ("Client info: $info\n");
    $info = mysql_get_host_info ()
        or die ("Could not get host info\n");
    print ("Host info: $info\n");
    $info = mysql_get_proto_info ()
        or die ("Could not get protocol info\n");
    print ("Protocol info: $info\n");
    $info = mysql_get_server_info ()
        or die ("Could not get server info\n");
    print ("Server info: $info\n");
    $info = mysql_stat ()
        or die ("Could not get status info\n");
    print ("Status info: $info\n");
    $info = mysql_thread_id ()
        or die ("Could not get thread ID\n");
    print ("Thread ID: $info\n");
?>
```

Many of these routines correspond to C API functions of the same name. See the descriptions for those functions in Appendix F for more information.

- string
  mysql_get_client_info (void);

  Returns a string indicating the current client library version.

  mysql_get_client_info() was introduced in PHP 4.0.5.

- string
  mysql_get_host_info ([resource conn_id]);

  Returns a string describing the given connection, such as "Localhost via UNIX socket", "cobra.snake.net via TCP/IP", or ". via named pipe".

  mysql_get_host_info() was introduced in PHP 4.0.5.

- `int`
  mysql_get_proto_info (`[resource conn_id]`);

  Returns a number indicating the client/server protocol version used for the given connection.

  `mysql_get_proto_info()` was introduced in PHP 4.0.5.

- `string`
  mysql_get_server_info (`[resource conn_id]`);

  Returns a string describing the server version, for example, `"4.0.2-alpha-log"`. The value consists of a version number, possibly followed by one or more suffixes. The suffix values are listed in the description of the `VERSION()` function in Appendix C, "Operator and Function Reference."

  `mysql_get_server_info()` was introduced in PHP 4.0.5.

- `string`
  mysql_info (`[resource conn_id]`);

  Returns information about queries that affect multiple rows. The format of the string is described in the entry for the `mysql_info()` function in Appendix F.

  `mysql_info()` was introduced in PHP 4.3.0.

- `string`
  mysql_stat (`[resource conn_id]`);

  Returns a string containing server status information. The format of the string is described in the entry for the `mysql_stat()` function in Appendix F.

  `mysql_stat()` was introduced in PHP 4.3.0.

- `int`
  mysql_thread_id (`[resource conn_id]`);

  Returns the thread identifier that the server associates with the given connection.

  `mysql_thread_id()` was introduced in PHP 4.3.0.

- `string`
  mysql_character_set_name (`[resource conn_id]`);

  Returns the name of the default character set for the given connection.

  `mysql_character_set_name()` requires MySQL 3.23.21 or later. It was introduced in PHP 4.3.0.

Deprecated Routines

The routines in this section are deprecated in favor of the preferred alternatives indicated in the routine descriptions.

- bool
  mysql_create_db (string db_name
                       [, resource conn_id]);

  Creates a database with the given name and returns true if the database was created successfully or false if an error occurred. You must have the CREATE privilege on the database to create it.

  It is preferable to use mysql_query() to issue a CREATE DATABASE statement rather than using mysql_create_db().

- resource
  mysql_db_query (string db_name,
                     string query
                     [, resource conn_id]);

  mysql_db_query() is like mysql_query() except that it takes an additional database name argument and makes it the default database before executing the query.

  It is inefficient to select a database each time you issue a query, so mysql_db_query() should be avoided. It is preferable to use mysql_select_db() to select a database and mysql_query() to issue queries after that.

- bool
  mysql_drop_db (string db_name
                     [, resource conn_id]);

  Drops (removes) the database with the given name and returns true if the database was removed successfully, or false if an error occurred. You must have the DROP privilege on the database to remove it.

  Be careful with this function; if you drop a database, it's gone. You can't get it back.

  It is preferable to use mysql_query() to issue a DROP DATABASE statement rather than using mysql_drop_db().

PHP also supports a number of older function names for backward compatibility. As indicated in Table H.5, these are aliases to newer function names. (But note that some of the "newer" functions are deprecated.)

Table H.5 **Backward-Compatibility Function Aliases**

Old Name	New Name
mysql_createdb()	mysql_create_db()
mysql_dbname()	mysql_db_name()
mysql_dropdb()	mysql_drop_db()
mysql_fieldflags()	mysql_field_flags()
mysql_fieldlen()	mysql_field_len()
mysql_fieldname()	mysql_field_name()
mysql_fieldtable()	mysql_field_table()
mysql_fieldtype()	mysql_field_type()
mysql_freeresult()	mysql_free_result()
mysql_listdbs()	mysql_list_dbs()
mysql_listfields()	mysql_list_fields()
mysql_listtables()	mysql_list_tables()
mysql_numfields()	mysql_num_fields()
mysql_numrows()	mysql_num_rows()
mysql_selectdb()	mysql_select_db()

I

Internet Service Providers

Many people have full-time access over a fast connection to the Internet in general and to a MySQL server in particular. This is especially common in university environments and in businesses that have their own computing services departments. But for many others this is not true, and access to online services comes through an Internet Service Provider (ISP). In addition to basic Internet connectivity for services such as email and Web browsing, many ISPs offer other services, such as access to MySQL, a Web server, and programming languages like Perl and PHP.

This chapter provides a guide to choosing an ISP appropriately for your requirements. You may need both a way to connect to the Internet and a host on which MySQL services are provided. Alternatively, you may already have MySQL running on your machine and need only a provider that can provide the connectivity necessary to enable incoming connections from the Internet to reach your machine.

One way to find candidate providers is to visit the Web sites for the packages you require to see if they have a page about ISPs that host the service. For example, the PHP Web site has a search page intended for finding ISPs that have PHP service. One of the search criteria allows you to look for providers that have MySQL. There is also a site that lists MySQL providers. You can visit these sites at the following addresses:

```
http://hosts.php.net/search.php
http://www.wix.com/mysql-hosting/
```

ISPs are not all the same, so it's important to do a comparative analysis before picking one. Choose carefully; a bad ISP can take all the pleasure out of using MySQL, whereas a good one can help you immeasurably. It's more work to shop around, but if you don't, you may make a bad choice and then you'll have to invest the time necessary to make a comparison later anyway.

Most of the criteria presented in this chapter must be assessed on a relative basis. You may not be able to find an ISP that satisfies all your requirements completely, but you should be able to find one that satisfies most of them better than other ISPs.

As you shop, try to maintain your perspective. Internet Service Providers are not all bad guys looking to bleed you for as much money as possible while offering as little real value as possible. But they're not all good guys either. It's important to do your homework so that you can find one of the ISPs that does know its stuff and can help you accomplish your goals. As you proceed in your investigation, be wary of an ISP that evades specific questions about its business practices or technical capabilities. Also watch out for ISPs that give only general answers when you press for details.

A Note to Service Providers

MySQL represents a service that you can offer to your customers, with a much lower financial outlay than almost any other relational database system. In addition, you can use MySQL for your own purposes internally (for example, to assist you in keeping track of customer records). If you are considering installing MySQL, read this chapter from the reverse perspective. That is, where it says "Ask the ISP such-and-such a question," ask yourself whether you could answer the question. If not, why not? Where the chapter says, "Does the ISP provide this or that service?" ask yourself whether you provide it. If not, what would be required for you to be able to do so?

Getting Ready to Shop for an ISP

Your first step in finding a service provider is to assess your needs. Before you can choose a provider that meets your requirements, you must know what your requirements are for services and bandwidth. Perhaps that is stating the obvious, but unfortunately it's not unusual for people to look for an ISP with nothing more than the vague idea that they want to "get connected." That's a difficult goal to accomplish satisfactorily; it leaves many questions unanswered because they aren't even asked. Connected for what purpose? To pursue which activities? What cost is considered reasonable?

When you know what you want, you can approach ISPs with a common set of questions and you'll be much better equipped to compare the answers you receive. If you don't figure out what you want in advance, you'll be learning what questions to ask with each successive ISP, you'll get incomplete information, and it will be more difficult to perform a meaningful comparison.

As one part of your evaluation, you might consider making a few preliminary calls to see if you can find an ISP or two that offers an assessment service to help you determine what you need. If the service actually is geared toward helping you specify your requirements (as opposed to being simply another sales technique for pushing services you don't want or need), you may have found a provider with at least one strength—customer service.

Keep in mind as you shop that many organizations that provide services such as MySQL access and Web site hosting do not provide basic connectivity services. You may actually be best served by using two providers—one that allows you to access the Internet yourself and another that hosts your database and Web servers. For example, you might choose a local ISP that provides cable modem, DSL, or dialup connectivity allowing you to connect to the Internet, and a national ISP that focuses exclusively on Web hosting. The following sections that discuss bandwidth and services describe the types of concerns that are most appropriately addressed by each type of ISP.

Bandwidth

Providers offer various options, from dedicated lines (faster) to dialup modem connections (slower). In general, the tradeoff is between cost and speed; Fast access costs more. If you're going to shuttle a lot of data through the connection between your computer and your ISP, dialup access likely will be too slow. In certain cases, however, you may be able to get by with a slower connection between the ISP and yourself. Suppose that most of the network activity sustained on your MySQL host is due to other people accessing your database. For example, these might be customers accessing information you provide through a Web server running on the MySQL host. In that case, the majority of your database-related traffic will be directed upstream from the ISP to those people rather than downstream toward you.

Services

The most obvious requirement for any candidate ISP is that it provides MySQL, but the following services might be necessary or desirable as well:

- **An email address.** This is essential for communicating with the ISP's technical support staff, and you can use it to join one or more of the MySQL mailing lists. Many ISPs offer multiple email addresses per account, which may be useful if you have employees or are working in collaboration with other people.

- **Access to a shell account.** This gives you the ability to log in on your server host and run programs from the command prompt. These programs include standard UNIX utilities as well as MySQL command-line clients, such as `mysql`, `mysqldump`, and `mysqlimport`. You may also be able to install your own software. Access to a shell account typically is provided via SSH (secure shell) or Telnet. SSH is preferable to Telnet because it is more secure.

- **Additional MySQL-related services.** These might include Web site hosting and access to programming languages, such as Perl and PHP, so that you can write your own Web scripts.

- **scp or FTP.** This is useful for transferring files between your computer and the ISP's machine. (`scp` uses SSH, so it is preferable as a more-secure alternative to FTP.) For example, you'll likely have some data files that you want to load into your database to populate it initially, or you may generate output from the database that you want to manipulate on your own machine. You may also want to give other people the ability to download files via FTP.

- **Domain name registration and virtual hosting.** These services give you email and Web site addresses under your own domain name rather than under the domain of your ISP. This is a desirable service if you want to establish a Web presence under a name that can be readily identified with your organization or business. An email address like `you@yourbiz.com` is more distinctive than `you@yourbiz.some-isp.com`, just as a URL of `http://www.yourbiz.com` is more distinctive than `http://yourbiz.some-isp.com`. Having your own domain also provides more continuity should it be necessary to change ISPs. If your name is tied to your ISP's name, switching from one ISP to another requires you to re-establish your identity as `you@yourbiz.other-isp.com` and `http://yourbiz.other-isp.com`. This works against the stability that people want when they need to reach you or your Web site.

Assessing an ISP—General Considerations

This section enumerates general criteria that are useful for evaluating candidate ISPs. The following section deals with issues that pertain specifically to MySQL. As you approach a new ISP, determine the answers to these questions:

- How easy is it to get information?
- What are the costs?
- What kind of client access software does the ISP provide?
- What kind of initial assistance do you receive from the ISP?
- What are the ISP's customer connectivity options?
- Does the provider have good upstream connectivity and bandwidth?
- What kind of technical support does the ISP provide?
- Are there quotas? If so, what are they?
- What kind of hardware does the ISP use?
- How do they handle privacy and security issues?
- What kind of reputation do they have?
- How long has the provider been in business?
- What are their plans for growth?

Let's consider each of these questions in more detail.

- **How easy is it to get information?** When you call to inquire about the services an ISP provides, does anyone answer? If you have difficulty getting through, maybe it's an operation run by someone out of a garage during the evening. If you reach an answering machine, does the ISP return your call? If you send email, do you receive a prompt reply?

  Do customer service representatives have the answers to your questions? If not, do they find someone within their organization who does, or do they try to convince you that the issues you're raising are unimportant? ("Oh, sure, we can handle that—don't worry.") If you can't get answers to questions before they have your money, how will they treat you after they do?

  Does the ISP staff communicate with you in terms you understand? If their only language is marketing drivel, you may be in contact with an outfit that's long on selling themselves and short on hard technical knowledge. On the other hand, if they overpower you with jargon, you might be dealing with a bunch of geeks that have their technical know-how down pat but who can't communicate well with "normal people."

Visit the provider's Web site. Is it clear, informative, and easy to understand? Putting together a good home page is much easier than managing a well-run service. If they can't do the easier thing well, do you suppose they'll do the harder one any better?

- **What are the costs?** This can vary considerably because it depends on so many factors. Is there an initial signup/setup fee in addition to the usual monthly fee? Is the monthly fee fixed or sliding? What does the fee include? Do you get unlimited connect time, or is there some hourly limit? If you exceed the limit, what happens? Do they simply refuse connections (which is inconvenient, but you incur no extra fee)? Or is there a surcharge on top of your normal monthly rate? If there is a charge, does it include disk space?

For dialup connections, the ISP presumably has a local number for use within the calling area. But if you live in a rural area, make sure that ISP access doesn't involve a toll call.

Does the ISP provide an 800 number that you can use when you're away from home for checking your email and accessing the Web? If you travel with a laptop and require Internet access as you travel, you'll probably be better served by a national ISP rather than a local one. If an 800 number is available, is it free? (Some are not.)

ISPs often include a modest amount of disk space in the basic fee (a few megabytes) with an option to purchase a larger allocation as needed. Get specific information about disk charges if you expect your database to be large or if you plan on hosting a Web site (particularly if it will be graphics heavy).

If you establish a Web presence on the ISP's host, how does the ISP charge for bandwidth when people access your Web pages or download files? Some ISPs impose a quota and shut you off until the next time period begins if you exceed the limit. Others may include a sliding fee based on download volume in your bill. Still others may reclassify you as a commercial customer (probably at a higher rate). Find out what your options are.

Is technical support free or is there a charge? If it's free, is that only for a limited time, such as your first 30 days? If there is a charge, do you pay a flat rate or a per-incident rate? Can you pay an extra fee to get premium support with a guaranteed short response time?

If you are presented with a fee prepayment plan, evaluate it with an eye to the history and reputation of the company. Prepayment options are sometimes used by startups as a means of raising operating capital, but such ISPs are also the most likely to fold, and if they do, your prepaid fees are likely to be unrecoverable.

Do you have to sign a long-term contract (a year or more)? If you're uncertain about an ISP's capabilities, you want to be able to back out after a month or two. It might be easy to get signed up; how easy is it to get out if you decide you don't like them? Can you get back the unused portion of your contract?

Perhaps you can get a free or low-cost trial account that will allow you to assess the ISP's technical competence and support services. Keep in mind that such an account typically will include limitations on your activities. For example, disk space constraints will limit the size of any trial database you may create.

- **What kind of client access software does the ISP provide?** Do they support your platform? Some ISPs may specify that they support only certain systems. This is less likely than it used to be, but it still happens. If the ISP does support only a single platform, it's likely to be Windows. That doesn't help you if you're running UNIX or Mac OS.

  Does the ISP provide an email client and Web browser? If so, are you required to use them, or can you use others if you prefer?

- **What kind of initial assistance do you receive from the ISP?** Do they offer help in getting you connected and getting your account working? Is there a fee for this service (which is likely if you have complex requirements)?

- **What are the ISP's customer connectivity options?** If you'll be connecting by modem, you don't want to get a busy signal when you try to reach the service provider. You can ask candidate providers what their customer/modem ratio is, but that depends on customer activity. Residential customers who connect briefly to check email don't tie up the modem pool as much as commercial customers who camp out on a connection all day to conduct business. It's better to ask how often you'll get a busy signal, particularly at the time of day you typically expect to be connecting.

  You can test this for yourself before signing up. Dial the ISP's number on a regular phone and listen for a modem screeching on the other end. Perform this test several times on different days. How often do you get a busy signal or no answer? Assess modem availability against your activities. If you're a business, you want to be sure you can connect whenever you want. For personal purposes, you may not mind the occasional busy signal.

To avoid the hassles of dialup, you may prefer to get an always-on connection, such as that provided by a cable modem or DSL line. These are also much faster than dialup. Does the ISP offer these higher-speed options? Note that cable or DSL connections typically require some sort of high-speed modem or router. Does the ISP provide it, or are you expected to? You may have fewer installation problems if the ISP provides the equipment. If you expect to be moving large amounts of traffic between your site and the ISP, you might even want to set up a dedicated line. Will the ISP help you with that?

If you get a line that is always up, you may have the option of supporting incoming connections to your own machine, and thus of hosting your own Web site if you feel comfortable doing that. But for that to work, other people need to be able to find you reliably and to make connections to your servers. Many ISPs provide dynamic rather than static IP addresses by default and may filter your incoming traffic. A static IP is almost a necessity if you want to support incoming connections because it's difficult for people to reach you when your address changes periodically. You'll also need to verify that incoming connections to the ports used by your servers won't be blocked. It's not uncommon for ISPs to filter traffic to SMTP, HTTP, and FTP ports, for example. (Usually, the purpose of this is precisely to prevent customers from setting up servers and hogging bandwidth.) Some providers offer the option of a static IP with no filtering, but you can expect to pay more; ISPs know that customers who require that type of connection tend to generate more traffic.

- **Does the provider have good upstream connectivity and bandwidth?** How close is the provider to the Internet backbone? Are they directly connected, or do they go through another provider to get there? Do they have redundant connections in case of connection outage?

  How big is the "pipe" between the ISP and the backbone? The type of connection determines its bandwidth—that is, the maximum amount of traffic the ISP can handle between the backbone and its own installation. High-bandwidth trunks like OC3, T-3, or T-1 lines provide fast connections. If the provider's link to the Internet is made through some lower-bandwidth connection, that's a bottleneck and transmission rates will suffer. For example, an ISP that is attempting to host dozens of Web sites through a DSL line won't provide much throughput to any given client.

Evaluate the amount of bandwidth with regard to the size of the customer base served by the ISP. Ask how much traffic they're actually moving over their connection—how much of their capacity is used? If you're sharing a connection to the backbone with many other active users, the bandwidth that is available to you decreases. If the ISP hosts your Web site, a saturated link slows down people attempting to connect, with the result that your site appears to be unresponsive.

- **What kind of technical support does the ISP provide?** Is it available at all times or only during normal business hours? You may plan to connect only during the day, but if you don't, will someone be there to answer your questions? What about weekends? Do they provide both phone and email access to technical support staff? You want phone support because you can't send email if you can't log on. But you want email, too, so that you can mail technical information or program output to the support staff to avoid trying to describe it over the phone. Do they promise a response within a certain amount of time? (The problem may not necessarily be resolved within that time, but requests at least should be acknowledged promptly so that you know they're working on them.)

  Is there online help? Is it clear and to the point or confusing and vague? Can you navigate it easily to find the information you need? Is it searchable?

  You can assess technical support availability for yourself the same way you test the dialup access numbers—call them. You might feel foolish doing this before you have an account with the ISP, but it can be instructive to find out whether you get put in a phone queue and for how long. Also, ask how many technical support personnel there are or what the customer-to-technician ratio is.

- **Are there quotas? If so, what are they?** Are there quotas for disk space or processing time? Are there time constraints on scripts executed by the Web server? It's not unreasonable for the ISP to put some limits on customer activities to prevent monopolization of resources shared by other customers, but you want to know what those limits are. If you approach quota limits, what happens? Does the ISP notify you so that you can modify your usage, or do they silently start applying a surcharge when you go over limit that you find out about only when you get your next bill?

  Does the provider place a limit on the size of email messages? If you routinely send or receive large attachments, make sure that the provider's limit is high enough to allow your messages to pass through without truncation.

- **What kind of hardware does the ISP use?** It's possible to run basic Internet services on an old 386-class PC, but it won't be suitable for large numbers of users, to say nothing of trying to run more computationally intensive services, such as MySQL. MySQL doesn't hog system resources the same way large database systems do, but you still want an ISP that runs hardware with some muscle. What kinds of load can the system handle comfortably?

    Where is the server located? In someone's garage or basement? A provider located in a commercial district is likely to have an easier time getting the phone company to run additional trunk lines as capacity demands increase.

    How does the ISP deal with equipment failure? Is there a recovery plan in place, or are you just knocked offline until the equipment is repaired or replaced? What is their actual uptime percentage over the past several months? What accounts for the downtime incidents? Do they perform file system backups. If so, how often, or does the ISP consider that your responsibility?

    Are there expected downtimes (for scheduled maintenance or backups, for example)? Does the ISP inform customers when those will be? If you run a Web server, you probably prefer that it be available 24 hours a day.

- **How do they handle privacy and security issues?** Do they have a policy regarding privacy of your files? What measures do they take to prevent your account from being compromised?

- **What kind of reputation do they have?** What other customers do they have, and how well are those customers satisfied? Word of mouth can be useful; ask around to see if your acquaintances are familiar with candidate ISPs. You can ask the ISP for references, but they probably will refer you to people who are satisfied with their service. It might be informative to ask for opinions on the MySQL mailing list as well, where you're more likely to hear from people willing to relate experiences with an ISP—both good and bad.

- **How long has the provider been in business?** The ISP industry has a phenomenal number of failed or short-lived startups because it's easy to get started and difficult to do well. A provider with some longevity is more likely to be around in the not-so-near future and be able to help you for the long term.

- **What are their plans for growth?** How big are they? You probably don't want to use a tiny new startup, but the biggest services aren't necessarily better. Smaller companies can be more in touch with the needs of their customers.

  How fast are they growing? How many customers do they have now? A month ago? A year ago? You might want to go with a company that's prospering, but growth puts pressure on resources for bandwidth, customer access, and technical support. What is their policy for dealing with increased load?

> **Don't Have Unreasonable Expectations of an ISP**
> You won't get unlimited access, unlimited disk space, and unlimited tech support for $20 a month. Are you willing to pay for good service and support? You want something for your money, but ISPs expect to be reasonably compensated for the services they provide, too.

Assessing an ISP—MySQL-Specific Considerations

The preceding section gives you a way to assess an ISP's general capabilities. This section discusses criteria for evaluating an ISP more specifically with regard to MySQL and related services, such as Apache, Perl, and PHP.

- What MySQL-related services does the ISP provide?
- What version of MySQL is installed?
- What is the ISP policy on updating MySQL?
- Are there known problems with MySQL on the ISP's operating system?
- Can you install your own software?
- Is the ISP concerned about privacy and security of your database?
- Do they help you get started?
- What kind of MySQL-specific technical support is provided?
- How many of their customers use MySQL?

Let's consider each of these questions in more detail.

- **What MySQL-related services does the ISP provide?** The provider should have MySQL installed already, as well as any other related packages you need. The exception might be that you've already got an ISP with which you're otherwise satisfied but that doesn't have MySQL. In this case, you might want to simply ask whether they'd be willing to install it for you. You'll probably need to make some sort of business case for doing so, and you may have to agree that any such installation is done with the understanding that MySQL is not supported at the same level as email or Web hosting.

Visit the ISP's Web site. Do they provide information in any detail about their MySQL services? Does it sound like they have any technical understanding, or is the site strong on the marketing language? Is the site easy to navigate? Do they provide an area with answers to common questions customers have about using their services so that you can look up information for yourself?

- **What version of MySQL is installed?** Is it a recent version, or is it some really old release that hasn't been touched since its installation? Check the change notes appendix in the *MySQL Reference Manual* to see what features have been added after the version the ISP runs. Do you require any of those additional features?

- **What is the ISP policy on updating MySQL?** The ISP has to balance the need for stability and known behavior with existing MySQL applications against customers' desire to take advantage of new features in recent releases. This isn't necessarily an easy issue to resolve, so don't treat an ISP's concerns about it as trivial. But you will want to know that there is at least some possibility for upgrades, perhaps on a separate host devoted to test purposes. If you offer to serve as a guinea pig for newer releases, you may be able to reach a cooperative solution because you'll be providing your ISP with a valuable testing service.

- **Are there known problems with MySQL on the ISP's operating system?** Check the installation chapter in the *MySQL Reference Manual* to see if there are limitations that may affect you. Often there are workarounds to circumvent these problems.

- **Can you install your own software?** This allows you to enhance your own MySQL capabilities with third-party software or programs you've written yourself.

- **Is the ISP concerned about privacy and security of your database?** In addition to the ISP's general measures to protect customer data, does the ISP take any steps to protect MySQL data in particular? Do you get your own MySQL server? This is better from the customer's point of view because you can control who gets to see the contents of your database. But it's more work on the ISP's part, and it puts more of a resource burden on the server host. The same considerations apply to the Web server. It's more secure to have your own than to share one, but more of a processing load. You may be faced with a tradeoff between shared database and Web servers that cost less and your own servers at a higher cost.

- **Do they help you get started?** Don't expect the provider to teach you SQL or to show you how to write your queries, but you need to be able to connect to the MySQL server. Do they tell you what you need to know to make a connection? Do you get a sample script you can run to verify that you can access your database?

- **What kind of MySQL-specific technical support is provided?** I've heard a number of stories from people having ISP-related difficulties getting MySQL to run properly, and I've noticed that it's fairly common for ISPs to point a finger at the customer as the source of problems. As in many disputes, there often is fault on both sides of the issue, but sometimes its clear that an ISP has little idea how to deal with MySQL and is just guessing how to solve the problem. For this reason, it's important to determine ahead of time that an ISP candidate has administrative or technical staff with a decent grasp of MySQL. Question them about their level of technical expertise. The ISP should be familiar with the material in Part III, "MySQL Administration," of this book. Ask if they have a MySQL support contract (that's an indication that they take MySQL seriously and stand ready to assist you with problems that may arise) or do they just say, "Go ask the mailing list?"

  You'll need to assess the technical support provided against the control that the ISP gives you over your resources. If you want complete control over your MySQL server, and the ISP gives it to you, it's reasonable for the ISP to expect you to be capable of administering the server. In this case, you'll want the ISP to allow you to provide a script that will start your server at system boot time so that you need not do it manually each time the machine is restarted.

- **How many of their customers use MySQL?** If MySQL is used actively by many customers, there's a better chance that the ISP will provide good support for it than if just one or two customers use it.

Beware the Absentee Administrator

Watch out for ISPs that simply install MySQL so that they can add it to their list of services to attract customers. You don't want the kind of administrator that tries to get away with knowing as little as possible in performing administrative duties.

Index

Symbols

G

H

L

M

N

T

W

Your Guide
to Computer
Technology

www.informit.com

Developer's Library

Essential references for programming professionals

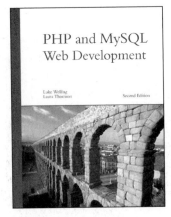

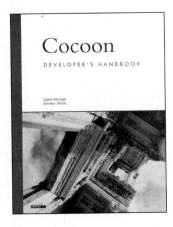

PHP and MySQL Web Development

Luke Welling
Laura Thomson

ISBN: 0-672-32525-X
$49.99 US/$77.99 CAN

Cocoon

DEVELOPER'S HANDBOOK

Lajos Moczar
Jeremy Aston

ISBN: 0-672-32257-9
$49.99 US/$77.99 CAN

PostgreSQL

Korry Douglas
Susan Douglas

ISBN: 0-7357-1257-3
$49.99 US/$77.99 CAN

OTHER DEVELOPER'S LIBRARY TITLES

MySQL and Perl for the Web

Paul DuBois
ISBN: 0-7357-1054-6
$44.99 US/$67.95 CAN

PHP

DEVELOPER'S COOKBOOK

Sterling Hughes
Andrei Zmievski

ISBN: 0-672-32325-7
$39.99 US/$59.95 CAN

PostgreSQL

DEVELOPER'S HANDBOOK

Ewald Geschwinde
and Hans–Jürgen
Schönig

ISBN: 0-672-32260-9
$44.99 US/$67.95 CAN

mod_perl

DEVELOPER'S COOKBOOK

Geoffrey Young
Paul Lindner
Randy Kobes

ISBN: 0-672-32240-4
$39.99 US/$62.99 CAN

PRICES SUBJECT TO CHANGE

DEVELOPER'S LIBRARY

www.developers-library.com